Introduction to Homeland Security

Fifth Edition

Introduction to Homeland Security

Principles of All-Hazards Risk Management

Fifth Edition

Jane A. Bullock

George D. Haddow

Damon P. Coppola

AMSTERDAM • BOSTON • HEIDELBERG • LONDON
NEW YORK • OXFORD • PARIS • SAN DIEGO
SAN FRANCISCO • SINGAPORE • SYDNEY • TOKYO

Butterworth-Heinemann is an imprint of Elsevier

Acquiring Editor: Sara Scott
Editorial Project Manager: Hilary Carr
Project Manager: Punithavathy Govindaradjane
Designer: Mark Rogers

Butterworth-Heinemann is an imprint of Elsevier
225 Wyman Street, Waltham, MA 02451, USA

Notices
Knowledge and best practice in this field are constantly changing. As new research and experience broaden our understanding, changes in research methods, professional practices, or medical treatment may become necessary.

Practitioners and researchers must always rely on their own experience and knowledge in evaluating and using any information, methods, compounds, or experiments described herein. In using such information or methods they should be mindful of their own safety and the safety of others, including parties for whom they have a professional responsibility.

To the fullest extent of the law, neither the Publisher nor the authors, contributors, or editors, assume any liability for any injury and/or damage to persons or property as a matter of products liability, negligence or otherwise, or from any use or operation of any methods, products, instructions, or ideas contained in the material herein.

ISBN: 978-0-12-802028-9

British Library Cataloguing-in-Publication Data
A catalogue record for this book is available from the British Library

Library of Congress Cataloging-in-Publication Data
A catalogue record for this book is available from the Library of Congress

For information on all BH publications,
visit our website at store.elsevier.com

Printed and bound in Canada

Dedication

The authors dedicate this book to Pam Chester as an expression of sincere gratitude for all of the advice, expertise, and support she provided in each of the previous editions of this textbook. Pam's knowledge of the publishing world makes her a consummate professional. But it is her ability to understand and accommodate the idiosyncrasies of her authors without losing her wonderful sense of humor that made the production of each edition enjoyable. A huge thank you to our editor and our friend.

Contents

Acknowledgments

The authors of this book would like to express their appreciation for the continued support and encouragement we have received from Dr. Jack Harrald, Dr. Joseph Barbera, and Dr. Greg Shaw. In addition to contributing a large dose of practical advice and humor, these three individuals provide outstanding leadership to institutions and governments in designing and implementing homeland security projects.

We would like to acknowledge the many individuals whose research, analysis, and opinions helped to shape the content of this volume.

We would also like to thank Sara Scott, Hilary Carr, and Marisa LaFleur at Elsevier for their assistance in making the fifth edition of this text possible and for their patience and faith in us. Our gratitude also extends to Barbara Johnson, Ryan Miller, Ehren Ngo, Irmak Renda-Tanali, Matt Foster, Bridger McGaw, Don Goff, Jack Suwanlert, Sarp Yeletaysi, Erdem Ergin, Lissa Westerman, Terry Downes, Steve Carter, Audra Kiesling, Jeff Dailey, Phillip Schertzing, Lawrence Nelson, Babak Akhgar, Dale Suiter, and David Gilmore.

Finally, we recognize the thousands of professionals and volunteers who, through their daily pursuits, are creating a more secure and safe homeland.

Introduction

It has been almost 15 years since the September 11 terrorist attacks occurred, forever changing the way Americans and their government perceive and approach domestic security. These events set in motion a series of decisions and actions that have transformed the function of domestic security in ways that could never have been imagined prior to these attacks. The reorganization of the federal government as a result of the Homeland Security Act of 2002 represented one of the largest reorganizations of government in the nation's history and certainly the largest involving nonmilitary agencies. Congress established the National Commission on Terrorist Attacks Upon the United States (informally known as "the 9/11 Commission") to better understand how these attacks could have happened and what would reduce the future likelihood of similar events, and their findings continue to influence the direction of federal organization and policy. The passage of the USA Patriot Act, which sought to increase the abilities of US law enforcement agencies to identify, track, and apprehend terrorists, challenged the concepts of freedom and privacy for Americans, forcing them to choose between civil liberties and security. The nation engaged in multiple wars to address the growing worldwide threat of terrorism and has continued to seek out and develop partnerships in action with traditional and new allies alike.

These acts and actions have resulted in significant progress in the movement to establish security and disrupt terrorist and criminal threats to the country. Terrorist cells have been infiltrated and their attacks disrupted, as demonstrated by the disruption of a planned attack in New York's Times Square in 2009 and the killing of al-Qaeda leader Osama bin Laden in 2011. However, the threat evolves and in some cases surprises us, as evidenced by the 2013 Boston Marathon bombings and the emergence of the Khorasan Group and ISIS as a legitimate threat to the security of the United States and its interests abroad.

With the US government's increased focus on terrorism came a change in the manner in which we view the all-hazards risk profile. The perception of threats from natural hazards has shifted in response to events in relation to the terrorist threat, all dictated by fleeting memories and media agendas. All the while, natural disasters have continued to impact thousands of our communities, reminding us that the likelihood of a natural disaster far exceeds a terrorist event at least in terms of actualized occurrence. The aftermath of Hurricane Katrina brought sweeping legislative changes to the Federal Emergency Management Agency (FEMA), within DHS, and served to remind officials of the exacting toll natural disasters can take on public safety and our social and economic security. The devastating wildfires, floods, weather, and drought problems that impacted the nation in 2011 and Hurricane Sandy in 2012 each furthered this trend, and the response from FEMA/DHS and other partners was much improved in each case. Striking the right balance between the various hazards; looking for commonalities among the hazards in mitigation, preparedness, response, and recovery; and adopting a more all-hazards approach to homeland security remain priorities for the officials responsible for public safety.

At the same time, issues related to the impacts of illegal and legal immigration, especially in terms of the economic and social stability of American communities, continue to emerge. These concerns are most acute in the border communities where the bulk of DHS land-based interdiction efforts occur. The Coast Guard (CG) is vigilant in maintaining territorial waters and safety and security at our ports that are of the highest priority to ensure that homeland commerce can continue.

Seaside Heights, NJ, February 25, 2013. The end of the 630-foot long Casino Pier collapsed during Hurricane Sandy causing the Jet Star roller coaster to plunge into the ocean. (Photo by Steve Zumwalt/FEMA.)

Galveston Island, TX, September 20, 2008. The US Coast Guard patrol boat USCGC Manowar continues missions in the intercoastal waterway after Hurricane Ike. (Photo by Jocelyn Augustino/FEMA.)

New emerging and evolving threats require greater attention to cybersecurity, preventing cybercrime, and protecting our critical infrastructure. The complexities and speed with which the cyber environment changes require diligence and a level of cooperation and coordination between the government and the private sector not evidenced before. As more of our daily lives are dependent on the continual operation of computers and computer systems, for example, transportation, energy, and banking systems, preventing an attack on these systems becomes a critical priority for homeland security officials.

This fifth edition reflects the ongoing changes to the environment within which homeland security must establish itself. It includes details about the many structural changes that have occurred and in turn served to influence the nation's focus on traditional and emerging domestic security threats (e.g., cybersecurity). It explains several new public policy initiatives and provides a broad overview of the hazards, context, and the historic and organizational bases that continue to dictate the directions that the department and other agencies and entities at the national, state, and local levels have taken to address each.

The first chapter is intended to introduce the concept of homeland security and how that concept has changed in the years since the events of September 11.

The second chapter provides a historical perspective on the terrorist events that preceded September 11 and how the government's mechanisms to respond to emergencies have evolved, including descriptions of the statutory actions that were taken in reaction to September 11 and in support of preventing future attacks.

The book continues with complete descriptions and fact sheets on the types of hazards and risks that make up the potential homeland security vulnerabilities from future terrorist events, natural hazards, or human-made hazards. This section is followed by an overview presentation of the organization of DHS so that subsequent chapters and discussions will have a structural context.

In the revised format, we have developed chapters that describe the programs and actions being undertaken by government agencies, organizations, and the private sector to reduce or minimize the threat. We have focused chapters on the areas of intelligence and counterterrorism, border security and immigration, transportation safety and security, and cybersecurity and critical infrastructure protection.

A significant section is devoted to all-hazards response and recovery as these responsibilities are now recognized as a primary focus for DHS. In this chapter, we describe the current state of the art in first responder applications and discuss the changes that are under way within the national response and recovery system network. This is followed with a chapter focused on mitigation, prevention, and preparedness.

Recognizing the critical role that communications now play in our everyday lives and the use of social media in emergencies are now highlighted in a separate chapter, as are advancements in science and technology that support the homeland security enterprise mission.

We have included more case studies to demonstrate practical application to the materials being presented. In addition, we have included full texts of critical guidance documents, directives, and legislation for use and reference. Wherever possible, budget and resource charts show past allocations and future projections through 2015.

The volume concludes with a chapter that examines potential future and still unresolved issues that are relative to the disciplines of homeland security, with more of focus on public safety and emergency management that must be addressed as we meet the challenges of establishing a secure homeland.

Homeland security is a still-evolving discipline, changing to adapt to new threats and challenges. This book was written at a particular point in time, and changes to programs, activities, and even organizations occur regularly. For that reason, we have included online references wherever possible so the reader will have access to websites that can provide up-to-date information on program or organization changes, new initiatives, or simply more detail on specific issues.

The authors' goal in writing this book was to provide a source of history, practical information, programs, references, and best practices so that any academic, homeland security official, emergency manager, public safety official, community leader, or individual could understand the foundations of homeland security and be motivated to engage in actions to help make their communities safer and more secure. The homeland security function clearly is an evolving discipline that will continue to change in reaction to the steps we take to reduce the impacts of known hazards and as new threats are identified.

In the end, achieving homeland security will not be accomplished by the federal government but by each individual, each organization, each business, and each community working together to make a difference.

1

Homeland Security: The Concept, the Organization

What You Will Learn

- What the history behind the establishment of homeland security was
- How events have altered the concept of homeland security
- What the homeland security enterprise (HSE) is
- How other agencies and entities besides DHS contribute to the homeland security enterprise

Introduction

In the immediate aftermath of the September 11, 2001, attacks, as search and rescue teams were still sifting through the debris and wreckage for survivors in New York, Pennsylvania, and Virginia, the federal government was analyzing what had just happened and what it could quickly do to begin the process of ensuring such attacks could not be repeated. It was recognized that nothing too substantial could take place without longer-term study and congressional review, but the circumstances mandated that real changes begin without delay.

The idea of homeland security was primarily the result of the White House's, the federal government's, and the US Congress' reactions to the September 11 events. However, the movement to establish such broad-sweeping measures was initiated long before those attacks took place. Domestic and international terrorists have been striking Americans, American facilities, and American interests, both within and outside the nation's borders, for decades—though only fleeting interest was garnered in the aftermath of these events. Support for counterterrorism programs and legislation was, therefore, rather weak, and measures that did pass rarely warranted front-page status. Furthermore, the institutional cultures that characterized many of the agencies affected by this emerging threat served as a resilient barrier to the fulfillment of goals. Only the spectacular nature of the September 11 terrorist attacks was sufficient to boost the issue of terrorism to primary standing on all three social agendas: the public, the political, and the media.

Out of the tragic events of September 11, an enormous opportunity for improving the social and economic sustainability of our communities from all threats, but primarily terrorism, was envisioned and identified as homeland security. Public safety officials and emergency managers championed the concept of an all-hazards approach, and despite some unique characteristics, they felt terrorism could be incorporated into that approach as well (Figure 1-1).

However, in the immediate aftermath of 9/11, the single issue of preventing a future terrorist attack was foremost in the minds of federal officials and legislators. On September 20, 2001, just 9 days after the attacks, President George W. Bush announced that an Office of Homeland Security would be established within the

FIGURE 1-1 New York City, New York, October 13, 2001—New York firefighters at the site of the World Trade Center. *Photo by Andrea Booher/FEMA News Photo.*

White House by executive order. Directing this office would be Pennsylvania Governor Tom Ridge. Ridge was given no real staff to manage, and the funding he would have at his disposal was minimal. The actual order, cataloged as Executive Order 13228, was given on October 8, 2001. In addition to creating the Office of Homeland Security, this order created the Homeland Security Council, "to develop and coordinate the implementation of a comprehensive national strategy to secure the United States from terrorist threats or attacks."

Four days later, on September 24, 2001, President Bush announced that he would be seeking passage of an act entitled "Uniting and Strengthening America by Providing Appropriate Tools Required to Intercept and Obstruct Terrorism," which would become better known as the PATRIOT Act of 2001. This act, which introduced a large number of controversial legislative changes in order to significantly increase the surveillance and investigative powers of law enforcement agencies in the United States (as it states) to "...deter and punish terrorist acts in the United States and around the world," was signed into law by the president on October 26 after very little deliberation in Congress.

On October 29, 2001, President Bush issued the first of many homeland security presidential directives (HSPDs), which were specifically designed to "record and communicate presidential decisions about the homeland security policies of the United States" (HSPD-1, 2001). The sidebar "Homeland Security Presidential Directives" lists the HSPDs and their stated purposes.

The legislation to establish a Department of Homeland Security (DHS) was first introduced in the US House of Representatives by Texas Representative Richard K. Armey on June 24, 2002. A similar legislation was introduced into the Senate soon after. After the differences between the two bills were quickly ironed out, the Homeland Security Act of 2002 (Public Law 107-296) was passed by both houses and signed into law by President Bush on November 25, 2002.

Select Homeland Security Presidential Directives

Homeland Security Presidential Directives are issued by the President on matters pertaining to Homeland Security.

- **HSPD-1**: Organization and Operation of the Homeland Security Council. Ensures coordination of all homeland security-related activities among executive departments and agencies and promotes the effective development and implementation of all homeland security policies.
- **HSPD-2**: Combating Terrorism Through Immigration Policies. Provides for the creation of a task force which will work aggressively to prevent aliens who engage in or support terrorist activity from entering the United States and to detain, prosecute, or deport any such aliens who are within the United States.
- **HSPD-3**: Homeland Security Advisory System. Establishes a comprehensive and effective means to disseminate information regarding the risk of terrorist acts to Federal, State, and local authorities and to the American people.
- **HSPD-4**: National Strategy to Combat Weapons of Mass Destruction. Applies new technologies, increases emphasis on intelligence collection and analysis, strengthens alliance relationships, and establishes new partnerships with former adversaries to counter this threat in all of its dimensions.
- **HSPD-5**: Management of Domestic Incidents. Enhances the ability of the United States to manage domestic incidents by establishing a single, comprehensive national incident management system.
- **HSPD-6**: Integration and Use of Screening Information. Provides for the establishment of the Terrorist Threat Integration Center.
- **HSPD-7**: Critical Infrastructure Identification, Prioritization, and Protection. Establishes a national policy for federal departments and agencies to identify and prioritize United States critical infrastructure and key resources and to protect them from terrorist attacks.
- **Presidential Policy Directive/PPD-8**: National Preparedness. Aimed at strengthening the security and resilience of the United States through systematic preparation for the threats that pose the greatest risk to the security of the nation, including acts of terrorism, cyber attacks, pandemics, and catastrophic natural disasters.
- **HSPD-8 Annex 1**: National Planning. Rescinded by PPD-8: National Preparedness, except for paragraph 44. Individual plans developed under HSPD-8 and Annex 1 remain in effect until rescinded or otherwise replaced.
- **HSPD-9**: Defense of United States Agriculture and Food. Establishes a national policy to defend the agriculture and food system against terrorist attacks, major disasters, and other emergencies.
- **HSPD-10**: Biodefense for the Twenty-First Century. Provides a comprehensive framework for our nation's biodefense.

- **HSPD-11**: Comprehensive Terrorist-Related Screening Procedures. Implements a coordinated and comprehensive approach to terrorist-related screening that supports homeland security, at home and abroad. This directive builds upon HSPD-6.
- **HSPD-12**: Policy for a Common Identification Standard for Federal Employees and Contractors. Establishes a mandatory, government-wide standard for secure and reliable forms of identification issued by the federal government to its employees and contractors (including contractor employees).
- **HSPD-13**: Maritime Security Policy. Establishes policy guidelines to enhance national and homeland security by protecting US maritime interests.
- **HSPD-14**: Domestic Nuclear Detection.
- **HSPD-15**: US Strategy and Policy in the War on Terror.
- **HSPD-16**: Aviation Strategy. Details a strategic vision for aviation security while recognizing ongoing efforts, and directs the production of a national strategy for aviation security and supporting plans.
- **HSPD-17**: Nuclear Materials Information Program. (Classified)
- **HSPD-18**: Medical Countermeasures Against Weapons of Mass Destruction. Establishes policy guidelines to draw upon the considerable potential of the scientific community in the public and private sectors to address medical countermeasure requirements relating to CBRN threats.
- **HSPD-19**: Combating Terrorist Use of Explosives in the United States. Establishes a national policy, and calls for the development of a national strategy and implementation plan, on the prevention and detection of, protection against, and response to terrorist use of explosives in the United States.
- **HSPD-20**: National Continuity Policy. Establishes a comprehensive national policy on the continuity of federal government structures and operations and a single national continuity coordinator responsible for coordinating the development and implementation of federal continuity policies.
- **HSPD-20 Annex A**: Continuity Planning. Assigns executive departments and agencies to a category commensurate with their COOP/COG/ECG responsibilities during an emergency.
- **HSPD-21**: Public Health and Medical Preparedness. Establishes a national strategy that will enable a level of public health and medical preparedness sufficient to address a range of possible disasters.
- **HSPD-22**: Cyber Security and Monitoring.
- **HSPD-23**: National Cyber Security Initiative.
- **HSPD-24**: Biometrics for Identification and Screening to Enhance National Security. Establishes a framework to ensure that federal executive departments use mutually compatible methods and procedures regarding biometric information of individuals, while respecting their information privacy and other legal rights.
- **HSPD-25**: Arctic Region Policy. Establishes the policy of the United States with respect to the Arctic region and directs related implementation actions.

Source: Homeland Security Digital Library (2014).

Creating DHS would provide the United States with a huge law enforcement capability that would deter, prepare, and prevent any future September 11-type events. Agencies such as the Federal Emergency Management Agency (FEMA) became part of DHS because it was responsible for dealing with the consequences to our communities of natural and technological disasters and had played a major role in providing federal assistance to recover from the previous terrorist events on the US soil: the 1993 World Trade Center bombing and the Murrah Federal Building bombing.

Prior to 9/11, the majority of FEMA's efforts and funding were focused on the mitigation of, preparedness for, response to, and recovery from natural disasters. Much of this changed with the establishment of DHS. Many, if not all, of the grant programs established within the new DHS focused on terrorism. FEMA programs and funding were diverted or reduced to support terrorism. The all-hazards concept was not embraced in the early years of DHS. State and local governments, who were more concerned about their flooding or hurricane threat, had to focus on terrorism. Just like in the 1980s, when FEMA insisted that to be eligible for FEMA grants, state and local governments had to engage in nuclear attack planning, DHS insisted that terrorism planning was the top priority for recipients of funding.

The decision of the 1980s to focus on nuclear attack planning led to the botched response to Hurricane Andrew, under the first Bush administration. The decision by the leadership of DHS to focus on terrorism, at the expense of other threats, and to diminish the role of FEMA led directly to the horrible events and aftermath of Hurricane Katrina (Figure 1-2).

Hurricane Katrina, which struck on August 29, 2005, and resulted in the death of over 1800 people (and the destruction of billions of dollars in housing stock and other infrastructure), exposed significant problems with the United States' emergency management framework. Clearly, the terrorism focus had been maintained at the expense of preparedness and response capacity for other hazards, namely, the natural disasters that have proved to be much more likely to occur. FEMA and likewise DHS were highly criticized by the public and by Congress in the months following the 2005 hurricane season. In response, Congress passed the Post-Katrina Emergency Management Reform Act (H.R. 5441, Public Law 109-295), signed into law by the president on October 4, 2006.

FIGURE 1-2 New Orleans, LA, September 8, 2005—Neighborhoods and roadways throughout the area remain flooded as a result of Hurricane Katrina. *Photo by Jocelyn Augustino/FEMA News Photo.*

This law established several new leadership positions within the Department of Homeland Security, moved additional functions into (several were simply returned) FEMA, created and reallocated functions to other components within DHS, and amended the Homeland Security Act in ways that directly and indirectly affected the organization and functions of various entities within DHS. The changes were required to have gone into effect by March 31, 2007. Transfers that were mandated by the Post-Katrina Emergency Management Reform Act included (with the exception of certain offices as listed in the act) the following:

- United States Fire Administration (USFA)
- Office of Grants and Training (G&T)
- Chemical Stockpile Emergency Preparedness Division (CSEP)
- Radiological Emergency Preparedness Program (REPP)
- Office of National Capital Region Coordination (NCRC)

In passing this act, Congress reminded DHS that the natural disaster threats to the United States were every bit as real as the terrorist threats and required changes to the organization and operations of DHS to provide a more balanced approach to the concepts of homeland security in addressing the threats impacting the United States.

Upon taking office in January 2009, the Obama administration once again made responding to major disaster events a top priority for DHS and FEMA. The appointment by President Obama of Craig Fugate, the then director of the Florida Division of Emergency Management, as FEMA administrator marked only the second time that FEMA has been led by an experienced emergency manager. FEMA successfully managed the response by the federal government in support of state and local governments in 11 states to Hurricane Sandy in 2012. In April 2013, DHS, FBI, and other federal law enforcement agencies responded effectively to the Boston Marathon bombings, working in close support of the Boston Police Department and the Massachusetts State Police in identifying and capturing the bombing suspects.

The Obama administration is building on the past efforts of the Bush administration to understand and implement a more balanced, universal approach to homeland security. This balanced approach is reflected in the first-ever Quadrennial Homeland Security Review (QHSR) published by the Obama administration and DHS in February 2010. A second Quadrennial Homeland Security Review was completed in June 2014. In the years since the events of September 11 and the establishment of DHS, knowledge and recognition of the real scope of threats and hazards to the United States have greatly increased.

When we look at how fast ideas, goods, and people move around the world and through the Internet, we recognize that this flow of materials is critical to the economic stability and the advancement of the US interests. However, this globalization of information and commerce creates new security challenges that are borderless and unconventional. As evidenced by the US and European economic recession and the Arab Spring in 2011 and the rise of the Islamic state also known as ISIS or ISIL in 2014, entire economies and groups organized through social media, and the criminal networks and terrorist organizations now have the ability to impact the world with far-reaching effects, including those that are potentially disruptive and destructive to our way of life.

The 2014 QHSR acknowledges that the threats and challenges facing DHS continue to evolve noting, "In this report, we conclude that we will continue to adhere to the five basic homeland security missions set forth in the first Quadrennial Homeland Security Review report in 2010, but that these missions must be refined to reflect the evolving landscape of homeland security threats and hazards. The Deepwater Horizon oil spill in 2010, Hurricane Sandy in 2012, and the Boston Marathon bombing in 2013 illustrate these evolving threats and hazards. We must constantly learn from them and adapt. The terrorist threat is increasingly decentralized and may be harder to detect. Cyber threats are growing and pose ever-greater concern to our critical infrastructure systems as they become increasingly interdependent. Natural hazards are becoming more costly to address, with increasingly variable consequences due in part to drivers such as climate change and interdependent and aging infrastructure" (DHS, 2014).

As noted in the sidebar "Drivers of Change and Prevailing Challenges," homeland security is certainly becoming tied to the impacts of globalization.

Drivers of Change and Prevailing Challenges

Drivers of Change	Prevailing Challenges
• Evolving terrorist threat	• Evolving terrorist threat
• Information and communications technology	• Growing cyber threats
• Natural disasters, pandemics, and climate change	• Biological concerns
• Interdependent and aging critical infrastructure systems and networks	• Nuclear terrorism
• Flows of people and goods: increasing volume and speed	• Transnational criminal organizations
• Budget drivers	• Natural hazards

Source: DHS (2014).

Critical Thinking

Can you identify the reasons why FEMA should not have been incorporated into the new DHS?

A New Concept of Homeland Security

Reflecting the increasingly complex issues surrounding homeland security, the 2010 QHSR revised the definition of homeland security to incorporate a more global and comprehensive approach. The department now identifies with the "homeland security enterprise (HSE)."

Then DHS Secretary Janet Napolitano, in her letter in the 2010 QHSR, describes the HSE as "the Federal, State, local, tribal, territorial, nongovernmental, and private-sector entities, as well as individuals, families, and communities who share a common national interest in the safety and security of America and the American population. DHS is one among many components of this national enterprise. In some areas, like securing our borders or managing our immigration system, the Department possesses unique capabilities and, hence, responsibilities. In other areas, such as critical infrastructure protection or emergency management, the Department's role is largely one of leadership and stewardship on behalf of those who have the capabilities to get the job done. In still other areas, such as counterterrorism, defense, and diplomacy, other Federal departments and agencies have critical roles and responsibilities, including the Departments of Justice, Defense, and State, the Federal Bureau of Investigation, and the National Counterterrorism Center. Homeland security will only be optimized when we fully leverage the distributed and decentralized nature of the entire enterprise in the pursuit of our common goals."

The Executive Summary of the 2010 QHSR elaborates on the definition of homeland security as "the intersection of evolving threats and hazards with traditional governmental and civic responsibilities for civil defense, emergency response, law enforcement, customs, border control, and immigration. In combining these responsibilities under one overarching concept, homeland security breaks down longstanding stovepipes of activity that have been and could still be exploited by those seeking to harm America. Homeland security also creates a greater emphasis on the need for joint actions and efforts across previously discrete elements of government and society" (DHS, 2010).

By creating this broader definition of homeland security, DHS is stressing the diversity of organizations and individuals who have responsibility for, and interest in, the safety and security of the United States—from the president, as commander in chief; to the secretary of DHS and secretaries of other federal departments and agencies (D&As); to governors, mayors, city council chairs, business leaders, nongovernmental leaders, educators, first responders, and neighborhood watch captains; to each and every citizen. Under this definition, with the diversity of stakeholders, no single person or entity is wholly responsible for achieving homeland security; it is a shared responsibility.

DHS defined the following three concepts as the foundation for a comprehensive approach to homeland security:

1. *Security*: Protect the United States and its people, vital interests, and way of life.
2. *Resilience*: Foster individual, community, and system robustness, adaptability, and capacity for rapid recovery.
3. *Customs and exchange*: Expedite and enforce lawful trade, travel, and immigration.

The 2010 QHSR noted the following about security: "Homeland security relies on our shared efforts to prevent and deter attacks by identifying and interdicting threats, denying hostile actors the ability to operate within our borders, and protecting the Nation's critical infrastructure and key resources. Initiatives that strengthen our protections, increase our vigilance, and reduce our vulnerabilities remain important components of our security. This is not to say, however, that security is a static undertaking. We know that the global systems that carry people, goods, and data around the globe also facilitate the movement of *dangerous* people, goods, and data, and that within these systems of transportation and transaction, there are key nodes—for example, points of origin and transfer, or border crossings—that represent opportunities for interdiction. Thus, we must work to confront threats at every point along their supply chain—supply chains that often begin abroad. To ensure our homeland security then, we must engage our international allies, and employ the full breadth of our national capacity—from the Federal Government, to State, local, tribal, and territorial police, other law enforcement entities, the Intelligence Community, and the private sector—and appropriately enlist the abilities of millions of American citizens" (Figure 1-3) (DHS, 2010).

On resilience, the 2010 QHSR had the following explanation of resilience "to foster individual, community, and system robustness, adaptability, and capacity for rapid recovery. Our country and the world are underpinned by interdependent networks along which the essential elements of economic prosperity—people, goods and resources, money, and information—all flow. While these networks reflect progress and increased efficiency, they are also sources of vulnerability. The consequences of events are no longer confined to a single point; a disruption in one place can ripple through the system and have immediate, catastrophic, and multiplying consequences across the country and around the world" (Figure 1-4) (DHS, 2010).

The third concept in the foundation of the HSE as discussed in the 2010 QSHR is customs and exchange. Under this concept, DHS seeks to "expedite and enforce lawful trade, travel, and immigration. The partners and stakeholders of the HSE are responsible for facilitating and expediting the lawful

FIGURE 1-3 A Customs and Border Protection (CBP) officer directs a truck with a seaport container to an inspection area at a port. *DHS photo by James R. Tourtellotte. http://www.cbp.gov/xp/cgov/newsroom/multimedia/photo_gallery/afc/field_ops/inspectors_seaports/cs_photo26.xml.*

FIGURE 1-4 Greensburg, KS, May 16, 2007—The center of town 12 days after it was hit by an F5 tornado with 200 mph winds. Debris removal is moving at a record pace, but reconstruction will likely take years. *Photo by Greg Henshall/FEMA News Photo.*

movement of people and goods into and out of the United States. This responsibility intersects with and is deeply linked to the enterprise's security function. We need a smarter, more holistic approach that embeds security and resilience directly into global movement systems. Strengthening our economy and promoting lawful trade, travel, and immigration must include security and resilience, just as security and resilience must include promoting a strong and competitive US economy, welcoming lawful immigrants, and protecting civil liberties and the rule of law. We view security along with customs and exchange as mutually reinforcing and inextricably intertwined through actions such as screening, authenticating, and maintaining awareness of the flow of people, goods, and information around the world and across our borders" (Figure 1-5) (DHS, 2010).

In his opening letter to the 2014 QHSR, DHS Secretary Jeh Johnson noted, "Since taking office as Secretary of DHS on December 23, 2013, I have reviewed this report, and I concur with its recommendations. Reflecting deep analysis of the evolving strategic environment and outlining the specific strategic shifts necessary to keep our Nation secure, this report reflects the more focused, collaborative Departmental strategy, planning, and analytic capability that is necessary for achieving Departmental unity" (DHS, 2014).

The 2014 QHSR builds on the work of the 2010 QHSR and states that "In this report, we conclude that we will continue to adhere to the five basic homeland security missions set forth in the first Quadrennial Homeland Security Review report in 2010, but that these missions must be refined to reflect the evolving landscape of homeland security threats and hazards. The Deepwater Horizon oil spill in 2010, Hurricane Sandy in 2012, and the Boston Marathon bombing in 2013 illustrate these evolving threats and hazards. We must constantly learn from them and adapt. The terrorist threat is increasingly decentralized and may be harder to detect. Cyber threats are growing and pose ever-greater concern to our critical infrastructure systems as they become increasingly interdependent. Natural hazards are becoming more costly to address, with increasingly variable consequences due in part to drivers such as climate change and interdependent and aging infrastructure.

Meanwhile, this Nation's homeland security architecture has matured over the past four years, and we are determined that this progress continue. For example, our law enforcement and intelligence communities

FIGURE 1-5 A Border Patrol agent uses a computer word translator to assist in determining the needs of this illegal immigrant. *DHS photo by James Tourtellotte. http://www.cbp.gov/xp/cgov/newsroom/multimedia/photo_gallery/afc/bp/32.xml.*

are becoming increasingly adept at identifying and disrupting terrorist plotting in this country. Programs such as TSA Pre✓™ and Global Entry demonstrate the effectiveness and efficiency of risk-based security that can be achieved within budget constraints. It is also worth noting that, in late 2013, DHS received its first unqualified or 'clean' audit opinion; this occurred just 10 years after the Department's formation, which was the largest realignment and consolidation of Federal Government agencies and functions since the creation of the Department of Defense in 1947" (DHS, 2014).

The 2014 QHSR identified the five basic homeland security missions. Descriptions of these missions from the 2014 QHSR are presented in the two sidebars "DHS's Five Basic Homeland Security Missions" and "Fire Core Missions and Goals Identified by DHS."

DHS's Five Basic Homeland Security Missions

Prevent Terrorism and Enhance Security: Preventing terrorist attacks on the Nation is and should remain the cornerstone of homeland security. Since the last quadrennial review in 2010, the terrorist threat to the Nation has evolved, but it remains real and may even be harder to detect. The Boston Marathon bombing illustrates the evolution of the threat. Through the US Government's counterterrorism efforts, we have degraded the ability of al-Qa'ida's senior leadership in Afghanistan and Pakistan to centrally plan and execute sophisticated external attacks. But since 2009, we have seen the rise of al-Qa'ida affiliates, such as al-Qa'ida in the Arabian Peninsula, which has made repeated attempts to export terrorism to our Nation. Additionally, we face the threat of domestic-based "lone offenders" and those who are inspired by extremist ideologies to radicalize to violence and commit acts of terrorism against Americans and the Nation. These threats come in multiple forms and, because of the nature of independent actors, may be hardest to detect. We must remain vigilant in detecting and countering these threats. Given the nature of this threat, engaging the public and private sectors through campaigns, such as "If You See Something, Say Something™" and the Nationwide Suspicious Activity Reporting Initiative, and through partnering across federal, state, local, tribal, and territorial law enforcement will, over the next 4 years, become even more important.

Secure and Manage Our Borders: We must continue to improve upon border security, to exclude terrorist threats, drug traffickers, and other threats to national security, economic security, and public safety. We will rely on enhanced technology to screen incoming cargo at ports of entry and will work with foreign partners to monitor the international travel of individuals of suspicion who seek to enter this country. We will continue to emphasize risk-based strategies that are smart, cost-effective, and conducted in a manner that is acceptable to the American people. We must remain agile in responding to new trends in illegal migration, from Central America or elsewhere. Meanwhile, we recognize the importance of continuing efforts to promote and expedite lawful travel and trade that will continue to strengthen our economy.

Enforce and Administer Our Immigration Laws: We will continually work to better enforce our immigration laws and administer our immigration system. We support common-sense immigration reform legislation that enhances border security, prevents and discourages employers from hiring undocumented workers, streamlines our immigration processing system, and provides an earned pathway to citizenship for the estimated 11.5 million undocumented immigrants in this country. It is indeed a matter of homeland security and common sense that we encourage those physically present in this country to come out of the shadows and to be held accountable. Offering the opportunity to these 11.5 million people—most of whom have been here 10 years or more and, in many cases, came here as children—is also consistent with American values and our Nation's heritage. We will take a smart, effective, and efficient risk-based approach to border security and interior enforcement and continually evaluate the best use of resources to prioritize the removal of those who represent threats to public safety and national security.

Safeguard and Secure Cyberspace: We must, over the next 4 years, continue efforts to address the growing cyber threat, illustrated by the real, pervasive, and ongoing series of attacks on our public and private infrastructure. This infrastructure provides essential services such as energy, telecommunications, water, transportation, and financial services and is increasingly subject to sophisticated cyber intrusions, which pose new risks. As the Federal Government's coordinator of efforts to counter cyber threats and other hazards to critical infrastructure, DHS must work with both public and private sector partners to share information, help make sure new infrastructure is designed and built to be more secure and resilient, and continue advocating internationally for openness and security of the Internet and harmony across international laws to combat cybercrime. Further, DHS must secure the Federal Government's information technology systems by approaching federal systems and networks as an integrated whole and by researching, developing, and rapidly deploying cybersecurity solutions and services at the pace that cyber threats evolve. And finally, we must continue to develop cyber law enforcement, incident response, and reporting capabilities by increasing the number and impact of cybercrime investigations, sharing information about tactics and methods of cyber criminals gleaned through investigations, and ensuring that incidents reported to any federal department or agency are shared across the US Government. In addition, the Federal Government must continue to develop good working relationships with the private sector, lower barriers to partnership, develop cybersecurity best practices, promote advanced technology that can exchange information at machine speed, and build the cyber workforce of tomorrow for DHS and the Nation.

Strengthen National Preparedness and Resilience: Acting on the lessons of Hurricane Katrina, we have improved disaster planning with federal, state, local, tribal, and territorial governments, as well as nongovernmental organizations and the private sector; pre-positioned a greater number of resources; and strengthened the Nation's ability to respond to disasters in a quick and robust fashion. Seven years after Katrina, the return on these investments showed in the strong, coordinated response to Hurricane Sandy. We must continue this progress.

Source: DHS (2014).

Five Core Missions and Goals Identified by DHS

Mission 1: Prevent Terrorism and Enhance Security

- **Goal 1.1:** Prevent Terrorist Attacks
- **Goal 1.2:** Prevent and Protect Against the Unauthorized Acquisition or Use of Chemical, Biological, Radiological, and Nuclear Materials and Capabilities
- **Goal 1.3:** Reduce Risk to the Nation's Critical Infrastructure, Key Leadership, and Events

Mission 2: Secure and Manage Our Borders

- **Goal 2.1:** Secure US Air, Land, and Sea Borders and Approaches
- **Goal 2.2:** Safeguard and Expedite Lawful Trade and Travel
- **Goal 2.3:** Disrupt and Dismantle Transnational Criminal Organizations and Other Illicit Actors

Mission 3: Enforce and Administer Our Immigration Laws

- **Goal 3.1:** Strengthen and Effectively Administer the Immigration System
- **Goal 3.2:** Prevent Unlawful Immigration

Mission 4: Safeguard and Secure Cyberspace

- **Goal 4.1:** Strengthen the Security and Resilience of Critical Infrastructure
- **Goal 4.2:** Secure the Federal Civilian Government Information Technology Enterprise
- **Goal 4.3:** Advance Law Enforcement, Incident Response, and Reporting Capabilities
- **Goal 4.4:** Strengthen the Ecosystem

Mission 5: Strengthen National Preparedness and Resilience

- **Goal 5.1:** Enhance National Preparedness
- **Goal 5.2:** Mitigate Hazards and Vulnerabilities
- **Goal 5.3:** Ensure Effective Emergency Response
- **Goal 5.4:** Enable Rapid Recovery

Source: DHS (2014).

As noted in the 2010 QHSR, public safety officials, including police, fire, public health, emergency management, and border security, will continue to be in the forefront of mitigation, preparedness, response, and recovery from the potential threat of terrorism, natural hazards, and other man-made hazards. However, the new concept of an HSE broadened the spectrum of responsibility to include risk managers, computer analysts, public policy officials, health and environmental practitioners, economic development leaders, educators, the media, businesses, and other elected officials responsible for the safety of their communities. Each and every individual is now responsible for helping to achieve the HSE.

The 2014 QHSR builds on this inclusive message calling for the full involvement of the whole community in addressing the evolving threats and hazards facing our country. This doctrine is in line with FEMA's "Whole Community" concept and significantly increases the involvement of the public, the private sector, and nongovernmental organizations in the nation's homeland security efforts.

Not everyone is enamored with the new HSE. Several individuals and organizations have questioned whether it is just another example of the DHS trying to rebrand an organization that is not well understood by the public. The main public/DHS interface is either being subjected to TSA security at airports or reading about immigration raids and Border Patrol problems. Perspectives on the 2010 and 2014 QHSRs are presented in the following sidebars: "America's Failing 'Homeland Security Enterprise'" and "DHS Releases Quadrennial Homeland Security Review."

Another Voice: America's Failing "Homeland Security Enterprise" by Tom Barry, Border Lines Blog, February 2010

They don't know what it is, so they call it an "enterprise."

In the tradition of the Defense Department's quadrennial review, Janet Napolitano, secretary of the Department of Homeland Security, released the department's first *Homeland Security Quadrennial Review* on February 1. As part of an attempt to address the department's deep-seated identity problem and to distinguish it from its DOD big brother, DHS now refers to itself as a "Homeland Security Enterprise."

George W. Bush will be remembered as the president who created this unwieldy new federal bureaucracy as part of his "Global War on Terror." But Democratic Party security hardliners like Sen. Joe Lieberman of Connecticut were some of the original proponents of a homeland security department, and the new Democratic Party administration of Barack Obama has unconditionally embraced the department as a core government institution.

Rather than using the review (mandated by Congress in 2007 in the midst of rising criticism of DHS) as an opportunity to reexamine the wisdom of creating this amalgam of 22 separate agencies organized around the homeland security theme, the Obama administration is allowing the department to consolidate and expand. Last year the administration moved ahead with plans to construct a $3.4 billion building to house this sprawling admixture of disparate agencies. The newly released *Quadrennial Review* now outlines plans for "maturing and strengthening the homeland security enterprise," and the department's budget will rise 2% in 2011.

Faced with persistent criticism about management, oversight, and its lack of a unifying mission, DHS is putting a new spin on its diffuse identity. In the *Quadrennial Review*, DHS states: "Homeland security is a distributed and diverse national enterprise."

According to DHS, the term enterprise "refers to the collective efforts and shared responsibilities of Federal, State, local, tribal, territorial, nongovernmental, and private-sector partners—as well as individuals, families, and communities—to maintain critical homeland security capabilities. It recognizes the diverse risks, needs, and priorities of these different stakeholders, and connotes a broad-based community with a common interest in the public safety and well-being of America and American society."

Politics and a rush to create a new font of security-related funding were largely responsible for the ill-considered creation of DHS; and the continuing search for meaning and definition at DHS, as illustrated by this new DHS report, underscores the department's fundamental and continuing dysfunction.

It's worth recalling that, as part of his aggressive but badly focused response to the September 11 attacks, President Bush created at first not a department but rather a new White House office—the Office of Homeland Security. However, the homeland security office, headed by Pennsylvania governor Tom Ridge, was short-lived. Congressional Democrats, led by Senator Lieberman, insisted that the country needed more than an executive office to monitor domestic security.

According to Lieberman, the country needed a full-fledged homeland security department to organize domestically against terrorism. Lieberman, a leading Senate hawk and foreign policy neoconservative, also began beating the drums of war. He campaigned for the launching of wars against Iraq and Iran in the aftermath of September 11, as well as for boosting the Pentagon's budget and its domestic response capabilities.

President Bush—although increasingly won over by the neoconservative foreign policy agenda promoted by Lieberman and others—initially rejected the senator's demand for the creation of a homeland security department, arguing that bureaucratic expansion was a typically big-government Democratic response. But nine months after September 11, President Bush reversed course, tacitly accepting the proposals of congressional Democrats led by Lieberman to establish a new department.

In announcing his plan to establish the department on June 6, 2002, President Bush declared that the government should "be reorganized to meet the new threats of the 21st century" and that the new department would involve "the most extensive reorganization of the federal government since the 1940s."

Although the Homeland Security Act of 2002 was largely his proposal, it did not bear Lieberman's name but was sold to Congress as the president's initiative. But having succeeded in his mission to expand the nation's security apparatus, Lieberman didn't begrudge the president and the Republicans for having adopted his proposal. Instead, he began pushing hard for the other parts of his security agenda.

In a speech to the Progressive Policy Institute (an affiliate of the center-right Democratic Leadership Council) on June 26, 2002, Lieberman not only reiterated his vision for a domestic defense department but also proposed adopting a new vision of the Pentagon's role in the domestic response to terrorism. With respect to the need for a homeland security department, Lieberman proclaimed:

> *Our challenge and our responsibility after September 11th is to meet the deadly fervor of our terrorist enemies by adapting, responding, and reforming to protect our people from future attacks.*
>
> *For the U.S. Congress today, that means taking the disconnected pieces of a disorganized federal bureaucracy and reordering them into a unified, focused domestic defense department. While we create the new department, we must also develop a coherent and comprehensive homeland security strategy that can and will safeguard the American people—and that the new department can implement as soon as it is up and running.*

But the core of Lieberman's speech concerned not this new "domestic defense department" but the Defense Department itself. As Lieberman told his fellow Democrats:

> *Today I want to talk to you about what should be one of the core components of such a larger strategy: maximizing the use of our military resources here at home. Our Department of Defense has more tools, training, technology, and talent to help combat the terrorist threat at home than any other federal agency. Our military has proven capable of brilliance beyond our borders. Now, we must tap its expertise and its resources within our country—by better integrating the Defense Department into our homeland security plans.*

Lieberman went on to sketch out his proposal for the Pentagon's own role in domestic defense, with the homeland security department as its new junior partner. He set forth his vision of a well-funded security sector at home, including expanded domestic use of the National Guard by the Pentagon, funding for a new array of security technologies, and stepped-up intelligence operations.

This post-September 11 rush to create a new security department and at the same time beef-up the Pentagon's and intelligence community's role in counterterrorism at home rose in part from a new bipartisan fervor to protect the homeland and strike out against Islamist terrorists.

But the birthing of DHS cannot be explained without also considering how military contractors and their politician partners had begun rallying around proposals calling for Congress and the White House to unleash vast sums of federal revenues in new homeland security-related contracts, issued either by the new department or by the Pentagon and the intelligence agencies.

Source: Barry (2010).

DHS's Missing Mission

From its conception, the Department of Homeland Security was a hodgepodge without a clear mission or clear authority. It brought together 22 agencies and more than a hundred bureaus and subagencies. The decision as to which agencies to include was based more on political bargaining than on any clarity about the department's mission or what it would take to create a cohesive department.

The one entity that had already had a mission somewhat aligned with the notion of homeland security was the National Guard, but it was reported that White House officials couldn't figure out how to extract the Guard from the DOD. It was also likely that both the Democratic Party architects of homeland security and White House officials saw from the beginning that DHS in counterterrorism matters would always be subservient to the DOD, the intelligence agencies, and to a certain extent the FBI.

Organizational and mission problems plagued DHS from the start, as excellently reported by the *Washington Post* in its December 22, 2005, investigative article, "Department's Mission Undermined from the Start." Reporters Susan B. Glasser and Michael Grunwald concluded:

> *DHS was initially expected to synthesize intelligence, secure borders, protect infrastructure and prepare for the next catastrophe. For most of those missions, the bipartisan Sept. 11 commission recently gave the Bush administration D's or F's. To some extent, the department was set up to fail. It was assigned the awesome responsibility of defending the homeland without the investigative, intelligence and military powers of the FBI, CIA and the Pentagon; it was also repeatedly undermined by the White House that initially opposed its creation. But the department has also struggled to execute even seemingly basic tasks, such as prioritizing America's most critical infrastructure.*

The DHS's *Quadrennial Review* strains to formulate a strategic framework for the HSE. The creation of DHS added another vast bureaucracy—with a $50 billion-plus department—and to its security apparatus without bothering to explain to voters and taxpayers why such a multidepartmental complex is necessary.

As was to be expected, the initial strategic foundation of DHS was counterterrorism—warding off and responding to attacks on the homeland. The founding National Strategy for Homeland Security, issued on July 2002, declared that the department's mission was to "mobilize and organize our nation to secure the US homeland from terrorist attacks." The strategy statement defined homeland security as "a concerted national effort to prevent terrorist attacks within the United States, reduce America's vulnerability to terrorism, and minimize the damage and recover from attacks that do occur."

One problem with such a formulation was that in the first two of these three functions, the new department played only a supporting role to the FBI, DOD, and intelligence community. Another problem became startlingly clear on August 2005 when DHS flailed in face of the disaster left in the wake of Hurricane Katrina. DHS, organized around a counterterrorism mission—albeit for politically opportunistic reasons and in a shockingly reckless fashion—grossly failed its first test.

Another Voice: "DHS Releases Quadrennial Homeland Security Review" by Dan Verton, FedScoop, June 20, 2014

The Homeland Security Department Thursday released its strategic vision and priorities for the next 4 years as part of a process required by Congress known as the Quadrennial Homeland Security Review.

The release of the 103-page document, however, met stiff resistance in the House, where members of the House Homeland Security Committee held a hearing Friday criticizing the department for delivering the report six months late—well after it could have helped guide the president's 2015 budget request—and for its failure to address significant management deficiencies that many argue have prevented DHS from becoming a more integrated and agile agency capable of keeping up with a rapidly changing threat landscape.

"Year after year, DHS has ranked at or near the bottom of federal agencies and many public sector agency performance rankings," Rep. Jeff Duncan, R-S.C., chairman of the Subcommittee on Oversight and Management Efficiency, said during a hearing to examine the DHS strategy document. "There seems to be a lack of aligning resources with strategic priorities. While the QHSR briefly mentions budget drivers, in general it does not link specific mission areas to the actual budget."

House Homeland Security Committee chairman Rep. Michael McCaul, R-Texas, said the latest DHS strategy guidance is "more important than ever" given the increasing threats from resurgent terrorist groups overseas, continued border security weaknesses and the constant barrage of major cyber attacks against critical infrastructures.

"While I am encouraged by the emphasis of public-private partnerships and a risk-based approach to homeland security outlined in the QHSR, I am concerned that once again the Department has failed to make a link between their strategy and the resources necessary to implement," McCaul said in a statement. "In addition, the QHSR's lack of focus on management initiatives within the Department is troubling. To strengthen the Department, workforce challenges must also be addressed," he said.

Stewart Baker, a partner at the law firm Steptoe & Johnson LLP and the first Assistant Secretary for Policy at DHS, said the quality and depth of the QHSR has improved significantly since the first review was issued in 2010, but there are areas that lack proper attention.

"With respect to cyber security, the 2014 QHSR has little new to say about the need to recruit and develop a skilled cyber security workforce," Baker said in his testimony. "It also does not appropriately prioritize the importance of protecting critical U.S. infrastructure from espionage. To be sure, there are parts of the QHSR that need work. Nonetheless, on balance the report is an improvement over its predecessor."

But at a more fundamental and tactical level, DHS needs to be able to respond quicker to emerging threats, said Frank Cilluffo, director of the Homeland Security Policy Institute at The George Washington University and a former special assistant to President George W. Bush on homeland security issues. "We can't wait four years for strategies," Cilluffo said. "You need a department that's agile. I recommended an Office of Net Assessment along the lines of what the [Defense Department] has. That has played a significant role in protecting our country from a defense perspective. I think DHS would be well served if it had something that was nimble, agile and doesn't have to wait four years to put together a strategy when the world changes so dramatically overnight."

Source: Verton (2014).

Critical Thinking

What do you think were the reasons for DHS establishing the HSE?

Based on your current knowledge of homeland security, describe the responsibilities a mayor, a nongovernmental organization leader, or a citizen would have for achieving homeland security.

The Department of Homeland Security

On November 25, 2002, President Bush signed into law the Homeland Security Act of 2002 (HS Act) (Public Law 107-296) and announced that former Pennsylvania Governor Tom Ridge would become secretary of a new DHS to be created through this legislation. This act, which authorized the greatest federal government reorganization since President Harry Truman joined the various branches of the armed forces under the Department of Defense, was charged with a threefold mission of protecting the United States from further terrorist attacks, reducing the nation's vulnerability to terrorism and minimizing the damage from potential terrorist attacks and natural disasters.

The sweeping reorganization into the new department, which officially opened its doors on January 24, 2003, joined more than 179,000 federal employees from 22 existing federal agencies under a single, cabinet-level organization. The legislation, which was not restricted to the newly created department, also transformed several other federal agencies that at first glance may have appeared only remotely affiliated with the homeland security mission. To the affected government employees, millions of concerned American citizens, the entire world media, and even the terrorists themselves, it was clear that the US government was entering a new era.

The creation of the DHS was the culmination of an evolutionary legislative process that began largely in response to criticism that increased interagency cooperation between federal intelligence organizations could have prevented the September 11 terrorist attacks. Based on the findings of several pre-September 11 commissions, it appeared that the country needed a centralized federal government agency whose primary reason for existence would be to coordinate the security of the "homeland" (a term that predated the attacks). The White House and Congress were both well aware that any homeland security czar position they conceived would require both an adequate staff and a large budget to succeed. Thus, in early 2002, deliberations began to create a new cabinet-level department that would fuse many of the security-related agencies dispersed throughout the federal government.

For several months during the second half of 2002, Congress jockeyed between differing versions of the homeland security bill in an effort to establish legislation that was passable yet effective. Lawmakers were particularly mired on the issue of the rights of the 179,000 affected employees—an issue that prolonged the legislative process considerably. Furthermore, efforts to incorporate many of the intelligence-gathering and investigative law enforcement agencies, namely, the National Security Agency (NSA), the Federal Bureau of Investigation (FBI), and the Central Intelligence Agency (CIA), into the legislation failed.

Despite these delays and setbacks, after the 2002 midterm elections, the Republican seats that were gained in both the House and Senate gave the president the leverage he needed to pass the bill without further deliberation (House of Representatives, 299-121 on November 13, 2002; Senate, 90-9 on November 19, 2002). While the passage of this act represented a significant milestone, the implementation phase to come presented a tremendous challenge.

Critical Thinking

Do you think that the CIA should have been moved into DHS? If so, why, or if not, why not?

The Department of Transportation's Office of Lifeline Safety was not moved into DHS. What would the reasons be to keep it in the Department of Transportation and not move it to DHS?

Department of Homeland Security Establishment Timeline

September 11, 2001—Terrorist attacks occurred in Washington, DC, New York, and Pennsylvania.

September 20, 2001—In an address to Congress, President Bush announced the creation of the Office of Homeland Security (OHS) and the appointment of Tom Ridge as director.

October 8, 2001—President Bush swore in Tom Ridge as assistant to the president for homeland security and issued an executive order creating the OHS.

October 9, 2001—President Bush swore in General Wayne Downing as director of the Office of Combating Terrorism (OCT) and issued an executive order creating the OCT.

October 16, 2001—President Bush issued an executive order establishing the president's Critical Infrastructure Protection Board to coordinate and have cognizance of federal efforts and programs that relate to protection of information systems.

October 26, 2001—President Bush signed the USA PATRIOT Act.

October 29, 2001—President Bush chaired the first meeting of the Homeland Security Council (HSC) and issued Homeland Security Presidential Directive No. 1 (HSPD-1), establishing the organization and operation of the HSC and HSPD-2, establishing the Foreign Terrorist Tracking Task Force, and increasing immigration vigilance.

November 8, 2001—President Bush announced that the Corporation for National and Community Service (CNCS) will support homeland security, "mobilizing more than 20,000 Senior Corps and AmeriCorps participants."

November 8, 2001—President Bush created the Presidential Task Force on Citizen Preparedness in the War against Terrorism to "help prepare Americans in their homes, neighborhoods, schools, workplaces, places of worship and public places from the potential consequences of terrorist attacks."

November 15, 2001—FEMA announced the Individual and Family Grant program for disaster assistance.

January 30, 2002—President Bush issued an executive order establishing the USA Freedom Corps, encouraging all Americans to serve their country for the equivalent of at least 2 years (4000 h) over their lifetimes.

February 4, 2002—President Bush submitted the president's budget for FY 2003 to Congress, directing $37.7 billion to homeland security (up from $19.5 billion in FY 2002).

March 12, 2002—President Bush established the Homeland Security Advisory System (HSPD-3).

March 19, 2002—President Bush issued an executive order establishing the president's Homeland Security Advisory Council.

September 17, 2002—President Bush declared the National Strategy to Combat Weapons of Mass Destruction (HSPD-4).

November 25, 2002—President Bush signed the Homeland Security Act of 2002 (HR 5005) as Public Law 107-296. Tom Ridge was announced as secretary, Navy Secretary Gordon England was nominated as deputy secretary of the DHS, and Drug Enforcement Agency (DEA) Administrator Asa Hutchinson was nominated as the undersecretary of border and transportation security.

January 24, 2003—Sixty days after it was signed, the Homeland Security Act became effective.

February 28, 2003—President Bush called for the creation of the National Incident Management System (NIMS) through HSPD-5.

March 1, 2003—Most affected federal agencies were incorporated into the DHS.

June 1, 2003—All remaining affected federal agencies were incorporated into the DHS.

Source: Compiled from Multiple Sources, by Damon Coppola, January 2003.

The Department of Homeland Security is a massive agency, juggling numerous responsibilities between a staggeringly wide range of program areas, employing approximately 240,000 people (as of November 2014), and managing a massive $50+ billion-dollar budget and an ambitious list of tasks and goals. The department leverages resources within federal, state, and local governments, coordinating the ongoing transition of multiple agencies and programs into a single, integrated agency focused on protecting the American people and their homeland. In total, more than 87,000 different governmental jurisdictions at the federal, state, and local levels have homeland security responsibilities.

At the federal level, the DHS organizational composition remains in a state of flux. Scattered readjustments have occurred throughout its first years of existence, with multiple offices being passed between the department's components. Though it seemed by the end of DHS Secretary Tom Ridge's years of service that the basic organizational makeup had been established, incoming DHS Secretary Chertoff proposed several fundamental changes to the department's organization, which were implemented under Secretary Chertoff's reorganization plan. Again, the department was reorganized following the 2005 hurricane season according to the requirements of the Post-Katrina Emergency Management Reform Act (PKEMRA) of 2006.

The Obama administration has retained the fundamental organizational structure as mandated by the PKEMRA at the agency and subcomponent level, adding one new subcomponent, an Office of Intergovernmental Affairs. At the subcomponent level, some minor changes were made. There was hope within the emergency management community that President Obama might move FEMA out of DHS and return it to its former status as an independent agency. That did not happen nor does it look like it will ever happen. FEMA's successful response to Hurricane Sandy may have put this idea to rest.

Critical Thinking

Should President Obama have taken FEMA out of DHS and made it an independent agency? Discuss the pros and cons of your opinion.

Other Federal Departments Responsible for the Homeland Security Enterprise

Appendix A of the 2014 QHSR details the roles and responsibilities of the other federal agencies in the HSE. They are summarized below:

- The Department of Justice (DOJ), led by the attorney general, is responsible for the prosecution of federal crimes. The attorney general has lead responsibility for criminal investigations of terrorist acts or terrorist threats by individuals or groups inside the United States or directed at US citizens or institutions abroad, as well as for related intelligence collection activities within the United States. The attorney general leads the Department of Justice, which also includes the Federal Bureau of Investigation, Drug Enforcement Administration, and Bureau of Alcohol, Tobacco, Firearms, and Explosives, each of which has key homeland security responsibilities.
- The Department of State is the lead US foreign affairs agency, and the secretary of state is the president's principal foreign policy adviser. The secretary of state has the responsibility to coordinate activities with foreign governments and international organizations related to the prevention, preparation, response, and recovery from a domestic incident and for the protection of US citizens and US interests overseas. The Department of State also adjudicates and screens visa applications abroad.
- The Department of Defense (DOD) military services, defense agencies, and geographic and functional commands defend the United States from direct attack; deter potential adversaries; foster regional stability; secure and assure access to sea, air, space, and cyberspace; and build the security capacity of key partners. The DOD also provides a wide range of support to civil authorities at the direction of the secretary of defense or the president when the capabilities of state and local authorities to respond effectively to an event are overwhelmed.
- The Department of Health and Human Services leads the coordination of all functions relevant to Public Health Emergency Preparedness and Disaster Medical Response. Additionally, the Department of Health and Human Services (HHS) incorporates steady-state and incident-specific activities as described in the National Health Security Strategy.
- The Department of the Treasury works to safeguard the US financial system, combat financial crimes, and cut off financial support to terrorists, WMD proliferators, drug traffickers, and other national security threats.

- The Department of Agriculture (USDA) provides leadership on food, agriculture, natural resources, rural development, and related issues based on sound public policy, the best available science, and efficient management. The US Department of Agriculture (USDA) is the sector-specific agency for the Food and Agriculture Sector, a responsibility shared with the Food and Drug Administration with respect to food safety and defense.
- Office of the Director of National Intelligence (ODNI). The director of national intelligence serves as the head of the intelligence community (IC), acts as the principal adviser to the president and National Security Council for intelligence matters relating to national security, and oversees and directs the implementation of the National Intelligence Program. In addition to IC elements with specific homeland security missions, the Office of the Director of National Intelligence maintains a number of mission and support centers that provide unique capabilities for homeland security partners, including the National Counterterrorism Center (NCTC) and the National Counterproliferation Center.
- The Department of Commerce promotes job creation, economic growth, sustainable development, and improved standards of living for all Americans. The Department of Commerce is a member of the Mitigation Framework Leadership Group and the coordinating agency and a primary agency for the Economic Recovery Support Function.
- The Department of Education oversees discretionary grants and technical assistance to help schools plan for and respond to emergencies that disrupt teaching and learning. The Department of Education supports the National Health Security Strategy and is a primary agency for the Health and Social Services Recovery Support Function.
- The Department of Energy (DOE) maintains stewardship of vital national security capabilities, from nuclear weapons to leading-edge research and development programs. The DOE is the designated federal agency to provide a unifying structure for the integration of federal critical infrastructure and key resources' protection efforts specifically for the energy sector. It is also responsible for maintaining continuous and reliable energy supplies for the United States through preventive measures and restoration and recovery actions.
- The Environmental Protection Agency (EPA) is charged with protecting human health and the environment.
- The Department of Housing and Urban Development is the coordinator and primary agency for the Housing Recovery Support Function and a member of the Mitigation Framework Leadership Group.
- The Department of the Interior (DOI) develops policies and procedures for all types of hazards and emergencies that impact federal lands, facilities, infrastructure, and resources; tribal lands; and insular areas. The DOI, together with the Department of Agriculture, also operates the National Interagency Fire Center.
- The Department of Transportation (DOT) collaborates with DHS on all matters relating to transportation security and transportation infrastructure protection and in regulating the transportation of hazardous materials by all modes (including pipelines).
- The General Services Administration is a member of the Mitigation Framework Leadership Group.
- The Department of Labor supports the National Health Security Strategy and is a primary agency for the Economic and Health and Social Services Recovery Support Functions. The Department of Labor/Occupational Safety and Health Administration is the coordinating agency for the Worker Safety and Health Support Annex under the National Response Framework.

- The Department of Veterans Affairs is a primary agency for the Health and Social Services Recovery Support Function.
- The Small Business Administration is a member of the Mitigation Framework Leadership Group and a primary agency for the Economic Recovery Support Function.
- Other federal agencies contribute to the homeland security mission in a variety of ways. This includes agencies responsible for either supporting efforts to assure a resilient homeland or collaborating with the departments and agencies noted above in their efforts to secure the homeland.
- The American Red Cross is chartered by Congress to provide relief to survivors of disasters and help people prevent, prepare for, and respond to emergencies (DHS, 2014).

Critical Thinking

After DHS, which federal entity has the most critical role in the HSE and what are the factors that support your choice?

In addition, the 2014 QHSR defines the roles of state and local governments and the private sector, which are summarized in the following sidebar.

Roles and Responsibilities of Nonfederal Government Organizations in Homeland Security

In addition to the roles and responsibilities of federal departments and agencies, other homeland security participants include the following:

- *Private sector entities*, including businesses, industries, private schools, and universities, are integral parts of the community, and they play a wide range of critical roles. The majority of the nation's infrastructure is owned and operated by private sector entities. They take action to align relevant planning, training, exercising, risk management, and investments in security as a necessary component of prudent business planning and operations. During times of disaster, private sector partners provide response resources—including specialized teams, essential services, equipment, and advanced technologies—through public-private emergency plans/partnerships, or mutual aid and assistance agreements, or in response to requests from government and from nongovernmental-volunteer initiatives. In addition, the private sector has a role in building community resiliency by preparing for, responding to, and recovering from emergencies affecting their businesses.
- *Governors* are responsible for overseeing their state's threat prevention activities and the state's response to any emergency or disaster and take an active role in ensuring that other state officials and agencies address the range of homeland security threats, hazards, and challenges. During an emergency, governors will play a number of roles, to include serving as the state's chief communicator and primary source of information on the scope of the disaster, the need for evacuations, and the availability of assistance. Governors are commanders of their National Guards and are able to activate them to assist under state active duty during a disaster and also retain command over their National Guard under Title 32 status. During a

disaster, governors also will need to make decisions regarding the declaration of emergencies or disasters, requests for mutual aid, and calls for federal assistance.

- *State and territorial governments* supplement the activities of cities, counties, and intrastate regions. States administer federal homeland security grants (in certain grant programs) to local and tribal governments, allocating key resources to bolster their prevention and preparedness capabilities. State agencies conduct law enforcement and security activities, protect the governor and other executive leadership, and administer state programs that address the range of homeland security threats, hazards, and challenges. State government officials lead statewide disaster planning and mitigation planning. During response, states coordinate resources and capabilities throughout the state and are responsible for requesting and obtaining resources and capabilities from surrounding states. States often mobilize these substantive resources and capabilities to supplement the local efforts before, during, and after incidents.
- *Tribal leaders* are responsible for the public safety and welfare of their membership. They can serve as both key decision-makers and trusted sources of public information during incidents.
- *Tribal governments*, which have a special status under federal laws and treaties, ensure the provision of essential services to members within their communities and are responsible for developing emergency response and mitigation plans. Tribal governments may coordinate resources and seek assistance from neighboring jurisdictions, states, and the federal government. Depending on location, land base, and resources, tribal governments provide law enforcement, fire, and emergency services and public safety to their members. During a disaster, tribal governments make decisions regarding whether to request a presidential emergency or major disaster declaration independent of the state within which the tribal lands are located.
- *Mayors and other local elected and appointed officials* are responsible for ensuring the public safety and welfare of their residents, serving as their jurisdiction's chief communicator and a primary source of information for homeland security-related information, and are responsible for ensuring their governments are able to carry out emergency response activities. Officials serve as key decision-makers and trusted sources of public information during incidents. In some states, elected officials such as sheriffs or judges also serve as emergency managers, search and rescue officials, and chief law enforcement officers.
- *Local governments* are responsible for the public safety, security, health, and welfare of the people who live in their jurisdictions. Local governments promote the coordination of ongoing protection plans and the implementation of core capabilities and engagement and information sharing with private sector entities, infrastructure owners and operators, and other jurisdictions and regional entities. Local governments also address unique geographic issues, dependencies, and interdependencies among agencies and enterprises and, as necessary, the establishment of agreements for cross jurisdictional and public-private coordination. Local governments provide frontline leadership for local law enforcement, fire, public safety, environmental response, public health, and emergency medical services for preventing, protecting, mitigating, and responding to all manners of hazards and emergencies. They are also responsible for ensuring all citizens receive timely information in a variety of accessible formats and coordinate resources and capabilities during disasters with neighboring jurisdictions, nongovernmental organizations, the state, and the private sector.
- *Nongovernmental organizations* provide sheltering, emergency food supplies, counseling services, and other vital services to support response and promote the recovery of disaster survivors. They often provide specialized services and advocacy that help individuals with

special needs, including those with disabilities, and provide resettlement assistance and services to arriving refugees. They also provide for evacuation, rescue, shelter, and care of animals, including household pets and service animals. Nongovernmental organizations are key partners in preparedness activities to include response and recovery operations.

- *Communities* are unified groups that share goals, values, or purposes, rather than geographic boundaries or jurisdictions. These groups may possess the knowledge and understanding of the threats and hazards, local response capabilities, and requirements within their jurisdictions and have the capacity to alert authorities of those emergencies, capabilities, or needs. During an incident, these groups may be critical in passing along vital communications to individuals and families and supporting response activities in the initial stages of a crisis.
- *Individuals, families, and households* take protective actions and the basic steps to prepare themselves for emergencies, including understanding the threats and hazards that they may face, reducing hazards in and around their homes, preparing an emergency supply kit and household emergency plans (which include care for animals, including household pets and service animals), monitoring emergency communications, volunteering with established organizations, enrolling in training courses, and practicing what to do in an emergency. These preparedness activities help to strengthen community resilience and mitigate the impact of disasters. In addition, individual vigilance and awareness can help communities remain safer and bolster prevention efforts by contacting local law enforcement and sharing information within their communities.

Source: DHS (2014).

DHS has determined that in order to "mature and strengthen" homeland security and the agency itself, it must focus its effort on several strategic areas growing out of each mission area as described in the sidebar. These are the following:

- Integrate intelligence, information sharing, and operations.
- Enhance partnerships and outreach.
- Conduct homeland security research and development.
- Train and exercise frontline operators and first responders.
- Strengthen service delivery and manage DHS resources.

Mature and Strengthen Homeland Security

The strategic aims and objectives for Maturing and Strengthening Homeland Security are drawn from the common themes that emerge from each of the homeland security mission areas.

Integrate Intelligence, Information Sharing, and Operations

- Enhance unity of regional operations coordination and planning.
- Share homeland security information and analysis, threats, and risks.
- Integrate counterintelligence.
- Establish a common security mind-set.
- Preserve civil liberties, privacy, oversight, and transparency in the execution of homeland security activities.

Enhance Partnerships and Outreach

- Promote regional response capacity and civil support.
- Strengthen the ability of federal agencies to support homeland security missions.
- Expand and extend governmental, nongovernmental, domestic, and international partnerships.
- Further enhance the military-homeland security relationship.

Conduct Homeland Security Research and Development

- Scientifically study threats and vulnerabilities.
- Develop innovative approaches and effective solutions.
- Leverage the depth of capacity in national labs, universities, and research centers.

Train and Exercise Frontline Operators and First Responders

- Enhance systems for training, exercising, and evaluating capabilities.
- Support law enforcement, first responder, and risk management training.

Strengthen Service Delivery and Manage DHS Resources

- Recruit, hire, retain, and develop a highly qualified, diverse, effective, mission-focused, and resilient workforce.
- Manage the integrated investment life cycle to ensure that strategic and analytically-based decisions optimize mission performance.

Source: DHS (2014).

The future existence of the DHS seems very safe under the Obama administration. In recent years, DHS and the nation have been tested by the Deepwater Horizon oil spill in 2010, Hurricane Sandy in 2012, and the Boston Marathon bombings in 2013. The massive response to Hurricane Sandy has been judged successful in most quarters, and the coordinated response between federal, state, and local law enforcement to the Boston Marathon bombings illustrated the progress that has been made in marshaling and managing an effective law enforcement response to a domestic terrorist act. DHS has a lot more to do to become an effective federal department on a par with the FEMA of the 1990s, but since 2011, it appears to be making some strides to becoming a mature, disciplined, and effective federal department.

Conclusion

The 2010 QHSR report established a vision for the future of homeland security in the United States. The 2014 QHSR builds on the vision and mission set forth for DHS in the 2010 QHSR. Both documents reflect lessons learned from the past that homeland security is not just about terrorism. While building protections, securing our borders, or preventing terrorism, measures are all critical to homeland security; it encompasses so much more. To be successful, DHS needs to acknowledge and focus on threats other than terrorism, both natural and man-made, that have had devastating impacts on the United States in the past decade. It must recognize and build protective mechanisms for new and evolving threats such as cybercrime. Fundamentally, DHS and homeland security are about protecting the American way of life and ensuring our resilience in a challenging world.

As the DHS matures and critical funding continues, we should have better-trained and better-equipped first responders; a stronger, less vulnerable national infrastructure; more rational immigration and border policies; an enhanced delivery system for public health and new technologies; and mechanisms to improve and safeguard our information, communications, and cyber networks.

DHS is one among many components. It is a department with unique expertise such as securing our borders or managing our immigration system. In many other areas, such as emergency management, the department's role is largely one of leadership among the governmental families to get the job done. In counterterrorism, defense, and diplomacy, other federal departments and agencies have critical roles and responsibilities, including the Departments of Justice, Defense, and State, the Federal Bureau of Investigation, and the National Counterterrorism Center.

As the 2010 QHSR states, "The effectiveness of the evolving concept of homeland security will only be accomplished when we leverage the capabilities of our partners at all levels of government, within the private sector, and among our citizens to achieve the goals of the homeland security enterprise" (DHS, 2010).

The 2014 QHSR concluded, "Four years ago, the first quadrennial review defined homeland security for America in the 21st century as a concerted national effort to ensure a Nation that is safe, secure, and resilient against terrorism and other hazards where American interests, aspirations, and way of life can thrive. Since then, we have developed capabilities and processes to become more risk based, more integrated, and more efficient. This second quadrennial review describes how those capabilities and processes inform us of what challenges lie ahead and how to strategically posture ourselves to address those challenges" (DHS, 2014).

Key Terms

Critical Infrastructure: Critical infrastructure includes any system or asset that, if disabled or disrupted in any significant way, would result in catastrophic loss of life or catastrophic economic loss. Some examples of critical infrastructure include the following:
Public water systems
Primary roadways, bridges, and highways
Key data storage and processing facilities, stock exchanges, or major banking centers
Chemical facilities located in close proximity to large population centers
Major power generation facilities
Hydroelectric facilities and dams
Nuclear power plants

Executive Order: A declaration issued by the president or by a governor that has the force of law. Executive orders are usually based on existing statutory authority and require no action by Congress or the state legislature to become effective.

Federal Response Plan: The FRP was developed to establish a standard process and structure for the systematic, coordinated, and effective delivery of federal assistance to address the consequences of any major disaster or emergency declared under the Robert T. Stafford Disaster Relief and Emergency Assistance Act, as amended. This plan was later replaced by the National Response Plan.

Homeland Security Enterprise: A new concept defined as "the Federal, State, local, tribal, territorial, nongovernmental, and private-sector entities, as well as individuals, families, and communities who share a common national interest in the safety and security of America and the American population."

National Incident Management System: This is a system mandated by Homeland Security Presidential Directive (HSPD) 5 that provides a consistent nationwide approach for governments, the private sector, and nongovernmental organizations to work effectively and efficiently together to prepare for, respond to, and recover from domestic incidents, regardless of cause, size, or complexity.

Presidential Directive: A form of executive order issued by the president that establishes an action or change in the structure or function of the government (generally within the Executive Office). Under President Bush, directives have been termed *Homeland Security Presidential Directives* (HSPDs) and *National Security Presidential Directives* (NSPDs). Under President Clinton, they were termed *Presidential Decision Directives* (PDDs) and *Presidential Review Directives* (PRDs).

Quadrennial Homeland Security Review (QHSR): A comprehensive report published by DHS in February 2010 that establishes the future direction of the DHS and the discipline of homeland security.

Statutory Authority: The legally granted authority, bestowed on the named recipient by a legislature, that provides a government agency, board, or commission the power to perform the various functions, expenditures, and actions as described in the law.

Review Questions

1. What is the Quadrennial Homeland Security Review?
2. What legislation required DHS to undertake the QHSR?
3. What changes to the definition of *homeland security* were manifested in the 2010 QHSR?
4. What are the visionary goals set forth in the 2014 QHSR?
5. How has the PKEMRA influenced the QHSR and DHS?
6. Discuss the role of federal agencies other than DHS in homeland security.
7. Discuss the role of state and local governments in homeland security.
8. Discuss how DHS hopes to mature and strengthen homeland security.

References

Barry, T., 2010. Border Lines blog. http://www.borderlinesblog.blogspot.com/2010/02/Americas-failing-homelandsecurity.html.

Department of Homeland Security, 2010. Quadrennial homeland security review report: a strategic framework for a secure homeland. http://www.dhs.gov/xlibrary/assets/qhsr_report.pdf.

Department of Homeland Security, 2014. The 2014 quadrennial homeland security review. http://www.dhs.gov/quadrennial-homeland-security-review-qhsr (June 18, 2014).

Homeland Security Digital Library, 2014. The Naval Postgraduate School Center for Homeland Defense and Security. https://www.hsdl.org/?search=&page=1&all=HSPD&searchfield=&collection=limited&submitted=Search

Verton, D., 2014. FedScoop. http://fedscoop.com/dhs-releases-quadrennial-homeland-security-review/ (June 20, 2014).

2

Historic Overview of the Terrorist Threat

What You Will Learn

- The evolution of the federal government in responding to emergencies, disasters, and terrorist threats before September 11
- Measures taken to address the terrorism hazard within the United States following the September 11 terrorist attacks
- Significant statutory measures taken before and after September 11
- The actions taken by DHS to address the recommendations in the 9/11 Commission Report and results of the 9/11 Commission 10th anniversary report

Introduction

Harry Truman once said, "The only thing new is the history we don't know." For many Americans, the rush of activities by the government to pass new laws, reorganize government institutions, and allocate vast sums of money in the aftermath of the September 11, 2001, terrorist attacks may have seemed unprecedented. The reality is that similar actions in terms of both type and scope have happened in the past, and these historical experiences can provide insight into the prospect of the ultimate success or failure of the actions that have been taken since the September 11 attacks occurred.

The purpose of this chapter is to provide a historic perspective of the evolution of the programs, policies, and organizations established to address the problem of terrorism, nuclear threats, and other emergencies in the United States. It will examine the chronology of events and actions leading up to and beyond September 11, 2001. This perspective will help frame the issues to be discussed in subsequent chapters of this book, which will detail the legislative, organizational, and operational underpinnings of America's homeland security structure.

This chapter provides summaries of terrorist events aimed at the US government outside its shores including the Khobar Towers bombing and the attack of the USS Cole. Information is provided for the two terrorist incidents prior to September 11: the 1993 World Trade Center (WTC) bombing and the 1995 Oklahoma City bombing of the Murrah Federal Building. There is an extensive section of the tragic events of September 11 including updated statistics and timelines and information on the 9/11 Commission and the July 2011 Department of Homeland Security (DHS) report on Implementing 9/11 Commission Recommendations.

New material will include brief profiles of the April 15, 2013, Boston Marathon bombings and subsequent capture of one of the bombers and the response to the 2012 Hurricane Sandy, information from the 10th anniversary report of the 9/11 Commission.

Before It Was Called Homeland Security: From the 1800s to the Creation of FEMA

The US government has a long history of responding to all types of threats and emergencies before terrorism became an emerging threat in the 1990s. A brief history of the evolution of government's role is outlined below, primarily focusing on the evolution of government response to these threats. It is important to note that each major change was event-driven, just as the attacks of September 11 drove the adoption of homeland security.

In 1803, a congressional act was passed to provide financial assistance to a New Hampshire town devastated by fire. This is the first example of the federal government becoming involved in a local disaster.

During the 1930s, the Reconstruction Finance Corporation and the Bureau of Public Roads both were granted the authority to make disaster loans available for repair and reconstruction of certain public facilities after disasters. The Tennessee Valley Authority (TVA) was created during this era to produce hydroelectric power and, as a secondary purpose, to reduce flooding in the region.

The next notable period of evolution occurred during the 1950s. The Cold War era presented the potential for nuclear war and nuclear fallout as the principal disaster risk. Civil defense programs proliferated across communities during this time. Individuals and communities alike were encouraged to and did build bomb shelters to protect themselves and their families from a nuclear attack by the Soviet Union.

Federal support for these activities was vested in the Federal Civil Defense Administration (FCDA), an organization with few staff and limited financial resources whose main role was to provide technical assistance. A companion office to the FCDA, the Office of Defense Mobilization, was established in the Department of Defense (DOD). The primary functions of this office were to allow for the quick mobilization of materials and the production and stockpiling of critical materials in the event of war. In 1958, these two offices were merged into the Office of Civil and Defense Mobilization.

As the 1960s began, three major natural disasters occurred. In a sparsely populated area of Montana in 1960, the Hebgen Lake earthquake struck, measuring 7.3 on the Richter scale, calling attention to the fact that the nation's earthquake risk extended far beyond California's borders. Later that year, Hurricane Donna hit the west coast of Florida, and in 1961, Hurricane Carla blew across Texas. The incoming Kennedy administration decided to change the federal approach to disasters. In 1961, it created the Office of Emergency Preparedness inside the White House to deal with these large-scale events. It distinguished these activities from the civil defense responsibilities, which remained in the Office of Civil Defense within DOD.

During the remainder of the 1960s, the United States was struck by a series of major natural disasters. In 1964, in Prince William Sound, Alaska, an earthquake, measuring 9.2 on the Richter scale, killed 123 people and generated a tsunami that affected beaches as far south as the Pacific coast of California. Hurricane Betsy struck in 1965 and Hurricane Camille in 1969, together killing and injuring hundreds and causing hundreds of millions of dollars in damage along the Gulf Coast. The response to these events, as with previous disasters, was the passage of ad hoc legislation for funds. However, the financial losses resulting from Hurricane Betsy brought about the passage of the National Flood Insurance Act of 1968, which in turn created the National Flood Insurance Program (NFIP) that allowed the government to provide low-cost flood insurance to individuals.

During the 1970s, responsibility for dealing with different threats was allotted to more than five separate federal departments and agencies, including the Department of Commerce (weather, warning, and fire protection), the General Services Administration (continuity of government, stockpiling, and federal preparedness), the Department of the Treasury (import investigation), the Nuclear Regulatory Commission (power plants), and the Department of Housing and Urban Development (HUD) (flood insurance and disaster relief).

With the passage of the Disaster Relief Act of 1974, prompted by the previously mentioned hurricanes and the San Fernando earthquake of 1971, the Department of HUD possessed the most significant authority for natural disaster response and recovery through the NFIP, which it administered under the Federal Insurance Administration (FIA) and the Federal Disaster Assistance Administration (FDAA). On the military side, there existed the Defense Civil Preparedness Agency (nuclear attack) and the US Army Corps of Engineers (flood control).

In the 1970s, a partial release of radioactive materials occurred at the Three Mile Island nuclear power plant in Pennsylvania, requiring the evacuation of thousands of residents. This accident brought national media attention to the lack of adequate off-site preparedness around commercial nuclear power plants and the role of the federal government in responding to such an event.

On June 19, 1978, President Carter transmitted to Congress the Reorganization Plan Number 3 (3 CFR 1978, 5 US Code 903). The intent of this plan was to consolidate emergency preparedness, mitigation, and response activities into a single federal emergency management organization. The president stated that the plan would provide for the establishment of the Federal Emergency Management Agency (FEMA) and that the FEMA director would report directly to the president.

Reorganization Plan Number 3 transferred the following agencies or functions to FEMA: National Fire Prevention and Control Administration (Department of Commerce), Federal Insurance Administration (HUD), Federal Broadcast System (Executive Office of the President), Defense Civil Preparedness Agency (DOD), Federal Disaster Assistance Administration (HUD), and the Federal Preparedness Agency (GSA).

After congressional review and concurrence, the FEMA was officially established by Executive Order 12127 of March 31, 1979 (44 FR 19367, 3 CFR, Compilation, p. 376). A second executive order, Executive Order 12148, mandated reassignment of agencies, programs, and personnel into this new entity.

The early and middle 1980s saw a renewed interest and concern for threats from the Soviet Union, causing the federal efforts to once again focus on civil defense and nuclear attack planning. There were no significant natural disasters, and a robust program for commercial nuclear power preparedness was begun as part of the new Nuclear Regulatory Commission (NRC) licensing process so that threat was believed to have dissipated.

As Congress debated and finally passed major reform of federal disaster policy as part of the Stewart McKinney-Robert Stafford Act, FEMA, the agency responsible for responding to any threat, natural or man-made, was having severe problems with leadership and organization, and its ability to support a national threat response remained in doubt. It was in conflict with its partners at the state and local levels over agency spending and priorities for nuclear attack planning when they wanted to plan for natural hazards. In 1989, two devastating natural disasters, Hurricane Hugo and the Loma Prieta earthquake, called into question the continued existence of FEMA. In 1992, Hurricane Andrew struck Florida and Louisiana and Hurricane Iniki struck Hawaii within months of each other (Figure 2-1). FEMA wasn't ready, and neither were FEMA's partners at the state level. The agency's failure to respond was witnessed by Americans all across the country as major news organizations followed the crisis. It was not just FEMA that failed during Hurricane Andrew; it was the whole federal emergency management process and system. Investigations by the General Accountability Office (GAO) and other governmental and nongovernmental watchdog groups called for major reforms. None of this was lost on the incoming Clinton administration. President Clinton

FIGURE 2-1 Hurricane Andrew, Florida, August 24, 1992—Many houses, businesses, and personal effects suffered extensive damage from one of the most destructive hurricanes ever recorded in America. One million people were evacuated, and 54 died in this hurricane. *Source: FEMA News Photo.*

appointed James Lee Witt to be director of FEMA with a mandate to make the agency ready to respond to any threat or disaster facing the country. Witt was a seasoned state director of Arkansas Department of Emergency Management and ex-local elected official, who had been through numerous natural and man-made disasters.

The threat of a major natural disaster or even multiple disasters was the US government's concern as the United States started the 1990s. Other threats from man-made incidents such as the Valdez oil spill or a nuclear attack seemed remote. There was an increasing awareness of an ever-growing terrorist threat throughout the world, but it hadn't really impacted the US mainland or its property. US intelligence agencies were monitoring an increase in terrorist attacks all over. Within the United States, there were many incidents of bombings, but they were perpetrated by homegrown citizens and rarely for ideological reasons. This was to change with the first terrorist attack on US soil on the World Trade Center (WTC) in 1993.

Critical Thinking

In light of the events that have transpired, how would you apportion the amount of federal effort and funding between natural hazards and man-made hazards and terrorism?

World Trade Center Bombing

The 1993 bombing of the WTC presented a new threat on US soil, that is, the first large-scale terrorist attack. Prior to this, bombings that occurred at post offices, medical facilities, etc., were considered to be criminal acts by individuals. This bombing changed that. On February 23, 1993, a massive explosion occurred in the basement parking lot of the WTC in New York City. Six adults and one unborn child were killed and more than 1000 people sustained injuries. The explosive device, which weighed more than 1000 pounds, caused extensive damage to seven of the building's floors, six of which were below grade. A blast crater that resulted from the explosion measured 130 ft in width by 150 ft in length. More than 50,000 people were evacuated, 25,000 of whom were in the Twin Towers of the World Trade Center. The entire evacuation process required approximately 11 hours to complete (Fusco, 1993).

Fire Department City of New York Responds to World Trade Center Bombing

At the time, the response to the bombing was described as being the largest incident that the Fire Department City of New York (FDNY) had ever managed in its 128-year history. In terms of the number of fire units that responded, the event was described as being "the equivalent of a 16-alarm fire" (Fusco, 1993). The following list provides a summary of relevant data from the bombing event:

- Deaths: 6
- Injuries: 1042
- Firefighter injuries: 85 (one requiring hospitalization)
- Police officers injured: 35
- EMS workers injured: 1
- Firefighter, police, and EMS deaths: 0
- Number of people evacuated from WTC complex: approximately 50,000
- FDNY engine companies responding: 84
- FDNY truck companies responding: 60
- FDNY special units responding: 26
- FDNY personnel responding: 28 battalion chiefs and 9 deputy chiefs
- Percentage of FDNY on duty staff responding: 45% (Fusco, 1993)

This incident resulted in increased efforts to address the terrorist threat. Shootings in California and the botched raid in Waco, Texas, added to public concern over terrorism and crime in general. Through the work of the Joint Terrorism Task Force, four suspects were arrested and convicted of the WTC bombing. In response to these incidents, the Congress passed and President Clinton signed the Violent Crime Control and Law Enforcement Act of 1994. This was the most comprehensive crime legislation in US history. Among the provisions of this act was an expanded application of the death penalty to "acts of terrorism or the use of weapons of mass destruction." It included a 10-year ban on assault weapons, which was later allowed to expire, programs to fight violence against women, and significant increases in funding for the Immigration and Naturalization Service (INS), Border Patrol, Drug Enforcement Agency (DEA), and the Federal Bureau of Investigation (FBI).

Murrah Federal Building Bombing

The bombing of the Murrah Federal Building represented the next incident of domestic terrorism. On April 19, 1995, a massive truck bomb exploded outside of the Alfred P. Murrah Federal Building in downtown Oklahoma City. All told, 168 people died, including 19 children attending a daycare program in the

FIGURE 2-2 Oklahoma City, Oklahoma, April 26, 1995—Search-and-rescue crews work to save those trapped beneath the debris after the Oklahoma City bombing. *Source: FEMA News Photo.*

building. A total of 674 people were injured. The Murrah building was destroyed, 25 additional buildings in the downtown area were severely damaged or destroyed, and another 300 buildings were damaged by the blast. The ensuing rescue and recovery effort during the next 16 days involved, among many other resources, the dispatch of 11 FEMA urban search-and-rescue teams (see sidebar "FEMA Urban Search and Rescue at Murrah Building Bombing in Oklahoma City, 1995") from across the country to assist local and state officials' search first for survivors and, ultimately, for victims' bodies (Figure 2-2) (City of Oklahoma City Document Management, 1996).

FEMA Urban Search and Rescue at Murrah Building Bombing in Oklahoma City, 1995

At 9:02 on the morning of April 19, 1995, a bomb exploded from inside a Ryder truck under the Alfred P. Murrah Federal Building in Oklahoma City. The blast caused a partial collapse of all nine floors of the 20-year-old building, and 168 people died.

Rescuers from the Oklahoma City Fire Department entered the building unsure of whether the building would continue to support its own weight. Most of the steel support system had been blown out.

Within 5 h of the blast, the first FEMA urban search-and-rescue task force was deployed. By 6 pm the task force was in the building, searching for victims. One of the first assignments was to search the second floor nursery for victims.

Teams with search-and-rescue dogs began the search in the nursery. The dogs are trained to bark when they find live victims. No dogs barked that night.

Eleven of FEMA's 27 USAR (US Army Reserve) task forces worked in the building, with representation from virtually every task force in the country. The FEMA teams coordinated with local fire departments, police departments, and military and federal agencies during the search-and-rescue effort.

The rescue effort involved extensive stabilization of the fragmented building, rescuing of people trapped within tight spaces, rescues from high angles, and breaking through concrete and hazardous materials analysis and removal.

An innovative plan was developed to help rescuers deal with the psychological and emotional trauma of such a grisly scene. The plan allowed workers to be briefed in advance and prepared for what they were to experience; extensive debriefing sessions were also included.

Source: FEMA, www.fema.gov

At this time, Congress was debating the Nunn-Lugar-Domenici legislation that was aimed at better preparing this nation and its responsible organizations for a terrorist attack. The Nunn-Lugar-Domenici legislation provided the primary authority and focus for domestic federal preparedness activities for terrorism. Several agencies—including the FEMA, Department of Justice (DOJ), Department of Health and Human Resources (DHHS), DOD, and the National Guard—were involved in the terrorism issue, and all were jockeying for the leadership position. Several attempts at coordination among these various agencies were launched, but in general, each agency pursued its own agenda. The single factor that provided the greatest distinction between these agencies related to the levels of funding they received, with DOD and DOJ controlling the majority of what was allocated. State and local governments generally found themselves confused by the federal government's approach and likewise felt unprepared as a result. Although many of these state and local agencies appealed to the federal government to recognize local vulnerabilities and to establish stronger systems to accommodate anticipated needs, the majority rarely considered the possibility of an attack at all. The Oklahoma City bombing tested this thesis and set the stage for interagency disagreements over which agency would be in charge of terrorism.

The Nunn-Lugar legislation of 1995 (Defense against Weapons of Mass Destruction Act of 1996) left open the question as to who would be the lead agency in terrorism. Many fault FEMA leadership for not quickly claiming that role and the late 1990s was marked by several different agencies and departments assuming various roles in terrorism planning. The question of who should respond first to a terrorism incident—fire or police department, emergency management, or emergency medical personnel (the FBI, DOJ, or FEMA)—was closely examined, but no clear answers emerged. The state directors looked to FEMA to claim the leadership role. In an uncharacteristic way, the leadership of FEMA vacillated on this issue. Terrorism was certainly part of the all-hazards approach to emergency management championed by FEMA, but the resources and technologies needed to address specific issues, such as weapons of mass destruction and the consequences of a chemical/biological attack, seemed well beyond the reach of the current disaster structure.

Critical Thinking

Was there an obvious federal agency to be named as lead? If so, which one and what is the rationale for naming that agency?

Khobar Towers Bombing, Saudi Arabia

On June 25, 1996, a truck bomb was detonated at the US Army Forces Command in the Khobar Towers building in Riyadh. The force of the bomb damaged or destroyed six high-rise buildings within the compound. The blast was felt 20 miles away. Some security measures that had been previously erected including Jersey barriers and the marble construction of the building minimized damages. The quick actions of an Air Force sentry, noticing the suspicious actions of the terrorists and alerting security, minimized the deaths and injuries. In anonymous communications to the United States prior to the attack, there were indications that some level of attack would occur as an impetus to get the US troops out of the country. In the aftermath of the attack, the US military and different members of the intelligence-gathering community were criticized for the lack of preparation for such an event. Most people viewed this as an intelligence failure.

The Three Commissions

In 1998, President Clinton and House Speaker Newt Gingrich petitioned Congress to form a 14-member panel called the US Commission on National Security/21st Century (USCNS/21), also known as the Hart-Rudman Commission, to make strategic recommendations on how the US government could ensure the nation's security in the coming years. The independent panel, created by Congress, was tasked with conducting a comprehensive review of American security with the goal of designing a national security strategy.

The commission's report, titled "Road Map for National Security: Imperative for Change," dated January 31, 2001, recommended the creation of a new independent National Homeland Security Agency (NHSA) with responsibility for planning, coordinating, and integrating various US government activities involved in homeland security. This agency would be built on the FEMA, with the Coast Guard, the Customs Service, and the US Border Patrol (now part of US Customs and Border Protection (CBP) within the DHS) transferred into it. NHSA would assume responsibility for the safety of the American people as well as oversee the protection of critical infrastructure, including information technology. Obviously, the commission's recommendations were not heeded before 2001, but many of its findings would later be integrated into the justification and legislation behind the creation of the DHS.

Two other commissions were established to study the terrorist threat during these years: the Gilmore Commission and the Bremer Commission, as discussed next.

The Gilmore Commission, also known as the Advisory Panel to Assess Domestic Response Capabilities for Terrorism Involving Weapons of Mass Destruction, produced a series of annual reports beginning in 1999 (with the final report released in 2003). Each of these reports presented a growing base of knowledge concerning the weapons of mass destruction (WMD) risk faced by the United States and a recommended course of action required to counter that risk.

The Bremer Commission, also known as the National Commission on Terrorism, addressed the issue of the international terrorist threat. The commission was mandated by Congress to evaluate the nation's laws, policies, and practices for preventing terrorism and for punishing those responsible for terrorist events. Its members drafted a report titled "Countering the Changing Threat of International Terrorism." This report, issued in 2000, arrived at the following conclusions:

- International terrorism poses an increasingly dangerous and difficult threat to America.
- Countering the growing danger of the terrorist threat requires significantly stepping up the US efforts.
- Priority one is to prevent terrorist attacks. US intelligence and law enforcement communities must use the full scope of their authority to collect intelligence regarding terrorist plans and methods.
- US policies must firmly target all states that support terrorists.

- Private sources of financial and logistical support for terrorists must be subjected to the full force and sweep of US and international laws.
- A terrorist attack involving a biological agent, deadly chemicals, or nuclear or radiological material, even if it succeeds only partially, could profoundly affect the entire nation. The government must do more to prepare for such an event.
- The president and Congress should reform the system for reviewing and funding departmental counterterrorism programs to ensure that the activities and programs of various agencies are part of a comprehensive plan.

Each of these conclusions and recommendations would take on new meaning in the aftermath of the September 11 attacks and would guide many of the changes incorporated into the Homeland Security Act of 2002. However, in the absence of a greater recognition of a terrorist threat within the borders of the United States, no major programs were initiated to combat the growing risk.

Critical Thinking

President Clinton and Congress were concerned enough about terrorism in the late 1990s that they chose to form and fund the three terrorism commissions. Do you feel that the US public was adequately concerned or aware of the threat of terrorism during this time and leading up to the September 11 terrorist attacks? Do you believe that the US government was adequately concerned during this same time period? Explain your answer.

Presidential Decision Directives 62 and 63

As these commissions were conducting their research, President Clinton was addressing other recognized and immediate needs through the passage of several presidential decision directives (PDDs). Terrorist attacks continued to occur throughout the world, aimed at US government, military, and private interests. In 1996, terrorists carried out a suicide bombing at US military barracks (Khobar Towers) in Saudi Arabia, and in 1998, simultaneous bombings were carried out at the US diplomatic missions in Kenya and Tanzania.

In May 1998, President Clinton issued PDD-62, "Combating Terrorism," which called for the establishment of the office of the National Coordinator for Security, Infrastructure Protection, and Counterterrorism. The directive's primary goal was to create a new and more systematic approach to fighting the terrorist threat. PDD-62 reinforced the mission of many US agencies involved in a wide array of counterterrorism activities. The new national coordinator was tasked with overseeing a broad variety of relevant policies and programs including counterterrorism, critical infrastructure protection, WMD preparedness, and consequence management.

Soon after this directive, President Clinton issued PDD-63, "Protecting America's Critical Infrastructures." This directive tasked all of the departments of the federal government with assessing the vulnerabilities of their cyber and physical infrastructures and with working to reduce their exposure to new and existing threats.

Attorney General's Five-Year Interagency Counterterrorism and Technology Crime Plan

In December 1998, as mandated by Congress, the DOJ, through the FBI, began a coordinated project with other agencies to develop the Attorney General's Five-Year Interagency Counterterrorism and Technology

Crime Plan. The FBI emerged as the federal government's principal agency for responding to and investigating terrorism. Congress had intended the plan to serve as a baseline for the coordination of a national strategy and operational capabilities to combat terrorism. This plan represented a substantial interagency effort, including goals, objectives, and performance indicators, and recommended specific agency actions to help resolve interagency problems. It clearly did not, however, tear down the walls that prevented interagency sharing of information, as evidenced by the failures that resulted in the success of the 9/11 terrorists.

General Accountability Office (GAO) Findings on Terrorism

The DOJ asserted that the Attorney General's Five-Year Interagency Counterterrorism and Technology Crime Plan, considered together with related PDDs as described earlier, represented a comprehensive national strategy to address the terrorist threat. However, after a thorough review, the General Accountability Office (GAO), Congress' investigative arm, concluded that additional work remained that would build on the progress that the plan represented. The GAO contended that a comprehensive national security strategy was lacking.

The GAO report "Combating Terrorism: Comments on Counterterrorism Leadership and National Strategy" (GAO-01-55T), released March 27, 2001, stated that the DOJ plan did not have measurable outcomes and suggested, for example, that it should include goals that improve state and local response capabilities. The report argued that without a clearly defined national strategy, the nation would continue to miss opportunities to focus and shape counterterrorism programs to meet the impending threat. It also made the criticism that the DOJ plan lacked a coherent framework to develop and evaluate budget requirements for combating terrorism since there was no single focal point. The report claimed that no single entity was acting as the federal government's top official accountable to both the president and the Congress for the terrorism hazard and that fragmentation existed in both coordination of domestic preparedness programs and efforts to develop a national strategy.

The GAO released another report in early September 2001 titled "Combating Terrorism: Selected Challenges and Related Recommendations" (GAO-01-822), which it finalized in the last days before the terrorist attacks occurred in Washington and New York. The report stated that the federal government was ill equipped and unprepared to counter a major terrorist attack, claiming also that—from sharing intelligence to coordinating a response—the government had failed to put in place an effective critical infrastructure system. It further stated that

> *Federal efforts to develop a national strategy to combat terrorism ... have progressed, but key challenges remain. The initial step toward developing a national strategy is to conduct a national threat and risk assessment ... at the national level (agencies) have not completed assessments of the most likely weapon-of-mass destruction agents and other terrorist threats....*

To prevent terrorist attacks, the GAO recommended the following:

- A national strategy to combat terrorism and computer-based attacks
- Better protection for the nation's infrastructure
- A single focal point to oversee coordination of federal programs
- Completion of a threat assessment on likely WMD and other weapons that might be used by terrorists

- Revision of the Attorney General's Five-Year Interagency Counterterrorism and Technology Crime Plan to better serve as a national strategy
- Coordination of research and development to combat terrorism

In a later report regarding homeland security, "Key Elements to Unify Efforts Are Underway But Uncertainty Remains" (GAO-02-610), the GAO called for more of the same in terms of needing central leadership and an overarching strategy that identifies goals and objectives, priorities, measurable outcomes, and state and local government roles in combating terrorism since the efforts of more than 40 federal entities and numerous state and local governments were still fragmented. It also called for the term *homeland security* to be defined properly since to date it had not.

USS Cole Bombing, Yemen

On October 12, 2000, while refueling in the port of Aden in Yemen the US Navy destroyer, the USS Cole sustained a suicide bomb attack. The terrorist organization al-Qaeda claimed responsibility for the attack that took the lives of 17 Navy sailors with an additional 39 injured. However, evidence of al-Qaeda involvement was inconclusive. The 9/11 Commission Report does indicate that in December 2000, the Central Intelligence Agency (CIA) had made a preliminary conclusion that al-Qaeda may have supported the attack. Intelligence agencies produced videos showing al-Qaeda members and Osama Bin Laden celebrating the bombing of the USS Cole. Further intelligence indicated Bin Laden expressing disappointment that the United States did not retaliate for the attack. There was thought to be complicity by the government of the Sudan, and a US judge determined that Sudan was liable for the attack. At the time, then President Clinton declared it an "act of terrorism." However, some people have questioned whether an attack against a military installation meets the legal definition of "terrorism" as opposed to an act of war. Both the Clinton and, later, the Bush administrations have been criticized for not responding with military force on this attack before the September 11 attack. The Navy, however, was quick to act. They opened an Anti-Terrorism and Force Protection Warfare Center and aggressively implemented stronger random antiterrorism measures (RAM) to their security posture. The attack on the USS Cole added to an already heightened terrorism profile within the federal government, especially within the intelligence community.

September 11 Attacks on the World Trade Center and the Pentagon

The concept of homeland security was born on September 11, 2001. On that day, terrorists hijacked four planes and crashed them into the Twin Towers of the WTC in New York City, the Pentagon in Washington, DC, and a field in Pennsylvania (see sidebar "September 11, 2001, Terrorist Attacks Timeline for the Day of the Attacks"). These actions resulted in the collapse of both the Twin Towers, the collapse of a section of the Pentagon, and the crash of a domestic airliner that resulted in unprecedented deaths and injuries:

- Total deaths for all 9/11 attacks: 2974 (not counting the 19 terrorists)
- Total injured for all 9/11 attacks: 2337
- Total deaths in the World Trade Center towers: 2603

- Total injured at the World Trade Center: 2261
- Total firefighter deaths at the World Trade Center: 343
- Total police deaths at World Trade Center: 75
- Total deaths at the Pentagon: 125
- Total injured at the Pentagon: 76
- Total deaths, American Airlines Flight 77, the Pentagon: 59
- Total deaths, United Airlines Flight 93, Pennsylvania: 40
- Total deaths, American Airlines Flight 11, WTC North Tower: 88
- Total deaths, United Airlines Flight 175, WTC South Tower: 59 (from www.september11news.com/911Art.htm and http://en.wikipedia.org/wiki/September_11,_2001_Terrorist_Attack)

September 11, 2001, Terrorist Attacks Timeline for the Day of the Attacks

Note: All times in New York time (EDT). This is 4 h (GMT) before Tuesday, September 11, 2001.

7:58 am: American Airlines Flight 11, a fully fueled Boeing 767 carrying 81 passengers and 11 crew members, departs from Boston Logan International Airport, bound for Los Angeles, California.

8:00 am: United Airlines Flight 175, another fully fueled Boeing 767, carrying 56 passengers and 9 crew members, departs from Boston's Logan International Airport, bound for Los Angeles, California.

8:10 am: American Airlines Flight 77, a Boeing 757 with 58 passengers and 6 crew members, departs from Washington's Dulles International Airport for Los Angeles, California.

8:40 am: The Federal Aviation Administration (FAA) notifies North American Aerospace Defense Command (NORAD) about the suspected hijacking of American Airlines Flight 11.

8:42 am: United Airlines Flight 93, a Boeing 757, takes off with 37 passengers and 7 crew members from Newark Liberty International Airport bound for San Francisco, following a 40 min delay caused by congested runways. Its flight path initially takes it close to the World Trade Center.

8:43 am: The FAA notifies NORAD about the suspected hijacking of United Airlines Flight 175.

8:46:26 am: American Airlines Flight 11 crashes with a speed of roughly 490 miles per hour into the north side of the north tower of the World Trade Center, between floors 94 and 98. (Many accounts have given times that range between 8:45 am and 8:50 am). The building's structural type, pioneered in the late 1960s to maximize rentable floor space and featuring lightweight tubular design with no masonry elements in the facade, allows the jetliner to literally enter the tower, mostly intact. It plows to the building core, severing all three gypsum-encased stairwells and dragging combustibles with it. A massive shock wave travels down to the ground and up again. The combustibles, as well as the remnants of the aircraft, are ignited by the burning fuel. Because the building lacks a traditional full-cage frame and depends almost entirely on the strength of a narrow structural core running up the center, the fire at the center of the impact zone is in a position to compromise the integrity of all internal columns. People below the severed stairwells in the north tower start to evacuate. Officials in the south tower tell people shortly afterward by megaphone and office announcements that they are safe and can return to their offices. Some don't hear it; some ignore it and evacuate anyway; and others congregate in common areas such as the 78th-floor sky lobby to discuss their options.

9:02:54 am: United Airlines Flight 175 crashes with a speed of about 590 miles per hour into the south side of the south tower, banked between floors 78 and 84 in full view of media cameras. Parts of the plane leave the building at its east and north sides, falling to the ground six blocks away. A passenger on the plane, Peter Hanson, had called his father earlier from the plane reporting that hijackers were stabbing flight attendants in order to force the crew to open the cockpit doors.

8:46 am to 10:29 am: At least 20 people, primarily in the north tower, trapped by fire and smoke in the upper floors, jump to their deaths. There is some evidence that large central portions of the floor near the impact zone in the north tower collapsed soon after the plane hit, perhaps convincing some people that total collapse was imminent. One person at street level, firefighter Daniel Thomas Suhr, is hit by a jumper and dies. No form of airborne evacuation is attempted because the smoke is too dense for a successful landing on the roof of either tower, or New York City lacks helicopters specialized for horizontal rescue.

9:04 am (approximately): The FAA's Boston Air Route Traffic Control Center stops all departures from airports in its jurisdiction (New England and eastern New York State).

9:06 am: The FAA bans takeoffs of all flights bound to or through the airspace of New York center from airports in that center and the three adjacent centers—Boston, Cleveland, and Washington. This is referred to as a first-tier ground stop and covers the Northeast from North Carolina north and as far west as eastern Michigan.

9:08 am: The FAA bans all takeoffs nationwide for flights going to or through New York center airspace.

9:24 am: President George W. Bush is interrupted with the news of the second crash as he participates in a class filled with Florida schoolchildren. He waits out the lesson and then rushes into another classroom commandeered by the Secret Service. Within minutes, he makes a short statement, calling the developments "a national tragedy," and is hurried aboard Air Force One.

9:24 am: The FAA notifies NORAD's Northeast Air Defense Sector about the suspected hijacking of American Airlines Flight 77. The FAA and NORAD establish an open line to discuss American Airlines Flight 77 and United Airlines Flight 93.

9:26 am: The FAA bans takeoffs of all civilian aircraft regardless of destination—a national ground stop.

9:37 am: American Airlines Flight 77 crashes into the western side of the Pentagon and starts a violent fire. The section of the Pentagon hit consists mainly of newly renovated, unoccupied offices. Passenger Barbara K. Olson had called her husband, Solicitor General Theodore Olson, at the Department of Justice twice from the plane to tell him about the hijacking and to report that the passengers and pilots were held in the back of the plane. As bright flames and dark smoke envelop the west side of America's military nerve center, all doubts about the terrorist nature of the attacks are gone.

9:45 am: US airspace is shut down. No civilian aircraft are allowed to lift off, and all aircraft in flight are ordered to land at the nearest airport as soon as practical. All air traffic headed for the United States is redirected to Canada. Later, the FAA announces that civilian flights are suspended until at least noon, September 12. The groundings last until September 14, but there are exemptions for Saudi families who fear retribution if they stay in the United States. Military and medical flights continue. This is the fourth time all commercial flights in the United States have been stopped and the first time a suspension was unplanned. All previous suspensions were military-related (Sky Shield I-Sky Shield III) and took place from 1960 to 1962.

9:45 am: The White House and the Capitol are closed.

9:50 am (approximately): The Associated Press reports that American Airlines Flight 11 was apparently hijacked after departure from Boston's Logan International Airport. Within an hour, this report is confirmed for both Flight 11 and United Airlines Flight 175.

9:57 am: President Bush is moved from Florida.

9:59:04 am: The south tower of the World Trade Center collapses. A vast TV and radio audience reacts primarily with horrified astonishment. It is later widely reported that the collapse was not directly caused by the jetliner's impact but that the intense sustained heat of the fuel fire was mostly or wholly responsible for the loss of structural integrity. Later, a growing number of structural engineers assert that the fire alone would not have caused the collapse. Both towers made use of external load-bearing minicolumns, and on one face of each building, approximately 40 of these were severed by the jetliners. Had they been intact to efficiently distribute the increasing gravity load as the bunched core columns and joist trusses weakened in the fires, the towers might have stood far longer or perhaps indefinitely. Concrete in the towers' facades might have prevented most of the debris and fuel from reaching the building core. Investigations that may radically change skyscraper design (or result in a radical retreat to full-cage construction with high concrete-to-steel ratios as in pre-1960s skyscrapers) are ongoing.

10:03 am: United Airlines Flight 93 crashes southeast of Pittsburgh in Somerset County, Pennsylvania. Other reports say 10:06 or 10:10. According to seismographic data readings, the time of impact was 10:06:05. The first reports from the police indicate that none on board survived. Later reports indicate that passengers speaking on cell phones had learned about the World Trade Center and Pentagon crashes and at least three were planning on resisting the hijackers. It is likely that the resistance led to the plane crashing before it reached its intended target. Reports stated that an eyewitness saw a white plane resembling a fighter jet circling the site minutes after the crash. These reports have limited credibility, although fighter jets had been scrambled to defend the Washington, DC, region earlier. These jets, however, stayed within the immediate DC area.

10:10 am: Part of the Pentagon collapses.

10:13 am: Thousands are involved in an evacuation of the United Nations complex in New York.

10:15 am (approximately): The Democratic Front for the Liberation of Palestine is reported to have taken responsibility for the crashes, but this is denied by a senior officer of the group soon after.

10:28:31 am: The north tower of the World Trade Center collapses from the top down, as if being peeled apart. Probably, as a result of the destruction of the gypsum-encased stairwells on the impact floors (most skyscraper stairwells are encased in reinforced concrete), no one above the impact zone in the north tower survives. The fact that the north tower stood much longer than the south one is later attributed to three facts: The region of impact was higher (which meant that the gravity load on the most damaged area was lighter), the speed of the airplane was lower, and the fireproofing in the affected floors had been partially upgraded. Also, the hottest part of the fire in the south tower burned in a corner of the structure, perhaps leading to a more concentrated failure of columns or joist trusses or both. The Marriott Hotel, located at the base of the two towers, is also destroyed.

10:35 am (approximately): Police are reportedly alerted about a bomb in a car outside the State Department in Washington, DC. Later reports claim that nothing happened at the State Department.

10:39 am: Another hijacked jumbo jet is claimed to be headed for Washington, DC. F-15s are scrambled and patrol the airspace above Washington, DC, while other fighter jets sweep the airspace above New York City. They have orders, first issued by Vice President Cheney and later confirmed by President Bush, to shoot down any potentially dangerous planes that do not comply with orders given to them via radio.

10:45 am: CNN reports that a mass evacuation of Washington, DC, and New York has been initiated. The UN headquarters are already empty. A few minutes later, New York's mayor orders an evacuation of Lower Manhattan.

10:50 am: Five stories of part of the Pentagon collapse as a result of the fire.

10:53 am: New York's primary elections are canceled.

11:15 am (approximately): Reports surfaced that the F-15s over Washington had shot something down. There was no later confirmation of these reports.

11:16 am: American Airlines confirms the loss of its two airplanes.

11:17 am: United Airlines confirms the loss of Flight 93 and states that it is "deeply concerned" about Flight 175.

11:53 am: United Airlines confirms the loss of its two airplanes.

11:55 am: The border between the United States and Mexico is on highest alert, but has not been closed.

12:00 pm (approximately): President Bush arrives at Barksdale Air Force Base in Louisiana. He was on a trip in Sarasota, Florida, to speak about education but is now presumed to be returning to the capital. He makes a brief and informal initial statement to the effect that terrorism on US soil will not be tolerated, stating that "freedom itself has been attacked and freedom will be protected."

12:02 pm: The Taliban government of Afghanistan denounces the attacks.

12:04 pm: Los Angeles International Airport, the intended destination of Flight 11, Flight 77, and Flight 175, is shut down.

12:15 pm: San Francisco International Airport, the intended destination of United Airlines Flight 93, is shut down.

12:15 pm (approximately): The airspace over the 48 contiguous United States is clear of all commercial and private flights.

1:00 pm (approximately): At the Pentagon, fire crews are still fighting fires. The early response to the attack had been coordinated from the National Military Command Center, but that location had to be evacuated when it began to fill with smoke.

1:04 pm: President Bush puts the US military on high alert worldwide. He speaks from Barksdale Air Force Base and leaves for the Strategic Air Command bunker in Nebraska.

1:27 pm: Mayor Anthony A. Williams of Washington, DC, declares a state of emergency; the DC National Guard arrives on site.

2:30 pm: Senator John McCain characterizes the attack as an "act of war."

2:49 pm: At a press conference in New York, Mayor Rudy Giuliani is asked to estimate the number of casualties at the World Trade Center. He replies, "More than any of us can bear."

4:00 pm: National news outlets report that high officials in the federal intelligence community are stating that Osama bin Laden is the primary suspect in the attacks.

4:25 pm: The New York Stock Exchange, NASDAQ, and the American Stock Exchange report that they will remain closed on Wednesday, September 12.

5:20 pm: Salomon Brothers 7, commonly referred to as "7 World Trade Center," a 47-story building that had sustained what was originally thought to be light damage in the fall of the Twin Towers and was earlier reported on fire, collapses. Structural engineers are puzzled, and the investigation continues. The building was not designed by the same team responsible for the Twin Towers. The building contained New York's special emergency center, which may well have been intended for such a disaster as September 11.

6:00 pm: Explosions and tracer fire are reported in Kabul, the capital of Afghanistan, by CNN and the BBC. The Northern Alliance, involved in a civil war with the Taliban government, is later reported to have attacked Kabul's airport with helicopter gunships.

6:00 pm: Iraq announces that the attacks are the fruit of "US crimes against humanity" in an official announcement on state television.

6:54 pm: President Bush finally arrives at the White House. Executive authority through much of the day had rested with Vice President Cheney.

7:00 pm: Frantic efforts to locate survivors in the rubble that had been the Twin Towers continue. Fleets of ambulances have been lined up to transport the injured to nearby hospitals. They stand empty. "Ground zero" is the exclusive domain of the FDNY and NYPD, despite volunteer steel and construction workers who stand ready to move large quantities of debris quickly. Relatives and friends displaying enlarged photographs of the missing printed on home computer printers are flooding downtown. The New York Armory, at Lexington Avenue and 26th Street, and Union Square Park, at 14th Street, become centers of vigil.

7:30 pm: The US government denies any responsibility for reported explosions in Kabul.

8:30 pm: President Bush addresses the nation from the White House. Among his remarks: "Terrorist attacks can shake the foundations of our biggest buildings, but they cannot touch the foundation of America. These acts shatter steel, but they cannot dent the steel of American resolve."

9:00 pm: President Bush meets with his full National Security Council, followed roughly half an hour later by a meeting with a smaller group of key advisers. Bush and his advisers have evidence that Osama bin Laden is behind the attacks.

11:00 pm: There are reports of survivors buried in the rubble in New York making cell phone calls. These rumors were later proved to be wrong (www.wikipedia.com).

The response to these attacks by fire, police, and emergency medical teams was immediate, and their combined efforts saved hundreds if not thousands of lives, especially at the WTC. The following facts provide additional insight into the situation faced by the responders that day:

- Year the World Trade Center was built: 1970
- Number of companies housed in the World Trade Center: 430
- Number working in the World Trade Center on average working day before September 11: 50,000
- Average number of daily visitors: 140,000
- Maximum heat of fires, in degrees Fahrenheit, at the World Trade Center site: 2300

- Number of days underground fires at the World Trade Center continued to burn: 69
- Number of days that workers dug up debris at ground zero, searching for body parts: 230
- Number of body parts collected: 19,500
- Number of bodies discovered intact: 291
- Number of victims identified by New York medical examiner: 1102
- Number of death certificates issued without a body at request of victims' families: 1616
- Number of people still classified as missing from the World Trade Center that day: 105
- Number of people who survived the collapse of the towers: 16 (http://observer.guardian.co.uk/waronterrorism/story/0,1373,776451,00.html and www.snopes.com/rumors/survivor.htm)

The addition of another stairway in each tower, the widening of existing stairways, and regular evacuation drills—actions implemented in the aftermath of the 1993 WTC bombing—are all credited with facilitating the evacuation of thousands of office workers in the towers before they collapsed. Federal, state, and nongovernmental groups (e.g., Red Cross and Salvation Army) also responded quickly, establishing relief centers and dispensing critical services to victims and first responders. The following list illustrates the relief efforts that ensued:

- Cases opened: 55,494
- Mental health contacts made: 240,417
- Health services contacts made: 133,035
- Service delivery sites opened: 101
- Shelters opened: 60
- Shelter population: 3554
- Meals/snacks served: 14,113,185
- Response vehicles assigned: 292
- Disaster workers assigned: 57,434 (www.redcrossalbq.org/04a_911statistics.html)

In addition to the stunning loss of life and the physical destruction caused by the attacks, two other losses are significant for their size and impact. First, 343 New York City firefighters and 75 New York City police officers were lost in the WTC when the towers collapsed, setting a record for the highest number lost in a single disaster event in the United States. Their untimely deaths brought extraordinary attention to America's courageous and professional firefighters, police officers, and emergency medical technicians. They became the heroes of September 11, and this increased attention has resulted in increased funding for government programs that provide equipment and training for first responders. It has also resulted in a reexamination of protocols and procedures in light of the new terrorist threat.

The second significant aspect of the September 11 attacks is the magnitude and the scope of the losses resulting from the attacks. The total economic impact on New York City alone is estimated to be between \$82.8 and \$94.8 billion. This estimate includes \$21.8 billion in lost buildings, infrastructure, and tenant assets; \$8.7 billion in the future earnings of those who died; and \$52.3 to \$64.3 billion gross city product (Curci, 2004). The economic impact of the attacks was felt throughout the United States and the world, causing jobs to be lost and businesses to fail in communities hundreds and thousands of miles from ground zero:

- Value of US economy: \$11 trillion
- Estimated cost of attacks to United States based solely on property losses and insurance costs: \$21 billion

- Amount of office space lost, in square feet: 13.5 million
- Estimated number of jobs lost in Lower Manhattan area following September 11: 100,000
- Estimated number of jobs lost in the United States as a result of the attacks, by the end of 2002: 1.8 million
- Number of jobs lost in US travel industry in the final 5 months of 2001: 237,000
- Amount allocated by Congress for emergency assistance to airline industry in September 2001: $15 billion (http://observer.guardian.co.uk/waronterrorism/story/0,1373,776451,00.html)

The federal government costs were extraordinary, and spending by FEMA on these events easily exceeded its spending on past natural disasters and disasters that have happened since (see also Table 2-1):

- Direct emergency assistance from FEMA: $297 million
- Aid to individuals and families: $255 million
- Direct housing: 8957 applications processed and 5287 applications approved (59%)
- Mortgage and rental assistance: 11,818 applications processed and 6187 applications approved (52%)
- Individual and family grant program: 43,660 applications processed and 6139 applications approved (14%)

Table 2-1 Top Ten Natural Disasters (Ranked by FEMA Relief Costs)

Event	Year	FEMA Funding
Hurricane Katrina (AL, LA, and MS)	2005	$7.2 billion[a]
Northridge earthquake (CA)	1994	$6.961 billion
Hurricane Georges (AL, FL, LA, MS, PR, and VI)	1998	$2.251 billion
Hurricane Ivan (AL, FL, GA, LA, MS, NC, NJ, NY, PA, TN, and WVA)	2004	$1.947 billion[b]
Hurricane Andrew (FL and LA)	1992	$1.813 billion
Hurricane Charley (FL and SC)	2004	$1.559 billion[b]
Hurricane Frances (FL, GA, NC, NY, OH, PA, and SC)	2004	$1.425 billion[b]
Hurricane Jeanne (DE, FL, PR, VI, and VA)	2004	$1.407 billion[b]
Tropical Storm Allison (FL, LA, MS, PA, and TX)	2001	$1.387 billion
Hurricane Hugo (NC, SC, PR, and VI)	1989	$1.307 billion

[a]Amount obligated from the President's Disaster Relief Fund for FEMA's assistance programs, hazard mitigation grants, federal mission assignments, contractual services, and administrative costs as of March 31, 2006. Figures do not include funding provided by other participating federal agencies, such as the disaster loan programs of the Small Business Administration and the Department of Agriculture's Farm Service Agency. Note: Funding amounts are stated in nominal dollars, unadjusted for inflation.

[b]Amount obligated from the President's Disaster Relief Fund for FEMA's assistance programs, hazard mitigation grants, federal mission assignments, contractual services, and administrative costs as of May 31, 2005. Figures do not include funding provided by other participating federal agencies, such as the disaster loan programs of the Small Business Administration and the Department of Agriculture's Farm Service Agency. Note: Funding amounts are stated in nominal dollars, unadjusted for inflation.

Source: Federal Emergency Management Agency (FEMA). Top ten natural disasters: ranked by FEMA relief costs. http://www.fema.gov/hazard/topten.shtm.
Last modified: Wednesday, August 11, 2010, 14:38:40 EDT.

- Disaster unemployment: 6657 claims processed and 3210 claims approved (48%)
- Crisis counseling: $166 million
- Aid to government and nonprofits: $4.49 billion
- Debris removal: $437 million
- Overtime for New York City Police Department (NYPD): $295.4 million
- Overtime for the Fire Department City of New York: $105.6 million (Federal Emergency Management Agency, 2003)

The insurance losses resulting from the September 11 events were also extraordinary, especially when considered in light of the relatively small amount of physical property that was directly affected by the events themselves. Despite the fact that many natural hazards affect hundreds, if not thousands and even tens of thousands, of square miles of inhabited and developed land, thereby affecting thousands of structures and infrastructure components, these terrorist attacks that were isolated to one neighborhood in New York City and one building in Arlington, Virginia, exceeded all but two events worldwide in terms of their insurance-related disaster losses (Tables 2-2 and 2-3). This comprehensive terrorist attack illustrates the far-reaching indirect, intangible consequences of terrorism and their potential for damaging a nation's economy:

- Amount of federal aid New York received within 2 months of the September 11 events: $9.5 billion
- Amount collected by the September 11 fund: $501 million

Table 2-2 The Ten Most Costly World Insurance Losses, 1970-2013[a] (2013 $ Millions)

Rank	Date	Country	Event	Insured Loss[b]
1	Aug. 25, 2005	United States, Gulf of Mexico, Bahamas, North Atlantic	Hurricane Katrina, storm surge, levee failure, damage to oil rigs	$80,373
2	Mar. 11, 2011	Japan	Earthquake (Mw 9.0) triggers tsunami, aftershocks	37,665
3	Oct. 24, 2012	United States, etc.	Hurricane Sandy, storm surge	36,890
4	Aug. 23, 1992	United States, Bahamas	Hurricane Andrew, floods	27,594
5	Sep. 11, 2001	United States	Terror attacks on WTC, Pentagon, and other buildings	25,664
6	Jan. 17, 1994	United States	Northridge earthquake (M 6.6)	22,857
7	Sep. 6, 2008	United States, Caribbean, Gulf of Mexico, etc.	Hurricane Ike, floods, offshore damage	22,751
8	Sep. 2, 2004	United States, Caribbean, Barbados, etc.	Hurricane Ivan, damage to oil rigs	17,218
9	Jul. 27, 2011	Thailand	Floods caused by heavy monsoon rains	16,519
10	Feb. 22, 2011	New Zealand	Earthquake (Mw 6.3), aftershocks	16,142

[a]Property and business interruption losses, excludes life and liability losses and includes flood losses in the United States insured via the National Flood Insurance Program.
[b]Adjusted to 2013 dollars by Swiss Re.
Source: Swiss Re, *sigma*, No. 1/2014.
Note: Loss data shown here may differ from figures shown elsewhere for the same event due to differences in the date of publication, the geographical area covered and other criteria used by organizations collecting the data.

Table 2-3 The Ten Most Costly Catastrophes, the United States[a] ($ Millions)

Rank	Date	Peril	Estimated Insured Property Losses	
			Dollars When Occurred	**In 2013 Dollars[b]**
1	Aug. 2005	Hurricane Katrina	$41,100	$47,622
2	Sep. 2001	Fire, explosion: World Trade Center, Pentagon terrorist attacks	18,779	23,895
3	Aug. 1992	Hurricane Andrew	15,500	23,386
4	Oct. 2012	Hurricane Sandy	18,750	19,033
5	Jan. 1994	Northridge, CA earthquake	12,500	18,038
6	Sep. 2008	Hurricane Ike	12,500	13,426
7	Oct. 2005	Hurricane Wilma	10,300	11,934
8	Aug. 2004	Hurricane Charley	7475	8939
9	Sep. 2004	Hurricane Ivan	7110	8502
10	Apr. 2011	Flooding, hail and wind including the tornadoes that struck Tuscaloosa and other locations	7300	7540

[a]Property coverage only. Excludes flood damage covered by the federally administered National Flood Insurance Program.
[b]Adjusted for inflation through 2013 by ISO using the GDP implicit price deflator.
Source: The Property Claim Services® (PCS®) unit of ISO®, a Verisk Analytics® company.

- Percentage of fund used for cash assistance and services such as grief counseling for families of victims and survivors: 89
- Quantity, in pounds, of food and supplies supplied by September 11 fund at ground zero: 4.3 million
- Number of hot meals served to rescue workers by September 11 fund: 343,000
- Number of displaced workers receiving job referrals: 5000
- Amount of compensation sought by the families of civilian casualties of US bombing in Afghanistan from the US government: $10,000
- Amount of compensation sought for reckless misconduct and negligence from American Airlines by husband of September 11 victim: $50 million (http://observer.guardian.co.uk/waronterrorism/story/0,1373,776451,00.html)

The Creation of the Department of Homeland Security: 2001–2004

In the immediate aftermath of the September 11 attacks, as search-and-rescue teams were still sifting through the debris and wreckage for survivors in New York, Pennsylvania, and Virginia, the federal government was analyzing what had just happened and what it could quickly do to begin the process of ensuring such attacks could not be repeated. It was recognized that nothing too substantial could take place without longer-term study and congressional review, but the circumstances mandated that real changes begin without delay.

On September 20, 2001, just 9 days after the attacks, President George W. Bush announced that an Office of Homeland Security would be established within the White House by executive order. Directing this office would be Pennsylvania Governor Tom Ridge. Ridge was given no real staff to manage, and the funding he would have at his disposal was minimal. The actual order, cataloged as Executive Order 13228, was given on October 8, 2001. In addition to creating the Office of Homeland Security, this order created the Homeland Security Council, "to develop and coordinate the implementation of a comprehensive national strategy to secure the United States from terrorist threats or attacks."

Four days later, on September 24, 2001, President Bush announced that he would be seeking passage of an act titled "Uniting and Strengthening America by Providing Appropriate Tools Required to Intercept and Obstruct Terrorism," which would become better known as the PATRIOT Act of 2001. This act, which introduced a large number of controversial legislative changes in order to significantly increase the surveillance and investigative powers of law enforcement agencies in the United States (as it states) to "… deter and punish terrorist acts in the United States and around the world," was signed into law by the president on October 26 after very little deliberation in Congress.

On October 29, 2001, President Bush issued the first of many homeland security presidential directives (HSPDs), which were specifically designed to "record and communicate presidential decisions about the homeland security policies of the United States" (HSPD-1, 2001). On March 21, 2002, President Bush signed Executive Order 13260 establishing the President's Homeland Security Advisory Council (PHSAC) and Senior Advisory Committees for Homeland Security.

In the flurry of legislation and presidential directives that were enacted immediately after September 11, the PATRIOT Act was clearly the most controversial. The PATRIOT Act of 2001 (Public Law 107-56) was signed into law by President Bush on October 26, 2001. This legislation was introduced in the US House of Representatives by Representative F. James Sensenbrenner, Jr. (R-WI), on October 23, 2001, "to deter and punish terrorist acts in the United States and around the world, to enhance law enforcement investigatory tools, and for other purposes" (Library of Congress, 2003).

Under normal circumstances, legislation, especially that that has broad-sweeping reach and that brings into question constitutional rights, requires years and even decades of deliberation before it is finally passed—if that day ever comes. Considering the PATRIOT Act was passed less than a month after the event that inspired it, with almost no significant deliberation, it can be regarded as an anomalous case and one that, considering its comprehensive nature and its impact on civil liberties, deserves more detailed description.

The principal focus of the PATRIOT Act is to provide law enforcement agencies with the proper legal authority to support their efforts to collect information on suspected terrorists, to detain people suspected of being or aiding terrorists and terrorist organizations, to deter terrorists from entering and operating within the borders of the United States, and to further limit the ability of terrorists to engage in money-laundering activities that support terrorist actions. The major provisions of the PATRIOT Act are as follows:

- The act relaxes restrictions on information sharing between US law enforcement and intelligence officers on the subject of suspected terrorists.
- The act makes it illegal to knowingly harbor a terrorist.
- The act authorizes "roving wiretaps," which allows law enforcement officials to get court orders to wiretap any phone a suspected terrorist would use. The provision was needed, advocates said, with the advent of cellular and disposable phones.
- The act allows the federal government to detain non-US citizens suspected of terrorism for up to 7 days without specific charges (original versions of the legislation allowed for the holding of suspects indefinitely).
- The act allows law enforcement officials greater subpoena power for e-mail records of terrorist suspects.

- The act triples the number of border patrol personnel, customs service inspectors, and INS inspectors at the northern border of the United States and provides $100 million to improve technology and equipment on the US border with Canada.
- The act expands measures against money laundering by requiring additional record keeping and reports for certain transactions and requiring identification of account holders.
- The act eliminates the statute of limitations for prosecuting the most egregious terrorist acts but maintains the statute of limitation on most crimes at 5–8 years.

The PATRIOT Act immediately sparked concern among citizens and organizations involved in protecting the civil rights and liberties of all Americans, although this concern only became more vocal as the time between the attacks increased due to the emotional sensitivities associated with what had transpired. The critics that have emerged and that continue to emerge in growing numbers as the act is repeatedly renewed have questioned the constitutionality of several of the act's provisions and have expressed grave concerns regarding the methods by which some of those new authorities will be used by law enforcement agencies in their pursuit of terrorists.

The US attorney general at the time, John Ashcroft, and the DOJ that operated under his direction countered that these authorities are necessary if the US government is to more effectively track and detain terrorists. Regardless, the act very quickly began generating lawsuits, resistance from community officials, and concern about the way its provisions were being used and abused outside of their intended scope in a way that affected everyday Americans with no association with terrorist activities. The position paper titled "Debating the USA PATRIOT Act" presents both positive and negative perspectives on the PATRIOT Act.

Conclusion: An excerpt from "Debating the USA PATRIOT Act," by Donna L. Point

The US Army manual defines terrorism as "the calculated use of violence or threat of violence to attain goals that are political, religious or ideological in nature" (Chomsky, 2003, pp. 605–606). This act of terrorism is carried out in various ways such as intimidation, coercion, or instilling fear. Being safe and being free are not mutually exclusive. We do not gain one by giving up the other. The Constitution of the United States of America has survived many threats, including civil insurrections and world wars. It is precisely during times of crisis that rights must be most steadfastly defended. The protection of constitutional liberties need not, and indeed should not, deprive the government of the authority necessary to vigorously apprehend terrorists, prosecute them, and defend the homeland. America's credibility in the world has been dangerously compromised by the Bush administration's blatant disregard for the rule of law. The doctrine of preventive war, which was used to launch the "War on Terror," accords the Bush administration the sovereign right to take military action at will to control and destroy any challenge it perceives (Chomsky, 2003). The Bush doctrine is in essence a return to the claim of right to use force or any other means necessary to pursue national interests (O'Connell, 2003).

This is not the first time in American history that political leaders advocated and justified the suspension of civil liberties by emphasizing national security and evoking feelings of nationalism. As Benjamin Franklin once noted, "If we surrender our liberty in the name of security, we shall have neither" (Thornburgh, 2005). In order to regain respect in the eyes of the world, the president must comply with all international agreements to which the United States is a party. Additionally, the

United States must comply with customary international law, including the Geneva Conventions and the Convention against Torture and Other Cruel, Inhuman or Degrading Treatment or Punishment. When we adopt the principle of universality, we adhere to the premise: if an action is right or wrong for others, it is right or wrong for us as well. Those who do not rise to the minimal moral level of applying to themselves the standards they apply to others cannot be taken seriously when they speak of right and wrong or good and evil. Only by respecting and obeying the law, as we compel others to do, can the United States enlist international cooperation in the "War on Terror" (Center for American Progress, 2005; Chomsky, 2002).

The USA PATRIOT Improvement and Reauthorization Act was signed into law on March 9, 2006. The Bush administration succeeded in avoiding the introduction of any restrictive judicial controls over permanent measures. Many of the provisions that had a "sunset" clause, meaning that once the clear and present danger dissipated, they would disappear, did not happen. Instead, 14 temporary measures, adopted in 2001 as emergency procedures, were made a permanent part of the act. The "new" act authorizes the imprisonment, for an indefinite period of time, of foreigners suspected of terrorism, without trial or indictment. It also establishes widespread surveillance of the entire population. It left unchecked the provisions that grant "sneak and peek" warrants and national security letters, among others. Government actions and official proceedings should be as transparent as possible in times of war and peace. The government should be held accountable for its actions through our system of checks and balances as the founding fathers intended. Measures undertaken by the government should be narrowly tailored to the goal of enhancing our security not threatening our civil liberties. President Bush has been quoted as saying that "There's no telling how many wars it will take to secure freedom in the homeland." We are now in the midst of a new political order. We have moved from a state of emergency into a permanent state of exception with no end in sight. It is very difficult to tell if one is a terrorist or not until they have committed a terrorist act. Unwarranted suspicion renders even a perfect procedure useless and may push the associative guilt beyond the legislative intent. This "war" has not divided the terrorists; it has divided the allies (Paye, 2006).

See the companion website for this book for the complete text and full bibliography of this position paper.

Source: Excerpt taken from the following website: http://www.ccclr.org/documents/ccclrpositionpaper.htm.

Critical Thinking

Do you feel that the USA PATRIOT Act counters the basic freedoms bestowed upon Americans by the drafters of the Constitution? Why or why not? Would you be willing to give up some of your freedom for increased security from terrorism?

In the years since the act's passage, numerous communities across the country have passed resolutions opposing parts or all of the act's contents. These resolutions began appearing as early as January 2002, when the city of Ann Arbor, Michigan, voiced its opposition to what they saw as an attack on the basic freedoms and rights that Americans considered sacred. As of December 2007, these resolutions continued to appear, with the latest passed in the city of Wichita Falls, Texas, on December 4.

The American Civil Liberties Union (ACLU), which monitors these actions, registered 414 local, county, and state resolutions in 43 states that had been passed as of January 1, 2008, with another 275 efforts currently under debate (to see a complete list of resolutions passed, see https://www.aclu.org/national-security/list-communities-have-passed-resolutions or http://www.aclu.org/resolutions). Similar resolutions have been passed in the cities of Dallas, Denver, Detroit, Honolulu, Minneapolis, and Seattle and at the state level in Vermont, Montana, Maine, Hawaii, and Alaska (ACLU, 2004).

Update on the PATRIOT Act, *New York Times*, Friday, August 12, 2011

A *New York Times* article on October 2, 2001, described its passage as "the climax of a remarkable 18-hour period in which both the House and the Senate adopted complex, far-reaching antiterrorism legislation with little debate in an atmosphere of edgy alarm, as federal law enforcement officials warned that another attack could be imminent." Final passage came in October 24, and President George W. Bush signed it into law 2 days later.

It has been the subject of debate ever since, as civil liberty advocates have fought to rein in some of the powers it granted. It has been amended but its basic policies have been little changed.

Here is how the Congressional Research Service summarized the law shortly after its passage:

> *The Act gives federal officials greater authority to track and intercept communications, both for law enforcement and foreign intelligence gathering purposes. It vests the Secretary of the Treasury with regulatory powers to combat corruption of U.S. financial institutions for foreign money laundering purposes. It seeks to further close our borders to foreign terrorists and to detain and remove those within our borders. It creates new crimes, new penalties, and new procedural efficiencies for use against domestic and international terrorists. Although it is not without safeguards, critics contend some of its provisions go too far. Although it grants many of the enhancements sought by the DOJ, others are concerned that it does not go far enough.*

In May 2011, Congress voted to extend three provisions of the law that would have otherwise expired. They allow investigators to get "roving wiretap" court orders allowing them to follow terrorism suspects who switch phone numbers or providers; to get orders allowing them to seize "any tangible things" relevant to a security investigation, like a business' customer records; and to get national security wiretap orders to monitor noncitizen suspects who are not believed to be connected to any foreign power.

The Senate passed the extension 72 to 23 late in the afternoon of the day on which the provision would expire and within hours the House approved it 250 to 153. In an unusual move, a White House spokesman said that President Obama, who was in Europe, would "direct the use" of an autopen machine to sign the bill into law without delay.

During the debate, two senators, Ron Wyden and Mark Udall, claimed that the Department of Justice had secretly interpreted the act in a twisted way, enabling domestic surveillance activities that many members of Congress do not understand.

In March 2002, President Bush took another major step and signed Homeland Security Presidential Directive-3 (HSPD-3), which stated that

> *The Nation requires a Homeland Security Advisory System to provide a comprehensive and effective means to disseminate information regarding the risk of terrorist acts to Federal, State, and local authorities and to the American people. Such a system would provide warnings in the form of a set of graduated "Threat Conditions" that would increase as the risk of the threat increases. At each Threat Condition, Federal departments and agencies would implement a corresponding set of "Protective Measures" to further reduce vulnerability or increase response capability during a period of heightened alert.*

This system is intended to create a common vocabulary, context, and structure for an ongoing national discussion about the nature of the threats that confront the homeland and the appropriate measures that should be taken in response. It seeks to inform and facilitate decisions appropriate to different levels of government and to private citizens at home and at work.

The product outcome of this directive was the widely recognizable color-coded Homeland Security Advisory System (HSAS). The HSAS has been called on repeatedly since its inception to raise and lower the nation's alert levels between elevated (yellow) and high (orange), although the frequency of these movements has decreased over time as standards for such movements have been developed.

On April 20, 2011, the HSAS was replaced by the National Terrorism Advisory System (NTAS). In announcing the NTAS, DHS noted:

> *Under NTAS, DHS will coordinate with other federal entities to issue detailed alerts to the public when the federal government receives information about a credible terrorist threat. NTAS alerts provide a concise summary of the potential threat including geographic region, mode of transportation, or critical infrastructure potentially affected by the threat, actions being taken to ensure public safety, as well as recommended steps that individuals, communities, businesses, and governments can take to help prevent, mitigate, or respond to a threat. NTAS Alerts will include a clear statement on the nature of the threat, which will be defined in one of two ways:*
>
> - "Elevated Threat": Warns of a credible terrorist threat against the United States
> - "Imminent Threat": Warns of a credible, specific, and impending terrorist threat against the United States
>
> *DHS (2011)*

On November 25, 2002, President Bush signed into law the Homeland Security Act of 2002 (HS Act) (Public Law 107-296) and announced that former Pennsylvania Governor Tom Ridge would become secretary of a new DHS to be created through this legislation. This act, which authorized the greatest federal government reorganization since President Harry Truman joined the various branches of the armed forces under the DOD, was charged with a threefold mission of protecting the United States from further terrorist attacks, reducing the nation's vulnerability to terrorism, and minimizing the damage from potential terrorist attacks and natural disasters.

The sweeping reorganization into the new department, which officially opened its doors on January 24, 2003, joined more than 179,000 federal employees from 22 existing federal agencies under a single, cabinet-level organization. Since that time, there have been many additions, movements, and changes to both the organizational makeup of the department and its leadership. See Chapter 1 for a detailed timeline of the establishment of DHS.

Critical Thinking

Were members of Congress justified in making such a sweeping reform of the federal government as they did in the aftermath of the September 11 attacks? What could have, or should have, been done differently now that the benefit of hindsight exists?

The 9/11 Commission

As a result of the September 11 attacks, President Bush established the National Commission on Terrorist Attacks Upon the United States, informally known as the 9/11 Commission. He asked former Congressman Lee Hamilton and former New Jersey Governor Thomas Keane to chair the commission. Members included a broad range of people including former congressmen and senators and officials from previous administrations. The commission was charged with looking at the events leading up to the September 11 attacks and the actions that were taken immediately following the attack and making recommendations to the president and the Congress. The major finding of the commission's report was that there were government failures in policy, capabilities, and management. The main areas they focused on were unsuccessful diplomacy, problems within the intelligence community, problems with the FBI, permeable borders and aviation security, lack of command and control in the response, and underfunding of programs to combat terrorism. The intelligence community, the CIA, and the FBI were highly criticized. Congress also came in for criticism for its failure to financially support counterterrorism programs and the confusion over oversight and jurisdictions within its committee structure.

The final report of the 9/11 Commission was issued on July 22, 2004. The specific recommendations were encompassed in the following categories:

- Attack terrorists and their organizations.
- Prevent the continued growth of Islamist terrorism.
- Protect against and prepare for terrorist attacks.
- Establish a National Counterterrorism Center.
- Appoint a Director of National Intelligence.
- Encourage the sharing of information among government agencies and with state and local officials.

A copy of the Final Report is available at http://www.911commission.gov/report/911report.pdf.

On July 22, 2014, members of the 9/11 Commission released a follow-up report entitled "Today's Rising Terrorist Threat and the Danger to the United States: Reflections on the Tenth Anniversary of The 9/11 Commission Report." 9/11 Commission members noted at the time of the new report's release, "A decade later, we are struck by how dramatically the world has changed. In the United States, federal, state, and local authorities have implemented major security reforms to protect the country. Overseas, the United States and allies went on the offensive against al Qaeda and related terrorist organizations. Ten years ago, many feared that al Qaeda would launch more catastrophic attacks on the United States. That has not happened. While homegrown terrorists struck Fort Hood and the Boston Marathon, with tragic results, and while major attempted attacks on aviation have been disrupted, no attack on a scale approaching that of 9/11 has taken place" (9/11 Commission, 2014). See report highlights in sidebar.

Today's Rising Terrorist Threat and the Danger to the United States: Reflections on the Tenth Anniversary of the 9/11 Commission Report, July 2014

Ten years ago, as members of the National Commission on Terrorist Attacks Upon the United States, we issued the 9/11 Commission Report, the official account of the horrific attacks of September 11, 2001. A decade later, we have reconvened, as private citizens, to reflect on the changes of the past decade and the emerging threats we face as a country. In recent months, we have spoken with some of the country's most senior current and recently retired national security leaders.

Here, in brief, is what we have learned:

- The struggle against terrorism is far from over—rather, it has entered a new and dangerous phase. Al-Qaeda-affiliated groups are now active in more countries than before 9/11. The world has become more dangerous over the past few years.
- The American people remain largely unaware of the daily onslaught of cyberattacks against our nation's most sensitive and economically important electronic networks. Unfortunately, cyber readiness lags far behind this rapidly growing threat.
- Data collection and analysis are vital tools for preventing terrorist attacks, but must be tempered by appropriate measures to protect civil liberties. To date, the government has done a poor job explaining to the public—with specificity, not generalities—what is being done and why. Government leaders must verify, and persuade a skeptical public, that data collection is no broader than necessary to keep the country safe.
- Congress has proved resistant to needed reforms in its oversight of homeland security and intelligence.
- Counterterrorism fatigue and a waning sense of urgency among the public threaten US security.

The terrorist threat, while altered, remains very dangerous, and we still need vigorous and proactive counterterrorism efforts to protect the United States. In that spirit, we offer the following recommendations.

Sustaining Counterterrorism Authorities and Budgets

- National security leaders must communicate to the public—in specific terms—what the state of the threat is, how the threat is evolving, and what measures are being taken to address it.
- Congress and the president should update the September 2001 Authorization for Use of Military Force. Continuing to rely indefinitely on that authorization without further congressional action threatens to erode the constitutionally mandated separation of powers.

Congressional Oversight

- Congress should oversee and legislate for DHS through one primary authorizing committee in each house.

National Intelligence Program Budget

- Congress should fund the entire National Intelligence Program (NIP) through a unitary appropriations bill. Routing all NIP appropriations through ODNI will improve the DNI's ability to manage the Intelligence Community as a cohesive entity.

Office of the Director of National Intelligence

- Future DNIs should replicate the current DNI's focus on (1) coordinating the work of the various intelligence agencies, rather than replicating that work or turning ODNI itself into an operational entity; (2) advancing interagency information-sharing, unified IT capabilities, joint duty, and other Community-wide initiatives; and (3) providing centralized budgetary planning.
- The DNI should continue his efforts to instill counterterrorism information-sharing throughout the Intelligence Community.

Defending the Cyber Domain

- Government officials should explain to the public—in clear, specific terms—the severity of the cyber threat and what the stakes are for the country. Public and private sector leaders should also explain what private citizens and businesses can do to protect their systems and data.
- Congress should enact cybersecurity legislation to enable private companies to collaborate with the government in countering cyber threats. Companies should be able to share cyber threat information with the government without fear of liability. Congress should also consider granting private companies legal authority to take direct action in response to attacks on their networks.
- The administration should determine and communicate through appropriate channels what the consequences of cyberattacks against the United States will be and then act on the basis of those statements. And we should work with our allies to establish norms of cyberspace, clearly defining what is considered an attack by one country on another.
- The administration and Congress need to clearly delineate the respective responsibilities of the various agencies in the cyber realm. DHS and other domestic agencies need to complement, rather than attempt to replicate, the technical capabilities of the NSA.

Transparency

- The National Archives and Records Administration should work expeditiously to make all remaining 9/11 Commission records available to the public.

Bipartisanship in National Security

- The 9/11 Commission's recommendations would not have been taken up with such urgency had its report been less than unanimous or perceived as partisan.
- Bipartisanship in national security is no less important today. America remains under terrorist threat, and it will take bipartisan trust and cooperation to develop counterterrorism policies that can be sustained until the struggle is won.

Source: National Security Program and Homeland Security Project (2014).

A copy of this new 9/11 Commission Report is available at http://bipartisanpolicy.org/library/rising-terrorist-threat-9-11-commission/.

Critical Thinking

How has the work of the 9/11 Commission members continued to shine a spotlight onto America's and DHS's ongoing homeland security efforts? Are the results positive or negative?

Homeland Security Focus on Terrorism Results in a Disaster: Hurricane Katrina and Its Aftermath

In the first few years following the creation of the DHS, the nation worked through many of the growing pains associated with such a drastic bureaucratic overhaul. The TSA certainly experienced growing pains as the public was faced with ever more restrictive and evasive security policies. Of the many new and changing policies related to both national security and emergency management, one that sparked significant concern was that the focus of emergency management at all levels of government was being led away from the all-hazards philosophy to that of the single terrorism hazard. Floods, tornadoes, and other events continued to occur, although there were several mild hurricane seasons. However, several members of Congress still proposed legislation to remove the FEMA from DHS, although their efforts were ultimately rebuffed.

In late August 2005, Hurricane Katrina veered into the Gulf Coast states of Louisiana, Mississippi, and Alabama, dealing a blow considered by many emergency planners to be a worst-case scenario. At the last minute, the category 5 storm weakened to a category 3, and its track turned just slightly askew, thus preventing a direct hit on the city of New Orleans, but the damage that followed this glancing blow was still enough to completely overwhelm all mitigation and preparative measures that had been taken to protect the city and its residents. The storm's impact covered a broad geographic area stretching from Alabama, across coastal Mississippi and southeast Louisiana, spanning an estimated 90,000 square miles. As of January 2007, the official death toll attributable to the storm stood at 1836 with another 705 individuals listed as missing (Figure 2-3).

By any account, Hurricane Katrina was a massive storm, both deadly and destructive. But it was the failed response that followed, which exposed severe cracks that had developed in the nation's emergency management system and its ability to respond to a catastrophic event. Both government and independent after-action reports, and several media accounts, judged the overall response an outright failure—with the ongoing recovery phase receiving the same poor evaluation. Many of the problems of the immediate response exposed the impacts of a priority focus on terrorism and homeland security that had developed

FIGURE 2-3 Biloxi, Mississippi, April 1, 2006—After Hurricane Katrina, demolition is the only choice for many buildings such as this one along Highway 90. After 7 months, it is still difficult to comprehend the degree of devastation the Mississippi coast area has sustained. *Photo by George Armstrong/FEMA.*

in preceding years, which had likely been a major contributing factor in the decrease in local, state, and national capacities and capabilities.

Congress immediately tackled the apparent emergency management shortfalls, drawing up legislation aimed at patching many of the holes that had been exposed and developing new systems that were hoped would reduce overall risk for the future. For the moment, at least, it seemed as if the nation's emergency management focus was willing to regain its all-hazards approach. The resulting legislation, the Post-Katrina Emergency Reform Act (PKEMRA), was signed into law by the president on October 4, 2006. This law served to reconfigure the leadership hierarchy of the DHS and to return many functions that were stripped from FEMA back into the agency.

This law established several new leadership positions within the DHS, moved additional functions into (several were simply returned) the FEMA, created and reallocated functions to other components within DHS, and amended the Homeland Security Act in ways that directly and indirectly affected the organization and functions of various entities within DHS. The changes were required to have gone into effect by March 31, 2007. Transfers that were mandated by the Post-Katrina Emergency Management Reform Act included (with the exception of certain offices as listed in the act) the following:

- US Fire Administration (USFA)
- Office of Grants and Training (G&T)
- Chemical Stockpile Emergency Preparedness Division (CSEP)
- Radiological Emergency Preparedness Program (REPP)
- Office of National Capital Region Coordination (NCRC)

The law determined that the head of FEMA would take on the new title of administrator. This official would now be supported by two deputy administrators. One is the deputy administrator and chief operating officer, who serves as the principal deputy and maintains overall operational responsibilities at FEMA. The other is the deputy administrator for National Preparedness Division, a new department created within FEMA.

The National Preparedness Division under FEMA included several existing FEMA programs and several programs that were moved into the former National Preparedness Directorate. This division focuses on emergency preparedness policy, contingency planning, exercise coordination and evaluation, emergency management training, and hazard mitigation (with respect to the CSEP and REPP programs). The National Preparedness Division oversees two new divisions: Readiness, Prevention, and Planning (RPP) and the National Integration Center (NIC). RPP is now the central office within FEMA handling preparedness policy and planning functions. The NIC maintains the National Incident Management System (NIMS) and the National Response Plan (NRP) and coordinates activities with the US Fire Administration.

The existing Office of Grants and Training was moved into the newly expanded FEMA and was renamed the "Office of Grant Programs." The Training and Systems Support Divisions of the Office of Grants and Training was transferred into the NIC. The Office of the Citizen Corps was transferred into the FEMA Office of RPP.

Additional headquarters' positions created at FEMA by the new law included a Disability Employment Program coordinator (located in the FEMA Office of Equal Rights), a small state and rural advocate, a law enforcement advisor to the administrator, and a National Advisory Council.

This act specifically excluded certain elements of the former DHS Preparedness Directorate from transfer into FEMA. The Preparedness Directorate was renamed the National Protection and Programs Directorate (NPPD), and it remained under the direction of a DHS undersecretary.

And finally, the law created the Office of Health Affairs (OHA). OHA is led by the chief medical officer, who was given the title of Assistant Secretary for Health Affairs and Chief Medical Officer. The Office of Health Affairs has three main divisions:

- WMD and Biodefense
- Medical Readiness
- Component Services

Critical Thinking

Several legislators and key emergency management officials proclaimed that, in order to truly reform emergency management in the United States, FEMA would have to be removed from DHS and returned to its cabinet-level status. Do you agree or disagree with their sentiments, and why?

Obama Administration

With the election of President Barak Obama in November 2008, many people expected dramatic change relative to homeland security issues. As a senator, Mr. Obama voted against the war in Iraq and expressed concerns about civil liberties lost in the aftermath of 9/11. During the campaign, he spoke of wanting to close Guantanamo Bay prison where hundreds of suspected al-Qaeda conspirators were being kept. There were also some thoughts that the new administration might take FEMA out of DHS and restore it to its independent agency status. Recognizing that the permeable border remains an issue, President Obama nominated Janet Napolitano, governor of Arizona, to be secretary of DHS. She was quickly confirmed by the Senate and was committed to addressing issues facing the department as well as aggressively tackling the emerging threats such as cybersecurity. Among the high-priority issues were problems with immigration programs, the Transportation Security Administration (TSA) cybersecurity, and critical infrastructure. The TSA was created to address the need for heightened airport security after the hijacking of the planes during 9/11 and has had a mixed record in accomplishing its mission.

On December 25, 2009, a Nigerian national, Umar Farouk Abdulmutallab, on a flight from Amsterdam to Detroit, attempted to explode a plastic device hidden in his underwear. It didn't work and he was immediately arrested when the plane landed. His connections were traced to Yemen and an organized terrorist's organization, possibly al-Qaeda. This event was a clear blot on the TSA security operations. Initially, Secretary Napolitano said the system "worked," but the next day, she acknowledged that somewhere the system had failed.

DHS in 2011 published a report on their accomplishments in meeting the recommendations of the 9/11 Commission including in the areas of airline security. Airports now include full body screeners that, hopefully, will prevent any future underwear bombers, but these additional security measures are not popular with the general public.

On July 21, 2011, Secretary of DHS Janet Napolitano released a report that highlighted the progress DHS has made in fulfilling the 9/11 Commission recommendations. In releasing the report, the Secretary said, "Now 10 years after the worst terrorist attacks ever on American soil, America is stronger and more resilient than ever before. But threats from terrorism persist. And challenges remain. Over the past decade, we have made great strides to secure our nation against a large attack or disaster, to protect our critical infrastructure and cyber networks, and to engage a broader range of Americans in the shared responsibility for security." (See "Implementing the Recommendations of the 9/11 Commission: Progress Report 2011," http://www.dhs.gov/files/publications/implementing-9-11-commission-recommendations.shtm or access specific recommendations on the companion website for this book.)

The most significant success for the Obama administration and the intelligence community of homeland security was the capture and subsequent killing of Osama bin Laden on May 2, 2011. The US intelligence community, led by the CIA, began an extensive effort starting in 2002 that culminated in a surveillance program on what was thought to be the al-Qaeda's leader's compound in 2010. Operation Neptune Spear was authorized by President Obama and executed by the CIA and US Navy SEALs. The raid on bin Laden's compound in Pakistan started in Afghanistan. After the successful raid, bin Laden's body was taken back to Afghanistan to be verified and then buried at sea. Following this event, other al-Qaeda operatives were arrested and the general opinion in the intelligence community was that al-Qaeda was severely wounded and it would be hard to recover. An account of the operation, "Getting Bin Laden" by Schmidle (2011), appeared in the August 8, 2011, issue of *The New Yorker*.

Many people have been disappointed by the Obama administration's adoption of Bush-era homeland security practices, including the lack of progress on comprehensive immigration reform, support for continuation of certain segments of the PATRIOT Act, and the failure to resolve issues on the closing of Guantanamo Bay prison. The passage of health-care legislation, the problems with unemployment, and a lackluster economy have dominated the administration's agenda, although continuing issues with TSA and airport security, along with significant natural disaster activity, have required some focus on DHS issues.

In May 2011, the Obama administration proposed comprehensive cybersecurity legislation. The highlights in this legislation include consolidating the 47 different state laws that require businesses to report breaches of their cybersystems to consumers and DHS will work with industry to prioritize most important cyber threats and vulnerabilities; provide clear authority to allow the federal government to provide assistance to state and local governments when there has been a cyber breach; provide immunity to industry and state and local government when sharing cybersecurity information with DHS; and provide for a new framework to protect individuals' privacy and civil liberties. A more thorough discussion of this legislation is found in Chapter 8.

Jeh Johnson became the fourth secretary of the Department of Homeland Security in December 2013 succeeding Janet Napolitano. Secretary Johnson previously served as general counsel at the Department of Defense. See sidebar "DHS Secretary Jeh Johnson."

DHS Secretary Jeh Johnson

Jeh Charles Johnson was sworn in on December 23, 2013, as the fourth secretary of Homeland Security. Prior to joining DHS, Secretary Johnson served as general counsel for the Department of Defense, where he was part of the senior management team and led the more than 10,000 military and civilian lawyers across the department. As general counsel of the Department of Defense, Secretary Johnson oversaw the development of the legal aspects of many of our nation's counterterrorism policies, spearheaded reforms to the military commissions system at Guantanamo Bay in 2009, and coauthored the 250-page report that paved the way for the repeal of "Don't Ask, Don't Tell" in 2010.

Secretary Johnson's career has included extensive service in national security, law enforcement, and as an attorney in private corporate law practice. Secretary Johnson was general counsel of the Department of the Air Force from 1998 to 2001, and he served as an Assistant US Attorney for the Southern District of New York from 1989 to 1991.

In private law practice, Secretary Johnson was a partner with the New York City-based law firm of Paul, Weiss, Rifkind, Wharton, and Garrison LLP. In 2004, Secretary Johnson was elected a fellow in the prestigious American College of Trial Lawyers, and he is a member of the Council on Foreign Relations.

Secretary Johnson graduated from Morehouse College in 1979 and received his law degree from Columbia Law School in 1982.

Source: DHS (2014a).

As of November 2014, the two most significant domestic events to occur during the Obama administration from an emergency management and homeland security perspective are the 2012 Hurricane Sandy and the 2013 Boston Marathon bombings. Hurricane Sandy struck the East Coast of the United States on October 29, 2012, killing 117 people and causing an estimated $68 billion in damages across parts of 11 states. By most reports, the well-coordinated response by federal, state, and local government emergency management organizations, including FEMA, and their voluntary and private sector partners was successful. The debacle that marked the response to Hurricane Katrina was not repeated. More on the Hurricane Sandy response and recovery can be found in Chapter 9.

On April 15, 2013, two bombs were detonated within seconds of each other at the finish line area of the annual Boston Marathon. Three people were killed and 264 injured. The quick response by bystanders and race medical officials to the injured helped to prevent further deaths. The ensuing efforts by state and local law enforcement officials with support from federal law enforcement agencies resulted in the quick identification of two bombing suspects. One suspect was killed in a shoot-out with police that resulted in the death of a police officer, and the second suspect was captured after a massive manhunt encompassing the Boston metropolitan area. More on the Boston Marathon bombings can be found in Chapter 9.

These two events share two significant things in common. One, the response to both events illustrated a newfound ability for coordination and support among the myriad federal, state and local agencies, voluntary organizations, and the private sector involved in the response. Two, both events witnessed the emergence of social media as a growing mechanism for responding officials to provide the public with timely and accurate information during and after the events occurred and for these same officials to gleam valuable information from individual postings on social media sites, such as Facebook, Twitter, and YouTube, that they used to identify problems and allocate resources. In Boston, the police department made effective use of social media in identifying, tracking, and capturing the second bombing suspect. More on the emerging role of social media in emergencies can be found in Chapter 11.

In addition to these two major events, two other stories dominated discussions in and out of government in the realm for homeland security. One was the release of thousands of top secret documents by Edward Snowden in June 2013. Many of these documents concerned massive surveillance of American citizens at home and abroad by the National Security Agency (NSA). The second event is ongoing and entails discussions within the administration and the Congress concerning the ethics about the use of the NSA wiretaps of millions of Americans. The ramifications of both of these events will be felt in the homeland security community for years and possibly decades to come.

Finally, two new sets of threats/hazards came to prominence in 2013/2014. First, DHS and DOD have acknowledged that the future consequences of climate change could impact homeland security and defense capabilities and infrastructures. DHS has developed a series of sustainability and infrastructure protection plans designed to address potential future climate change impacts (DHS, 2014b). DOD released its "2014 Climate

Change Adaptation Roadmap" that calls for "integrating climate change considerations into our (DOD) plans, operations, and training across the Department so that we can manage associated risks" (DOD, 2014). Second, the faulty initial response to a patient presenting himself to a Dallas hospital with Ebola-like symptoms in October 2014 has reminded the nation that a pandemic remains a serious threat to our population and led to reviews of hospital protocols and procedures with the Centers for Disease Control and Prevention (CDC) taking the lead for the federal government. Both of these threats/hazards require further study and an ongoing effort to inform and prepare the public and public health workers concerning how to deal with them.

Conclusion

The terrorist attacks of September 11 have forever changed America and, in many ways, the world. This event has been termed the most significant disaster since the attack on Pearl Harbor and the first disaster that affected the United States on a national scale. It seemed that every American knew someone or knew of someone who perished in the attacks, and surely, every citizen felt the economic impact in the form of lost jobs, lost business, and an immediate reduction in the value of college savings and retirement accounts.

Does the killing of Osama bin Laden negate the need for such a focus on terrorism in homeland security? Terrorist organizations that dislike the US government and its policies exist outside of al-Qaeda as the Islamic State or ISIS proved in 2014. The Boston Marathon bombings clearly illustrate that domestic terrorism is still a real threat to our communities and citizens. So being vigilant is important and the intelligence community becomes ever more critical in achieving this goal.

But there are new forms of terrorism—in cybersecurity—with which major corporations such as Sony and Lockheed Martin have had their systems compromised. The DOD experienced a major cybersecurity attack, when one of its defense contractors with documentation on a new weapon system was hacked into. Critical computer systems used by major credit card companies, large retailers, and major banks have been hacked.

Natural hazards continue to beset a good portion of our nation and impact our economic and social stability. In 2011, record floods impacted the Midwest, whereas in 2010, wildfires destroyed forests and threatened communities. In 2012, Hurricane Sandy struck areas in 11 states, and in 2014, nearly every county in California is experiencing an extreme drought. Severe winter storms and temperatures struck communities across the country in 2013 and 2014 with Buffalo, NY, besieged by 7 ft of snow in November 2014. At the other extreme, record high temperatures are becoming the norm every summer with 2013 tied with 2003 as the fourth warmest year globally since records began in 1880. The impacts of a changing climate are affecting communities and individuals across the United States.

The threat portfolio under the area of terrorism has only expanded, thereby presenting the nation with a whole new set of hazards about which to worry (e.g., biological, chemical, radiological, and nuclear weapons), as well as infectious diseases, and which must now be studied and understood in much greater detail in order to best prepare. These significant changes are reflected not only in the daily lives of the American people but also in the way in which the country's government functions.

The concept of homeland security is impacted by each event that happens—natural or man-made—the level of impact of the event has determined its influence, so the concept of homeland security is still, clearly, a work in progress, reacting to events as opposed to strategically anticipating future events.

Key Terms

Cold War: A struggle for power waged between the United States and the Soviet Union, which lasted from the end of World War II until the Soviet Union ultimately collapsed. This war was defined as being "cold" because the aggression was ideological, economic, and diplomatic rather than a direct military conflict.

Critical infrastructure: Critical infrastructure includes any system or asset that, if disabled or disrupted in any significant way, would result in catastrophic loss of life or catastrophic economic loss. Some examples of critical infrastructure include the following:

Public water systems
Primary roadways, bridges, and highways
Key data storage and processing facilities, stock exchanges, or major banking centers
Chemical facilities located in proximity to large population centers
Major power generation facilities
Hydroelectric facilities and dams
Nuclear power plants

Cybersecurity: The prevention of damage to, unauthorized use of, or exploitation of, and, if needed, the restoration of electronic information and communications systems and the information contained therein to ensure confidentiality, integrity, and availability. It includes protection and restoration, when needed, of information networks and wire line, wireless, satellite, public safety answering points, and 911 communications systems and control systems (NIPP).

Department of Homeland Security: A federal agency whose primary mission is to help prevent, protect against, and respond to acts of terrorism on US soil.

Emergency management: The discipline dealing with the identification and analysis of public hazards, the mitigation of and preparedness for public risk, and the coordination of resources in response to and recovery from associated emergency events.

Executive order: A declaration issued by the president or by a governor that has the force of law. Executive orders are usually based on existing statutory authority and require no action by Congress or the state legislature to become effective.

Homeland Security Presidential Directive (HSPD): Policy decisions, issued by the president, on matters that pertain to homeland security. As of January 2008, there have been 21 HSPDs issued by the president.

National Incident Management System: This is a system mandated by HSPD-5 that provides a consistent nationwide approach for governments, the private sector, and nongovernmental organizations to work effectively and efficiently together to prepare for, respond to, and recover from domestic incidents, regardless of cause, size, or complexity.

Presidential directive: A form of executive order issued by the president that establishes an action or change in the structure or function of the government (generally within the executive office). Under President Bush, directives have been termed HSPDs and National Security Presidential Directives (NSPDs). Under President Clinton, they were termed PDDs and Presidential Review Directives (PRDs).

Statutory authority: The legally granted authority, bestowed on the named recipient by a legislature, that provides a government agency, board, or commission the power to perform the various functions, expenditures, and actions as described in the law.

Review Questions

1. What role does the US Constitution define for federal, state, and local governments in the area of emergencies and public safety?
2. What were the first indications that terrorism might be something that the US government had to deal with?
3. What events precipitated President Clinton to sign the Violent Crime Control and Law Enforcement Act of 1994?

4. Was enactment of the PATRIOT Act justified?
5. What were the areas of recommendations identified by the 9/11 Commission for preventing future attacks, and how did commission members assess these efforts in their 10th anniversary report?
6. What are the most significant emerging threats to homeland security?

Bibliography for Conclusion

Center for American Progress, 2005. Securing America, protecting our freedoms after September 11. In: Progressive Priorities: An Action Agenda for America, pp. 217–234.

Center for Democracy Technology, 2006. The nature and scope of governmental electronic surveillance activity. http://www.cdt.org/wiretap/wiretap_overview.html (July 2006).

Chomsky, N., 2003. Commentary: moral truisms, empirical evidence, and foreign policy. Rev. Int. Studies 29, 605–620.

Chomsky, N., 2002. Terror and just response. ZNet. http://www.chomsky.info/articles/20020702.htm (July 2, 2002).

O'Connell, M.E., 2003. Lawful and unlawful wars against terrorism. Law in the War on International Terrorism, pp. 79–96.

Paye, J.-C., 2006. A permanent state of emergency. Monthly Review 29–37.

Thornburgh, D., 2005. Balancing civil liberties and homeland security: does the USA PATRIOT act avoid Justice Robert H. Jackson's suicide pact? Albany Law Review (September).

References

9/11 Commission, 2014. Today's rising terrorist threat and the danger to the United States: reflections on the Tenth Anniversary of The 9/11 Commission report. In: A Nation Remembers, A Nation Recovers. FEMA, Washington, DC. http://bipartisanpolicy.org/library/rising-terrorist-threat-9-11-commission/ (July 22, 2014).

ACLU, 2004. American Civil Liberties Union. List of Communities That Have Passed Resolutions. https://www.aclu.org/national-security/list-communities-have-passed-resolutions.

City of Oklahoma City Document Management, 1996. Final report: Alfred P. Murrah Federal Building Bombing April 19, 1995. Department of Central Services Central Printing Division, Stillwater.

Curci, Lt.Col.M.A., 2004. Transnational terrorism's effect on the U.S. economy. In: United States Army War College Strategy Research Project. United States Army, Carlisle Barracks, PA.

DHS, 2011. http://www.dhs.gov/news/2011/04/20/secretary-napolitano-announces-implementation-national-terrorism-advisory-system.

DHS, 2014a. Secretary Jeh Johnson. http://www.dhs.gov/secretary-jeh-johnson.

DHS, 2014b. Sustainability performance plan. http://www.dhs.gov/publication/sustainability-performance-plan.

DOD, 2014. 2014 Climate change adaptation roadmap. http://www.acq.osd.mil/ie/download/CCARprint.pdf.

Federal Emergency Management Agency (FEMA), 2003. A Nation Remembers, A Nation Recovers. FEMA, Washington, DC.

Fusco, A.L., 1993. The World Trade Center Bombing: report and analysis. U.S. Fire Administration, Emmitsburg, MD.

Library of Congress, 2003. www.congress.gov (July 21).

National Security Program, Homeland Security Project, 2014. Bipartisan Policy Center. http://bipartisanpolicy.org/wp-content/uploads/sites/default/files/files/%20BPC%209-11%20Commission.pdf.

Schmidle, N., 2011. Getting Bin Laden. The New Yorker (August 8). http://www.newyorker.com.reporting/2011/08/110808fa_fact_schmidle.

3
Hazards

What You Will Learn

- The various hazards that often result in major emergencies and disasters, including natural hazards, technological hazards, and terrorism (including chemical, biological, radiological, nuclear, and explosive weapons)
- The reason why it is so difficult to assess and evaluate the likelihood of terrorist attacks, both within the United States and elsewhere in the world

Introduction

While most Americans associate the Department of Homeland Security (DHS) with terrorism and the terrorist threat, the relatively new Federal agency is actually responsible for the preparation for, the prevention of, the mitigation of, and the response to a much wider portfolio of natural, technological, and intentional hazards. Any destabilizing incident, condition, or factor, be it at the hands of humans or otherwise, is a threat to the security of the nation. Historically, the United States has suffered significantly more deaths, injuries, damages, and losses due to natural disasters than it has at the hands of terrorists. Of course, many will argue that the ever-growing threat of a terrorist's use of a weapon of mass destruction provides some parity between natural and man-made events as our cities, states, and country look to the future.

The nation's natural hazard profile remained relatively unchanged for decades with regard to its composition. However, due to urbanization, increasing social complexity, greater dependence on infrastructure, and the effects of climate change, the likelihood and severity of disaster events have gradually increased. Capacity-exceeding events are now occurring much more frequently, and with far more damaging outcomes, thereby demanding greater and greater attention from the government and society at all administrative levels. What is abundantly clear is that in the United States, just as is true elsewhere in the world, without concerted action, such trends will not reverse course.

For most of the nation's municipalities, urban and rural alike, the threat or risk posed by terrorism has expanded the standard set of hazards. These new hazards fall into four principal categories often referred to by the acronym CBRNE: chemical, biological, radiological/nuclear, and explosive. CBRNE hazards must now be allotted the same attention and consideration as the myriad natural and technological hazards that have menaced communities for decades and in some case centuries. And in doing such, these communities must further strain the limited financial, equipment, and human resources they possess.

There are two significant differences between these new hazards and the more traditional ones. First, there exists a wealth of both tacit knowledge and explicit knowledge for the traditional hazards as a result of years of research and actual response to and recovery from them. For instance, it is now possible to predict with a fair amount of accuracy the track of a hurricane. We know enough about the limits of a tornado's destructive force to design and build effective safe rooms. We have spent the better part of a century trying, with increasing success, to control flooding. We have developed building codes and standards that protect structures from earthquakes, fires, and wind damage. We have enough experience in responding to disaster events caused by these hazards to ensure that our first responders have sufficient protective gear and are trained and exercised in the best response protocols and practices.

But for CBRNE hazards, knowledge is more sparse and direct experience is, thankfully, much less common. The general understanding of the properties and the destructive qualities of the various chemical and biological threats is limited at best, even among the many response agencies that will be called upon to manage the consequences of their deployment in an attack. The first responder community, the state and local emergency managers, and the general public all remain almost completely ill informed about these hazards and have little or no experience in limiting their consequences. The same is largely true with community and national leaders and the news media who influence or are actually among the decision-making elite. Achieving baseline fluency levels in managing the traditional mix of natural and technological disasters required many decades of work. Understandably, it will take some time before we have reached an adequate degree of comfort with regard to our knowledge of the new hazards.

The second notable difference between the traditional hazards and the new hazards of terrorism is the manner in which we encounter each. Traditional hazards occur because of natural processes, whether geologic, meteorologic, or hydrologic, or because of some human accident, oversight, or negligence. Hurricanes, tornadoes, and earthquakes are inherently natural forces that have existed for eons, regardless of the presence of humans. Technological hazards, including HazMat spills, unintentional releases at nuclear power plants, and transportation accidents, for example, have traditionally been just that—accidents. The new terrorism hazards differ from these natural and technological hazards in that their genesis is intentional and their primary purpose is maximized death and destruction. These hazards are weapons in every sense of the word, set apart from military resources in that they target civilian populations and the greater social consciousness for purposes of advancing political, ideological, or religious agendas. No hurricane or earthquake has ever struck in pursuit of a human agenda.

The Hazards

A *hazard* is a physical condition that has the potential to cause fatalities, injuries, property damage, infrastructure damage, agricultural loss, damage to the environment, interruption of business, or other types of harms or losses (FEMA, 1997). Each hazard carries an associated risk, which is represented by the likelihood of the hazard leading to an actual disaster event and the consequences of that event should it occur. The product of realized hazard risk is an emergency event, which is typically characterized as a situation exhibiting negative consequences that require the efforts of one or more of the emergency services (fire, police, emergency medical services (EMS), public health, and others) to manage. When the response requirements of an emergency event exceed the capabilities of those established emergency services in one or more critical areas (e.g., shelter, fire suppression, and mass care), the event is classified as a disaster.

Each hazard is distinct with regard to its characteristics. However, there are three umbrella groupings into which all hazards may be sorted that include natural hazards, technological hazards, and terrorist (intentional) hazards.

Natural Hazards

Natural hazards are those that exist in the natural environment as a result of hydrologic, meteorologic, seismic, geologic, volcanic, mass movement, or other natural processes and that pose a threat to human populations and communities. Natural hazard risk is often magnified by human activities, including development and modification of the landscape and changes in the atmosphere. As individuals and collectively as societies, humans consciously expose themselves to the risks posed by natural hazards in order to achieve some other benefit or gain, such as access to land or fisheries, aesthetics, and access to commerce and transportation, to name a few. The following is a list of those hazards that possess the greatest potential to impact humans on a community-wide or greater scale.

Floods

A flood is an overabundance of water that engulfs land and property that is normally dry (see Figure 3-1). Floods are caused by a number of factors, including sustained or heavy rainfall, melting snow, an obstruction of a natural waterway, destruction of water containment structures, and other generative means. Floods usually occur from large-scale weather systems associated with prolonged rainfall or onshore winds, but they may also result from locally intense thunderstorms, snowmelt, ice jams, and dam failures. Floods are capable of undermining buildings and bridges, eroding shorelines and riverbanks, tearing out trees, washing out access routes, and causing loss of life and injuries. Flash floods occur when intense storms drop large amounts of rain within a brief period, providing little or no warning and reaching peak levels in a matter of minutes.

FIGURE 3-1 FEMA is completing aerial preliminary damage assessments over Tennessee following the severe storms and floods that have damaged or destroyed homes and businesses in May 2010. *Source: David Fine/FEMA. http://1.usa.gov/1p4wIQq (May 3, 2010).*

Floods are the most frequent and widespread disaster in the United States, primarily the result of human development in the floodplain. The close relationship that exists between societies and water is the result of commerce, agriculture, and access to drinking water. As development and urbanization rates increase, so does the incidence of flooding in large part as a result of this relationship. FEMA estimates that approximately 10 million households are at risk from flooding in the United States. These households have sustained an average of $8.2 billion in damages each year during the period from 1983 to 2013 (NOAA, 2014). Since FEMA's National Flood Insurance Program began in 1978, it has paid out over $50.9 billion for flood insurance claims and related losses (FEMA, 2014a) (see sidebar "Flood Facts").

Flood Facts

- In the past 5 years (2009–2014), all 50 states have experienced floods or flash floods.
- Everyone lives in a flood zone.
- Most homeowner's insurance does not cover flood damage.
- Just a few inches of water from a flood can cause tens of thousands of dollars in damage.
- Flash floods often bring walls of water 10–20 ft high.
- A car can easily be carried away by just 2 ft of floodwater.
- Hurricanes, winter storms, and snowmelt are common (but often overlooked) causes of flooding.
- New land development can increase flood risk, especially if the construction changes natural runoff paths.
- Federal disaster assistance is usually a loan that must be paid back with interest. For a $50,000 loan at 4% interest, your monthly payment would be around $240 a month ($2880 a year) for 30 years. Compare that to a $100,000 flood insurance premium, which is about $400 a year ($33 a month).
- You are eligible to purchase flood insurance as long as your community participates in the National Flood Insurance Program.
- In most cases, it takes 30 days after purchase for a policy to take effect, so it's important to buy insurance before the storm approaches and the floodwaters start to rise.
- In a high-risk area, your home is more likely to be damaged by flood than by fire.
- From 2003 to 2012, total flood insurance claims averaged nearly $4 billion per year.
- More than 5.5 million people currently hold flood insurance policies in more than 21,800 communities across the United States.

Source: FEMA (2014b).

Floods are typically measured according to their elevation above standard water levels (of rivers or coastal water levels). This elevation is translated into the annualized likelihood of reaching such heights. For example, a flood depth that has a 1% chance of being reached or could be expected to occur once across a 100-year period would be considered a "100-year flood event." Typically, structures that are contained within areas likely to experience flooding in a 100-year flood event are considered to be within the floodplain. River and stream gauges are maintained to monitor floodwater elevations and to provide information on rising water for use in sandbagging and dike construction. Such information also allows for early warning and evacuation to occur.

Earthquakes

An earthquake is a sudden, rapid shaking of the Earth's surface that is caused by the breaking and shifting of tectonic (crustal) plates. This shaking can affect both the natural and built environments, with even moderate events leading to the collapse of buildings and bridges; disruptions in gas, electric, and phone services; landslides; avalanches; fires; and tsunamis. Structures constructed on unconsolidated landfill, old waterways, or other unstable soil are generally at greatest risk unless seismic mitigation has been utilized. Seismicity is not seasonal or climate-dependent and can therefore occur at any time of the year.

Earthquakes are sudden, no-notice events despite scientists' and soothsayers' best efforts to predict when they will occur. Seismic sensing technology is effective at measuring and tracking seismic activity, but it has yet to accurately predict a major seismic event with any degree of accuracy.

Each year, hundreds of earthquakes occur in the United States, though the vast majority of these are barely perceptible. As earthquake strength increases, its likelihood of occurrence decreases. Major events, which are those reaching or exceeding 6.5 magnitude on the Richter scale, strike the country only once every decade or so, but such events have led to some of its most devastating disasters. The 1994 Northridge (California) earthquake, for instance, is the country's second most expensive natural disaster as ranked by FEMA relief costs. It resulted in almost $7 billion in federal funding (and second only to Hurricane Katrina). It is anticipated that a major earthquake along the New Madrid Fault could cause catastrophic damage across eight states and result in indirect damages throughout the entire country that would significantly impact the nation's economy.

The strength and effects of earthquakes are commonly described by the Richter and Modified Mercalli Intensity (MMI) Scales. The Richter scale, designed by Charles Richter in 1935, assigns a single number to quantify the strength and effect of an earthquake across the entire area affected according to the strength of ground waves at its point of origin (as measured by a seismograph). Richter magnitudes are logarithmic and have no upper limit. The MMI also measures the effects of earthquakes, but rather than applying a single value to the event, it allows for site-specific evaluation according to the effects observed at each location. The MMI (Table 3-1) rates event intensity using Roman numerals I through XII. Determinations are generally made using reports by people who felt the event and observations of damages sustained by structures.

Hurricanes

Hurricanes are cyclonic storms that occur in the Western Hemisphere where the majority of the US land is located. When these storms affect the Pacific Island territories, such as Guam, American Samoa, and the Northern Mariana Islands (among others), they are called *cyclones*. These very strong wind storms begin as tropical waves and grow in intensity and size as they progress to become tropical depressions and tropical storms (as determined by their maximum sustained wind speed). The warm-core depression becomes a tropical storm when the maximum sustained surface wind speeds fall between 39 and 73 miles per hour (mph). Tropical cyclonic storms are defined by their low barometric pressure, closed-circulation winds originating over tropical waters, and an absence of wind shear. Cyclonic storm winds rotate counterclockwise in the Northern Hemisphere and clockwise in the Southern Hemisphere.

Table 3-1 Modified Mercalli Intensity Scale

MMI Intensity	Damages Sustained and Sensations Experienced	Richter Scale Equivalent
I-IV (instrumental to moderate)	No damage sustained. Sensation ranges from imperceptible to that of a heavy truck striking the building. Standing motor cars may rock	<4.3
V (rather strong)	Felt by nearly everyone; many awakened. Some dishes and windows broken. Unstable objects overturned. Pendulum clocks may stop	4.4–4.8
VI (strong)	Felt by all; many frightened. Some heavy furniture moved; a few instances of fallen plaster. Damage slight	4.9–5.4
VII (very strong)	Damage negligible in buildings of good design and construction; slight to moderate in well-built ordinary structures; considerable damage in poorly built or badly designed structures; some chimneys broken	5.5–6.1
VIII (destructive)	Damage slight in specially designed structures; considerable damage in ordinary substantial buildings with partial collapse. Damage great in poorly built structures. Fall of chimneys, factory stacks, columns, monuments, walls. Heavy furniture overturned	6.2–6.5
IX (ruinous)	Damage considerable in specially designed structures; well-designed frame structures thrown out of plumb. Damage great in substantial buildings, with partial collapse. Buildings shifted off foundations	6.6–6.9
X (disastrous)	Most masonry and frame structures/foundations destroyed. Some well-built wooden structures and bridges destroyed. Serious damage to dams, dikes, embankments. Sand and mud shifting on beaches and flatland	7.0–7.3
XI (very disastrous)	Few or no masonry structures remain standing. Bridges destroyed. Broad fissures in ground. Underground pipelines completely out of service. Widespread earth slumps and landslides. Rails bent greatly	7.4–8.1
XII (catastrophic)	Damage nearly total. Large rock masses displaced. Lines of sight and level are distorted. Objects are thrown into the air	>8.1

Source: USGS (2009).

A *hurricane* is a cyclonic tropical storm with sustained winds measuring 74 mph or more. Hurricane winds extend outward in a spiral pattern as much as 400 miles around a relatively calm center of up to 30 miles in diameter known as the *eye*. Hurricanes are fed by warm ocean waters. As these storms make landfall, they often push a wall of ocean water known as a *storm surge* over coastal zones. Once over land, hurricanes cause further destruction by means of torrential rains and high winds. A single hurricane can last for several weeks over open waters and can run a path across the entire length of the eastern seaboard.

Hurricane season runs annually from June 1 to November 30. August and September are peak months during the hurricane season. Hurricanes are commonly described using the Saffir-Simpson Hurricane Scale (Table 3-2). Hurricanes are capable of causing great damage and destruction over vast areas. Hurricane

Table 3-2 The Saffir Simpson Hurricane Scale

Category	Conditions	Effects
1	Wind speed: 74-95 mph Storm surge: 4-5 ft above normal	Primary damage to unanchored mobile homes, shrubbery, and trees. Some coastal flooding and minor pier damage. Little damage to building structures
2	Wind speed: 96-110 mph Storm surge: 6-8 ft above normal	Considerable damage to mobile homes, piers, and vegetation. Coastal and low-lying area escape routes flood 2-4 h before arrival of hurricane center. Buildings sustain roofing material, door, and window damage. Small craft in unprotected mooring break moorings
3	Wind speed: 111-130 mph Storm surge: 9-12 ft above normal	Mobile homes destroyed. Some structural damage to small homes and utility buildings. Flooding near coast destroys smaller structures; larger structures damaged by floating debris. Terrain continuously lower than 5 ft above sea level (ASL) may be flooded up to 6 miles inland
4	Wind speed: 131-155 mph Storm surge: 13-18 ft above normal	Extensive curtain wall failures, with some complete roof structure failure on small residences. Major erosion of beaches. Major damage to lower floors of structures near the shore. Terrain continuously lower than 10 ft ASL may flood (and require mass evacuations) up to 6 miles inland
5	Wind speed: over 155 mph Storm surge: over 18 ft above normal	Complete roof failure on many homes and industrial buildings. Some complete building failures. Major damage to lower floors of all structures located less than 15 ft ASL and within 500 yards of the shoreline. Massive evacuation of low-ground, residential areas may be required

Source: FEMA.

Floyd in 1999 first threatened the states of Florida and Georgia, made landfall in North Carolina, and damaged sections of South Carolina, North Carolina, Virginia, Maryland, Delaware, New Jersey, New York, Connecticut, Massachusetts, and Maine. The damage was so extensive in each of these states that they all qualified for federal disaster assistance. To date, the costliest disaster in US history is Hurricane Katrina that occurred in August of 2005 and required over $29 billion in federal funding. In comparison, the next costliest disaster is the 9/11 attacks on America, which required only $8.8 billion (less than one-third of Katrina's costs). In total dollar figures, this hurricane was estimated to have resulted in over $80 billion in losses (Finn, 2009) and was one of the deadliest in terms of lives lost (1836 killed). Many of the Gulf Coast areas—especially hard-hit New Orleans—are still reeling from this disaster event, with full recovery years or even decades away.

In recent years, significant advances have been made in hurricane tracking technology and computer models. The National Hurricane Center in Miami, Florida, now tracks tropical waves from the moment they form off the coast of West Africa through their development as a tropical depression. Once the tropical depression grows to the strength of a tropical storm, the Hurricane Center assigns the storm a name. After the sustained wind speed exceeds 74 mph, the storm officially becomes a hurricane. The National Hurricane Center uses aircraft to observe and collect meteorologic data on the hurricane and to track its movements across the Atlantic Ocean. It also uses several sophisticated computer models to predict the storm's path.

These predictions are provided to local and state emergency officials to help them make evacuation decisions and to predeploy response and recovery resources.

Historically, high winds and storm surge-related flooding have been the principal contributors to the loss of life and injuries and the property and infrastructure damage caused by hurricanes. Inland flooding caused by hurricane rainfall has also resulted in large losses of life and severe property damage, especially in zones of hilly or mountainous topography. Damage to the environment is another important factor related to hurricane-force winds and flooding. For instance, storm surges cause severe beach erosion, most notably on fragile barrier islands. Inland flooding from Hurricane Floyd inundated waste ponds on hog farms in North Carolina, washing the hog waste into the Cape Fear River and ultimately into the ocean. Storm surges caused by Hurricanes Katrina and Sandy had profound impacts on the environment—in some cases, completely erasing or altering coastal areas. Dauphin Island was literally pushed toward the land by the force of Katrina's surge, and the Chandeleur Islands were completely destroyed. Breton National Wildlife Refuge, 1 of 16 wildlife refuges damaged by the storm, lost over half of its area. Much of this land lost served as breeding grounds for marine mammals, reptiles, birds, and fish.

Storm Surges

Storm surges, defined as masses of water that are pushed toward the shore by meteorologic forces, are a primary cause of the injuries, deaths, and structural damages associated with hurricanes, cyclones, northeasters, and other coastal storms. When the advancing surge of water coincides with high tides, the resulting rise in sea level is further exacerbated. Storm surges may reach several dozen feet under the right conditions, as was the case in Hurricane Katrina. Even moderate storm surges, such as the 12 foot surge caused by Hurricane Sandy that was pushed into New York and New Jersey, are capable of causing profound impacts when major metropolitan areas are affected. Storm surge impacts may be exacerbated by wind-driven turbulence, which becomes superimposed on the storm tide and further damages inundated structures by means of wave action (each cubic yard of water results in 1700 lb of pressure on affected structures). The surge height at landfall is ultimately dictated by the expanse and intensity of the storm, the height of the tide at the time of landfall, and the slope of the seafloor approaching land. The longer and shallower the seafloor, the greater the storm surge will be. Because much of the United States' densely populated Atlantic and Gulf Coast coastlines lie less than 10 ft above mean sea level, storm surge risk is extreme.

Tornadoes

A *tornado* is a rapidly rotating vortex or funnel of air extending groundward from a cumulonimbus cloud, exhibiting wind speeds of up to 300 mph. Approximately 1200 tornadoes are spawned by thunderstorms each year in the United States. Most tornadoes remain aloft, but the few that do touch the ground are devastating to everything in their path. The forces of a tornado's wind are capable of lifting and moving huge objects, destroying or moving whole buildings, and siphoning large volumes from bodies of water and ultimately depositing them elsewhere. Because tornadoes typically follow the path of least resistance, people living in valleys have the greatest exposure to damage.

Tornadoes have been measured using the Fujita-Pearson Tornado Intensity Scale since its creation in 1971 (Table 3-3). In 2006, research indicated that tornado damage was occurring from winds of much weaker intensity than previously thought, so the National Weather Service created an enhanced scale to measure them (Table 3-4). First used in January 2007, this scale expands upon the original system's measure of damage to homes by adding 18 new damage indicators, including those that affect trees, mobile homes,

Table 3-3 Original Fujita-Pearson Tornado Intensity Scale

Category	Conditions	Effects
F-0	40–72 mph	Chimney damage, tree branches broken
F-1	73–112 mph	Mobile homes pushed off foundation or overturned
F-2	113–157 mph	Considerable damage, mobile homes demolished, trees uprooted
F-3	158–205 mph	Roofs and walls torn down, trains overturned, cars thrown
F-4	207–260 mph	Well-constructed walls leveled
F-5	261–318 mph	Homes lifted off foundation and carried considerable distances, autos thrown as far as 100 m

Table 3-4 Enhanced Fujita-Pearson Tornado Intensity Scale

Category	Conditions	Effects
F-0	65–85 mph	Minor to light damage to structures and vegetation
F-1	85–110 mph	Moderate damage to structures and vegetation
F-2	111–135 mph	Heavy damage to structures and vegetation
F-3	136–165 mph	Severe damage to structures and vegetation
F-4	166–200 mph	Extreme damage to structures and vegetation
F-5	Over 200 mph	Complete destruction of structures and vegetation

and several other structures (giving a total of 28 indicators studied in the classification of a tornado). Under the enhanced Fujita-Pearson Tornado Intensity Scale, a tornado that does not affect houses can still be classified.

Tornado damage occurs only when the funnel cloud touches down on land. The states with the greatest tornado risk are Texas, Oklahoma, Arkansas, Missouri, and Kansas, which together occupy what is commonly known as "Tornado Alley." In recent years, however, tornadoes have struck cities that are not regularly frequented by tornadoes, including Miami, Nashville, and Washington, DC. Tornadoes can also touch down in several places in succession, as occurred in Washington, DC, in 2001. In that event, a single tornado first touched down in Alexandria, Virginia, just south of the city and then again in College Park, Maryland, just north of DC. Tornado "outbreaks," which are occurrences wherein multiple tornadoes result from a single weather system, can extend over hundreds of miles of land. A tornado outbreak that occurred over the course of 4 days in April of 2014 included 84 tornadoes and resulted in 35 deaths, over 300 injuries, and over a billion dollars in damage in states spanning over a dozen states.

Tornado season generally falls between March and August, although tornadoes can occur at any time of the year. Tornadoes tend to occur in the afternoon and evening, with more than 80% of all tornadoes striking between noon and midnight. Collapsing buildings and flying debris are the principal factors behind the deaths and injuries tornadoes cause. Early warning is key to surviving tornadoes, as warned citizens can protect themselves by moving to structures designed to withstand tornado-force winds. Doppler radar and other meteorologic tools have drastically improved the ability to detect tornadoes and the amount of advance warning time available before a tornado strikes. Improved communications and new technologies have also been critical to giving people advance warning.

Buildings that are directly in the path of a tornado have little chance of surviving unless they are specifically designed to withstand not only the force of the winds but also the force of the debris "missiles" that are thrown about. "Safe room" technology developed by FEMA and Texas Tech University, which retrofits a portion of a structure to withstand such winds through engineered resistant design and special resilient materials, offers those in the path of a tornado much greater survival likelihoods. Safe rooms are often the most cost-effective way to mitigate tornado risk in communities that are already heavily developed, since they can be built into an existing (or new) structure for a small cost (estimated between $3000 and $5000).

In order to greatly expand the mitigation benefits of safe rooms, similar technology is being developed for use in community mass-care shelters. New technologies in building design and construction are also being developed by FEMA and others to reduce the damage to buildings and structures not located directly in the path of a tornado. Many of the same wind-resistant construction techniques used effectively in high-risk hurricane areas have been found to be equally effective when applied to new and retrofitted structures located in tornado-prone areas.

Wildfires

Wildfires (often called "wildland fires") are classified into three categories: surface fires, the most common type, which burn along the floor of a forest, moving slowly and killing or damaging trees; ground fires, which are usually started by lightning and burn on or just below the forest floor; and crown fires, which burn through the forest canopy high above the ground and therefore spread much more rapidly due to wind and direct contact with nearby trees. Wildland fires are an annual and increasing hazard due to the air pollution (primarily smoke and ash that travel for miles, causing further hazards to health and mechanical or electrical equipment), risk to firefighters, environmental effects, and property destruction they cause.

As residential areas expand into relatively untouched wildlands (called the *wildland-urban interface*), the threat to the human population increases dramatically. Protecting structures located in or near the wildland poses special problems and often stretches firefighting resources beyond capacity. Wildland fires also cause several secondary hazards. For instance, when heavy rains follow a major fire, landslides, mudflows, and floods can strike on or downhill from the newly unanchored soil. These fires can also severely scorch the land, destroying animal habitats and causing barren patches that may persist for decades, increasing the likelihood of long-term erosion.

Several terms are used to classify the source and behavior of wildland fires:

- *Wildland fires*: Fueled almost exclusively by natural vegetation, these fires typically occur in national forests and parks, where federal agencies are responsible for fire management and suppression (see Figure 3-2).
- *Interface or intermix fires*: These fires occur in or near the wildland-urban interface, affecting both natural and built environments and posing a tactical challenge to firefighters concerned with the often conflicting goals of firefighter safety and property protection.
- *Firestorms*: Events of such extreme intensity that effective suppression is virtually impossible, firestorms occur during extreme weather and generally burn until conditions change or the available fuel is exhausted.
- *Prescribed fires and prescribed natural fires*: These are fires that are intentionally set or selected natural fires that are allowed to burn for the purpose of reducing available natural fuel.

Severe drought conditions and the buildup of large quantities of "fuel" (dead trees and flammable vegetation) on the forest floors have led to a steady increase in the prevalence of wildfires in the United States. Since the National Interagency Fire Center began tracking the number and acreage of fires in 1960, the

FIGURE 3-2 Helicopters drop water and fire retardant on the Harris fire, near the Mexican border, to stop the wildfire from advancing. Currently, the fires in Southern California have burned nearly 350,000 acres. *Source: Andrea Booher/FEMA. http://1.usa.gov/1r2WuQM (October 24, 2007).*

average number of fires has fallen (presumably due to fire prevention programs), while the annual acreage burned has risen. In other words, the fewer fires that are occurring are larger and more destructive on average. Before 2004, no year had seen more than 7 million acres burned, and few experienced greater than 4 or 5 million acres burned. Yet, from 2004 to 2013, acres burned in 6 of the 10 years exceeded 8 million (NIFC, 2014).

Mass Movements

The general category of mass movements includes several different hazards caused by the horizontal or lateral movement of large quantities of physical matter. Mass movements cause damage and loss of life through several different processes, including the pushing, crushing, or burying of objects in their path, the damming of rivers and waterways, the subsequent movement of displaced bodies of water (typically in the form of a tsunami), destruction or obstruction of major transportation routes, and alteration of the natural environment in ways in which humans are negatively impacted. Mass movement hazards are most prevalent in areas of rugged or varied topography, but they can occur even on level land, as in the case of subsidence. The following are the categories of mass movement hazards:

- *Landslides*: Landslides occur when masses of relatively dry rock, soil, or debris move in an uncontrolled manner down a slope. Landslides may be very highly localized or massive in size, and they can move at a creeping pace or at very high speeds. Many areas have experienced landslides repeatedly since prehistoric times. Landslides are activated when the mechanisms by which the material was anchored become compromised (e.g., through a loss of vegetation or seismic activity).

- *Mudflows*: Mudflows are water-saturated rivers of rock, earth, and other debris that are drawn downward by the forces of gravity. These phenomena develop when water rapidly accumulates in the material that is moved, like during heavy rainfall or rapid snowmelt. Under these conditions, solid or loose earth can quickly change into a flowing river of mud, or "slurry." These flows move rapidly down slopes or through channels, following the path of least resistance, and often strike with little or no warning. Mudflows have traveled several miles in many instances, growing in size as they pick up trees, cars, and other materials along the way. The March 22, 2014, Oso mudslide in Washington state, which completely destroyed 49 homes and resulted in the deaths of 43 people, occurred after 45 days of rainfall that doubled the average precipitation in the affected area (see Figure 3-3).
- *Lateral spreads*: Lateral spreads occur when large quantities of accumulated earth or other materials spread downward and outward due to gradual hydrologic and gravitational forces. Spreads can affect rock, but they also occur in fine-grained, sensitive soils such as clays.
- *Liquefaction*: When saturated solid material becomes liquid-like in constitution due to seismic or hydrologic activity, it can exacerbate lateral spreading.
- *Rockfalls*: Rockfalls occur when masses of rock or other materials detach from a steep slope or cliff and descend by freefall, rolling, or bouncing. Topples consist of the forward rotation of rocks or other materials about a pivot point on a hillslope. Rockfalls can occur spontaneously when fissures in rock or other materials cause structural failure or due to seismic or other mechanical activity (including explosions or the movement of heavy machinery).

FIGURE 3-3 Specialized canine recovery teams search the Snohomish County mudslide disaster site in an effort to aid recovery operations. *Source: Marty Bahamonde/FEMA. http://1.usa.gov/1uGKw2W (April 4, 2014).*

- *Avalanches*: An avalanche is a mass of ice or snow that moves downhill at a high velocity. Avalanches can shear trees, cover entire communities and highway routes, and level buildings in their path. Avalanches are triggered by a number of processes, including exceeding critical mass on a steep slope and disturbances caused by seismicity or human activity. As temperatures increase and snowpack becomes unstable, the risk of avalanches increases. The primary negative consequences associated with avalanches are loss of life (mostly to backcountry skiers, climbers, and snowmobilers) and obstruction of major transportation routes. Around 10,000 avalanches are reported each year in the United States. Since tracking began in 1790, an average of 144 people have become trapped in avalanches annually, and of these, an average of 14 sustain injuries and 14 die. In the last decade, this number has increased to an average of 28 deaths per year (Colorado Avalanche Information Center, 2014). The average annual value of structural damage is $500,000, though the secondary costs associated with disrupted commerce can be much greater.
- *Land subsidence*: Land subsidence is the loss of surface elevation caused by the removal of subsurface support. Subsidence can range from broad, regional lowering of large landmasses to severe localized collapses. The primary cause of this hazard is human activity, including underground mining, extraction of groundwater or petroleum, and the drainage of organic soils. Although statistics are not maintained on the annual cost of land subsidence in the United States, in 1991, the National Research Council estimated the direct damages to be at least $125 million per year (USGS, 1999) with costs associated with the loss of resources and property value likely increasing this number severalfold.
- *Expansive soils*: Soils and soft rock that tend to swell or shrink when their moisture content changes are referred to as *expansive soils*. These changes are extremely detrimental to transportation routes (including highways, streets, and rail lines) and structures that are built above the affected soils. The most extensive damage affects highways and streets. Two rock types that are particularly prone to expansion and that are prevalent in the United States (primarily in the West) are aluminum silicates (e.g., ash, glass, and rocks of volcanic origin) and sedimentary rocks (e.g., clay and shale).

Tsunamis

A *tsunami* is a wave or series of waves that are generated by a mass displacement of sea or lake water. The most common generative factor behind tsunamis is undersea earthquakes that cause ocean floor displacement, but large tsunamis have been caused by volcanic eruptions and landslides as well. Tsunami waves travel outward as movements of kinetic energy (rather than traveling water) at very high speeds in all directions from the area of the disturbance, much like the ripples caused by a rock thrown into a pond. As the waves approach shallow coastal waters, wave speed quickly decreases and the water is drawn upward and onto land. Tsunamis can strike at heights of up to and over 100 ft and extend onto land for a mile or more (depending upon topography). The force of the water causes near total destruction of everything in its path.

The areas at the greatest risk from tsunamis are those lying less than 50 ft above sea level and within 1 mile of the shoreline. Successive crests (high water) and troughs (low water) can occur anywhere from 5 to 90 min apart. Tsunamis travel through deep water at approximately 450 mph, so the areas closest to the point of origin experience the greatest destruction and have the least amount of forewarning. Most tsunami-related deaths are the result of drowning, while the loss of services and related health problems associated with the incredible destruction of the infrastructure (including the loss of hospitals and clinics, water pollution, contaminated food and water stocks, and damaged transmission lines) add to these statistics.

Volcanic Eruptions

A volcano is a break in the Earth's crust through which molten rock from beneath the Earth's surface (magma) erupts. Over time, volcanoes will grow upward and outward, forming mountains, islands, or large, flat plateaus called *shields*. Volcanic mountains differ from mountain chains formed through plate tectonics (movement of the Earth's crustal plates) because they are built through the accumulation of materials (lava, ash flows, and airborne ash and dust) rather than being pushed up from below. When volcanic material exits the Earth, it is called *lava*, and the nature of its exit determines the land formations that result. Thinner lava typically moves quickly away from the source and becomes a large shield (as in the case of the Hawaiian Islands), while thicker lava and other materials form steeper volcanic formations.

When pressure from gases and molten rock becomes strong enough to cause an explosion, violent eruptions may occur. Gases and rock shoot up through the opening and spill over or fill the air with lava fragments. Volcanoes cause injuries, death, and destruction through a number of processes, including direct burns, suffocation from ash and other materials, trauma from ejected rocks, floods and mudflows from quickly melted snow and ice, burial under burning hot "pyroclastic" burning ash flows, and others. Airborne ash can affect people hundreds of miles away from the eruption and influence global climates for years afterward.

Volcanic ash contaminates water supplies, causes electrical storms, and can cause roofs to collapse under the weight of accumulated material. Eruptions may also trigger tsunamis, flash floods, earthquakes, and rockfalls. Sideways-directed volcanic explosions, known as *lateral blasts*, can shoot large pieces of rock at very high speeds for several miles. These explosions can kill by impact, burial, or heat. They have been known to knock down entire forests. Most deaths attributed to the Mount St. Helens eruption were a result of lateral blast that was strong enough to topple a large swath of forest. Despite the destructive power of volcanoes, the ash that is created can provide value in that it may be used for construction or road building, in abrasives and cleaning agents, and as a raw material in many chemical and industrial products. Ash-covered land is also rich in mineral nutrients and ideal for agricultural production.

Severe Winter Storms

Severe winter storms occur when extremely cold atmospheric conditions coincide with high airborne moisture content, resulting in rapid and heavy precipitation of snow and/or ice. When combined with high winds, the event is known as a *blizzard*. In the United States, these hazards originate from four distinct sources:

- In the Northwest, cyclonic weather systems originate in the North Pacific Ocean or the Aleutian Islands region.
- In the Midwest and Upper Plains, Canadian and Arctic cold fronts push ice and snow deep into the heart of the nation—in some instances, traveling as far south as Florida.
- In the Northeast, lake-effect snowstorms develop when cold weather fronts pass over the relatively warm surfaces of the Great Lakes.
- The eastern and northeastern states are affected by extratropical cyclonic weather systems in the Atlantic Ocean and the Gulf of Mexico that produce snow, ice storms, and occasional blizzards.

On January 1, 2006, the federal government began using a new scale to measure severe winter storms that is similar to those used to measure the magnitude and intensity of hurricanes and tornadoes. The Northeast Snowfall Impact Scale (NESIS) provides a numerical value to storms based on the geographic

Table 3-5 NESIS Values

Category	NESIS Value	Description
1	1–2.499	Notable
2	2.5–3.99	Significant
3	4–5.99	Major
4	6–9.99	Crippling
5	10.0+	Extreme

Source: NOAA (2006).

area affected, the amount of snow accumulation, and the number of people affected. The minimum threshold for a storm's inclusion in the scale is 10 in. of snow falling over a wide area.

NESIS values range from 1 to 5 and include associated descriptors (from most to least severe) of extreme, crippling, major, significant, and notable. The NESIS scale differs from other meteorologic indices in that it considers population data. It uses the following formula:

$$\text{NESIS} = \underset{n=4}{\overset{n=30}{S}}\left[n/10\left(A_n / A_{\text{mean}} + P_n / P_{\text{mean}}\right)\right]$$

where *A* equals the area affected and *P* equals the population affected. Table 3-5 shows the categories assigned to severe winter storms using this formula.

Drought

Drought is defined as a prolonged shortage of available water, primarily due to insufficient rain and other precipitation or because exceptionally high temperatures and low humidity cause a drying of agriculture and a loss of stored water resources. Drought hazards differ from other natural hazards in three ways:

1. A drought's onset and conclusion are difficult to determine because the effects accumulate slowly and may linger even after the apparent termination of an episode.
2. There is no precise or universally accepted determination of what conditions constitute official drought conditions or the degree of drought severity.
3. The drought's effects are less obvious and spread over a larger geographic area.

The Climate Prediction Center of the National Weather Service monitors nationwide drought conditions and provides visual reports on a weekly basis and seasonal reports on a monthly basis. A report of current drought conditions in the United States, referred to as the *United States Drought Monitor*, can be viewed at http://bit.ly/1uwz3F6.

Extreme Temperatures

Major diversions in average seasonal temperatures can cause injuries, fatalities, and major economic impacts when they are prolonged or coincide with other natural or technological events. Extreme heat, called a *heat wave*, occurs when temperatures of 10 or more degrees above the average high temperature persist across a geographic region for several days or weeks. Humid or muggy conditions, which add to the discomfort of high temperatures, can occur when a "dome" of high atmospheric pressure traps hazy, damp air close to the ground. Excessively dry conditions that coincide with extreme heat can provoke wind and dust storms.

When little rain occurs in conjunction with extreme heat, droughts are likely to occur. Prolonged periods of heat have resulted in hundreds of thousands of deaths in single instances, including 600 in the Chicago area in 1995 and almost 37,500 in Europe in 2003. In most years, over 1500 people die from exposure to excessive heat in the United States, making it the number one weather-related killer of humans.

While there is no widely accepted standard for extreme cold temperatures, periods of colder than normal conditions exhibit a range of negative consequences, depending on where they occur and exactly how cold temperatures fall. Any time temperatures fall below freezing, there is the risk of death from hypothermia to humans and livestock, with the degree to which populations are accustomed to those temperatures a primary factor in resilience. Extreme cold can also lead to serious economic damages from frozen water pipes; the freezing of navigable rivers, which halts commerce and can cause ice dams; and the destruction of crops.

Thunderstorms

Thunderstorms are meteorologic events that bring heavy rains, strong winds, hail, lightning, and tornadoes. Thunderstorms are generated by atmospheric imbalance and turbulence caused by a combination of several conditions, including unstable, warm air rising rapidly into the atmosphere; sufficient moisture to form clouds and rain; and upward lift of air currents caused by colliding weather fronts (cold and warm), sea breezes, or mountains.

A thunderstorm is classified as severe if its winds reach or exceed 58 mph, it produces a tornado, or it drops surface hail at least 1 in. (quarter-sized) in diameter. Thunderstorms may occur singly, in clusters, or in lines. Thus, it is possible for several thunderstorms to affect one location in the course of a few hours. These events are particularly devastating when a single thunderstorm affects one location for an extended period. Such conditions lead to oversaturation of the ground and subsequent flash flooding and slope erosion.

Lightning is a major secondary threat associated with thunderstorms. In the United States, between 75 and 100 Americans are hit and killed by lightning each year. Many air disasters have been linked to thunderstorms due to the unpredictable and turbulent wind conditions they cause and the threat of electronic or mechanical failure caused by lightning strikes. When humans or structures are hit by lightning, the effect is devastating to both.

Hail

Hail is frozen atmospheric water that falls to the Earth. Moisture in clouds becomes frozen into crystals at high temperatures and begins to fall under its own weight. Typically, these crystals melt at lower temperatures, but in the right conditions, they pick up more moisture as they fall and are then lifted to cold elevations, which causes refreezing. This cycle may continue until the individual hailstones reach several inches in diameter under the right conditions. Because of the strength of severe thunderstorms and tornadoes, both can cause this cyclic lifting, and therefore, they are often accompanied by hail. Hailstorms occur more frequently during late spring and early summer when the jet stream migrates northward across the Great Plains. When they fall, they can damage crops, break windows, destroy cars and other exposed properties, collapse roofs, and cause other destruction totaling nearly $1 billion each year in the United States.

Critical Thinking

Why do Americans seem to be more concerned with terrorist hazards than natural hazards? How do our perceptions of risk affect the way that we manage them? Do individuals have a greater personal responsibility to protect themselves from natural hazards than they do from other technological or terrorist hazards?

Technological Hazards

Technological hazards, or "man-made" hazards as they are often called, are an inevitable product of technological innovation and human development. These hazards, which can occur after the failure of or damage to the many structures and systems upon which humans rely, tend to be much less understood than their natural counterparts. Additionally, as technology advances with each passing year, the number of associated disasters increases, and their scope expands. The most common technological hazards arise from systems and structures related to transportation, infrastructure, industry, and construction.

Structural Fires

Studies have shown that civilizations have been fighting structural fires using coordinated governmental resources since the first century AD (Coppola, 2011). Structural fires can be triggered or exacerbated by both natural processes, including lightning, high winds, earthquakes, volcanoes, and floods, and by human origins, including accidents and arson, for example. Lightning is the most significant natural contributor to fires affecting the built environment. Buildings with rooftop storage tanks for flammable liquids are particularly susceptible. There were 1,240,000 fires reported in the United States in 2013. Of these, 45.5% of these were outside and "other" fires, 39.3% were structure fires, and 15.2% were vehicle fires (NFPA, 2014).

Residential fires may not typically result in disasters (as defined earlier in this chapter and by the Department of Homeland Security), but together, they result in 85% of the roughly 3000 civilian deaths that occur each year and 75% of the 17,000 injuries that occur. They are also a major contributor to the 75,000-85,000 firefighter injuries that occur annually (National Fire Protection Association, 2010).

Transportation Accidents

Transportation is a technology on which the entire world depends for travel, commerce, and industry. The vast system of land, sea, and air transportation involves complex and expensive infrastructure, humans or machines to conduct that infrastructure, and laws and policies by which the whole system is guided. A flaw or breakdown in any one of these components can and often does result in a major disaster involving loss of life, injuries, property and environmental damage, and economic consequences. Transportation accidents can cause mass casualty incidents, as well as major disruptions to society and commerce, when they occur in any of the transportation sectors (including air travel, sea travel, rail travel, bus travel, and roadways). The accidents do not need to be the result of the vehicles themselves. For instance, the collapse of the I-35 Mississippi Bridge in Minneapolis (August 4, 2007) resulted in 13 fatalities, 145 injuries, and severe financial implications given that 140,000 daily commuters had to find alternate means of crossing the river (see Figure 3-4). Transportation systems and infrastructure are considered a top terrorist target due to these severe consequences.

FIGURE 3-4 Cars and roadway litter the river where the I-35 bridge collapsed in Minneapolis. *Source: FEMA/Todd Swain. (August 4, 2007).*

Infrastructure Failures

Infrastructure hazards are another type of technological hazard and are primarily related to critical systems of utilities, services, and other assets (both state-run and private) that serve the public. The consequences of infrastructure hazards may include loss of vital services, injury, death, property damage, or a combination of these. As technological innovation, global communication, and global commerce increase, nations are becoming much more dependent upon their critical infrastructure. One of the most common types of infrastructure failures, the power outage (or "blackout"), is the number one concern of businesses and has been estimated to be causing between $80 and $188 billion in economic losses each year (Fahey, 2013). The frailty of the electrical grid was highlighted by a 2011 blackout, which was the largest in the State's history and resulted in over 7 million people losing power, caused by an error made by a service technician (Los Angeles Times, 2011). The primary types of infrastructure hazards include power failures, telecommunications system failures, computer network failures, critical water or sewer system failures, and major gas distribution line breaks.

Dam Failures

Dams are constructed for many purposes, the most common being flood control and irrigation. When dams retaining large quantities of water fail, there exists the potential for large-scale uncontrolled release of stored water downstream. Dam failures pose the most extreme flood risk due to the sudden and severe impacts that can result. Dams most often fail as a result of maintenance neglect, overtopping (as in the case of a flood), poor design, or structural damage caused by a major event such as an earthquake, collision, or blast. However, dams are also considered a critical terrorist risk due to the fact that dam failure would result in immediate and significant deaths and property destruction and would provide little hope for warning those in the resulting torrent's path. Dams are both publicly and privately owned and maintained, so their monitoring can pose a challenge to offices of emergency management and homeland security charged with assessing associated hazard risk. The United States as a nation boasts the second greatest number of dams worldwide, exceeded only by China.

Hazardous Materials Incidents

Hazardous materials are chemical substances that if released or misused can pose a threat to people and the environment. Chemicals are prevalent in many industries and products, including agriculture, medicine, research, and consumer product development. These materials may be explosive, flammable, corrosive, poisonous, radioactive, or otherwise toxic or dangerous. Releases typically occur as a result of transportation accidents or accidents at production and storage facilities. Depending on the nature of the chemical, the result of a release or spill can include death, serious injury, long-lasting health effects, and damage to buildings, homes, and other property.

The majority of hazardous materials incidents occur in homes, and the quantities released are almost always too small to cause more than a highly localized hazard. However, it is the transportation or industrial use of these same products that leads to major disaster events when releases occur due to the massive volumes or quantities involved. At present, hazardous materials are manufactured, used, or stored at an estimated 4.5 million facilities in the United States—from major industrial plants to local dry cleaning establishments or gardening supply stores. Since the Oklahoma City and World Trade Center bombings, monitoring of many of these chemicals has increased. However, it was in the wake of September 11, with recognition of the terrorist potential at a great many other facility types, that tracking became institutional. This is discussed in greater detail later in this chapter as well as in Chapter 8.

Nuclear Accidents

Radioactive materials have provided significant benefits since their discovery, including the generation of power, scientific treatments and experiments, new detection, and imaging technologies, among many others. However, because the radiation emitted from these materials can cause immediate and lasting tissue damage to humans and animals upon exposure, these materials must be handled and contained using specialized techniques, materials, and facilities. National and international law strictly dictates who may possess these materials, how they can be used, and how and where they must be disposed of.

Exposure to radiation can be the result of an accidental or intentionally caused spill, breach of the containment vessel, escape of gases, or an explosion. Nuclear material remains radioactive until it has shed all of its ionizing particles, called *radionuclides*. This process, called *radioactive decay*, is the primary source of health risk to life. When released quickly, dust or gases may rise into the atmosphere in a characteristic plume, which carries the contaminants far from the point of origin with atmospheric currents, depositing it as radioactive fallout along its course.

In the United States, the greatest threat of exposure to radioactive materials comes from an accident or sabotage at one of the nation's many nuclear power plants. As the distance to a nuclear power plant decreases, the risk of exposure increases, and the likelihood of surviving in the event of a large-scale release of materials decreases. Since 1980, utilities operating commercial nuclear power plants in the United States have been required to maintain on- and off-site emergency response plans as a condition of maintaining their operating licenses. On-site emergency response plans are approved by the Nuclear Regulatory Commission (NRC). Off-site plans (which are closely coordinated with the utility's on-site emergency response plan) are evaluated by FEMA and provided to the NRC, who must consider the FEMA findings when issuing or maintaining a license.

A catastrophic failure of a nuclear reactor is called a *meltdown*, indicative of the failure of the reactor's containment due to the incredibly high heat caused by a runaway nuclear reaction. The worst nuclear accident to date was the result of a reactor core meltdown that occurred in the Chernobyl Nuclear Power Plant in Ukraine on April 26, 1986. So great was the radioactive plume and resultant fallout, which traveled as far as and landed primarily in neighboring Belarus, that over 336,000 people had to be evacuated and permanently resettled. Over 20 years later, the area is still uninhabitable. The more recent failure of containment vessels at the Fukushima Daiichi Nuclear Power Plant in Japan, which occurred when the plant was inundated in the March 11, 2011, tsunami, highlights the vulnerability of all nuclear plants to the effects of natural disasters. This accident will require decades to overcome, with contamination condemning thousands to permanent displacement and possible long-term health effects. It has also caused all nuclear nations to consider the safety of their own plants and to reconsider whether the risk associated with nuclear power is justified. Three years after this accident, all 48 of Japan's nuclear power plants remained shuttered, costing the nation billions of dollars in increased power costs associated with importing fossil fuels (Humber, 2014).

In the United States, the most dangerous radioactive event, which was ultimately contained (thereby preventing any realized threat to human life), was the partial core meltdown at the Three Mile Island Nuclear Generating Station in Pennsylvania on March 28, 1979. The accident happened when a system that cooled the nuclear reactor, and therefore controlled the temperature of the reactor core, failed to operate correctly. While some nuclear material was released, the effect on people exposed was similar to that of receiving one or two medical X-rays. The public reaction to this event, however, significantly changed the course of the nuclear power industry in the United States, as expansion abruptly ended. In 2011, in major part due to the events in Japan, the nation turned its attention to two Nebraska-based nuclear power plants located on the banks of the then-flooding Missouri River. Images of the Fort Calhoun Station plant, which was completely surrounded by floodwater, caused understandable concern for nearby residents. In recognition that the Japan incident was caused by a loss of power to cooling systems, the Nebraska plants arranged for multiple backup power systems including newly installed overhead lines and diesel-powered generators.

Terrorism (Intentional) Hazards

Terrorism hazards, or "intentional hazards" as they are often called, are the means or mechanisms through which terrorists are able to carry out their attacks. Chapter 2 described the motivational factors behind terrorists' actions, which the terrorists feel are justified by the need to achieve their goals. This section describes the mechanisms employed, including what they are, how they function, and the likely consequences that result. The greatest achievement in managing the consequences of terrorist attacks will come from gaining a better understanding of how these hazards influence risk, how America's society and structures are vulnerable to attacks, and how individuals, communities, and countries can minimize their impacts.

This section presents basic information about the four primary categories of terrorist hazards summarized in the acronym CBRNE, namely, chemical, biological, radiological/nuclear, and explosive.

Coordinated assaults, which are not typically considered "weapons of mass destruction," will also be addressed. Cyberterrorism, a driver for cybersecurity, is addressed in Chapter 8.

Critical Thinking

Will it ever be possible to accurately predict terrorist attacks, whether in the United States or elsewhere? Why or why not? What tools, skills, and other options may be used to increase the accuracy of predictions? What is so different about the assessment of terrorist risk versus other hazard types?

Conventional Explosives and Secondary Devices

Conventional explosives have existed for centuries, since the explosive precursor to gunpowder, invented by the Chinese for use in firecrackers, was modified for use in weaponry. Traditional (manufactured) and improvised explosive devices (IEDs) are generally the easiest weapons to both obtain and use. In fact, instructions for their assembly and deployment are widely available in print and on the Internet, as well as through the transfer of institutional knowledge within informal criminal networks. These widely available weapons, when skillfully used, can inflict massive amounts of destruction to property and can cause significant injuries and fatalities to humans. Conventional explosives are most troubling as weapons of mass destruction (WMD) in light of their ability to effectively disperse chemical, biological, or radiological agents.

Conventional explosives and IEDs can be either explosive or incendiary in nature. Explosives use the physical destruction caused by the expansion of gases that results from the ignition of "high- or low-filler" explosive materials to inflict damage or harm. Examples of explosive devices include simple pipe bombs, made from common plumbing materials; satchel charges, which are encased in a common looking bag such as a backpack and left behind for later detonation; letter or package bombs, delivered through the mail; or a car bomb, which can be used to deliver a large amount of explosives. On April 18, 2013, the Tsarnaev brothers detonated improvised explosive devices crafted out of pressure cookers and other easily obtainable materials near the finish line of the Boston Marathon (see Figure 3-5). They claim to have learned how to make these bombs through an online magazine published by an al-Qaeda cell based in Yemen. The explosions killed 3 people and injured another 264 more, many of whom lost limbs because the bombs contained bolts, nails, and other shrapnel to maximize human impacts (House Homeland Security Committee, 2014). Incendiary devices, also referred to as firebombs, rely on the ignition of fires to cause damage or harm. Examples include Molotov cocktails (gas-filled bottles capped with a burning rag), napalm bombs, and fuel-air explosives (thermobaric weapons).

Explosions and conflagrations can be delivered via a missile, or projectile device, such as a rocket, rocket-propelled grenade (RPG), mortar, or air-dropped bomb. Nontraditional explosive delivery methods are regularly discovered and include the use of fuel-filled commercial airliners flown into buildings as occurred on September 11, 2001, bombs hidden in the soles of shoes, bombs crafted to look like everyday objects (e.g., a bomb crafted to mimic a printer cartridge), and even a bomb integrated into a pair of underwear. Because explosives rely on easily obtainable technology and are relatively easy to craft, transport, and deliver, they are the most common choice of terrorists. Although suicide bombings, in which bombers manually deliver and detonate the device on or near their person, are becoming more common, most devices are detonated through the use of timed, remote (radio or cell phone), or other methods of transmission (light sensitivity, air pressure, movement, electrical impulse, etc.).

Although almost 50% of terrorist attacks involve the use of conventional explosives, less than 5% of actual and attempted bombings are preceded by any kind of threat or warning. These devices can

FIGURE 3-5 Members of the FBI arrive on the scene of the bombings at the Boston Marathon. *Source: Robert Rose/FEMA. http://1.usa.gov/1v0gE2Z (April 14, 2013).*

be difficult to detect because most easily attainable explosive materials are untraceable except in the rare instance where highly specialized detection equipment is being utilized. Commercial explosives in the United States are now required to contain a chemical signature that can be used to trace their source should they be used for criminal means, but this accounts for only a fraction of materials available to terrorists. What is particularly troubling about these devices is that the physical and psychological impacts can be magnified by detonating multiple explosives at once or in succession. Secondary explosives have been used in this manner to target bystanders and officials who are responding to the initial, often smaller, explosion. Because of the graphic nature of the carnage resulting from explosives, as well as the apparent ease and frequency of their use, even the threat of explosive weapons is effective at inflicting fear (FEMA, 2002).

Critical Thinking

Conventional explosives can be manufactured using ingredients commonly found in hardware stores, pharmacies, and other sources available to the general public. What can be done to prevent terrorists from using these much-needed materials for sinister purposes short of banning them entirely?

Chemical Agents

Like explosives, chemical weapons have existed for centuries and have been used repeatedly throughout history. Evidence has been found in what is now Syria of an AD 256 incident where an attack by the Persian army on Roman troops killed at least 20 soldiers by burning sulfur and bitumen, which creates a toxic smoke (Jacobs, 2013). The first large-scale organized application and the most significant modern use of chemical weapons occurred during World War I. German troops conducting an attack against allied forces in Belgium released 160 tons of chlorine gas into the air, killing more than 10,000 soldiers and injuring another 15,000. In total, it is estimated that about 113,000 tons of chemical weapons was used in World War I, resulting in the deaths of more than 90,000 people and injury to over 1.3 million.

Chemical weapons are created for the sole purpose of killing, injuring, or incapacitating people. They can enter the body through inhalation, ingestion, or the skin or eyes. Many different kinds of chemicals have been developed as weapons, falling under six general categories that are distinguished according to their physiological effects on victims:

1. Nerve agents (sarin and VX)
2. Blister agents (mustard gas and lewisite)
3. Blood agents (hydrogen cyanide)
4. Choking/pulmonary agents (phosgene)
5. Irritants (tear gas and capsicum (pepper) spray)
6. Incapacitating agents (BZ and Agent 15)

Terrorists can deliver chemical weapons by means of several different mechanisms. Aerosol devices spread chemicals in liquid, solid (generally powdered), or gas form by causing tiny particulates of the chemical to be suspended into the air. Explosives can also be used to disperse the chemicals through the air in this manner. Devices that contain chemicals, for either warfare or everyday use (such as a truck or train tanker), can be breached, thereby exposing the chemical to the air. Chemicals can also be mixed with water or placed into food supplies. Chemicals that are easily absorbed through the skin can be placed directly onto a victim to cause harm or death.

Chemical attacks, in general, are recognized immediately (some indicators of the possible use of chemical agents are listed in the sidebar "General Indicators of Possible Chemical Agent Use"), although it may be unclear to victims and responders until further testing has taken place that an attack has occurred (see Figure 3-6), and whether the attack was chemical or biological in nature. Chemical weapons may be persistent (remaining in the affected area for long after the attack) or nonpersistent (evaporating quickly, due to their lighter-than-air qualities, resulting in a loss of ability to harm or kill after ~10 or 15 min in open areas). In unventilated rooms, however, any chemical can linger for a considerable time.

General Indicators of Possible Chemical Agent Use

- Stated threat to release a chemical agent
- Unusual occurrence of dead or dying animals—for example, lack of insects or dead birds
- Unexplained casualties
    - Multiple victims
    - Surge of similar 911 calls

  - Serious illnesses
  - Nausea, disorientation, difficulty breathing, or convulsions
  - Definite casualty patterns
- Unusual liquid, spray, vapor, or powder
  - Droplets, oily film
  - Unexplained odor
  - Low-lying clouds/fog unrelated to weather
- Suspicious devices, packages, or letters
  - Unusual metal debris
  - Abandoned spray devices
  - Unexplained munitions

Source: FEMA (2002).

The effect of chemical weapons on victims is usually fast and severe. Identifying what chemical has been used presents special difficulties, and responding officials (police, fire, EMS, HAZMAT) and hospital staff treating the injured are at risk from their effects. Without proper training and equipment, there is little these first response officials can do in the immediate aftermath of a chemical terrorist attack to identify or treat the consequences.

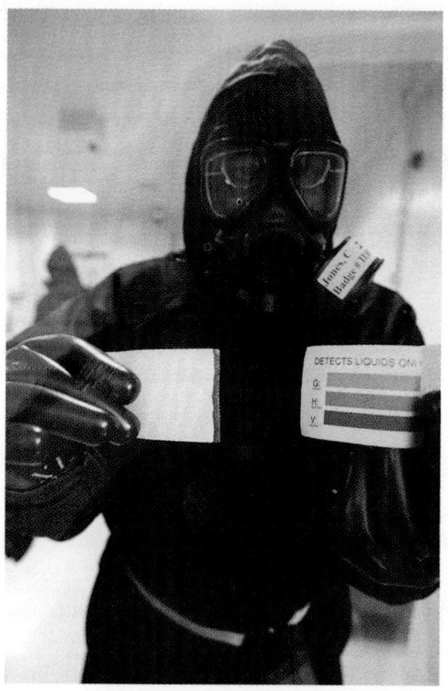

FIGURE 3-6 Todd Jones, superintendent of the Center for Domestic Preparedness (CDP), demonstrates a positive result for nerve agent during training at the CDP's Chemical, Ordnance, Biological, and Radiological (COBRA) Training Facility. *Source: Shannon Arledge/FEMA. http://1.usa.gov/1HtbSAn (August 3, 2011).*

A simple list of agents compiled by the CDC is presented in the sidebar "List of Chemical Agents." Fact sheets about cyanide, sulfur mustard (mustard gas), sarin, ricin, and chlorine, which have been compiled from the CDC website, are presented in the companion website for this book.

List of Chemical Agents

- Abrin
- Adamsite (DM)
- Agent 15
- Ammonia
- Arsenic
- Arsine (SA)
- Benzene
- Bromobenzyl cyanide (CA)
- BZ
- Cannabinoids
- Chlorine (CL)
- Chloroacetophenone (CN)
- Chlorobenzylidenemalononitrile (CS)
- Chloropicrin (PS)
- Cyanide
- Cyanogen chloride (CK)
- Cyclohexyl sarin (GF)
- Dibenzoxazepine (CR)
- Diphenylchlorarsine (DA)
- Diphenylcyanoarsine (DC)
- Diphosgene (Do P)
- Distilled mustard (HD)
- Ethyldichloroarsine (ED)
- Ethylene glycol
- Fentanyls and other opioids
- Hydrofluoric acid
- Hydrogen chloride
- Hydrogen cyanide (AC)
- Lewisite (L, L-1, L-2, L-3)
- LSD
- Mercury
- Methyldichloroarsine (MD)
- Mustard gas (H) (sulfur mustard)
- Mustard/lewisite (HL)
- Mustard/T
- Nitrogen mustard (HN-1, HN-2, HN-3)
- Nitrogen oxide (NO)
- Paraquat
- Perfluoroisobutylene (PHIB)
- Phenyldichloroarsine (PD)
- Phenothiazines
- Phosgene (CG)
- Phosgene oxime (CX)
- Phosphine
- Potassium cyanide (KCN)
- Red phosphorus (RP)
- Ricin (considered to be both a chemical and biological weapon)
- Sarin (GB)
- Sesqui mustard
- Sodium azide
- Sodium cyanide (NaCN)
- Soman (GD)
- Stibine
- Strychnine
- Sulfur mustard (H) (mustard gas)
- Sulfur trioxide-chlorosulfonic acid (FS)
- Superwarfarin
- Tabun (GA)
- Teflon and perfluoroisobutylene (PHIB)
- Thallium
- Titanium tetrachloride (FM)
- VX
- White phosphorus
- Zinc oxide (HC)

Source: CDC (2013).

Biological Agents

Biological or "germ" weapons are live organisms (either bacteria or viruses) or the toxic by-products generated by living organisms that are manipulated in order to cause illness, injury, or death in humans, livestock, or plants. Although awareness of the potential for use of bacteria, viruses, and toxins as weapons existed long before Bruce Edward Ivins used the US mail system to launch a series of anthrax attacks in 2001—killing and injuring several people—these events certainly put the threat on the forefront of the public and political agendas.

Evidence of the use of biological weapons in warfare exists as early as the fourteenth century, when the Mongols used plague-infected corpses to spread disease among their enemies. Since that time, their use has been documented in dozens of instances. Additionally, scientific discovery has enabled a significant increase in the ability of governments and terrorists alike to manufacture and deploy these weapons, and with more devastating and far-reaching results. What makes these weapons so terrifying to responders and citizens alike is that there is an almost complete lack of direct experience in responding to them, coupled with an extreme sense of dread that surrounds the graphic and horrifying nature of their possible consequences. In terms of pure statistical risk, the likelihood of their use causing a major event is very low simply because it is so difficult and comparatively very expensive for small-scale terrorist elements to manufacture, store, and deploy them when considered in light of the wider range of attack options available. Simply speaking, it is easier to make a bomb than it is to grow and weaponize anthrax. That being said, preparedness is still warranted given that they have been used with success in the past and the consequences of any successful intentional deployment have catastrophic potential.

Bioweapons may be dispersed overtly or covertly by perpetrators. When covertly applied, bioweapons are extremely difficult to recognize because their negative consequences can take hours, days, or even weeks to emerge. This is especially true with bacteria and viruses, although toxins (which are, in essence, poisons) generally elicit an immediate reaction. Attack recognition is made through a range of methods, including identification of a credible threat, the discovery of weapons materials (dispersion devices, raw biological material, or weapons laboratories), and correct diagnosis of affected humans, animals, or plants. Detection is most successful when there exist a collaborative public health monitoring system, trained and aware physicians, patients who elect to seek medical care, and equipment suitable for confirming diagnoses. Bioweapons are unique in this regard in that detection is likely to be made not by a first responder, but by members of the public health community.

The devastating potential of bioweapons is confounded by the fact that people normally have no idea that they have been exposed. During the incubation period, when they do not exhibit symptoms but are contagious to others, they can spread the disease by direct contact or through aerosolized particles. Incubation periods differ by agent and can be as short as several hours to as long as several weeks. These delays in the onset of obvious symptoms allow for wider geographic transmission—especially in light of the efficiency modern travel affords. While not linked to terrorism, the rapid and expansive spread of the SARS virus throughout all continents of the world provides evidence of this phenomenon.

Biological weapons are also effective at disrupting economic and industrial components of society, even when they only target animals or plants. Terrorists could potentially spread a biological agent over a large geographic area, undetected, causing significant destruction of crops. If the agent spreads easily, as is often the case with natural diseases such as Dutch elm disease, the consequences could be devastating to an entire industry. Cattle diseases such as foot and mouth disease and mad cow disease, which occur naturally, could be used for sinister purposes with little planning, resources, or technical knowledge. In 1916 and 1917, the German army did just this, spreading anthrax and other diseases through exported livestock and animal feed as well as other means (Albarelli, 2001). With globalization, such actions would require much less effort to conduct.

The primary defense against the use of biological weapons is recognition, which is achieved through proper training of first responders and public health officials. Early detection, before the disease or illness has spread to critical limits, is key to preventing a major public health emergency.

Biological agents are grouped into three categories, designated by the letters A, B, and C. *Category A agents* are those that have great potential for causing a public health catastrophe and that are capable of being disseminated over a large geographic area. Examples of *Category A agents* are anthrax, smallpox, plague, botulism, tularemia, and viral hemorrhagic fevers. *Category B agents* are those that have low mortality rates but that may be disseminated over a large geographic area with relative ease. *Category B agents* include salmonella, ricin, Q fever, typhus, and glanders. *Category C agents* are common pathogens that have the potential for being engineered for terrorism or weapon purposes. Examples of *Category C agents* are hantavirus and tuberculosis (CDC, 2014a).

Critical Thinking

Why do chemical and biological agents instill such fear? Should Americans be any more or less fearful of these agents? Why or why not? Do you think that most people overestimate or underestimate their actual risk from such agents? What can be done to correct misperceptions of risk? What is most likely causing misperceptions?

Some Indicators of Biological Attack

- Stated threat to release a biological agent
- Unusual occurrence of dead or dying animals
- Unusual casualties
  - Unusual illness for region/area
  - Definite pattern inconsistent with natural disease
- Unusual liquid, spray, vapor, or powder
  - Spraying, suspicious devices, packages, or letters

Source: FEMA (2002).

For indicators of biological attack and a list of biological agents, see the sidebars of the same respective titles. Fact sheets compiled from the CDC website for the following selected biological agents are available as files with matching titles on this book's companion website, together with FEMA information on cyanide, sulfur mustard, sarin, ricin, and chlorine:

- Anthrax
- Smallpox
- Plague
- Botulism
- Tularemia

List of Biological Agents

- Anthrax (*Bacillus anthracis*)
- Botulism (*Clostridium botulinum* toxin)
- Brucellosis (*Brucella* species)
- Cholera (*Vibrio cholerae*)
- *E. coli* O157:H7 (*Escherichia coli*)
- Epsilon toxin (*Clostridium perfringens*)
- Emerging infectious diseases such as Nipah virus and hantavirus
- Glanders (*Burkholderia mallei*)
- Melioidosis (*Burkholderia pseudomallei*)
- Typhoid fever (*Salmonella typhi*)
- Typhus fever (*Rickettsia prowazekii*)
- Plague (*Yersinia pestis*)
- Psittacosis (*Chlamydia psittaci*)
- Q fever (*Coxiella burnetii*)
- Ricin (considered to be both a chemical and biological weapon)
- Salmonellosis (*Salmonella* species)
- Smallpox (*Variola major*)
- Staphylococcal enterotoxin B
- Tularemia (*Francisella tularensis*)
- Viral encephalitis (alphaviruses (e.g., Venezuelan equine encephalitis, eastern equine encephalitis, and western equine encephalitis))
- Viral hemorrhagic fevers (filoviruses (e.g., Ebola and Marburg) and arenaviruses (e.g., Lassa and Machupo))
- Water safety threats (e.g., *Vibrio cholerae*, shigellosis (*Shigella*), and *Cryptosporidium parvum*)

Source: CDC (2014b).

The Difficulties of Preventing or Treating Biological Attacks with Vaccines

Unlike chemical, radiological, nuclear, or other WMDs, biological weapons may be prevented before an attack and in some cases limited during an attack with the use of vaccines. Vaccines work by helping the body to recognize and destroy a biological agent, thereby developing immunity to it. Vaccines have been used for over two centuries to prevent or eradicate common diseases, first appearing in 1796 when English physician Edward Jenner developed a vaccine that was effective at preventing smallpox. Since then, several other diseases have been limited or eradicated through widespread

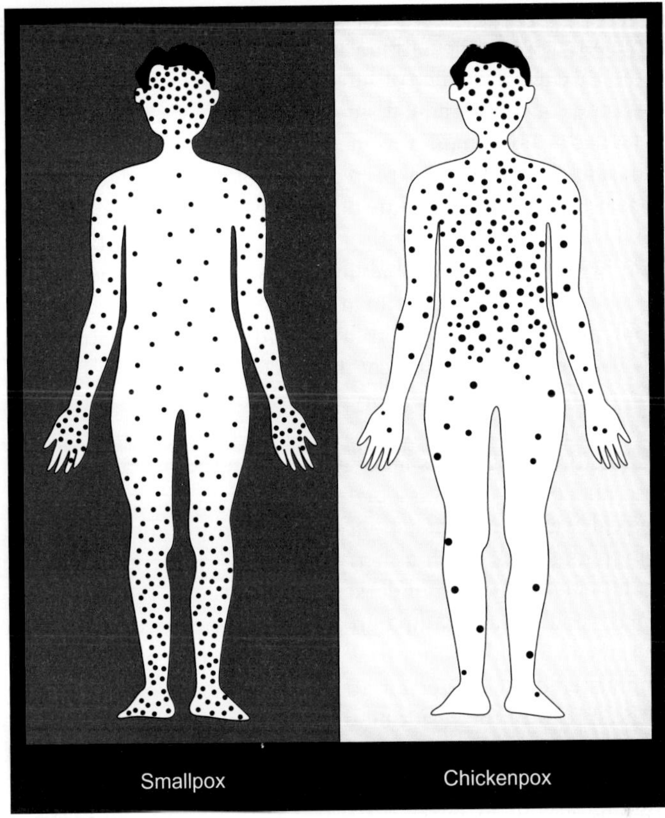

FIGURE 3-7 Rash distribution in (left) smallpox and (right) chickenpox.

vaccination programs, including polio, measles, mumps, rubella, typhoid fever, Japanese encephalitis, hepatitis, and many other once-common diseases.

Vaccines, however, often come at a high cost. Their development requires significant investments in research, testing, and public relations. For some diseases, including HIV and Ebola, expensive, drawn-out campaigns to develop vaccines have thus far proved fruitless despite heavy investment in cash and human resources and decades of time. A second cost of vaccines is the risk associated with administering them. Almost without exception, vaccines carry associated health risks for recipients. For instance, it is estimated that one in every million people given the smallpox vaccine will die as a result of complications directly related to the vaccine itself. In addition to fatalities caused by the vaccine, 1 in 10,000 vaccine recipients experienced one or many other adverse effects directly related to the vaccine itself. These include corneal scarring (blindness), eczema, generalized smallpox-like reaction, and encephalitis (Figure 3-7).

For many of the biological weapons that are considered to be viable threats, including anthrax and smallpox, there already exist vaccines that could offer a much higher level of resistance in the human population. However, because of the aforementioned costs and risks associated with these vaccines, policymakers are faced with determining whether the vaccine-related injuries and deaths outweigh the potential deaths and injuries that would occur in the event that a terrorist was able to effectively use a biological weapon containing the agent in question. For instance, if the threat of a smallpox attack spurred a renewed vaccination campaign in the United States, and 40 million people received the vaccine, the vaccines incidence of fatal reactions (1 per million doses) would result in 40 deaths regardless of whether or not an actual smallpox attack ever occurred. Using this baseline, we can then determine whether or not a mass vaccination program is worth the expected vaccine-related fatalities only if we can safely say that the expected result of not vaccinating the population would be a fatality rate greater than 40. To calculate this number, we must first estimate the number of people that would likely be exposed in an attack, multiply this number by 30% (the fatality rate of smallpox), and multiply this again by the expected probability of an attack over the lifetime of the population. So, let's just say that 100,000 people are estimated to be infected in a scenario (a figure chosen for illustrative purposes only). This number would likely lead to 30,000 deaths given the fatality rate of the disease. But if it is determined, for instance, that there is only a 1 in 1000 chance that an attack like that could happen, then the expected fatality rate based upon the scenario is only 30 deaths—10 fewer deaths than would be guaranteed in a mass evacuation campaign. Under this scenario, the risk associated with the vaccination program is more deadly than the risk associated with an attack.

Because of these and other costs associated with the vaccination of the entire population against certain biological warfare agents, policy has generally dictated that only those specific people who have an individual risk (such as active members of the military, public health officials, laboratory workers, and emergency responders) should have the benefit of vaccination; there has never been a single mass vaccination campaign for a biological weapon. Instead, the US government, as well as governments of other countries, has chosen instead to stockpile large amounts of the vaccine to be administered only after an attack is imminent or has already occurred, for the purposes of limiting the spread of the resulting disease. This too has presented problems, however, because the expensive stockpiles quickly expire, and it is doubtful that vaccine programs can be effectively managed in the panic and uncertainty that would result in the aftermath of a biological attack. Further compounding this problem is the fact that weaponized forms of certain biological agents can render the protective benefits of vaccines useless, as is postulated in the case of weaponized anthrax.

For more information about the ongoing efforts to develop vaccines against smallpox, see the 2013 World Health Organization article entitled *Summary Report on the First, Second, and Third Generation Smallpox Vaccines* by H. Meyer (http://bit.ly/1u7tVGi).

Nuclear/Radiological Weapons

Nuclear and radiological weapons are those that involve the movement of energy through space and material. There are three primary mechanisms by which terrorists can use radiation to carry out an attack: detonation of a nuclear bomb, dispersal of radiological material, or an attack on a facility housing nuclear material (power plant, research laboratory, storage site, etc.).

Nuclear weapons have the greatest devastating potential of the three attack mechanisms through which nuclear and radiological weapons may be deployed. They are also the most difficult to develop or acquire and thus are considered the lowest threat of the three in terms of terrorist potential (likelihood). A nuclear weapon causes damage to property and harm to life through two separate processes. First, a blast is created by the detonation of the bomb. An incredibly large amount of energy is released in the explosion, which is the result of an uncontrolled chain reaction of atomic splitting. The initial shock wave, which destroys all built structures within a range of up to several miles, is followed by a heat wave reaching tens of millions of degrees close to the point of detonation. High winds accompany the shock and heat waves.

The second process by which nuclear weapons inflict harm is through harmful radiation. This radiation and radiological material is most dangerous close to the area of detonation, where high concentrations can cause rapid death, but particles reaching high into the atmosphere can pose a threat several hundreds of miles away under the right meteorologic conditions. Radiation can also persist for years after the explosion occurs.

Radiological dispersion devices (RDDs) are simple explosive devices that spread harmful radioactive material upon detonation, without the involvement of a nuclear explosion. These devices are often called "dirty bombs." Radiological dispersion devices also exist that do not require explosives for dispersal. Although illnesses and fatalities very close to the point of dispersal are likely, these devices are more likely to be used to spread terror. Like many biological and chemical weapons, it may be difficult to initially detect that a radiological attack has occurred. Special detection equipment and the training to use it are a prerequisite. See the sidebar "General Indicators of Possible Nuclear Weapon/Radiological Agent Use."

General Indicators of Possible Nuclear Weapon/Radiological Agent Use

- Stated threat to deploy a nuclear or radiological device
- Presence of nuclear or radiological equipment
- Spent fuel canisters or nuclear transport vehicles
- Nuclear placards/warning materials along with otherwise unexplained casualties

Source: FEMA (2002).

A third scenario involving nuclear/radiological material entails an attack on a nuclear facility. There are many facilities throughout the United States that manufacture, use, or store nuclear material including nuclear power plants, hazardous materials storage sites, hospitals and medical research facilities, military installations, and industrial and manufacturing plants. An attack on any one of these could result in a release of radiological material into the community or the atmosphere, either of which has the potential to harm life and would certainly cause fear among those who live in close proximity.

If a radiological or nuclear attack were to occur, humans and animals would experience both internal and external effects. External exposure results from any contact with radioactive material on the skin or in the eyes, while internal exposure requires ingestion, inhalation, or injection of radiological materials. Radiation sickness results from high doses of radiation and can result in death if the dosage is high enough. Other effects of radiation exposure can include redness or burning of the skin and eyes, nausea, damage to the body's immune system, and an elevated lifetime risk of developing cancer (FEMA, 2002).

Information developed by the CDC on a radiation event is presented on the companion website in the document "Facts about a Radiation Emergency."

Combined Hazards

By combining two or more methods of attack, terrorists can achieve a synergistic effect. And in doing so, they often increase the efficacy of each agent in terms of its potential to destroy, harm, or kill, thereby creating a sum total consequence much more devastating than had each agent been used independently. The dirty bomb, in which radiological material is added to a conventional explosive, is an example of a combined terrorist weapon. The explosives in the weapon cause physical damage through the expansion of gases, while the radiological material inflicts harm by inducing a range of adverse health effects on those who are exposed. The combination of the two results in an attack that not only causes both physical damage and harmful exposure to radiation but also disperses the radiological material over a much larger area, contaminates both the crime scene and the surrounding structures and environment, and instills a sense of fear into the entire affected population and far beyond that area as well. "Facts about Dirty Bombs," available on the companion website for this book, comprises a fact sheet compiled by the CDC describing dirty bombs and their effects.

Explosives can also be used to deliver chemical or biological weapons in a similar manner. This presents a dangerous scenario in that the trauma resulting from the explosion will demand immediate attention from responders, who may enter a contaminated attack scene without first recognizing or taking the time to check if a biological or chemical agent is present. Victims who are rushed to hospitals can cause secondary infections or injuries to EMS and hospital staff. Additionally, contaminated debris can help to spread certain viruses that may not otherwise have so easily entered the body (Patel et al., 2012). There have even been reports of HIV-positive suicide bombers passing their infection to victims struck with bits of shrapnel and bone, though no actual evidence of transmission has ever been confirmed.

When multiple chemicals, biological agents, or a combination of the two is used in an attack, the consequences can confound even seasoned experts. The combination of symptoms resulting from multiple injuries or infections will make recognition extremely difficult because diagnoses often depend on the existence of a defined set of effects. The multiple agents will cause physiological effects in humans, animals, or plants that do not fit any established models. The extra time required for identification of the agents used will undoubtedly cause an overall increase in the efficacy of the terrorist attack.

Other Armed Attacks Using Firearms or Other Tactics

In addition to deploying the CBRNE weapons described above, terrorists may also employ a range of tactical methods to instill terror and inflict death and destruction. In fact, of the 9707 attacks that took place in 2013, while 57% of those involved the use of bombs, incendiary devices, or suicide bomb attacks, the remaining 43% of attacks involved armed assaults, kidnapping, assassinations, attacks on infrastructure, and other methods (US Department of State, 2014a). Table 3-6 illustrates how the 2013 attacks were distributed by method of attack.

Terrorists generally use the weapons that best meet their budget, expertise, target, and the resources they have accessible. Based on these statistics, it is clear that terrorists favor weapons other than CBRNE weapons, and of the CBRNE weapons that are used, the overwhelming majority are explosive or incendiary in nature. Judging by the number of fatalities caused by these explosive attacks, they are much more effective at causing the fatalities sought by the perpetrators. However, it is undeniable that terrorist attacks using simpler methods of attack can be devastatingly effective. FEMA describes several of these other terrorism hazards in their guide "FEMA 452: Risk Assessment: A How-To Guide to Mitigate Potential Terrorist Attacks," displayed in Table 3-7.

Table 3-6 Worldwide Terrorist Attacks by Attack Type, 2013

Method of Terrorist Attack	Number of Attacks Using the Method[a]
Bombing	6678
Facility/infrastructure attack	607
Hijacking	17
Unknown	290
Armed Assault	3149
Hostage taking/kidnapping	657
Unarmed assault	40
Assassination	840

[a]Note that there is some double counting due to the fact that multiple methods were used in many attacks.
Source: US Department of State (2014a).

Table 3-7 Selected Terrorism Hazards

Threat	Application Mode	Duration	Extent of Effects: Static/Dynamic	Exacerbating Conditions
Armed attack—ballistics (small arms) and stand-off weapons (rocket-propelled grenades, mortars)	Tactical assault or sniper attacks from a remote location	Generally minutes to days	Varies, based on the perpetrator's intent and capabilities	Inadequate security can allow easy access to target, easy concealment of weapons, and undetected initiation of an attack
Cyber attacks	Electronic attack using one computer system against another	Minutes to days	Generally, no direct effects on built environment	Inadequate security can facilitate access to critical computer systems, allowing them to be used to conduct attacks
High-altitude electromagnetic pulse (HEMP)	An electromagnetic energy field produced in the atmosphere by the power and radiation of a nuclear explosion. It can overload computer circuitry, causing damage much more swiftly than a lightning strike	It can be induced hundreds to a few thousand kilometers from the detonation	Affects electronic systems. There is no effect on people. It diminishes with distance, and electronic equipment that is turned off is less likely to be damaged	To produce maximum effect, a nuclear device must explode very high in the atmosphere. Electronic equipment may be hardened by surrounding it with protective metallic shielding that routes damaging electromagnetic fields away from highly sensitive electrical components

Continued

Table 3-7 Selected Terrorism Hazards—Cont'd

Threat	Application Mode	Duration	Extent of Effects: Static/Dynamic	Exacerbating Conditions
High-power microwave (HPM) EMP	A nonnuclear radio-frequency energy field. Radio-frequency weapons can be hidden in an attaché case, suitcase, van, or aircraft. Energy can be focused using an antenna, or emitter, to produce effects similar to HEMP, but only within a very limited range	An HPM weapon has a shorter possible range than HEMP, but it can induce currents large enough to melt circuitry, or it can cause equipment to fail minutes, days, or even weeks later. HPM weapons are smaller scale, are delivered closer to the intended target, and can sometimes be emitted for a longer duration	Vulnerable systems include electronic ignition systems, radars, communications, data processing, navigation, and electronic triggers of explosive devices. HPM capabilities can cause a painful burning sensation or other injury to a person directly in the path of the focused power beam or can be fatal if a person is too close to the microwave emitter	Very damaging to electronics within a small geographic area. A shock wave could disrupt many computers within a 1 mile range. Radio-frequency weapons have ranges from tens of meters to tens of kilometers. Unlike HEMP, however, HPM radiation is composed of shorter wave forms at higher frequencies, which make it highly effective against electronic equipment and more difficult to harden against

Source: FEMA 452: risk assessment: a how-to guide to mitigate potential terrorist attacks. http://1.usa.gov/1rAZtmK.

Critical Thinking

What is the difference between a terrorist attack and an act of war? Do you think that the terrorist attacks that occur in Iraq are terrorism? Are terrorist attacks against military installations terrorism? Why or why not? Will it ever be possible to eradicate terrorism entirely? Why or why not?

Selected Examples of Chemical, Biological, Radiological, and Nuclear Incidents

- **August 2013:** A poisonous gas, most likely a nerve agent, was delivered to civilian areas of Damascus by rockets. It is suspected that the Syrian military is behind the attacks, which killed approximately 1430 people and sickened another 2200.
- **May 2013:** Actress Shannon Richardson mailed a series of letters containing ricin to the White House and New York City Mayor Michael Bloomberg. She was arrested in June of that year and convicted in 2014.
- **April 2013:** A letter containing highly refined ricin was sent to the US Capitol and to the White House, both of which were intercepted at off-site mail processing facilities. Everett Dutschke was indicted in June of 2013 in relation to the letters, which caused no injuries or deaths.

- **April 2012–June 2013:** A series of 23 poisoning incidents at girl's schools in Afghanistan using pesticides or other chemical agents resulted in over 1950 students becoming sickened. Islamic extremists are suspected to have carried out the attacks.
- **February 2008:** Ricin was discovered in a hotel room occupied by a man who suddenly fell into a coma. The man had produced the toxin years earlier and had been storing it since, but claimed to have never used it for purposes of terrorism.
- **June 2007:** A car bomb rigged with canisters of chlorine gas was detonated outside a US military base located in Diyala, Iraq, sickening 62 soldiers but causing no fatalities.
- **May 2007:** Bombs rigged with chlorine were detonated in two separate incidents in Iraq: one in an open-air market in the Diyala province, killing 32 and injuring 50 people, and the other at a police checkpoint in the Zangora district, killing as many as 11 people (though most if not all fatalities in both incidents were attributed to the effects of the explosives, not the chemicals).
- **April 2007:** Three separate incidents involving truck bombs rigged with chlorine occurred in Iraq: one incident at a Ramadi police checkpoint, killing 27 and injuring 30; another at a checkpoint outside Baghdad, killing 1 and injuring 2; and a third near a restaurant in Ramadi, killing 6 and wounding 10 (though most if not all fatalities in all three incidents were attributed to the effects of the explosives, not the chemicals).
- **March 2007:** Four attacks involving the detonation of tankers or other trucks containing chlorine occurred in Iraq: an attack at a Ramadi checkpoint wounded 2 people, an attack in Fallujah killed 2 and injured hundreds, an attack in Fallujah killed 6 and injured 250, and a fourth injured 71.
- **February 2007:** Three attacks involving the detonation of explosives and the release of chlorine occurred in Iraq: a suicide bomber in Ramadi killed 2 and injured 16, the detonation of a tanker truck near Baghdad killed 9 and injured 148, and a truck bomb in Baghdad killed 5 and hospitalized over 50.
- **January 2007:** A truck bomb in Iraq rigged with chlorine gas canisters was detonated in Ramadi, killing 16.
- **November 2006:** Alexander Litvinenko, a former Russian Federal Security Service official, was poisoned in a suspected assassination in London with radioactive polonium-210.
- **October 2006:** A car bomb rigged with mortar shells and chlorine gas canisters was detonated in Ramadi, wounding four people.
- **February 2004:** US Senate Majority Leader Bill Frist received a letter containing ricin powder. Several staff members needed decontamination, but no injuries or fatalities occurred as a result of the attack.
- **October 2003:** A metallic container was discovered at a Greenville, South Carolina, postal facility with ricin in it. The small container was in an envelope along with a threatening note. Authorities did not believe this was a terrorism-related incident. The note expressed anger against regulations overseeing the trucking industry.
- **November, 2002:** 193 children at a school in Changde, China, were sickened when their breakfast was tainted with rat poison. Two men were arrested about a month later, and it was determined they carried out the attack after losing a catering contract with the school.
- **August 2002:** Ansar al-Islam, a Sunni militant group, was reported to have tested ricin powder as an aerosol on animals such as donkeys and chickens and perhaps even an unwitting human subject. Additional specific details have not been released.

- **February 2002:** Italian authorities arrested as many as nine Moroccan nationals who may have been plotting to poison the water supply of the US embassy in Rome. Authorities confiscated a detailed map of Rome's underground water system, highlighting the location of the US embassy's pipes. The suspects also had 4 kg of potassium ferrocyanide in their possession.
- **December 2001:** According to press reports, the military wing of HAMAS (Palestinian Islamic Resistance Movement) claimed that the bolts and nails packed into explosives detonated by a suicide bomber had been dipped in rat poison.
- **October 2001:** US and international law enforcement authorities stepped up investigations in the United States and abroad to determine the sources of confirmed cases of anthrax exposures in Florida, New York, and Washington, DC. In the past several years, there have been hundreds of hoaxes involving anthrax in the United States. In the aftermath of the September 11 terrorist attacks against the United States, these anthrax scares have spread across the globe and have exacerbated international concerns. The confirmed anthrax cases involved letters sent through the mail to the US Congress and several media organizations. More than 50 individuals were exposed to *B. anthracis* spores, including 18 who became infected, and 5 people died from inhalation anthrax—the first reported cases in the United States in 25 years. US and international health organizations have treated thousands of individuals associated with these incidents.
- **September 2001:** Colombian police accused the Revolutionary Armed Forces of Colombia (FARC) of using improvised grenades filled with poisonous gas during an attack on the city of San Adolfin, Huila Department. According to media accounts, four policemen died and another six suffered respiratory problems from the attack.
- **January 2000:** According to press reports, a Russian general accused Chechen rebels of delivering poisoned wine and canned fruit to Russian soldiers in Chechnya.
- **November 1999:** Raw materials for making ricin were seized by law enforcement authorities during the arrest of a US citizen who threatened to poison two Colorado judges.
- **June 1998:** US law enforcement authorities arrested two members of the violent secessionist group called the Republic of Texas for planning to construct a device with toxins to kill selected government officials. A US federal court convicted them in October 1998 for threatening to use a weapon of mass destruction.
- **December 1996:** Sri Lankan press noted that government authorities warned the military in the northern region not to purchase food or stamps from local vendors, because some stamps had been found laced with cyanide.
- **August 1995:** An MIT Center for Cancer Research employee ingested radioactive phosphorus-32, in what was believed to be a deliberate attempt to poison him.
- **July 1995:** Four improvised chemical devices (ICDs) were found in restrooms at the Kayabachō, Tokyo, and Ginza subway stations and the Japanese railway's Shinjuku station. Each device was slightly different but contained the same chemicals.
- **May 1995:** An ICD was left in Shinjuku station in Tokyo. The device consisted of two plastic bags, one containing sodium cyanide and the other sulfuric acid. If the device had not been neutralized, the chemicals would have combined to produce a cyanide gas.
- **May 1995:** A US citizen, and member of the neo-Nazi Aryan Nations, acquired three vials of *Y. pestis*, the bacteria that causes plague, from a Maryland lab. Law enforcement officials recovered the unopened material and arrested the individual. No delivery system was recovered, and no information indicated the subject's purpose in obtaining the bacteria.

- **March 20, 1995:** Members of the Japanese cult Aum Shinrikyo used ICDs to release sarin nerve gas in the Tokyo subway station. Twelve people died, and thousands of others were hospitalized or required medical treatment.
- **March 15, 1995:** Three briefcases were left at locations in the Kasumigaseki train station in Tokyo. No injuries resulted, but an Aum Shinrikyo member later confessed that this was a failed biological attack with botulinum toxin.
- **January 1995:** Tajik opposition members laced champagne with cyanide at a New Year's celebration, killing six Russian soldiers and the wife of another soldier and sickening other revelers.
- **June 27, 1994:** A substance identified as sarin was dispersed using a modified van in a residential area near Matsumoto; 7 people died, and more than 200 people were injured. Reportedly, an Aum Shinrikyo member confessed that the cult targeted three judges who lived there to prevent them from returning an adverse decision against the cult.
- **1993:** A US citizen was detained by the Canadian Customs Service as he attempted to enter Canada from Alaska. A white powdery substance was confiscated and later identified through laboratory analysis as ricin. The individual, traveling with a large sum of cash, told officials that he was carrying the poison to protect his money.
- **1992:** Four individuals were convicted by a US federal court for producing ricin and advocating the violent overthrow of the government. The subjects, who had espoused extremist, antigovernment, antitax ideals, specifically had targeted a deputy US marshal who previously had served papers on one of them for tax violations.
- **1984:** An outbreak of *Salmonella* poisoning that occurred in Oregon during a 2-week period was linked to the salad bars of eight restaurants. More than 700 people were affected, but no fatalities occurred. Investigators of the outbreak determined that two members of the Rajneesh religious sect produced and dispensed *Salmonella* bacteria in the restaurants in order to influence a local election by incapacitating opposition voters.

Source: CIA (2002), CNN (February 4, 2004), CNS reports (2004), BBC News (2015), and Johnston (2014).

Difficulty of Predicting Terror Attacks in the United States

A risk index published on August 18, 2003, by the World Markets Research Center (WMRC), a business intelligence firm based in London, ranked the United States fourth among the top five countries most likely to be targeted for a terrorist attack within the 12-month period that followed (www.wmrc.com). The index also predicted that "another September 11-style terrorist attack in the United States is highly likely." Colombia, Israel, and Pakistan ranked in the top three positions, respectively. After the United States, the Philippines, Afghanistan, Indonesia, Iraq, India, and Britain, which tied with Sri Lanka, rounded out the top 10. North Korea ranked as the least likely country to experience a terrorist attack within that next year. The index, which assessed the risk of terrorism to some 186 countries and their interests, was based on five criteria: "motivation of terrorists, the presence of terror groups, the scale and frequency of past attacks, efficacy of the groups in carrying out attacks, and how many attacks were thwarted by the country." Explaining the US ranking, the index stated that while the presence of militant Islamic networks within the United States is less extensive than in Western Europe, "U.S.-led military action in Afghanistan and Iraq has exacerbated anti-U.S. sentiment" (Homeland Security Monitor, August 19, 2003).

That year's ranking for terrorism risk in the United States made issues such as detection, containment, control, quarantine, and vaccination—to name just a few—significant factors in developing new response and recovery practices for first responders. Political affairs and events across the globe have factored heavily in efforts to prepare populations and to mitigate the impacts of these new hazards on those populations and on critical infrastructure, communities, economies, and the normality of daily life.

During the months that followed the WMRC risk prediction, the actual incidence of terrorism followed drastically different patterns than expected. Who, for instance, could have foreseen that the Maoist insurgency in Nepal would have heated up so quickly, with such deadly consequences? And who could have guessed that Islamic separatists in the southern provinces of Thailand would have resorted to such brutal measures that the country was elevated to a place near the top of the terrorism target list for many years to follow? The ongoing conflict in Iraq, by far the statistical leader in both the number of attacks conducted and fatalities associated with those attacks, spiraled out of control much faster than anyone could have imagined, thanks to the presence of foreign fighters who imported deadly and effective terrorism methods and materials. The differences in what was predicted and what transpired highlight the difficulty of analyzing and evaluating intentional hazards such as terrorism that are dynamic and that respond to unforeseeable social, political, economic, and other anthropologically generated factors. Table 3-8 presents the top 10 countries ranked by number of people killed in terrorist attacks in 2005 and 2013, adapted from studies conducted by the National Counterterrorism Center (NCTC), the Federal Bureau of Investigation (FBI), and the Department of State. This table illustrates how great uncertainty factors into any terrorism risk predictions over time.

Table 3-8 Top 10 Countries Ranked by Number of Terrorism-Related Fatalities in 2005 and 2013

Country	Rank in 2005	Number of Fatalities	Rank in 2013 (Change)	Number of Fatalities
Iraq	1	8262	1 (0)	6378
India	2	1361	7 (−5)	405
Colombia	3	813	N/A	N/A
Afghanistan	4	684	2 (+2)	3111
Thailand	5	498	10 (−5)	131
Nepal	6	485	N/A	N/A
Pakistan	7	338	3 (+4)	2315
Russia	8	238	N/A	N/A
Sudan	9	157	N/A	N/A
DPR Congo	10	154	N/A	N/A
The Philippines	N/A	N/A	9 (+2)	279
Yemen	N/A	N/A	8	291
Nigeria	N/A	N/A	4	1817
Syria	N/A	N/A	5	1074
Somalia	N/A	N/A	6	408

Source: US Department of State (2014b).

A general lack of experience with and knowledge about these new hazards, and the realization that they could be deliberately used to harm or kill US citizens, has resulted in a significant yet waning perception among nearly all American communities that they are potential terrorist targets (see sidebar "Where Will Terrorists Strike?"). And unlike hurricanes or tornadoes, which tend to have geographic boundaries, the terrorism threat in general as well as each of the specific terrorist weapons is each considered to affect the United States on a national level. People in Montana do not worry about hurricanes, and it rarely floods in the desert of Nevada. There have been few if any tornadoes reported in Maine. But residents of all states may consider themselves, however remotely, the next possible victims of terrorism, thereby reinforcing what has become a skewed perception of risk. The open nature of our governance system and our society has resulted in widespread press coverage of WMD risk analyses at the federal level, especially in relation to belief among various government officials not only that terrorists will acquire WMD technologies in the near future but also that the heartland of America (e.g., small towns, shopping malls, restaurants, and other locations away from major, obvious, and hardened targets) is the most likely next target. The appearance of such weapons in literature, in the cinema, and in the media, as actual events occur around the world (a list of selected chemical, biological, radiological, and nuclear incidents is presented in the sidebar "Selected Examples of Chemical, Biological, Radiological, and Nuclear Incidents"), buttresses the exaggerated perception of individual risk.

Where Will Terrorists Strike? Different Theories…

One of the greatest problems the Department of Homeland Security faces is trying to determine where terrorists will strike next. Major US cities are considered the most likely targets for terrorist attacks, as evidenced by risk-based funding for terrorism that has clearly targeted urban centers with the greatest amount of counterterrorism-related funding. There are, however, opinions that conflict with this majority assessment.

In 2003, Deputy Secretary of Health and Human Services Claude Allen stated that rural America should be considered among the most likely sites for the next terror attack in the United States, especially a bioterrorism attack. Deputy Secretary Allen stated that "[s]ome rural communities are among the most vulnerable to attack, simply because of their proximity to a missile silo or to a chemical stockpile. Other rural communities are vulnerable simply because they mistakenly believe that terrorism is an urban problem and they are safe from attack." While Allen said the federal government has increased funding for bioterrorism preparedness, he also noted that rural areas are vulnerable given their "limited infrastructure for public health as well as fewer health care providers and volunteer systems."

In March 2004, CSO Online, an industry journal for security executives, conducted a survey that asked where in the United States terrorists would likely strike next. The results of the poll indicated that these industry experts felt the next target would be the airline industry (3%), a seaport (7%), a large public event (23%), an urban mass transit system (27%), or a "different and unexpected target" (41%). Considering the efforts that are under way to block an attack on known or expected targets, it would follow in this line of thinking that terrorists would seek to exploit an unknown target that would likely be "soft," or more vulnerable to attack. Citing another major area of vulnerability, a Princeton University research group found that most Internet experts feel that a devastating cyber attack will occur within the next 10 years, possibly affecting business, utilities, banking, communications, and other Internet-dependent components of society.

On June 23, 2005, the US Senate Committee on Foreign Relations released a report stating that there was a 50% chance of a major WMD-based attack, between 2005 and 2010, somewhere in the world. The report was based on a poll of 85 national security and nonproliferation experts. The reports found that the risks of biological or chemical attacks were comparable to or slightly higher than the risk of a nuclear attack but that there is a "significantly higher" risk of a radiological attack.

Time proved several, though not all, of these predictions true—most notably that a large-scale public event would be attacked as occurred in the 2013 Boston Marathon bombing. Added to this event are at least 30 incidents that were thwarted in various stages of planning and development, the most significant of these include the following:

- Shoe Bomber Richard Reid (2001)—Unsuccessful attempt to destroy a commercial airline in flight
- Jose Padilla (2002)—Planning to use a dirty bomb
- Lackawanna Six (2002)—Attended jihadist training in Pakistan to learn how to attack Americans
- Iyman Faris (2003)—Planning to destroy the Brooklyn Bridge
- Virginia Jihad Network (2003)—Planning undetermined attacks against Americans
- Nuradin Abdi (2003)—Planning to bomb a shopping mall
- Dhiren Barot (2004)—Planning to attack the New York Stock Exchange
- James Elshafay and Shahawar Matin Siraj—Planning to bomb a New York subway station
- Yassin Aref and Mohammed Hossain (2004)—Planning to assassinate a Pakistani diplomat in New York City
- Levar Haley Washington, Gregory Vernon Patterson, Hammad Riaz Samana, and Kevin James (2005)—Planning to attack National Guard facilities, synagogues, and other targets in the Los Angeles area
- Michael Reynolds (2005)—Planning to blow up a natural gas refinery in Wyoming
- Narseal Batiste, Patrick Abraham, Stanley Grant Phanor, Naudimar Herrera, Burson Augustin, Lyglenson Lemorin, and Rothschild Augustine (2006)—Planning to destroy the Chicago Sears Tower, FBI offices, and other government buildings
- Assem Hammoud (2006)—Planning to attack underground transit links between New York City and New Jersey
- Derrick Shareef (2006)—Planning to set off hand grenades in a Chicago-area shopping mall
- Fort Dix Plot (2007)—Six men planned to attack Fort Dix Army post in New Jersey using assault rifles and grenades
- JFK Airport Plot (2007)—Four men planned to blow up aviation fuel tanks and pipelines at the John F. Kennedy International Airport in New York City
- Christopher Paul (2008)—Planning to use weapons of mass destruction against Americans
- Synagogue Terror Plot (2009)—Four men planned to attack Jewish centers in New York and planes at a nearby military base
- Najibullah Zazi (2009)—Planning to detonate explosives on the New York City subway
- Hosam Maher Husein Smadi (2009)—Planning to plant a bomb in a Dallas skyscraper
- Michael Finton (2009)—Attempting to detonate a car bomb in downtown Springfield, IL

- Tarek Mehanna and Ahmad Abousamra (2009)—Planning to kill US politicians, American troops in Iraq, and civilians in local shopping malls
- Umar Farouk Abdulmutallab (2009)—Attempted to detonate a bomb hidden in his underwear on a US-bound international flight as the plane began to land
- Printer bomb (2010)—Bombs disguised as printer cartridges and shipped on a US-bound cargo plane (originating in Dubai) to locations in the Chicago area, which were found before they could be detonated (but not until after they reached the United Kingdom) when a caller tipped off security officials

Conclusion

Terrorism has caused communities throughout the United States to manage an expanded hazard profile. Many of these new hazards have existed elsewhere in the world for decades or even centuries, but due to the changing nature of terrorism, they are just now starting to be perceived as a legitimate threat to the typical American community. Concern for these hazards has spurred significant investments in increasing public preparedness through education and expanding local officials' response capacities. The media has likewise given greater attention to the threat of terrorism, and Americans have in turn become as familiar with and knowledgeable about these new hazards as they have been about the natural and technological hazards they have been dealing with for far longer.

Managing the expanded community hazard profile demands investment in training, protective equipment and gear, specialized technical capabilities, and enhancements to public health networks. But this threat has also presented a unique opportunity to integrate many of the different and often disparate groups that have always been key stakeholders in the effort to mitigate, prepare for, respond to, and recover from disasters, including the public health service. These community assets would likely assist not only in terrorist events but also in just about any devastating disaster that might occur. It has given us the opportunity to include many of these public health concerns into general disaster planning efforts and has increased cooperation with the private sector in emergency management systems and efforts (often because privately owned and maintained financial and communications infrastructures are primary terrorist targets). The research and development efforts associated with these new hazards, described in greater detail in Chapter 12, have already begun to result in advances spanning a broad spectrum of human activities from medicine to communications technology and have led to the development of safer personal protective equipment, vaccines, and other defenses for the first responders that must manage attack consequences. Most importantly, these new hazards, and the benefits enjoyed as a result of the financial outlays their presence has garnered, serve to remind us that the best systems are those that maintain an all-hazards, risk-based approach.

Key Terms

Aerosol device: A tool, apparatus, or machine that converts liquid or solid matter into a gaseous state or otherwise airborne suspension.

Biological weapon: A warfare or terrorism device capable of projecting, dispersing, or disseminating a biological warfare agent (bacteria, virus, or toxin).

Blister agent: Also known as a vesicant, a blister agent is any chemical compound that, upon contact with exposed skin, eyes, or other tissue, causes severe pain and irritation.

Blood agent: Any chemical compound that is inhaled, ingested, or absorbed, which prevents otherwise normal blood cells from carrying oxygen.

Category A biological weapon: Organisms that can be easily disseminated or transmitted from person to person; result in high mortality rates and have the potential for major public health impact; might cause public panic and social disruption; and require special action for public health preparedness.

Category B biological weapon: Second highest-priority agents, including those that are moderately easy to disseminate, result in moderate morbidity rates and low mortality rates, and require specific enhancements of diagnostic capacity and enhanced disease surveillance.

Category C biological weapon: Third highest-priority agents, including emerging pathogens that could be engineered for mass dissemination in the future because of availability, ease of production and dissemination, and potential for high morbidity and mortality rates and major health impact.

CBRNE: Weapons that are chemical, biological, radiological/nuclear, or explosive in nature, often referred to as "weapons of mass destruction."

Chemical weapon: A warfare or terrorist device capable of projecting, dispersing, or disseminating a chemical warfare agent.

Choking/pulmonary agent: A chemical weapon affecting the lungs, designed to impede a victim's ability to breathe (ultimately resulting in their suffocation).

Containment: The prevention of spread of biological, chemical, or radiological materials.

Cyberterrorism: The use or destruction of computing or information technology resources aimed at harming, coercing, or intimidating others in order to achieve a greater political or ideological goal.

Detection: Recognition of the existence of a WMD agent, or the consequences of such an attack. Detection is often achieved through various public health services working together to recognize trends in disease symptoms and geographic coverage.

Drought: A prolonged shortage of available water.

Earthquake: A sudden, rapid shaking of the Earth's surface that is caused by the breaking and shifting of tectonic plates.

Explosive weapon (conventional explosives): A device relying on the expansion of gases and/or the propelling of bits of metal, glass, and other materials, to achieve bodily harm, death, and destruction.

Flood: An overabundance of water that engulfs dryland and property that is normally dry.

Hazard: A source of danger that may or may not lead to an emergency or disaster.

Hazardous materials: Chemical substances that, if released or misused, can pose a threat to people and the environment.

High-filler explosive: An explosive that combusts nearly instantaneously, thereby producing a violent, shattering effect. High-filler explosives, which are most often used by the military in shells and bombs, may be detonated by a spark, flame, or by impact or may require the use of a detonator. Examples include TNT, RDX, and HBX.

Hurricane: A cyclonic atmospheric storm occurring in the Western Hemisphere, characterized by sustained wind speeds exceeding 74 mph.

Incapacitating agent: A chemical warfare agent that produces a temporary disabling condition (physiological or psychological) that persists. Oftentimes, incapacitating agents result in death to those exposed due to unexpected physical reactions.

Incendiary weapon: A weapon that disperses a chemical weapon that causes fire. Napalm bombs, used extensively in the Vietnam War to reduce forest coverage, are one example.

Irritant: A noncorrosive chemical that causes a reversible inflammatory effect on living tissue at the site of contact (skin, eyes, or respiratory tract).

Low-filler explosives: Also called "low explosives," a low-filler explosive is a mixture of a combustible substance and an oxidant that decomposes rapidly once ignited. Under normal conditions, low explosives undergo combustion rates that vary from a few centimeters per second to approximately 400 m/s. It is possible, however, for low-filler explosives to combust so quickly as to produce an effect similar to detonation (see high-filler explosive) as often occurs when ignited in a confined space. Gunpowder and pyrotechnics (including flares and fireworks) are generally low explosives.

Mass movement: Hazard characterized by a horizontal or lateral movement of large quantities of physical matter.

Natural hazard: A hazard that exists in the natural environment as a result of hydrologic, meteorologic, seismic, geologic, volcanic, mass movement, or other natural processes and that poses a threat to human populations and communities.

Nerve agent: A chemical weapon that is absorbed through the skin, eyes, or lungs that disrupts the body's nervous system.

Nuclear weapon: A weapon whose destructive force is derived from the energy produced and released during a fission or fusion reaction.

Persistent chemical: A chemical agent or weapon that maintains its toxic properties for an extended period of time following release into the atmosphere (several hours or days).

Quarantine: The imposed isolation placed upon people, animals, or objects that are confirmed or suspected of being contaminated or infected with a chemical or biological agent, for the purpose of limiting the spread of exposure.

Radiological dispersion device: A bomb or other weapon used to spread radiological waste across a wide area for the purpose of causing contamination and bodily harm (often called a "dirty bomb").

Radiological weapon: See "radiological dispersion device."

Satchel charge: A powerful yet portable explosive device traditionally used by infantry forces but which has become a terrorist weapon of choice in that they blend easily for effective concealment in public places.

Storm surge: Masses of water that are pushed toward the shore by meteorologic forces.

Synergistic effect: Simultaneous action of separate things that have a greater total effect than the sum of their individual effects.

Tornado: A rapidly rotating vortex or funnel of air extending groundward from a cumulonimbus cloud.

Tsunami: A wave or series of waves generated by a mass displacement of sea or lake water.

Vaccination: The process of administering weakened or dead pathogens to a healthy person or animal, with the intent of conferring immunity against a targeted form of a related disease agent.

Volcano: A break in the Earth's crust through which molten rock from beneath the Earth's surface erupts.

Wildfire: Large fires that spread throughout the natural environment, whether at the surface, close to the ground, or in the forest crown.

Review Questions

1. Discuss the two major differences between traditional hazards (e.g., hurricanes, floods, tornadoes, earthquakes, and hazardous materials incidents) and the new hazards associated with terrorism.
2. What are five major hazards associated with terrorism?

3. Discuss the appropriate responses to the new hazards associated with terrorism. For each hazard, when is it appropriate to shelter in place, evacuate, and/or quarantine?
4. Understanding the new hazards associated with terrorism will be critical to reducing the fear among the public of these hazards. This was done very successfully in the past in understanding and dispelling the fear surrounding traditional hazards. How would you design and implement a public education campaign concerning the new hazards? What information would you present and how?
5. If you were a member of the Congress, what role would you foresee for the federal government in researching these new hazards, identifying appropriate response and preparedness measures, and educating the public? What role would you have if you were a governor? What role would you have if you were a mayor or county executive?

References

Albarelli, H.P., 2001. The secret history of anthrax. WND (November 6). http://bit.ly/1sJL3mU.

BBC, 2015. Timeline: Iraq. BBC Website. Accessed March 2015. http://bbc.in/1EzsOnA.

Centers for Disease Control and Prevention, 2013. Chemical agents. CDC website: http://1.usa.gov/1jlpeDh.

Centers for Disease Control and Prevention, 2014a. Bioterrorism agents/diseases. Emergency preparedness and response. CDC website: http://1.usa.gov/1nxVCHD.

Centers for Disease Control and Prevention, 2014b. Bioterrorism agents/diseases. CDC website: http://1.usa.gov/1fwFuCe.

Central Intelligence Agency (CIA), 2002. Terrorism: Guide to Chemical, Biological, Radiological, and Nuclear Weapons Indicators. Interagency Intelligence Committee on Terrorism. Washington, DC.

Colorado Avalanche Information Center, 2014. Statistics and reporting. CAIC website: http://bit.ly/YE8r7k.

Coppola, D., 2011. Introduction to International Disaster Management, second ed. Butterworth Heinemann, Burlington, MA.

Fahey, J., 2013. US Power Grid Costs to Rise, But Service Slips. Associated Press, New York. http://bit.ly/1qNgHbt March 5.

Federal Emergency Management Agency, 2002. Interim Planning Guide for State and Local Government: Managing the Emergency Consequences of Terrorist Incidents. FEMA, Washington, DC. http://1.usa.gov/1DQvAE8.

Federal Emergency Management Agency (FEMA), 2002. Managing the Emergency Consequences of Terrorist Incidents—Interim Planning Guide for State and Local Governments. FEMA, Washington, DC.

FEMA, 1997. Multihazard Identification and Assessment. Washington, DC.

FEMA, 2014a. Loss Statistics from Jan. 1, 1978 through July 31, 2014. National Flood Insurance Program. http://1.usa.gov/1Czq3QU.

FEMA, 2014b. Resources: flood facts. FloodSmart website: http://1.usa.gov/1mF8aw3.

Finn, K., 2009. Obama Officials Vow to Cut Red Tape After Katrina. Reuters. March 5. http://reut.rs/1EnmrFw.

House Homeland Security Committee, 2014. The road to Boston: counterterrorism challenges and lessons from the marathon bombings. US House of Representatives. http://1.usa.gov/1nxlNgC.

Humber, Y., 2014. Nuclear Power-less Japan must pay for fuel imports in Weak Yen. Bloomberg Business Yen (September 18). http://buswk.co/1pBmH6R.

Jacobs, S., 2013. Chemical warfare, from Rome to Syria: a timeline. National Geographic (August 22). http://bit.ly/1rBjDgu.

Johnston, W.R., 2014. Summary of historical attacks using chemical or biological weapons. Johnston Archive website: http://bit.ly/1CD7qeP.

Los Angeles Times, 2011. Arizona power company baffled by events that led to outage. http://lat.ms/1rxd26P (September 9).

National Fire Protection Association, 2010. Fire Loss in the United States During 2010. NFPA Report. http://bit.ly/1DTE9v5.

National Fire Protection Association, 2014. Fires in the U.S. NFPA website: http://bit.ly/1uwzxeC.

National Interagency Fire Center, 2014. Total wildland fires and acres (1960–2013). http://1.usa.gov/1oppgd1.

NOAA, 2006. Regional Snowfall Index (RSI). National Climatic Data Center Website. Accessed March 2015. http://1.usa.gov/1rqczEA.

NOAA, 2014. Hydrologic Information Center: Flood loss data. National Weather Service. http://1.usa.gov/1ywfK1p.

Patel, H.D.L., Dryden, S., Gupta, A., Stewart, N., 2012. Human body projectiles implanted in victims of suicide bombings and implications for health and emergency care providers: the 7/7 experience. Ann. R. Coll. Surg. Engl. 96, 313–317. http://1.usa.gov/1CCjQ6H.

Turnbull, W., Abhayaratne, P., 2002. 2002 WMD Terrorism Chronology: Incidents Involving Sub-National Actors and Chemical, Biological, Radiological, and Nuclear Materials. Center for Nonproliferation Studies (CNS). http://bit.ly/1Bc9KdU.

US Department of State, 2014. Statistical information on terrorism in 2013. Bureau of Counterterrorism website: http://1.usa.gov/ZmAHfN.

US Department of State, 2014. Country reports on terrorism 2013. Statistical information on terrorism in 2013. http://1.usa.gov/ZmAHfN.

United States Geological Survey, 1999. Land subsidence in the United States. Circular 1182. http://on.doi.gov/1qN6dsS.

USGS, 2009. Magnitude/intensity comparison. Earthquake hazards program. http://on.doi.gov/1rqcjFM.

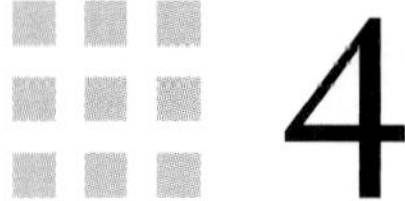

4 Governmental Homeland Security Structures

What You Will Learn

- The organizational structure and individual components of the Department of Homeland Security, including the function of each component and other interesting facts and figures
- The instigating causes and characterization of the major organizational changes that have occurred within the Department of Homeland Security since it was established in 2002
- The federal agencies other than the Department of Homeland Security that participate in traditional homeland security activities and the nature of their work
- The various homeland security-related activities that the nation's state and local organizations participate in and what types of assistance they provide their constituent members

Introduction

The Department of Homeland Security is a massive agency, juggling numerous responsibilities between a staggeringly wide range of program areas, employing approximately 240,000 people (DHS, 2014a), and managing a massive multibillion dollar budget and an ambitious list of tasks and goals. The department leverages resources within federal, state, and local governments, coordinating the ongoing transition of multiple agencies and programs into a single integrated agency focused on protecting the American people and their homeland.

The function of homeland security, however, is not unique to this one federal department. In fact, there are more than 87,000 different governmental jurisdictions at the federal, state, and local levels that have homeland security responsibilities (DHS, 2007b).

This chapter presents the structure and makeup of the Department of Homeland Security as it exists today, explains the organizational positioning of its many components, and details how this organizational structure has changed through time. These components are presented according to three organizational groupings, which include components falling within the Office of the Secretary, preexisting offices (which have maintained their structural integrity within the new department), and new offices and directorates. This chapter also explains several other areas within the federal government and at the state and local levels, where homeland security functions exist.

Department of Homeland Security Organizational Chart

At the federal level, the Department of Homeland Security (DHS) organizational composition continues to experience regular transition and as such remains in a constant state of flux. Several readjustments and

The United States Department

United States Coast Guard: Admiral Thomas Collins
The USCG has been kept intact within DHS, maintaining its historic mission of ensuring maritime safety, national defense, maritime security, mobility, and protection of natural resources.

United States Secret Service: W. Ralph Basham
The USSS has been kept intact within DHS, maintaining its mission of protecting the President and other senior executive personnel, protecting the nation's currency and financial infrastructure, and providing security for designated national events.

Office of the Secretary
Secretary: Michael Chertoff

Chief of Staff

Management Directorate
Under Secretary: Janet Hale

Responsible for budget, appropriations, expenditure of funds, accounting and finance, procurement, human resources and personnel, information technology systems, facilities, property, equipment and other material resources, and identification and tracking of performance measures relating to the responsibilities of the Department of Homeland Security. Management is also be responsible for all immigration statistics of the Bureau of Border Statistics and the Bureau of Citizenship and Immigration Services.

Office of the Deputy Secretary
Deputy Secretary: Michael Jackson

Border and Transportation Security Directorate
Under Secretary: Randy Beardsworth

Goal
To secure the air, land, and sea borders, and to secure the nation's land, sea, and air transportation systems.

Border and Transportation Security Tasks
- Prevent the entry of terrorists and the instruments of terrorism, drugs, and unlawful commerce, while simultaneously ensuring the efficient flow of lawful traffic and commerce.
- Secure the borders, territorial waters, ports, terminals, waterways, and air, land, and sea transportation systems.
- Establish and administer rules governing entry into the US.
- Establish national immigration enforcement policies and priorities, and enforce these policies.
- Administer the customs laws of the United States.
- Conduct the inspection and administrative functions of the Animal and Plant Health Inspection Service.

Domestic Preparedness Tasks
- Coordinate preparedness efforts at the Federal level, and work with all State, local, and private emergency response providers on all matters pertaining to terrorism.
- Coordinate and/or consolidate homeland security communications and communications systems, at all levels.
- Direct and supervise federally funded terrorism preparedness grant programs.
- Provide agency-specific training for agents and analysts within DHS, other federal agencies, and State, local, and international agencies.
- Cooperate closely with EP&R to prepare for and mitigate the effects of non-terrorist related disasters in the US.
- Assist the director in conducting risk analysis and risk management consistent with the mission and functions of BTS

Incorporates:
The US Customs Service, Animal and Plant Health Inspection Service, Transportation Security Administration, Office for Domestic Preparedness, Federal Protective Service, Federal Law Enforcement Training Center, and INS Enforcement Division.

Science & Technology Directorate
Under Secretary: Charles E. McQueary

Goal
To facilitate the nation's research, development, and enhancement of emergent practice and technology geared towards the prevention and mitigation of chemical, biological, radiological, nuclear, and other terrorist threats.

Homeland Security Advanced Research Projects Agency
- Award competitive, merit-reviewed grants, cooperative agreements or contracts to public or private entities, including businesses, federally funded research and development centers, and university.
- Support basic and applied homeland security research to promote revolutionary changes in technologies that would promote homeland security.
- Advance the development, testing and evaluation, and deployment of critical homeland security technologies.
- Accelerate the prototyping and deployment of technologies that would address homeland security vulnerabilities.

To fulfill these research tasks, the Acceleration Fund for Research and Development of Homeland Security Technologies (The Fund) will be established within the directorate.

Incorporates:
CBRN (Chemical, Biological, Radiological, Nuclear) Countermeasures Program, Environmental Measures Laboratory, National BioWeapon Defense Analysis Center, and Plum Island Animal Disease Center.

Bullock & Haddow, LLC

August 15, 2005

FIGURE 4-1 Original DHS organizational chart, with leadership figures holding office in July of 2005. *Designed by Damon Coppola for Bullock & Haddow, funding provided by the Annie E. Casey Foundation.*

reorganizations occurred during the course of its first decade, with multiple offices and responsibilities being passed between the departments and many functional components. Though it seemed by the end of first DHS Secretary Tom Ridge's years of service that the basic organizational makeup had been established (see Figure 4-1), the agency's second secretary, Michael Chertoff, proposed and implemented several fundamental changes to the department's organization under his widely publicized reorganization plan. The department was again reorganized following the 2005 hurricane season according to the requirements of the Post-Katrina Emergency Management Reform Act (PKEMRA) of 2006.

There remain a number of factors that keep the department's structure in a state of flux as it progresses through its second decade. The first is the long-delayed and uncertain plans for the physical consolidation of the department's many agencies into a new "campus" of buildings currently under construction in the Washington, DC, area. The department broke ground for this new massive facility on September 9, 2009, on the site of a former psychiatric institution in the city's southeast quadrant. The facility was originally

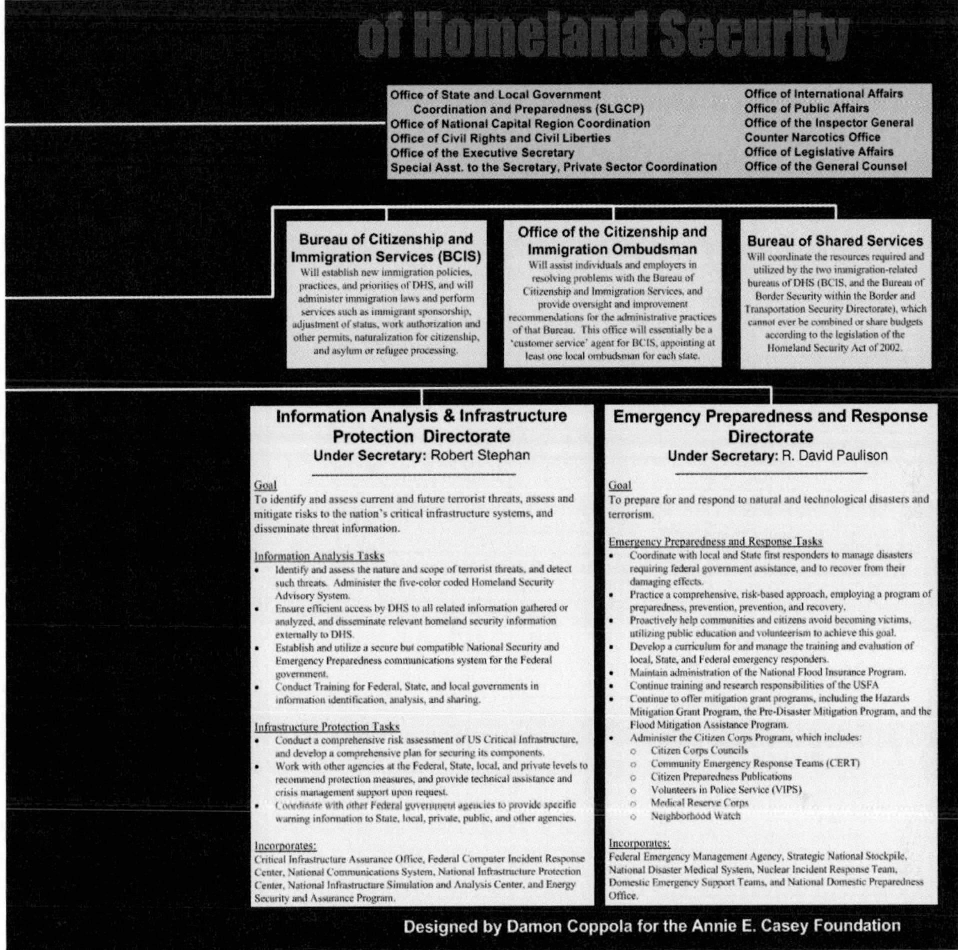

FIGURE 4-1 (Continued)

scheduled for completion in 2016 but has since been delayed at least until 2026 and its budget ballooned from $3 to $4.5 billion. At completion, it is expected that most of the 22,000 department employees that are currently scattered across the metropolitan area in more than fifty different buildings will be collocated. As of 2015, only one building, housing employees of the Coast Guard, had opened. Former DHS Secretary Chertoff, who led the effort to develop the site, felt that consolidation was needed to streamline communications, evolve the department's culture, and ultimately ensure that it is able to enhance national security. Such action might also result in the conglomeration of different offices, though it remains to be seen if the facility will ever open at all (Markon, 2014).

A second factor is the completion of the second Quadrennial Homeland Security Review and the release of the corresponding report in July of 2014. This study was conducted to identify and track all of the department's functions and to assess how efficiently its various components are carrying out these functions in their present form. The findings of this study were summarized as follows: "we conclude that we will continue to adhere to the five basic homeland security missions set forth in the first Quadrennial Homeland

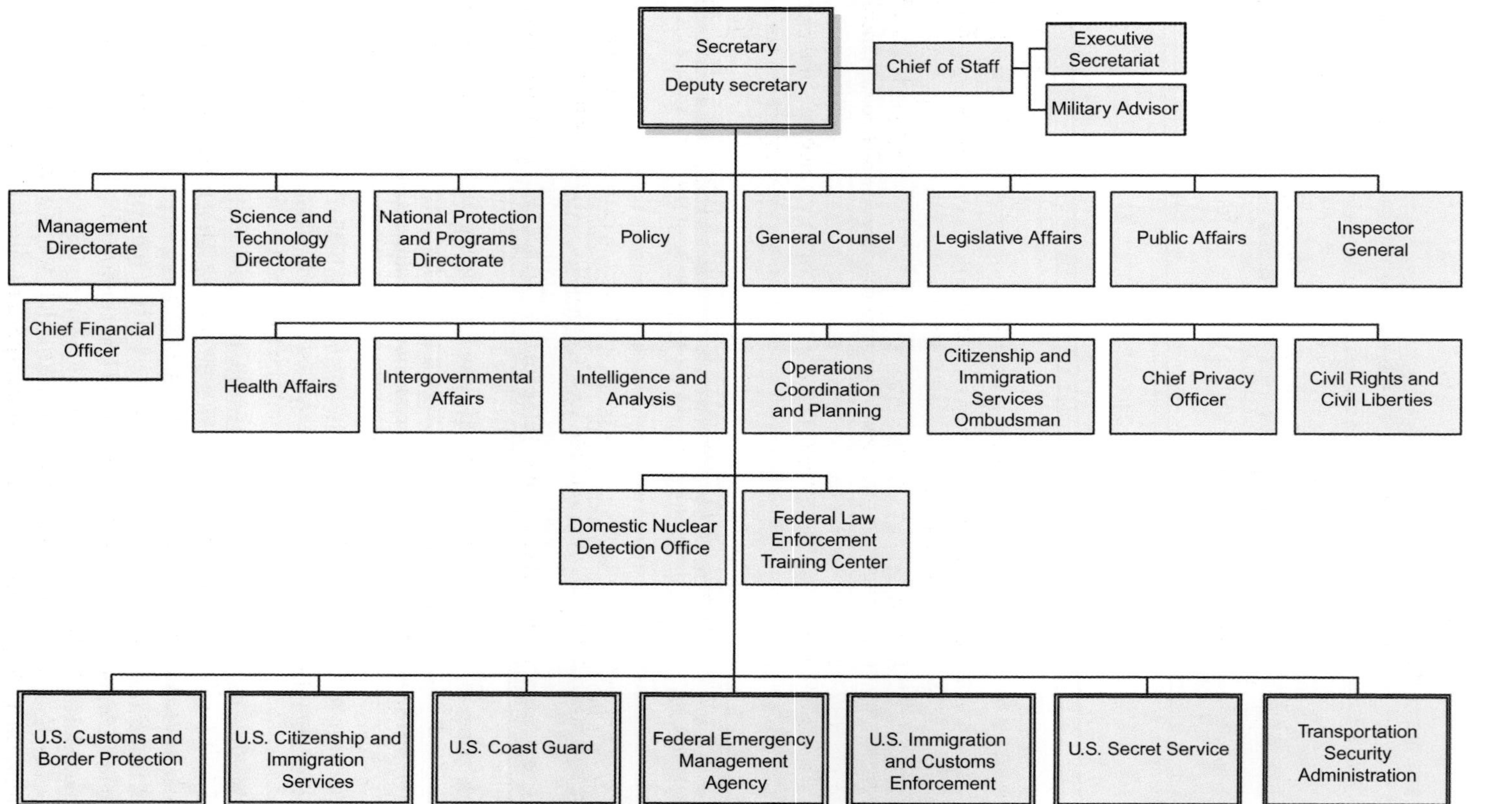

FIGURE 4-2 Current DHS organizational chart. *Source: DHS (2014e).*

Security Review report in 2010, but that these missions must be refined to reflect the evolving landscape of homeland security threats and hazards" (DHS, 2014b). The release of this report comes just 6 months following the arrival of the department's fourth secretary of homeland security, Jeh Charles Johnson. The QHSR process is required to assess the department's organizational alignment with the stated homeland security strategies and mission areas, which includes its organizational structure. Since the last major realignment, which followed Hurricane Katrina, there have been several small organizational "tweaks," and there is always the possibility that pattern will continue. This might include the consolidation of various components, the exchange of functions and budgets, or the creation of new offices. The current organization of the department is provided in Figure 4-2.

The Office of the Secretary of Homeland Security

The secretary of homeland security is a cabinet-level official, within the executive branch, who leads the department. The first DHS secretary, who served from the department's opening day in March 2003 until February 2005, was former Pennsylvania Governor Tom Ridge. Tom Ridge was followed by Michael Chertoff, who formerly served as a US circuit judge for the Third Circuit Court of Appeals and who served as secretary from February 2005 to January 21, 2009. Former Arizona Governor Janet Napolitano took over the office immediately upon Chertoff's departure and held that position until September 6, 2013. Rand Beers served as acting Secretary of Homeland Security until Jeh Johnson was confirmed and instated as the current secretary in December of 2013.

The secretary and his or her staff are responsible for managing the overall direction of the department and overseeing all department activities. In conjunction with other entities and stakeholders at the federal, state, and local levels (including private and NGO sector entities), the Office of the Secretary sets the direction for intelligence analysis and infrastructure protection, improved use of science and technology to counter weapons of mass destruction, and the creation of comprehensive response and recovery initiatives.

Within the Office of the Secretary are multiple-program and issue-related divisions that support the overall homeland security mission. These offices and their purposes include the following:

- *The Privacy Office*: This office was created to develop and maintain policies that minimize the impact of the DHS mission on the privacy of individuals—particularly with respect to respecting and securing their personal information and protection of their dignity. Privacy remains a major concern of citizens' advocacy groups due to the types of personally identifiable information collected by the department from US citizens, as well as the acts and actions citizens are subject to in the course of security checks (e.g., at airport security checkpoints). The Congress required by statute that DHS maintain a privacy office—something they had never done previously with any other federal agency. In addition to protecting the privacy of US citizens, this office also designs and implements department information management systems and fulfills Freedom of Information Act (FOIA) requests.
- *Office of Civil Rights and Civil Liberties*: This office provides legal and policy advice to DHS leadership on civil rights and civil liberties issues, investigates and resolves complaints related to civil rights and civil liberties, and provides leadership to Equal Employment Opportunity Programs. Many of these programs, such as Accessible Systems and Technologies, relate to the ability of employees and citizen end users with functional needs to be able to access and use information and data. Even more so than privacy concerns, civil liberties advocates have argued that the actions of the department (especially with regard to transportation security, investigations, and

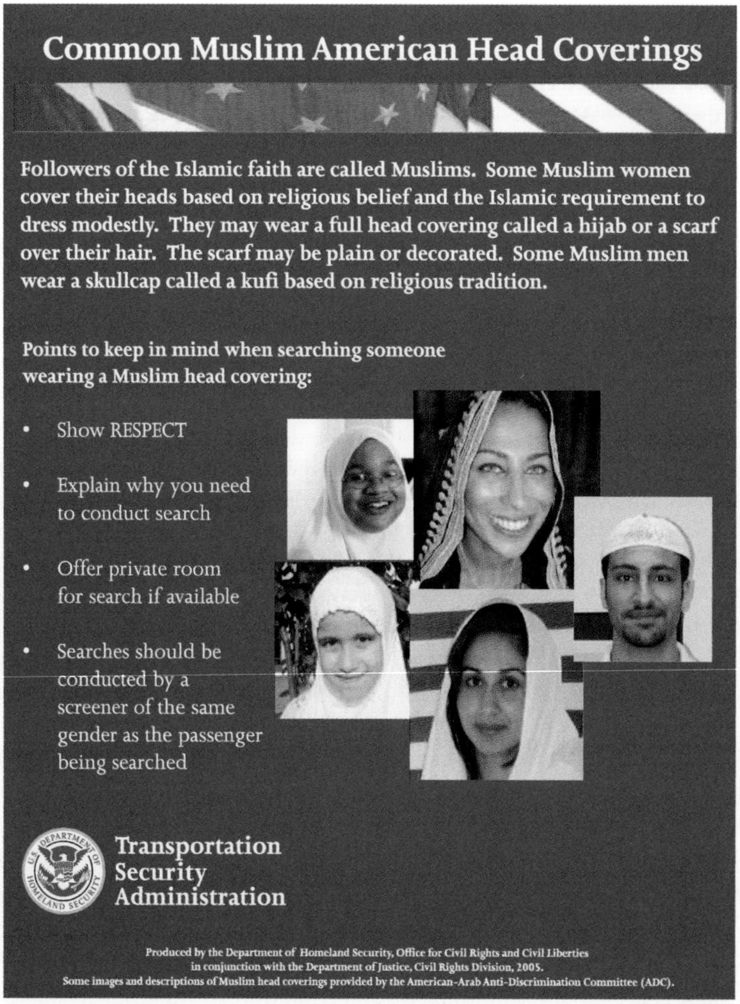

FIGURE 4-3 Transportation Security Administration training poster describing common Muslim-American head coverings. *Source: DHS (2005).*

counterterrorism measures) have infringed upon the civil liberties and constitutional rights of American citizens. This office tracks those concerns and provides a dedicated staff to the resolution of such issues as they arise and provides department-wide training to help manage incidents and reduce the number of incidents that arise. Through its Programs Branch, this office directs the Civil Rights and Civil Liberties Institute, which works closely with the Department of Justice Bureau of Justice Assistance in developing and providing training to DHS personnel. Figure 4-3 is an example of a training poster that explains common Muslim-American head coverings to staff and provides tips for conducting security searches of a person wearing a head covering.

- *Office of the Inspector General*: Federal civilian and military agencies commonly maintain an inspector general's office in order to conduct audits of agency or department operations, looking for fraud, misconduct, or waste. They may be congressionally mandated or not, and they can differ with regard to who they report to. The DHS Office of the Inspector General was established by the original Homeland Security Act of 2002, and the inspector general (IG) is appointed by the president and requires Senate confirmation. The DHS IG reports to both the secretary of homeland security and the Congress. Audits can arise from one of the following three sources: congressional mandates, congressional and departmental requests, and self-initiation. Considering the massive changes that have resulted from the creation of DHS, and the billions of dollars that have been dedicated to the department's mission, an office such as this is critical. In 2014, the OIG maintained a staff of 725 people. The OIG budget has remained relatively constant during the period of FY 2004 to FY 2006, with an allocation of approximately $83 million. In FY 2007, this jumped by nearly 25% to $103 million, as the perceived need for greater oversight was confirmed. This amount rose again in FY 2008 to $109 million. The 2015 OIG budget request was $145 million, representing less than 1% of the total DHS budget. Clark Kent Ervin left the post of inspector general on December 8, 2004, and was replaced by Assistant Inspector General Richard L. Skinner. Mr. Skinner retired in January 2011, and the seat was filled by Acting IG Charles K. Edwards until 2014 when John Roth assumed office.

- *Office of Citizenship and Immigration Services Ombudsman*: This office provides recommendations for resolving individual and employer problems with the US Citizenship and Immigration Services (USCIS) in order to ensure that both the national security and the integrity of the legal immigration system are maintained. The work of this office is a major concern of employers, especially in the agriculture and construction industries, who rely heavily upon a foreign workforce and who have had to dramatically increase their filing and tracking requirements. This office is also tasked with improving the interface that exists between the department and foreign applicants seeking permission to immigrate to the United States or to become a US citizen.
- *Office of Legislative Affairs*: This office is tasked with liaising between the Office of the DHS secretary and Congress, the White House and Executive Branch, and other federal agencies and governmental entities. Legislative Affairs staff members work to ensure that information is shared accurately and effectively between DHS and other key government agencies involved in homeland security.
- *Office of General Counsel*: This office works to integrate the efforts of approximately 1700 lawyers positioned throughout the department into what they term to be an "effective, client-oriented, full-service legal team" (DHS, 2007a).
- *Office of Public Affairs*: This office is tasked with informing the public, the press, and other individuals and groups about DHS activities and priorities (including general information about the department). Because the Federal Emergency Management Agency (FEMA) is located within the DHS structure, the Office of Public Affairs also serves as the lead Public Information Office (PIO) when FEMA becomes involved in an emergency or disaster.
- *Executive Secretariat*: This office ensures that all DHS officials are included in the correspondence drafting and policymaking process through a managed clearance and control system.
- *Military Advisor's Office*: This office provides advice to the DHS secretary and other executive staff whenever department operations relate to, influence, are influenced by, or otherwise involve the Department of Defense.
- *Office of Intergovernmental Affairs*: This office is the primary point of contact with other government agencies at all government levels (including federal, state, local, and tribal governments), integrating the work of the department with that of each of these other entities in their national security efforts.

The Office of the Secretary also maintains a number of advisory panels and committees, which help to form direction and policy on a number of issues deemed critical to the department's mission. These may be the result of presidential requests, statutory requirements, or discretionary spending:

- The Homeland Security Advisory Council (HSAC) is a discretionary advisory committee that provides advice and recommendations to the secretary on matters related to homeland security. This council is composed of leaders from state and local governments, first-responder communities, the private sector, and the academia. This council oversees a number of task forces, which address topics including border security, community resilience, and department sustainability and efficiency.
- The National Infrastructure Advisory Council (NIAC) is a presidential advisory committee that provides advice to the secretary and the president on the security of information systems for the public and private institutions managing or owning critical infrastructure. Topics addressed include threats to infrastructure, mitigation of infrastructure disruption, establishing resilience standards and goals, understanding and managing infrastructure interdependencies, and the impact of chemical, biological, radiological/nuclear, and explosive (CBRNE) hazards on infrastructure components.
- The Experts Panel on Cost Estimating for the Public Assistance Program is a statutory advisory committee that evaluates the FEMA disaster assistance program that supports the repair and reconstruction of public and nonprofit facilities and infrastructure in order to ensure that estimated project costs are accurate and that the proper technical expertise is used to develop project budgeting techniques.

The full list of DHS Federal Advisory Committees is as follows:
Presidential

- National Infrastructure Advisory Council (NIAC)
- President's National Security Telecommunications Advisory Committee (NSTAC)

Statutory

- Board of Visitors for the National Fire Academy (BOV NFA)
- Commercial Fishing Safety Advisory Committee (CFSAC)
- Advisory Committee on Commercial Operations of the Customs and Border Protection (COAC)
- Expert Panel on Cost Estimating for the Public Assistance Program
- Great Lakes Pilotage Advisory Committee (GLPAC)
- Houston/Galveston Navigation Safety Advisory Committee (HOGANSAC)
- Lower Mississippi River Waterway Safety Advisory Committee (LMRWSAC)
- Merchant Mariner Medical Advisory Committee (MEDMAC)
- National Advisory Council (NAC)
- Navigation Safety Advisory Council (NAVSAC)
- National Boating Safety Advisory Council (NBSAC)
- National Maritime Security Advisory Committee (NMSAC)
- Federal Emergency Management Agency Technical Mapping Advisory Council (TMAC)
- Towing Safety Advisory Committee (TSAC)

- US Customs and Border Protection Airport and Seaport Inspections User Fee Advisory Committee
- US Customs Service COBRA Fees Advisory Committee

Discretionary

- Aviation Security Advisory Committee (ASAC)
- Chemical Transportation Advisory Committee (CTAC)
- Data Privacy and Integrity Advisory Committee (DPIAC)
- Homeland Security Academic Advisory Council (HSAAC)
- Homeland Security Advisory Council (HSAC)
- Homeland Security Information Network Advisory Committee (HSINAC)
- Homeland Security Science and Technology Advisory Committee (HSSTAC)
- Merchant Marine Personnel Advisory Committee (MERPAC)
- National Security Telecommunications Advisory Committee (NSTAC)
- National Offshore Safety Advisory Committee (NOSAC)

Preexisting Offices Moved into DHS in 2002

Several agencies that existed elsewhere in the federal government prior to September 11 were transferred with few or no structural changes into the DHS when it was established. The leadership and staff of each of these agencies now report directly to the Office of the Secretary. Most notable of these agencies are the US Coast Guard (USCG) and the US Secret Service. FEMA was originally integrated into one of four original directorates, but after the bungled response to the post-Katrina 2007 reorganization, FEMA was reinstated as a stand-alone agency reporting directly to the DHS secretary. The Federal Law Enforcement Training Center (FLETC) was similarly incorporated into a DHS entity in 2002 but restored to its independent status under the DHS secretary as part of this 2002 reorganization. These intact agencies are described individually in the following subsections.

The US Coast Guard

The US Coast Guard (USCG), under the direction of Commandant Thad W. Allen, was transferred to the DHS as an intact agency on March 1, 2003. Today, the Coast Guard is led by Admiral Paul Zukunft. The primary function of the Coast Guard within the DHS remains consistent with its historic mission, as identified in the following eleven mission areas:

- Ports, waterways, and coastal security
- Drug interdiction
- Aids to navigation
- Search and rescue
- Living marine resources
- Marine safety
- Defense readiness
- Migrant interdiction

- Marine environment protection
- Ice operations
- Other law enforcement

As lead federal agency for maritime safety and security, the USCG protects several of the nation's vital interests, the personal safety and security of the American population, the natural and economic resources of the United States, and the territorial integrity of the country from both internal and external threats, natural and human-made. As a maritime military service, the USCG is responsible for a full range of humanitarian, law enforcement, regulatory, diplomatic, and national defense services (Figure 4-4).

The USCG was recognized after September 11 as being a well-equipped military force with established jurisdiction within the US territory. Immediately following September 11, the importance of this fact was not lost on federal government officials who witnessed how, as naval ships were quickly leaving the nation's ports to protect themselves, the Coast Guard's ships were moving into position inside those same ports.

Since entering DHS, the USCG has received a significant boost in its budget allocation, which has been used primarily to update a fleet of ships and aircraft that was considered outdated in relation to the other armed services (as part of the ongoing $24 billion Integrated Deepwater System Program). Additionally, many more employees have been added to the agency's payroll. As of 2014, the Coast Guard employed 41,416 active duty military members and 8131 civilian employees, for a total of 49,547 people. In addition to these, the USCG maintains 7000 selected reserve and 30,472 auxiliary employees. Between FY 2004 and FY 2015, the USCG saw its budget rise from $6.994 to $9.797 billion. This represents 16% of the total FY2015 DHS budget authorization (see Figure 4-5).

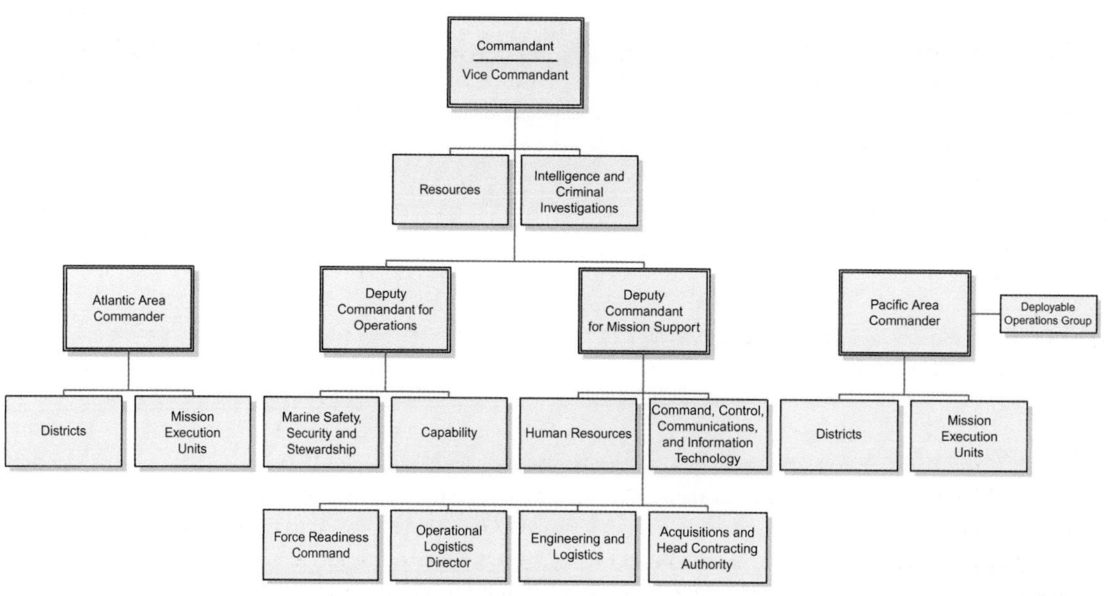

FIGURE 4-4 US Coast Guard organizational chart. *Source: DHS (2014f).*

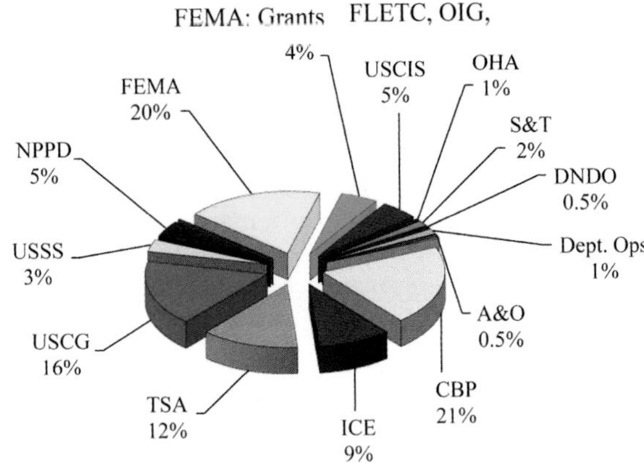

FIGURE 4-5 DHS: Percent of total budget authority by organization. *Source: DHS (2014g).*

US Secret Service

The US Secret Service (USSS), under the leadership of W. Ralph Basham, was transferred to the DHS as an intact agency on March 1, 2003. The Secret Service was able to continue its historic mission of protecting the president and senior executive personnel, in addition to protecting the country's currency and financial infrastructure and providing security for designated national events (e.g., the Super Bowl and the Olympics). The USSS is also responsible for the protection of the vice president, immediate family members of these senior officials, the president-elect and vice president-elect, or other officers next in the order of succession to the Office of the President and members of their immediate families, presidential candidates, visiting heads of state and their accompanying spouses, and, at the direction of the president, other distinguished foreign visitors to the United States and official representatives of the United States performing special missions abroad. Former presidents, their spouses, and minor children are also offered USSS protection for life.

The USSS also protects the executive residence and grounds in the District of Columbia, buildings in which White House offices are located, the official residence and grounds of the vice president in the District of Columbia, foreign diplomatic missions located in the Washington metropolitan area, the headquarters buildings and grounds of the DHS and Department of the Treasury, and such other areas as directed by the president. The USSS is also responsible for telecommunications fraud, computer and telemarketing fraud, fraud relative to federally insured financial institutions, and other criminal and noncriminal cases. The Secret Service is organized into two major components, one focused on protection and the other focused on investigation.

All people, places, and events that are protected represent key components of the nation's government and heritage. They are all, in addition to their intended roles, symbols of the country and therefore considered potential terrorist targets. The loss of any of these, whether due to terrorist or other means, could threaten the security of the nation, and therefore, their protection is considered integral to the homeland security mission.

The Secret Service experienced a series of high profile scandals and security lapses under the direction of its second and third directors (under DHS), Mark J. Sullivan and Julia Pierson. Sullivan largely weathered the pressure though Pierson retired soon after a man was successful in gaining access into the East Room of the White House. As of publication, the Secret Service remained under the leadership of Acting Director Joseph Clancy.

In 2014, the USSS employed 6572 people. The Secret Service budget allocation has gained slightly each year, rising from $1.334 billion in FY 2004 to $1.896 billion in FY 2015. This accounts for about 3% of the total FY 2015 DHS budget.

Federal Emergency Management Agency

The Federal Emergency Management Agency (FEMA) is the government agency responsible for leading national efforts to mitigate the risk of and prepare for the response to all types of disasters, whether they are natural, technological, or terrorism-related (Figure 4-6). In this effort, FEMA leads several important risk reduction programs including the National Flood Insurance Program, the National Earthquake Hazards Reduction Program, and others. FEMA is also tasked with managing the federal response and recovery efforts to support affected states and jurisdictions included in presidentially declared disasters.

FEMA maintains a fluctuating full-time staff that stood at 14,844 employees in April of 2014. Of this number, all but 5000 are funded through the Disaster Relief Fund (i.e., are associated with the response and recovery of specific disaster events). These employees work at FEMA headquarters in Washington, DC, at regional and area offices across the country (including 10 regional offices, 3 permanent area offices, and a varying number of recovery offices), at the Mount Weather Emergency Operations Center, and at the National Emergency Training Center in Emmitsburg, Maryland.

While FEMA's central mission has remained the same since it was incorporated into DHS, its various functions have been transferred into and out of the agency during various organizational iterations that have occurred in the intervening years. One of its primary missions, as stated by DHS in its earliest days, is to "further the evolution of the emergency management culture from one that reacts to disasters to one that proactively helps communities and citizens avoid becoming victims" (Library of Congress, 2014). In addition, the directorate develops and manages a national training and evaluation system, designs curriculums, sets standards, and rewards performance in local, state, and federal training efforts.

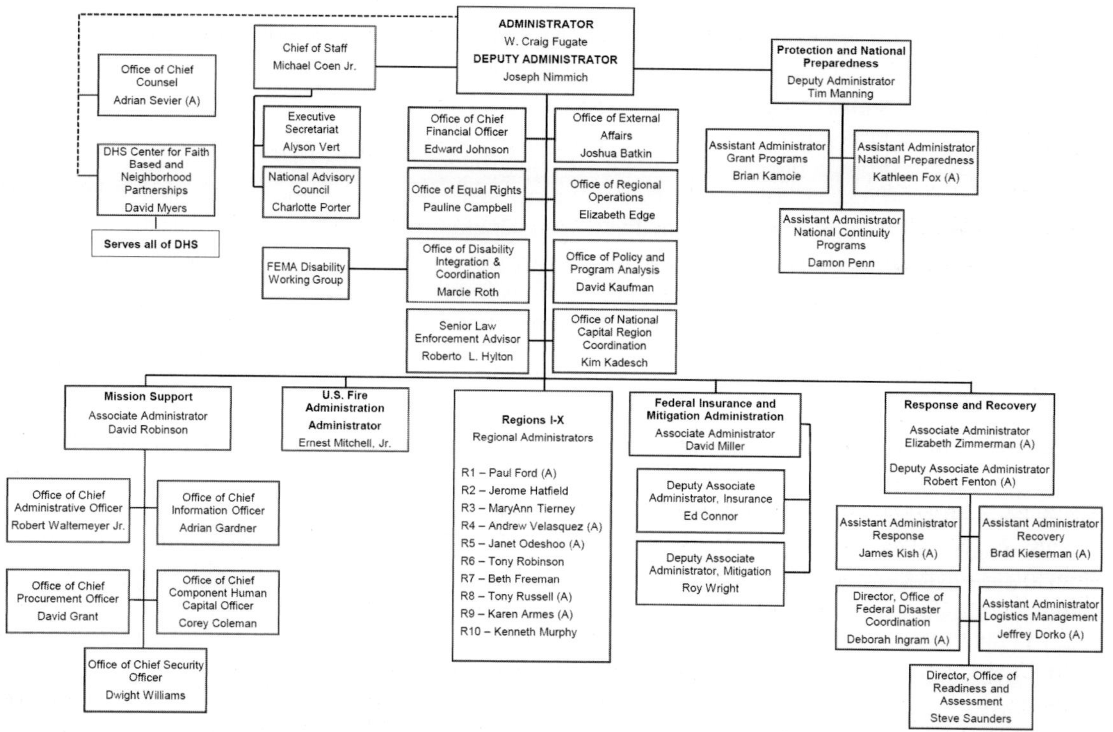

FIGURE 4-6 FEMA organizational chart. *Source: FEMA (2014).*

Through the Disaster Relief Fund, FEMA provides assistance to individuals, the public sector, and nongovernmental organizations to help families and communities impacted by disasters rebuild and recover. FEMA also administers hazard mitigation programs to prevent or to reduce the risk to life and property from floods and other hazards. In addition to administering the National Incident Management System (NIMS), in FY 2007, FEMA's role as the lead federal agency for incident management, preparedness, and response was expanded to include the administration of DHS's grant programs and the US Fire Administration (USFA). The inclusion of these programs was intended to reinforce the nation's all-hazards preparedness, response, and recovery capacity at all levels of government including federal, state, tribal, and local.

FEMA maintains a leadership role to manage the DHS response to any sort of natural, technological, or terrorist attack disaster, per the National Response Framework (NRF) and the Robert T. Stafford Disaster Relief and Emergency Assistance Act. The agency is also in charge of coordinating the involvement of other federal response teams, such as the National Guard, in the event of a major incident. In accordance with the NRF and the National Disaster Recovery Framework (NDRF), FEMA also leads federal government relief and recovery efforts that follow major declared disasters. These response and recovery processes are illustrated in much greater detail in Chapter 9.

FEMA funds and administers the Citizen Corps program. Citizen Corps funding supports the formation and training of local Citizen Corps Councils (CCCs), which increase local involvement (in CCCs), develop community action plans, help in the performance of threat assessments and the identification of local resources for homeland security, and locally coordinate the Citizen Corps programs. The existing programs, administered by several federal agencies both internal and external to homeland security, involve leaders from law enforcement, fire, and emergency medical services; businesses; community-based institutions; schools; places of worship; health-care facilities; public works; and other key community sectors. Current Citizen Corps programs include the following (Citizen Corps activities are documented in greater detail in Chapter 9 of this book):

- Community Emergency Response Teams (CERTs), administered by DHS
- Volunteers in Police Service (VIPS) program, administered by DOJ (Department of Justice)
- Medical Reserve Corps (MRC), administered by HHS (Department of Health and Human Services)
- USAOnWatch (Neighborhood Watch) programs, administered by DOJ
- Fire Corps Program, administered by the USA Freedom Corps and several nongovernmental partners
- Citizen-preparedness publications, which are public education guides that seek to increase individual knowledge and preparedness for crime, terrorism, and disasters at home, in neighborhoods, at places of work, and in public spaces

FEMA saw its budget (as a component of the former Emergency Preparedness and Response Directorate until 2006) rise from $5.554 billion in FY 2004 to $7.541 billion in FY 2005, mostly because of biodefense funding. However, biodefense funding was cut from the FEMA budget in FY 2006, dropping the amount the agency received to $5.365 billion. With the introduction of the FEMA Grants Program in 2008, this amount as requested stood at $9.639 billion. In FY 2015, the FEMA budget request was $10.562 billion. This amount accounts for 20% of the total DHS budget, of which 22% is reallocated outside of FEMA in the form of grants and 70% goes to the Disaster Relief Fund. The FEMA budget can be increased by the Congress through emergency appropriations to cover the costs of catastrophic disasters, as occurred following the September 11 attacks and the Hurricane Katrina response. In 2013, following Hurricane Sandy, over $11 billion in supplemental funding was added to the FEMA budget—an amount that exceeded its entire regular budget allocation that year.

Critical Thinking

Do you believe that FEMA is appropriately placed within the DHS bureaucracy in its current position under the secretary of homeland security, or should it have been placed somewhere else within the federal structure outside of DHS? Explain your answer.

Critical Thinking

Does it make sense to fund the Disaster Relief Fund on an annual basis using levels that do not account for major disasters (as is currently the practice) and then passing supplemental funding bills to cover shortfalls, or should the Disaster Relief Fund have a large enough buffer built in to its funding levels to ensure that FEMA is able to quickly disburse funding even when major disasters occur? Explain your answer.

Federal Law Enforcement Training Center

The Federal Law Enforcement Training Center (FLETC) serves as the federal government's principal provider of federal law enforcement personnel training. The FLETC provides for the training needs of over 85 federal agencies that carry out law enforcement responsibilities. The center also provides training and technical assistance to state and local law enforcement entities and plans, develops, and presents formal training courses and practical exercise applications related to international law enforcement training. The center offers numerous basic law enforcement training programs of varying lengths, designed specifically for the duties and responsibilities of the personnel to be trained, and conducts numerous advanced and specialized training programs found nowhere else in the country.

The FLETC currently operates four training sites throughout the United States. Its headquarters and primary training site is located in Glynco, Georgia. Two other field locations, both of which provide both basic training and advanced training, are located in Artesia, New Mexico, and Charleston, South Carolina. The fourth training site, in Cheltenham, Maryland, provides in-service and requalification training for officers and agents in the Washington, DC, area. In cooperation with the Department of State, the FLETC also operates International Law Enforcement Academies in Gaborone, Botswana; Bangkok, Thailand; and throughout the world through collaboration with US embassies and consulates abroad. The FLETC maintained a staff of 1092 in FY 2014 and saw budget allocations rise from $192 million in FY 2004 to $260 million in FY 2014 (representing <1% of the DHS budget).

Transportation Security Administration

The Transportation Security Administration (TSA) was created just 2 months after the September 11 terrorist attacks (on November 19, 2001), through the Aviation and Transportation Security Act (ATSA—Public Law 107-071). TSA protects the nation's transportation systems in order to ensure the freedom of movement for both people and commercial goods and services. ATSA was passed in recognition of failures in private security systems and placed overall aviation transportation security under the direction and responsibility of the federal government. The agency it created was tasked with identifying risks to the transportation sector, prioritizing them, and managing them to acceptable levels (Figure 4-7).

The TSA began as an agency focused on airline security, which was understandable considering that the September 11 terrorists capitalized on lax aviation security measures to attack the nation. The agency's focus has steadily expanded to address other transportation modes such as intercity buses, rail travel, and ferry travel, but in terms of both dollars and people, its primary focus clearly remains on aviation security.

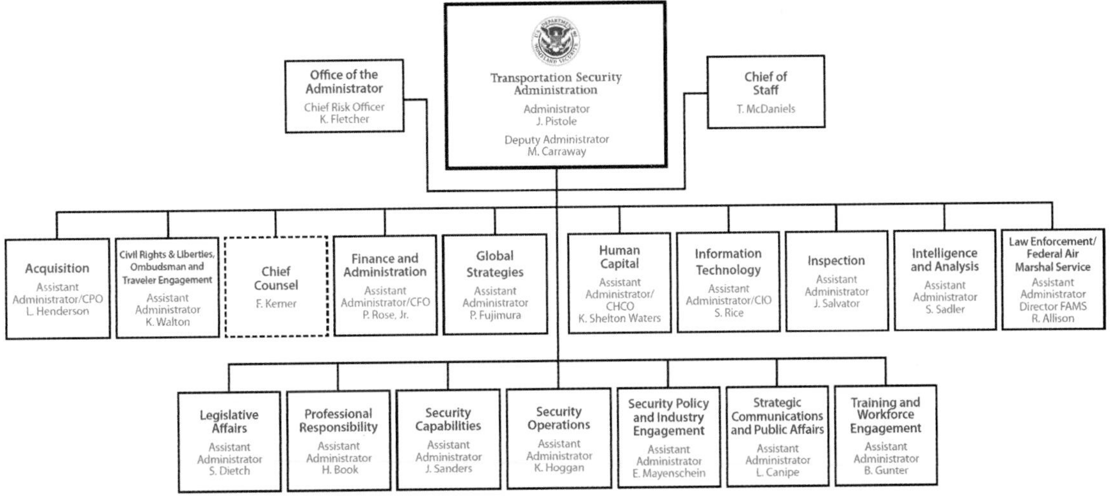

FIGURE 4-7 TSA organizational chart. *Source: TSA (2014).*

The TSA's specific responsibilities include ensuring thorough and efficient screening of all airline passengers and baggage through an appropriate mix of federalized and privatized screeners and technology. This screener workforce consists primarily of 50,000 passenger and baggage screeners located at more than 450 commercial and privatized airports throughout the country.

US air carriers transport over 10 million tons of cargo, of which about 30% is flown on board commercial passenger planes (with the rest transported via cargo planes that are not inspected to the same degree as passenger carriers). TSA has been given the responsibility to devise and implement a system to screen, inspect, or otherwise ensure the security of all cargo that is to be transported aboard aircraft—a task that will likely require many years and significant financial investment. The importance of screening air cargo was highlighted in October 2010 when al-Qaeda terrorists successfully shipped bombs disguised as printers on both passenger and cargo planes bound for the United States. It is almost certain that the bombs would not have been detected had Saudi intelligence officials not sounded an alert to perform a thorough inspection. These bombs were so advanced in their design that they evaded detection by visual and manual inspection from a bomb squad, inspection by bomb-sniffing dogs, and X-ray inspection (Cruickshank et al., 2012).

TSA is also tasked with managing the security risk to the US surface transportation systems. They are confronted with the paradox of trying to ensure the freedom of movement of people and commerce while preventing the same for terrorists. These transportation systems include approximately 751 million passengers traveling on buses each year and over 10 billion passenger trips on mass transit per year; over 168,000 mi of railroad (of which 120,000 mi is privately owned); 3.9 million mi of roads (46,717 mi of Interstate highway and 114,700 mi of National Highway System roads), 604,000 bridges over 20 ft of span, 366 tunnels over 1000 ft in length, and nearly 2.6 million miles of pipeline; and nearly 800,000 shipments of hazardous materials transported every day (95% by truck) (Pistole, 2014).

As part of Secretary Chertoff's reorganization plan, the Federal Air Marshal Service was transferred from the US Immigration and Customs Enforcement (ICE) office to TSA, where it was originally located before being removed in 2003 under the original framework of DHS.

John Pistole is the current administrator of TSA. The TSA maintained an employee base of 53,670 in FY 2014 (primarily federal airport security screeners) and saw its budget rise steadily from $4.578 billion in FY 2004 to $7.305 billion in FY 2015 (of which $5. 6083 billion was dedicated to aviation security). The TSA budget represents 12% of the total DHS budget.

New Offices and Directorates

Many new offices have been created within the DHS to manage the wide range of functions that directly and indirectly support national security. Over the past decade, the number of offices has gone up and down as functions arise, are eliminated, or are consolidated. Among these offices, DHS currently maintains three major multifunctional divisions, which have been termed directorates. Each directorate is led by an undersecretary. Each of the directorates and offices is described in this section.

Directorate for National Protection and Programs

The Directorate for National Protection and Programs serves to accomplish the risk-reduction mission that is central to DHS. This directorate was newly created in 2007 as a result of the PKEMRA, thereby assuming several functions that had existed previously in other areas spread throughout DHS. This office is led by acting DHS Undersecretary Suzanne Spaulding and maintains a full-time staff of 3463 employees. The NPPD budget has increased from $1.177 billion in FY 2008 to $2.858 billion in FY 2015, representing 5% of the DHS budget request and an increase of more than 100% over FY 2008 amounts.

Prior to NPPD, the DHS Preparedness Directorate fulfilled three critical department-wide needs:

1. To strengthen national risk management efforts for critical infrastructure
2. To define and synchronize DHS-level doctrine for homeland security protection initiatives that entail aggressive coordination internally within DHS, in planning and integration work across the federal government, and with state, communities, and the private sector
3. To deliver grants and related preparedness program and training activities

Of these three functions, the third was transferred to FEMA, while NPPD assumed the status as a "department-level focal point" for the ongoing management of the first two. In addition, NPPD provides management support and direction for US-VISIT, an immigration tracking and technology program. NPPD is also the lead office for federal efforts to protect and prevent attacks on critical infrastructure, and as such, it works to improve cybersecurity and communications system resilience. NPPD is the office that interacts with the private sector and with state and local government leaders to ensure that the full range of department-wide programs and policies is effectively integrated. This office is also working to standardize DHS risk management efforts. The NPPD responsibilities include the following:

- Identifying threats and vulnerabilities to the nation's cyber infrastructure and mitigating against the consequences of a cyber attack
- Protecting and strengthening the nation's national security and emergency communications capabilities' reliability, survivability, and interoperability at the federal, state, local, and tribal levels
- Integrating and disseminating critical infrastructure and key resources' threat, consequence, and vulnerability information and developing risk mitigation strategies that enhance protection and resilience through coordination with critical infrastructure and key resources' owners
- Developing and ensuring implementation of the National Infrastructure Protection Plan (NIPP) for the nation's infrastructure through sector-specific plans
- Ensuring a safe and secure environment in which federal agencies can conduct business by reducing threats posed against approximately 9000 federal facilities nationwide
- Providing biometric and biographical identity management and screening services to other departmental entities as well as to other federal, state, local, and international stakeholders for immigration and border management

- Leading the department's effort to develop, implement, and share a common framework addressing the overall analysis and management of homeland security risk

The five components of NPPD include the following:

- *The Office of Cybersecurity and Communications (CS&C)*: This office works to ensure the security, resiliency, and reliability of the nation's cyber and communications infrastructure in collaboration with the public and private sectors, including international partners. Specifically, CS&C is focused on preparing for and responding to catastrophic incidents that could degrade or overwhelm the networks, systems, and assets that operate US information technology and communications infrastructure—especially the ".gov" domain. CS&C partners with the private sector to help protect the ".com" domain. The five divisions that carry out the work of this office include
  - the Office of Emergency Communications,
  - the National Cybersecurity and Communications Integration Center,
  - Stakeholder Engagement and Cyber Infrastructure Resilience,
  - Federal Network Resilience,
  - Network Security Deployment.
- *The Office of Infrastructure Protection (IP)*: This office leads the coordinated national effort to reduce risk to critical infrastructure and key resources posed by terrorism. IP facilitates the identification, prioritization, coordination, and protection of these resources in support of federal, state, local, territorial, and tribal governments, as well as the private sector and international entities. IP shares this information with partners at the state, local, and private levels, communicating threats, vulnerabilities, incidents, potential security measures, and best practices that enhance the mitigation of risks to and protection of infrastructure, response to events that impact infrastructure, and the restoration of infrastructure when impacted by a disaster or other event. IP functions are guided by the National Infrastructure Protection Plan (NIPP), which was updated in 2013 and can be found by accessing http://1.usa.gov/1sEEFwx.
- *The Federal Protective Service (FPS)*: This office provides security and law enforcement services to federally owned and leased buildings, facilities, properties, and other assets nationwide. FPS employs 1371 federal staff (including 900 law enforcement security officers, criminal investigators, police officers, and support personnel) and 15,000 contract guard staff to secure over 9000 buildings and safeguard their occupants. In October of 2009, FPS was transferred into NPPD from US ICE, another DHS component described later in this chapter.
- *The Office of Cyber and Infrastructure Analysis (OCIA)*: In 2014, OCIA was separated out of the Office of Infrastructure Protection (IP), where it was formerly called the Infrastructure Analysis and Strategy Division (IASD). OCIA supports critical infrastructure protection by providing risk analysis on the consequences of infrastructure disruptions, whether from natural or intentional causes. The goal of these efforts is to help public and private owners and operators of infrastructure to become better prepared to take action and to institute necessary measures that will increase the protection of their facilities and operations. The information it uses comes from other DHS components, such as the Homeland Infrastructure Threat and Risk Analysis Center (HITRAC) and the National Infrastructure Simulation and Analysis Center (NISAC).
- *The Office of Biometric Identity Management (OBIM)*: The US Visitor and Immigrant Status Indicator Technology (US-VISIT) program was created in 2003 to more accurately record the entry and exit of travelers to the United States. The program's focus was to collect biographical and biometric information, such as digital fingerprints and photographs, so that visitors to the United States could be tracked on their way in and out of the country. In 2013, US-VISIT became the Office of Biometric Identity Management (OBIM). The office is responsible for ensuring that ports of entry and other data

intake centers have the equipment required to collect and store biometric data and provides analysis of that data as needed to identify risks. OBIM maintains a watchlist of travelers suspected of criminal or terrorist activities and, more importantly, helps to ensure that the data on visitors maintained by different DHS components associated with immigration and border protection are adequately linked.

Science and Technology Directorate

The Science and Technology (S&T) Directorate provides leadership for directing, funding, and conducting research, development, test, and evaluation (RDT&E) and procurement of technologies and systems that can prevent the importation of weapons of mass destruction and the materials that can be used to produce them. S&T also supports the development of solutions for the response to incidents involving these weapons.

The Office of Science and Technology formerly existed within the National Institute of Justice, which still exists within the DOJ today. The HS Act of 2002 effectively abolished that office and transferred all applicable functions to the new S&T Directorate within DHS. In its current organization, S&T is composed of four groups that address basic research through advanced technology development and transition, spanning six primary divisions that address critical homeland security needs (Figure 4-8). These lead groups include the following:

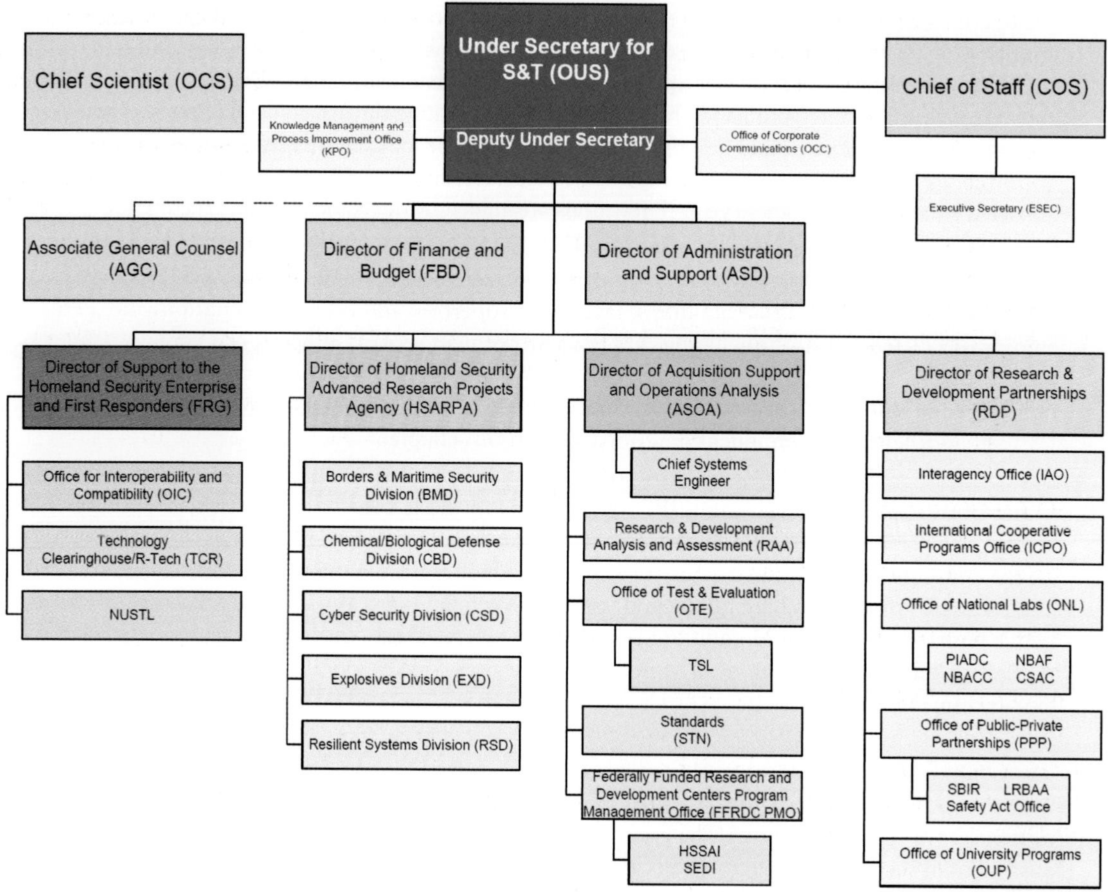

FIGURE 4-8 Science and technology directorate. *Source: DHS (2014h).*

- *The Support to the Homeland Security Enterprise and First Responders Group (FRG)*: This group identifies, validates, and facilitates the fulfillment of first-responder requirements through the use of existing and emerging technologies, knowledge products, and the acceleration of standards. The group manages a number of working groups, teams, and stakeholder outreach efforts that seek to better understand the requirements of first responders. FRG manages the following offices:
  - Office of Interoperability and Compatibility
  - Technology Clearinghouse/R-Tech
  - National Urban Security Technology Laboratory (NUSTL)
- *The Homeland Security Advanced Research Projects Agency (HSARPA)*: This organization manages a portfolio of highly innovative programs that are transforming the future mission of homeland security. HSARPA manages the following technical divisions that address customer-identified needs through scientific projects:
  - *Borders and Maritime Security Division*: Develops and transitions tools and technologies that improve the security of our nation's borders and waterways, without impeding the flow of commerce and travel.
  - *Chemical/Biological Defense Division*: Works to increase the nation's preparedness against chemical and biological threats through improved threat awareness, advanced surveillance and detection, and protective countermeasures.
  - *Cyber Security Division*: Works to address the security of the nation's computer networks against crime and/or terrorist attacks.
  - *Explosives Division*: Develops the technical capabilities to detect, interdict, and lessen the impacts of nonnuclear explosives used in terrorist attacks against mass transit, civil aviation, and critical infrastructure.
  - *Resilient Systems Division*: Supports the FEMA "Whole Community" concept by developing systems and solutions that help to reduce the vulnerability of individuals and communities. The program's four "thrust areas" include
    - Adaptive risk mitigation (tools and processes that enable adaptation to changing or evolving threats),
    - Agile disaster management (advanced situational awareness and real-time decision support),
    - Resilience infrastructure (disaster-resilient design and standards for critical infrastructure),
    - Effective training, education, and performance.
- *Acquisition Support and Operations Analysis (ASOA)*: This office supports other DHS components developing technical or analytic requirements or documents related to acquisition. This might include testing new technologies or products and providing an analysis of their usefulness in meeting needs. ASOA maintains a chief systems engineer and operates through the following components:
  - Research and Development Analysis and Assessment (RAA)
  - Standards (STN)
  - Office of Test & Evaluation (OTE)
  - Federally Funded Research and Development Centers Program Management Office (FFRDC PMO)
- *The Research and Development Partnerships (RDP)*: This group conducts stakeholder outreach and engagement through close partnerships with seven department science and technology groups. The RDP groups include the following:
  - The Interagency Office
  - The International Cooperative Programs Office
  - The Office of National Laboratories, which includes the following:

- Plum Island Animal Disease Center (PIADC)
- National Biodefense Analysis and Countermeasures Center (NBACC)
- National Bio- and Agro-Defense Facility (NBAF)
- Chemical Security Analysis Center (CSAC)
- The Office of Public-Private Partnerships, which includes the following:
  - Small Business Innovative Research Office (SBIR)
  - Long-Range Broad Agency Announcement (LRBAA) Office
  - Office of SAFETY Act Implementation
  - Commercialization Office
- The Office of University Programs
- The Homeland Security Science and Technology Advisory Committee (HSSTAC)
- The Special Projects Office

The S&T Directorate maintained a staff of 467 full-time employees in FY 2014. The S&T budget allocation began at $913 million in FY 2004 and has fluctuated both above and below this amount since. In FY 2015, the budget stood at $1072 billion, accounting for 2% of that year's total DHS budget. The S&T Directorate is expanded on in much greater detail in Chapter 12.

Directorate for Management

The undersecretary for management (USM) is responsible for budget, appropriations, expenditure of funds, accounting, and finance; procurement; human resources and personnel; information technology systems; facilities, property, equipment, and other material resources; and identification and tracking of performance measurements relating to the responsibilities of the DHS. The Office of the USM requested a budget of $195 million in FY 2015 and a staff of 854, which represented a continued steady decrease in both that has existed for several years. The Office of the USM is but one component of the function termed departmental management and operations. This function, which came under a blanket request of $748 million in FY 2015, provides leadership, direction, and management to the whole department and is composed of separate appropriations, which include (in addition to the Management Directorate) the following:

- Office of the Secretary and Executive Management (OSEM)
- Office of the Chief Financial Officer (OCFO)
- Office of the Chief Information Officer (OCIO)
- DHS Headquarters Consolidation Project (HQ)

The OSEM provides central leadership, management, direction, and oversight of all the department's components. The secretary serves as the top representative of the department to the president, the Congress, and the general public.

The Management Directorate includes the Office of the Under Secretary for Management, the Office of the Chief Human Capital Officer, the Office of the Chief Procurement Officer, the Office of the Chief Administrative Officer, and the Office of the Chief Security Officer. The directorate's primary mission is to deliver administrative support services and provide leadership and oversight for all departmental management and operations functions that include IT, budget and financial management, procurement and acquisition, human capital, security, and administrative services.

The OCFO is composed of the Budget Division, the Program Analysis and Evaluation Division, the Office of Financial Operations Division, the Financial Management and Policy Division, the Internal Control Management Division, the Resource Management Transformation Office (Financial Systems Division), the Grants Policy and Oversight Division, the Departmental Audit Liaison Office, and the Workforce Development Division. The OCFO is responsible for the fiscal management, integrity, and accountability of DHS. The mission of the OCFO is to provide guidance and oversight of the department's budget, financial management, financial operations for all departmental management and operations, the DHS Working Capital Fund, grants and assistance awards, and resource management systems to ensure that funds necessary to carry out the department's mission are obtained, allocated, and expended in accordance with the department's priorities and relevant law and policies.

The OCIO consists of five program offices: Executive Front Office, Information Security Office, Enterprise Business Management Office, Office of Applied Technology, and the Information Technology Services Office. OCIO is responsible for all the information technology projects in the department. The OCIO provides information technology leadership, as well as products and services, to ensure the effective and appropriate use of information technology across DHS. The OCIO coordinates acquisition strategies to minimize costs and improve consistency of the information technology infrastructure. The OCIO enhances mission success by partnering with other DHS components to leverage the best available information technologies and management practices. The OCIO is the lead organization in providing the capability for DHS to partner in the sharing of essential information to federal, state, tribal, and local governments as well as private industry and regular US citizens for the protection of the homeland. The OCIO coordinates the planning and design structure to ascertain the best IT practices, processes, and systems to support both the OCIO and component missions in accordance with the department's overall goals. The OCIO is the lead organization in developing and maintaining the DHS Information Security Program, which includes oversight and coordination of activities associated with the Federal Information Security Management Act (FISMA). The OCIO is also responsible for providing performance metrics and overall evaluation of DHS component IT programs as related to DHS and Government Performance and Results Act (GPRA) goals.

The DHS HQ Consolidation Project is responsible for the collocation and consolidation of the department through lease consolidation and build-out of the St. Elizabeth's campus. The DHS Management Directorate provides the coordination, planning, policy, guidance, operational oversight and support, and innovative solutions for the management needs of the entire department for the "One DHS" culture. As previously described, this project is currently more than 10 years behind schedule and more than 50% overbudget. Conservative estimates place full consolidation in the St. Elizabeth's site at the year 2026, long past the original 2016 projected date.

US Citizenship and Immigration Services

The US Citizenship and Immigration Services (USCIS) is the DHS component responsible for facilitating the legal immigration of people seeking to enter, reside, or work in the United States. The office, led by Director León Rodríguez, is responsible for "providing accurate and useful information to our customers, granting immigration and citizenship benefits, promoting an awareness and understanding of citizenship, and ensuring the integrity of our immigration system" (DHS, 2014c). USCIS has established six strategic goals in accomplishing this mission:

1. Strengthening the security and integrity of the immigration system
2. Providing effective customer-oriented immigration benefit and information services
3. Supporting immigrants' integration and participation in American civic culture
4. Promoting flexible and sound immigration policies and programs
5. Strengthening the infrastructure supporting the USCIS mission
6. Operating as a high-performance organization that promotes a highly talented workforce and a dynamic work culture

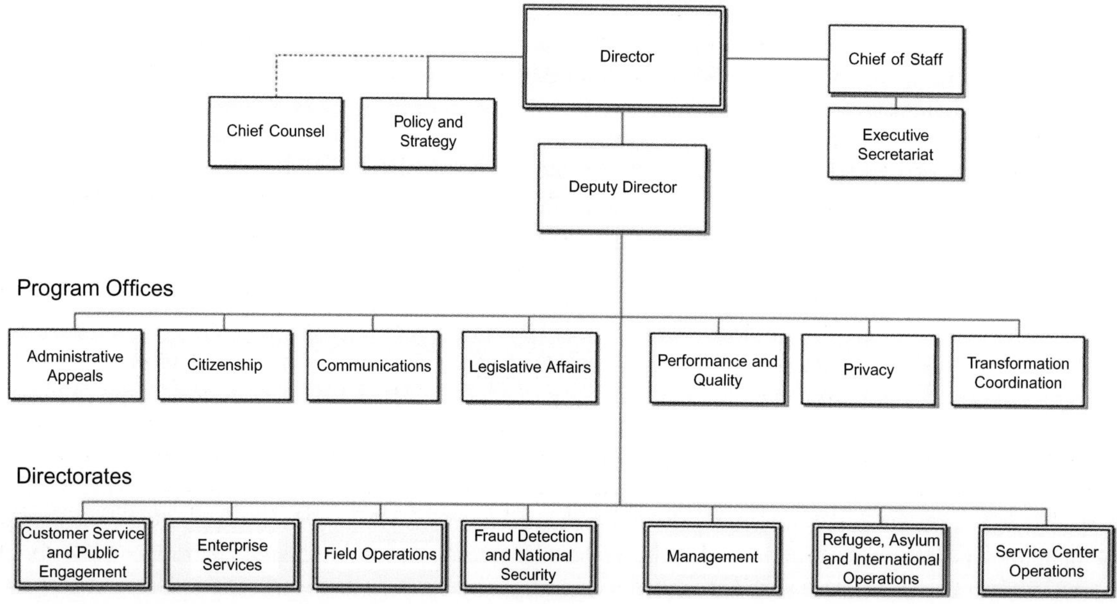

FIGURE 4-9 US Citizenship and Immigration Services organizational chart. *Source: USCIS (2014).*

Before September 11, all immigration issues were handled by the US Department of State through the Consular Services section and by the Immigration and Naturalization Service (INS) of the Department of Justice. The Department of State has maintained the authority to grant or deny permission to applicants applying to enter the United States from overseas despite the major reorganization of government since the September 11 attacks. The INS, however, which handled the creation and enforcement of immigration policy within the United States, was absorbed into DHS and further dismantled into three distinct offices. USCIS maintains responsibility for immigration services (applications for residence, for instance), ICE is responsible for enforcing immigration law within the United States, and Customs and Border Protection (CBP) enforces those same laws at the US ports of entry and the borders (Figure 4-9).

USCIS processes more than 25 million applications each year at over 220 locations worldwide. In 2013, the USCIS office maintained a staff of 13,196 full-time employees and almost 6000 contractors in FY 2014 and saw their budget rise from $1.550 billion in FY 2004 to $4.260 billion in FY 2015. The FY 2014 budget appropriation for USCIS represents 5% of the department's total budget.

US Customs and Border Protection

US Customs and Border Protection (CBP) is responsible for protecting the nation's borders, at and between official ports of entry. CBP works to ensure that all people and cargo that come into the country do so in both a legal and safe manner. CBP inspectors are strategically positioned to limit the cross border smuggling of contraband like illegal narcotics and other controlled substances, weapons of mass destruction (WMDs), and illegal plants and animals. They also ensure that people traveling or immigrating to the United States have all of the documents required to do so legally. Other tasks include the prevention of illegal currency (and other negotiable financial assets or instruments) export, the export of stolen property (e.g., automobiles), and the export of strategically sensitive technologies that could be used by other groups or governments to compromise either the security or the strategic and economic position of the United States. CBP maintains control of the country's 7500 miles of land borders between ports of entry through the efforts of the Border Patrol, which it directs. The Border Patrol also assists the Coast Guard in its efforts to control the 95,000 miles of maritime border.

CBP preempts border breaches by deploying officials overseas at major international seaports, through application of the Container Security Initiative (CSI). This project was established in 2002 to allow the prescreening of shipping containers before they arrive in the United States in order to detect and interdict WMDs and other illicit material early in the supply chain. To date, there are 58 CSI ports located worldwide, covering over 80% of inbound maritime containers.

CBP's entry specialists and trade compliance personnel enforce US trade and tariff laws and regulations in order to ensure that a fair and competitive trade environment exists for the United States. CBP's Air and Marine Operations Division patrols the nation's borders to interdict illegal drugs and terrorists before entry into the United States and provides surveillance and operational support to special national security events.

CBP officers process approximately 25 million shipping containers and make direct contact with more than 360 million people crossing the borders through ports each year and with tens of thousands of shippers, drivers, pilots, and importers associated with more than 25 million officially declared trade entries. In FY 2014, CBP maintained a staff of 65,552 and saw budgets rise steadily from $5.997 billion in FY 2004 to $13.097 billion in FY 2015. The FY 2015 budget request represents the single greatest item on the DHS budget, accounting for 21% of the total.

US Immigration and Customs Enforcement

As the largest investigative arm of DHS, the US Immigration and Customs Enforcement (ICE) enforces federal immigration and customs laws. ICE is tasked with protecting the country and upholding public safety by identifying and dismantling criminal organizations at the nation's borders. ICE agents and investigators identify, apprehend, and remove (deport) criminal and other illegal aliens. It does this through the following organizational divisions (Figure 4-10):

- Enforcement and Removal Operations (ERO) is responsible for enforcing the nation's immigration laws. This includes the identification of unlawful aliens and the detention and removal of those identified (as necessary). Given the scope of illegal immigration in the United States, ERO focuses its efforts on those people who pose the greatest threat to national security, including convicted criminals, fugitives, and suspected or known terrorists. Repeat offenders are also prioritized. Once detained, ERO is responsible for caring for and transporting illegal aliens until their case is settled. Some of those interdicted may be seeking asylum, and in such cases, ERO is responsible for providing access to legal resources and advocacy group representatives. The Secure Communities Program was recently moved into ERO. This office helps ICE agents to target their efforts more effectively by using emerging technologies and by connecting the DHS and FBI databases that contain arrest and other relevant data (e.g., fingerprints).
- Homeland Security Investigations (HSI) is, as its name suggests, the immigration and customs investigative arm of DHS. HSI agents investigate the illegal movement of and trafficking of people and goods into and out of the United States, as well as within its borders. Investigations also look into criminal immigration activities, illegal drug and weapons smuggling, trafficking in persons, financial crimes, cybercrime, and more. One of the most difficult yet important functions of this office is to investigate and prevent intellectual property right (IPR) violations. Piracy of American goods by Chinese companies alone was estimated by the US Congress to cost US businesses upwards

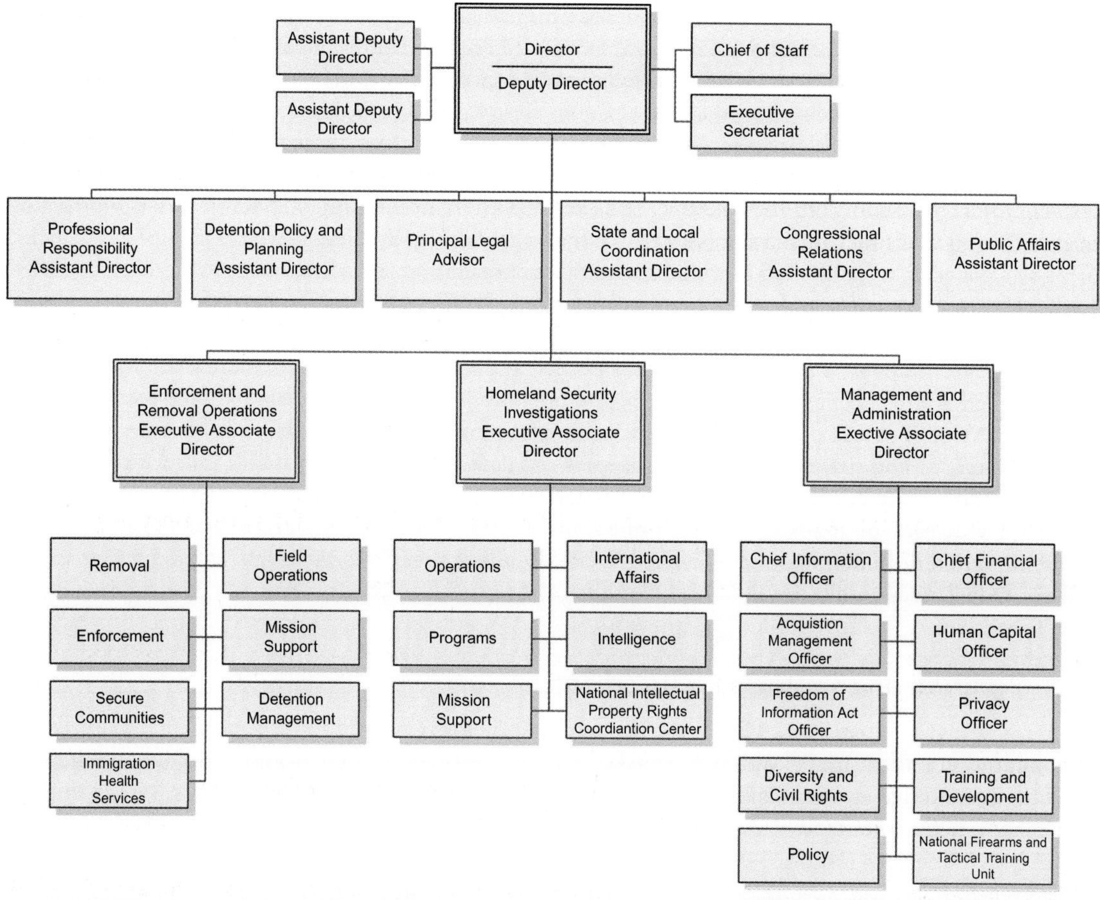

FIGURE 4-10 US Immigration and Customs Enforcement organizational chart. *Source: DHS (2014i).*

of $48 billion each year (US Senate Committee on Finance, 2011). The International Affairs Operations and Intelligence, which was formerly an independent unit within ICE, is now managed by HSI. Through this function, HSI agents are located in 47 countries worldwide.

- Management and Administration is the third component and is responsible for setting and administering the ICE budget, spending, accounting, procurement, human resources, information technology, and other administrative tasks.

ICE is led by Acting Director Thomas Winkowski. In FY 2014, ICE employed 19,332 employees. The office saw allocations rise steadily from $3.616 billion in FY2004 to $5.359 billion as requested in FY 2015. This allocation represents 9% of the department's 2015 budget.

Office of Policy

The Office of Policy, led by Acting Assistant Secretary for Policy Alan Bersin, formulates and coordinates homeland security policy and procedures for the department. This office helps the expansive and functionally diverse DHS to maintain a centralized, coordinated focus as it pursues its various missions, which include counterterrorism efforts; disaster preparedness; prevention, response, and recovery; weapons of mass destruction; border security; and immigration. This office helps the various components to align their efforts where they are shared, which can be a challenging task especially where cultures and missions may differ (e.g., with regard to infrastructure risk assessment and protection where FEMA, the USCG, and NPPD are concerned). Its existence ensures that there is a central office through which these crossover policies may be developed and communicated across the multiple departmental components and helps to ensure that strategic and budgetary planning efforts are coordinated.

The Office of Policy operates through the actions of the following offices:

- *Office of Policy Implementation and Integration*: Provides policy development and analysis across all DHS mission areas, including Counterterrorism Policy, Screening Coordination, Resilience Policy, Immigration Policy, CBRN Policy, and Transborder Policy
- *Office of Strategy, Planning, Analysis, and Risk*: Articulates the department's long-term vision, designs and refines strategic planning processes, and ensures that leadership is equipped with the necessary information
- *Office for State and Local Law Enforcement*: Leads the coordination of department-wide policies relating to state, local, and tribal law enforcement's role in preventing acts of terrorism and also serves as the primary liaison between law enforcement agencies across the country and the department
- *Office of International Affairs*: Develops DHS's strategy for promoting the department's mission overseas and actively engages foreign allies to improve international cooperation for immigration policy, visa security, aviation security, border security and training, law enforcement, and cargo security
- *Private Sector Office*: Provides the nation's private sector with a direct line of communication (to DHS), utilizes information received from the private sector, and promotes DHS policies to the private sector
- *Homeland Security Advisory Council*: Leverages the experience, expertise, and national and global connections of its members to provide the DHS secretary with real-time, real-world, sensing and independent advice to support decision making for homeland security operations

This office was created in 2007 and previously fell under the Directorate for Management. It has since been elevated in status and falls directly under the Office of the Secretary and Executive Management (OSEM). Its budget therefore is included in the $128 million requested in 2015 for OSEM.

Office of Health Affairs

The Office of Health Affairs (OHA) coordinates all DHS medical activities to ensure appropriate preparation for and response to incidents having medical significance. OHA serves as the principal medical adviser for the DHS secretary and FEMA administrator by providing timely incident-specific management guidance for the medical consequences of disasters. Additionally, OHA leads the department's biodefense and chemical defense activities; leads the department's food, agriculture, and veterinary defense; works with partner agencies to ensure medical readiness for catastrophic incidents; and supports the DHS mission through department-wide standards and best practices for the occupational health and safety of employees. During the 2014 Ebola epidemic, this office was integral to new screening policies at ports of entry that sought to limit the introduction of the virus by checking the health of those arriving from designated high-risk countries. This office was created in 2007 and is led by the chief medical officer who maintains the title of assistant secretary for health affairs and chief medical officer. The office is currently held by Acting Assistant Secretary Dr. Kathryn Brinsfield.

The OHA has two main divisions:

- *The Health Threats Resilience Division*: Strengthens the nation's ability to prepare for, recognize, and respond to the health impacts of diseases and other natural and intentional threats (including CBRN weapons). These activities are conducted through the efforts of five divisions, which include Detection; Food, Agriculture, and Veterinary Diseases; Health Incident Surveillance; Planning and Exercise Support; and State and Local Initiatives.
- *The Workforce Health and Medical Support Division*: Ensures coordination of medical first responders by providing operational medical support; enhances occupational health in the department by developing strategy, policy, requirements, and metrics for the medical aspects of an occupational health and safety program; and ensures medical quality assurance.

The FY 2015 budget request for this relatively new office, which maintained a full-time staff of 99 employees in FY 2014, is $126 million. Given the concerns related to the Ebola scare, and the congressional attention paid to ensuring Ebola and similar diseases can be stopped at the nation's borders, it is likely this budget will increase.

Offices of Intelligence and Analysis (I&A) and Operations Coordination and Planning (OPS)

The Office of Intelligence and Analysis (I&A), created in 2007 in response to the changes brought about by the PKEMRA, is responsible for using the information and intelligence gleaned from the myriad sources throughout the federal government to identify and assess current and future threats to the United States. I&A is also responsible for the department's intelligence and information-gathering and information-sharing capabilities for and among all components of DHS; state, local, and private sector partners; and the IC. I&A serves as the primary federal interface with state and local fusion centers, providing for reciprocal intelligence and information sharing in support of homeland security operations across all levels of government and the private sector. The undersecretary for intelligence and analysis (ASIS), currently Francis X. Taylor, leads this office and serves as the DHS chief intelligence officer (CINT). I&A ensures that information is gathered from all relevant DHS field operations and is fused with information from throughout the IC to produce intelligence reports (and other products) for officials who require them inside and outside of DHS.

The Office of Operations Coordination is responsible for monitoring US security on a daily basis and coordinating activities within DHS and with governors, homeland security advisors, law enforcement partners, and critical infrastructure operators in all 50 states and more than 50 major urban areas nationwide. Information is shared daily by the two halves of the office, referred to as the “Intelligence Side” and the “Law Enforcement Side.” Each half is identical and functions in tandem with the other but operates under different security clearance standards for information access purposes. The Intelligence Side focuses on pieces of highly classified intelligence and how the information contributes to the current threat picture for any given area. The Law Enforcement Side is dedicated to tracking the different enforcement activities across the country that may have terrorist significance. The two pieces fuse together to create a real-time picture of the nation's threat environment.

Operations Coordination oversees the National Operations Center (NOC), which collects and collates information from more than 35 federal, state, territorial, tribal, local, and private sector agencies.

Through the NOC, the office provides real-time situational awareness and monitoring of the nation, coordinates incidents and response activities, and, in conjunction with the I&A, issues advisories and bulletins concerning threats to homeland security, as well as specific protective measures. The NOC—which is always operational—coordinates information sharing to help deter, detect, and prevent terrorist acts and to manage domestic incidents. Information on domestic incident management is shared with emergency operations centers at all levels through the Homeland Security Information Network (HSIN). This office, also created in 2007 in response to the changes brought about by the PKEMRA, is led by Director for Operations Coordination Richard Chavez.

These two offices operate under a joined budget, termed Analysis and Operations, for which $302 million was requested in 2015. Together, these offices employed 845 people in FY 2014.

Domestic Nuclear Detection Office

The Domestic Nuclear Detection Office (DNDO) is tasked with enhancing the abilities of federal, state, territorial, tribal, and local governments and private sector agencies to be able to detect nuclear and radiological threats and to ensure that the response to such threats is coordinated. DNDO was established April 15, 2005, in response to an increase in the assessed likelihood that terrorists might try to import, possess, store, develop, or transport nuclear or radiological material for use in a terrorist attack. The objectives of the office are to

- develop the global nuclear detection and reporting architecture;
- develop, acquire, and support the domestic nuclear detection and reporting system;
- characterize detector system performance before deployment;
- facilitate situational awareness through information sharing and analysis.
- establish operational protocols to ensure detection leads to effective response;
- conduct a transformational research and development program;
- provide centralized planning, integration, and advancement of US government nuclear forensics programs (DHS, 2014d).

The DNDO is led by Director Huban Gowadia and employed 127 people in FY 2014. The DNDO budget fell from $317 million in FY 2006 to $285 million in FY 2014. The FY 2014 budget request for DNDO is $304 million.

Critical Thinking

Do you believe that it is possible to effectively lead a single federal department like the DHS, with over 240,000 employees, or does its existence combine too many unrelated functions under a single organizational mission? Explain your answer.

Agency Reorganization

Several reorganizations have been necessary during the first 14 years of the department's existence. On an ongoing basis, offices have been added or expanded and reduced or eliminated. Branches and departments have been moved under other existing offices or elevated in stature. And in a number of cases, multiple offices have been joined into a single function, while others have been split. Among all of these large and small changes, there are two specific instances for which the nature of the reorganizations that occurred is of such great scope that it is called out as a notable event. These include the reorganization that occurred as a result of Secretary (Michael) Chertoff's DHS reorganization plan and the changes that occurred following passage of the Post-Katrina Emergency Management Reform Act (PKEMRA). Each is described below.

Secretary Chertoff's DHS Reorganization Plan

On July 13, 2005, DHS Secretary Michael Chertoff released a six-point agenda that was used to guide the first of two major reorganizations that have occurred within DHS. This effort was aimed at streamlining what was considered to be an inefficient and cumbersome operation. The agenda followed an initial comprehensive review of department business that Chertoff initiated immediately upon assuming his office. The review closely examined the department in search of ways in which leadership could better manage risk in terms of threat, vulnerability, and consequence; prioritize policies and operational missions according to this risk-based approach; and establish a series of preventive and protective steps that would increase security. According to the six-point agenda, the changes that resulted from this study were meant to accomplish the following:

- Increasing overall national preparedness, particularly for catastrophic events
- Creating better transportation security systems that would more securely and effectively move people and cargo
- Strengthening border security, enforcement of immigration within the nation's borders, and the overall immigration process
- Enhancing information sharing (among partners)
- Improving financial management, human resource development, procurement, and information technology within the department
- Realigning the department's organization to maximize mission performance

Secretary Chertoff initiated several new policy initiatives that were tied to the department's overhaul, including the following:

- Instituting new border security approaches, accomplished by adding personnel, pursuing new technologies, investing in infrastructure, and conducting more comprehensive enforcement. These efforts were to be coupled with a drive to reduce the demand for illegal border migration by helping migrants to seek work through regulated legal channels.
- Restructuring the current immigration process with a focus on enhancing security while at the same time improving the interface between the agency and its "customers."
- Reaching out to the state homeland security officials in order to improve information exchange protocols, refine the (now defunct) Homeland Security Advisory System, and support state and regional data fusion centers.
- Investing in DHS personnel by providing professional career training and other development efforts.

One of the most significant changes that occurred as result of the six-point agenda was an organizational restructuring of the department. Chertoff asserted that these changes were made "to increase [the Department's] ability to prepare, prevent, and respond to terrorist attacks and other emergencies." Changes included the following:

- A new Directorate of Policy was created "to centralize and improve policy development and coordination." This directorate was led by an undersecretary and served as the primary department-wide coordinator for policies, regulations, and other initiatives. It was created to ensure the

consistency of policy and regulatory development across various parts of the department and to perform long-range strategic policy planning. This directorate, which later became the Office of Policy in 2007, included many of the same offices that exist today, which is indicative of what Chertoff saw as being absent from the organization. These include
- the Office of International Affairs,
- the Office of Private Sector Liaison,
- the Homeland Security Advisory Council,
- the Office of Immigration Statistics,
- the Senior Asylum Officer.

- The Office of Intelligence and Analysis, which still exists in the current structure of DHS as described previously, was created to "strengthen intelligence functions and information sharing."
- The Operations Coordination, and a corresponding position Director for Operations Coordination, was created. This office also remains in the current structure of DHS.
- The Information Analysis and Infrastructure Protection Directorate was renamed the Preparedness Directorate, which consolidated preparedness assets from across the department. The Preparedness Directorate was created to facilitate grants and oversee nationwide preparedness efforts specifically as they supported first-responder training, citizen awareness, public health, infrastructure security, and cybersecurity. Special emphasis was to be placed on what were considered high-risk targets. Many of this directorate's functions, several of which were removed from FEMA in accordance with Secretary Chertoff's reorganization plan, were later returned to that and other agencies and offices spread across the department in 2007 following the passage of PKEMRA (see section "The Post-Katrina Emergency Management Reform Act" later in this chapter).
- FEMA was removed from the Emergency Preparedness and Response Directorate that was created under the original DHS structure and was given a direct reporting responsibility to the secretary of homeland security. When this change occurred, it was felt that FEMA should be separated from its preparedness functions in order to focus on response and recovery. As such, when the agency was elevated in status, it lost its preparedness and risk reduction offices. Following Hurricane Katrina, it was determined that this was not an ideal approach and these functions were ultimately returned to FEMA as it exists in its current state.
- The Federal Air Marshal Service was moved from ICE to TSA, which is where it was originally housed prior to the creation of DHS in 2002 when it had been separated out.
- A new Office of Legislative and Intergovernmental Affairs was created, which merged the functions of the original Offices of Legislative Affairs and of State and Local Government Coordination. This was done to streamline intergovernmental relations and improve upon information sharing between DHS, Congress, and state and local officials. This office was later split into two distinct offices, both of which are located within the Office of the Secretary.
- The Office of Security, which develops, implements, and oversees the security policies, programs, and standards within DHS, was moved into the Directorate for Management "in order to better manage information systems, contractual activities, security accreditation, training and resources." This office, led by the chief security officer, remains there today.

Of the changes that were made in accordance with Secretary Chertoff's reorganization plan, there was one change that stood out above the rest as being particularly troubling—the disassembly of the Emergency Preparedness and Response (EP&R) Directorate. Although it made perfect sense that FEMA should exist as a stand-alone agency within the department—especially considering the fact that the functions of FEMA fully dominated this original directorate—it was somewhat inexplicable as to why FEMA would be stripped of its preparedness and mitigation functions. This action was clearly a complete reversal in the 30-year trend toward the comprehensive approach to emergency management's four functions: mitigation, preparedness, response, and recovery.

United Press International reported that critics both within FEMA and outside of DHS, especially from within the first-responder community, felt that the change was a sure sign that DHS was making a significant departure from the traditional "all-hazards" approach to emergency management that would consider terrorism to be but one of many hazards encompassing the community hazard profile. Following the poor response to Katrina, members of the Congress redressed this apparent mistake by reinstating all of the functions withdrawn from FEMA back under the direction of its administrator.

Critical Thinking

Do you believe that the problems attributed to FEMA in the response to Hurricane Katrina would have happened regardless of Secretary Chertoff's reorganization plan or that it was something about this structure that caused the inefficiencies and shortfalls that were observed? Or were the problems entirely unrelated to the DHS structure? Explain your answer.

The Post-Katrina Emergency Management Reform Act

Hurricane Katrina, which struck on August 29, 2005, and resulted in the death of over 1800 people (and the destruction of billions of dollars in housing stock and other infrastructure), exposed significant problems with the US emergency management framework. Clearly, the terrorism focus had been maintained at the expense of preparedness and response capacity for other hazards, namely, the natural disasters that have proven to be much more likely to occur. FEMA, and likewise DHS, was highly criticized by the public and by the Congress in the months following the 2005 hurricane season. In response, the Congress passed the Post-Katrina Emergency Management Reform Act (PKEMRA) (H.R. 5441, Public Law 109-295), signed into law by the president on October 4, 2006.

This law established several new leadership positions within DHS, moved additional functions into (several were simply returned to) the FEMA, created and reallocated functions to other components within DHS, and amended the Homeland Security Act in ways that directly and indirectly affected the organization and functions of various entities within DHS. The changes were required to have gone into effect by March 31, 2007. Transfers into FEMA that were mandated by PKEMRA included (with the exception of certain offices as listed in the act):

- the US Fire Administration (USFA),
- Office of Grants and Training (OGT),
- Chemical Stockpile Emergency Preparedness Division (CSEP),
- Radiological Emergency Preparedness Program (REPP),
- Office of National Capital Region Coordination (NCRC).

The law determined that the head of FEMA, at the time R. David Paulison, would take on the new title of administrator. This official would be supported by two deputy administrators. One was the deputy administrator and chief operating officer, who served as the principal deputy and maintained overall operational responsibilities at FEMA. The other was the deputy administrator for National Preparedness, a new division that was created within FEMA and which today exists as Protection and National Preparedness (whose director is the sole deputy administrator under the current FEMA structure). The new National Preparedness Division incorporated several existing FEMA programs and several programs that had been moved into the former Preparedness Directorate. This division focused on emergency preparedness policy, contingency planning, exercise coordination and evaluation, emergency management training, and hazard mitigation (with respect to the CSEP and REPP programs). The National Preparedness Division oversaw two new divisions: Readiness, Prevention and Planning (RPP) and the National Integration Center (NIC)—both of which have since been moved elsewhere within FEMA.

The existing Office of Grants and Training (OGT) was moved into the newly expanded FEMA and was renamed the "Office of Grant Programs." The training and systems support divisions of the OGT were transferred into the NIC. The Office of the Citizen Corps was transferred into the FEMA Office of Readiness, Prevention and Planning.

Additional headquarters positions created at FEMA by the new law included a disability coordinator (located in the FEMA Office of Disability Integration and Coordination), a small state and rural advocate, a law enforcement advisor to the administrator, and a national advisory council.

This act specifically excluded certain elements of the former DHS Preparedness Directorate from its transfer into FEMA. The Preparedness Directorate was renamed the National Protection and Programs Directorate (NPPD), and it remained under the direction of a DHS undersecretary (currently Suzanne Spaulding).

And finally, the law created the OHA, which is described in detail in the preceding section.

DHS Budget

Table 4-1 details the FY 2015 DHS budget proposed by department function or component.

Other Agencies Participating in Community-Level Funding

As mentioned in the Introduction, the DHS may be the most recognized embodiment of federal homeland security action and has the most central role in its implementation, but it is not alone in the federal government by any means in this mission. Several other federal agencies outside of the new department have both maintained existing programs and created entirely new programs, each addressing some aspect of homeland security. Many of these also fund or support homeland security efforts at the state and local levels as well. While many of these programs are well established and have been performing these functions since before the creation of DHS, several remain in either a transitional or developmental phase.

The White House (the Executive Office of the President)

The president of the United States and the White House (i.e., the Executive Office of the President) play an important homeland security role because they are the primary drivers of federal policy and because the president is the nation's commander in chief. Through the National Security Council and the Domestic Policy Council, the Executive Office of the President provides overall direction and coordination on many issues that are central to the homeland security mission and goals. As a result of Presidential Study Directive 1 (2009), which directed an examination of ways to reform the White House organization for counterterrorism and homeland security, the White House merged the staffs of the National Security Council and the Homeland Security Council into a single new integrated National Security Staff (NSS). The new NSS supports all White House policymaking activities related to international, transnational, and homeland

Table 4-1 FY 2015 Proposed DHS Budget ($ in Thousands)

Budget Item	FY 2013	FY 2014	FY 2015 Proposed	Year Over Year Change	Year Over Year (%)
Departmental Operations	708,695	728,269	748,024	19,755	2.7
Analysis and Operations (A&O)	301,853	300,490	302,268	1778	0.6
Office of the Inspector General (OIG)	137,910	139,437	145,457	6020	4.3
US Customs and Border Protection (CBP)	11,736,990	12,445,616	12,764,835	319,219	2.6
US Immigration and Customs Enforcement (ICE)	5,627,660	5,614,361	5,359,065	(255,296)	−4.5
Transportation Security Administration (TSA)	7,193,757	7,364,510	7,305,098	(59,412)	−0.8
US Coast Guard (USCG)	9,972,425	10,214,999	9,796,995	(418,004)	−4.1
US Secret Service (USSS)	1,808,313	1,840,272	1,895,905	55,633	3.0
National Protection and Programs Directorate (NPPD)	2,638,634	2,813,213	2,857,666	44,453	1.6
Office of Health Affairs (OHA)	126,324	126,763	125,767	(996)	−0.8
Federal Emergency Management Agency (FEMA)	11,865,196	11,553,899	12,496,517	942,618	8.2
FEMA: Grant Programs	2,373,540	2,530,000	2,225,469	(304,531)	−12.0
US Citizenship and Immigration Services (USCIS)	3,378,348	3,219,142	3,259,885	40,743	1.3
Federal Law Enforcement Training Center (FLETC)	243,111	258,730	259,595	865	0.3
Science and Technology Directorate (S&T)	794,227	1,220,212	1,071,818	(148,394)	−12.2
Domestic Nuclear Detection Office (DNDO)	302,981	285,255	304,423	19,168	6.7
Total budget authority:	59,209,964	60,655,168	60,918,787	263,619	0.4
Mandatory, fee, and trust funds	(11,308,307)	(11,526,210)	(11,890,496)	(364,286)	3.2
Gross discretionary budget authority	47,901,657	49,128,958	49,028,291	(100,667)	−0.2
Discretionary offsetting fees	(3,553,282)	(3,733,428)	(4,414,798)	(681,370)	18.3
Net discount budget authority	44,348,375	45,395,530	44,613,493	(782,037)	−0.2
Less FEMA Disaster Relief Fund	(6,075,554)	(5,626,386)	(6,437,793)	(811,407)	14.4
Less rescission of prior-year carryover—regular appropriations	(151,463)	(543,968)	-	543,968	−100
Adjusted net discount budget authority	38,121,358	39,225,176	38,175,700	(1,049,476)	−2.7
Supplemental	11,483,313				

security matters. The NSS was established under the direction of the National Security Advisor. The NSS is maintained as the principal venue for interagency deliberations on national security issues including terrorism, WMDs, and natural disasters, among others. Within the NSS, a number of new directorates and positions were created to deal with new and emerging threats including cybersecurity, WMD terrorism, transborder security, information sharing, and resilience.

Immigration policy is guided by the Domestic Policy Council. Topics relevant to immigration policy managed by this group of leaders include border security, immigration enforcement, the earning of citizenship, streamlining the immigration process, and impacts of immigration on the economy. Immigration reform, which will have a significant impact on DHS operations, remains high on the policy agenda for years to come.

US Department of Agriculture

Considering the varied and wide-reaching impacts that both terrorism and other natural disasters (such as plant and animal diseases) could have on both the US food supply and the US economy, agriculture has assumed a very important role in the overall homeland security approach of the United States. Shortly after September 11, the US Department of Agriculture (USDA) formed a Homeland Security Council (within USDA) to develop a department-wide plan and coordinate efforts among all USDA agencies and offices. Their efforts focused on three key areas of concern:

- Ensuring the safety and security of the food supply and agricultural production
- Protection of USDA facilities
- Emergency preparedness for USDA staff

The USDA contributes to an ongoing DHS effort of protecting the nation's food supply by keeping foreign agricultural pests and diseases from entering the country. In this vein, there has been a drastic increase in the number of veterinarians and food import surveillance officers that have been posted at borders and ports of entry. Although approximately 2600 members of the USDA border inspection force were transferred to DHS as stipulated in the Homeland Security Act of 2002, the USDA has continued to train inspectors and set policy for plants, animals, and commodities entering the United States.

In March 2004, the former DHS Bureau of Customs and Border Protection's Border Patrol (BP) announced the 2004 Arizona Border Control Initiative. This initiative was aimed at securing the border with Mexico. The initiative required increased cooperation between the DHS and the USDA Forest Service in allowing more access to public lands on the border. Forest Service resource managers continue to help DHS enhance border security in such a way as to avoid disturbing the environment, and Forest Service law enforcement personnel have assisted DHS in deterring illegal activities on National Forest System lands.

In 2010, the USDA Office of Homeland Security and Emergency Coordination (OHSEC) was established within USDA Departmental Management (DM) to handle all security and emergency response activities. This office coordinates all such activities throughout the department, which has a wide variety of agencies and offices where security and safety are relevant to their work. OHSEC maintains six divisions, which include the following:

- *Continuity and Planning Division (CPD)*: Coordinates USDA planning and preparedness activities, including continuity of operations planning, developing response plans and procedures, and advising leadership on a range of homeland security issues
- *Emergency Programs Division (EPD)*: Manages the USDA Emergency Operations Center when it is mobilized and leads the USDA response according to the USDA mission and their role in the National Response Framework or in line with USDA disaster declarations
- *Personnel and Documents Safety Division (PDSD)*: Protects information related to US agriculture that, if released, could threaten national security and manages programs that determine the suitability of employment for certain jobs that require a security clearance
- *Physical Security Division*: Provides protection for employees, facilities, and assets that fall under USDA control and exist outside the Washington, DC area
- *Radiation Safety Division (RSD)*: Oversees policies related to the use and protection of radioactive materials by USDA employees and in USDA facilities and issues permits related to its use
- *Executive Protection Operations Division (EPO)*: Provides protection for the secretary of agriculture whenever necessary

Protecting the Health and Safety of Farm Animals, Crops, and Natural Resources

The USDA created a National Surveillance Unit within its Animal and Plant Health Inspection Service's (APHIS) Veterinary Services program in 2003. The unit provides a focal point for the collection, processing, and delivery of surveillance information used to make risk analyses and to take further action when needed. The unit designs surveillance strategies and coordinates and integrates surveillance activities in order to protect the health of and enhance the marketability of livestock and poultry. NSU oversees the National Animal Health Surveillance System (NAHSS), which integrates the information coming in from and going out to the various animal health monitoring programs throughout the country, and the National Animal Health Reporting System (NAHRS), which provides information on diseases and outbreaks.

The USDA appointed a National Surveillance System Coordinator whose purpose is to more efficiently lead the agency's animal health surveillance efforts. The USDA also works with universities and state veterinary diagnostic laboratories to create plant and animal health laboratory networks that help to increase the nation's capability to respond in an emergency. The USDA developed guidance documents to help remind farmers and ranchers of steps that they can take to secure their operations.

The USDA Food Safety and Inspection Service (FSIS) is responsible for ensuring that the commercial supply of meat, poultry, and egg products in the United States is safe. This office works to prevent, prepare for, respond to, and recover from nonroutine emergencies resulting from intentional and unintentional contamination affecting these products. FSIS assesses vulnerabilities to the US food supply, monitors the food supply to detect intentional contamination, works with other government agencies to conduct a response to a contamination emergency, and helps to facilitate recovery from contamination events.

The USDA has provided tens of millions of dollars to states, universities, and tribal lands to increase homeland security prevention, detection, and response efforts. The USDA has also continued to perform research on rapid identification tests for biological agents considered to pose the most serious threats to our agricultural system, including foot and mouth disease, rinderpest, and soybean and wheat rust.

Ensuring a Safe Food Supply

The USDA has enhanced security at all food safety laboratories around the country and expanded its abilities to test for "nontraditional" biological, chemical, and radiological agents. The FSIS Food Defense and Emergency Response division serves as the lead coordinating body in the development of the infrastructure and capacity to prevent, prepare for, and respond to terrorism aimed at the US food supply. The USDA also drafted and distributed guidance for field and laboratory personnel about what to do when National Terrorism Advisory System alerts are issued.

New import surveillance liaison inspectors have been hired by the department, who are stationed around the United States to enhance surveillance of imported products. The USDA has conducted training for employees, veterinarians, and inspectors on threat prevention and preparedness activities according to a food security plan developed by the department following 9/11. USDA food safety labs have maintained a lead role in creating a network to integrate the US laboratory infrastructure and surge capacity at the local, state, and federal levels.

Protecting Research and Laboratory Facilities

The USDA has provided millions of dollars in grants aimed at security assessments, background investigations, physical security upgrades, and additional security personnel at research and laboratory facilities. Security countermeasures have been implemented based on the findings of these assessments. Furthermore, all USDA laboratories where dangerous agents and toxins are used are held to the requirements of the Agricultural Bioterrorism Protection Act of 2002.

Emergency Preparedness and Response

The USDA serves as the coordinator and primary agency for two Emergency Support Functions: ESF #4 (Firefighting) and ESF #11 (Agriculture and Natural Resources). The USDA, together with the Department of the Interior (DOI), also operates the National Interagency Fire Center. The USDA firefighting resources are maintained within the US Forest Service. The Forest Service responds to tens of thousands of forest fires that burn on public land each year. To do this, the Forest Service hires approximately 8400 temporary wildland firefighters on a seasonal basis. In the aftermath of major fires, the Forest Service Burned Area Emergency Response (BAER) program addresses the environmental impacts to ensure that no lasting hazards remain.

To address responses to the food supply, FSIS has developed a department-specific incident management system called the FIMS Incident Management System (FIMS), which is a web-based platform that ensures a common operating picture is available throughout the department. FSIS has also developed a number of agriculture-specific emergency response plans that are updated on an annual basis.

The construction of an APHIS Emergency Operations Center (AEOC), which is used to coordinate and support emergency response within APHIS, has been completed. The AEOC, which enhances APHIS's ability to provide leadership during national emergencies, has already been utilized on several occasions, including the exotic Newcastle disease outbreak, the monkey pox outbreak, and the confirmations of bovine spongiform encephalopathy (BSE) in both Canada and the United States.

Protecting Other Infrastructure

The USDA Forest Service's law enforcement officers continue to conduct security assessments of research facilities and air tanker bases nationwide. The USDA's Forest Service continues to enhance efforts to protect National Forest System lands and facilities, including dams, reservoirs, pipelines, water treatment plants, power lines, and energy production facilities on government property.

Department of Commerce

The Department of Commerce promotes homeland security through actions conducted in three of its many offices and agencies. These include

- Bureau of Industry and Security,
- National Institute for Standards and Technology,
- National Oceanographic and Atmospheric Administration.

Bureau of Industry and Security

The mission of the Bureau of Industry and Security (BIS) is to advance US national security, foreign policy, and economic interests. BIS's activities include regulating the export of sensitive goods and technologies and enforcing export control and public safety laws, cooperating with and assisting foreign countries on export control, helping the US industry to comply with international arms control agreements, and monitoring the US defense industrial base to ensure that it is capable of handling national and homeland security needs. This agency gained more notoriety after September 11, when concerns about certain technologies and arms that could be used by terrorists abroad were raised. The bureau has enjoyed an increase in funding as a result of these changes.

National Institute for Standards and Technology

The National Institute for Standards and Technology (NIST) has provided significant contributions to the homeland security of the nation by assisting in the measurement infrastructure used to establish safety and security standards. NIST labs have enjoyed an increase in funding levels since September 11 and have developed technologies that are used for such actions as establishing standards for and measuring the safety and security of buildings, for the development of biometric identification systems, and for various radiation detection systems utilized at US and foreign ports, among many others. NIST laboratories involved, at least partially, in homeland security include the following:

- Building and Fire Research Laboratory
- Chemical Science and Technology Laboratory
- Materials Science and Engineering Laboratory
- Physics Laboratory
- Technology Services

NIST also investigates disaster and failure studies of buildings and other man-made structures. This program helps architects and builders to better understand what besides gravity will destroy a building, such as wind forces, the force of a blast or explosion, seismic forces, or fire. It also investigates how poor design, errors in design, inadequate or improper materials, or other problems might lead to spontaneous collapse or vulnerability to the aforementioned hazards. And finally, NIST looks at how evacuation and emergency response might take place given the building's design and the associated infrastructure. Most of these activities occur outside of disaster scenarios for the purpose of future disaster risk reduction, though it is not uncommon in the aftermath of a disaster for NIST to investigate why a building might have failed. The purpose of all of this work is to establish and improve upon construction codes, which serve to reduce disaster risk. NIST lists the following examples of events that led to code changes:

- Following the 9/11 attacks on the World Trade Center, a total of 40 code changes were made as a result of NIST recommendations.
- The 2003 Station nightclub fire in Rhode Island led to standards adjustments for sprinklers, restricted festival seating, crowd management, and egress inspection record-keeping requirements for new and existing facilities.
- The 1997 Jarrell, TX, tornado led to the adoption of the enhanced Fujita (EF) Tornado Intensity Scale by the NOAA National Weather Service.
- The 1994 Northridge earthquake led to adoption of design guidelines for seismic rehabilitation of existing welded steel frame buildings by the American Institute of Steel Construction.
- Hurricane Andrew in 1992 led to the adoption of upgraded wind load provisions in HUD's Manufactured Home Construction and Safety Standards.
- The 1986 Dupont Plaza Hotel fire in San Juan PR led to the passage of the Hotel-Motel Sprinkler Act.
- The 1982 collapse of the L' Ambiance Plaza in Hartford CT led to improvements in OSHA's safety and inspection requirements for lift slab construction (NIST, 2014).

The Department of Commerce is also involved in disaster response and recovery as a coordinating agency for a number of Emergency Support Functions. These include the following:

- ESF#1: Transportation
- ESF#2: Communications
- ESF#3: Public Works and Engineering
- ESF#4: Firefighting
- ESF#5: Information and Planning

- ESF#7: Logistics
- ESF#8: Public Health and Medical Services
- ESF#9: Search and Rescue
- ESF#10: Oil and Hazardous Materials
- ESF#11: Agriculture and Natural Resources
- ESF#12: Energy
- ESF#15: External Affairs

National Oceanographic and Atmospheric Administration

The National Oceanographic and Atmospheric Administration (NOAA) has been involved in disaster management since long before the creation of DHS. NOAA monitors meteorologic conditions, makes forecasts about storm risks, and recommends preparedness measures to FEMA and other federal, state, and local government agencies. The NOAA National Weather Service (NWS), under which the All-Hazards Radio Warning Network is managed, is another vital component to the overall homeland security needs of the nation. Although not focused on terrorism, the weather radio system is capable of being activated in the event of any type of disaster, regardless of its origin, to provide timely warning to people who may be in danger.

Department of Education

The Department of Education is responsible for, among other things, taking a leadership position in establishing standards and technical assistance for school safety. Schools not only are vulnerable to the effects of natural and technological disasters but also have been identified by many terrorism experts to be a primary target for terrorist activities due to the emotional factor involved with the injury or death of children. Both before and since September 11, there have been many terrorist or other attacks in schools throughout the world, including in Beslan, Russia, and in Cambodia—both of which resulted in fatalities—and elsewhere. Attacks on schools, exemplified by those in 1999 in Littleton, Colorado, and in 2012 in Newtown, Connecticut (among many others), provide further justification of the required homeland security role that is assumed by the Department of Education.

The office of Safe and Drug-Free Schools was created in September 2002 to manage all Department of Education activities related to safe schools, crisis response, alcohol and drug prevention, and health and well-being of students. Until recently, this office was responsible for leading the homeland security efforts of the department, and millions of dollars in funding had been made available to schools on an annual basis to help them to better address emergency planning issues.

In 2012, the Congress eliminated funding for most of this program's initiatives. Today, the program is called the Office of Safe and Healthy Students (OSHS), and it performs many of the same roles as its predecessor office. OSHS is divided into three sections, which include the following:

- Safe and Supportive Schools Group (S3), which administers programs that help to ensure that schools are drug- and violence-free.
- Healthy Students Group, which promotes violence and alcohol abuse and addresses problems related to students' health.
- Center for School Preparedness, which maintains a number of programs focused on increasing the capacity of schools to respond to and recover from disasters effectively. This is also the program that manages all homeland security issues for the Department of Education and coordinates the department's response under the National Response Framework.

The Department of Education administers a number of grant programs that support homeland security, including Emergency Management for Higher Education, Readiness and Emergency Management for Schools, Emergency Planning Grants, the Safe Schools-Healthy Students Initiative, and the Safe and Drug-Free Schools and Communities State Grants program.

Emergency planning guidance and technical assistance are major concerns of the Department of Education, and this area of expertise is also handled through the Office of Safe and Healthy Students. Through the maintenance of a website (http://1.usa.gov/1F2hf8p), the Department of Education has created a "one-stop shop" for schools to locate information to plan for all types of disasters, whether they are natural, terrorist, or others.

The Environmental Protection Agency

The Environmental Protection Agency's (EPA) charge to protect human health and the environment links it closely to the homeland security mission. Since long before DHS existed, the EPA has played a very important role in facilitating emergency management and ensuring the nation's security, most notably with regard to the water sector. The EPA was one of the signatory agencies of the original Federal Response Plan (FRP), and today, it plays a major role in the National Response Framework (NRF).

The agency is primarily concerned with emergencies that involve the release, or threatened release, of oil, radioactive materials, or hazardous chemicals that have the potential to affect communities and the surrounding environment. These releases may be accidental, deliberate, or the result of a natural disaster. In fulfilling this mission to prevent, prepare for, and respond to spills and other environmental emergencies, the EPA works with a variety of private and public partners. The agency's website provides information that these entities can use to reduce the likelihood of spills and releases and to better respond to them when they occur.

The EPA is also responsible for the nation's efforts to prepare for and respond to terrorist threats that involve the release of chemical, biological, or nuclear/radiological materials into the air or water. Because of its inherent role in protecting human health and the environment from possible harmful effects of these hazardous materials, the EPA is actively involved in counterterrorism planning and response efforts. The agency supports such programs through the following four actions:

1. Helping state and local responders to plan for emergencies
2. Coordinating with key federal partners
3. Training first responders
4. Providing resources in the event of a terrorist incident

EPA and the National Response Framework

The EPA becomes involved in the response to Presidentially Declared Disasters under the National Response Framework whenever there are hazardous materials releases or oil spills associated with the event. The EPA may respond under the authority of the National Contingency Plan (NCP) or the National Response Framework (NRF). In such instances, the EPA is the coordinating agency for ESF#10 (Oil and Hazardous Materials). It is also the supporting agency for a number of other ESFs, including the following:

- ESF#3: Public Works and Engineering
- ESF#4: Firefighting
- ESF#5: Emergency Management

- ESF#8: Public Health and Medical Services
- ESF#11: Agriculture and Natural Resources
- ESF#13: Public Safety and Security
- ESF#15: External Affairs

In the event that a hazardous materials spill or release occurs, it cannot be assumed that the federal government will automatically respond. In fact, there exists a hierarchy of responsibility for response that differs somewhat from other typical hazards. This order progresses as follows:

1. The company responsible for the release first assumes responsibility.
2. The company responsible may invoke an existing or initiate a new contract with response contractors to handle the cleanup.
3. The local fire and police departments may be called or deployed to assist if the company is not able to handle the response themselves, even with contract crews.
4. The local emergency response system may need to be activated in order to bring other government and contract resources into play.
5. State resources may be called in if the local government is not able to address the response requirements.
6. The federal government may be called in to assist if the state is not able to handle the response.

Oftentimes, governmental emergency response agencies resist getting involved because the costs of response may be excessive and may not be reimbursed by the company. The EPA Local Governments Reimbursement Program provides local governments up to $25,000 per incident for their efforts in such cases. And when the quantity of hazardous materials that were released exceeds the established reporting triggers established by the National Response Center (NRC), the NRC notifies a predesignated EPA or USCG On-Scene Coordinator (OSC) (as determined by the accident or spill location). The OSC assesses the situation and determines whether or not federal involvement is needed. Regardless of what is decided, it becomes the job of the OSC to ensure the cleanup is appropriate, efficient, and effective regardless of who is ultimately responsible for performing the required actions. However, the OSC is authorized to assume response command if any of the following situations occur:

- The responsible party is unknown or uncooperative.
- The event is beyond the capacity of the company, local, or state responders to manage.
- The incident is an oil spill, and the size and character of the incident appears to present a substantial threat to public health or welfare.

Within the EPA, there are two offices in particular that are involved in homeland security efforts. They include

- the Office of Solid Waste and Emergency Response (OSWER),
- the Office of Air and Radiation (OAR).

The Office of Solid Waste and Emergency Response

The Office of Solid Waste and Emergency Response (OSWER) has an expansive list of responsibilities related to the accidental, intentional, and disaster-related release of hazardous chemicals and waste. It oversees the following suboffices.

Office of Emergency Management

The EPA Office of Emergency Management (OEM) works with other federal government emergency management partners. Its purpose is to reduce the risk of accidents resulting in the release of hazardous materials, as well as to maintain the agency's emergency and disaster response capabilities. OEM generates and distributes information about these response capabilities, as well as regulations, tools, and research that will help the community of government entities, businesses, and private citizens whose actions are EPA-regulated to prevent, prepare for, and respond to emergencies. OEM also administers the Oil Pollution Act and several other environmental statutes that relate to the prevention of and response to environmental emergencies involving this resource.

In 1985, 1 year after the Bhopal, India, chemical accident that killed thousands of people, the EPA established the Chemical Emergency Preparedness and Prevention Office (CEPPO). Through this office, the EPA assumed a leading role within the federal government in building programs to respond to and prevent chemical accidents. CEPPO worked with numerous federal, state, local, and tribal governments; industry groups; environmental groups; labor organizations; and community groups to help them better understand the risks posed by chemicals in their communities, to manage and reduce those risks, and to deal with emergencies.

CEPPO also worked with its state and local partners to develop new approaches to deal with emergency preparedness and accident prevention. They assisted local emergency planning committees (LEPCs) and state emergency response commissions (SERCs) by providing leadership, issuing regulations, developing technical guidance, and enabling these committees to develop their own unique emergency planning systems appropriate to their individual needs.

Today, the roles of CEPPO fall within the new Office of Emergency Management. This office addresses a number of areas related to the prevention of and preparedness for hazard events and the response and recovery actions required when events actually occur. These programs include the following:

- *The Chemical, Biological, Radiological, and Nuclear Consequence Management Advisory Division (CMAD)*: CMAD provides technical assistance during the response to actual incidents. This group assists responding agencies or offices by providing a number of scientific support tools like sampling and screening, monitoring, and decontamination. It has a mobile laboratory called the Portable High Throughput Integrated Laboratory Identification System (PHILIS) that brings on-site capabilities to incidents. CMAD also maintains a 16-person technical team whose members are located in six key geographic areas that can deploy to major incidents on short notice.
- *The Environmental Response Laboratory Network (ERLN)*: The ERLN was established to assist in addressing chemical, biological, and radiological threats during major disaster events. The ERLN is a national network of laboratories that can be ramped up as needed to support large-scale environmental responses by providing analytic capabilities, response capacity, and systematic, coordinated data as needed. The ERLN integrates capabilities of existing public sector laboratories with accredited private sector labs to support environmental responses. The ERLN's mission is to provide consistent analytic capabilities, capacities, and quality data to federal, state, and local decision makers.
- *The Emergency Planning and Community Right-To-Know Act (EPCRA) Requirements*: The EPCRA requirements help communities prepare for and respond to chemical accidents by requiring facilities to report chemical storage and release information and communities to develop emergency response plans. EPCRA stipulates that every community in the United States must be part of a comprehensive emergency response plan. SERCs oversee the implementation

of EPCRA requirements in each state. LEPCs work to understand chemical hazards in the community, develop emergency plans in case of an accidental release, and look for ways to prevent chemical accidents. LEPCs are made up of emergency management agencies, responders, industry, and the public.

- *Emergency Response and Cleanup Actions*: Each year, more than 20,000 emergencies involving the release (or threatened release) of oil and hazardous substances are reported in the United States, potentially affecting both communities and the surrounding natural environment. Emergencies range from small-scale spills to large events requiring prompt action and evacuation of nearby populations. The EPA coordinates and implements a wide range of activities to ensure that adequate and timely response measures are taken in communities affected by hazardous substances and oil releases where state and local first-responder capabilities have been exceeded or where additional support is needed. The EPA's emergency response program responds to chemical, oil, biological, and radiological releases and large-scale national emergencies, including homeland security incidents. EPA conducts time-critical and non-time-critical removal actions when necessary to protect human health and the environment by either funding response actions directly or overseeing or enforcing actions conducted by potentially responsible parties.
- *Facility Response Plan (FRP) Rule*: A Facility Response Plan (FRP) demonstrates a facility's preparedness to respond to a worst-case oil discharge. Under the Clean Water Act, as amended by the Oil Pollution Act, certain facilities that store and use oil are required to prepare and submit these plans. As part of the Oil Pollution Prevention regulation, the FRP rule addresses
  - who must prepare and submit an FRP,
  - what must be included in an FRP,
  - potential to cause "substantial harm" in the event of a discharge.
- *Local Governments Reimbursement (LGR) Program*: In the event of a release (or threatened release) of hazardous substances, the EPA may reimburse local governments for expenses related to the release and associated emergency response measures. The LGR Program provides a safety net of up to $25,000 per incident to local governments that do not have funds available to pay for response actions.
- *National Contingency Plan (NCP) Subpart J*: Subpart J provides for a schedule of dispersants, other chemicals, and other spill-mitigating devices and substances that may be authorized for use on oil discharges.
- *Risk Management Plans (RMPs)*: RMPs require certain facilities to tell the public and the EPA what they are doing to prevent accidents and how they plan to operate safely and manage their chemicals in a responsible way. Under the authority of section 112(r) of the Clean Air Act, the chemical accident prevention provisions require facilities that produce, handle, process, distribute, or store certain chemicals to develop a Risk Management Program, prepare an RMP, and submit the RMP to EPA. Covered facilities were initially required to comply with the rule in 1999, and the rule has been amended on several occasions since then, most recently in 2004.
- *Spill Prevention, Control, and Countermeasure (SPCC) Rule*: The SPCC Rule includes requirements for oil spill prevention, preparedness, and response to prevent oil discharges to navigable waters and adjoining shorelines. The rule requires specific facilities to prepare, amend, and implement SPCC plans. The SPCC rule is part of the Oil Pollution Prevention regulation, which also includes the FRP rule.

Office of Superfund Remediation and Technology Innovation

The Office of Superfund Remediation Technology Innovation (OSRTI), called the Office of Emergency and Remedial Response (OERR) until 2003, manages the Superfund program. The Superfund program was created to protect citizens from the dangers posed by abandoned or uncontrolled hazardous waste sites. The Congress established Superfund in 1980 by passing the Comprehensive Environmental Response, Compensation, and Liability Act (CERCLA). CERCLA gives the federal government the authority to respond to hazardous substance emergencies and to develop long-term solutions for the nation's most serious hazardous waste problems.

Office of Air and Radiation

The Office of Air and Radiation (OAR) develops national programs, technical policies, and regulations for controlling air pollution and radiation exposure. OAR is concerned with energy conservation and pollution prevention, indoor and outdoor air quality, industrial air pollution, pollution from vehicles and engines, radon, acid rain, stratospheric ozone depletion, and radiation protection. With regard to homeland security, this office is responsible for emergency response to radiation disasters, helping to design and implement air protection measures, monitoring ambient air, and maintaining a national air monitoring system.

The Department of Justice

The Department of Justice has led responsibility for criminal investigations of terrorist acts or terrorist threats by individuals or groups inside the United States or directed at US citizens or institutions abroad, as well as for related intelligence collection activities within the United States. This makes them a key homeland security player in that their agents and operatives help to prevent terrorist attacks and then capture those responsible for carrying out attacks that succeed.

Following a terrorist threat or an actual incident that falls within the criminal jurisdiction of the United States, the attorney general identifies the perpetrators and makes every effort through the various DOJ agencies to bring those perpetrators to justice. DOJ also works with INTERPOL, the international police organization that is represented by over 190 countries including the United States, to locate perpetrators of attacks that are residing outside of the United States and supports immigration by assisting in investigations.

- *Federal Bureau of Investigation (FBI)*: The FBI has a broad homeland security mandate. FBI agents investigate and arrest individuals and organizations involved in terrorism, counterintelligence, and cyber crime, in addition to other criminal acts. The FBI is a self-described "Intelligence-driven and threat-focused national security organization with both intelligence and law enforcement responsibilities" (FBI, 2014). Their focus is on national threats that are either out of the local and state jurisdiction or too large or complex for these agencies to handle on their own. The FBI currently has 13,598 special agents and 21,746 support staff. They are located throughout the United States and at various locations worldwide. In 2014, the FBI budget was $8.3 billion, which reflects the relative importance of the FBI mission.
- *Drug Enforcement Administration (DEA)*: The DEA is responsible for enforcing laws that pertain to controlled substances, including illegal drugs. Terrorist organizations have found significant funding through the manufacture and sale of narcotics, and as such, the DEA mission intersects with the homeland security mission. Additionally, gangs involved in the manufacture and distribution of narcotics have been known to perform acts classified as terrorism in their bid to gain territory or intimidate citizens.

- *Bureau of Alcohol, Tobacco, Firearms and Explosives (ATF)*: This office contributes to homeland security by regulating the firearms and explosives industries and investigating crimes related to the use of both. Because these are the weapons of choice in most terrorist attacks, ATF plays a key role in the prevention of terrorist attacks.
- *Executive Office for Immigration Review (EOIR)*: The immigration function of government sat in the Department of Justice Immigration and Naturalization Service (INS) prior to its transfer to DHS. Today, DOJ adjudicates cases involving immigration law.

The Department of State

The Department of State has the responsibility to coordinate activities with foreign governments and international organizations related to the prevention, preparation, response, and recovery from domestic disasters and for the protection of US citizens and US interests overseas. The Department of State political officers located at the various embassies and consulates, found throughout all countries of the world maintaining diplomatic relations with the United States, monitor emerging and known threats through establishment of local contacts and monitoring of events. The Department of State also provides direction to the Office of the President on areas where diplomatic pressure may be utilized to control emerging and known threats to domestic security (see sidebar "Diplomatic Pressure"). Foreign Service Officers posted in almost every country, and often in multiple cities within each country, work with local counterparts to address common problems including those related to national security. The Department of State also has an important counterterrorism role through its adjudication of visa applications, which helps to prevent easy access to the nation for possible terrorists (as identified through the various intelligence efforts).

Diplomatic Pressure

Through the US Department of State, the US government works to develop allies in the fight against terrorism around the world. As a major world power, and the leading provider of international development assistance, the United States is able to influence the actions of other nations through the application of diplomatic pressure when the White House feels that such actions are necessary to maintain national security. An example of this pressure occurred in the summer of 2011 when the US government threatened to significantly reduce the amount of military aid it provided to Pakistan, a major ally in the fight against terrorism. Several consecutive events initiated this action, the most significant of which happened in the spring of 2011 when the US military, working in conjunction with the Central Intelligence Agency, located and killed al-Qaeda leader Osama bin Laden. When it was discovered that bin Laden had been living unnoticed in the shadow of a significant military facility in Abbottabad, Pakistan, many US lawmakers felt that Pakistan was not doing enough to battle terrorist extremists. After the military operation took place, Pakistan retaliated against what it called a "violation of its sovereignty" by refusing entry of various military support personnel and by releasing the names of key CIA officials operating in the country. These events marked a significant change in the working relationship that existed between the two countries and were a sign that Pakistan may not be taking a hard enough line against terrorism to achieve the outcomes that the US government would like to see (with regard to a reduction in national security risks). In response, Pakistan was threatened with a reduction of approximately $800 billion in the ongoing military assistance the United States had been providing to Pakistan for years. The move was clearly a message to the South Asian country that their actions were moving away from what was felt by the White House to be in the best interests of the national security of the United States (Associated Press, 2011).

For more information, see The Guardian (2011); http://bit.ly/1zhoV6h.

The Department of Defense

The Department of Defense (DOD) ensures the security of the United States both by acting as a military deterrent to nations and groups who might otherwise wish to attack American soil and by pursuing and eliminating threats around the world. DOD military services, defense agencies, and geographic and functional commands also work to ensure regional stability by participating in conflict around the globe; securing and assuring access to sea, air, space, and cyberspace; and building the security capacity of key partners. DOD supports civil authorities in disaster events, at the direction of the secretary of defense or the president, when the capabilities of state and local authorities to respond effectively to an event are overwhelmed. Military forces also pursue and attack terrorists and terrorist organizations operating outside the borders of the United States. The Department of Defense only became directly involved in the conflict in Syria when it was feared that the Islamic State in Syria and the Levant (ISIL, also called ISIS) might try to attack the United States or American interests abroad. And it was the US military that conducted the strike that killed Osama bin Laden in Pakistan once the CIA determined his whereabouts.

The National Guard is the one military force that regularly responds to homeland security and disaster incidents in the United States. Although the National Guard falls under the command of the secretary of defense, there are 54 different National Guard organizations representative of the 50 states, the District of Columbia, Guam, the US Virgin Islands, and Puerto Rico. National Guard forces are attached to their state or territorial unit and fall under the command of an adjutant general. They can be mobilized into service for either state or federal duty and are often on the front lines of disaster response given that they are the chief resource for the State government in such incidents.

While it is common to see National Guard troops present during responses to disasters, terrorist attacks, or other incidents and events that impact national security (e.g., the Boston Marathon bombings), it is not common to see national-level military forces (e.g., the Army, Air Force, Navy, or Marines). The 2006 Military Commissions Act provided the president with increased authority to utilize the US military for domestic operations in times of disaster, though this has not been required to any significant degree even during events like Hurricanes Katrina and Sandy. Additionally, per the Posse Comitatus Act, the US military can only provide domestic support and cannot perform any law enforcement functions. Additionally, it must be determined that local, state, and federal resources are together unable to meet response or recovery requirements before these forces are called upon. The Northern Command of the US military, created in 2002 and headquartered in Colorado Springs, CO, was given the territory that encompasses Canada, the United States, Mexico, the Bahamas, and parts of the Caribbean. Forces operating under this command would respond to a domestic incident if the Department of Defense was tasked with response. As such, the

Northern Command is actively involved in intelligence sharing and communication with domestic homeland security agencies, and its units participate in many US-based exercises. The specific units through which NORTHCOM operates include the following:

- *US Special Operations Command, North*: A provisional command, also known as SOCNORTH, which enhances command and control of special operations forces throughout the NORTHCOM area of responsibility. SOCNORTH also supports interagency counterterrorism operations.
- *US Marine Forces Northern Command*: Executes antiterrorism program and force protection responsibilities, plans for the use of US Marine Corps (USMC) Forces and advises on the proper employment of USMC Forces, coordinates with and supports USMC Forces when attached to USNORTHCOM within USNORTHCOM's area of responsibility in order to conduct homeland defense operations, and provide defense support to civil authorities.
- *US Fleet Forces Command (USFF)/US Navy North (USNN)*: The Navy component of NORTHCOM, located at Norfolk, Virginia. USFF's mission is to provide maritime forces prepared to conduct homeland defense, civil support operations, and theater security cooperation activities when directed by NORTHCOM.
- *Air Forces Northern*: Air Forces Northern is headquartered in Panama City, FL, and has sole responsibility for ensuring the aerospace control and air defense of the continental United States, US Virgin Islands, and Puerto Rico. First Air Force is also the designated air component for NORTHCOM. When tasked, it conducts homeland defense and Defense Support of Civil Authorities operations in the NORTHCOM area of responsibility.
- *US Army North (ARNORTH)*: The Army component of USNORTHCOM, located at Fort Sam Houston, Texas. ARNORTH's mission is to conduct homeland defense, civil support operations, and theater security cooperation activities. On order, US Army North commands and controls deployed forces as a joint task force or Joint Force Land Component Command.
- *Joint Task Force North (JTF North)*: The DOD organization, located in Fort Bliss, TX, tasked with supporting federal law enforcement agencies in the interdiction of suspected transnational threats within and along the approaches to the continental United States. Transnational threats are those activities conducted by individuals or groups that involve international terrorism, narcotrafficking, alien smuggling, weapons of mass destruction, and the delivery systems for such weapons that threaten the national security of the United States.
- *Joint Task Force Civil Support (JTF-CS)*: This task force, headquartered at Fort Eustis, VA, and originally formed as a standing task force under US Joint Forces Command, was transferred to NORTHCOM when it was established.
- *Joint Task Force Alaska (JTF-AK)*: This task force is a subordinate command of NORTHCOM headquartered at Elmendorf Air Force Base, Alaska. It is composed of soldiers, sailors, airmen, and Department of Defense (DOD) civilian specialists. JTF-AK's mission is to deter, detect, prevent, and defeat threats within the Alaska Joint Operations Area (AK JOA) in order to protect US territory, citizens, and interests and, as directed, conduct civil support.
- *Joint Force Headquarters National Capital Region (JFHQ-NCR)*: This task force, based at Fort McNair, Washington, DC, is responsible for land-based homeland defense, defense support of civil authorities (DSCA), and incident management in the National Capital Region. JFHQ-NCR is responsible for protecting the District of Columbia and neighboring counties and cities of Maryland and Virginia, including Loudoun, Fairfax, and Prince William Counties in Virginia. JFHQ-NCR draws together the existing resources of the Army, Navy, Air Force, Marine Corps, Coast Guard,

and NORAD into a single point headquarters for planning, coordination, and execution of the mission in the National Capital Region (NORTHCOM, 2014).

In October of 2014, the Department of Defense created a special military medical incident support team to provide additional public health capacity in the event of an outbreak of Ebola in the United States. See the sidebar below.

Pentagon to Create Medical Support Team for US Ebola Response

US Defense Secretary Chuck Hagel has ordered the creation of a 30-member expeditionary medical support team to provide emergency help in a US domestic Ebola response, a Pentagon spokesman said on (October 19, 2014). The team of 5 doctors, 20 nurses, and 5 trainers could respond on short notice to help civilian medical professionals, a statement from Rear Admiral John Kirby. It would not be deployed to West Africa or elsewhere overseas.

Source: Reuters (2014).

The Department of Health and Human Services

The Department of Health and Human Services (HHS) leads the coordination of all functions relevant to Public Health Emergency Preparedness and Disaster Medical Response. Additionally, HHS incorporates steady-state and incident-specific activities as described in the National Health Security Strategy. HHS is the coordinator and primary agency for NRF Emergency Support Function (ESF) #8 (Public Health and Medical Services) providing the mechanism for coordinated federal assistance to supplement state, local, tribal, and territorial resources in response to a public health and medical disaster or potential or actual incident requiring a coordinated federal response and/or during a developing potential health and medical emergency. Through the Office of the Assistant Secretary for Preparedness and Response (ASPR), HHS leads the federal government effort to prevent, respond to, and recover from all events that involve a public health component, including terrorism. Given the all-hazards role of DHS, it is important to note that this agency also considers natural hazard response, given that there is often a public health component of them as well. However, it is the Centers for Disease Control and Prevention (CDC) that is the agency's most recognizable homeland security-focused office. CDC monitors and responds to disease outbreaks throughout the world and provides epidemic control support both domestically and abroad. One of the most important roles of the CDC is to prepare local and state public health departments for new and emerging threats, such as was required to respond to the worldwide Ebola outbreak that began in early 2014.

The Department of the Treasury

The Department of the Treasury (Treasury) works to safeguard the US financial system, combat financial crimes, and cut off financial support to terrorists, WMD proliferators, drug traffickers, and other national security threats. After the 9/11 terrorist attacks, Treasury initiated the Terrorist Finance Tracking Program (TFTP) to identify, track, and pursue terrorists and terror networks (e.g., al-Qaeda). The Department of the Treasury is uniquely positioned to track terrorist money flows and assist in broader US government efforts to uncover terrorist cells and map terrorist networks here at home and around the world. As the policy development and outreach office for Terrorism and Financing Intelligence (TFI), the Office of Terrorist Financing and Financial Crimes (TFFC) works across all elements of the national security community—including the law enforcement, regulatory, policy, diplomatic, and intelligence communities—and with the private sector and foreign governments to identify and address the threats presented by all forms of illicit finance to the international financial system. TFFC advances this mission by developing initiatives and strategies to deploy a full range of financial authorities to combat money laundering, terrorist financing, WMD proliferation, and other criminal and illicit activities both at home and abroad. These include not only systemic initiatives to enhance the transparency of the international financial system but also threat-specific strategies and initiatives to apply and implement targeted financial measures to the full range of national security threats. Through the Office of Foreign Assets Control, the Department of the Treasury works to seize property owned by terrorist organizations and prevent US entities from conducting business with those associated with those organizations (or with the organizations themselves). A list of those individuals and organizations monitored by the program can be found at http://1.usa.gov/10ck331. And finally, the Department of the Treasury is instrumental in the development of insurance protection from acts of terrorism. The department was specified under the 2002 Terrorism Risk Insurance Act as being the lead agency responsible for the new Terrorism Risk Insurance Program. This program provides reinsurance to support private insurance providers in the event of a large-scale terrorist attack that results in over $100 million in covered expenses. The program is authorized to provide up to $100 billion per fiscal year. This program is set to expire at the end of calendar year 2014 without an extension. As of publication, the Senate had passed legislation to extend the act until the end of 2021, but no matching bill had been passed by the House of Representatives. The Senate bill divided terrorist attacks into two categories—one for CBRN attacks and another for non-CBRN attacks. For the former, the co-pay would be 15% and the trigger $100 million, while for non-CBRN attacks, the co-pay would rise to 20% and the trigger to $500 million.

The Director of National Intelligence

The Director of National Intelligence (DNI) serves as the head of the IC, acts as the principal advisor to the president and National Security Council for intelligence matters relating to national security, and oversees and directs implementation of the National Intelligence Program. The IC, composed of 16 elements across the US government, functions consistent with law, executive order, regulations, and policy to support the national security-related missions of the US government. The homeland security role of DNI is explained in much greater detail in Chapter 5.

Department of Energy

The Department of Energy (DOE) maintains stewardship of vital national security capabilities, from nuclear weapons to research and development programs. The DOE is the designated federal agency to provide a unifying structure for the integration of federal critical infrastructure and key resources' protection efforts, specifically for the energy sector. It is also responsible for maintaining continuous and reliable energy supplies for the United States through preventive measures and restoration and recovery actions. The DOE is the coordinator and primary agency for ESF #12 (Energy) when disasters are declared by the president.

The Department of Housing and Urban Development

The Department of Housing and Urban Development (HUD) is a coordinating and primary agency of the Housing Recovery Support Function (RSF) under the National Disaster Recovery Framework (NDRF) and a supporting organization for the Community Planning and Capacity Building RSF. The NDRF, which provides a mechanism for coordinating federal support to state, tribal, regional, and local governments, nongovernmental organizations (NGOs), and the private sector to enable community recovery from the long-term consequences of major disaster events, is described in greater detail in Chapter 9.

Department of the Interior

The DOI develops policies and procedures for all types of hazards and emergencies that impact federal lands, facilities, infrastructure, and resources; tribal lands; and insular areas. The DOI is also a primary agency for ESF #9 (Search and Rescue), providing specialized lifesaving assistance to state, tribal, and local authorities when activated for incidents or potential incidents requiring a coordinated federal response. The DOI, together with the Department of Agriculture, also operates the National Interagency Fire Center.

Department of Transportation

The Department of Transportation (DOT) collaborates with DHS on all matters relating to transportation security and transportation infrastructure protection and in regulating the transportation of hazardous materials by all modes (including pipelines). The secretary of transportation is responsible for operating the national airspace system. The DOT is the coordinating agency for ESF #1 (Transportation) in the event of disasters declared by the president.

The Corporation for National and Community Service

The Corporation for National and Community Service (CNCS) is a government agency that administers several individual volunteer-based but grant-funded programs that contribute to homeland security and emergency management, including AmeriCorps, Senior Corps, and Learn and Serve America. Together, these programs reach more than 5 million people each year:

- AmeriCorps is a network of national service programs that recruit and hire more than 75,000 Americans each year to address critical needs in the areas of education, public safety, health, and the environment. AmeriCorps members serve through more than 3000 nonprofit and nongovernment agencies, public agencies, and faith-based organizations, tutoring and mentoring youth, building affordable housing, teaching computer skills, cleaning parks and streams, running after-school programs, and helping communities respond to disasters. Since CNCS became a supporting agency under both the NRF and the NDRF, AmeriCorps members have been receiving training in emergency response and recovery activities and have been deployed to a number of major disaster declarations. AmeriCorps service members help local governments to satisfy local match requirements by providing full-time equivalent work hours.
- Senior Corps is a network of programs that recruit senior citizens in order to benefit from their experience, skills, and talents in order to better address the challenges faced by the community. It includes three programs: Foster Grandparents, Senior Companions, and the Retired and Senior Volunteer. More than a half-million Americans aged 55 and older assist local nonprofit agencies,

public agencies, and faith-based organizations in carrying out their missions, together having provided over one billion volunteer hours nationwide.

- Learn and Serve America is a program that "supports service-learning programs in schools and community organizations that help nearly one million students from kindergarten through college meet community needs, while improving their academic skills and learning the habits of good citizenship." Service learning is defined as an educational method by which participants learn and develop through active participation in service that is conducted in and meets the needs of a community.

In July 2002, CNCS awarded 43 grants totaling $10.3 million to increasing citizen participation in homeland security in communities, government agencies, and voluntary organizations. Since that time, CNCS has continued to support community-level homeland security projects. In response to and recovery from the 2005 Gulf Coast hurricanes, CNCS became highly involved in the cleanup and rebuilding of the affected communities through volunteer participation. CNCS grantee programs from throughout the country sent volunteer participants. CNCS volunteers provided millions of hours of service in relief and recovery areas such as "mucking out" flooded houses, demolition, construction, tarping of damaged roofs, victim case management, counseling, and much more. The postdisaster assistance provided by various CNCS programs in a more recent disaster is described in the sidebar "National Service Responds to May 2014 Severe Weather Disaster."

The CNCS leads its disaster response activities through the efforts of the Disaster Services Unit (DSU). In 2012, FEMA and CNCS created a partnership to build and maintain a specialized AmeriCorps team focused on disaster work called FEMA Corps. There are 1600 available slots for FEMA Corps members within the larger grouping called AmeriCorps National Civilian Community Corps (NCCC). FEMA Corps members work on projects in preparedness, mitigation, response, and recovery—not just postdisaster assistance.

National Service Responds to May 2014 Severe Weather Disaster

In response to severe weather that struck in early May 2014, which included tornadoes and flooding across the central United States and the Mississippi Valley, 230 national service members were deployed to Alabama, Arkansas, Florida, Kansas, and Mississippi. Statistics on each location follow.

Alabama—71 Members Deployed

- 2 Senior Corps RSVP volunteers. The Calhoun County RSVP project of Jacksonville, AL, opened a Volunteer Reception Center in Sardis City, AL, with the support of two RSVP participants and 300 community volunteers. Volunteers delivered food to families, disaster workers, and responders, coordinated volunteer and donation management, and helped with debris removal.
- 25 Senior Corps RSVP volunteers. The Tuscaloosa County Voluntary Organizations Active in Disasters (VOAD) activated and the RSVP sponsor, FOCUS On Senior Citizens, served as the site of the Volunteer Reception Center where they managed affiliated and unaffiliated volunteers.
- In Athens, AL, Senior Corps RSVP volunteers worked with the United Way and the VRC, cutting trees and assisting with debris removal. RSVP volunteers and staff also conducted telechecks with seniors to identify needs in the aftermath of the storms.
- 44 FEMA Corps members (5 teams) were deployed to AL (Southern, Atlantic, and Pacific campuses) to support FEMA.

Arkansas—31 Members Deployed

- 3 AmeriCorps members with the Seattle Red Cross were deployed to Little Rock, AR, to assist with client casework.
- 2 AmeriCorps members with the Red Cross in Columbus, OH, were deployed to Little Rock, AR, to assist with client casework.
- 26 FEMA Corps members (three teams) supported FEMA operations in Arkansas.

Florida—33 Members Deployed

- 24 FEMA Corps members (3 teams) supported FEMA operations in Pensacola, FL.
- 3 AmeriCorps members with AmeriCorps Financial Empowerment Services assisted Pensacola, FL, with assessments in neighborhoods that had not been reached after the flooding.
- 6 Florida AmeriCorps VISTA and AmeriCorps project staff were deployed to the Escambia County EOC.

Kansas—40 Members Deployed

- 2 AmeriCorps members with the Red Cross NPRC were deployed to Baxter Springs, KS.
- 2 AmeriCorps members with the Michigan Red Cross were deployed to Baxter Springs, KS, to assist with client casework.
- 4 AmeriCorps St. Louis members were deployed to Kansas to assist VOADs with operating multiagency resource center and volunteer reception centers.
- 2 St. Bernard Project Rebuilding Joplin AmeriCorps members supported volunteer reception center operations in Baxter Springs, Kansas.
- 30 members from Kansas Outdoor AmeriCorps Action Team were deployed on weekends to assist with debris removal.

Mississippi—55 Members Deployed

- 13 AmeriCorps NCCC members were deployed to Tupelo, MS, to support NECHAMA in cleanup efforts and debris removal.
- 13 Southern Region AmeriCorps NCCC were deployed to Mantachie, MS, to assist in volunteer reception center operations.
- 16 (2 teams) FEMA Corps members supported FEMA disaster survivor assistance efforts in Louisville, MS.
- 1 AmeriCorps member with the Michigan Red Cross was deployed to Mississippi to assist in relief efforts.
- 7 AmeriCorps members with the Red Cross NPRC were deployed to Mississippi.
- 3 AmeriCorps members with the Seattle Red Cross were deployed to Tupelo, MS, to assist with client casework.
- 1 AmeriCorps member with the Red Cross in Columbus, OH, was deployed to Tupelo, MS, to provide assessment and casework.
- 1 AmeriCorps State member (FoodCorps) displaced from regular service was redirected to perform volunteer reception center operations in Louisville, MS.

Source: CNCS (2014).

Citizen Corps Program

Citizen Corps is a FEMA-administered program that provides opportunities for citizens who want to help make their communities more secure. Since its January 2002 establishment, tens of thousands of people from all 50 states and US territories have volunteered to work with one or more of the Citizen Corps programs. These include the following:

- Citizen Corps Councils (CCCs) were established at the state and local levels to promote, organize, and run the various programs that fall under the Citizen Corps umbrella. Funding for these councils is provided by the federal government through grant awards. As of November 2014, there were CCCs in 56 states and US territories and 1242 local communities, all of which serve 65% of the total population of the United States.
- Community Emergency Response Teams (CERTs) began in 1983 in Los Angeles, California. City administrators there recognized that in most emergency situations, average citizens—neighbors, coworkers, and bystanders, for example—were often on scene during the critical moments before professional help arrives. These officials acted on the belief that by training average citizens to perform basic search and rescue, first aid, and other critical emergency response skills, they would increase the overall resilience of the community. Additionally, should a large-scale disaster like an earthquake occur, where first response units would be stretched very thin, these trained citizens would be able to augment official services and provide an important service to the community. Beginning in 1993, FEMA began to offer CERT training on a national level, providing funding to cover start-up and tuition costs for programs. By 2008, CERT programs had been established in more than 2915 communities in all 50 states, the District of Columbia, and several US territories. Today, that number has fallen to 2538, mostly due to falling funding levels. CERT teams remain active in the community before a disaster strikes, sponsoring events such as drills, neighborhood cleanup, and disaster-education fairs. Trainers offer periodic refresher sessions to CERT members to reinforce the basic training and to keep participants involved and practiced in their skills. CERT members also offer other nonemergency assistance to the community with the goal of improving the overall safety of the community.
- Volunteers in Police Service (VIPS) was created in the aftermath of September 11, 2001, to address the increased demands on state and local law enforcement. The basis of the program is that civilian volunteers are able to support police officers by doing much of the behind-the-scenes work that does not require formal law enforcement training, thereby allowing officers to spend more of their already strained schedules on the street. Although the concept is not new, the federal support for such programs is. VIPS draws on the time and recognized talents of civilian volunteers. Volunteer roles may include performing clerical tasks, serving as an extra set of "eyes and ears," assisting with search-and-rescue activities, and writing citations for accessible parking violations, just to name a few. As of November 2014, there were 2288 official VIPS programs registered throughout the United States.
- The Medical Reserve Corps (MRC) was founded after the 2002 State of the Union Address to establish teams of local volunteer medical and public health professionals who can contribute their skills and experience when called on in times of need. The program relies on volunteers who are practicing and retired physicians, nurses, dentists, veterinarians, epidemiologists, and other health professionals, as well as other citizens untrained in public health but who can contribute to the community's normal and disaster public health needs in other ways (which may include

interpreters, chaplains, and legal advisers). Local community leaders develop their own MRC units and recruit local volunteers that address the specific community needs. For example, MRC volunteers may deliver necessary public health services during a crisis, assist emergency response teams with patients, and provide care directly to those with less serious injuries and other health-related issues. MRC volunteers may also serve a vital role by assisting their communities with ongoing public health needs (e.g., immunizations, screenings, health and nutrition education, and volunteering in community health centers and local hospitals). The MRC unit decides, in concert with local officials (including the local CCC), on when the community MRC is activated during a local emergency. As of November 2014, there were 980 MRC programs established throughout the United States.

- The Neighborhood Watch Program has been in existence for more than 30 years in cities and counties throughout the United States. The program is based on the concept that neighbors who join together to fight crime will be able to increase security in their surrounding areas and, as a result, provide an overall better quality of life for residents. Understandably, after September 11, when terrorism became a major focus of the US government, the recognized importance of programs like Neighborhood Watch took on much greater significance. The Neighborhood Watch Program is not maintained by the National Sheriff's Association, which founded the program initially. At the local level, the CCCs help neighborhood groups that have banded together to start a program to carry out their mission. Many printed materials and other guidance are available for free to help them carry out their goals. Neighborhood Watch Programs have successfully decreased crime in many of the neighborhoods where they have been implemented. In addition to serving a crime prevention role, Neighborhood Watch has been used as the basis for bringing neighborhood residents together to focus on disaster preparedness and terrorism awareness, to focus on evacuation drills and exercises, and even to organize group training, such as the CERT training.
- Fire Corps was created in 2004 under the umbrella of USA Freedom Corps and Citizen Corps. The purpose of the program, like the VIPS program with the police, was to enhance the ability of fire departments to utilize citizen advocates and provide individuals with opportunities to support their local fire departments with both time and talent. Fire Corps was created as a partnership between the International Association of Fire Chiefs' Volunteer and Combination Officers Section (VCOS), the International Association of Fire Fighters (IAFF), and the National Volunteer Fire Council (NVFC). By participating in the program, concerned and interested citizens can assist in their local fire department's activities through tasks such as administrative assistance, public education, fund-raising, data entry, accounting, public relations, and equipment and facility maintenance, just to name a few examples. Any fire department that allows citizens to volunteer support service is considered a Fire Corps Program, but programs can become official through registering with a local, county, or state CCC, if one exists. Official Fire Corps Programs will be provided with assistance on how to implement a nonoperational citizen advocates program or improve existing programs. A Fire Corps National Advisory Committee has been established under the program in order to provide strategic direction and collect feedback from the field. As of November 2014, there were 1098 established Fire Corps Programs throughout the United States and the US territories. Although some of these programs are relatively new, some, such as Neighborhood Watch, have been in place for more than a decade. More information on these programs is provided in Chapter 9.

NRF Participant Agencies

Many other federal agencies other than those just listed are involved in homeland security efforts, although most of these actions occur as a result of their contractual obligations set out in NRF. Although these actions will be described in greater detail in Chapter 9, the following is a list of the federal agencies that participate in the response to disasters within the United States:

- Corporation for National and Community Service
- Department of Agriculture
- Department of Commerce
- Department of Defense
- Department of Education
- Department of Energy
- Department of Health and Human Services
- Department of Homeland Security
- Department of Housing and Urban Development
- Department of the Interior
- Department of Justice
- Department of Labor
- Department of State
- Department of Transportation
- Department of the Treasury
- Department of Veterans Affairs
- Central Intelligence Agency
- Environmental Protection Agency
- Federal Bureau of Investigation
- Federal Communications Commission
- General Services Administration
- National Aeronautics and Space Administration
- National Transportation Safety Board
- Nuclear Regulatory Commission
- Office of Personnel Management
- Small Business Administration
- Social Security Administration
- Tennessee Valley Authority
- US Agency for International Development
- US Postal Service

Critical Thinking

Why do you think certain homeland security-related functions are still performed by other federal agencies that were not incorporated into DHS? Should they have been? Why or why not?

Activities by State and Local Organizations

State and local governments have expended considerable human and financial resources to secure their jurisdictions from the perceived threat of terrorism. Although large quantities of federal dollars have been provided to state and local agencies as they have prepared for terrorist threats, many of their efforts have been performed without any federal compensation. And each time a threat is identified or an alert is issued, or a major event is identified as being a potential terrorist target, local leaders in the affected jurisdictions must divert already sparse financial and human resources away from other areas of need to adequately address the new threats. These collective strains have prompted the many organizations representative of state and local governments to become actively engaged in the homeland security debate, from the passage of the Homeland Security Act of 2002 until today.

As early as September 2002, the municipal organizations, which include the US Conference of Mayors (USCM), the National League of Cities (NLC), the National Association of Counties (NACo), and the National Governors Association (NGA), and the emergency management organizations, which include the National Emergency Management Association (NEMA) and the International Association of Emergency Managers (IAEM), began fighting for first-responder funding for state and local governments and about the way the money was allocated—whether it would be to the states or directly to the local municipalities. Clearly, these organizations were and continue to be involved in informing the federal government's approach to funding state and local homeland security efforts. Each of these organizations is discussed next.

US Conference of Mayors

The US Conference of Mayors (USCM) is the official nonpartisan organization of the nation's 1393 US cities with populations of 30,000 or more. Each city is represented in the conference by its chief elected official, the mayor. The primary roles of the USCM are to

- promote the development of effective national urban/suburban policy,
- strengthen federal-city relationships,
- ensure that federal policy meets urban needs,
- provide mayors with leadership and management tools,
- create a forum in which mayors can share ideas and information.

The conference has historically assumed a national leadership role, calling early attention to serious urban problems and pressing successfully for solutions.

In December 2001, just 3 months after the 9/11 attacks, the USCM released "A National Action Plan for Safety and Security in America's Cities." The document was prepared as part of the Mayors Emergency Safety and Security Summit held in Washington, DC, on October 23–25, 2001. It contained recommendations in four priority areas: transportation security, emergency preparedness, federal-local law enforcement, and economic security. In this document, the mayors made the following critical point:

> *It is important to understand that while the fourth area, economic security, is viewed as the ultimate goal of a nation, it cannot be achieved in the absence of the first three. That is, securing our transportation system, maximizing our emergency response capability, and coordinating our law enforcement response to threats and incidents at all levels are viewed as prerequisites to eliminating the anxiety that has accelerated the nation's economic downturn, and to achieving economic security for the nation.*

The principal areas of concern in federal-local law enforcement for the mayors are communications, coordination, and border-city security. In the transportation security section, the mayors' paper presents recommendations concerning security issues in each of the major transportation modes: airport, transit, highway, rail, and port.

The USCM leadership has repeatedly expressed concern that a significant amount of funding from the federal government has not reached the cities for combating terrorism. The mayors expressed that they have been working on initiatives related to homeland security, largely without any federal assistance. Select initiatives, related to communities, that they mentioned include the following: (1) conducting exercises to help prepare for emergencies and improve response capabilities, (2) expanding public information and education efforts, and (3) conducting vulnerability assessments of potential key targets.

Funding for cities has remained a principal focus of the USCM in the area of homeland security. In September 2003, the USCM released a report titled, "First Mayors' Report to the Nation: Tracking Homeland Security Funds Sent to the 50 State Governments" (U.S. Conference of Mayors, 2003). Through release of the report, the USCM website announced that 90% of cities had not received funds from the largest federal homeland security program designed to assist first responders by the federally set deadline of August 1, 2003. The report also found that more than half of the cities either had not been consulted or had no opportunity to influence state decision making about how to use and distribute funding.

The USCM established a Homeland Security Monitoring Center (no longer active) to monitor the flow of homeland security funds from the federal government to states and localities. This focus on funding was at the heart of a March 12, 2004, message from Tom Cochran, executive director of the USCM, in a website column that stated, "Our goal is to do one thing: get the money down to our first responders on the front line in cities throughout America" (U.S. Conference of Mayors, 2004). In June 2004, the USCM released a report of a survey that was conducted to assess the flow of federal homeland security funds through the states to the cities. Their study found that 52% of the 231 cities surveyed had not received any money at all, nor had they been notified that they would receive money from the state block grant program, which is the largest homeland security program designed to assist first responders.

In 2006, the USCM conducted a survey to determine levels of emergency and disaster readiness at the city level in the United States. The results of this survey were issued in a report titled "Five Years Post 9/11 and One Year Post Hurricane Katrina: The State of America's Readiness." Results at the time showed that cities lacked the readiness to address a variety of disaster-related response and recovery needs. The USCM has continued to fight for municipal homeland security issues in the years since. In January 2007, the mayors released a 10-point legislative agenda that included a section on homeland security. This plan identified three areas of concern for the cities, many of which remain relevant to this day. These included the following:

- *Interoperable communications*: The mayors called for a well-funded, stand-alone, federal emergency communications grant program designed to improve interoperable communications, including flexible direct grants to cities and first responders.
- *Transit security*: The mayors called for a flexible federal transit security initiative to improve security in the areas of communications, surveillance, detection systems, personnel, and training. Because of the negative experiences cities had previously encountered trying to find money locally to cover these kinds of expenses, and in trying to receive the actual funds once granted by the federal government, the mayors requested that there be no local or state match and that security funds would go directly to the operator of the system or the jurisdiction providing the security.

- *Funding mechanism*: The mayors contend that improvements must be made in the application process and delivery mechanism for federal homeland security grant resources to make sure that the process is more user-friendly, the funding reaches cities quickly, and the funding is flexible enough to meet local needs.

The mayor's influence was felt by the Congress, and many of their 10-Point Plan requests were honored in the 9/11 Bill that was passed on August 3, 2007. For instance, the Urban Area Security Initiative (UASI), which is designed to assist high-risk urban areas in preventing, preparing for, protecting against, and responding to terrorism, was altered to meet the mayors' preferences. For FY 2008, $850 million was authorized, with an additional $150 million every year thereafter. Eligible city governments were given the opportunity to present what they feel is relevant information about their city's threat, vulnerability, and likely consequences of a terrorist attack and details about the intended allocation of funds within the local government. If approved, awards are still distributed to the state (a point of contention for the mayors), but the state is required to pass at least 80% of the funds to the appropriate urban area within 45 days. Any remaining amounts retained by the states must be put toward "items, services, or activities that benefit the high-risk urban area." Under the law, the 100 most populous metropolitan areas in the United States are eligible for UASI grants. If a region is not ranked within the 100 most populous metropolitan areas, DHS can still determine it to be a high-risk urban area based on a risk formula, and DHS can designate regions consisting of more than one metropolitan area into several high-risk urban areas. Finally, a high-risk urban area can, with DHS permission, expand its jurisdiction to include additional regions.

The law also changed the Homeland Security Grant Program (HSGP), which seeks to enhance statewide homeland security management, personnel, training, and equipment. The new bill reduced the minimum amount of total funding each state would receive from 0.75% to 0.375% in FY 2008, 0.365% in FY 2009, and 0.360% for FY 2010 and thereafter. Today, that has dropped further, to 0.35% for each state and territory and just 0.08% for American Samoa, Guam, the Northern Mariana Islands, and the US Virgin Islands. Like the Urban Areas Security Initiative (UASI), the state is responsible for allocating at least 80% of the funds to local governments within 45 days of receiving the grant. The factors that will ultimately determine the sums awarded to the states are risk level and the quality of the anticipated effectiveness of the proposal. The most important change to this grant that affects the mayors is the absence of a local match requirement, which had been included in earlier versions of the legislation and was opposed by the Conference of Mayors.

1. The new 9/11 Bill was to have increased the authorization for the Emergency Management Performance Grants Program to $400 million for FY 2008, $535 million in FY 2009, $680 million in FY 2010, $815 million in FY 2011, and $950 million in FY 2012. However, in 2011, those figures fell to $329 million once the budget was approved, rising to $350 million in 2012. In 2014, the program was given $988 million, though this was actually a reduction in total homeland security grant dollars to state and local agencies because several grant programs including the Urban Areas Security Initiative had been incorporated into the HSGP.

The USCM also saw its transit security recommendation in the 10-Point Plan integrated in the final version of the 9/11 Bill. Through a partnership between the DHS and the DOT, the bill created the National Strategy for Public Transportation and Security that sought to minimize security threats to the public transportation system and maximize recovery ability. The Public Transportation Security Assistance Program, which has since ended, made grants available for security improvements to transportation agencies that have performed a security assessment or have drawn up a security plan.

National League of Cities

The NLC is the oldest and largest national organization representing municipal governments throughout the United States. The NLC serves as a resource to and is an advocate for the more than 19,000 cities, villages, and towns it represents. More than 2000 municipalities of all sizes pay dues to NLC and actively participate as leaders and voting members in the organization. The NLC provides numerous benefits to its network of members, including the following:

- Advocates for cities and towns in the Washington, DC, area through full-time lobbying and grassroots campaigns
- Promotes cities and towns through an aggressive media and communications program that draws attention to city issues and enhances the national image of local government
- Provides programs and services that give local leaders the tools and knowledge to better serve their communities
- Keeps leaders informed of critical issues that affect municipalities and warrant action by local officials
- Strengthens leadership skills by offering numerous training and education programs
- Recognizes municipal achievements by gathering and promoting examples of best practices and honoring cities and towns with awards for model programs and initiatives
- Partners with state leagues to supplement resources and strengthen the voice of local government in the nation's capital and all state capitals
- Promotes cities and towns through an aggressive media and communications program that draws attention to city issues and enhances the national image of local government

Like the USCM, the NLC has also focused on the first-responder funding issue. It conducted a letter-writing campaign to the White House and Congress to build support for the original allocation of first-responder funds. In 2002, NLC proposed a $75.5 billion stimulus package that would include $10 billion for unmet homeland security needs.

In January 2003, then NLC President Karen Anderson appointed the special Working Group on Homeland Security to serve as NLC's frontline resource on the subject. That group worked to prepare resources to help city officials in carrying out their new roles as the "frontline of hometown defense."

The NLC has continued to lobby the Congress and the Executive Office to increase or maintain funding support to strengthen "hometown" and homeland security and develop extensive policy on these issues. The NLC reports the results of surveys on municipal responses to terrorism regarding vulnerable targets and the need for federal guidance and support. A variety of publications that the NLC generates offer practical guidance to local officials to assist in their ongoing efforts to develop and refine local and regional homeland security plans.

In 2005, homeland security remained a top priority for the NLC. The two primary NLC issues were first-responder funding and public safety communications. Presented in the sidebar "2005 Advocacy Priority" is text from an NLC document detailing advocacy policy regarding funding for first responders.

In 2005, the NLC developed a policy statement on homeland security that was included in its "National Municipal Policy." The policy statement addresses the following topics:

- Prevention, planning, and mitigation
- Disaster response and recovery
- Training and technical assistance
- Disaster insurance
- Domestic terrorism

- Border security
- Immigration enforcement
- Profiling

In support of these policies, the NLC developed a publication, "Protecting Hometown America: Lessons Learned from and for Small Cities and Towns," available on this book's companion website.

2005 Advocacy Priority: The Issue—Funding for First Responders

The nation's cities and towns need a well-funded, improved grant program to respond to terrorism threats in highly populated and high-threat areas. Local governments seek funding that allows jurisdictions to prepare for possible terrorist threats, with flexibility to use the funds for a range of risks based on their state homeland security plans.

Message to the Congress

- Preserve direct funding. Preserve direct funding to local governments and regions based on the congressionally mandated 80% pass-through requirement from states to local governments.
- Improve homeland and hometown security. Improve security by increasing funding for Urban Area Security Grants and the State Homeland Security Grant Program.
- Preserve funding. Preserve funding for both homeland security programs such as Law Enforcement Terrorism Prevention grants, the Urban Search and Rescue program and the Metropolitan Medical Response System, and traditional first-responder and emergency management programs that existed before September 11, 2001.
- Provide flexibility. Provide flexibility for local governments to use homeland security funds to offset overtime expenditures during national high alerts, counterterrorism activities, and training exercises.
- Create a federal clearinghouse. Create a web-based federal clearinghouse of best practices and updated voluntary national consensus standards.
- Waive cost-sharing requirements. Waive matching or cost-sharing requirements for local governments.

Request to the Congress

- Enact an authorization bill that provides funding for first responders to target terrorism threats in highly populated and high-threat areas, with maximum flexibility to use the funds for a range of risks based on their state homeland security plans.
- Fully fund the State Homeland Security Grant Program, Urban Area Security Grants, and other critical homeland security programs.

Source: National League of Cities.

In 2013, the NLC issued a press release to describe their analysis of the future of homeland security grants to American communities, which is presented in the sidebar "Funding Homeland Security Grants."

Funding Homeland Security Grants: The House, the Senate, and the Administration Take Different Approaches

As if sequestration and the various continuing resolutions weren't confusing enough, we now have to deal with the fiscal year 2014 budget proposals developed separately by the House, Senate and Administration. Based on their various budget documents we now know that federal anti-terrorism funds will be appropriated and allocated in very different ways if the House, Senate and Administration have their ways.

The Senate appears prepared to retain the current grant structure with separate funding for the State Homeland Security Program (SHSP), the Urban Areas Security Initiative (UASI), and Operation Stonegarden (OPSG). The House may be willing to consolidate dozens of homeland security programs into one, based upon language in its budget resolution that points to the presence of numerous duplicative and overlapping programs. And the Administration has called on Congress to consolidate SHSP, UASI and OPSG into a single block grant named the National Preparedness Grant Program (NPGP).

Overall post-sequestration funding for fiscal year 2013 for SHSP, UASI and OPSG will be about $800 million. About $270 will go to the SHSP program for state based emergency preparedness work; about $450 million has been appropriated to the Urban Areas Security Initiative (UASI) program; and about $45 million has been appropriated for the Stonegarden Program.

The UASI grants are of particular importance to cities and towns. According to DHS, these funds are designed to "address the unique planning, organization, equipment, training, and exercise needs of high-threat, high-density urban areas, and assists them in building an enhanced and sustainable capacity to prevent, protect against, mitigate, respond to, and recover from acts of terrorism." The Stonegarden Program helps border state communities better coordinate their local anti-terror activities.

If the Senate prevails, we can expect the current funding structure to remain in place, though the actual funding levels for each of the programs remains unclear and will not be known until the Homeland Security Appropriations Committee decides what the funding levels should be.

If the House prevails, we can expect that many homeland security programs will be rolled into a single block grant that could result in a substantial reduction in funding.

If the Administration prevails we can expect funding to remain relatively level in fiscal year 2014, but what were once three separate programs will be merged into the NPGP.

While the possible changes coming from the House remain vague—the House Budget Resolution does make note of what it calls the numerous duplicative Homeland Security programs but offers no specific solution—the Administration has been very clear as to what it wants to do and achieve. According to the Department of Homeland Security (DHS), the NPGP "would eliminate the redundancies and requirements placed on both the Federal Government and the grantees resulting from the current system of multiple individual, and often disconnected, grant programs."

DHS also claims that this grant program would not impact local funding since 80% of the appropriated funds would have to be passed through to localities. In support of the proposed changes, DHS has launched a major campaign in support of this new funding mechanism. It has been reaching out to members of Congress as well as state and local elected officials urging them to support the new mechanism. It is too early to know whether Congress is amenable to the Administration's approach.

Despite this, NLC will continue to oppose this proposal, in part, because block grants of the sort proposed often result in reduced funding, and, in part, because the current grant program structure is working well by funneling funds to local areas to develop and implement local and regional responses to terrorism and other potential catastrophes.

Source: Bomberg (2013).

Several years ago, the NLC developed a number of publications to assist local governments in participating in homeland security. Two of these include

- "Homeland Security: Practical Tools for Local Governments" (http://bit.ly/1vALW0f),
- "Why Can't We Talk?" Emergency Communications Interoperability Guide (http://bit.ly/ZLldlb).

In July 2007, NLC representatives met with DHS officials to exchange views and perspectives on homeland security in towns and cities. At this meeting, the NLC reiterated that all emergency situations are local events and that local elected officials involved in the day-to-day operations of local government shoulder the burden of ensuring that public safety resources are available to citizens in times of emergency or disaster. NLC highlighted the following seven topics as priorities for local elected officials:

1. Emergency communications
2. Emergency Management Assistance Compacts (EMACs)/Mutual Aid
3. All-hazards planning
4. Federalization of the National Guard
5. Intragovernmental collaboration and communication
6. Full funding of federal mandates
7. Immigration/border security

National Association of Counties

NACo was created in 1935 and remains the only national organization that represents county governments in the United States. NACo maintains a membership of more than 2300 counties (over 75% of the US population) but represents all of the nation's 3069 counties to the White House and to the Congress.

NACo is a full-service organization that provides many services to its members, including legislative, research, technical, and public affairs assistance. The association acts as a liaison with other levels of government, works to improve public understanding of counties, serves as a national advocate for counties, and provides them with resources to help them find innovative methods to meet the challenges they face. NACo is involved in a number of special projects that deal with such issues as the environment, sustainable communities, volunteerism, and intergenerational studies.

In 2001, NACo created the "Policy Agenda to Secure the People of America's Counties." This policy paper stated that "[c]ounties are the first responders to terrorist attacks, natural disasters and major emergencies" (National Association of Counties, 2002). NACo established a 43-member NACo Homeland

Security Task Force that, on October 23, 2001, prepared a set of 20 recommendations in four general categories concerning homeland security issues: public health, local law enforcement and intelligence, infrastructure security, and emergency planning and public safety. Since that time, NACo has continued to release policy recommendations, with the 2007–2008 policy resolutions titled "NACo Homeland Security Policy Resolutions ..." available on this book's companion website.

Like the other municipal organizations listed earlier, NACo is vitally interested in homeland security funding issues and works to help its member counties to locally address the complex issues. In addition to advocacy, NACo develops toolkits and other publications that counties can use to decipher the flood of information that exists. In 2014, NACo issued a press release describing their analysis and stance on homeland security grants, presented in the sidebar "President's Budget Proposes Consolidation of DHS State and Local Grants."

President's Budget Proposes Consolidation of DHS State and Local Grants

President Obama's recently released FY15 budget proposes the consolidation of U.S. Department of Homeland Security's (DHS) state and local preparedness grant programs into one grant program, called the National Preparedness Grant Program (NPGP).

Not included in the consolidation are the Emergency Management Performance Grants and fire grants. While the president's budget has suggested this type of consolidation in two previous budget proposals this year, DHS has submitted legislative language to accompany the consolidation proposal.

NACo has identified the following concerns with the proposed legislative language:

The definition of "unit of local government" would be expanded to include nonprofit organizations, transit agencies and port areas

Local governments could no longer be direct FEMA grantees; counties would be considered as "subgrantees" under one state application

"State-centric" program application and administration

Uncertainty around mandatory pass-through to local governments, and

Consolidation of the Urban Area Security Initiative (UASI) into the NPGP.

The administration for the NPGP relies heavily on states as states are the only eligible entities that are able to apply for grants under the NPGP. Currently, counties can apply directly to FEMA for grants like the pre-disaster mitigation grant program. Under the proposed language for the NPGP, counties would not be able to directly apply to FEMA but must coordinate their request under the state's application.

DHS Secretary Jeh Johnson appeared before the House Appropriations Committee's Subcommittee on Homeland Security on March 11 and was questioned by Rep. David Price (D-N.C.) about the rationale for proposing the NPGP consolidation. Johnson acknowledged the opposition to the consolidation and cited increased efficiency of federal oversight as a justification for the proposal. He also said he was inclined to defer to the judgment of FEMA Administrator Craig Fugate, who was said to be a "big believer" in the consolidation of the grant programs.

On March 18, NACo, joined by members from several local government, emergency management and law enforcement groups, met with both majority and minority staff on the House Homeland Security Committee's Subcommittee on Emergency Preparedness, Response and Communications regarding the consolidation of these programs. The coalition reiterated concerns over state-centric program administration and changing the definition of "unit of local government."

Given that midterm elections are on the horizon, it is unlikely that this proposal will be implemented this year. NACo supports a collaborative effort between states and all levels of local government regarding priority funding decisions within DHS funding. NACo will continue to monitor the progress of the NPGP proposal.

Source: Jang (2014).

The following is an example of the homeland security toolkits and other relevant publications released by NACo:

- *NIMS Guide for County Officials*: A guide to help county officials understand what NIMS is and the role counties play in planning to prepare for and respond to emergencies of any type and of any scale (http://1.usa.gov/1DrOWyl)

NACo has made a considerable effort to assist US counties in preventing cyber terrorism and crime through their cybersecurity programs. NACo is now an official partner of DHS in the "Stop. Think. Connect." Campaign, which is described in Chapter 8. NACo created the cyber guidebook to help county governments understand, prevent, and prepare for acts of cyberterrorism, which can be found at http://bit.ly/1tEmw3c. The organization also facilitates a series of webinars on cybersecurity and has produced podcasts on the topic—all available on the organization's website. The program is maintained by a cybersecurity task force.

National Governors Association

The NGA—the bipartisan organization of the nation's governors—promotes visionary state leadership, shares best practices, and speaks with a unified voice on national policy. Its members are the governors of the 50 states and 5 territories. The NGA bills itself as the collective voice of the nation's governors and one of Washington, DC's most respected public policy organizations. NGA provides governors and their senior staff members with services that range from representing states on Capitol Hill and before the administration on key federal issues to developing policy reports on innovative state programs and hosting networking seminars for state government executive branch officials. The NGA Center for Best Practices focuses on state innovations and best practices on issues that range from education and health to technology, welfare reform, and the environment. The NGA also provides management and technical assistance to both new and incumbent governors.

In August 2002, the Center for Best Practices of the NGA released "States' Homeland Security Priorities." A list of 10 major priorities and issues was identified by the NGA center through a survey of states' and territories' homeland security offices (NGA Center for Best Practices, 2002). These priorities clearly illustrated the main concerns of the state leadership in light of the massive changes that were occurring at the federal level and included the following:

- Coordination must involve all levels of government.
- The federal government must disseminate timely intelligence information to the states.

- The states must work with local governments to develop interoperable communications between first responders, and an adequate wireless spectrum must be set aside to do the job.
- State and local governments need help and technical assistance to identify and protect critical infrastructure.
- Both the states and federal government must focus on enhancing bioterrorism preparedness and rebuilding the nation's public health system to address twenty-first-century threats.
- The federal government should provide adequate federal funding and support to ensure that homeland security needs are met.
- The federal government should work with states to protect sensitive security information, including restricting access to information available through "freedom of information" requests.
- An effective system must be developed that secures points of entry at borders, airports, and seaports without placing an undue burden on commerce.
- The National Guard has proven itself to be an effective force during emergencies and crises. The mission of the National Guard should remain flexible, and Guard units should primarily remain under the control of the governor during times of crises.
- Federal agencies should integrate their command systems into existing state and local incident command systems (ICS) rather than requiring state and local agencies to adapt to federal command systems (NGA Center for Best Practices, Issue Brief, August 19, 2002).

The NGA Center for Best Practices (NGAC) provides support to the governors in their management of new homeland security challenges as they arise and the overall homeland security domain that exists as a result of September 11 attacks. NGAC provides these officials with technical assistance and policy research and facilitates their participation in national discussions and initiatives. Center activities focus on states' efforts to protect critical infrastructure, develop interoperable communications capabilities, and prepare for and respond to bioterrorism, agroterrorism, nuclear and radiological terrorism, and cyberterrorism (as it impacts the government's ability to obtain, disseminate, and store essential information). The NGA does recognize that, while terrorism must be a priority, natural and human-made disasters will continue to demand timely and coordinated responses from local, state, and federal government agencies.

In late 2013, the NGO Homeland Security and Public Safety Committee adopted a policy on Homeland Security and Emergency Management. This is presented in the sidebar "NGA Policy on Homeland Security and Public Safety."

NGA Policy on Homeland Security and Public Safety

Preamble

Providing for the safety and security of citizens is a high priority for governors. With the constantly evolving threat of terrorism and increased occurrences of natural disasters, governors must maintain and continually update state strategies to prevent, prepare for, respond to, and recover from emergencies. Protecting the public requires close coordination among all levels of government, as well as with the private sector. Governors offer the following recommendations to address several of today's homeland security and emergency management challenges.

Preparedness and Response: Principles

- National plans and strategies should be developed collaboratively between federal, state, and local governments.
- Any federal law requirements imposed upon the states should be properly funded.
- Federal agencies should proactively work with state resources, including the robust network of state and local fusion centers.
- States should have maximum flexibility in how grant funds are utilized and funds should be coordinated through the state.
- The federal government, in collaboration with states, should enhance efforts to secure critical infrastructure, transportation systems, and food supply chains, including increased use of advanced technology.

Disaster Assistance: Principles

- The Congress and the Administration should ensure that the Disaster Relief Fund has funds available to assist in response and recovery to federally declared disasters.

Cybersecurity: Principles

- The federal government should work with states to share threat information and to provide technical support to protect computer networks and other related critical infrastructure.

Immigration: Principles

- The federal government must fulfill its responsibility to secure the borders and enforce existing immigration laws.

NGA Survey

For 6 years, from 2004 to 2009, the NGA surveyed state homeland security advisors to capture the homeland security priorities of 56 states and territories. The state and territorial homeland security advisors collectively comprise the Governors Homeland Security Advisors Council. In 2007, the top five priorities for states were, in order, the following:

- Developing interoperable communications
- Coordinating state and local efforts
- Protecting critical infrastructure
- Developing state fusion centers
- Strengthening citizen preparedness

The survey also revealed that

- states continue to report unsatisfactory progress in their relationship with the federal government, specifically with the Department of Homeland Security (DHS);
- in the view of the states, federal homeland security grant programs are not adequately funded and do not strike an adequate balance among preparedness, prevention, response, and recovery;
- the majority of states said DHS should coordinate policies with the states prior to the release or implementation of those policies;
- states need federal funding to support personnel to implement and sustain initiatives that are national in scope but that are carried out locally;

- federal agencies should coordinate their security clearances to ensure that a clearance issued by one agency is recognized by other agencies;
- only about one-third of states have at least 75% of their National Guard forces available to respond to natural or man-made disasters;
- more than half the states have "significantly" involved local governments in the development of strategic plans, including grant funding allocation plans.

In 2010, the NGA released the results of the sixth and latest survey, which found that the five priorities that year included the following:

- Coordinating the efforts of state and local agencies
- Developing interoperable communications for emergency responders
- Identifying and protecting critical infrastructure
- Strengthening citizen preparedness
- Using exercises and simulations to improve preparedness

This shows very little change between 2007 and 2009. The survey also revealed the following:

- Due to the H1N1 pandemic, pandemic influenza preparedness reemerged as a priority after falling from the list of priorities in 2008.
- More than half of states had placed their homeland security operations within a broader cabinet-level department, and more than half of respondents had positioned their state's primary fusion center under the command of the homeland security director.
- Communications from DHS to the states continued to improve in 2009, with 98% of respondents reporting satisfaction with the information received from DHS. About two-thirds of respondents said they are satisfied with the timeliness of the intelligence they receive from the federal government.
- Seventy-five percent of respondents believed DHS should improve the grant allocation process and work with the Congress to permanently restore allowable management and administration funding to 5%.
- States reported that they were struggling to sustain their capabilities with the amount of grant funding that is available to them and are hoping for some relief from the administrative burdens that come with that funding.

Full results from the 2009 survey can be found at http://bit.ly/ZMbn2r.

Source: NGA (2013).

National Emergency Management Association

The National Emergency Management Association (NEMA) is a nonpartisan, nonprofit association that works to enhance public safety. NEMA is focused on the all-hazards approach to emergency management. NEMA began in 1974 when state directors of emergency services first united in order to exchange information on common emergency management issues in their constituencies. State emergency management directors form the core membership, but members also include key state staff, homeland security advisers, federal agencies, nonprofit organizations, private-sector companies, and concerned individuals.

NEMA's mission is to

- provide national leadership and expertise in comprehensive emergency management,
- serve as a vital emergency management information and assistance resource,
- advance continuous improvement in emergency management through strategic partnerships, innovative programs, and collaborative policy positions.

Following September 11, NEMA created the National Homeland Security Consortium, which includes key state and local organizations, elected officials, the private sector, and others with roles and responsibilities for homeland security prevention, preparedness, response, and recovery activities. Participating organizations began meeting in 2002, and today, there are 21 national-level organization members. The consortium is an outgrowth of those initial discussions regarding the need for enhanced communication and coordination between disciplines and levels of government. The consortium is now recognized by DHS and works in partnership with other federal agencies such as the Centers for Disease Control and Prevention. The mission of the consortium is to provide a forum wherein key ideas on homeland security can be shared among and between various levels of government. In 2011, the NHSC surveyed their members to track their homeland security priorities. The results of that research are found in the sidebar "2010–2011 National Homeland Security Consortium Member Priorities."

2010–2011 National Homeland Security Consortium Member Priorities

Adjutants General Association of the United States (AGAUS)

1. State control of domestic military operations (unity of effort)
2. More robust state-based chemical, biological, radiological, nuclear, and explosive response forces
3. End strength; full-time staff; trainees, transients, holdees, and students (TTHS) account
4. Personnel capacity, the need for nondeployable assets, and Army and Air Guard recapitalization
5. Military construction funding (despite having 22% of the facilities, the Guard only receives 8% of MilCon funding)

American Public Works Association (APWA)

1. Designate public works as a first responder
2. Disaster assistance (supporting an all-hazards approach to assistance)
3. Interoperable communications and D-Block allocation (D-Block refers to the 700 MHz band on the mobile wireless network, which has been explored as a possible solution for interoperable communications)
4. Protection of critical infrastructure systems
5. Cyber security (particularly the integration of cyber systems in public works GIS systems)

Council of State Governments (CSG)

1. Public safety communications (D-Block reallocation and development of standards)
2. Federal-state partnership for homeland security policy (consistent state and local input into federal decisions)

3. Sustained resources for state and local governments (shift of disaster costs to the state level)
4. Border security (enhanced international coordination and better port inspections)
5. PASS ID/REAL ID (develop alternatives to REAL ID)

Governors Homeland Security Advisors Council (GHSAC)

1. Coordinate the efforts of state and local agencies
2. Improve information sharing and fusion center coordination (includes FEMA regions and coordination with the DHS component agencies)
3. Interoperable communication for emergency responders with D-Block allocation and sustained grant funding
4. Identify and protect critical infrastructure
5. Strengthening citizen preparedness
6. Ensure the transition of new homeland security advisors

Association of State and Territorial Health Officials (ASTHO)

1. Fiscal Solvency (multiyear funding to prevent potential downfall of preparedness programs)
2. National Health Security Strategy (NHSS) implementation
3. Pandemic and All-Hazards Preparedness Act reauthorization
4. Public health performance measures
5. Completion of the emergency management cycle by ensuring inclusive after-action evaluations

International Association of Emergency Managers (IAEM-USA)

1. Support for local emergency management and leadership development
2. Emergency Management Performance Grant funding and stand-alone status
3. Full implementation of the Post-Katrina Emergency Management Reform Act (PKEMRA)
4. Coordinating Stafford Act amendments and reauthorization of mitigation programs
5. Support for the Emergency Management Institute

International Association of Fire Chiefs (IAFC)

1. Timely FEMA reimbursement to locals
2. D-Block allocation
3. Key Information sharing with first responders/fire service (resolve issues surrounding obtaining clearances)
4. Defining resilience at the local level
5. Clarifying the role of DoD in major disasters

International City/County Management Association (ICMA)

1. Recovery and response issues (specifically long-term recovery issues regarding surge capacity)
2. Financial constraints and capacity questions (including impact on essential services)
3. Cyber security
4. Immigration
5. D-Block allocation
6. Stafford Act amendments

Major City Chiefs (MCC)

1. D-Block allocation
2. Continued development of and sustained funding for the fusion center system

3. Nationwide implementation of Department of Justice-sponsored suspicious activity reporting system
4. Local law enforcement involvement in immigration enforcement
5. Continued erosion of local budgets of the National Association of Counties (NACo)

National Association of Counties (NACo)

1. Allocation of D-Block spectrum
2. Sustained funding by DHS for state and local programs
3. Long-term reauthorization of National Flood Insurance Program
4. Reauthorize Pre-Disaster Mitigation Grant program
5. Enact Comprehensive Immigration Reform

National Association of City and County Health Officials (NACCHO)

1. Strengthen local public health preparedness infrastructure (multiyear and sustained funding)
2. Develop evidence-based performance metrics for public health preparedness
3. Promote all-hazards preparedness
4. Strengthen public health preparedness workforce development
5. Build and strengthen community resilience

National Association of State EMS Officials (NASEMSO)

1. Base funding as opposed to sustained funding
2. EMS recognized as a healthcare professional official
3. Medicare reimbursement (specifically for ambulance providers)
4. Standardization of equipment, communications, and training by 2013
5. Recruitment and retention

National Conference of State Legislatures (NCSL)

1. D-Block reallocation
2. Immigration reform and REAL ID
3. Preservation of state authority to enforce chemical security standards
4. Funding for Homeland Security Grant Programs

National Emergency Management Association (NEMA)

1. Turnover of state emergency management directors and Homeland Security Advisors (HSA)
2. Establishment of performance measure for preparedness
3. Disaster declaration reform by the federal government
4. Critical infrastructure and systems interdependencies
5. Impact of changing weather patterns on emergency management

National Governors Association (NGA)

1. D-Block allocation
2. Council of governors—support to civil authorities recognized in legislation and DoD decisions
3. Fusion centers and information sharing (sustained funding and baseline capability review)
4. Cyber security
5. Grants administration, reporting, and performance measures
6. PASS ID (explore alternative way forward)

National League of Cities (NLC)

1. Hiring and funding for key local government employees and stabilized funding
2. Strengthen and stabilize the housing market and invest in transportation infrastructure
3. Support local energy efficiency and conservation efforts
4. D-Block allocation
5. Legislative reforms (Stafford Act and immigration)

Naval Postgraduate School (NPS)

1. Acceptance that "homeland security" is a permanent and pervasive component of our culture for the foreseeable future.
2. Prevention of terrorist acts deserves a "whole of governments" priority beyond law enforcement and federal agencies.
3. The era of selflessness and rallying to a common goal has waned in the years since 9/11.
4. "All hazards" and "all disasters are local" have become misleading concepts and create division between governments and disciplines.
5. What do we want the country to "look like" after the next attack or catastrophic incident and what is in place to realize that vision?

National Sheriffs' Association (NSA)

1. Support nationwide implementation of suspicious activity reports (SARS)
2. D-Block allocation and dedicated funding
3. Comprehensive Immigration Reform (including strong border security)
4. Federal funding for law enforcement (fusion centers and local jails that house illegal immigrants)
5. Medical Countermeasures Programs (distribution issues)

US Chamber of Commerce

1. Cyber security (currently developing a guide due to the Fall of 2011)
2. Global supply chain security (and how it affects national security while keeping trade moving)
3. Emergency Preparedness and Response (ensure members have the tools to know what to do in the event of an attack)
4. Chemical security
5. Critical infrastructure protection (including improvements to information sharing)

Business Executives for National Security (BENS)

1. Cyber security
2. Global supply chain security (working with DoD to encourage private sector engagement)

Source: NEMA (2011).

International Association of Emergency Managers

The International Association of Emergency Managers (IAEM) is a nonprofit organization dedicated to promoting the goals of saving lives and protecting property during emergencies and disasters. Founded in 1952 as the US Civil Defense Council, it became the National Coordinating Council on Emergency Management in 1985 and changed its name to the IAEM in 1998.

The association brings together emergency managers and disaster response professionals from all levels of government, as well as the military, the private sector, and volunteer organizations in the United States and around the world. The purpose of IAEM is to serve the emergency management community by

- encouraging the development of disaster-resistant communities to reduce the effect of disasters on life and property,
- acting as a clearinghouse for information on comprehensive management issues,
- providing a forum for creative and innovative problem solving on emergency management issues,
- maintaining and expanding standards for emergency management programs and professionals,
- fostering informed decision making on public policy in the emergency management arena.

The IAEM often issues policy briefs that relay the position of the nation's and the world's emergency managers about salient issues being debated or considered in the Congress.

Homeland Security Activity of State and Tribal Governments

Each governor is responsible for overseeing and ensuring the prevention of hazard risk within that state, including the assessment of threats and vulnerability, the mitigation of hazard risks, the funding and coordination of local offices of emergency management, and the coordination with federal emergency management agencies and entities. The governor is also tasked with leading the state's response to any emergency or disaster and must therefore take an active role in ensuring that other state officials and agencies are able to address these many hazards and ongoing challenges.

During a disaster event, the governor will likely take on a number of roles, including the state's principal source of information to the public. This might include the issuance of evacuations, details about the scope of the disaster, and availability of assistance. Governors command the state's National Guard resources and maintain the authority to mobilize them in times of disaster (as stipulated by Title 32 of the US Code). During disasters, it is the responsibility of the governor to assess the need for a disaster declaration and to make that request to the president and/or mutual aid partners if such a determination for need is made.

The state or territorial government itself is tasked with coordinating the activity of cities, counties, and intrastate regions. States administer federal homeland security grants to local and tribal (in certain grant programs) governments, allocating key resources to bolster their prevention and preparedness capabilities. Several state agencies and offices are tasked with ensuring the enforcement of state and federal law and for carrying out other security activities. State government agencies have expanded their roles with regard to the homeland security function since 9/11 as many key components of critical infrastructure, as well as key resources, exist or are maintained at the state level. Moreover, because many risk reduction and other emergency management/homeland security programs are coordinated and funded at the state level, the state government is tasked with providing the necessary direction and guidance for these efforts. During actual disaster events, states must often mobilize their various response resources, as stipulated in the state emergency plan, and help to coordinate federal and other resources as they are provided.

Like governors, tribal leaders are responsible for the public safety and welfare of their membership. They can serve as both key decision makers and trusted sources of public information during incidents. Tribal governments, which have a special status under federal laws and treaties, ensure the provision of essential services to members within their communities and are responsible for developing emergency response and mitigation plans. Tribal governments may coordinate resources and capabilities with neighboring jurisdictions and establish mutual aid agreements with other tribal governments, local jurisdictions, and state governments. Depending on location, land base, and resources, tribal governments provide law enforcement, fire, and emergency services as well as public safety to their members.

A good indicator of the manner in which each of the state governments approaches the terrorism issue is the priorities set by their emergency managers. A survey of state homeland security structures by NEMA conducted in June 2002 found that all 50 states maintain primary point of contact for antiterrorism/homeland security efforts. At that time, these contacts were located in the following state government offices:

- Governor/Lieutenant Governor's office—14 states
- Military/adjutant general—12 states
- Public safety/law enforcement—12 states
- Office of Homeland Security/Emergency Management—10 states
- Attorney general—2 states
- Land commissioner—1 state (National Conference of State Legislatures, 2005)

In January 2008, these numbers had changed significantly, reflecting an approach that gave much more weight to homeland security as a stand-alone function in the overall context of state government affairs. Many states had even created dedicated homeland security offices. These figures were as follows:

- Office of Homeland Security/Emergency Management—34 states
- Military/adjutant general—8 states
- Public safety/law enforcement—7 states
- Governor's office—2 states

However, by August 2011, possibly as a result of shrinking budgets or because of the changing nature of homeland security and emergency management (especially with regard to the nature of natural versus terrorist-based threats), there was a major reversal in the trends toward state government homeland security structuring. The trend continues, and as of November 2014, NEMA tracked the state homeland security and emergency management directorship positionings as follows (not all states listed):

- Governor's Office—8 states and 1 territory (Alabama, Florida, Georgia, Illinois, Louisiana, Mississippi, Oklahoma, Pennsylvania, and the Northern Marianna Islands)
- Military/adjutant general—17 states and 1 territory (Alaska, Arizona, Hawaii, Idaho, Iowa, Kansas, Kentucky, Maine, Maryland, Montana, Nebraska, North Dakota, Oregon, Rhode Island, South Carolina, Tennessee, Washington, Wisconsin, and the US Virgin Islands)
- Combined Office of Homeland Security and Emergency Management—7 states, 3 territories, and the District of Columbia (Arkansas, California, Connecticut, District of Columbia, Indiana, Louisiana, New Mexico, New York, American Samoa, Guam, and the US Virgin Islands)
- Office of Public Safety—14 states (Colorado, Massachusetts, Minnesota, Missouri, Nevada, New Hampshire, North Carolina, Ohio, South Dakota, Texas, Utah, Vermont, Virginia, and West Virginia)
- State Police—2 states (Michigan and New Jersey) (NEMA, 2014a)

Shrinking budgets have been a major concern of state directors of homeland security, who feel that the task of preparing for hazards and maintaining national security is causing incredible strain on state budgets. NEMA reports that the FY 2014 operating budgets for state emergency management were as large as $50 million, though the average was $6.1 million and the median $2.9 million. This amount was a reduction from the FY 2009 median of $3,406,500. In 2014, 39 states received 60% or more of their homeland security funding from federal dollars. On average, states depend on federal funding for approximately 76% of their homeland security capability (NEMA, 2014b).

Local Government Homeland Security Activities

Like their counterpart governors at the state level, mayors and other local elected and appointed officials (such as city managers) are responsible for ensuring the public safety and welfare of their residents. Local chief elected officials serve as their jurisdiction's chief communicator and a primary source of information for homeland security-related information and ensure their governments are able to carry out emergency response activities. They are typically the key decision makers in times of disaster as stipulated in the local emergency operations plan.

The local government manages a number of key government functions, many of which pertain directly to emergency management and homeland security. These include, for example, law enforcement, fire safety and suppression, public safety, environmental response, public health, and emergency medical services. In times of disaster, this role is put to the forefront as the local government maintains operational control of incidents in accordance with the US federal system of government.

Through individual cooperation, as well as support by other state and federal programs (such as the UASI program), cities and counties address multijurisdictional planning and operations, equipment support and purchasing, and training and exercises in support of high-threat, high-density urban areas. Federal grant money helps local governments to build and sustain their homeland security capabilities. Local governments coordinate resources and capabilities during disasters with neighboring jurisdictions, NGOs, the state, and the private sector.

County leaders serve as chief operating officers of county governments, in a fashion similar to what exists at the local level. The role of the county (or parish in the case of Louisiana) changes from state to state. This role typically includes supporting and enabling the county governments to fulfill their responsibilities to constituents, including public safety and security. County governments provide frontline leadership for local law enforcement, fire, public safety, environmental response, public health, and emergency medical services for all manner of hazards and emergencies. County governments coordinate resources and capabilities during disasters with neighboring jurisdictions, NGOs, the state, and the private sector. (Note that Connecticut and Massachusetts counties maintain almost no governmental functions.)

Emergency preparedness, mitigation, response, and recovery all occur at the local community level. It is at the local level that the critical planning, communications, technology, coordination, command, and spending decisions matter the most. The priorities of groups such as the US Conference of Mayors and the National Association of Counties are to represent these very concerns shared by local communities about what is necessary for them to become resilient from the threat of terrorism. The drive toward a reduction in vulnerability from terrorism has spawned a series of new requirements in preparedness and mitigation planning for most local-level officials that, prior to September 11, rarely considered such issues.

Policy papers by both NACo and the USCM identified issues in the areas of command, coordination, communications, funding and equipment, training, and mutual aid. These two organizations recognized and relayed the local concerns about protecting critical community infrastructure, including the public health system, most of which is maintained and secured at the local level by local government law enforcement, fire, and health officials.

The September 11 events brought to the surface the notion that the security of community infrastructure, which was suddenly recognized as a potential target for terrorist attacks, was vital to the security of the nation as a whole. Community infrastructure has always been vulnerable to natural and other technological disaster events—so much so that FEMA's largest disaster assistance program, Public Assistance, is designed to fund the rebuilding of community infrastructure damaged by a disaster event. However, local government officials and local emergency managers were suddenly finding themselves dedicating a greatly increased amount of funding and personnel to protecting and securing community infrastructure from the increased threat of terrorist attack. They have also had to boost the abilities of the local public health system, which has been recognized by the federal government as the most likely area where an outbreak caused by a bioterrorism agent will be identified.

To illustrate several of the new issues that local governments, most notably the smaller, rural governments, have had to consider in light of the new terrorist threat, the following checklist designed for the City of Boone, North Carolina, is provided. This checklist is excerpted from that municipality's technological annex developed for the town's All-Hazards Planning and Operations Manual:

- Identify the types of terrorist events that might occur in the community
- Plan emergency activities in advance to ensure a coordinated response to terrorist attacks
- Build capabilities necessary to respond effectively to the consequences of terrorism
- Identify the type or nature of a terrorist attack when it does happen
- Implement the planned response quickly and efficiently
- Recover from the incident

The response to terrorism is similar in many ways to that of other natural or human-made disasters for which Boone has already prepared. Through additions and modifications, the development of a completely separate system could be avoided. Training and public education have been vital to enhancing preparedness, and understanding the process by which available federal financial assistance is acquired has drastically increased local capacity. The general types of activities that Boone has needed to take to meet the above-mentioned objectives follow:

- Strengthen information and communications technology
- Establish a well-defined incident command structure that includes the FBI.
- Strengthen local working relationships and communications
- Educate health-care and emergency response communities about identification of bioterrorist attacks and agents
- Educate health-care and emergency response communities about medical treatment and prophylaxis for possible biological agents
- Educate local health department about state and federal requirements and assistance
- Maintain locally accessible supply of medications, vaccines, and supplies
- Address health-care worker safety issues
- Designate a spokesperson to maintain contact with the public
- Develop comprehensive evacuation plans
- Become familiar with state and local laws relating to isolation/quarantine
- Develop or enhance local capability to prosecute crimes involving WMD or the planning of terrorism events
- Develop, maintain, and practice an infectious diseases' emergency response plan
- Practice with surrounding jurisdictions to strengthen mutual agreement plans
- Outline the roles of federal agency assistance in planning and response

- Educate the public in recognizing events and ways to respond as individuals
- Stay current (Town of Boone, All-Hazards Planning and Operations Manual, Technological Hazards Annex. Boone, NC: Town of Boone, March 2007)

Critical Thinking

Terrorism prevention and preparedness have added significant strain to already stretched local budgets. Do you feel that the local governments should determine their risk and act accordingly, or should they be expected to prescribe a minimum level of preparedness regardless of the effect it has on other local programs that may suffer as a result of budget reallocations?

Role of Private Sector in Homeland Security and Changes in Business Continuity and Contingency Planning

The September 11 terrorist attacks affected thousands of private businesses, not just businesses in New York or near the Pentagon, but businesses that were as far away as Hawaii and Seattle. The attacks killed nearly 3000 people, most of whom were employees of private corporations that had offices in or near the World Trade Center (WTC). Some companies lost hundreds of employees. In downtown Manhattan, almost 34.5 million square feet of office space was destroyed. Totaling \$50 billion to \$70 billion in insured losses, the WTC attack became one of the costliest disasters in US history. Most of these direct economic losses were incurred by the private sector. In addition to the physical resources and systems lost by businesses in the WTC, changes in public behavior following the attacks had a severe impact on travel, tourism, and other businesses. Because the biggest portion of the impact was absorbed by the private sector, the September 11 attacks were a sudden wake-up call for disaster preparedness, business continuity planning, and corporate crisis management.

The changes in private-sector disaster preparedness after September 11 can be analyzed from two perspectives: (1) the direct involvement of the private sector in disaster preparedness and response in coordination with the DHS and as foreseen by the NRF and the NIMS and (2) the self-reassessment of the private sector in terms of corporate crisis management and business continuity as a competitive requirement as opposed to cost of business. Our reference point in addressing the changing expectations of the federal government from the private sector will be several major federal documents and strategies, such as the National Strategy for Homeland Security and official press releases from relevant departments and agencies. While addressing the change of internal processes and procedures among the private sector, we will refer to publications and press releases that address changes in particular companies and try to find general trends between different approaches.

Expectations of DHS from the Private Sector

The National Strategy for Homeland Security defines the basic approach of DHS and briefly describes the characteristics of the partnership the department is planning to achieve with the private sector. Given the fact that almost 85% of the infrastructure of the United States is owned or managed by the private sector, there is no doubt that the private sector must be included as a major stakeholder in homeland security. Reducing the vulnerabilities and securing the private sector means the same as securing the vast portion of US infrastructure and economic viability.

According to the National Strategy for Homeland Security, a close partnership between the government and private sectors is essential in ensuring that existing vulnerabilities of critical infrastructures to terrorism are identified and eliminated as quickly as possible. The private sector is expected to conduct risk assessments on their holdings and invest in systems to protect key assets. The internalization of these costs is interpreted by the DHS as not only a matter of sound corporate governance and good corporate citizenship but also an essential safeguard of economic assets for shareholders, employees, and the nation.

The National Strategy for the Physical Protection of Critical Infrastructure and Key Assets provides more direct clues about what the DHS expects from the private sector as a partner and stakeholder in homeland security. The strategy defines the private sector as the owner and operator of the bulk of US critical infrastructures and key assets and mentions that private-sector firms prudently engage in risk management planning and invest in security as a necessary function of business operations and customer confidence. Moreover, since in the present threat environment the private sector generally remains the first line of defense for its own facilities, the DHS expects private-sector owners and operators to reassess and adjust their planning, assurance, and investment programs to better accommodate the increased risk presented by deliberate acts of violence (Figure 4-11).

Since the September 11 events, many businesses have increased their threshold investments and undertaken enhancements in security in an effort to meet the demands of the new threat environment. For most enterprises, the level of investment in security reflects implicit risk-versus-consequence trade-offs, which are based on (1) what is known about the risk environment, (2) what is economically justifiable and sustainable in a competitive marketplace or in an environment of limited government resources, (3) potential consequences of disasters, and (4) priorities for the protection of human capital, processes, physical infrastructure, organizational reputation, stakeholder confidence, and vital records that require immediate attention. Given the dynamic nature of the terrorist threat and the severity of the consequences associated with many potential attack scenarios, the private sector naturally looks to the government for better information to help make its crucial security investment decisions. The private sector is continuing to look for better data, analysis, and assessment from DHS to use in the corporate decision-making process.

Similarly, the private sector looks to the government for assistance when the threat at hand exceeds an enterprise's capability to protect itself beyond a reasonable level of additional investment. In this light, the federal government promises to collaborate with the private sector (and state and local governments) to ensure the protection of nationally critical infrastructures and assets; provide timely warning and ensure the protection of infrastructures and assets that face a specific, imminent threat; and promote an environment in which the private sector can better carry out its specific protection responsibilities.

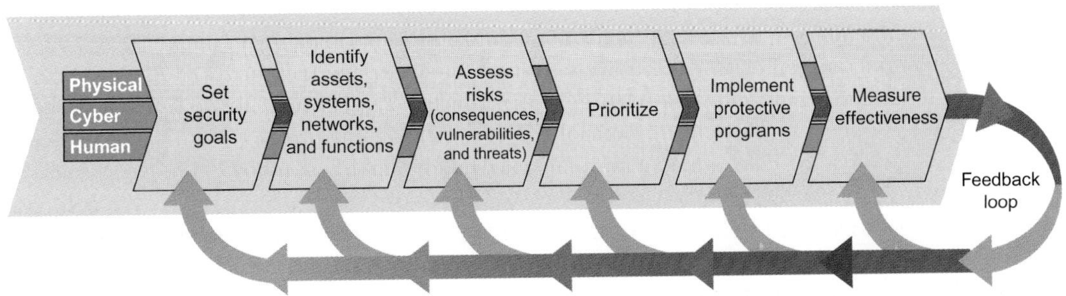

FIGURE 4-11 Operational framework for critical infrastructure and key assets protection. *Source: National Infrastructure Protection Plan.*

A good example of partnership between the private sector and DHS is the sectoral Information Sharing and Analysis Centers (ISACs). ISACs are established by the owners and operators of a national critical infrastructure to better protect their networks, systems, and facilities within the coordination of DHS. ISACs serve as central points to gather, analyze, sanitize, and disseminate private-sector information to both the industry and DHS. These centers also analyze and distribute information received from DHS to the private sector. The objectives of this program are to seek participation from all sector segments/entities, representation of all segments on ISAC advisory board in order to establish a two-way, trusted information sharing program between ISAC entities and DHS and to provide cleared industry expertise to assist DHS in evaluating threats and incidents. Currently, ISACs exist and are being created in a variety of critical infrastructure sectors. The DHS document that defines the relationships between the private sector and DHS is the 2013 National Infrastructure Protection Plan (NIPP). This document defines mechanisms that serve to build those relationships and create a system where the government and private entities can work in harmony to achieve a higher level of protection for critical infrastructures and key resources of the United States. Table 4-2 gives a list of operating ISACs, their ISAC title, and their purpose.

Table 4-2 Operating Status of Sectoral ISACs as of 2008

Sector	ISAC	Function
Aviation	A-ISAC	Provides an aviation-focused information sharing and analysis function to help protect aviation businesses, operations, and services globally. Analyzes and shares timely, relevant, and actionable information as it pertains to threats, vulnerabilities, and incidents
Financial services	DIB-ISAC	Created to secure the DIB supply chain from hazard risks and to provide assistance in responding to and recovery from manmade and natural disasters
Financial services	FS-ISAC	An industry forum for collaboration on critical security threats facing the financial services sector. Members receive timely notification and authoritative information specifically designed to help protect critical systems and assets from physical and cyber security threats
Real estate	RE-ISAC	Works with government officials to prevent, detect, and respond to terrorist threats and malicious incidents. RS-ISAC is a nonprofit organization and a public-private partnership between the US real estate industry and federal homeland security officials
Water	Water-ISAC	Keeps drinking water and wastewater utility managers informed about potential risks to the nation's water infrastructure from contamination, terrorism, and cyber threats and helps utilities respond to and recover from all hazards
Oil and natural gas	ONG-ISAC	The central reservoir of cyber threat information for the oil and natural gas industry. It protects the industry's exploration and production, transportation, refining, and delivery systems from cyber-attacks through the analysis and sharing of timely and trusted cyber intelligence
Emergency services	EMR-ISAC	To collect and analyze critical infrastructure protection and resilience information having potential relevance for Emergency Services Sector departments and agencies and to synthesize and disseminate the information to leaders, owners, and operators of the emergency services
Electricity	ES-ISAC	Facilitates communications between electricity sector participants, federal governments, and other critical infrastructures and promptly disseminates threat indications, analyses, and warnings, together with interpretations, to assist electricity sector participants take protective actions

(Continued)

Table 4-2 (Continued)

Sector	ISAC	Function
Maritime	Maritime ISAC	A nonprofit, member-driven organization representing ocean carriers, cruise lines, port facilities and terminals, logistics providers, importers, exporters, and related maritime industries. Its mission is to advance the security of the United States and the international maritime community by representing maritime interests before government bodies; acting as liaison between industry and government; disseminating timely information; encouraging and assisting in the development of industry-specific technologies; and convening educational and informational conferences for our membership and government partners
State and local government	MS-ISAC	The Multi-State Information Sharing and Analysis Center (MS-ISAC) is a collaborative state and local government-focused cyber security entity that is significantly enhancing cyber threat prevention, protection, and response, and recovery. Its mission is to provide a common mechanism for raising the level of cyber security readiness and response in each state/territory and with local governments. The MS-ISAC provides a central resource for gathering information on cyber threats to critical infrastructure and providing two-way sharing of information between and among the states and territories and with local government
Information technology	IT-SAC	A community of specialists dedicated to protecting information technology infrastructure by identifying threats and vulnerabilities and sharing best practices on how to quickly and properly address them. IT-ISAC also communicates with other sector specific ISACs, enabling members to understand physical threats, in addition to cyber-based threats
National health care	NH-ISAC	Protects the nation's health-care and public health critical infrastructure against security threats and vulnerabilities; its mission is to ensure and preserve the public trust by advancing the integrity and cybersecurity protection of the nation's health care and public health sector's critical infrastructure
Nuclear energy	NEI	The Nuclear Energy Institute (NEI) is the policy organization of the nuclear energy and technologies industry and participates in both the national and global policymaking process. NEI's objective is to ensure the formation of policies that promote the beneficial uses of nuclear energy and technologies in the United States and abroad
Research and education	REN-ISAC	Aids and promotes cyber security operational protection and response within the higher education and research (R&E) communities. Also serves as the R&E trusted partner for served networks, the formal US ISAC community, and in other commercial, governmental, and private security information sharing relationships
Public transit	PT-ISAC	Provides its constituency a 24/7 security operating capability that establishes the sector's specific information/intelligence requirements for incidences, threats, and vulnerabilities. It collects, analyzes, and disseminates alerts and incident reports to members. PT-ISAC also helps government agencies understand impacts for their sector
Supply chain	SC-ISAC	Offers the most comprehensive forum for collaboration on critical security threats, incidents, and vulnerabilities to the global supply chain. Its mission is to facilitate communication among supply chain dependent industry stakeholders, foster a partnership between the private and public sectors to share critical information, collect, analyze and disseminate actionable intelligence to help secure the global supply chain, and provide an international perspective through private sector subject matter experts and help protect US critical infrastructure
Surface transportation	ST-ISAC	Provides a secure cyber and physical security capability for owners, operators, and users of critical infrastructure. Security and threat information is collected from worldwide resources and then analyzed and distributed to members to help protect their vital systems from attack

Source: National Council of ISACs (2014).

As mentioned earlier, the primary building block of this relationship is the formation of sectoral ISACs, which promote the coordination, cooperation, best practices, lessons learned, information flow, and information sharing among sector-specific entities. The NIPP defines another coordination body for the achievement of the public-private integration. Those coordinating bodies are called Critical Infrastructure and Key Resources Sector Coordinating Councils. They are private-sector coordinating mechanisms that comprise private-sector infrastructure owners and operators and supporting associations, as appropriate. Sector coordinating councils bring together the entire range of infrastructure protection activities and issues to a single entity.

The roles of the sector coordinating councils are to identify, establish, and support the information sharing mechanisms (ISMs) that are most effective for their sector, drawing on existing mechanisms (e.g., ISACs) or creating new ones as required. The NIPP also creates Critical Infrastructure and Key Resources Government Coordinating Councils, which are government coordinating councils for each sector composed of representatives from DHS, the sector-specific agency (SSA), and the appropriate supporting federal departments and agencies. The government coordinating councils work with and support the efforts of the sector coordinating councils to plan, implement, and execute sufficient and necessary broad-based sector security, planning, and information sharing to support the nation's homeland security mission.

As indicated by the NIPP, the private sector will be engaged by DHS, in collaboration with the relevant SSAs, to promote awareness of and feedback on the NIPP framework and to solicit their involvement in the national CIP program. The private sector will also be working with the appropriate SSAs to begin implementation of the sector-specific plans (SSPs) for their sectors. As the interim NIPP is implemented, the private sector will be provided with more coordinated data calls from government agencies, enhanced engagement through sector coordinating councils, and subsequent versions of the NIPP, and SSPs will reflect discussions among DHS, the SSAs, and other stakeholders, including the private sector. The NIPP serves as a guide for the private sector to identify and implement the procedures to protect the critical infrastructure against specific threats and the general threat environment. There are five major goals identified in the plan:

- Assess and analyze threats to, vulnerabilities of, and consequences to critical infrastructure to inform risk management activities.
- Secure critical infrastructure against human, physical, and cyber threats through sustainable efforts to reduce risk while accounting for the costs and benefits of security investments.
- Enhance critical infrastructure resilience by minimizing the adverse consequences of incidents through advance planning and mitigation efforts and employing effective responses to save lives and ensure the rapid recovery of essential services.
- Share actionable and relevant information across the critical infrastructure community to build awareness and enable risk-informed decision making.

Promote learning and adaptation during and after exercises and incidents. These goals are to be achieved using the critical infrastructure risk management framework as defined by the NIPP.

DHS has acknowledged that it is well known that effective protection of the critical infrastructure in the United States is only achievable through direct involvement of and strong partnership with the private sector. The private sector not only is an integral part of the national infrastructure protection effort but also lies in the center of all protection strategies designed by DHS. That said, DHS is responsible for creating the environment where public- and private-sector entities talk to each other and work together to achieve a well-established national goal. Understanding the needs of each sector, building trust among officials and decision makers, making plausible assumptions, and setting realistic milestones are all key success factors. The real challenge is addressing cross sectoral vulnerabilities due to interdependencies where involvement of multiple sectors is necessary for sustainable protection of a critical infrastructure and creation of realistic recovery objectives and procedures. Creation of cross sectoral vulnerability assessment teams and utilization of multiple-sector expertise are critical to successfully plan for contingencies that may simultaneously hit interdependent critical infrastructures.

Corporate Crisis Management, Business Continuity, and Contingency Planning: The New Cost of Doing Business

September 11 was the most devastating day in modern history for American corporations. The attack in New York City was a direct attack on not only the symbols of corporate America but also the businesses themselves. The private sector lost human resources, expertise, buildings, office space, data, records, and revenue. Some of these losses were irreplaceable, such as people. The affected companies also suffered time-dependent and continuous losses such as business interruption, loss of customer trust, and employee loyalty. The property and human losses could not have been prevented because the private sector itself could not have stopped the hijacked planes from crashing into the towers. However, effective corporate crisis management and business continuity planning absolutely could have, and in many places did, minimize the continuous losses.

To put this discussion in perspective, the statistics and charts shown in Figure 4-12 illustrate the vulnerability of the private sector in terms of terrorist actions. The Department of State report Patterns of Global Terrorism reports on the total number of facilities struck by international terrorist attacks. The statistics show attacks with respect to the year they occurred and the type of facility struck (e.g., private sector, government, diplomatic, or military). These figures are important because they show changing trends in the types of facilities terrorists have chosen to attack. There is a common belief that terrorists are more likely to attack military and government facilities, because of the stated political ideologies of the terrorist groups. However, the facts prove this theory wrong. In actuality, it is the soft-target private-sector facilities that have most commonly been victimized by the scourge of terrorism.

Clearly, a reduction in the number of attacks on businesses worldwide occurred after 2001. This reduction may be attributable to several factors that have changed since that time. One of these factors is the increased global effort to reduce terrorist acts. This effort is primarily led by the United States and its allies, which are the most likely targets but which also have spent billions on preventing such attacks. As terror cells become more and more international and decentralized, international cooperation and intelligence sharing become critical to prevent acts of terrorism. Since 2001, significant amounts of resources have been allocated to achieve this goal, and this may serve as a contributing factor to the reduced number of terrorist attacks.

However, the preceding explanation does not account for why the reduction in the total number of attacks to businesses is steeper compared to other potential targets. As seen in Figure 4-12, the number of terrorist attacks aimed at businesses was reduced from 408 in 2001, to 122 in 2002, to 93 in 2003, whereas such reductions were not as significant for diplomatic facilities, government buildings, or military or other facilities.

Businesses have historically been targets of terrorists primarily because they have been perceived as soft targets that are easier to attack and minimally protected. After the 9/11 attacks, the vulnerability of businesses to disasters such as terrorism became obvious. Businesses learned through tragic experience that they constitute a potential target for terrorists. So they began to invest more into their security, risk management, crisis management, and business continuity programs. Research shows that all sophisticated terrorists carefully observe their prospective targets before deciding on their actual target.

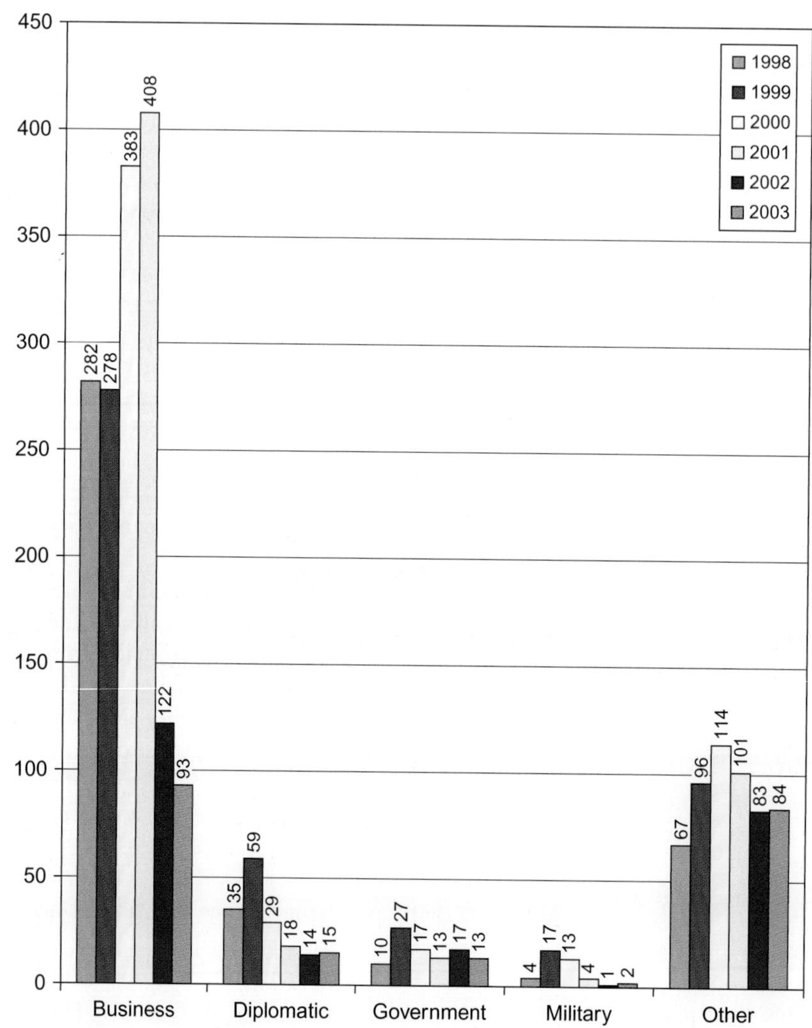

FIGURE 4-12 Total facilities attacked by terrorists (worldwide), 1998–2003. *Source: Department of State (2003).*

Another Voice: Safety and Security Concerns in the Private Sector

Security in Public Versus Private Sectors

The phone rang at 15 min before 3 am. It was January 26, 2007. Sound asleep, I instinctively reached for my phone, wondering who could be calling at this hour. It was little surprise to me that it was my boss on the line. He was notifying me that an explosion had just occurred outside the entrance of one of our hotels in South Asia. An unidentified man attempted to penetrate hotel security. Strapped with a homemade explosive device, he was confronted by our guards who prevented access to the property. A scuffle ensued and the bomber detonated the device. The security guard was killed instantly alongside the bomber and seven bystanders were injured.

Through the system we had established years earlier, all of our crisis management team members were on a conference call within 15 min. We concluded the conference call an hour later with tasks assigned to each member. The team convened again a few hours later to report on their assignments. Since the damage to the hotel's building structure was minimal, the hotel was able to resume its normal operations later that day. Later, a relief fund was set up to help the deceased employee's family.

This is an example of one of those phone calls you do not wish to receive, regardless of the time of day. A phone call like this precipitates a crisis lasting anywhere from 1 day to several weeks. Everyone in the security department will be tested dealing with this on a 24-h basis. It is our employee, our company, our reputation, after all.

There is little distinction between the security responsibilities of government agencies and private sector entities. Both protect people, facilities, assets, and reputation. However, the ramifications are far more complex for the private sector when it comes to dealing with the aftermath of a crisis. When working in the government sector, there is little concern about the stock performance, shareholders, a potential increase in insurance premiums, public relations disasters, or lawsuits by customers. These elements can be extremely challenging for someone who makes the decision to cross over into the private sector.

In a corporate crisis environment, pressure comes from many areas. It most often manifests itself from stockholders, legal advisors, consultants, rank-and-file employees, customers, and, naturally, competitors. Everyone is a stakeholder.

If FEMA had been a privately owned company and its directors performed in much the same manner that they did during Hurricane Katrina, FEMA's stock would have plunged and no insurance company would have dared to insure them again. Senior executives in the parent company (which would be the Department of Homeland Security in this example) and its board of directors would have fired them all, and needless to say, the PR department would have their own crisis trying to mitigate the negative publicity.

The Hurricane Katrina story could have been very different if it had been handled in an effective and efficient manner. When such disasters occur, mass evacuations and major rescue operations require extensive efforts. In this case, government waste was rampant and communication between agencies broke down. Politics obfuscated good judgment. Conversely, a private company has to be self-sufficient. Its contingency plans need to cover all aspects from start to finish. If a private company fails to manage a crisis effectively, profits will plunge, customers will not return, stock holders will sell, and the company will eventually go under.

Private companies have to have a strategic focus, think ahead, and prepare resources. They should assess the situation from the perspective of each stakeholder. Hurricane plans should include shelters both inside and outside of the facility, prenegotiated contracts with chartered airlines, and supplies such as food, beds, and toilets. Having these plans and provisions in place will boost customer confidence, increase business, please shareholders, and drive revenue. Everyone is happy.

Another aspect to consider is that many companies are global, thereby expanding the horizon and adding more elements to the crisis plan. Different parts of the world involve various kinds of threats that might not exist in corporate America. Wars, government instability, foreign languages, customs, laws, and restrictions need to be considered and evaluated in order to allow for fast and seamless reaction during a crisis.

A private company's plan needs to be all-encompassing, including preventative methods as well as solutions. A comprehensive review of the business continuity plan is always needed after a crisis comes to an end.

Last but not least, cooperation from company executives is the key. Without it, no crisis plan can function as they always require top-down support, money, time, and resources.

Jack Suwanlert, Director—International Loss Prevention, Marriott International Inc.

Corporate Security

Terrorists often select targets they consider to be soft—that is, those that are easy to hit. Therefore, it is not only the operational benefits gained by corporate security programs but also their visibility that serves as a deterrent for terrorists. For example, if a terrorist organization aims to damage a country's tourism sector, it may attempt to detonate a bomb in a hotel. As terrorists determine which hotel to attack, they will likely consider several alternatives and select that which has the least visible security. Overall, business sector preparedness is much greater today than it was in 2001, which is one obvious explanation for why attacks on business targets have decreased. This reduction can be attributed to businesses "hardening" themselves against their former "soft-target" image.

Another factor that is changing private-sector perceptions is insurance and losses. The Insurance Information Institute has plotted the distribution of different types of insured damages from the September 11 attacks and it presents some interesting facts (see Figure 4-13). The most notable figure in this graph is the amount of damage from business interruption: $9.8 billion (30% of all estimated damage). This is

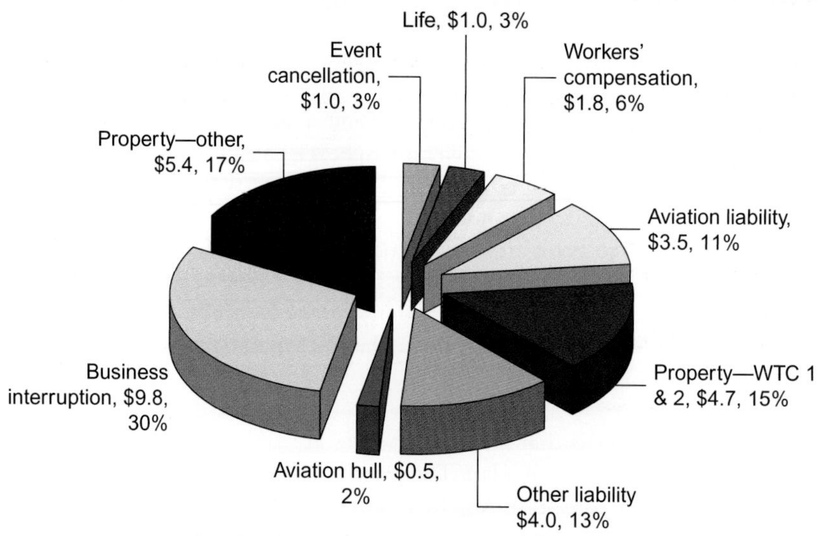

FIGURE 4-13 September 11, 2001, distribution of losses by insurance type ($ in billions). *Source: Hartwig (2014).*

a significant portion of the damage, one over which we have some degree of control if adequate business impact analysis and business continuity planning activities can be established before the crisis. One needs to remember that despite significant losses in the 2001 attack, due to the 1993 WTC bombing and the potential Y2K threat, private-sector members located inside the WTC complex were among the more prepared stakeholders compared to private organizations in other parts of the nation.

Insurance companies are taking into account the existence of preparedness programs as they calculate the premiums and business interruption insurance coverage for private corporations. Due to the heavy losses they incurred after 9/11, insurance companies looked for ways to limit their exposure to potential future catastrophic losses caused by acts of terrorism. Since reinsurers were also hit hard with the costly claims of 9/11, one option was to exclude terrorism coverage completely from the portfolio of available insurance product. At this point, the US government intervened and passed the Terrorism Risk Insurance Act of 2002 (TRIA). This act essentially mandated enrolled insurance companies to offer terrorism insurance, and in exchange, the US government would backstop any potential losses with reinsurances as long as certain criteria were met. The act was designed as a temporary provision to the insurance industry until it figures out a feasible way to offer terrorism insurance and was initially set to expire by the end of 2005. However, the act was amended in both 2005 and 2007, extending its current benefits to consumers until 2014. In July of 2014, the Senate voted to extend the provisions of this act until the end of 2021, but at the time of publication, the House of Representatives had not yet passed the bill.

The latest version of the act is governed by the following rules:

- The insurance companies enrolled have to make terrorism insurance available to all commercial customers if demanded. The customers may opt to exclude terrorism if they wish to reduce the premiums of their insurance coverage.
- The definition of an "act of terrorism" is that of the secretary of treasury.
- The US government is ensuring assistance to the industry of up to $100 billion a year for terrorism-related insurance claims for which the program trigger criteria have been met.
- For a specific incident to qualify for protection by the US government, the combined losses of the incident should exceed $100 million (in the new bill, non-CBRN events would need to see over $500 million in losses).
- The insurance companies agree to pay up to 15% of the direct earned premium for each year per claim before federal assistance becomes available. The government agrees to pay 85% of the portion of the claim that exceeds the insurer's deductibles (in the new bill, insurers would pay a co-pay of 20% for non-CBRN incidents).

With the launch of the Terrorism Risk Insurance Act, in a sense, the US government agreed to act as a reinsurer of insurance companies by guaranteeing to absorb a significant amount of losses after terrorist incidents that qualify to trigger the program. The most significant change in this legislation came in 2007, when lawmakers added "domestic" terrorism events to those that are eligible for coverage (Government Accountability Office, 2004; NCCI, 2015).

The "Another Voice" section by Jack Suwanlert provides a comparison of how security is handled differently by public and private entities.

Other Homeland Security Structures

The maintenance of a safe and secure nation depends upon the actions and activities of many more organizations and individuals than those associated with government (as detailed in the preceding text of this chapter). The role of these "other" organizations has been known for quite some time but was officially recognized in the NRF, which expanded its treatment to include nongovernmental groups. These include the private sector, faith-based organizations, community organizations, voluntary organizations, and individuals, among others.

The American Red Cross is probably one of the most significant of these other supporting entities. The American Red Cross is a key player in US emergency management preparedness and response and is currently a supporting agency to the mass care functions of ESF #6 (Mass Care, Emergency Assistance, Housing, and Human Services) under the NRF. As the nation's largest mass care service provider, the American Red Cross provides sheltering, feeding, bulk distribution of needed items, basic first aid, welfare information, and casework, among other services, at the local level as needed. In its role as a service provider, the American Red Cross works closely with local, tribal, and state governments to provide mass care services to victims of every disaster, large and small, in an affected area.

VOADs, or voluntary organizations active in disasters, are associations of NGOs who have a common goal of assisting in major emergencies and who work together to better coordinate their efforts in times of need. At the national level, the National Voluntary Organizations Active in Disaster (NVOAD) is a consortium of approximately 58 national organizations and 55 state and territory equivalents that typically send representatives to the FEMA's National Response Coordination Center to represent the voluntary organizations and assist in response coordination. Members of NVOAD form a coalition of nonprofit organizations that respond to disasters as part of their overall mission. Each state maintains a VOAD, which includes organizations that work statewide, and to a growing degree, communities are establishing community VOADs.

Individual NGOs are becoming a vital part of the nation's response and recovery network, providing shelter, emergency food supplies, counseling services, and other services to support official emergency management organizations and agencies. They often provide specialized services that help individuals with special needs, including those with disabilities, and provide resettlement assistance and services to arriving refugees. NGOs also play key roles in engaging communities to integrate lawful immigrants into American society and reduce the marginalization or radicalization of these groups. Through the communities, and in some cases official community organizations, many homeland security needs are met. There are a number of established community-based organizations that act toward this common goal, including Neighborhood Watch, the CERTs, and other civic and professional organizations (such as the Lions Club or Rotary International.) These groups may possess the knowledge and understanding of the threats, local response capabilities, and special needs within their jurisdictions and have the capacity necessary to alert authorities of those threats, capabilities, or needs. Additionally, during an incident, these groups may be critical in passing along vital incident communications to individuals and families and to supporting critical response activities in the initial stages of a crisis.

Finally, individuals and families take the basic steps to prepare themselves for emergencies, including understanding the threats and hazards that they may face, reducing hazards in and around their homes, preparing an emergency supply kit and household emergency plans (that include care for pets and service animals), monitoring emergency communications carefully, volunteering with established organizations, mobilizing or helping to ensure community preparedness, enrolling in training courses, and practicing what to do in an emergency. These individual and family preparedness activities strengthen community resilience and mitigate the impact of disasters. In addition, individual vigilance and awareness can help communities remain safer and bolster prevention efforts (DHS, 2010).

Conclusion

Emergency management in the United States was forever changed by the events of September 11, 2001. While some claim the increased funding to support emergency management has allowed a true professionalization in the field, others would say that the movement of FEMA into the Department of Homeland Security negatively impacted the all-hazards emergency management mission. These opinions remain in wide dispute, for a variety of reasons that are unique to each successive level of government. Regardless, it is undeniable that emergency management, and now homeland security, has been thrust to the forefront of the public and the policy agendas and is one of many primary concerns of federal, state, and local administrators.

For local governments, terrorism is a new threat that greatly expands their already strained safety and security requirements and adds to a long list of needs and priorities. But the threat of terrorism is one that cannot be ignored, and state and local governments have not done so. At these local levels, the dramatic increase in funding that has provided training and equipment to local first responders has been greeted with mixed emotion. Many recipients feel it has remained singular in focus, addressing mainly the terrorism threat. Historically, and including the 2001 terrorist attacks, natural disasters have taken many more lives and have caused much more financial harm. These natural and technological hazards will continue to pose a threat and will continue to result in disaster. It is undeniable that a more comprehensive approach to building the capacity of the local government to respond would provide more long-term benefits. Whether or not these local government agencies will be better prepared overall remains to be seen. If the actions of the Boston Police Department and other responding agencies are any indication, it would appear that the efforts are paying off.

At the state level, governors and state emergency management directors have resisted the push toward local control and have been accused on many occasions of holding out federal homeland security funding from the local governments for which it was intended. In many circumstances, it was determined that these accusations were correct. But state officials feel the same concerns about the terrorist threat as do the locals and have called for better coordination, new communications technologies, and, as always, more and more funding.

At the federal government level, the changes that have resulted with regard to emergency management have been the most visible—and the most dramatic. The creation in 2002 of the DHS, which absorbed FEMA and most of the former federal government disaster management programs, has resulted in DHS taking the lead in addressing these new issues. This new agency has been tested on several occasions, as is displayed throughout this chapter, and has enjoyed relatively mixed but primarily positive success. Under the leadership of DHS, many federal disaster response, recovery, and mitigation programs have so far fared well, although their priorities have seen a drastic shift to accommodate the new terrorist concern. In general, the United States has taken the typical response to a new problem in that it reorganized and committed huge amounts of funding to reducing the newly recognized problem.

Sidebar "Select Websites for Additional Information" lists websites about the organizations discussed in this chapter.

Select Websites for Additional Information

AmeriCorps: http://www.americorps.org
Animal and Plant Health Inspection Service: http://www.aphis.usda.gov
Citizen Corps: http://www.citizencorps.gov
Corporation for National and Community Service: http://www.nationalservice.org
Department of Homeland Security: http://www.dhs.gov

Federal Emergency Management Agency: http://www.fema.gov
Medical Reserve Corps: http://www.medicalreservecorps.gov
National Association of Counties: http://www.naco.org
National Governors Association: http://www.nga.org
National League of Cities: http://www.nlc.org
Neighborhood Watch: http://www.usaonwatch.org
Senior Corps: http://www.seniorcorps.org
Transportation Security Administration: http://www.tsa.gov
United States Coast Guard: http://www.uscg.mil
United States Conference of Mayors: http://www.usmayors.org
United States Customs Service: http://www.cbp.gov
United States Secret Service: http://www.secretservice.gov
Volunteers in Police Service: http://www.theiacp.org/VIPS

Key Terms

Adjutant general: The chief administrative officer of a major military unit (the National Guard, in the case of the state government)
Civil Rights: The rights belonging to an individual by virtue of citizenship
Cybersecurity: The protection of data and systems in networks that are connected to the Internet
Directorate (DHS): A major division within the Department of Homeland Security that oversees several offices addressing a similar broad-reaching topic (like Science and Technology, for instance)
Ombudsman: A person or an office that investigates complaints and mediates fair settlements
Superfund: Another name for the Comprehensive Environmental Response, Compensation, and Liability Act of 1980 (CERCLA), which sought to define liability for individual toxic waste sites and then clean up those sites from a fund built from taxes and fines

Review Questions

1. What is the principal role of emergency management in homeland security? Identify the other major players and their roles in homeland security.
2. Identify the three directorates of the Department of Homeland Security and discuss their respective missions.
3. Discuss the homeland security role of federal agencies other than DHS.
4. Make the case for retaining an all-hazards approach to emergency management that includes terrorism and its associated hazards as one of many hazards. Discuss the pros and cons of such an approach as it relates to all four phases of emergency management: mitigation, preparedness, response, and recovery.
5. If you had been in charge of establishing the Department of Homeland Security (DHS), would you have included the Federal Emergency Management Agency in DHS or would you have retained it

as an independent executive branch agency reporting directly to the president? Discuss the possible ramifications of moving FEMA into DHS in terms of FEMA's mission, programs, and reporting structure. The director of FEMA no longer reports directly to the president; will this be a problem in future natural and terrorist-related disasters? What will the impact of FEMA's inclusion in DHS be on the nation's emergency management system?

References

Associated Press, 2011. In sign of tougher line with Pakistan, Obama administration suspends $800 million in military aid. The Washington Post (July 9).

Bomberg, N., 2013. Funding Homeland Security Grants – The House, The Senate, and the Administration Take Different Approaches. National League of Cities Press Release. http://bit.ly/1y9SdPP (April 29).

CNCS, 2014. National service responds to severe weather. CNCS Press Release. http://bit.ly/1olnCid (May 9, 2014).

Cruickshank, P., Robertson, N., Shiffman, K., 2012. How safe is the cargo on passenger flights? CNN (February 19). http://cnn.it/ZXyxn.

Department of State, 2003. Patterns of Global Terrorism.

DHS, 2005. http://1.usa.gov/ZpdlFz.

Department of Homeland Security, 2007a. Department subcomponents and agencies. DHS website: http://1.usa.gov/1yUdOyX.

Department of Homeland Security, 2007b. DHS annual financial report. Fiscal year 2007. Washington, DC. http://1.usa.gov/1vX5v1l.

DHS, 2010. Quadrennial Homeland Security Review. DHS website: http://1.usa.gov/1t7w9qd.

Department of Homeland Security, 2014a. 2015 Budget in brief. Washington, DC. http://1.usa.gov/1w12899.

Department of Homeland Security, 2014b. The 2014 quadrennial homeland security review. Washington, DC. http://1.usa.gov/1sGKYyB.

DHS, 2014c. USCIS: about us. Mission Statement. USCIS website: http://1.usa.gov/1yBdaq0 (accessed October 15, 2014).

DHS, 2014d. About the Domestic Nuclear Detection Office. DHS website: http://1.usa.gov/1EWn0EA (accessed October 15, 2014).

DHS, 2014e. http://1.usa.gov/ZMkWyh.

DHS, 2014f. http://1.usa.gov/1v6ot72.

DHS, 2014g. FY 2015 Budget in Brief. http://1.usa.gov/1z6icMn.

DHS, 2014h. http://1.usa.gov/1qqgBYm.

DHS, 2014i. http://1.usa.gov/1w1tr4a.

FBI, 2014. Quick facts. FBI website: http://1.usa.gov/1y8WBi3 (accessed October 20, 2014).

FEMA, 2014. http://1.usa.gov/1p7SyNF.

Government Accountability Office, 2004. Terrorism Insurance: Effects of the Terrorism Risk Insurance Act of 2002.

Hartwig, R., 2014. Terrorism Risk: A Constant Threat; Impacts for Property/Casualty Managers. Insurance Information Institute (III). http://bit.ly/1FmM1Y2.

Jang, Y., 2014. President's budget proposes consolidation of DHS state and local grants. NACo Press Release. http://bit.ly/ZLq4CO (April 7).

Library of Congress, 2014. Archived websites. DHS organization. http://1.usa.gov/1nk4AI2 (March 14, 2003).

Markon, J., 2014. Planned homeland security headquarters, long delayed and over budget, now in doubt. Washington Post (May 20). http://wapo.st/11dF8KB.

National Association of Counties (NACo), 2002. Counties and Homeland Security: Policy Agenda to Secure the People of America's Counties. NACo, Washington, DC.

National Conference of State Legislatures, 2005. State offices of homeland security. NCSL website. No longer available.

National Council of ISACs, 2014. Member ISACs. National Council of ISACs website: http://bit.ly/1roW99S (accessed October 21, 2014).

National Governors Association Center for Best Practices (NGAC), 2002. Issue Brief: States' Homeland Security Priorities. NGAC, Washington, DC August 19.

NCCI, 2015. Frequently asked questions for the terrorism risk insurance act. NCCI website: http://bit.ly/1A5nSlj (accessed October, 2015).

NEMA, 2011. 2010–2011 National Homeland Security Consortium Member Priorities. http://bit.ly/1ziFezF.

NEMA, 2014a. State emergency management organizations. NEMA website: http://bit.ly/1x36VXU.

NEMA, 2014b. State emergency management agency budgets. Funding for State Homeland Security Offices. NEMA website: http://bit.ly/1nxujgl (accessed October 21, 2014).

NGA, 2013. HSPS – 01: homeland security and emergency management. NGA Winter Meeting 2013. http://bit.ly/1wkVwCN.

NIST, 2014. About disaster and failure studies. Department of Commerce website: http://1.usa.gov/1stuRTn (accessed October 16, 2014).

NORTHCOM, 2014. About Northcom. Northcom website: http://bit.ly/10fUb6q (accessed October 21, 2014).

Pistole, J., 2014. Statement before the Committee on Appropriations Subcommittee on Homeland Security. US House of Representatives. http://1.usa.gov/1v6KBhp (March 25).

Reuters, 2014. Pentagon to create medical support team for US Ebola response. October 19.

The Guardian, 2011. Sixty years of US aid to Pakistan: get the data. Poverty Matters Blog. http://bit.ly/1pwmNhi.

TSA, 2014. http://1.usa.gov/1sKA7DX.

U.S. Conference of Mayors, 2003. Homeland security report: 90 percent of cities left without funds from largest federal homeland security program. http://bit.ly/1pwnJCm (September 29).

U.S. Conference of Mayors, 2004. Executive director's column. http://bit.ly/1tHBsNN (March 12).

US Senate Committee on Finance, 2011. Baucus, Hatch, Grassley Demand China End Intellectual Property Rights Infringement. Press Release. http://1.usa.gov/1patPs7 (May 18).

USCIS, 2014. http://1.usa.gov/1EVPEpp.

5

Intelligence Counterterrorism

What You Will Learn

- Elements, structure, and purpose of the intelligence community
- The purpose and types of intelligence and the process by which intelligence is requested, gathered, and shared
- Detailed overview of essential intelligence agencies and entities such as the DNI, CIA, NSA, NRO, and NGA
- New coordination body of national intelligence: Office of the Director of National Intelligence
- The impact of intelligence leaks and calls for greater privacy protections

Introduction

On September 20, 2001, only 9 days after the 9/11 attacks, President George W. Bush initiated what was to become one of the most significant governmental transformations in the nation's history. It was on this day that he announced the establishment of the Office of Homeland Security within the White House and appointed Tom Ridge, who was serving as governor of Pennsylvania at the time, as homeland security chief. Some months later, after having originally rejected the idea, President Bush proposed the creation of a cabinet-level department of homeland security whose primary purpose would be to unify those agencies responsible for homeland security missions and to achieve greater accountability in the execution of those missions. Driving this effort was a desire among lawmakers to prevent the information-sharing failures that occurred prior to the 9/11 attacks, between the many disparate government intelligence agencies, which prevented a complete picture of the pending attacks from being understood. On November 19, 2002, the US Senate voted overwhelmingly to create the Department of Homeland Security (DHS), spurring the most extensive reorganization of the federal government since the 1940s. Despite that so many iterations of this new department's structure centered around the conglomeration of these many intelligence agencies, in the end, not one of them was incorporated. Intelligence, however, has remained on the forefront of homeland security and as such is integral to its mission. This chapter explores the role of intelligence in homeland security and describes the various governmental agencies that are involved in intelligence and counterterrorism activities.

The Intelligence Community

The US Intelligence Community (IC) is made up of 16 agencies and organizations that operate within the executive branch and work both independently and collaboratively to gather the intelligence necessary to conduct national security activities (among other activities). The IC works to collect and convey essential security-related information to the president and members of the policy making, law enforcement, and military communities as they need to carry out their required functions and duties. Within the US government, the IC has developed in a manner that has resulted in its many components being spread out across the vast range of civilian and military departments (Figure 5-1). While the number of actual agencies has expanded and contracted over time, today, 16 agencies perform this function. These agencies include

- Air Force Intelligence, Surveillance and Reconnaissance Agency,
- Army Intelligence,
- Central Intelligence Agency,
- Coast Guard Intelligence,
- Defense Intelligence Agency,
- Department of Energy's Office of Intelligence and Counterintelligence,
- Department of Homeland Security's Office of Intelligence and Analysis,
- Bureau of Intelligence and Research,
- Department of the Treasury's Office of Terrorism and Financial Intelligence's Office of Intelligence and Analysis,
- Drug Enforcement Administration's Office of National Security Intelligence,
- Federal Bureau of Investigation's National Security Branch,
- Marine Corps Intelligence,

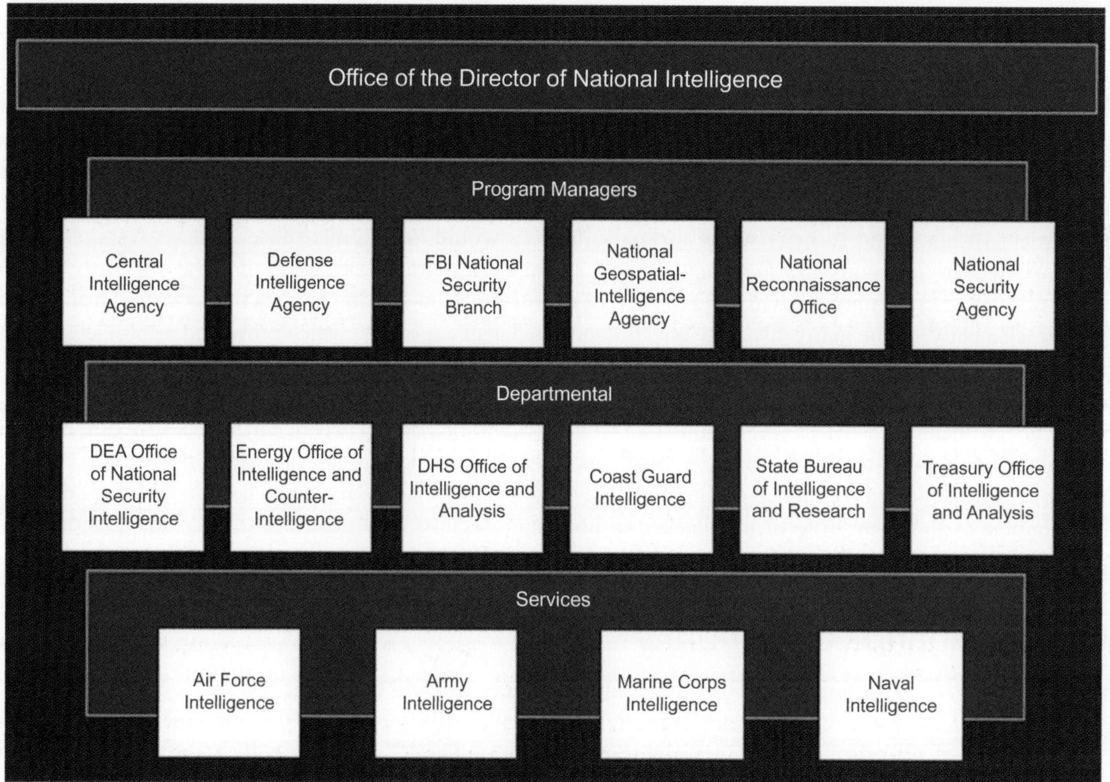

FIGURE 5-1 The US Intelligence Community. *Source: Intelligence.Gov (2014a).*

- National Geospatial-Intelligence Agency,
- National Reconnaissance Office,
- National Security Agency,
- Office of Naval Intelligence.

These agencies are tasked to varying degrees with the collection and assessment of information regarding national security issues that may include

- terrorism;
- weapon (viz., nuclear) proliferation, including technologies;
- chemical warfare;
- biological warfare;
- information infrastructure attack;
- narcotics trafficking;
- hostile activities by foreign powers, organizations, persons, and their agents;
- foreign intelligence activities directed against the United States;
- other special activities required to protect US security interests against domestic and foreign threats (as directed by the president).

Like most countries' national governments, the US government has always performed some form of intelligence-gathering and intelligence analysis activities. However, the extensive IC as we know it today is largely the result of expansion during the Cold War era. The cadre of federal employees that form the intelligence function of the government grew by the mid-1980s to include more than 100,000 people disbursed throughout 25 organizations and specializing in different aspects of the collection and analysis of information. The amount of the federal budget dedicated to these employees and the activities they conducted grew to more than $30 billion, which was considerable at the time given the relative speed with which these agencies came to prominence. However, considering the highly secretive and critical information needs of the government during this period of showdown among the world's great superpowers, such growth was not surprising.

After the end of the Cold War, the number of agencies and employees was reduced by consolidation of activities and reduction in budgetary allocations. The military intelligence services saw the steepest cuts. Total reductions in the employee base were about 20%. However, because intelligence capacity grew so large during the Cold War era, a vast intelligence capacity remains despite these cuts.

The IC was established to identify and head off plans for attacks like those that were carried out on September 11, 2001. Unfortunately, because there existed a number of intelligence disconnects and other weaknesses, the attacks were not prevented (or even adequately anticipated). The 9/11 Commission was formed in the aftermath of the attacks to study these weaknesses in the structure and effectiveness of US intelligence, to form a better understanding of how the Intelligence Community functions, and to identify areas for improvement. The commission's findings have since profoundly impacted both the IC's budgets and the nature of its members' work and collaboration. Specifically, the commission found six problems pertaining to the IC for which it made recommendations for change. Actions pertaining to these changes include (with commentary drawn from the 9/11 Commission Report) (9/11 Commission, 2004):

1. *Structural barriers to performing joint intelligence work*: National intelligence is still organized around the collection disciplines of the home agencies, not the joint mission. The importance of integrated, all-source analysis cannot be overstated. Without it, it is not possible to "connect the dots." No one component holds all the relevant information.

2. *Lack of common standards and practices across the foreign-domestic divide*: The leadership of the IC should be able to pool information gathered overseas with information gathered in the United States, holding the work—wherever it is done—to a common standard of quality in how it is collected, processed, reported, shared, and analyzed. A common set of personnel standards for intelligence can create a group of professionals better able to operate in joint activities, transcending their own service-specific mind-sets.
3. *Divided management of national intelligence capabilities*: While the CIA was once "central" to the national intelligence capabilities, following the end of the Cold War, it has been less able to influence the use of the nation's imagery and signals intelligence capabilities in three national agencies housed within the Department of Defense: the National Security Agency, the National Geospatial-Intelligence Agency, and the National Reconnaissance Office. One of the lessons learned from the 1991 Gulf War was the value of national intelligence systems in precision warfare. Helping to orchestrate this transformation is the undersecretary of defense for intelligence, a position established by Congress after the 9/11 attacks. An unintended consequence of the developments has been the far greater demand made by defense on technical systems, leaving the Director of Central Intelligence (DCI) less able to influence how these technical resources are allocated and used.
4. *Weak capacity to set priorities and move resources*: The agencies are mainly organized around what they collect or the way they collect it. But the priorities for collection are national. As the DCI makes hard choices about moving resources, he or she must have the power to reach across agencies and reallocate effort.
5. *Too many jobs*. The DCI now has at least three jobs: He or she is expected to run a particular agency, the CIA. He or she is expected to manage the loose confederation of agencies, that is, the IC. He or she is expected to be the analyst-in-chief for the government, sifting evidence and directly briefing the president as his or her principal intelligence adviser. No recent DCI has been able to do all three activities effectively. Usually, what loses out is the management of the IC, a difficult task even in the best case because the DCI's current authorities are weak. With so much to do, the DCI often has not used even the authority he or she has.
6. *Too complex and secret*: Over the decades, the agencies and the rules surrounding the IC have accumulated to a depth that practically defies public comprehension. There are now 15 agencies or parts of agencies in the IC. The IC and the DCI's authorities have become arcane matters, understood only by initiates after long study. Even the most basic information about how much money is actually allocated to or within the IC and most of its key components is shrouded from public view.

Soon after publication of the 9/11 Commission Report, Congress passed the Intelligence Reform and Terrorism Prevention Act (IRTPA) of 2004 (S. 2845, December 7, 2004). This act prescribed far-reaching reforms for the IC, both specific to and in addition to those recommendations made by the 9/11 Commission. Of particular relevance within this act is the first of its eight sections that is aptly titled "Reform of the IC." Of particular note within the verbiage of this section is a call for the creation of two intelligence entities, both of which are described in detail later in this chapter and together have helped to address many of the coordination and information-sharing problems that were identified by the commission. These two entities are

- Office of the Director of National Intelligence and
- National Counterterrorism Center

At present, the IC is structured to maximize the effectiveness of intelligence collection and dissemination among its 17 member agencies. Each agency is authorized to operate under its own directive, but all share the common intelligence mission as stated in the IRTPA to collect and convey essential information to the president and other key stakeholders. The current structure of the IC is represented in the organizational chart shown in Figure 5-1.

The government intelligence capacity involves a full range of activities and operations related to intelligence gathering, analysis, and sharing. Through systems and procedures, the various intelligence agencies convert the information they acquire into clear, comprehensible intelligence and deliver it to end users as required (generally, the president, policy makers, and military commanders). Key to this effort is delivering it in a form that can be utilized. The IC performs this role according to what is commonly referred to as the "intelligence cycle."

The Intelligence Cycle

The intelligence cycle begins with the identification of key issues that interest policy makers and defining the answers they require in order to make educated decisions on action and policy (see sidebar "What Intelligence Can and Cannot Do"). The individual agencies, under the direction of the Office of the Director of National Intelligence, determine how they will acquire needed information and then act on those plans. Once attained, the intelligence is sorted and analyzed, and any necessary reports and recommendations are prepared and delivered. These reports often reveal other areas of concern, which in turn lead to more questions. In this way, the end of one cycle effectively leads to the start of the next.

The steps of the intelligence cycle include (Figure 5-2) the following:

- *Planning*: During the planning step, decisions are made regarding what types of information to collect and how to collect it. The IC relies upon the National Intelligence Priorities Framework (NIPF—see sidebar below) to articulate what issues are important, which then determines how to prioritize the use of intelligence resources. The intelligence end users participate in this step by ensuring that their information needs are included in the NIPF process.

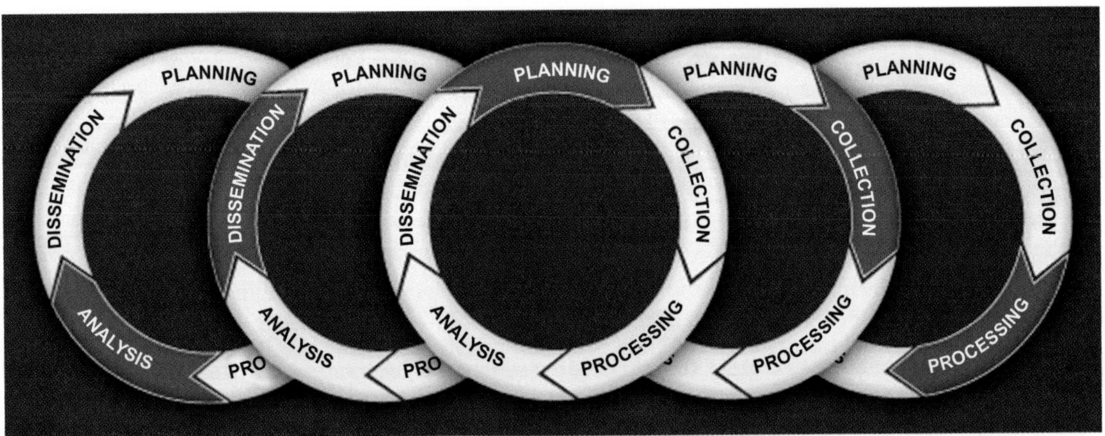

FIGURE 5-2 The intelligence cycle. *Source: Intelligence.Gov (2014b).*

- *Collection*: During the collection step, the IC gathers the raw data used to produce finished intelligence products. Collection can be from one or more of the source types (listed below), which may be open source or clandestine. End users are able to share their scientific and/or substantive expertise and information in this process.
- *Processing*: In the processing step, information that is collected is converted into a usable format, such as by language translation or decryption.
- *Analysis*: In the analysis step, intelligence officers analyze processed information to turn it into finished intelligence. This may include drafting reports, evaluating the reliability of different sources of information, resolving data conflicts, and other analytic services. Intelligence reports typically integrate multiple sources of intelligence and the experience and knowledge of many different members of the IC. Many end user organizations have their own analytic capabilities that better meet internal needs and subject matter experts who have specialized knowledge not typically found in the IC. Oftentimes, the intelligence gathered merely supports a much wider understanding held by the end user—an understanding that likely exceeds that of the individuals who collected and processed the data.
- *Dissemination*: In the dissemination step, intelligence products are provided to those who request or otherwise need them.

The IC information-gathering effort draws from a number of different source types, which include the following:

- *Open-source intelligence* (OSINT): This is the publicly available information appearing in print or electronic forms, including radio, television, newspapers, journals, the Internet, commercial databases, videos, graphics, and drawings.
- *Human intelligence* (HUMINT): This is the intelligence derived from information collected and provided by human sources. This intelligence includes overt data collected by personnel in diplomatic and consular posts and unobtainable information collected via clandestine sources of information, debriefings of foreign nationals and US citizens who travel abroad, official contacts with foreign governments, and direct observation.
- *Signals intelligence* (SIGINT): This is the information gathered from data transmissions, including communications intelligence (COMINT), electronic intelligence (ELINT), and foreign instrumentation signals intelligence (FISINT).
- *Geospatial intelligence* (GEOINT): This is the information describing, visually depicting, and accurately locating physical features and human activities on the Earth. Examples of GEOINT products include imagery, analyses, maps, and navigation charts. Imagery intelligence (IMINT), sometimes called photo intelligence (PHOTINT) is a subset of GEOINT.
- *Measurement and signature intelligence* (MASINT): This is the information produced by quantitative and qualitative analysis of physical attributes of targets and events in order to characterize and identify them.

  Source: Office of the Director of National Intelligence (2009) and FBI (2014).

The National Intelligence Priorities Framework (NIPF)

The NIPF is the Office of the Director of National Intelligence's guidance to the IC on the national intelligence priorities approved by the president.

The NIPF is the DNI's sole mechanism for establishing national intelligence priorities. The NIPF consists of the following:

- Intelligence topics reviewed by the National Security Council Principals Committee and approved by the president.
- A process for assigning priorities to countries and nonstate actors relevant to the approved intelligence topics.
- A matrix showing these priorities. The NIPF matrix reflects consumers' priorities for intelligence support and ensures that long-term intelligence issues are addressed.

The NIPF is updated semiannually in coordination with IC elements, the National Intelligence Council, and other internal components of the Office of the Director of National Intelligence. Ad hoc adjustments may also be made to reflect changes in world events and policy priorities.

The Office of the Director of National Intelligence and IC elements use the NIPF to guide allocation of collection and analytic resources. In addition, IC elements associate intelligence collection requirements and analytic production with NIPF priorities and report to the Office of the Director of National Intelligence on their coverage of NIPF priorities.

Source: Office of the Director of National Intelligence (DNI) (2011).

What Intelligence Can (and Cannot) Do

Intelligence Can

- provide an advantage in dealing with foreign adversaries by supplying information and analysis that can enhance the intelligence consumer's understanding,
- warn of potential threats and opportunities,
- provide insight into the causes and consequences of current events,
- enhance situational awareness,
- assess long-term strategic issues and alternative futures,
- assist in preparation for international or planning meetings,
- inform official travelers of security threats,
- report on specific topics, either as part of routine reporting or upon request.

What Intelligence Cannot Do

Intelligence cannot predict the future or know about everything.

- Intelligence can provide assessments of likely scenarios or developments, but it cannot provide predictions of what will happen with absolute certainty. The IC's resources and capabilities are limited by
  - numerous priorities competing for finite budget dollars, personnel, and capabilities;
  - limited access to denied areas;
  - technological limitations of IC systems.

- The IC must maintain its ability to obtain useful information. The need to protect information and intelligence sources and methods may limit the sharing or use of some reports.

  Intelligence cannot violate US law or the US constitution

- The activities of the US IC must be conducted in a manner consistent with all applicable laws and executive orders. The IC is particularly aware of the importance of ensuring
  - civil liberties and the privacy of US citizens and lawful US residents,
  - confidentiality of sources and the identities of IC personnel and protection of privileged information,
  - appropriate conduct of IC personnel and activities.

Source: DNI (2013a).

Intelligence Oversight

The IC agencies and offices fall within the executive branch. However, due to the nature of their work, they are subject to external oversight from the executive and legislative branches. The IC provides a vital service of ensuring that both policy and decision makers and lawmakers are equally informed of the intelligence related to national security issues, and Congress is authorized to maintain oversight of the IC intelligence activities. Executive organizations involved in oversight of the IC include

- The President's Intelligence Advisory Board,
- The President's Intelligence Oversight Board,
- The Office of Management and Budget.

Within the Congress, principal oversight responsibility rests with the following two entities:

- The Senate Select Committee on Intelligence
- The House Permanent Select Committee on Intelligence

Office of the Director of National Intelligence

The National Commission on Terrorist Attacks upon the United States (the 9/11 Commission) recommended the following in its final report:

> *The current position of Director of Central Intelligence should be replaced by a National Intelligence Director with two main areas of responsibility: (1) to oversee national intelligence centers on specific subjects of interest across the U.S. government and (2) to manage the national intelligence program and oversee the agencies that contribute to it.*

In efforts to move forward with the commission's recommendation, Senators Susan Collins and Joe Lieberman and Speaker of the House of Representatives Dennis Hastert separately introduced legislation to create the Office of the Director of National Intelligence (DNI) position. Both bills sought to establish a presidentially nominated, Senate-confirmed position of DNI, who would serve as the head of the IC's distinct intelligence agencies. Both bills also sought to establish a separate Senate-confirmed director of central intelligence, who would manage the CIA and would be prohibited from serving simultaneously as the DNI.

The House of Representatives passed the Collins-Lieberman Intelligence Reform and Terrorism Prevention Act on December 7, 2004, by a vote of 336 to 75. On December 8, 2004, the bill was approved by an 89-to-2 vote in the US Senate and was sent to the president for his signature. The president signed the bill and nominated John Negroponte, the former US ambassador to the United Nations and recently the US ambassador to Iraq, for the position of national intelligence director on February 17, 2005. John Negroponte was confirmed by the Senate on April 21, 2005, and was officially sworn in on May 18, 2005.

The primary goals of this new position were to ensure coordination and cooperation among all intelligence communities in the United States and to unify the national intelligence effort in place of the director of central intelligence. The new DNI was given the authority to perform the following critical tasks and activities according to the act:

- Creating national intelligence centers to incorporate capabilities from across the IC in order to accomplish intelligence missions
- Controlling the national intelligence budget in terms of dollar amounts and distribution among different intelligence agencies
- Transferring personnel and funds to ensure that the IC is flexible and can respond to emerging threats
- Creating the Privacy and Civil Liberties Oversight Board to protect privacy and civil liberties concerns potentially created by proposals to fight terrorism
- Establishing an information-sharing network to break down the stovepipes that currently impede the flow of information between federal, state, and local agencies and the private sector (Congressional Research Service, 2004a,b)

In its first 3 years of existence, the new office accomplished some of the goals mentioned above, but more importantly, this period was marked as one of transition in the IC. It included the creation of new functions, the reshaping of others, and the several changes in the role of key officials.

On October 13, 2005, approximately 6 months after taking the office, Director Negroponte together with the director of central intelligence created the National Clandestine Service within the CIA to boost the nation's human intelligence capabilities. Within the same timeframe, the directorate released the National Intelligence Strategy, a document that details the national intelligence framework and established goals, priorities, and measures of effectiveness in adapting to the changing intelligence needs of the United States in the aftermath of the 9/11 attacks. The implementation of the strategy kicked off with the creation of DNI Open Source Center in an attempt to better exploit openly available information (such as websites, reports, videos, radio, television, and books) for intelligence-gathering and intelligence analysis purposes. Shortly before the end of 2005, the DNI created the DNI National Counterproliferation Center (NCPC). The office is tasked with the unification of efforts to prevent the proliferation of weapons of mass destruction (WMDs).

On February 17, 2006, the Drug Enforcement Administration became the 16th member of the IC. In May 5, CIA, Chief Porter Goss resigned and the media reported that the cause of the resignation was a combination of differences between Goss's and DNI Negroponte's management styles and the changes made in the direction of the IC that Goss did not agree with. Later in the same month, General Mike Hayden

(US Air Force) was sworn in as the new chief of CIA. General Hayden previously served as the first principal deputy director of National Intelligence, which is the highest-ranking intelligence post within the US Armed Forces.

2007 saw another change of key officials when President Bush announced that DNI John Negroponte would be moving to the Department of State as the deputy secretary of state, and nominated Admiral Mike McConnell as his replacement. Although McConnell was holding a senior management position with a private consulting company focusing on intelligence and national security prior to his appointment as the DNI, he had previously served as the director of the National Security Agency (NSA). As his first major move in his new post, McConnell created the Information Sharing and Safeguarding Steering Committee within the DNI to further improve coordination and collaboration among different members of the IC. Within this new setting, every member of the IC must appoint an information-sharing executive who works closely with the committee to share vital information processed by his or her agency. Just a few days after the announcement of the creation of the new committee, the DOD chief information officer (CIO) and the ODNI CIO signed an agreement that created the Unified Cross Domain Management Office to enhance information sharing between the DOD and the IC. On March 27, 2007, the DNI announced the release of the National Counterintelligence Strategy, which details the IC's goals and priorities toward a reduction in intelligence threats aimed at the United States.

Today, the DNI serves as the head of the IC and is the principal advisor to the president, the National Security Council, and the Homeland Security Council (HSC) for intelligence matters related to national security. Also, the DNI oversees and directs the implementation of the National Intelligence Program. The DNI's responsibilities, among others, are to

- lead the IC,
- oversee the coordination of foreign relationships between elements of the IC and intelligence services of foreign governments,
- establish requirements and priorities for collection, analysis, production, and dissemination of national intelligence,
- coordinate reform of security clearance and acquisition processes,
- achieve auditable financial statements,
- support legislative, legal, and administrative requirements,
- ensure compliance with statutory and presidentially mandated responsibilities,
- transform the IC into a unified, collaborative, and coordinated enterprise.

The DNI organization is composed of the DNI leadership, six centers, and fifteen offices. The core mission offices, which are guided by a Deputy DNI for Intelligence Integration (DDNI/II), include the following:

- *National Counterterrorism Center* (NCTC): This office serves as the primary US government organization for integrating and analyzing all intelligence pertaining to terrorism possessed or acquired by the US government (except purely domestic terrorism).
- *Office of the National Counterintelligence Executive* (ONCIX): This office produces threat assessments for foreign counterintelligence efforts and damage assessments related to these activities of other governments and develops counterintelligence strategies and awareness reports and other guidance. It is staffed by senior counterintelligence and other specialists from across the national intelligence and security communities. Its mission is to exploit and defeat adversarial intelligence activities directed against US interests; protect the integrity of the US intelligence system; provide

incisive, actionable intelligence to decision makers at all levels; protect vital national assets from adversarial intelligence activities; and neutralize and exploit adversarial intelligence activities targeting the armed forces.

- *National Counterproliferation Center* (NCPC): It is responsible for coordinating strategic planning within the IC to enhance intelligence support to US efforts to stem the proliferation of WMDs and related delivery systems. NCPC works toward five principle objectives: discouraging the efforts of states, terrorists, or armed groups aimed at building or using WMDs; limiting the abilities of these groups to acquire WMD capabilities; limiting or eliminating programs that enable WMDs; deterring the use of WMDs by those that possess them; and mitigating the risk of WMD use against the United States and its allies.
- *Intelligence Advanced Research Projects Activity* (IARPA): It invests in high-risk/high-payoff research that has the potential to provide the United States with an overwhelming intelligence advantage over future adversaries.
- *National Intelligence Council* (NIC): It is the IC's center for mid-term and long-term strategic analysis. The NIC supports the DNI in his or her roles as the head of the IC and principal advisor for intelligence matters to the president and the National Security and Homeland Security Councils and serves as the senior intelligence advisor representing the IC's views within the US government. The NIC also provides key products and services, such as the National Intelligence Estimates assessing future trends on a wide range of global issues.
- *The Information Sharing Environment* (ISE): It ensures that the wider stakeholder group of intelligence producers and end users is able to share data and information. The information-sharing environment is one of collaboration in addition to merely passing information back and forth, and it is the challenge of this office to ensure that such an environment is possible yet secure.

The DNI offices, which provide support, oversight, and other functions, include the following:

- Acquisition, Technologies, and Facilities (AT&F) leads the IC effort to acquire the systems, equipment, and facilities necessary to remain competitive while fulfilling the IC mission.
- Office of the Chief Financial Officer (CFO) justifies the IC budget and oversees broader financial management efforts.
- IC Chief Human Capital Office (CHCO) provides analysis, guidance, and leadership to oversee human resources across the wider IC.
- The Civil Liberties and Privacy Office (CLPO) works to limit how much the IC activities infringe upon the civil liberties, privacy, and freedom of American citizens as guaranteed by the Constitution and by Federal law.
- Office of the IC Chief Information Officer (IC CIO) oversees the information technology (IT) requirements of the IC to ensure effective information sharing among its members (thereby connecting "people to people, data to people, and data to data") (DNI, 2014b).
- Office of the Deputy Chief Management Officer (DCMO) oversees the internal administrative functions of the DNI, including such things as personnel management and financial management.
- Office of Equal Employment Opportunity and Diversity (EEOD) guides IC hiring and employment practices to ensure they are fair, equitable, and aligned with applicable laws and statutes.
- Office of IC Inspector General (IC IG) conducts audits across the wider IC, addressing systemic risks, vulnerabilities, and deficiencies.

- Office of the Deputy Director of National Intelligence for Intelligence Integration (DDII) works to address the disconnects that existed across the wider IC prior to 9/11 and resulted in the associated intelligence failures and oversees the National Intelligence Council (NIC), which is the IC's center for mid-term and long-term strategic analysis.
- Office of General Counsel (OGC) is the chief legal officer for the Office of the Director of National Intelligence.
- Legislative Affairs Office (LAO) is the principal interface between Congress and the Office of the Director of National Intelligence.
- Office of Public Affairs (OPA) supports both internal and external communications for the Office of the Director of National Intelligence.
- Partner Engagement (PE) is the primary interface between the IC and the external stakeholders including those within and outside the United States and those in the private sector.
- Office of Policy and Strategy (P&S) develops the National Intelligence Strategy and evaluated the overall progress and trajectory of the IC.
- Office of Systems and Resource Analysis (SRA) helps to "shape intelligence capabilities by enabling proactive, balanced, and effective resource decisions on issues of national importance" (DNI, 2014c).

Central Intelligence Agency

The recognized intelligence needs of modern warfare that surfaced during World War II resulted in the creation of America's first central intelligence organization, the Office of Strategic Services (OSS). The OSS was created to perform a variety of functions, including traditional espionage, covert action (ranging from propaganda to sabotage), counterintelligence, and intelligence analysis. The OSS represented a revolution in US intelligence, not only because of the varied functions performed by a single, national agency but also because of the breadth of its intelligence interests and its use of scholars to produce finished intelligence.

In the aftermath of World War II, the OSS was disbanded, officially ceasing all operations on October 1, 1945, by executive order from President Truman. However, several of its branches were retained and were distributed among other governmental departments. For instance, the X-2 (counterintelligence) and Secret Intelligence branches were transferred to the War Department to form the Strategic Services Unit, and the Research and Analysis branch was transferred to the Department of State (Smith, 1983).

As Truman was ordering the termination of the OSS, he was also commissioning studies to determine the requirements of and changes to the US intelligence structure in the post-World War II climate. Based on these studies, the National Intelligence Authority (NIA) and its operational element, the Central Intelligence Group (CIG), were created. The CIG was initially responsible for coordinating and synthesizing the reports produced by the military service intelligence agencies and the FBI, but it soon after assumed the task of secret intelligence collection.

National security needs and the intelligence reorganization were addressed by the National Security Act of 1947. The CIA was established as an independent agency within the executive office of the president to replace the CIG. According to the act, the CIA was to have five functions:

1. To advise the National Security Council in matters concerning such intelligence activities of the government departments and agencies as related to national security
2. To make recommendations to the National Security Council for the coordination of such intelligence activities of the departments and agencies of the government as related to national security

3. To correlate and evaluate the intelligence relating to national security and to provide for the appropriate dissemination of such intelligence within the government using, where appropriate, existing agencies and facilities
4. To perform for the benefit of existing intelligence agencies such additional services of common concern that, as the National Security Council determines, can be more effectively accomplished centrally
5. To perform other such functions and duties related to intelligence affecting the national security as the National Security Council may from time to time direct

The organizational structure of the CIA as it exists today began to take shape in the early 1950s under Director Walter Bedell Smith. In 1952, the Office of Policy Coordination was transferred under CIA control and merged with the secret intelligence-gathering Office of Special Operations to form the Directorate of Plans. That same year, the offices involved in intelligence research and analysis were placed under the Directorate of Intelligence. A third unit, the Directorate of Administration, was established to perform administrative functions.

The principal functions of the Directorate of Plans were clandestine collection and covert action. A separate directorate was later formed to perform technical collection operations, but before that time, the Directorate of Plans was heavily involved in the development and operation of overhead collection systems like the U-2 spy plane and CORONA reconnaissance satellite. In 1973, the Directorate of Plans became the Directorate of Operations. On October 13, 2005, the creation of the National Clandestine Service was announced by the director of central intelligence and the director of national intelligence, which absorbed all functions of the Directorate of Operations (Figure 5-3). Today, its functions within the National Clandestine Service include clandestine collection, covert action, counternarcotics and counterterrorism activities, and counterintelligence. On the day of the establishment of this new function within the CIA, John Negroponte, the first Director of National Intelligence, stated that the National Clandestine Service would significantly improve the nation's HUMINT capabilities.

A fourth directorate, the Directorate of Research, was established in 1962. This directorate consolidated into a single-unit all-agency components involved in technical collection activities. In 1963, it was renamed the Directorate of Science and Technology and assumed control of scientific intelligence analysis. Its present functions include the following:

- Developing technical collection systems
- Collecting intelligence from embassy sites (in cooperation with the NSA)
- Recording foreign radio and television broadcasts (through its Foreign Broadcast Information Service)
- Developing and producing technical devices (such as bugging devices, hidden cameras, and weaponry) for agents and officers
- Providing research and development in support of intelligence collection and analysis

Until late 1996, the directorate also managed the National Photographic Interpretation Center (NPIC), which interpreted satellite and aerial reconnaissance imagery. NPIC was absorbed by the newly established National Imagery and Mapping Agency (NIMA) (Richelson et al., 2003).

Another vital directorate of the CIA is the Intelligence and Analysis Directorate (Figure 5-3). This directorate is primarily in charge of analyzing the intelligence data and information collected to make sense out of it for the development of more comprehensive intelligence products. The next section briefly covers the specific duties of different offices within the Intelligence and Analysis Directorate.

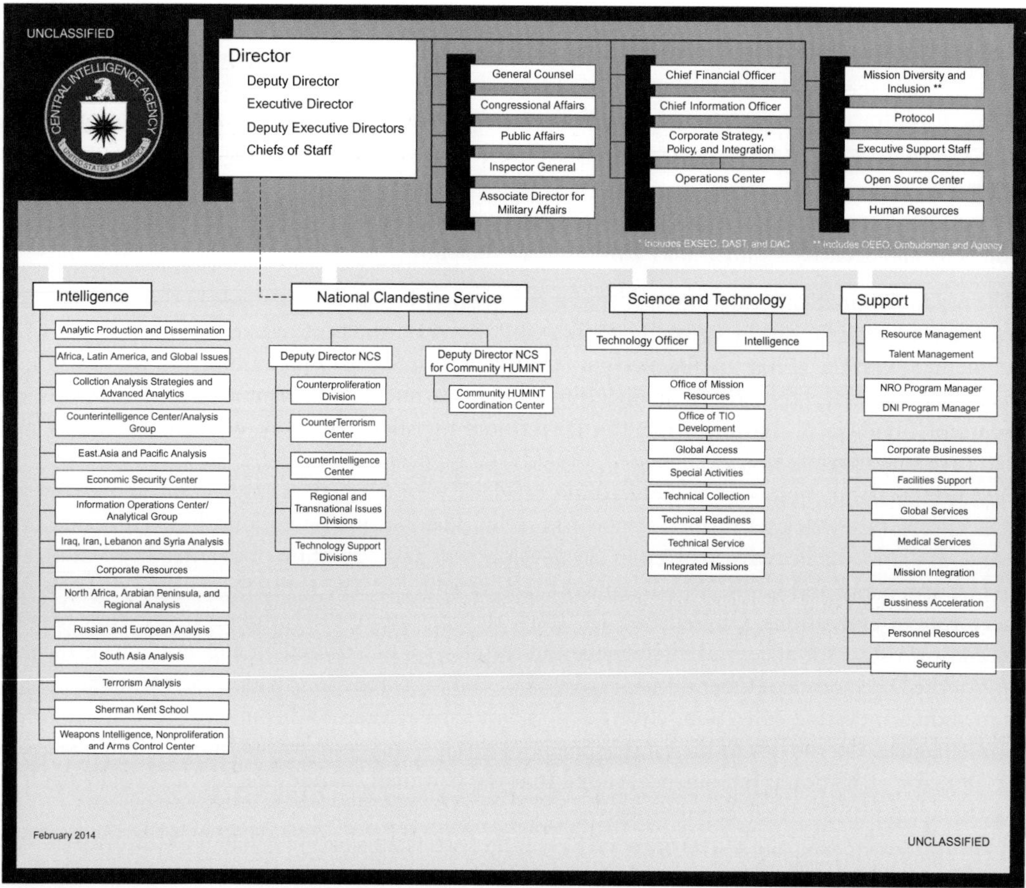

FIGURE 5-3 CIA organizational chart. *Source: CIA (2014). http://1.usa.gov/1rK6Ncu.*

Crime and Narcotics Center

The Crime and Narcotics Center (CNC) focuses on international narcotics trafficking and organized crime for policy makers and the law enforcement community. CNC's workforce is diverse, utilizing individuals with a variety of backgrounds, experience, and specialties. The CNC strategic analysts research long-term trends and keep US policy makers informed about new developments. They estimate the impact of the drug trade and of organized crime on US national security, uncover trafficking trends and routes, and monitor relationships among organized crime groups, traffickers, and terrorists. Targeting analysts use technology to identify key people, organizations, trends, and components in criminal organizations. Operational support specialists and program managers provide fast-paced operational research, management, and support to colleagues overseas. They develop substantive expertise on organized crime and narcotics issues and often travel to support operations or collect information. Analysts specializing in technologies such as remote sensing and geographic information systems capitalize on those tools to locate and estimate quantities of illegal crops in countries where those plants are known to be grown.

Counterintelligence Center/Analysis Group

The Counterintelligence Center/Analysis Group (CIC/AG) identifies, monitors, and analyzes the efforts of foreign intelligence entities against US persons, activities, and interests. The CIC/AG analysts focus on two specific types of counterintelligence threats to US national security: transnational threats, such as the counterintelligence aspect of terrorism, and the threats posed by emerging or changing technologies to the US government's intelligence operations and information systems. The CIC/AG also tracks threats posed by foreign intelligence services and monitors their activities.

Information Operations Center/Analysis Group

The Information Operations Center/Analysis Group (IOC/AG) evaluates foreign threats to US computer systems, particularly those that support critical infrastructures. The group provides its analysis to the president; his senior advisers; high-level officials on cyber issues in the Departments of Defense, State, and Treasury; and senior private-sector officials responsible for operating critical infrastructures. The IOC/AG analysts consider potential threats from state and nonstate actors and evaluate a wide array of information, including foreign intentions, plans, and capabilities.

Office of Asian Pacific, Latin American, and African Analysis

The Office of Asian Pacific, Latin American, and African Analysis (APLAA) studies the political, economic, leadership, societal, and military developments in Asia, Latin America, and sub-Saharan Africa.

Office of Collection Strategies and Analysis

The Office of Collection Strategies and Analysis (CSAA) provides comprehensive intelligence collection expertise to the DCI, a wide range of senior agency and IC officials, and key national policy makers. The CSAA staff work with analysts in the CIA's National Clandestine Service and Directorate of Science and Technology, the DOD, the NSA, the NGA, the NRO, and other IC agencies to craft new approaches to solving complex collection issues.

Office of Iraq, Iran, Syria, and Lebanon Analysis

The Office of Iraq, Iran, Syria, and Lebanon Analysis is the newest office within the Intelligence and Analysis Directorate. This office was created in November 2003 at a point in time when the collection and analysis of intelligence from Iraq became increasingly important in the aftermath of the war. Since its creation, the analysis workforce of the office has covered important events such as the captures of Saddam Hussein and many other top Iraqi officials, the rise of the Iraqi insurgency, the nation's first post-Saddam elections, and Iraqi economic development. It has since expanded to encompass other threats in the region, specifically those in Syria, Iran, and Lebanon.

Office of Near Eastern and South Asian Analysis

The Office of Near Eastern and South Asian Analysis (NESA) provides policy makers with comprehensive analytic support on Middle Eastern and North African countries and on the South Asian nations of India, Pakistan, and Afghanistan.

Office of Policy Support

The Office of Policy Support customizes defense intelligence analysis and presents it to a wide variety of policy, law enforcement, military, and foreign liaison recipients.

Office of Russian and European Analysis

The Office of Russian and European Analysis (OREA) provides intelligence support on a large set of countries that have long been of crucial importance to the United States as allies or as adversaries and are likely to continue to occupy a key place in US national security policy. OREA officers are a mix of generalists and specialists who concentrate on issues ranging from ethnic conflict in the Balkans to the US-Russian relationship. Previous historical events covered by analysts include the Solidarity movement in Poland, the breakup of the former Soviet Union, the fall of the Berlin Wall, NATO expansion, and numerous wars in the Balkans. Some current focus areas are arms control negotiations and treaty-monitoring efforts, analysis of potential benefits and challenges of EU enlargement, and reporting on the political and economic landscape of central Asia.

Office of Corporate Resources

The Office of Corporate Resources oversees support to the directorate on a wide variety of issues, including budget, contracts, diversity programs, equal employment opportunity, facilities management, human resources, and resource planning.

Office of Terrorism Analysis

The Office of Terrorism Analysis (OTA) informs policy makers and supports the intelligence, law enforcement, homeland security, and military communities by performing the following tasks:

- Tracking terrorists and the activities of states that sponsor them and assessing terrorist vulnerabilities by analyzing their ideology and goals, capabilities, associates, and locations
- Analyzing worldwide terrorist threat information and patterns to provide warnings aimed at preventing terrorist attacks
- Monitoring worldwide terrorism trends and patterns, including emerging and nontraditional terrorist groups, evolving terrorist threats or operational methods, and possible collusion between terrorist groups
- Identifying, disrupting, and preventing international financial transactions that support terrorist networks and operations

Office of Transnational Issues

The Office of Transnational Issues (OTI) produces analytic assessments on critical intelligence-related issues that transcend regional and national boundaries. Drawing on a broad range of experts in engineering, science, and social science disciplines, OTI's analysis addresses energy and economic security, illicit financial activities, societal conflicts, humanitarian crises, and the long-term military and economic strategic environment.

Weapons Intelligence, Nonproliferation, and Arms Control Center

The Weapons Intelligence, Nonproliferation, and Arms Control Center (WINPAC) provides intelligence support aimed at protecting the United States and its interests from all foreign weapon threats. WINPAC officers are a diverse group with a variety of backgrounds and work experiences and include mathematicians, engineers (nuclear, chemical/biological, mechanical, and aerospace, among others), physicists, economists, political scientists, computer specialists, and physical scientists. On any given day, those analysts could be answering a question from the president, assessing information about a foreign missile test, or developing new computational models to determine blast effects. A key part of its mission includes studying the development of the entire spectrum of threats, from WMDs (nuclear, radiological, chemical, and biological weapons) to advanced conventional weapons such as lasers, advanced explosives, and armor and all types of missiles, including ballistic, cruise, and surface-to-air missiles. The center studies systems from their earliest development phase to production, deployment, and transfers to other countries and monitors strategic arms control agreements. The WINPAC also supports military and diplomatic operations.

Today, the CIA is the largest producer of national security intelligence for senior US policy makers. The director of the CIA (DCIA) is the national HUMINT manager and serves on behalf of the DNI as the national authority for coordination, deconfliction, and evaluation of clandestine HUMINT operations across the IC, consistent with existing laws, executive orders, and interagency agreements.

The CIA is probably the most widely recognized of the various US intelligence agencies, primarily because of its celebrated and cinematized involvement in covert action and also because of the central role it plays in providing intelligence to the president. However, as noted before, there are several US intelligence agencies, some of which rival the CIA in influence and exceed it in budget. Each of these is described in detail next.

Defense Intelligence Agency

The Defense Intelligence Agency (DIA) is a major producer and manager of foreign military intelligence for the DOD. The DIA was established on October 1, 1961, and was designated a combat support agency in 1986. The DIA's mission is to provide timely, objective, all-source military intelligence to policy makers, to US Armed Forces around the world, and to the US acquisition community and force planners to counter a variety of threats and challenges across the spectrum of conflict.

The director of DIA is a three-star military officer who serves as the principal advisor on substantive military intelligence matters to the secretary of defense and the chairman of the Joint Chiefs of Staff. Additionally, he or she is the program manager for the General Defense Intelligence Program that funds a variety of military intelligence programs at and above the corps level. The director also serves as the program manager for the department's Foreign Counterintelligence Program and is the chairman of the Military Intelligence Board that examines key intelligence issues such as information technology architectures, program and budget issues, and defense intelligence inputs to National Intelligence Estimates.

DIA is headquartered in the Pentagon, but the agency employs more than 15,000 civilian and military personnel around the world. The largest facilities include the following:

- The Defense Intelligence Analysis Center (DIAC) at Bolling Air Force Base in Washington, DC
- The Missile and Space Intelligence Center (MSIC) at Redstone Arsenal in Huntsville, Alabama
- The National Center for Medical Intelligence (NCMI) at Fort Detrick, Maryland

The DIA also deploys military and civilian personnel worldwide during crises or conflicts to support military forces. In December 2007, the DIA established the Defense Intelligence Operations Coordination Center (DIOCC) to seamlessly integrate all defense intelligence resources on the transnational threats to US national security and to enhance defense intelligence collaboration. The DIOCC collaborates with the DOD and national intelligence resources to manage risk and resource requirements. It integrates and synchronizes all-source military and national-level intelligence capabilities in support of the warfighters. Working closely with the DIOCC to help manage risk and intelligence resources is the Joint Functional Component Command for Intelligence, Surveillance and Reconnaissance (JFCC-ISR). To support DOD efforts in the global war on terrorism, the DIA established the Joint Intelligence Task Force for Combating Terrorism to consolidate and produce all-source terrorism-related intelligence.

The DIA director is the commander of the US Strategic Command organization. The agency is organized as follows:

- The Directorate for Analysis (DI) assesses foreign militaries. Its focuses include WMDs, missile systems, terrorism, infrastructure systems, and defense-related medical issues.
- The Directorate for Intelligence, Joint Staff (J2), provides foreign military intelligence to the Joint Chiefs of Staff and senior DOD officials.
- The Directorate for Human Intelligence (DH) conducts worldwide strategic HUMINT collection operations. The DH oversees the Defense Attaché System, which conducts representational duties on behalf of the DOD and advises US ambassadors on military matters.
- The Directorate for MASINT and Technical Collection (DT) is the defense intelligence center for MASINT. It collects and analyzes MASINT and also develops new MASINT capabilities.
- The Directorate for Information Management and Chief Information Officer (DS) serves as DIA's information technology component. It manages the Department of Defense Intelligence Information System (DODIIS) and operates the Joint Worldwide Intelligence Communications System (JWICS).

DIA also maintains a specialized research and analysis center. The Underground Facilities Analysis Center (UFAC) uses a range of intelligence resources to locate and assess tunnels, bunkers, and other underground facilities used by US adversaries. This center coordinates all such activities across the entire IC, and the director of the center reports jointly to the secretary of defense and the DNI.

The Federal Bureau of Investigation (Department of Justice)

The Federal Bureau of Investigation (FBI) is a law enforcement organization that exists at the federal level. However, it is also a threat-based, intelligence-driven national security organization that protects the United States from critical threats while safeguarding civil liberties. As both a component of the Department of Justice and a full member of the US IC, the FBI serves as a vital link between intelligence and law enforcement communities.

The FBI's top priority is combating the threat of terrorism, counterintelligence, and cybercrime. As to counterterrorism, the FBI gives particular attention to terrorist efforts to acquire and use WMDs. FBI agents have been credited with disrupting a number of terrorist plots in various stages of development, and the nature of these threats continues to evolve. In response, the FBI continuously adapts to trends in terrorist recruitment, financing, and training and terrorists' development of new weapons.

The FBI also maintains a counterintelligence role, addressing the threat of foreign intelligence services that attempt to infiltrate the US government. A similar threat comes from foreign business interests and students and scientists seeking to steal technology on behalf of foreign governments or commercial interests. Their investigations include economic espionage, financial crimes, export control violations, cyber intrusions, and the compromise of US strategic intellectual property.

Cyberterrorism and crime are on the forefront of the FBI intelligence efforts. Of greatest concern are terrorists or foreign state-sponsored elements targeting national information infrastructure and criminal enterprises and individuals who illegally access computer systems or spread malicious code. Other areas receiving priority focus are crimes that undermine the health of the economy, including large-scale financial institution frauds, securities and commodities fraud or bank fraud, environmental crimes, health-care fraud, and telemarketing fraud. In the area of violent crimes, the FBI focuses on increasingly sophisticated national and transnational gangs, dangerous fugitives, and kidnappers. The FBI leverages partnerships with over 800,000 state, local, and tribal law enforcement agencies through task forces and fusion centers to collect and disseminate intelligence, serving as a unique link between the intelligence and law enforcement communities.

Federal law, attorney general authorities, and executive orders give the FBI jurisdiction to investigate all federal crimes not assigned exclusively to another federal agency and to investigate threats to the national security. Additionally, there are other laws that give the FBI responsibility to investigate specific crimes. This combination of authorities gives the FBI the unique ability to address national security and criminal threats that are increasingly intertwined and to shift between the use of intelligence tools such as surveillance or recruiting sources and law enforcement tools of arrest and prosecution. Regardless of which tools are employed, law and policy require that the FBI's information-gathering activities use the least intrusive techniques possible to accomplish the objective and cannot be based solely on activities protected by the First Amendment.

The organization of the FBI intelligence operation is as follows:

- The National Security Branch (NSB) oversees the FBI's national security programs. It includes four divisions plus the Terrorist Screening Center (TSC).
- The Counterterrorism Division (CTD) focuses on both domestic and international terrorism. It oversees the Joint Terrorism Task Forces (JTTFs), which serve to coordinate the efforts of law enforcement agencies at the local, state, and federal levels to detect and disrupt terrorist activities.
- The Counterintelligence Division (CD) prevents and investigates foreign intelligence activities within the United States and espionage activities in the United States and overseas.
- The Directorate of Intelligence (DI) is the FBI's intelligence analysis component. It has embedded employees at FBI headquarters and in each field office through Field Intelligence Groups (FIGs) and fusion centers.
- The Weapons of Mass Destruction Directorate (WMDD) prevents individuals and groups from acquiring WMD capabilities and technologies for use against the United States and links all operational and scientific/technology components to accomplish this mission.
- The Terrorist Screening Center (TSC) was created to consolidate the US government's approach to terrorist screening and create a single, comprehensive watch list of known or suspected terrorists. The TSC helps ensure that federal, local, state, and tribal terrorist screeners have ready access to information and expertise.

National Geospatial-Intelligence Agency

By the mid-1990s, imagery was the basis for both imagery intelligence and map-based imagery products, and the IC wished to centralize the management of both of these functions. The NIMA, formally proposed by the secretary of defense and the director of the CIA in November 1995, was established on October 1, 1996. Through this creation, the NIMA joined five existing imagery interpretation and mapping organizations: the NPIC, the Defense Mapping Agency, the CIA's Office of Imagery Analysis, the DIA's Office of Imagery Analysis, and the Central Imagery Office. Other offices absorbed into the new agency include the Defense Dissemination Program Office and elements of the Defense Airborne Reconnaissance Office and National Reconnaissance.

Initially, the NIMA was organized into three main directorates: operations, systems and technology, and corporate affairs. Three key units within the Operations Directorate were Imagery Analysis, Geospatial Information and Services, and the Central Imagery Tasking Office. The latter was responsible for allocating targets to imagery collection systems and determining when the imagery was obtained.

Formed from several defense and intelligence agencies, the NIMA merged imagery, maps, charts, and environmental data to produce what has been called *geospatial intelligence*. The Imagery Analysis Unit combined the activities of the NPIC and the CIA and DIA imagery analysis organizations, while the Geospatial Information and Services Unit provided the mapping, charting, and geodesy products formerly provided by the DMA. The unit was responsible for producing strategic and tactical maps, charts, and databases and specialized products to support current and advanced weapons and navigation systems (Richelson et al., 2003).

Between 1995 and 1998, the NIMA products helped resolve many national and international issues, including long-standing border disputes between Peru and Ecuador and between Israel and southern Lebanon. The NIMA products also supported the Dayton Peace Accord efforts in the Balkans. In February 2000, the space shuttle Endeavor's Shuttle Radar Topography Mission (SRTM) provided the most detailed measurements of the planet's elevation ever gathered—data that will prove invaluable in supporting the NGA's geospatial-intelligence efforts.

The NIMA played a critical role in homeland security following the attacks of September 11. In the response and recovery phases of the disaster in New York City, the NIMA partnered with the US Geological Survey (USGS) to survey the World Trade Center site and determine the extent of the destruction. Then, in 2002, the NIMA partnered with federal organizations to provide geospatial assistance to the 2002 Winter Olympics in Utah.

On November 24, 2003, the president signed the 2004 Defense Authorization Bill, which included a provision to change the NIMA's name to the National Geospatial-Intelligence Agency (NGA). Today, the NGA develops imagery and map-based intelligence for national defense, homeland security, and navigation safety purposes. The NGA maintains a headquarters in Bethesda, Maryland, and major facilities in Washington, DC, Northern Virginia, and St. Louis, Missouri. NGA activities are organized under the five mission offices and four operations offices. The mission offices include the following:

- *Source Operations and Management Directorate*: The Source Operations and Management Directorate discovers, acquires, produces, delivers, and manages the data and information used to produce geospatial intelligence. This directorate manages the end-to-end execution of geospatial-intelligence information requirements. This provides the foundation for the "information superiority" needed by the president and executive office agencies, Congress, and the military.
- *Information Technology Services Directorate*: The IT Services Directorate is responsible for day-to-day systems operations and leveraging technology to ensure and protect the NGA's mission by operating the National System for Geospatial Intelligence (NSG—a unified community of geospatial-intelligence experts, producers, and users) and providing enterprise, corporate, dissemination, and information services.
- *Analysis and Production Directorate*: The Analysis and Production Directorate provides geospatial intelligence and services to policy makers, military decision makers, and operational "warfighters" and tailored support to civilian federal agencies and international organizations. This geospatial intelligence is derived from many sources.
- *InnoVision Directorate*: The InnoVision office forecasts future environments, defines future needs, establishes plans to align resources, and provides technology and process solutions to help NGA, end users, and partners. The InnoVision also provides the focal point in NGA to address the future; leads NGA into the future by developing comprehensive plans and technology initiatives based on analysis of intelligence trends, technology advances, and emerging customer and partner concepts; and helps to guide the agency as it adapts to new needs and the needs of the IC.

- *Xperience Directorate*: The Xperience Directorate, also called the X Directorate, is considered the "customer service" focus of the agency (Finn, 2013). Until 2013, this office was called the Online GEOINT Services offices. It is responsible for marketing the agencies' products and services in order to simplify and clarify access. The directorate merges several former web-based interface platforms into a single interface.

  The four operations offices maintained by NGA include

- Human Development,
- International Affairs,
- Military Support,
- Security and Installations.

  The NGA also provides imagery in support of major disasters as noted in the following sidebar.

National Geospatial-Intelligence Agency Responds to US Disasters

NGA's mission includes the following verbiage: "Know the Earth ... Show the Way ... Understand the World." The agency lives up to this mission in part by providing geospatial-intelligence support for global world events, disasters, and military actions. Examples of the natural disasters and other national security-related functions served by NGA products include the following:

- *2010 Deepwater Horizon Oil Spill*: During the greatest environmental disaster in US history, wherein over 210 million gallons of oil poured into the Gulf of Mexico, NGA mobilized and led a crisis action team that included staff from throughout the agency. The team provided intelligence analysis and geospatial-intelligence products in support of US Coast Guard operations. Support included unclassified commercial satellite imagery and geospatial products that focused on the Mississippi Delta and surrounding Gulf Coast areas—inclusive of three-dimensional models of Gulf Coast infrastructure, operational planning map atlases, and other graphic illustrations of the spill (Figure 5-4).
- *2008 Midwest Flooding*: In spring 2008, NGA partnered with the US Federal Emergency Management Agency (FEMA) to provide direct support for those affected by the Midwest floods. NGA used geospatial information and commercial imagery to determine the extent of the damage. NGA posted imagery and mapping products on our nga-earth.org website for residents and first responders to see the damage and watch recovery efforts.
- *2007 California Wildfires*: In the fall of 2007, NGA provided over 150 geospatial-intelligence products to FEMA to lend support in combating the California wildfires. NGA supplied damage assessments of major infrastructure in the area, assessments of areas still on fire and areas where the fire had been extinguished. This information was uploaded to the nga-earth.org website as a way for the public to see the damage without returning to the area. Our products greatly assisted firefighters and other first responders with relief efforts (Figure 5-4).
- *Hurricane Katrina*: NGA supported recovery efforts for hurricanes Katrina and Rita in 2005. NGA sent a team of analysts to the region to support FEMA and other first

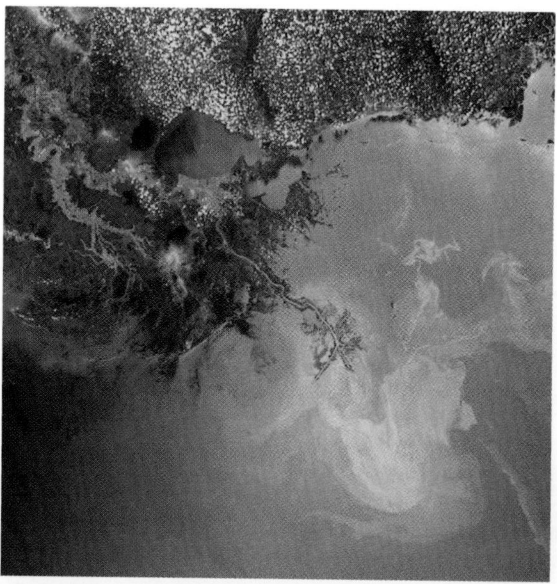

FIGURE 5-4 Deepwater horizon oil spill. *Source: NGA (2010).*

FIGURE 5-5 Hurricane Katrina. *Source: NGA (2006).*

responders. NGA provided imagery from commercial and US government satellites and from airborne platforms. NGA created the nga-earth.org website to show residents the extent of the damage and progress of the recovery efforts. As a result of our hard work, NGA was highlighted in the US government after action report on Hurricane Katrina under "What was Done Right" (Figure 5-5).

- *2004 Olympics*: NGA provided substantial support to the Olympic Games in Athens, Greece, in 2004 and Torino, Italy, in 2006. NGA deployed a team of analysts to assist each event with force protection and security issues. NGA lends its geospatial knowledge in helping officials create geospatial products including maps of the locations used for the events and surrounding key infrastructure.

Source: NGA (2011).

Perhaps the most well-known efforts of the agency, and the event that opened most peoples' eyes to its existence, is that of providing imagery in support of the raid on Osama bin Laden's compound in Abbottabad, Pakistan. NGA supported the Department of Defense and other agencies within the IC that were part of the operation by providing the imagery used to locate, monitor, and map the compound. NGA analysis also assisted in the creation of scale and full-size replicas of the compound for planning and practice.

National Reconnaissance Office

The National Reconnaissance Office (NRO) was established on September 6, 1961, to coordinate CIA reconnaissance activities with those of the DOD. The NRO's primary function has been to oversee the research and development, procurement, deployment, and operation of imaging, signals intelligence, and ocean surveillance satellites. It awards contracts, oversees the research and development efforts of contractors, supervises the launch of the payloads, and, in conjunction with the CIA and the NSA, operates these spacecraft. It has also been involved in the research, development, and procurement of selected aerial reconnaissance systems, such as the SR-71. From its inception until September 18, 1992, when its existence was formally acknowledged, the NRO operated as a classified organization. A major restructuring of the NRO also began to be implemented in 1992, which turned the NRO into a functional organization instead of a stand-alone organization (Richelson et al., 2003).

In its current setting, the NRO designs, builds, and operates the nation's reconnaissance satellites. NRO products, provided to an expanding list of customers such as the CIA and the DOD, can warn of potential trouble spots around the world, help plan military operations, and monitor the environment. The NRO is a DOD agency and is staffed by DOD and CIA personnel (Figure 5-6). The NRO has historically been one of the most clandestine intelligence organizations in the United States, but many parts of its operations have now been declassified. For example, the location of its headquarters, in Chantilly, Virginia, was declassified in 1994. In February 1995, CORONA, a photoreconnaissance program in operation from 1960 to 1972, was declassified, and 800,000 CORONA images were transferred to the National Archives and Records Administration. The NRO is known as the "nation's eyes and ears in space."

NRO intelligence-gathering and intelligence analysis activities are conducted at the request of the secretary of defense and/or the DNI. The director of National Reconnaissance Office (DNRO) is selected by the secretary of defense with the concurrence of the DNI and also serves as the assistant to the secretary of the Air Force (Intelligence Space Technology). The NRO's workforce of approximately 3000 includes personnel primarily from the Air Force, the CIA, and the Navy.

The NRO systems provide the foundation for global situational awareness and address many of the nation's most significant intelligence challenges. For instance, the NRO systems are the only collectors able

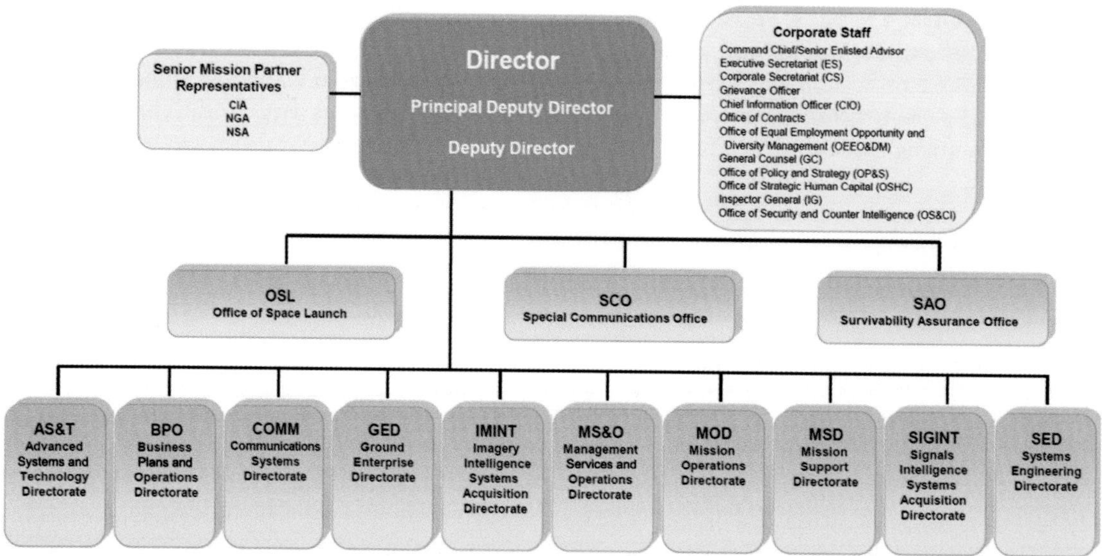

FIGURE 5-6 NRO organizational chart. *Source: NRO (2012) and NRO (2014).*

to access critical areas of interest, and data from overhead sensors provide unique information and perspectives not available from other sources.

The NRO systems

- monitor the proliferation of WMDs,
- track international terrorists, drug traffickers, and criminal organizations,
- develop highly accurate military targeting data and bomb damage assessments,
- support international peacekeeping and humanitarian relief operations,
- assess the impact of natural disasters, such as earthquakes, tsunamis, floods, and fires.

Together with other Department of Defense satellites, the NRO systems play a crucial role in providing global communications, precision navigation, early warning of missile launches and potential military aggression, signals intelligence, and near-real-time imagery to US forces to support the war on terrorism and other continuing operations. The NRO satellites also support civil customers in response to disaster relief and environmental research. Scientists created a global environment database using NRO imagery to help predict climate change, assess crop production, map habitats of endangered species, track oil spills, and study wetlands. Finally, the NRO data form the basis for products that help depict and assess the devastation in areas affected by natural disasters.

National Security Agency

On May 20, 1949, Secretary of Defense Louis Johnson established the Armed Forces Security Agency (AFSA) and placed it under the command of the Joint Chiefs of Staff. In theory, the AFSA was to direct the communications intelligence and electronic intelligence activities of the military service signals intelligence units (at that time, the Army Security Agency, Naval Security Group, and Air Force Security Service). In practice, however, the AFSA had little power, and its functions were characterized as activities not performed by the service units.

On October 24, 1952—the same day that he sent a (now-declassified) top-secret eight-page memorandum entitled "Communications Intelligence Activities" to the Secretaries of State and Defense—President Truman abolished the AFSA and transferred its personnel to the newly created National Security Agency (NSA). As its name indicates, the new agency was to have national, not just military, responsibilities. In 1971, the NSA became the National Security Agency/Central Security Service (NSA/CSS). The second half of NSA's title, which is rarely used, refers to its role in coordinating the signals intelligence activities of the military services (Richelson, 1999). Today, the NSA has two primary responsibilities: information assurance and signals intelligence.

The NSA is organized as follows:

- The Information Assurance Directorate (IAD) operates under the authority of the secretary of defense and ensures the availability, integrity, authentication, confidentiality, and nonrepudiation of national security and telecommunications and information systems (national security systems). The IAD is dedicated to providing information assurance solutions that serve to protect US information systems from harm. This mission involves many activities, including the following:
  - Detecting, reporting, and responding to cyber threats
  - Making encryption codes to securely pass information between systems
  - Embedding information assurance measures directly into the emerging global information grid
  - Building secure audio and video communications equipment
  - Making tamper-proof products
  - Providing trusted microelectronics solutions
  - Testing the security of its partners' and customers' systems
  - Providing operational security assistance
  - Evaluating commercial software and hardware against set standards
- The Signals Intelligence Directorate is responsible for understanding end users' intelligence information needs and for the collection, analysis and production, and dissemination of SIGINT. The NSA's SIGINT mission provides military leaders and policy makers with intelligence to ensure national defense and to advance US global interests, and the information attained is specifically limited to that that focuses on foreign powers, organizations, or persons and international terrorists.
- The Central Security Service (CSS) oversees the function of the military cryptological system, develops policy and guidance on the contributions of military cryptology to the Signals Intelligence/Information Security (SIGINT/INFOSEC) enterprise, and manages the partnership of the NSA and the Service Cryptologic Components. The NSA as a whole is known as "NSA/CSS."
- The NSA/CSS Threat Operations Center (NTOC) monitors the operations of the global network to identify network-based threats and protect the United States and allied networks.
- The National Security Operations Center (NSOC) is a 24 h a day/7 days a week operations center that, on behalf of the NSA/CSS, provides total situational awareness across the NSA/CSS enterprise for both foreign signals intelligence and information assurance, maintains cognizance of national security information needs, and monitors unfolding world events.
- The Research Directorate conducts research on signals intelligence and on information assurance for the US government.

DHS Office of Intelligence and Analysis

The original thinking behind the creation of DHS was to align the efforts of the various IC members. While this did not happen, DHS remains integral to the IC mission in that it drives the policy and leads the efforts aimed at ensuring US security by reducing the risk from terrorist attacks and responding to those attacks

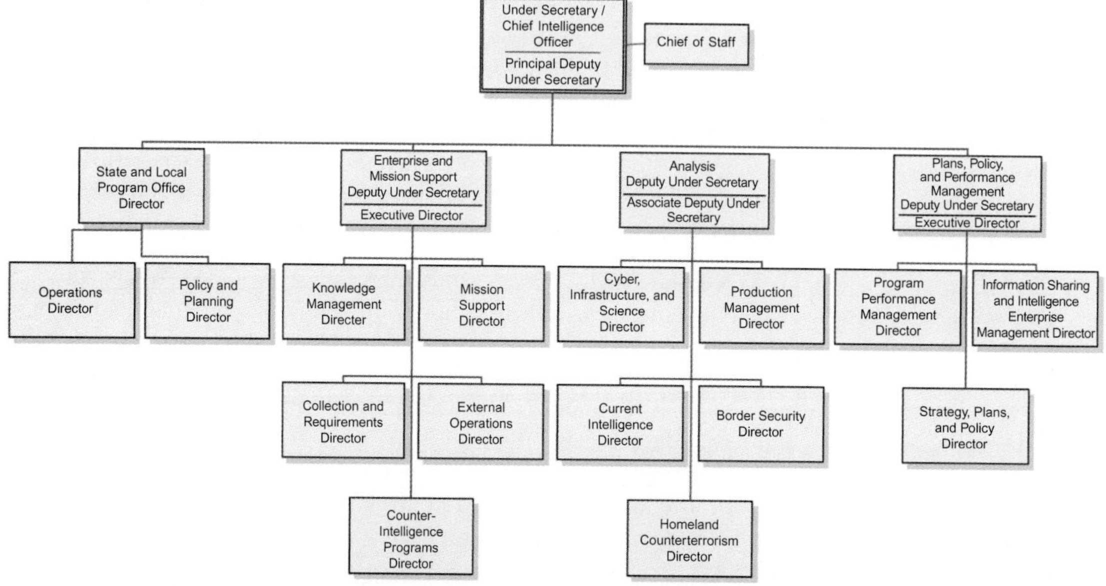

FIGURE 5-7 Office of Intelligence and Analysis organizational chart. *Source: DHS (2014).*

that do occur. It is through the Office of Intelligence and Analysis (I&A) that DHS interfaces most directly with the IC. I&A is an IC member and is the DHS intelligence function located at DHS headquarters in Washington, DC. It is led by the undersecretary for Intelligence and Analysis and is guided by both the Homeland Security Council and the Homeland Security Intelligence Council. As an IC member, I&A is tasked with identifying, gathering, and applying intelligence products from throughout the greater IC in order to better understand and assess domestic security risks. I&A also contributes to security by producing and sharing actionable intelligence to, in support of DHS leadership, partners at the state, local, and tribal levels, with the private sector, and among the other federal agencies involved in security and intelligence activities.

In line with the mission of its umbrella agency, I&A focuses on threats related to border security; chemical, biological, radiological, and nuclear (CBRN) issues, to include explosives and infectious diseases; critical infrastructure protection; extremists within the homeland; and travelers entering the homeland. Several other DHS subcomponents, including US Immigration and Customs Enforcement, Customs and Border Protection, Transportation Security Administration, Secret Service, and Citizenship and Immigration Services, maintain intelligence-gathering and intelligence-sharing functions despite that they are not part of the IC (Figure 5-7).

Department of State Bureau of Intelligence and Research

The Department of State Bureau of Intelligence and Research (INR) provides expert intelligence analysis to the secretary of state and senior policy makers on decisions regarding the protection of American interests around the world. INR serves as the Department of State focal point for all policy issues and activities involving the IC. INR assistant secretary reports directly to the secretary of state and serves as his or her principal adviser on all intelligence matters.

INR foreign affairs analysts utilize all-source intelligence, diplomatic reporting, public opinion polling, and interaction with US and foreign scholars, in conjunction with intelligence gathered by all IC partners, to formulate intelligence products. Their strong regional and functional backgrounds allow them to respond rapidly to changing policy priorities and to provide early warning and analysis of events and trends. INR analysts—a combination of Foreign Service Officers often with extensive in-country experience and civil service specialists with in-depth expertise—cover all countries and regional or transnational issues.

INR provides daily briefings, reports, and memoranda to the secretary of state and other department principals. INR also briefs members of Congress and their staffs as appropriate. INR products cover the world on foreign relations issues such as political/military developments, terrorism, narcotics, and trade. INR develops intelligence policy for the Department of State and works to harmonize all agencies' intelligence.

The INR Humanitarian Information Unit (HIU) serves as a nucleus for unclassified information related to complex emergencies and provides a coordinating mechanism for data sharing among the US government, the United Nations, nongovernmental organizations, and foreign governments. The bureau also administers the Title VIII Grant Program, an initiative funded by Congress for senior-level academic research in Russian, Eurasian, and East European studies.

Debate Over the Reach of Intelligence Activities

In 2013, Booz Allen Hamilton contractor Edward Snowden stole thousands of classified documents while working at a National Security Administration facility in Hawaii. Snowden traveled to Hong Kong before releasing a number of these documents to several media outlets based both within and outside the United States.

The release of these documents exposed a number of classified intelligence programs and practices and in turn initiated a debate on how much Americans are willing to allow themselves to be subject to surveillance by their own government in the name of heightened security. The source of the debate stemmed from the fact that several of these programs were found to have inadvertently or intentionally collected personal information on US citizens—a practice that is strictly limited by the US Constitution. The most prominent of these programs include

- PRISM, a data mining program that functioned by collecting Internet communications including e-mail, chat, videoconferencing, and voice-over-IP calls,
- MAINWAY, an NSA database of mobile phone metadata for calls made on the AT&T and Verizon networks,
- DISHFIRE, a program that intercepts text messages from throughout the world,
- XKEYSCORE, a program that is believed to enable undetected surveillance of Internet browsing, communications, and other activities across the wider spectrum of users (rather than requiring specific targeting) (Franceschi-Bicchierei, 2014).

The leaks also led to increased public knowledge about the existence of the Foreign Intelligence Surveillance Court (FISC). The FISC is a specialized, secret court that considers requests for permission to perform surveillance on foreign targets. These courts were originally created in the 1970s in response to similar fears about unchecked government surveillance. The courts were created under the Foreign Intelligence Surveillance Act (FISA), which passed in 1978. This court is unique in that its jurisdiction is so highly limited to the granting of these requests. It operates in secret, and its judges are selected by a process that differs considerably from the regular appointment method (the 11 judges are appointed by the Chief Justice of the Supreme Court). The revelations have caused Congress and the American public to question how these courts operate given that all contested programs were given permission to proceed (Nolan and Thompson, 2014).

Snowden's leaks also led to a national debate on the limits of IC activities, which were repeated in many other countries where similar programs were revealed to have been occurring. The US government maintains that while there may have been incidents where American citizens were inadvertently targeted by these programs, their intent was to monitor communications between foreign targets or communications directly between two people located on opposite sides of the US border. The Department of Defense and many security professionals contend that the leaks did more harm than good in that they enabled terrorists, adversarial governments, and other criminals to more easily avoid US efforts to monitor them (Dilanian and Serrano, 2014). Privacy activists argued that the leaks enabled a discussion about Internet and communications privacy that might not otherwise have been possible.

In terms of actual changes, it is doubtful that the IC will cease collecting communications information, but there will likely be greater oversight of such programs and more stringent protections to ensure that surveillance does not infringe upon constitutional rights. In September 2014, President Obama announced that the government would no longer be storing mass amounts of metadata on calls as it had before, but would rather require mobile phone carriers to store that information at their facilities. The USA FREEDOM Act was also passed by the Senate in order to address this issue. If enacted, the act would create new mechanisms by which telephone metadata were collected such that bulk collection was no longer needed (nor permitted) (DNI, 2014a). As of publication, Edward Snowden remains in Russia where he has been granted asylum status until 2017. He is wanted in the United States for a number of charges that stem from the misuse of classified information.

Conclusion

Despite that Congress and President Bush were not able to consolidate the various intelligence agencies under a single department "roof," there has been significant improvement in the collection, analysis, and dissemination of intelligence since the 9/11 attacks. This coordination among various agencies has also led to some failures that otherwise may not have occurred, such as Bradley Manning's 2009 release of over 250,000 diplomatic cables to WikiLeaks, which was only possible after the classified computer systems of the Department of State (which produced the cables) and the Department of Defense (which is where Manning worked when he stole the cables) became linked. Stark differences between the security procedures at the Department of State (whose policies on the handling of classified materials would never have allowed for such a leak to have occurred) and those of the Department of Defense (which allowed a low-level employee to not only access information that had no pertinence to his position but also download the information onto a removable drive without detection) were never rectified. The changes that have occurred thus far have been credited by those in the IC to have helped prevent or deter a number of terrorist plots in both the United States and overseas. Intelligence is not capable of stopping every threat, as the Boston Marathon bombings illustrate, but they have certainly been instrumental in disrupting many terrorist networks including that of al-Qaeda. The question about how far Americans are willing to allow their government to watch and listen to their activities in the name of increased security remains unanswered. It is likely that, like most other aspects of risk management, the direction this topic takes will depend upon whether or not American's perceive themselves to remain in the sights of the foreign and domestic terrorists such programs are designed to monitor.

Key Terms

Consequence: The result of a terrorist attack or other hazard that reflects the level, duration, and nature of the loss. For the purposes of the NIPP, consequences are divided into four main categories: public health and safety, economic, psychological, and governance impacts.

Crisis Management: A proactive management effort to avoid crisis and the creation of strategy that minimizes adverse impacts of crisis to the organization when it could not be prevented. Effective crisis management requires a solid understanding of the organization, its strategy, liabilities, stakeholders, and legal framework combined with advanced communication, leadership, and decision-making skills to lead the organization through the crisis with minimizing potential loss.

Director of Central Intelligence (DCI): Director of the Central Intelligence Agency. In the aftermath of the 9/11 intelligence reform, the DCI is reporting to the Office of the Director of National Intelligence for overall intelligence coordination purposes.

Information Sharing and Analysis Center (ISAC): ISACs are sectoral information analysis and information-sharing centers that bring together representatives and decision makers of a given sector for the purposes of critical infrastructure protection and disaster preparedness.

Intelligence: Intelligence is a secret state activity to understand or influence foreign entities (CIA).

Intelligence Community: The collective body of US government agencies that have been tasked with the responsibility of collecting, analyzing, or acting upon intelligence.

Office of the Director of National Intelligence (DNI): The statutory authority created on the basis of the recommendations of the 9/11 Commission and tasked by the president to coordinate the holistic intelligence of the United States. Directors of member agencies of the IC report to the DNI. The DNI is also responsible for establishing budget priorities for the overall US intelligence effort.

Review Questions

1. What are the key intelligence agencies in the United States? Briefly comment on their roles in terms of homeland security.
2. Describe how intelligence has evolved in the United States.
3. Is the Office of the National Director of Intelligence a viable alternative for the consolidation of intelligence agencies under one government "roof," as was originally proposed in the early days following the 9/11 attacks?
4. What are the various steps in the intelligence cycle, and what is involved in each?
5. What are the different categories of intelligence?

References

9/11 Commission, 2004. The 9/11 commission report. http://bit.ly/1DoQNC7.

Central Intelligence Agency, 2014. Offices of CIA. CIA website: http://1.usa.gov/1rwWEyH (accessed 10/28/2014).

Congressional Research Service, 2004a. RL32506—The Proposed Authorities of a National Intelligence Director: Issues for Congress and Side-by-Side Comparison of S. 2845, H.R. 10, and Current Law. http://bit.ly/1nMaUs5.

Congressional Research Service, 2004b. RS21948—The National Intelligence Director and Intelligence Analysis. http://bit.ly/1tDmw2I.

DHS, 2014. Office of Intelligence & Analysis organizational chart. DHS website: http://1.usa.gov/ZVCKas (accessed 10/28/2014).

Dilanian, K., Serrano, R., 2014. Snowden leaks severely hurt US security, two house members say. Los Angeles Times (January 9). http://lat.ms/1yGeepT.

Director of National Intelligence (DNI), 2013. US National Intelligence: An Overview. DNI website: http://1.usa.gov/1u2jy8Q (April 19).

DNI, 2014a. Joint statement from the ODNI and the US DOJ on the declassification of renewal of collection under Section 501 of the FISA. DNI Press Release (September 12). http://1.usa.gov/12ZMi66.

DNI, 2014b. Chief Information Officer. DNI website: http://1.usa.gov/1wuD3Vh (accessed 10/27/14).

DNI, 2014c. Systems & resource analysis. DNI website: http://1.usa.gov/1pPPFBs (accessed 10/27/14).

FBI, 2014. Intelligence Gathering Disciplines. Directorate of Intelligence. FBI website http://1.usa.gov/1rJcdob (accessed 10/27/14).

Finn, K., 2013. Xperience NGA. Pathfinder Fall, 6–8. http://1.usa.gov/1sxgDh7.

Franceschi-Bicchierei, L., 2014. The ten biggest revelations from Edward Snowden's leaks. Mashable June 4, http://on.mash.to/1zef0gX.

Intelligence.Gov, 2014a. Organization. IC website: http://1.usa.gov/1tvsTVI (accessed 10/27/14).

Intelligence.Gov, 2014b. The intelligence cycle. IC website: http://1.usa.gov/12O5nbk (accessed 10/27/14).

NGA, 2006. Hurricane Katrina. NGA in history. NGA website: http://1.usa.gov/1DnMs25.

NGA, 2010. Deepwater horizon oil spill. NGA in history. NGA website: http://1.usa.gov/1wCVbgz.

NGA, 2011. National Geospatial Intelligence Agency responds to U.S. disasters. NGA website. What We Do (accessed October 2011).

Nolan, A., Thompson, II R.M., 2014. Reform of the federal intelligence surveillance courts: procedural and operational changes. Congressional Research Service, R43362.

NRO, 2012. Organizational chart. NRO website: http://1.usa.gov/1nLlui6 (accessed 10/28/14).

NRO, 2014. NRO organization. NRO website: http://1.usa.gov/1nLlui6 (accessed 20/28/2014).

Office of the Director of National Intelligence, 2009. National Intelligence: A Consumer's Guide. Intelligence Overview. Office of the Director of National Intelligence, Washington, DC.

Office of the Director of National Intelligence (DNI), 2011. National intelligence: an overview. http://1.usa.gov/1rJdmMm.

Richelson, J.T., 1999. The U.S. Intelligence Community, fourth ed. Westview Press, Boulder, CO.

Richelson, J.T., Gefter, J., Waters, M., et al., 2003. U.S. espionage and intelligence, 1947–1996. Digital National Security Archive. Mfiche 2552 GRN–MTXT.

Smith, B.F., 1983. The Shadow Warriors: OSS, and the Origins of the CIA. Basic Books, New York.

6

Border Security, Immigration, and Customs Enforcement

What You Will Learn

- A detailed overview of the immigration and customs functions of government and the purposes each serves with regard to homeland security and economic vitality
- The importance of national borders and the functions of the government that pertain to the movement of people and goods across these borders
- The role of various homeland security organizations in performing immigration and customs enforcement services

Introduction

A nation's borders are of critical strategic importance because of the critical role they play in its economic vitality and commerce. They are the foundation of the nation-state concept, help to establish national identity, and enable protection of state sovereignty. However, the nature of borders is changing as increases in the globalization of economic systems and the interconnectedness of transportation networks have linked every American community with the outside world. The vast system of airports, seaports, pipelines, roadways, railways, and waterways has posed incredible challenges to the border concept. The nation's sea, land, and air borders remain gateways for imported and exported goods and for the transit of people. And to a growing extent, their effectiveness and efficiency are thus vital to enabling the country's trade capacity and capabilities.

Borders are not perfect and, in fact, have been found to be very porous. In few places, they are much more than a fence or a physical feature and therefore do not inherently limit movement into and out of the country through clandestine entry or exit points. This is true not only for illegal immigrants but also for illegal or illicit goods. Therefore, the security and control of borders is of utmost importance in the drive to mitigate the risk posed by the penetration of unwanted or dangerous people and goods into the country. Human traffickers, smugglers, drug dealers, criminals, terrorists, illegal drugs, conventional weapons, undeclared or counterfeit products, biological agents, and weapons of mass destruction (WMDs) are but a small sample of the many possible individuals and items that together mandate the existence of strong national borders.

The Department of Homeland Security (DHS) has been tasked with managing the legal movement of goods and people through the nation's borders and with protecting these same borders from illegal infiltration. This chapter explores the DHS functions of border protection, immigration, and customs enforcement.

Knowledge Check

What does a nation risk in failing to protect its borders? What are the economic repercussions? What are the security considerations? What other problems might arise?

Border Security

The United States shares 5525 miles of border with Canada and 1989 miles with Mexico. The maritime border includes 95,000 miles of shoreline and a 3.4 million square miles of exclusive economic zone. Each year, more than 500 million people cross these borders to enter the United States, and approximately 330 million of them are foreign nationals.

Entry points into the country are not limited to its external borders, however. International seaports and airports can be hundreds of miles from neighbors Canada or Mexico and may be far upriver from any international body of water. Each international airport, and each major seaport, therefore serves as another doorway for foreign visitors and goods and, likewise, another opportunity for illegal immigration and illicit products and materials. The concept of border security must not be limited in one's mind to a guarding of the nation's perimeter and that of its various territories.

The United States has actively maintained border control since the turn of the twentieth century. The first border patrols were conducted by US Immigration Service watchmen on horseback, who began their mission to curb illegal border crossings in 1904. At that time, patrols were unpredictable, irregular, and limited by the availability of uncertain resources. Border patrol agents, called mounted guards, were based in El Paso, Texas. At most times, approximately 75 mounted guards (and oftentimes far fewer) were tasked with the responsibility of patrolling the entire length of the Mexico border. Their primary function was to stave off illegal immigrants who were arriving from China.

Congress authorized a separate group of mounted guards in 1915 called the mounted inspectors. This unit operated on horseback, in cars, and in boats. Like the mounted guards, the mounted inspectors focused their efforts on illegal immigrants from China. During that time, US military troops were similarly tasked with patrolling the US-Mexico border in support of the mounted guards and inspectors. When military units interdicted illegal aliens, they were brought to immigration inspection sites staffed by mounted inspectors. Texas Rangers were the fourth group assigned patrol duties in Texas, and they were found to be highly effective in supporting the border protection effort.

Given the economic importance of international commerce and the prospect of foreign military threats that characterized early twentieth-century America, the US government was much more concerned with customs violations and espionage than the trickle of people trying to illegally enter the country in search of employment. However, the government agencies and officials charged with inspecting the people and products that entered and left the United States through established border crossings felt that their efforts were ineffective without proper enforcement between these official inspection stations. In 1917, the US government issued a higher head tax and introduced a literacy requirement for entry into the country, and the motive for illegal immigration grew almost instantaneously. The number of illegal crossing attempts (and successes) quickly followed suit.

Most Americans are familiar with the role the 18th Amendment statutes had in banning the production and sale of alcohol. However, most are not aware that this same amendment also introduced finite limits on the number of people permitted to immigrate to the United States (as guided by the Immigration Acts of 1921 and 1924). The enforcement of the nation's borders received newfound interest among lawmakers and bureaucrats in the wake of these changes given that the new limits dramatically increased the number of people attempting illegal entry—especially those for which legal means proved inadequate or otherwise unsuccessful.

FIGURE 6-1 Del Rio Border Patrol inspectors gathered near vehicles in 1925. *Source: US Customs and Border Protection. http://1.usa.gov/1BT3F85.*

Congress passed the Labor Appropriation Act of 1924 on May 28 of that year, thereby establishing the US Border Patrol for the purpose of securing the nation's borders between the established inspection stations. In 1925, the Border Patrol's duties were expanded to include the seacoast boundaries as well. The size of this agency was rapidly expanded to a staff of 450 officers tasked with meeting the law's requirements (see Figure 6-1). Recruits were drawn from organizations familiar with the task including the Texas Rangers, local sheriffs' departments, and appointees from the Civil Service Register of Railroad Mail Clerks. The government initially provided each agent a badge and revolver, but these officials did not officially begin wearing standard uniforms until 1928.

In 1932, the Border Patrol split management responsibility between the Mexican and Canadian borders, with a director in charge assigned to each. Because alcohol smuggling was the primary concern at this point, most of the Border Patrol's staff were assigned to the Canadian border and were headquartered in Detroit.

In 1933, President Franklin D. Roosevelt joined together the Bureau of Immigration and the Bureau of Naturalization into what became the Immigration and Naturalization Service (INS). One year later, the first Border Patrol Academy opened as a training school at Camp Chigas in El Paso, TX. Just 7 years later, the new INS was transferred out of the Department of Labor (where it was first placed due to the nature of immigration prior to that time) and into the Department of Justice. The agency's human resource base more than doubled to 1531 INS officers by the end of World War II. During the same time, the Border Patrol saw its ranks grow to over 1400 employees in both law enforcement and civilian positions. During World War II, the Border Patrol expanded its duties to include the guarding of alien detention camps, protecting diplomats, and assisting the US Coast Guard (USCG) in searching for enemy saboteurs. It was at this time that aircraft became an integral part of operations.

In 1952, new legislation expanded the power of the Border Patrol to include the boarding and search of conveyances for illegal immigrants anywhere in the United States, not just at the points of entry. In that initial year, US agents deported 52,000 illegal immigrants to Mexico. When the program lost its budget after just 1 year, the Mexican government began offering train rides from the border for its deported nationals—yet this program also ended after less than a year. Many more iterations of deportation programs followed within a few years and included the use of planes, trains, and buses, among the means of conveyance, to remove illegal immigrants from the country. In all cases, it was found that the cost of deportation was prohibitively expensive and most deportees would simply return soon after being deported on account of the weak monitoring capacity that typified the southern border.

In the late 1950s, some immigrants turned their attention to private aircraft to enter the United States, and in the decade that followed, the nation saw a spate of hijacked commercial aircraft used in such efforts. In response, Border Patrol agents began working with the airline industry by accompanying flights to prevent illegal immigrants from taking control of planes. This increased pressure gave rise to a more robust alien smuggling industry as people turned to "expert" assistance in helping them to avoid the growing layers of protection.

With the assistance of organized smuggling and an increasing economic draw, illegal immigration spiraled out of control in the 1980s and 1990s. In turn, the Border Patrol requested and received increased funding to support growth in terms of both manpower and technology. Through the use of infrared imaging (night vision), seismic sensors (to detect walking and vehicle movement), and modern computing power, Border Patrol agents were better equipped to locate, apprehend, and process intending illegal immigrants.

The INS initiated a program called "Operation Hold the Line" in 1993 to begin to stave off the unchecked flow of illegal immigrants. This program, which was highly successful, concentrated agents and equipment in high-risk areas and increased the level of visibility of the agency for deterrence purposes. In 1994, "Operation Gatekeeper" was implemented in San Diego using similar tactics, resulting in a reduction of successful illegal immigrant crossings by 75%. A defined and strategic national border control plan was introduced at this time, which established a long-term course of action for the Border Patrol.

Following the 9/11 terrorist attacks, weaknesses in the nation's border security and immigration systems were exposed. It was recognized that these two functions were vital to national security and were therefore a natural fit in the new DHS. Like most other agencies that were moved into DHS, the Border Patrol became part of the new agency on March 1, 2003 (in the US Customs and Border Protection (CBP)).

Immigration

Immigration is defined as the act of entering and settling permanently in another country and/or becoming a permanent resident or a legal citizen of that country. The United States is a nation that was founded on the principles of open immigration, and all but a few of its present-day citizens trace their roots back to immigrants that arrived from other countries. Understandably, immigration is closely tied to that of border security, given that a nation's borders exist to ensure that only those transiting legal channels are able to enter the nation. It is through the function of immigration that foreign citizens gain such access.

The granting of residency and citizenship of foreign nationals is guided by a nation's immigration laws. Over the course of America's history, these laws have changed often, reflecting the volatility of national attitudes about the value of open doors in relation to the need to address a growing workforce. There has always existed a global demand for residency and citizenship in the United States given the strength of its economy, the high standard of living, the availability of jobs, and the prospect of a better life for many who have struggled fruitlessly in their native countries. At the same time, many US businesses have looked outward to meet manpower needs as the strength of the US economy has made certain low-wage and seasonal jobs harder to fill.

In America's first two hundred years, spanning from about 1600 to 1800, it is estimated that less than 1 million people migrated to thc colonies or the newly independent United States. During this period, law only permitted citizenship to those deemed Caucasian (with expansion to other races added in the nineteenth and twentieth centuries). Then, beginning in about 1820 with the advent of industrialization, immigration rates increased. For the next 100 years, about 30 million people migrated to the United States, increasing the nation's population 30-fold.

Immigration law aimed at limiting residency or citizenship for foreign nationals who first appeared during this time. The Immigration Act of 1882 levied a tax of 50 cents on each immigrant to the United States, which helped to generate revenue to support the enforcement of immigration provisions through a new immigration service. The Immigration Act of 1891 established the Office of the Superintendent of Immigration within the Department of Treasury, which was responsible for admitting, rejecting, and processing intending immigrants. Immigration inspectors were recruited and stationed at major US ports of entry (POEs) to track passengers as they arrived on incoming ships. The immigration station at Ellis Island in New York, which opened in January 1892, is the most famous of these (see Figure 6-2).

Legislation in March 1895 upgraded the Office of Immigration to the Bureau of Immigration and changed the agency head's title from Superintendent of Immigration to Commissioner General of Immigration. The bureau's first task was to standardize basic operating and regulatory procedures. For example, inspectors queried arrivals about their suitability for permanent entry and recorded their admission or rejection on manifest records. Detention guards cared for those who were detained until their cases were decided and, if the decision was negative, until they were deported. Inspectors served on boards of special inquiry that reviewed each exclusion case.

In 1913, the Department of Commerce and Labor reorganized into two separate cabinet departments (as they exist today). The Bureau of Immigration and Naturalization also separated into two distinct bureaus, but they were reunited in 1933 by executive order into today's INS. President Roosevelt moved

FIGURE 6-2 The registry room at Ellis Island. *Source: National Park Service.*

the INS from the Department of Labor to the Department of Justice in 1940, thereby changing the nature of immigration to reflect its national security implications. In fact, it is the INS that was tasked with organizing and managing the internment camps and detention facilities of aliens and US citizens considered to be from "enemy" nations.

Prior to the creation of the INS, the 1921 Emergency Quota Act was passed, which restricted the number of immigrants annually from any country to 3% of the number of residents from that country already living in the United States (per the most recent census). This was followed by the Immigration Act of 1924, which lowered the 1921 quota to 2%, further restricted immigrants from southern and eastern Europe, and prohibited the immigration of people from East Asia and India. The War Brides Act of 1945 facilitated admission of the spouses and families of returning American soldiers. The Displaced Persons Act of 1948 and the Refugee Relief Act of 1953 allowed many refugees, displaced by the war and unable to enter the United States under regular immigration procedures, to be admitted. With the onset of the Cold War, the Hungarian Refugee Act of 1956, the Refugee-Escapee Act of 1957, and the Cuban Adjustment Act of 1966 did much the same, offering a new home to the "huddled masses" who sought freedom, opportunity, and escape from tyranny.

In 1965, the Immigration and Nationality Act (INA) amendments removed any quotas related to specific nationalities. This legislation served to significantly change the nature of the US population in the years to come, with those of European lineage falling from 60% in 1970 to less than 15% in 2000. During the half century that followed this act, immigration grew and grew, doubling in size each decade. However, the Immigration Reform and Control Act of 1986 expanded the INS's responsibilities, giving it more law enforcement powers. One of the most important provisions in this regard was that it charged the agency with enforcing sanctions against American employers who hired undocumented aliens.

In 1990, the Immigration Act of 1990 increased this rate almost overnight by about 40% by raising the statutory limit from 500,000 per year to 700,000 per year and by instituting a new "visa lottery program" that helped people from poorer countries to attain citizenship. Annual immigration rates continued to rise over time despite recommendations from presidential commissions that recommended curtailing rates significantly, and in the first years of the twenty-first century, well over 1 million people per year were granted citizenship. In 2013, the most recent year for which complete records are available, 990,553 people were granted permanent residency—the first time it had dropped below 1 million in over a decade (likely representative of the relatively high unemployment that existed during that time).

The emphasis on controlling illegal immigration for reasons of economic and national security and crime control fostered INS's growth in the late twentieth century. The INS workforce grew from 8000 in the 1940s to more than 30,000 in 1998. The one-time force of immigrant inspectors became a corps of officers specializing in inspection, examination, adjudication, legalization, investigation, patrol, and refugee and asylum issues. In 2003, as a direct result of the 9/11 terrorist attacks, the INS was transferred to DHS. Rather than transferring as a distinct unit, the INS divisions were broken into three DHS agencies, namely, the US Citizenship and Immigration Services, US Immigration and Customs Enforcement (ICE), and the US Customs and Border Protection.

Immigration enforcement in the United States is conducted through the following functions, each of which is described in the context of specific DHS components in this chapter:

- Inspections
- Border Patrol
- Investigations
- Detention and removal

Customs Enforcement

Nations protect their national economic interests within the greater global economy by levying import taxes, called *duties*, on foreign goods and by controlling the rate of flow and quantity of specific goods that enter the country. The inspection of goods collection of duties is performed by a customs agency or office, which remains a traditional function of government.

The United States initiated its customs service function soon after declaring independence in 1776. The right to collect duties was a major factor in the call for declaration and was subsequently a way for the new government to generate significant revenue. The first official action relevant to customs was the Tariff Act of July 4, 1789, signed by George Washington, which authorized the collection of duties on imported goods. Only 4 weeks later, Congress established the Customs Service and identified the nation's POE. Established were 59 collection districts, which were also POEs, and 116 ports of delivery. The legislation provided for presidential appointment of 59 collectors, 10 naval officers, and 33 surveyors. The organization fell under the direct authority of the Secretary of Treasury.

For 125 years, the collection of customs generated almost all of the government's revenue and fueled the nation's rapid growth. By 1835, the revenue collected on imported goods had helped to fully eliminate the national debt. The work of the Customs Service funded all other executive department agencies and functions and paid all military and civilian government employee salaries. As such, the Customs Service became the largest federal agency at that time, and even in 1792, it represented 80% of the staff of the US Department of Treasury (500 employees).

The United States remains a major importer of foreign goods, and at present, almost 16% of the national budget is supported by income from customs. The US Customs Service ensures that all imports and exports comply with US laws and regulations. The Customs Service collects and protects the revenue, guards against smuggling, and is responsible for the following:

- Assessing and collecting customs duties, excise taxes, fees, and penalties due on imported merchandise
- Interdicting and seizing contraband, including narcotics and illegal drugs
- Processing persons, baggage, cargo, and mail and administering certain navigation laws
- Detecting and apprehending persons engaged in fraudulent practices designed to circumvent customs and related laws
- Protecting American business and labor and intellectual property rights by enforcing US laws intended to prevent illegal trade practices, including provisions related to quotas and the marking of imported merchandise—the Anti-Dumping Act—and by providing customs recordation fees for copyrights, patents, and trademarks
- Protecting the general welfare and security of the United States by enforcing import and export restrictions and prohibitions, including the export of critical technology used to develop WMD and money laundering
- Collecting accurate import and export data for compilation of international trade statistics

Border Security, Immigration, and Customs in the Department of Homeland Security

In its initial organization, DHS consolidated the various agencies responsible for the safety, security, and control of the borders under the Directorate of Border and Transportation Security (BTS). These agencies include the ICE agency (previously the INS), the CBP (previously the Customs Service), the USCG, and the

US Citizenship and Immigration Services (USCIS). With the reorganization effort initiated in the latter half of 2005, the Directorate of Border and Transportation Security was replaced with the Directorate of Policy Planning, and its policy functions were transferred to the new directorate. In today's DHS, the agencies mentioned above have direct reporting responsibility to the secretary of Homeland Security.

The increasing urgency for more effective customs and border protection measures has forced government agencies to come up with new initiatives to minimize border breaches. The challenge has been in minimizing the entry of illegal immigrants and substances into the United States while concurrently preserving the efficient travel of legal people and goods into the country.

The three functions described in the preceding text of this chapter (pp. 232–237) are today managed throughout DHS, but the most direct responsibilities fall within four specific functional elements:

- The US Customs and Border Protection
- The US Immigration and Customs Enforcement
- The US Coast Guard
- The US Citizenship and Immigration Services

The US Customs and Border Protection

The US Customs and Border Protection (CBP) is the only agency responsible for protecting the sovereign borders of the United States at and between the official POE. CBP is considered the front line in protecting the nation against terrorist attacks. The CBP also ensures national economic security by regulating and facilitating the lawful movement of goods and persons across US borders. CBP is one of DHS's largest and most complex components (Figure 6-3).

The Border Patrol

The mission of the Border Patrol is to prevent terrorists and their weapons (including WMD) from entering the United States while ensuring that the flow of legal immigration and goods is maintained. The Border Patrol is specifically responsible for patrolling nearly 6000 miles of Mexican and Canadian international land borders and over 2000 miles of coastal waters surrounding the Florida peninsula and the island of Puerto Rico.

As described earlier in this chapter (pp. 234–236), the Border Patrol has grown from a handful of mounted agents in the early twentieth century to a dynamic workforce of over 21,000 agents employed today. Border Patrol agents carry out their mission by maintaining surveillance, following up leads, responding to electronic sensor alarms and aircraft sightings, and interpreting and following tracks. Some of the major activities include maintaining traffic checkpoints along highways leading from border areas and conducting city patrol and transportation checks and antismuggling investigations.

In many places, the US border traverses remote landscapes, oftentimes through uninhabited deserts, canyons, or mountains. To address the associated challenges, the Border Patrol has to employ specialized equipment and methods that enable it to accomplish its mission despite the inhospitable conditions. Electronic sensors have been placed at strategic locations along the border to detect people or vehicles entering the country illegally, and video monitors and night vision scopes are used regularly to detect illegal entries. Agents patrol the border in vehicles, in boats, and, when required, on foot. In some areas, Border Patrol agents ride horses or drive all-terrain motorcycles, bicycles, and snowmobiles (see section "Examples of Border Patrol Tactics").

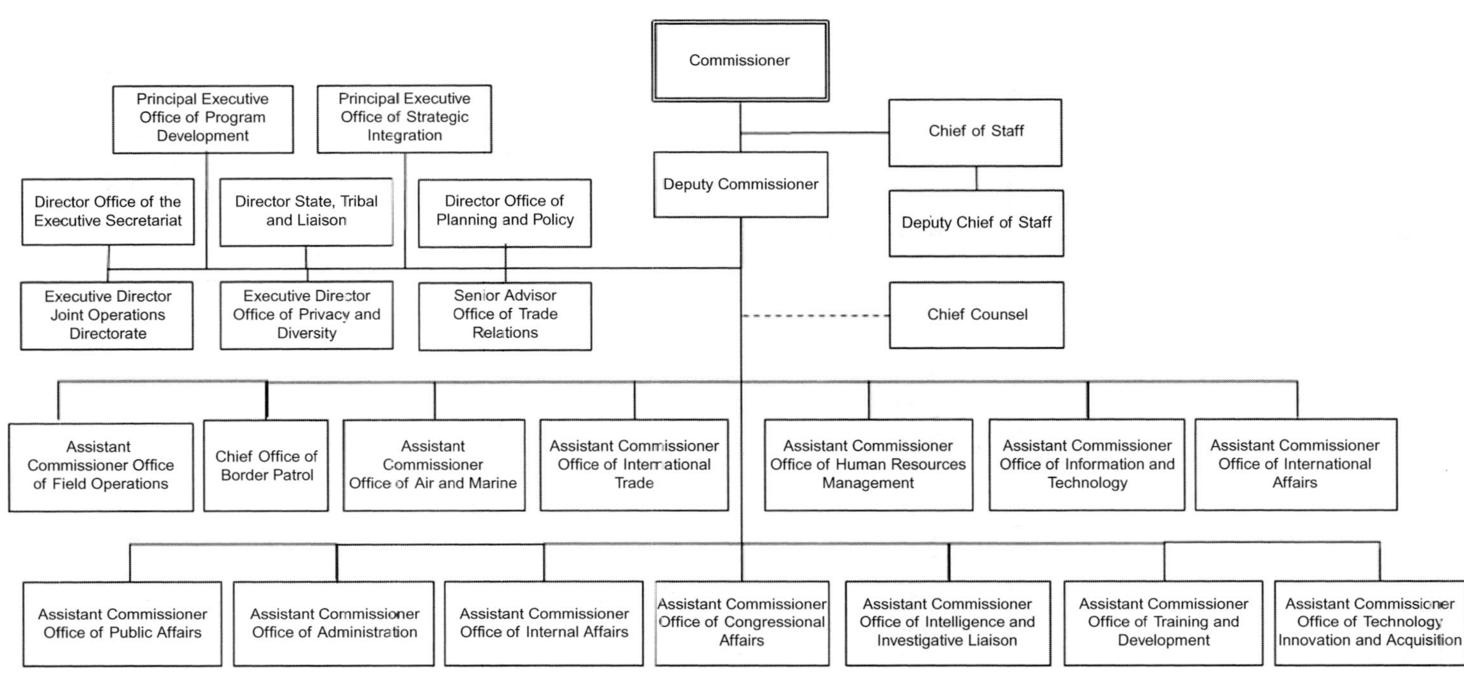

FIGURE 6-3 Customs and Border Protection organizational chart. *Source: CBP (2014f).*

Examples of Border Patrol Tactics

- *Linewatch operations*: Linewatch operations are conducted near international boundaries and coastlines in areas of Border Patrol jurisdiction to prevent the illegal entry and smuggling of aliens into the United States and to intercept those who do enter illegally before they can escape from border areas.
- *Sign-cutting operations*: Sign-cutting is the detection and the interpretation of any disturbances in natural terrain conditions that indicate the presence or passage of people, animals, or vehicles.
- *Traffic checks*: Traffic checks are conducted on major highways leading away from the border (1) to detect and apprehend illegal aliens attempting to travel farther into the interior of the United States after evading detection at the border and (2) to detect illegal narcotics.
- *Transportation checks*: Transportation checks are inspections of interior-bound conveyances, which include buses, commercial aircraft, passenger and freight trains, and marine craft.
- *Marine patrol*: Along the coastal waterways of the United States and Puerto Rico and interior waterways common to the United States and Canada, the Border Patrol conducts border control activities from the decks of marine craft of various sizes. The Border Patrol maintains over 109 vessels, ranging from blue-water craft to inflatable-hull craft, in 16 sectors, in addition to headquarters' special operations components.
- *Horse and bike patrol*: Horse units patrol remote areas along the international boundary that are inaccessible to standard all-terrain vehicles. Bike patrol aids city patrol and is used over rough terrain to support linewatch.

Source: USCBP (2014b).

In FY 2013, Border Patrol agents apprehended over 420,000 people entering the country illegally. Apprehensions have been on the decline for the past several years as a result of improved enforcement, improved infrastructure, and new technologies. Interestingly, while the number of apprehensions of people from Mexico has remained relatively constant, the number of people apprehended who are from countries other than Mexico—most notably those in Central America—rose by more than 50% (USCBP, 2014a).

Cross-border movement of drugs has always been a problem, and the Border Patrol is tasked with limiting such movement. In fact, CBP is considered the lead organization for drug interdiction along the southwest border, and their role continues to expand. The Border Patrol's heightened presence of Border Patrol agents along the southwest border has greatly affected narcotics traffickers and alien smugglers. In FY 2013, Border Patrol agents seized more than 4600 pounds of cocaine and over 2.4 million pounds of marijuana. More than $106 million in unreported currency was also seized, much of which is associated with the drug trade. Programs aimed at reducing demand on the US side of the border are also being conducted, including *Operation Detour*, which puts Border Patrol agents in border area high schools and middle schools to educate students about the dangers of the cross-border drug trade.

Critical Thinking

Given the mission of the Border Patrol, do you feel it is appropriately positioned within DHS (as opposed to being an independent agency or under some other federal agency or department)?

The CBP Office of Air and Marine

The mission of the CBP Office of Air and Marine (OAM) is to protect people and critical infrastructure through the coordinated use of integrated air and marine forces. AOM agents support border security by detecting, interdicting, and preventing acts of terrorism and the unlawful movement of people, illegal drugs, and other contrabands toward or across US borders. OAM is reputed to be the world's largest aviation and maritime law enforcement organization. It supports border security through the efforts of approximately 1200 federal agents, 250 aircraft, and 280 marine vessels. AOM operations are launched from 83 different locations distributed throughout the country.

During FY 2013, OAM performed the following:

- The apprehension of 63,562 undocumented aliens
- The seizure of over 1 million pounds of marijuana, valued at over $2.6 billion
- The seizure of over 155,000 pounds of cocaine valued at over $11.6 billion
- Seized over $25.3 million in currency
- Seized almost 2200 weapons (USCBP, 2014c)

Examples of AOM Operations

AOM conducts operations in support of border protection, law enforcement, search and rescue, emergency response, and other tasks. The following is a sample of notable achievements the agency has highlighted for the FY2013 period:

- On December 4, 2012, a P-3 aircraft stationed at National Air Security Operations Center-Corpus Christi participated in the interdiction of a self-propelled semisubmersible (SPSS). The crew of the SPSS scuttled the vessel, which was later recovered with 13,164 pounds of cocaine with an estimated street value of $985 million.
- On November 22, 2012, while conducting an airborne night patrol, a San Diego Air and Marine Branch AS-350 helicopter detected a suspect panga-type vessel approximately 300 ft offshore near Carlsbad, California. The OAM helicopter was able to successfully direct an OAM interceptor vessel to intercept and follow the panga. As the suspect vessel fled from the OAM vessel, Marine Interdiction Agents (MIAs) fired two warning shots and a subsequent disabling round. MIAs then boarded the disabled vessel, arresting the two occupants and seizing approximately 2570 pounds of marijuana.
- In February 2013, OAM flew in support of the search for Christopher Dorner, the former Los Angeles Police Department officer who was charged in connection with a series of shootings and attacks on police officers and their families. A Riverside Air Unit-based PC-12

fixed-wing aircraft participated in the initial high-level search for the suspect, and as the search progressed to a more detailed area in mountainous terrain, the unit launched an AS-350 helicopter to provide a low-level live video feed to the tactical operations center. These live videos were critical to supporting local law enforcement on the ground with important images that contributed to agent and officer safety in the resolution of the incident.

- On April 19, 2013, the National Air Security Operations Center-National Capital Region (NASOC-NCR) deployed aircraft in response to the Boston Marathon explosions. During the resulting law enforcement efforts, a NASOC-NCR AS-350 helicopter was able to relieve a Massachusetts State Police aircraft that was low on fuel and provide electro-optical/infrared coverage on the boat where the bombing suspect was hiding. Additionally, a NASOC-NCR S-76 helicopter transported the Bureau of Alcohol, Tobacco, Firearms and Explosives Special Response Team to Boston to assist in the apprehension of the suspect.
- *Hurricane Sandy relief efforts*: OAM flew over 230h in response to Hurricane Sandy and used numerous fixed-wing aircraft, including P-3s, C-550s, C-206s, and C-12s, and rotary-wing aircraft, such as S-76s, UH-60s, UH-1Hs, and AS-350s. OAM aircrews provided logistic support and personnel transport and conducted damage assessment and reconnaissance flights. Additionally, agents from the El Paso Air Branch, Miami Air and Marine Branch, and the National Air Security Unit-New York (NASU-NY) coordinated with NASOC-NCR and FEMA to participate in recovery efforts after Hurricane Sandy battered the New Jersey and New York coastline. Throughout the recovery effort, OAM personnel at the FEMA Emergency Operations Center in New Jersey worked with FEMA's Air Operations Coordinators. OAM also provided air support to DOD and EPA.

Source: USCBP (2014c).

OAM operates a number of unmanned aircraft systems (UAS; otherwise known as "drones") in support of law enforcement and homeland security missions at the nation's borders. The CBP drone program focuses operations on helping to identify and intercept potential terrorists and illegal cross-border activity. These aircraft have also been used to support disaster relief operations for assessment purposes. The remotely piloted aircraft allow OAM staff to safely conduct missions in areas that are difficult to access or otherwise too high risk for manned aircraft or CBP ground personnel. In 2013, OAM UAS operators logged over 5100h, adding to a total of over 23,000h of flight time for the aircraft since they were introduced into the agency. The associated missions resulted in the seizure of over 2600 pounds of cocaine and 56,000 pounds of marijuana. The missions also resulted in the apprehension of 2525 people and the seizure of 116 weapons (CBP, 2014c).

The CBP Office of Technology Innovation and Acquisition (OTIA) (Formerly the Secure Border Initiative)

DHS Secretary Michael Chertoff established the Secure Border Initiative (SBI) in 2005 as a comprehensive, multiyear plan to better secure the nation's borders. The SBI program was established within CBP to manage the development, deployment, and integration of SBI acquisition programs and integrate and coordinate border security programs within CBP.

Evaluations found that the SBI program was rife with problems and was not found to be as effective as hoped. In 2011, the then-DHS Secretary Janet Napolitano canceled the program. This was not a surprise considering many of its functions had been superseded by a new Office of Technology Innovation and Acquisition (OTIA), which was established under CBP in 2010. OTIA was created to seek out, develop, and acquire technological solutions to the problems that CBP is tasked with addressing. This includes establishing acquisition policies, maintaining an acquisition workforce, assessing the cost and effectiveness of the technologies that are requested, and assessing their performance in the field. The construction of pedestrian and vehicle fences falls under this office (Figures 6-4 and 6-5).

Secure Freight Initiative

On December 7, 2006, DHS announced the launch of the Secure Freight Initiative (SFI). The purpose of the program is to deploy a network of radiation detection and container imaging equipment to be operated in seaports worldwide for the purpose of preventing terrorists from using nuclear or other radiological materials to attack the global maritime supply chain or using cargo containers to bring the resources for such an attack to the United States.

SFI uses modern imagery and scanning systems to inspect maritime container cargo. Containers arriving at the six participating overseas seaports are scanned with both nonintrusive radiographic imaging and passive radiation detection equipment placed at terminal arrival gates. Optical scanning technology is used to identify containers and classify them by destination. Relay cargoes (containers being moved from one ship to another) are also inspected with the technology. Sensor and image data gathered in the US ports are

FIGURE 6-4 US Border Patrol agent Martin Hernandez stands at the 18 ft tall pedestrian fence at the Santa Teresa port of entry in New Mexico. *CPB Photo Gallery, 2013. http://1.usa.gov/1A2PpbY.*

FIGURE 6-5 Vehicle fence in El Paso Sector, New Mexico. *CPB Photo Gallery, 2013. http://1.usa.gov/1wZsKbZ.*

encrypted and transmitted near real time to the CBP National Targeting Center for final assessment and risk classification. If the scanning data indicate concerns, the specific container is sent to secondary inspection according to response protocols established in agreement with the port's host government. Participating host governments have immediate access to all scanning data collected, including any scans conducted on non-US-bound containers. If there is a cause for concern, DHS requests that the host government open and inspect US-bound container contents or instruct carriers under existing regulations to refuse to load the container until the risk is fully resolved.

To date, the six ports that are participating are as follows:

- Port Qasim in Pakistan
- Puerto Cortés in Honduras
- Southampton in the United Kingdom
- Port of Salalah in Oman
- Port of Singapore
- Port of Busan in Korea

Of these six, the first three are actively using scanning equipment, and the latter three are in the process of integrating scanning technology into their operations.

The program seeks to eventually have in place a global network of equipment and information that allows instantaneous information sharing, including imagery, ownership, and inventories, between ports and their governments. SFI is building risk assessment capabilities such that containers and their freight may be better prioritized such that the highest-risk containers get the most attention, while low-risk freight moves through more easily thereby freeing up resources (DHS, 2012b).

Container Security Initiative

The Container Security Initiative (CSI) was created by the US Customs Service soon after the 9/11 attacks. It was recognized at that time that, like the use of airlines as weapons in 2001, containers could be used by terrorists to easily deliver a WMD device. CSI was created to address the threat to border security and global trade posed by this potential terrorist methodology.

CSI proposes a security regime to ensure all containers that pose a potential risk for terrorism are identified and inspected at foreign ports before they are placed on vessels destined for the United States. CBP has stationed multidisciplinary teams of US officers from both CBP and ICE to work together with the host foreign government counterparts. Their mission is to target and prescreen containers and to develop additional investigative leads related to the terrorist threat to cargo destined for the United States.

The three core elements of CSI are as follows:

- Identify high-risk containers. CBP uses automated targeting tools to identify containers that pose a potential risk for terrorism, based on advance information and strategic intelligence.
- Prescreen and evaluate containers before they are shipped. Containers are screened as early in the supply chain as possible, generally at the port of departure.
- Use technology to prescreen high-risk containers to ensure that screening can be done rapidly without slowing down the movement of trade. This technology includes large-scale X-ray and gamma ray machines and radiation detection devices.

Through CSI, CBP officers work with host customs administrations to establish security criteria for identifying high-risk containers. Those administrations use nonintrusive inspection and radiation detection technology to screen high-risk containers before they are shipped to US ports. CSI offers its participant countries the opportunity to send their customs officers to major US ports to target oceangoing containerized cargo to be exported to their countries. Likewise, CBP shares information on a bilateral basis with its CSI partners. Japan and Canada currently station their customs personnel in some US ports as part of the CSI program.

CSI is now operational at ports in North America, Europe, Asia, Africa, the Middle East, and Latin and Central America. These include the following (* indicates SFI port):

The Americas

- Montreal, Vancouver, and Halifax, Canada
- Santos, Brazil
- Buenos Aires, Argentina
- Puerto Cortés,* Honduras
- Punta Caucedo, the Dominican Republic
- Kingston, Jamaica
- Freeport, The Bahamas
- Balboa, Colón, and Manzanillo, Panama
- Cartagena, Colombia

Europe

- Rotterdam, the Netherlands
- Bremerhaven and Hamburg, Germany
- Antwerp and Zeebrugge, Belgium

- Le Havre and Marseille, France
- Gothenburg, Sweden
- La Spezia, Genoa, Naples, Gioia Tauro, and Livorno, Italy
- Felixstowe, Liverpool, Thamesport, Tilbury, and Southampton, United Kingdom
- Piraeus, Greece
- Algeciras, Barcelona, and Valencia, Spain
- Lisbon, Portugal

Asia and the Middle East

- Singapore*
- Yokohama, Tokyo, Nagoya, and Kobe, Japan
- Hong Kong
- Busan* (Pusan), South Korea
- Port Klang and Tanjung Pelepas, Malaysia
- Laem Chabang, Thailand
- Dubai, United Arab Emirates (UAE)
- Shenzhen and Shanghai
- Kaohsiung and Chi-Lung
- Colombo, Sri Lanka
- Port of Salalah,* Oman
- Port Qasim, Pakistan
- Ashdod, Israel
- Haifa, Israel

Africa

- Alexandria, Egypt
- Durban, South Africa

CBP's 58 operational CSI ports now make approximately 86% of all maritime containerized cargo imported into the United States subject to prescreening prior to importation. CSI continues to expand to strategic locations around the world. The World Customs Organization (WCO), the European Union (EU), and the G8 support CSI expansion and have adopted resolutions implementing CSI security measures introduced at ports throughout the world (CBP, 2011).

Agricultural Inspection

Agriculture contributes about one percent of the US economy. While this doesn't seem like a large amount, it represents over 1 percent of jobs and over $173 billion in the economy. But more importantly, the agriculture sector is the major source of food for the American public, and because the United States is a net exporter of food, other countries depend upon these commodities as well.

Despite this rich agricultural bounty, the United States still imports millions of pounds of food products (including fruits and vegetables), as well as flowers, plants, and other plant products. Parasites, diseases, or other sources of harm carried by these imported products could spell devastation to the US economy and security where they are to be released upon their arrival.

Agricultural inspection has been part of the DHS mission since the Animal and Plant Health Inspection Service was transferred from the Department of Agriculture to DHS under CBP in 2003. CBP agents work in collaboration with inspection agents from the US Department of Agriculture to prevent the introduction of harmful pests into the United States, whether through the products themselves or the containers and vehicles that transport them (see sidebar "CBP Intercepts Asian Gypsy Moth at Port of Honolulu"). CBP agricultural specialists have extensive training and experience in agricultural and biological inspection and are also able to recognize and prevent the entry of organisms that could be used for biological warfare or terrorism.

CBP employs more than 2300 agriculture specialists at 160 ports of entry who intercept thousands of shipments of prohibited meat, plant materials, or animal products each day at POE. The CBP continues to work in close consultation with USDA, both in training the inspection force and in setting regulations and policies for which plants, animals, and other commodities may legally enter the country.

CBP agriculture specialists use detector dogs (canine teams) to sniff out hidden prohibited agricultural items. CBP agriculture specialists and canine teams work at key US ports of entry, including international airports, land borders, and international mail facilities, inspecting both commercial cargo and passengers/pedestrians. There are currently 114 agricultural canine inspection teams (CBP, 2014a).

All agricultural items are subject to inspection.

CBP Intercepts Asian Gypsy Moth at Port of Honolulu (CBP Press Release Dated October 7, 2014)

US Customs and Border Protection agriculture specialists (CBPAS) stationed at Honolulu seaport recently intercepted 11 Asian Gypsy Moth (AGM) egg masses on a ship from Taiwan. Each of these masses can contain hundreds of eggs of this devastating plant pest. The interception marks the first time the destructive pest's eggs have been discovered in the islands.

"CBP's primary mission is protecting our nation's borders from anything that could do us harm, no matter what form it takes," said Brian J. Humphrey, CBP Director of Field Operations in San Francisco. "The introduction of AGM could have devastating effects on our agriculture industry."

In late September, CBPAS inspected the foreign flag merchant vessel for AGM. During the deck sweep, the agriculture specialists discovered 11 AGM egg masses on various surfaces of the vessel superstructure. The egg masses were carefully scraped off and the areas treated (Figure 6-6). After a further intensive inspection, CBP determined that the AGM risk had been mitigated and the vessel was permitted to process the cargo.

CBP has taken a strategic, proactive approach to combat this threat. AGM (*Lymantria dispar*) is a voracious pest that can eat the foliage of more than 600 different species of forest trees, shrubs, and other plants. This pest is of particular concern because AGM has the potential to spread quickly since the female moth can fly up to 25 miles. If established in the United States, AGM could decimate America's forest resources and agriculture production.

FIGURE 6-6 Asian Gypsy Moth found in Hawaii. *Source: CBP (2014b).*

Source: CBP (2014b).

CBP Immigration Inspection Program

Travelers and other individuals seeking to enter the United States must pass through an immigration inspection station at all US POE, including international airports. CBP officers inspect their documents and determine their admissibility. The inspection process includes all work performed in connection with the entry of aliens and US citizens into the United States, including preinspection performed by the immigration inspectors outside the United States. The visa process, wherein permission is granted to travel to a US port for entry examination, is conducted by the US Department of State at overseas missions (embassies and consulates). However, it is DHS that maintains the final say on whether or not the person is able to enter. The CBP officer is responsible for determining the nationality and identity of each person who presents and must prevent the entry of ineligible aliens, including criminals, terrorists, and drug traffickers, among others. CBP agents will automatically admit US citizens upon verification of citizenship.

Under the authority granted by the Immigration and Naturalization Act of 1952 (INA), as amended, a CBP officer may question, under oath, any person coming into the United States to determine his or her admissibility. In addition, an inspector has authority to search without warrant the person and effects of any person seeking admission, when there is a reason to believe that the grounds of exclusion exist, which would be disclosed by such search. The INA is based on the law of presumption: An applicant for admission is presumed to be an alien until he or she shows evidence of citizenship; an alien is presumed to be an immigrant until he or she proves that he or she fits into one of the nonimmigrant classifications.

The mission of the inspections program is to control and guard the boundaries and borders of the United States against the illegal entry of aliens in a way that (CBP, 2015)

- functions as the initial component of a comprehensive immigration enforcement system;
- prevents the entry of terrorists, drug traffickers, criminals, and other persons who may subvert the national interest;
- deters illegal immigration through the detection of fraudulent documents and entry schemes;
- initiates prosecutions against individuals who attempt or aid and abet illegal entry;
- cooperates with international, federal, state, and local law enforcement agencies to achieve mutual objectives;
- contributes to the development and implementation of foreign policy related to the entry of persons;
- facilitates the entry of persons engaged in commerce, tourism, and/or other lawful pursuits;
- respects the rights and dignity of individuals;
- examines individuals and their related documents in a professional manner;
- assists the transportation industry to meet its requirements;
- responds to private sector interests, in conformance with immigration law;
- continues to employ innovative methods to improve the efficiency and cost-effectiveness of the inspection process.

CBP maintains a number of "trusted-traveler" programs that allow preapproved, low-risk travelers to expedite their immigration inspection through the use of dedicated lines and kiosks. These include the following:

- Global Entry (worldwide) (http://1.usa.gov/1wLDedY)
- Free and Secure Trade for Commercial Vehicles (FAST) driver cards (between the United States and Canada and the United States and Mexico) (http://1.usa.gov/1E7DLeK)
- NEXUS alternative inspection prescreening program (between the United States and Canada) (http://1.usa.gov/1zPXosQ)
- Secure Electronic Network for Travelers Rapid Inspection (SENTRI) (between the United States and Mexico) (http://1.usa.gov/1DCWCMx)

On a Typical Day in Fiscal Year 2013

CBP Fact Sheet: On a Typical Day in Fiscal Year 2013

Processed

- 992,243 passengers and pedestrians
- 280,059 incoming international air passengers and crew
- 48,994 passengers and crew on arriving ship/boat
- 663,190 incoming land travelers
- 67,337 truck, rail, and sea containers
- 269,753 incoming privately owned vehicles

Conducted

- 1153 apprehensions between US ports of entry
- 22 arrests of wanted criminals at US ports of entry
- 366 refusals of inadmissible persons at US ports of entry

Discovered

- 440 pests at US ports of entry and 4379 materials for quarantine—plant, meat, animal by-product, and soil

Seized

- 11,945 pounds of drugs
- $291,039 in undeclared or illicit currency
- $4.7 million worth of products with intellectual property rights violations

Identified

- 137 individuals with suspected national security concerns

Intercepted

- 48 fraudulent documents

Employed 59,969 men and women, including

- 21,650 CBP officers
- 2382 CBP agriculture specialists
- 20,979 Border Patrol agents
- 766 Air Interdiction agents (pilots)
- 343 Marine Interdiction agents
- 116 Aviation Enforcement officers

Deployed

- More than 1500 canine teams and 250 horse patrols

Flew

- 169h enforcement missions over the United States

Conducted operations at

- 328 ports of entry
- 136 Border Patrol stations and five substations within 20 sectors, with 35 permanent checkpoints
- 22 Air and Marine Branches, five National Security Operations, and one Air and Marine Operations Center

---

Source: CBP (2014d,e).

US Immigration and Customs Enforcement

Immigration and Customs Enforcement (ICE) is the principal investigative arm of DHS and the second largest investigative agency in the federal government. ICE was created in 2003 when the US Customs Service and INS investigative and nonborder (interior) enforcement units were joined and placed into the new DHS. Today, there are more than 20,000 ICE employees operating in all 50 states and in 48 foreign countries.

The agency's primary mission is to promote homeland security and public safety through the criminal and civil enforcement of federal laws governing border control, customs, trade, and immigration. The agency has an annual budget of about $6 billion, primarily devoted to its two principal operating components—Homeland Security Investigations (HSI) and Enforcement and Removal Operations (ERO). Traditionally, the primary mission of the customs enforcement component of ICE was to combat various forms of smuggling. Over time, however, this mission has been expanded to other violations of law involving terrorist financing, money laundering, arms trafficking (including WMD), technology exports, commercial fraud, and child pornography, to name a few.

In total, ICE enforces more than 400 different laws and regulations, including those of 40 other agencies. Within ICE, there are several distinct offices that carry out separate tasks related to the general agency mission. Many of these programs and offices are described below.

ICE Enforcement and Removal Operations

ERO is charged with the enforcement of US immigration laws. It identifies and apprehends removable aliens (see sidebar "Definitions of Immigration Enforcement Terms"), detains them if necessary, and removes (deports) them from the country. ERO prioritizes the apprehension, arrest, and removal of convicted criminals who pose a threat to national security, fugitives, and recent illegal border crossers.

ERO officers and staff transport the illegal aliens they have apprehended, manage them while they are being held or allowed to stay in an "alternative to detention" program, ensure that they have adequate access to and representation from legal and advocacy groups, and remove those people who have been given a deportation order following adjudication of their case. These functions are performed at six service processing centers, seven contract detention facilities, and over 240 facilities under intergovernmental service agreements where aliens are housed. The ERO staff base includes law enforcement officers, medical professionals, administrative specialists, and many others given the broad nature of the agency's mission.

ERO on a Given Day in FY 2012

The following occurred on an average day (relative to ERO operations) in FY 2012:

- ERO housed an average of 34,260 illegal aliens in these various facilities nationwide.
- ERO personnel managed over 1.71 million aliens in the various stages of immigration removal proceedings.
- ERO processed 1305 aliens into detention centers. The intake process includes an initial health care screening that is completed within 12 h of arrival at the facility, followed by a comprehensive health assessment that includes a physical examination and the completion of a detailed medical history within 14 days of arrival.
- ERO health care professionals conducted approximately 603 intake health care screenings in facilities staffed by ERO health care providers.
- ERO facilitated 285 physical examinations and 95 dental examinations.
- Health care professionals conducted 372 chronic disease interventions and 151 mental health interventions.
- Facility clinics received 377 detainees during sick call and 896 prescriptions were filled at facilities staffed by ERO health care providers.

- Health care personnel saw 44 detainees for urgent care, and there were 46 emergency room or off-site referrals.
- ERO responded to 250 calls placed by detainees, family members, and community stakeholders received through the ICE Community and Detainee Helpline.
- ERO personnel monitored 23,034 aliens enrolled in the Alternatives to Detention program under the Intensive Supervision Appearance Program II (ISAP II).
- ERO employees procured 246 travel documents.
- ERO employees processed 363 bond actions.
- ERO removed 1120 aliens from the United States to countries around the globe, including 616 criminal aliens.
- ERO processed and removed 382 cases as a result of reinstated final orders.
- Thirty-seven aliens were removed via commercial airlines and 788 aliens were removed via government aircraft.
- Thirty-one children were placed with the Office of Refugee Resettlement in the Department of Health and Human Services.
- ERO officers arrested 471 convicted criminal aliens through its enforcement efforts.
- ERO worked with US Attorneys' offices, who accepted 25 cases for criminal prosecution.

Source: ICE (2014a).

ICE ERO operates according to national performance-based detention standards, which clarify exactly how detainees are to be treated and processed. These standards are called the Performance-Based National Detention Standards 2011 (PBNDS 2011) and were created to ensure that immigration law could be enforced without the US government violating human rights. Concerns are regularly raised about the treatment of detainees, and the federal government must continue to ensure that its procedures are just and humane. The PBNDS provides guidance on the following topics:

- Safety
- Security
- Order
- Care
- Activities
- Justice
- Administration and management

The full text of these standards can be found at http://1.usa.gov/1s6gsub.

The On-Site Detention Compliance Oversight Program was established in 2009 within ERO to enhance oversight and care of detainees in the ICE custody as part of the agency's commitment to immigration detention reform. Detention oversight inspectors work at each of the detention facilities and assess the actions of both government officers and contractors. Forty detention monitors are embedded in ICE detention facilities so that they are able to assess potential problems and address them before they occur or, at least, to ensure that corrective actions are taken in a timely manner.

Critical Thinking

How is the management of lawful immigration efforts related to the security of the nation? How could people harm the country or its citizens by misusing the lawful immigration mechanisms?

Definitions of Immigration Enforcement Terms

- *Administrative removal*: The removal of an alien not admitted for permanent residence or an alien admitted for permanent residence on a conditional basis, under a DHS order based on the determination that the individual has been convicted of an aggravated felony. The alien may be removed without a hearing before an immigration court.
- *Deportable alien*: An alien who has been admitted into the United States but who is subject to removal under INA § 237.
- *Detention*: The seizure and incarceration of an alien in order to hold him or her while awaiting judicial or legal proceedings or return transportation to his or her country of citizenship.
- *Expedited removal*: The removal of an alien who is inadmissible because the individual does not possess valid entry documents or attempted to enter the United States by fraud or misrepresentation of material fact. The alien may be removed without a hearing before an immigration court.
- *Inadmissible alien*: An alien seeking admission into the United States who is ineligible to be admitted according to the provisions of INA § 212.
- *Reinstatement of final removal orders*: The removal of an alien based on the reinstatement of a prior removal order, where the alien departed the United States under an order of removal and illegally reentered the United States. The alien may be removed without a hearing before an immigration court.
- *Removal*: The compulsory and confirmed movement of an inadmissible or deportable alien out of the United States based on an order of removal. An alien who is removed has administrative or criminal consequences placed on subsequent reentry owing to the fact of the removal.
- *Return*: The confirmed movement of an inadmissible or deportable alien out of the United States not based on an order of removal.

Source: Simanski (2014).

Secure Communities Program

It is part of the homeland security and immigration strategies to prioritize the detention and removal of those illegal aliens who pose a unique or significant public safety threat and those who are repeat immigration violators. The Secure Communities program was created to support this mission, relying upon an information-sharing partnership that already existed between ICE and the Federal Bureau of Investigation (FBI). Through this program, agencies involved in immigration enforcement are able to access the information they need to quickly identify those criminal aliens that pose this special risk without imposing new or additional requirements on state and local law enforcement agencies.

The Secure Communities program functions as follows: The FBI collects and sends the fingerprints of people who are arrested and processed by local police departments to ICE, which checks these prints against the immigration databases it maintains. The FBI has been working with local agencies on fingerprint cross-referencing for decades, so the FBI/local partnership is not new. Once ICE processes the prints, they can determine if the arrested individual is residing illegally and therefore deportable under current regulations. In such cases, ICE has the authority to begin removal operations. The individuals identified by this program are moved to the "front of the line" in terms of priority for deportation given that they pose more than a simple economic threat to the nation.

DHS has expanded Secure Communities from 14 jurisdictions in 2008 to all 3181 US jurisdictions in all states and territories as well as the District of Columbia. The expansion to all jurisdictions was completed on January 22, 2013. Thus far, there have been over 283,000 convicted criminal aliens removed from the United States as a result of the Secure Communities program. And these represent just a portion of all prioritized removals. In FY 2013 alone, more than 368,000 priority illegal aliens were deported. Secure Communities is important because ICE only receives enough funding to remove a portion of the more than 10 million individuals estimated to be in the United States illegally or who are removable because of criminal convictions. This program ensures that security is improved, given the nature of how deportation is focused.

ICE Homeland Security Investigations

The ICE HSI directorate is tasked with investigating various domestic and international activities that are related to the illegal movement of people and goods into, within, and out of the United States. HSI investigates the following:

- Financial crimes, money laundering, and bulk cash smuggling
- Commercial fraud and intellectual property theft
- Cybercrimes
- Human rights violations
- Human smuggling and trafficking
- Immigration, document, and benefit fraud
- Narcotics and weapons smuggling/trafficking
- Transnational gang activity
- Export enforcement
- International art and antiquity theft (HSI, 2014)

ICE special agents conduct investigations aimed at protecting critical infrastructure industries that are vulnerable to sabotage, attack, or exploitation. In addition to ICE criminal investigations, HSI oversees the agency's international affairs operations and intelligence functions. HSI consists of more than 10,000 employees, consisting of 6700 special agents, who are assigned to more than 200 cities throughout the United States and 46 countries around the world.

HSI is made up of eight key divisions, which include

- Domestic Operations
- HSI-Led National Intellectual Property Rights Coordination Center
- Information Management
- Office of Intelligence

- International Operations
- Investigative Programs
- Mission Support
- National Security Investigations

ICE Project Shield America

Project Shield America is an ICE program aimed at preventing WMD trafficking by illegal exporters, targeted foreign countries, terrorist groups, and international criminal organizations. This program also works to stop organized criminal and state-sponsored efforts from obtaining and illegally exporting licensable commodities, technologies, conventional munitions, and firearms; exporting stolen property; and engaging in financial transactions that support these activities or violate US sanctions and embargoes.

The US government protects both the economic and national security interests of the country in this regard. Foreign adversaries regularly attempt to acquire and steal technologies developed in the United States by both legal and illegal means. Those who succeed in acquiring such technologies often do so without having to expend great amounts of resources required by the innovative US company or governmental or nongovernmental agency. Moreover, such technologies can be used against the country to jeopardize national security and/or the US economy.

Examples of strategic technology sought by foreign adversaries (and, in some cases, allies) include

- modern manufacturing technology for the production of microelectronics, computers, digital electronic components, and signal processing systems;
- technology necessary for the development of aircraft, missile, and other tactical weapon delivery systems;
- all types of advanced signal and weapon detection, tracking, and monitoring systems;
- technology and equipment used in the construction of nuclear weapons and materials;
- biological and chemical warfare agents and precursors and associated manufacturing equipment.

Project Shield America was designed and implemented to work in concert with the four-pronged effort of its Export Enforcement Program:

- *Inspection/interdiction*—Specially trained US CBP inspectors stationed at high-threat ports selectively inspect suspect export shipments.
- *Investigations*—ICE agents deployed throughout the country initiate and pursue high-quality cases that result in the arrest, prosecution, and conviction of offenders of the Export Administration Act, Arms Export Control Act, Trading with the Enemy Act, International Emergency Economics Powers Act, and other related statutes. ICE investigations aim to detect and disrupt illegal exports before they can cause damage to the national security interests of the United States.
- *Industry outreach*—ICE agents conduct outreach visits with industry officials to educate them about US export laws and to solicit their assistance in preventing illegal foreign acquisition of their products.
- *International cooperation*—ICE international attaché offices enlist the support of their host governments to initiate new investigative leads and to develop information in support of ongoing domestic investigations (ICE, 2009).

The Joint Terrorism Task Force

The National Security Investigations Division (NSID) National Security Unit (NSU) oversees ICE participation on the Joint Terrorism Task Force (JTTF). The JTTF investigates, detects, interdicts, prosecutes, and removes terrorists and dismantles terrorist organizations. ICE is involved in almost every foreign terrorism investigation related to cross-border crime. ICE is the largest federal contributor to the JTTF through active participation in each of the 104 local JTTFs nationwide. The agency also plays a critical leadership role on the national JTTF. Examples of ICE participation in the JTTF include the following:

- ICE JTTF agents in Philadelphia led an undercover weapons smuggling investigation resulting in the arrests of 31 subjects, most notably a reputed procurement officer for an overseas terrorist organization.
- ICE JTTF special agents arrested and indicted multiple targets involved in an organized import/export scheme with an OFAC-designated Hezbollah front company in South America's triborder area, resulting in guilty pleas to export smuggling and conspiracy.
- An ICE JTTF special agent led the investigation, arrest, conviction, and ultimate removal from the United States of the Brooklyn imam accused of tipping off Najibullah Zazi and his coconspirators days prior to the attempted attack against the New York subway system in September 2009. ICE agents in Denver developed immigration fraud charges against Amanullah Zazi, a family member of Najibullah Zazi, and placed him into removal proceedings in November 2009. Amanullah Zazi later pleaded guilty to conspiracy to obstruct justice and abetting others to receive military training from a foreign terrorist organization.
- More than 30 ICE special agents were the first criminal investigators to respond to the attempted Christmas Day attack of Northwest Airlines Flight 253. They rapidly disseminated lead information to other ICE and JTTF special agents throughout the country.
- ICE JTTF special agents were influential in identifying the would-be Times Square bomber in May 2010 and utilized unique immigration authorities to arrest an alleged hawaladar who allegedly provided funds to execute the attack.
- An ICE JTTF special agent authored the criminal complaint against Brahim Lajqi, a citizen of Kosovo who intended to engage in acts of terrorism targeting four major US cities. Lajqi ultimately pleaded guilty to fraud/misuse of visas (ICE, 2014b).

Border Enforcement Security Task Force

In response to the dramatic increase in cross-border crime and violence in recent years (due in part to feuds between Mexican drug cartels and criminal smuggling organizations), ICE partnered with federal, state, local, and foreign law enforcement counterparts to create the Border Enforcement Security Task Force (BEST). The program was created in 2005, but has been bolstered as a result of the signing of the Jaime Zapata Border Enforcement Security Task Force (BEST) Act, which occurred on December 7, 2012. BEST is made up of multiagency teams that have been developed to identify, disrupt, and dismantle criminal organizations posing significant threats to border security. Several international law enforcement agencies serve as key members of the team.

On the southwest border, the participation of the Mexican Secretaría de Seguridad Pública (SSP) is vital. On the northern border, Canadian law enforcement agencies like the Canada Border Services Agency, the Royal Canadian Mounted Police, the Ontario Provincial Police, the Niagara Regional Police Service, the Toronto Metropolitan Police, the Windsor Police Service, and the Amherstburg Police Service are active members. The Argentinean customs agency is part of the Miami BEST and the Colombian National Police is part of both the Miami BEST and New York-New Jersey BEST. Currently, there are 35 BEST with locations around the United States and in Mexico, which include

- Arizona (Phoenix, Tucson, Nogales, Yuma, and Casa Grande),
- California (Imperial Valley, Port of Los Angeles, Port of San Diego, San Ysidro, and Port of San Francisco),
- Florida (Miami Seaport, Fort Lauderdale Seaport),
- Michigan (Detroit),

- New Mexico (Albuquerque, Deming, and Las Cruces),
- New York (Buffalo, Massena, and New York seaport),
- New Jersey (Port Newark),
- Texas (El Paso, Laredo, Rio Grande Valley, Port of Houston, and Big Bend),
- Washington (Blaine and Seattle Port),
- Louisiana (Port of New Orleans),
- Alabama (Port of Mobile),
- Mississippi (Port of Gulfport),
- South Carolina (Port of Charleston),
- Georgia (Port of Savannah),
- Virginia (Hampton Roads),
- Puerto Rico (Port of San Juan),
- Hawaii (Port of Honolulu) (ICE, 2014c).

Since BEST's inception, investigators have collectively initiated more than 10,600 cases. These actions have resulted in more than

- 12,718 criminal arrests,
- 7245 administrative arrests.
- The seizure of more than
  - 110,711 pounds of cocaine,
  - 5517 pounds of ecstasy,
  - 1764 pounds of heroin,
  - 1,036,749 pounds of marijuana,
  - 6325 pounds of methamphetamine,
  - 2,988,561 rounds of ammunition,
  - 4657 vehicles,
  - $130.2 million in US currency,
  - 15,062 weapons (ICE, 2014c).

Counterterrorism and Criminal Exploitation Unit

The Counterterrorism and Criminal Exploitation Unit (CTCEU) prevents terrorists and other criminals from exploiting US immigration. CTCEU staff also review the immigration status of known and suspected terrorists, combat criminal exploitation of the Student and Exchange Visitor Program (SEVP), and leverage HSI's expertise to identify national security threats.

CTCEU is composed of two sections:

- SEVIS Exploitation Section (SES)
- Terrorist Tracking Pursuit Group (TTPG)

SES analyzes and refers educational/school fraud criminal investigation leads to the respective ICE field office. It implements and manages the Agent/SEVIS School Outreach Program that educates others about SEVP exploitation. The program also improves communication between designated school officials and HSI field agents and provides subject matter expertise to partnering agencies when exploitation is suspected.

TTPG leverages ICE expertise across partnering agencies dedicated to promoting national security. This group leads the Targeted Enforcement Program (TEP), an initiative with US CBP that tracks how long individuals identified as security risks stay in the United States. The program works jointly with the FBI's Foreign Terrorist Tracking Task Force (FTTTF) that also proactively identifies known or suspected terrorists. TTPG also initiates high-priority nonimmigrant overstay investigations as dictated by the Compliance Enforcement Advisory Panel (CEAP).

Counterproliferation Investigations

ICE is the only federal law enforcement agency with full statutory authority to investigate and enforce criminal violations of all US export laws related to military items, controlled "dual-use" commodities, and sanctioned or embargoed countries. The magnitude and scope of such threats increase significantly each year. ICE agents in the field who conduct counterproliferation investigations (CPI) focus on the trafficking and illegal export of the following commodities and services:

- WMD materials
- Chemical, biological, radiological, and nuclear (CBRN) materials
- Military equipment and technology
- Controlled dual-use commodities and technology
- Firearms and ammunition
- Financial and business transactions with sanctioned and embargoed countries and terrorist organizations

The US Coast Guard

The US Coast Guard (USCG) is one of the five armed forces of the United States and the only military organization within the DHS. The USCG protects the maritime economy and the environment, defends the nation's maritime borders, and rescues those in peril. The USCG is simultaneously and at all times an armed force and federal law enforcement agency (Figure 6-7).

The USCG was created on August 4, 1790, by congressional authorization of the construction of ten vessels to enforce federal tariff and trade laws and to prevent smuggling. Known variously through the nineteenth and early twentieth centuries as the Revenue Marine Bureau and the Revenue Cutter Service, the USCG expanded in size and responsibilities as the nation grew. The service received its present name in 1915 under an act of Congress that merged the Revenue Cutter Service with the Life-Saving Service, thereby providing the nation with a single maritime service dedicated to saving life at sea and enforcing the nation's maritime laws. The USCG began to maintain the country's aids to maritime navigation, including operating the nation's lighthouses, when President Franklin Roosevelt ordered the transfer of the Lighthouse Service to the USCG in 1939. In 1946, Congress permanently transferred the Commerce Department's Bureau of Marine Inspection and Navigation to the USCG, thereby placing merchant marine licensing and merchant vessel safety under the USCG purview.

The USCG has always served to provide a national defense function and that mission is unchanged within DHS. What differs from other military branches is that the USCG has a significant domestic peacetime role as it exists within the umbrella function of homeland security under DHS. In this vein, the USCG is the nation's frontline agency for enforcing the US law at sea; protecting the marine environment, coastlines, and ports; and providing lifesaving assistance when required. Organizationally, DHS falls under the direction of the Secretary of Homeland Security, but in times of war or at the discretion of the president, it falls under the command of the Department of the Navy.

For over two centuries, the USCG has guarded US maritime interests domestically, in the ports, at sea, and around the globe. The USCG has nearly 42,000 men and women on active duty today. By law, the

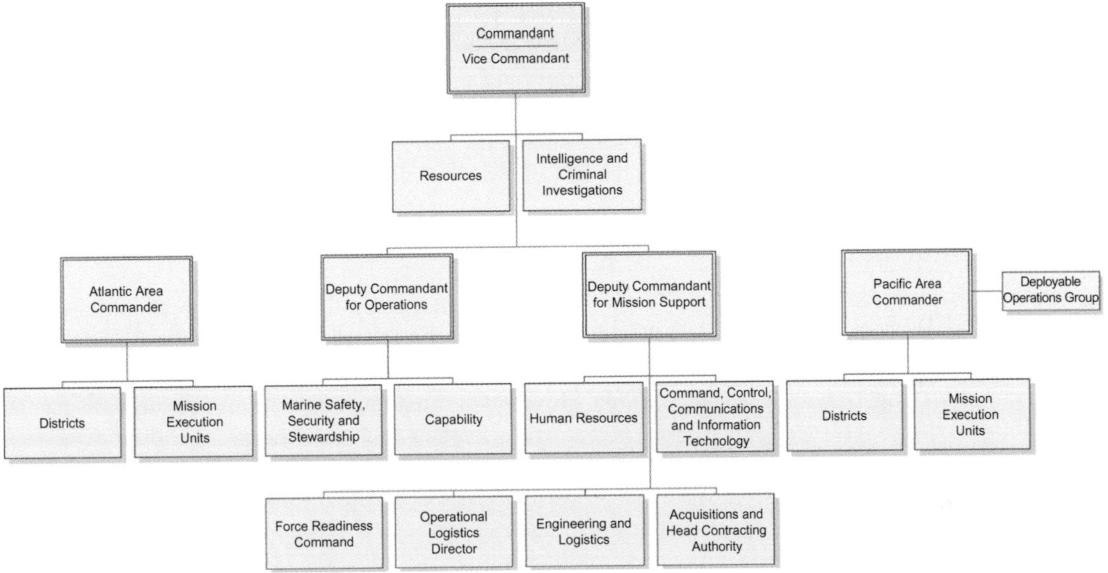

FIGURE 6-7 The US Coast Guard organizational chart. *Source: DHS (2011b).*

USCG has 11 missions (three of which are starred, representing an association with border security, customs, or immigration, and which are described in greater detail below). By law, the USCG has 11 missions, which include the following:

- Ports, waterways, and coastal security
- Drug interdiction*
- Aids to navigation
- Search and rescue
- Living marine resources
- Marine safety
- Defense readiness
- Migrant interdiction*
- Marine environmental protection
- Ice operations
- Other law enforcement*

Drug Interdiction

The USCG is the lead federal agency for maritime drug interdiction and shares lead responsibility for air interdiction with the US Customs Service. As such, it is a key player in combating the flow of illegal drugs to the country. The USCG's drug interdiction mission is to reduce the supply of drugs from the source by denying smugglers the use of air and maritime routes in the Transit Zone, a 6 million square mile area that includes the Caribbean, the Gulf of Mexico, and eastern Pacific. In meeting the challenge of patrolling this vast area, the USCG coordinates closely with other federal agencies and countries within the region to disrupt and deter the flow of illegal drugs. The USCG drug interdiction accounts for nearly 52% of all US government seizures of cocaine each year.

The USCG has been conducting drug interdiction missions since the late nineteenth century, when Chinese drug smugglers began illegally importing opium on ships. In the prohibition days, the USCG saw a rather large increase in resources and funding to fight alcohol smuggling, which included the chasing of now-legendary rum-runners. Today, maritime drug smuggling is a very significant problem, and smugglers are using new technologies to evade capture (including submersible ships that are very difficult to detect). Since its first drug seizures in the early 1970s, the USCG has seized well over 1.1 million pounds of cocaine and marijuana.

Migrant Interdiction

The USCG is responsible for the daunting task of preventing illegal immigration to the United States via maritime routes—namely, the Atlantic and Pacific Oceans and the Gulf of Mexico. Human trafficking and smuggling operations that utilize sea routes are well established, and thousands of people try to illegally enter the country along its many miles of coastline. However, if intending migrants are captured before they reach land, they can be returned to their point of departure, or their country of origin, without having to go through the lengthy and costly immigration hearings.

The USCG migrant interdiction role began in earnest in 1980 during the mass exodus from Cuba that followed Mariel Boatlift. Immigration by sea surged again between 1991 and 1995, this time from Haiti. The tide of immigrants by sea ebbs and flows, with other sources including the Dominican Republic, China, and elsewhere (see Table 6-1 and Figure 6-8).

Table 6-1 USCG Maritime Migrant Interdictions by Country and Year

Fiscal Year	Haiti	Dominican Republic	China	Cuba	Mexico	Ecuador	Others	Total
2014	949	293	0	2059	48	0	29	3378
2013	508	110	5	1357	31	1	82	2094
2012	977	456	23	1275	79	7	138	2955
2011	1137	222	11	985	68	1	50	2474
2010	1377	140	0	422	61	0	88	2088
2009	1782	727	35	799	77	6	41	3467
2008	1583	688	1	2216	47	220	65	4825
2007	1610	1469	73	2868	26	125	167	6338
2006	1198	3011	31	2810	52	693	91	7886
2005	1850	3612	32	2712	55	1149	45	9455
2004	3229	5014	68	1225	86	1189	88	10,899
2003	2013	1748	15	1555	0	703	34	6068
2002	1486	177	80	666	32	1608	55	4104
2001	1391	659	53	777	17	1020	31	3948
2000	1113	499	261	1000	49	1244	44	4210
1999	1039	583	1092	1619	171	298	24	4826
1998	1369	1097	212	903	30	0	37	3648
1997	288	1200	240	421	0	0	45	2194
1996	2295	6273	61	411	0	2	38	9080
1995	909	3388	509	525	0	0	36	5367

Source: USCG (2014).

FIGURE 6-8 Twelve Cuban migrants in a modified 1951 Chevrolet truck. *Photo by Anthony Neste, USCG. 2003. http://bit.ly/1ty3REB.*

Other Border-Area Law Enforcement Roles

Countries need to protect their commercial fishing interests as a matter of economic, environmental, and food supply security. Commercial fishery zones extending from the nation's borders are protected by federal and international laws, and the USCG is tasked with enforcing these laws. USCG vessels prevent illegal foreign fishing vessels from entering and exploiting the US "exclusive economic zone" (EEZ) encroachment as part of the USCG's mission. In addition, the USCG is tasked with the duty of enforcing international agreements aimed at controlling illegal, unreported, and unregulated (IUU) fishing activity on the high seas. In FY 2013, the USCG boarded over 5000 US-flagged fishing vessels and detected 184 incursions by foreign fishing vessels into the US EEZ.

An Average Day for the US Coast Guard

In an average day, the USCG accomplishes the following:

- Saves 13 lives
- Responds to 64 search and rescue cases
- Rescues 77% of mariners in imminent danger
- Keeps 959 pounds of cocaine off the streets
- Saves $260,000 in property
- Interdicts 10 undocumented migrants trying to enter the United States
- Services 49 buoys and fixes 21 discrepancies (such as buoys moved by a hurricane)

- Provides a presence in all major ports
- Screens 679 commercial vessels and 170,000 crew and passengers
- Issues 200 credentials to merchant mariners
- Inspects 70 containers
- Inspects 33 vessels for compliance with air emissions standards
- Performs 30 safety and environmental examinations of foreign vessels entering US ports
- Boards 15 fishing boats to ensure compliance with fisheries laws
- Investigates 12 marine accidents
- Responds to and investigates 10 pollution incidents
- Performs security boardings of 5 high-interest vessels
- Escorts 4 high-value US Navy vessels transiting US waterways
- Identifies one individual with terrorism associations
- Maintains 6 patrol boats and 400 personnel who protect Iraq's offshore oil infrastructure, train Iraqi naval forces, and keep sea lanes secure in the Arabian Gulf

Source: USCG (2010).

US Citizenship and Immigration Services

The US Citizenship and Immigration Services (USCIS) is the DHS component that oversees lawful immigration to the United States. USCIS is tasked with ensuring the security of the nation by providing accurate and useful information to intending immigrants, granting immigration and citizenship benefits, promoting an awareness and understanding of citizenship, and ensuring the integrity of the US immigration system (Figure 6-9).

The USCIS currently employs 19,000 people, many of whom are contractors, at approximately 225 locations throughout the world. USCIS employees facilitate the immigration process, which can be cumbersome, time-consuming, and at times technically challenging (due to the requirements under US immigration law). Because intelligence has shown terrorists to be interested in exploiting the US immigration system to gain entry to the United States, USCIS faces an ongoing challenge to maintain system integrity and innovation. At the same time, to serve the millions of people who are adhering to all immigration policies and laws, USCIS must ensure the immigration system is effective, flexible, and customer-oriented.

Services provided by USCIS include the following:

- *Citizenship (including citizenship through naturalization)*: Intending immigrants who wish to become US citizens submit applications to USCIS. USCIS determines each applicant's eligibility, processes his or her applications, and, if approved, schedules the applicant for a ceremony to take the Oath of Allegiance. USCIS also determines eligibility and provides documentation of US citizenship for people who acquired or derived US citizenship through their parents.
- *Family member immigration*: USCIS manages the process that allows current permanent residents and US citizens to bring close relatives to live and work in the United States.

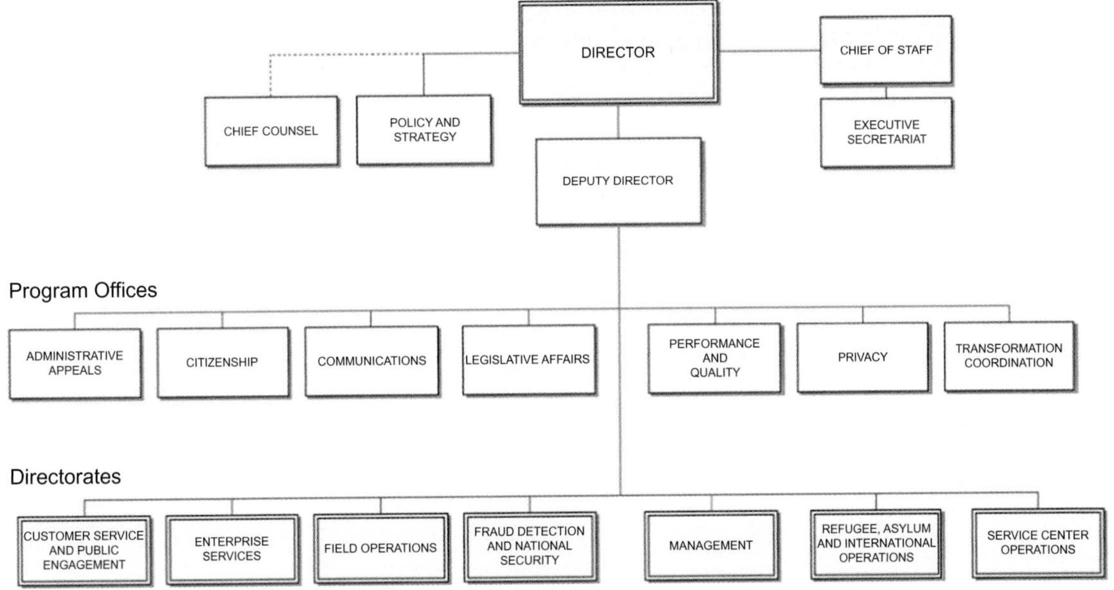

FIGURE 6-9 US Citizenship and Immigration Services organizational chart. *Source: USCIS (2014).*

- *Employment for foreign nationals*: USCIS manages the process that allows individuals from other countries to work in the United States.
- *Verifying an individual's legal right to work in the United States (E-Verify)*: USCIS maintains the E-Verify system, which allows employers to electronically verify an employee's employment eligibility.
- *Humanitarian programs*: USCIS administers programs that provide protection to individuals inside and outside the United States who are displaced by war, famine, and civil and political unrest and those who are forced to flee their countries to escape the risk of death and torture.
- *Adoptions*: USCIS manages the first step in the process for US citizens to adopt children from other countries. Approximately 20,000 adoptions take place each year.
- *Civic integration*: USCIS promotes instruction and training on citizenship rights and responsibilities and provides immigrants with the information and tools necessary to successfully integrate into American civic culture.

Office of Citizenship

The Office of Citizenship engages and supports the citizenship process by helping new immigrants to succeed in their adoptive country. This includes promotion of the English language and education on the rights and responsibilities of citizenship. The Office of Citizenship is tasked with the following activities:

- Developing and enhancing educational products and resources that welcome immigrants, promote English language learning and education on the rights and responsibilities of citizenship, and prepare immigrants for naturalization and active civic participation

- Leading initiatives to promote citizenship awareness and demystify the naturalization process for aspiring citizens
- Supporting national and community-based organizations that prepare immigrants for citizenship by providing grants, educational materials, and technical assistance
- Building collaborative partnerships with state and local governments and nongovernmental organizations to expand integration and citizenship resources in communities
- Conducting training workshops and enhancing professional development and classroom resources for educators and organizations preparing immigrants for citizenship
- Promoting integration policy dialogue among different sectors of society and coordinating with stakeholders at all levels to foster integration and community cohesion

The Office of Citizenship is divided into three divisions:

- Testing, Education, and Training
- Policy and Programs
- Grants

Fraud Detection and National Security Directorate

The Fraud Detection and National Security (FDNS) directorate was created within USCIS in 2004 to strengthen ongoing efforts to ensure that immigration benefits are not granted to individuals who pose a threat to national security or public safety or who seek to defraud the US immigration system. In 2010, FDNS became a directorate, which elevated the profile of this work within USCIS. FDNS officers are located in every USCIS center, district, field, and asylum office. FDNS officers are also located in other government agencies. FDNS staff enhance USCIS's ability to detect and remove known and suspected fraud from the application process without hampering the process by which legitimate applications are processed. FDNS officers also perform checks of USCIS databases and public information, as well as other administrative inquiries, to verify information provided on, and in support of, applications and petitions. Administrative inquiries may include

- fraud assessments (determine the types and volumes of fraud in certain immigration benefits programs),
- compliance reviews (reviews of certain types of applications or petitions to ensure the integrity of the immigration benefits system),
- targeted site visits (inquiries conducted in cases where fraud is suspected).

FDNS uses the fraud detection and national security data system (FDNS-DS) to identify fraud and track potential patterns. In July 2009, FDNS implemented the Administrative Site Visit and Verification Program (ASVVP) to conduct unannounced site inspections to verify information contained in certain visa petitions.

Refugee, Asylum, and International Operations Directorate

The Refugee, Asylum, and International Operations (RAIO) directorate operates both within and outside the United States to provide protection, humanitarian, and other immigration benefits to legitimate foreign citizen applicants while, at the same time, ensuring that these benefits are not exploited by terrorists or criminals. Refugees and asylum seekers are people who are typically characterized as

- fleeing oppression, persecution, and torture because of their race, religion, nationality, membership in a particular social group, or political opinion;
- confronting an urgent humanitarian situation and needing authorization to enter the United States on a temporary basis.

RAIO also provides immigration services to certain groups of foreign citizens who should not or cannot apply for citizenship or immigration permission within the United States itself. These include

- active duty members of the US Armed Forces serving overseas who seek to become naturalized citizens,
- lawful permanent residents who are overseas and have lost documentation that would enable them to lawfully return to the United States,
- individuals who live overseas and seek to be reunified with relatives in the United States.

RAIO maintains two Washington, DC, offices, which include the RAIO headquarters and the refugee corps. These are supported by

- 25 international field offices;
- 8 domestic asylum offices;
- 2 domestically located branches of the International Operations (IO) Division tasked with the adjudication of overseas applications not requiring interview;
- An IO office in Miami responsible for administering a cooperative agreement that provides resettlement and orientation benefits to Cuban and Haitian parolees;
- RAIO officers who deploy on "circuit rides" overseas to adjudicate refugee benefits, frequently in remote locations, and domestically to adjudicate asylum benefits.

RAIO is made up of three divisions, which include the following:

- *The Refugee Affairs Division*: It is responsible for providing the humanitarian benefit of refugee resettlement to applicants in need of protection throughout the world while diligently protecting US homeland through careful national security screening.
- *The Asylum Division*: It manages the US affirmative asylum process, which permits individuals already in the United States, or at a port of entry, who are not in immigration proceedings, to request asylum if they are unable or unwilling to return to their country of origin due to past persecution or a well-founded fear of future persecution.
- *The International Operations Division*: It extends immigration benefits to eligible individuals located overseas.

A Typical Day at USCIS

On an average day at USCIS,

- more than 375,000 people visit the USCIS Web site;
- 310 refugee applications from around the world are processed, and 55 people already in the United States are granted asylum;

- USCIS staff answer 44,000 phone calls to the USCIS toll-free customer service line, and 9500 customers are served at 84 local offices;
- the employment eligibility of more than 58,000 new hires in the United States is confirmed;
- 15,000 applicants are fingerprinted and photographed at 136 Application Support Centers;
- 148,000 national security background checks are conducted;
- 23,000 applications for various immigration benefits are completed;
- 2600 applications to sponsor relatives and fiancées are processed, and the American parents of 78 foreign-born orphans are assisted in their adoption processes;
- 2040 petitions filed by employers to bring workers to the United States are processed;
- permanent residence is granted to 2400, people and 6100 permanent resident cards are issued;
- 3200 new citizens are welcomed (approximately 35 of whom are already serving in the US Armed Forces).

Source: USCIS (2014) and http://1.usa.gov/13ybKjq.

Office of Biometric Identity Management (OBIM)

The Office of Biometric Identity Management (OBIM) is a program that tracks the movement of noncitizens into and out of the United States using biometric information (namely, fingerprints and photographs). OBIM replaced the Office of the US Visitor and Immigrant Status Indicator Technology (US-VISIT) in 2013. US-VISIT was a biometric tracking program that was designed to provide biometric identification services to federal, state, and local government decision makers in order to help them accurately identify people they encounter and to determine whether those people pose a risk to the United States. It functioned by associated fingerprint and photograph data with each passport and visa to ensure that these documents were not used on multiple immigrants and that the individuals who possessed them left the country within the time limit they were allotted.

Implementation of US-VISIT began in 2004 at 115 airports. Over the years that followed, the biometric machines were installed at US embassies and consulates throughout the world. Applicants used the machine to digitally scan their fingerprints, and the generated images were saved in a database where other relevant data about the applicants are located. The fingerprints were later used to verify thc identity of a visitor when he or she entered or left the country.

On arrival in the United States, as part of the enhanced procedures, most visitors traveling on visas had two fingerprints scanned by an inkless device and a digital photograph taken. All of the data and information were then used to assist the border inspector in determining whether or not to admit the traveler. These enhanced procedures added only seconds to the visitor's overall processing time.

All data obtained from the visitor are securely stored as part of the visitor's travel record. This information was made available only to authorized officials and selected law enforcement agencies on a need-to-know basis in their efforts to help enforce immigration and provide for security and safety.

The most notable change for international visitors was the new exit procedure. Most visitors who required a visa needed to verify their departure. This checkout process was completed by the use of automated self-service workstations in the international departure areas of airports and seaports. By scanning travel documents and capturing fingerprints on the same inkless device, the system validated the visitor's identity, verified his or her departure, and confirmed his or her compliance with US immigration policy (DHS, 2011a).

OBIM falls under the DHS National Protection and Programs Directorate (NPPD). Under OBIM, visitor tracking will likely become more comprehensive given the importance of this information to the integrity of the immigration system. This might include such things as iris scans as well as greater interconnectivity of databases.

State and Local Role in Customs and Immigration Enforcement

Enforcement of immigration and customs law falls squarely within the jurisdiction of the federal government and its applicable agencies and offices. This is because immigration status does not concern any single state, but rather that of the relationship between the United States and other countries and their citizens. State and local governments do not dictate whether or not a foreign citizen may enter the country, nor may they decide how long they are allowed to remain once they do. In fact, state and local law enforcement agencies must be certain that their actions, relative to the enforcement of state and local laws and statutes, do not interfere with the ability of the federal government to enforce immigration and customs law. This is especially true with regard to detention and deportation of illegal aliens.

That being said, it is expected that state and local government law enforcement agencies will "cooperate" with the federal government in the enforcement of these laws and will provide assistance as they are able to ensure that the pursuit of the federal homeland security mission with regard to immigration and customs enforcement is possible. The interpretation of what the term cooperate means forms the basis of how state and local agencies participate in immigration and customs enforcement actions. The following sidebar illustrates the difference between cooperating with the federal government on these issues and performing them outright.

Permitted and Impermissible Immigration and Customs Enforcement Actions of State and Local Governments

Permitted actions

- State and local law enforcement officers participating in joint task forces with DHS immigration officers (among other possible US and international partners), where one purpose of the task force includes identifying and apprehending individuals suspected of being in violation of federal immigration law
- State and local law enforcement officers providing assistance to DHS immigration officers in the execution of a civil or criminal search or arrest warrant for individuals suspected of being in violation of federal immigration law—for example, by providing tactical officers to join the federal officials during higher-risk operations or providing perimeter security for the operation (e.g., blocking off public streets)
- State and local governments providing state equipment, facilities, or services for use by federal immigration officials for official business
- Where independent state or local law grounds provide a basis for doing so, state and local law enforcement officers seizing evidence or initiating a stop of an individual at the request of DHS immigration officers where the seizure or stop would aid an ongoing federal investigation into possible violations of federal immigration law

- Allowing federal immigration officials access to state and local facilities for the purpose of identifying detained aliens not only who are held under the state or local government's authority but also who may be of interest to the federal government
- Where state government officials learn in the normal course of state business of possible violations of federal immigration law, referring those possible violations to DHS immigration officials on a case-by-case basis. State or local governments sharing information related to immigration matters with DHS—whether this occurs by state or local governments utilizing standing information-sharing programs established by DHS, developing relationships with local DHS offices through which information is shared on a regular basis, or making calls to DHS on a case-by-case basis
- A state or local government exercising certain immigration authorities delegated to it by DHS pursuant to a written agreement

Impermissible actions

- State and local governments attempting to independently remove an alien from the United States or imposing sanctions on an alien due to a suspected violation of federal immigration law
- State and local governments establishing programs under which aliens currently in foreign countries may seek permission to enter the United States or state or local governments independently facilitating the entry of aliens into the United States
- State governments mandating that state or local law enforcement officers inquire into the immigration status of a specified group or category of individuals
- State governments requiring aliens, because of their status as aliens, to perform certain tasks or satisfy certain criteria that the INA and federal law neither requires nor expressly authorizes, in order for those aliens to avoid sanctions by state officials
- State or local governments creating state prohibitions or imposing civil or criminal sanctions for conduct that is within the scope of the INA, even if not prohibited by the INA—for example, penalizing aliens present in the United States without lawful status, penalizing aliens who are in violation of federal registration requirements, or prohibiting aliens who do not have work authorization from the federal government to seek work within a state
- State or local government officials consistently referring certain classes of individuals or matters to DHS for some action to such an extent as to risk burdening limited DHS resources and personnel either after being asked by DHS not to refer those matters or where such referrals fall outside of DHS priorities
- State and local governments creating a program that authorizes aliens to work in their jurisdictions without regard to whether the aliens have work authorization from the federal government
- State and local governments proscribing or penalizing the use of consular identification cards or other documents, in circumstances where their use would be reasonably related to fulfilling the United States' treaty-based obligation to inform arrested or detained aliens that they may have their country's embassy or consulate notified and that officials from the embassy or consulate must be allowed access to them upon request

---

Source: DHS (2012a).

Conclusion

The nation's security and economic stability are contingent upon effective maintenance of secure borders, effective enforcement of immigration laws, and enforceable customs policies and procedures. These three tasks are monumental in their scope, requiring the dedication of hundreds of thousands of government employees, cutting-edge technologies, intergovernmental cooperation, and billions upon billions of dollars in budget allocations. By consolidating these functions under the DHS umbrella, the various agencies involved in their conduct have increased the effectiveness of each, and as a result, the nation is likely safer and more secure. While legal immigrants and legitimate commerce do form both the foundation and ongoing prosperity of our nation, the truth remains that criminals and terrorists will continue to seek out new and better ways to evade our systems of protection.

Key Terms

Asylum: The protection granted by a nation to a person who has left their native country as a refugee (and would therefore face imminent danger were they to return to that country).

Border: A line that defines geographic and political boundaries or legal jurisdictions.

Containerization: The transportation of cargo in standardized containers that can be seamlessly transferred between oceangoing (ships), rail (trains), and highway (trucks) vehicles without having to unload contents.

Customs: The government function tasked with collecting duties levied on imported goods.

Deportation: The act of forcibly expelling a foreign national from one country to their own country or to a third country willing to accept them.

Drone aircraft: A powered, pilotless, unmanned aircraft that is typically flown remotely by an operator on the ground.

Duties: Taxes imposed upon goods imported into one country from another, typically imposed for the purposes of protecting domestic business interests, equalizing the charges imposed by other countries on exported goods, and/or generating government revenue.

Excise tax: Tax imposed on the use or consumption of certain products.

Immigration: The act of a foreign citizen coming to another country for the purposes of residing there permanently, either by legal or by illegal means.

Linewatch operations: Operations that are conducted near international boundaries and coastlines in areas of Border Patrol jurisdiction to prevent the illegal entry and smuggling of aliens into the United States and to intercept those who do enter illegally before they can escape from border areas.

Marine patrol: Border Patrol activities conducted along the coastal waterways of the United States and Puerto Rico and interior waterways common to the United States and Canada. Marine patrol activities are typically conducted from the decks of marine craft.

Naturalization: The process under national law by which a foreign-born person is granted citizenship.

Refugee: A person who has been forced to leave their country due to war, persecution, or other reasons for which they fear for their life and safety.

Sign-cutting operations: The detection and interpretation of any disturbances in natural terrain conditions that indicate the presence or passage of people, animals, or vehicles.

Visa: An endorsement on a passport that indicates the holder is allowed to enter, exit, and/or stay for a predetermined amount of time in a country. There are numerous classes of visas that each bestows different privileges.

Review Questions

1. How do the nation's borders serve to maintain economic and physical security?
2. What DHS offices are involved in each of the following, and what specific actions do they perform?
   a. Immigration
   b. Border security
   c. Customs enforcement
3. How does DHS balance the protection of the nation's borders with the freedom of movement of legitimate travelers and goods across the borders?

References

CBP, 2014a. Fulfilling CBP's Agricultural Mission. CBP Press Release. http://1.usa.gov/1wLoID3.

CBP, 2014b. CBP intercepts Asian Gypsy Moth at Port of Honolulu. CBP Press Release (October 7). http://1.usa.gov/108DHvW.

CBP, 2014c. Unmanned aircraft system MQ-9 predator B. CBP fact sheet. http://1.usa.gov/1s7100U.

CBP, 2014d. On a typical day in FY2013. USCBP website: http://1.usa.gov/106LcUt (accessed 11/03/2014).

CBP, 2014e. On a typical day in fiscal year 2013. CBP fact sheet. CBP website: http://1.usa.gov/106LcUt (accessed 10/31/2014).

CBP, 2014f. CBP organizational chart. CBP website: http://1.usa.gov/1wN7Dfp (accessed 10/30/2014).

DHS, 2011a. Securing America's borders: CBP fiscal year 2010 in review fact sheet (March 15).

DHS, 2011b. USCG organizational chart. DHS website: http://1.usa.gov/1v6ot72 (accessed 11/03/2014).

DHS, 2012a. Guidance on State and Local Governments' Assistance in Immigration Enforcement and Related Matters. Department of Homeland Security, Washington. http://1.usa.gov/1DPUr8q.

DHS, 2012b. Secure freight initiative. DHS website: http://1.usa.gov/1rV7IH1 (accessed 10/30/2014).

Customs and Border Protection (CBP), 2011. Container Security Initiative In Summary. Brochure. May. http://1.usa.gov/18Zrhfc.

Customs and Border Protection (CBP), 2015. Immigration Inspection Program. Overview. CBP Website. http://1.usa.gov/1Mhebbg (accessed March 2015).

Homeland Security Investigations Directorate (HSI), 2014. HSI – a diverse, global force. DHS website: http://1.usa.gov/10Mwu5O (accessed 11/03/2014).

ICE, 2009. Shield America: a partnership to protect America. ICE brochure. http://1.usa.gov/1wqQPJM.

ICE, 2014a. A day in the life of ICE enforcement and removal operations. DHS website: http://1.usa.gov/1EbYBcl (accessed 11/03/2014).

ICE, 2014b. Joint Terrorism Task Force. DHS website: http://1.usa.gov/1Gd04BB (accessed 11/03/2014).

ICE, 2014c. Border Enforcement Security Task Force (BEST). DHS website: http://1.usa.gov/1pgwbLH (accessed 11/03/2014).

Simanski, J., 2014. Immigration Enforcement Actions 2013. Office of Immigration Statistics. http://1.usa.gov/1FoWLFj.

USCBP, 2014a. CBP FY 2013 in review. CBP website: http://1.usa.gov/1u9uotD (accessed 11/30/2014).

USCBP, 2014b. Border patrol overview. CBP website: http://1.usa.gov/1slPaJi (accessed 10/30/2014).

USCBP, 2014c. Fiscal year 2014 milestones and achievements. Air and marine. CBP website: http://1.usa.gov/1zhCPEw (accessed 10/30/2014).

USCG, 2010. Coast Guard 2010 snapshot. http://www.uscg.mil/top/about/doc/uscg_snapshot.pdf.

USCG, 2014. US Coast Guard maritime migrant interdictions. Alien migration interdiction. USCG website: http://bit.ly/1tS0A2x (accessed 11/03/2014).

USCIS, 2014. USCIS organizational chart. USCIS website: http://1.usa.gov/1tyaDdu (accessed 11/03/2014).

7 Transportation Safety and Security

What You Will Learn

- The various modes of transportation in the US transportation network
- The roles and responsibilities of the Transportation Security Administration and its many different program offices

Introduction

Transportation is the general term that refers to the movement of things or people from one location to another. However, in today's modern world, where transportation systems are intertwined into a global network that moves billions of people and products throughout the world on a daily basis, such simple definitions are insufficient to express the complexity that exists in this sector. Furthermore, when considering the safety and security programs and measures required to address this complex sector, one must expand their consideration of what transportation is beyond simple modes and efforts of conveyance.

Historically, the United States has relied on the private sector for both the transportation network and the promise of domestic transportation safety and security. The events of September 11, 2001, however, illustrated the vulnerabilities of the nation's transportation systems and subsequently spurred a massive change in the existing approaches. Transportation security, namely, the identification, assessment, and reduction of vulnerabilities within and threats to the vast transportation network, has expanded greatly, experiencing great change and challenge along the way. These actions are far from complete, and the complexity of the system continues to pose a great hindrance to pursuits at all government levels as well as in the private sector where many of the networks reside. Terrorists will continue to target the transportation network given its inherent vulnerabilities and high-value outcomes, yet people have no choice but to continue using it given the deep and irreversible reliance that has developed.

In the United States, the Department of Homeland Security (DHS) Transportation Security Administration (TSA) is the primary government body tasked with addressing the security of transportation systems and infrastructure. The Coast Guard (within DHS) and the Department of Transportation support the role of the TSA in these efforts. Transportation security is also the responsibility of the companies that maintain components of the transportation network and of the state and local jurisdictions through which such networks traverse.

This chapter provides an overview of the various components of the nation's transportation network and describes the agencies and programs that exist to ensure their protection.

The Transportation Network

Transportation is a catch-all term that refers to a very wide range of systems, structures, vehicles, and actions. The transportation of people and things (viz., goods) takes many forms and affects every American's life in some way or another. Modern economies are interconnected at local, national, regional, and global levels and would all collapse were transportation systems and networks significantly disrupted. Even minor disruptions to the transportation network—such as gridlock or disruption of a rail line—cause hardship to those impacted. Examples of more severe disruptions, such as grounding of all commercial airlines for almost a week following the September 11, 2001, terrorist attacks, can range into the billions of dollars and cause many expected and unexpected national security threats. Each of the nation's transportation network components is thus critical to the functioning of American society and therefore a component of the nation's critical infrastructure.

There are a number of distinct components that make up the nation's transportation network, and these include the following:

Freight Rail

The US freight railroad network is intertwined throughout the country, reaching within miles of almost every community. It is still a viable and marketable alternative to roadway or air freight, and the economy remains heavily dependent on it for the transport of both raw materials and marketable goods. In fact, the freight rail network is a $60 billion per year industry that still connects many of the nation's distribution hubs and shipping ports.

At present, there is approximately 140,000 miles of active railroad track that is utilized by 565 common carrier freight railroads. These railroads serve nearly every industrial, wholesale, retail, and resource-based sector of the US economy and are responsible for transporting a majority of the goods and commodities Americans depend on. This system includes both large and small independent companies. In the absence of one single coast-to-coast freight rail operator, these carriers have developed various interchange, joint services, and voluntary access agreements that allow for the transfer of rail cars between carriers, as well as the operation of one carrier's train on the tracks of another. This type of system has maintained a high level of operational efficiency for the railroads and has helped to further lower transportation costs. It does, however, increase the complexity of the security operation needed to support it.

Freight railroads are divided into three classes based on their size and operating revenues:

- **Class I:** Railroads that operate over large areas, in multiple states, and concentrate on the long-haul, high-density, intercity traffic lines with annual revenues over $250 million
- **Class II:** Railroads that operate on at least 350 miles of active lines and have annual revenues between $20 and $250 million
- **Class III:** Railroads that operate on less than 350 miles of line and generate less than $20 million in annual revenues

Highways, Roadways, and Motor Carrier Networks

All Americans depend on the US highway and roadway systems directly through the facilitation of personal transport and indirectly through the transport of goods and services upon which they depend. This massive infrastructure network includes the following:

- 47,714 miles of interstate highway
- 164,000 miles of other National Highway System roads
- 4,000,000 miles of other roads
- 607,378 bridges over 20 feet of span
- 366 US highway tunnels over 100 m in length

The scope of personal reliance on US roads becomes fully apparent when considering that, through 2013, the total number of private and commercial vehicles registered in the United States exceeded 253 million. This includes 118 million trucks, 666,000 buses, 126 million passenger cars, and 8.4 million motorcycles.

The National Highway System

The National Highway System (NHS) is composed of approximately 160,000 miles of roadway, including the Interstate Highway System. It was developed by DOT in cooperation with the Department of Defense (DoD), the States, local officials, and metropolitan planning organizations (MPOs). The NHS includes the following subsystems of roadways (Figure 7-1):

- *The Eisenhower Interstate Highway System* (system that retains a separate identity within the NHS)
- *Other Principal Arterials* (major roadways that provide access between an arterial and a major port, airport, public transportation facility, and/or other intermodal transportation facilities)

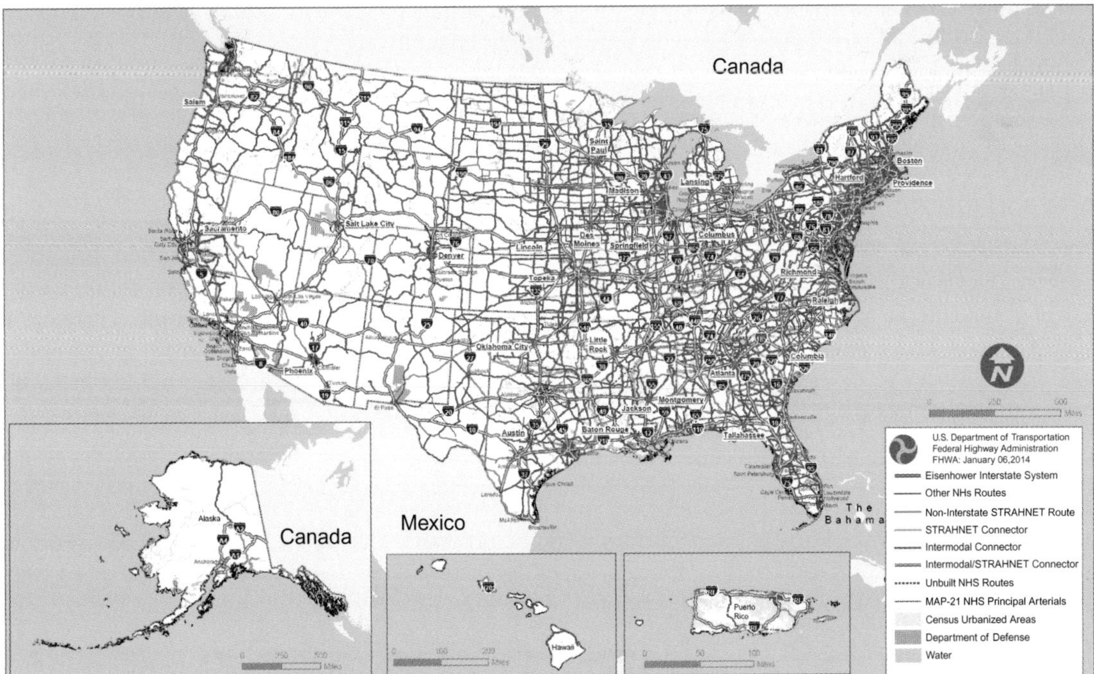

FIGURE 7-1 National Highway System. *Source: Department of Transportation (2013).*

- *Strategic Highway Network (STRAHNET)* (a network of highways that are important to the strategic defense policy of the United States and that provide defense access, continuity, and emergency capabilities for defense purposes)
- *Major Strategic Highway Network Connectors* (highways that provide access between major military installations and highways that are part of the STRAHNET)
- *Intermodal Connectors* (highways that provide access between major intermodal facilities and the other four subsystems making up the NHS)

Source: DOT (2013).

The motor carrier industry, which does not include intracity or mass transit buses, consists of three primary components:

- *The US motor coach industry*: 3623 bus companies operate 35,354 motor coach buses. These provide 132,900 jobs (71,600 full-time) and make 637 million passengers trips each year (ABA, 2014).
- *The pupil transportation (school bus) industry*: The nation's 480,000 school buses represent the largest fleet of public vehicles in the United States. They serve 19,000 US school districts and transport 26 million students each day. Collectively, these buses conduct 10 billion student trips per year (ST News, 2009).
- *The motor carrier freight industry*: In the United States, there are approximately 409,000 active motor carrier companies. These companies employ 6.8 million people, 3 million of whom are commercial vehicle drivers, who operate 26.4 million commercial trucks and 5.7 million commercial trailers. The industry moves 9.2 billion tons of freight annually, representing about 67% of the nation's shipped freight total. 61,000 of the trucking companies transport 2 billion tons of hazardous materials (HAZMATs) each year (ATA, 2014).

Ports and Intermodal Freight Transport

In the United States, 99% of imports and exports are conducted by ship through the nation's system of seaports. The US seaport infrastructure is a massive network that is owned and operated by multiple stakeholders at the federal, state, and local levels and in both the private and the public domains. There are 32 states that have active public ports, and there are 327 official ports of entry in the United States and 15 preclearance offices in Canada and the Caribbean. More information about ports is provided in Section "Ports and Shipping Security."

Mass Transit

US law defines *mass transit* to be "transportation by a conveyance that provides regular and continuing general or special transportation to the public, but does not include school bus, charter, or sightseeing transportation" (US Code Title 49, Subtitle III, Chapter 53, §5302). Modes of mass transit in the United States typically include (APTA, 2014) the following:

- *Intracity bus*: Also called *motor buses*. They are characterized by roadway vehicles powered by diesel, gasoline, battery, or alternative fuel engines contained within the vehicle; vehicles operate on streets and roadways in fixed-route or other regular services.

- *Trolleybus*: Also called *trolley coach*. It uses vehicles propelled by a motor drawing current from overhead wires via connecting poles called trolley poles from a central power source not on board the vehicle.
- *Commuter rail*: Also called *metropolitan rail*, *regional rail*, or *suburban rail*. It is characterized by an electric- or diesel-propelled railway for urban passenger train service consisting of local short-distance travel operating between a central city and adjacent suburbs; intercity rail service is excluded, except for that portion of such service that is operated by or under contract with a public transit agency for predominantly commuter services.
- *Demand response service*: Also called *paratransit* or *dial-a-ride*. It is characterized by the use of passenger automobiles, vans, or small buses operating in response to calls from passengers or their agents to the transit operator, who then dispatches a vehicle to pick up the passengers and transport them to their destinations.
- *Heavy rail*: Also called *metro*, *subway*, *rapid transit*, or *rapid rail*. It is operating on an electric railway with the capacity for a heavy volume of traffic and characterized by high-speed and rapid acceleration passenger rail cars operating singly or in multicar trains on fixed rails, separate rights-of-way from which all other vehicular and foot traffic are excluded, sophisticated signaling, and high platform loading.
- *Light rail*: Also called *streetcar*, *tramway*, or *trolley*. It is operating passenger rail cars singly or in short, usually two-car or three-car, trains, on fixed rails in right-of-way that is often separated from other traffic for part or much of the way; vehicles are typically driven electrically with power being drawn from an overhead electric line via a trolley or a pantograph, are driven by an operator on board the vehicle, and may have either high platform loading or low-level boarding using steps.
- *Automated guideway transit*: Also called *personal rapid transit*, *group rapid transit*, or *people mover*. Automated guideway transit includes electric railways (single or multicar trains) of guided transit vehicles operating without an onboard crew.
- *Cable cars*: A railway with individually controlled transit vehicles attached while moving to a moving cable located below the street surface and powered by engines or motors at a central location not on board the vehicle.
- *Monorails*: An electric railway of guided transit vehicles operating singly or in multicar trains. Vehicles are suspended from or straddle a guideway formed by a single beam, rail, or tube.
- *Ferries*: Vessels carrying passengers and in some cases vehicles over a body of water and that are generally steam- or diesel-powered. When at least one terminal is within an urbanized area, it is urban ferryboat service, such service excludes international, rural, rural interstate, island, and urban park ferries.

Each year, almost 10.3 billion passenger rides are conducted on mass transit systems in the United States. To facilitate these trips, over 141,000 vehicles are required, of which about 48% are buses. The nation's passenger rail system, Amtrak, also operates a nationwide rail transportation network of 21,000 miles of track and provides 30 million passenger trips per year at more than 500 stations. Interconnectivity of these systems has been fostered such that several different mass transit systems share terminals and other facilities. Ownership of mass transit systems is unique, with many smaller systems independently owned and operated and most medium-to-large-size agencies owned and operated by governmental or quasigovernmental organizations (APTA, 2013).

Ferries continue to serve as a vital component of the US transportation system. At present, there are 38 major ferry systems that together provide approximately 80 million passenger trips each year (APTA, 2013). Due to the nature of many waterways, ferries often travel between states, and in certain locations near Mexico and Canada, across international borders. Ferry-related accidents tend to be spectacular in nature given the unique aspect of drowning, and in many historical events, dozens and even hundreds to thousands of people have died. As such, ferries have been and continue to be seen as a high-priority target for terrorists throughout the world.

Pipeline Security

As a conveyor of goods from place to place, the oil and gas pipeline network that spans the nation is considered a component of the transportation infrastructure (Figure 7-2). The national pipeline system is somewhat unique with regard to its status as a transportation system and as such has unique infrastructure security characteristics and requirements. Pipelines have been a regular target of terrorism throughout the world, and intelligence has found evidence that terrorists consider the US pipeline system a high-value target. Additionally, accidents or other disruptions to the pipeline infrastructure can cause significant impacts to property and to humans, and the economic impacts may be far-reaching.

Virtually all the critical pipeline infrastructure is owned or operated by private entities. There are

- 182,166 miles of hazardous liquid pipelines operated by over 350 operators,
- 342,832 miles of natural gas transmission pipelines operated by over 1000 operators,
- 2.1 million miles of natural gas distribution pipelines operated by over 1285 operators (DOT, 2014).

Perhaps, the most significant risk to the nation's pipeline network is the age of its infrastructure components. Following World War II, there was a major push to develop infrastructure, and over 50% of the US interstate pipeline network was built at this time. The Department of Transportation estimates

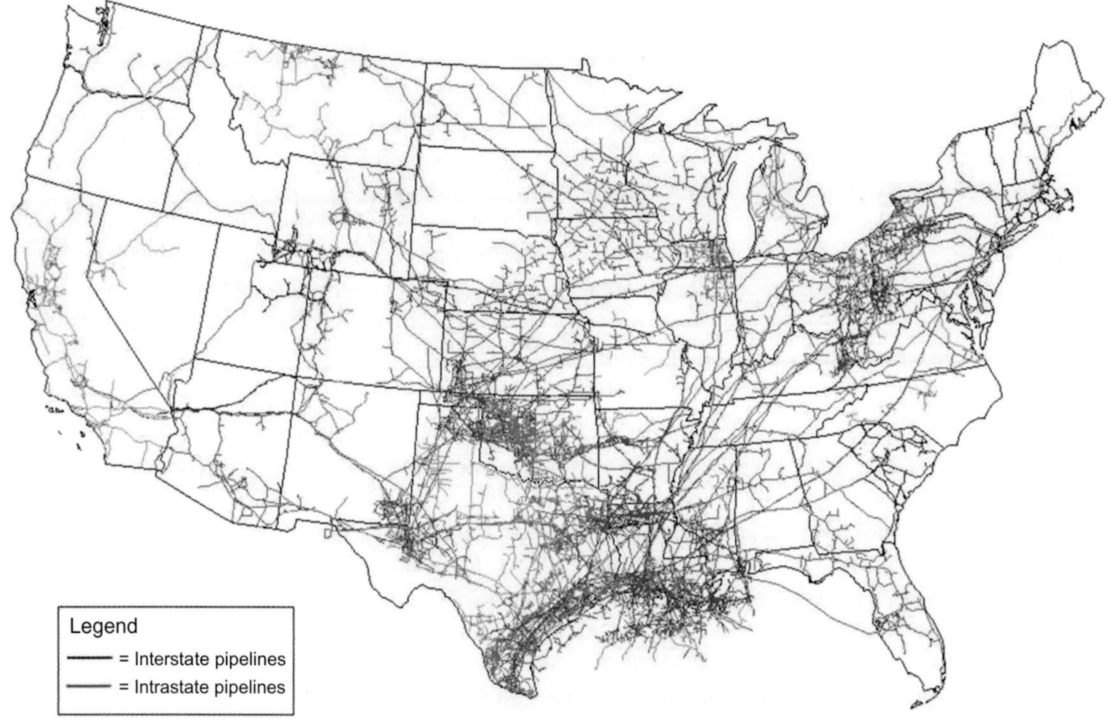

FIGURE 7-2 US natural gas pipeline infrastructure. *Source: Energy Information Administration (2009).*

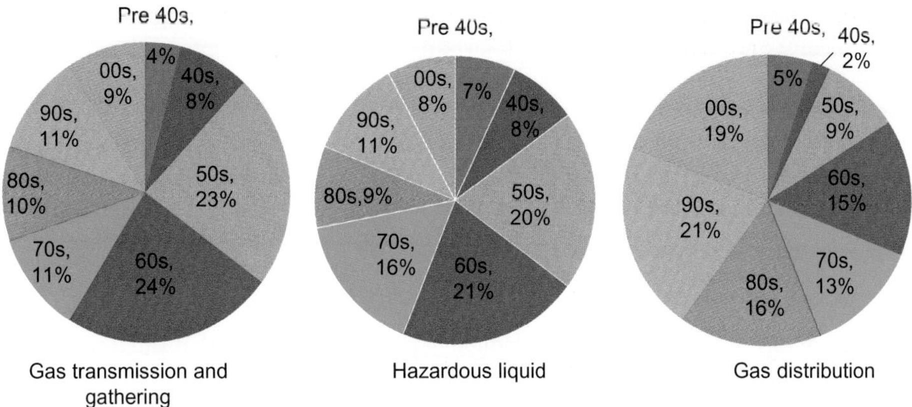

FIGURE 7-3 Age of US pipeline infrastructure by resource type. *Source: Department of Transportation (2014a).*

that at least 3% of gas distribution lines were put in place prior to 1950 and are made of cast or wrought iron. Furthermore, at least 12% of interstate gas and hazmat transmission pipelines were built prior to 1950, many using welding and connection technologies and solutions that are no longer considered durable (Figure 7-3) (DOT, 2014a).

Pacific Gas and Electric Pipeline Rupture in San Bruno, CA

On September 9, 2010, at 6:11 pm, a 30 in. diameter natural gas transmission pipeline in San Bruno, CA, ruptured and released vast quantities of natural gas. The escaping gas ignited and initiated structure fires in the community surrounding the pipeline. Local emergency responders utilized air drops of fire retardant and water to limit the spread of the fire. At 7:40 pm, PG&E completed the isolation of the ruptured pipeline from sources of gas supply by closing valves upstream and downstream of the rupture site. Approximately 5 h after the rupture, PG&E reported the pipeline rupture to the National Response Center (NRC). The consequences of the rupture and fire were devastating. Eight people lost their lives, 51 people required in-patient hospitalization, and 38 homes were destroyed. PG&E has estimated the property damage from the rupture to be over $220 million.

Source: DOT (2014b).

Air Freight

In 2011, approximately 17 million tons of freight (or "cargo") was transported within the United States and between the United States and other countries using commercial aircraft. The air freight industry is vital given the speed and efficiency it can provide, both of which are vital for products that are needed immediately or for which the risk of spoilage exists. This includes over 300 foreign and domestic air cargo carriers, which operate out of approximately 450 airports. The top five US-international country gateways for freight in this period included Japan, South Korea, Germany, the United Kingdom, and Taiwan. Air freight presents a unique security challenge due to its sheer quantity and the methods by which it is transported. Air freight is shipped both on dedicated freight-carrying airplanes and on passenger planes in the cargo hold. When transported on passenger aircraft, passengers are exposed to the risk of these goods, which may be used to conduct terrorist attacks.

Commercial and General Aviation

Commercial aviation has been operating in the United States since 1914. At that time, and in the years that followed, the airline industry was accessible only to the most privileged clients and served very few locations. Today, more than 28,000 flights take off or land in the United States each day, representing about half of the world's commercial airline traffic. Of approximately 20,000 airports that are registered in the United States, approximately 500 are certified to serve commercial flights. These commercial airports serve hundreds of millions of passengers each year, with some of the largest serving tens of millions of passengers each (Atlanta's Hartsfield-Jackson International Airport, for instance, served 95.5 million passengers in 2012, making it the busiest in the world) (Hartsfield-Jackson Airport, 2013).

General aviation (GA) is a vital component of the aviation sector and the national economy that accounts for some 77% of all flights in the United States. It encompasses a wide range of activities, from pilot training to flying for business and personal reasons, delivery of emergency medical services, and sightseeing. Operations range from short-distance flights in single-engine light aircraft to long-distance international flights in corporate-owned wide bodies and from emergency aeromedical helicopter operations to airships seen at open-air sporting events. The sole characteristic that GA operations have in common is that flights are not routinely scheduled; they are on demand.

Postal and Shipping Services

In 2013, the postal and shipping services sector was moved into the transportation sector as a result of Presidential Policy Directive 21 (also known as Critical Infrastructure Security and Resilience), which was issued on February 13 of that year. This sector differs from cargo and freight in that its focus is what we think of as "flat" mail—letters, envelopes, magazines, and small packages. This sector is responsible for moving approximately 575 pieces of mail that fit this description on a daily basis. The postal and shipping stakeholders serve over 150 million distinct addresses in fulfilling this mission.

The Transportation Security Domain

The following is a snapshot of the transportation network that exists in the United States:

- 3.9 million miles of public roads
- 1.2 million trucking companies operating 15.5 million trucks including 42,000 HAZMAT trucks
- 10 million licensed commercial vehicle drivers including 2.7 million HAZMAT drivers

- 2.2 million miles of hazardous liquid and natural gas pipeline
- 120,000 miles of major railroads
- Nearly 15 million daily riders on mass transit and passenger rail systems nationwide
- 25,000 miles of commercial waterways
- 361 ports
- 9.0 million containers through 51,000 port of calls
- 11.2 million containers via Canada and Mexico
- 19,576 general aviation airports, heliports, and landing strips
- 459 federalized commercial airports
- 211,450 general aviation aircraft

Source: TSA (2013b).

The National Infrastructure Protection Plan

In 2006, the Department of Homeland Security released the first of a series of National Infrastructure Protection Plans (NIPPs). The NIPP was developed to outline how the federal government viewed the role of each partner involved in critical infrastructure ownership, operation, and protection. It also described the strategy by which critical infrastructure protection would be carried out. This plan is described in greater detail in Chapter 8.

The NIPP addresses the protection of 16 specific infrastructure sectors by means of sector-specific annexes, each led by a Sector-Specific Agency (SSA). The 16 sectors include the following:

1. Chemical Sector
2. Commercial Facilities Sector
3. Communications Sector
4. Critical Manufacturing Sector
5. Dams Sector
6. Defense Industrial Base Sector
7. Emergency Services Sector
8. Energy Sector
9. Financial Services Sector
10. Food and Agriculture Sector
11. Government Facilities Sector
12. Healthcare and Public Health Sector
13. Information Technologies Sector
14. Nuclear Reactors, Materials, and Waste Sector
15. Transportation Systems Sector
16. Water and Wastewater Systems Sector

The Transportation Systems Sector is coled by SSA's Department of Transportation and Department of Homeland Security. Under the NIPP, protective actions focused on the various components that fall within the sector's domain have been organized according to the plan's four general goals, which include

1. Preventing and deterring acts of terrorism using, or against, the transportation system,
2. Enhancing the all-hazards preparedness and resilience of the global transportation system to safeguard US national interests,
3. Improving the effective use of resources for transportation security,
4. Improving sector situational awareness, understanding, and collaboration (DHS, 2009).

The NIPP vision for the transportation sector is for there to be "*A secure and resilient transportation system, enabling legitimate travelers and goods to move without significant disruption of commerce, undue fear of harm, or loss of civil liberties*" (DHS, 2009). This pursuit is led and coordinated by a Government Coordinating Council (GCC), which includes representatives from the federal, state, local, and tribal governments and which works with (but is not represented by) the private and NGO communities.

Department of Transportation Offices Involved in Transportation Infrastructure Protection

- *Federal Aviation Administration (FAA)*: FAA is charged with safely and efficiently operating and maintaining the nation's aviation system. The FAA's major roles include regulating civil aviation to promote safety; encouraging and developing civil aeronautics, including new aviation technology; developing and operating a system of air traffic control and navigation for both civil and military aircraft; researching and developing the National Airspace System; developing and conducting programs to control aircraft noise and other environmental effects of civil aviation; and regulating US commercial space transportation.
- *Federal Highway Administration (FHWA)*: FHWA is charged with the responsibility of ensuring that America's roads and highways continue to be the safest and most technologically up to date. Although state, local, and tribal governments own most of the nation's highways, FHWA provides financial and technical support to them for constructing, improving, and preserving America's highway system through the administration of the Federal-Aid and Federal Lands Highway Programs.
- *Federal Motor Carrier Safety Administration (FMCSA)*: The primary mission of the FMCSA is to reduce crashes, injuries, and fatalities involving large trucks and buses. FMCSA also has responsibility for overseeing safe and secure highway transportation of hazardous materials and compliance of household goods movements. FMCSA accomplishes its mission through a strong partnership with law enforcement in the United States.
- *Federal Railroad Administration (FRA)*: FRA promulgates and enforces railroad safety regulations, administers railroad assistance programs, conducts research and development in support of improved railroad safety and national railroad transportation policy, provides for the rehabilitation of Northeast Corridor railroad passenger service, and consolidates government support of railroad transportation activities.
- *Federal Transit Administration (FTA)*: As part of the effort to secure transit infrastructure, FTA has undertaken an aggressive nationwide security program, receiving full cooperation and support from every transit agency. FTA has conducted risk and vulnerability assessments and deployed

technical assistance teams to help strengthen security and emergency preparedness plans and has funded emergency response drills conducted in conjunction with local fire, police, and emergency responders. FTA has also implemented programs to improve public transit focusing on three priorities: training all transit employees and supervisors, improving emergency preparedness, and increasing public awareness of security issues.

- *Maritime Administration (MARAD)*: MARAD promotes the development and maintenance of a marine transportation system (MTS) sufficient to move the nation's waterborne commerce and capable of serving the deployment requirements of the DoD. It engages in outreach and coordination activities in order to assist the maritime industry in emergency preparedness and response and recovery efforts related to maritime transportation security incidents and natural disasters. The outreach and coordination activities include interaction with MTS stakeholders in planning and training forums, conferences, workshops, exercises, and real-world response and recovery efforts. MARAD provides a range of MTS information and emergency coordination capabilities through its Gateway Offices, Division Offices, and the Office of Emergency Preparedness. Disaster response and recovery missions closely parallel the Ready Reserve Force (RRF) military support mission. RRF ships have inherent capabilities to support response and recovery efforts including provision of storage for petroleum or potable water, large areas suitable for shelters or field-grade hospitals, electric power generation capability, emergency communications, dining facilities, command and control platforms, and room to carry large equipment. These RRF ships are available in appropriate circumstances to aid in response and recovery efforts.
- *National Highway Traffic Safety Administration (NHTSA)*: NHTSA's mission is to save lives, prevent injuries, and reduce economic costs due to road traffic crashes through education, research, safety standards, and enforcement activity. NHTSA also serves as the lead federal agency for emergency medical services coordination and houses the National 9-1-1 Implementation Coordination Office, which are vital to our preparedness and response to all hazards.
- *Office of Intelligence, Security, and Emergency Response (S-60)*: S-60 serves as DOT's focal point for leadership and direction on intelligence and security matters and executes the secretary's delegated authorities for DOT emergency management. Further, S-60 has overall department lead responsibility for the development and implementation of all responsibilities under the NRF and NIPP. As DOT's leading office on transportation emergency management, S-60 directs DOT's overall prevention, preparedness, response, and recovery efforts to include providing support for the DOT Crisis Coordinator; providing transportation threat notifications; directing the intra- and interagency emergency coordination efforts at the regional level; developing and maintaining DOT's emergency management strategy, policies, and plans; and operating DOT's Crisis Management Center.
- *Pipeline and Hazardous Materials Safety Administration (PHMSA)*: PHMSA oversees the safety of more than 1.2 million daily shipments of hazardous materials in the United States and 2.3 million miles of pipeline through which two-thirds of the nation's energy supply is transported. PHMSA is dedicated solely to working toward the elimination of transportation-related deaths and injuries in hazardous materials and pipeline transportation and the promotion of transportation solutions that enhance the resilience of communities and protect the natural environment.
- *Research and Innovative Technologies Administration (RITA)*: RITA coordinates DOT research programs and is charged with advancing the deployment of crosscutting technologies to

improve our nation's transportation system. As directed by Congress in its founding legislation, RITA leads DOT in coordinating, facilitating, and reviewing the department's R&D programs and activities; advancing innovative technologies, including intelligent transportation systems; performing comprehensive transportation statistics research, analysis, and reporting; and providing education and training in transportation and transportation-related fields.
- *Saint Lawrence Seaway Development Corporation (SLSDC)*: SLSDC, a wholly owned government corporation and an operating administration of DOT, is responsible for the operations and maintenance of the US portion of the St. Lawrence Seaway between Montreal and Lake Erie. This responsibility includes managing vessel traffic control in areas of the St. Lawrence River and Lake Ontario, as well as maintaining and operating the two US Seaway locks located in Massena, NY. The SLSDC coordinates its activities with its Canadian counterpart, the St. Lawrence Seaway Management Corporation, to ensure that the US portion of the St. Lawrence Seaway, including the two US locks, is available for commercial transit during the navigation season (usually late March to late December of each year). Additionally, the SLSDC performs trade development activities designed to enhance the utilization of the Great Lakes St. Lawrence Seaway System.

Source: DHS (2009).

The Transportation Security Administration

The Aviation and Transportation Security Act (Public Law 107-71), signed by President Bush on November 19, 2001, created the TSA within the Department of Transportation. This new office operated in that location until the 2003 opening of the DHS when TSA was absorbed into the now-dissolved Directorate for Border and Transportation Security. Since that time, TSA has been returned to its independent status as a stand-alone agency within DHS.

The 2001 Aviation and Transportation Security Act is notable in that it made many fundamental changes in the way transportation security is performed and managed in the United States. For instance, for the first time, this law made aviation security a direct federal responsibility. In addition, it consolidated all transportation security activities under the umbrella of one agency. Because of the nature of the September 11 terrorist attacks, aviation security has received the highest priority among TSA responsibilities (in terms of both staff and budget), and the agency commits significant human and financial resources toward developing strategies and implementing necessary technologies to prevent any future terrorist events connected to the abuse of the aviation system and air transportation (Table 7-1 illustrates the internal budget allocations of the TSA, illustrating its heavy emphasis toward aviation security). It is likely that in light of the continuing threat posed by terrorists to all public transportation systems, these trends will change and the spending gap between aviation security and other types of transportation security will diminish over time.

Since its initial full year of funding in 2003, TSA has accomplished several important projects that seek to improve air transportation security. The 2003 budget for TSA totaled \$4.8 billion, an increase of more than \$3.5 billion from 2002 funding levels. The 2003 budget included the costs of well over 30,000 airport security personnel, including screeners, law enforcement personnel, and screener supervisors.

Table 7-1 The TSA Budget

	FY 2013 Revised Enacted[a]		FY 2014 Enacted		FY 2015 Pres. Budget[b]		FY 2015±FY 2014	
	FTE	$000	FTE	$000	FTE	$000	FTE	$000
Aviation Security	51,378	$4,766,114	52,580	$4,982,735	50,318	$5,683,304	(2262)	$700,569
Surface Transportation Security	634	122,015	668	108,618	860	127,637	192	19,019
Intelligence and Vetting	416	267,537	449	237,489	736	307,131	287	69,642
Transportation Security Support	1701	908,417	2001	962,061	1750	932,026	(251)	(30,035)
Federal Air Marshals	-	874,557	-	818,607	-	-	-	(818,607)
Gross Discretionary	54,129	$6,938,640	55,698	$7,109,510	53,664	$7,050,098	(2034)	($59,412)
Mandatory, Fees, and Trust Fund	4	255,117	6	255,000	6	255,000	-	-
Total Budget Authority	54,133	$7,193,757	55,704	$7,364,510	53,670	$7,305,098	(2034)	($59,412)
Less prior year Rescissions		(25,035)		(59,209)				
Total	54,133	$7,168,722	55,704	$7,305,301	53,670	$7,305,098	(2034)	($59,412)

[a] FY 2013 Revised Enacted funding includes 0.132% across-the-board rescissions and sequestration for appropriated funds. The fees represent actual collections in FY 2013 and are not reduced for sequestration. The FTE reflects actual FTE used in FY 2013.
[b] The FY 2015 Request proposes to realign funding for the Federal Air Marshal Service under the Aviation Security appropriation. The Request also proposes to realign Intelligence funding from the Transportation Security Support appropriation to the Intelligence and Vetting (formerly known as Transportation Threat Assessment and Credentialing) appropriation.
FTE, full-time employees.
Source: DHS (2014a).

The budget also included funding for the purchase of explosive detection systems that had to be in place to screen all checked baggage and the maintenance of that equipment. The 2003 budget was also the first year reflecting full funding of the greatly expanded Federal Air Marshal Program. The president's budget request of $4.82 billion for TSA in FY 2004 was over $1 billion more than the previous year. The FY 2004 budget was spent primarily on four programs, among which the aviation security program was the largest at $4.22 billion (86%) of overall funds. The aviation security program consisted of a passenger screening program for which $1.80 billion was allocated, a baggage screening program with a budget of $944 million, and a security direction and enforcement program for which $1.47 billion was allocated (TSA, 2005).

When TSA celebrated its fifth anniversary on November 19, 2006, it had accomplished several of its congressionally mandated goals and responsibilities. During that time period, TSA detected and removed more than 40 million items that are prohibited onboard airplanes. TSA installed advanced explosive detection systems in all major airports and redesigned the air cargo rules to ensure that air cargo transported within US airspace on a daily basis is safe. TSA officials assisted the air evacuation of 25,000 hurricane victims in the aftermath of Hurricane Katrina. During that same 5-year period, TSA grew its National Explosives Detection Canine Team Program to 425 teams at more than 80 airports and 11 public transportation systems in the nation (TSA, 2006).

Today, TSA's security focus is on identifying risks, prioritizing them, managing these risks to acceptable levels, and mitigating the impact of potential incidents that may arise as result of these risks. Sharing of information among agencies and stakeholders—including intelligence information—has become a cornerstone of its risk management model. TSA has needed to adapt to the complex and unique requirements of both passenger and cargo security, in recognition of the many differences that exist between transportation modes, and to instill confidence in the security of the transportation system. TSA's stated guiding principle is that it will focus on the leveraging of prevention services, new technologies, best practices, public education, stakeholder outreach, and regulation compliance across transportation modes.

Today, approximately 50,000 transportation security officers (TSOs) provide screening and other security services at approximately 450 airports throughout the United States. They are trained and certified in constantly evolving rules, methods, and technologies that detect the presence of threats against people and the infrastructure required to maintain safe travel for nearly 2 million passengers each day. Additionally, US air carriers annually transport approximately 12.5 million tons of cargo, 2.8 million tons of which is now secured on passenger planes. The remaining 9.7 million tons of freight, which is shipped in cargo planes, also remains a unique threat to the nation given the destructive physical and psychological impact of a large plane crash.

The full scope of TSA's security mandate is staggering and encompasses a jurisdiction that rivals that of any other federal agencies. This mandate includes more than 10 billion passenger trips per year on the nation's mass transit systems, more than 161,000 miles of interstate and national highways and their integrated bridges and tunnels, and nearly 800,000 shipments of hazardous materials (95% of which are made by truck). While the United States may not have had another successful attack on its transportation infrastructure in the 14 years that have followed the 9/11 events, there have been several attempts. Transportation systems remain on the forefront of the security domain in light of the global terrorism experience—much of which has focused on various transportation systems and components (including the 2004 Manila ferry bombing, the 2004 Madrid train bombings, the 2005 London subway and bus attacks, the 2006 Mumbai train bombing, the 2010 West Bengal train sabotage and derailment, the 2010 Moscow subway attack, and the 2011 Belarus subway attack, among many, many more).

TSA Transportation Network Management Role

For each of the US transportation systems, TSA addresses these security responsibilities in partnership with other components of the DHS as well as the Department of Transportation and other departments. TSA's Office of Transportation Sector Network Management is tasked with leading the national-level effort to protect and secure the US transportation and transport systems. By establishing strategies for protecting and securing each of these different forms of transportation, this office ensures the safe movement of passengers and promotes the free flow of commerce. The Office of Transportation Sector Network Management is developed and is in the process of executing a strategy to ensure effective, efficient, and standardized operations within and among transportation modes. The strategy calls for the following:

- Completion of transportation industry threat, vulnerability, and consequence assessments
- Development of baseline security standards
- Assessment of operator security status versus existing standards

- Development of plan to close gaps in security standards
- Enhancement of transportation security systems

TSA Components

The TSA ensures transportation security through four mechanisms, each of which is described below. These include the following (see Figure 7-4):

- Transportation security grants
- Law enforcement program
- Security programs
- Security screening

Transportation Security Grants

Since 2006, DHS has awarded over $1.9 billion in special grants that target the nation's transportation systems. TSA oversees the department's transportation security grant program, which is provided to help mass transit and passenger rail systems, intercity bus companies, freight railroad carriers, ferries, and the trucking industry better secure the nation's critical transportation infrastructure against acts of terrorism and other large-scale events. The grants are designed to support "high-impact" security projects that serve to reduce the risk faced by the various transportation systems.

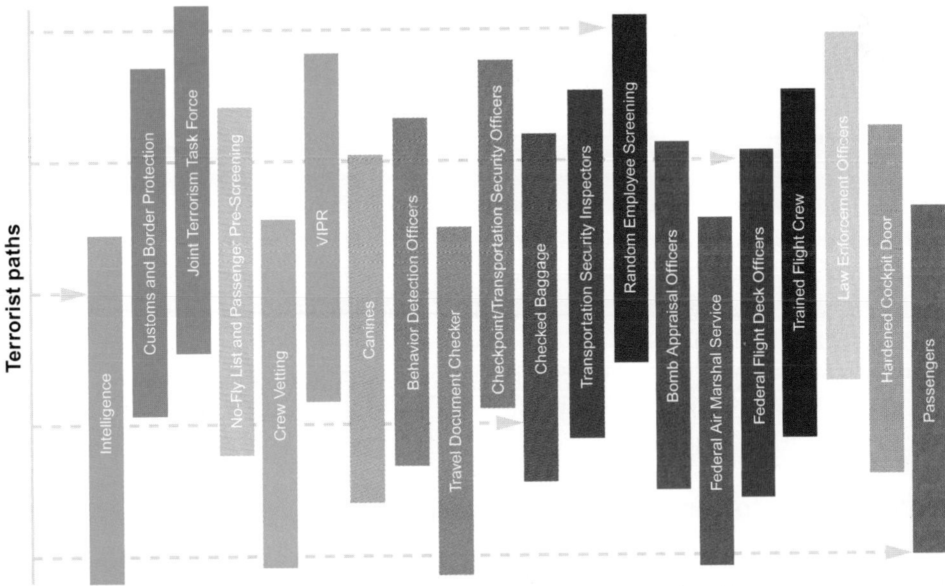

FIGURE 7-4 Layers of aviation security. *Source: Department of Homeland Security (2014).*

Until 2012, grants were provided through several vehicles specific to individual modes of transportation. These included the following:

- *The Freight Rail Security Grant Program*—created to increase security levels within the freight rail industry by funding vulnerability assessments and security plans, providing funding for security training and exercises for frontline personnel, purchasing and installing Global Positioning System (GPS) tracking on railroad cars, and hardening of bridges that are used for freight rail transportation.
- *The Intercity Bus Security Grant Program*—created to support the work of operators of fixed-route intercity and charter bus services servicing high-risk urban areas and designed to strengthen the infrastructure upon which these operators depend and to protect the traveling public against risks associated with potential terrorist attacks.
- *Transit Security Grant Program*—provides funds to owners and operators of transit systems, including intracity bus, commuter bus, certain ferry systems, and all forms of passenger rail. Grants are intended to protect critical surface transportation infrastructure and the traveling public from acts of terrorism.

In 2012, all of TSA's grant programs were eliminated except for the Transit Security Grant Program (TSGP). In FY 2013, the grant program was funded at a level of $94.2 million, of which $83.7 million was dedicated to a wide range of surface transportation providers and $9.49 million was set aside for Amtrak. The Top Transit Asset List (TTAL) assets are considered priority for this program. DHS drafted the TTAL support of the TSGP to identify those things it considers critical to surface transportation. This prioritized list was developed by examining the highest, criticality-type assets at the highest-risk regions and by examining existing intelligence. The assets were analyzed on the basis of threats, vulnerabilities, and consequences. Remediation projects for assets on the TTAL are given priority funding consideration over other capital projects. Priority is also given to "shovel-ready" projects that have complete designs/remediation plans and can be implemented quickly. Funding priorities in this fiscal year focused on addressing vulnerabilities to the transportation infrastructure and its networks. The $83.7 million was to be used for the following:

- *Priority A*: Operational activities—Training, public awareness, drills and exercises, and security planning
- *Priority B*: Top Transit Asset List (TTAL) remediation—Hardening of assets on the TTAL (a list DHS has created that identifies assets considered critical to surface transportation) that have complete remediation plans, including Environmental and Historic Preservation (EHP) documentation and are in progress or considered "shovel-ready"
- *Priority C*: Operational Packages (OPacks)/Surge Patrols—Development of new capabilities and sustainment of existing capabilities to enhance visible, unpredictable deterrence efforts in transit, including canine teams, antiterrorism teams, mobile explosive detection screening teams, patrols on overtime, equipment, and other support
- *Priority D*: All other projects—All other capital projects not included in the above priorities, with priority given to "shovel-ready" projects (TSA, 2013a)

TSA Office of Law Enforcement/Federal Air Marshal Service

TSA is best known for passenger and baggage screening at airport security checkpoints. However, the agency also maintains a number of law enforcement functions across a fairly wide jurisdiction of transportation infrastructure components. TSA law enforcement also includes the training of transportation employees in the knowledge and skills required to maintain the safety and security of the transportation network.

The Federal Air Marshal Service

The Federal Air Marshal Service is a TSA-managed law enforcement agency charged with securing the civil aviation system from both criminal and terrorist acts. Federal air marshals are specially trained federal security officers who travel inconspicuously on commercial flights for the purpose of quickly thwarting an attempted criminal or terrorist attack (or to neutralize a potentially dangerous situation involving unruly passengers) (see sidebar "Key Aviation Risk Mitigation Activities"). Awareness of the role of air marshals, as they are often called, has grown considerably since terrorists overtook four airplanes as part of a concerted attack on America on September 11.

The Federal Air Marshal Service existed long before TSA was created in the aftermath of the September 11 attacks, however. The roots of this organization actually date back to the 1960s and 1970s, when several US commercial flights were hijacked (for both political and asylum-related purposes). To address the growing threat to air travel, the Federal Air Marshal Service was created within the US Customs Service (as the "Customs Air Security Officers Program" or the "Sky Marshal Program"). Under the original program, over 1700 men and women were given special tactical training at the US Army's Fort Belvoir.

Placed on American aircraft dressed as typical passengers, the customs air security officers were flying armed and ready. The program lost support and therefore ceased operations, in mid-1974 when X-ray screening equipment was introduced in the nation's airports.

In 1985, TWA Flight 847 was hijacked, and in response, the then president Ronald Reagan directed the secretary of transportation to explore expansion of the armed Sky Marshal Program aboard international flights for US air carriers. Congress responded by passing the International Security and Development Cooperation Act (Public Law 99-83), which provided the statutes that supported the Federal Air Marshal Service. When the terrorists took over the four planes on September 11, 2001, the air marshal program consisted of less than 50 armed marshals who, by statute, flew only on international flights flown by US air carriers. In the aftermath of these events, President George W. Bush quickly enhanced the role of the agency in greatly expanding its ranks to include thousands of new marshals.

Today, federal air marshals serve as the primary law enforcement entity within TSA. Officers are deployed on flights both within the United States and elsewhere in the world. While their primary mission of protecting air passengers and crew has not changed much over the years, federal air marshals have an ever-expanding role in homeland security and work closely with other law enforcement agencies to accomplish their mission. Currently, air marshals staff several positions at different organizations such as the National Counterterrorism Center, the National Targeting Center, and the FBI's Joint Terrorism Task Forces. In addition, they are also distributed among other law enforcement and homeland security liaison assignments during times of heightened alert or special national events.

Due to the nature of their assignment, federal air marshals operate in almost complete independence, without any chance of calling in additional support if needed. The close quarters of the airplane cabin, where any mistake could easily cost an innocent passenger's health or life, demand a standard of firearms' accuracy that exceeds that seen in almost all other law enforcement services. They must remain undercover given the importance of surprise to prevent intending terrorists from knowing whether or not a federal air marshal is on a particular flight.

National Explosives Detection Canine Team

The TSA National Explosives Detection Canine Team Program is tasked with preparing dogs and their handlers to quickly locate and identify dangerous materials that may present a threat to transportation systems. The threat of a cargo- or luggage-based explosive has mandated the need for increased security measures on both cargo and passenger airplanes, but these measures have come at the cost of shipping speed and efficiency. However, trained explosive detection dogs are able to quickly rule out the presence of dangerous materials in unattended packages, structures, or vehicles, allowing the free and efficient flow of commerce.

The TSA Explosives Detection Canine Handler Course is held at Lackland Air Force Base in San Antonio, Texas. Law enforcement officers from throughout the United States travel to this location for training and are paired with a dog from the TSA "Puppy Program" at that time (dog breeds used for this function include German Shepherds, Belgian Malinois, Vizslas, and other types of dogs with exceptional abilities to smell trace amounts of explosive residue). Dogs are given 10 weeks of training, wherein they learn how to locate and identify a wide variety of dangerous materials inclusive of search techniques for aircraft, baggage, vehicles, and transportation structures, as well as procedures for identifying dangerous materials and alerting or letting the handler know when these materials are present.

Crew Member Self-Defense Training Program

The Federal Air Marshal Service manages a program to reduce terrorism risk in airplanes called Crew Member Self-Defense Training (CMSDT). This training, which is available to all US carrier crew members, is provided at 22 locations distributed among TSA sites found throughout the country to maximize access for the various airlines and their employees. The course takes 1 day and is provided free of charge. Crew members are trained in hand-to-hand combat, self-defense techniques, and other skills such as how to detain an unruly passenger or potential terrorist until the plane has landed. CMSDT is delivered in two parts. First, the participating crew members review a self-paced, interactive DVD and student manual designed to familiarize them with self-defense concepts and techniques. After completing the review, the crew members schedule and attend the 1-day hands-on training. Crew members may repeat the training as often as they would like. Crew members trained under this program regularly use their training to restrain intoxicated, belligerent, and otherwise hostile passengers aboard flights originating and/or terminating in the United States.

Key Aviation Risk Mitigation Activities

- Security vetting of workers, travelers, and shippers
- Securing of critical physical infrastructure
- Implementation of risk mitigating operational practices
- Implementation of unpredictable operational deterrence
- Screening of workers, travelers, and cargo
- Security awareness and response training
- Preparedness and response exercises

- Awareness and preparedness
- Leveraging of technologies
- Transportation industry security planning
- Security programs and vulnerability assessments
- Securing of critical cyber security

Source: DHS (2009).

Armed Security Officer Program

The Armed Security Officer Program is a very specialized transportation security program that focuses on Ronald Reagan Washington National Airport (DCA) in Arlington, Virginia (just minutes to downtown Washington, DC). Because of this airport's proximity to the nation's capital and many key US landmarks, there are a number of special security considerations associated with flights in and out of the facility, namely, that it would be very difficult to thwart another attack like the September 11 attack (given that very little warning would be possible). While commercial flights regularly fly in and out of this airport, general aviation flights require much less security and are therefore more difficult to track, and there remains a concern that terrorists will again try to use aircraft as weapons. In order to allow a small number of general aviation flights to use this facility, the Armed Security Officer Program was created under TSA in partnership with DHS and Department of Defense agencies. The DCA Access Standard Security Program (DASSP), as it is called, allows a total of 48 general aviation flights a day to leave from or fly to designated gateway airports with an Armed Security Officer (ASO) onboard.

Federal Flight Deck Officers Program

The Federal Flight Deck Officers program further strengthens commercial flights from crime or terrorism by increasing the likelihood that certain cockpit-based flight crew members are able to withstand an attack. Under this program, eligible flight crew members are authorized to use firearms to defend against an act of criminal violence or air piracy attempting to gain control of an aircraft. A flight crew member may be a pilot, flight engineer, or navigator assigned to the flight. This program has since been expanded to include cargo pilots and certain other flight crew members. Each participating crew member is trained by the Federal Air Marshal Service on the use of firearms, use of force, legal issues, defensive tactics, the psychology of survival, and program standard operating procedures.

Law Enforcement Officers Flying Armed Program

Related to the Federal Flight Deck Officers program is the Law Enforcement Officers Flying Armed training program. This TSA-maintained program is provided to all law enforcement officers who will be flying armed. Under Code of Federal Regulation (CFR) 1544.219 (Carriage of Accessible Weapons), certain law enforcement officers are able to declare their firearms to the airline and bring them onto the flight to increase the security presence that exists. Attendees in the program are given a structured lesson plan that includes protocols in the handling of prohibited items, prisoner transport, and dealing with an act of criminal violence aboard an aircraft. To qualify to fly armed, the Code of Federal Regulation states that an officer must meet the following basic requirements:

- Be a federal law enforcement officer (LEO) or a full-time municipal, county, or state LEO who is a direct employee of a government agency.
- Be sworn and commissioned to enforce criminal statutes or immigration statutes.
- Be authorized by the employing agency to have the weapon in connection with assigned duties.
- Have completed the training program "Law Enforcement Officers Flying Armed."

TSA Security Programs

TSA is also charged with ensuring the secure operation of various transportation networks. The following are examples of these programs:

Air Cargo Security

Air cargo has remained a major security concern since it was discovered that terrorists considered, and even attempted without success, destroying cargo planes over populated areas as an attack method (Associated Press, 2010). The TSA Air Cargo Security Program is composed of two distinct areas, namely,

1. the Office of Security Policy and Industrial Engagement Air Cargo Division (charged with the strategic development of programs),
2. the Office of Security Operations (OSO) (charged with program compliance).

The TSA Air Cargo Division is responsible for coordinating the different actions required to bring about a secure air cargo industry, which includes agencies and partners both within and outside of DHS. This division considers a number of threats and systems, both internationally and within the United States, and develops corresponding air cargo regulations, technological solutions, and policies. The challenge is in maintaining constant vigilance while ensuring that commerce is able to continue unimpeded. Examples of the approaches used to secure cargo include the following:

- Vetting companies that ship and transport cargo on passenger planes to ensure they meet TSA security standards
- Maintaining and staffing Certified Cargo Screening Facilities (CCSFs) that physically screen cargo using approved screening methods and technologies
- Employing random and risk-based assessments to identify high-risk cargo that requires increased scrutiny
- Inspecting industry compliance with security regulations through the deployment of TSA inspectors (TSA, 2013c)

TSA worked closely with Congress in 2007 to formulate the components of the 9/11 Bill that relate to air cargo. Since the law went into effect, TSA has increased the amount of cargo currently screened to almost 100% (with 100% of the cargo on 96% of the flights originating in the United States being screened, which means that 85% of passengers flying each day from US airports are on planes where all of the cargo has been fully screened). In late 2008, TSA completed a required milestone of screening 100% of cargo being flown on narrow-body airplanes. TSA conducts surprise cargo security inspections called *strikes*, covert testing, security directives, and 100% screening at 250 smaller airports. In 2008, TSA eliminated all exemptions to screening of air cargo for the first time and increased the amount of cargo that is subject to mandatory screening.

TSA employs 620 cargo transportation security inspectors (TSIs), who are exclusively dedicated to the oversight of air cargo. TSA also maintains 460 canine teams, of which 120 are specifically assigned to the screening of air cargo at the nation's highest cargo volume airports. This presence has significantly increased the amount of cargo screening TSA is able to conduct (TSA, 2012).

Flight School Security Awareness Training Program

Federal law (the Interim Final Rule, Flight Training for Aliens and Other Designated Individuals; Security Awareness Training for Flight School Employees) requires flight schools to ensure that their employees who have direct contact with students (including flight instructors, ground instructors, chief instructors, and administrative personnel) receive both initial security awareness training and recurrent security awareness training. Flight schools may choose either to use TSA's security awareness training program or to develop their own program. If a flight school chooses to develop its own program, the program must adhere to standards in the rule. Flight staff employed by a flight school must complete their initial training no later than 60 days after their date of hire. Recurrent training must be provided to employees each year in the same month as the month they received initial training. TSA and the Aircraft Owners and Pilots Association (AOPA) have collaborated to create an online General Aviation Security course in order to better facilitate these new security requirements placed on flight schools.

I-STEP Program

The TSA Intermodal Security Training and Exercise Program (I-STEP) provides exercise, training, and security planning tools and services to the transportation community. The program serves the port and intermodal, aviation, mass transit, freight rail, highway and motor carrier, and pipeline industries. This program enables these TSA security partners to

- enhance security capabilities through participation in or conduct of exercises and training that strengthen security plans, test emergency procedures, and sharpen skills in incident management;
- build partnerships by collaborating with stakeholder partners, law enforcement personnel, first responders, health and medical professionals, government transportation and homeland security leaders, and industry representatives to address challenges in transportation security;
- gain insights into transportation security by ensuring that needs are aligned with federal grant opportunities and allowing partners to gain a deeper understanding of lessons learned and best practices.

The I-STEP program coordinates public and private sector partners for exercise, training, and information sharing and to address transportation security issues focused on protecting travelers, commerce, and infrastructure. TSA is pilot testing an online transportation security portal called the Exercise Information System (EXIS) that guides users through a step-by-step exercise planning process, provides exercise planning and evaluation tools, and helps to ensure that lessons learned are shared.

TSA Security Screening

Over 600 million people fly each year and carry with them a quantity of baggage and other items that number in the billions. TSA inspectors are responsible for checking each passenger and each item that will be accompanying them onto a commercial aircraft. Screeners work at over 700 security checkpoints and nearly 7000 baggage screening areas throughout the United States (Figure 7-5).

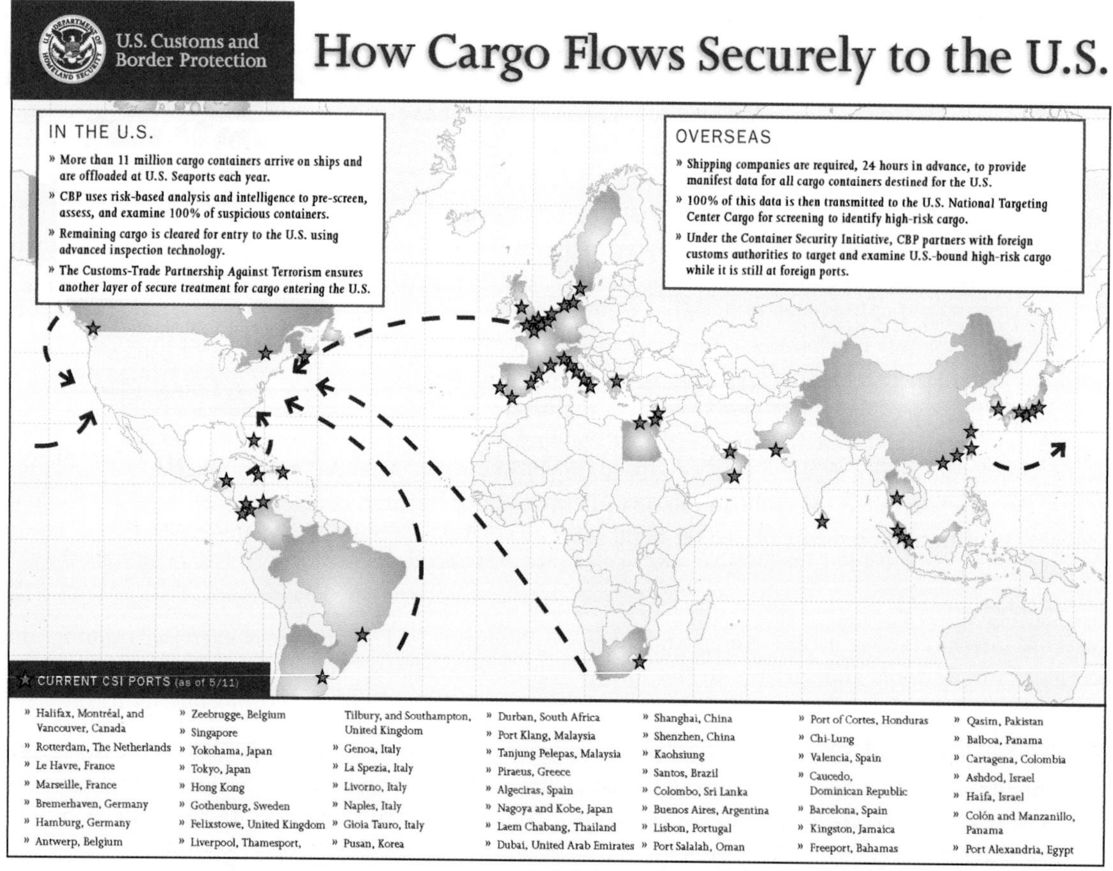

FIGURE 7-5 New Orleans, Louisiana, August 30, 2008—TSA officials check evacuees and baggage with security scanners at the airport during Hurricane Gustav. *Photo by Jacinta Quesada/FEMA News Photo.*

Passenger Screening

TSA received a legal mandate in 2001, soon after (and as a direct consequence of) the 9/11 terrorist attacks, to screen all air travelers. This role was formerly conducted by private security guards employed by each airport. However, in what is one of the largest single-recruitment campaigns in the civilian government, TSA took over airport passenger screening duties and created a workforce of tens of thousands in just a few months. Today, TSA is best known to Americans through the 43,000 transportation security officers who are stationed at airports throughout the country. In conjunction with over 1000 credentialed security inspectors, the TSA transportation security officers screen over 2 million passengers each day. TSA transportation security officers also lead and support security operations in other transportation systems, including mass transit and maritime vessels, although these roles cannot be compared in scope to the role of TSA in the airline industry.

In recent years, TSA has attempted to utilize new technologies to detect weapons and other banned items possessed by passengers. Some feel the use of these technologies has come at the expense of civil liberties and infringes upon the personal rights, privacy, and dignity of passengers. For instance, backscatter devices, which can create imagery that displays what appears underneath a passenger's clothing, have been a matter of contention given the discomfort many passengers have with screeners seeing what they feel to be "pictures of them without their clothes on." Attempts have been made to adapt the technology such that the images do not display anatomical details, but the debate continues (and the devices continue to be used).

Some of the search methods utilized by TSA transportation security officers have also come under scrutiny, including the patting-down of children, senior citizens, and the infirm. Examples of these events, which highlight the sensitive nature of conducting such personal searches and which have served to mar the TSA image, include the following:

- **November 2010:** A breast cancer survivor was asked to remove a prosthetic breast to prove to the TSA screener it was what she claimed it to be.
- **March 2011:** A cancer survivor who wears a urostomy (urine collection) bag was publicly humiliated when TSA screeners in Detroit burst the bag during a pat-down, causing it to soak his clothing in front of other passengers.
- **April 2011:** Parents of a 6-year-old child videotaped TSA officers patting-down the visibly shaken child at a New Orleans airport.
- **June 2011:** TSA screeners in Florida forced an elderly woman suffering from leukemia to remove her adult diaper when a screening showed what appeared to be a suspicious spot on the undergarment.

Baggage Screening

TSA maintains a suite of sophisticated technology and equipment that has been developed in recent years to ensure that luggage and other cargo passengers take onto planes are free from terrorist and other potential hazards (such as flammable liquids, aerosols, and radio equipment that may interfere with the flight). TSA transportation security officers electronically screen millions of bags for explosives and other dangerous items each day at over 7000 baggage screening locations and at over 450 airports nationwide.

Covert Testing

Covert testing is a process by which trained security officials test the effectiveness of screening systems by attempting to successfully board airplanes (or to check baggage on airplanes) while carrying (or packing) banned substances and devices. This can and does typically involve the use of actual explosives and/or weapons. The purpose of covert testing is to ensure that there are no omissions or unknown loopholes in security systems and to ensure that employees are maintaining high-security standards at all times. Testers try to think like a terrorist or a criminal and devise new ways in which to fool current screening systems. Whenever they are successful in moving banned substances and devices past security checkpoints, new processes and procedures are developed to prevent such breaches in the future. The details of covert testing are typically kept secret given the need to maintain an element of surprise for screeners. However, the following are general examples of the types of tests that are employed:

- *Threat Image Projection (TIP)*: The TIP system randomly superimposes images of bombs and bomb parts into real carry-on bags. These images may be superimposed on any of the millions of carry-on bags at checkpoints across the country, at any time of day or night. There are tens of thousands of TIP images and the system is updated with the latest intelligence-driven threats added on a regular basis. Officers are evaluated on the images they detect and training is tailored to drive improvement in the detection of threats across the system.

- *Aviation Screening Assessment Program (ASAP)*: ASAP assessments test the screening process by inserting inert bombs, bomb parts, and other threat items into the screening process to identify weaknesses. The assessments test both the technologies and the abilities of the screeners to identify the items. Items are placed on TSA or local, state, and federal employees or in carry-on or checked bags, not on unwitting passengers. Thousands of these assessments are conducted each year.
- *TSA's Office of Inspection (TSA OI)*: TSA's Office of Inspection, also called the "Red Team," conducts no-notice covert tests to assess the effectiveness of screening operations. Testers are trained in bomb and weapons smuggling techniques, which are gleaned from intelligence gathered from actual terrorist groups and from actual experience throughout the transportation security system. All airports are subject to no-notice testing by TSA OI. The morning of testing, local police are notified (to protect the testers and passengers in the area), and once testing has begun, the local TSA management is informed of the ongoing process. Upon completion of the test, training is conducted to address any weaknesses in the system that are identified. A Red Team inspection wherein TSA screeners at Newark Airport failed to locate an inert bomb made national news in March of 2013. In this incident, the tester had a simulated improvised explosive device hidden in his pants. The tester was able to pass both the magnetic testing (metal detector) and a physical pat-down before boarding an airplane. This test highlighted the difficulties faced by inspectors who are screening millions of passengers each day with equipment that terrorists are constantly looking for new ways to deceive (Messing, 2013).
- *DHS Office of Inspector General (DHS IG) testing*: The DHS IG conducts hundreds of covert tests at airports from coast to coast and acts completely independently from TSA. DHS IG agents measure the effectiveness of screening protocols and communicate these results to TSA and DHS management to increase screening and security effectiveness.
- *Government Accountability Office (GAO) testing*: GAO conducts independent tests of airport security to ensure these systems are reviewed by a true independent, external entity. GAO employees report their findings to Congress and share results with TSA. GAO results have led to increases in security through enhanced training and use of technology.

Trucking Security

Security within the nation's commercial trucking industry is a very important component of homeland security given that a significant portion of the nation's hazardous materials (HAZMATs) are transported by these trucks on public highways and roads. Incidents where hazardous materials are spilled or released as a result of commercial truck accidents are fairly common. Moreover, the threat always exists that a terrorist will use a truck carrying some dangerous chemical or other materials to cause significant human, property, and environmental damages. Releases involving the volumes or weights of materials contained in these vehicles can have catastrophic effects.

A serious HAZMAT incident is defined by DOT's Research and Special Programs Administration (RSPA) as

- an incident that involves a fatality or major injury caused by the release of a hazardous material,
- the evacuation of 25 or more persons as a result of release of a hazardous material or exposure to fire,
- a release or exposure to fire that results in the closure of a major transportation artery,
- the alteration of an aircraft flight plan or operation,

- the release of radioactive materials from type B packaging,
- the release of over 11.9 gallons or 88.2 pounds of a severe marine pollutant,
- the release of a bulk quantity (over 119 gallons or 882 pounds) of a hazardous material.

Table 7-2 illustrates the number of these serious incidents that occurred in the major transportation modes in the United States in 2013 (including air, highway, railway, and waterway).

The Office of Hazardous Materials Safety of DOT/RSPA is responsible for coordinating a national safety program for the transportation of hazardous materials by air, rail, highway, and water in the United States. The Code of Federal Regulations (CFR) 49 Part 107 documents the steps being taken to enhance hazardous material transportation security. Subchapter C, Part 107, specifically discusses regulations for HAZMAT transportation on US highways. The subparts of the document include information about regulations for loading and unloading of HAZMAT transportation vehicles, segregation and separation of HAZMAT vehicles and shipments in transit, accidents, and regulations applying to hazardous material on motor vehicles carrying passengers for hire. To supplement safety efforts, the DHS Office of Screening

Table 7-2 HAZMAT Summary by Mode of Transportation/Cause for 2013

Mode of Transportation	Cause	Incidents	Hospitalized	Nonhospitalized	Fatalities	Damages
Air	Abrasion	4	0	0	0	$0
	Broken component or device	2	0	0	0	$6500
	Cause not reported	630	0	6	0	$133,555
	Commodity self-ignition	1	0	0	0	$0
	Conveyer or material handling equipment mishap	20	0	0	0	$0
	Corrosion—interior	1	0	0	0	$0
	Defective component or device	50	0	0	0	$0
	Deterioration or aging	1	0	0	0	$0
	Dropped	168	0	0	0	$0
	Fire, temperature, or heat	2	0	0	0	$0
	Forklift accident	27	0	0	0	$3050
	Freezing	3	0	0	0	$0
	Human error	171	0	5	0	$0
	Impact with sharp or protruding object (e.g., nails)	31	0	0	0	$0
	Improper preparation for transportation	183	0	1	0	$0
	Inadequate blocking and bracing	1	0	0	0	$0
	Inadequate preparation for transportation	37	0	0	0	$0
	Inadequate procedures	4	0	0	0	$0
	Loose closure, component, or device	17	0	0	0	$0
	Missing component or device	1	0	0	0	$0
	Overpressurized	8	0	0	0	$0
	Overfilled	4	0	0	0	$0

(Continued)

Table 7-2 (Continued)

Mode of Transportation	Cause	Incidents	Hospitalized	Nonhospitalized	Fatalities	Damages
	Too much weight on package	15	0	0	0	$0
	Valve open	56	0	0	0	$0
	Vandalism	1	0	0	0	$0
	Vehicular crash or accident damage	3	0	0	0	$0
	Water damage	5	0	0	0	$0
Highway	Abrasion	78	1	0	0	$232,960
	Broken component or device	233	0	4	0	$302,572
	Cause not reported	2231	2	15	2	$3,703,089
	Commodity polymerization	2	0	0	0	$61,299
	Commodity self-ignition	10	0	0	0	$8300
	Conveyer or material handling equipment mishap	37	0	0	0	$37,600
	Corrosion—exterior	27	0	0	0	$27,416
	Corrosion—interior	34	1	0	0	$120,159
	Defective component or device	677	0	2	0	$994,358
	Deterioration or aging	130	0	1	0	$404,755
	Dropped	1131	0	4	0	$25,702
	Fire, temperature, or heat	29	9	6	1	$2,338,144
	Forklift accident	1422	1	7	0	$672,150
	Freezing	26	0	0	0	$30,191
	Human error	1429	1	19	0	$3,710,561
	Impact with sharp or protruding object (e.g., nails)	754	0	8	0	$1,153,875
	Improper preparation for transportation	751	0	6	0	$360,660
	Inadequate accident damage protection	12	0	1	0	$2200
	Inadequate blocking and bracing	1671	0	3	0	$525,229
	Inadequate maintenance	10	0	0	0	$0
	Inadequate preparation for transportation	611	0	5	0	$237,218
	Inadequate procedures	87	0	2	0	$62,359
	Inadequate training	7	0	0	0	$10,548
	Incompatible product	1	0	0	0	$340,000
	Incorrectly sized component or device	7	0	0	0	$0
	Loose closure, component, or device	1694	0	6	0	$358,824
	Misaligned material, component, or device	21	0	0	0	$3500
	Missing component or device	17	0	0	0	$32,500
	Overpressurized	61	1	1	1	$386,650
	Overfilled	124	0	2	0	$666,742
	Rollover accident	124	0	1	1	$17,878,481

Table 7-2 (Continued)

Mode of Transportation	Cause	Incidents	Hospitalized	Nonhospitalized	Fatalities	Damages
	Threads worn or cross threaded	7	0	0	0	$10,700
	Too much weight on package	295	0	16	0	$99,227
	Valve open	86	0	2	0	$20,173
	Vandalism	4	0	0	0	$85,725
	Vehicular crash or accident damage	156	5	8	6	$16,900,949
	Water damage	3	0	0	0	$0
Railway	Abrasion	8	0	0	0	$18,514
	Broken component or device	25	0	0	0	$53,308
	Cause not reported	13	1	0	0	$801,750
	Corrosion—exterior	1	0	0	0	$2500
	Corrosion—interior	10	1	0	0	$125,115
	Defective component or device	85	0	0	0	$273,567
	Derailment	21	0	0	0	$34,450,363
	Deterioration or aging	72	0	3	0	$123,467
	Dropped	2	0	0	0	$5540
	Fire, temperature, or heat	1	0	0	0	$2,285,200
	Forklift accident	4	0	0	0	$8020
	Freezing	3	0	0	0	$25,000
	Human error	27	0	1	0	$440,262
	Impact with sharp or protruding object (e.g., nails)	13	0	0	0	$49,734
	Improper preparation for transportation	51	0	0	0	$131,322
	Inadequate blocking and bracing	13	0	0	0	$35,794
	Inadequate maintenance	6	0	0	0	$36,106
	Inadequate preparation for transportation	50	0	0	0	$139,900
	Inadequate procedures	3	0	0	0	$17,250
	Incorrectly sized component or device	2	0	0	0	$10,000
	Loose closure, component, or device	235	4	1	0	$864,514
	Misaligned material, component, or device	35	0	0	0	$88,568
	Missing component or device	28	0	0	0	$130,398
	Overpressurized	12	0	0	0	$17,368
	Overfilled	13	0	0	0	$73,644
	Rollover accident	2	0	0	0	$0
	Threads worn or cross threaded	5	0	0	0	$6710
	Too much weight on package	5	0	0	0	$19,070
	Valve open	58	0	0	0	$150,504
	Vandalism	1	0	0	0	$2500
	Vehicular crash or accident damage	2	0	0	0	$86,500

(Continued)

Table 7-2 (Continued)

Mode of Transportation	Cause	Incidents	Hospitalized	Nonhospitalized	Fatalities	Damages
Water	Cause not reported	56	0	2	0	$7100
	Forklift accident	2	0	0	0	$0
	Human error	3	0	0	0	$8613
	Impact with sharp or protruding object (e.g., nails)	1	0	0	0	$3000
	Improper preparation for transportation	1	0	0	0	$8613
	Loose closure, component, or device	1	0	0	0	$8613
	Overfilled	1	0	0	0	$0

Note: Due to multiple causes being involved in a single incident, the totals above may not correspond to the totals in the other reports.
PHMSA revised the definition of a serious incident in 2002. This is the current definition: a fatality or major injury caused by the release of a hazardous material, the evacuation of 25 or more persons as a result of release of a hazardous material or exposure to fire, a release or exposure to fire that results in the closure of a major transportation artery, the alteration of an aircraft flight plan or operation, the release of radioactive materials from type B packaging, the release of over 11.9 gallons or 88.2 pounds of a severe marine pollutant, or the release of a bulk quantity (over 119 gallons or 882 pounds) of a hazardous material.
Source: USDOT (2013).

Coordination and Operations (SCO) within the (former) BTS Directorate initiated hazardous materials trucker background checks in 2005 in an effort to secure the highways and trucks. Since then, the office's name has been changed to the Screening Coordination Office, and it has been tasked with the coordination of all screening activities and systems administered and maintained by DHS. It is currently housed within the DHS Office of Policy.

In fiscal years 2005 and 2006, TSA provided grants through the Trucking Security Program (TSP) totaling $4.8 million to trucking companies. This funding level increased to $11.6 million in fiscal year (FY) 2007 and again to $15.5 million for FY 2008.

The funding priorities for 2008 were the following:

- *Participant identification and recruitment*: Identification and recruitment of highway professionals, such as truckers, school bus drivers, motor coach drivers, highway workers, and first responders to participate in highway security efforts, and development of a 5-year strategic plan.
- *Planning*: Development of emergency response and contingency plans based on identified high-risk scenarios (e.g., truck hijacking and HAZMAT) and conducting hazard analysis and risk assessment in an effort to improve the plan.
- *Training*: Development of a web-based security training system to train highway professionals, specialized HAZMAT drivers, and state and local law enforcement organizations and design of an evaluation methodology for all training programs and the development of a 5-year strategic plan for training.

- *Communications*: Maintain a full-service (24/7) communications/call center staffed with well-trained responders who will provide nationwide first responder/enforcement contact numbers and electronic linkage to registered participants and the development of a 5-year strategic plan for communications.
- *Information analysis and distribution*: The applicant will provide management consulting services and oversight in cooperation with ODP leadership to maintain the Highway Information Sharing and Analysis Center (ISAC), located at the Transportation Security Operations Center (TSOC) in Herndon, Virginia. This center is dedicated exclusively to highway and highway transport-related security needs and issues. The applicant will provide recommendations, implementation strategies, and a completed plan for continued Highway ISAC operations. Responsibilities may include identification of the appropriate role of a highway-specific ISAC, identification of benefits of highway-specific ISAC separation from existing rail or other centers, optimal configuration and location of a new ISAC, and optimal staffing or implementation strategies (DHS, 2005, 2006, 2007; TSA, 2007).

In 2009, the Trucking Security Grant Program funding fell to $7 million, and in 2010, direct funding for the program was eliminated altogether.

Ports and Shipping Security

DHS considers the securing of goods imported and exported via maritime transport to be a critical task. Each year, more than 11 million shipping containers arrive from overseas at US ports. Given the significance of containerization and maritime commerce on the US economy, it is clear that a successful terrorist attack on a major US port could result in not only significant loss of life and tremendous physical damage but also serious disruption to the economy of the United States and its trade partners. The SAFE Port Act of October 2006 tasked DHS with the responsibility of assuring maritime transport security and protecting the nation's ports. This is accomplished through risk mitigation, vulnerability analysis, and the establishment of preventive measures in those facilities. The SAFE Port Act also tasked DHS with the creation of a resumption plan to minimize the disruption to economic activity in the case of a major terrorist attack on these seaports.

The USCG is the lead federal agency for maritime homeland security efforts and is integral to DHS's port and shipping security efforts (see sidebar "USCG MARSEC Levels"). The USCG adheres to its own maritime homeland security strategy that defines duties, responsibilities, and strategic missions. Under this strategy, the USCG homeland security mission is declared to be the protection of the US maritime domain and the US marine transportation system, the denial of their use and exploitation by terrorists as a means for attacks on US territory, population, and critical infrastructure; and the preparation for and, in the event of attack, conduct of emergency response operations. In accomplishing its homeland security mission, the strategic goals of the Coast Guard are as follows:

- Increasing maritime domain awareness
- Conducting enhanced maritime security operations
- Closing port security gaps
- Building critical security capabilities
- Leveraging partnerships to mitigate security risks
- Ensuring readiness for homeland defense operations

USCG MARSEC Levels

The USCG has a three-tiered system of Maritime Security (MARSEC) levels to reflect the prevailing threat environment to the maritime elements of the national transportation system. MARSEC levels are designed to provide a means to easily communicate preplanned scalable responses to increased threat levels (see Figure 7-6):

- Level 1 indicates the level for which minimum appropriate security measures shall be maintained at all times.
- Level 2 indicates the level for which appropriate additional protective security measures shall be maintained for a period of time as a result of a heightened risk of a transportation security incident (TSI).
- Level 3 indicates the level for which specific protective security measures shall be maintained for a limited period of time when a TSI is probable and imminent or has occurred, although it may not be possible to identify the specific target.

The commandant of the USCG sets MARSEC levels, but because of the unique nature of the maritime industry, MARSEC levels will align closely with DHS National Terrorism Advisory System (NTAS). The international community also uses a three-tiered advisory system specified by the International Ship and Port Facility Security (ISPS) Code. MARSEC levels are consistent with the international three-tiered advisory system.

FIGURE 7-6 USCG MARSEC levels. *Source: DHS (2009).*

Source: USCG (2014a).

FEMA supports port security through its Grant Programs Directorate (GPD). This directorate has assumed responsibility of the Port Security Grant Program (PSGP), which has existed in one form or another since the beginning of DHS. In fact, between 2002 and 2014, DHS awarded almost $3 billion in grants to port owners, operators, and service providers in order to shore up the vulnerabilities that have been identified by the USCG and by other means. While the focus of these grants changes from year to year, the 2014 priorities are indicative of the maturity of this effort and include

- improving port-wide maritime security risk management,
- enhancing maritime domain awareness,
- supporting maritime security training and exercises,
- maintaining or reestablishing maritime security mitigation protocols that support port recovery and resiliency capabilities.

Funding levels have dropped considerably and were at $100 million for FY 2014. The list of eligible port facilities was increased, however, from the original 52 ports considered to be most critical to 146 (grouped into 90 "discrete port funding areas"). Certain ferry operators are also eligible as long as they do not also apply to the transportation security grant program (DHS, 2014b).

Assuring the security of seaports is a unique challenge due to the importance of commerce that passes through them and the relatively complex supply chain operations involved. This complexity is the result of both the multistep process that is required of each cargo item as it navigates its way to the intended recipient and the varied nature of the different stakeholders involved in the process (inclusive of private companies and foreign governments). Figure 7-7 provides a simplified overview of the process for a typical container shipped to the United States from a foreign destination.

Several of the typical security steps in the shipment of maritime cargo to the United States occur outside the jurisdiction of US authorities. In other words, they occur at foreign ports or on the ships themselves while in international waters. This presents a challenge to DHS in that all security steps must be performed in order for the assurance of security to be maintained. To address the challenge of jurisdiction and control, DHS has developed cooperative security-focused relationships and partnerships with a number of foreign governments and their corresponding port authorities, under which each government allows the other to inspect facilities and carry out specific counterterrorism and other inspection measures as the materials weave their way through the shipment process. For instance, in many key foreign ports, DHS officials perform daily audits and inspections of containers bound for the United States and work with their foreign counterparts to ensure that chemicals, biological agents, nuclear materials, and explosives that may be hidden in containers are detected and interdicted before they pose a threat to life and commerce. While partner government agencies are invited to conduct the same level of inspection at US ports for materials bound for their own ports, only a handful actually accept.

In light of these challenges, the risk intervention and port security efforts of DHS may be grouped into three distinct phases, namely,

- overseas vulnerability reduction efforts,
- in-transit vulnerability reduction,
- vulnerability reduction in US waters and on US shores.

Examples of the various initiatives that occur in each phase are the following:

Initiatives That Address Overseas Vulnerability Reduction

1. *The 24-h Advance Manifest Rule*: All sea carriers with the exception of bulk carriers and approved break bulk cargo are required to provide proper cargo descriptions and valid consignee addresses

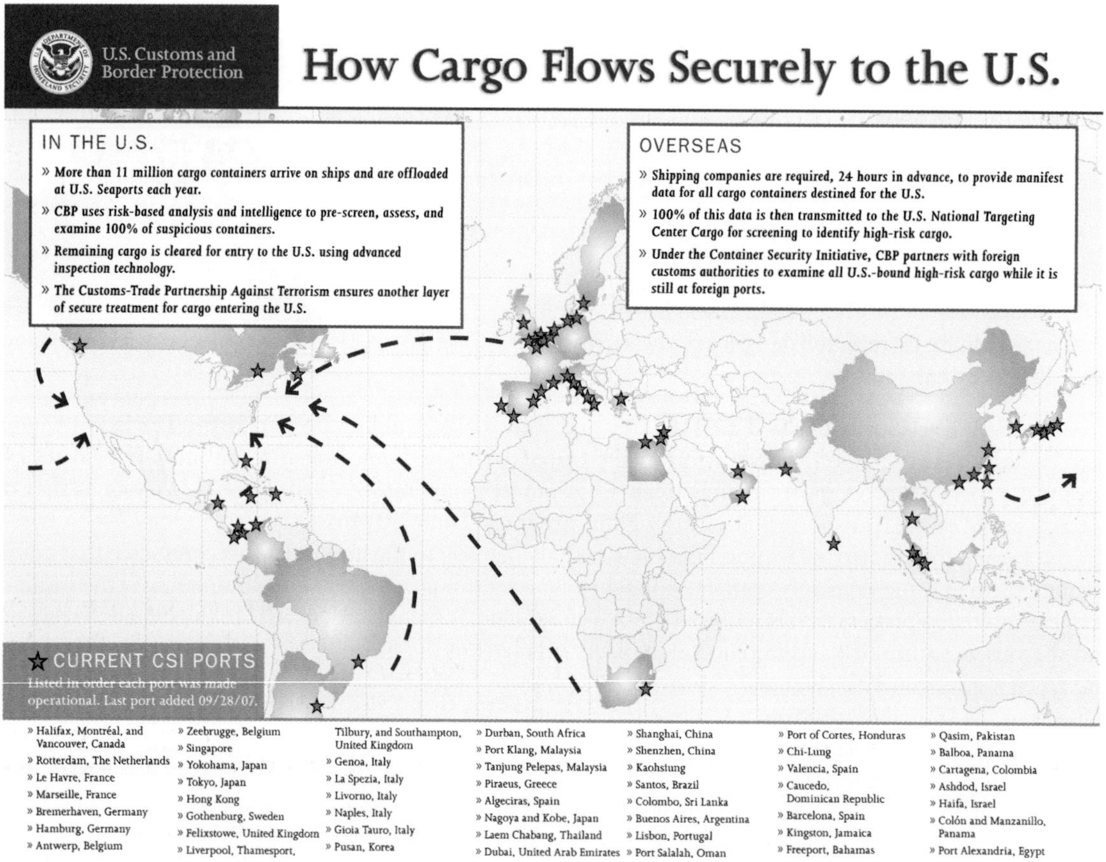

FIGURE 7-7 How cargo flows securely to the United States. *Source: Department of Homeland Security (2011).*

24 h before a cargo is loaded at the foreign port for shipment to the United States through the Sea Automated Manifest System. Failure to meet the 24-h Advanced Manifest Rule results in a "do not load" message and other penalties. The information collected by the Customs and Border Patrol (CBP) is analyzed and the cargo deemed as high risk is inspected at the port of origin before it starts its journey into the United States.

2. *Container Security Initiative (CSI)*: The screening of containers that pose a risk for terrorism is accomplished by teams of CBP officials deployed to work in concert with their host nation counterparts through the CSI program. As of 2014, there were 58 international ports participating in CSI, which prescreen over 80% of all transatlantic and transpacific cargoes imported into the United States subject to preload screening. A full list of all participating CSI ports is given in Table 7-3.
3. *Customs-Trade Partnership against Terrorism (C-TPAT)*: C-TPAT is a voluntary government business initiative aimed at strengthening and improving international supply chain and US border security. Through this initiative, DHS asks businesses to ensure the integrity of their security practices and to communicate and verify the security guidelines of their business partners within the supply chain. Thousands of importers, carriers, brokers, forwarders, ports and terminals, and foreign manufacturers,

Table 7-3 Ports in CSI

Currently Operational Ports
In the Americas and Caribbean
• Montreal, Vancouver, and Halifax, Canada
• Santos, Brazil
• Buenos Aires, Argentina
• Puerto Cortes, Honduras
• Caucedo, Dominican Republic
• Kingston, Jamaica
• Freeport, the Bahamas
• Balboa, Colón, and Manzanillo, Panama
• Cartagena, Colombia
In Europe
• Rotterdam, the Netherlands
• Bremerhaven and Hamburg, Germany
• Antwerp and Zeebrugge, Belgium
• Le Havre and Marseille, France
• Gothenburg, Sweden
• La Spezia, Genoa, Naples, Gioia Tauro, and Livorno, Italy
• Felixstowe, Liverpool, Thamesport, Tilbury, and Southampton, the United Kingdom
• Piraeus, Greece
• Algeciras, Barcelona, and Valencia, Spain
• Lisbon, Portugal
In Asia and the East
• Singapore
• Yokohama, Tokyo, Nagoya, and Kobe, Japan
• Hong Kong
• Pusan, South Korea
• Ports Klang and Tanjung Pelepas, Malaysia
• Laem Chabang, Thailand
• Dubai, United Arab Emirates (UAE)
• Shenzhen and Shanghai
• Kaohsiung and Chi-Lung
• Colombo, Sri Lanka
• Port Salalah, Oman
• Port Qasim, Pakistan
• Port of Ashdod, Israel
• Port in Haifa, Israel
In Africa
• Durban, South Africa
• Alexandria, Egypt

Source: U.S. Customs and Protection (2014).

most of whom are private companies, have participated. In turn, business participants providing verifiable security information are eligible for special benefits, including more expeditious transit of goods through a reduction in the number of inspections, priority processing, specially assigned C-TPAT inspectors who work directly with the company, eligibility in a self-inspection program, and invitations to security seminars. Through C-TPAT efforts, CBP is able to devote its resources to high-risk shipments. As of 2014, more than 10,650 companies had enrolled in the program.

4. *International Ship and Port Facility Security (ISPS) Code*: The ISPS Code requires large vessels operating internationally and port facilities that serve them to conduct security assessments, to develop security plans, and to hire security officers. By establishing a standard for security, the world trade community has increased its ability to prevent maritime-related attacks by making ports around the world more aware of unusual or suspicious activity. In the United States, the code is followed by the enactment of provisions of the Marine Transportation Security Act of 2002 and by aligning domestic marine security regulations with the guidelines of ISPS.
5. *International Port Security Program (IPS)*: IPS is a program maintained by the US Coast Guard. It was created in 2003 as a component of the US Maritime Transportation Security Act. The program's objective is to engage in bilateral or multilateral discussions with trading nations around the world to exchange information and share best practices to align port security programs. This is done through the implementation of the ISPS Code and other international maritime security standards. Under this effort, the US Coast Guard engages with foreign governments to evaluate the trade partner countries' overall compliance with the ISPS Code. USCG then uses the information they gain from these site visits to improve the United States' own security practices and to determine if additional security precautions are required for vessels arriving from other countries (e.g., boarding the vessel). The program allows reciprocity from participating countries, who may apply the same standards to US ships entering their own ports.
6. *Secure Freight Initiative (SFI)*: The Secure Freight Initiative was launched in 2006 through partnership with DHS and the Department of Energy to prevent terrorists' use of global commerce to carry out a nuclear or radiological attack. Through the program, which was described in detail in Chapter 6, containers are scanned using special imaging and detection equipment while they are still at foreign ports and inspected further while still overseas if concerns arise. The first countries that participated in the program were Honduras and Pakistan, and these have been followed by the United Kingdom, Oman, Singapore, and Korea.
7. *Operation Safe Commerce (OSC)*: Operation Safe Commerce was a program funded by Congress that seeks to improve methods of analyzing security in the commercial supply chain and testing new security technologies and solutions. Technologies tested through OSC enhance maritime cargo security, protect the global supply chain, and facilitate the flow of commerce. The ports of Seattle and Tacoma, Los Angeles, and Long Beach and the Port Authority of New York and New Jersey as well as selected international ports participated in the program. OSC was completed in 2004, after over $200 million in grants had been awarded. The findings, outcomes, and lessons learned in the pilot project have since been incorporated into DHS safe commerce strategies.

Initiatives That Address "In-Transit" Vulnerability Reduction

1. *Smart Box Initiative*: Through CSI, smarter, tamper-evident containers that better secure containerized shipping have been developed. Designed to be "tamper-evident," smart boxes couple an internationally approved mechanical seal affixed to an alternate location on the container door

with an electronic container security device designed to deter and detect tampering. If someone attempts to open the cargo door after it has been sealed, the smart box device on the door records the attempted or successful intrusion. The container security market has grown rapidly since the initiative began, and today, there is a wide selection of smart box devices available on the market with different capabilities and technologies (radio frequency, cellular, and satellite). More recent options allow for the identification of the container's contents and the exporter's shipping patterns and even to identify atypical movements of the container.

2. *Ship Security Alert System (SSAS)*: Like a silent alarm in a bank, an SSAS allows a vessel operator to send a covert alert to shore for incidents involving acts of violence (such as piracy and terrorism), indicating the security of the ship is under threat or has been compromised. The International Maritime Organization requires all vessels of 500 gross tons or larger to have SSAS onboard to ensure covert alerting of a designated authority, ensuring a timely response during a threat.
3. *Automated Targeting System (ATS)*: CBP's ATS is a tool that allows the performance of transactional risk assessments and the evaluation of potential national security risks posed by cargo and passengers arriving by sea, air, truck, and rail. Using prearrival information and input from the intelligence community, this rule-based system identifies high-risk targets before they arrive in the United States. ATS consists of six modules that provide selectivity and targeting capability to support CBP inspection and enforcement activities. These include the following:
   a. *ATS-Antiterrorism (ATS-AT)*: Outbound cargo and staff
   b. *ATS-N*: High-risk inbound cargo, including the following:
      i. *ATS-International (ATS-I)*: Cargo targeting for CBP's collaboration with foreign customs authorities
      ii. *Cargo Enforcement Reporting and Tracking System (CERTS)*: Provides a single point of entry for examination data
      iii. *ATS-Trend Analysis and Analytical Selectivity Program (ATS-TAP) 2000*: Allows easy analysis of importer and exporter trends
   c. *ATS-Land (ATS-L)*: Private vehicles arriving by land
   d. *ATS-Passenger (ATS-P)*: Travelers and conveyances (air, ship, and rail)
   e. *ATS-Targeting Framework (ATS-TF)*: Allows the tracking of information of targeting interest regarding passengers and cargo
4. *96-h Advance Notice of Arrival*: Foreign ships must notify the Coast Guard 96 h before arriving in a US port and provide detailed information on the crew, passenger, cargo, and voyage history. This information is analyzed using databases and intelligence information, including reviewing previous security problems with the vessel or illegal activity on the part of the crew. Part of this analysis will also account for the security environment in previous ports of call. By obtaining this information well in advance of a vessel's arrival, the US Coast Guard is able to make determinations about which vessels require additional attention, including security precautions such as an at-sea boarding or armed escort during transit to and from port.

Initiatives That Address Vulnerability Reduction "in US Waters and on US Shores"

1. *National Targeting Center (NTC)*: The priority mission of CBP's NTC is to provide tactical targeting and analytic research support for CBP antiterrorism efforts. Experts in passenger and cargo targeting at the NTC operate around the clock using tools like the Automated Targeting System (ATS) to identify tactical targets and support intradepartmental and interagency

antiterrorist operations. The NTC also supports operations in the field, including the Container Security Initiative (CSI) personnel stationed at critical foreign ports throughout the world.

2. *Maritime Intelligence Fusion Centers*: Located in Norfolk, Virginia, and Alameda, California, these units compile and synthesize intelligence products from the federal, state, and local levels dealing with maritime security. The intelligence is then disseminated to homeland security professionals across the country responsible for securing ports and waterways to more effectively perform their security functions.
3. *High-Interest Vessel Boarding*: Before they are allowed to enter port, all vessels are screened for the security risk they pose to the United States based on information about the vessel's cargo, size, voyage, security history, and any intelligence information. Those identified as higher risk are targeted for offshore boarding to ensure potential security issues are addressed prior to entry into port. In addition, the Coast Guard randomly selects vessels for security boarding to ensure an element of unpredictability and thus deterrence. Specially trained Coast Guard teams board the boats through traditional water-based methods or via fast roping from helicopters.
4. *Nationwide Automatic Identification System (NAIS)*: The Nationwide Automatic Identification System (NAIS) is based on the International Maritime Organization's Automatic Identification System (AIS), which uses digital VHF communications to continually transmit and receive voiceless data. Communication is ship-to-ship and ship-to-shore. Through AIS, detailed ship information and tracking data are automatically sent to other ships and shore-based agencies, allowing for comprehensive, virtually instantaneous vessel tracking and monitoring. This program effectively increases security and safety in shipping channels. The IMO's International Convention for the Safety of Life at Sea (SOLAS) requires AIS equipment to be fitted on international voyaging ships with a gross weight exceeding 300 tons, and all passenger ships regardless of size. It is estimated that more than 40,000 ships currently carry AIS equipment. Most vessels required to use this technology are large vessels on international voyages. NAIS was initiated as a result of the Maritime Transportation Security Act of 2002. It functions by combining AIS data with other sensor- and cargo-specific data to paint a more complete picture than is otherwise available through AIS alone. The system has been implemented in 58 ports and 11 coastal areas and currently receives 92 million AIS messages per day from almost 13,000 vessels (USCG, 2014b).
5. *Area Maritime Security Committees*: The Coast Guard has established committees at each of the nation's ports to coordinate the activities of the stakeholders involved. This includes other federal, local, and state government agencies, industry partners, and the boating public. Each committee is tasked with collaborating on plans to secure the port so that the different resources that exist in and around the port can be best used to deter, prevent, and respond to terrorism risk.
6. *Maritime Security Risk Assessment Model (MSRAM)*: The Port Security Assessment Program was a maritime risk assessment program that began in 2003. The purpose of the program was to increase the information and best practices available to port officials across the country in order to help them make decisions about how to reduce vulnerability. Through the use of the Port Security Risk Assessment Model, the Coast Guard prioritized the examination of key infrastructure in the nation's 55 most economically and strategically important ports for potential vulnerabilities from the period 2003 to 2005. A Government Accountability Office study identified inadequate project planning and delayed implementation regarding the USCG GIS project, and it was soon replaced by MSRAM. Since its development and implementation in 2005, the USCG has utilized the standardized risk assessment methodology to assess maritime infrastructure, inclusive of HAZMAT sites (e.g., chemical facilities, oil refineries, and cargo vessels). The methodology

enables prioritization of risk reduction efforts by enabling the comparison of local-, regional-, and national-level targets. In total, more than 28,000 possible maritime targets have been assessed (GAO, 2011).

7. *Nonintrusive Inspection (NII) technology*: NII technologies allow US Customs and Border Protection to screen a larger portion of the stream of commercial traffic in less time while facilitating legitimate trade. CBP officers use large-scale gamma ray and X-ray imaging systems to safely and efficiently screen conveyances for contraband, including weapons of mass destruction. These units can scan the interior of a full-size 40 foot container within a minute. Inspectors also use personal radiation detectors to scan for signs of radioactive materials as well as special high-tech tools such as density meters and fiber-optic scopes to peer inside suspicious containers. Finally, if necessary, containers are opened and unloaded for a more intensive manual inspection.
8. *Maritime Safety and Security Teams (MSSTs)*: MSSTs are a Coast Guard rapid response force assigned to vital ports and capable of nationwide deployment via air, ground, or sea transportation to meet emerging threats. MSSTs were created in direct response to the terrorist attacks on September 11, 2001, through the Maritime Transportation Security Act of 2002. They have unique capabilities, including explosive detection dogs, personnel trained to conduct fast-roping deployments from a helicopter to a hostile vessel, and antiterrorism/force protection small boat handling training. As of 2014, there are 12 distinct MSSTs within the US Coast Guard, each with approximately 75 personnel. They include the following:
   a. Seattle, WA
   b. Chesapeake, VA
   c. Los Angeles/Long Beach, CA
   d. Houston/Galveston, TX
   e. San Francisco, CA
   f. Fort Wadsworth, NY
   g. Honolulu, HI
   h. St. Marys, GA
   i. San Diego, CA
   j. Boston, MA
   k. New Orleans, LA
   l. Miami, FL
   m. An Anchorage, AK-based team was dismantled in 201.
9. *Guarding in between the ports*: Coast Guard, US CBP, and US Immigration and Customs Enforcement's Air and Marine Operations units are responsible for patrolling and securing the nation's borders between the ports of entry.
10. *Transportation Worker Identification Credential (TWIC)*: The TSA was directed by the Maritime Transportation Security Act of 2002 to develop a biometric, common credentialing system for all individuals who require unescorted access to secure areas of port facilities or the ships themselves. Through TWIC, a secure uniform credential now exists, which helps reduce the risk that terrorists are able to easily access certain sensitive areas of port facilities where they could do significant harm. The biometric identifiers make them difficult to counterfeit. TSA kicked off the first TWIC credentialing in October 2007 at the Port of Wilmington, Delaware, and since then expanded throughout the nation to over 262 enrollment centers. As of July 2014, over 3 million people were enrolled in the program, and over 1.9 million active cards were in use (TSA, 2014a).

Another Voice: VB-IEDS by Don Goff (CSTAR Systems)

The initial attack on December 7, 1941, came not, as we usually think, by aircraft, but from five small two-man submarines that tried to enter Pearl Harbor ahead of the planes. More recently, attacks on the MS Achille Lauro and the USS Cole, piracy off of Somalia, and the terrorist incursion in Mumbai remind us that seaborne attacks by small craft remain a real threat. Within the continental United States, the convergence of transportation, energy, and communication systems provides potential terrorists with numerous targets accessible by small boat. As in the attack on the USS Cole, a small boat filled with explosives maneuvered alongside a target can inflict substantial damage. Obtaining and operating a small boat is both affordable and easily learned. Termed "vessel-borne improvised explosive devices" or VB-IEDs, this attack vector creates a highly challenging scenario and causes more than a few sleepless nights for those charged with maritime defense and law enforcement.

Vulnerabilities

Attacks across water can, of course, occur anywhere along the United States' Atlantic, Pacific, Caribbean, and Great Lakes coast lines—some 88,000 miles long, including Alaska and Hawaii. The vulnerabilities of the great port cities have been looked at in terms of point targets such as container facilities, nuclear plants, and liquid natural gas (LNG) terminals. A great deal of effort has gone on post 9/11 to identify, assess, and prioritize such vulnerability points. Less obvious are the cities on the inland waters. Of all the major cities in the United States, only Indianapolis is not positioned on a navigable body of water. All of these cities, both coastal and inland, have a large concentration of critical infrastructure, and most are transportation hubs for air, rail, and motor transport, as well as for communications, energy, and power distribution.

Using open-source materials, it is relatively easy to identify critical points in the transportation, energy, and communication infrastructure that, if attacked, could not only create chaos and physical damage but also lead to substantial economic and environmental problems, using relatively small quantities of conventional explosives. Many of these open-source materials that can be used for target analysis are unclassified online resources that are just as readily available to potential terrorists as to casual surfers.

Examples of such convergence points are fairly intuitive. In the past several decades, railroads have struggled to remain profitable. Since at least the 1980s, they have augmented their revenue by leasing out their rights-of-way to other carriers such as telecommunications and gas and oil pipelines. When railroad bridges cross waterways, they may have cables and pipes attached to them or channeled under them. These points of infrastructure convergence exist in numerous locations around the country. Using global information system freeware on the Internet, it is fairly easy to spot these particular vulnerabilities. Current satellite photography resolution openly published allows even a casual observer to see these points with great ease and clarity.

Threats

We have seen such attacks in other instances, but not in the United States to date. The ready availability of small recreational watercraft and the shortage of law enforcement and Coast Guard coverage of all possible avenues of approach create great difficulties for detection. The ability of the potential terrorist to be "hiding in plain sight" makes this a particularly onerous threat. Think about the crowds of recreational boaters on the waterway on a given weekend driving small, white, fiberglass outboard runabouts. Think about the difficulty of detecting a specific such boat within those crowds of weekend sailors and you get a sense for the law enforcement challenges, though, as we will see below, a number of countermeasures and mitigations are in play.

What is less clear is whether a potential terrorist would want to attack such targets simply because they are available. To date, most attacks have been included within a fairly narrow target window. The terrorists appear to believe they will score more political points by attacking symbolic targets than by imposing substantial physical damage to property. Lives matter more than things, fortunately. But the human impact of infrastructure damage could create a more significant impact, leaving longer-term consequences.

Consequences

Conducting a kinetic attack against a single point of failure could not only produce damage at that point but also trigger a cascading effect. Attacks on the telecommunications infrastructure are relatively self-healing. Attacks on the energy distribution system are more problematic. In addition to the loss of a power cable or a gas pipeline, the impact of a seaborne attack could also produce ecological consequences, such as pollution of a river or bay, fouling of water intake ducts for public water supplies, or destroying wetlands.

With modern "just-in-time" delivery methods, the disruption of energy and transportation has a rapid and growing effect on manufacturing processes, food distribution, and other aspects of the economy, which are dependent on those infrastructures. In studies simulating the importation of a series of "dirty bombs" through a West Coast port, the economic impact grew steadily while the port was closed, with economic effects felt for several weeks and even months after the port was reopened. One study identified port closures as costing the US economy about $1 billion for each of the first 5 days and then rising exponentially.

Risk Mitigation

The Maritime Transportation Security Act of 2002 (MTSA) was enacted to address port and waterway security. It focuses on vessels and port facilities conducting vulnerability assessments and developing security methods related to screening procedures, security patrols, restricted areas, personnel identification, access controls, and surveillance equipment. It is primarily focused on the ocean ports.

The MTSA security regulations use risk management methods to identify, prioritize, and focus on those sectors of maritime industry with a higher risk of involvement in a transportation security incident, such as offshore oil and gas platforms, fuel terminals, and port facilities that handle certain kinds of dangerous cargo or service the vessels that carry such cargoes.

MTSA also created Area Maritime Security Committees (AMSCs) to coordinate the activities of all maritime stakeholders, including other federal, local, and state agencies, industry, and recreational and commercial boaters. The AMSCs collaborate on identifying key locations that would present a risk, evaluate and prioritize those risks, and develop mitigation plans to deter, prevent, and respond to terror threats.

A large number of these area studies of seaborne attacks have been conducted by the Coast Guard, port authorities, and Area Maritime Security Committees; however, the inland waters have more limited security coverage and critical points are often at the jurisdictional boundaries of federal, state, and local governments. Entities such as the US Coast Guard, Customs and Border Protection, the Federal Emergency Management Agency, and state and local law enforcement and emergency planners collaborate to focus preventive measures on key points of vulnerability and to maximize the effectiveness of response.

Additional legislation was adopted 4 years later called the Security and Accountability For Every Port Act of 2006 (SAFE Port Act). This act added certain requirements to prevent foreign ownership of US ports, required worker identification measures, and created a grant program.

It also clarified the responsibilities of the Coast Guard's companion agencies within the Department of Homeland Security, Customs and Border Patrol (CBP), and the Transportation Security Administration (TSA).

CBP has added to efforts to counter terrorist efforts by creating the Container Security Initiative (CSI) and the Customs Trade Partnership against Terrorism (C-TPAT). These programs provide incentives to shippers to increase their security procedures and to focus on containers.

In addition, the Maritime Administration in the Department of Transportation has regulatory authority over both vessels and nonvessel operating container cargo, that is, the companies that own the containers but not the ships hauling them.

Finally, the Coast Guard has organized America's Waterway Watch, a sort of marine neighborhood watch, to encourage recreational and commercial boaters to develop situational awareness and to report suspicious behaviors through a toll-free telephone number. This program is really the only program focused on the threat from VB-IEDs.

The primary focus of these government actions has been upon the major ports and upon container cargo and individual screenings. The problem is that none of these programs have focused on or provided major resources to analyze the threat and identify mitigation procedures for VB-IEDs, merely to look for them incidentally.

Don Goff has over 40 years' experience in business, education, and public policy. He is a nationally recognized subject matter expert on security and critical infrastructure issues and has served on the Area Maritime Security Committees for the National Capital Region and for Maryland and the Chesapeake Bay. He is currently the president of CSTAR Systems, Inc. Dr. Goff holds a PhD from Northwestern University.

Bus Transportation Security

Bus transportation safety is an often-neglected link in the nation's transportation infrastructure and represents a substantial homeland security vulnerability. In the first edition of this book, we described the issue of bus transportation security as follows: "The bus transportation system is likely to eventually become a target of terrorists because the system has comparatively less protection against terrorist attacks, which makes it 'soft' for terrorists searching for less risky but high-consequence attacks." On July 7, 2007, a terrorist detonated a bomb in a London double-decker bus in a coordinated attack on the bus and rail networks of that city, killing 13 people and injuring many more. The incident highlighted the vulnerability of the bus transportation system, despite that the majority of transportation security efforts focus on air and sea transport. In 2011, TSA Administrator John Pistole announced that DHS has become aware of increased terrorist surveillance of bus systems given their inherent ease of access and underscored at the time that buses remain a preferred terrorist target worldwide. TSA released a bulletin to law enforcement agencies at this time citing the statistic that there had been 725 attacks on buses worldwide between the years 2004 and 2009 and stressing that this far exceeded attacks on airlines (Herridge, 2011). Securing the bus system remains an extremely challenging task as public ground transportation is much more dynamic and state-changing than other types of transport. With multiple stops and frequently changing passengers over short periods of time, securing the bus system becomes a very resource-intensive and, in some instances, impractical process. However, there are ways to reduce the vulnerabilities even if the security risks of bus transport cannot be eliminated to the degree as exists in other transportation sectors.

To support the intercity bus transportation sector, DHS established the Intercity Bus Security Grant Program under its Infrastructure Protection Program, as described previously in this chapter. DHS used this program to provide funding to intercity bus companies for the improvement of their transport security measures. In FY 2012, the Intercity Bus Security Grant Program was discontinued.

Railway Transportation Security

The railroad system is another highly utilized and valuable component of the US transportation infrastructure that requires protective measures to address the growing threat of terrorist attacks and other hazard-related vulnerabilities. DHS made its most noticeable references to the protection of the railway system in the first version of the National Strategy for the Physical Protection of Critical Infrastructure and Key Assets and in the 2003 announcement of Operation Liberty Shield. This national strategy document refers to potential vulnerabilities of the rail system and expands upon possible terrorist attack scenarios. At that time, four priorities for improvement in the railroad security were identified:

1. The need to develop improved decision-making criteria regarding the shipment of hazardous materials: DHS and DOT, coordinating with other federal agencies, state and local governments, and industry, facilitated the development of an improved process to ensure informed decision making with respect to hazardous materials shipments.
2. The need to develop technologies and procedures to screen intermodal containers and passenger baggage: DHS and DOT worked with sector counterparts to identify and explore technologies and processes to enable screening of rail passengers and baggage, especially at intermodal stations.
3. The need to improve security of intermodal transportation: DHS and DOT worked with sector counterparts to identify and facilitate the development of technologies and procedures to secure intermodal containers and detect threatening content. DHS and DOT also worked with the rail industry to devise hazardous materials identification to support first responders.
4. The need to clearly delineate roles and responsibilities regarding surge requirements: DHS and DOT worked with industry to delineate infrastructure protection roles and responsibilities to enable the rail industry to address surge requirements for resources in the case of catastrophic events. DHS and DOT also convened a working group consisting of government and industry representatives to identify options for the implementation of surge capabilities, including access to federal facilities and capabilities in extreme emergencies.

The national physical protection strategy clearly identifies the transportation of HAZMAT within the railroad infrastructure as the greatest vulnerability of the system. This assessment was reiterated by Admiral James Loy, former TSA administrator, in a meeting with the North American Rail Shippers Association where he identified the following as the primary threats to the railway system: (1) hazardous material, (2) nuclear and radiological material, (3) food and livestock, and (4) intermodal containers. In response to Admiral Loy's assessment, the DOT and DHS released a document regarding the HAZMAT transportation vulnerability and measures to be taken to minimize the terrorist threat to the system. This document provides background information on the improvements accomplished in the railroad system since September 11. It discusses the security task force established by the Association of American Railroads (AAR) to assess vulnerabilities in several critical areas, such as physical assets, information technology, chemicals and hazardous materials, defense shipments, train operations, and passenger security. In March 2003, DHS announced Operation Liberty Shield, which included the following steps to enhance railway security:

1. *To improve rail bridge security*: State governors were asked to provide additional police or National Guard forces at selected bridges.
2. *To increase railroad infrastructure security*: Railroad companies were asked to increase security at major facilities and key rail hubs.
3. *AMTRAK security measures*: AMTRAK implemented security measures consistent with private rail companies.
4. *To increase railroad hazardous material safety*: At the request of the Department of Transportation, private railroad companies will monitor shipments of hazardous material and increase surveillance of trains carrying this material.

On April 8, 2004, the Senate Commerce, Science, and Transportation Committee approved the Rail Security Act of 2004, which authorized an increase in rail security funding by $1.1 billion, over the initial funding of only $65 million. The Rail Security Act, as proposed, required DHS to conduct a vulnerability assessment of the nation's rail systems and report back to Congress with its findings. The vulnerability assessment requires a review of freight and passenger rail transportation, including the identification and evaluation of critical assets and infrastructures; threats to those assets and infrastructures; vulnerabilities that are specific to rail transportation of hazardous materials; and security weaknesses. Based on the assessment, conducted through the Surface Transportation Security Inspection Program (STSIP), DHS developed prioritized recommendations for improving the security of rail infrastructure and facilities, terminals, tunnels, bridges, and other at-risk areas; deploying weapons detection and surveillance equipment; training employees; and conducting public outreach campaigns. The results of the DHS freight and passenger rail transportation vulnerability assessment are also used to distribute future funding for the Rail Security Grant Program. The Baseline Assessment for Security Enhancement is a part of this effort (see sidebar "Baseline Assessment for Security Enhancement (BASE)").

Baseline Assessment for Security Enhancement (BASE)

Under the Baseline Assessment for Security Enhancement (BASE) program, TSA transportation security inspectors (TSIs) assess the security posture of mass transit and passenger rail agencies in 17 Security and Emergency Management Action Items. The action items cover a range of areas that are foundational to an effective security program. The specific purpose is to evaluate, across multiple areas with a thorough checklist and narrative responses, the effectiveness of security programs, procedures, and measures developed and implemented by mass transit and passenger rail agencies. The results are used to develop risk mitigation priorities and security enhancement programs and to determine grant allocations. The assessments are conducted on a voluntary basis and with emphasis on the 100 largest systems based on passenger volume, which collectively account for over 80% of all public transportation users. TSA originally set a performance standard of 90% average across the 17 action items, with no category under 70%. There are three levels of security that could result:

1. If a transit agency achieves a BASE score of 90% or greater with no one action item less than 70%, then they are scheduled for the next BASE in 3 years and are considered to have achieved the gold standard.

2. If a transit agency achieves a BASE score between 70% and 89% with no one action item less than 70%, then they are scheduled for the next BASE in 2 years and are considered to be In Compliance.
3. If a transit agency achieves a BASE score of less than 70%, then they are scheduled for the next BASE the following year, and they are considered to be Not in Compliance. These properties will be visited on a regular basis until they are In Compliance and will have a Performance Improvement Action Plan on file at TSA.

The 17 action items are as follows:

1. Establish written system security programs and emergency management plans.
2. Define roles and responsibilities for security and emergency management.
3. Ensure that operations and maintenance supervisors, forepersons, and managers are held accountable for security issues under their control.
4. Coordinate security and emergency management plan(s) with local and regional agencies.
5. Establish and maintain a security and emergency training program.
6. Establish plans and protocols to respond to the DHS Homeland Security Advisory System threat levels.
7. Implement and reinforce a public security and emergency awareness program.
8. Conduct tabletop and functional drills.
9. Establish and use a risk management process to assess and manage threats, vulnerabilities, and consequences.
10. Participate in an information-sharing process for threat and intelligence information.
11. Establish and use a reporting process for suspicious activity (internal and external).
12. Control access to security-critical facilities with identification badges for all visitors, employees, and contractors.
13. Conduct physical security inspections.
14. Conduct background investigations of employees and contractors.
15. Control access to documents of security-critical systems and facilities.
16. Implement a process for handling and access to sensitive security information.
17. Conduct security program audits.

Source: TSA (2014b) and DHS OIG (2010).

The Association of American Railroads coordinated and conducted a comprehensive risk analysis covering the entire railway industry. The scope of this risk assessment included the train operations, communication and cybersecurity aspects, identification and protection of critical assets, transportation of hazardous materials, and identification of a military liaison. The association worked closely with the federal intelligence community and security experts and identified and prioritized more than 1300 critical assets. As a result of the vulnerability analysis, more than 50 permanent changes were made to procedures and operations, including restricted access to facilities, increased tracking of certain shipments, enhanced employee security training, and cybersecurity improvements. In addition to those measures, it was decided that one rail police officer should sit on the FBI's National Joint Terrorism Task Force and two rail analysts should sit in the DHS intelligence offices to help evaluate data at the top-secret level. The association created a DOD-certified, full-time operations center, working at the secret level to monitor and evaluate intelligence on potential threats and communicate with railroads through the Railway Alert Network (RAN) (see sidebar "Railway

Alert Network"). A Surface Transportation Information Sharing and Analysis Center (ST-ISAC)—operating at the top-secret level—was also created to collect, analyze, and disseminate information on physical and cybersecurity threats.

Railway Alert Network and Surface Transportation ISAC

Since 2001, the Association of American Railroads (AAR) Security Operations Center has provided full-time security support to include threat warning and incident reporting. The security operations center supports the Railroad Alert Network (RAN), and provides oversight and direction to the Surface Transportation ISAC (ST-ISAC) (see Chapter 4 for more information on ISACs). The ST-ISAC provides a secure cyber and physical security capability for owners, operators, and users of critical surface transportation infrastructure. Security and threat information is collected from world-wide resources, then analyzed, and distributed to members to help protect their vital systems from attack. The ST-ISAC also provides a vehicle for the anonymous or attributable sharing of incident, threat, and vulnerability data among the members. Members have access to information and analytic reporting provided by other sources, such as US and foreign governments, law enforcement agencies, technology providers, and international computer emergency response teams. An example of a RAN "Situational Alert Message" follows:

Railway Alert Network (RAN) Situational Awareness Message: Suspicious Incidents Involving Two Persons Claiming to be FRA Employees

July 26, 2011

Dissemination of the Transit and Rail Intelligence Awareness Daily (TRIAD) that presented details of a suspicious incident prompted identification by another railroad of similar activity and advisories to rail police and employees to assure awareness and reinforce fundamental security procedures.

The July 19 TRIAD conveyed the report that Canadian Pacific (CP) made to TSA's Transportation Security Operations Center (TSOC) on suspicious activity at a rail bridge. In summary, at approximately 1335 h, Central time on July 16, two individuals approached CP's Menomonee Bridge in Milwaukee, WI. As they came up to the bridge tender, the two men identified themselves as Federal Railroad Administration (FRA) employees and stated they were there to "inspect" the bridge. The alert rail employee responded by asking the pair for their identification—precisely the right action. In reaction, the two men returned to their vehicle, ostensibly to obtain their identification. Instead, they reentered the vehicle and drove away from the area.

The CP employee immediately reported the incident, providing CP police special agents with a description of the two individuals and the vehicle—a gray sedan. Though he was not able to discern the license plate number, his timely reporting, with as much detail as observations allowed, again represents precisely the right action.

CP properly reported the incident to TSOC to meet the applicable regulatory requirement at 49 CFR Section 1580.105. This report informed the July 19 TRIAD article that, on broader dissemination, implicated a similar incident that had occurred on Union Pacific (UP) property in the greater Los Angeles, CA, area.

Though the activity there remains under investigation, some details can be conveyed. At approximately 2030 h Pacific time on July 17—about 31 h after the incident at the CP bridge in Milwaukee—a UP manager of yard operations in Long Beach observed two male subjects sitting in a gray, four-door sedan watching UP train crews switching tank cars. After monitoring the pair for a period of time, the yard operations manager drove his vehicle toward the two individuals and, from his vehicle, asked them who they were. In response, they stated they were with the FRA and were there to watch the crews work. The manager asked the two men for their identification and then moved his vehicle to park it safely and get out to review the credentials. As he was turning to park, the two subjects drove away from the scene.

The manager contacted FRA, which stated it did not have any of its personnel on official duty in the area. Apparently, the FRA notified the TSOC of this impersonation incident.

Though they may be unrelated, the similarities between these two incidents warrant attention. In each case, two males, operating a gray sedan, observed rail operations or sought access to rail property, claiming they were FRA employees. In each case, FRA is adamant that it had no employees on official duties in either area.

In light of these events, in a model likely emulated by other railroads, UP has provided awareness briefings to employees, describing the similar incidents and reinforcing the importance of essential security procedures:

- Request credentials of *any* person claiming to be an official government inspector or employee (FRA, TSA, DHS, or other agencies).
- When observing a suspect vehicle, write down or otherwise record the description (type, color, make, model, and number of doors) and license plate number.
- Stay vigilant for suspicious people, behaviors, activities, and objects at and near rail operations and infrastructure.
- Report these potential security concerns to the railroad's communications or operations center, in accordance with standing procedures.
- Review those procedures in awareness briefings with employees to ensure familiarity.

Source: DHS (2009) and American Association of Railroads (2009).

Perhaps, the greatest threat from freight rail is the terrorist use of hazardous materials rail cars, notably those containing toxic inhalation hazards (TIH) such as chlorine or phosgene, as delivery mechanisms for chemical weapons attacks. In fact, rail cars would not even have to be in motion, or under the control of the terrorists, for an attack to take place. By detonating an explosive device on a chemical freight tanker car, or perhaps even shooting the tanker with a high caliber weapon from a distance, those in the surrounding area could be in immediate and severe danger. Accidental freight rail incidents that have involved the release of poisonous gas plumes highlight the threat. A train crash that occurred in 2005 in Graniteville, SC, was of moderate size yet resulted in significant impacts. In this incident, two trains collided resulting in the breach of a tank car loaded with 90 tons of chlorine. The single ruptured tank car released 60 tons of chlorine as a gas plume into the surrounding community. Nine people died at the scene, and another 250 or more people in nearby areas required treatment for exposure. The wider area, which was home to over 5000 people, remained under evacuation order for almost 2 weeks during which time cleanup took place. This was the result of one tank car being breached in a relatively unpopulated area. The same incident in or near an urban center could easily result in catastrophic consequences. Several DHS risk assessments have noted this risk, thereby resulting in risk mitigation, procedures, rules, and standards as well as a number of specific programs (e.g., the TIH Risk Reduction Program and the Tank Car Vulnerability Assessment Project). These focus on limiting the amount of time TIH-containing rail cars in urban population centers, in unsecure storage, or in other vulnerable situations. Research has been identifying other solutions as well, including ballistic tanks (tanks able to withstand gunfire) and self-sealing mechanisms if breached (the Tank Car Hardening Project).

As rail security grew in stature following the 9/11 attacks, TSA provided the top 10 mass transit and passenger rail agencies with TSA-certified explosive detection canine teams to aid in the identification of explosive materials within the mass transit/rail transportation system. The pilot inspection program was named the Transit and Rail Inspection Pilot (TRIP), which is a first-time rail security technology study conducted by DHS in cooperation with several other entities. TRIP was conducted in three phases. TRIP phase I occurred at the New Carrollton, Maryland, rail station and evaluated the use of technologies for screening rail passengers and their baggage prior to boarding a train. TRIP phase II occurred at Union Station in Washington, DC, and tested the use of screening equipment for checked baggage and cargo prior to their loading onto an Amtrak passenger train, as well as screening of unclaimed baggage and temporarily stored items inside Union Station. TRIP phase III occurred onboard a Shore Line East commuter rail car. The goal of phase III was to evaluate the use of existing technologies installed on a rail car to screen passengers and their baggage for explosives, while the rail car is in transit. By 2007, DHS increased its deployment and coverage of explosive detection and canine teams to 13 mass transit systems and a total of 53 canine teams. In addition to the TRIP program, TSA hired and deployed 100 surface transportation (rail) inspectors to enhance the level of national transportation security by leveraging private and public partnerships through a consistent national program of compliance reviews, audits, and enforcement actions pertaining to required standards and directives.

The DHS FY 2011 Freight Rail Security Program was appropriated with total funds of $10 million. The funding priorities for the program were as follows:

1. *GPS tracking*: Owners and offerors of railroad cars used in the transportation of poisonous by inhalation/toxic inhalation hazardous (TIH) materials may apply for funds to acquire, install, and operate satellite GPS tracking on those railroad cars for the period of performance.
2. *Infrastructure hardening on rail bridges*: Owners of rail bridges that are used for freight rail transportation may apply for infrastructure hardening capabilities. Infrastructure hardening is defined as the act of applying security to the infrastructure including but not limited to access control systems, video monitoring systems, and physical barriers.
3. *Vulnerability assessments and security plans*: Freight railroad vulnerability assessments provide a broader picture of the mode's preparedness, as well as security risks that need to be mitigated. Security plans help target resources and mitigation strategies toward gaps in the mode's security identified by the vulnerability assessments. The information captured in the vulnerability assessments and security plans (including any mitigation strategies) can be used to form the basis of funding priorities for this grant program in future years, as appropriate. Only class II and class III railroad carriers are eligible to apply for vulnerability assessment and security planning funds.
4. *Security training and exercises for railroad frontline employees*: Effective employee training programs address individual employee responsibilities and provide heightened security awareness. Training should cover assessment and reporting of incidents, employee response, crew communication and coordination, and incident evacuation procedures.

Conclusion

Transportation safety and security are key concepts in the scope of homeland security given the high valuation of these systems to terrorists, the importance of the systems to freedom of movement, and the US economy and because of the high vulnerability these systems have with regard to natural hazards (out of their sheer scope and size). The complexity of each of these systems and their related infrastructure, and the interconnectedness of each of these systems upon which we depend each day, increases our overall vulnerability and increases the difficulty of mitigating the risks we face. In dealing with those distinct vulnerabilities, homeland security agencies at all government levels, and security agencies within the transit authorities and in the private sector, must coordinate on a level that surpasses most other areas of security. The proportional budget appropriation dedicated to transportation security is indicative of these challenges and the growing risk we face as infrastructure ages, as populations move and expand, and as climate change brings about more frequent and devastating events.

Key Terms

Hazardous material (HAZMAT): Materials, substances, or chemicals that are deemed to have adverse effects on human health and the environment. Typical examples of HAZMAT include but are not limited to biological, chemical, and radiological agents and materials. HAZMAT incidents may be intentional (terrorism) or unintentional (man-made/technological). Oil spills, poisonous gas releases, nuclear waste incidents, and dirty bombs are examples of HAZMAT-related incidents.

Smart box: Designed to be "tamper-evident," the smart box couples an internationally approved mechanical seal affixed to an alternate location on the container door with an electronic container security device designed to deter and detect tampering of the container door.

Transportation Worker Identification Credential (TWIC): TWICs are tamper-resistant biometric credentials that will be issued to workers who require unescorted access to secure areas of ports, vessels, outer-continental-shelf facilities, and all credentialed merchant mariners.

Review Questions

1. What are the different transportation modes in the United States?
2. How does the US government protect each?
3. Discuss what types of criteria should be used for prioritizing budgets for protecting different transportation modes.

References

American Association of Railroads, 2009. Railway alert network situational alert message. Suspicious incidents involving two persons claiming to be FRA employees (July 29).

American Bus Association, 2014. Motorcoach census 2013. ABA Foundation (February 27). http://bit.ly/1odaAD7.

American Public Transportation Association, 2014. Ridership report 2014. Definitions. http://bit.ly/1qmRO86.

American Trucking Association, 2014. Industry data. ATA website: http://bit.ly/10PYrdc (accessed 11/04/2014).

American Public Transport Association, 2013. 2013 Public Transportation Fact Book. American Public Transport Association, Washington, DC. http://bit.ly/1t7uUkS.

Associated Press, 2010. US knew for years that cargo planes were terror targets. http://fxn.ws/1uHNtjD (November 9).

Department of Homeland Security, 2005. FY 2006 critical infrastructure protection program. http://bit.ly/11I5kTl.

Department of Homeland Security, 2006. FY 2007 critical infrastructure protection program. http://bit.ly/1vv6Yip.

Department of Homeland Security, 2007. FY 2008 critical infrastructure protection program. http://bit.ly/1uNCOpj.

Department of Homeland Security, 2011. How cargo flows securely to the United States. US Customs and Border Protection website: http://1.usa.gov/1Ehc1UZ (accessed 11/05/2014).

Department of Homeland Security, 2014. Layers of US aviation security. TSA. DHS website: http://1.usa.gov/1sbmvxs.

Department of Transportation, 2013. National Highway System. Federal Highway Administration website: http://1.usa.gov/1GwgdCj (accessed 11//07/2014).

Department of Transportation, 2014a. Pipeline incidents and mileage reports. Office of pipeline safety awareness. http://1.usa.gov/1ySYDDm.

Department of Transportation, 2014b. Pacific gas & electric pipeline rupture in San Bruno, CA. Office of pipeline safety awareness. http://1.usa.gov/1x4ALvt.

DHS, 2009. NIPP Transportation Sector Specific Plan. DHS, Washington, DC.

DHS, 2014a. DHS Budget in Brief Fiscal Year 2015. Department of Homeland Security, Washington, DC.

DHS, 2014b. FY 2014 Port Security Grant Program. Grant Program Guidance. DHS website: http://1.usa.gov/1wwgWyR (accessed 11/05/2014).

DHS Office of the Inspector General, 2010. TSA's preparedness for mass transit and passenger rail emergencies. OIG-10-68. http://1.usa.gov/10CTNyr (March).

Energy Information Administration, 2009. U.S. Natural Gas Pipeline Network, 2009. Office of oil and gas, natural gas division. Gas transportation information system. http://1.usa.gov/1odAIha.

GAO, 2011. Security risk model meets DHS criteria, but more training could enhance its use for managing programs and operations. GAO-12-14 (November).

Hartsfield-Jackson Airport, 2013. Hartsfield-Jackson still "World's Busiest Airport" in 2012. Press Release (February 5). http://bit.ly/1uoOsIB.

Herridge, C., 2011. Authorities warn terrorists increasingly eyeing attacks on buses over other transit targets. Fox News (November 11). http://fxn.ws/1vGXtY6.

Messing, P., 2013. TSA screeners allow fed agent with fake bomb to pass through security at Newark Airport. New York Post (March 8). http://bit.ly/1xWnZPl.

School Transportation News, 2009. School bus safety data. STOnline (October 19). http://bit.ly/1qmQwtM.

Transportation Security Administration, 2005. TSA FY 2004 budget briefing. http://1.usa.gov/1yxpleV (June 2005).

Transportation Security Administration, 2006. TSA Turns Five. Department of Homeland Security, Washington, DC (Out of print).

Transportation Security Administration, 2007. FY 2008 trucking security program fact sheet. http://1.usa.gov/1qF01tV.

TSA, 2012. Office of security operations. Air Cargo, security programs. TSA website: http://1.usa.gov/1x2TOXV (accessed 11/04/2014).

TSA, 2013a. Transit security grant program fact sheet. http://1.usa.gov/10nGnWI.

TSA, 2013b. Intermodal transportation systems. TSA website: http://1.usa.gov/10njPp8 (accessed 11/04/2014).

TSA, 2013c. Air Cargo. Office of security policy and industry engagement. TSA website: http://1.usa.gov/1xWcsju (accessed 11/04/2014).

TSA, 2014a. TWIC Dashboard as of July 2014. Cumulative Program Statistics. TSA website: http://1.usa.gov/13GqNrr (accessed 11/5/2014).

TSA, 2014b. Baseline Assessment for Security Enhancements (BASE) program. Mass transit and passenger rail programs and initiatives. DHS website: http://1.usa.gov/1110Scl (accessed 11/07/2014).

U.S. Customs and Border Protection, 2014. CSI ports. DHS website: http://1.usa.gov/1utXzYC (accessed 11/5/2014).

USCG, 2014a. US Coast Guard Maritime Security (MARSEC) levels. USCG website: http://bit.ly/1xhDrlx (accessed 11/07/2014).

USCG, 2014b. Nationwide automatic identification system. Acquisition Directorate. USCG website: http://bit.ly/1tZ6EGz (accessed 11/05/2014).

USDOT, 2013. Hazardous materials information system. HAZMAT intelligence portal. Incidents by mode. http://1.usa.gov/1AeDM1Y.

8

Cybersecurity and Critical Infrastructure Protection

What You Will Learn

- The meaning of key cybersecurity terms and the difference between cyberterrorism, cyberwarfare, cyberespionage, and cybercrime
- The nature of the cybersecurity threat and the different cyber weapons that exist
- What makes infrastructure critical, and how the various infrastructure sectors differ
- The roles of various federal government agencies in maintaining cybersecurity and protecting critical infrastructure
- Cybersecurity and critical infrastructure protection roles and responsibilities of state, local, tribal, and territorial governments and of the private sector

Introduction

Perhaps, the most appropriate characterization of the twenty-first century is that of an age when all people and, to a growing degree, all things are interconnected. This is an era of technology, for the sake of convenience, capacity, and capability. Communications, commerce, finance, and all forms of information management and access can be achieved from almost anywhere, using devices so compact that they fit in our pockets. Engineers can simultaneously and remotely monitor and control operations at multiple facilities, surgeons can conduct operations on patients thousands of miles away, and manufacturers can detect when one of their automobiles has been involved in an accident within seconds of it occurring. Bolstered by the expansion of the Internet and wireless data networks, it is the interconnectivity of so much data and so many devices that has quickly become the foundation of modern society. We can barely imagine how things must have been done before. And in fact, we often forget that many call the present period "The Information Age." It is a unique era in human history that began back in the 1970s with the advent of the computer and progressing in its innovation at a lightning pace ever since. This has caused us to become a knowledge-based society that relies heavily on technology to perform or support tasks or functions. We are undoubtedly a more capable society as a result. But we are also a much more vulnerable one.

The scope of our vulnerability results from the fact that so much of what we do is supported at some point by the entry, storage, and retrieval of data and information on an interconnected network of hard drives and data servers, whether local or remotely located. And at each of these junctures, there exists the opportunity to steal, circumvent, manipulate, or sabotage. And this doesn't even account for the risk related to unintentional incidents arising from human error, system failures, incompatibilities, or other unexpected issues and "acts of god."

The security of these computer—or "cyber"—systems is thus a matter of national security. In fact, so great are these threats that more and more security experts are claiming that the protection of cyber systems and data is a bigger concern than terrorism given the scope of the threat (with regard to the onslaught of cyberattacks) and the actual damage that is caused on an annual basis (as well as the possible consequences if certain systems and structures are compromised) (Bruinius, 2014). Hackers have proved themselves capable of defacing government and business websites, stealing personal data to fuel a multibillion dollar credit theft industry, altering traffic signal patterns, speeding up and slowing down trains, and much more. State-sponsored cyber teams have achieved even more significant results, including the self-destruction of dozens of centrifuges maintained by Iran's nuclear program. The threat was succinctly stated in the second Quadrennial Homeland Security Review wherein it was stated that "*Cyberspace is particularly difficult to secure due to a number of factors: the ability of malicious actors to operate from anywhere in the world, the linkages between cyberspace and physical systems, and the difficulty of reducing vulnerabilities and consequences in complex cyber networks*" (DHS, 2014a).

We are therefore faced with the fact that a nation, group, or even an individual armed with nothing more than a complex computer virus or knowledge of a weakness in a software package or hardware system can quietly and from a great distance away cause great social or economic disruption or, worse, physical destruction, injuries, and deaths. There is evidence, for instance, that an unknown group has been trying to break into the control systems of US natural gas pipeline networks for years (Crooks, 2012). Oppressive governments have sought to infiltrate the communications and networking of human rights groups, including those located in the United States (Freeze, 2014). And the National Oceanic and Atmospheric Administration announced in late 2014 that hackers in China had successfully hacked into and disrupted US weather satellite networks, which in turn resulted in a loss of services that support disaster planning, aviation, shipping, and other industries for several days (Flaherty et al., 2014).

But our nation's cyber infrastructure is just one of many important systems and networks that make our modern society possible. In fact, government and society are both completely dependent on the functioning of various infrastructure systems and components. The loss of any of these different critical infrastructure elements can easily translate to a loss of movement for people and things, disruption of trade and commerce, breaks in communication across both short and great distances, a loss of power generation and transmission, inadequate access to healthcare, and much more. Government itself is considered a component of critical infrastructure. Great investments in each of these and other infrastructure sectors translated to increases in development and an upward progression of quality of life measures. But like what was true with information networks, it is our increasing dependence on this infrastructure that is the source of a great and growing vulnerability associated with infrastructure disruption or loss.

Due to their widespread physical presence, many infrastructure components are vulnerable to the effects of natural disasters. Roads, power transmission lines, communications nodes, pipelines, sewers, and other networked systems receive significant damage during earthquakes, ice storms, floods, tornadoes, hurricanes, and other wide-scale hazards. But given their value to the society, they are also a desirable target for terrorists. Attacking the infrastructure network can oftentimes cause more financial damage and affect more people, than directly attacking people or structures. Security experts have for decades considered and made efforts to protect against the terrorist targeting of municipal water supplies (in 2002, an actual plot to poison the water supply for US Embassy in Rome, Italy, was discovered and thwarted). In 2014, snipers attacked a power transfer station in California, disabling 19 of the transformers that feed power to Silicon Valley. The area power utility was able to reroute power from other locations to compensate for the disabled station, which was offline for almost a month following the attack (Smith, 2014). It requires little imagination to consider the long-term impacts that could have resulted had the attackers included more area substations in their assault. For homeland security, infrastructure is and will remain a primary concern.

Cybersecurity

Cybersecurity is defined by the United States Computer Emergency Readiness Team (US-CERT) as being "the activity or process, ability or capability, or state whereby information and communications systems and the information contained therein are protected from and/or defended against damage, unauthorized use or modification, or exploitation." This definition is comprehensive in that it describes the primary focus of cybersecurity efforts. However, we have to think of the practice also in terms of the secondary, tertiary, and even more distant systems, equipment, and processes that are protected. For instance, we don't often think of a valve on an oil pipeline as being part of an "information and communications system" or according to the "information contained therein," yet with the right tools and knowledge, a cyberterrorist could cause a pipeline leak to go undetected, thereby resulting in an environmental and economic disaster, by manipulating the control mechanisms of certain valves and meters. As such, the discipline of cybersecurity is one that requires a full appreciation of the complexity and reach of modern information systems and control mechanisms.

Entities Posing a Significant Threat to Cybersecurity

- Cyberterrorists
- Cyberspies
- Cyberthieves
- Cyberwarriors
- Cyberhacktivists

Source: Fischer et al. (2013).

While there are many different goals that drive the efforts of cybercriminals and cyberterrorists, the focus of their disruptive or destructive behavior is the same—the nation's vast and growing cyber infrastructure. Cyber infrastructure includes all of the information and communications systems and services; the hardware components and software systems that process, store, and communicate that information; and different combinations of these different components that are arranged in a manner as to perform one or more tasks or provide one or more services. Elaborating on this definition, we can think of processing as being the step in the process where data and information are created, accessed, modified, or destroyed. Storage of data within the cyber infrastructure might be in magnetic form, as in the following: Processing includes the creation, access, modification, and destruction of information. Storage occurs using magnetic, optical, mechanical, electronic encoding, printed (as in barcodes or QR codes), and otherwise. Communications includes any process through which information is transmitted, shared, or otherwise distributed. Cyberspace is a related term and refers to the global network of information technology infrastructure, inclusive of the Internet, the telecom network, systems of servers and computers, electronic control mechanisms, and the embedded processes in microchips and other semiconductors. All of this translates to a monumental area of coverage for the cybersecurity function.

Cyberwarfare and Cyberterrorism

Cyberterrorism is the newest of all terrorist attack methods, and it is defined as the use or destruction of computing or information technology resources aimed at harming, coercing, or intimidating others in order to achieve a greater political or ideological goal. Richard Clark, a cybersecurity expert and former White House special advisor for cyberspace security, coined the term "infowarfare" in the late 1990s to refer to the threat, perhaps in recognition of the fact that the most serious attacks that pose a legitimate threat to national security were those that were conducted by or otherwise supported by national governments rather than by groups or individuals (Tech and Law Center, 2014). Information warfare is also regularly termed "cyberwarfare." And following the logic of this system of nomenclature, cyberterrorism would therefore include actions that similarly targeted the information systems, computers and computer networking systems, and other associated computer components that were owned and operated by nonmilitary entities and that were conducted by groups or individuals not associated with any national government, for the purpose of achieving some ideological goal. This is an extrapolation from the definitions of the terms "cyber infrastructure" and "terrorism." And both of these terms must be further differentiated from cybercrime, which seeks only personal gain or notoriety and is described next in this chapter.

The Stuxnet computer virus/worm is one of the most successful known examples of cyberwarfare. In this widely publicized example, some highly sophisticated entity, speculated to be the government of the United States and/or Israel, developed and deployed a highly sophisticated self-replicating program that appears to have directly targeted Iran's nuclear enrichment program. Stuxnet functioned by feeding instructions to the control mechanisms of the highly sensitive nuclear centrifuges that resulted in their destruction while simultaneously feeding information to the technicians operating these centrifuges that the systems were operating normally. The virus was knowingly or unwittingly introduced into the information network to which all of the centrifuges were connected using a USB drive device (such as a USB storage device), and from there, it spread itself onto any piece of equipment that had the control software it was targeting. It is believed that as many as one-fifth of Iran's nuclear centrifuges were destroyed as a result of the attack. While this could be a case of terrorism, it is more likely the act of one or several governments that target another government, especially considering that the software was designed to erase itself if it did not recognize the specific software used on the Iranian centrifuges and only allowed itself to be replicated three times from each newly infected computer (thereby limiting its spread) (Schneier, 2010). And while it is not as obvious an act of war as perhaps a cruise missile targeting the same facilities might be, there is still destruction albeit in this case limited to the mechanical devices affected.

In 2014, NSA head Mike Rogers announced that the NSA has detected the existence of viruses and other malware on the US computer infrastructure that could have a debilitating impact on critical infrastructure if it were activated in a particular targeted and coordinated manner. Rogers stated that his agency believes that many of these viruses are the work of hackers sponsored by China and other governments, presumably including Russia. The point of Rogers' argument, which was presented in testimony before Congress, was that China and as many as two other countries currently have the ability to fully take down the US electrical grid and impact other infrastructure sectors as well (Crawford, 2014). Such an attack if tied to a particular government would surely amount to a declaration of war given that it would have devastating impacts on the US economy and would cause an unknown yet significant degree of harm to human life and disruption of public safety.

Related to cyberwarfare is the act of cyberespionage or cyberspying as it is also referred. Governments have conducted overt and covert surveillances on each other and on each others' citizens for centuries, so it goes without saying that the cyber infrastructure would be an attractive target for any nation's surveillance capability. The Edward Snowden leaks (see below) highlighted the extensive nature of the United States' cyberespionage program and capabilities. Michael Hayden, former director of both the CIA and NSA, recently explained the nature and purpose of US cyberespionage efforts in stating that "We steal stuff. We make no apologies about it. But we steal things to keep our citizens free and keep our citizens safe" (The Washington Post, 2014). But the United States government is also regularly on the receiving end of cyberespionage attacks as well, many of which are of such great sophistication and consequence that one has to assume state sponsorship. A recent spate of these incidents, which began in early fall of 2014, targeted key US government agencies. These agencies were each able to recognize that their networks had been breached by hackers, who had gained access to significant parts of their information networks. This included the White House (on at least two different occasions), the United States Postal Service, the National Oceanographic and Atmospheric Administration, and the US Department of State (Perlroth, 2014). The attacks required these agencies to close down their networks, shut down e-mail and Internet access to tens of thousands of employees, and disrupt or even suspend the internal and external services they provide until security patches could be implemented. The purpose and the source of these attacks may never be fully discovered, but the impacts on operations are extreme, given the reliance of so many different systems and services on the Internet and information network access.

The fact remains that states will continue to spy on each other using cyber networks. Defense remains a high priority for these activities. China has long been a suspect in high-profile cases of data theft from US defense contractors, including the contractor responsible for developing the highly secretive F-35 Joint Strike Fighter. A report released in September 2014 by the US Senate Armed Services Committee claimed that China infiltrated US defense contractors more than 20 times in a yearlong period between 2012 and 2013 (Volz, 2014). Intrusions like these, if verified, are at best clear-cut cases of espionage, but under the right circumstances, it would not be far-fetched for a nation to accuse another or incite war by means of cyberattack. There is clearly an ongoing economic war, and very little is done to hide the fact that tens if not hundreds of thousands of attacks on US companies occur on an annual basis, which originate from China, Russia, and elsewhere (with strong accusations from the US government that a number of these are directly supported by the government of China) (The Washington Post, 2014). These attacks target intellectual property, internal communications, and negotiation tactics, among other information, and are believed to cost US businesses billions of dollars in revenues each year (Martina, 2014) (note that this activity is included in this section on cyberespionage rather than cybercrime simply because of the state sponsorship aspect of the attacks).

Cyberterrorism differs from cyberwarfare and cyberespionage on account of differences in the nature of the perpetrators and/or the victims. As of the writing of this book, there had yet to occur even a single verified act of cyberterrorism, as the act is commonly defined. This does not, however, discount the potential that exists for terrorists to cause physical or economic harm for the purpose of furthering an ideological goal by means of accessing, disrupting, and/or controlling computer or information systems. As was previously mentioned, there are certainly many examples of attempts to perform such actions that have been identified. Furthermore, as our reliance on computer systems continues to grow, the opportunities to launch such attacks, and the likelihood that an attack will ultimately be carried out with some degree of success, likewise grow. There are already reports that hackers could take over the control of an automobile using mobile network systems such as Sync and Onstar or by simply attaching a device to the car's computer system (Greenberg, 2013). And with the likelihood of driverless cars in the not-so-distant future, operating almost entirely off of data received remotely, the prospect of such attacks becomes a frightening reality.

For certain, terrorists and terror organizations are exploiting the cyber infrastructure to further their goals and objectives. A group of cybersecurity analysts contends that there are multiple categories, or "clusters," of cyberterrorism (Brickey, 2012). The most worrisome of these is destructive cyberterrorism, though this is the most difficult to carry out and is the least likely to occur as a result. Incidents in this category involve the terrorists' use of cyberattack methods to inflict damage on physical structures, systems, or equipment or the attempt on the part of terrorists to damage or manipulate data in order to inflict physical or economic harm. One could imagine a terrorist manipulating a water treatment plant's operating systems such that untreated or contaminated water supplies were introduced into the water distribution network of pipelines that supply the population in a given community or city. Likewise, terrorists might try to manipulate a company's client data in order to financially devastate the company or to cause a loss of trust among the customer base. As previously mentioned, there are no verifiable cases of this type of attack, but the likelihood of one occurring is almost a certainty.

The second cluster is disruptive cyberterrorism. Disruptive events are those that utilize electronic means to attack the credibility of groups or individuals, those that expose groups or individuals for the purpose of causing danger or embarrassment, or those that deny access to a website, communications system, or other components of the cyber infrastructure. For instance, the activist hacking collective known as Anonymous posted in 2014 the names, contact information, and in some cases the social security numbers of police officers and political officials associated with the shooting of teenager Mike Brown in Ferguson, MO. This release led to numerous cases of identity theft, credit fraud, and threats (Barr, 2014; Hunn, 2014) (note that the activities of Anonymous differ from but are closely related to cyberactivism, which also uses the cyber infrastructure (including the Internet and social media) to further a cause, raise awareness, gain support, and other means, but the actions are conducted in a manner that is in accordance with the law.)

And the third cluster is enabling cyberterrorism. In this grouping, terrorist groups use information networks and technology to recruit members or to communicate their messages and threats. Terrorist-designated groups like the Islamic State have used sleek production videos posted on mainstream social media sites including YouTube and Facebook to both recruit new members and to make calls for new attacks. Terrorists have also utilized the Internet to distribute instructions for weapons that could be used to carry out terrorist attacks, including the types of bombs that were utilized in the 2013 Boston Marathon bombings. Several terrorist groups, including al-Qaeda, have released newspapers on the Internet in order to spread propaganda, push for radicalization of followers, and recruit new members.

Cybercrime

Cybercrime differs from cyberwarfare, cyberespionage, and cyberterrorism in that its purpose is personal gain or advantage. By some broad legal definitions, any crime that involves the use of computers or the Internet is said to have a cybercrime element. However, the term cybercrime is generally reserved for those events wherein the computer hardware or information component is central to the nature of the crime (i.e., researching "how to rob a bank" using Internet search engines, and then subsequently robbing the bank in person, is not a cybercrime even though it contains some involvement of the cyber network) (see sidebar "FBI 10 Most Wanted Cyber Criminals"). Cybercrime is increasing at a pace that so far appears to be outpacing every effort to contain it (Lewis, 2014). Cybercriminals have attacked and gained access to the networks and information of some of the nation's largest companies, including Target, Home Depot, Neiman Marcus, Adobe, eBay, AOL, CNET, and more. Because of these security breaches, hundreds of millions of Americans have been affected. An attack on JP Morgan's systems resulted in the theft of information on more than 76 million households (Glazer and Yadron, 2014). The Target breach resulted in the theft of names, credit card numbers, and other contact information of as many as 110 million customers (Kosner, 2014). And a recent attack on the US Postal Service resulted in the theft of information on almost a million employees, managers, and customers that in many cases included social security numbers, which are critical to identity theft and credit card fraud (Stevens et al., 2014). The Associated Press recently reported that hackers have since 2006 gained access to the personal information and account data of as many as 255 million retail business customers, 212 million financial and industry sector customers, 13 million employees in the education sector, and many more (Bruinius, 2014). A 2014 Ponemon Institute study further highlighted the extent of the problem in finding that 43% of American companies had experienced a data breach in just the year preceding the study (Weise, 2014).

Cybercriminals also seek to steal intellectual property (IP) for their own use. By doing so, they are able to benefit from the high cost of research, and development companies have dedicated to their products without having to make any major capital investments in such requirements themselves. IP theft is widely publicized in the music, film, software, and publishing industries because these depend on the sale of licensed products to achieve a return on their investment. Hackers often break into the systems that contain master files on each of these or crack the codes that prevent duplication and sell copied (or "pirated") versions for a greatly reduced price that undercuts the IP owner or agent. But IP theft also affects the biotech, defense, automotive, manufacturing, oil exploration, and many other industries in a similar manner. Trade secrets are often stolen by overseas groups of hackers that operate with little to no fear of prosecution given that they are not even physically present in the country where their victims are located. This threat is incredibly damaging to the companies it affects, and the number of attacks doubles each year on average (Kuchler, 2013).

Cybercriminals often seek no other purpose than to gain notoriety. In fact, the earliest viruses were created simply to cause chaos and, in doing so, allow the programmer of the virus to proclaim their prowess. This behavior, often termed a "malicious attack," is similar in many ways to graffiti tagging in that it truly brought no financial gain to the perpetrator yet caused disruption and damage. These early viruses, which functioned (and continue to do so) by exploiting some weakness or feature in software and which often self-propagate by tricking users into installing them on their devices, resulted in the early emergence of antivirus software packages that exist on virtually all computers. Viruses are still a major and growing problem, of course, and their sophistication (as well as the domain to which they are able to do their damage) has likewise grown significantly. The impact of viruses that provide no benefit to the programmer can of course be significant, especially when they render key systems useless. The infamous "Sasser" virus, which was a special variant of a virus called a "worm" (see attack methods below), had a worldwide impact and shut down over 140 major corporations and agencies including those involved in air travel, banking, insurance, healthcare, national defense, and academia, among others (Coren, 2005). The worm was ultimately linked to a German teenager who confessed to all aspects of the attack, which occurred when he was only 17 years old (Blau, 2005).

FBI 10 Most Wanted Cyber Criminals

1. NICOLAE POPESCU

Crime: *Conspiracy to Commit Wire Fraud, Money Laundering, Passport Fraud, and Trafficking in Counterfeit Service Marks*

Nicolae Popescu is wanted for his alleged participation in a sophisticated Internet fraud scheme where criminal enterprise conspirators, based in Romania and elsewhere in Europe, posted advertisements on Internet auction market sites for merchandise for sale. Such advertisements contained images and descriptions of vehicles and other items for sale, but those items did not really exist. Conspirators posing as sellers then negotiated via e-mail with unsuspecting buyers in the United States. These "sellers" sent fraudulent invoices that appeared to be from legitimate online payment services to the victim buyers, with instructions for payment to bank accounts held by other conspirators in the United States. These conspirators opened US bank accounts under false identities using fraudulent passports made in Europe by other conspirators. When victims wired money to an account identified on the false invoices, the conspirator associated with that account would be notified and then would withdraw the proceeds and send them via wire transfer to another conspirator based on e-mailed instructions.

2. EVGENIY MIKHAILOVICH BOGACHEV

Crime: *Conspiracy to Participate in Racketeering Activity; Bank Fraud; Conspiracy to Violate the Computer Fraud and Abuse Act; Conspiracy to Violate the Identity Theft and Assumption Deterrence Act; Aggravated Identity Theft; Conspiracy; Computer Fraud; Wire Fraud; Money Laundering; Conspiracy to Commit Bank Fraud*

Evgeniy Mikhailovich Bogachev, using the online monikers "lucky12345" and "slavik," is wanted for his alleged involvement in a wide-ranging racketeering enterprise and scheme that installed, without authorization, malicious software known as "Zeus" on victims' computers. The software was used to capture bank account numbers, passwords, personal identification numbers, and other information necessary to log into online banking accounts. While Bogachev knowingly acted in a role as an administrator, others involved in the scheme conspired to distribute spam and phishing e-mails, which contained links to compromised websites. Victims who visited these websites were infected with the malware, which Bogachev and others utilized to steal money from the victims' bank accounts. This online account takeover fraud has been investigated by the FBI since the summer of 2009. Starting in September 2011, the FBI began investigating a modified version of the Zeus Trojan, known as Gameover Zeus (GOZ). It is believed that GOZ is responsible for more than one million computer infections, resulting in financial losses in the hundreds of millions of dollars.

3. SUN KAILIANG

Crime: *Conspiring to Commit Computer Fraud; Accessing a Computer Without Authorization for the Purpose of Commercial Advantage and Private Financial Gain; Damaging Computers Through the Transmission of Code and Commands; Aggravated Identity Theft; Economic Espionage; Theft of Trade Secrets*

On May 1, 2014, a grand jury in the Western District of Pennsylvania indicted five members of the People's Liberation Army (PLA) of the People's Republic of China (PRC) for 31 criminal counts, including conspiring to commit computer fraud; accessing a computer without authorization for the purpose of commercial advantage and private financial gain; damaging computers through the transmission of code and commands; aggravated identity theft; economic espionage; and theft of trade secrets. The subjects, including Sun Kailiang, were officers of the PRC's Third Department of the General Staff Department of the People's Liberation Army (3PLA), Second Bureau, Third Office, Military Unit Cover Designator (MUCD) 61398, at some point during the investigation. The activities executed by each of these individuals allegedly involved in the conspiracy varied according to his specialties. Each provided his individual expertise to an alleged conspiracy to penetrate the computer networks of six American companies while those companies were engaged in negotiations or joint ventures or were pursuing legal action with, or against, state-owned enterprises in China. They then used their illegal access to allegedly steal proprietary information including e-mail exchanges among company employees and trade secrets related to technical specifications for nuclear plant designs. Sun, who held the rank of captain during the early stages of the investigation, was observed both sending malicious e-mails and controlling victim computers.

4. HUANG ZHENYU

Crime: *Conspiring to Commit Computer Fraud; Accessing a Computer Without Authorization for the Purpose of Commercial Advantage and Private Financial Gain; Damaging Computers Through the Transmission of Code and Commands; Aggravated Identity Theft; Economic Espionage; Theft of Trade Secrets*

Huang Zhenyu's activity is related to that of Sun Kailiang (see above). Huang was a computer programmer who managed the domain accounts used by the others.

5. WEN XINYU

Crime: *Conspiring to Commit Computer Fraud; Accessing a Computer Without Authorization for the Purpose of Commercial Advantage and Private Financial Gain; Damaging Computers Through the Transmission of Code and Commands; Aggravated Identity Theft; Economic Espionage; Theft of Trade Secrets*

Wen Xinyu's activity is related to that of Sun Kailiang (see above). Wen controlled victim computers.

6. SHAILESHKUMAR P. JAIN

Crime: *Wire Fraud; Conspiracy to Commit Computer Fraud; Computer Fraud*

Shaileshkumar P. Jain, along with his coconspirator, Bjorn Daniel Sundin (see below), is wanted for his alleged involvement in an international cybercrime scheme that caused Internet users in more than 60 countries to purchase more than one million bogus software products, resulting in consumer loss of more than $100 million. It is alleged that from December 2006 to October 2008, through fake advertisements placed on legitimate companies' websites, Jain and his accomplices deceived Internet users into believing that their computers were infected with "malware" or had other critical errors in order to encourage them to purchase "scareware" software products that had limited or no ability to remedy the purported defects. Jain and his coconspirators allegedly deceived victims, through browser hijacking, multiple fraudulent scans, and false error messages, into purchasing full paid versions of software products offered by their company, Innovative Marketing, Inc. The proceeds of these credit card sales were allegedly deposited into bank accounts controlled by the defendant and others around the world and were then transferred to bank accounts located in Europe. When customers complained that their purchases were actually fraudulent software, call center representatives were allegedly instructed to lie or provide refunds in order to prevent fraud reports to law enforcement or credit companies.

7. THE JABBERZEUS SUBJECTS

Crime: *Conspiracy to Participate in Racketeering Activity; Bank Fraud; Conspiracy to Violate the Computer Fraud and Abuse Act; Conspiracy to Violate the Identity Theft and Assumption Deterrence Act; Aggravated Identity Theft*

These three individuals, thought to be located in Russia and Ukraine, are wanted for their involvement in a wide-ranging racketeering enterprise and scheme that installed, without authorization, malicious software known as "Zeus" on victims' computers. The malicious software was used to capture bank account numbers, passwords, personal identification numbers, and other information necessary to log into online banking accounts. These subjects were then able to coordinate unauthorized transfers of funds from victims' accounts.

8. BJORN DANIEL SUNDIN

Crime: *Wire Fraud; Conspiracy to Commit Computer Fraud; Computer Fraud*

Bjorn Daniel Sundin is accused of the same crimes as his coconspirator Shaileshkumar P. Jain (see above).

9. ALEXANDR SERGEYEVICH BOBNEV

Crime: *Conspiracy to Commit Wire Fraud; Conspiracy to Commit Money Laundering*

Alexandr Sergeyevich Bobnev was indicted for his alleged participation in a money-laundering scheme involving unauthorized access to the accounts of a major provider of investment services. Bobnev allegedly accessed compromised accounts and wire transferred funds out of these accounts to money mules in the United States. These mules were then responsible for transferring the money back to Bobnev. Between June 2007 and August 2007, Bobnev allegedly wired or attempted to wire over $350,000 from compromised accounts.

10. CARLOS ENRIQUE PEREZ-MELARA

Crime: *Not Listed*

Carlos Enrique Perez-Melara is wanted for his alleged involvement in manufacturing spyware that was used to intercept the private communications of hundreds, if not thousands, of victims. As part of the scheme, Perez-Melara ran a website offering customers a way to "catch a cheating lover" by sending spyware masqueraded as an electronic greeting card. Victims who opened the greeting card would unwittingly install a program onto their computers. The program collected keystrokes and other incoming and outgoing electronic communications on the victims' computers. The program would periodically send e-mail messages back to the purchasers of the service containing the acquired communications, including the victims' passwords, lists of visited websites, intercepted e-mail messages, and keystroke logs. The program in question was initially called "Email PI" and renamed "Lover Spy" in July/August 2003. Perez-Melara allegedly hosted the website and created the computer program. He ran the operation from his San Diego residence in 2003.

Source: FBI (2014a).

Cyber Threats

Agents of cyberwarfare, cybercriminals, and cyberterrorists have a broad arsenal of weapons to use in their pursuits. These differ considerably in terms of the level of engagement required by the perpetrator, the sophistication of the tool, the mechanisms for protection, and many other factors. Achieving cybersecurity, however, requires individuals, businesses, and government agencies to ensure that they are prepared and able to defend their own data and networks from any and all forms given that even the most advanced technological solutions can be bypassed by a hacker that is able to trick an employee into giving up their login information.

The most common methods are listed and briefly described here:

- *Malicious website*: The most common form of attack, resulting in over one billion incidents per year, is the malicious website or malicious uniform resource locator (URL) as it is also referred. These websites work by exploiting the manner in which web browsers work. When a user clicks on a website, pictures, files, and programs are downloaded onto the user's devices during the time of browsing (and may be cached thereafter). Malicious sites exploit this process by enabling the downloading of damaging software onto the user's computer. This is sometimes called "drive-by-downloading." These often utilize common web interface programs like Java, Flash, or ActiveX but can use a number of other less common platforms as well. The regularity of updates on these programs is driven by the speed at which hackers develop piggyback methods to exploit them in order to attack web users.

- *Virus*: Viruses are programs that operate unseen and undetected on a computer or other hardware in order to influence the manner in which the device's operating system functions. They are typically, though not always, destructive or damaging in their function. Their name is derived from their ability to replicate and spread to other devices using a number of common methods of interaction (such as e-mail attachments).
- *Trojan horse*: Like a virus, a Trojan horse is a program that exists to influence the manner in which a component of a hardware or a software program operates. Unlike the virus, however, the Trojan horse is disguised to appear like a useful program, which the affected user knowingly installs on their system or device.
- *Worm*: A worm is a type of virus that is able to replicate itself on an infected system without any human action. Many worms will send themselves to every user in an infected computer's stored contact lists (e.g., on an e-mail platform). Many worms have an intended target and simply pass through all other systems until they reach that target. The Stuxnet virus is a classic example of a worm.
- *Spyware*: Spyware programs are installed on a system or device without the user's knowledge for the purpose of gathering information and transmitting it to the source of the attack. Many spyware programs only seek to better understand the web-browsing habits of the user, but a certain class of spyware called crimeware seeks to collect and transmit to the attacker sensitive information that is stored in programs or databases. This might be just user IDs and passwords, but crimeware has also been used to collect financial account data or other information valuable to a cyber criminal seeking to defraud victims.
- *Keystroke logger (keylogger)*: Keyloggers are programs or physical devices that record each key pressed by the user in ordered succession. Many, though not all, keystroke loggers are able to transmit the recorded information back to the person or group that deployed them, via the Internet or other communications method. Others must be physically collected in order to access the recorded information.
- *Malware*: Malware is a catchall name for any program that seeks to compromise, disrupt, or steal from a device or system. It is also referred to as malicious code or malicious software.
- *DOS/DDOS attack*: Denial of service (DOS) attacks prevent the access to or use of a website or information management system. Attackers conduct DOS attacks for many purposes, such as to punish a company or group they consider to be an adversary, to prevent a company or group from serving their customers, or simply to cause havoc. In a distributed denial of service (DDOS) attack, the attackers use multiple devices to stage an attack simultaneously, thereby increasing its impact. Oftentimes, DDOS attacks will involve the hijacking of unwitting users' computers to simultaneously flood a particular website or system with data or requests in order to crash that system. These types of attacks are common and can prevent access to a website for hours or even days at a time.
- *Bot*: A bot is a computer that has been remotely taken over by an attacker, almost exclusively through its Internet connection. Bots typically rely upon previous installation of malware that enables the attacker, called a bot master or bot herder, to perform the attack. The term "botnet" is used to describe the network of computers that are being simultaneously controlled by the bot master in the course of their attack. Botnets are typically the source of a DDOS attack (see sidebar "FBI-Taking Down Botnets").

- *Hack*: A hack is a successful gaining of entry into an information or computer system using nefarious means. Hacks are performed by hackers, who might steal passwords from users by tricking them, by accessing password records, or by other methods of fooling security access points.
- *Phishing*: Phishing is a method hackers use to gain the identification and password information of an unwitting target. Phishing schemes use social engineering tricks to deceive, such as sending an e-mail that appears to be from a network administrator or a trusted friend or colleague. Oftentimes, phishing schemes will include copied website images or logos to fool the victim into believing they are logging into a legitimate site when in fact, they are simply giving their sensitive information to the hacker. The Target and Home Depot breaches in which a combined 200 million customers' data were ultimately stolen were both the result of an employee of the company falling for a phishing scheme.
- *Spoofing*: Spoofing is a method often used in phishing schemes wherein a hacker is able to masquerade their own e-mail address to look like one that would be trusted by their target. It can also be used to bypass system filters that would otherwise block the sender's e-mail. Spoofing is also used to create fake Internet protocol (IP) addresses, which in effect hide the identity of the sending computer, thereby making the attack much harder to trace. This method is often used for DDOS attacks because the information returned from each phony request does not in turn flood the attacking computer. Websites can also be spoofed in order to conduct phishing attacks, although there is almost always a slight variation in the website address or URL. In more sophisticated attacks, a method called URL cloaking where the URL is masked to look legitimate is often used.
- *DNS poisoning (or DNS spoofing)*: Domain Name System (DNS) poisoning attacks are a form of hacking wherein the hacker is able to divert traffic from a legitimate website to their own, thereby giving them access to all of the data that users would normally provide to the legitimate owner of the website (e.g., a business or a government entity). Hackers often use a phishing method called "domain slamming" to fool the website owner into transferring the registrar of their website to that of the hacker under the pretense that the hacker is actually a domain name registration service. Domain squatting is a related method wherein a hacker or simply a person seeking a profit legitimately purchases a website that is so similar to that of the name of the legitimate entity that they are able to gain traffic simply because people enter the wrong website address. The squatter either acts like the legitimate entity in order to fool the victim into providing information, or they use the ownership of the domain to charge extortionist prices to the legitimate entity to buy it from them. This is also done with social media services like Facebook and Twitter.
- *Exploit*: An exploit is a hacking method that allows a hacker to gain entry to a secure system by taking advantage of a bug or an unknown vulnerability in the software or system. Exploits are often the target of viruses and worms. Software patches and updates are used to fix the software code that allowed the exploit to occur. Exploits are particularly dangerous because they can allow hacks to go undetected. A "zero-day exploit" is one that takes advantage of unknown or unpatched vulnerabilities. It is considered zero-day until the patch exists and it is then incumbent upon the users to apply the patch and address the vulnerability.
- *Clickjacking*: Clickjacking is a hacking method wherein the hacker tricks a target into clicking on something that appears legitimate but in fact directs them to another website or attempts to install malicious software on their computer. This form of attack has been used to trick targets into unwittingly turn on their computer's camera, liking a certain person or entity on Facebook, following a certain person or entity on Twitter, altering computer security settings, and more.

- *Cookies*: Cookies are small packets of information that a website stores on a user's computer in order to track, store, and then return information to the website for the purpose of understanding previous activity. For legitimate websites, cookies are useful to both the user and the website, such as storing items that have been placed into a retail website's shopping cart. However, cookies can be used by hackers to better understand a target's broader web-browsing habits for the purpose of performing phishing or other social engineering methods. Some cookies can store information that is entered into web-based forms, including bank account or credit card information, for instance, and then return that information to the hacker. Users can protect themselves by deleting cookies often or even every time they close down their browsing session, but a class of cookies called zombie cookies store parts of their code in other parts of the operating system and then recreate themselves each time the browser is opened.
- *SQL injection*: SQL injection is a hacking method wherein the hacker enters code into a database interface, or other data-driven program, in order to command the program to send them some or all of the information that the system is storing. SQL injection relies upon the existence of security exploits. Hackers have been able to receive personal information stored by many online retailers and service websites using this method, including a famous 2008 attack on the Oklahoma Sexual and Violent Offender Registry Database that resulted in the theft of over 10,000 offenders' social security numbers. Other attacks have resulted in tens and hundreds of millions of user's data being stolen.
- *Skim*: A skim is an action where personal data are collected from a credit card during an in-person transaction without the owner's knowledge. ATM and debit cards are also affected. Skimmers are machines that can be attached over the slot on an ATM, such that users voluntarily pass their card through the skimmer on its way into the machine. Hidden cameras capture the victim typing their pin into the keypad. Sometimes, criminals hide skimmers behind a counter or at a wait station as in the case of a restaurant. When handed the card, they do the legitimate transaction first and then, at some point when the victim is not paying attention, pass the card through the skimmer that records all the key data.
- *Social engineering*: Social engineering methods use psychological or other nontechnical means to trick victims into voluntarily or unwittingly handing over their personal information, including login information and passwords. Kevin Mitnick, a hacker that has since begun consulting with the security industry, recently stated that it was easier to trick a person into giving up their password information than trying to hack into their system (Mitnick, 2003). In social engineering schemes, people call or present posing as someone who would warrant the information they are asking for, and oftentimes, victims simply give it up believing that they are doing the right thing. Some social engineers do nothing other than stand too close to a person and look over their shoulder.
- *Ransomware*: Ransomware, cyber ransom, and cyber blackmail are tools and actions wherein a cyber criminal alters or corrupts the data on a target system and then instructs an individual in charge of the targeted material to provide a ransom payment in exchange for repair of the data. Cyber ransom has also been utilized in situations where compromising information, oftentimes pictures, has been stolen from a target's computer, and the cyber criminals threaten to post the information publically unless a payment is made. Several celebrities have been targeted by the images. In one particularly disturbing case, the cyber criminal was able to turn on the victim's webcam and record images and videos of her without her knowledge that anything was happening.

FBI: Taking Down Botnets

The following is an extract from the testimony of Joseph Demarest, Assistant Director of the FBI Cyber Division before the Senate Judiciary Committee Subcommittee on Crime and Terrorism, July 15, 2014:

Good morning Senator Whitehouse. I thank you for holding this hearing today, and I look forward to discussing the progress the FBI has made on campaigns to disrupt and disable significant botnets. As you well know, we face cyber threats from state-sponsored hackers, hackers for hire, organized cyber syndicates, and terrorists. They seek our state secrets, our trade secrets, our technology, and our ideas—things of incredible value to all of us. They may seek to strike our critical infrastructure and our economy. The threat is so dire that cyber security has topped the Director of National Intelligence list of global threats for the second consecutive year.

Cyber criminal threats pose very real risks to the economic security and privacy of the United States and its citizens. The use of botnets is on the rise. Industry experts estimate that botnet attacks have resulted in the overall loss of millions of dollars from financial institutions and other major US businesses. They also affect universities, hospitals, defense contractors, government, and even private citizens. The "weapons" of a cyber criminal are tools, like botnets, which are created with malicious software that is readily available for purchase on the Internet. Criminals distribute malicious software, also known as malware, that can turn a computer into a "bot." When this occurs, a computer can perform automated tasks over the Internet, without any direction from its rightful user. A network of these infected computers—numbering in the hundreds of thousands or even millions—is called a botnet (robot network), and each computer becomes connected to a command-and-control server operated by the criminal.

Once the botnet is in place, it can be used in distributed denial of service (DDoS) attacks, proxy and spam services, malware distribution, and other organized criminal activity. Botnets can also be used for covert intelligence collection, and terrorists or state-sponsored actors could use a botnet to attack Internet-connected critical infrastructure. And they can be used as weapons in ideology campaigns against their target to instigate fear, intimidation, or public embarrassment.

A botnet typically operates without obvious visible evidence and can remain operational for years. Our personal computers can become part of a botnet—it only takes one wrong click for a home user to download malicious code. For example, you might get an unsolicited e-mail promoting a dating website or a work-at-home arrangement or an e-mail that appears to come from your bank containing a seemingly harmless link. You could be sent a link by a friend asking you to view a great video, which was actually sent because your friend's computer is already infected. You could see a link on a webpage that seems to be soliciting donations for a recent tragedy. And you might even visit a fraudulent website—or a legitimate one that's been compromised—and download videos, pictures, or a document containing malicious code.

Once the malware is on your computer, it's hard to detect. In addition to your computer being commanded to link up with other compromised computers to facilitate criminal activity, the bot can also collect and send out your personally identifiable information—like credit card numbers, banking information, and passwords—to the criminals running it. Those criminals will take advantage of the information themselves or offer it for sale on cyber criminal forums.

The impact of this global cyber threat has been significant. According to industry estimates, botnets have caused over $9 billion in losses to US victims and over $110 billion in losses globally. Approximately 500 million computers are infected globally each year, translating into 18 victims per second.

The FBI, with its law enforcement and private sector partners, has had success in taking down a number of large botnets. But our work is never done, and by combining the resources of government and the private sector, and with the support of the public, we will continue to improve cyber security by identifying and catching those who threaten it.

Source: FBI (2014b).

The Threat of Rogue Insiders

One of the most destructive cybersecurity threats, and quite possibly the most difficult to prevent, is the rogue employee or contractor who has full or partial access to the company's or entity's data systems. This person is already trusted and is therefore in possession of all that is needed to access the systems and infrastructure that hackers must go to great lengths to supersede. Perhaps, the most notorious rogue insiders in recent history are Bradley Manning and Edward Snowden. These two individuals used their security clearances to download and release hundreds of thousands of classified government documents whose release revealed top-secret government security programs and reportedly endangered the lives of US citizens and other foreign nationals who had been secretly working with US intelligence services overseas. Agencies and businesses can only protect against being "breached" by an insider source by instituting certain policies that would in effect make it impossible for a single person or a small group of people that have network access from stealing data, leaking information, sabotaging information, or causing other disruption, destruction, or loss. For instance, in the case of Bradlee Manning, who downloaded hundreds of thousands of classified documents onto his personal computer, differences in the manner in which different agencies protected classified information are what led to such a severe internal data breach. The Department of State, which owned the breached documents, maintains strict access procedures that would have prevented employees from accessing such a great number of documents, from having the capability to download them locally, and from being able to record them on removable devices. Data-sharing protocols between DOD and other agencies are what permitted Manning, a DOD employee, to access the files. However, DOD did not have in place the same security procedures, and as such, Manning was able to perform a data theft that no Department of State employee ever could, even though they managed the systems (PBS, 2013).

Rogue employee thefts are not isolated to activists or spies within government. In fact, rogue employees regularly steal information or compromise systems in order to gain some financial payout or to avail themselves to a competitor who will reward them. In some cases, revenge is the motivation. There are countless cases of employees selling the data of customers, of patients, or of clients. Examples of companies affected include Aventura Hospital (over 80,000 patients' data stolen), Compuserve (sensitive company data), Bank of America ($10 million in customer funds), and Tufts Health Plan (8800 employees' health-related data). There are a number of reasons a rogue insider might take such destructive insider action, such as disagreements with company or agency policy, personal debt or greed, an impending departure from the company, or possibly a personal disagreement. Amanuel Tsighe of File Open Systems describes a number of policies that often increase vulnerability to insider breaches such as the following:

- Overly generous document access privileges
- Decentralized storage of sensitive information

- Allowing legacy access to documents
- Allowing unfettered access on take-home devices
- Trusting high-level employees too much
- Failing to monitor document usage (Tsighe, 2014)

A Georgia Tech Institute of Technology report found that insider attacks were harder to detect and costlier to investigate and can be expensive to resolve as well. Because employees need access to operate and overclassification of information can actually impede progress if not performed correctly, creative mechanisms that differ significantly from protection of external breaches are required. For instance, the George Tech study suggested enforceable two-person security systems that would prevent damage from rogue employees that were truly acting alone. Another option is behavior modeling, using "anomaly detection systems" that identify and alert supervisors when actions that could potentially hurt the company occur (Lee and Rotoloni, 2014). Whether for retail sales, for government intelligence, or simply within social and personal relationships, insider threats are always the most difficult to detect, and the same is certainly true for any situation pertaining to the cyber network.

Cybersabotage: The Case of Sony

On December 1, 2014, Sony Entertainment became the target of a highly sophisticated cyberattack. Hackers used a variety of methods, including malware that had been downloaded onto company computers, hijacking of command and control servers, and the use anonymous public wireless networks (to conceal identities), among others. Once the Sony network was breached, the hackers took a number of steps to harm the company, its employees, and its clients, including

- defacing company websites with images of skeletons and with political messages;
- releasing personal information of company employees, including contract and salary information, home addresses, and social security numbers (including for employees that had left the company more than a decade prior);
- erasing information and data stored on company hard drives.

The hackers used sophisticated methods and launched their attack from a hotel in Bangkok, Thailand, where they presumably knew that subsequent tracing of clues would be very difficult for investigators. Like the coding found in the Stuxnet virus, the coding of the malware used in the Sony attack was written specifically for Sony's networks.

What is interesting about the case is that while it follows patterns seen in many cybercrime incidents, the manner in which the data were leaked publicly seems to suggest that the attack was conducted to hurt the Sony brand or image rather than provide any financial benefit for the attackers. This has resulted in speculation that the attack was state-sponsored, and North Korea has emerged as the most likely culprit were that theory to be proved correct. Sony had recently produced a movie (The Interview) that portrayed the assassination of North Korean leader Kim Jong-Un, which certainly serves as a possible motive. Additionally, the methods of attack are similar to several other cybersecurity incidents for which North Korea has been implicated, including attacks using the same hijacked servers used in the Sony attack and coding that closely matched that used in previous attacks against North Korea's traditional adversaries.

Were this attack found to be linked to a national government or to be supported by one, it would significantly intensify the nature of cyber threats against individuals and private-sector organizations. Attacks with government involvement are rare and exclusively targeted other government and military networks and systems. This attack represents a break from that norm and therefore changes the nature of the risk to which the private sector has calibrated their cybersecurity programs. This event will have prompted many companies' executives to consider the fact that they do not have security programs in place capable of preventing attacks by groups with state-sponsored levels of sophistication. And the balance between increased investments in protection and risking embarrassment and revenue loss has again shifted towards the former of these two options.

Source: Robertson et al. (2014) and Arce (2014).

Using the Cyber Network as a Security Tool

The cyber network and our reliance on it for almost all functions of government and society have certainly introduced monumental vulnerabilities that must continue to be addressed given the new and increasing risks that are regularly discovered, acted upon, and addressed. But we must not overlook the fact that the cyber infrastructure has also been a boon for agencies tasked with protecting national security. The cyber network enables communication, surveillance, tracking, information sharing, and much more, to a degree that was unimaginable just a few decades ago.

Like all organizations, terrorists and criminals also use mobile phones, computers, e-mail, SMS chat, Twitter, Facebook, and more. In fact, the terrorists who planned and carried out the devastating terror attacks in Mumbai that killed over 150 people in 2008 used Google Earth to plan their method of attack. Several terrorist organizations maintain online magazines and newsletters, such as the al-Qaeda online newsletter "Inspire" and the online magazine of the Islamic State "Dabiq." Terrorist organizations also regularly post videos on YouTube and other outlets for propaganda purposes. At each step of the way, information is created that counterterrorism officials are able to gather to begin painting a more complete picture (including identifying people and locations).

For governments and the companies that own and operate the systems behind this infrastructure, the processes by which cyber network information is "tapped into" are quite a bit different than what has been discussed thus far in this chapter (in most cases). If there is evidence that a crime is being committed or an attack is being planned, officers can work within the bounds of the law and request issuance of a search warrant to access records from the company or companies maintaining the data in question. This might include records of past Internet activity, logs of e-mail messages and contact lists, full texts of phone messages and all sender/recipient information, the sources of the computer or the Internet outlet from which postings were made on blog or other social media sites, and the sources of websites or newsletters, among many other things. Because terrorist financing provides such strong legal authority to investigate, many online surveillance efforts involve tracking the movement of money to and from groups known to be associated with terrorist organizations and individuals, which in turn allows for the freezing of the person's or the group's funds.

In fact, many terrorists are so acutely aware of the level of ongoing electronic surveillance being conducted to intercept their communications, determine their plans, and locate their whereabouts, that they avoid using the Internet if at all possible. It was the willingness to stay off the cyber infrastructure completely, among other moves, which enabled Osama bin Laden to survive as long as he did without capture. Bin Laden chose instead to use a human currier who handed delivered messages or traveled great distances to make phone calls.

But not all information requires a warrant. In fact, a great amount of the online activity conducted by terrorists and terror organizations is done so in the wide open spaces of the Internet. Investigators are constantly tracking activity and reading publicly posted online materials on websites associated with terror and criminal organizations or groups. Terrorists are prevalent on online chat rooms and message boards where they attempt to push forward their ideology and recruit for support. And in some cases, the investigators are posing as terrorists themselves in order to engage directly with those with established or fledgling terrorist intentions.

The Patriot Act greatly increased the ability of Federal law enforcement officers to monitor communications between, to, and from known and suspected terrorists, though the program itself has led to significant concerns about privacy. The revelations that came out of the Snowden leaks, which are explained in more detail in Chapter 5 and describe situations where Americans with no ties to terrorism have had their data monitored or recorded, have only fueled this fire. As the time since September 11 grows, the willingness of Americans to relax their security preferences in the name of national security has waned, and the result on actual security levels has yet to be understood.

Executive Order 13636: Improving Critical Infrastructure Cybersecurity

On February 12, 2013, President Obama issued Executive Order 13636, entitled *Improving Critical Infrastructure Cybersecurity*. The order was issued in response to growing calls for more action to counteract the threat to all US sectors, especially that of critical infrastructure, and tasked government to develop and implement a more holistic method of dealing with threats to the nation's cyber infrastructure. The language of the executive order directed the executive branch agencies to do the following (DHS, 2013a):

- Develop a voluntary cybersecurity framework that was "technology-neutral" (i.e., organizations of any technological sophistication can benefit from it, and it does not prescribe specific technologies that could have the unintended effect of stifling innovation).
- Increase the adoption of good cybersecurity practices by promoting effective methods and developing incentives.
- Improve the sharing of information on threats to the cyber infrastructure, including its reach, its timeliness, and its quality.
- Ensure that cybersecurity measures adhere to privacy standards and protect civil liberties.
- Explore the use of existing regulation to promote cybersecurity.

This policy action indicated that the federal government recognizes that cybersecurity protection is not possible without adequate public-private partnership, especially as regards to critical infrastructure that exists in the private-sector domain. Of particular note is the requirement that a cybersecurity framework be developed, with the National Institute of Standards and Technology (NIST) at the lead.

The Cybersecurity Framework

On February 12, 2014, the White House announced the release of the nation's cybersecurity framework, a direct result of Executive Order 13636. The framework was developed to guide and/or supplement the efforts of private- and public-sector owners and operators of critical infrastructure components, but much of what is contained in this framework is applicable to all sectors and stakeholders. Its foundation is the building and maintaining of public-private partnerships, thereby recognizing that there exists a sharing of the cybersecurity burden between both sectors as was previously mentioned. Most importantly, it is a risk-based approach that helps those facing cybersecurity threats to take a systematic look at what they are (people, information, facilities, etc.), what threatens them (and what the possible consequences of those threats might be), what can be done to address those threats and to respond to them, and what can be done to ensure a rapid recovery.

There are three main parts to the framework, which include the following:

- The Framework Core, described as a set of cybersecurity activities and informative references that are common across critical infrastructure sectors. The cybersecurity activities are grouped by five functions, each of which provides a high-level view of an organization's management of cyber risks. These include (NIST, 2014) (see Figure 8-1) the following:
  - *Identify*: Develop the organizational understanding to manage cybersecurity risk to systems, assets, data, and capabilities. Understanding the business context, the resources that support critical functions, and the related cybersecurity risks enables an organization to focus and

Function Unique Identifier	Function	Category Unique Identifier	Category
ID	Identify	ID.AM	Asset Management
		ID.BE	Business Environment
		ID.GV	Governance
		ID.RA	Risk Assessment
		ID.RM	Risk Management Strategy
PR	Protect	PR.AC	Access Control
		PR.AT	Awareness and Training
		PR.DS	Data Security
		PR.IP	Information Protection Processes and Procedures
		PR.MA	Maintenance
		PR.PT	Protective Technology
DE	Detect	DE.AE	Anomalies and Events
		DE.CM	Security Continuous Monitoring
		DE.DP	Detection Processes
RS	Respond	RS.RP	Response Planning
		RS.CO	Communications
		RS.AN	Analysis
		RS.MI	Mitigation
		RS.IM	Improvements
RC	Recover	RC.RP	Recovery Planning
		RC.IM	Improvements
		RC.CO	Communications

FIGURE 8-1 Cybersecurity framework functions and categories. *Source: NIST (2014).*

prioritize its efforts, consistent with its risk management strategy and business needs. Examples of outcome categories within this function include asset management, business environment, governance, risk assessment, and risk management strategy.

- *Protect*: Develop and implement the appropriate safeguards to ensure delivery of critical infrastructure services. The Protect function supports the ability to limit or contain the impact of a potential cybersecurity event. Examples of outcome categories within this function include access control, awareness and training, data security, information protection processes and procedures, maintenance, and protective technology.
- *Detect*: Develop and implement the appropriate activities to identify the occurrence of a cybersecurity event. The Detect function enables timely discovery of cybersecurity events. Examples of outcome categories within this function include anomalies and events, security continuous monitoring, and detection processes.
- *Respond*: Develop and implement the appropriate activities to take action regarding a detected cybersecurity event. The Respond function supports the ability to contain the impact of a potential cybersecurity event. Examples of outcome categories within this function include response planning, communications, analysis, mitigation, and improvements.
- *Recover*: Develop and implement the appropriate activities to maintain plans for resilience and to restore any capabilities or services that were impaired due to a cybersecurity event. The Recover function supports timely recovery to normal operations to reduce the impact from a cybersecurity event. Examples of outcome categories within this function include recovery planning, improvements, and communications.

- The Profiles, which "help organizations align their cybersecurity activities with business requirements, risk tolerances, and resources." It was envisioned that private-sector entities, especially those that own or operate critical infrastructure, would use these profiles to better understand how cyber threats affect them, how they are vulnerable, and how they should prioritize their efforts and measure their successes.
- Tiers (see sidebar "Cybersecurity Framework Tiers"), which enable stakeholders in the public and private sectors to assess how they are managing their cyber risk and to better understand how those actions measure up to what is considered effective. There are four tiers, which are described as "partial" at the low end and "adaptive" at the high end. The tiers include general descriptions of how much attention is being provided to risk management, the degree to which these activities are linked to the needs of the business, and how much integration cybersecurity enjoys across the greater operations of the enterprise or organization (White Housc., 2014).

Cybersecurity Framework Tiers

Tier 1: Partial

- *Risk management process*: Organizational cybersecurity risk management practices are not formalized, and risk is managed in an ad hoc and sometimes reactive manner. Prioritization of cybersecurity activities may not be directly informed by organizational risk objectives, the threat environment, or business/mission requirements.

- *Integrated risk management program*: There is limited awareness of cybersecurity risk at the organizational level, and an organization-wide approach to managing cybersecurity risk has not been established. The organization implements cybersecurity risk management on an irregular, case-by-case basis due to varied experience or information gained from outside sources. The organization may not have processes that enable cybersecurity information to be shared within the organization.
- *External participation*: An organization may not have the processes in place to participate in coordination or collaboration with other entities.

Tier 2: Risk Informed

- *Risk management process*: Risk management practices are approved by management but may not be established as organizational-wide policy. Prioritization of cybersecurity activities is directly informed by organizational risk objectives, the threat environment, or business/mission requirements.
- *Integrated risk management program*: There is an awareness of cybersecurity risk at the organizational level, but an organization-wide approach to managing cybersecurity risk has not been established. Risk-informed, management-approved processes and procedures are defined and implemented, and staff has adequate resources to perform their cybersecurity duties. Cybersecurity information is shared within the organization on an informal basis.
- *External participation*: The organization knows its role in the larger ecosystem but has not formalized its capabilities to interact and share information externally.

Tier 3: Repeatable

- *Risk management process*: The organization's risk management practices are formally approved and expressed as policy. Organizational cybersecurity practices are regularly updated based on the application of risk management processes to changes in business/mission requirements and a changing threat and technology landscape.
- *Integrated risk management program*: There is an organization-wide approach to manage cybersecurity risk. Risk-informed policies, processes, and procedures are defined, implemented as intended, and reviewed. Consistent methods are in place to respond effectively to changes in risk. Personnel possess the knowledge and skills to perform their appointed roles and responsibilities.
- *External participation*: The organization understands its dependencies and partners and receives information from these partners that enables collaboration and risk-based management decisions within the organization in response to events.

Tier 4: Adaptive

- *Risk management process*: The organization adapts its cybersecurity practices based on lessons learned and predictive indicators derived from previous and current cybersecurity activities. Through a process of continuous improvement incorporating advanced cybersecurity technologies and practices, the organization actively adapts to a changing cybersecurity landscape and responds to evolving and sophisticated threats in a timely manner.
- *Integrated risk management program*: There is an organization-wide approach to managing cybersecurity risk that uses risk-informed policies, processes, and procedures to address potential cybersecurity events. Cybersecurity risk management is part of the organizational culture and evolves from an awareness of previous activities,

information shared by other sources, and continuous awareness of activities on their systems and networks.

- *External participation*: The organization manages risk and actively shares information with partners to ensure that accurate, current information is being distributed and consumed to improve cybersecurity before a cybersecurity event occurs.

Source: NIST (2014).

DHS Cybersecurity Efforts

Through presidential directives, the Department of Homeland Security (DHS) was tasked with leading and managing the nation's cyberterrorism threat through its risk management division, the Directorate for National Protection and Programs. In the first Quadrennial Homeland Security Review published in February 2010, the fourth stated mission of the department was safeguarding and securing cyberspace. In this document, they state (DHS, 2010a):

"Our vision is a cyberspace that supports a secure and resilient infrastructure, that enables innovation and prosperity, and that protects privacy and other civil liberties by design. It is one in which we can use cyberspace with confidence to advance our economic interests and maintain national security under all conditions. We will achieve this vision by focusing on two goals: (1) helping to create a safe, secure, and resilient cyber environment; and (2) promoting cybersecurity knowledge and innovation. We must enhance public awareness and ensure that the public both recognizes cybersecurity challenges and is empowered to address them. We must create a dynamic cyber workforce across government with sufficient capacity and expertise to manage current and emerging risks. We must invest in the innovative technologies, techniques, and procedures necessary to sustain a safe, secure, and resilient cyber environment. Government must work creatively and collaboratively with the private sector to identify solutions that take into account both public and private interests, and the private sector and academia must be fully empowered to see and solve ever larger parts of the problem set. Finally, because cybersecurity is an exceedingly dynamic field, we must make specific efforts to ensure that the nation is prepared for the cyber threats and challenges of tomorrow, not only of today. To do this, we must promote cybersecurity knowledge and innovation. Innovation in technology, practice, and policy must further protect—not erode—privacy and civil liberties."

2010 QHSR Cybersecurity Goals Defined

Goal 4.1 Create a Safe, Secure, and Resilient Cyber Environment
Ensure that malicious actors are unable to effectively exploit cyberspace, impair its safe and secure use, or attack the nation's information infrastructure.

Goal 4.1 Objectives

- *Understand and prioritize cyber threats*: Identify and evaluate the most dangerous threats to federal civilian and private-sector networks and the nation
- *Manage risks to cyberspace*: Protect and make resilient information systems, networks, and personal and sensitive data
- *Prevent cybercrime and other malicious uses of cyberspace*: Disrupt the criminal organizations and other malicious actors engaged in high-consequence or wide-scale cybercrime
- *Develop a robust public-private cyber incident response capability*: Manage cyber incidents from identification to resolution in a rapid and replicable manner with prompt and appropriate action

Goal 4.2 Promote Cybersecurity Knowledge and Innovation

Ensure that the nation is prepared for the cyber threats and challenges of tomorrow.

Goal 4.2 Objectives

- *Enhance public awareness*: Ensure that the public recognizes cybersecurity challenges and is empowered to address them
- *Foster a dynamic workforce*: Develop the national knowledge base and human capital capabilities to enable success against current and future threats
- *Invest in innovative technologies, techniques, and procedures*: Create and enhance science, technology, governance mechanisms, and other elements necessary to sustain a safe, secure, and resilient cyber environment

Source: DHS (2010a).

This mission was furthered 4 years later in the 2014 Quadrennial Homeland Security Review, wherein it was stated that "*In light of the risk and potential consequences of cyber events, strengthening the security and resilience of cyberspace has become an important homeland security mission*" (DHS, 2014a). DHS is but one agency of many, however, that address the cybersecurity threat. In addition to private-sector partners who have to implement the cybersecurity measures within their own operations and who are the source of many of the security software, hardware, and other solutions that are developed, DHS works with partners at the federal level. The Department of Justice is tasked with investigating, disrupting, and prosecuting cybercrimes and other threats involving the cyber infrastructure; the Department of Defense and the Intelligence Community work to gather foreign cyber threat information and ensure that the nation's cyber infrastructure is safe from attack; and the Department of Commerce is tasked with developing cybersecurity standards through the efforts of NIST.

National Cyber Incident Response Plan

The president's cybersecurity policy review called for "a comprehensive framework to facilitate coordinated responses by Government, the private sector, and allies to a significant cyber incident." DHS coordinated the interagency, state and local governments, and private-sector working group that developed the National Cyber Incident Response Plan. This plan was created to enable DHS to coordinate the response of multiple federal agencies, state and local governments, international partners, and private industry to incidents at all levels and is designed to be flexible and adaptable to allow synchronization of response activities across jurisdictional lines. The NCIRP is developed in accordance with the standards and principles upon which the National Response Framework is based in order to provide consistency in response procedures and mechanisms. In that vein, the National Response Framework has a cyber incident annex (dubbed the "CIA"), which has not been updated since its inclusion in the former National Response Plan (NRP) in 2004. However, the NCIRP expands upon and updates the information contained in the CIA in recognition that special actions and procedures are required that fall outside the normal scope of NRF operations. Like the NRF, this plan outlines the roles and responsibilities of each tasked federal agency and organizes these tasks into incident management "lanes" (which include homeland security, intelligence, defense, and law enforcement—see Figure 8-2). DHS maintains that any agency involved in the NCIRP should also be familiar with the workings of the NRF, the CIA, and the NIMS considering that cyber incidents could easily have physical consequences that require a more concerted and complex federal response, possibly involving a presidential disaster declaration. The NCIRP is tested through the conduct of the Cyber Storm national exercise program, which simulates large-scale attacks on the nation's critical information infrastructure (see sidebar "Cyber Storm Exercises").

Cyber Storm Exercises

Cyber Storm is the name given to a series of response exercises that focus on the cybersecurity threat. The exercises were conducted every 2 years between 2006 and 2010 and then again in 2013 with the conduct of Cyber Storm IV. The exercises are intended to do the following:

- Examine organizations' capability to prepare for, protect from, and respond to cyberattacks' potential effects.
- Exercise strategic decision making and interagency coordination of incident response(s) in accordance with national-level policy and procedures.
- Validate information-sharing relationships and communications paths for collecting and disseminating cyber incident situational awareness, response, and recovery information.
- Examine means and processes through which to share sensitive information across boundaries and sectors without compromising proprietary or national security interests.

Cyber Storm I was conducted in February 2006. It involved domestic agencies only and involved over 115 different organizations in a number of sectors including information technology, communications, energy, and air transportation. Indicative of the threats at the time, the exercise focused on breakdowns in communications and disruptions in coordination structures between agencies and other actors.

Cyber Storm II was conducted in March 2008. This exercise included international partners and government agencies at all administrative levels. As was true in Cyber Storm I, several private-sector partners were also invited to participate. In this exercise, the sectors impacted were the

Coordination of Cyber Incident Management

Coordinating Agency
DHS—responsible for coordinating incident management activities across the breadth of the incident and across all partners.

Coordinating Center
NCCIC—the point of integration for all information from Federal departments and agencies, State, Local, Tribal, and Territorial Governments, and the private sector related to situational awareness, vulnerabilities, intrusions, incidents, and mitigation activities.

Support to External Stakeholders
NCCIC—provides multi-directional information sharing across all partners.

Homeland Security

- **DHS**—works with all partners to establish and maintain Nationally-integrated cybersecurity and communications situational awareness.
- **DHS**—serves as the National focal point for Cyber Incident management and coordination during cyber-specific incidents.

Coordinating Centers
- NCCIC
  - US-CERT
  - NCC
  - ICS-CERT
- NOC
  - NICC
  - NRCC

Associated D/As
- Cabinet departments
- Independent agencies and government corporations

Support to External Stakeholders
- **State, Local, Tribal, and Territorial**—Upon request, coordinate and assist with incident response.
- **Private Sector**—coordinate on the collection, analysis, and sharing of such data in real-time, to help prioritize actions and resource allocation.

Intelligence

- **IC**—provides attack sensing and warning capabilities to characterize the cyber threat and attribution of attacks and forestall future incidents.

Coordinating Centers
- IC-IRC
- NTOC
- NCIJTF

Associated D/As
- Cabinet departments
- Independent agencies and government corporations

Support to External Stakeholders
- **State, Local, Tribal, and Territorial and Private Sector**—share appropriate classified intelligence with cleared CIKR crisis management and threat intelligence groups at the lowest classification possible to allow the provision of sector impact assessments and response coordination.

Defense

- **DOD**—establishes and maintains shared situational awareness and directs the operation and defense of the .mil network.
- **DOD**—works with partners to gain attribution of the cyber threat, offer mitigation techniques, and take action to deter or defend against cyber attacks which pose an imminent threat to national security.
- **National Guard Bureau**—communicates and coordinates the synchronization of NG forces (to include but not limited to cyberspace, communications, and signals organizations) in response to cyber incidents

Coordinating Centers
- JTF-GNO/CYBERCOM
- NTOC
- DC3

Associated D/As
- Cabinet departments
- Independent agencies and government corporations

Support to External Stakeholders
- **State, Local, Tribal, and Territorial**—DOD coordinates DSCA when requested

Law Enforcement

- **DOJ**—maintains and shares situational awareness about law enforcement activities
- **AG**—lead for criminal investigations
- **DOJ**—leads the national effort to investigate and prosecute cybercrime.

Coordinating Centers
- NCIJTF
- DC3

Associated D/As
- FBI
- USSS

Support to External Stakeholders
- **State, Local, Tribal, and Territorial**—DOJ/FBI/NCIJTF coordinates with law enforcement.
- **Private Sector**—FBI coordinates with InfraGard efforts and works with the private sector regarding the investigation and prosecution of cybercrime.

FIGURE 8 2 Federal cyber incident "lanes" from the NCIRP. *Source: DHS (2010b).*

chemical industry, information technology, communications, and rail and pipeline transportation. The focus of this exercise was testing the processes, procedures, and tools that had been developed since the first exercise 2 years earlier.

Cyber Storm III was conducted in September 2010 and involved a much larger group of stakeholders, including 12 countries, 60 private-sector organizations, 11 state governments, and 8 cabinet-level agencies. The primary purpose of the exercise was to test the new National Cyber Incident Response Plan and the National Cybersecurity and Communications Integration Center.

Cyber Storm IV was conducted in November 2013 and was code-named Evergreen. This exercise was actually a number of different exercises conducted simultaneously at different administrative levels and involved a simulated cyberattack targeting local-level infrastructure. It was unique in that the participants worked at their regular workstations, which created a realistic attack response simulation.

Source: DHS (2014b).

Cybersecurity Within the Department of Homeland Security

Cybersecurity operations within DHS are focused within the Office of Cybersecurity and Communications (CS&C), which falls under the National Protection and Programs Directorate (NPPD). CS&C is tasked with "enhancing the security, resilience, and reliability of the Nation's cyber and communications infrastructure" (DHS, 2014e). CS&C has five primary divisions, which include

- Network Security Deployment,
- Federal Network Resilience,
- Stakeholder Engagement and Cyber Infrastructure Resilience,
- The National Cybersecurity and Communications Integration Center,
- The Office of Emergency Communications.

The Network Security Deployment (NSD) division and the Federal Network Resilience work to address the critical cybersecurity requirements of the federal government, including such things as contracting, acquisitions of new equipment and systems, and interagency networking. The Stakeholder Engagement and Cyber Infrastructure Resilience (SECIR) division is tasked with managing the interface and engagement between DHS and its governmental and nongovernmental partners on national security emergency preparedness and cybersecurity efforts. And the Office of Emergency Communications is primarily concerned with the interoperability of emergency responder communications systems as described later in this text. It is the National Cybersecurity and Communications Integration Center, or NCCIC, where the bulk of cybersecurity efforts to address wider national cybersecurity threats occur.

National Cybersecurity and Communications Integration Center (NCCIC)

The NCCIC is a 24 h, DHS-led coordinated watch and warning center that serves as the nation's principal hub for organizing cyber response efforts and maintaining the national cyber and communications common operational picture. The NCCIC provides information to the public- and private-sector partners that it serves, in order to provide an improved awareness of the threats that exist and that are constantly emerging. It was created to reduce national vulnerability to cyberattacks, by reducing both the number of attacks that occur and the consequences of those that do. In addition to the NCCIC operations and integration office, NCCIC oversees three more branches that include the following:

1. The US Computer Emergency Readiness Team (US-CERT)

US-CERT was established in 2003. It is charged with protecting the US cyber infrastructure by coordinating the nation's defense against and response to cyberattacks. It is responsible for analyzing and reducing cyber threats and vulnerabilities, disseminating warnings and other threat information, and coordinating incident response activities. US-CERT interacts with federal agencies, industry, the research community, state and local governments, and others to disseminate reasoned and actionable cybersecurity information to the public. Its services are available to any interested end user, whether governmental, private-sector, individual, and even international partners. Through its National Cyber Awareness System, US-CERT issues alerts about existing and emerging threats, which include current threats and activity, information about exploits and vulnerabilities, weekly cybersecurity summaries (called "bulletins"), and tips about common security issues. End users are able to subscribe to any or all of these different information resources through the US-CERT subscription system, which is found at http://bit.ly/1xNUlxp. US-CERT also develops and distributes guidance publications on topics related to cybersecurity, examples of which include the following:

- Playing it Safe: Avoiding Online Gaming Risks
- Protecting Aggregated Data
- The Risks of Using Portable Devices
- Cyber Threats to Mobile Phones
- Understanding and Protecting Yourself Against Money Mule Schemes
- Socializing Securely: Using Social Networking Services
- Understanding Voice over Internet Protocol (VoIP)
- Banking Securely Online
- Ten Ways to Improve the Security of a New Computer
- Password Security, Protection, and Management
- Recovering from a Trojan Horse or Virus

Users can subscribe to news feeds that US-CERT distributes through the National Cyber Awareness System (NCAS). These alerts help to increase awareness of cybersecurity threats as they are emerging so that attacks may be limited considering that even with the existence of patches, vulnerabilities will persist until users implement them. The team receives its information from its end users, who report incidents or vulnerabilities using an online incident reporting system, which is located at www.us-cert.gov/forms/report.

2. The Industrial Control Systems Cyber Emergency Response Team (ICS-CERT)

ICS-CERT is the office within NCCIC that is specifically concerned with the control mechanisms of key infrastructure components. These include such things as the computers that control switches, motors, valves, robots, and other automated machines and devices. One of the more serious cyber threats is the terrorist or criminal control of these automated devices that run the nation's critical infrastructure given the destruction that could result if they were damaged or incorrectly operated. ICS-CERT is a team that is tasked with addressing this problem by performing the following tasks and functions (DHS, 2014c):

- Responding to and analyzing control systems-related incidents
- Conducting vulnerability, malware, and digital media analysis
- Providing onsite incident response services
- Providing situational awareness in the form of actionable intelligence
- Coordinating the responsible disclosure of vulnerabilities and associated mitigations
- Sharing and coordinating vulnerability information and threat analysis through information products and alerts

DHS established the Industrial Control Systems Joint Working Group (ISCJWG) to increase information sharing among those stakeholders who use or manufacture industrial control mechanisms. In conjunction with the efforts of this group, ICS-CERT issues alerts and advisories for new and emerging

FIGURE 8-3 Organization of the Office of Cybersecurity and Communications. *Source: DHS (2014e).*

threats; produces instructional documentation, fact sheets, and white papers to facilitate cybersecurity operations at critical facilities; and provides training.

3. The National Coordinating Center for Communications (NCC)

The NCC is a component of the NCCIC that is specifically concerned with ensuring the security of the nation's communications infrastructure. It is tasked with monitoring developing incidents within the United States and throughout the world that have the potential to impact communications systems and components, including terrorist attacks, natural disasters, and other threats. Cybersecurity plays a large role, though this office is not a uniquely cyber-oriented unit. It is the organizational makeup of DHS, which ties cybersecurity and communications together, that explains the nature of this office (see Figure 8-3). The NCC predated the NCCIC and has been a vital component of the nation's emergency response system since the 1990s.

The EINSTEIN Program

EINSTEIN is a DHS-administered program that began in 2000 and that is designed to provide all federal civilian government agencies with the ability to detect intrusions into their networks. It is designed to provide near-real-time identification of the malicious activity and automatically disrupt it when detected. EINSTEIN included several iterations and is currently operating under the third such iteration. The first iteration, dubbed EINSTEIN 1, was developed in 2003. It was designed to automate the collection and analysis of computer network security information from participating agency and government networks to help analysts identify and combat malicious cyber activity that poses a threat to network systems, data protection, and communications infrastructure. *EINSTEIN 2* is the second iteration and was developed in 2008. It uses intrusion detection capabilities and is also provided to the Internet service providers that serve federal agencies to assist them with protecting their computers, networks, and information. On average, this component of the program registers 5.4 million detected intrusions per year or over 450,000 per month. *EINSTEIN 3*, released in 2013, is the third and latest iteration and includes an intrusion prevention capability that provides DHS with the ability to automatically detect and disrupt malicious activity before harm is done to critical networks and systems.

Cybersecurity Role of Other Federal Agencies

As lead on domestic security issues, DHS maintains the most outwardly visible cybersecurity presence in the federal government. However, DHS role is just one of many. Of course, all federal agencies have been faced with the integration of cybersecurity practices into their ongoing operations and programs, including such things as employee training, threat reduction practices (e.g., instituting policies on removable storage devices), and continuity of operations planning. However, several have more distinct roles that play into the nation's cybersecurity strategy. The development and maintenance of the National Cybersecurity Workforce Framework, for instance, which was described previously in this chapter and which is the result of an executive order issued by President Obama in 2013, were tasked to the NIST within the Department of Commerce. Several other federal agencies also contribute to national security in the domain of cyberspace, as described below.

The Federal Bureau of Investigation

As described in Chapter 4, the FBI is the federal government's investigative law enforcement agency. And in addition to the many different categories of crime addressed by the bureau, the FBI has become heavily involved in the investigation and prosecution of crimes that involve a cybersecurity component in their regular work. For many of these cases, cybercrime is the principal focus of investigations.

FBI investigators cooperate with other federal, state, and local law enforcement partners in investigations through the 56 FBI field offices that are spread throughout the nation and via the National Cyber Investigative Joint Task Force (NCIJTF). The FBI also maintains a full-time command center for cyber incidents called "CyWatch," which helps to coordinate these investigative efforts and efforts put forth in the event of an emerging cyber threat or attack.

The FBI supports the private sector in their cybersecurity efforts through a number of projects including the following:

- The Domestic Security Alliance Council
- InfraGard: Through its InfraGard program, the FBI develops partnerships and working relationships with experts in the private, academic, nonprofit, and other sectors in order to increase national capabilities to protect critical infrastructure. The program functions by promoting dialog and fostering communication among the base of member SMEs, which stood at 25,863 in April 2014 (Quinn, 2014).
- The National Cyber-Forensics & Training Alliance: The National Cyber-Forensics & Training Alliance (NCFTA) is an FBI-established quasigovernmental nonprofit agency that began operations in 1997 in Pittsburgh, PA. Its purpose is to allow for greater coordination between law enforcement, private industry, and academia for the purpose of sharing information on cyber threats. Its original focus was reducing spam e-mail, but it has since expanded its focus to include more serious cyber threats including viruses, stock manipulation schemes, telecommunication scams, and other financial fraud. The NCFTA is designed to provide early warning, with notification coming from stakeholder institutions like banking system investigators. NCFTA also facilitates training for its membership, thereby increasing overall capacity to recognize and deal with attacks.

The FBI's Key Partnership Engagement Unit (KPEU) is tasked with conducting targeted outreach to the leadership of large corporations where the risk for cybercrime and cyber espionage is greatest. Because many companies are reticent to share information about attacks for fear of damaging shareholder confidence, these types of relationships are critical to understanding and neutralizing the threat before attacks become more widespread or cause more damage.

The FBI also maintains legal attaché offices at US embassies and consulates abroad, which help to coordinate cybersecurity investigations with foreign governments, when necessary, and help to address issues of jurisdiction when crimes affecting individuals, companies, or government offices in the United States are committed by groups residing outside of the country. These offices provide reports called Joint Indicator Bulletins (JIBs) to help increase the reach of threat information and to enhance international cooperation in identifying and stopping threats.

FBI Cyber Division

The FBI dedicates resources to the investigation of cyber-related incidents through its Cyber Division, which was established in 2002. Cyber Division investigators take on cases that involve everything from cyberterrorism to extortion, crime, and espionage. There are several units within this division that provide specialized services. For instance, the FBI's **Cyber Initiative and Resource Fusion Unit (CIRFU)** maximizes and develops intelligence and analytic resources received from law enforcement, academia, international, and critical corporate private-sector subject matter experts to identify and combat significant actors involved in current and emerging cyber-related criminal and national security threats. **Cyber Action Teams**, or CATs, are specialized teams of investigators with training in computer forensics and cybercrime that respond worldwide to emerging incidents, oftentimes in partnership with other countries' governments. By deploying overseas, they are better able to conduct the necessary on-the-ground investigations of servers and other hardware that might not be possible from the United States, despite that the attacks focused on domestic targets. They can also assist in the operations through which foreign citizen perpetrators of cybercrimes are arrested and charged with the offenses that impacted US interests. **Cyber Task Forces** are also specially trained teams, but in this case, they operate out of the 56 FBI field offices, offering specialized knowledge required to investigate and prosecute cybercrimes.

The **Internet Crime Complaint Center (IC3)** is a resource maintained by the Cyber Division that was established in 1999 to serve as a conduit between victims of Internet-related crime and the law enforcement agencies that investigate and prosecute the crimes reported. The center receives complaints from both within and outside the United States, which number in the hundreds of thousands per year. In 2013, the NC3 received 262,813 complaints, which was down from the all time high of 336,655 received in 2009.

How the IC3 Internet Crime Reporting System Works

The process begins when victims file a complaint with the IC3. Complaints are entered into an extensive tracking database. From there, IC3's analysts review each complaint, identify key characteristics, and group the complaints according to characteristic similarities. They are then collated and referred to the appropriate federal, state, local, tribal, and/or international law enforcement agencies for investigation when required. IC3 analysts also collect relevant case information from other public and protected information sources. The analysts use automated matching systems to identify links and commonalities between different complaints and combine the respective complaints into referral groups for law enforcement. Because IC3 can be remotely accessed, its data are available to law enforcement officers anywhere and anytime. This level of access allows end users in the law enforcement community to aggregate victims and losses to substantiate criminal activity within the user's agency area of jurisdiction and to enhance the development of their cases. Even when the complaints do not result in referrals, they help to identify trends and build statistical reports. Trends are then posted on IC3's website for viewing by the public in order to increase public awareness of the threats that exist.

Source: FBI (2014c).

Critical Thinking

Based on what you have read, do you think that DHS is the appropriate federal entity to lead the government's cybersecurity programs? If so, why; if not, what other agencies would be more appropriate and what is your reasoning?

Based on your knowledge, what do you think are the biggest cybersecurity threats to the United States and why?

The Department of Defense (DOD)

The twenty-first-century military is fully dependent upon cyberspace to function. In fact, it was the US military that in the 1960s funded research that ultimately resulted in the development of what is today's Internet. Intelligence gathering and sharing, operational command and awareness, weapons targeting and deployment, communications, and much more would cease were there to be a disruption. Cyberspace has also proved to be a warfighting theater and a recruiting domain for the United States, its allies, and its adversaries.

In 2009, US Cyber Command was established within the DOD under the US Strategic Command to serve as the central strategic center for DOD cyber operations. It is located in Fort Meade, Maryland. The mission of this new command reads as follows: "USCYBERCOM plans, coordinates, integrates, synchronizes and conducts activities to: direct the operations and defense of specified Department of Defense information networks; and prepare to, and when directed, conduct full spectrum military cyberspace operations in order to enable actions in all domains, ensure US/Allied freedom of action in cyberspace and deny the same to our adversaries" (DOD, 2014).

In March 2011, hackers broke into DOD and contractor information networks and stole approximately 24,000 files documenting new weapons systems that were under development. The attack was believed to have been the work of a foreign intelligence organization (Wyler, 2011). In response, the DOD announced in July 2011 its first comprehensive strategy on cybersecurity entitled Department of Defense Strategy for Operating in Cyberspace. The strategy covers both cybersecurity and cyberwar and establishes the Internet as a domain of war. The blueprint was produced by the new US Cyber Command.

This strategy addresses the cyber domain by means of five specific initiatives, which include (DOD, 2011)

1. treating cyberspace as an operational domain to organize, train, and equip so that DoD can take full advantage of cyberspace's potential;
2. employing new defense operating concepts to protect DoD networks and systems;

3. partnering with other US government departments and agencies and the private sector to enable a whole-of-government cybersecurity strategy;
4. building robust relationships with US allies and international partners to strengthen collective cybersecurity;
5. leveraging the nation's ingenuity through an exceptional cyber workforce and rapid technological innovation.

There remains controversy over the decision to identify cyberspace as a military domain, like what is true with land or sea. To address these concerns, the White House prepared draft guidance to assist agencies in the careful application of the use of the word, indicating its preference for the use of the term *cyberspace*. The DOD has pushed forward with the development of cyber weapons and is considered one of only a handful of countries with cyberwarfare capabilities. The global leaders include the United States, China, and Russia. To a lesser extent, Great Britain, Germany, Israel, and Taiwan also have cyberwarfare capabilities, and there are reports that Iran has developed and deployed damaging viruses (Wilking, 2013). It has developed systems that are used to deter adversaries from using computer hacking or other computer means to attack the United States and has developed viruses that can be used to corrupt critical networks outside of the United States and possibly destroy components of critical infrastructure.

The Department of State

The Department of State handles all direct diplomatic interactions with other countries. As such, the Department of State handles international efforts to address cybersecurity concerns and works to build partnerships with or elicit action on the part of other countries' governments. Cybersecurity operations most often involve attacks that begin overseas, and as such, the State Department must serve as the liaison between the US agencies involved and the counterpart agencies in the foreign country.

The National Science Foundation

The National Science Foundation is the nation's preeminent provider of government research support. In this role, it supports cybersecurity research and development in concert with the National Telecommunications and Information Administration. Within its Directorate for Computer and Information Science & Engineering, NSF maintains a program area "Secure and Trustworthy Cyberspace" (SaTC). In 2011, in conjunction with the National Science and Technology Council (NSTC), NSF issued a strategic plan to guide the nation's cybersecurity research and development efforts. This document, released in December of that year and entitled "Trustworthy Cyberspace: Strategic Plan for the Federal Cybersecurity Research and Development Program," was published by the White House and can be found at http://1.usa.gov/1EYJfXC.

SaTC Proposal Guidelines

The Secure and Trustworthy Cyberspace (SaTC) program welcomes proposals that address cybersecurity from a Trustworthy Computing Systems (TWC) perspective and/or a Social, Behavioral, and Economic Sciences (SBE) perspective or from the Secure, Trustworthy, Assured and Resilient Semiconductors and

Systems (STARSS) perspective. In addition, we welcome proposals that integrate research addressing all of these perspectives. Proposals may be submitted in one of the following three categories:

- *Small projects*: up to $500,000 in total budget, with durations of up to 3 years
- *Medium projects*: $500,001 to $1,200,000 in total budget, with durations of up to 4 years
- *Large projects*: $1,200,001 to $3,000,000 in total budget, with durations of up to 5 years

Projects with Trustworthy Computing Systems and/or Social, Behavioral and Economic Sciences perspectives may include a Transition to Practice (TTP) option, described in a supplementary document of no more than five pages. This document should describe how successful research results are to be further developed, matured, and experimentally deployed in organizations or industries, including in networks and end systems used by members of the NSF science and engineering communities. Proposals with a TTP option may exceed the above-stated funding maxima by up to $167,000 for small projects, $400,000 for medium projects, and $750,000 for large projects.

For small hardware security proposals, the Secure, Trustworthy, Assured and Resilient Semiconductors and Systems (STARSS) perspective is focused specifically on hardware research innovation that addresses SaTC goals and includes the opportunity to collaborate closely with industry. STARSS proposals may not include either the TWC or SBE perspective but may include a TTP option following the same guidelines as above.

In addition, the SaTC program seeks proposals focusing entirely on cybersecurity education with total budgets limited to $300,000 and durations of up to 2 years.

Source: NSF (2014).

National Institute for Standards and Technology (NIST), Department of Commerce

In addition to leading the development of the cybersecurity framework, NIST was central in the development of the National Initiative for Cybersecurity Education (NICE). The NICE initiative supports the building of a knowledge base required to reduce cyber threats, which is provided in a number of different environments. This includes federal government employees, students in all grades from kindergarten to postgraduate school, and those in the private-sector workforce and elsewhere. The program's goal is to establish an operational, sustainable, and continually improving cybersecurity education program for the nation to promote the use of sound practices in relation to the cyber network—for the purpose of protecting national security. NICE has grown to include over 20 federal departments and agencies. NIST is also the lead of the National Strategy for Trusted Identities in Cyberspace. The purpose of this program is to reduce the ability of cyber criminals, terrorists, or other entities to hide or disguise their identities online.

Critical Thinking

Based on what you have read, does the proliferation of government committees and initiatives in cybersecurity make sense and do you think there are other actions that they should consider taking? What are your thoughts on DOD making cyberspace a new area, or domain, requiring military vigilance?

Private-Sector Cybersecurity

The private sector, including individuals, businesses, and private-sector owners and operators of critical infrastructure, is subject to regular cyberattacks. There is no way that the federal government could take action that would provide any level of protection from cyber criminals, cyber terrorists, and cyberspies, which would negate the need for private-sector entities and individuals to take action to protect themselves, their systems, and their data.

For individuals, the key lies in behavior and software protections. Understanding the threats that exist and how the individuals are vulnerable to them is the first step. Anyone with an Internet connection and an e-mail address is exposed to cyber threats, regardless of their browsing preferences or activities. Even legitimate websites, or e-mails from trusted sources, are regularly compromised, and this results in exposure. Additionally, social engineering schemes like phishing can be so well crafted as to fool even the most tech-savvy user. There are a number of options available to individuals to increase protection from cyber threats, including virus protection for all devices, secure access to wireless networks, and enhanced login security for online banking or other important transactions, among other options. Unfortunately, even with all of these in place, many users still become victimized because they encountered an emergent threat or simply because a retailer they used was compromised and their data were stolen in the conduct of that attack.

For businesses, the same is true. Businesses are targeted by criminals seeking to obtain their customer data, their trade secrets and intellectual property, and their negotiation tactics or simply to disrupt their operations or tarnish their reputation. Many businesses are increasing their network security resources to account for the increase in risk and are collaborating with government agencies to ensure that their operations are protected. In the event of a breach, businesses are finding that they face the prospect of devastating financial consequences, especially if they are found to be responsible through negligence. Target, which experienced a breach that involved the personal and financial data of over 100 million customers, lost a significant amount of business during the key holiday shopping season and incurred the expense of providing credit protection services to most of the customers whose data had been stolen. It took months for the company to regain the trust of their customer base, and there may always be an association of vulnerability associated with the company name given the scope of the attack. Because of the reputation risk associated with cyber breaches, many companies have been reluctant to announce when their data have been stolen or even when a breach has been identified. The FBI and DHS have been working with the private sector to establish a reporting system that is built upon trust and confidentiality in order to better limit the consequence of these attacks and identify those responsible (as well as to enable impacted customers to protect their finances). The release of the National Cybersecurity Workforce Framework is the guiding document for these efforts.

DHS "Stop. Think. Connect." Campaign

The Stop.Think.Connect. Campaign is a national public awareness campaign aimed at increasing the understanding of cyber threats and empowering the American public to be safer and more secure online. The campaign was launched on October 4, 2010, in conjunction with National Cyber Security Awareness Month. It is part of a coordinated multistakeholder effort to reduce vulnerability to cyber threats and likewise reduce the financial losses they cause. DHS serves as the government lead for the campaign.

The message of the campaign is as follows:

STOP

- Stop hackers from accessing your accounts—set secure passwords.

- Stop sharing too much information—keep your personal information personal.
- Stop—trust your gut. If something doesn't feel right, stop what you are doing.

THINK
- Think about the information you want to share before you share it.
- Think how your online actions can affect your offline life.
- Think before you act—don't automatically click on links.

CONNECT
- Connect over secure networks.
- Connect with people you know.
- Connect with care and be on the lookout for potential threats.

The campaign has developed instructional and marketing materials for a number of different stakeholder types, including students, parents and educators, young professionals, older Americans, government, industry, small business, and law enforcement. Several social marketing materials are provided by the campaign, including posters and bookmarks. One of these is provided as Figure 8-4.

FIGURE 8-4 Stop.Think.Connect. Campaign poster. *Source: DHS (2014f).*

Critical Infrastructure Protection

The nation's infrastructure is extensive and includes all of the basic physical and organizational structures, systems, services, and facilities that are required for the society to operate. The construction and expansion of infrastructure represent a principal driver in any nation's development trajectory given that it serves as the foundation of its society, the vehicle for commerce and governance, and many other factors. The quality and reach of infrastructure are so closely tied to a nation's development progress simply because it is so expensive both to build and to maintain. And any subsequent advancement in infrastructure development represents additional up-front costs and an ongoing budgetary burden. Moreover, as nations expand and improve their infrastructure, their national security vulnerabilities likewise expand given the prospect of growing dependencies and consequences of outage or loss.

The various components, or sectors, that make up a nation's infrastructure are both interconnected and interdependent. They collectively provide the functional framework for political, social, and economic operations. The different infrastructure sectors vary greatly in their characteristics but generally fall into two classes: object-oriented and network-oriented. Object-oriented infrastructure components are made up of stand-alone units, even if multiple units of that infrastructure exist. Hospitals, for example, are individual "objects" that contribute to a nation's health infrastructure. Network-oriented infrastructure is intrinsically more interconnected and often relies upon transmission lines traversing great distances. Pipelines, communication wires, power transmission lines, and roadways, for example, each support different network-oriented infrastructure sectors (Studer, 2000).

Critical infrastructure, or CI, is a subcategory of infrastructure that includes those assets, systems, and networks, whether physical or virtual, which are so vital that their failure or destruction would have a debilitating impact on security, governance, public health and safety, public confidence, commerce, or other societal factors (DHS, 2008). CI sectors in the United States are provided in the sidebar "Critical Infrastructure Sectors."

Critical Infrastructure Sectors

The 2013 US National Infrastructure Protection Plan (NIPP) defines 16 different CI sectors. This number has been reduced from 18 as different categories have been merged together (e.g., a category "Postal and Shipping" was merged into Transportation.) The 16 current CI sectors include the following:

- Food and Agriculture
- Commercial Facilities
- Dams
- Energy
- Information Technology
- Banking and Finances
- Communications
- Defense Industrial Base
- Government Facilities
- Transportation Systems (including Postal and Shipping)
- Chemical
- Critical Manufacturing

- Emergency Services
- Healthcare and Public Health
- Nuclear Reactors, Materials, and Waste
- Water

Source: DHS (2014d).

Communities, particularly urban ones, have become increasingly dependent on all infrastructure categories. Despite their high cost, the intrinsic value of CI to the successful functioning of society far exceeds the direct expenditures associated with their physical structures and facilities. Their true worth is better measured in terms of the quality of life enhancements and increased efficiency of commerce and governance enjoyed by the societies they serve. When considering the total value of such infrastructure with regard to investments in their protection, these less tangible benefits must be accounted for. CI loss can quite easily translate to the loss of commerce, security, safety, movement, life-sustaining goods replenishment, and other primary and secondary impacts. Owing to the strategic role CI plays in the operation of these systems and the complexity and interconnectedness of these systems, associated risk considerations are numerous and unique. These include the following:

- *Criticality*: The vital nature of CI, in terms of its role in ensuring the safe, secure, and efficient functioning of society, requires that great efforts be made to protecting it from identified hazards or threats. In the event of loss or disruption, immediate correction is necessary even in the earliest phases of response given that failure to do so exacerbates consequences and precludes many response and recovery functions.
- *Exposure*: The placement of infrastructure typically mirrors that of human settlement patterns. As such, the physical vulnerability of the population can often translate to that of infrastructure. The dispersed nature of networked infrastructure often means that it is impacted in some manner no matter where in the community or the country the disaster occurs. Moreover, disasters affecting great geographic ranges will have profound impacts on CI, notably that of networked infrastructure.
- *Redundancy*: Infrastructure complexity and cost can hinder the availability of redundancy systems. However, consider the loss of a single critical bridge or the destruction of a major regional seaport—both of which would isolate thousands and devastate the economy—and the importance of redundancy quickly becomes apparent.
- *System complexity*: Infrastructure systems are complex and interconnected. The failure or loss of just one CI system can rapidly cascade across multiple infrastructure sectors as dependency lines are severed. System complexities can be understood through mapping and the use of event and fault tree analyses, but only to a limited degree in the absence of actual experience.
- *Infrastructure as a risk source*: Infrastructure damage or loss is a common disaster consequence. However, such losses can occur irrespective of initiating events and can in turn result in significant and immediate life-threatening conditions arising. For instance, the failure of a dam can result in no-notice, extreme flooding. Contamination from nuclear power plant emergencies or hazardous materials releases (e.g., freight rail accident or oil spills) can have widespread and long-lasting impacts. Emergency managers must understand not only the service interruption ramifications of each infrastructure component's loss but also the hazardous conditions that may present from their damage or failure.

- *Geographic range and populations served*: The world is urbanizing, including in the United States. People are moving into denser living conditions, with populations reaching up to and exceeding 50,000 people/mi^2. In these and all urban centers, CI disruptions affecting even small geographic ranges can significantly impact millions of people. Infrastructure systems are also notable in that they may provide service across great distances. Disruptions can therefore extend tens to hundreds of miles beyond the impacted area.
- *Jurisdiction*: Infrastructure systems are owned, operated, and/or regulated by government agencies, private-sector entities, and quasigovernment or public-private partnerships with shared responsibility. This may present risk management challenges given the differences in jurisdiction and responsibility of public-sector officials and the motivation to and/or ability of owners and operators to take risk-reduction measures. When infrastructure is privately owned, it may still fall upon government to fund or support risk reduction and/or reconstruction as national security and social recovery are both at stake. Private infrastructure also presents significant public risk, with dams being an obvious example.
- *Terrorist and saboteur valuation*: CI is a preferred terrorist and saboteur target given the physical and symbolic impact successful attacks achieve. Attacks on transportation are common and often result in mass casualties. Government, energy, communications, and other CI components are also sought given the significant consequences such attacks generate. As described earlier in this chapter, cyberattacks on infrastructure are growing in number across all infrastructure sectors, oftentimes targeting the computer control mechanisms of chemical, electricity, water, and transportation systems.

Sources of Infrastructure Risk and Vulnerability

The primary sources of CI risk and hazard exposure closely mirror the hazards and risks that affect the community or the country where the infrastructure components or networks are located. Additionally, infrastructure failure itself, even in the absence of an external force, is an additional and significant hazard. Infrastructure risk and vulnerability factors are closely tied, and understanding each enables risk reduction to occur. The typical sources of critical infrastructure risk are numerous, oftentimes involving one or more of the following categories (IRP, 2010):

- *Poor or misguided land use planning*: Improper siting is the most likely source of infrastructure vulnerability. While ignorance of hazard exposure accounts for a small number of siting issues, many factors drive the intentional siting of infrastructure on high-risk land including (among others) proximity to resources (e.g., water), proximity to populations, specific land requirements (e.g., long swaths of level land for airport runways), or the availability of undeveloped or low-cost land. Network-oriented infrastructure may have no option for low-risk siting given the requirement to extend continuously from node to node. Other influential factors include inadequate control of surrounding land, changes in hazard exposure over time, and changes in risk awareness.
- *Poor, weak, or inappropriate construction materials and inappropriate design*: IC must be constructed with materials capable of resisting likely hazard forces and designed to withstand those forces. Older infrastructure may have been built without the benefit of modern technologies or using construction codes that are now outdated. This is especially true with the nation's transportation infrastructure, which is quickly aging as described in Chapter 7.

- *Neglected, deferred, or improper maintenance*: As IC facilities, equipment, and networks age, exposure to the elements, gravity, and wear and tear from use cause them to weaken. Their ability to withstand even ordinary natural forces eventually drop as a result. Maintenance must be conducted to counteract deterioration and prevent unexpected failure. Improperly maintained infrastructure can and often does fail even in the absence of a precipitating disaster.
- *Cascading failure*: The complex dependencies between various infrastructure components create vulnerability. Weakness of one infrastructure component can easily translate to vulnerability in all other infrastructure systems and components that depend on or are otherwise associated with it (see sidebar "Squirrels and Infrastructure Risk").
- *Climate change*: Changes in the global climate are significantly altering the nature of IC hazard risk. Stronger storms, more severe flooding, and greater temperature extremes all result in increased stresses. Roadways, pipelines, transmission lines, facilities, and other components of infrastructure have all incurred impacts at rapidly increasing rates over time due to these global changes.
- *Urbanization and remoteness*: Urbanization concentrates people and wealth into small, often vulnerable pockets. When disasters impact urban areas, the likelihood that a significant portion of IC, industrial output, and governance will be affected greatly increases. Remote, isolated rural areas also exacerbate IC risk. Even minor impacts to infrastructure can have profound impacts on remote populations living far outside the reaches of standard national and regional government services.
- *Regulation*: Effective regulation must be in place where private-sector CI ownership and/or operation exists. The absence of such measures may encourage businesses to place profits over safety given the typically high costs of risk reduction. However, social, political, and economic vulnerabilities are all tied to the ability of infrastructure owners/operators to prevent damage and loss of service, to manage actual incidents, and to effectively and quickly recover from events.

Squirrels and Infrastructure Risk

A 2014 event on cybersecurity hosted by the Brookings Institution included a discussion on the true threat posed by cyber terrorists, especially in relation to other relative risks. In this discussion, it was noted that terrorists have yet to take down the nation's infrastructure by means of cyberattack. On the other hand, each and every year, there are hundreds of incidents that involve squirrels inadvertently knocking out power to populations that at times number into thousands of people. These outages have also affected the Internet and telephone communications networks. Panelists felt that these data suggest the nation approaches infrastructure protection in an unbalanced manner that does not accurately account for statistical risk in its prioritization.

Source: Dews (2014) and Mooallem (2013).

Before the creation of DHS, the Clinton administration grew increasingly concerned about US critical infrastructure risk following the bombings of two US embassies and various overseas military facilities. In May 1998, President Clinton issued Presidential Decision Directive/NSC-63, "Critical Infrastructure Protection," to spur government action to address the protection of infrastructure and key resources. This directive was comprehensive in its language and called for the development of what has become the foundation of today's federal government strategy for preserving and protecting national critical infrastructure assets. Many of the ideas and programs espoused by PDD-63 and subsequently developed or put into action were continued even after the transition into the Bush administration. The terrorist attacks of September 11, 2001, only added new depth to the notion of the national security implications of critical infrastructure protection. The full text of this directive is available at http://bit.ly/1u9Ojlw.

In the wake of September 11, the focus on CI protection policy expanded. Two major documents released in a relatively short timeframe provided the federal government significant authority to expand activities centered around the protection of critical infrastructure. These included the Homeland Security Act of 2002 and Homeland Security Presidential Directive 7 (HSPD-7), "Critical Infrastructure Identification, Prioritization, and Protection."

The Homeland Security Act of 2002 provided primary authorization for and directed the creation of the Department of Homeland Security. It also assigned DHS the responsibility for developing a comprehensive plan to secure critical infrastructure and required that the new department develop recommendations for measures to protect the nation's key resources and critical infrastructure of the United States.

HSPD 7 expanded upon the tasking of the 2002 legislation by requiring the establishment of a framework by which the new department and its partners would be able to identify, prioritize, and protect the critical infrastructure that existed in every community from the increasing risk of terrorist attack (and later expanded to include all hazards). For each of the critical infrastructure sectors mentioned in sidebar "Critical Infrastructure Sectors" located earlier in this chapter, the directive designated a federal "Sector-Specific Agency" (SSA) that was on the hook to lead the development and oversight of protection and resilience-building programs and activities in their particular sector of influence. The directive further required DHS to identify gaps in terms of what sectors were critical and how those sectors should be organized, establishing new sectors to fill such gaps when necessary. In March 2008, DHS did just that by establishing the Critical Manufacturing Sector.

In February 2013, almost 10 years following the issuance of HSPD-7, President Obama signed Presidential Policy Directive-21 (PPD-21), "Critical Infrastructure Security and Resilience." This latest directive builds upon each of the previous ones by stating that an inclusive national strategy involving all stakeholders at all government levels and in the private and nongovernmental sectors is required to adequately address the risks that threaten critical infrastructure. It also further clarifies the infrastructure protection roles of a number of federal agencies, including DHS and the SSAs, that had previously played a less significant role. The directive listed three "Strategic Imperatives" that are indicative of where the Obama administration felt infrastructure protection deficiencies were greatest. These include (White House, 2013) the following:

1. Refine and clarify functional relationships across the federal government to advance the national unity of effort to strengthen critical infrastructure security and resilience
2. Enable efficient information exchange by identifying baseline data and systems requirements for the federal government
3. Implement an integration and analysis function to inform planning and operational decisions regarding critical infrastructure

Sector-Specific Agencies

PPD-21 identifies the following roles and responsibilities for the SSAs (see Figure 8-5).

Each critical infrastructure sector has unique characteristics, operating models, and risk profiles. The Federal SSA or co-SSA assigned to each sector has institutional knowledge and specialized expertise about its sector(s). Recognizing existing statutory or regulatory authorities of specific federal departments and agencies and leveraging existing sector familiarity and relationships, SSAs

- coordinate with DHS and other relevant federal departments and agencies and collaborate with critical infrastructure owners and operators, where appropriate with independent regulatory agencies and with state, local, tribal, and territorial (SLTT) entities, as appropriate to implement PPD-21;
- serve as a day-to-day federal interface for the dynamic prioritization and coordination of sector-specific activities;
- carry out incident management responsibilities consistent with statutory authority and other appropriate policies, directives, or regulations;
- provide, support, or facilitate technical assistance and consultations for that sector to identify vulnerabilities and help mitigate incidents, as appropriate; and
- support the secretary of Homeland Security's statutory reporting requirements by providing, on an annual basis, sector-specific critical infrastructure information.

Sector-Specific Agency	Critical Infrastructure Sector
Department of Agriculture[a] Department of Health and Human Services	Food and Agriculture
Department of Defense[b]	Defense Industrial Base
Department of Energy[c]	Energy[d]
Department of Health and Human Services	Healthcare and Public Health
Department of the Treasury	Financial Services
Environmental Protection Agency	Water and Wastewater Services
Department of Homeland Security	▪ Chemical ▪ Commercial Facilities ▪ Communications ▪ Critical Manufacturing ▪ Dams ▪ Emergency Services ▪ Information Technology ▪ Nuclear Reactors, Materials, and Waste
Department of Homeland Security, General Services Administration	Government Facilities[e]
Department of Homeland Security, Department of Transportation	Transportation Systems

FIGURE 8-5 Sector-Specific Agencies. a—The Department of Agriculture is responsible for agriculture and food (meat, poultry, and processed egg products). b—The Department of Health and Human Services is responsible for food other than meat, poultry, and processed egg products. c—Nothing in this plan impairs or otherwise affects the authority of the Secretary of Defense over the Department of Defense (DoD), including the chain of command for military forces from the president as commander in chief, to the Secretary of Defense, to the commander of military forces or military command and control procedures. d—The Energy Sector includes the production, refining, storage, and distribution of oil, gas, and electric power. The Department of Homeland Security is the SSA for commercial nuclear power facilities and for dams. e—The Department of Education is the SSA for the Education Facilities Subsector of the Government Facilities Sector; the Department of the Interior is the SSA for the National Monuments and Icons Subsector of the Government Facilities Sector. *Source: DHS (2013b).*

Source: DHS (2013b).

The National Infrastructure Protection Plan

Since 2006, the federal government has organized its diverse infrastructure protection policies according to a comprehensive plan dubbed the National Infrastructure Protection Plan, or NIPP. To date, there have been three iterations of this plan, the latest of which was released in late 2013 on the heels of PPD-21. This latest plan updates the document's 2009 version, which had at the time replaced an original version released in 2006. Each version has helped to define the mission, goals, and objectives of national CI protection policy and has provided a description of the mechanisms through which the federal government would support infrastructure protection. The roles of the various governmental and nongovernmental stakeholders have been described in very high-level language, and priorities for action have been stated. The subtitle of this latest version, "Partnering for Critical Infrastructure Security and Resilience," is indicative of the recognized need for collaborative action to achieve any meaningful levels of resilience.

Protection under the NIPP as stated has included a wide range of activities such as improving security protocols; hardening facilities; building resiliency and redundancy; incorporating hazard resistance into facility design; initiating active or passive countermeasures; installing security systems; leveraging "self-healing" technologies; promoting workforce surety programs; implementing cybersecurity measures, training, and exercises; and business continuity planning, among others. Protection includes actions to mitigate the overall risk to critical infrastructure assets, systems, networks, functions, or their interconnecting links resulting from exposure, injury, destruction, incapacitation, or exploitation.

To focus the pursuit of critical infrastructure protection activities, the 2013 NIPP lists five central goals, including

- assessing and analyzing threats to, vulnerabilities of, and consequences to critical infrastructure to inform risk management activities;
- securing critical infrastructure against human, physical, and cyber threats through sustainable efforts to reduce risk while accounting for the costs and benefits of security investments;
- enhancing critical infrastructure resilience by minimizing the adverse consequences of incidents through advance planning and mitigation efforts and employing effective responses to save lives and ensure the rapid recovery of essential services;
- sharing actionable and relevant information across the critical infrastructure community to build awareness and enable risk-informed decision making; and
- promoting learning and adaptation during and after exercises and incidents (DHS, 2013b).

Roles and Responsibilities Under the 2013 NIPP

The 2013 NIPP organizes critical infrastructure into 16 sectors and designates a federal department or agency as the lead coordinator—Sector-Specific Agency (SSA)—for each sector. There are also a number of coordinating councils that structure the action of the different stakeholders involved in each of these sectors. These include (also see Figure 8-6) the following:

- *Sector Coordinating Councils (SCCs)*: Self-organized, self-run, and self-governed private-sector councils consisting of owners and operators and their representatives, which interact on a wide range of sector-specific strategies, policies, activities, and issues. SCCs serve

		Critical Infrastructure Partnership Advisory Council		
Critical Infrastructure Sector	**Sector-Specific Agency**	**Sector Coordinating Councils (SCCs)**	**Government Coordinating Councils (GCCs)**	**Regional Consortia**
Chemical	Department of Homeland Security	✓	✓	
Commercial Facilities (i)		✓	✓	
Communications (i)		✓	✓	
Critical Manufacturing		✓	✓	
Dams		✓	✓	
Emergency Services (i)		✓	✓	
Information Technology (i)		✓	✓	
Nuclear Reactors, Materials & Waste		✓	✓	
Food & Agriculture	Department of Agriculture, Department of Health and Human Services	✓	✓	
Defense Industrial Base (i)	Department of Defense	✓	✓	
Energy (i)	Department of Energy	✓	✓	
Healthcare & Public Health (i)	Department of Health and Human Services	✓	✓	
Financial Services (i)	Department of the Treasury	Uses separate coordinating entity	✓	
Water & Wastewater Systems (i)	Environmental Protection Agency	✓	✓	
Government Facilities	Department of Homeland Security, General Services Administration	Sector does not have an SCC	✓	
Transportation Systems (i)	Department of Homeland Security, Department of Transportation	Various SCCs are broken down by transportation mode or subsector.	✓	

(i) Indicates that a sector (or a subsector within the sector) has a designated information-sharing organization.

FIGURE 8-6 Sector and cross sector coordinating structures. *Source: DHS (2013b).*

as principal collaboration points between the government and private-sector owners and operators for critical infrastructure security and resilience policy coordination and planning and a range of related sector-specific activities.

- *Critical Infrastructure Cross-Sector Council*: Consisting of the chairs and vice chairs of the SCCs, this private-sector council coordinates cross sector issues, initiatives, and interdependencies to support critical infrastructure security and resilience.
- *Government Coordinating Councils (GCCs)*: Consisting of representatives from across various levels of government (including federal, state, local, tribal, and territorial), as appropriate to the operating landscape of each individual sector, these councils enable interagency, intergovernmental, and cross jurisdictional coordination within and across sectors and partner with SCCs on public-private efforts.
- *Federal Senior Leadership Council (FSLC)*: Consisting of senior officials from the SSAs and other federal departments and agencies with a role in critical infrastructure security and resilience, the FSLC facilitates communication and coordination on critical infrastructure security and resilience across the federal government.
- *State, Local, Tribal, and Territorial Government Coordinating Council (SLTTGCC)*: Consisting of representatives from across state, local, tribal, and territorial (SLTT) government entities, the SLTTGCC promotes the engagement of SLTT partners in national critical infrastructure security and resilience efforts and provides an organizational structure to coordinate across jurisdictions on state and local government guidance, strategies, and programs.
- *Regional Consortium Coordinating Council (RC3)*: This council comprises regional groups and coalitions around the country engaged in various initiatives to advance critical infrastructure security and resilience in the public and private sectors.
- *Information-sharing organizations*: Organizations including Information Sharing and Analysis Centers (ISACs) serve operational and dissemination functions for many sectors, subsectors, and other groups and facilitate sharing of information.

Source: DHS (2013b).

The basic framework of the NIPP focuses on managing risk, organizing and partnerships, information sharing, and program sustainability. To support managing risks, the plan defines a process that includes steps to identify, assess, and prioritize risks; implement protective measures; and measure the effectiveness of those measures. The 2013 NIPP presents a risk management approach that is similar to other risk management guidelines previously ascribed by DHS and FEMA to address hazard risk management needs in other areas of need (e.g., for community emergency planning purposes or for the development of a hazard mitigation plan), though there is instruction that is specific to the infrastructure sectors. The five steps of the NIPP risk management process include

1. setting infrastructure goals and objectives,
2. identifying infrastructure,
3. assessing and analyzing risks,

4. implementing risk management activities,
5. measuring effectiveness.

The 2006 and 2009 versions of the NIPP called for the development of sector-specific plans (SSPs), which detail the application of the NIPP framework to the unique characteristics of each sector. Each SSP does the following for the sector it applies to:

- Defines the various security partners, statutory authorities, regulatory bases, roles and responsibilities, and interdependencies
- Establishes new procedures or institutionalizes those that already exist in the sector regarding interaction between sector stakeholders, information sharing, coordination, and partnership
- Establishes security goals and objectives
- Identifies any international considerations
- Defines or otherwise documents any sector-specific risk management approaches or methodologies the SSAs will use (DHS, 2013c)

Critical Thinking

Under the Clinton PDD-63, sector responsibility was spread among the federal agencies, but now, the DHS has assumed lead responsibilities for many of the critical infrastructure sectors. Do you have an opinion on which approach is better?

Under the DHS approach, do you think any of these could be better done by another agency, for example, assigning nuclear reactors, materials, and waste to the Nuclear Regulatory Commission?

DHS Office of Infrastructure Protection

Within the DHS National Protection and Programs Directorate is the Office of Infrastructure Protection (IP). It is through this office that the federal government's critical infrastructure protection programs and policies are organized and directed. IP directs the development of guidance for the owners and operators of critical infrastructure as they assess and address their vulnerabilities and risks and monitors infrastructure threats in order to provide alerts and warnings. IP is organized according to five divisions, which include (see Figure 8-7) the following:

- The Infrastructure Information Collection Division (IICD)

This office leads the federal government's efforts to gather and manage information on critical infrastructure inventory, vulnerabilities, and risks. It supports these efforts by providing data collection standards and tools. Until 2014, IICD maintained the Automated Critical Asset Management System (ACAMS) to store and provide access to data related to these needs, though this program has since been canceled (the Infrastructure Protection Gateway (IP Gateway), which is a single IP-hosted knowledge management interface for all CI partners, still hosts all of the legacy ACAMS data). IICD also manages the collection of data to inform the National Critical Infrastructure Prioritization Program (NCIPP), which enables the federal government and state, local, tribal, and territorial governments to prioritize their protection needs.

- The Infrastructure Security Compliance Division (ISCD)

This office has a specific function related to the chemical infrastructure sector. ISCD implements the Chemical Facility Anti-Terrorism Standards (CFATS), which provides minimum protection standards for chemical facilities that are vulnerable to terrorism, sabotage, crime, or other threats. Protection at chemical

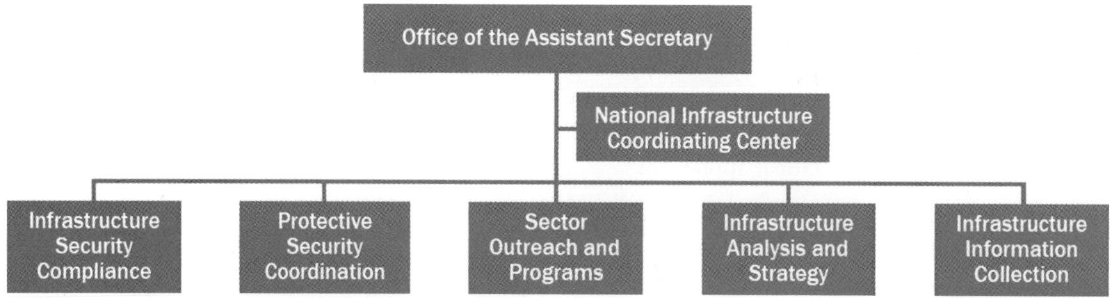

FIGURE 8-7 Office of Infrastructure Protection organizational chart. *Source: DHS (2012).*

facilities is particularly important because a breach could quickly lead to widespread death, injuries, or environmental damage depending on the chemicals that were involved.

- The National Infrastructure Coordination Center (NICC)

  The NICC is a full-time fully staffed facility that fosters information sharing among the various CI stakeholders and serves as the central incident management coordination center for DHS, the SSAs, and the owners and operators of critical infrastructure components. The NICC collects and shares real-time information on threats and hazards, enables information sharing between the IC stakeholders, evaluates the infrastructure data and information that is collected for accuracy, and provides decision support on actions that stakeholders need to take (relating to security, response, and recovery.)

- The Protective Security Coordination Division (PSCD)

  PSCD supports risk management for the CI stakeholders. In addition to supporting the hazard identification, vulnerability assessment, and capability assessment processes, PSCD helps CI owners and operators to identify threat reduction options and supports them if they ever must respond to or recover from an incident. PSCD staff are positioned throughout the country in all 50 states and Puerto Rico. These Regional Directors and Protective Security Advisors work directly with state and local governments and the infrastructure owners and operators themselves. The Office for Bombing Prevention is a special office within this division that assists IC owners and operators with the assessment and management of attacks involving explosive devices.

- The Sector Outreach and Programs Division (SOPD)

  SOPD is tasked with the partnership-building efforts outlined in the NIPP. It also serves as the SSA in the 6 critical infrastructure sectors for which DHS is designated, which includes Chemical, Commercial Facilities, Critical Manufacturing, Dams, Emergency Services, and Nuclear Reactors, Materials, and Waste.

The Infrastructure Analysis and Strategy Division, pictured in the current organizational chart (see Figure 8-7), was elevated to "office" status within NPPD and renamed the Office of Cyber and Infrastructure Analysis (OCIA). OCIA now supports critical infrastructure protection specifically in terms of the cyber threats and vulnerabilities that exist. This move was made as a direct result of PPD-21 and EO 13636, both of which called for the identification of convergence areas between the two issues (i.e., where cybersecurity influenced critical infrastructure protection and vice versa).

State and Local Governments

Under the NIPP, state, local, tribal, and territorial governments are responsible for implementing the CI protection goals and objectives as described and in line with their jurisdictional authority. These roles fall in line with their responsibility to protect public safety and welfare and to ensure the provision of essential services to communities and industries within their jurisdictions. State and local activities are coordinated through the cross sector coordination structures previously listed, specifically that of the State, Local, Tribal, and Territorial Government Coordinating Council (SLTTGCC). The NIPP language specific to the SLTT role is provided in sidebar "SLTTGCC NIPP Roles and Responsibilities."

SLTTGCC NIPP Roles and Responsibilities

SLTT governments implement the homeland security mission, protect public safety and welfare, and ensure the provision of essential services to communities and industries within their jurisdictions. They also ensure the security and resilience of critical infrastructure under their control and that owned and operated by other parties within their jurisdictions. Their efforts are critical to the effective planning and implementation of critical infrastructure security and resilience activities. Since SLTT officials are often the first on the scene of an incident, they are critical to time-sensitive, postevent critical infrastructure response and recovery activities. State, territorial, and tribal governments are also conduits for requests for federal assistance when a threat or incident situation exceeds the capabilities of public- and private-sector partners at lower jurisdictional levels.

Critical infrastructure security and resilience programs form an essential component of SLTT homeland security strategies, particularly with regard to establishing funding priorities and informing security and resilience investment decisions. To facilitate effective critical infrastructure security and resilience and performance measurement, these programs should address all core elements of this *national plan*, where appropriate, including key cross jurisdictional security and information-sharing linkages and specific critical infrastructure security and resilience activities focused on risk management. These programs play a primary role in the identification and protection of critical infrastructure regionally and locally and also support DHS and SSA efforts to identify, ensure connectivity with, and enable the security and resilience of critical infrastructure of national significance within the jurisdiction.

State and territorial governments establish partnerships, facilitate coordinated information sharing, and enable planning and preparedness for critical infrastructure security and resilience within their jurisdictions. They are crucial coordination hubs, bringing together prevention, protection, mitigation, response, and recovery authorities, capabilities, and resources among local jurisdictions, across sectors, and between regional entities. States and territories receive critical infrastructure information from the federal government to support national and state critical infrastructure security and resilience programs. In addition, states and territories provide information to DHS, as part of the grants process or through homeland security strategy updates, regarding state or territorial priorities, requirements, and critical infrastructure-related funding needs.

States and territories should work with state- and territorial-level sector-specific agencies to support the vision, mission, and goals of this *national plan* within those sectors, as appropriate, and engage subject matter experts at the sector level to assist with this effort.

State and territorial programs should address all relevant aspects of critical infrastructure security and resilience, leverage support from homeland security assistance programs that apply across the homeland security mission area, and reflect priority activities in their strategies to ensure that resources are effectively allocated. Effective statewide and regional critical infrastructure security and resilience efforts should be integrated into the overarching homeland security program framework at the state or territorial level to ensure that prevention, protection, mitigation, response, and recovery efforts are synchronized and mutually supportive.

Critical infrastructure security and resilience at the state or territorial level must cut across all sectors present within the jurisdiction and support national, state, and local priorities. The program also should explicitly address unique geographic issues, including transborder concerns, and interdependencies among sectors and jurisdictions within those geographic boundaries.

Local governments provide critical public services and functions in conjunction with private-sector owners and operators. In some sectors, local government entities, through their public works departments, own and operate critical infrastructure such as water, storm water, and electric utilities. Most disruptions or natural hazards that affect critical infrastructure begin and end as local situations. Local authorities typically shoulder the weight of initial response and recovery operations until coordinated support from other sources becomes available, regardless of who owns or operates the affected asset, system, or network. As a result, local governments are key players within the critical infrastructure partnership. They drive emergency preparedness and local participation in critical infrastructure security and resilience across a variety of jurisdictional partners, including government agencies, owners and operators, and private citizens in the communities that they serve.

Specific activities for critical infrastructure security and resilience at the state, territorial, and local level may include, but are not limited to,

- acting as a focal point for and promoting the coordination of security, resilience, and emergency response activities, preparedness programs, and resource support among relevant jurisdictions, regional organizations, private-sector partners, and citizens;
- developing a consistent approach to critical infrastructure identification, risk determination, mitigation planning, prioritized security investment, and exercising preparedness among all relevant stakeholders within their jurisdictions;
- identifying, implementing, and monitoring a risk management approach and taking corrective actions, as appropriate;
- participating in significant national, regional, and local awareness programs to encourage appropriate management and security of cyber systems;
- facilitating the exchange of security information, including threat assessments and other analyses, attack indications, warnings, and advisories, within and across entities and sectors within their jurisdictions;
- participating in the critical infrastructure partnership, including sector-specific GCCs; the State, Local, Tribal, and Territorial Government Coordinating Council (SLTTGCC); and other relevant critical infrastructure governance and planning efforts;
- ensuring that funding priorities are addressed and that resources are allocated efficiently and effectively;
- sharing information on infrastructure deemed significant from a national, state, regional, local, tribal, and/or territorial perspective to enable prioritized security and restoration of critical public services, facilities, utilities, and lifeline functions within the jurisdiction;
- documenting and applying lessons learned from predisaster mitigation efforts, exercises, and actual incidents;

- coordinating with partners to promote education, training, and awareness of critical infrastructure security and resilience to motivate increased participation by owners and operators;
- providing response and security support, as appropriate, where there are gaps and where local entities lack the resources needed to address those gaps;
- identifying and communicating to DHS the requirements for critical infrastructure-related R&D; and
- working with state and territorial cabinet agencies to ensure that all pertinent critical infrastructure partners are represented.

Tribal government roles and capabilities regarding critical infrastructure security and resilience generally mirror those of state and local governments as detailed above. Tribal governments are responsible for the public health, welfare, and safety of tribal members and the security of critical infrastructure and the continuity of essential services under their jurisdiction. Within the critical infrastructure partnership, tribal governments coordinate with federal, state, local, and international counterparts to achieve synergy in the implementation of critical infrastructure security and resilience frameworks within their jurisdictions. This is particularly important in the context of information sharing, risk analysis and management, awareness, preparedness planning, and security and resilience program investments and initiatives.

Regional partnerships include a variety of public-private sector initiatives that cross jurisdictional and/or sector boundaries and focus on prevention, protection, mitigation, response, and recovery within a defined geographic area. Specific regional initiatives range in scope from organizations that include multiple jurisdictions and industry partners within a single state to groups that involve jurisdictions and enterprises in more than one state and across national borders. In many cases, state governments also collaborate through the adoption of interstate compacts to formalize regionally based partnerships. Partners leading or participating in regional initiatives are encouraged to capitalize on the larger area- and sector-specific expertise and relationships to

- promote collaboration among partners in implementing critical infrastructure risk assessment and management activities;
- facilitate education and awareness of critical infrastructure security and resilience efforts occurring within their geographic areas;
- participate in regional exercise and training programs, including a focus on critical infrastructure security and resilience collaboration across jurisdictional and sector boundaries;
- support threat-initiated and ongoing operations-based activities to enhance security and resilience and to support mitigation, response, and recovery;
- work with SLTT and international governments and the private sector, as appropriate, to evaluate regional and cross sector critical infrastructure interdependencies, including cyber considerations;
- conduct appropriate regional planning efforts and undertake appropriate partnership agreements to enable regional critical infrastructure security and resilience activities and enhanced response to emergencies;
- facilitate information sharing and data collection between and among regional initiative members and external partners;

- share information on progress and critical infrastructure security and resilience requirements with DHS, the SSAs, state and local governments, and other critical infrastructure partners, as appropriate; and
- participate in the critical infrastructure partnership.

An array of boards, commissions, authorities, councils, and other entities at the state, local, tribal, and regional levels perform regulatory, advisory, policy, or business oversight functions related to various aspects of critical infrastructure operations and security within and across sectors and jurisdictions. Some of these entities are established through state- or local-level executive or legislative mandates with elected, appointed, or voluntary membership. These groups include, but are not limited to, transportation authorities, public utility commissions, water and sewer boards, park commissions, housing authorities, public health agencies, and many others. These entities may serve as state-level sector-specific agencies and contribute expertise, assist with regulatory authorities, or help facilitate investment decisions related to critical infrastructure security and resilience efforts within a given jurisdiction or geographic region.

Source: DHS (2013b).

Critical Thinking

Consider the community you live in and identify the critical infrastructure that exists within that community. Choose one critical infrastructure asset and describe its potential vulnerabilities.

Private Sector

The private sector is especially critical since significant portions of the United States' critical infrastructure are owned or managed by the private sector. The issue of a private company sharing information with the federal government has not been completely resolved, though each successive NIPP has sought to increase information-sharing capabilities. Since the events of September 11, many businesses have increased their threshold investments and undertaken enhancements in security in an effort to meet the demands of the new threat environment (see sidebar "Another Voice: Safety and Security Concerns in the Private Sector," which describes the concerns of a private-sector entity in the Commercial Facilities critical infrastructure sector). For most enterprises, the level of investment in security reflects implicit risk-versus-consequence trade-offs, which are based on (1) what is known about the risk environment, (2) what is economically justifiable and sustainable in a competitive marketplace or in an environment of limited government resources, (3) potential consequences of disasters, and (4) priorities for the protection of human capital, processes, physical infrastructure, organizational reputation, stakeholder confidence, and vital records that require immediate attention. Given the dynamic nature of the terrorist threat and the severity of the consequences associated with many potential attack scenarios, the private sector naturally looks to the government for better information to help make its crucial security investment decisions. The private sector is continuing to look for better data, analysis, and assessment from DHS to use in the corporate decision-making process.

Similarly, the private sector looks to the government for assistance when the threat at hand exceeds an enterprise's capability to protect itself beyond a reasonable level of additional investment. In this light, the federal government promises to collaborate with the private sector (and state and local governments) to ensure the protection of nationally critical infrastructures and assets; to provide timely warning and ensure the protection of infrastructures and assets that face a specific, imminent threat; and to promote an environment in which the private sector can better carry out its specific protection responsibilities.

Private owners have an economic interest in protecting their investments and ensuring a continuity of operations of their facilities and systems from a variety of threats both internal and external. Private owners and operators are usually best able to assess what risks they face and how to set some priorities among the risks for prevention purposes. For many private-sector enterprises, the level of investment in security reflects risk-versus-consequence trade-offs that are based on two factors: (1) what is known about the risk environment and (2) what is economically justifiable and sustainable in a competitive marketplace or within resource constraints. The NIPP details the role of the private sector as detailed in sidebar "Private-Sector NIPP Roles and Responsibilities."

Private-Sector NIPP Roles and Responsibilities

Critical infrastructure owners and operators in the public and private sectors develop and implement security and resilience programs for the critical infrastructure under their control while taking into consideration the public good as well. Owners and operators take action to support risk management planning and investments in security as a necessary component of prudent business planning and operations. In today's risk environment, these activities generally include reassessing and adjusting business continuity and emergency management plans, building increased resilience and redundancy into business processes and systems, protecting facilities against physical and cyberattacks, reducing the vulnerability to natural disasters, guarding against insider threats, and increasing coordination with external organizations to avoid or minimize the impact on surrounding communities or other industry partners.

For many private-sector enterprises, the level of investment in security reflects risk-versus-consequence trade-offs that are based on two factors: (1) what is known about the risk environment and (2) what is economically justifiable and sustainable in a competitive marketplace or within resource constraints. In the context of the first factor, the federal government is uniquely positioned to help inform critical infrastructure investment decisions and operational planning across the sectors. Owners and operators may look to the government and information-sharing and information analysis organizations like ISACs as a source of security-related best practices and for attack or natural hazard indications, warnings, and threat assessments.

In relation to the second factor, owners and operators may rely on government entities or participate in collective efforts with other owners and operators to address risks outside of their property or in situations in which the current threat exceeds an enterprise's capability to protect itself or requires an unreasonable level of additional investment to mitigate risk. In this situation, public- and private-sector partners at all levels collaborate to address the security and resilience of national-level critical infrastructure, provide timely warnings, and promote an environment in which critical infrastructure owners and operators can carry out their specific responsibilities.

Critical infrastructure owners and operators participate in many risk mitigation activities including cybersecurity information-sharing efforts (e.g., sector-specific cyber working groups, the Cross Sector Cybersecurity Working Group, and the Industrial Control Systems Joint Working Group), cyber risk assessments, cybersecurity exercises, cyber incident response and recovery efforts, and cyber metrics development. The roles of specific owners and operators vary widely within and across sectors. Some sectors have statutory and regulatory frameworks that affect private-sector security operations within the sector; however, most are guided by a voluntary focus on security and resilience or adherence to industry-promoted best practices.

Within this diverse landscape, critical infrastructure owners and operators may contribute to national critical infrastructure security and resilience efforts through a range of activities. These activities may include but are not limited to performing critical infrastructure risk assessments, understanding dependencies and interdependencies, developing and coordinating emergency response plans with appropriate federal and SLTT government authorities, establishing continuity plans and programs that facilitate the performance of lifeline functions during an incident, participating in critical infrastructure-focused training and exercise activities with public- and private-sector partners, and contributing technical expertise to the critical infrastructure security and resilience efforts of DHS and the SSAs.

Source: DHS (2013b).

ANOTHER VOICE: Safety and Security Concerns in the Private Sector

Security in Public Versus Private Sectors

The phone rang at 15 min before 3 am. It was January 26, 2007. Sound asleep, I instinctively reached for my phone, wondering who could be calling at this hour. It was little surprise to me that it was my boss on the line. He was notifying me that an explosion had just occurred outside the entrance of one of our hotels in South Asia. An unidentified man attempted to penetrate hotel security. Strapped with a homemade explosive device, he was confronted by our guards who prevented access to the property. A scuffle ensued and the bomber detonated the device. The security guard was killed instantly alongside the bomber and seven bystanders were injured.

Through the system, we had established years earlier; all of our crisis management team members were on a conference call within 15 min. We concluded the conference call an hour later with tasks assigned to each member. The team convened again a few hours later to report on their assignments. Since the damage to the hotel's building structure was minimal, the hotel was able to resume its normal operations later that day. Later, a relief fund was set up to help the deceased employee's family.

This is an example of one of those phone calls you do not wish to receive, regardless of the time of day. A phone call like this precipitates a crisis lasting anywhere from 1 day to several weeks.

Everyone in the security department will be tested dealing with this on a 24 h basis. It is our employee, our company, and our reputation, after all.

There is little distinction between the security responsibilities of government agencies and private-sector entities. Both protect people, facilities, assets, and reputation. However, the ramifications are far more complex for the private sector when it comes to dealing with the aftermath of a crisis. When working in the government sector, there is little concern about the stock performance, shareholders, a potential increase in insurance premiums, public relations disasters, or lawsuits by customers. These elements can be extremely challenging for someone who makes the decision to cross over into the private sector.

In a corporate crisis environment, pressure comes from many areas. It most often manifests itself from stockholders, legal advisors, consultants, rank-and-file employees, customers, and, naturally, competitors. Everyone is a stakeholder.

If FEMA had been a privately owned company and its directors performed in much the same manner that they did during Hurricane Katrina, FEMA's stock would have plunged and no insurance company would have dared to insure them again. Senior executives in the parent company (which would be the Department of Homeland Security in this example) and its board of directors would have fired them all, and needless to say, the PR department would have their own crisis trying to mitigate the negative publicity.

The Hurricane Katrina story could have been very different if it had been handled in an effective and efficient manner. When such disasters occur, mass evacuations and major rescue operations require extensive efforts. In this case, government waste was rampant and communication between agencies broke down. Politics obfuscated good judgment. Conversely, a private company has to be self-sufficient. Its contingency plans need to cover all aspects from start to finish. If a private company fails to manage a crisis effectively, profits will plunge, customers will not return, stock holders will sell, and the company will eventually go under.

Private companies have to have a strategic focus, think ahead, and prepare resources. They should assess the situation from the perspective of each stakeholder. Hurricane plans should include shelters both inside and outside of the facility, prenegotiated contracts with chartered airlines, and supplies such as food, beds, and toilets. Having these plans and provisions in place will boost customer confidence, increase business, please shareholders, and drive revenue. Everyone is happy.

Another aspect to consider is that many companies are global, thereby expanding the horizon and adding more elements to the crisis plan. Different parts of the world involve various kinds of threats that might not exist in corporate America. Wars, government instability, foreign languages, customs, laws, and restrictions need to be considered and evaluated in order to allow for fast and seamless reaction during a crisis.

A private company's plan needs to be all encompassing, including preventative methods and solutions. A comprehensive review of the business continuity plan is always needed after a crisis comes to an end.

Last but not least, cooperation from company executives is the key. Without it, no crisis plan can function as they always require top-down support, money, time, and resources.

Jack Suwanlert, Director—International Loss Prevention, Marriott International Inc.

International

The federal government and private-sector corporations have a significant number of facilities located outside the United States that may be considered critical infrastructure. The NIPP addresses international critical infrastructure protection, including interdependencies and vulnerabilities based on threats (and associated consequences) that originate outside the country or pass through it. The federal government and the private sector work with foreign governments and international/multinational organizations to enhance the confidentiality, integrity, and availability of cyber infrastructure and products. High priority is placed on the protection of assets, systems, and networks that operate across or near the borders with Canada and Mexico or rely on other international aspects to enable critical functionality. These also include any assets that require coordination with and planning and/or sharing resources among neighboring governments at all levels and private-sector critical infrastructure owners and operators.

The NIPP recognizes several areas where special considerations exist: first, when critical infrastructure is extensively integrated into an international or global market (e.g., financial services, agriculture, energy, transportation, telecommunications, or information technology) or when a sector relies on inputs that are not within the control of US entities and, second, when government facilities and functions are directly affected by foreign-owned and foreign-operated commercial facilities.

The federal government, working in close coordination and cooperation with the private sector, launched the Critical Foreign Dependencies Initiative in 2007 to identify assets and systems located outside the United States, which, if disrupted or destroyed, would critically affect public health and safety, the economy, or national security. The initiative produced a strategic compendium that guides the engagement with foreign countries in the critical infrastructure protection mission.

Conclusion

It is clear that cybersecurity remains the latest homeland security frontier. It is an area where new questions and challenges arise each day and where the threat to our evolving way of life adapts in response to our every effort. For the nation's critical infrastructure, many of these emergent threats are the same given the interdependencies that exist between cyber infrastructure and critical infrastructure. And like cyber infrastructure, there is a need for collaboration between the public and the private sectors. The federal government has acknowledged the fact that while it is making significant efforts to enhance cybersecurity and provide protections for critical infrastructure, it can accomplish neither on its own. But as the 9/11 investigations and subsequent report have shown, sharing information with the private sector is not an area where the past is flush with success stories. There will need to be a willingness on the part of each of the relevant federal agencies to work with the private sector as described in the cybersecurity and infrastructure strategies. Giving the speed with which the treats are evolving, there is no doubt that the coming years will test that willingness.

Key Terms

ACAMS: ACAMS is a web-enabled information services portal that helps state and local governments build critical infrastructure programs.

CFATS: The Chemical Facilities Anti-Terrorism Standards (CFATS) were established by DHS to provide guidance on hardening the facilities that produce, utilize, or store chemical substances, both public and private, throughout the United States.

Critical infrastructure: It refers to the assets, systems, and networks, whether physical or virtual, so vital to the United States that the incapacity or destruction of such assets, systems, or networks would have a debilitating impact on security, national economic security, public health or safety, or any combination of those matters (Source: NIPP).

Critical Infrastructure (and Key Resources) Government Coordinating Council (GCC): The GCC brings together diverse federal, state, local, and tribal interests to identify and develop collaborative strategies that advance critical infrastructure protection. GCCs serve as a counterpart to sector coordinating councils for each critical infrastructure sector. They provide interagency coordination around critical infrastructure strategies and activities and policy and communication across government and between government and the sector to support the nation's homeland security mission. Government-coordinating councils for each sector are composed of representatives from DHS, the SSA, and the appropriate supporting federal departments and agencies.

Cybersecurity: It is the prevention of damage to, unauthorized use of, or exploitation of, and, if needed, the restoration of electronic information and communications systems and the information contained therein to ensure confidentiality, integrity, and availability. It includes protection and restoration, when needed, of information networks and wire line, wireless, satellite, public safety answering points, and 911 communications systems and control systems.

Federal Energy Regulatory Commission (FERC): The FERC regulates and oversees energy industries in the economic, environmental, and safety interests of the American public.

Information and communications systems: They are composed of hardware and software that process, store, and communicate data of all types.

Information Sharing and Analysis Center (ISAC): ISACs are sectorial information analysis and information-sharing centers that bring together representatives and decision makers of a given sector for the purposes of critical infrastructure protection and disaster preparedness.

Information technology (IT) critical functions: They are sets of processes that produce, provide, and maintain products and services. IT critical functions encompass the full set of processes (e.g., R&D, manufacturing, distribution, upgrades, and maintenance) involved in transforming supply inputs into IT products and services.

National Infrastructure Protection Plan (NIPP): It is a US government plan that lays the framework for critical infrastructure and key asset protection activities. The plan is complemented with sector-specific annexes that detail sector-specific planning, response, and coordination bodies for effective disaster preparedness and incident response.

National Response Coordination Center (NRCC): The NRCC is FEMA's primary operations center during disaster response. The center is also vital for resource coordination between different emergency support functions.

National Response Team (NRT): The US National Response Team is an organization of 16 federal departments and agencies responsible for coordinating emergency preparedness and response to oil and hazardous substance pollution incidents. The Environment Protection Agency (EPA) and the US Coast Guard (USCG) serve as chair and vice chair, respectively.

Sector Coordinating Councils: These councils are private-sector counterparts to the GCCs. They are self-organized, self-run, and self-governed organizations that are representative of a spectrum of key stakeholders within a sector. SCCs serve as the government's principal point of entry into each sector for developing and coordinating a wide range of critical infrastructure protection activities and issues.

Sector-Specific Agency (SSA): It is the federal agency designated to lead identification, assessment, protection, and resilience-building programs and activities for each CI sector.

US Computer Emergency Readiness Team (US-CERT): Established in 2003 to protect the nation's Internet infrastructure, US-CERT coordinates defense against and responses to cyberattacks across the nation.

Vulnerability: It is the vector of physical, social, geographic, and political factors that influence or define the combined susceptibility to a disaster of a given person, place, or other physical entities.

Review Questions

1. Who has the lead role for cybersecurity in the federal government?
2. What are the differences between cyberwarfare, cyberterrorism, cyber espionage, and cybercrime?
3. What is the role of the private sector in cybersecurity? What are your suggestions to improve private-sector participation and coordination with the DHS in cybersecurity?
4. Why are public-private partnerships so important in both cybersecurity and critical infrastructure protection?
5. Identify three of the sixteen critical infrastructure sectors. For each, name which agency is the SSA, and describe in general terms the purpose of an SSA.
6. What is the difference between object-oriented and network-oriented infrastructures? How does the nature of risk differ for these two classes of infrastructure?

References

Arce, N., 2014. North Korea Deems Sony pictures hack and celebs data leak 'Righteous Deed': here's why. Tech Times (December 8). http://bit.ly/1yxFmFw.

Barr, D., 2014. Hackers targeted Ferguson officials. St. Louis Business Journal (November 3). http://bit.ly/1oUsZow, Morning edition.

Blau, J., 2005. German teen confirms he created the sasser worm. PC World (July 5). http://bit.ly/1qHyEd8.

Brickey, J., 2012. Defining Cybeterrorism: Capturing a Broad Range of Activities in Cyberspace. Combating Terrorism Center, West Point Academy. http://bit.ly/11n8RB3 (August 23).

Bruinius, H., 2014. Feds hacked: is cybersecurity a bigger threat than terrorism? Christ. Sci. Monitor (November 10). http://bit.ly/1sHOOQn.

Coren, M., 2005. Experts: cyber-crime bigger threat than cyber-terror. CNN (January 24). http://cnn.it/1x0dvRt.

Crawford, J., 2014. The U.S. Government thinks China could take down the power grid. CNN (November 20). http://cnn.it/1uZKFzZ.

Crooks, Ed, 2012. Hackers target US natural gas pipelines. Financial Times (May 8). http://on.ft.com/1wviXHW.

Department of Defense, 2011. Department of Defense Strategy for operating in cyberspace. http://1.usa.gov/1p0TqZR.

Department of Defense, 2014. U.S. cyber command. DOD fact sheet. http://bit.ly/1xOjqYX.

Department of Homeland Security (United States), 2008. A Guide to Critical Infrastructure and Key Resources Protection at the State, Regional, Local, Tribal, and Territorial Level. http://1.usa.gov/1vokkwJ.

Dews, F., 2014. Squirrels – A Bigger Threat Than Cyber Terrorists? The Brookings Institute (January 6).

DHS, 2010a. 2010 Quadrennial Homeland Security Review. http://1.usa.gov/1xKL6Op.

DHS, 2010b. National Cyber Incident Response Plan – Interim. Department of Homeland Security, Washington, DC.

DHS, 2012. National Protection and Programs Directorate Office of infrastructure protection strategic plan 2012–2016. http://1.usa.gov/1F6p5gk.

DHS, 2013a. Executive order (EO) 13636 Improving critical infrastructure cybersecurity and presidential policy directive (PPD) – 21 critical infrastructure security and resilience. DHS fact sheet. http://1.usa.gov/1xKzZVJ.

DHS, 2013b. National Infrastructure Protection Plan. Department of Homeland Security. http://bit.ly/1uAeXYB.

DHS, 2013c. National infrastructure protection plan sector specific plans. Fact sheet. http://1.usa.gov/1HoV2Ct.

DHS, 2014a. 2014 Quadrennial Homeland Security Review. Department of Homeland Security. http://1.usa.gov/1sGKYyB.

DHS, 2014b. Cyber storm: security cyber space. DHS fact sheet. http://1.usa.gov/11naHBb.

DHS, 2014c. Office of Cybersecurity and Communications. DHS website: http://1.usa.gov/1HdW9Fc (accessed 11/18/2014).

DHS, 2014d. Critical infrastructure sectors. DHS website: http://1.usa.gov/1uHuo2K (accessed 11/19/2014).

DHS, 2014e. Organizational Chart of the Office of Cybersecurity and Communications. DHS website: http://1.usa.gov/1vlCklg (accessed 11/18/2014).

DHS, 2014f. Stop. Think. Connect. Promotional materials. DHS website: http://1.usa.gov/1tmYIKz (accessed 11/21/2014).

FBI, 2014a. Cyber's most wanted. Wanted by the FBI. FBI website: http://1.usa.gov/11AIB6z (accessed 11/19/2014).

FBI, 2014b. Taking down botnets. Testimony of Joseph Demarest. Senate Judiciary committee subcommittee on crime and terrorism. FBI fact sheet. July 15.

FBI, 2014c. 2013 internet crime report. Federal bureau of investigation report. Washington, DC.

Fischer, E., Liu, E., Rollins, J., Theohary, C., 2013. The 2013 cybersecurity executive order: overview and considerations for congress. Congressional research service. Report R42984. http://bit.ly/1t0Dbbw.

Flaherty, M.P., Samenow, J., Rein, L., 2014. Chinese hack U.S. weather systems, satellite network. The Washington Post (November 14). http://wapo.st/1u7N9dJ.

Freeze, C., 2014. State-sponsored hackers target human rights groups, study says. The Globe and Mail (November 11). http://bit.ly/1qGDaIX.

Glazer, E., Yadron, D., 2014. J.P. Morgan says about 76 million households affected by cyber breach. Wall St. J. (October 2). http://on.wsj.com/1tPSTFF.

Greenberg, A., 2013. Hackers reveal nasty new car attacks. Forbes (July 24). http://onforb.es/1uj8UsJ.

Hunn, D., 2014. How hackers wreaked havoc in St. Louis, MO. St. Louis Post Dispatch (November 3).

International Recovery Platform, 2010. Guidance Note on Recovery: Infrastructure. UN International Strategy for Disaster Reduction, Kobe, Japan. http://bit.ly/11BlTv7.

Kosner, A., 2014. Actually two attacks in one, target breach affected 70 to 110 million customers. Forbes (January 17). http://onforb.es/1yErXwR.

Kuchler, H., 2013. Symantec chief warns over cyber threat to intellectual property. Financial Times Technology (November 25). http://on.ft.com/115hXBK.

Lee, W., Rotoloni, B., 2014. Emerging cyber threats report 2015. Georgia Tech Institute of Technology. Cybersecurity Summit 2014. http://bit.ly/1yLNmEn.

Lewis, J.A., 2014. The arms race in cyberspace. The Washington Post. Cybersecurity: a special report. October 10.

Martina, M., 2014. China angered after FBI head says Chinese hacking costs billions. Reuters (October 9). http://reut.rs/1yEoGh0.

Mitnick, K., 2003. The Art of Deception. Wiley, Indianapolis.

Mooallem, J., 2013. Squirrel power. The New York Times (August 31). http://nyti.ms/1xUfoPP, Sunday Review. Opinion.

NIST, 2014. Framework for Improving Critical Infrastructure Cybersecurity. Version 1.0. http://1.usa.gov/1wMKqoD.

NSF, 2014. Secure and trustworthy cyberspace. NSF website: http://1.usa.gov/11BdAzd (accessed 11/19/2014).

PBS, 2013. How does the government manage workers with access to classified information. Newshour (June 11). http://to.pbs.org/1qO8iGq.

Perlroth, N., 2014. State Department targeted by hackers in 4th agency computer breach. The New York Times. http://nyti.ms/1qNKS3Z November 16.

Quinn, R., 2014. The FBI Role in Cyber Security. Statement Before the House Homeland Security Committee, Subcommittee on Cyber Security, Infrastructure Protection, and Security Technologies. April 16.

Robertson, J., Lawrence, D., Strohm, C., 2014. Sony's breach stretched from Thai hotel to Hollywood. Bloomberg (December 7). http://bloom.bg/1A9GTUn.

Schneier, B., 2010. The story behind the stuxnet virus. Forbes (October 7). http://onforb.es/1xyjCvd.

Smith, R., 2014. Assault on California power station raises alarm on potential for terrorism. Wall St. J. (February 5). http://on.wsj.com/1urJ2KW.

Stevens, L., Yadron, D., Barrett, D., 2014. U.S. postal service says it was victim of data breach. Wall St. J. (November 10). http://on.wsj.com/11ngEyT.

Studer, J.A., 2000. Vulnerability of Infrastructure. Studer Engineering, Zurich, Switzerland. http://bit.ly/1t3U9Wr.

Tech and Law Center, 2014. Cyberwar and cyberterrorism. Tech and Law Center website: http://bit.ly/1EJ0JZG (accessed 11/14/2014).

The Washington Post, 2014. Cybersecurity: a special report. http://wapo.st/1uo5iEf (October 10).

The White House, 2013. Presidential policy directive-critical infrastructure security and resilience. White House Press Release (February 12). http://1.usa.gov/1p17VNf.

Tsighe, A., 2014. Minimizing insider threats: the rogue employee. File Open Systems. http://bit.ly/1BHNt9V (accessed 11/17/2014).

Volz, D., 2014. Report: China hacked defense contractors 20 times in one year. Natl. J. (September 17). http://bit.ly/1xyqF7j.

Weise, E., 2014. 43% of companies had a data breach in the past year. USA Today (September 24). http://usat.ly/1qDi8AA.

White House, 2014. Launch of the cybersecurity framework. White House Press Release (February 12). http://1.usa.gov/11cTs5U.

Wilking, R., 2013. Expert: US in cyberwar arms race with China, Russia. NBC News (February 20). http://nbcnews.to/1tcvw9f.

Wyler, G., 2011. Pentagon admits 24,000 files were hacked, declares cyberspace a theater of war. Business Insider (July 14). http://read.bi/1p0TFnu.

Further Reading

CRS Reports and Other CRS Products: Cybersecurity Policy

Fischer, E.A. Federal laws relating to cybersecurity: overview and discussion of proposed revisions. CRS report R42114.

Stevens, G. The Obama administration's cybersecurity proposal: criminal provisions. CRS report R41941.

Fischer, E.A., et al. The 2013 cybersecurity executive order: overview and considerations for congress. CRS report R42984.

Sargent, Jr. J.F. A federal chief technology officer in the Obama administration: options and issues for consideration. CRS report R40150.

Liu, E.C., et al. Cybersecurity: selected legal issues. CRS report R42409.

Figliola, P.M., Fischer, E.A. Overview and issues for implementation of the federal cloud computing initiative: implications for federal information technology reform management. CRS report R42887.

Thompson II, R.M. Cloud computing: constitutional and statutory privacy protections. CRS report R43015.

Thompson II, R.M. House intelligence committee marks up cybersecurity bill CISPA. CRS legal sidebar WSLG478.

Chu, V.S. Can the president deal with cybersecurity issues via executive order? CRS legal sidebar WSLG263.

CRS Reports: Critical Infrastructure

Moteff, J.D. Critical infrastructure resilience: the evolution of policy and programs and issues for congress. CRS report R42683.

Moteff, J.D. Critical infrastructures: background, policy, and implementation. CRS report RL30153.

Parfomak, P.W. Pipeline cybersecurity: federal policy. CRS report R42660.

Parfomak, P.W. Keeping America's pipelines safe and secure: key issues for congress. CRS report R41536.

Campbell, R.J. The smart grid and cybersecurity—regulatory policy and issues. CRS report R41886.

Murrill, B.J., Liu, E.C., Thompson II, R.M. Smart meter data: privacy and cybersecurity. CRS report R42338.

Figliola, P.M. The federal networking and information technology research and development program: background, funding, and activities. CRS report RL33586.

Kruger, L.G. Internet domain names: background and policy issues. CRS report 97-868.

Fischer, E.A., Theohary, C.A., Rollins, J.W. Open-source software and cybersecurity: the heartbleed bug. CRS report IN10027.

CRS Reports and Other CRS Products: Cybercrime and National Security

Doyle, C. Cybercrime: an overview of the federal computer fraud and abuse statute and related federal criminal laws. CRS report 97-1025.

Doyle, C. Extraterritorial application of american criminal law. CRS report 94-166.

Doyle, C. Cybersecurity: cyber crime protection security act (S. 2111, 112th congress)—a legal analysis. CRS report R42403.

Stevens, G., Doyle, C. Privacy: an overview of federal statutes governing wiretapping and electronic eavesdropping. CRS report 98-326.

Figliola, P.M. Spyware: background and policy issues for congress. CRS report RL32706.

Yeh, B.T. Illegal internet streaming of copyrighted content: legislation in the 112th congress. CRS report R41975.

Yeh, B.T. Online copyright infringement and counterfeiting: legislation in the 112th congress. CRS report R42112.

Finklea, K. Identity theft: trends and issues. CRS report R40599.

Finklea, K. The interplay of borders, turf, cyberspace, and jurisdiction: issues confronting U.S. law enforcement. CRS report R41927.

Smith, A.M. Protection of children online: federal and state laws addressing cyberstalking, cyberharassment, and cyberbullying. CRS report RL34651.

Finklea, K., Theohary, C.A. Cybercrime: conceptual issues for congress and U.S. law enforcement. CRS report R42547.

Fischer, E.A. Data security and credit card thefts: CRS experts. CRS report R43382.

Nolan, A. Legal barriers to an expanded role of the military in defending against domestic cyberattacks. CRS legal sidebar WSLG399.

Liu, E.C., Liu, E.C. Obstacles to private sector cyber threat information sharing. CRS legal sidebar WSLG483.

Murphy, M.M. Online banking fraud: liability for unauthorized payment from business checking account. CRS legal sidebar WSLG672.

Seitzinger, M.V. Federal securities laws and recent data breaches. CRS legal sidebar WSLG831.

Doyle, C. Hackers cannot always be tried where third-party victims reside. CRS legal sidebar WSLG 906.

StevensObst, G. In the matter of LabMD: the FTC must publicly disclose its data security standards. CRS legal sidebar WSLG 959.

9

All-Hazards Emergency Response and Recovery

What You Will Learn

- How large-scale emergencies are declared at each level of government and what kinds of declarations are made
- Legislative actions taken since the 9/11 terrorist attacks that affect the nation's response capabilities
- The many federal homeland security grant programs that are available to states and local communities
- The response roles assumed by each level of government, from local to national (including those of the Department of Homeland Security and other federal agencies and offices), and by private and nonprofit organizations
- What homeland security volunteer programs exist, what each does, and how they are distributed across the country
- How the National Incident Management System and the National Response Framework guide all hazards emergency response to major incidents in the United States
- How the National Disaster Recovery Framework functions

Introduction

When a natural disaster such as a flood, earthquake, or hurricane occurs or when a technological incident or terrorist attack happens, local police, fire, and emergency medical personnel are generally the first to respond. Their mission is to rescue and attend to victims, suppress any secondary fires that may have resulted, secure and police the disaster area, and begin the process of restoring order. They are supported in this effort by local emergency management personnel and community government officials.

The adage that "practice makes perfect" comes to mind when considering the unprecedented number of natural and man-made disasters the past decade has presented, which have together tested the capacity of these first responders and the nation's response system as a whole. In the vast majority of cases, both the systems in place and the participants responding were considered efficient and effective. However, the unexpected terrorist attacks of September 11, 2001, the anthrax events that followed shortly thereafter, and the poor response to Hurricane Katrina all revealed certain weaknesses in this system that clearly needed to be addressed. Although the immediate responses to the World Trade Center attacks were typical of an effective national response system (the most advanced in the world at the time), there still followed an unprecedented loss of lives among both civilians and first responders (Figure 9-1). Several of the primary support systems

FIGURE 9-1 New York City, New York, September 27, 2001—An aerial view of the rescue and recovery operations under way in lower Manhattan at the site of the collapsed World Trade Center. *Photo by Bri Rodriguez/FEMA News Photo.*

in place at the time performed far below expectations, and many established procedures were not followed or were not deemed suitable for the catastrophic scenario that presented. Hurricane Katrina, just 4 years later, exposed yet more remaining and several new systemic shortfalls that the terrorism-focused efforts could not have possibly addressed.

The 9/11 attacks were truly a watershed event in emergency management history. In their shadow, agencies at the national, state, and local government levels were prompted to initiate evaluations that sought to improve existing response procedures and protocols in light of the vast new knowledge and experience that had been attained. The spectacular nature of the attacks, and the apparent threat of subsequent events of equal or greater magnitude, mandated the generation of after-action reports that spurred many changes and improvements in the procedures and protocols that first responders have since applied to their emergency management efforts. Considering the devious and dangerous potential posed by future terrorism events, many of these evaluations focused their attention on what appeared to be a relatively new concept for most of the agencies involved: how best to protect first responders from harm in future attacks.

The federal government responded to this shift in response procedures by updating the Federal Response Plan (FRP). A new prescriptive and functional document, the National Response Plan (NRP), was the product of these efforts. This change was justified under the belief that, because the nature of threats facing the United States had become more complex and because the effect of future natural, technological, and terrorist events could cause detriment to the American way of life, a unified national effort was required to prepare for the response to these events before they occur again. The team members assembled to create this document were charged with making this new national response system as efficient and effective as possible and to focus on utilizing a unified approach to managing incidents that would result in a significant reduction in the vulnerability of the United States to all hazards.

The NRP, which resulted from these collective efforts and which was released in January 2005, was billed as an all-discipline, all-hazards plan. The NRP was designed to establish a single, comprehensive framework for the management of domestic incidents, which would likely involve many participants from all government levels. The plan directly addressed the prevention of terrorist attacks, as well as the reduction in vulnerability to all natural and man-made hazards. Finally, it attempted to offer guidance on minimizing the damage and assisting in the recovery from any type of incident that occurred.

Although the plan placed a clear emphasis on retaining the primary responsibility for initial incident response at the local level, with the locally available assets and special capabilities for prevention, it included a more aggressive integration between agencies in charge and sought to establish a workable, unified approach to the management of incidents, especially those involving the criminal element of terrorism.

To carry out the coordinated response approach prescribed in the NRP, the federal government created the National Incident Management System (NIMS). On March 1, 2004, former Department of Homeland Security (DHS) Director Tom Ridge announced the release of NIMS and stated that it was created in order to "provide a consistent nationwide approach for federal, state, and local governments to work effectively and efficiently together to prepare for, respond to, and recover from domestic incidents, regardless of cause, size, or complexity."

Hurricane Katrina (2005) exposed several problems that existed within the new NRP, the most significant reported to be its sheer length. In response, the federal government developed a much more concise National Response Framework (NRF), based heavily upon the systems and organization contained within the original NRP. Upon draft release in early September 2007, the NRF came under heavy criticism due to the fact that it had been created largely devoid of local or state response agency involvement, and many emergency managers felt that it lacked the detailed operational guidance they had hoped for. After a period of comment and adjustment that was expanded far beyond its initial 30 days, a final NRF was released on January 22, 2008.

Overall, the changing nature of the terrorist threat (e.g., greater population exposure and possible use of weapons of mass destruction (WMDs)) has been the motivator for developing a new approach to response operations. This new approach has sought to initiate a profound transformation on the response community at the state and local levels through implementation of the following four goals:

- To unify crisis and consequence management (CM) as a single, integrated function, rather than two separate functions, and integrate all existing federal emergency response plans into a single document (the NRF)
- To provide interoperability and compatibility among federal, state, and local capabilities (through NIMS)
- To enhance response and preparedness capabilities of first responders and state and local governments against all kinds of hazards and threats by providing extensive funding for equipment, training, planning, and exercises
- To integrate the private sector and the business communities at a greater extent into response activities and responsibilities in order to increase resources in hand

In January 2009, President Barack Obama entered office, and in May 2009, President Obama appointed Craig Fugate as the new FEMA administrator. Fugate had served as the director of the Florida Division of Emergency Management and was considered as one of the top state emergency managers in the country. According to his bio on the FEMA website,

> *Fugate served as the Florida State Coordinating Officer for 11 Presidentially-declared disasters including the management of $4.5 billion in federal disaster assistance. In 2004, Fugate managed the largest federal disaster response in Florida history as four major hurricanes impacted the state in quick succession; Charley, Frances, Ivan and Jeanne. In 2005, Florida was again*

impacted by major disasters when three more hurricanes made landfall in the state; Dennis, Katrina and Wilma. The impact from Hurricane Katrina was felt more strongly in the gulf coast states to the west but under the Emergency Management Assistance Compact or EMAC, Florida launched the largest mutual aid response in its history in support of those states.

FEMA (2014h)

Under Fugate's leadership, FEMA has regained its status as a federal agency that can be relied on to successfully fulfill its mission. FEMA's response to Hurricane Sandy in 2012 was considered a major success especially considering the size and breadth of the storm. FEMA has adopted a "Whole Community" approach to emergency management, strengthened partnerships with volunteer community, further integrated the private sector into the nation's emergency management system and supported the creation of the National Business Emergency Operations Center, supported state and local efforts to plan and implement climate change adaptation actions, and developed and implemented the National Disaster Recovery Framework. As of November 2014, FEMA and its partners are in the nation's emergency management system functioning at full capacity and very effectively in responding to major disaster events across the country (FEMA, 2014h).

On April 15, 2013, two bombs exploded at the finish line area of the Boston Marathon. The response to this terrorist incident was immediate with bystanders, race officials, and on-site medical personnel rushing to help the wounded. The resulting search for the bombers occurred over the next 4 days until the capture of the second suspect on April 19, 2013, which was a coordinated effort led by the Boston Police Department and including law enforcement officials from multiple local jurisdictions, the state police, and federal authorities including DHS and the FBI. The response of law enforcement in this incident was no accident but the result of years of relationship building, exercising, and accepting the Incident Command System. See sidebars "Testimony of Former Boston Police Commissioner Edward F. Davis III and Edward P. Deveau, Chief of Police, Watertown (MA) Police Department" and "Testimony of Herman B. 'Dutch' Leonard and Eliot I. Snider."

Testimony of Former Boston Police Commissioner Edward F. Davis III and Edward P. Deveau, Chief of Police, Watertown (MA) Police Department

On April 9, 2014, former Boston Police Commissioner Edward Davis and Watertown (MA) Police Chief Edward Deveau testified before the US House of Representatives Committee on Homeland Security in a hearing on "The Boston Marathon Bombings, One Year On: A Look Back to Look Forward." They testified about the roles of their police departments in the response to the 2013 Boston Marathon Bombings and the manhunt and ultimately the death of one suspect and the capture of the second suspect. Presented below are excerpts from their testimony that focus on how their respective police departments functioned during the period from April 15, 2013, when the bombs exploded at the marathon finish line area, to April 19, 2015, when the second suspect was arrested.

Testimony from Former Boston Police Commissioner Edward Davis, III
Excerpt 1

In the weeks after last April's attack, many questions were raised about who knew what when, and what kind of information was being shared between law enforcement agencies.

I am here to tell you that throughout this past year, the level of inter-agency cooperation and information-sharing that has occurred between local, state, and federal law enforcement agencies has been critical to ensuring that we have found answers to as many questions as we could pose.

Within the first few minutes of hearing about the explosions on Boylston Street, my first phone call was to my friend and colleague Rick Deslauriers at the FBI. He and I worked side-by-side throughout the ensuing week, and I consider him a staunch friend and ally. He offered all of the services of the FBI and other agencies to make sure that we not only apprehended the terrorists responsible for this crime, but also to ensure that our inter-agency collaboration affords all of our agencies the critical amount of information-sharing needed for our organizations to operate at peak efficiency.

What all of us learned that week and in the ensuing 12 months, though, is just how big our community is beyond the partnerships within the levels of government. Our law enforcement community is obvious. With me today are some of my colleagues from the neighboring Watertown Police Department, the community where the manhunt came to an end and a community that found its neighborhoods under siege like never before in our country's history.

Make no mistake about this—Boston Police, Watertown police—none of our agencies could have enjoyed the successes we achieved without the involvement of a much larger community, one that felt personally victimized by the attacks. That is the community which has come to be known as Boston Strong.

Excerpt 2

This is the same community who waited anxiously as the largest manhunt in New England history played out over 4 days. When law enforcement decided to release the photos of the two suspects, we knew the dissemination of information into the hands of the public would be one of the most effective ways we could apprehend the individuals we wanted.

As we saw it play out on Thursday and Friday of that week, when the suspects took to the run, and began endangering innocents in other communities, we had to take the unprecedented action of asking more than half a million people to shelter in place while we search for these two men, who were throwing bombs at the police officers trying to catch them.

And for that historic Friday after the marathon, when we asked our communities to work with us and remain at home to keep the streets clear so we could do our job, they listened.

They listened because they shared a common goal, of wanting us to catch the men responsible. They listened because they trusted law enforcement, and by extension, their government, to take care of them.

As anyone who has followed my career with the Boston and Lowell Police Departments knows, I believe in community policing, and the critical role that our residents play in helping to keep a community safe. It was relationships built before the marathon attacks that allowed us to implement such drastic measures, and those relationships only grew stronger when our communities saw the professional responses from their police agencies.

Excerpt 3

Beyond the successes we have achieved with the cooperation of the media agencies that cover our agencies, we also learned quickly what a valuable information tool our social media networks could be to us as that week unfolded last April. Systems that remain in place a year later, and allow our agencies to more effectively and more rapidly communicate directly with the men and women we are sworn to serve and protect.

Testimony from Watertown (MA) Police Chief Edward Deveau

Excerpt 1

I am here today to talk about the events that occurred in Watertown in the early morning hours of April 19th. That seemingly quiet overnight shift suddenly turned into a warzone. For the first time in America, police officers were attacked with guns and bombs and it happened on a quiet backstreet in my community. Those two brothers were trying to kill my police officers and had plans to kill and injure more innocent people.

Excerpt 2

Mr. Chairman, during those trying days last April two individuals attempted to strike fear and take down a city. They attempted to terrorize us all. In the end they accomplished nothing. What they will never know is that when America gets knocked down we pick ourselves up and become even stronger. We will not be intimidated. Watertown is stronger, Boston is stronger, and in my opinion the entire country is more united and stronger. The strength, resilience and defiance is what made Boston Strong and I know if an attack occurs in any city within our country they will respond in a similar way.

The Watertown police officers on duty that night stopped these terrorists from leaving with their car full of weapons to carry out their next deadly plan. In the following 18 h our entire department of 65 officers was tested and worked around the clock to keep our community safe. We received unprecedented support from surrounding police departments and federal agencies. As a result the second Boston Marathon bombing suspect was finally captured.

Source: Committee on Homeland Security (2014).

Testimony of Herman B. "Dutch" Leonard and Eliot I. Snider

On April 9, 2014, Harvard University Professors Herman B. "Dutch" Leonard and Eliot I. Snider testified before the US House of Representatives Committee on Homeland Security in a hearing on "The Boston Marathon Bombings, One Year On: A Look Back to Look Forward." They testified about the results of the research they had conducted "to understand the sources of the strengths and weaknesses of the response to the marathon bombing." Presented below are excerpts from their testimony that examine the response actions taken in the aftermath of the bombings on April 15, 2013. Additional excepts from their testimony focused on preparations made by law enforcement officials before the bombings occurred and how they impacted the response are included in a sidebar in Chapter 10. Recommendations for future actions to improve response are presented in this sidebar and recommendations to improve preparedness in the future are presented in the sidebar in Chapter 10.

Excerpt 1: Incident Command

I have two simple messages for you today.

The first message is about the *first responder* part of Boston Strong that was on display last April.

That message is this: It works! *Incident command* works! When you build it in advance and use it in the moment, incident command is effective. The *National Incident Management System* is starting to work.

It has been a long time in coming and it is long overdue—but we've made a lot of progress nationally, and the events in Boston last year put that vividly on display.

For something like 50 years, starting in the 1960s and continuing with greater energy after a devastating fire in California in 1970, people of goodwill in emergency management sought to develop and promulgate an effective, unified, coherent doctrine of incident management so that agencies and organizations that find themselves having to work together on terrible and dark days can efficiently and smoothly combine their capabilities and resources. The central purpose of having a single, unified approach is to enable a sudden team to produce the best performance reasonably possible given the nature of the challenge and the capacities that they have available. Too many times we have watched while vitally needed and clearly existing capabilities were not marshaled or effectively deployed—but instead were idled by a lack of ability to organize, coordinate, and execute across agencies, jurisdictional boundaries, and levels of government.

Finally, Congress—through the House Select Committee on Homeland Security, the original inception of this committee, in Part 5 of Section 502 of Public Law 107-296, the Homeland Security Act of 2002—mandated that the Secretary of Homeland Security build "a comprehensive national incident management system with Federal, State, and local government personnel, agencies, and authorities, to respond to ... attacks and disasters." In 2004, the Department of Homeland Security duly issued instructions to those it could command directly (and created incentives for those it could not) to organize themselves for emergency response purposes in compliance with the structures and precepts and procedures of that system. FEMA has since worked to develop the system further and to help federal and other agencies implement the structures, procedures, and training associated with making this doctrine a practical reality.

Excerpt 2: Effective Response

There were some quite remarkably effective elements of the response in the aftermath of the bombing in Boston. As an example, the bombs caused literally dozens of fatal injuries, but, mercifully, there were only three fatalities on that terrible day. All of the seriously injured people were removed from the scene within 22 min. Every person who left the scene alive is alive today. The scene was rapidly secured and swept for additional explosive devices. It was then secured as a crime scene, collaboratively, using FBI and local and state assets, and the investigation was launched. Video from private and public surveillance cameras was quickly collected, additional photographic evidence (mainly from media and bystanders who volunteered their photographs and videos) was obtained, and an exhausting search through the video and photographic evidence began. Meanwhile, the public was informed by individual agencies and through a series of organized press conferences.

Taken together, that seems like a very good performance. We can all point to elements where it could be further improved. But the standard can't be an unrealistic expectation of perfection. Our question has to be this: did the response accomplish what could reasonably have been expected, given the intrinsic nature of the event itself—the surprise, the physical and emotional shock, and the inevitable chaos of the immediate aftermath. *We believe that the response in Boston was as good as one could reasonably have hoped*. This then begs explanation, and forms the basic question of our research: ***Why*** were people and organizations able to provide as effective a response as this was? What were the strengths of that response, and what enabled them? And where were the weaknesses—and what can we do to further minimize them? These were the questions at the heart of our research.

I want to emphasize three elements of our research findings about where these features of the response "came from"—that is, what caused or created them:

> First, *the core underlying reason for the effectiveness of the response in the moment was the rapid formation of an effective command and coordination structure* that oversaw and directed all elements of the response. Senior officials from a wide range of

agencies—federal, state, local, and private—felt an immediate need to find one another and join into a concerted and unified command structure and were then able to do so reasonably quickly.

Second, *none of that was due to chance*—it resulted from literally tens of thousands of hours of joint work, planning, exercises and operations combining numerous agencies over many years in the planning for and production of fixed events ranging from the Democratic National Convention in 2004 (an event that got particularly attentive focus because it was the first national political convention after 9/11) to the Boston Marathon to the July 4th concert and fireworks on the Esplanade to Patriots and Red Sox and Bruins and Celtics victory parades. Each of those events provided an opportunity—and opportunity that was *taken*—to practice the process of planning and doing things together. This built knowledge of one another's assumptions and priorities and procedures, fostering understanding and mutual respect of individual and organizational competence and capabilities across agencies. This was the infrastructure that enabled command and coordination to be established quickly and to function effectively after the bombs exploded.

Third, *others can do this, too*. To be sure, some of the features that contributed to the effectiveness of the response in Boston were unique to Boston. Boston has eight Level I trauma centers, for example, and by happenstance they are arrayed in every direction around the area where the bombs went off, so the injured could be transported in many different directions, reducing congestion among emergency vehicles. Some other elements were unique to the moment—for example, the fact that the marathon takes place on a state holiday, when hospitals are open and fully staffed, but are not doing elective surgery, meant that dozens of operating rooms were immediately available. A shift change was underway at the time of the bombing, which increased availability of skilled hands when they were needed. So there were elements of good fortune that reduced the terrible consequences on that awful day. *But most of what made the response as effective as it was can be undertaken by other communities as readily and as well as it was by Boston*. Any community can engage in joint planning across its agencies for any major fixed event—from a high school football victory parade to a Fourth of July celebration. Any community can find opportunities to engage in joint planning with other jurisdictions, and with other levels of government—both federal and state.

On a good day, joint planning and practicing inter-agency coordination—and carrying that out through an incident command structure—is helpful in making events go more smoothly. Paying your dues on the good days by building the infrastructure of interagency familiarity, respect, knowledge, and trust thus has an immediate payoff—and if a bad day ever comes, that infrastructure is literally a life-saver.

The single most important lesson of our research is that routine and constant practice and use of incident command is one of the best investments a community can make in its present well-being and against any future dark day that might arise.

Excerpt 3: Recommendations Future Responses

Our full report contains more detail about the events and further discussion of the key implications and lessons about the challenges of organizing and operating command and coordination in events like this. For purposes of my testimony here, let me now enumerate more completely the main recommendations from our research:

Strategic Command

- *Senior leaders should participate in a unified command at the strategic level and avoid being pulled back into making tactical decisions and directly overseeing basic operations.* While some engagement with rapidly evolving tactical matters is necessary, top commanders should concentrate on working with their peers in other organizations to establish an integrated, cross-agency, policy perspective that looks at the big picture context and a longer time frame.
- *The management of intra-organizational, tactical matters should be undertaken by the next tier of institutional leaders*, who should be carefully prepared *in advance* through training, exercises, and actual experience to assume these responsibilities during crises.
- *To help ensure leaders' strategic focus and opportunity for effective coordination with peers, contingency plans for fixed events like the Marathon should provide for well-equipped, secure facilities for top commanders to work together in the event of an emergency.* This command post should be close to but separate from the location of subordinates who manage tactical operations.
- *Organizations must develop sufficient depth of leadership so that they can rotate personnel regularly during extended events; otherwise, they will inevitably falter from fatigue.* By Friday evening, many of the people managing the overall event had been awake for 36 or more hours and, more generally, had been sleep deprived since Monday's bombing. Both they and their deputies had been more than fully deployed throughout the event, leaving no unused (rested) capacity in the system. Failure to provide for sufficient downtime for senior officials inevitably degrades their judgment, ability to comprehend information, and performance of even normal tasks. Allowing for regular rotation requires creating more personnel depth in these leadership positions.
- *Senior leaders should not to be unduly exposed to the enormous flow of raw information, lest their attention be diverted from strategic issues and problems.* In an event with 24/7 news and social media saturation, there is an enormous amount of information circulating at any given time, much of which is misleading or wrong. This stream of data needs to be filtered and organized for top level leaders so they can concentrate on interpretation and strategic issues.

Tactical/Local Command

- *Response organizations must develop procedures and practices to better control "self-deployment" by individual personnel to the scene of emergency action.* Dangerous situations that threatened both responders and bystanders developed at the scene of the Thursday night shootout and Friday apprehension of the second suspect in Watertown, in part because of an overload of individual public safety officers operating as individuals rather than in disciplined units.
- *Public safety organizations should develop improved doctrine, better training, and practice through exercises to ensure effective "micro-command" in crises.* While officers typically look for command authority when operating at a scene with groups from their own agencies, they are less likely to do so when they have deployed as individuals and arrive at an emergency site on their own. Except for situations when near-instantaneous action is required to preserve life, doctrine should be developed and officers should be trained to look for authority at a scene of mass action, even if command is taken by someone from another organization.
- *Improved discipline and training is needed to control weapons fire when public safety officers from many organizations are present.* Control over fields of fire and authorization to fire is another critical micro-command issue in any rapidly-evolving, high-stress, emotion-laden event. It is dramatically more complicated when a "sudden team" of people from different agencies are thrown together under circumstances where there is no pre-determined command structure.

- *Improved protocols and control systems for parking emergency vehicles at an actual or potential emergency site must be developed and effectively communicated/emphasized to officers by dispatchers and on-scene commanders during an event to prevent obstruction of further movement that may be required.*
- *In complex, multi-agency events, teams of responders in the field should be structured to take advantage of both the local knowledge of conditions that the "home" organization possesses and the quantity and specialized resources that outside reinforcements can bring.*

Public Communication

- *Maintaining regular and open communication with the public—through traditional and social media—should be a high priority for senior officials, even when confidential investigations are ongoing.* When accurate, frequent, official communications were absent, news and social media filled the gap, sometimes with speculation and misinformation. Development of protocols for crisis communication, incorporating utilization of social media, should be part of the planning for fixed events. This should include improving practices for dispelling widely disseminated, inaccurate information or rumors.
- *Systems for coordinating and communicating information to families of individuals missing or injured in a crisis need to be improved*, perhaps including revision of HIPAA rules governing the release of personal information about patients receiving care during public safety emergencies.

Herman B. "Dutch" Leonard is the George F. Baker, Jr., professor of Public Management and faculty codirector, Program on Crisis Leadership, John F. Kennedy School of Government at Harvard University, and Eliot I. Snider is the family professor of Business Administration and faculty cochair, Social Enterprise Initiative, Harvard Business School at Harvard University.

Source: Committee on Homeland Security (2014).

It is the purpose of this chapter to describe the functional and operational performance of the US response system, to identify and describe the changes brought about by the creation of the DHS and the actions of DHS and Congress, and to discuss their consequences. The chapter highlights in this regard include legislative and budgetary issues; local and state response capacities; volunteer group response mechanisms; an overview of the Incident Command System (ICS) and the NIMS, NRP, and NRF; and the National Disaster Recovery Framework (NDRF) and the various programs available to assist in recovery.

Critical Thinking

Should the federal emergency management role be crafted by the Department of Homeland Security, by the state and local emergency management organizations that ultimately benefit from the federal assistance provided, or by collaboration among all levels? What benefits and shortcomings would result from each of these three different planning scenarios?

Response Processes

Whenever the national emergency number 911 is called, in any event ranging from a simple traffic accident, to a tornado sighting, to someone showing signs of a viral disease, the first responders that answer the call are always local officials. But when the size of the incident grows so large that response requirements exceed these local capabilities and the costs of inflicted damage surpass what the local government can manage, the mayor or county executive must turn to the governor and state government resources for assistance in responding to the event and in helping the community to recover. Each state then calls upon an established system whereby the governor crafts a response that combines various personnel (including the state emergency management agency and the state National Guard), equipment, and funding. And should the disaster exceed the state's abilities to manage, then it is likely that a national disaster has occurred and federal emergency management efforts are required.

The new National Response Framework (NRF), like that of its predecessors, dictates the rules by which states initiate an appeal for assistance and by which that assistance is granted should the president choose to declare a disaster. The new disaster reporting process is similar to that which was stipulated under the original FRP, although fundamental changes have certainly occurred. The following gives a brief overview of the declaration process that exists under the NRF, which is described in much greater detail later in this chapter.

Should the governor decide, based on information and damage surveys generated by community and state officials or predictions of impending disaster or terrorist threat, that the size of the actual or anticipated disaster event has exceeded or will exceed the state's capacity to respond, the governor will make a formal request to the president for a presidential major disaster declaration or an emergency declaration. This request is prepared by state officials in cooperation with regional staff from the Federal Emergency Management Agency (FEMA).

At the federal level, the governor's request is analyzed first by FEMA's regional administrator, who evaluates the damage and requirements for federal assistance and makes a recommendation to the FEMA administrator. The FEMA administrator, acting through the secretary of the DHS, may then recommend a course of action to the president.

The president considers the FEMA administrator's recommendation and decides whether or not to declare the disaster a presidential major disaster declaration or an emergency declaration. What constitutes each of these is described in the sidebar "Types of Presidential Declarations."

Types of Presidential Declarations

Presidential Major Disaster Declaration

A Presidential Major Disaster Declaration (Major Declaration) is defined by FEMA to be "any natural catastrophe (including any hurricane, tornado, storm, high water, wind-driven water, tidal wave, tsunami, earthquake, volcanic eruption, landslide, mudslide, snowstorm, or drought), or, regardless of cause, any fire, flood, or explosion, in any part of the United States, which in the determination of the President causes damage of sufficient severity and magnitude to warrant major disaster assistance under the [Stafford] Act to supplement the efforts and available resources of States, local governments, and disaster relief organizations in alleviating the damage, loss, hardship, or suffering caused thereby."

A Presidential major disaster declaration puts into motion long-term Federal recovery programs, some of which are matched by State programs, and designed to help disaster victims, businesses, and public entities.

Emergency Declaration
An Emergency Declaration is defined by FEMA to be "any occasion or instance for which, in the determination of the President, Federal assistance is needed to supplement State and local efforts and capabilities to save lives and to protect property and public health and safety, or to lessen or avert the threat of a catastrophe in any part of the United States."

An emergency declaration is more limited in scope and without the long-term Federal recovery programs of a major disaster declaration. Generally, Federal assistance and funding are provided to meet a specific emergency need or to help prevent a major disaster from occurring.

Source: FEMA (2014d).

Once a presidential declaration has been made, the FEMA administrator, acting on behalf of the secretary of the DHS, or the senior staff designated by the FEMA administrator determines the need to activate components of the NRF to conduct further assessment of the situation, initiate interagency coordination, share information with affected jurisdictions, and/or initiate the deployment of resources. At this time, federal departments and agencies are notified by the DHS National Operations Center (NOC) and may be called on to staff the National Response Coordination Center (NRCC) or the National Infrastructure Coordinating Center (NICC).

If an incident has already occurred, the NRF priority shifts to immediate- and short-term response activities. The purpose of these activities is to preserve lives, protect property, and prevent further harm to the environment. The social, economic, and political structures of the affected community or communities are protected as well. Response actions could include the participation of law enforcement officers, fire officials, emergency medical services (mass care, public health, and medical services), officials involved in infrastructure restoration, environmental protection officials, and more.

Either during (if appropriate) or immediately following the response phase, the long-term recovery is initiated (Figure 9-2).

When a major disaster strikes in the United States or when the threat of disaster is imminent, the aforementioned chronology describes how the most sophisticated and advanced emergency management system in the world responds and begins the recovery process. The fundamental pillars on which the system is built are, and continue to be, coordination and cooperation among a significant number of federal, state, and local government agencies, volunteer organizations, and, more recently, the business community.

Critical Thinking

When the Federal Response Plan (FRP) was replaced by the National Response Plan (NRP), the president gained the power to initiate a federal response in support of the states, under specific circumstances as outlined in the plan, regardless of a request from a governor. This power was transferred into the new National Response Framework (NRF). Do you feel that this takes too much authority away from the states or that this is a necessary tool?

FIGURE 9-2 Tuscaloosa, AL, May 25, 2011—FEMA Community Relations (CR) Specialist Tony Bronk speaks with a storm survivor at a disaster benefit concert. FEMA CR outreach efforts attempt to get FEMA registration and other helpful recovery information to survivors of the deadly April tornado. *Photo by George Armstrong/FEMA.*

Legislative Actions

The establishment of the state of homeland security as it exists today involved several bills and laws, essentially determined by homeland and national security presidential directives delivered during the years following the 9/11 attacks. The most significant include the following:

- The US PATRIOT Act of 2001
- The Aviation and Transportation Security Act of 2001
- The SA 4470 Amendment
- The Public Health Security and Bioterrorism Preparedness and Response Act of 2002
- The Enhanced Border Security and Visa Entry Reform Act of 2002
- The Maritime Transportation Security Act of 2002
- The Homeland Security Act of 2002

These laws, among many other goals, attempted to clearly define the mission and organization of emergency management and terrorism preparedness in the United States. The single greatest change that resulted from these laws in the spectrum of emergency management—and also in terms of the changes that have occurred within the federal government itself—was the creation of the DHS. The new department, which integrated 22 existing federal agencies under the direction of a single cabinet-level official for the purpose of streamlining emergency management and counterterrorism activities, was vigorously debated, but finally came into existence in March 2003.

FEMA, which was included in this transfer and which retained its pre-DHS trademark name, was transferred largely intact to form one of five directorates that existed under the original DHS organization, the Directorate of Emergency Preparedness and Response (EP&R). The EP&R mission as defined by the Homeland Security Act of 2002 was similar to that of FEMA prior to its incorporation (to ensure that the nation is prepared for catastrophes—whether natural or technological disasters or terrorist assaults), although there was clearly a new focus that considered more carefully the terrorism hazard. This new directorate supported the original federal government national response and recovery strategy and dedicated much of its resources to enhancing the abilities of first responders at the local level to carry out that same mission. For several years, however, many of its original (and central) mitigation and preparedness functions were removed from the agency and transferred elsewhere within DHS, only to be returned to FEMA per legislation passed in the aftermath of Hurricane Katrina.

DHS has emphasized through its public relations efforts that it continues to make every effort to support FEMA's original mission of comprehensive emergency management. They assure that FEMA, within DHS, will continue in its efforts to reduce the loss of life and property and to protect the nation's institutions from all types of hazards through risk-based emergency management. In a continuation of FEMA's mitigation role, but using new nomenclature, DHS has asserted it will further the evolution of the emergency management culture from one that reacts to disasters to one that proactively helps communities and citizens avoid becoming victims—with *prevention* being the term of choice to replace *mitigation*.

The Homeland Security Act of 2002 describes the responsibilities of FEMA, within DHS, as follows:

- Helping to ensure the preparedness of emergency response providers for terrorist attacks, major disasters, and other emergencies
- Establishing standards, conducting exercises and training, evaluating performance, and providing funds in relation to the Nuclear Incident Response Team (defined in Section 504 of the bill)
- Providing the federal government's response to terrorist attacks and major disasters
- Aiding the recovery from terrorist attacks and major disasters
- Working with other federal and nonfederal agencies to build a comprehensive national incident management system
- Consolidating existing federal government emergency response plans into a single, coordinated national response plan
- Developing comprehensive programs for developing interoperable communications technology and ensuring that emergency response providers acquire such technology

The responsibility of providing the federal government's response to terrorist attacks and major disasters—third item above—is explained in detail in the act and includes the following:

- Coordinating the overall response to terrorist attacks
- Directing the Domestic Emergency Support Team (DEST), the Strategic National Stockpile (SNS), the National Disaster Medical System (NDMS), and the Nuclear Incident Response Team (each described later in this chapter)
- Overseeing the Metropolitan Medical Response System (MMRS) and coordinating other federal response resources

It is important to note that the new responsibilities of FEMA are not intended to detract from other important functions transferred to DHS, such as those of the US Fire Administration (USFA). In almost all areas, DHS has fully preserved the authority to carry out the original functions of FEMA, including support for community initiatives that promote homeland security.

The following agencies were transferred to DHS and were integrated into FEMA as a result, through the provisions of the Homeland Security Act of 2002:

- The Integrated Hazard Information System of the National Oceanic and Atmospheric Administration (NOAA), which was renamed "FIRESAT"
- The National Domestic Preparedness Office (NDPO) of the Federal Bureau of Investigation (FBI)
- The Domestic Emergency Support Teams (DEST) of the Department of Justice (DOJ)
- The Office of Emergency Preparedness (OEP), the National Disaster Medical System (NDMS), and the Metropolitan Medical Response System (MMRS) of the Department of Health and Human Services (HHS) (the NDMS was transferred back into HHS in 2007)
- The Strategic National Stockpile (SNS) of HHS

Other legislation that addresses local response issues are presented briefly in Table 9-1.

Table 9-1 Local Response-Related Legislation

Bill	Title	Homeland Purpose
HR 3153	State Bioterrorism Preparedness Act of 2001	To assist states in preparing for, and responding to, biological or chemical terrorist attacks
HR 3435	Empowering Local First Responders to Fight Terrorism Act of 2001	To provide for grants to local first-responder agencies to combat terrorism and be a part of homeland defense
HR 3615	Protecting Our Schools Homeland Defense Act of 2002	To amend the Public Health Service Act to direct the Secretary of Health and Human Services to make grants to train school nurses as "first responders" in the event of a biological or chemical attack
HR 5169	Wastewater Treatment Works Security Act of 2002	To improve the defense and response of publicly owned water treatment plants against terrorist attacks by assessing risks and locating vulnerabilities
S 1520	State Bioterrorism Preparedness Act of 2002	To assist states in preparing for, and responding to, biological or chemical attack
S 1602	Chemical Security Act of 2001	To protect the public against the threat of a chemical terrorist attack
S 1746	Nuclear Security Act of 2001	To strengthen security at sensitive nuclear facilities
S 2664	First Responder Terrorism Preparedness Act of 2002	To establish an Office of National Preparedness to coordinate terrorism preparedness and response
HR 727	Trauma Care Systems Planning and Development Act of 2007	To amend the Public Health Service Act to add requirements regarding trauma care and for other purposes
HR 1	Implementing Recommendations of the 9/11 Commission Act of 2007	To provide for implementation of the recommendations of the National Commission on Terrorist Attacks Upon the United States
HR 1674	Tsunami Warning and Education Act	To authorize and strengthen the tsunami detection, forecast, warning, and mitigation program of the National Oceanic and Atmospheric Administration, to be carried out by the National Weather Service, and to establish tsunami warning centers, among other things, to disseminate forecasts and tsunami warning bulletins to federal, state, and local government officials and the public

Table 9-1 (Continued)

Bill	Title	Homeland Purpose
HR 5136	National Integrated Drought Information System Act of 2006	To establish a National Integrated Drought Information System that (1) provides an effective drought early warning system, (2) coordinates and integrates as practicable, federal research in support of such a system, and (3) builds on existing forecasting and assessment programs and partnerships
HR 23	Tornado Shelters Act	To amend the Housing and Community Development Act of 1974 to authorize communities to use community development block grant funds for the construction of tornado-safe shelters in manufactured home parks
HR 5419	Commercial Spectrum Enhancement Act	To amend the National Telecommunications and Information Administration Organization Act to facilitate the reallocation of spectrum from governmental to commercial users; to improve, enhance, and promote the nation's homeland security, public safety, and citizen-activated emergency response capabilities through the use of enhanced 911 services; to further upgrade public safety answering point capabilities and related functions in receiving E-911 calls; and to support in the construction and operation of a ubiquitous and reliable citizen-activated system
S 3678	Pandemic and All-Hazards Preparedness Act	A bill to amend the Public Health Service Act with respect to public health security and all-hazards preparedness and response and for other purposes
S 1152	Firefighting Research and Coordination Act	A bill to reauthorize the United States Fire Administration and for other purposes (including directing the administrator to (1) provide technical assistance and training to state and local fire service officials to establish nationwide and state mutual aid systems for dealing with national emergencies and (2) develop and make model mutual aid plans for both intrastate assistance and interstate assistance available to state and local fire service officials)
S. 2735	Dam Safety Act of 2006	A bill to amend the National Dam Safety Program Act to reauthorize the national dam safety program, and for other purposes

Source: American Corporate Counsel Association ACCA (2002) and http://www.govtrack.us.

Budget

The DHS receives one of the largest shares of the federal budget. Each year since its creation, its associated budget requests and funds granted have only increased in size. In 2004, this amounted to $35.6 billion, rising to $38.5 billion in 2005, to $40.4 billion in 2006, again to $43.0 billion in 2007, again to $47.0 billion in 2008, again to $52.7 billion in FY 2009, to $56 billion in FY 2010, down to $55.6 in FY 2011, back up to $56.9 billion in FY 2012, to $59.2 billion in FY 2013, and to $60.6 billion in FY 2014. In FY 2015, the president has requested $60.9 billion for DHS. Of this total allocation, approximately $14.7 billion is targeted for emergency management through FEMA. A breakdown of the various components that make up the FEMA budget, including changes from the period FY 2013 to FY 2015 (as proposed) can be found online in the DHS Budget Overview (p. 130) (DHS, 2014).

Local Response

On an operational level, minor disasters occur daily in communities around the United States. Local fire, police, and emergency medical personnel respond to these events in a routine, systematic, and well-planned course of action (Figure 9-3). Firefighters, police officers, and emergency medical technicians respond to the scene and take immediate actions. Their job is to secure the scene and maintain order, rescue and treat those who are injured, contain and suppress fire or hazardous conditions, and retrieve the dead. Some notable facts about first responders who assert their role as the real front line in the nation's defense from disasters of all categories are as follows:

- There are an estimated 1,129,250 firefighters in the United States, of whom approximately 783,300 (69%) are volunteers (NFPA, 2014).
- There about 780,000 police officers and detectives working in the United States (Department of Labor, http://www.bls.gov/ooh/protective-service/police-and-detectives.htm).
- There are 3080 sheriffs' offices in the United States with about 291,000 full-time employees, including about 186,000 sworn personnel (National Sheriff's Association, http://www.sheriffs.org/content/about-nsa).
- There are an estimated 239,100 emergency medical technicians (EMTs) (Department of Labor, http://www.bls.gov/ooh/healthcare/emts-and-paramedics.htm).

Critical Thinking

The nation's system of emergency management relies predominantly upon the efforts of unpaid volunteer first responders. Is this type of system sustainable? Why or why not? What could be done to improve it, and at what cost?

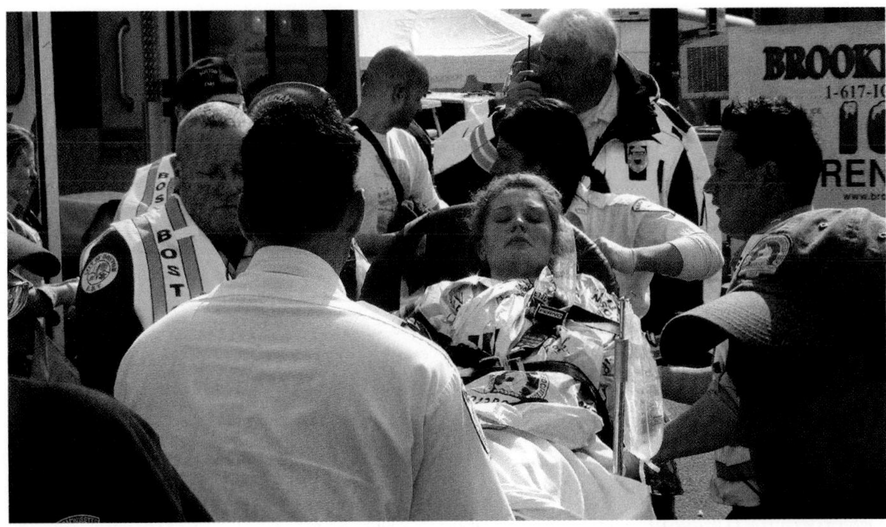

FIGURE 9-3 New York City, NY, October 5, 2001—Rescue workers continue their efforts at the World Trade Center. *Photo by Andrea Booher/FEMA News Photo.*

The actions of local first responders are driven by procedures and protocols developed by the responding agencies themselves (e.g., fire, police, and emergency medical). Most communities in the United States have developed community-wide emergency plans, mandated by the Disaster Mitigation Act of 2000 (DMA2000), which incorporate these procedures and protocols. In the aftermath of the 9/11 terrorist events, many communities have reworked their community emergency plans to include new and improved methodologies for responding to all forms of terrorist attacks including bioterrorism and other WMDs. These changes are most often driven by available federal and state funds (including grants that require such changes for fund eligibility) and to mirror new programs that have been designed at these two higher levels of government (see "Fiscal Year (FY) 2014 Homeland Security Grant Program (HSGP) Fact Sheet," https://www.fema.gov/media-library/assets/documents/97228)

The federal government has continued to support local-level first responders heavily through funding, as described earlier in the discussion of budgets. This funding support has been provided to address four primary areas of focus:

- *Planning*: Support of state and local governments in developing comprehensive plans to prepare for and respond to a terrorist attack
- *Equipment*: Assistance for state and local first-responder agencies for the purchase of a wide range of equipment needed to respond effectively to a terrorist attack, including personal protective equipment, chemical and biological detection systems, and interoperable communications gear
- *Training*: Resources to train firefighters, police officers, and emergency medical technicians to respond and operate in response to terrorist attacks, most notably for those that result in a chemically or biologically hazardous environment
- *Exercises*: Support for a coordinated, regular program of exercises that improve response capabilities, practice mutual aid, and assess operational improvements and deficiencies

First-Responder Roles and Responsibilities

The roles and responsibilities of first responders are usually detailed in the community emergency operations plan (EOP). Citing the responsibilities of first responders after a terrorist incident provides a useful example of the scope of the changes that these officials are experiencing, as displayed in the following list detailing several of the main objectives for the first responders to a terrorist incident:

- Protect the lives and safety of the citizens and other first responders
- Isolate, contain, and/or limit the spread of any cyber, nuclear, biological, chemical, incendiary, or explosive devices
- Identify the type of agent and/or devices used
- Identify and establish control zones for the suspected agent used
- Ensure emergency responders properly follow protocol and have appropriate protective gear
- Identify the most appropriate decontamination and/or treatment for victims
- Establish victim services
- Notify emergency personnel, including medical facilities, of dangers and anticipated casualties and proper measures to be followed
- Notify appropriate state and federal agencies

- Provide accurate and timely public information
- Preserve as much evidence as possible to aid in the investigation process
- Protect critical infrastructure
- Oversee fatality management
- Develop and enhance medical EMS
- Protect property and environment (Bullock & Haddow LLC, 2003)

Local Emergency Managers

It is primarily the responsibility of the designated local emergency manager to develop and maintain community-level emergency plans. Often, this individual shares a dual responsibility in local government, such as fire or police chief, and serves only part-time as the community's emergency manager. The emergency management profession, and the professional skill and knowledge of the local emergency manager, has progressively matured since the 1980s. Today, there are far more opportunities for individuals to receive formal training in emergency management than ever before, including as recently as 5 years ago. According to the FEMA Higher Education College List, as of November 2014, there are currently 296 junior college, undergraduate, and graduate programs that offer courses and degrees in emergency management and 154 Homeland Security/Defense and Terrorism Higher Education Programs. Additionally, FEMA's Emergency Management Institute (EMI) located in Emmitsburg, Maryland, offers emergency management courses on campus and through distance learning programs. EMI has also worked closely with junior colleges, colleges, universities, and graduate schools to develop course work and curriculums in emergency management. Details of EMI's Certified Emergency Manager Program are as follows:

- The International Association of Emergency Managers (IAEM) created the Certified Emergency Manager (CEM) program to raise and maintain professional standards. It is an internationally recognized program that certifies achievements within the emergency management profession.
- CEM certification is a peer-reviewed process administered through the IAEM. An individual does not have to be an IAEM member to be certified. Certification is maintained in 5-year cycles.
- The CEM program is served by a CEM commission that is composed of emergency management professionals, including representatives from allied fields, education, the military, and private industry.
- Development of the CEM program was supported by FEMA, the National Emergency Management Association (NEMA), and a host of allied organizations (International Association of Emergency Managers, www.iaem.org).

The roles and responsibilities of the county emergency manager are defined by the County EOP. The job descriptions of these individuals exhibit the same levels of variance as those in the local first-responder community, primarily on the account of the broadening incident threat spectrum that likewise poses a threat at the county level. Although no specific guidelines are given for the new roles of either local or county emergency managers, the essential differences between legacy and more modern EOPs are based on the following requirements:

- Changes in established procedures for handling terrorist incidents
- Changes in necessary response equipment

- Changes in the structure of responding agencies and protocols of operations and interagency cooperation
- Changes in neighboring local, state, and federal emergency operation plans

Funding for First Responders

As of early 2008, the federal government had spent more than $16 billion on funding for first responders since the 9/11 terrorist attacks. This funding has come not only in the clear recognition of the importance of first responders in managing the new terrorist risk but also in the acknowledgment of their role in protecting citizens from all forms of disaster. Since 2001, this support has come through the provision of several grant programs, which often change from year to year as needs and priorities are evaluated, adjusted, and reevaluated. Several of these programs and their associated funding levels from recent years are discussed below.

The administration authority for the various first-responder and other state homeland security and emergency management grant programs has been transferred time and again since the establishment of DHS. Before its creation, this funding (which existed at much lower levels) was administered through several different federal agencies—the most significant portion of which was managed by FEMA. After the 2002 establishment of DHS, funding was consolidated under the EP&R directorate. In 2004, the Office of State and Local Government Coordination and Preparedness (SLGCP) was established within DHS to streamline and coordinate all homeland security-based funding to the states and territories—which included first-responder grant programs. Grants were managed by an office within this office, appropriately titled the Office for Domestic Preparedness (ODP). One of the greatest accomplishments of ODP was the consolidation of six individual grant programs, including the State Homeland Security Program (SHSP), the Urban Areas Security Initiative (UASI), the Law Enforcement Terrorism Prevention Program (LETPP), the Citizen Corps Program (CCP), the Emergency Management Performance Grants (EMPGs), and the Metropolitan Medical Response System Program Grants. All six programs were integrated into the Homeland Security Grant Program (HSGP). Finally, in 2007, when DHS was reorganized yet again according to the Post-Katrina Emergency Management Reform Act of 2006, grant administration authority was once again returned to the newly reestablished FEMA.

First-responder grant amounts have varied significantly from year to year. The federal government provided a total of $5.056 billion in grants to state and local governments during FY 2003, but this amount dropped to $4.366 billion during FY 2004. These grants targeted state and local responders, public health agencies, and emergency managers, in their efforts to prepare for disasters. There was considerable dispute between the states during these years, addressed at the congressional level, about how this funding should be disbursed among the states and territories. There existed two schools of opposing thought—one that felt funding should include a minimum amount per state, based on the assumption that nobody can say for sure where the terrorists will strike next, and another that felt funding should be risk-based, going to those states with populated urban centers containing obvious terrorist targets. The calculation that determined the amount allocated to each state as a factor of how many people reside in that state—the "per capita funding"—was often used to illustrate how states like Alaska were receiving much more funding per person than states believed to be obvious targets, such as New York or California. In 2005, it was decided by Congress that risk factors would be considered in the determination of funding levels for each state. The amount of funding, however, has wavered since its record high of $5.056 billion in FY 2003 to $1.043 billion in FY 2014.

Fiscal Year (FY) 2014 Homeland Security Grant Program (HSGP)

State Homeland Security Program (SHSP)

- *Total Funding Available in FY 2014*: $401,346,000
- *Purpose*: SHSP supports the implementation of risk driven, capabilities-based State Homeland Security Strategies to address capability targets set in Urban Area, State, and regional Threat and Hazard Identification and Risk Assessments (THIRAs). The capability targets are established during the THIRA process, and assessed in the State Preparedness Report (SPR) and inform planning, organization, equipment, training, and exercise needs to prevent, protect against, mitigate, respond to, and recover from acts of terrorism and other catastrophic events.
- *Eligible Applicants*: The State Administrative Agency (SAA) was the only entity eligible to apply to FEMA for SHSP funds. Eligible applicants included all 50 states, the District of Columbia, Puerto Rico, American Samoa, Guam, the Northern Mariana Islands, and the US Virgin Islands.
- *Program Awards*: The allocation methodology for FY 2014 SHSP was based on three factors: minimum amounts as legislatively mandated, DHS' risk methodology, and anticipated effectiveness of proposed projects. The anticipated effectiveness was assessed based on the applicant's description of how the proposed projects, as outlined in the Investment Justification (IJ), aligned with the State THIRA and SPR results. Each State and territory received a minimum allocation under SHSP using the thresholds in the *Homeland Security Act of 2002*, as amended. All 50 States, the District of Columbia, and Puerto Rico received 0.35% of the total funds allocated for grants under *Section 2003 and Section 2004 of the Homeland Security Act of 2002*, as amended. Four territories (American Samoa, Guam, the Northern Mariana Islands, and the US Virgin Islands) received a minimum allocation of 0.08% of the total funds allocated for grants under *Section 2003 and 2004 of the Homeland Security Act of 2002*, as amended.

Urban Areas Security Initiative (UASI)

- *Total Funding Available in FY 2014*: $587,000,000
- *Purpose*: The UASI program funds addressed the unique risk driven and capabilities-based planning, organization, equipment, training, and exercise needs of high-threat, high-density Urban Areas based on the capability targets identified during the THIRA process and associated assessment efforts; and assists them in building an enhanced and sustainable capacity to prevent, protect against, mitigate, respond to, and recover from acts of terrorism.
- *Eligible Applicants*: The SAA was the only entity eligible to apply to FEMA for UASI funds. A total of high-threat, high-density urban areas were eligible for funding under the FY 2014 UASI program. Eligible candidates for the FY 2014 UASI program were determined through an analysis of relative risk of terrorism faced by the 100 most populous metropolitan statistical areas in the United States, in accordance with the 9/11 Act.
- *Program Awards*: The allocation methodology for FY 2014 UASI was based on DHS' risk methodology and anticipated effectiveness of proposed projects. The anticipated effectiveness is assessed based on the applicant's description of how the proposed projects, as outlined

in the IJ, aligned with the Urban Area THIRA. Eligible candidates for the FY 2014 UASI program have been determined through an analysis of relative risk of terrorism faced by the 100 most populous metropolitan statistical areas (MSAs) in the United States, in accordance with the Homeland Security Act of 2002, as amended. Detailed information on MSAs is publicly available from the United States Census Bureau at http://www.census.gov/population/www/metroareas/metrodef.html

Operation Stonegarden (OPSG)

- *Total Funding Available in FY 2014*: $55,000,000
- *Purpose*: OPSG funds are intended to enhance cooperation and coordination among local, tribal, territorial, state, and Federal law enforcement agencies in a joint mission to secure the United States' borders along routes of ingress from international borders to include travel corridors in States bordering Mexico and Canada, as well as states and territories with international water borders.
- *Eligible Applicants*: The SAA was the only entity eligible to apply to FEMA for OPSG funds. Local units of government at the county level and federally recognized tribal governments in the states bordering Canada, southern states bordering Mexico, and states and territories with International water borders were eligible to apply for FY 2014 OPSG funds through their SAA.
- *Program Awards*: FY 2014 OPSG funds were allocated based on risk-based prioritization using a US Customs and Border Protection (CBP) Sector-specific border risk methodology. Factors considered included, but were not limited to, threat, vulnerability, miles of border, and other border-specific "law enforcement intelligence," as well as feasibility of FY 2014 Operation Orders to designated localities within the United States border States and territories.

Source: FEMA (2014c).

Critical Thinking

If you could design any grant program to increase the nation's preparedness to cope with all forms of hazards, what types of items or actions would that grant program support? How would you craft the program regarding eligibility? At what levels would your program need to be funded in order for it to make an actual difference in performance levels nationwide?

State Response

States make up the second tier of emergency response in the United States. State emergency management provides mitigation and preparedness support throughout the year, but comes into play only when called upon by an overwhelmed community, county, or region. Each of the 50 states and 6 territories that make up the United States maintains a state government office of emergency management. However, where the emergency management office resides within the government structure varies from state to state. In California, the California Emergency Management Agency reports to the governor's office. In Tennessee, the Tennessee Emergency Management Agency (TEMA) reports to the adjutant general. In Florida, the emergency management function is located in the Office of Community Affairs. Today, the National Guard adjutant generals manage state emergency management offices in less than one-quarter of the states and territories, a number that has fallen from more than 50% only 5 years ago. Civilian employees lead all other state emergency management offices, a growing trend that recognizes the comprehensive intergovernmental organizational role that is central to the office of emergency management.

Funding for state emergency management offices is provided principally through a combination of DHS support and state budgets. In recent years, FEMA has provided up to $350 million annually to the states to fund state and local government emergency management activities. This money is used by state emergency management agencies to hire staff, conduct training and exercises, and purchase equipment. A segment of this funding is targeted for local emergency management operations as designated by the state. State budgets provide funding for emergency management operations, but this funding historically has been inconsistent, especially in those states with minimal annual disaster activity. The principal resource available to governors in responding to a disaster event in their state is the National Guard. The resources of the National Guard that are used for disaster response include personnel, communications systems and equipment, air and road transport, heavy construction and earth-moving equipment, mass care and feeding, equipment, and emergency supplies such as beds, blankets, and medical supplies.

Not surprisingly, response capabilities and capacities are strongest in those states and territories that experience the highest levels of annual disaster activity. All states and territories, however, being in possession of critical assets and resources, find themselves suddenly striving to reinforce their capabilities against the possibility of a terrorist incident. North Carolina is a state that regularly manages the risk of and response to hurricanes and floods. How the North Carolina Department of Emergency Management describes its response process presents a good example of some of the individual aspects of a mature state response function. The sidebar "North Carolina State Emergency Management Response Process" details that function.

North Carolina State Emergency Management Response Process

The [State's] emergency response functions are coordinated in a proactive manner from the State Emergency Operations Center located in Raleigh, North Carolina. Proactive response strategies used by the division include the following:

- Area commands that are strategically located in an affected region to assist with local response efforts using state resources
- Central warehousing operations managed by the state that allow for immediate delivery of bottled water, ready-to-eat meals, blankets, tarps, and the like
- Field deployment teams manned by division and other State agency personnel that assist severely affected counties; coordinate and prioritize response activity
- Incident action planning that identifies response priorities and resource requirements 12–24 h in advance

The State Emergency Response Team (SERT), which is comprised of top-level management representatives of each State agency involved in response activities, provides the technical expertise and coordinates the delivery of the emergency resources used to support local emergency operations.

When resource needs are beyond the capabilities of State agencies, mutual aid from other unaffected local governments and States may be secured using the Statewide Mutual Aid agreement or Emergency Management Assistance compact. Federal assistance may also be requested through the Federal Emergency Response Team, which collocates with the SERT during major disasters.

Source: North Carolina Department of Emergency Management, https://www.ncdps.gov/Search.cfm?q=response+functions.

The changes that continue to occur regarding the roles and responsibilities of the state emergency managers are based on the same principles as those occurring at the local level (i.e., changes in procedures to handle terrorist incidents, response equipment, responding agencies and protocols of cooperation, and in local/state/federal operation plans). The sidebar "State, Territorial, or Tribal Emergency Management Responsibilities as Described in the National Response Framework" summarizes the responsibilities of the various political entities for the public safety and welfare of the residents of each, as stated in the NRF.

State, Territorial, or Tribal Emergency Management Responsibilities as Described in the National Response Framework

States, territories, and tribal nations have the primary responsibility for the public health and welfare of their citizens (under the NRF, the term "State" and discussion of the roles and responsibilities of States typically include those responsibilities that apply to US territories and possessions and tribal nations). State and local governments are closest to those impacted by natural disasters, and have always had the lead in response and recovery. States are sovereign entities, and the Governor has the primary responsibility for the public safety and welfare of residents. US territories and possessions and tribal nations also have sovereign rights and hold special responsibilities.

States have significant resources of their own, including State emergency management and homeland security agencies, State Police, health agencies, transportation agencies, and the National Guard. The role of the State government in incident response is to supplement local efforts before, during, and after incidents. During incident response, States play a key role coordinating resources and capabilities from across the State and obtaining resources and capabilities from other States. If a State anticipates that its resources may become overwhelmed, each Governor can request assistance from the Federal government or from other States through mutual aid and assistance agreements such as the Emergency Management Assistance Compact.

A primary role of State government in incident management is to supplement and facilitate local efforts before, during, and after incidents. The State provides direct and routine assistance to its local jurisdictions through emergency management program development, coordinating routinely in these efforts with Federal preparedness officials. States must be prepared to maintain or accelerate services and to provide new services to local governments when local capabilities fall short of demands.

States are also responsible for requesting Federal emergency assistance for communities and tribes within their area of responsibility. Thus, States help by coordinating federal assistance to the local level. In response to an incident, the State helps coordinate and integrate resources and applies them to local needs.

As a State's chief executive, the Governor is responsible for the public safety and welfare of the people of his or her State. The Governor (for the purposes of the NRF, any reference to a State Governor also references the chief executive of US territories):

- Is responsible for coordinating State resources needed to prevent, prepare for, respond to and recover from emergency incidents of all types.
- In accordance with State law, may be able to make, amend or suspend certain orders or regulations in support of the incident response.
- Communicates to the public and helps people, businesses and organizations cope with the consequences of any type of emergency.
- Commands the State military forces (National Guard and State militias).
- Arranges help from other States through interstate mutual aid and assistance compacts, such as the Emergency Management Assistance Compact (EMAC).
- Requests federal assistance including, if appropriate, a Stafford Act Presidential declaration of an emergency or disaster, when it becomes clear that State or interstate mutual aid capabilities will be insufficient or have been exceeded.
- Coordinates with impacted tribal nations within the State and initiates requests for a Stafford Act Presidential emergency or disaster declaration on behalf of an impacted tribe when appropriate.

Before being sworn in, each new Governor should:

- Avoid vacancies in key homeland security positions such as the State homeland security director or the State emergency manager. A newly elected Governor should work with his or her transition team to identify these key personnel early to minimize vacancies and encourage overlap with the outgoing administration. As soon as a new Governor selects people for these positions, the department or agency they are about to lead should be informed.
- Ensure that a staff able to manage a disaster response operation is in place on their inauguration day.
- Task their incoming gubernatorial staff, particularly the legal counsel, with reviewing the procedures necessary for them to declare a State emergency and use their emergency powers.

The State Homeland Security Advisor serves as counsel to the Governor on homeland security issues and serves as a liaison between the Governor's office, the State homeland security structure, DHS and other organizations both inside and outside of the State. The advisor often chairs a committee composed of representatives of relevant State agencies, including public safety, the National Guard, emergency management, public health and others charged with developing preparedness and response strategies.

All States have laws mandating establishment of a State emergency management agency and the EOP coordinated by that agency. The Director of the State emergency management agency ensures that the State is prepared to deal with large-scale emergencies and is responsible for coordinating the State response in any major emergency or disaster. This includes supporting local governments as needed or requested, and coordinating assistance with the federal government. If the community's resources are not adequate, local authorities can seek additional assistance from the county or State emergency manager. The State emergency management agency may dispatch personnel to the scene to assist in the response and recovery effort. If a community requires resources beyond those available in the State, local agencies may request certain types of federal assistance directly. For example, under the Oil Protection Act or the Comprehensive Environmental Response, Compensation, and Liability Act (CERCLA), local and tribal governments can request assistance directly from the Environmental Protection Agency and/or the US Coast Guard without having to go through the State. However, only the Governor can request a Presidential declaration under the Stafford Act.

Heads of other State departments and agencies and their staff develop and train to internal policies and procedures to meet response and recovery needs. They should also participate in interagency training and exercising to develop and maintain the necessary capabilities.

Source: DHS (2008).

Critical Thinking

Should the states take a more active role in emergency management at the local level? Do you feel there is anything that the states could do to improve local capacities without infringing on their jurisdictional rights?

Volunteer Group Response

Volunteer groups are often on the front line of disaster response. National groups such as the American Red Cross and the Salvation Army maintain rosters of local chapters of volunteers who are trained in emergency response. These organizations work collaboratively with local, state, and federal authorities to address the immediate needs of disaster victims. They provide shelter, food, and clothing to disaster victims who have had to evacuate or lost their homes to disasters large and small. Each year, the range of response and recovery functions assumed by volunteer groups in lieu of traditional government response agency efforts only grows.

In addition to the Red Cross and the Salvation Army, there are numerous volunteer groups across the country that provide aid and comfort to disaster victims. The National Voluntary Organizations Active in Disaster (NVOAD) is composed of an association of 58 national member organizations, 56 state and territorial VOADs, and a quickly growing number of county, community, regional, and other local VOADs that are involved in disaster response and recovery operations around the country and abroad. Formed in 1970, NVOAD helps member groups at a disaster location to coordinate and communicate in order to provide the most efficient and effective response. The following is a list of the NVOAD member organizations:

- ACTS World Relief (Foundation of Hope)
- Adventist Community Services
- All Hands Volunteers, Inc.
- Alliance of Information and Referral Systems (AIRS)
- AmeriCares
- American Radio Relay League
- The American Red Cross
- Billy Graham Rapid Response Team
- Brethren Disaster Ministries

- Buddhist Tzu Chi Foundation
- Catholic Charities USA
- Churches of Scientology Disaster Response
- Church World Service
- CityTeam Ministries
- Convoy of Hope
- Cooperative Baptist Fellowship
- Direct Relief
- Episcopal Relief & Development
- Feeding America
- Feed the Children
- Habitat for Humanity International
- Headwaters Relief Organization
- Heart to Heart International
- HOPE Animal-Assisted Crisis Response
- HOPE Coalition America (Operation HOPE)
- Hope Force International
- HOPE *worldwide*
- Humane Society of the United States
- ICNA Relief USA
- Islamic Relief
- International Critical Incident Stress Foundation
- International Relief & Development
- The Jewish Federations of North America, Inc.
- Latter-Day Saints Charities
- Lutheran Disaster Response
- Mennonite Disaster Service
- Mercy Medical Angels
- National Association of Jewish Chaplains
- National Baptist Convention, USA, Inc.
- National Organization for Victim Assistance
- Nazarene Disaster Response
- NECHAMA—Jewish Response to Disaster
- Noah's Wish
- Operation Blessing
- Presbyterian Church in America—Mission to North America
- Presbyterian Disaster Assistance
- Rebuilding Together
- Samaritan's Purse
- Save the Children

- Society of St. Vincent de Paul
- Southern Baptist Convention/North American Mission Board
- The Salvation Army
- Team Rubicon
- ToolBank Disaster Services
- United Church of Christ
- United Methodist Committee on Relief
- United Way Worldwide
- World Vision (NVOAD, 2014)

DHS Volunteer Programs

Volunteerism has been an integral part of life in the United States for decades. After the 9/11 terrorist attacks, this attribute only expanded. What also occurred was that many people who already volunteered in their communities, and many people who had not volunteered but were suddenly drawn to do so, sought out ways in which they could contribute to making their communities more secure. The federal government responded to their outpouring of concern through the creation of USA Freedom Corps, which was created "in an effort to capture those opportunities [to contribute to community security] and to foster a culture of service, citizenship, and responsibility."

Citizen Corps is the arm of USA Freedom Corps that provides opportunities for citizens who want to help make their communities safer and more secure. In the first 5 years of its existence, following a call by President George W. Bush for 2 years of volunteer service from every American citizen, almost 24,000 people from all 50 states and US territories volunteered to work with one or more of the Citizen Corps programs. Since then, the numbers have increased. The programs contained within Citizen Corps include the following:

- Citizen Corps Councils
- Community Emergency Response Team (CERT)
- Volunteers in Police Service (VIPS)
- Medical Reserve Corps (MRC)
- Neighborhood Watch
- Fire Corps

Although some of these programs are new, others, such as Neighborhood Watch, have been in place for more than a decade. Brief information about the programs and their response component follows, along with section "Citizen Corps Facts," which includes various facts about the Corps reported by DHS (FEMA, 2014e).

Citizen Corps Facts

- There are now 51 state/territory Citizen Corps Councils and 1246 county/local/tribal councils.
- There are now 2543 Community Emergency Response Teams (CERT) active in communities across the country.
- There are currently more than 244,000 volunteers registered with the Volunteers in Police Service program and over 2288 registered programs. Volunteers provide well over 1 million hours of service a year.

- Since its inception in 2002, the Medical Reserve Corps has grown to over 147,000 volunteer members. There are 980 communities with federally funded Medical Reserve Corps units.
- Fire Corps was started in May 2004. In its first year of existence, almost 300 Fire Corps programs were created. Today, there are 1098 throughout the United States.
- Based on the 2000 Census, Citizen Corps, VIPS, CERT, and MRC programs serve 67% of the US populations (190,548,299 citizens).

Citizen Corps Councils

Citizen Corps Councils (CCCs) are established at the state and local levels to promote, organize, and run the various programs that fall under the Citizen Corps umbrella. Funding for these councils is provided by the federal government through grant awards. As of November 2014, there were CCCs in 51 states and US territories and 1246 local communities, all of which serve 67% of the total population of the United States. Figure 9-4 displays the geographic coverage of the CCCs.

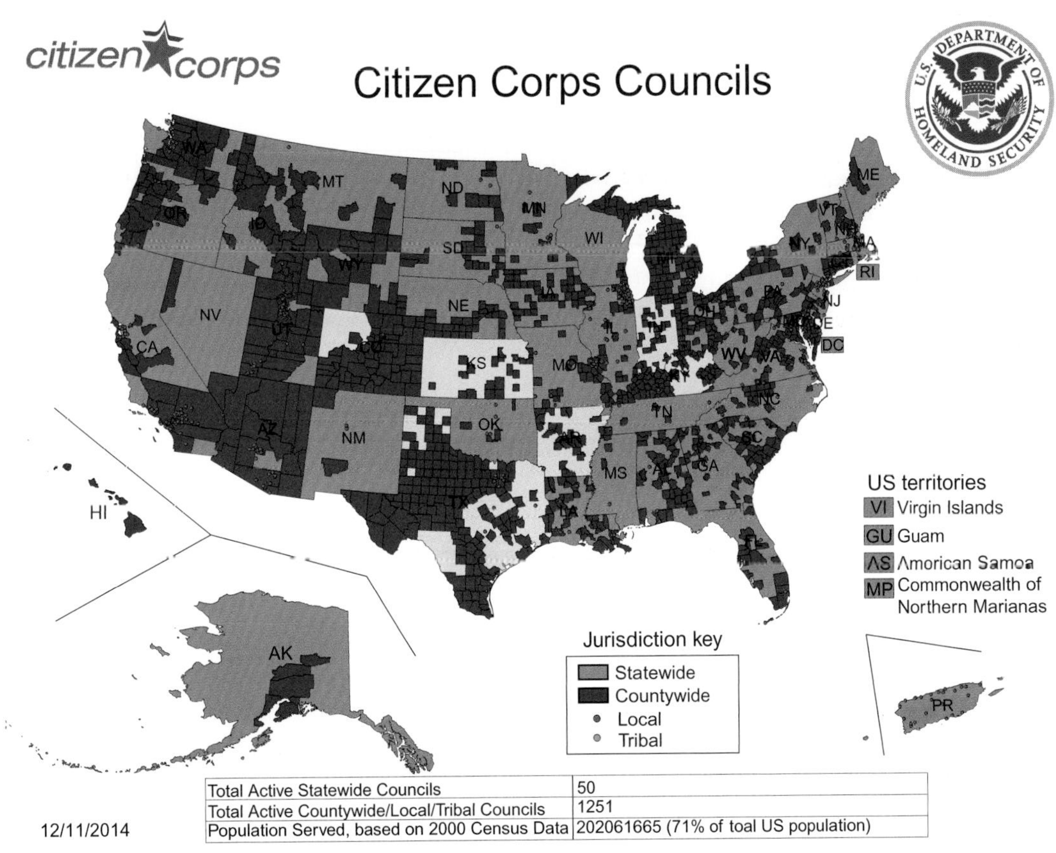

Total Active Statewide Councils	50
Total Active Countywide/Local/Tribal Councils	1251
Population Served, based on 2000 Census Data	202061665 (71% of toal US population)

FIGURE 9-4 Map of Citizen Corps Councils in the United States and its territories. *Source: Citizen Corps (2011).*

Community Emergency Response Teams

The Community Emergency Response Team (CERT) program began in Los Angeles, California, in 1983. City administrators there recognized that in most emergency situations, average citizens—neighbors, co-workers, and bystanders, for example—were often on the scene during the critical moments before professional help arrived. These officials acted on the belief that, by training average citizens to perform basic search and rescue, first aid, and other critical emergency response skills, they would increase the overall resilience of the community. Additionally, should a large-scale disaster like an earthquake occur, where first-response units would be stretched very thin, these trained citizens would be able to augment official services and provide an important service to the community.

Beginning in 1993, FEMA began to offer CERT training on a national level, providing funding to cover start-up and tuition costs for programs. As of November 2014, CERT programs had been established in more than 2543 active programs in communities in all 50 states, the District of Columbia, and several US territories. CERT teams remain active in the community before a disaster strikes, sponsoring events such as drills, neighborhood cleanup, and disaster-education fairs. Trainers offer periodic refresher sessions to CERT members to reinforce the basic training and to keep participants involved and practiced in their skills. CERT members also offer other nonemergency assistance to the community with the goal of improving the overall safety of the community. Figure 9-5 illustrates the geographic coverage of CERT in the United States.

Volunteers in Police Service Program

Since September 11, 2001, the demands on state and local law enforcement have increased dramatically. Limited resources at the community level have resulted from these increased demands, and regular police work has ultimately suffered. To address these shortfalls, the Volunteers in Police Service (VIPS) program was created. The basis of the program is that civilian volunteers are able to support police officers by doing much of the behind-the-scenes work that does not require formal law enforcement training, thereby allowing officers to spend more of their already strained schedules on the street. Although the concept is not new, federal support for such programs is.

The VIPS draws on the time and recognized talents of civilian volunteers. Volunteer roles may include performing clerical tasks, serving as an extra set of eyes and ears, assisting with search and rescue activities, and writing citations for accessible parking violations, just to name a few. As of November 2014, there were 2288 official VIPS programs registered throughout the United States. Figure 9-6 illustrates the geographic coverage of VIPS in the United States.

Medical Reserve Corps Program

The Medical Reserve Corps (MRC) was founded after the 2002 State of the Union Address, to establish teams of local volunteer medical and public health professionals who can contribute their skills and experience when called on in times of need. The program relies on volunteers who are practicing and retired physicians, nurses, dentists, veterinarians, epidemiologists, and other health professionals and other citizens untrained in public health but who can contribute to the community's normal and disaster public health needs in other ways (which may include interpreters, chaplains, and legal advisors).

Local community leaders develop their own MRC units and recruit local volunteers who can address the specific community needs. For example, MRC volunteers may deliver necessary public health services during a crisis, assist emergency response teams with patients, and provide care directly to those with less serious injuries and other health-related issues. MRC volunteers may also serve a vital role by assisting

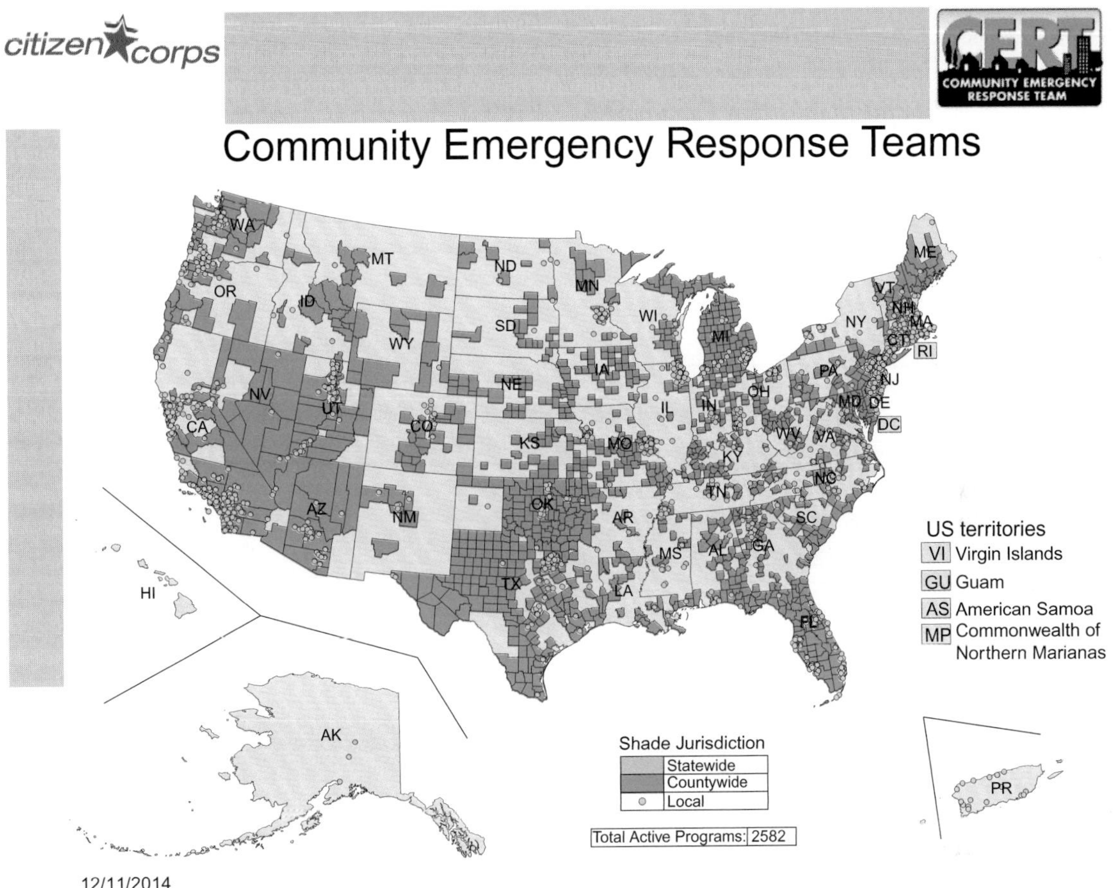

FIGURE 9-5 CERT programs in the United States and its territories. *Source: Citizen Corps (2011).*

their communities with ongoing public health needs (e.g., immunizations, screenings, health and nutrition education, and volunteering in community health centers and local hospitals). The MRC unit decides, in concert with local officials (including the local CCC), on when the community MRC is activated during a local emergency. As of November 2014, there were 980 MRC programs established throughout the United States (see Figure 9-7).

Neighborhood Watch Program

The Neighborhood Watch program has been in existence for more than 30 years in cities and counties throughout the United States. The program is based on the concept that neighbors who join together to fight crime will be able to increase security in their surrounding areas and, as a result, provide an overall better quality of life for residents. Understandably, after September 11, 2001, when terrorism became a major focus of the US government, the recognized importance of programs like Neighborhood Watch took on much greater significance.

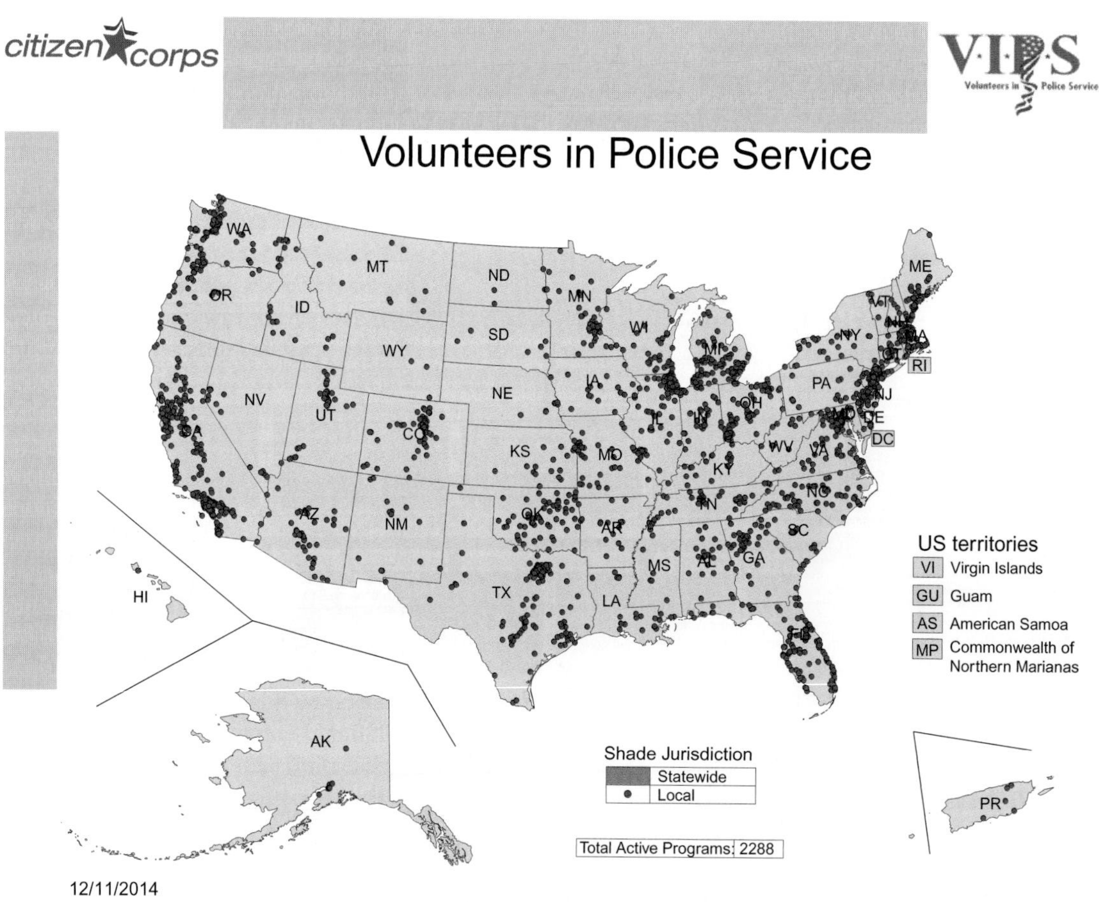

FIGURE 9-6 VIPS programs in the United State and its territories. *Source: Citizen Corps, 2011.*

The Neighborhood Watch program is not maintained by the National Sheriff's Association, which founded the program initially. At the local level, the CCCs help neighborhood groups who have banded together to start a program to carry out their mission. Many printed materials and other guidance are available for free to help them carry out their goals.

Neighborhood Watch programs have successfully decreased crime in many of the neighborhoods where they have been implemented. In total, as of January 2008, there were 14,791 programs spread out throughout the United States and the US territories. In addition to serving a crime prevention role, Neighborhood Watch has also been used as the basis for bringing neighborhood residents together to focus on disaster preparedness and terrorism awareness, to focus on evacuation drills and exercises, and even to organize group training, such as the CERT training.

Fire Corps

The Fire Corps was created in 2004 under the umbrella of USA Freedom Corps and Citizen Corps. The purpose of the program, like the VIPS program with the police, was to enhance the ability of fire departments to

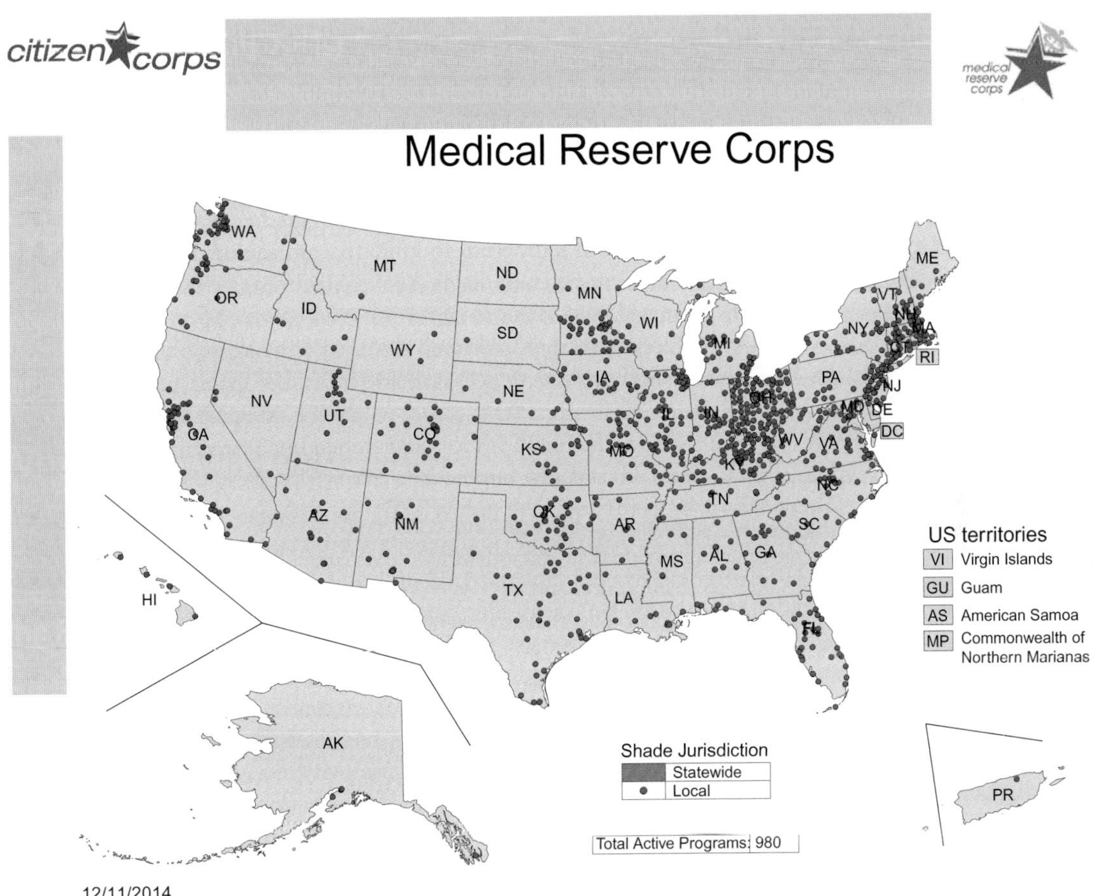

FIGURE 9-7 Medical Reserve Corps in the United States and its territories. *Source: Citizens Corps (2011).*

utilize citizen advocates and provide individuals with opportunities to support their local fire departments with both time and talent.

Fire Corps was created as a partnership between the International Association of Fire Chiefs' Volunteer and Combination Officers Section (VCOS), the International Association of Fire Fighters (IAFF), and the National Volunteer Fire Council (NVFC). By participating in the program, concerned and interested citizens can assist in their local fire department's activities through tasks such as administrative assistance, public education, fund-raising, data entry, accounting, public relations, and equipment and facility maintenance, to name just a few.

Any fire department that allows citizens to volunteer support service is considered a Fire Corps program, but programs can become official through registering with a local, county, or state CCC, if one exists. Official Fire Corps programs will be provided with assistance on how to implement a nonoperational citizen advocates program or how to improve existing programs. A Fire Corps National Advisory Committee has been established under the program in order to provide strategic direction and collect feedback from the field. As of August 2011, there were 1098 established Fire Corps programs throughout the United States and US territories.

DHS Response Agencies

With the passage of the Homeland Security Act of 2002, several government agencies and offices that managed components of the nation's response framework were consolidated into the DHS. Originally, these various components were brought into DHS and merged together to form an EP&R directorate, composed most prominently by the functions of the original FEMA. During the course of the DHS's nearly 13-year history, several of these components have moved within the structure of DHS—many falling under the direction of the newly reformed FEMA—while others have since been removed from the department entirely or are facing permanent closure. These agencies and offices, each of which is described in detail below, include the following:

The Federal Emergency Management Agency (FEMA)
The National Domestic Preparedness Office of the Federal Bureau of Investigation
Domestic Emergency Support Teams of the Department of Justice
Office of Emergency Management
National Disaster Medical System
Metropolitan Medical Response System
Strategic National Stockpile

Federal Emergency Management Agency

The Federal Emergency Management Agency—a former independent agency that became part of the new DHS in March 2003—is tasked with responding to, planning for, recovering from, and mitigating against disasters. The FEMA Response Division provides the core operational and logistical disaster response capability of the federal government, which is called upon to save and sustain lives, minimize suffering, and protect property in a timely and effective manner in communities that become overwhelmed by natural disasters, acts of terrorism, or other emergencies. FEMA response program activities encompass the coordination of all federal emergency management response operations, response planning, and logistics programs and integration of federal, state, tribal, and local disaster programs. This coordination is designed to facilitate the delivery of immediate emergency assistance to individuals and communities impacted and overwhelmed by emergency and disaster events (see Figure 9-8).

FEMA's disaster response responsibilities within DHS, which are very similar to those maintained by the agency prior to its incorporation into DHS, include (among others)

- coordinating with local and state first responders to manage disasters requiring federal assistance and to recover from their effects (as stipulated in the NRF);
- administering the Disaster Relief Emergency Fund;
- maintaining the administration of the National Flood Insurance Program;
- administering the training and other responsibilities of the US Fire Administration;
- offering mitigation grant programs, including the Hazards Mitigation Grant Program, the Pre-Disaster Mitigation Program, and the Flood Mitigation Assistance program;
- administering the Citizen Corps program.

National Domestic Preparedness Office

The National Domestic Preparedness Office (NDPO), within the DOJ, coordinated all federal efforts, including those of the DOD, FEMA, the HHS, the Department of Energy (DOE), and the Environmental

FIGURE 9-8 Joplin, MO, August 3, 2011—Damage sustained at St. John's Regional Medical Center after the May 22 EF-5 tornado that struck the city. FEMA is working to provide assistance to those affected by the tornado. *Photo by Elissa Jun/FEMA.*

Protection Agency (EPA), to assist state and local first responders with planning, training, equipment, and exercises necessary to respond to a conventional or nonconventional WMD incident.

NDPO's various functions were transferred into the new DHS and placed under the direction of the FEMA-dominated EP&R directorate. Among the functions of the NDPO transferred were to

- serve as a single program and policy office for WMD to ensure that federal efforts are in harmony and represent the most effective and cost-efficient support to the state and local first-responder community;
- coordinate the establishment of training curriculum and standards for first-responder training to ensure consistency based on training objectives and to tailor training opportunities to meet the needs of the responder community;
- facilitate the efforts of the federal government to provide the responder community with detection, protection, analysis, and decontamination equipment necessary to prepare for, and respond to, an incident involving WMD;
- provide state and local governments with the resources and expertise necessary to design, conduct, and evaluate exercise scenarios involving WMD;
- communicate information to the state and local emergency response communities.

Domestic Emergency Support Team

The Domestic Emergency Support Team (DEST) is designed to be an interagency team of experts, operating on a standby basis, which can be quickly mobilized. This team, even within DHS (and directed by FEMA per the Stafford Act), is led by the FBI to provide an on-scene commander (OSC) (special agent in charge) with advice and guidance in situations involving WMDs or other significant domestic threats. The DEST guidance can range from information management and communications support to instructions on how to best respond to the detonation of a chemical, biological, or nuclear weapon or a radiological dispersal device (RDD). As specialized predesignated teams, DEST has no permanent staff at DHS, the FBI, or any other federal agency.

Office of Emergency Preparedness

The Office of Emergency Preparedness (OEP) was responsible for oversight, coordination, and management of EP&R and recovery activities in the HHS prior to its transfer to DHS. There were two principal programs of OEP that now exist within DHS under separate functional units. They are the NDMS and the MMRS and are described in further detail later.

Before its move into DHS, OEP served as the lead for Emergency Support Function (ESF) #8 within the FRP—Public Health and Medical Services. Under the NRF, HHS has maintained this responsibility under the new ESF #8, Public Health and Medical Services. The tasks performed by the NDMS and MMRS, which were fulfilled within ESF #8, are still performed as before but under a different direction.

National Disaster Medical System

The National Disaster Medical System (NDMS), which originally resided within the Office of Emergency Preparedness of HHS, was transferred to the DHS EP&R directorate per the Homeland Security Act of 2002, but now falls back under the direction of HHS as stipulated in the Post-Katrina Emergency Management Reform Act of 2006 (including its $33.8 million budget). NDMS is a federally coordinated system that is responsible for supporting federal agencies in the management and coordination of the federal medical response to major emergencies and federally declared disasters. In doing so, it establishes a single, integrated national medical response capability for assisting state and local authorities in dealing with the medical and health effects of major disasters. NDMS also cares for casualties of US military operations overseas who have been airlifted back to the United States.

NDMS consists of more than 8000 volunteer health professionals and support personnel organized into disaster assistance teams that can be activated and deployed anywhere in the country to assist state and local emergency medical services. Several operational units within NDMS assist in this function:

- *Disaster Medical Assistance Team (DMAT)*: A DMAT is a group of professional and paraprofessional medical personnel, supported by logistical and administrative staff, designed to provide medical care during a disaster or other event. Each team has a sponsoring organization, such as a major medical center, public health or safety agency, nonprofit, public, or private organization that signs a Memorandum of Agreement (MOA) with DHS. The DMAT sponsor organizes the team and recruits members, arranges training, and coordinates the dispatch of the team.
- *Disaster Mortuary Operational Response Team (DMORT)*: DMORTs, like DMATs, are composed of private citizens, each with a particular field of expertise, who are activated in the event of a disaster. During an emergency response, DMORTs work under the guidance of local authorities

by providing technical assistance and personnel to recover, identify, and process deceased victims. Teams are composed of funeral directors, medical examiners, coroners, pathologists, forensic anthropologists, medical records technicians and transcribers, fingerprint specialists, forensic odontologists, dental assistants, X-ray technicians, mental health specialists, computer professionals, administrative support staff, and security and investigative personnel. Their duties include setting up temporary morgue facilities, victim identification, forensic dental pathology, forensic anthropology, and processing, preparation, and disposition of remains.

- *International Medical Surgical Response Team (IMSURT)*: The International Medical Surgical Response Team (IMSURT) is a National Disaster Medical System (NDMS) team of medical specialists who provide surgical and critical care during a disaster or public health emergency. Originally conceived to address the needs of US citizens injured overseas, the IMSURT role has expanded over the years to include both domestic deployments, including the World Trade Center Bombings and Hurricane Katrina, and international deployments, including the earthquakes in Bam, Iran, and Port au Prince, Haiti. IMSURT personnel are Federal employees used on an intermittent basis to deploy to the site of a disaster or public health emergency and provide high quality, life saving surgical and critical care.
- *Veterinary Medical Assistance Team (VMAT)*: VMATs are composed of private citizens who are activated in the event of a disaster. During an emergency response, VMATs work under the guidance of local authorities by providing technical assistance and veterinary services. Teams are composed of clinical veterinarians, veterinary pathologists, animal health technicians (veterinary technicians), microbiologist/virologists, epidemiologists, toxicologists, and various scientific and support personnel. It is the primary Federal resource for the treatment of injured or ill animals affected by disasters. These responsibilities include assessing the veterinary medical needs of the community, veterinary medical support to working animals (including horses) which might include search and rescue dogs and animals used for law enforcement, treatment of injured and ill large and small animals post disasters, veterinary medical support for sheltered animals, veterinary health screening at points of embarkation and debarkation for any animals, veterinary public health support including environmental and zoonotic disease assessment, research animal support (Lab animals), and support for an outbreak in livestock and poultry (USDA led).

Metropolitan Medical Response System

The Metropolitan Medical Response System (MMRS) provides funding to cities that upgrade and improve their own planning and preparedness to respond to mass casualty events. The concept for the program began in 1995 in the Washington, DC, metropolitan area with the creation of the Metropolitan Medical Strike Team (MMST). This first team, which pooled resources from several adjoining jurisdictions, was created primarily for the response to chemical incidents, but was able to provide on-site emergency health and medical services following WMD terrorist incidents.

The MMST concept was expanded to several cities under the guidance and funding of the federal government through the authority of the Defense Against Weapons of Mass Destruction Act of 1996 (Nunn-Lugar-Domenici legislation). The program's name was changed to the Metropolitan Medical Response System to highlight its national system-oriented approach. The program has grown from the 25 teams created in 1995 to almost 124 municipalities.

The sidebar "MMRS Capabilities and Impacts" provides a detailed description of capabilities and the difference the MMRS makes at the local level.

MMRS Capabilities and Impacts

MMRS Capabilities

- Initial identification of agents
- Ability to perform operations in OSHA levels A, B, and C personal protective equipment, avoiding secondary responder casualties
- Enhanced triage, treatment, and decontamination capabilities at the incident site and definitive care facilities
- Maintenance of local caches sufficient to treat 1000 patients exposed to chemical agents
- Ability to transport uncontaminated/decontaminated patients to area hospitals for definitive care
- Ability to maintain a viable health system
- Ability to transport patients to participating NDMS hospitals throughout the nation
- Mechanisms to activate mutual aid support from local, state, and federal emergency response agencies
- Ability to integrate additional response assets into the ongoing incident command structure

MMRS Local Level Impacts

- Requires development of response plans unique for each city
- Creates integrated immediate response structure
- Creates additional local and regional support networks
- Integrates with local mass casualty plans
- Brings together and encourages city planning agencies to interact where they never interacted before
- Encourages and initiates hospital WMD planning
- Encourages local health-care providers to develop appropriate medical treatment protocols

Source: HHS, www.hhs.gov.

Strategic National Stockpile

The Strategic National Stockpile (SNS) began in 1999, when Congress charged HHS and Centers for Disease Control and Prevention (CDC) with the establishment of the capability to provide a resupply of large quantities of essential medical material to states and communities during an emergency within 12 h of the federal decision to deploy to that region. The system that was developed was called the National Pharmaceutical Stockpile (NPS).

As stipulated in the Homeland Security Act of 2002, on March 1, 2003, the NPS was transferred from HHS to DHS and was given the new title Strategic National Stockpile. The program was established so that it could be managed jointly by DHS and HHS and be able to work with governmental and nongovernmental partners to continually seek ways to upgrade the nation's public health capacity to respond to national emergencies. With the signing of the BioShield legislation, however, the SNS program was returned to HHS for oversight and guidance.

During a national emergency, state, local, and private stocks of medical material will be depleted quickly. The SNS is designed to help all state and local first responders bolster their response to a national emergency, through the provision of specially designed 12-h push packages, private vendors, or a combination of both, depending on the situation. Like most federal response programs, the SNS is not a first-response tool, but one that supplements the initial local response efforts.

The SNS is a national repository of antibiotics, chemical antidotes, antitoxins, life-support medications, IV administration supplies, airway maintenance supplies, and medical/surgical items. The SNS is designed to supplement and resupply state and local public health agencies in the event of a national emergency anywhere and at any time within the United States or its territories. The system is also set up to allow for the acquisition of additional pharmaceuticals and/or medical supplies not maintained directly by the SNS through the use of private vendors (which can ship supplies to arrive within 24–36 h of the request). In some areas, the vendors, which are preregistered under the program, can actually provide the first wave of supplies that arrive.

The sidebar "The Strategic National Stockpile" gives an overview of how the SNS functions and how its components interact with local and state organizations.

The Strategic National Stockpile

The Strategic National Stockpile (SNS) program is committed to have 12-h Push Packages delivered anywhere in the United States or its territories within 12 h of a Federal decision to deploy. The 12-h Push Packages have been configured to be immediately loaded onto either trucks or commercial cargo aircraft for the most rapid transportation. Concurrent to SNS transport, the SNS program will deploy its Technical Advisory Response Unit (TARU). The TARU staff will coordinate with State and local officials so that the SNS assets can be efficiently received and distributed on arrival at the site.

DHS will transfer authority for the SNS materiel to the State and local authorities once it arrives at the designated receiving and storage site. State and local authorities will then begin the breakdown of the 12-h Push Package for distribution. SNS TARU members will remain on-site in order to assist and advise State and local officials in putting the SNS assets to prompt and effective use.

The decision to deploy SNS assets may be based on evidence showing the overt release of an agent that might adversely affect public health. It is more likely, however, that subtle indicators, such as unusual morbidity and/or mortality identified through the nation's disease outbreak surveillance and epidemiology network, will alert health officials to the possibility (and confirmation) of a biological or chemical incident or a national emergency. To receive SNS assets, the affected State's Governor's office will directly request the deployment of the SNS assets from CDC or DHS. DHS, HHS, CDC, and other Federal officials will evaluate the situation and determine a prompt course of action.

The SNS program is part of a nationwide preparedness training and education program for State and local health-care providers, first responders, and governments (to include Federal officials, Governors' offices, State and local health departments, and emergency management agencies). This training explains the SNS program's mission and operations and also alerts State and local emergency response officials to the important issues they must plan for in order to receive, secure, and distribute SNS assets.

To conduct this outreach and training, CDC and SNS program staff are currently working with DHS, HHS agencies, regional emergency response coordinators at all of the US Public Health Service regional offices, State and local health departments, State emergency management offices, the Metropolitan Medical Response System cities, the Department of Veterans Affairs, and the Department of Defense.

Source: Centers for Disease Control and Prevention, http://www.cdc.gov/phpr/stockpile/stockpile.htm.

Urban Search and Rescue

The concept of formally maintained Urban Search and Rescue (US&R or USAR) teams was introduced in the early 1980s. The Fairfax County Fire and Rescue, Virginia, and the Metro-Dade County Fire Department, Florida, each created specialized search and rescue teams trained for rescue operations in collapsed buildings. US&R involves the location, rescue (extrication), and initial medical stabilization of victims trapped in confined spaces. Structural collapse is most often the cause of victims being trapped, but victims may also be trapped in transportation accidents, mines, and collapsed trenches. The initial teams created to carry out these tasks were so successful in this specialty that they were often sent abroad on missions, representing the US government relief efforts, through the support of the Department of State and the Office of US Foreign Disaster Assistance (OFDA) of the US Agency for International Development (USAID). These teams have been deployed to Mexico City, the Philippines, and Armenia, providing vital search and rescue support in earthquake-induced disasters in each of these areas (see Figure 9-9).

FIGURE 9-9 Sabine Pass, Texas, September 14, 2008—FEMA Urban Search and Rescue team conducts searches in areas impacted by Hurricane Ike. *Photo by Jocelyn Augustino/FEMA.*

Beginning in 1991, US&R became a component of federal response operations under the FRP, when the US&R concept was incorporated as an individual ESF. From that starting point, the size of the US&R system grew considerably, with FEMA sponsoring the creation of 25 national US&R task forces. Today, there are 28 national task forces staffed and equipped to conduct round-the-clock search-and-rescue operations following earthquakes, tornadoes, floods, hurricanes, aircraft accidents, hazardous materials spills, and catastrophic structure collapses. These task forces, complete with necessary tools and equipment and required skills and techniques, can be deployed by FEMA for the rescue of victims of structural collapse.

In 2003, when FEMA was transferred into DHS, the US&R system transferred with FEMA, intact. FEMA, under DHS, maintains its primary agency designation under ESF #9, Search and Rescue.

How the teams are structured and operate is discussed in the sidebars "Urban Search and Rescue (US&R) Teams" and a "Profile of a Rescue."

Urban Search and Rescue (US&R) Teams

- If a disaster event warrants national US&R support, DHS will deploy the three closest task forces within 6 h of notification and additional teams as necessary. The role of these task forces is to support State and local emergency responders' efforts to locate victims and manage recovery operations.
- Each task force consists of two 31-person teams, four canines, and a comprehensive equipment cache. For every US&R task force, there are 62 positions. To ensure that a full team can respond to an emergency, the task forces have at the ready more than 130 highly trained members.
- A task force is really a partnership between local fire departments, law enforcement agencies, Federal and local governmental agencies, and private companies.
- A task force is totally self-sufficient for the first 72 h of a deployment.
- The equipment cache used to support a task force weighs nearly 60,000 pounds and is worth about $1.4 million. Add the task force members to the cache, and you can completely fill a military C-141 transport or two C-130s.
- US&R task force members work in four areas of specialization: search, to find victims trapped after a disaster; rescue, which includes safely digging victims out of tons of collapsed concrete and metal; technical, made up of structural specialists who make rescues safe for the rescuers; and medical, which cares for the victims before and after a rescue.
- In addition to search and rescue support, the DHS provides hands-on training in search and rescue techniques and equipment, technical assistance to local communities, and in some cases Federal grants to help communities better prepare for US&R operations.
- The bottom line in US&R: Some day, lives may be saved because of the skills these rescuers gain. These first responders consistently go to the front lines when the nation needs them most.
- Not only are these first responders a national resource that can be deployed to a major disaster or structural collapse anywhere in the country, they are also the local firefighters and paramedics who answer local 911 calls.
- Events such as the 1995 bombing of the Alfred P. Murrah Federal Office Building in Oklahoma City, the Northridge earthquake, the Kansas grain elevator explosion in 1998, and earthquakes in Turkey and Greece in 1999 underscore the need for highly skilled teams to rescue trapped victims.

- What the task force can do: Conduct physical search and rescue in collapsed buildings; provide emergency medical care to trapped victims; deploy search and rescue dogs; assess and control gas, electric service, and hazardous materials; and evaluate and stabilize damaged structures.

Source: Federal Emergency Management Agency, www.fema.gov and Department of Homeland Security, www.dhs.gov.

Profile of a Rescue

While every search-and-rescue assignment is unique, a rescue might go something like this:

- Response always begins at the local level. Local fire departments, emergency management, and local and state law enforcement are the first to arrive at the scene and begin rescue and response.
- Following a disaster, the local emergency manager may request assistance from the state; if the need is great, the state may in turn request federal assistance; in the event of a major disaster, FEMA deploys three of the closest task forces.
- After arriving at the site, structural specialists, who are licensed professional engineers charged with making the rescue safe for the rescuers, provide direct input to the FEMA task force members about structural integrity of the building and the risk of secondary collapses.
- Heavy equipment is used to remove large rubble and debris that could injure rescue workers and impede rescue operations.
- The search team ventures around and into the collapsed structure, carefully shoring up structures while attempting to locate trapped victims. Rescuers use electronic listening devices, extremely small search cameras and specially trained search dogs to help locate victims.
- Once a victim is located, the search group begins the daunting task of breaking and cutting through thousands of pounds of concrete, metal, and wood to reach the victims. They also stabilize and support the entry and work areas with wood shoring to prevent further collapse.
- Medical teams, composed of trauma physicians, emergency room nurses and paramedics, provide medical care for the victims as well as the rescuers. A fully stocked mobile emergency room is part of the task force equipment cache. Medics may be required to enter the dangerous interior of the collapsed structure to render immediate aid.
- Throughout the effort, hazardous materials specialists evaluate the disaster site, and decontaminate rescue and medical members who may be exposed to hazardous chemicals or decaying bodies.
- Heavy rigging specialists direct the use of heavy machinery, such as cranes and bulldozers. These specialists understand the special dangers of working in a collapsed structure, and help to ensure the safety of the victims and rescuers inside.
- Technical information and communication specialists ensure that all team members can communicate with each other and the task force leaders, facilitating search efforts and coordinating evacuation in the event of a secondary collapse.

- Logistics specialists handle the more than 16,000 pieces of equipment to support the search and extrication of the victims. The equipment cache includes such essentials as concrete cutting saws, search cameras, medical supplies, and tents, cots, food and water to keep the task force self-sufficient for up to 4 days.

Source: FEMA (2014f).

Maritime Search and Rescue

The USCG is one of only two federal agencies (including the US Secret Service) that transferred into the new DHS as an independent entity, thus reporting directly to the secretary of the DHS as opposed to one of the five directorates. The USCG maintains several distinct missions within DHS, but one of those, search and rescue, has resulted in the strong cooperation with FEMA and the EP&R directorate. Specifically, USCG maintains the authority and responsibility for the various tasks related to maritime search and rescue.

Maritime search and rescue (SAR) is one of the Coast Guard's oldest missions. Minimizing the loss of life, injury, property damage, or loss by rendering aid to persons in distress and property in the maritime environment has always been a Coast Guard priority. Coast Guard SAR response involves multiple-mission stations, cutters, aircraft, and boats linked by communications networks. The Coast Guard is the SAR coordinator for US aeronautical and maritime search and rescue regions that are near America's oceans, including Alaska and Hawaii. To meet this responsibility, the Coast Guard maintains SAR facilities on the East, West, and Gulf Coasts; in Alaska, Hawaii, Guam, and Puerto Rico; and on the Great Lakes and inland US waterways.

The USCG maintains that, in performing their SAR goal, they are guided by two program objectives:

1. Save at least 93% of those people at risk of death on waters over which the Coast Guard has SAR responsibility.
2. Prevent the loss of at least 80% of the property that is at risk of destruction on the waters over which the Coast Guard has SAR responsibility.

Additionally, the USCG maintains standards of operation by which they plan to fulfill these goals and objectives:

Readiness: Search and rescue unit ready to proceed within 30 min of notification of a distress.

Transit: Search and rescue unit on scene, or within the search area, within 90 min of getting under way.

VHF-FM Distress Net Standard: 100% VHF-FM continuous coverage to receive a 1 W signal out to 20 nautical miles around the US Atlantic, Pacific, Gulf of Mexico, and Great Lakes coasts. This is the primary distress alerting and SAR communications method for US coastal waters.

406 MHz Emergency Position Indicating Radio Beacon (EPIRB): Maximum use of the 406 MHz EPIRB in the offshore environment. The beacon's superior alerting, position indicating, and signaling capabilities significantly improve system effectiveness and efficiency. Beacon registration provides useful SAR response information and mitigates false alarm response costs. Currently, about 70% of US beacons are registered.

Command and Control Standard: Initiate action within 5 min of initial notification of a distress incident. Process and evaluate information about the SAR incident and determine appropriate action.

Computer-Assisted Search Planning (CASP) System Standard: Use CASP for planning guidance for all cases involving incidents outside the 30 fathom mark when

- the duration of an incident has or could have exceeded 24 h,
- there is uncertainty concerning the incident time, incident location, or type of search object(s) involved.

Automated Mutual-Assistance Vessel Rescue (AMVER) System Standard: Use AMVER for identification of rescue resources for all cases involving incidents on the high seas. The Coast Guard actively seeks to increase participation in this voluntary reporting system. Each year, more vessels participate in the system and more lives are saved.

SAR Planner Training Standard for SAR Mission Coordinators: 100% attendance and completion of resident SAR planner training at the National SAR School for Area, District, Section, and Group SAR planners.

The Coast Guard currently maintains six separate programs under the SAR, as briefly described in the sidebar "US Coast Guard Search and Rescue Programs."

US Coast Guard Search and Rescue Programs

Rescue 21

The Coast Guard currently uses the National Distress and Response System to monitor for maritime distress calls and coordinate response operations. The system consists of a network of VHF-FM antenna sites with analog transceivers that are remotely controlled by regional communications centers and rescue boat stations providing coverage out to approximately 20 nautical miles from the shore in most areas.

Salvage Assistance and Technical Support

The Marine Safety Center Salvage Assistance and Response Teams provide on-scene technical support during maritime catastrophes in order to predict events and mitigate their impact.

Operational Command, Control, and Communications

The National Strike Force Coordination Center (NSFCC) provides oversight and strategic direction to the strike teams, ensuring enhanced interoperability through a program of standardized operating procedures for response, equipment, training, and qualifications. The NSFCC conducts at least six major government-led spill response exercises each year under the National Preparedness for Response Exercise Program; maintains a national logistics network, using the Response Resource Inventory; implements the Coast Guard Oil Spill Removal Organization program; and administers the National Maintenance Contract for the Coast Guard's $30 million inventory of prepositioned spill response equipment.

AMVER

AMVER (Automated Mutual-Assistance Vessel Rescue) is a ship-reporting system for search and rescue. It is a global system that enables identification of other ships in the area of a ship in distress, which could then be sent to its assistance. AMVER information is used only for search and rescue and is made available to any rescue coordination center in the world responding to a search and rescue case. The Coast Guard actively seeks to increase participation in this voluntary reporting system. Each year, more vessels participate in the system and more lives are saved. Currently, ships from more than 143 nations participate.

AMVER represents "free" safety insurance during a voyage by improving the chances for aid in an emergency. By regular reporting, someone knows where a ship is at all times on its voyage in the event of an emergency. AMVER can reduce the time lost for vessels responding to calls for assistance by orchestrating a rescue response, utilizing ships in the best position or with the best capability to avoid unnecessary diversions in response to a Mayday or SOS call.

Pollution Control

The Response Operations Division develops and maintains policies for marine pollution response. They also coordinate activities with the international community, intelligence agencies, and the federal government in matters concerning threats or acts of terrorism in US ports and territorial waters.

National Strike Force

The National Strike Force (NSF) was established in 1973 as a direct result of the Federal Water Pollution Control Act of 1972. The NSF's mission is to provide highly trained, experienced personnel and specialized equipment to Coast Guard and other federal agencies to facilitate preparedness and response to oil and hazardous substance pollution incidents in order to protect public health and the environment. The NSF's area of responsibility covers all Coast Guard districts and federal response regions.

The strike teams provide rapid response support in incident management, site safety, contractor performance monitoring, resource documentation, response strategies, hazard assessment, oil spill dispersant and operational effectiveness monitoring, and high-capacity lightering and offshore-skimming capabilities.

Source: Department of Homeland Security, www.dhs.gov.

Other Response Agencies

Each of the agencies listed in the preceding section operates under the management of DHS and, in several cases, under FEMA, regardless of whether or not a disaster declaration has occurred. However, there are several other agencies within the federal government that bring emergency response capabilities to the federal response system, in many cases operating in their respective organizations without any clear day-to-day contact with DHS outside of a declared disaster. As stipulated in the NRF, these agencies can all be called upon to provide their services in times of need, under the coordination efforts of FEMA, in response to major disasters that require federal support (namely, presidentially declared disasters and emergencies). These departments and agencies are discussed individually.

Federal Bureau of Investigation

The Federal Bureau of Investigation (FBI), part of the Department of Justice, is the lead federal agency (LFA) for crisis management and investigation of all terrorism-related matters, including incidents involving a WMD. Within the FBI's role as LFA, the FBI federal on-scene commander (OSC) coordinates the overall federal response until the attorney general transfers the LFA role to FEMA (Figure 9-10). The primary response-related units within the FBI include the following:

- *FBI Domestic Terrorism/Counterterrorism Planning Section (DTCTPS)*: The DTCTPS serves as the point of contact (POC) to the FBI field offices and command structure and other federal agencies in incidences of terrorism, the use or suspected use of WMDs, and/or the evaluation of threat credibility. If the FBI's Strategic Information and Operations Center (SIOC) is operational for exercises or actual incidents, the DTCTPS will provide staff personnel to facilitate the operation of SIOC.
- *FBI Laboratory Division*: Within the FBI's Laboratory Division reside numerous assets, which can be deployed to provide assistance in a terrorism/WMD incident. The Hazardous Materials Response Unit (HMRU) personnel are highly trained and knowledgeable and are equipped to direct and assist in the collection of hazardous and/or toxic evidence in a contaminated environment.
- *FBI Critical Incident Response Group (CIRG)*: The Crisis Management Unit (CMU), which conducts training and exercises for the FBI and has developed the concept of the Joint Operations Center (JOC), is available to provide on-scene assistance to the incident and integrate the concept of the JOC and the ICS to create efficient management of the situation.

FIGURE 9-10 New York, N.Y., September 18, 2001—FBI members look on towards the wreckage at the World Trade Center. *Photo by Andrea Booher/FEMA News Photo.*

Department of Defense

In the event of a terrorist attack or an act of nature on American soil resulting in the release of chemical, biological, radiological, or nuclear material or high-yield explosive (CBRNE) devices, the local law enforcement, fire, and emergency medical personnel who are first to respond may become quickly overwhelmed by the magnitude of the attack. The Department of Defense (DOD) has many unique war-fighting support capabilities, both technical and operational, that could be used in support of state and local authorities, if requested by DHS, as the LFA, to support and manage the consequences of such a domestic event.

When requested, the DOD will provide its unique and extensive resources in accordance with the following principles. First, the DOD will ensure an unequivocal chain of responsibility, authority, and accountability for its actions to ensure the American people that the military will follow the basic constructs of lawful action when an emergency occurs. Second, in the event of a catastrophic CBRNE, the DOD will always play a supporting role to the LFA in accordance with all applicable law and plans. Third, DOD support will emphasize its natural role, skills, and structures to mass mobilize and provide logistical support. Fourth, the DOD will purchase equipment and provide support in areas that are largely related to its war-fighting mission. Fifth, reserve component forces are the DOD's forward-deployed forces for domestic CM.

All official requests for DOD support to CBRNE consequence management (CM) incidents are made by the LFA to the executive secretary of the DOD. Although the LFA may submit the requests for DOD assistance through other DOD channels, immediately upon receipt, any request that comes to any DOD element shall be forwarded to the executive secretary. In each instance, the executive secretary will take the necessary action so that the deputy secretary can determine whether the incident warrants special operational management. In such instances, upon issuance of secretary of defense guidance to the chairman of the Joint Chiefs of Staff (CJCS), the joint staff will translate the secretary's decisions into military orders for these CBRNE-CM events, under the policy oversight of the ATSD(CS). If the deputy secretary of the DOD determines that DOD support for a particular CBRNE-CM incident does not require special CM procedures, the secretary of the Army will exercise authority as the DOD executive agent through the normal director of Military Support and Military Support to Civil Authorities (MSCA) procedures, with policy oversight by the ATSD(CS).

Additionally, the DOD has established 10 Weapons of Mass Destruction Civil Support Teams (WMD-CSTs), each composed of 22 well-trained and equipped full-time National Guard personnel. Upon the secretary of the DOD certification, one WMD-CST will be stationed in each of the 10 FEMA regions around the country, ready to provide support when directed by their respective governors. Their mission is to deploy rapidly, assist local responders in determining the precise nature of an attack, provide expert technical advice, and help pave the way for the identification and arrival of follow-up military assets. By congressional direction, the DOD is in the process of establishing and training an additional 17 WMD-CSTs to support the US population. Interstate agreements provide a process for the WMD-CST and other National Guard assets to be used by neighboring states. If national security requirements dictate, these units may be transferred to federal service.

In August 2005, the DOD announced that it had, for the first time, created operational plans of war that included US territory, primarily for use in the response to a major terrorist attack within the nation's borders. The plans are based on 15 possible attack scenarios that assume simultaneous attacks throughout the country. Northern Command, a new military sector created in 2002 whose territory includes the United States, developed these domestic war plans. In the event of military involvement in a domestic disaster, as stipulated in these plans, ground troop responsibilities would range from crowd control to high-end, full-scale disaster management following attacks that utilize WMDs. What is important to note about these plans, which are the first of their kind, is that they maintain in explicit verbiage that military assets utilized in a domestic incident will be provided in support of civilian response units, including police, fire, and EMS officials. They do allow, however, for the military to assume command in mass casualty situations where local response units are clearly overwhelmed and no longer able to adequately perform their duties.

These military plans are based on two separate documents, entitled CONPLAN 2002 and CONPLAN 0500 (CONPLAN is short for "Concept Plan"). CONPLAN 2002 was drafted to centralize missions of domestic basis into a single document, covering land, sea, and air operations. The plan covers the pre- and postattack time frames, which enables the military to help prevent terrorist attacks from occurring (either within or outside the United States). CONPLAN 0500, on the other hand, covers the organizational response to the 15 hypothetical scenarios mentioned earlier. These two plans have yet to gain approval of the secretary of the DOD.

These plans represent a great advancement for military involvement in domestic disaster response. Though it was always assumed that the military may have to lend support in response to a large-scale terrorist attack within the United States, no formalized plans had been created to dictate how that would be carried out. Through these plans, the military will be able to formalize both its responsibilities and its capabilities and will likely be able to exercise in this role before its members are required to perform.

Organizations that are concerned with civil liberties have raised alarm about the idea of greater military involvement in homeland security operations. These groups feel that such defined military involvement would run counter to the 1878 Posse Comitatus Act, which prevents military forces from participating in domestic law enforcement in any form (this act was reiterated in the Homeland Security Act of 2002). However, military drafters of the two CONPLANs assert that the military role would fall under Article 2 of the Constitution, which allows the president to use the military to defend the nation as he or she sees fit, which is allowable under the Posse Comitatus Act (Washington Post, 2005).

Department of Energy

Through its Office of Emergency Response, the Department of Energy (DOE) manages radiological emergency response assets that support both crisis and CM response in the event of an incident involving a WMD. The DOE is prepared to respond immediately to any type of radiological accident or incident with its radiological emergency response assets.

Through its Office of Nonproliferation and National Security, DOE coordinates activities in nonproliferation, international nuclear safety, and communicated threat assessment. DOE maintains the following capabilities that support domestic terrorism preparedness and response:

- *Aerial Measuring System (AMS)*: AMS is an aircraft-operated radiation detection system that uses fixed-wing aircraft and helicopters equipped with state-of-the-art technology instrumentation to track, monitor, and sample airborne radioactive plumes and/or detect and measure radioactive material deposited on the ground.
- *Atmospheric Release Advisory Capability (ARAC)*: ARAC is a computer-based atmospheric dispersion and deposition modeling capability operated by Lawrence Livermore National Laboratory (LLNL), and its role in an emergency begins when a nuclear, chemical, or other hazardous material is, or has the potential of being, released into the atmosphere. ARAC consists of meteorologists and other technical staff using three-dimensional computer models and real-time weather data to project the dispersion and deposition of radioactive material in the environment.
- *Accident Response Group (ARG)*: ARG is DOE's primary emergency response capability for responding to emergencies involving US nuclear weapons. ARG members will deploy with highly specialized, state-of-the-art equipment for weapons' recovery and monitoring operations. ARG advance elements focus on initial assessment and provide preliminary advice to decision-makers.
- *Federal Radiological Monitoring and Assessment Center (FRMAC)*: For major radiological emergencies affecting the United States, the DOE established an FRMAC. The center is the control point for all federal assets involved in the monitoring and assessment of off-site radiological

conditions. FRMAC provides support to the affected states, coordinates federal off-site radiological environmental monitoring and assessment activities, maintains a technical liaison with tribal nations and state and local governments, responds to the assessment needs of the LFA, and meets the statutory responsibilities of the participating federal agency.

- *Nuclear Emergency Search Team (NEST)*: NEST is the DOE's program for dealing with the technical aspects of nuclear or radiological terrorism. Response teams vary in size from a five-person technical advisory team to a tailored deployment of dozens of searchers and scientists who can locate and then conduct or support technical operations on a suspected nuclear device.
- *Radiological Assistance Program (RAP)*: Under RAP, the DOE provides, upon request, radiological assistance to DOE program elements; other federal agencies; state, tribal, and local governments; private groups; and individuals. RAP provides resources (trained personnel and equipment) to evaluate, assess, advise, and assist in the mitigation of actual or perceived radiation hazards and risks to workers, the public, and the environment.
- *Radiation Emergency Assistance Center/Training Site (REAC/TS)*: The REAC/TS is managed by DOE's Oak Ridge Institute for Science and Education in Oak Ridge, Tennessee, and it maintains a 24h response center staffed with personnel and equipment to support medical aspects of radiological emergencies.
- *Communicated Threat Credibility Assessment*: DOE is the program manager for the Nuclear Assessment Program (NAP) at LLNL. The NAP is a DOE-funded asset specifically designed to provide technical, operational, and behavioral assessments of the credibility of communicated threats directed against the US government and its interests.
- *Nuclear Incident Response*: This program provides expert personnel and specialized equipment to a number of federal emergency response entities that deal with nuclear emergencies, nuclear accidents, and nuclear terrorism. The emergency response personnel are experts in such fields as device assessment, device disablement, intelligence analysis, credibility assessment, and health physics.

Department of Health and Human Services

The Department of Health and Human Services (HHS), as the LFA for ESF #8 (Health and Medical Services), provides coordinated federal assistance to supplement state and local resources in response to public health and medical care needs following a major disaster or emergency. Additionally, HHS provides support during developing or potential medical situations and has the responsibility for federal support of food, drug, and sanitation issues. Resources are furnished when state and local resources are overwhelmed and public health and/or medical assistance is requested from the federal government.

HHS, in its primary agency role for ESF #8, coordinates the provision of federal health and medical assistance to fulfill the requirements identified by the affected state/local authorities having jurisdiction. Included in ESF #8 are overall public health response; triage, treatment, and transportation of victims of the disaster; and evacuation of patients out of the disaster area, as needed, into a network of military services, veterans affairs, and preenrolled nonfederal hospitals located in the major metropolitan areas of the United States.

ESF #8 utilizes resources primarily available from

1. within HHS,
2. ESF #8 support agencies,
3. the National Disaster Medical System,
4. specific nonfederal sources (major pharmaceutical suppliers, hospital supply vendors, international disaster response organizations, and international health organizations).

Other than the agencies integrated under FEMA, the CDC may also be used in response activities. CDC is the federal agency responsible for protecting the public health of the country through prevention and control of diseases and response to public health emergencies. CDC works with national and international agencies to eradicate or control communicable diseases and other preventable conditions. The CDC's Bioterrorism Preparedness and Response Program oversees the agency's effort to prepare state and local governments to respond to acts of bioterrorism. In addition, the CDC has designated emergency response personnel throughout the agency who are responsible for responding to biological, chemical, and radiological terrorism. The CDC has epidemiologists trained to investigate and control outbreaks or illnesses, as well as laboratories capable of quantifying an individual's exposure to biological or chemical agents.

Environmental Protection Agency

The Environmental Protection Agency (EPA) is chartered to respond to WMD releases under the National Oil and Hazardous Substances Pollution Contingency Plan (NCP) regardless of the cause of the release. EPA is authorized by the Comprehensive Environmental Response, Compensation, and Liability Act (CERCLA); the Oil Pollution Act; and the Emergency Planning and Community Right-to-Know Act to support federal, state, and local responders in counterterrorism.

EPA will provide support to the FBI during crisis management in response to a terrorist incident. In its crisis management role, the EPA on-scene commander (OSC) may provide the FBI special agent in charge (SAC) with technical advice and recommendations, scientific and technical assessments, and assistance (as needed) to state and local responders. The EPA's OSC will support DHS during consequence management for the incident. The EPA carries out its response according to the FRP's ESF #10, Oil and Hazardous Materials. The OSC may request an environmental response team that is funded by the EPA if the terrorist incident exceeds available local and regional resources. The EPA chairs the National Response Team (NRT).

Department of Agriculture

It is the policy of the US Department of Agriculture (USDA) to "be prepared to respond swiftly in the event of national security, natural disaster, technological, and other emergencies at the national, regional, state, and county levels to provide support and comfort to the people of the United States." USDA has been charged with ensuring the safety of the nation's food supply. Since September 11, the concern that bioterrorism will impact agriculture in rural America, namely, crops in the field, hoofed animals, and food-safety issues in the food chain between the slaughterhouse and/or processing facilities and the consumer, has only grown. USDA offices that address this concern include the following:

- *Office of Crisis Planning and Management (OCPM)*: This USDA office coordinates the emergency planning, preparedness, and crisis management functions and the suitability for employment investigations of the department.
- *USDA State Emergency Boards (SEBs)*: The SEBs have the responsibility for coordinating USDA emergency activities at the state level.
- *Farm Service Agency*: This USDA agency develops and administers emergency plans and controls covering food processing, storage, and wholesale distribution; distribution and use of seed; and manufacture, distribution, and use of livestock and poultry feed.
- *Food and Nutrition Service (FNS)*: This USDA agency provides food assistance in officially designated disaster areas on request by the designated state agency. Generally, the food assistance

response from FNS includes authorization of Emergency Food Stamp Program benefits and use of USDA-donated foods for emergency mass feeding and household distribution, as necessary. FNS also maintains a current inventory of USDA-donated food held in federal, state, and commercial warehouses and provides leadership to the FRP under ESF #11, Agriculture and Natural Resources.

- *Food Safety and Inspection Service*: This USDA agency inspects meat and meat products, poultry and poultry products, and egg products in slaughtering and processing plants; assists the Food and Drug Administration in the inspection of other food products; develops plans and procedures for radiological emergency response in accordance with the Federal Radiological Emergency Response Plan (FRERP); and provides support, as required, to the FRP at the national and regional levels.
- *Natural Resources Conservation Service*: This USDA agency provides technical assistance to individuals, communities, and governments relating to the proper use of land for agricultural production; provides assistance in determining the extent of damage to agricultural land and water; and provides support to the FRP under ESF #3, Public Works and Engineering.
- *Agricultural Research Service (ARS)*: This USDA agency develops and carries out all necessary research programs related to crop or livestock diseases; provides technical support for emergency programs and activities in the areas of planning, prevention, detection, treatment, and management of consequences; provides technical support for the development of guidance information on the effects of radiation, biological, and chemical agents on agriculture; develops and maintains a current inventory of ARS-controlled laboratories that can be mobilized on short notice for emergency testing of food, feed, and water safety; and provides biological, chemical, and radiological safety support for USDA.
- *Economic Research Service*: This USDA agency, in cooperation with other departmental agencies, analyzes the impacts of the emergency on the US agricultural system, as well as on rural communities, as part of the process of developing strategies to respond to the effects of an emergency.
- *Rural Business-Cooperative Service*: This USDA agency, in cooperation with other government agencies at all levels, promotes economic development in affected rural areas by developing strategies that respond to the conditions created by an emergency.
- *Cooperative State Research, Education, and Extension Service (CSREES)*: This USDA agency coordinates the use of land-grant and other cooperating state college and university services and other relevant research institutions in carrying out all responsibilities for emergency programs.
- *Rural Housing Service*: This USDA agency will assist the Department of Housing and Urban Development by providing living quarters in unoccupied rural housing in an emergency situation.
- *Rural Utilities Service*: This USDA agency will provide support to the FRP under ESF #12, Energy, at the national level.
- *Office of Inspector General (OIG)*: This USDA office is the department's principal law enforcement component and liaison with the FBI. The OIG, in concert with appropriate federal, state, and local agencies, is prepared to investigate any terrorist attacks relating to the nation's agriculture sector, to identify subjects, to interview witnesses, and to secure evidence in preparation for federal prosecution. As necessary, the OIG will examine USDA programs regarding counterterrorism-related matters.
- *Forest Service (FS)*: This USDA agency will prevent and control fires in rural areas in cooperation with state, local, and tribal governments and appropriate federal departments and agencies. They will determine and report requirements for equipment, personnel, fuels, chemicals, and other materials needed for carrying out assigned duties.

Nuclear Regulatory Commission

The Nuclear Regulatory Commission (NRC) is the LFA (in accordance with the FRERP) for facilities or materials regulated by NRC or by an NRC agreement. NRC's counterterrorism-specific role, at these facilities or material sites, is to exercise the federal lead for radiological safety while supporting other federal, state, and local agencies in crisis and CM. Emergency management assistance that is provided by the NRC includes the following:

- *Radiological safety assessments*: NRC provides facilities (or materials users) with technical advice to ensure on-site measures are taken to mitigate negative "off-site" consequences. NRC serves as the primary federal source of information regarding on-site radiological conditions and off-site radiological effects. The commission supports the technical needs of other federal agencies by providing descriptions of devices or facilities containing radiological materials and assessing the safety impact of terrorist actions and of proposed tactical operations of any responders. Safety assessments are coordinated through an NRC liaison at the Domestic Emergency Support Team (DEST), Strategic Information and Operations Center (SIOC), Command Post (CP), and Joint Operations Center (JOC).
- *Protective action recommendations*: NRC contacts state and local authorities and offers them advice and assistance on the technical assessment of radiological hazards and, if requested, provides advice on protective actions for the public. NRC coordinates any recommendations for protective actions through an NRC liaison at the CP or JOC.
- *Responder radiation protection*: NRC assesses the potential radiological hazards to any responders and coordinates with the radiation protection staff of an affected facility (or disaster site) to ensure that personnel responding to the scene are observing the appropriate precautions.
- *Information coordination*: NRC supplies other responders and government officials with timely information concerning the radiological aspects of an event. NRC liaises with the Joint Information Center (JIC) to coordinate information concerning the federal response.

Critical Thinking

How does the involvement of the Department of Defense in the nation's emergency management system differ from all other federal agencies? Why is this difference significant? Do you feel that anything should be done to change the way the military supports domestic emergency management?

National Incident Management System

A difficult issue in any response operation is determining who is in charge of the overall response effort at the incident. This concept of control, or leadership, is most commonly referred to in the emergency management community as *incident command*. With the significant shift in legislation brought about by the creation of DHS, and the new emphasis on terrorism, the issue of incident command was in danger of becoming even more difficult and, likewise, confusing and even conflicting. To address the concerns that many officials at the local, state, and federal levels expressed in light of the changes that were occurring in the emergency management world, President George W. Bush called on the secretary of the DHS, by means of Homeland Security Presidential Directive (HSPD)-5, to develop a nationally based ICS. The purpose of this system, it was assumed, was to provide a consistent nationwide approach for federal, state, tribal, and local governments to work together to prepare for, prevent, respond to, and recover from domestic incidents—regardless of their cause, size, or complexity.

On March 1, 2004, following the collective efforts of state and local government officials, representatives from a wide range of public safety organizations, and DHS, the product result of HSPD-5 was released. The NIMS, as it is called, incorporated existing knowledge, lessons learned, and best practices into a new comprehensive national approach to domestic incident management and command that appeared to fully account for the many recent changes in federal response requirements that resulted for the reasons mentioned above. This document was created such that it addressed all jurisdictional levels and all functional disciplines involved in emergency management.

The NIMS represents a core set of doctrine, principles, terminology, and organizational processes to enable the management of disasters at all government levels. One very important aspect of this new framework is that it recognized the value of an existing system, the ICS, and stressed the importance of effective incident command as a way of better managing disaster events. The well-known National Commission on Terrorist Attacks Upon the United States (the 9/11 Commission) identified ICS as an answer to many of the coordination problems that arose during the response to the 9/11 attacks and recommended a national adoption of ICS to enhance command, control, and communications capabilities during disaster response (Figure 9-11).

To better understand the processes by which NIMS helps in the management of events requiring multiple levels of government, it is necessary to have a brief understanding of the ICS. The ICS was developed in California in 1970 after a devastating wildfire. During the after-action analysis of the response to the fire, which caused hundreds of millions of dollars in damage, killed 16 people, and left hundreds of families without homes, it was recognized that problems with communications and with coordination between different agencies made operations much less effective than they could have been. Following this analysis, Congress mandated that a system be created to address these coordination issues, and the result was a system called FIRESCOPE ICS, developed by the US Forest Service, the California Department of Forestry and Fire Protection, the Governor's Office of Emergency Services, and several local and county fire departments.

FIGURE 9-11 New York City, NY, September 21, 2001—Rescue operations continue far into the night at the World Trade Center. *Photo by Andrea Booher/FEMA News Photo.*

FIRESCOPE ICS effectively standardized the response to wildfires in California. It resulted in a common terminology being used by all responding agencies, which significantly reduced the confusion. It established common procedures to be applied to firefighting, which significantly reduced the amount of time needed to coordinate between two or more agencies that would be working together on attacking a fire. Several field tests had shown that the system was effective, and by 1981, it was being applied throughout southern California. So effective was FIRESCOPE ICS at standardizing coordination to wildfire events that departments began to apply its methods to other events unrelated to wildfires. It was soon recognized as being effective for the response to floods, hazardous materials' spills and leaks, earthquakes, and even major transportation accidents.

There are multiple functions in the ICS, including the common use of terminology, integrated communications, a unified command (UC) structure, resource management, and action planning. A planned set of directives includes assigning one coordinator to manage the infrastructure of the response and assigning personnel, deploying equipment, obtaining resources, and working with the numerous agencies that respond to the disaster scene. In most instances, the local fire chief or fire commissioner is designated the incident commander.

The ICS was designed to remain effective at each of the following three levels of incident escalation:

1. Single jurisdiction and/or single agency
2. Single jurisdiction with multiagency support
3. Multijurisdictional and/or multiagency support

There are five major management systems within the ICS. They include command, operations, planning, logistics, and finance. Each is described here:

- *Command*: The command section includes developing, directing, and maintaining communication and collaboration with the multiple agencies on site, as well as working with local officials, the public, and the media to provide up-to-date information regarding the disaster.
- *Operations*: The operations section handles the tactical operations, coordinates the command objectives, develops tactical operations, and organizes and directs all resources to the disaster site.
- *Planning*: The planning section provides the necessary information to the command center to develop the action plan to accomplish the objectives. This section also collects and evaluates information as it is made available.
- *Logistics*: The logistics section provides personnel, equipment, and support for the command center. This section handles the coordination of all services that are involved in the response from locating rescue equipment to coordinating the response for volunteer organizations such as the Salvation Army and the Red Cross.
- *Finance*: The finance section is responsible for the accounting for funds used during the response and recovery aspect of the disaster. This section monitors costs related to the incident and provides accounting procurement time recording cost analyses.

Under the ICS, there is almost always a single incident commander. However, even under this single command figure, the ICS allows for something called a *unified command* (UC). UC is often used when there is more than one agency with incident jurisdiction or when incidents cross multiple political jurisdictions. Within this UC framework, agencies are able to work together through the designated members of the UC, often with a senior official from each agency or discipline participating in the UC, to establish a common set of objectives and strategies and a single plan of action. Due to the nature of disasters, multiple government agencies often need to work together to monitor the response and manage a large number of personnel responding to the scene. ICS allows for the integration of the agencies to operate under a single response management.

Although NIMS was built upon this ICS system, the new system extends far beyond the initial scope of ICS. This is to be expected, of course, considering the exponentially greater size of the incidents regularly managed under NIMS (despite that NIMS was designed to be effectively used to manage small, single-jurisdictional events such as house fires or automobile accidents). NIMS establishes standardized incident management processes, protocols, and procedures that all responders, whether they are federal, state, tribal, or local, can use to coordinate and conduct their cooperative response actions. Using these standardized procedures, it is presumed that all responders will be able to share a common understanding and will be able to work together with very little mismatch. The following are the key components of the new incident management system:

- *Incident Command System (ICS)*: NIMS establishes ICS as a standard incident management organization with five functional areas—command, operations, planning, logistics, and finance/administration—for the management of all major incidents. To ensure further coordination, and during incidents involving multiple jurisdictions or agencies, the principle of UC has been universally incorporated into NIMS. This UC not only coordinates the efforts of many jurisdictions but also provides for and ensures joint decisions on objectives, strategies, plans, priorities, and public communications.
- *Communications and Information Management*: Standardized communications during an incident are essential, and NIMS prescribes interoperable communications systems for both incident and information management. NIMS recognizes that responders and managers across all agencies and jurisdictions must have common access to the full operational picture, thereby allowing for efficient and effective incident response.
- *Preparedness*: Preparedness incorporates a range of measures, actions, and processes accomplished before an incident happens. NIMS preparedness measures include planning, training, exercises, qualification and certification, equipment acquisition and certification, and publication management. NIMS stresses that each of these measures helps to ensure that preincident actions are standardized and consistent with mutually agreed-on doctrine. NIMS further places emphasis on mitigation activities to enhance preparedness. Mitigation includes public education and outreach; structural modifications to reduce the loss of life or destruction of property; code enforcement in support of zoning rules, land management, and building codes; and flood insurance and property buyout for frequently flooded areas.
- *Joint Information System (JIS)*: The Joint Information System provides the public with timely and accurate incident information and unified public messages. This system employs JICs and brings incident communicators together during an incident to develop, coordinate, and deliver a unified message. This is performed under the assumption that it will ensure that federal, state, and local levels of government are releasing the same information during an incident.
- *NIMS Integration Center (NIC)*: To ensure that NIMS remains an accurate and effective management tool, a NIMS NIC will be established by the DHS Secretary to assess proposed changes to NIMS, capture and evaluate lessons learned, and employ best practices. The NIC will provide strategic direction and oversight, supporting both routine maintenance and continuous refinement of the system and its components over the long term. It will also develop and facilitate national standards for NIMS education and training, first-responder communications and equipment, typing of resources, qualification and credentialing of incident management and responder personnel, and standardization of equipment maintenance and resources. Finally, the NIC will continue to use the collaborative process of federal, state, tribal, local, multidisciplinary, and private authorities to assess prospective changes to NIMS.

Figure 9-12 illustrates how NIMS was developed on the structure originally outlined in the ICS. The NRP, which guides the federal support of state, county, tribal, and local response to disasters, was built on the NIMS framework. Together, these three coordinated concepts have likely helped to further eliminate coordination problems that may have existed before in the absence of such complementary systems.

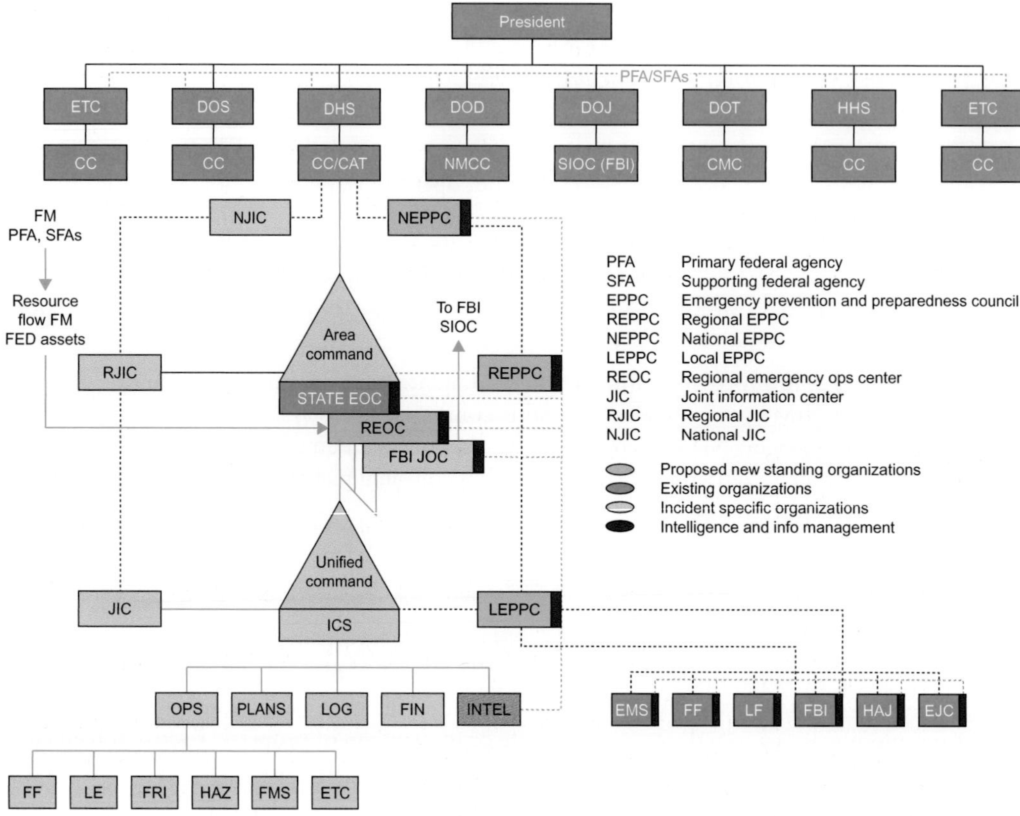

FIGURE 9-12 National structure for NIMS operations.

Federal Response

Almost every facet of the nation's emergency response system has undergone change to some degree as a result of the reaction to the 9/11 terrorist attacks on America. Although some of the more significant adjustments have occurred at the federal level—most notably the creation of DHS—all state and most local agencies have followed this lead. As for the response to major disasters, namely, those requiring action by multiple levels of government, these changes have resulted in a shift toward increased federal control and direction. This shift is most notable with regard to events that involve a criminal element such as exists with intentional disasters (e.g., sabotage or civil unrest) and terrorist-driven threats or events. These changes have all been formalized through the transformation of the federal response framework from the old Federal Response Plan (FRP), which was successfully applied during several terrorist event responses including the Murrah Federal Building bombing and the 9/11 attacks, to the National Response Plan (NRP) in the years immediately following the 9/11 attacks, to the National Response Framework (NRF), released January 2008 in response to criticisms and shortcomings of the NRP.

It has traditionally been the case that a federal response may be initiated in two ways: a governor can request a presidential disaster declaration and the president can declare a presidential emergency upon damage to federal entities (as was the case for the *Discovery* tragedy). Today, however, there is a third mechanism. The president, through FEMA, can predeploy resources (personnel and equipment) to a location where a disaster declaration is imminent due to an impending disaster. These authorities first appeared in the NRP and remain unchanged under the NRF. It is important to note that, although a formal declaration does not have to be signed by the president for the federal government to begin response, the governor of the affected state must make a formal request for assistance to occur and must specify in the request the specific needs of the disaster area. Under the new NRF, the president may unilaterally declare a major disaster or emergency if extraordinary circumstances exist. For summaries of procedures on disaster declaration by the president and assistance without the president's declaration, see the sidebars "Declaration Process Fact Sheet" and "Federal Assistance Without a Presidential Declaration," respectively.

Declaration Process Fact Sheet

The Emergency Response Process

Preliminary Damage Assessments/The Declarations Process/Primary Considerations for Declarations

Local emergency and public works personnel, volunteers, humanitarian organizations, and other private interest groups provide emergency assistance required to protect the public's health and safety and to meet immediate human needs.

If necessary, a governor can declare a state of emergency and invoke the state's emergency plan to augment individual and public resources as required.

A governor may determine, after consulting with local government officials, that the recovery appears to be beyond the combined resources of both the state and local governments and that federal assistance may be needed. In requesting supplemental Federal assistance under the Robert T. Stafford Disaster Relief and Emergency Assistance Act, 42 USC §§ 5121-5206 (Stafford Act), the Governor must certify that the severity and magnitude of the disaster exceed state and local capabilities; certify that Federal assistance is necessary to supplement the efforts and available resources of the state and local governments, disaster relief organizations, and compensation by insurance for disaster related losses; confirm execution of the state's emergency plan; and certify adherence to cost sharing requirements.

Under the declaration process and to assist a governor to determine if a request for assistance should be made, a preliminary damage assessment is conducted. These assessments are conducted in counties affected by the disaster event. The Federal Emergency Management Agency (FEMA) works with the State's emergency management agency to accomplish these assessments.

The Preliminary Damage Assessment

This preliminary damage assessment team is comprised of personnel from FEMA, the State's emergency management agency, county and local officials and the US Small Business Administration (SBA). The team's work begins with reviewing the types of damage or emergency costs incurred by the units of government, and the impact to critical facilities, such as public utilities, hospitals, schools, and fire and police departments. They will also look at the effect on individuals and businesses, including the number damaged, the number of people displaced, and the threat to health and safety caused by the storm event. Additional data from the Red Cross or other local voluntary agencies may also be reviewed. During the assessment the team will collect estimates of the expenses and damages.

This information can then be used by the Governor to support a declaration request—showing the cost of response efforts, such as emergency personnel overtime, other emergency services, and damage to citizens, is beyond state and local recovery capabilities. The information gathered during the assessment will help the Governor certify that the damage exceeds state and local resources.

The Declaration Process

As set forth in the Stafford Act, a governor seeks a presidential declaration by submitting a written request to the President through the FEMA regional office. In this request the Governor certifies that the combined local, county and state resources are insufficient and that the situation is beyond their recovery capabilities. Following a FEMA regional and national office review of the request and the findings of the preliminary damage assessment, FEMA provides the President an analysis of the situation and a recommended course of action.

Criteria Used by FEMA

The federal disaster law restricts the use of arithmetical formulas or other objective standards as the sole basis for determining the need for federal supplemental aid. As a result, FEMA assesses a number of factors to determine the severity, magnitude and impact of a disaster event. In evaluating a Governor's request for a major disaster declaration, a number of primary factors, along with other relevant information, are considered in developing a recommendation to the President for supplemental disaster assistance. Primary factors considered include:

- Amount and type of damage (number of homes destroyed or with major damage);
- Impact on the infrastructure of affected areas or critical facilities;
- Imminent threats to public health and safety;
- Impacts to essential government services and functions;
- Unique capability of Federal government;
- Dispersion or concentration of damage;
- Level of insurance coverage in place for homeowners and public facilities;
- Available assistance from other sources (Federal, State, local, voluntary organizations);
- State and local resource commitments from previous, undeclared events
- Frequency of disaster events over recent time period.

The very nature of disasters—their unique circumstances, the unexpected timing, and varied impacts—precludes a complete listing of factors considered when evaluating disaster declaration requests. However, the above lists most primary considerations.

FEMA's mission is to support our citizens and first responders to ensure that as a nation we work together to build, sustain, and improve our capability to prepare for, protect against, respond to, recover from, and mitigate all hazards.

Source: FEMA (2014b).

Federal Assistance Without a Presidential Declaration

In many cases, assistance may be obtained from the Federal government without a Presidential declaration. For example, FEMA places liaisons in State EOCs and moves commodities near incident sites that may require Federal assistance prior to a Presidential declaration. Additionally, some types of assistance, such as Fire Management Assistance Grants—which provide support to States experiencing severe wildfires—are performed by Federal departments or agencies under their own authorities and do not require Presidential approval. Finally, Federal departments and agencies may provide immediate lifesaving assistance to States under their own statutory authorities without a formal Presidential declaration.

Source: FEMA (2008).

Under the NRF, the president maintains the ultimate discretion in making a disaster declaration. There are no set criteria by which he or she is bound and no government regulations to guide which events are declared disasters and which are not. FEMA has developed a number of factors it considers in making its recommendation to the president, including individual property losses per capita, level of damage to existing community infrastructure, level of insurance coverage, repetitive events, and other subjective factors. But in the end, the decision to make the declaration is the president's alone. One major change in the verbiage of the plan, as changed in the NRP, concerns the prevention of terrorist attacks. In situations where the Homeland Security Operations Center determines that a terrorist threat exists for which federal intervention is required to prevent an incident from occurring, DHS provides support as necessary under the direction of the attorney general, through the FBI.

A presidential disaster declaration can be made in as short a time as a few hours, as was the case in the 1994 Northridge earthquake, the 1995 Oklahoma City bombing, and the 9/11 World Trade Center attacks. Sometimes, it takes weeks for damages to be assessed and the capability of state and local jurisdictions to fund response and recovery efforts to be evaluated. Should the governor's request be turned down by the president, the governor has the right to appeal, an appeal that will be considered, especially if new damage data become available and are included in the appeal.

Presidential declarations are routinely sought for such events as floods, hurricanes, earthquakes, and tornadoes. In recent years, governors have become more inventive and have requested presidential disaster declarations for snow removal, drought, West Nile virus, and economic losses caused by failing industries, such as the Northwest salmon-spawning decline.

Once a disaster declaration has been made, the full range of federal government resources becomes available to assist the affected state or states. The federal assistance is guided through the invocation of the National Response Framework (NRF), which is detailed later in this chapter. Through this plan, and under the guidance of the DHS, 32 signatory federal agencies and the American Red Cross provide all forms of assistance as dictated under the 15 ESFs (also detailed later in this chapter). A declaration also paves the way for federal funding to pay for response activities at all government levels (including reimbursing the expenses of federal agencies that do respond) and certain recovery costs to individuals, businesses, nonprofit agencies, and public entities.

From January 1953 to November 2014, there have been 2191 presidential disaster declarations, averaging 36 declarations per year (Table 9-2). As an illustration of disaster declaration activity in a single year, in 2012 there were 47 major disaster declarations in 34 states:

- 15 for hurricanes (11 alone for Hurricane Sandy)
- 5 for severe storms and straight-line winds
- 5 for severe storms, tornadoes, straight-line winds, and flooding
- 4 for severe storms and flooding
- 3 for wildfires
- 3 for severe storms
- 2 for severe storms, tornadoes, flooding, mudslides, and landslides
- 1 for severe storm and snowstorm
- 1 for severe storms, straight-line winds, flooding, and landslides
- 1 for severe storms, straight-line winds, and flooding
- 1 for flooding

Table 9-2 Total Major Disaster Declarations, 1953-2011 (as of July)

Year	Declarations
1953	13
1954	17
1955	18
1956	16
1957	16
1958	7
1959	7
1960	12
1961	12
1962	22
1963	20
1964	25
1965	25
1966	11
1967	11
1968	19
1969	29
1970	17
1971	17
1972	48
1973	46
1974	46
1975	38

Table 9-2 (Continued)

Year	**Declarations**
1976	30
1977	22
1978	25
1979	42
1980	23
1981	15
1982	24
1983	21
1984	34
1985	27
1986	28
1987	23
1988	11
1989	31
1990	38
1991	43
1992	45
1993	32
1994	36
1995	32
1996	75
1997	44
1998	65
1999	50
2000	45
2001	45
2002	49
2003	46
2004	68
2005	48
2006	52
2007	63
2008	75
2009	59
2010	81
2011	99
2012	47
2013	62
2014 (as of November)	44
Total	2191
Average	36

Source: FEMA (2014a).

- 1 for tropical Storm Debby
- 1 for severe storms, flooding, and landslides
- 1 for severe winter storm, flooding, landslides, and mudslide flooding
- 1 for severe storms, tornadoes, and flooding
- 1 for severe storms, flooding, mudslides, and landslides
- 1 for straight-line winds and tornadoes

Before the creation of the NRP, and subsequent NRF, there were several individual response plans that guided the government response to several different kinds of emergencies or disasters. However, HSPD-5 directed DHS to develop the NRP such that all existing federal plans were integrated into that one document or directly linked through formal coordination mechanisms—giving it the distinction of serving as the single guide for federal response. The following list contains the various plans and operation guidelines integrated or linked under the NRP:

- Federal Response Plan (FRP)
- Federal Radiological Emergency Response Plan (FRERP)
- Domestic Terrorism Concept of Operations Plan (CONPLAN)
- Mass Mitigation Emergency Plan (Distant Shore)
- National Oil and Hazardous Substances Pollution Contingency Plan (NCP)

The NRP essentially replaced the FRP and accommodated the needs of events covered under the FRERP, CONPLAN, Distant Shore, and NCP, as well as several newly identified or newly addressed issues through the development of various *incident annexes*. These annexes, which have not yet been developed for the new NRF and are therefore still applicable in their original NRP format, include the following (described in much greater detail later in this chapter):

- Biological incident
- Catastrophic incident
- Cyber incident
- Food and agriculture incident
- Nuclear/radiological incident
- Oil and hazardous materials incident
- Terrorism incident law enforcement and investigation

National Response Framework

The National Response Framework (NRF) was developed to be a single document by which emergency management efforts at all levels of government could be structured. The NRF has been described by FEMA as being "a guide to how the Nation conducts all-hazards response." It is meant to be scalable, flexible, and adaptable in coordinating the key roles and responsibilities of response participants throughout the country, at all levels of the government. It describes specific authorities and practices for managing incidents that range from serious local events to large-scale national-level terrorist attacks or catastrophic natural disasters. The NRF was built directly upon the structure of the NIMS, itself developed to provide a consistent template for managing incidents.

The NRF is the latest iteration in a progression of emergency response documents guiding federal emergency management action. The first in this series of documents was the FRP, released in 1992, which focused most specifically on the roles and responsibilities of the federal government in assistance to overwhelmed state and local jurisdictions. Following the 9/11 attacks, it was determined that the document guiding national response required a more comprehensive approach in order to define the state, local, and other roles in the greater scheme of major disaster response and recovery. As a result, the NRP was released in 2004, thereby replacing the FRP. Nine months after Katrina's landfall, however, a notice of change to the NRP was released, incorporating preliminary lessons learned from the 2005 hurricane season. These changes were based upon suggestions of various emergency management stakeholders, many of whom felt that the NRP was overly bureaucratic, repetitive, and national in focus. FEMA officials felt that one of the greatest criticisms was that users did not consider the NRP to be a "plan" as its name suggested, but rather a framework guiding the types of actions that could be taken in response to the variety of possible incidents that might occur. In response, the DHS developed and released the NRF in September of 2007 and provided a period for comments by local and state stakeholders. Changes were made to the draft framework based upon these comments, and on January 22, 2008, the final NRF was released. The document became official 60 days following its release, thereby superseding the NRP.

In May 2013, FEMA published "National Response Framework: Second Edition May 2013" that supersedes the NRF that was issued in January 2008. This document sets forth the following rationale, goal, and objectives of the NRF.

NRF Rationale

The National Response Framework (NRF) is an essential component of the National Preparedness System mandated in Presidential Policy Directive 8 (PPD-8): National Preparedness. PPD-8 is aimed at strengthening the security and resilience of the United States through systematic preparation for the threats that pose the greatest risk to the security of the nation. PPD-8 defines five mission areas—prevention, protection, mitigation, response, and recovery—and mandates the development of a series of policy and planning documents to explain and guide the nation's collective approach to ensuring and enhancing national preparedness. The NRF sets the doctrine for how the nation builds, sustains, and delivers the response core capabilities identified in the National Preparedness Goal (the goal). The goal establishes the capabilities and outcomes the nation must accomplish across all five mission areas in order to be secure and resilient.

NRF Goal

The NRF is a guide to how the nation responds to all types of disasters and emergencies. It is built on scalable, flexible, and adaptable concepts identified in the National Incident Management System (NIMS) to align key roles and responsibilities across the nation. The NRF describes specific authorities and best practices for managing incidents that range from the serious but purely local to large-scale terrorist attacks or catastrophic natural disasters.

The term "response," as used in the NRF, includes actions to save lives, protect property and the environment, stabilize communities, and meet basic human needs following an incident. Response also includes the execution of emergency plans and actions to support short-term recovery. The NRF describes doctrine for managing any type of disaster or emergency regardless of scale, scope, and complexity. This framework explains common response disciplines and processes that have been developed at all levels of the government (local, state, tribal, territorial, insular area, and federal) and have matured over time.

NRF Objectives

To support the Goal, the objectives of the NRF are to:

- Describe scalable, flexible, and adaptable coordinating structures, as well as key roles and responsibilities for integrating capabilities across the whole community, to support the efforts of local, state, tribal, territorial, insular area, and Federal governments in responding to actual and potential incidents
- Describe, across the whole community, the steps needed to prepare for delivering the response core capabilities
- Foster integration and coordination of activities within the Response mission area
- Outline how the Response mission area relates to the other mission areas, as well as the relationship between the Response core capabilities and the core capabilities in other mission areas
- Provide guidance through doctrine and establish the foundation for the development of the supplemental Response Federal Interagency Operational Plan (FIOP).

Source: FEMA (2013)

A significant difference between the 2008 version and the 2013 Second Edition of the NRF is the inclusion in the 2013 document of FEMA's "Whole Community" doctrine. The 2013 document defines the "Whole Community" doctrine as, "Whole community includes: individuals, families, households, communities, the private and nonprofit sectors, faith-based organizations, and local, state, tribal, territorial, and Federal governments." Whole community is defined in the National Preparedness Goal as "a focus on enabling the participation in national preparedness activities of a wider range of players from the private and nonprofit sectors, including nongovernmental organizations and the general public, in conjunction with the participation of Federal, state, and local governmental partners in order to foster better coordination and working relationships." The National Preparedness Goal may be found online at http://www.fema.gov/ppd8 (FEMA, 2013).

The NRF is built upon the template established under the NIMS, which was called for by HSPD-5 in the aftermath of the 9/11 terrorist attacks. NIMS enables all levels of government, the private sector, and nongovernmental organizations (NGOs) to work together during an emergency or disaster event. The NRF and NIMS, working together, seek to ensure that all stakeholders are operating under a common set of emergency management principles.

The NRF can be either partially or fully implemented in the lead-up or response to an emergency or disaster threat, thereby allowing for what is considered a "scaled" response that tasks only those agencies and resources that are actually needed.

The NRF is risk-based and built on the "following principles establish fundamental doctrine for the Response mission area: (1) engaged partnership, (2) tiered response, (3) scalable, flexible, and adaptable operational capabilities, (4) unity of effort through unified command, and (5) readiness to act. These principles are rooted in the Federal system and the Constitution's division of responsibilities between state and federal governments. These principles reflect the history of emergency management and the distilled wisdom of responders and leaders across the whole community" (FEMA, 2013).

Organization of NRF

The NRF is composed of:

- *a core document* that describes the principles that guide national response roles and responsibilities, response actions, response organizations, and planning requirements that together work to achieve an effective national response to any incident that occurs;

- *Emergency Support Function (ESF) Annexes* that group federal resources and capabilities into functional areas that are most frequently needed in a national response (e.g., transportation, firefighting, and mass care);
- *Support Annexes* that describe essential supporting aspects that are common to all incidents (e.g., financial management, volunteer and donations management, and private-sector coordination);
- *Incident Annexes* that address the unique aspects of how we respond to seven broad incident categories (e.g., biological, nuclear/radiological, cyber, and mass evacuation).

The NRF describes the roles and responsibilities not only of public-sector agencies but also of the private sector, NGOs, and individuals and households. Communities, tribes, states, the federal government, NGOs, and the private sector are each informed of their respective roles and responsibilities and how their actions complement each other. Each governmental level is tasked with developing capabilities needed to respond to incidents, including the development of plans, conducting assessments and exercises, providing and directing resources and capabilities, and gathering lessons learned.

The scope of the NRF includes domestic incidents of all sizes, regardless of state or federal involvement. The NRF can be partially or fully implemented in response to or anticipation of a natural or technological hazard, or a terrorist threat. By defining what is called *selective implementation*, the NRF allows for a scaled response. In this manner, events that start out small but grow larger in scope can be applicable to the plan from the moment they begin. This also allows for what is considered a more seamless transition from local, to state, to ultimately federal involvement as incidents grow in size. One of the greatest changes between the NRF and previous versions of the response document is that no formal declaration is required before the NRF may be invoked.

For the NRF doctrine, see the sidebar "National Response Framework Response Doctrine."

National Response Framework Response Doctrine

The National Response Framework is a guide to how the Nation responds to all types of disasters and emergencies. It is built on scalable, flexible, and adaptable concepts identified in the National Incident Management System to align key roles and responsibilities across the Nation. This Framework describes specific authorities and best practices for managing incidents that range from the serious but purely local to large-scale terrorist attacks or catastrophic natural disasters. The National Response Framework describes the principles, roles and responsibilities, and coordinating structures for delivering the core capabilities required to respond to an incident and further describes how response efforts integrate with those of the other mission areas. This Framework is always in effect, and elements can be implemented at any time. The structures, roles, and responsibilities described in this Framework can be partially or fully implemented in the context of a threat or hazard, in anticipation of a significant event, or in response to an incident. Selective implementation of National Response Framework structures and procedures allows for a scaled response, delivery of the specific resources and capabilities, and a level of coordination appropriate to each incident.

The Response mission area focuses on ensuring that the Nation is able to respond effectively to all types of incidents that range from those that are adequately handled with local assets to those of catastrophic proportion that require marshaling the capabilities of the entire Nation. The objectives of the Response mission area define the capabilities necessary to save lives, protect property and the environment, meet basic human needs, stabilize the incident, restore basic services and community functionality, and establish a safe and secure environment moving toward the transition to recovery. The Response mission area includes 14 core capabilities: planning, public information and warning, operational coordination, critical transportation, environmental response/health and safety, fatality management services, infrastructure systems, mass care services, mass search and rescue operations, on-scene security and protection, operational communications, public and private services and resources, public health and medical services, and situational assessment.

The priorities of response are to save lives, protect property and the environment, stabilize the incident and provide for basic human needs. The following principles establish fundamental doctrine for the Response mission area: engaged partnership, tiered response, scalable, flexible, and adaptable operational capabilities, unity of effort through unified command, and readiness to act.

Scalable, flexible, and adaptable coordinating structures are essential in aligning the key roles and responsibilities to deliver the Response mission area's core capabilities. The flexibility of such structures helps ensure that communities across the country can organize response efforts to address a variety of risks based on their unique needs, capabilities, demographics, governing structures, and non-traditional partners. This Framework is not based on a one-size-fits-all organizational construct, but instead acknowledges the concept of tiered response which emphasizes that response to incidents should be handled at the lowest jurisdictional level capable of handling the mission.

In implementing the National Response Framework to build national preparedness, partners are encouraged to develop a shared understanding of broad-level strategic implications as they make critical decisions in building future capacity and capability. The whole community should be engaged in examining and implementing the strategy and doctrine contained in this Framework, considering both current and future requirements in the process.

Source: DHS (2013).

Roles and Responsibilities Defined by the NRF

The NRF Core Document provides an overview of the roles and responsibilities of key emergency management stakeholders at the local, tribal, state, and federal levels who are involved in the implementation of the NRF, including the private sector and NGOs. The following section describes exactly who is involved with the NRF at each jurisdictional level and what each must do to build and maintain emergency response capabilities.

Local Level

Disaster response almost always begins locally and remains local in terms of actual incident command and control responsibility. This responsibility rests both with the individual members of the community themselves and with the public officials elected by them in the county and city governments. The responsibilities of the following individuals are specifically mentioned in the NRF.

Chief Elected or Appointed Official

A mayor, city manager, or county manager, as a jurisdiction's chief executive officer, is responsible for ensuring the public safety and welfare of the people of that jurisdiction. Specifically, this official provides strategic guidance and resources during preparedness, response, and recovery efforts by

- establishing strong working relationships with local jurisdictional leaders and core private-sector organizations, voluntary agencies, and community partners (this official must get to know, coordinate with, and train with local partners in advance of an incident and to develop mutual aid and/or assistance agreements for support in response to an incident);
- leading and encouraging local leaders to focus on preparedness by participating in planning, training, and exercises;
- supporting participation in local mitigation efforts within the jurisdiction and, as appropriate, with the private sector;
- understanding and implementing laws and regulations that support emergency management and response;
- ensuring that local emergency plans take into account the needs of
  - the jurisdiction, including persons, property, and structures;
  - individuals with special needs, including those with service animals;
  - individuals with household pets;
- encouraging residents to participate in volunteer organizations and training courses;
- working closely with members of Congress during incidents and on an ongoing basis regarding local preparedness capabilities and needs.

Emergency Manager

The local emergency manager has the day-to-day authority and responsibility for overseeing emergency management programs and activities. They must work with chief elected and appointed officials to ensure that there are effective emergency plans in place and activities being conducted. The local emergency manager's duties often include

- advising elected and appointed officials during a response;
- conducting response operations in accordance with the NIMS;
- coordinating the functions of local agencies;
- coordinating the development of plans and working cooperatively with other local agencies, community organizations, private-sector entities, and NGOs;
- developing and maintaining mutual aid and assistance agreements;
- coordinating resource requests during an incident through the management of an emergency operations center;
- coordinating damage assessments during an incident;
- advising and informing local officials and the public about emergency management activities during an incident;
- developing and executing accessible public awareness and education programs;
- conducting exercises to test plans and systems and obtain lessons learned;
- coordinating integration of the rights of individuals with disabilities, individuals from racially and ethnically diverse backgrounds, and others with access and functional needs into emergency planning and response (FEMA, 2013).

Department and Agency Heads

The local emergency manager is assisted by, and coordinates the efforts of, employees in departments and agencies that perform emergency management functions. The emergency management responsibilities of department and agency heads include

- collaborating with the emergency manager during the development of local emergency plans and providing key response resources;
- participating in the planning process to ensure that specific capabilities (e.g., firefighting, law enforcement, emergency medical services, public works, and environmental and natural resources agencies) are integrated into a workable plan to safeguard the community;
- developing, planning, and training on internal policies and procedures to meet response and recovery needs safely;
- participating in interagency training and exercises to develop and maintain the necessary capabilities.

Individuals and Households

Although not formally a part of emergency management operations, individuals and households are considered as playing an important role in the overall emergency management strategy under the NRF. Specifically, the NRF states that community members can contribute by

- reducing hazards in and around their homes,
- preparing an emergency supply kit and household emergency plan,
- monitoring emergency communications carefully,
- volunteering with an established organization,
- enrolling in emergency response training courses.

Private-Sector and Nongovernmental Organizations (NGOs)

In almost every large-scale emergency incident, and some small-scale ones, the government must work together with the private-sector and NGO groups as partners in emergency management. Examples of key private sector activities include:

- Addressing the response needs of employees, infrastructure, and facilities
- Protecting information and maintaining the continuity of business operations
- Planning for, responding to, and recovering from incidents that impact their own infrastructure and facilities
- Collaborating with emergency management personnel to determine what assistance may be required and how they can provide needed support
- Contributing to communication and information sharing efforts during incidents
- Planning, training, and exercising their response capabilities
- Providing assistance specified under mutual aid and assistance agreements
- Contributing resources, personnel, and expertise;
- helping to shape objectives; and
- receiving information about the status of the community (FEMA, 2013).

Participation of the private sector varies based on the nature of the organization and the nature of the incident. The four distinct roles that private-sector organizations play are summarized in Table 9.3.

The NRF states that "NGOs play vital roles at the local, state, tribal, territorial, insular area government, and national levels in delivering important services, including those associated with the response core capabilities. NGOs include voluntary, racial and ethnic, faith-based, veteran-based, and nonprofit organizations that provide sheltering, emergency food supplies, and other essential support services. NGOs are inherently independent and committed to specific interests and values." NGOs provide shelters, emergency food supplies, counseling services, and other vital support services to support response and promote the recovery of disaster victims. These groups often provide specialized services that help individuals with special needs, including those with disabilities. NGOs bolster and support government efforts at all levels—for response operations and planning. NGOs impacted by a disaster may also need government assistance. NGOs collaborate with responders, governments at all levels, and other agencies and organizations. Examples of NGO contributions include

- training and managing volunteer resources;
- identifying physically accessible shelter locations and needed supplies to support those displaced by an incident;
- providing emergency commodities and services, such as water, food, shelter, assistance with family reunification, clothing, and supplies for postemergency cleanup;
- supporting the evacuation, rescue, care, and sheltering of animals displaced by the incident;

Table 9.3 Private-Sector Response Role Under NRF

Category	Role in This Category
Affected organization/component of the nation's economy	Private-sector organizations may be affected by direct or indirect consequences of an incident. Such organizations include entities that are significant to local, regional, and national economic recovery from an incident. Examples include major employers and suppliers of key commodities or services. As key elements of the national economy, it is important for private-sector organizations of all types and sizes to take every precaution necessary to boost resilience, to stay better in business, or to resume normal operations quickly
Affected infrastructure	Critical infrastructure—such as privately owned transportation and transit, telecommunications, utilities, financial institutions, hospitals, and other health regulated facilities—should have effective business continuity plans
Regulated and/or responsible party	Owners/operators of certain regulated facilities or hazardous operations may be legally responsible for preparing for and preventing incidents and responding when an incident occurs. For example, federal regulations require owners/operators of nuclear power plants to maintain emergency plans and to perform assessments, notifications, and training for incident response
Response resource	Private-sector entities provide response resources (donated or compensated) during an incident—including specialized teams, essential service providers, equipment, and advanced technologies—through local public-private emergency plans or mutual aid and assistance agreements or in response to requests from government and nongovernmental-volunteer initiatives

Source: Federal Emergency Management Agency (2013).

- providing search and rescue, transportation, and logistics services and support;
- identifying those whose needs have not been met and helping to provide assistance;
- providing health, medical, mental health, and behavioral health resources;
- assisting, coordinating, and providing disability-related assistance and Functional Needs Support Services (FNSS);
- providing language assistance services to individuals with limited English proficiency (FEMA, 2013).

State, Territorial, and Tribal Governments

The primary emergency management role of state, territorial, and tribal governments is to supplement and facilitate local efforts before, during, and after an emergency incident occurs. These government agencies provide direct and routine assistance to their local jurisdictions through emergency management program development and by routinely coordinating these efforts with federal officials. They must be prepared to maintain or accelerate the provision of commodities and services to local governments when local capabilities fall short of demands. The roles and responsibilities of the following individuals are described in greater detail in the NRF.

Governor

The public safety and welfare of a state's citizens are fundamental responsibilities of the governor. The governor

- is responsible for coordinating state resources and providing the strategic guidance needed to prevent, mitigate, prepare for, respond to, and recover from incidents of all types;
- may be able to make, amend, or suspend, in accordance with state law, certain orders or regulations associated with response;
- communicates to the public and helps people, businesses, and organizations cope with the consequences of any type of incident;
- commands the state military forces (National Guard personnel not in federal service and state militias);
- coordinates assistance from other states through interstate mutual aid and assistance compacts, such as the EMAC;
- requests federal assistance including, if appropriate, a Stafford Act presidential declaration of an emergency or major disaster, when it becomes clear that state capabilities will be insufficient or have been exceeded;
- coordinates with impacted tribal governments within the state and initiates requests for a Stafford Act presidential declaration of an emergency or major disaster on behalf of an impacted tribe when appropriate.

State Homeland Security Advisor

The State Homeland Security Advisor serves as a counsel to the governor on homeland security issues and may serve as a liaison between the governor's office, the state homeland security structure, DHS, and other organizations both inside and outside of the state. The adviser often chairs a committee composed of representatives of relevant state agencies, including public safety, the National Guard, emergency management, public health, and others charged with developing prevention, protection, response, and recovery strategies. This also includes preparedness activities associated with these strategies.

Director, State Emergency Management Agency

All states have laws mandating the establishment of a state emergency management agency and the emergency plans coordinated by that agency. The state director of emergency management ensures that the state is prepared to deal with large-scale emergencies and is responsible for coordinating the state response in any incident. This includes supporting local governments as needed or requested and coordinating assistance with other states and/or the federal government. If local resources are not adequate, authorities can seek additional assistance from the county emergency manager or the state director of emergency management. The state emergency management agency may dispatch personnel to the scene to assist in the response and recovery effort.

National Guard

The National Guard is an important state and federal resource available for planning, preparing, and responding to natural or man-made incidents. National Guard members have expertise in critical areas, such as emergency medical response; communications; logistics; search and rescue; civil engineering; chemical, biological, radiological, and nuclear response and planning; and decontamination (FEMA, 2013).

The governor may activate elements of the National Guard to support state domestic civil support functions and activities. The state adjutant general may assign members of the National Guard to assist with state, regional, and federal civil support plans (FEMA, 2013).

Other State Departments and Agencies

State department and agency heads and their staff develop, plan, and train on internal policies and procedures to meet response and recovery needs. They also participate in interagency training and exercises to develop and maintain the necessary capabilities. "They are vital to the state's overall emergency management program, as they bring expertise spanning various response functions and serve as core members of the state emergency operations center (EOC) and incident command posts (ICP). Many of them have direct experience in providing accessible and vital services to the whole community during response operations. State departments and agencies typically work in close coordination with their Federal counterpart agencies during joint state and Federal responses, and under some Federal laws, they may request assistance from these Federal partners" (FEMA, 2013).

Tribes

The United States has a trust relationship with federally recognized Indian tribes and recognizes their right to self-government. Tribal governments are responsible for coordinating resources to address actual or potential incidents. When tribal response resources are inadequate, tribal leaders may seek assistance from states or the federal government. For certain types of federal assistance, tribal governments work with the state in which they are located. For other types of federal assistance, as sovereign entities, tribal governments can elect to work directly with the federal government.

Tribes are encouraged to build relationships with local jurisdictions and their states as they may have resources most readily available. The NRF's Tribal Relations Support Annex outlines processes and mechanisms that tribal governments may use to request direct federal assistance during an incident regardless of whether or not the incident involves a Stafford Act presidential declaration (FEMA, 2013).

Territories/Insular Areas

Territorial and insular area governments are responsible for coordinating resources to address actual or potential incidents. Due to their remote locations, territories and insular area governments often face unique challenges in receiving assistance from outside the jurisdiction quickly and often request assistance from neighboring islands; other nearby countries and states; the private sector or NGO resources; or the federal government. Federal assistance is delivered in accordance with pertinent federal authorities (e.g., the Stafford Act or through other authorities of federal departments or agencies).

Tribal/Territorial/Insular Area Leader

The tribal/territorial/insular area government leader is responsible for the public safety and welfare of the people of his or her jurisdiction. As authorized by the tribal, territorial, or insular area government, the leader:

- Coordinates resources needed to respond to incidents of all types
- In accordance with the law, may make, amend, or suspend certain orders or regulations associated with the response
- Communicates with the public in an accessible manner and helps people, businesses, and organizations cope with the consequences of any type of incident
- Commands the territory's military forces
- Negotiates mutual aid and assistance agreements with other tribes, territories, insular area governments, states, or local jurisdictions
- Can request Federal assistance under the Stafford Act (FEMA, 2013)

Federal Government

When an incident occurs that exceeds or is anticipated to exceed local or state resources—or when an incident is managed by federal departments or agencies acting under their own authorities—the federal government uses the NRF to involve all necessary department and agency capabilities, organize the federal response, and ensure coordination with response partners. Under the NRF, the federal government's response structures are adaptable specifically to the nature and scope of a given incident. The principles of UC are applied at the headquarters, regional, and field levels to enable diverse departments and agencies to work together effectively. Using UC principles, participants share common goals and synchronize their activities to achieve those goals.

Coordination of Federal Responsibilities

The president leads the federal government response effort to ensure that the necessary coordinating structures, leadership, and resources are applied quickly and efficiently to large-scale and catastrophic incidents. The president's Homeland Security Council (HSC) and National Security Council (NSC), which bring together cabinet officers and other department or agency heads as necessary, provide national strategic and policy advice to the president during large-scale incidents that affect the nation.

Federal assistance can be provided to state, tribal, and local jurisdictions and to other federal departments and agencies, in a number of different ways through various mechanisms and authorities. Federal assistance does not require coordination by DHS and can be provided without a presidential major disaster or emergency declaration (as is the case with the National Oil and Hazardous Substances Pollution Contingency Plan, the Mass Migration Emergency Plan, the National Search and Rescue Plan, and the National Maritime Security Plan).

When the overall coordination of federal response activities is required, it is implemented through the secretary of the DHS. Other federal departments and agencies carry out their response authorities and responsibilities within this authority and direction. Several presidential directives outline the following primary lanes of responsibility that guide federal support at national, regional, and field levels.

Incident Management

The secretary of the DHS is the principal federal official for domestic incident management. By presidential directive and statute, the secretary is responsible for coordination of federal resources utilized in the prevention of, preparation for, response to, or recovery from terrorist attacks, major disasters, or other emergencies. The role of the secretary of the DHS is to provide the president with an overall architecture for domestic incident management and to coordinate the federal response, when required, while relying upon the support of other federal partners. Depending on the incident, the secretary also contributes elements of the response consistent with DHS's mission, capabilities, and authorities.

The FEMA administrator, as the principal advisor to the president, the secretary, and the HSC on all matters regarding emergency management, helps the secretary in meeting these responsibilities. Federal assistance for incidents that do not require DHS coordination may be led by other federal departments and agencies consistent with their authorities. The secretary of the DHS may monitor such incidents and may activate specific NRF mechanisms to provide support to departments and agencies without assuming overall leadership for the federal response to the incident. The following four criteria define situations for which DHS shall assume overall federal incident management coordination responsibilities within the NSF and implement the NSF's coordinating mechanisms:

- A federal department or agency acting under its own authority has requested DHS assistance.
- The resources of state and local authorities are overwhelmed and federal assistance has been requested.
- More than one federal department or agency has become substantially involved in responding to the incident.
- The secretary has been directed by the president to assume incident management responsibilities.

Law Enforcement

- The attorney general is the chief law enforcement officer of the United States. Generally acting through the FBI, the attorney general has the lead responsibility for criminal investigations of terrorist acts or terrorist threats by individuals or groups inside the United States or directed at US citizens or institutions abroad, as well as for coordinating activities of the other members of the law enforcement community to detect, prevent, and disrupt terrorist attacks against the United States. This includes actions that are based on specific intelligence or law enforcement information. In addition, the attorney general approves requests submitted by state governors pursuant to the Emergency Federal Law Enforcement Assistance Act for personnel and other federal law enforcement support during incidents. The attorney general also enforces federal civil rights laws and will provide expertise to ensure that these laws are appropriately addressed.

National Defense and Defense Support of Civil Authorities

The primary mission of the DOD and its components is national defense. Because of this critical role, resources are committed after approval by the secretary of the DOD or at the direction of the president. Many DOD components and agencies are authorized to respond to save lives, protect property and the environment, and mitigate human suffering under imminently serious conditions, as well as to provide support under their separate established authorities, as appropriate. The provision of the DOD support is evaluated by its legality, lethality, risk, cost, appropriateness, and impact on readiness. When federal military and civilian personnel and resources are authorized to support civil authorities, command of those forces will remain with the secretary of the DOD. DOD elements in the incident area of operations and National Guard forces under the command of a governor will coordinate closely with response organizations at all levels.

International Coordination

The secretary of state is responsible for managing international preparedness, response, and recovery activities relating to domestic incidents and the protection of US citizens and US interests overseas.

Intelligence

The director of National Intelligence leads the intelligence community, serves as the president's principal intelligence advisor, and oversees and directs the implementation of the National Intelligence Program.

Other Federal Departments and Agencies

Under the NRF, various federal departments or agencies may play primary, coordinating, and/or supporting roles based on their authorities and resources and the nature of the threat or incident. In situations where a federal department or agency has responsibility for directing or managing a major aspect of a response being coordinated by DHS, that organization is part of the national leadership for the incident and is represented in the field at the JFO in the Unified Coordination Group and at headquarters through the NOC and the NRCC, which is part of the NOC. In addition, several federal departments and agencies have their own authorities to declare disasters or emergencies. For example, the secretary of the Department of Health and Human Services can declare a public health emergency. These declarations may be made independently or as part of a coordinated federal response. Where those declarations are part of an incident requiring a coordinated federal response, those federal departments or agencies act within the overall coordination structure of the NSF.

Response Actions under the NRF

The NRF was created to strengthen, organize, and coordinate emergency response actions across all levels of the government and with all involved stakeholders. The NRF reiterates the long-standing notion that incident response should begin and continue at the lowest jurisdictional level capable of handling the required actions. The NRF applies to incidents of all types, including acts of terrorism, major disasters, and other emergencies. The NRF core document describes and outlines key tasks related to the three phases of an effective response capacity, namely, prepare, respond, and recover. An overview of the key tasks associated with response is provided below.

Depending on the size, scope, and magnitude of an incident, communities, states, and, in some cases, the federal government will be called to action. Four key actions typically occur in support of a response.

Gain and Maintain Situational Awareness

Baseline Priorities

Situational awareness requires continuous monitoring of relevant sources of information regarding actual and developing incidents. The scope and type of monitoring vary based on the types of incidents being evaluated and needed reporting thresholds. Critical information is passed through established reporting channels according to established security protocols. Priorities are summarized as follows:

Providing the right information at the right time: For an effective national response, jurisdictions must continuously refine their ability to assess the situation as an incident unfolds and rapidly provide accurate and accessible information to decision-makers in a user-friendly manner. It is essential that all levels of the government, the private sector (in particular, owners/operators of critical infrastructure and key resources (CIKR)), and NGOs share information to develop a common operating picture and synchronize their response operations and resources.

Improving and integrating national reporting: Situational awareness must start at the incident scene and be effectively communicated to local, tribal, state, and federal governments and the private sector, to include CIKR. Jurisdictions must integrate existing reporting systems to develop an information and knowledge management system that fulfills national information requirements.

Linking operations centers and tapping subject-matter experts: Local governments, tribes, states, and the federal government have a wide range of operations centers that monitor events and provide situational awareness. Based on their roles and responsibilities, operations centers should identify information requirements, establish reporting thresholds, and be familiar with the expectations of decision-makers and partners. Situational awareness is greatly improved when experienced technical specialists identify critical elements of information and use them to form a common operating picture.

Local, Tribal, and State Actions

Local, tribal, and state governments can address the inherent challenges in establishing successful information-sharing networks by

- creating fusion centers that bring together into one central location law enforcement, intelligence, emergency management, public health, and other agencies, as well as private-sector and NGOs when appropriate, and that have the capabilities to evaluate and act appropriately on all available information;
- implementing the National Information Sharing Guidelines to share intelligence and information and improve the ability of systems to exchange data;
- establishing information requirements and reporting protocols to enable effective and timely decision-making during response to incidents (terrorist threats and actual incidents with a potential or actual terrorist link should be reported immediately to a local or regional Joint Terrorism Task Force).

Federal Actions

The NOC serves as the national fusion center, collecting and synthesizing all source information, including information from state fusion centers, across all-threats and all-hazards information covering the spectrum of homeland security partners. Federal departments and agencies should report information regarding actual or potential incidents requiring a coordinated federal response to the NOC. Such information may include

- the implementation of a federal department or agency emergency plan;
- actions to prevent or respond to an incident requiring a coordinated federal response for which a federal department or agency has responsibility under law or directive;
- submission of requests for coordinated federal assistance to, or receipt of a request from, another federal department or agency;
- requests for coordinated federal assistance from state, tribal, or local governments, the private sector, and NGOs;
- suspicious activities or threats, which are closely coordinated among the DOJ/FBI SIOC, the NOC, and the National Counterterrorism Center (NCTC).

The primary reporting method for information flow is the Homeland Security Information Network (HSIN). Additionally, there are threat-reporting mechanisms in place through the FBI where information is assessed for credibility and possible criminal investigation. Each federal department and agency must work with DHS to ensure that its response personnel have access to and are trained to use the HSIN common operating picture for incident reporting.

Alerts

When notified of a threat or an incident that potentially requires a coordinated federal response, the NOC evaluates the information and notifies appropriate senior federal officials and federal operations centers: the NRCC, the FBI SIOC, the NCTC, and the National Military Command Center (NMCC). The NOC serves as the primary coordinating center for these and other operations centers. The NOC alerts department and agency leadership to critical information to inform decision-making. Based on that information, the secretary of the DHS coordinates with other appropriate departments and agencies to activate plans and applicable coordination structures of the NRF as required. Officials should be prepared to participate, either in person or by secure video teleconference, with departments or agencies involved in responding to the incident. The NOC maintains the common operating picture that provides overall situational awareness for incident information. Each federal department and agency must ensure that its response personnel are trained to utilize these tools.

Operations Centers

Federal operations centers maintain active situational awareness and communications within and among federal departments and agency regional, district, and sector offices across the country. These operations centers are often connected with their state, tribal, and local counterparts and can exchange information and draw and direct resources in the event of an incident.

Activate and Deploy Resources and Capabilities

Baseline Priorities

When an incident or potential incident occurs, responders assess the situation, identify and prioritize requirements, and activate available resources and capabilities to save lives, protect property and the environment, and meet basic human needs. In most cases, this includes the development of incident objectives based on incident priorities, development of an incident action plan by the incident command in the field, and development of support plans by the appropriate local, tribal, state, and/or federal government entities. Key activities are summarized in the following:

Activating people, resources, and capabilities: Across all levels, initial actions may include activation of people and teams and establishment of incident management and response structures to organize and coordinate an effective response. The resources and capabilities deployed and the activation of supporting incident management structures should be directly related to the size, scope, nature, and complexity of the incident. All responders should maintain and regularly exercise notification systems and protocols.

Requesting additional resources and capabilities: Responders and capabilities may be requested through mutual aid and assistance agreements, the state, or the federal government. For all incidents, especially large-scale incidents, it is essential to prioritize and clearly communicate incident requirements so that resources can be efficiently matched, typed, and mobilized to support operations.

Identifying needs and prepositioning resources: When planning for heightened threats or in anticipation of large-scale incidents, local or tribal jurisdictions, states, or the federal government should anticipate resources and capabilities that may be needed. Based on asset availability, resources should be prepositioned and response teams and other support resources may be placed on alert or deployed to a staging area. As noted above, mobilization and deployment will be most effective when supported by planning that includes prescripted mission assignments, advance readiness contracting, and staged resources.

Local, Tribal, and State Actions

In the event of, or in anticipation of, an incident requiring a coordinated response, local, tribal, and state jurisdictions should

- identify staff for deployment to the EOC, which should have standard procedures and call-down lists to notify department and agency points of contact;
- work with emergency management officials to take the necessary steps to provide for continuity of operations;
- activate incident management teams (IMTs) as required (IMTs are incident command organizations made up of the command and general staff members and appropriate functional units of an ICS organization, and the level of training and experience of the IMT members, coupled with the identified formal response requirements and responsibilities of the IMT, are factors in determining the "type," or level, of the IMT);
- activate specialized response teams as required (jurisdictions may have specialized teams including search and rescue teams, crime scene investigators, public works teams, hazardous materials response teams, public health specialists, and veterinarians/animal response teams);
- activate mutual aid and assistance agreements as required.

Federal Actions

In the event of, or in anticipation of, an incident requiring a coordinated federal response, the NOC, in many cases acting through the NRCC, notifies other federal departments and agencies of the situation and specifies the level of activation required. After being notified, departments and agencies should

- identify and mobilize staff to fulfill their department's or agency's responsibilities, including identifying appropriate subject-matter experts and other staff to support department operations centers;
- identify staff for deployment to the NOC, the NRCC, FEMA Regional Response Coordination Centers (RRCCs), or other operations centers as needed, such as the FBI's Joint Operations Center (these organizations have standard procedures and call-down lists and will notify the department or agency points of contact if deployment is necessary);
- identify staff who can be dispatched to the JFO, including federal officials representing those departments and agencies with specific authorities, lead personnel for the JFO sections (operations, planning, logistics, and administration and finance), and the ESFs;
- begin activating and staging federal teams and other resources in support of the federal response as requested by DHS or in accordance with department or agency authorities (Figure 9-13);
- execute prescripted mission assignments and readiness contracts, as directed by DHS.

FIGURE 9-13 Joplin, MO, May 25, 2011—An applicant services specialist assists one of the survivors of the Joplin tornado with the FEMA registration process. Disaster Recovery Centers, like this one in a local Methodist church, are set up for survivors to register for assistance and get questions answered about the recovery process. Registering with FEMA starts the process for survivors to receive aid. *Photo by Jace Anderson/FEMA.*

Coordinate Response Actions

Baseline Priorities

Coordination of response activities occurs through response structures based on assigned roles, responsibilities, and reporting protocols. Critical information is provided through established reporting mechanisms. The efficiency and effectiveness of response operations are enhanced by the full application of the NIMS with its common principles, structures, and coordinating processes. Specific priorities include the following:

Managing emergency functions: Local, tribal, and state governments are responsible for the management of their emergency functions. Such management includes mobilizing the National Guard, prepositioning assets, and supporting communities. Local, tribal, and state governments, in conjunction with their voluntary organization partners, are also responsible for implementing plans to ensure the effective management of the flow of volunteers and goods in the affected area.

Coordinating initial actions: Initial actions are coordinated through the on-scene incident command and may include immediate law enforcement, rescue, firefighting, and emergency medical services; emergency flood fighting; evacuations; transportation detours; and emergency information for the public. As the incident unfolds, the on-scene incident command develops and updates an incident action plan, revising courses of action based on changing circumstances.

Coordinating requests for additional support: If additional resources are required, the on-scene incident command requests the needed support. Additional incident management and response structures and personnel are activated to support the response. It is critical that personnel understand roles, structures, protocols, and concepts to ensure clear, coordinated actions. Resources are activated through established procedures and integrated into a standardized organizational structure at the appropriate levels.

Identifying and integrating resources and capabilities: Resources and capabilities must be deployed, received, staged, and efficiently integrated into ongoing operations. For large, complex incidents, this may include working with a diverse array of organizations, including multiple private-sector entities and NGOs through prearranged agreements and contracts. Large-scale events may also require sophisticated coordination and time-phased deployment of resources through an integrated logistics system. Systems and venues must be established to receive, stage, track, and integrate resources into ongoing operations. Incident command should continually assess operations and scale and adapt existing plans to meet evolving circumstances.

Coordinating information: Effective public information strategies are essential following an incident. Incident command may elect to establish a JIC, a physical location where the coordination and dissemination of information for the public and media concerning the incident are managed. JICs may be established locally, regionally, or nationally depending on the size and magnitude of an incident. In the event of incidents requiring a coordinated federal response, JICs are established to coordinate federal, state, tribal, local, and private-sector incident communications with the public. By developing media lists, contact information for relevant stakeholders, and coordinated news releases, the JIC staff facilitates the dissemination of accurate, consistent, accessible, and timely public information to numerous audiences.

Local, Tribal, and State Actions

Within communities, NIMS principles are applied to integrate response plans and resources across jurisdictions and departments and with the private sector and NGOs. Neighboring communities play a key role in providing support through a framework of mutual aid and assistance agreements. These agreements are formal documents that identify the resources that communities are willing to share during an incident. Such agreements should include

- definitions of key terms used in the agreement;
- roles and responsibilities of individual parties;
- procedures for requesting and providing assistance;
- procedures, authorities, and rules for allocation and reimbursement of costs;
- notification procedures;
- protocols for interoperable communications;

- relationships with other agreements among jurisdictions;
- treatment of workers' compensation, liability, and immunity;
- recognition of qualifications and certifications.

States provide the majority of the external assistance to communities. The state is the gateway to several government programs that help communities prepare. When an incident grows beyond the capability of a local jurisdiction and responders cannot meet the needs with mutual aid and assistance resources, the local emergency manager contacts the state. Upon receiving a request for assistance from a local government, immediate state response activities may include

- coordinating warnings and public information through the activation of the state's public communications strategy and the establishment of a JIC;
- distributing supplies stockpiled to meet the emergency;
- providing needed technical assistance and support to meet the response and recovery needs of individuals and households;
- suspending existing statutes, rules, ordinances, and orders by the governor for the duration of the emergency, to the extent permitted by law, to ensure timely performance of response functions;
- implementing state donations management plans and coordinating with NGOs and the private sector;
- ordering the evacuation of persons from any portions of the state threatened by the incident, giving consideration to the requirements of special needs populations and those with household pets or service animals;
- mobilizing resources to meet the requirements of people with special needs, in accordance with the state's preexisting plan and in compliance with federal civil rights laws.

In addition to these actions, the governor may activate elements of the National Guard. The National Guard is a crucial state resource, with expertise in communications, logistics, search and rescue, and decontamination. National Guard forces employed under state active duty or Title 32 status are under the command and control of the governor of their state and are not part of federal military response efforts. Title 32 Full-Time National Guard Duty refers to federal training or other duty, other than inactive duty, performed by a member of the National Guard. Title 32 is not subject to posse comitatus restrictions and allows the governor, with the approval of the president or the secretary of the DOD, to order a guard member to

- perform training and other operational activities;
- conduct homeland defense activities for the military protection of the territory or domestic population of the United States, or of the infrastructure or other assets of the United States determined by the secretary of the DOD to be critical to national security, from a threat or aggression against the United States.

State-to-State Assistance

If additional resources are required, the state should request assistance from other states by using interstate mutual aid and assistance agreements such as the EMAC. Administered by the NEMA, EMAC is a congressionally ratified organization that provides form and structure to the interstate mutual aid and assistance process. Through EMAC or other mutual aid or assistance agreements, a state can request and receive assistance from other member states. Such state-to-state assistance may include

- invoking and administering a statewide mutual aid agreement, as well as coordinating the allocation of resources under that agreement;
- invoking and administering EMAC and/or other compacts and agreements and coordinating the allocation of resources that are made available to and from other states.

Requesting Federal Assistance

When an incident overwhelms or is anticipated to overwhelm state resources, the governor may request federal assistance. In such cases, the affected local jurisdiction, tribe, state, and the federal government will collaborate to provide the necessary assistance. The federal government may provide assistance in the form of funding, resources, and critical services. Federal departments and agencies respect the sovereignty and responsibilities of local, tribal, and state governments while rendering assistance. The intention of the federal government in these situations is not to command the response, but rather to support the affected local, tribal, and/or state governments.

Robert T. Stafford Disaster Relief and Emergency Assistance Act

When it is clear that state capabilities will be exceeded, the governor can request federal assistance, including assistance under the Robert T. Stafford Disaster Relief and Emergency Assistance Act (Stafford Act). The Stafford Act authorizes the president to provide financial and other assistance to state and local governments, certain private nonprofit organizations, and individuals to support response, recovery, and mitigation efforts following presidential emergency or major disaster declarations. The Stafford Act is triggered by a presidential declaration of a major disaster or emergency, when an event causes damage of sufficient severity and magnitude to warrant federal disaster assistance to supplement the efforts and available resources of state, local governments, and the disaster relief organizations in alleviating the damage, loss, hardship, or suffering.

Proactive Response to Catastrophic Incidents

Prior to and during catastrophic incidents, especially those that occur with little or no notice, the state and federal governments may take proactive measures to mobilize and deploy assets in anticipation of a formal request from the state for federal assistance. Such deployments of significant federal assets would likely occur for catastrophic events involving chemical, biological, radiological, nuclear, or high-yield explosive WMDs; large-magnitude earthquakes; or other catastrophic incidents affecting heavily populated areas. The proactive responses are utilized to ensure that resources reach the scene in a timely manner to assist in restoring any disruption of normal function of state or local governments. Proactive notification and deployment of federal resources in anticipation of or in response to catastrophic events will be done in coordination and collaboration with state, tribal, and local governments and private-sector entities when possible.

Federal Assistance Available Without a Presidential Declaration

In many cases, assistance may be obtained from the federal government without a presidential declaration. For example, FEMA places liaisons in state EOCs and moves commodities near incident sites that may require federal assistance prior to a presidential declaration. Additionally, some types of assistance, such as Fire Management Assistance Grants—which provide support to states experiencing severe wildfires—are performed by federal departments or agencies under their own authorities and do not require presidential approval. Finally, federal departments and agencies may provide immediate lifesaving assistance to states under their own statutory authorities without a formal presidential declaration.

Other Federal or Federally Facilitated Assistance

The NRF covers the full range of complex and constantly changing requirements in anticipation of, or in response to, threats or actual incidents, including terrorism and major disasters. In addition to Stafford Act support, the NRF may be applied to provide other forms of support to federal partners. Federal departments and agencies must remain flexible and adaptable in order to provide the support that is required for a particular incident.

Federal-to-Federal Support

Federal departments and agencies execute interagency or intraagency reimbursable agreements, in accordance with the Economy Act or other applicable authorities. The NRF's Financial Management Support Annex contains additional information on this process. Additionally, a federal department or agency responding to an incident under its own jurisdictional authorities may request DHS coordination to obtain additional federal assistance. In such cases, DHS may activate one or more ESF to coordinate required support. Federal departments and agencies must plan for federal-to-federal support missions, to identify additional issues that may arise when providing assistance to other federal departments and agencies and to address those issues in the planning process. When providing federal-to-federal support, DHS may designate a federal resource coordinator to perform the resource coordination function.

International Assistance

A domestic incident may have international and diplomatic implications that call for coordination and consultations with foreign governments and international organizations. An incident may also require direct bilateral and multilateral actions on foreign affairs issues related to the incident. The Department of State has responsibility for coordinating bilateral and multilateral actions and for coordinating international assistance. International coordination within the context of a domestic incident requires close cooperative efforts with foreign counterparts, multilateral/international organizations, and the private sector. Federal departments and agencies should consider in advance what resources or other assistance they may require or be asked to accept from foreign sources and address issues that may arise in receiving such resources. Detailed information on coordination with international partners is further defined in the International Coordination Support Annex.

Response Activities

Specific response actions will vary depending on the scope and nature of an incident. Response actions are based on the objectives established by the incident command and JFO's Unified Coordination Group. Detailed information about the full range of potential response capabilities is contained in the Emergency Support Function Annexes, Incident Annexes, and Support Annexes.

Department and Agency Activities

Federal departments and agencies, upon receiving notification or activation requests, implement their specific emergency plans to activate resources and organize their response actions. Department and agency plans should incorporate procedures for

- the designation of department or agency representatives for interagency coordination and identification of state, tribal, and local points of contact;
- activation of coordination groups managed by the department or agency in accordance with roles and responsibilities;
- activation, mobilization, deployment, and ongoing status reporting for resource-typed teams with responsibilities for providing capabilities under the NRF;
- readiness to execute mission assignments in response to requests for assistance (including prescripted mission assignments) and to support all levels of department or agency participation in the response, at both the field and the national levels;
- ensuring that department or agency resources (e.g., personnel, teams, and equipment) fit into the interagency structures and processes set out in the framework.

Regional Response Activities

The FEMA regional administrator deploys a liaison to the state EOC to provide technical assistance and also activates the RRCC. Federal department and agency personnel, including ESF primary and support agency personnel, staff the RRCC as required. The RRCCs

- coordinate initial regional and field activities;
- deploy regional teams, in coordination with state, tribal, and local officials, to assess the impact of the event, gauge immediate state needs, and make preliminary arrangements to set up operational field facilities;
- coordinate federal support until a JFO is established;
- establish a JIC to provide a central point for coordinating emergency public information activities.

Incident Management Assistance Team

In coordination with the RRCC and the state, FEMA may deploy an Incident Management Assistance Team (IMAT). IMATs are interagency teams composed of subject-matter experts and incident management professionals. IMAT personnel may be drawn from national or regional federal department and agency staff according to established protocols. IMAT teams make preliminary arrangements to set up federal field facilities and initiate the establishment of the JFO.

Emergency Support Functions

The NRCC or RRCC may also activate specific ESFs by directing appropriate departments and agencies to initiate the initial actions delineated in the ESF Annexes.

Demobilize

Demobilization is the orderly, safe, and efficient return of a resource to its original location and status. It should begin as soon as possible to facilitate the accountability of the resources and be fully coordinated with other incident management and response structures.

Local, Tribal, and State Actions

At the local, tribal, and state levels, demobilization planning and activities should include

- provisions to address and validate the safe return of resources to their original locations,
- processes for tracking resources and ensuring applicable reimbursement,
- accountability for compliance with mutual aid and assistance provisions.

Federal Actions

The Unified Coordination Group oversees the development of an exit strategy and a demobilization plan. As the need for full-time interagency response coordination at the JFO wanes, the Unified Coordination Group plans for selective release of federal resources, demobilization, transfer of responsibilities, and closeout. The JFO, however, continues to operate as needed into the recovery phase to coordinate those resources that are still active. ESF representatives assist in demobilizing resources and organizing their orderly return to regular operations, warehouses, or other locations.

Key NRF Concepts

The key concepts, systems, and components upon which the NRF was built were drawn directly from the NIMS. This close association has resulted in a core set of common concepts, principles, terminology, and technologies that exist throughout both documents. These key concepts, systems, and components are described in the following sections.

Incident Command System

The NIMS concept is modeled upon the Incident Command System (ICS), which was developed by the federal, state, and local wildland fire agencies during the 1970s. ICS is structured to facilitate activities in five major functional areas: command, operations, planning, logistics, and finance/administration. In some circumstances, intelligence and investigations may be added as a sixth functional area.

Multiagency Coordination System

The Multiagency Coordination System (MACS) is designed to help coordinate activities that occur above the field level and to prioritize demands for critical or competing resources. Examples of multiagency co-ordination include a state or county EOC, a state intelligence fusion center, the NOC, the FEMA National Response Coordination Center, the DOJ/FBI SIOC, the FBI Joint Operations Center, and the National Counterterrorism Center.

Unified Command

Unified command allows for more efficient multijurisdictional or multiagency management of emergency events. It enables agencies with different legal, geographic, and functional responsibilities to coordinate, plan, and interact with each other in an effective manner. UC allows all agencies with jurisdictional authority or functional responsibility for the incident to jointly provide management direction to an incident through a common set of incident objectives and strategies and a single incident action plan. Under a unified command, each participating agency maintains its authority, responsibility, and accountability.

Field-Level Incident Command

Under the NRF, local responders use ICS to manage response operations. ICS is designed to enable effective incident management by integrating a combination of facilities, equipment, personnel, procedures, and communications operating within a common organizational structure. A basic strength of ICS is that it is already widely adopted and used in incidents of any size. Typically, the incident command is structured to facilitate activities in five major functional areas: command, operations, planning, logistics, and finance/administration. ICS defines certain key roles for managing an ICS incident, as follows:

The incident commander is the individual responsible for all response activities, including the development of strategies and tactics and the ordering and release of resources. The incident commander has overall authority and responsibility for conducting incident operations and is responsible for the management of all incident operations at the incident site.

When multiple command authorities are involved, the incident may be led by a UC composed of officials who have jurisdictional authority or functional responsibility for the incident under an appropriate law, ordinance, or agreement. The UC provides direct, on-scene control of tactical operations.

The command staff consists of a public information officer, safety officer, liaison officer, and other positions. The command staff reports directly to the incident commander.

The general staff normally consists of an operations section chief, planning section chief, logistics section chief, and finance/administration section chief. An intelligence/investigations section may be established, if required, to meet response needs.

At the tactical level, on-scene incident command and management organization are located at an incident command post, which is typically composed of local and mutual aid responders.

Field-Level Area Command

If necessary, an area command may be established to assist the executive official that is responsible for providing management oversight for multiple incidents being handled by separate incident command posts or to oversee the management of a complex incident dispersed over a larger area. The area command does not have operational responsibilities and is activated only if necessary, depending on the complexity of the incident and incident management span-of-control considerations. The area command or incident command post provides information to, and may request assistance from, the local EOC.

Local Emergency Operations Center

Local EOCs are the physical locations where multiagency coordination occurs. EOCs are used to establish an operational "picture" of the incident, provide external coordination for OSCs, and secure additional resources as needed. The core functions of an EOC include coordination, communications, resource allocation and tracking, and information collection, analysis, and dissemination. EOCs may be permanent organizations and facilities staffed 24 h a day, 7 days a week, or they may be established only as required. Standing EOCs are typically directed by a full-time emergency manager. EOCs may be organized by major discipline (fire, law enforcement, medical services, etc.), by jurisdiction (city, county, region, etc.), by ESF (communications, public works, engineering, transportation, resource support, etc.), or, more likely, by some combination thereof. The chief elected or appointed official provides policy direction and supports the incident commander and emergency manager, as needed.

State Emergency Operations Center

State EOCs are the physical location where state agency emergency management coordination efforts occur. Every state maintains an EOC that can expand as necessary to manage events requiring state-level assistance. The local incident command structure directs on-scene emergency management activities and maintains command and control of on-scene incident operations, whereas state EOCs are activated only in support of local EOCs. The key function of state EOC personnel is to ensure that state agency personnel who are located at the scene have the necessary response resources.

Joint Information Center

To coordinate the release of emergency information and other public affairs functions, a JIC may be established. The JIC serves as a focal point for coordinated and timely release of incident-related information to the public and the media. Information about where to receive assistance is communicated directly to victims and their families in an accessible format and in appropriate languages.

Joint Field Office

Federal incident support to the state is generally coordinated through a JFO. The JFO provides the means to integrate diverse federal resources and engage directly with the state. Within the JFO, there is one key operational group and two key officials.

Unified Coordination Group

The Unified Coordination Group is composed of senior officials from the state and key federal departments and agencies and is established at the JFO. Using UC principles, this group provides national support to achieve shared emergency response and recovery objectives.

State Coordinating Officer

The SCO plays a critical role in managing the state response and recovery operations following presidential disaster declarations. The governor of the affected state appoints the SCO, and lines of authority flow from the governor to the SCO, following the state's policies and laws. For events in which a declaration has not yet occurred but is expected (such as with an approaching hurricane), the secretary of the DHS or the FEMA administrator may predesignate one or more federal officials to coordinate with the SCO to determine resources and actions that will likely be required and begin deployment of assets. The specific roles and responsibilities of the SCO include the following:

- Serving as the primary representative of the governor for the affected state or locality with the RRCC (see above) or within the JFO once it is established
- Working with the federal coordinating officer to formulate state requirements, including those that are beyond state capability, and to set priorities for employment of federal resources provided to the state
- Ensuring coordination of resources provided to the state via mutual aid and assistance compacts
- Providing a linkage to local government
- Serving in the Unified Coordination Group in the JFO

Governor's Authorized Representative

As the complexity of the response dictates, the NRF recognizes that the governor may empower a governor's authorized representative to

- execute all necessary documents for disaster assistance on behalf of the state, including certification of applications for public assistance;
- represent the governor of the impacted state in the Unified Coordination Group, when required;
- coordinate and supervise the state disaster assistance program to include serving as its grant administrator;
- identify, in coordination with the SCO, the state's critical information needs for incorporation into a list of essential elements of information (critical items of specific information required to plan and execute an operation).

Homeland Security Council and National Security Council

The Homeland Security Council (HSC) and National Security Council (NSC) advise the activities among executive departments and agencies and promote effective development and implementation of related policy. The HSC and NSC ensure unified leadership across the federal government. The assistant to the president for Homeland Security and Counterterrorism and the assistant to the president for National Security Affairs coordinate interagency policy for domestic and international incident management, respectively, and convene interagency meetings to coordinate policy issues. Both councils use well-established policy development structures to identify issues that require interagency coordination. To support domestic interagency policy coordination on a routine basis, HSC and NSC deputies and principals convene to resolve significant policy issues. They are supported by the two policy coordination committees at the assistant secretary level.

Domestic Readiness Group

The Domestic Readiness Group (DRG) is an interagency body convened on a regular basis to develop and coordinate preparedness, response, and incident management policy. This group evaluates various policy issues of interagency importance regarding domestic preparedness and incident management and makes recommendations to senior levels of the policymaking structure for decision. During an incident, the DRG may be convened by DHS to evaluate relevant interagency policy issues regarding response and develop recommendations as may be required.

Counterterrorism Security Group

The Counterterrorism Security Group (CSG) is an interagency body convened on a regular basis to develop terrorism prevention policy and to coordinate threat response and law enforcement investigations associated with terrorism. This group evaluates various policy issues of interagency importance regarding counterterrorism and makes recommendations to senior levels of the policymaking structure for decision.

National Operations Center

The National Operations Center (NOC) is the primary national hub for situational awareness and operations coordination across the federal government for incident management. It provides the secretary of the

DHS and other key officials with information necessary to make critical national-level incident management decisions. The NOC is a permanent, nonstop multiagency operations center. NOC staff monitor threat and hazard information from across the United States and abroad, supported by a 24/7 watch officer contingent, including

- NOC managers;
- selected federal interagency, state, and local law enforcement representatives;
- intelligence community liaison officers provided by the DHS chief intelligence officer;
- analysts from the Operations Division's interagency planning element;
- watch standers representing dozens of organizations and disciplines from the federal government and others from the private sector.

The NOC facilitates information-sharing and operations coordination with other federal, state, tribal, local, and nongovernmental partners. During emergency response, the NOC develops and distributes spot reports, situation reports, and other information-sharing tools. The following operational components of the NOC provide integrated mission support.

National Response Coordination Center

The National Response Coordination Center (NRCC) is FEMA's primary emergency management operations and resource coordination center. The NRCC constantly monitors potential or developing incidents and supports the efforts of regional and field components as needs arise. The NRCC can increase staffing in anticipation of or in response to an emergency by activating ESFs and other personnel in order to provide resources and policy guidance to a JFO or other local incident management structure. The NRCC conducts operational planning, deploys national-level entities, and collects and disseminates incident information as it is analyzed.

National Infrastructure Coordinating Center

The NICC monitors the nation's CIKR on an ongoing basis. During an incident, the NICC allows the sharing of information across the various components of critical infrastructure and key sectors through entities such as information-sharing and analysis centers and sector coordinating councils.

National Military Command Center

The National Military Command Center (NMCC) is the nation's focal point for continuous monitoring and coordination of worldwide military operations. It directly supports key military officials, including the chairman of the CJCS, the secretary of the DOD, and the president. The center participates in a wide variety of activities, ranging from missile warning and attack assessment to management of peacetime contingencies such as Defense Support of Civil Authorities (DSCA) activities. In conjunction with monitoring the current worldwide situation, the center alerts the joint staff and other national agencies to developing crises and will initially coordinate any military response required.

National Counterterrorism Center

The National Counterterrorism Center (NCTC) integrates and analyzes all intelligence pertaining to terrorism and counterterrorism for the federal government and conducts strategic operational planning using this information.

Strategic Information and Operations Center

The FBI SIOC is the focal point and operational control center for all federal intelligence, law enforcement, and investigative law enforcement activities related to domestic terrorist incidents or threats. The SIOC maintains direct communication with the NOC and serves as an information clearinghouse to help collect, process, vet, and disseminate information relevant to law enforcement and criminal investigation efforts.

Other DHS Operations Centers

Depending on the type of incident, the operations centers of other DHS operating components may serve as the primary operations management center in support of the secretary. These include the USCG, Transportation Security Administration, US Secret Service, and US Customs and Border Protection operations centers.

NRF Emergency Support Functions

Through the NRF, FEMA coordinates response support from across the federal government and certain NGOs by calling up, as needed, one or more of the 15 ESFs. The ESFs are coordinated by FEMA through its NRCC. ESFs are used to coordinate specific functional capabilities and resources provided by federal departments and agencies and with certain private sectors and NGOs when applicable. ESF functions are coordinated by a single agency but may rely on several agencies to provide resources specific to each functional area. The mission of the ESFs is to provide the greatest possible access to capabilities of the federal government regardless of which agency has those capabilities.

For each ESF, there is an ESF coordinator, a primary agency, and several support agencies (based upon authorities, resources, and capabilities). The categories of resources provided under the ESFs are consistent with those identified in the NIMS. ESFs may be selectively activated for both presidentially declared and nondeclared incidents as circumstances require, although not all incidents requiring federal support result in the activation of ESFs. FEMA has the ability to deploy assets and emergency management capabilities through the ESFs into an area in anticipation of an approaching storm or event that is expected to cause severe negative consequences.

A list of the 15 ESFs and a description of the scope of each are found in Table 9.4.

Once ESFs are activated, they may have a headquarters, regional, and field presence. At FEMA headquarters, the ESFs support decision-making and coordination of field operations within the NRCC. The ESFs deliver regional-level technical support and other services in the RRCs and in the JFO and incident command posts. At all levels, FEMA issues mission assignments to obtain resources and capabilities from across the ESFs in support of the affected states. At the headquarter, regional, and field levels, ESFs provide staff to support the incident command sections for operations, planning, logistics, and finance/administration, as requested, which enables the ESFs to work collaboratively. Similar structures organize response at the field, regional, and headquarters levels.

The Emergency Support Functions of the NRF are, in order, as follows:

- *ESF #1, Transportation (Coordinator: Department of Transportation)*: ESF #1 supports DHS by assisting federal, state, tribal, and local governmental entities; voluntary organizations; NGOs; and the private sector in the management of transportation systems and infrastructure during domestic threats or in response to incidents. ESF #1 also participates in prevention, preparedness, response, recovery, and mitigation activities. It carries out the Department of

Table 9.4 NRF Emergency Support Functions and Primary Responsibilities

ESF #1—Transportation
ESF coordinator: Department of Transportation
Aviation/airspace management and control
Transportation safety
Restoration and recovery of transportation infrastructure
Movement restrictions
Damage and impact assessment
ESF #2—Communications
ESF coordinator: DHS (National Communications System)
Coordination with telecommunications and information technology industries
Restoration and repair of telecommunications infrastructure
Protection, restoration, and sustainment of national cyber and information technology resources
Oversight of communications within the federal incident management and response structures
ESF #3—Public Works and Engineering
ESF coordinator: Department of Defense (US Army Corps of Engineers)
Infrastructure protection and emergency repair
Infrastructure restoration
Engineering services and construction management
Emergency contracting support for lifesaving and life-sustaining services
ESF #4—Firefighting
ESF coordinator: Department of Agriculture (US Forest Service)
Coordination of federal firefighting activities
Support to wildland, rural, and urban firefighting operations
ESF #5—Emergency Management
ESF coordinator: DHS (FEMA)
Coordination of incident management and response efforts
Issuance of mission assignments
Resource and human capital
Incident action planning
Financial management
ESF #6—Mass Care, Emergency Assistance, Housing, and Human Services
ESF coordinator: DHS (FEMA)
Mass care
Emergency assistance
Disaster housing
Human services
ESF #7—Logistics Management and Resource Support
ESF coordinators: General Services Administration and DHS (FEMA)
Comprehensive, national incident logistics planning, management, and sustainment capability
Resource support (facility space, office equipment and supplies, contracting services, etc.)
ESF #8—Public Health and Medical Services
ESF coordinator: Department of Health and Human Services
Public health
Medical

Table 9.4 (Continued)

Mental health services
Mass fatality management
ESF #9—Search and Rescue
ESF coordinator: DHS (FEMA)
Lifesaving assistance
Search and rescue operations
ESF #10—Oil and Hazardous Materials Response
ESF coordinator: Environmental Protection Agency
Oil and hazardous materials (chemical, biological, radiological, etc.) response
Environmental short- and long-term cleanup
ESF #11—Agriculture and Natural Resources
ESF coordinator: Department of Agriculture
Nutrition assistance
Animal and plant disease and pest response
Food safety and security
Natural and cultural resources and historic properties protection
Safety and well-being of household pets
ESF #12—Energy
ESF coordinator: Department of Energy
Energy infrastructure assessment, repair, and restoration
Energy industry utilities coordination
Energy forecast
ESF #13—Public Safety and Security
ESF coordinator: Department of Justice
Facility and resource security
Security planning and technical resource assistance
Public safety and security support
Support to access, traffic, and crowd control
ESF #14—Long-Term Community Recovery: superseded by the National Disaster Recovery Framework
ESF #15—External Affairs
ESF coordinator: DHS
Emergency public information and protective action guidance
Media and community relations
Congressional and international affairs
Tribal and insular affairs

Transportation's (DOT's) statutory responsibilities, including regulation of transportation, management of the nation's airspace, and ensuring the safety and security of the national transportation system.

- *ESF #2, Communications (Coordinators: DHS/National Protection and Programs/ Cybersecurity and Communication/National Communications System)*: ESF #2 supports the restoration of the communications infrastructure, facilitates the recovery of systems and applications from cyberattacks, and coordinates federal communications support to response efforts during incidents requiring a coordinated federal response. ESF #2 implements the provisions of the Office of Science and Technology Policy (OSTP) National Plan for Telecommunications Support (NPTS) in Non-Wartime Emergencies. ESF #2 also provides communications support to federal, state, tribal, and local governments and first responders when their systems have been impacted and provides communications and information technology (IT) support to the JFO and JFO field teams. The National Communications System (NCS) and the National Cyber Security Division (NCSD) work closely to coordinate the ESF #2 response to cyber incidents.

- *ESF #3, Public Works and Engineering (Coordinator: US Army Corps of Engineers)*: ESF #3 assists DHS by coordinating and organizing the capabilities and resources of the federal government to facilitate the delivery of services, technical assistance, engineering expertise, construction management, and other support to prepare for, respond to, and/or recover from a disaster or an incident requiring a coordinated federal response. Activities within the scope of this function include conducting preincident and postincident assessments of public works and infrastructure; executing emergency contract support for lifesaving and life-sustaining services; providing technical assistance to include engineering expertise, construction management, and contracting and real estate services; providing emergency repair of damaged public infrastructure and critical facilities; and implementing and managing the DHS/FEMA Public Assistance Program and other recovery programs.
- *ESF #4, Firefighting (Coordinator: US Forest Service)*: ESF #4 provides federal support for the detection and suppression of wildland, rural, and urban fires resulting from, or occurring coincidentally with, an incident requiring a coordinated federal response for assistance.
- *ESF #5, Emergency Management (Coordinator: FEMA)*: ESF #5 supports overall activities of the federal government for domestic incident management. ESF #5 serves as the coordination ESF for all federal departments and agencies across the spectrum of domestic incident management from hazard mitigation and preparedness to response and recovery. ESF #5 identifies resources for alert, activation, and subsequent deployment for quick and effective response. During the postincident response phase, ESF #5 is responsible for the support and planning functions. ESF #5 activities include those functions that are critical to support and facilitate multiagency planning and coordination for operations involving incidents requiring federal coordination. This includes alert and notification; staffing and deployment of DHS and FEMA response teams, as well as response teams from other federal departments and agencies; incident action planning; coordination of operations; logistics management; direction and control; information collection, analysis, and management; facilitation of requests for federal assistance; resource acquisition and management; federal worker safety and health; facilities management; financial management; and other support as required.
- *ESF #6, Mass Care, Emergency Assistance, Housing, and Human Services (Coordinator: FEMA)*: ESF #6 coordinates the delivery of federal mass care, emergency assistance, housing, and human services when local, tribal, and state response and recovery needs exceed their capabilities. When directed by the president, ESF #6 services and programs are implemented to assist individuals and households impacted by potential or actual disaster incidents (see Figure 9-14). ESF #6 is organized into four primary functions:

Mass care: Includes sheltering, feeding operations, emergency first aid, bulk distribution of emergency items, and collecting and providing information on victims to family members.

Emergency assistance: Assistance required by individuals, families, and their communities to ensure that immediate needs beyond the scope of the traditional "mass care" services provided at the local level are addressed. These services include support to evacuations

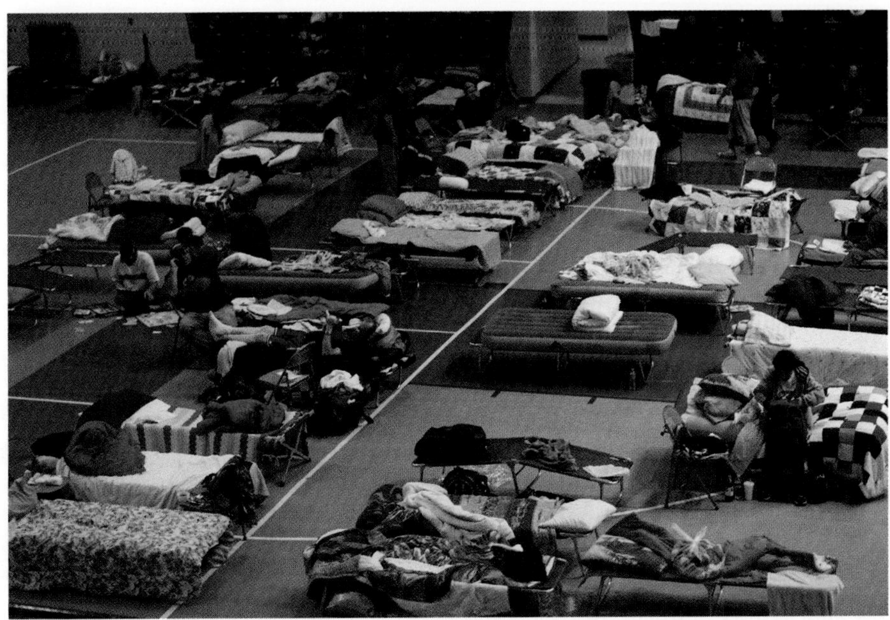

FIGURE 9-14 Minot, ND, June 24, 2011—Red Cross shelter in an auditorium that housed flood evacuees. Burleigh and Ward Counties were designated a federal disaster area, opening the way for federal disaster assistance from FEMA. *Photo by Andrea Booher/FEMA.*

(including registration and tracking of evacuees); reunification of families; provision of aid and services to special needs populations; evacuation, sheltering, and other emergency services for household pets and service animals; support to specialized shelters; support to medical shelters; nonconventional shelter management; coordination of donated goods and services; and coordination of voluntary agency assistance.

Housing: Includes housing options such as rental assistance, repair, loan assistance, replacement, factory-built housing, semipermanent and permanent construction, referrals, identification and provision of accessible housing, and access to other sources of housing assistance. This assistance is guided by the National Disaster Housing Strategy.

Human services: Includes the implementation of disaster assistance programs to help disaster victims recover their nonhousing losses, including programs to replace destroyed personal property, and obtain disaster loans, food stamps, crisis counseling, disaster unemployment, disaster legal services, support and services for special needs populations, and other federal and state benefits.

- *ESF #7, Logistics Management and Resource Support (Coordinators: General Services Administration, FEMA)*: ESF #7 assists DHS by

(FEMA) providing a national disaster logistics planning, management, and sustainment capability that harnesses the resources of federal logistics partners, key public and private stakeholders, and NGOs to meet the needs of disaster victims and responders;

(GSA) supporting federal agencies and state, tribal, and local governments that need resource support prior to, during, and/or after incidents requiring a coordinated federal response.

- *ESF #8, Public Health and Medical Services (Coordinator: HHS)*: ESF #8 provides the mechanism for coordinated federal assistance to supplement state, tribal, and local resources in response to a public health and medical disaster, potential or actual incidents requiring a coordinated federal response, and/or during a developing potential health and medical emergency. ESF #8, Public Health and Medical Services, includes responding to medical needs associated with mental health, behavioral health, and substance abuse considerations of incident victims and response workers. The services also cover the medical needs of members of the "at-risk" or "special needs" population. ESF #8, Public Health and Medical Services, includes behavioral health needs consisting of both mental health and substance abuse considerations for incident victims and response workers and, as appropriate, medical needs groups defined in the core document as individuals in need of additional medical response assistance and veterinary and/or animal health issues. ESF #8 provides supplemental assistance to state, tribal, and local governments in the following core functional areas:

  Assessment of public health/medical needs
  Health surveillance
  Medical care personnel
  Health/medical/veterinary equipment and supplies
  Patient evacuation
  Patient care
  Safety and security of drugs, biologics, and medical devices
  Blood and blood products
  Food safety and security
  Agriculture safety and security
  All-hazards public health and medical consultation, technical assistance, and support
  Behavioral health care
  Public health and medical information
  Vector control
  Potable water/wastewater and solid waste disposal
  Mass fatality management, victim identification, and decontaminating remains
  Veterinary medical support

- *ESF #9, Search and Rescue (SAR) (Coordinator: FEMA)*: ESF #9 rapidly deploys components of the federal SAR response system to provide specialized lifesaving assistance to state, tribal, and local authorities when activated for incidents or potential incidents requiring a coordinated federal response. The federal SAR response system is composed of the primary agencies that provide specialized SAR operations during incidents or potential incidents requiring a coordinated federal response. This includes the following:

  Structural Collapse (Urban) Search and Rescue (US&R)
  Waterborne Search and Rescue
  Inland/Wilderness Search and Rescue
  Aeronautical Search and Rescue

- *ESF #10, Oil and Hazardous Materials Response (Coordinator: EPA)*: ESF #10 provides federal support in response to an actual or potential discharge and/or uncontrolled release of oil or hazardous materials when activated. Response to oil and hazardous materials incidents is generally carried out in accordance with the National Oil and Hazardous Substances Pollution

Contingency Plan (NCP). Appropriate general actions under this ESF can include, but are not limited to, actions to prevent, minimize, or mitigate a release; efforts to detect and assess the extent of contamination (including sampling and analysis and environmental monitoring); actions to stabilize the release and prevent the spread of contamination; analysis of options for environmental cleanup and waste disposition; implementation of environmental cleanup; and storage, treatment, and disposal of oil and hazardous materials. In addition, ESF #10 may be used under appropriate authorities to respond to actual or threatened releases of materials not typically responded to under the NCP but that pose a threat to public health or welfare or to the environment.

- *ESF #11, Agriculture and Natural Resources (Coordinator: Department of Agriculture)*: ESF #11 supports state, tribal, and local authorities and other federal agency efforts to provide nutrition assistance; control and eradicate, as appropriate, any outbreak of a highly contagious or economically devastating animal or zoonotic disease, or any outbreak of an economically devastating plant pest or disease; ensure the safety and security of the commercial food supply; protect natural and cultural resources and historic properties (NCH); and provide for the safety and well-being of household pets during an emergency response or evacuation situation.
- *ESF #12, Energy (Coordinator: DOE)*: ESF #12 facilitates the restoration of damaged energy systems and components when activated for incidents requiring a coordinated federal response. ESF #12 is an integral part of the larger DOE responsibility of maintaining continuous and reliable energy supplies for the United States through preventive measures and restoration and recovery actions. ESF #12 collects, evaluates, and shares information on energy system damage and estimations on the impact of energy system outages within affected areas. Additionally, this function provides information concerning the energy restoration process such as projected schedules, percent completion of restoration, and geographic information on the restoration. It facilitates the restoration of energy systems through legal authorities and waivers. It also provides technical expertise to the utilities, conducts field assessments, and assists government and private-sector stakeholders to overcome challenges in restoring the energy system.
- *ESF #13, Public Safety and Security (Coordinator: Department of Justice)*: ESF #13 provides a mechanism for coordinating and providing federal-to-federal support; federal support to state, tribal, and local authorities; and/or support to other ESFs, consisting of law enforcement, public safety, and security capabilities and resources during potential or actual incidents requiring a coordinated federal response.
- *ESF #14, Long-Term Community Recovery—Superseded by the National Disaster Recovery Framework*
- *ESF #15, External Affairs (Coordinator: DHS)*: ESF #15 ensures that sufficient assets are deployed to provide accurate, coordinated, timely, and accessible information to the various groups affected by the disaster. ESF #15 provides the resource support and mechanisms to implement the NRF Incident Communications Emergency Policy and Procedures (ICEPP) described in the Public Affairs Support Annex. ESF #15 coordinates federal actions to provide the required external affairs support to federal, state, tribal, and local incident management elements to coordinate communications to their audiences. The JIC ensures the coordinated release of information under ESF #15. The planning and product component of ESF # 15, External Affairs, develops all external and internal communications strategies and products for the ESF #15 organization. And finally, ESF #15 provides the resources and structure for the implementation of the ICEPP.

NRF Support Annexes

The NRF Support Annexes describe how federal departments and agencies; state, tribal, and local entities; the private sector; volunteer organizations; and NGOs coordinate and execute the functional processes and administrative requirements necessary for the management of emergency and disaster incidents. The actions described in these annexes are applicable to nearly every type of incident that may occur, whether natural, technological, or intentional in origin. The annexes, which may be fully or partially implemented, may each support several ESFs, as needed.

As was true with the ESFs, there are roles and responsibilities assumed by federal departments and agencies, NGOs, and the private sector for each support annex. The overarching nature of functions covered by the annexes frequently involves either the support to or the cooperation of all departments and agencies involved in incident management efforts to ensure seamless transitions between preparedness, response, and recovery activities. Each annex is managed by one or more coordinating agencies and is supported by various cooperating agencies. The responsibilities of coordinating and cooperating agencies are identified below.

Coordinating Agency

Coordinating agencies are responsible for implementing the processes detailed in the annexes. These federal agencies support DHS incident management efforts by providing the leadership, expertise, and authority to implement critical and specific aspects of the response. When the functions of a particular support annex are required, the agency serving as the coordinator is responsible for

- orchestrating a coordinated delivery of those functions and procedures identified in the annex;
- providing staff for operations functions at fixed and field facilities;
- notifying and subtasking cooperating agencies;
- managing tasks with cooperating agencies, as well as appropriate state, tribal, or local agencies;
- working with appropriate private-sector organizations to maximize the use of available resources;
- supporting and keeping ESFs and other organizational elements informed of annex activities;
- planning for short- and long-term support to incident management and recovery operations;
- conducting preparedness activities such as training and exercises to maintain personnel who can provide appropriate support.

Cooperating Agencies

Cooperating agencies have specific expertise and capabilities that allow them to assist the coordinating agency in executing incident-related tasks or processes. When the procedures within a support annex are needed to support elements of an incident, the coordinating agency will notify cooperating agencies of the circumstances. Cooperating agencies are responsible for the following:

- Conducting operations, when requested by DHS or the coordinating agency, consistent with their own authority and resources
- Participating in planning for short- and long-term incident management and recovery operations and the development of supporting operational plans, standard operating procedures, checklists, or other job aids, in concert with existing first-responder standards

- Furnishing available personnel, equipment, or other resource support as requested by DHS or the support annex coordinator
- Participating in training and exercises aimed at continuous improvement of response and recovery capabilities

When requested, and upon approval of the secretary of the DOD, the DOD provides defense support of civil authorities during domestic incidents. Accordingly, the DOD is considered a cooperating agency for the majority of support annexes.

The support annexes of the NRF are as follows:

- *Critical Infrastructure and Key Resources (coordinator: DHS)*: Describes policies, roles and responsibilities, and the concept of operations for assessing, prioritizing, protecting, and restoring critical infrastructure and key resources (CIKR) during actual or potential domestic incidents. Specifically, this annex does the following:

    Describes roles and responsibilities for CIKR preparedness, protection, response, recovery, restoration, and continuity of operations

    Establishes a concept of operations for incident-related CIKR preparedness, protection, response, recovery, and restoration

    Outlines incident-related actions to expedite information-sharing and analysis of actual or potential impacts to CIKR and facilitate requests for assistance and information from public- and private-sector partners

- *Financial Management (coordinators: FEMA and others)*: Provides basic financial management guidance for all NRF departments and agencies providing assistance for incidents requiring a coordinated federal response. The financial management function is a component of ESF #5 (Emergency Management). The processes and procedures described ensure that funds are provided expeditiously and that financial operations are conducted in accordance with established federal laws, policies, regulations, and standards.
- *International Coordination (coordinator: Department of State)*: Provides guidance on carrying out responsibilities for international coordination in support of the federal government's response to a domestic incident with an international component. The NRF role of the Department of State is to fully support federal, state, tribal, and local authorities in effective incident management and preparedness planning. A domestic incident will have international and diplomatic impacts and implications that call for coordination and consultations with foreign governments and international organizations. An incident may also require direct bilateral and multilateral actions on foreign affairs issues related to the incident, for which DOS has independent and sole responsibility.
- *Private-Sector Coordination (coordinator: DHS)*: Describes the policies, responsibilities, and concept of operations for incident management activities involving the private sector during emergencies and disasters. The annex describes the activities necessary to ensure effective coordination and integration with the private sector, both for-profit and not-for-profit, including the nation's critical infrastructure, key resources, other business and industry components, and NGOs engaged in response and recovery. This annex applies incidents that involve the private sector in any of the following ways:

    Impacted organization or infrastructure

    Response resource

    Regulated and/or responsible party

    Member of the state emergency management organization

- *Public Affairs (coordinator: DHS)*: Describes the policies and procedures used to mobilize federal assets to prepare and deliver risk and emergency communications messages to the public. The annex is applicable to all federal departments and agencies responding under the NRF.
- *Tribal Relations (coordinator: DHS)*: Describes the policies, responsibilities, and concept of operations for coordination and interaction of federal incident management activities with those of tribal governments and communities during incidents requiring a coordinated federal response. Because tribal governments are fully integrated into the NRF, this annex addresses only those factors in the relationship between federal departments and agencies and the federally recognized tribes.
- *Volunteer and Donations Management (coordinator: FEMA)*: Describes the coordination processes used to support the state in ensuring the most efficient and effective use of unaffiliated volunteers, unaffiliated organizations, and unsolicited donated goods to support all ESFs, including offers of unaffiliated volunteer services and unsolicited donations to the federal government.
- *Worker Safety and Health (coordinator: Department of Labor/Occupational Safety and Health Administration)*: Provides federal support to response and recovery organizations in assuring response and recovery worker safety and health during emergency incidents. This annex describes the technical assistance resources, capabilities, and other support to ensure that response and recovery worker safety and health risks are anticipated, recognized, evaluated, communicated, and consistently controlled.

NRF Incident Annexes

The incident annexes address contingency or hazard situations requiring specialized application of the NRF. These annexes, which were not reengineered when the NRF was released and are therefore a carryover from the legacy NRP, describe the following components for each of the specialized incident types:

Policies: Each annex explains unique authorities pertinent to that incident, the special actions or declarations that may result, and any special policies that may apply.

Situation: Each annex describes the incident situation and the planning assumptions and outlines the approach that will be used if key assumptions do not hold (e.g., how authorities will operate if they lose communication with senior decision-makers).

Concept of operations: Each annex describes the concept of operations appropriate to the incident, integration of operations with NRF elements, unique aspects of the organizational approach, notification and activation processes, and specialized incident-related actions. Each annex also details the coordination structures and positions of authority that are unique to the type of incident, the specialized response teams or unique resources needed, and other special considerations.

Responsibilities: Each incident annex identifies the coordinating and cooperating agencies involved in an incident-specific response; in some cases, this responsibility is held jointly by two or more departments.

As is true with the support annexes described above, there are coordinating and cooperating agencies that have been identified for each incident annex. The responsibilities of these agencies in the incident annexes are identical to those detailed in the support annexes.

Each of the incident annexes is described below:

- *Biological Incident Annex (Coordinator: HHS)*: Outlines the actions, roles, and responsibilities associated with response to a disease outbreak of known or unknown origin requiring federal assistance, including threat assessment notification procedures, laboratory testing, joint investigative/response procedures, and activities related to recovery. The broad objectives of the federal government's response to a biological terrorism event, pandemic influenza, emerging infectious disease, or novel pathogen outbreak are to

detect the event through disease surveillance and environmental monitoring,
identify and protect the population(s) at risk,
determine the source of the outbreak,
quickly frame the public health and law enforcement implications,
control and contain any possible epidemic (including providing guidance to state and local public health authorities),
augment and surge public health and medical services,
track and defeat any potential resurgence or additional outbreaks,
assess the extent of residual biological contamination and decontaminate as necessary.

- *Catastrophic Incident Annex (Coordinator: DHS)*: Establishes the context and overarching strategy for implementing and coordinating an accelerated, proactive national response to a catastrophic incident (a more detailed NRF Catastrophic Incident Supplement (NRF-CIS), designated "For Official Use Only," has not been released for public view). A catastrophic incident is any natural or man-made incident resulting in extraordinary levels of mass casualties, damage, or disruption severely affecting the population, infrastructure, environment, economy, national morale, and/or government functions. Recognizing that federal and/or national resources are required to augment overwhelmed state, local, and tribal response efforts, the NRF-CIA establishes protocols to preidentify and rapidly deploy key essential resources (e.g., medical teams, US&R teams, transportable shelters, and medical and equipment caches) that are expected to be urgently needed/required to save lives and contain incidents. Accordingly, upon designation by the secretary of the DHS of a catastrophic incident, federal resources—organized into incident-specific "packages"—deploy in accordance with the NRF-CIS and in coordination with the affected state and incident command structure. An important factor associated with NRF-CIA-designated disasters is that federal assets unilaterally deployed in accordance with the NRF-CIS do not require a state cost-share. Departments and agencies assigned primary responsibility for one or more functional response areas under the NRF-CIS appendixes include the following:

Mass care: American Red Cross
Search and rescue: the Department of Homeland Security
Decontamination: the Department of Homeland Security, Environmental Protection Agency, and Department of Health and Human Services
Public health and medical support: the Department of Health and Human Services
Medical equipment and supplies: the Department of Health and Human Services
Patient movement: the Department of Health and Human Services and Department of Defense
Mass fatality: the Department of Health and Human Services
Housing: the Department of Homeland Security
Public and incident communications: the Department of Homeland Security
Transportation: the Department of Transportation
Private-sector support: the Department of Homeland Security
Logistics: the Department of Homeland Security

- *Cyber Incident Annex (Coordinators: DHS, DOD, and DOJ)*: Discusses policies, organization, actions, and responsibilities for a coordinated approach to prepare for, respond to, and recover from cyber-related emergency incidents impacting critical national processes and the national economy. A cyber-related emergency may take many forms: an organized cyberattack, an uncontrolled exploit such as a virus or a worm, a natural disaster with significant cyber consequences, and other incidents capable of causing extensive damage to critical infrastructure or key assets. Federal government responsibilities include the following:

  Providing indications and warning of potential threats, incidents, and attacks
  Information sharing both inside and outside the government, including best practices, investigative information, coordination of incident response, and incident mitigation
  Analyzing cyber vulnerabilities, exploits, and attack methodologies
  Providing technical assistance
  Conducting investigations, forensics analysis, and prosecution
  Attributing the source of cyberattacks
  Defending against the attack
  Leading national-level recovery efforts

- *Food and Agriculture Incident Annex (Coordinators: Department of Agriculture and HHS)*: Describes how the various involved agencies will respond to emergency incidents involving the nation's agriculture and food systems. A food and agriculture incident may threaten public health, animal nutrition, food production, aquaculture, livestock production, wildlife, soils, rangelands, and agricultural water supplies. Responding to the unique attributes of this type of incident requires separate planning considerations that are tailored to specific health and agriculture concerns and effects of the disease (e.g., deliberate contamination versus natural outbreaks and plant and animal versus processed food). The objectives of a coordinated federal response to an incident impacting food and agriculture are to

  detect the event through the reporting of illness, disease/pest surveillance, routine testing, consumer complaints, and/or environmental monitoring;
  establish the primary coordinating agency;
  determine the source of the incident or outbreak;
  control and contain the distribution of the affected source;
  identify and protect the population at risk;
  assess the public health, food, agriculture, and law enforcement implications;
  assess the extent of residual biological, chemical, or radiological contamination and decontaminate and dispose as necessary;
  support effective and coordinated communication between federal, state, and local responders to a potential or actual incident that requires a coordinated federal response impacting food and agriculture;
  minimize public health and economic impacts of a food- and agriculture-related incident;
  specify roles and responsibilities of coordinating federal agencies and departments;
  provide transition from response to rapid recovery following a food- and agriculture-related incident.

- *Nuclear/Radiological Incident Annex (Coordinators: DHS, DOD, DOE, EPA, National Aeronautics and Space Administration, and Nuclear Regulatory Commission)*: Facilitates an organized and coordinated response by federal agencies to terrorist incidents involving nuclear or radioactive materials and accidents or incidents involving such material. These nuclear/radiological incidents, which include sabotage and terrorist incidents, involve the release or potential release of radioactive material that poses an actual or perceived hazard to public health, safety, national security, and/or the environment (including the terrorist use of RDDs), or "dirty bombs," or improvised nuclear devices (INDs), reactor plant accidents (commercial or weapons production facilities), lost radioactive material sources, transportation accidents involving nuclear/radioactive material, and foreign accidents involving nuclear or radioactive material. This annex

provides planning guidance and outlines operational concepts for the federal response to any nuclear/radiological incident, including a terrorist incident that has actual, potential, or perceived radiological consequences within the United States or its territories, possessions, or territorial waters and that requires a response by the federal government;
describes federal policies and planning considerations on which this annex and federal agency-specific nuclear/radiological response plans are based;
specifies the roles and responsibilities of federal agencies for preventing, preparing for, responding to, and recovering from nuclear/radiological incidents;
includes guidelines for notification, coordination, and leadership of federal activities and coordination of public information, congressional relations, and international activities;
provides protocols for coordinating federal government capabilities to respond to radiological incidents. These capabilities include, but are not limited to,
the Interagency Modeling and Atmospheric Assessment Center (IMAAC), which is responsible for the production, coordination, and dissemination of consequence predictions for an airborne hazardous material release;
the Federal Radiological Monitoring and Assessment Center (FRMAC), established at or near the scene of an incident to coordinate radiological assessment and monitoring;
the Advisory Team for Environment, Food, and Health (known as "the Advisory Team"), which provides expert recommendations on protective action guidance.

- *Oil and Hazardous Materials Incident Annex (Coordinators: EPA and USCG)*: Describes the roles, responsibilities, and coordinating mechanisms for managing major oil and hazardous materials pollution incidents. This annex addresses those oil and hazardous materials incidents that are managed through concurrent implementation of the NRF and the National Oil and Hazardous Substances Pollution Contingency Plan (NCP), but are not ESF #10 (Oil and Hazardous Materials Response) activations. The NCP provides the organizational structure and procedures for federal response to releases of oil and hazardous materials and addresses incident prevention, planning, response, and recovery. The hazardous materials addressed under the NCP include certain substances considered weapons of mass destruction (i.e., chemical agents, biological agents, and radiological/nuclear material). The NCP establishes structures at the national, regional, and local levels that are used to respond to thousands of incidents annually. When an NRF incident does occur, these NCP structures remain in place to provide hazard-specific expertise and support. This annex describes how the NCP structures work with the NRF coordinating structures during major emergency or disaster incidents.
- *Terrorism Incident Law Enforcement and Investigation Annex (Coordinator: FBI)*: Facilitates a federal law enforcement and investigative response to all threats or acts of terrorism within the United States, regardless of whether they are deemed credible and/or whether they are major or minor in scope. This annex provides planning guidance and outlines operational concepts for the federal law enforcement and investigative response to a threatened or actual terrorist incident and acknowledges and outlines the unique nature of each threat or incident, the capabilities and

responsibilities of the local jurisdictions, and the law enforcement and investigative activities necessary to prevent or mitigate a specific threat or incident. The law enforcement and investigative response to a terrorist threat or incident within the United States is a highly coordinated, multiagency state, local, tribal, and federal responsibility. The attorney general holds the lead responsibility for criminal investigations of terrorist acts or terrorist threats by individuals or groups inside the United States or directed at US citizens or institutions abroad, under HSPD-5. Acting through the FBI, the attorney general, in cooperation with other federal departments and agencies engaged in activities to protect national security, also coordinates the activities of the other members of the law enforcement community to detect, prevent, preempt, and disrupt terrorist attacks. Although not formally designated under this annex, other federal departments and agencies may have authorities, resources, capabilities, or expertise required to support terrorism-related law enforcement and investigation operations. Agencies may be requested to participate in federal planning and response operations and may be requested to designate liaison officers and provide other support as required.

Partner Guides

Response Partner Guides were developed in conjunction with the NRF in order to provide local, tribal, state, federal, and private-sector response stakeholders with a reference of their key roles and actions in coordinated response. The Partner Guides include the following:

- Local Government Response Partner Guide
- State Response Partner Guide
- Private-Sector and Nongovernmental Response Partner Guide
- Federal Response Partner Guide

See the sidebar "NRF Federal-Level Operations Coordination" for a summary of the overall coordination.

NRF Federal-Level Operations Coordination

- The Secretary of Homeland Security is the principal federal official responsible for domestic incident management.
- All Federal departments and agencies may play significant roles in incident management and response activities, depending on the nature and size of an event. The policies, operational structures, and capabilities to support an integrated federal response are defined in the Emergency Support Functions (see below), and are coordinated through prescripted mission assignments, and formalized in interagency agreements.
- The FEMA administrator is the principal advisor to the president, the Secretary of Homeland Security, and the Homeland Security Council regarding emergency management. The FEMA administrator's duties include operation of the National Response Coordination Center, the effective support of all emergency support functions, and, more generally, preparation for, protection against, response to, and recovery from all-hazards incidents. Reporting to the Secretary of Homeland Security, the administrator also is responsible for management of the core DHS grant programs supporting homeland security.

- Other DHS agency heads have a lead response role or an otherwise significant role, depending on the type and severity of the event. For example, the US Coast Guard commandant has statutory lead authority for certain mass migration management scenarios and significant oil/hazardous substance spill incidents in the maritime environment.
- The DHS director of operations coordination is the Secretary's principal advisor for the overall departmental level of integration of incident management operations and oversees the National Operations Center.

Source: FEMA (2008).

Critical Thinking

The NRF is a comprehensive document, but it cannot possibly cover every possible need that may arise in every emergency incident. In light of the wide array of emergencies and disasters that could occur in your community, are there any specific community-level needs that might fall outside the spectrum of the NRF that are not explicitly detailed (e.g., the needs of children in emergencies)?

State to State Support: The Emergency Management Assistance Compact

The Emergency Management Assistance Compact (EMAC) is a national-level mutual aid program that has all fifty states, the District of Columbia, Puerto Rico, Guam, and the US Virgin Islands as its members. It was established in 1996. Through EMAC, states that have disasters declared by their governor can request assistance from other members in the forms of personnel, equipment, and commodities that are needed to respond to the disaster they are facing. EMAC has a unique dedicated governance structure composed of the International Association of Emergency Managers, an EMAC Committee, administration, an advisory group, an executive task force, and operational components. This distinguishes it from other mutual aid agreements that typically exist as agreements on paper. EMAC also benefits from its relationships with response organizations at all government levels.

States request assistance through EMAC using a five-phase process that provides the necessary systematic approach, form, and structure for assistance provision. These phases include the following:

1. *Preevent preparation*: Participant jurisdictions develop internal procedures for implementing the compact, incorporate lessons learned into their planning, perform resource typing and predetermine cost estimates, and conduct EMAC training and exercises in cooperation with their state emergency management agencies.
2. *Activation*: Affected jurisdictions identify needs and communicate them to the state office of emergency management. The state determines the appropriate course of action, whether that involves a presidential disaster declaration request, request from the private sector, from EMAC, or any other source.

3. *Request and offer*: State agencies use their in-state resource request procedures to route all requests, including those under EMAC, to their home state emergency management agency. Once a state emergency management agency identifies a need or receives a request for assistance and determines that those resources are best obtained through EMAC member states, the request and offer phases of the EMAC process begin.
4. *Response*: After all request requirements have been satisfied, including a contractual agreement between the assisting and requesting states, the movement of resources begins. Staff mobilize and deploy and tap into the coordination and the command and control systems in place.
5. *Reimbursement*: After the need for assistance has ended, the requesting state begins the process of reimbursing the assisting state for the agreed upon personnel, material, and service assistance that was provided.

For more information concerning the EMAC process, see http://www.emacweb.org/index.php/learnaboutemac/howemacworks.

EMAC offers the following benefits:

- EMAC assistance may be more readily available than other resources.
- EMAC allows for a quick response to disasters using the unique human resources and expertise possessed by member states.
- EMAC offers state-to-state assistance during governor-declared states of emergency and a responsive and straightforward system for states to send personnel and equipment to help disaster relief efforts in other states. When resources are overwhelmed, EMAC helps to fill the shortfalls.
- EMAC establishes a firm legal foundation: Once the conditions for providing assistance to a requesting state have been set, the terms constitute a legally binding contractual agreement that makes affected states responsible for reimbursement. Responding states can rest assured that sending aid will not be a financial or legal burden and personnel sent are protected under workers' compensation and liability provisions. The EMAC legislation solves the problems of liability and responsibilities of cost and allows for credentials to be honored across state lines.
- EMAC provides fast and flexible assistance: EMAC allows states to ask for whatever assistance they need for any type of emergency, from earthquakes to acts of terrorism. EMAC's simple procedures help states dispense with bureaucratic wrangling.
- EMAC can move resources such as medical provisions that other compacts cannot.

Recovery

The recovery function is not easy to classify; it often begins in the initial hours and days following a disaster event and can continue for months and in some cases years, depending on the severity of the event. Unlike the response function, where all efforts have a singular focus, the recovery function or process is characterized by a complex set of issues and decisions that must be made by individuals and communities. These issues include the following:

- Rebuilding homes
- Replacing property
- Resuming employment

- Restoring businesses
- Permanently repairing and rebuilding infrastructure

Because the recovery function has such long-lasting impacts and usually high costs, the participants in the process are numerous. They include all levels of the government, the business community, political leadership, community activists, and individuals. See sidebar "Hurricane Sandy: Two Years of Recovery."

Hurricane Sandy: Two Years of Recovery

Since Hurricane Sandy made landfall October 29, 2012, FEMA, in partnership with the federal family and state and local governments, has been on the scene helping individuals, government entities and eligible nonprofits as New Jersey recovers from the storm's devastation.

Two Years After Sandy—October 29, 2014
Billions of federal dollars have been expended during the past 2 years. The numbers below tell the story.

Amount	Funding Type
$6.67 million	Provided to the state of New Jersey for Hurricane Sandy Recovery
$422.9 million	Distributed to help survivors get back on their feet via temporary housing assistance, disaster unemployment and other needs assistance
$3.5 billion	Paid to policyholders for flood claims through FEMA's National Flood Insurance Program
$1.5 billion	Public Assistance funds has been obligated to communities and certain nonprofit organizations for debris removal, emergency work and permanent work
$279.5 million	Grants have been provided for projects to protect damaged facilities against future disasters
$123.9 million	Funding for property acquisitions, elevation and planning updates has been paid to New Jersey communities through the Hazard Mitigation Grant Program
$847.7 million	Approved by the Small Business Administration for SBA disaster loans to 10,726 individuals and 1718 small businesses

Source: FEMA (2014i).

Given that the federal government plays the largest role in providing the technical and financial support for recovery, this section focuses on the federal role and its relationships with state and local governments, nongovernmental organizations, the private sector, and individual communities as prescribed in the National Disaster Recovery Framework (NDRF) adopted by FEMA and the federal government in 2010.

National Disaster Recovery Framework

According to FEMA, "The National Disaster Recovery Framework (NDRF) is a guide designed to ensure coordination and recovery planning at all levels of government before a disaster, and defines how we will work together, following a disaster, to best meet the needs of states and communities in their recoveries.

This guide is the product of efforts to meet requirements from two key directives: first, the Post-Katrina Emergency Management Reform Act of 2006 requires FEMA to develop a National Disaster Recovery Strategy. Additionally, Presidential Policy Directive (PPD)-8, National Preparedness directs FEMA to work with interagency partners to publish a National Disaster Recovery Framework and supporting operational plans as an integral element of a National Preparedness System" (FEMA, 2014j).

FEMA states that, "The National Disaster Recovery Framework, for the first time, defines how, as a nation, we will approach recovery. The National Disaster Recovery Framework establishes coordination structures, leadership roles and responsibilities, and guides recovery planning at all levels of government before a disaster happens. The National Disaster Recovery Framework introduces recovery support functions that are led by designated federal coordinating agencies. These coordinating federal agencies support state, local, tribal and private sector groups with community planning and capacity building, regaining economic stability, rebuilding infrastructure, restoring health and social services, and natural and cultural resources and meeting the housing needs of residents displaced by disasters. In addition, the National Disaster Recovery Framework recommends and identifies key recovery leadership positions designed to allow for more concentrated focus on community recovery. These include State/Tribal disaster recovery coordinators and local disaster recovery managers, as well as a Federal Disaster Recovery Coordinator when needed for large-scale and catastrophic disasters" (FEMA, 2014j).

The NDRF incorporates FEMA's Whole Community concept and details how the federal government will work with its recovery partners. FEMA describes how the NRDF "establishes a clear structure for interagency and nongovernmental partners to align resources and work together to support recovery in a holistic, coordinated manner. The National Disaster Recovery Framework adds several new positions to the Joint Field Office structure for large-scale and catastrophic incidents, including the senior Federal Disaster Recovery Coordinator that will allow for more concentrated focus on community recovery. These new positions will have the flexibility to be assigned to some of the hardest hit areas as a result of large-scale and catastrophic disasters so that as a community and a team the federal government can ensure a speedy and seamless recovery process" (NDRF, 2014).

An overview of the NRDF developed by FEMA is provided in the sidebar "National Disaster Recovery Framework: Overview."

National Disaster Recovery Framework: Overview

The National Disaster Recovery Framework

The National Disaster Recovery Framework (NDRF) is a conceptual guide designed to ensure coordination and recovery planning at all levels of government before a disaster, and defines how we will work together, following a disaster, to best meet the needs of states, local and tribal governments and communities and individuals in their recoveries. For the first time, the framework establishes coordination structures, defines leadership roles and responsibilities, and guides coordination and recovery planning at all levels of government before a disaster happens. It involves better utilization of existing resources.

Recovery Support Functions

The National Disaster Recovery Framework introduces six recovery support functions that are led by designated federal coordinating agencies. The Recovery Support Functions (RSFs) comprise the coordinating structure for key functional areas of assistance. Their purpose is to support local governments by facilitating problem solving, improving access to resources and fostering coordination among state and federal agencies, nongovernmental partners and stakeholders. The Recovery Support Functions and designated federal coordinating agencies are:

- ***Community Planning and Capacity Building:*** *Federal Emergency Management Agency*
- ***Economic:*** *US Department of Commerce*
- ***Health and Social Services:*** *US Department of Health and Human Services*
- ***Housing:*** *US Department of Housing and Urban Development*
- ***Infrastructure Systems:*** *US Army Corps of Engineers*
- ***Natural and Cultural Resources:*** *US Department of Interior*

Leading Recovery

The framework identifies and recommends key recovery positions designed to allow for more concentrated focus on community recovery. These positions include a Federal Disaster Recovery Coordinator (when warranted in large-scale or catastrophic disasters), State/Tribal Disaster Recovery Coordinators and Local Disaster Recovery Managers.

Addressing the Needs of the Whole Community

The framework incorporates whole community values, with emphasis on core principles, such as individual and family empowerment and partnership and inclusiveness. The National Disaster Recovery Framework outlines how important state, local and tribal leadership and participation of community members in decision-making and coordinated engagement of a wide array of supporting organizations is critical for successful recovery.

Stakeholder Review and Comment

The framework was developed in partnership, and through extensive outreach, with Federal, state, local and tribal governments, private and non-profit partners who have a stake in immediate and ongoing recovery following a disaster. Outreach sessions that began in fall 2009 resulted in thousands of comments and recommendations from more than 600 stakeholders representing Federal, Tribal, state and local governments, public and private organizations, including communities recovering from disasters. This feedback informed the development of the draft National Disaster Recovery Framework.

In January 2010, the draft National Disaster Recovery Framework was published in the Federal Register for public comment. FEMA reviewed the more than 2000 comments to further refine the final version of the National Disaster Recovery Framework.

Summary

This framework, which helps to better define how we, as a Nation, will approach recovery, is not a finish line, but just one part of our ongoing mission to better meet the needs of disaster survivors. We will continue to work with all of our stakeholders on ways to improve our programs, and better partner with the entire team, in our common goal to support communities as they recover.

FEMA's mission is to support our citizens and first responders to ensure that as a nation we work together to build, sustain, and improve our capability to prepare for, protect against, respond to, recover from, and mitigate all hazards.

Source: FEMA (2014g).

Coordination of Disaster Recovery

The practical work of implementing the recovery process occurs at the JFO. Two organizational structures, or branches, divide the recovery assistance functions. These branches assess state and local recovery needs at the outset of the disaster and relevant time frames for program delivery. The human services branch coordinates assistance programs to help individuals, families, and businesses meet basic needs and return to self-sufficiency. It is responsible for the donations management function. The infrastructure support branch coordinates assistance programs to aid state and local governments and eligible private nonprofit organizations to repair or replace damaged public facilities. The two branches assist in identifying appropriate agency assistance programs to meet applicant needs, synchronizing assistance delivery and encouraging incorporation of mitigation measures where possible. In addition to the work of the DRCs, applicant briefings are conducted for local government officials and certain private nonprofit organizations to inform them of available recovery assistance and how to apply.

Federal disaster assistance available under a major disaster falls into three general categories: individual assistance, public assistance, and hazard mitigation assistance. Individual assistance is aid to individuals, families, and business owners. Public assistance is aid to public and certain private nonprofit entities for emergency services and the repair or replacement of disaster-damaged public facilities. Hazard mitigation assistance is funding available for measures designed to reduce future losses to public and private property. A detailed description of the first two types of assistance follows.

FEMA's Individual Assistance Recovery Programs

Individual Assistance Programs are oriented to individuals, families, and small businesses, and the programs include temporary housing assistance, individual and family grants, disaster unemployment assistance, legal services, and crisis counseling. The disaster victim must first register for assistance and establish eligibility. Three national centers provide centralized disaster application services for disaster victims. FEMA's National Processing Service Centers (NPSCs) are located in Denton, Texas; Berryville, Virginia; and Hyattsville, Maryland.

Since the first national center opened in 1994, more than 4 million applications have been processed and over 4.5 million calls have been taken for more than 300 major disasters. These NPSCs house an automated teleregistration service, through which disaster victims apply for Disaster Housing and the Individual and Family Grant program and through which their applications are processed and their questions answered.

This automated system provides automatic determination of eligibility for about 90% of Disaster Housing cases, usually within 10 days of application. The other 10% of cases, which may need documentation, take a little longer. Cases are also automatically referred to the state for possible grant assistance if the applicant's needs exceed the Disaster Housing program and the individual cannot qualify for a disaster loan from the Small Business Administration.

Following the 9/11 events, FEMA was concerned that many individuals and businesses had not sought help in the aftermath of the attack. Working with the Advertising Council and a volunteer ad agency, Muezzin Brown & Partners, a public service advertising campaign was developed to let viewers know that assistance was available by calling FEMA's toll-free registration number. The advertisements were distributed to electronic and media outlets in New York, New Jersey, Connecticut, Pennsylvania, and Massachusetts.

FEMA's individual assistance recovery programs are described in the following sections:

Disaster Housing Program

The Disaster Housing Program ensures that people whose homes are damaged by disaster have a safe place to live until repairs can be completed. These programs are designed to provide funds for expenses that are not covered by insurance and are available to homeowners and renters who are legal residents of the United States and who were displaced by the disaster:

- *Lodging expense reimbursement* provides a check for reimbursement for the costs of short-term lodging such as hotel rooms that were incurred because of damage to a home or an officially imposed prohibition against returning to a home.
- *Emergency minimal repair assistance* provides a check to help repair a home to a habitable condition.
- *Temporary rental assistance* provides a check to rent a place for the predisaster household to live.
- *Mortgage and rental assistance* provides a check to pay the rent or mortgage to prevent evictions or foreclosure. In order to qualify, the applicant must be living in the same house before and after the disaster and have a documented disaster-related financial hardship that can be verified by FEMA.

Individuals and Households Program

The Individuals and Households Program (IHP), formerly called the Individual and Family Grant (IFG) program, provides funds for the necessary expenses and serious needs of disaster victims that cannot be met through insurance or other forms of disaster assistance. The IHP is not designed to cover all of a victim's losses (home, personal property, and household goods) that resulted from the disaster, nor is it intended to restore damaged property to its condition before the disaster. Also, the IHP does not cover any business-related losses that resulted from the disaster. By law, the IHP cannot provide any money for losses that are covered by insurance.

IHP provides assistance for the following:

- *Temporary housing (a place to live for a limited period of time)*: Money is available to rent a different place to live or a government-provided housing unit when rental properties are not available.
- *Repairs*: Money is available to homeowners to repair damage from the disaster that is not covered by insurance. The goal is to make the damaged home safe, sanitary, and functional.
- *Replacements*: Money is available to homeowners to replace their home destroyed in the disaster that is not covered by insurance. The goal is to help the homeowner with the cost of replacing their destroyed home.
- *Permanent housing construction*: This involves either direct assistance or money for the construction of a home. This type of help occurs only in insular areas or remote locations specified by FEMA, where no other type of housing assistance is possible.
- *Other needs*: Money is available for necessary expenses and serious needs caused by the disaster. This includes medical, dental, funeral, personal property, transportation, moving and storage, and other expenses that are authorized by law.

The IHP covers only repair or replacement of items that are damaged as a direct result of the disaster that are not covered by insurance. Repairs or rebuilding may not improve a victim's home above its predisaster condition unless such improvements are required by current building codes.

Small Business Administration Disaster Loans

Following federally declared disasters, the US Small Business Administration (SBA) normally provides federally subsidized loans to repair or replace homes, personal property, or businesses that sustained damages not covered by insurance. For many individuals, the SBA disaster loan program is the primary form of disaster assistance. The SBA can provide three types of disaster loans to qualified homeowners and businesses:

- Home disaster loans to homeowners and renters to repair or replace disaster-related damage to home or personal property
- Business physical disaster loans to business owners to repair or replace disaster-damaged property, including inventory and supplies
- Economic injury disaster loans, which provide capital to small businesses and to small agricultural cooperatives to assist them through the disaster recovery period

Housing Needs

Money to repair a home is limited to making the home "safe and sanitary" so the victim can continue to live there. IHP will not pay to return a home to its predisaster condition. Grants may be used for housing needs to repair the following:

- Structural parts of your home (foundation, outside walls, and roof)
- Windows, doors, floors, walls, ceilings, and cabinetry
- Septic or sewage systems
- Wells or other water systems
- Heating, ventilating, and air conditioning system
- Utilities (electrical, plumbing, and gas systems)
- Entrance and exit ways from your home, including privately owned access roads
- Blocking, leveling, and anchoring of a mobile home and reconnecting or resetting its sewer, water, electrical, fuel lines, and tanks

Other Needs

Money to repair damaged personal property or to pay for disaster-related necessary expenses and serious needs is limited to items or services that help prevent or overcome a disaster-related hardship, injury, or adverse condition. Grants may be used to pay for the following:

- Disaster-related medical and dental costs
- Disaster-related funeral and burial cost
- Clothing, household items (room furnishings and appliances), tools (specialized or protective clothing and equipment) required for a job, and necessary educational materials (computers, school books, and supplies)

- Fuels for primary heat source (heating oil, gas, and firewood)
- Cleanup items (wet/dry vacuum, air purifier, and dehumidifier)
- Disaster-damaged vehicle
- Moving and storage expenses related to the disaster (moving and storing property to avoid additional disaster damage while disaster-related repairs are being made to the home)
- Other necessary expenses or serious needs as determined by FEMA

Money received from IHP for "housing" and "other" needs must be used for eligible expenses only, as identified by FEMA. If a grantee does not use the money for the reasons defined in the grant application, he or she may not be eligible for any additional help and may have to return any grant money provided. Grant money has the following features:

- Is usually limited to up to 18 months from the date the president declares the disaster
- Does not have to be repaid
- Is tax-free
- Is not counted as income or a resource in determining eligibility for welfare, income assistance, or income-tested benefit programs funded by the federal government
- Is exempt from garnishment, seizure, encumbrance, levy, execution, pledge, attachment, release, or waiver
- May not be reassigned or transferred to another person

FEMA pays 100% of the "housing" portion of the grant and 75% of the "other needs" portion. The state pays the remaining 25% of the "other needs" portion. The states may administer only the "other needs" portion of the grant. The total maximum amount of grant assistant for each family or individual in fiscal year 2005 is $25,000, and this amount is broken down further into the various types of assistance provided. For example, although up to $25,000 may be provided for home repairs, a maximum of $10,000 will be provided for replacement of "owner-occupied private residences."

Although some money often is made available through the IHP, most disaster aid from the federal government is provided in the form of loans from the Small Business Administration (SBA) that must be repaid. Applicants to IHP may be required to seek help from the SBA first before being considered for certain types of IHP help. The SBA can provide three types of disaster loans to qualified homeowners and businesses to repair or replace homes, personal property, or businesses that sustained damages not covered by insurance:

- *Home disaster loans* provide funds to homeowners and renters to repair or replace disaster-related damages to home or personal property.
- *Business physical disaster loans* provide funds to business owners to repair or replace disaster-damaged property, including inventory, and supplies.
- *Economic injury loans* provide capital to small businesses and to small agricultural cooperatives to assist them through the disaster recovery period. If the SBA determines that the individual is ineligible for a loan, or if the loan amount is insufficient to meet the individual's needs, then the applicant is referred to the IFG program.

Disaster Unemployment Assistance

The Disaster Unemployment Assistance (DUA) program provides unemployment benefits and reemployment services to individuals who have become unemployed because of major disasters and who are not eligible for disaster benefits under regular unemployment insurance programs.

Legal Services

The Young Lawyers' Division of the American Bar Association, through an agreement with FEMA, provides free legal assistance to low-income disaster victims. The assistance that the participating lawyers provide is for insurance claims; counseling on landlord/tenant problems; assistance in consumer protection matters, remedies, and procedures; and replacement of wills and other important legal documents destroyed in a major disaster. This assistance is intended for individuals who are unable to secure legal services adequate to meet their needs as a consequence of a major disaster.

Special Tax Considerations

Taxpayers who have sustained a casualty loss from a declared disaster may deduct that loss on the federal income tax return for the year in which the casualty occurred or through an immediate amendment to the previous year's return. Businesses may file claims with the Bureau of Alcohol, Tobacco, and Firearms (ATF) for payment of federal excise taxes paid on alcoholic beverages or tobacco products lost, rendered unmarketable, or condemned by a duly authorized official under various circumstances, including where a major disaster has been declared by the president.

Crisis Counseling

The Crisis Counseling Assistance and Training Program is designed to provide short-term crisis counseling services to people affected by a presidentially declared disaster. The purpose of the crisis counseling is to help relieve any grieving, stress, or mental health problems caused or aggravated by the disaster or its aftermath. These short-term services are provided by FEMA as supplemental funds granted to state and local mental health agencies. The American Red Cross, the Salvation Army, and other voluntary agencies, as well as churches and synagogues, also offer crisis counseling services.

Cora Brown Fund

Cora C. Brown of Kansas City, Missouri, died in 1977 and left a portion of her estate to the United States to be used as a special fund solely for the relief of human suffering caused by natural disasters. The funds are used to assist victims/survivors of presidentially declared major disasters for disaster-related needs that have not or will not be met by government agencies or other organizations.

Critical Thinking

Do you think that FEMA's individual grant programs provide enough assistance to individuals and families that are affected by disasters? Should federal assistance programs be available to all disaster victims regardless of their income or net worth? Why or why not?

FEMA's Public Assistance Grant Programs

FEMA, under the authority of the Stafford Act, administers the Public Assistance Program. The Public Assistance Grant Program provides federal assistance to state and local governments and to certain private nonprofit (PNP) organizations. These grants allow them to recover from the impact of disasters and to implement mitigation measures to reduce the impacts from future disasters. The grants are aimed at governments and organizations with the final goal to help a community and its citizens recover from devastating major disasters. The federal share of assistance is not less than 75% of the eligible cost for emergency measures and permanent restoration. The state determines how the nonfederal share is split with the applicants.

Eligible applicants include the states, local governments, and any other political subdivision of the state, Native American tribes, Alaska Native Villages, and certain PNP organizations. Eligible PNP facilities include educational, utility, irrigation, emergency, medical, rehabilitation, temporary or permanent custodial care, and other PNP facilities that are open to the public and provide essential services of a governmental nature to the general public. The work must be required as the result of the disaster, be located within the designated disaster area, and be the legal responsibility of the applicant. PNPs that provide critical services such as power, water, sewer, wastewater treatment, communications, or emergency medical care may apply directly to FEMA for a disaster grant. All other PNPs first must apply to the SBA for a disaster loan. If the loan is declined or does not cover all eligible damages, the applicant may reapply for FEMA assistance.

Work that is eligible for supplemental federal disaster grant assistance is classified as either emergency work or permanent work:

- *Emergency work* includes debris removal from public roads and rights-of-way and from private property when determined to be in the public interest. This may also include protective measures performed to eliminate or reduce immediate threats to the public.
- *Permanent work* is defined as work that is required to restore an eligible damaged facility to its predisaster design. This effort can range from minor repairs to replacement. Some categories for permanent work include roads, bridges, water control facilities, buildings, utility distribution systems, public parks, and recreational facilities. With extenuating circumstances, the deadlines for emergency and permanent work may be extended.

As soon as possible after the disaster declaration, the state, assisted by FEMA, conducts the applicant briefings for state, local, and PNP officials to inform them of the assistance that is available and how to apply for it (Figure 9-15). A Request for Public Assistance must be filed with the state within 30 days after the area is designated eligible for assistance. A combined federal, state, and local team work together to design and deliver the appropriate recovery assistance for the communities. Following the briefing, a "Kickoff Meeting" is conducted where damages are discussed, needs assessed, and a plan of action put in place. A team made up of federal, state, and local representatives initiates the project, including documenting the eligible facilities, the eligible work, and the eligible cost for fixing the damages to every public or PNP facility identified by state or local representatives. The team prepares a project worksheet (PW) for each project. Projects are grouped into the following categories:

- *Category A*: Debris removal
- *Category B*: Emergency protective measures
- *Category C*: Road systems and bridges
- *Category D*: Water control facilities
- *Category E*: Public buildings and contents
- *Category F*: Public utilities
- *Category G*: Parks, recreational, and others

FEMA reviews and approves the PWs and obligates the federal share of the costs (75% or more) to the state. The state then disburses funds to local applicants.

In determining the federal costs for the projects, private or public insurance can play a major role. For insurable buildings within special flood hazard areas (SFHAs) and damaged by floods, the disaster

FIGURE 9-15 Birmingham, AL, June 17, 2011—FEMA Associate Administrator William Carwile (center) listens to a report during a general staff meeting at the Joint Field Office, along with Alabama State Coordinating Officer Jeff Byard (left) and Federal Coordinating Officer Mike Byrne. The meetings help coordinate all of the state and federal resources to continue the recovery process. *Source: FEMA photo/Tim Burkitt.*

assistance is reduced by the amount of insurance settlement that would have been received if the building and its contents had been fully covered by a standard NFIP policy. For structures located outside of an SFHA, the amount is reduced by the actual or anticipated insurance proceeds.

Other Federal Agency Disaster Recovery Funding

Other federal agencies have programs that contribute to social and economic recovery. Most of these additional programs are triggered by a presidential declaration of a major disaster or emergency under the Stafford Act. However, the secretary of the Department of Agriculture and the administrator of the SBA have specific authority relevant to their constituencies to declare a disaster and provide disaster recovery assistance. All of the agencies are part of the structure of the NRF.

Conclusion

The motives behind the establishment of the DHS are almost as numerous as the number of agencies it involves and include politics, power, public relations, or a real need to improve the federal response and recovery systems because of the new spectrum of threats made apparent by the 9/11 attacks. For whatever reason or combination of reasons, a system that had demonstrated its operational capabilities in both natural disasters and terrorism events in Oklahoma City, New York City, and at the Pentagon became subject to significant and ongoing change. As a result of the integration of different agencies and the need for new procedural systems to operate together, the NRP was developed with the NIMS. NIMS and the NRF (which has since replaced the NRP) together serve as references and guidelines to determine how the nation's first responders and agencies involved in response operate.

The effort to include citizens and the private sector as active partners is commendable. Programs developed under the CCCs provide the opportunity to build strong communities. However, they have been poorly supported by the political leadership and are underfunded. Further collaboration with the business sector will allow for enhanced preparedness and protection of the critical infrastructure and provide a better understanding of its vulnerabilities and how to respond if it is attacked.

As a final point, it is essential to bear in mind that the massive integration of many agencies into one has its drawbacks: independence is compromised and the overall redundancy of the system decreases. The NRF and NIMS define how different agencies operate together but it should not jeopardize or change the agencies' own integrity and mission. Although redundancy is an attribute that all organizations try to get rid of, it is also what often saves the day during a crisis situation. "Too efficient" systems with minimal backup, no duplication of function, and low flexibility/adaptability have been shown to be more vulnerable to unexpected situations, to fail in a worse manner, and to be less agile when responding to and dealing with an emergency. Thus, an excessive integration to reduce redundancy can cause the involved agencies to depend on each other rather than empower each other—and this might lead the way for a catastrophic chain reaction of failure to occur in certain conditions.

CASE STUDY 1: THE LONDON TERROR ATTACKS, JULY 7, 2005

On Thursday, July 7, 2005, just before 9 a.m., four suicide bombers blew themselves up—three on London subway trains and one on a bus. The explosions resulted in the deaths of 56 people, including the bombers, and injured more than 700 others. The entire London subway system was closed for the remainder of the day, and cellular telephone systems were jammed, leading to commuter chaos. The following time line illustrates the attacks and the step-by-step response by British authorities:

8:50 a.m.—Three explosions occur almost simultaneously on three London underground trains: between Aldgate and Liverpool Street stations on the Circle Line, between Russell Square and King's Cross stations on the Piccadilly Line, and at Edgware Road station on the Circle Line. At first, police are only aware of the Aldgate/Liverpool Street train attack. The Russell Square/King's Cross blast was not reported until 8:56 and the Edgware blast at 9:17. A review of technical data and witness accounts showed that the three bombs actually went off within about 50 seconds of each other.

9:47—The No. 30 bus on Upper Woburn Place near Tavistock Square is destroyed by a fourth explosion. Pictures show the roof of the double-decker bus ripped off and witnesses report seeing body parts in the road, Reuters reports.

10:02—Scotland Yard says it is dealing with a "major incident."

10:20—Metropolitan Police post a message on their website reporting that a major transportation incident has happened in London and that it is responding to six metro stations and one confirmed explosion in a public bus. Cause, severity, and impact of the explosions are not known at this point.

10:47—Home Secretary Charles Clarke says multiple London blasts have caused "terrible injuries."

11:15—European Union commissioner for justice and security affairs Franco Frattini tells reporters in Rome that the blasts in London are terrorist attacks.

11:35—London police chief tells Reuters news agency there are "indications of explosives" at one of the blast sites.

12:00 p.m.—British Prime Minister Tony Blair says the "barbaric" London blasts are terrorist attacks and were designed to coincide with the G8 summit in Scotland. He will return to London.

12:15—A group calling itself the Group of al-Qaeda of Jihad Organization in Europe lays claim to the blasts, posting a statement on an Islamist website. The claim cannot be independently verified.

12:27—Police and hospital officials tell Reuters that a total of 185 people are wounded across London, 10 of them seriously, and 7 critically.

(Continued)

CASE STUDY 1: THE LONDON TERROR ATTACKS, JULY 7, 2005 (CONTINUED)

12:30—Metropolitan Police confirmed explosions in three metro stations and one public bus and continues its presence on the incident sites. At the time, the police did not provide numbers of casualties but underline that there are many.

12:51—Emergency services personnel tell CNN writer William Chamberlain that all survivors had been evacuated from King's Cross station, leaving the dead below ground "in the double digits."

12:53—Britain's Home Secretary Charles Clarke tells the House of Commons there were four explosions in central London and the underground system will be closed all day. They would decide later in the day whether to resume bus services. Earlier, six attacks were reported.

2:38—US law enforcement sources cite the British government as saying that at least 40 people have been killed. London hospitals report at least 300 wounded, the Associated Press reports.

3:26—London Deputy Police Chief Brian Paddick says police had no warning of the attacks and have not received any claims of responsibility. He says police are keeping an open mind over who carried out the attacks and that it is unclear whether a claim of responsibility by al-Qaeda is genuine or whether suicide bombers were involved. No arrests have been made in connection with the attacks.

3:41—Assistant chief ambulance officer Russell Smith says the service has treated 45 patients with serious or critical injuries. A further 300 patients have been treated for minor injuries.

4:30—London Police announce that the Metropolitan Police Service Casualty Bureau has been opened and ask the public to call the hotline if they are concerned about their loved ones who may have been affected by the incidents. The police announced the number of the confirmed fatalities as 33 for the first time and mentioned that the incidents were caused by terrorists.

4:32—Transport authorities say Docklands Light Railway services in east London and mainline rail services have resumed, except out of King's Cross and Victoria stations. Buses in central London are also returning to service. All underground services remain suspended.

5:43—The British Prime Minister Tony Blair says that Britain will not be intimidated by terrorism and promises intense police and security services action to bring those behind the bombings to justice. "I would also pay tribute to the stoicism and resilience of the people of London who have responded in a way typical of them," says Blair.

5:49—The United Nations Security Council passes a resolution condemning the London attacks and expressing "outrage and indignation at today's appalling terrorist attacks against the people of the United Kingdom that cost human life and caused injuries and immense human suffering."

7:15—Metropolitan police updates the number of confirmed fatalities as 37 and confirms that the incidents involved four explosive devices.

This time line is based on multiple sources including CNN and the London Metropolitan Police media releases:

www.cnn.com/2005/WORLD/europe/07/07/london.timeline/index.html,
www.met.police.uk/news/op_theseus/response1.htm,
www.met.police.uk/news/op_theseus/response2.htm,
www.met.police.uk/news/op_theseus/response3.htm, and
www.met.police.uk/news/op_theseus/response4.htm.

Observations and Comments on Incident

London Metropolitan Police: London Metropolitan Police immediately responded to all potential incident scenes and fulfilled their first-response responsibility. The unique aspect of the incident management by the Metropolitan Police was consistent and persistent behavior in terms of releasing information to the media and the public. The department did not speculate on the incidents and their outcomes and public impacts at any time. The Metropolitan Police chose to release factual information only when the validity of the information was confirmed by credible sources, in many cases its investigators or cooperating government officials. The first casualty numbers were announced about 4:30 p.m. by the department. Until then, various sources in the media were reporting a range of casualty numbers (between 2 and 90) (based on Multiple London Metropolitan Police Press Releases and media coverage on July 7, 2005).

London Fire Brigade: Around 200 firefighters were called to explosions at Aldgate, Edgware Road, and King's Cross London underground stations and an explosion on a bus at Tavistock Square on Thursday, July 7. Twelve fire appliances with 60 firefighters attended the incident at Edgware Road, 12 fire appliances with 60 firefighters attended the incident at King's Cross, 10 fire appliances with 50 firefighters attended the Aldgate incident, and 4 fire appliances with 20 firefighters were called to Tavistock Square. Throughout the morning, several new specialist fire rescue units were deployed to work with the other emergency services to evacuate casualties and make the incident locales safe (London Fire Brigade, http://www.london-fire.gov.uk/news/statement.asp).

London Emergency Medical Services: The response of the emergency medical service units to the bomb attacks in London has generally been assessed as "adequate" by experts. The incident claimed more than 50 lives, left more than 700 hurt, and kept about 100 overnight in hospital, 22 of whom were in critical condition as of July 8. Hospitals responding to the crisis included St. Mary's Hospital in Paddington, the Royal Free hospital in Hampstead, St. Thomas's Hospital, and Great Ormond Street Hospital for Children, which does not have an emergency department but took in 22 patients. Hospitals in London were put on major incident alert within minutes of the first explosion, which occurred at 0851 BST in the third carriage of an underground train traveling in a tunnel 100 meters from Liverpool Street station. Less than a mile away, at the Royal London Hospital in Whitechapel, medical staff implemented a well-rehearsed strategy to cope with the first of 208 patients. The shock waves from the blast were the cause of the most frequently seen injuries on that day, which are particularly traumatic for air-filled parts of the body. The waves can cause perforated eardrums, collapsed lungs, and perforated bowels. But the force can also devastate soft tissue—the blast was responsible for many of the limbs lost during the attacks. Smoke inhalation resulting in lung damage, burns, and ripped skin caused by debris such as glass shards were also common injuries ("Medical Teams Praised for Reaction to Bombings," www.newscientist.com/article.ns?id=dn7649).

Leadership and Crisis Communications

The British Prime Minister Tony Blair was participating in the G8 summit in Gleneagles, Scotland, when he learned about the terror attacks. At 12 p.m. that day, Blair appeared before the media in Gleneagles and gave a 3.5 min long speech about the day's terrorist incidents.

Blair's style of communication on that day has demonstrated his leadership skills and expertise in crisis communications. An analytic piece about the way he delivered his speech marks the following nuances in his speech as critical to conveying the right message in the right way:

- He demonstrated his passion for his people and did not choose to hide his emotions.
- He not only shared his emotions (grief) but also presented a strong image that communicated he and his government were there and ready to deal with the problem.
- He improvised his speech instead of reading it, which proved that it was not "business as usual" for him.
- He used many long pauses to communicate the gravity of the situation.
- He avoided speculations and focused on stating the limited number of facts he was informed about.
- He sincerely communicated his condolences to the families who lost loved ones in the attacks.
- He used strong and direct vocabulary to describe the events ("barbaric").

The analysis above is based on analysis by T.J. Walker ("Crisis Communications with Class," http://www.mediatrainingworldwide.com). For the video of the complete speech, see http://relay.westminsterdigital.co.uk/demand.php?c=number10/statements&m=statementFull2005-07-07.wmv&.wvx. For a transcript of the speech, see www.number-10.gov.uk/output/Page7853.asp.

CASE STUDY 2: RESPONSE TO TERRORISM: THE OKLAHOMA CITY BOMBING

On April 19, 1995, an explosion rocked the federal plaza in Oklahoma City. Within 45 min after notification from the Oklahoma Department of Civil Emergency Management, FEMA deployed staff to Oklahoma City. FEMA coordinated the federal response to the Oklahoma City bombing and later worked closely with state and local officials on recovery efforts. The president signed an emergency declaration within 8 h of the occurrence. This was the first time that Section 501(b) of the Stafford Act, granting FEMA the primary federal responsibility for responding to a domestic consequence management incident, was ever used. The president subsequently declared a major disaster on April 26, 1995. Because the disaster site was also a federal crime scene, FEMA appointed a liaison to the FBI to coordinate site access, support requirements, control public information, and other issues. The coordinated work among federal agencies in Oklahoma City led to the further clarification of agency and department roles in crisis and consequence management.

Harsh lessons were learned in Oklahoma City. A situation arose when local radio stations requested that all medical personnel should respond to the disaster area. A nurse who answered the call was killed by falling debris while trying to rescue victims in the building. A term constantly used after the bombing was the *Oklahoma Standard*. Oklahoma had personnel on the scene within 30 min. Federal officials were notified within minutes of the disaster. Volunteer services were immediate, and because this was a local disaster, everyone took responsibility to do whatever they could to help. Hospital personnel established an effective and efficient triage system. Phone numbers, Internet sites, and briefings were launched within hours of the disaster. The American Red Cross, as in all disasters, was quick to respond with personnel and supplies to help family members of those who were injured or killed in the bombing. The Salvation Army responded within hours with food and supplies. By the end of the day, the Salvation Army had deployed seven units to provide services to the workers and the victims. Law enforcement and EMS personnel had up-to-date training. Oklahoma had excellent coordination with the Public Works Department, the National Weather Service, and the National Guard. The Department of Public Safety also had a predetermined disaster plan in place.

CASE STUDY 3: THE RESPONSE TO HURRICANE KATRINA

By all accounts, the response to Hurricane Katrina represented a failure on all levels. According to the White House Report on the disaster, "The response to Hurricane Katrina fell far short of the seamless, coordinated effort that had been envisioned by President Bush when he ordered the creation of the National Response Plan in February 2003" (Townsend, 2006). The Senate report found that "the suffering [...] continued longer than it should have because of—and in some cases exacerbated by—the failure of government at all levels to plan, prepare for, and respond aggressively to the storm. These failures were not just conspicuous; they were pervasive" (Senate Committee on Homeland Security and Governmental Affairs, 2006). The report concluded that there were many coincident failures but that four among these deserved special placement given their important role in the disaster. These included the following:

1. Long-term warnings went unheeded, and government officials neglected their duties to prepare for a forewarned catastrophe.
2. Government officials took insufficient actions or made poor decisions in the days immediately before and after landfall.

3. Systems on which officials relied on to support their response efforts failed.
4. Government officials at all levels failed to provide effective leadership (Senate Committee on Homeland Security and Governmental Affairs, 2006).

The report developed by the House of Representatives to study the event also recognized that systemic weaknesses existed and that the agencies tasked with responding to catastrophic events were not prepared to do so; the command, control, and coordinate systems in place were not utilized effectively or to capacity; the defenses (levees) built to protect the city were not adequate to hold back the storm surges that occurred; and more. The report noted that the Hurricane Pam Exercise, which was conducted prior to Hurricane Katrina and which investigated what would happen and what response requirements were likely if a category 4 or 5 hurricane were to happen, should have been adequately informative for the decision-makers in place about the dangers that existed. On the positive side, the investigators concluded that the accuracy and timeliness of the National Weather Service and National Hurricane Center forecasts prevented further loss of life. Other key findings included the following:

- The failure of complete evacuations led to preventable deaths, great suffering, and further delays in relief.
- Massive communications damage and a failure to adequately plan for alternatives impaired response efforts, command and control, and situational awareness.
- The collapse of local law enforcement and lack of effective public communications led to civil unrest and further delayed relief.
- Medical care and evacuations suffered from a lack of advance preparations, inadequate communications, and difficulties coordinating efforts.
- Long-standing weaknesses and the magnitude of the disaster overwhelmed FEMA's ability to provide emergency shelter and temporary housing.
- FEMA logistics and contracting systems did not support a targeted, massive, and sustained provision of commodities.
- Contributions by charitable organizations assisted many in need, but the American Red Cross and others faced challenges due to the size of the mission, inadequate logistics capacity, and a disorganized shelter process (Select Bipartisan Committee to Investigate the Preparation for and Response to Hurricane Katrina, 2006).

In summary, these reports found that the government response lacked leadership at the top, was unprepared, operated on poor information and situational awareness, was poorly coordinated, and was incapable of communicating among the various responding agencies and with the general public. All of these factors added up to the confusion, violence, and suffering documented in the first weeks by the media and witnessed by billions across the globe.

Key Terms

Demobilization: The orderly, safe, and efficient return of a resource or resources to their original location and status.

Disaster declaration: The process by which the chief executive official of a jurisdiction (e.g., the mayor, governor, or president) identifies a situation as being beyond the capacity of that particular jurisdiction to be responded to. Under established statutory authorities at the state and federal levels, disaster declaration frees up various resources in support of the affected governments.

Emergency declaration: Any occasion or instance for which, in the determination of the president, federal assistance is needed to supplement state and local efforts and capabilities to save lives and to protect property and public health and safety or to lessen or avert the threat of a catastrophe in any part of the United States. An emergency declaration is more limited in scope and without the long-term federal recovery programs of a major disaster declaration. Generally, federal assistance and funding are provided to meet a specific emergency need or to help prevent a major disaster from occurring.

Emergency Support Function (ESF): Used by the federal government and many state governments as the primary mechanism at the operational level to organize and provide assistance. ESFs align categories of resources and provide strategic objectives for their use. ESFs exist within the NRF and in most state and local emergency operations plans. ESFs utilize standardized resource management concepts such as typing, inventorying, and tracking to facilitate the dispatch, deployment, and recovery of resources before, during, and after an incident.

Federal Response Plan: A plan guiding the overall delivery of federal assistance in Stafford Act (presidentially declared) disasters that was replaced by the National Response Plan in 2004.

Incident Command System (ICS): A system by which emergency incidents of all sizes are managed and developed by the federal, state, and local wildland fire agencies during the 1970s. ICS is structured to facilitate activities in five major functional areas: command, operations, planning, logistics, and finance/administration. In some circumstances, intelligence and investigations may be added as a sixth functional area.

Individual Assistance Programs: They are oriented to individuals, families, and small businesses, and the programs include the Individuals and Households Program, Small Business Administration loans, disaster unemployment assistance, legal services, special tax considerations, and crisis counseling. The disaster victim must first register for assistance and establish eligibility before receiving this assistance.

Joint Field Office: The JFO coordinates federal incident support to the state, allowing the integration of diverse federal resources. Within the JFO, there are one key operational group and two key officials, including the Unified Coordination Group and the state coordinating officer.

Joint Information Center (JIC): A JIC may be established in emergency situations in order to coordinate the release of emergency information and other public affairs functions. The JIC serves as a focal point for coordinated and timely release of incident-related information to the public and the media. Information about where to receive assistance is communicated directly to victims and their families in an accessible format and in appropriate languages.

Long-Term Recovery: This is the period that involves the restoration of lives and livelihoods beyond the emergency phase of the disaster, once lifelines and critical societal components have been restored or replaced. This phase falls squarely within the direction of Emergency Support Function #14, "Long-Term Community Recovery," and often continues for several months or years after the disaster has ended.

Multiagency Coordination System (MACS): A system designed to help coordinate activities that occur above the field level and to prioritize demands for critical or competing resources. Examples of multiagency coordination include a state or county emergency operations center, a state intelligence fusion center, the National Operations Center, the FEMA National Response Coordination Center, the Department of Justice/FBI Strategic Information and Operations Center, the FBI Joint Operations Center, and the National Counterterrorism Center.

National Incident Management System (NIMS): A system that provides a proactive approach guiding government agencies at all levels, the private sector, and nongovernmental organizations to work seamlessly to prepare for, prevent, respond to, recover from, and mitigate the effects of incidents, regardless of cause, size, location, or complexity, in order to reduce the loss of life or property and harm to the environment.

National Response Framework (NRF): A document released in 2008 to replace the National Response Plan that guides how the nation conducts all-hazards response. The framework documents the key response principles, roles, and structures that organize national response. It describes how communities, states, the federal government, and private-sector and nongovernmental partners apply these principles for national response. It also describes special circumstances where the federal government must exercise a larger role, including incidents where federal interests are involved and catastrophic incidents where a state would require significant support. It was designed to allow all response stakeholders to provide a unified national response.

National Response Plan: A plan released in 2004 to replace the Federal Response Plan that guided the response actions of local, state, and federal resources to major "incidents of national significance." This plan was replaced in 2008 by the NRF.

NRF Cooperating Agency: Cooperating agencies have specific expertise and capabilities that allow them to assist the coordinating agency in executing incident-related tasks or processes. When the procedures within a support annex are needed to support elements of an incident, the coordinating agency will notify cooperating agencies of the circumstances.

NRF Coordinating Agency: Coordinating agencies are responsible for implementing the processes detailed in NRF annexes. These federal agencies support DHS incident management efforts by providing the leadership, expertise, and authorities to implement critical and specific aspects of the response. When the functions of a particular support annex are required, the agency serving as the coordinator must carry out various responsibilities as stipulated in the NRF.

Posse Comitatus Act: A law passed in 1878 that restricts the use of the armed forces to perform domestic law enforcement.

Presidential major disaster declaration: Any natural catastrophe (including any hurricane, tornado, storm, high water, wind-driven water, tidal wave, tsunami, earthquake, volcanic eruption, landslide, mudslide, snowstorm, or drought) or, regardless of cause, any fire, flood, or explosion in any part of the United States that in the determination of the president causes damage of sufficient severity and magnitude to warrant major disaster assistance under the Stafford Act to supplement the efforts and available resources of states, local governments, and disaster relief organizations in alleviating the damage, loss, hardship, or suffering caused thereby.

Public Assistance: Public assistance, oriented to public entities, is designed to facilitate the repair, restoration, reconstruction, or replacement of public facilities or infrastructure damaged or destroyed by a federally declared disaster. Eligible applicants include state governments, local governments and any other political subdivision of a state, Native American tribes, and Alaska Native villages. Certain private nonprofit (PNP) organizations may also receive assistance, including educational, utility, irrigation, emergency, medical, rehabilitation, and temporary or permanent custodial care facilities, and other PNP facilities that provide essential services of a governmental nature to the general public.

Short-Term Recovery: This is the period when recovery actions that begin immediately upon occurrence of the disaster, which overlap with response actions, are taken. This phase includes actions such as providing essential public health and safety services, restoring interrupted utility and other essential services, reestablishing transportation routes, and providing food and shelter for those displaced by the incident. Although called *short term*, some short-term recovery activities may last for weeks. Short-term recovery actions are addressed in several functional areas of the NRF.

State Coordinating Officer (SCO): The SCO plays a critical role in managing the state response and recovery operations following presidential disaster declarations. The governor of the affected state appoints the SCO and lines of authority flow from the governor to the SCO, following the state's policies and laws. For events in which a declaration has not yet occurred but is expected (such as with an approaching hurricane), the secretary of the DHS or the FEMA administrator may predesignate one or more federal officials to coordinate with the SCO to determine resources and actions that will likely be required and begin deployment of assets.

Strategic National Stockpile: CDC's Strategic National Stockpile (SNS) consists of strategically placed repositories of medicine and medical supplies that can be called on to protect the public in the event of a public health emergency severe enough to deplete local supplies. Once federal and local authorities agree that the SNS is needed, medicines will be delivered to any state in the United States within 12 h. Each state has plans to receive and distribute SNS medicine and medical supplies to local communities as quickly as possible.

Unified Command: A system that allows for more efficient multijurisdictional or multiagency management of emergency events by enabling agencies with different legal, geographic, and functional responsibilities to coordinate, plan, and interact with each other in an effective manner. Unified command allows all agencies with jurisdictional authority or functional responsibility for the incident to jointly provide management direction to an incident through a common set of incident objectives and strategies and a single incident action plan. Under unified command, each participating agency maintains its authority, responsibility, and accountability.

Unified Coordination Group: The Unified Coordination Group is composed of senior officials from the states and key federal departments and agencies and is established at the JFO. Using unified command principles, this group provides national support to achieve shared emergency response and recovery objectives.

Urban Search and Rescue: Urban Search and Rescue (US&R) involves the location, rescue (extrication), and initial medical stabilization of victims trapped in confined spaces. Although structural collapse is the most common origin of trapped victims, transportation accidents, mines, and collapsed trenches may also cause such to occur. US&R is considered a "multihazard" discipline, as it may be needed for a variety of emergencies or disasters, including earthquakes, hurricanes, typhoons, storms and tornadoes, floods, dam failures, technological accidents, terrorist activities, and hazardous materials releases.

Zoonotic: A disease that can be spread between animals and people.

Review Questions

1. In your opinion, what are the most important differences between the NRF, the NRP, and the FRP?
2. Do you feel that the creation of the Department of Homeland Security has improved emergency response in the United States? Why or why not?
3. If you were an appointed local emergency manager, would you be satisfied with the actions of the federal government in terms of preparedness for large-scale emergency events? What would be

the greatest benefits and problems for you under this new structure (the NRF) from a response perspective? Answer the same question from a regional emergency manager officer and a FEMA high-level officer point of view.

4. What was the basis of the decision to create the National Incident Management System (NIMS)? Why wasn't the ICS used instead? What benefits are gained by having an NRF that is based on the NIMS?
5. The establishment of the Department of Homeland Security and the many subsequent changes to the national emergency management framework are seen by many local emergency managers as inhibiting their efforts to establish an effective all-hazards emergency response capacity. What are your opinions on this stance? Explain your answer.
6. Do you think the National Disaster Recovery Framework will help to facilitate and speed the delivery of federal recovery funding after future disaster events? Why or why not?

References

American Corporate Counsel Association (ACCA), 2002. In: 107th Congress Homeland Security Legislation.

Bullock & Haddow LLC, 2003. Personal interviews with the Chief of Staff and Deputy Chief of Staff of the Federal Emergency Management Agency. Unpublished.

Committee on Homeland Security, 2014. U.S. House of Representatives. http://homeland.house.gov/hearing/hearingthe-boston-marathon-bombings-one-year-look-back-look-forward (April 9, 2014).

Department of Homeland Security, 2007. FY 2007 Homeland Security Grant Program. http://www.dhs.gov/xlibrary/assets/grants_st-local_fy07.pdf.

DHS, 2008. The National Response Framework. DHS, Washington, DC. http://www.fema.gov/pdf/emergency/nrf/nrf-core.pdf.

DHS, 2013. National Response Framework. https://www.fema.gov/national-response-framework.

DHS, 2014. FY 2015 budget in brief. http://www.dhs.gov/publication/fy-2015-budget-brief.

Federal Emergency Management Agency, 2013. National Response Framework, second ed. Federal Emergency Management Agency, Washington, DC. https://www.fema.gov/media-library/assets/documents/32230 (May 2013).

Federal Emergency Management Agency, 2008. National Response Framework. Federal Emergency Management Agency, Washington, DC. http://www.fema.gov/pdf/emergency/nrf/nrf-overview.pdf.

FEMA, 2014a. https://www.fema.gov/disasters/grid/year.

Federal Emergency Management Agency, 2014b. Declaration Process Fact Sheet. https://www.fema.gov/declaration-process-fact-sheet.

FEMA, 2014c. FY 2014 Homeland Security Grant Program (HSGP). http://www.fema.gov/fy-2014-homeland-security-grant-program-hsgp.

Federal Emergency Management Agency (FEMA), 2014d. Disaster Process and Disaster Aid Programs. https://www.fema.gov/disaster-process-disaster-aid-programs.

FEMA, 2014e. http://www.citizencorps.fema.gov/cc/CouncilMapIndex.do.

Federal Emergency Management Agency, 2014f. http://www.fema.gov/profile-rescue.

FEMA, 2014g. National Disaster Recovery Framework: Overview. https://www.fema.gov/national-disaster-recovery-framework-overview.

Federal Emergency Management Agency, 2014h. William Craig Fugate. https://www.fema.gov/leadership/william-craig-fugate.

FEMA, 2014i. Hurricane Sandy: Two Years of Recovery. https://www.fema.gov/new-jersey-sandy-recovery-0/hurricane-sandy-two-years-recovery.

Federal Emergency Management Agency, 2014j. National Disaster Recovery Framework – Frequently Asked Questions. https://www.fema.gov/national-disaster-recovery-framework-frequently-asked-questions.

NDRF, 2014. National Disaster Recovery Framework. Federal Emergency Management Agency (FEMA). https://www.fema.gov/national-disaster-recovery-framework.

NFPA, 2014. National Fire Protection Association. http://www.nfpa.org/research/reports-and-statistics/the-fire-service/administration/us-fire-department-profile.

Senate Committee on Homeland Security and Governmental Affairs, 2006. Hurricane Katrina: A Nation Still Unprepared. S. Rept. 109–322. Government Printing Office. http://www.gpo.gov/fdsys/pkg/CRPT-109srpt322/pdf/CRPT-109srpt322.pdf.

Townsend. F.F., 2006. The Federal Response to Hurricane Katrina Lessons Learned. The White House. http://www.au.af.mil/au/awc/awcgate/whitehouse/katrina/katrina-lessons-learned.pdf.

Washington Post, 2005. War plans drafted to counter terror attacks in U.S. The Washington Post (August 8,)A1. http://www.washingtonpost.com/wp-.

NVOAD, 2014. http://www.nvoad.org/voad-network/national-members/.

10

Mitigation, Prevention, and Preparedness

What You Will Learn

- The definitions of mitigation, preparedness, and prevention
- Overview of mitigation and preparedness programs and frameworks
- Where terrorism fits in the classical life cycle of emergency management
- Overview of the National Terrorism Advisory System (NTAS)
- Preparedness for chemical, biological, and radiological incidents
- Community issues in preparedness
- Private sector involvement in mitigation and preparedness
- Exercise of scenario planning

Introduction

Mitigation and preparedness constitute one-half of the classic emergency management cycle, with response and recovery completing the sequence (Figure 10-1). Mitigation and preparedness generally occur before a disaster ever occurs, although postdisaster mitigation and preparedness, conducted in recognition that similar events are likely in the future, make these two activities somewhat general to the entire emergency management cycle. This is in contrast to response and recovery, which by definition are only possible in the aftermath of a disastrous event.

In its classical meaning, *mitigation* refers to a sustained action taken to reduce or eliminate risk to people and property from hazards and their effects. Mitigation activities address either or both of the two components of risk, which are probability (likelihood) and consequence. By mitigating either of these components, the risk becomes much less of a threat to the affected population. In the case of natural disasters, the ability of humans to limit the probability of a hazard is highly dependent on the hazard type, with some hazards such as hurricanes or tornadoes impossible to prevent, while avalanches, floods, and wildfires are examples of hazards for which limiting the rate of occurrence is possible.

In general, however, mitigation efforts for natural hazards tend to focus on improved consequence management. In terms of man-made disasters, however, there is a much greater range of opportunities to minimize both the probability and the consequences of potential incidents, and both are applied with equal intensity. Mitigation in terms of terrorism, which is a much more complicated process, is discussed later in this chapter.

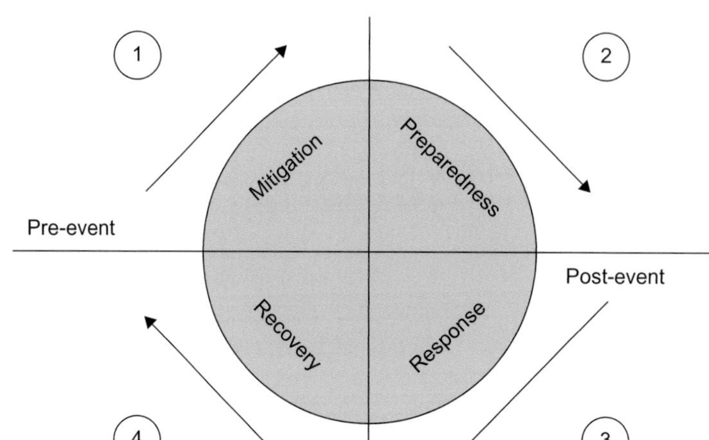

FIGURE 10-1 The four classical phases of disaster management.

Preparedness can be defined as a state of readiness to respond to a disaster, crisis, or any other type of emergency situation. In general, preparedness activities can be characterized as the human component of predisaster hazard management. Training and public education are the most common preparedness activities, and, when properly applied, they have great potential to help people survive disasters. Although preparedness activities do little to prevent a disaster from occurring, they are very effective at ensuring that people know what to do once the disaster has happened.

The concepts of mitigation and preparedness have been altered since September 11, 2001, when terrorism became viewed as the primary threat facing America. As such, terms like *terrorism prevention* and *terrorism preparedness* have become more popular. One must question, in light of these new terms, whether there is any real difference between the traditional definitions of *preparedness* and *mitigation* and what is being conducted in light of the new terrorism hazard.

Critical Thinking

Discuss the differences between preparedness and mitigation and why these differences are important.

The National Response Plan (NRP), released in December 2004 to replace the Federal Response Plan (FRP) as the operating plan for managing the response to major disasters by all federal government departments and agencies in support of state and local emergency managers, provided insight into this issue. Although this new plan did not directly define the phases of incident management, it introduced to users the sequential terminology of prevention, preparedness, response, recovery, and mitigation. The use of this terminology reflects two major changes with respect to the classical incident management approach in the United States. The first change is that mitigation is placed last in this cycle of incident management, which could indicate to readers that the activity (in the context of the plan) is perceived as a postincident one. This is significant mainly because it is altering a set terminology, which has already been widely understood and accepted within the emergency management discipline, feasibly resulting in unnecessary confusion. The second change, which is surely the more radical of the two, is the introduction of the term *prevention*, not only as a concept but also as a distinct phase in the incident management cycle. The plan defined prevention as "actions taken to avoid an incident or to intervene to stop an incident from occurring, which involve actions taken to protect lives and property." The NRP, like the FRP, was a comprehensive plan developed according to the all-hazards approach, but the inclusion of prevention as a separate incident phase (especially in light of the preceding definition) gave rise to the question of whether the NRP was focused primarily on terrorism incident management. Prevention does not seem applicable to most natural disasters.

In January 2008, the NRP was replaced by the National Response Framework (NRF), and as such, much of the emergency management terminology and functions have changed accordingly. The following section describes several of these changes as they relate to mitigation, prevention, and preparedness.

First, the document's title has been changed appropriately to reflect its true nature—namely, that it provides guidelines, rules of engagement, and an organizational framework for all stakeholders of a disaster response involving the federal government rather than offering specific steps of action as is typical in an emergency operations plan (EOP).

Second, the NRF does not attempt to redefine the phases of emergency management as occurred in the NRP. In the NRP, prevention was introduced as a distinct phase in the incident management cycle and, in many (but not all) references, as a replacement for mitigation. The NRF makes no direct reference to the emergency management cycle and refers more sensibly to the terms *prevention* and *mitigation*. *Mitigation* is used comfortably and consistently as part of the all-hazards approach, thereby providing clarity throughout the document. The choice not to push prevention as a distinct emergency management phase is consistent with former Department of Homeland Security (DHS) Secretary Michael Chertoff's vision to establish DHS as managing all hazards, rather than having a distinct focus on terrorism. The term *prevention* is most closely associated with terrorism and therefore finds little applicability in any generalized emergency management approach.

The third major difference relates to the adjustments made to general terms that better accommodate the involvement and partnership of nonfederal stakeholders. These entities are better defined in terms of their role with regard to the emergency support functions (ESFs). The final difference is that the framework commits the federal government to the development of specific emergency response plans based on the 15 incident scenarios identified by the Homeland Security Council. Because incident scenario planning tends to create a rigid response functionality, it is difficult to agree with the approach taken. In such an approach, flexibility is sacrificed and problems may arise when real incidents do not fit the expected parameters. Additionally, this should be seen as a departure from the all-hazards approach as so many of the scores of known hazards are omitted or disregarded, though it is true that these 15 scenarios may be useful as an exercise tool (FEMA, 2014b).

Whether we call it prevention or mitigation, proactive incident management is crucial for minimizing the loss of human life, injuries, financial losses, property damage, and interruption of business activities. Specific methods of prevention and mitigation change from hazard to hazard, and incident to incident, but the goals are the same.

Using the all-hazards approach, whether you are mitigating for earthquakes or floods or preparing for a potential terrorist threat, the classic mitigation planning process is an effective guide for the overall process. The traditional mitigation planning process, still conducted by the Federal Emergency Management Agency (FEMA) today under its DHS umbrella, consists of four stages: (1) identifying and organizing resources, (2) conducting a risk or threat assessment and estimating losses, (3) identifying mitigation measures that will reduce the effects of the hazards and creating a strategy to deal with the mitigation measures in priority order, and (4) implementing the measures, evaluating the results, and keeping the plan up-to-date. This chapter expands on these concepts.

Mitigation and preparedness are vital for sustainable emergency management because strategies geared strictly toward postdisaster response tend to be costlier than those accounting for predisaster opportunities.

However, it can be difficult to convince decision-makers to invest in mitigation and preparedness activities (see "Another Voice: Why Is Mitigation and Preparedness the Only Sustainable, Cost-Effective Way of Dealing with Emergencies?").

The next section focuses on mitigation, prevention, and preparedness activities in an effort to identify ongoing programs and new developments as they fit into each subject.

Critical Thinking

How did the evolution of federal disaster response planning from the Federal Response Plan (FRP) to the National Response Plan (NRP) to the current National Response Framework (NRF) impact the definition and application of preparedness and mitigation measures?

National Frameworks

In July 2014, FEMA released a report entitled "Overview of the National Planning Frameworks" that noted, "Presidential Policy Directive (PPD) 8: National Preparedness was released in March 2011 with the goal of strengthening the security and resilience of the United States through systematic preparation for the threats that pose the greatest risk to the security of the Nation. PPD-8 defines five preparedness mission areas—Prevention, Protection, Mitigation, Response, and Recovery—and mandates the development of a series of policy and planning documents to explain and guide the Nation's approach for ensuring and enhancing national preparedness. The National Planning Frameworks, which are part of the National Preparedness System, set the strategy and doctrine for building, sustaining, and delivering the core capabilities identified in the National Preparedness Goal. They describe the coordinating structures and alignment of key roles and responsibilities for the whole community and are integrated to ensure interoperability across all mission areas. The frameworks address the roles of individuals; nonprofit entities and nongovernmental organizations (NGOs); the private sector; communities; critical infrastructure; governments; and the Nation as a whole. This document is comprised primarily of excerpts from the National Planning Frameworks and presents a high-level introduction to each framework, as well as the key themes identified across the frameworks. The mission areas represent a spectrum of activity. They are highly interdependent and there is regular coordination among departments and agencies working to prevent, protect against, mitigate, respond to, and recover from all threats and hazards" (FEMA, 2014b). Descriptions of each of the five frameworks are presented in sidebar "Framework Overviews."

Framework Overviews

National Prevention Framework

The National Prevention Framework describes what the whole community—from community members to senior leaders in government—should do upon the discovery of intelligence or information regarding an imminent threat to the homeland in order to thwart an initial or follow-on terrorist attack. This Framework helps achieve the National Preparedness Goal of a secure and resilient Nation that is optimally prepared to prevent an imminent terrorist attack within the United States.

National Protection Framework

The National Protection Framework describes what the whole community—from community members to senior leaders in government—should do to safeguard against acts of terrorism, natural disasters and other threats or hazards. This Framework helps achieve the National Preparedness Goal of a secure and resilient Nation that is prepared to protect against the greatest risks in a manner that allows American interests, aspirations, and way of life to thrive. This Framework provides guidance to leaders and practitioners at all levels of government; the private and nonprofit sectors; and individuals.

National Mitigation Framework

The National Mitigation Framework establishes a common platform and forum for coordinating and addressing how the Nation manages risk through mitigation capabilities. It describes mitigation roles across the whole community. The Framework addresses how the Nation will develop, employ, and coordinate mitigation core capabilities to reduce loss of life and property by lessening the impact of disasters. Building on a wealth of objective and evidence-based knowledge and community experience, the Framework seeks to increase risk awareness and leverage mitigation products, services, and assets across the whole community.

National Response Framework

The National Response Framework (NRF) is a guide to how the Nation responds to all types of disasters and emergencies. It is built on scalable, flexible, and adaptable concepts identified in the National Incident Management System (NIMS) to align key roles and responsibilities across the Nation. The NRF describes specific authorities and best practices for managing incidents that range from the serious but purely local to large-scale terrorist attacks or catastrophic natural disasters. The NRF describes the principles, roles and responsibilities, and coordinating structures for delivering the core capabilities required to respond to an incident and further describes how response efforts integrate with those of the other mission areas. The NRF is always in effect, and elements can be implemented at any time. The structures, roles, and responsibilities described in the NRF can be partially or fully implemented in the context of a threat or hazard, in anticipation of a significant event, or in response to an incident. Selective implementation of NRF structures and procedures allows for a scaled response, delivery of the specific resources and capabilities, and a level of coordination appropriate to each incident.

National Disaster Recovery Framework

The National Disaster Recovery Framework (NDRF) is a guide to promote effective recovery, particularly for those incidents that are large-scale or catastrophic. The NDRF provides guidance that enables effective recovery support to disaster-impacted states, tribes, and local jurisdictions. It provides a flexible structure that enables disaster recovery managers to operate in a unified and collaborative manner. It also focuses on how best to restore, redevelop, and revitalize the health, social, economic, natural, and environmental fabric of the community and build a more resilient Nation.

Source: FEMA (2014b).

Mitigation Plans, Actions, and Programs

Mitigation activities include many different methods and strategies that have the common goal of reducing the risk associated with potential hazards. To provide a deeper understanding of mitigation, it is important to first understand the nature of natural, man-made, and terrorism risks.

There are many different definitions of *risk*, each of which may be appropriate within specific circumstances. Kaplan (1997), an acclaimed risk management expert, argues that rather than providing a full definition of *risk*, one must ask three major questions in considering a specific hazard: (1) What can happen? (2) How likely is it? (3) What are the consequences? This indirect definition provides a much more flexible starting point with which to begin our discussion of risk and how to mitigate it. It also sheds additional light on the complexity of treating risks, which are clearly dynamic in nature. How we consider those risks—and rank them according to our concern—is a factor of the combined answers of those three questions. For instance, although traffic accidents occur on a daily basis, their consequences tend to be relatively minor. Very large meteor strikes, on the other hand, are very rare, but when they do occur, their consequences are globally catastrophic. Each hazard must be considered for its individual characteristics, and it is up to the individual, community, or society that is making the analysis to determine what level of effort will be made to address each according to these individual risk components.

The uncertainty component of risk, contained within the probability of disastrous event occurrence, places the greatest burden on those who are treating a full portfolio of risks that must be compared in relation to each other. Uncertainty forces us to ask ourselves questions that are often difficult and based more on expert judgment than on concrete evidence, such as "What is the probability that a 7.0-magnitude earthquake will happen in San Francisco Bay within the next 10 years?" or "What is the probability that terrorists will attack and damage a nuclear power plant in the United States?" The probability component of risk is important because it is an equally weighted parameter that helps us to quantify and prioritize mitigation actions when dealing with multiple risks. The determination of probabilities for events is often a difficult and complicated process. Although several quantitative methods and tools are available that can be used to determine probabilities, these often tend to be too complex for communities to use. Qualitative methods have been developed to ease this problem, which in turn allows for much easier comparison of risk by communities that attempt to treat their risks. Sidebar "Qualitative Representation of Likelihood" illustrates but one example of a system of estimation used to establish qualitative risk likelihood rankings.

Qualitative Representation of Likelihood

This particular qualitative representation system uses words to describe the chance of an event occurring. Each word or phrase has a designated range of possibilities attached to it. For instance, events could be described as follows:

- *Certain*: >99% chance of occurring in a given year (one or more occurrences per year)
- *Likely*: 50%–99% chance of occurring in a given year (one occurrence every 1–2 years)
- *Possible*: 5%–49% chance of occurring in a given year (one occurrence every 2–20 years)
- *Unlikely*: 2%–5% chance of occurring in a given year (one occurrence every 20–50 years)
- *Rare*: 1%–2% chance of occurring in a given year (one occurrence every 50–100 years)
- *Extremely rare*: <1% chance of occurring in a given year (one occurrence every 100 or more years)

Note that this is just one of a limitless range of qualitative terms and values assigned that can be used to describe the likelihood component of risk. As long as all hazards are compared using the same range of qualitative values, the actual determination of likelihood ranges attached to each term does not necessarily matter.

The second component of risk, hazard consequence, is a detailed examination of the total unwanted impact of the disaster to the community, government, or the interested stakeholders. Consequence is often given an assigned monetary value in order to facilitate comparison with other hazards, but there are many intangible consequences that are very difficult to quantify in such absolute terms but have to be considered as well if a comprehensive risk analysis is expected (Table 10-1). Interestingly, the consequences of disasters also have a probabilistic nature. In practice, it is quite hard to assign a single monetary value to the expected damage; probability distributions are used to model the most likely damage estimates. For this reason, qualitative applications of consequence estimation have also been developed. An example is presented in sidebar "Qualitative Representation of Consequence."

Table 10-1 Tangible and Intangible Consequences of Disasters

Consequences	**Measure**	**Tangible Losses**	**Intangible Losses**
Deaths	Number of people	Loss of economically active individuals	Social and psychological effects on remaining community
Injuries	Number and injury severity	Medical treatment needs, temporary loss of economic activity by productive individuals	Social and psychological pain and recovery
Physical damage	Inventory of damaged elements by number and damage level	Replacement and repair cost	Cultural losses
Emergency operations	Volume of man power, person-days employed, equipment, and resources expended to relieve mobilization cost, investment in preparedness capability	Stress and overwork in relief participants	
Disruption to economy	Number of working days lost, volume of production lost	Value of lost production opportunities and in competitiveness and reputation	
Social disruption	Number of displaced persons, homeless	Temporary housing, relief, economic production	Psychological, social contacts, cohesion, community morale
Environmental impact	Scale and severity	Cleanup costs, repair costs	Consequences of poorer environment, health risks, risk of future disaster

Source: United Nations Development Programme (1994).

Qualitative Representation of Consequence

As was true with the qualitative representation of likelihood, words or phrases that have associated meanings can be used to describe the effects of a past disaster or the anticipated effects of a future one. These measurements can be assigned to deaths, injuries, or costs (often, the qualitative measurement of fatalities and injuries is combined). The following is one example of a qualitative measurement system for injuries and deaths:

- *Insignificant*: No injuries or fatalities
- *Minor*: Small number of injuries but no fatalities; first-aid treatment required
- *Moderate*: Medical treatment needed but no fatalities; some hospitalization
- *Major*: Extensive injuries, significant hospitalization; fatalities
- *Catastrophic*: Large number of fatalities and severe injuries; extended and large numbers requiring hospitalization

Once both of these factors (probability and consequence) have been determined, it is possible to compare risks against each other, primarily for the purposes of treating the risks through intervention measures. Normally, only limited funds exist for this purpose and, as such, not all risks can be treated. Risk comparison allows for a prioritization of risk, which can help those performing mitigation and preparedness ensure that they are spending their limited funds most wisely. Table 10-2 provides one example of a risk matrix that can be used to compare risks with each other.

Having provided a basic description of the components of risk, it is appropriate to move on to the mitigation of risk. In applying mitigation, risk managers try to minimize probability or consequence or both. In practice, however, it is not always easy, or even possible, to address both. And because each risk is unique, there are different strategies that must be identified, assessed, and applied for successful risk intervention. For example, assume one seeks to minimize the risk of an earthquake. How can one minimize the probability of its happening? In terms of modern science, unfortunately, there is no known way of doing so, and this is true for many natural hazards despite humankind's best efforts. However, one can still mitigate the risk of an earthquake by minimizing its consequences. For the earthquake risk, several known and proved strategies are available to minimize such consequences, such as adopting and enforcing earthquake-resistant building codes, educating the public about earthquakes, and developing robust earthquake response plans.

Table 10-2 Example of a Qualitative Risk-Level Analysis Matrix

Likelihood	Consequences				
	Insignificant	**Minor**	**Moderate**	**Major**	**Catastrophic**
Almost certain	High	High	Extreme	Extreme	Extreme
Likely	Moderate	High	High	Extreme	Extreme
Possible	Low	Moderate	High	Extreme	Extreme
Unlikely	Low	Low	Moderate	High	Extreme
Rare	Low	Low	Moderate	High	High

Source: Emergency Management Australia (2000).

Critical Thinking

What role does the calculation of risk play in decisions made by communities and individuals in preparing for or mitigating against a known hazard? Should a community with a known hazard design, implement and fund preparedness and mitigation programs that directly address this hazard despite the cost?

In dealing with the newly expanded terrorism risk, the mitigation strategy would likely take on a much different approach. In this case, the opportunity to minimize the likelihood of the event's occurrence is very possible and has been done countless times with great success. Through actionable intelligence collection on terrorist activity and by infiltration of its social and communication networks, it is possible to stop terrorists before they proceed with their plots. Therefore, theoretically, the probability component of terrorism risk can be reduced through mitigation (or "prevention"). Of course, minimizing this likelihood component is a very complex task, requiring governments to allocate significant resources to build and manage necessary systems, establish international partnerships, and build networks to identify and detain terrorists.

The consequence component of terrorism risk can also be mitigated. However, unlike most natural disasters that have a limited range of possible consequences, the options available to terrorists are limited only by their imagination. Terrorists have limitless targets, including facilities, infrastructures, and organizations, so many different strategies must be employed to minimize the impacts of terrorist attacks to each of these potential targets. In 2011, DHS revised and expanded a manual titled BIPS 06/FEMA 426: *Reference Manual to Mitigate Potential Terrorist Attacks against Buildings, 2nd Edition* (sidebar "BIPS 06/FEMA 426"). This manual discusses the importance of minimizing the impacts of potential terrorist attacks against buildings. Buildings, however, are but one target. Presumably, it may be impossible to mitigate all possible consequences only because to do so would surely exhaust even the richest nation's financial resources. It would seem, then, that the best measures would seek multiple-use solutions, such as building a robust mass-casualty public health system that would serve to mitigate not only the impact of terrorism on humans but also the consequences of other natural and technological hazards that also may affect the population.

BIPS 06/FEMA 426: Reference Manual to Mitigate Potential Terrorist Attacks against Buildings, 2nd Edition

In 2003, the Federal Emergency Management Agency (FEMA) developed the Reference Manual to Mitigate Potential Terrorist Attacks against Buildings to provide needed information on how to mitigate the effects of potential terrorist attacks. In 2011, FEMA revised and expanded this manual and retitled the manual "BIPS 06/FEMA 426: Reference Manual to Mitigate Potential Terrorist Attacks against Buildings, 2nd Edition." According to FEMA, "this manual is a revised and expanded version of FEMA 426. BIPS 06 provides an updated version of risk assessment techniques, a new concept on infrastructure resiliency, and identifies new protective measures and emerging technologies to protect the built environment. This manual provides design guidance to the building science community of architects and engineers, to reduce physical damage caused by terrorist assaults to buildings, related infrastructure, and people."

The intended audience includes the building sciences community of architects and engineers working for private institutions, and state and local government officials working in the building sciences community. The manual supports FEMA's Mission (Lead America to prepare for, prevent, respond to, and recover from disasters) and the Strategic Plan's Goal 3 (Prepare the nation to address the consequences of terrorism), all of which will be done within the all-hazards framework and the needs of homeland security.

The building science community, as a result of FEMA's efforts, has incorporated extensive building science into designing and constructing buildings against natural hazards (earthquake, fire, flood, and wind). To date, the same level of understanding has not been applied to manmade hazards (terrorism/intentional acts) and technological hazards (accidental events). Since September 11, 2001, terrorism has become a dominant domestic concern. Security can no longer be viewed as a standalone capability that can be purchased as an afterthought and put in place. Life, safety, and security issues must become a design goal from the beginning.

The objective of this manual is to reduce physical damage to structural and non-structural components of buildings and related infrastructure, and also to reduce resultant casualties during conventional bomb attacks, as well as attacks using chemical, biological, and radiological (CBR) agents.

Although the material and the risk assessment methodology in this manual can be applied to most building types, it is intended to assist with the design and management of facilities in eight designated sectors outlined in the DHS 2009 National Infrastructure Protection Plan (the NIPP):

- Banking and Finance
- Commercial Facilities
- Communications
- Critical Manufacturing
- Government Facilities
- Healthcare and Public Health
- Information Technology
- Postal and Shipping

The updated FEMA 426 delivers the following NIPP-defined and prioritized activities:

- Provide owners and operators of buildings and facilities timely, analytical, accurate, and useful information on a variety of threats to their assets.
- Articulate to corporate leaders, through education, training, and private communications, both the business and national security benefits of investing in security measures.
- Provide a rationale for creating a program of incentives for companies to adopt widely accepted and sound security practices voluntarily.
- Help private sector industry develop and clearly prioritize key missions, and enable their asset protection or restoration.
- Contribute materially to the emerging network for time-sensitive information sharing, restoration, and recovery support to facilities and services in the aftermath of incidents.

The manual is organized as follows:

- Chapter 1 presents the method for calculating risk for a building by assessing the threat or hazard, and determining the vulnerability and consequences.
- Chapter 2 presents guidance for site layout and design. In addition, it provides security design guidance for a number of site functions, such as access controls, gatehouses and security screening, parking, loading docks, and service areas.
- Chapter 3 discusses the risks from attacks with explosives and presents guidance for integrating protection techniques into building design, including structural, architectural, building envelope, and nonstructural aspects.

- Chapter 4 discusses the risks from attacks with CBR agents and presents guidance for integrating protection techniques against CBR hazards into the building design.
- Chapter 5 provides security systems design guidance, as well as concepts for integrating various security subsystems to create an effective integrated protective system approach. This chapter highlights electronic security.

Source: FEMA (2011a).

The threat of terrorism is not new. Throughout history, there have been terrorist organizations and terrorist attacks in all parts of the world, including North America, Europe, and Australia; however, the September 11 attacks resulted in such severe consequences that, not unexpectedly, terrorism became the primary issue on the US government's agenda.

Mitigating the terrorism risk is important in order to minimize potential damage that may result from what is known to be a very real threat, but it is vital to remember that combating terrorism is a complex and long-term task, one that requires both patience and sacrifice. Therefore, all stakeholders—including the government, the public, the private sector, the media, and the academia—need to appreciate the benefit of applying mitigation on an all-hazards approach such that all known risks are treated, not only terrorism. Clearly, as has been shown in the years following the September 11 attacks, there are much more likely hazards—hurricanes and floods being the greatest—that have much greater potential to cause harm in terms of both likelihood and consequence. Hurricane Katrina in 2005; the 2011 tornadoes that struck Joplin, MO, and Tuscaloosa, AL; and Hurricane Sandy in 2012 are just some of many recent examples.

DHS continues to provide funding for predisaster and postdisaster mitigation projects through FEMA and its other relevant directorates. Details of those initiatives are provided in the next sections.

Federal Insurance and Mitigation Administration

The Federal Insurance and Mitigation Administration (FIMA) is responsible for a vast majority of the US government's hazard mitigation activities, including the National Flood Insurance Program (NFIP). The FIMA performs several organizational activities that serve to promote protection, prevention, and partnerships at the federal, state, local, and individual levels. The overall mission of the FIMA is to protect lives and prevent the loss of property from natural and other hazards. The FIMA employs the all-hazards approach through a comprehensive risk-based emergency management program (see sidebar "What FIMA Does and Mitigation's Value to Society").

What FIMA Does and Mitigation's Value to Society

What FIMA Does

FIMA manages the National Flood Insurance Program (NFIP) and a range of programs designed to reduce future losses to homes, businesses, schools, public buildings, and critical facilities from floods, earthquakes, tornadoes, and other natural disasters.

Mitigation focuses on breaking the cycle of disaster damage, reconstruction, and repeated damage. Mitigation efforts provide value to the American people by creating safer communities and reducing loss of life and property. Mitigation includes such activities as:

- Complying with or exceeding NFIP floodplain management regulations.
- Enforcing stringent building codes, flood-proofing requirements, seismic design standards, and wind-bracing requirements for new construction or repairing existing buildings.
- Adopting zoning ordinances that steer development away from areas subject to flooding, storm surge or coastal erosion.
- Retrofitting public buildings to withstand hurricane-strength winds or ground shaking.
- Acquiring damaged homes or businesses in flood-prone areas, relocating the structures, and returning the property to open space, wetlands or recreational uses.
- Building community shelters and tornado safe rooms to help protect people in their homes, public buildings and schools in hurricane- and tornado-prone areas.

Mitigation's Value to Society

1. Mitigation creates safer communities by reducing losses of life and property.
2. Mitigation enables individuals and communities to recover more rapidly from disasters.
3. Mitigation lessens the financial impact of disasters on individuals, the Treasury, State, local and Tribal communities.

Source: FEMA (2014d).

The FIMA administers the nationwide risk reduction programs authorized by the US Congress and is composed of the following divisions:

The Risk Analysis Division applies engineering and planning practices in conjunction with advanced technology tools to identify hazards, assess vulnerabilities, and develop strategies to manage the risks associated with natural hazards. The division runs the following FEMA mitigation programs:

- Flood Map Modernization
- National Dam Safety Program
- Multi-Hazard Mitigation Planning Program

The Risk Reduction Division works to reduce risk to life and property through the use of land use controls, building practices, and other tools. These activities address risk in both the existing built environment and future development, and they occur in both pre- and postdisaster environments. The division is in charge of the following programs:

- National Earthquake Hazards Reduction Program (NEHRP).
- Hazard Mitigation Grant Program (HMGP).
- Flood Mitigation Assistance (FMA) Program.
- Pre-Disaster Mitigation (PDM) Program.
- Severe Repetitive Loss (SRL) Program—**07/2013**—The Biggert-Waters Flood Insurance Reform Act of 2012 eliminated the SRL program.

- Repetitive Flood Claims (RFC) Program—07/2013—The Biggert-Waters Flood Insurance Reform Act of 2012 eliminated the SRL program.
- Building Science.
- Community Rating System (CRS).

The Risk Insurance Division helps reduce flood losses by providing affordable flood insurance for property owners and by encouraging communities to adopt and enforce floodplain management regulations that mitigate the effects of flooding on new and improved structures. The Risk Insurance Division's prime responsibility is to run the NFIP, through which affordable flood insurance is provided to communities vulnerable to flood hazards, and impacts of floods are minimized through enforcement of floodplain management for new and altered buildings and structures (FEMA, 2011a). FEMA mitigation programs and their funding levels are described in subsequent sections.

Flood Map Modernization

Flood Map Modernization is a multiyear program to improve existing flood maps in the United States and to create new maps based on new technology and standards for those localities that require flood maps for which no previous maps exist. The need for Flood Map Modernization arises because of the dynamic nature of flood hazards that change with geography. Changing information management standards, improvements in information delivery methods such as the Internet, and advances in technologies such as a GIS (geographic information system) are other drivers behind Flood Map Modernization. Conventional flood maps involve paper-based cartographic maps that may be many years old, providing limited accuracy in a quickly changing physical environment. To make the updating, sharing, collaboration, and delivery of those maps more efficient, Flood Map Modernization is creating electronic maps based on GISs that adhere to the newest data management standards (i.e., GIS data models and metadata).

The resulting maps and data better serve the needs of all parties that use those maps. FEMA Risk Analysis Division takes the lead in this program and acts as the main integrator of data, the creator of geographic maps, and the clearinghouse for the dissemination of all flood map products. Community planners, public policy makers, local officials, developers, builders, insurance companies, and individual property owners can all benefit from those map products made available by the program. The improved flood maps provide more reliable information on flood risks and therefore help stakeholders make better-informed decisions related to their vulnerability to floods. In the long run, the use of those maps is expected to reduce the total costs of flood disasters, as communities and service providers make it a habit to check flooding risks before making land use decisions.

According to Congressional testimony by FEMA Administrator Craig Fugate, "FY 2015 request includes $84.4 million to continue FEMA's Flood Map Modernization Fund and its long-term efforts to address existing gaps in the flood hazard data inventory and address changes that continue to occur over time" (FEMA, 2014).

National Dam Safety Program

The National Dam Safety Program is an initiative of the FEMA Risk Analysis Directorate. The program was created by the Water Resources and Development Act of 1996 and has since been reauthorized twice with new legislation introduced in 2002 and 2006.

The primary goal of the program is to provide funding for states to be used in dam safety-related activities. In that scope, states use program funds to provide dam safety training, increase the frequency of dam safety inspections, create and test emergency response plans, and promote dam safety awareness through videos and other educative material. Between FY 1998 and FY 2004, the program provided approximately $22 million to states. Other components of the program include dam safety research and dam safety training.

As confirmed by the National Dam Safety Act of 2006 (Public Law 109-460), the program will continue to provide $38.7 million to states as dam safety grants, $9 million for dam safety research, and $3.25 million for dam safety training for FY 2007 to 2011; $7,134,100 FY 2013; est $7,575,055 FY 2014; and est $9,100,000 FY 2015 (Association of State Dam Safety Officials, 2005; FEMA, 2011a; American Society of Civil Engineers, 2007; Congressional Research Service, 2007; Catalog of Federal Domestic Assistance, 2014).

Multi-Hazard Mitigation Planning Program

The Multi-Hazard Mitigation Planning Program administered by FEMA's Risk Analysis Division creates multihazard mitigation planning manuals, how-to guidelines, and best practice documents. Since the program has an all-hazards mitigation scope, it works closely with several partners in different areas of interest and expertise. Some of the program partners include the American Planning Association, Association of State Floodplain Managers, Institute for Business and Home Safety, and National Institute of Building Sciences.

The purpose of mitigation planning is to identify policies and actions that can be implemented over the long term to reduce risk and future losses. Mitigation plans form the foundation for a community's long-term strategy to reduce disaster losses and break the cycle of disaster damage, reconstruction, and repeated damage. The planning process is as important as the plan itself. It creates a framework for risk-based decision-making to reduce damages to lives, property, and the economy from future disasters.

State, local, and tribal governments benefit from mitigation planning by

- identifying cost-effective actions for risk reduction that are agreed upon by stakeholders and the public;
- focusing resources on the greatest risks and vulnerabilities;
- building partnerships by involving people, organizations, and businesses;
- increasing education and awareness of hazards and risk;
- communicating priorities to state and federal officials;
- aligning risk reduction with other community objectives.

The program also works closely with the (postdisaster) HMGP and the PDM administered by FEMA's Risk Reduction Division (FEMA, 2014e).

National Earthquake Hazards Reduction Program

The NEHRP was established by the Earthquake Hazards Reduction Act of 1977 to "reduce the risks of life and property from future earthquakes in the United States." In 1980, the act was amended to include the National Institute of Standards and Technology (NIST; then the National Bureau of Standards) and to designate the newly created FEMA as the lead agency. FEMA coordinated with the NEHRP until 2003, when legislation transferred FEMA's management role in the program to the NIST. In this capacity, FEMA planned and managed the federal response to earthquakes, funded state and local preparedness exercises, and supported seismic design and construction techniques for new buildings and retrofit guidelines for existing buildings.

As part of this program, the US Geological Survey (USGS) conducts and supports earth science investigations into the origins of earthquakes, predicts earthquake effects, characterizes earthquake hazards, and disseminates earth science information. Additionally, the National Science Foundation (NSF) provides funding to earthquake engineering research, basic earth science research, and earthquake-related social science.

In addition to its lead management role for the program, the NIST conducts and supports engineering studies to improve seismic provisions of building codes, standards, and practices for buildings and lifelines (FEMA, "NEHRP," 2007b).

The NEHRP website describes the activities of the four agencies as follows:

The four NEHRP agencies work in close coordination to improve the Nation's understanding of earthquake hazards and to mitigate their effects. The missions of the four agencies are complementary, and the agencies work together to improve our understanding, characterization, and assessment of hazards and vulnerabilities; improve model building codes and land use practices; reduce risks through post-earthquake investigations and education; improve design and construction techniques; improve the capacity of government at all levels and the private sector to reduce and manage earthquake risk; and accelerate the application of research results. All four agencies are responsible for coordinating program activities with similar activities in other countries.

- *Federal Emergency Management Agency (FEMA)*: NEHRP responsibilities include: promoting the implementation of research results; promoting better building practices; providing assistance to enable states to improve earthquake preparedness, emergency response and management; supporting the implementation of an earthquake education and public awareness program; assisting NIST and others in the implementation of improved earthquake-resistant design guidance for building codes and standards for new and existing buildings, structures, and lifelines; aiding in the development of performance-based design procedures; developing, coordinating, and executing the National Response Plan when required following earthquakes; and, developing approaches to combine earthquake hazards reduction measures with measures for reducing hazards for other natural and technological hazards ("multi-hazard design").
- *National Institute of Standards and Technology (NIST)*: Designated as the lead NEHRP agency and has the primary responsibility for NEHRP planning and coordination. NIST conducts applied earthquake engineering research to provide the technical basis for building codes, standards, and practices, and is responsible for working with FEMA and others to implement improved earthquake-resistant design guidance for building codes and standards for new and existing buildings, structures, and lifelines. PL 108-360 assigns NIST significant new research and development (R&D) responsibilities to close the research-to-implementation gap and accelerate the use of new earthquake risk mitigation technologies based on the earth sciences and engineering knowledge developed through NEHRP efforts. These new responsibilities address a major technology transfer gap identified in the *NEHRP Strategic Plan 2001–2005* (PDF 217KB)—developed in partnership with the stakeholder community. This gap is the limited adaptation of basic research knowledge gained through NSF-sponsored research into practical application. At the request of NIST, the Applied Technology Council (ATC) developed an R&D roadmap in 2003 to address the research-to-implementation gap (visit *Summary Overview of the R&D Roadmap* for more information). NIST is also responsible for supporting the development of performance-based design tools for building codes, standards, and construction practices.
- *National Science Foundation (NSF)*: Supports fundamental research at the frontiers of science and engineering to advance the nation's health, welfare, and safety. NSF supports research in seismology, structural and geotechnical earthquake engineering, and social, behavioral, and economic sciences pertinent to preparation for, mitigation of, responses to, and recovery from earthquakes and related events such as tsunamis and landslides. NSF also supports research to improve the safety and performance of geomaterials, buildings, structures, and lifeline systems using the large-scale experimental facilities of the George E. Brown, Jr. *Network for Earthquake Engineering Simulation*

(NEES). Experimental and computational research is also supported at other institutions and through earthquake-related centers to develop a better understanding of the behavior of the Earth, foundations, buildings, bridges, and other structures, including the use of high-performance materials, advanced technologies, and smart structures for seismic hazard mitigation. NSF also supports post-earthquake reconnaissance, and collection of perishable data following a catastrophic event. NSF cooperates with USGS in the construction and operation of the Global Seismograph Network (GSN) and the *Advanced National Seismic System (ANSS)*, to provide accurate, thorough, and timely information about earthquake ground motions and related effects. These research activities also support the NSF priority of broadening participation in science and engineering. NSF emphasizes programs aimed at tapping the potential of underrepresented groups, and ensuring that the United States maintains a world-class science and engineering workforce.

- *United States Geological Survey (USGS)*: Provides the Nation with earthquake monitoring and notification, delivers regional and national seismic hazard assessments, conducts targeted geoscience research, and coordinates post-earthquake investigations. The USGS *Advanced National Seismic System (ANSS)* includes regional and national seismic networks and the *National Earthquake Information Center* (NEIC), which provides rapid reporting of global earthquake information. NSF and USGS jointly support the GSN, which provides high-quality seismic data to support earthquake and tsunami disaster response, hazards assessments, national security (through nuclear test treaty monitoring), and fundamental research into earthquake processes and the structure of the Earth. USGS develops and maintains national seismic hazard maps that form the basis for seismic provisions in building codes and performance-based structural design. The USGS program receives oversight and guidance from the external *Scientific Earthquake Studies Advisory Committee (SESAC)*, which was established in the 2000 reauthorization of NEHRP. (NEHRP, 2014)

The NEHRP is an essential program because of the susceptibility of the entire geography of the United States to earthquake disasters. Relative earthquake risks of US states can be viewed at the following website: http://www.fema.gov/hazard/earthquake/risk.shtm. There are multiple active faults throughout the United States. The San Andreas Fault in California and New Madrid Fault crossing parts of Illinois, Missouri, Arkansas, Kentucky, and Tennessee are but two examples. These faults are known to have the potential to generate very strong earthquakes. Had the 1906 San Francisco earthquake occurred today, it has been estimated that it would have affected nearly 10 million residents within a 19-county area and would have caused economic losses ranging from $90 to $120 billion. The earthquake could damage as many as 90,000 buildings and depending on the time of the day, 800–3400 people may lose their lives in collapsed buildings. Many of those consequences are preventable through effective earthquake hazard mitigation, thus the importance of the NEHRP (FEMA, 2007b).

FEMA's Mitigation Grant Programs

FEMA currently has five mitigation grant programs: the Hazard Mitigation Grant Program, Pre-Disaster Mitigation Grant Program, Flood Mitigation Assistance Grant Program, Severe Repetitive Loss (SRL) Grant Program, and Repetitive Flood Claims (RFC) Grant Program, all of which are administered by the Risk Reduction Division of the Mitigation Directorate.

Hazards Mitigation Grant Program

Authorized under Section 404 of the Stafford Act, the Hazard Mitigation Grant Program (HMGP) provides grants to states and local governments to implement long-term hazard mitigation measures after a major disaster declaration. The purpose of the program is to reduce the loss of life and property due to natural disasters and to enable mitigation measures to be implemented during the immediate recovery from a disaster declaration. HMGP funding is only available in states following a presidential disaster declaration. Eligible applicants follow

- state and local governments,
- Indian tribes or other tribal organizations,
- certain private nonprofit organizations.

Individual homeowners and businesses may not apply directly to the program; however, a community may apply on their behalf. HMGP funds may be used to fund projects that will reduce or eliminate the losses from future disasters. Projects must provide a long-term solution to a problem—for example, elevation of a home to reduce the risk of flood damages as opposed to buying sandbags and pumps to fight the flood. In addition, a project's potential savings must be more than the cost of implementing the project. Funds may be used to protect either public or private property or to purchase property that has been subjected to, or is in danger of, repetitive damage.

The HMGP is directly funded by FEMA's Disaster Relief Fund. The amount of HMGP funds that will be made available depends on the combined funding made available from the Disaster Relief Fund for the Public Assistance Program and the Individual Assistance Program. The Public Assistance Program makes funds available to communities for repairing or replacing roads, bridges, and other public infrastructure after a disaster occurs. The Individual Assistance Program provides grants for individuals and families in the aftermath of disasters.

According to FEMA's "Hazard Mitigation Assistance Unified Guidance: Hazard Mitigation Grant Program, Pre-Disaster Mitigation Program, and Flood Mitigation Assistance Program. July 12, 2013," "HMGP funding is allocated using a 'sliding scale' formula based on a percentage of the estimated total federal assistance under the Stafford Act, excluding administrative costs for each presidential major disaster declaration. Applicants with a FEMA-approved State or Tribal Standard Mitigation Plan may receive:

- Up to 15% of the first $2 billion of the estimated aggregate amount of disaster assistance;
- Up to 10% for the next portion of the estimated aggregate amount more than $2 billion and up to $10 billion; and
- 7.5% for the next portion of the estimated aggregate amount more than $10 billion and up to $35.333 billion.

Applicants with a FEMA-approved State or Tribal Enhanced Mitigation Plan are eligible for HMGP funding not to exceed 20% of the estimated total federal assistance under the Stafford Act, up to $35.333 billion of such assistance, excluding administrative costs authorized for the disaster" (FEMA, 2013).

As of November 2014, Louisiana was deemed eligible for $1.47 billion in HMGP funding. So far, 420 projects have been approved for a total of $873.2 million in obligated HMGP funding (FEMA, 2014f). As of October 6, 2014, 2 years after Hurricane Sandy struck the Northeast United States, FEMA reports that a total of $203 million in mitigation grants had been made in New Jersey and New York (FEMA, 2014g).

Pre-Disaster Mitigation Program

The Pre-Disaster Mitigation (PDM) Program was authorized by Section 203 of the Robert T. Stafford Disaster Relief and Emergency Assistance Act (as amended by Section 102 of the Disaster Mitigation Act of 2000). Funding for the program is provided through the National Pre-Disaster Mitigation Fund to assist state and local governments (including Indian tribal governments) in implementing cost-effective hazard mitigation activities that complement a comprehensive mitigation program. Recipients of this grant must be participating in the NFIP if they have been identified as being at special risk from flood hazards (i.e., have a "special flood hazard area") and must have a mitigation plan in effect. The president's FY 2015 includes "$400 million for the Pre-Disaster Mitigation program in the (President's) Opportunity, Growth, and Security Initiative" (FEMA, 2014h).

Flood Mitigation Assistance Program

The Flood Mitigation Assistance (FMA) Program provides funding to assist states and communities in implementing measures to reduce or eliminate the long-term risk of flood damage to buildings, manufactured homes, and other structures insurable under the NFIP. Three types of grants are available under the FMA: planning, project, and technical assistance grants. FMA planning grants are available to states and communities to prepare flood mitigation plans. NFIP-participating communities with approved flood mitigation plans can apply for FMA project grants. FMA project grants are available to states and NFIP-participating communities to implement measures to reduce flood losses. Ten percent of the project grant is made available to states as a technical assistance grant. These funds may be used by the state to help administer the program. Communities receiving FMA planning and project grants must be participating in the NFIP. An example of eligible FMA projects includes the elevation, acquisition, and relocation of NFIP-insured structures.

According to FEMA Administrator Fugate, "FEMA will also strive to reduce the risk associated with flood events via the Flood Mitigation Assistance Program. As a result of the unification of the Flood Mitigation Assistance, Repetitive Flood Claims and Severe Repetitive Loss grant programs under the Flood Mitigation Assistance Program, FEMA has been a more efficient delivery of flood-related grants to states, local and tribal communities, which has reduced future claims to NFIP. These grants provide funding to states, federally-recognized tribal governments, and communities for the reduction and elimination of the long-term risk flood damage poses. The grant also provides funds on an annual basis so that measures can be taken to reduce or eliminate risk of flood damage to buildings insured under the NFIP. These measures include the acquisition and demolition of flood prone structures, elevation of homes above expected flood levels and construction of minor drainage projects to reduce the impact of storms.

FEMA requests $150 million in FY 2015, an increase in $50 million over the FY 2014 request, for this activity so that important loss reduction measures are completed" (FEMA, 2014h).

Critical Thinking

Why do the bulk of the FIMA mitigation programs focus on floods? What do these programs hope to achieve?

Other FEMA Mitigation Directorate Programs

National Flood Insurance Program

Congress established the National Flood Insurance Program (NFIP) with the passage of the National Flood Insurance Act of 1968. The NFIP is a federal program enabling property owners in participating communities to purchase insurance as a protection against flood losses in exchange for state and community floodplain management regulations that reduce future flood damages. Flood insurance is designed to provide an alternative to disaster assistance to reduce the escalating costs of repairing damage to buildings and their contents caused by floods. Flood damage is reduced by nearly $1 billion a year through communities implementing sound floodplain management requirements and property owners' purchasing of flood insurance. Additionally, buildings constructed in compliance with NFIP building standards suffer approximately 80% less damage annually than those not built in compliance. And, every $3 paid in flood insurance claims saves $1 in disaster assistance payments (FEMA, 2005b).

The importance of flood insurance was again proved following Hurricanes Katrina, Rita, and Wilma in 2005, when the NFIP paid more than $16 billion in claims (Figure 10-2). As more communities meet floodplain management eligibility requirements and participate in the program, they will continue to minimize flood risk while enjoying greater financial protection from inevitable flood damages. As these benefits become more and more apparent to homeowners with each disaster that occurs, participation in the NFIP should continue to increase over time. Figure 10-3 provides an overview of the growth in the number of flood insurance policies issued by the NFIP.

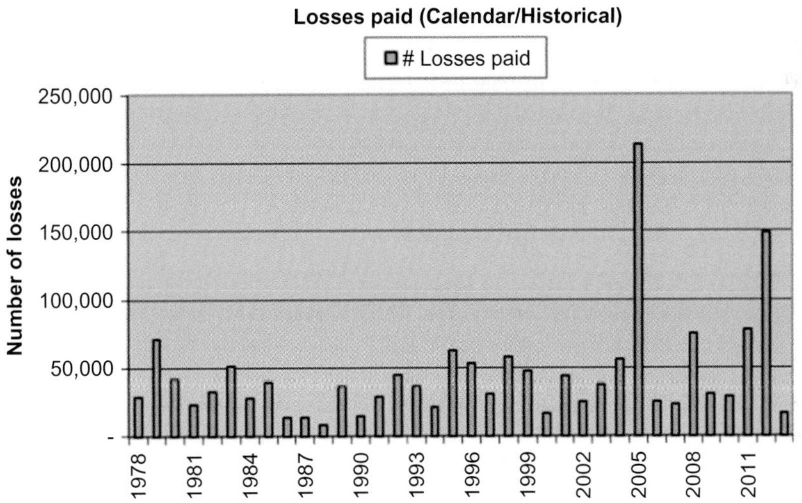

FIGURE 10-2 Losses paid by the National Flood Insurance Program by year. *Source: FEMA (2014j).*

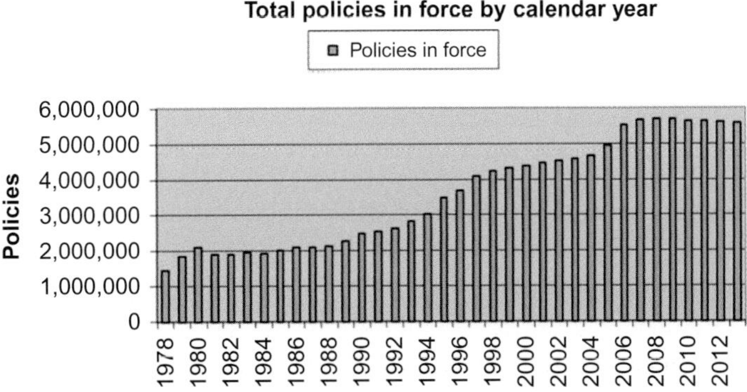

FIGURE 10-3 Growth in national flood insurance policies since 1978. *Source: FEMA (2014k).*

The Biggert-Waters Flood Insurance Act of 2012 was passed in an effort by Congress to control the cost of the NFIP that was over $20 billion in debt because of the impacts of Hurricanes Katrina and Sandy. The act resulted in the loss of subsidies for insurance premiums for many homeowners and businesses insured by the NFIP resulting in increased premiums for NFIP-backed flood insurance. As of November 2014, the implementation of these rate increases has been postponed, and it is uncertain if the rate increase will ever be enforced and how the act will ultimately impact the NFIP. For more information concerning the impacts of the Biggert-Waters Act, FEMA has developed a series of brochures and information briefs including the "Biggert-Waters Flood Insurance Reform Act of 2012 (BW12) Timeline" that can be accessed at https://www.fema.gov/media-library/resources-documents/collections/341

The president's FY 2015 budget request included $1.7 billion in discretionary funding for the program (DHS, 2014a).

Critical Thinking

How would the reduction of flood insurance policies in flood-risk areas around the country resulting from unaffordable policy premiums impact disaster relief costs from future flooding events? If the relief costs soar higher, would that be a legitimate reason to reform or eliminate the Biggert-Waters reforms of the NFIP?

Prevention Actions and Programs

Prevention refers to actions taken to avoid an incident or to intervene in an effort to stop an incident from occurring in order to protect lives and property. The draft National Incident Management System of August 2007 defines prevention as follows:

> *Actions to avoid an incident or to intervene to stop an incident from occurring. Prevention involves actions to protect lives and property. It involves applying intelligence and other information to a range of activities that may include such countermeasures as deterrence operations; heightened inspections; improved surveillance and security operations; investigations to determine the full nature and source of the threat; public health and agricultural surveillance and testing processes; immunizations, isolation, or quarantine; and, as appropriate, specific law enforcement operations aimed at deterring, preempting, interdicting, or disrupting illegal activity and apprehending potential perpetrators and bringing them to justice.*
>
> *Source: FEMA (2007a), p. 156*

National Prevention Framework

The National Prevention Framework describes what the whole community—from community members to senior leaders in government—should do upon the discovery of intelligence or information regarding an imminent threat to the homeland in order to thwart an initial or follow-on terrorist attack. This Framework helps achieve the National Preparedness Goal of a secure and resilient Nation that is optimally prepared to prevent an imminent terrorist attack within the United States.

The processes and policies described in this document will be conducted in accordance with existing laws and regulations (DHS, 2013).

This Framework provides guidance to leaders and practitioners at all levels of government; private and nonprofit sector partners; and individuals to prevent, avoid or stop a threatened or actual act of terrorism by:

- Describing the core capabilities needed to prevent an imminent act of terrorism
- Aligning key roles and responsibilities to deliver Prevention capabilities in time-sensitive situations
- Describing coordinating structures that enable all stakeholders to work together
- Laying the foundation for further operational coordination and planning that will synchronize Prevention efforts within the whole community and across the Protection, Mitigation, Response, and Recovery mission areas.

This Framework applies only to those capabilities, plans, and operations necessary to ensure the Nation is prepared to prevent an imminent act of terrorism against the United States, and does not capture the full spectrum of the Nation's efforts to counter terrorism. The seven Prevention core capabilities are planning; public information and warning; operational coordination; forensics and attribution; intelligence and information sharing; interdiction and disruption; and screening, search, and detection. This Framework sets out three principles that guide the development and execution of the core capabilities for Prevention: Engaged Partnerships; Scalability, Flexibility, and Adaptability; and Readiness to Act.

Having already established the ability to quickly collect, analyze, and further disseminate intelligence becomes critical in an imminent threat situation. In order to accomplish this, law enforcement, intelligence, homeland security professionals, and other members of the whole community must form engaged partnerships.[1] These partnerships allow for the seamless acquisition and passage of information. In addition to Federal Bureau of Investigation (FBI) Joint Terrorism Task Forces (JTTFs) and Field Intelligence Groups (FIGs), as well as state and major urban area fusion centers, a variety of analytical and investigative efforts support the ability to identify and counter terrorist threats by executing these prevention support activities. These efforts include other local, state, tribal, territorial, and Federal law enforcement agencies, and various intelligence centers and related efforts such as High Intensity Drug Trafficking Areas, Regional Information Sharing Systems Centers, criminal intelligence units, real-time crime analysis centers, and others.

Coordinating structures facilitate problem solving, improve access to resources, and foster coordination and information sharing. Departments or agencies, as well as private and nonprofit entities, with unique missions in Prevention, bring additional capabilities to bear through these structures. Coordinating structures can function on multiple levels, to include national-level coordinating structures, such as the Department of Homeland Security National Operations Center, the FBI Strategic Information and Operations Center, the Office of the Director of National Intelligence National Counterterrorism Center, the Department of Defense National Military Command Center, the FBI National Joint Terrorism Task Force, and others. Field coordinating structures, such as the FBI JTTFs and FIGs; state and major urban area fusion centers; state and local counterterrorism and intelligence units; and others also play a critical role as coordinating structures for the prevention of imminent acts of terrorism. These coordinating structures are scalable, flexible, and adaptable.

The responsibility for prevention builds from the individual and the community to local jurisdictions; state, tribal, territorial, and insular area governments; and the Federal Government. This Framework assists the whole community in thwarting initial or follow-on terrorist attacks.

This Framework provides individuals, communities, and governmental, private sector, and non-governmental decision makers with an understanding of the full spectrum of Prevention activities and what they can do to ensure the Nation is prepared to prevent imminent acts of terrorism. Initiatives based on Prevention mission activities and core capabilities help guide communities to create conditions for a safer, more secure, and more resilient Nation by enhancing prevention through operational coordination and information sharing.

The environment in which the Nation operates grows ever more complex and unpredictable. In implementing the National Prevention Framework to build national preparedness, partners are encouraged to develop a shared understanding of broad-level strategic implications as they make critical decisions in building future capacity and capability. The whole community should be engaged in examining and implementing the strategy and doctrine contained in this Framework, considering both current and future requirements in the process.

---

[1]These partnerships should support the development, implementation, and/or expansion of programs designed to partner with local communities to counter violent extremism in accordance with the *Strategic Implementation Plan for Empowering Local Partners to Prevent Violent Extremism in the United States* (December 2011).

Source: DHS (2013).

Several of the recommendations made by the 9/11 Commission, discussed in Chapter 2, also include prevention components. The following examples are provided:

Prevention of proliferation of weapons of mass destruction and their acquisition by terrorist groups: The 9/11 Commission underlines that about two dozen terrorist groups including al-Qaeda have attempted to acquire or develop chemical, biological, radiological, and nuclear weapons. Most of those weapons can be developed relatively inexpensively if the necessary knowledge is available to terrorists. The possible consequences of an attack involving those weapons are very likely to be devastating. Therefore, preventing the proliferation of such weapons or materials that are necessary in their development is a critical task that needs to be performed. The commission recommends that the United States has to work with the international community to get this done. The commission recommends that the United States should sustain its support for the Cooperative Threat Reduction Program, which aims to secure the weapons and highly dangerous materials still scattered in Russia and other countries of the Soviet Union.

Prevention of financial strength and flexibility of terrorist organizations: The United States and its allies made an effort to paralyze the financial networks of terrorists in the recent aftermath of 9/11. This effort aimed to reduce or eliminate the ability of terrorist groups to support their operations and maintain their existence. The experience showed that tracking and blocking of money that is potentially connected to terrorist groups is a very difficult job that demands not only international cooperation but also the convenience of national laws of international partners. Therefore, other innovative ways of reducing the financial strength and flexibility of terrorist organizations are necessary.

Prevention of terrorist travel: With the advancements in and increased frequency of international travel, terrorist groups were able to gain the mobility to conduct attacks in different parts of the world. This gives an opportunity to governments to identify the terrorist as they enter the transportation system or the country through its border checkpoints. This is a critical task that may prevent some terrorist attacks or at least the penetration of terrorists from one country to another one. But the fact that terrorists also use local resources and people in their activities makes the challenge even tougher.

Prevention of terrorist access to critical infrastructures and key assets: The 9/11 Commission recommends that the improvements being made to protect U.S. borders such as use of terrorist lists, biometric screening, biometric passports, and other threat-related information be shared with and implemented at access points to critical infrastructures and key assets. Such assets may include nuclear power plants, dams, and other infrastructures of national significance and consequences. (9/11 Commission, 2004)

In December 2011, FEMA introduced its Whole Community approach with the publication of a guidance document. According to the FEMA website, "A Whole Community Approach to Emergency Management: Principles, Themes, and Pathways for Action presents a foundation for increasing individual preparedness and engaging with members of the community as collaborative resources to enhance the resiliency and security of our Nation through a Whole Community approach. The document is intended to promote greater understanding of the approach and to provide a strategic framework to guide all members of the emergency management community as they determine how to integrate Whole Community into their daily practices." FEMA has incorporated the Whole Community concept into all its guidance documents for all four phases of emergency management—mitigation, preparedness, response, and recovery. More details on the Whole Community concept are provided in sidebar "Whole Community Engagement."

Whole Community Engagement

We fully recognize that a government-centric approach to emergency management is not enough to meet the challenges posed by a catastrophic incident. Whole Community is an approach to emergency management that reinforces the fact that FEMA is only one part of our nation's emergency management team; that we must leverage all of the resources of our collective team in preparing for, protecting against, responding to, recovering from and mitigating against all hazards; and that collectively we must meet the needs of the entire community in each of these areas. This larger collective emergency management team includes, not only FEMA and its partners at the federal level, but also local, tribal, state and territorial partners; non-governmental organizations like faith-based and non-profit groups and private sector industry; to individuals, families and communities, who continue to be the nation's most important assets as first responders during a disaster. Both the composition of the community and the individual needs of community members, regardless of age, economics, or accessibility requirements, must be accounted for when planning and implementing disaster strategies.

When the community is engaged in an authentic dialogue, it becomes empowered to identify its needs and the existing resources that may be used to address them. Collectively, we can determine the best ways to organize and strengthen community assets, capacities, and interests. This allows us, as a nation, to expand our reach and deliver services more efficiently and cost effectively to build, sustain, and improve our capability to prepare for, protect against, respond to, recover from, and mitigate all hazards.

Principles

As an ongoing component of the nation's larger, coordinated effort to enhance emergency planning and strengthen the nation's overall level of preparedness, FEMA engaged many of its emergency management partners—including local, tribal, state, territorial, and Federal representatives; academia; nongovernmental organizations; community members; and the private sector—in a national dialogue on a Whole Community approach to emergency management. Through this dialogue, three principles emerged that represent the foundation for Whole Community:

- Understand and meet the actual needs of the whole community. Community engagement can lead to a deeper understanding of the unique and diverse needs of a population, including its demographics, values, norms, community structures, networks, and relationships. The more we know about our communities, the better we can understand their real-life safety and sustaining needs and their motivations to participate in emergency management-related activities prior to an event.
- Engage and empower all parts of the community. Engaging the whole community and empowering local action will better position stakeholders to plan for and meet the actual needs of a community and strengthen the local capacity to deal with the consequences of all threats and hazards. This requires all members of the community to be part of the emergency management team, which should include diverse community members, social and community service groups and institutions, faith-based and disability groups, academia, professional associations, and the private and nonprofit sectors, while including government agencies who may not traditionally have been directly involved in emergency management. When the community is engaged in an authentic dialogue, it becomes empowered to identify its needs and the existing resources that may be used to address them.
- Strengthen what works well in communities on a daily basis. A Whole Community approach to building community resilience requires finding ways to support and strengthen the institutions, assets, and networks that already work well in communities and are working to address issues that are important to community members on a daily basis. Existing structures and relationships that are present in the daily lives of individuals, families, businesses, and organizations before an incident occurs can be leveraged and empowered to act effectively during and after a disaster strikes.

Source: FEMA (2014i).

Warning

On April 20, 2011, DHS Secretary Janet Napolitano announced the implementation of the National Terrorism Advisory System (NTAS). The NTAS took the place of the much-maligned color-coded Homeland Security Advisory System (HSAS) (Figure 10-4) that had been in place since 2002.

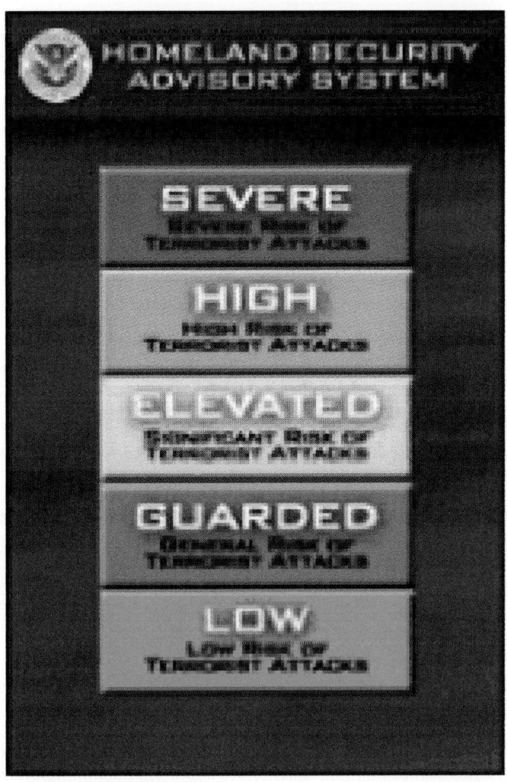

FIGURE 10-4 Homeland Security Advisory System (2002–2011).

Since its inception, concerns had been raised about the level of information provided through the HSAS. These concerns were shared by both the general public and members of the first-responder community (e.g., police, firefighters, and emergency medical technicians) and local officials responsible for ensuring public safety. The Partnership for Public Warning (PPW) was formed in January 2002 as a partnership among the private sector, academia, and government entities at the local, state, and federal levels for the purpose of better coordinating disaster warning programs. The PPW is a nonprofit entity with its stated mission to "promote and enhance efficient, effective, and integrated dissemination of public warnings and related information so as to save lives, reduce disaster losses and speed recovery" (Public Safety Canada, 2008). In May 2003, PPW published "A National Strategy for Integrated Public Warning Policy and Capability," which examined the current status of public warning systems, practices, and issues across the United States. The report stated, "Working together in partnership, the stakeholders should assess current warning capability, carry out appropriate research and develop the following:

- A common terminology for natural and man-made disasters
- A standard message protocol
- National metrics and standards

- National backbone systems for securely collecting and disseminating warnings from all official sources
- Pilot projects to test concepts and approaches
- Training programs
- A national multi-media education and outreach program" (Partnership for Public Warning, 2003)

In her announcement concerning the NTAS, Secretary Napolitano stated, "The terrorist threat facing our country has evolved significantly over the past ten years, and in today's environment—more than ever—we know that the best security strategy is one that counts on the American public as a key partner in securing our country." DHS released the document entitled "A Public Guide to the NTAS" as part of its effort to announce its establishment (DHS, 2011a). Additional information concerning the NTAS released by DHS in April 2011 is presented in sidebar "National Terrorism Advisory System (NTAS)."

National Terrorism Advisory System (NTAS)

Under NTAS, DHS will coordinate with other federal entities to issue detailed alerts to the public when the federal government receives information about a credible terrorist threat. NTAS alerts provide a concise summary of the potential threat including geographic region, mode of transportation, or critical infrastructure potentially affected by the threat, actions being taken to ensure public safety, as well as recommended steps that individuals, communities, businesses, and governments can take to help prevent, mitigate, or respond to a threat. NTAS Alerts will include a clear statement on the nature of the threat, which will be defined in one of two ways:

- "Elevated Threat": Warns of a credible terrorist threat against the United States
- "Imminent Threat": Warns of a credible, specific, and impending terrorist threat against the United States

Depending on the nature of the threat, alerts may be sent to law enforcement, distributed to affected areas of the private sector, or issued more broadly to the public through both official and social media channels—including a designated DHS webpage (www.dhs.gov/alerts), Facebook, and Twitter @NTASAlerts. NTAS alerts and posters will also be displayed in places such as transit hubs, airports, and government buildings.

NTAS threat alerts will be issued for a specific time period and will automatically expire. Alerts may be extended if new information becomes available or as a specific threat evolves.

Source: DHS (2011a).

As part of the announcement of the NTAS, DHS released the following information presented in sidebars "A Public Guide to the NTAS" and "Frequently Asked Questions of the NTAS." A sample NTAS alert is presented in Figure 10-5.

DATE & TIME ISSUED: XXXX

SUMMARY

The Secretary of Homeland Security informs the public and relevant government and private sector partners about a potential or actual threat with this alert, indicating whether there is an "imminent" or "elevated" threat.

DURATION

An individual threat alert is issued for a specific time period and then automatically expires. It may be extended if new information becomes available or the threat evolves.

DETAILS

- This section provides more detail about the threat and what the public and sectors need to know.
- It may include specific information, if available, about the nature and credibility of the threat, including the critical infrastructure sector(s) or location(s) that may be affected.
- It includes as much information as can be released publicly about actions being taken or planned by authorities to ensure public safety, such as increased protective actions and what the public may expect to see.

AFFECTED AREAS

- This section includes visual depictions (such as maps or other graphics) showing the affected location(s), sector(s), or other illustrative detail about the threat itself.

HOW YOU CAN HELP

- This section provides information on ways the public can help authorities (e.g. camera phone pictures taken at the site of an explosion), and reinforces the importance of reporting suspicious activity.
- It may ask the public or certain sectors to be alert for a particular item, situation, person, activity or developing trend.

STAY PREPARED

- This section emphasizes the importance of the public planning and preparing for emergencies before they happen, including specific steps individuals, families and businesses can take to ready themselves and their communities.
- It provides additional preparedness information that may be relevant based on this threat.

STAY INFORMED

- This section notifies the public about where to get more information.
- It encourages citizens to stay informed about updates from local public safety and community leaders.
- It includes a link to the DHS NTAS website http://www.dhs.gov/alerts and http://twitter.com/NTASAlerts

If You See Something, Say Something™. Report suspicious activity to local law enforcement or call 911.

The National Terrorism Advisory System provides Americans with alert information on homeland security threats. It is distributed by the Department of Homeland Security. More information is available at: **www.dhs.gov/alerts.** To receive mobile updates: **www.twitter.com/NTASAlerts**

If You See Something Say Something™ used with permission of the NY Metropolitan Transportation Authority.

FIGURE 10-5 A sample NTAS alert. *Source: DHS (2011b).*

A Public Guide to the NTAS

The National Terrorism Advisory System

The National Terrorism Advisory System, or NTAS, replaces the color-coded Homeland Security Advisory System (HSAS). This new system will more effectively communicate information about terrorist threats by providing timely, detailed information to the public, government agencies, first responders, airports and other transportation hubs, and the private sector.

It recognizes that Americans all share responsibility for the nation's security, and should always be aware of the heightened risk of terrorist attack in the United States and what they should do.

NTAS Alerts

Imminent Threat Alert: Warns of a credible, specific, and impending terrorist threat against the United States.

Elevated Threat Alert: Warns of a credible terrorist threat against the United States.

After reviewing the available information, the Secretary of Homeland Security will decide, in coordination with other Federal entities, whether an NTAS Alert should be issued.

NTAS Alerts will only be issued when credible information is available.

These alerts will include a clear statement that there is an imminent threat or elevated threat. Using available information, the alerts will provide a concise summary of the potential threat, information about actions being taken to ensure public safety, and recommended steps that individuals, communities, businesses and governments can take to help prevent, mitigate or respond to the threat.

The NTAS Alerts will be based on the nature of the threat: in some cases, alerts will be sent directly to law enforcement or affected areas of the private sector, while in others, alerts will be issued more broadly to the American people through both official and media channels.

NTAS Alerts contain a sunset provision indicating a specific date when the alert expires—there will not be a constant NTAS Alert or blanket warning that there is an overarching threat. If threat information changes for an alert, the Secretary of Homeland Security may announce an updated NTAS Alert. All changes, including the announcement that cancels an NTAS Alert, will be distributed the same way as the original alert.

The NTAS Alert—How can you help?

Each alert provides information to the public about the threat, including, if available, the geographic region, mode of transportation, or critical infrastructure potentially affected by the threat; protective actions being taken by authorities, and steps that individuals and communities can take to protect themselves and their families, and help prevent, mitigate or respond to the threat.

Citizens should report suspicious activity to their local law enforcement authorities. The "If You See Something, Say Something™" campaign across the United States encourages all citizens to be vigilant for indicators of potential terrorist activity, and to follow NTAS Alerts for information about threats in specific places or for individuals exhibiting certain types of suspicious activity. Visit www.dhs.gov/ifyouseesomethingsaysomething to learn more about the campaign.

Alert Announcements

NTAS Alerts will be issued through state, local and tribal partners, the news media and directly to the public via the following channels:

- Via the official DHS NTAS webpage—http://www.dhs.gov/files/programs/ntas.shtm
- Via email signup at—http://public.govdelivery.com/accounts/USDHS/subscriber/new?topic_id=USDHS_164
- Via social media
  - Facebook—http://www.facebook.com/NTASAlerts
  - Twitter—http://twitter.com/#!/NTASAlerts
- Via data feeds, web widgets and graphics
  - http://dhs.gov/files/programs/ntas-developer-resources.shtm

The public can also expect to see alerts in places, both public and private, such as transit hubs, airports and government buildings.

Source: DHS (2014c).

Frequently Asked Questions of the NTAS

The following are frequently asked questions regarding the National Terrorism Advisory System.

Q—What happened to the color-coded advisory system?

A—The National Terrorism Advisory System replaced the Homeland Security Advisory System that had been in place since 2002. The National Terrorism Advisory System, or NTAS, includes information specific to the particular credible threat, and does not use a color-coded scale.

Q—How does the new system work?

A—When there is credible information about a threat, an NTAS Alert will be shared with the American public. It may include specific information, if available, about the nature of the threat, including the geographic region, mode of transportation, or critical infrastructure potentially affected by the threat, as well as steps that individuals and communities can take to protect themselves and help prevent, mitigate or respond to the threat. The advisory will clearly indicate whether the threat is *Elevated*, if we have no specific information about the timing or location, or *Imminent*, if we believe the threat is impending or very soon.

Q—As a citizen, how will I find out that an NTAS Alert has been announced?

A— The Secretary of Homeland Security will announce the alerts publically. Alerts will simultaneously be posted at DHS.gov/alerts and released to the news media for distribution. The Department of Homeland Security will also distribute alerts across its social media channels, including the Department's blog, Twitter stream, Facebook page, and RSS feed.

Q—What should Americans do when an NTAS Alert is announced?

A—The NTAS Alert informs the American public about credible terrorism threats, and encourages citizens to report suspicious activity. Where possible and applicable, NTAS Alerts will include steps that individuals and communities can take to protect themselves to help prevent, mitigate or respond to the threat. Individuals should review the information contained in the alert, and based upon the circumstances, take the recommended precautionary or preparedness measures for themselves and their families.

Q—How should I report suspicious activity?
A—Citizens should report suspicious activity to their local law enforcement authorities. The "If You See Something, Say Something" campaign across the United States encourages all citizens to be vigilant for indicators of potential terrorist activity, and to follows NTAS Alert for information about threats in specific places or for individuals exhibiting certain types of suspicious activity.
Q—I get my news online, so how will I find out about an NTAS Alert?
A—Americans can go to DHS.gov/alerts to see the most recent advisories. Additionally, advisories will be sent out widely through social and mainstream media.
Q—How will NTAS Alerts be cancelled or updated?
A—The NTAS Alerts carry an expiration date and will be automatically cancelled on that date. If the threat information changes for an alert, the Secretary of Homeland Security may announce an updated NTAS Alert. All changes, including the announcement that cancels an NTAS Alert, will be distributed the same way as the original alert.
Q—Do these alerts apply to Americans in other countries?
A—NTAS Alerts apply only to threats in the United States and its possessions. The Department of State issues security advisory information for U.S. citizens overseas or traveling in foreign countries.

Source: DHS (2014d).

Preparedness Actions and Programs

Preparedness within the field of emergency management can best be defined as a state of readiness to respond to a disaster, crisis, or any other type of emergency situation. It includes those activities, programs, and systems that exist before an emergency that are used to support and enhance response to an emergency or disaster.

Preparedness is important to the overall emergency management cycle because it provides for the readiness and testing of all actions and plans before actual application occurs in response to a real incident or disaster. There is a close connection between mitigation and preparedness. Often, emergency managers argue over whether a specific action should be considered mitigation or preparedness. Oftentimes, the lines of distinction become fuzzy, and exact determination becomes impossible. In its most simple terms, preparedness is more about planning for the best response, whereas mitigation includes all the actions that are attempts to prevent the need for a disaster response or to minimize the scope of the needed response.

Examples of preparedness for natural hazards are organizing evacuation drills from buildings in case of fires or other threats, providing first-response training to employees so that they can assist each other and their neighbors in small emergencies (Figure 10-6), and preparing a family disaster plan that covers topics such as the designation of a location where family members will meet if they get separated during an event and what personal papers (e.g., prescriptions and insurance records) they might need in the aftermath of an event. More specific examples include the logistic planning for tugboats operating around oil refineries such that they become responsible for responding to fire emergencies in the refinery and providing training and relocating necessary hazardous materials (HAZMAT) teams to areas where the risk of radiological emergencies is higher, such as nuclear power plants.

FIGURE 10-6 Mays Landing, NJ, April 17, 2010—Community relations specialists Paul Williams and Joseph Bonaccorse (right) team up with Community Emergency Response Team members Nancy E. Neglia (left) and Dwight L. Neglia to inform residents of the flood-affected area of the FEMA registration process. FEMA community relations specialists are going door-to-door to inform residents about the assistance available. *Photo by Michael Medina-Latorre/FEMA.*

In the aftermath of September 11, terrorism preparedness has become a more pressing issue. The risk of terrorists gaining access to and using weapons of mass destruction (WMDs), such as biological, chemical, and radiological agents, forced the US government to establish an adequate response capability, capacity, and expertise to protect American citizens against a potential attack and respond to it in case these weapons are used. Citizens, who are the most likely targets of these attacks, must be adequately prepared if any response effort is to be successful. DHS has been given the responsibility for this task, although several other federal government agencies, including the Centers for Disease Control and Prevention (CDC) and the Department of Education, provide guidance on a full range of terrorism preparedness activities.

The effective response to the 2013 Boston Marathon bombings was built on the work done before the bombs exploded by federal, state, and local law enforcement officials in terms of using the Incident Command System and exercising their respective roles. See sidebar "Boston Marathon Bombings: Testimony of Herman B. 'Dutch' Leonard and Eliot I. Snider" to learn more about law enforcement preparations and recommendations from Harvard University researchers concerning how to improve preparations for future terrorist attacks.

Boston Marathon Bombings: Testimony of Herman B. "Dutch" Leonard and Eliot I. Snider

On April 9, 2014, Harvard University Professors Herman B. "Dutch" Leonard and Eliot I. Snider testified before the US House of Representatives Committee on Homeland Security in a hearing on "The Boston Marathon Bombings, One Year On: A Look Back to Look Forward." They testified about the results of the research they had conducted "to understand the sources of the strengths and weaknesses of the response to the marathon bombing." Presented in Chapter 9 are excerpts from their testimony that examine the response actions taken in the aftermath of the bombings on April 15, 2013, and recommendations for future actions to improve future response efforts. The excerpts from their testimony presented below focus on preparations made by law enforcement officials before the bombings occurred and how they impacted the response and recommendations concerning how to improve preparedness in the future.

Excerpt 1: Effective Response

There were some quite remarkably effective elements of the response in the aftermath of the bombing in Boston. As an example, the bombs caused literally dozens of fatal injuries, but, mercifully, there were only three fatalities on that terrible day. All of the seriously injured people were removed from the scene within 22 min. Every person who left the scene alive is alive today. The scene was rapidly secured and swept for additional explosive devices. It was then secured as a crime scene, collaboratively, using FBI and local and state assets, and the investigation was launched. Video from private and public surveillance cameras was quickly collected, additional photographic evidence (mainly from media and bystanders who volunteered their photographs and videos) was obtained, and an exhausting search through the video and photographic evidence began. Meanwhile, the public was informed by individual agencies and through a series of organized press conferences.

Taken together, that seems like a very good performance. We can all point to elements where it could be further improved. But the standard can't be an unrealistic expectation of perfection. Our question has to be this: did the response accomplish what could reasonably have been expected, given the intrinsic nature of the event itself—the surprise, the physical and emotional shock, and the inevitable chaos of the immediate aftermath. *We believe that the response in Boston was as good as one could reasonably have hoped.* This then begs explanation, and forms the basic question of our research: *Why* were people and organizations able to provide as effective a response as this was? What were the strengths of that response, and what enabled them? And where were the weaknesses—and what can we do to further minimize them? These were the questions at the heart of our research.

I want to emphasize three elements of our research findings about where these features of the response "came from"—that is, what caused or created them:

First, *the core underlying reason for the effectiveness of the response in the moment was the rapid formation of an effective command and coordination structure* that oversaw and directed all elements of the response. Senior officials from a wide range of agencies—Federal, State, local, and private—felt an immediate need to find one another and join into a concerted and unified command structure and were then able to do so reasonably quickly.

Second, *none of that was due to chance*—it resulted from literally tens of thousands of hours of joint work, planning, exercises, and operations combining numerous agencies over many years in the planning for and production of fixed events ranging from the Democratic National Convention in 2004 (an event that got particularly attentive focus because it was the first National political convention after 9/11) to the Boston Marathon to the July 4 concert and fireworks on the Esplanade to Patriots and Red Sox and Bruins and Celtics victory parades. Each of those events provided an opportunity—and opportunity that was *taken*—to practice the process of planning and doing things together. This built knowledge of one another's assumptions and priorities and procedures, fostering understanding and mutual respect of individual and organizational competence and capabilities across agencies. This was the infrastructure that enabled command and coordination to be established quickly and to function effectively after the bombs exploded.

Third, *others can do this, too*. To be sure, some of the features that contributed to the effectiveness of the response in Boston were unique to Boston. Boston has eight Level I trauma centers, for example, and by happenstance they are arrayed in every direction around the area where the bombs went off, so the injured could be transported in many different directions, reducing congestion among emergency vehicles. Some other elements were unique to the moment—for example, the fact that the marathon takes place on a state holiday, when hospitals are open and fully staffed, but are not doing elective surgery, meant that dozens of operating rooms were immediately available. A shift change was underway at the time of the bombing, which increased availability of skilled hands when they were needed. So there were elements of good fortune that reduced the terrible consequences on that awful day. *But most of what made the response as effective as it was can be undertaken by other communities as readily and as well as it was by Boston.* Any community can engage in joint planning across its agencies for any major fixed event—from a high school football victory parade to a Fourth of July celebration. Any community can find opportunities to engage in joint planning with other jurisdictions, and with other levels of government—both Federal and State.

On a good day, joint planning and practicing inter-agency coordination—and carrying that out through an incident command structure—is helpful in making events go more smoothly. Paying your dues on the good days by building the infrastructure of interagency familiarity, respect, knowledge, and trust thus has an immediate pay-off—and if a bad day ever comes, that infrastructure is literally a life-saver.

The single most important lesson of our research is that routine and constant practice and use of incident command is one of the best investments a community can make in its present well-being and against any future dark day that might arise.

Excerpt 2: Preparation for Future Crises

- *Robust development, practice, exercise, and application of incident management processes and skills (codified in the NIMS system) greatly enhance the ability of emergency responders to operate in complex, multi-organizational, cross-jurisdictional crises.* The great value of common systems and the understanding that these produce among responders who have never previously met or worked together should not be under-estimated. They can literally be life-savers for responders and others at a crisis scene.
- *"Fixed" or planned events can be effective platforms for practicing incident management skills even when no emergency occurs, and they are highly useful if emergency contingencies materialize at a fixed event as happened at and after the 2013 Boston Marathon.* Skills honed at such events can also prepare responders and response organizations to perform more effectively even in "no notice" emergencies that may occur at other times.
- *Because coordinating multiple agencies and disciplines will be particularly difficult in "no notice" events*, senior commanders should:
- Themselves form a unified command structure to make decisions and implement them,
- Identify a separate staging area to which deploying individuals and organizations should report and await before undertaking field operations.
- Establish protocols for the formation of "sudden" teams composed of individuals from different organizations that may not have previously worked together.
- *Community resilience should be systematically developed and celebrated.* In the face of the bombing, Boston showed strength, resilience, even defiance—and these were key drivers of the overall outcomes that is, of "Boston Strong." These qualities are latent in many

communities in the United States and elsewhere. Celebrating examples of community resilience—both local examples and from farther afield—may help to cultivate a culture of confidence and self-reliance.

Herman B. "Dutch" Leonard is the George F. Baker, Jr. Professor of Public Management and Faculty Co-Director, Program on Crisis Leadership at the John F. Kennedy School of Government, at Harvard University.

Eliot I. Snider is the Family Professor of Business Administration and Faculty Co-Chair of the Social Enterprise Initiative at Harvard Business School at Harvard University.

Source: Committee on Homeland Security (2014).

FEMA is responsible for preparing for and responding to natural and technological disasters and terrorism. As such, FEMA produces and publishes several documents that help citizens and businesses to take preparative action against each of these threats, including the new terrorism risk. Unfortunately, the arsenal of weapons available to the growing cadre of international terrorists is expanding, and as new weapons are identified and understood, the public must be educated accordingly. Sidebars "CDC Guidance for Evacuation Preparedness for Chemical Weapons," "FEMA 'Are You Ready' Protective Measures for a Nuclear Blast," and "DHS Ready.Gov Guidance on Explosions" presented in this chapter provide examples of the guidance provided by DHS, CDC, and FEMA for citizen preparedness against such weapons.

CDC Guidance for Evacuation Preparedness for Chemical Weapons

Some kinds of chemical accidents or attacks, such as a train derailment or a terrorist incident, may make staying put dangerous. In such cases, it may be safer for you to evacuate, or leave the immediate area. You may need to go to an emergency shelter after you leave the immediate area.

How to Know If You Need to Evacuate

You will hear from the local police, emergency coordinators, or government on the radio and/or television emergency broadcast system if you need to evacuate. If there is a "code red" or "severe" terror alert, you should pay attention to radio and/or television broadcasts so you will know right away if an evacuation order is made for your area.

What to Do

Act quickly and follow the instructions of local emergency coordinators, such as law enforcement personnel, fire departments, or local elected leaders. Every situation can be different, so local coordinators could give you special instructions to follow for a particular situation. Local emergency coordinators may direct people to evacuate homes or offices and go to an emergency shelter. If so, emergency coordinators will tell you how to get to the shelter. If you have children in school, they may be sheltered at the school. You should not try to get to the school if the children are being sheltered there.

The emergency shelter will have most supplies that people need. The emergency coordinators will tell you which supplies to bring with you, but you may also want to prepare a portable supply kit. Be sure to bring any medications you are taking. If you have time, call a friend or relative in another state to tell them where you are going and that you are safe. Local telephone lines may be jammed in an emergency, so you should plan ahead to have an out-of-state contact with whom to leave messages. If you do not have private transportation, make plans in advance of an emergency to identify people who can give you a ride.

Evacuating and sheltering in this way should keep you safer than if you stayed at home or at your workplace. You will most likely not be in the shelter for more than a few hours. Emergency coordinators will let you know when it is safe to leave the shelter and anything you may need to do to make sure it is safe to re-enter your home.

Source: CDC (2005a).

FEMA "Are You Ready" Protective Measures for a Nuclear Blast

Before a Nuclear Blast

To prepare for a nuclear blast, you should do the following:

- Find out from officials if any public buildings in your community have been designated as fallout shelters. If none have been designated, make your own list of potential shelters near your home, workplace and school. These places would include basements or the windowless center area of middle floors in high-rise buildings, as well as subways and tunnels.
- If you live in an apartment building or high-rise, talk to the manager about the safest place in the building for sheltering and about providing for building occupants until it is safe to go out.
- During periods of heightened threat increase your disaster supplies to be adequate for up to 2 weeks.
- Taking shelter during a nuclear blast is absolutely necessary. There are two kinds of shelters—blast and fallout. The following describes the two kinds of shelters:
- Blast shelters are specifically constructed to offer some protection against blast pressure, initial radiation, heat and fire. But even a blast shelter cannot withstand a direct hit from a nuclear explosion.
- Fallout shelters do not need to be specially constructed for protecting against fallout. They can be any protected space, provided that the walls and roof are thick and dense enough to absorb the radiation given off by fallout particles.

During a Nuclear Blast

The following are guidelines for what to do in the event of a nuclear explosion.

If an attack warning is issued:

- Take cover as quickly as you can, below ground if possible, and stay there until instructed to do otherwise.
- Listen for official information and follow instructions.

If you are caught outside and unable to get inside immediately:

- Do not look at the flash or fireball—it can blind you.
- Take cover behind anything that might offer protection.
- Lie flat on the ground and cover your head. If the explosion is some distance away, it could take 30 s or more for the blast wave to hit.
- Take shelter as soon as you can, even if you are many miles from ground zero where the attack occurred—radioactive fallout can be carried by the winds for hundreds of miles. Remember the three protective factors: Distance, shielding and time.

After a Nuclear Blast

Decay rates of the radioactive fallout are the same for any size nuclear device. However, the amount of fallout will vary based on the size of the device and its proximity to the ground. Therefore, it might be necessary for those in the areas with highest radiation levels to shelter for up to a month. The heaviest fallout would be limited to the area at or downwind from the explosion and 80% of the fallout would occur during the first 24 h. People in most of the areas that would be affected could be allowed to come out of shelter within a few days and, if necessary, evacuate to unaffected areas.

Returning to Your Home

Remember the following when returning home:

- Keep listening to the radio and television for news about what to do, where to go and places to avoid.
- Stay away from damaged areas. Stay away from areas marked "radiation hazard" or "HAZMAT." Remember that radiation cannot be seen, smelled or otherwise detected by human senses.

Source: Department of Homeland Security (2005). www.dhs.gov.

DHS Ready.Gov Guidance on Explosions

If There Is an Explosion

- Take shelter against your desk or a sturdy table.
- Exit the building ASAP.
- Do not use elevators.
- Check for fire and other hazards.
- Take your emergency supply kit if time allows.

If There Is a Fire

- Exit the building ASAP.
- Crawl low if there is smoke.

- Use a wet cloth, if possible, to cover your nose and mouth.
- Use the back of your hand to feel the upper, lower, and middle parts of closed doors.
- If the door is not hot, brace yourself against it and open slowly.
- If the door is hot, do not open it. Look for another way out.
- Do not use elevators.
- If you catch fire, do not run. Stop-drop-and-roll to put out the fire.
- If you are at home, go to a previously designated meeting place.
- Account for your family members and carefully supervise small children.
- Never go back into a burning building.

If You Are Trapped in Debris

- If possible, use a flashlight to signal your location to rescuers.
- Avoid unnecessary movement so that you don't kick up dust.
- Cover your nose and mouth with anything you have on hand. (Dense-weave cotton material can act as a good filter. Try to breathe through the material.)
- Tap on a pipe or wall so that rescuers can hear where you are.
- If possible, use a whistle to signal rescuers.
- Shout only as a last resort. Shouting can cause a person to inhale dangerous amounts of dust.

Source: FEMA (2005a).

Preparedness Against Biological and Chemical Attacks and Accidents

Preparedness against biological and chemical attacks and accidents poses a distinct challenge due to the unique consequences that they inflict and the relatively limited experience of emergency management professionals in dealing with them. This unique challenge is being addressed by many local, state, federal, private, and nonprofit agencies throughout the United States. In fact, the majority of preparedness funding under the Department of Homeland Security targets these WMD hazards.

Specific Challenges for Biological/Chemical Terrorism Incident Management

Deliberate biological or chemical incidents will present critical challenges to both the intended targets and those in charge of managing the incident that results. These agents, as with all WMDs, present public health threats that are not typically seen in either day-to-day or even major incidents of natural or accidental man-made nature. As such, the methods by which citizens and response officials can prepare for these attacks have only just begun to emerge in the past few years. Chemical incidents do occur with regularity, but it is very rare for them to deliberately target a human population.

Both chemical and biological agents, when used as weapons, have a significant potential to overwhelm the capabilities of the public health infrastructure. There have been several attempts to design a comprehensive framework to prepare for and manage mass-casualty medical incidents. The specific response challenges that those defining new preparedness methods must take into account are listed here:

- The existence of a chemical or biological attack may be hard to verify, due to delayed consequences or symptoms.
- The incident may involve multiple jurisdictions, which may make it much more difficult to organize a coordinated response.
- It may be time-consuming to identify and isolate the type and source of the chemical or biological agent present on site.
- The incident may have a pinpoint target where a specific crowd is targeted or may be designed to impact a larger geographic area and even larger crowds, both of which will likely create large crowds of morbidities if not mortalities.
- If a large number of the public are impacted by the incident, the demand for health care may quickly exceed local, or even regional, medical resources.
- The identification of the involved chemical(s) or biological agent(s) may consume the capacity of local medical laboratories making it mandatory to integrate use of neighboring laboratories.
- Resources of the medical system may be consumed not only by the victims but also by those who perceive themselves as possible victims who may not be real victims.
- The emergency management officials may have to make extremely difficult public policy decisions very quickly, where lives may have to be sacrificed to save other lives.
- It may be necessary to quarantine the impacted region to insulate the nonimpacted geographies from potential contamination.
- The medical units may have to triage arriving victims if the incoming demand dramatically exceeds the capacity of available resources.
- To decontaminate the impacted geographies and those who were contaminated by the release, necessary decontamination systems, equipment, and human resources may be necessary at multiple locations.
- The medical system may have to deal not only with the physical disease caused by the chemical or biological release but also with the mental impacts of the "mass paranoia" the incident may have triggered.

These are but a small subset of the potential challenges that must be met. Individual events will present individual response factors that may or may not be known beforehand. To address these issues, physical (equipment, tools, and technology), financial, knowledge, and human resources are all necessary. More importantly, a comprehensive system to address these challenges is necessary, and the adequate utilization of such a system demands the provision of training and exercises to those who will be dependent on such a system in a time of crisis (see sidebar "CDC's Strategic Plan for Preparedness and Response to Biological and Chemical Terrorism").

CDC's Strategic Plan for Preparedness and Response to Biological and Chemical Terrorism

The CDC has developed a plan, titled the "Strategic Plan for Preparedness and Response to Biological and Chemical Terrorism," that identifies preparedness and prevention, detection and surveillance, diagnosis and characterization of biological and chemical agents, response, and communication as the five focus areas for comprehensive mass casualty health incident management. Descriptions of each follow.

Preparedness and Prevention

Detection, diagnosis, and mitigation of illness and injury caused by biological and chemical terrorism is a complex process that involves numerous partners and activities. Meeting this challenge will require special emergency preparedness in all cities and states. CDC will provide public health guidelines, support, and technical assistance to local and state public health agencies as they develop coordinated preparedness plans and response protocols. CDC also will provide self-assessment tools for terrorism preparedness, including performance standards, attack simulations, and other exercises.

Detection and Surveillance

Early detection is essential for ensuring a prompt response to a biological or chemical attack, including the provision of prophylactic medicines, chemical antidotes, or vaccines. CDC will integrate surveillance for illness and injury resulting from biological and chemical terrorism into the U.S. disease surveillance systems, while developing new mechanisms for detecting, evaluating, and reporting suspicious events that might represent covert terrorist acts. As part of this effort, CDC and state and local health agencies will form partnerships with front-line medical personnel in hospital emergency departments, hospital care facilities, poison control centers, and other offices to enhance detection and reporting of unexplained injuries and illnesses as part of routine surveillance mechanisms for biological and chemical terrorism.

Diagnosis and Characterization of Biological and Chemical Agents

CDC and its partners will create a multilevel laboratory response network for bioterrorism (LRNB). The LRN and its partners will maintain an integrated national and international network of laboratories that are fully equipped to respond quickly to acts of chemical or biological terrorism, emerging infectious diseases, and other public health threats and emergencies.

Response

A comprehensive public health response to a biological or chemical terrorist event involves epidemiologic investigation, medical treatment and prophylaxis for affected persons, and the initiation of disease prevention or environmental decontamination measures. CDC will assist state and local health agencies in developing resources and expertise for investigating unusual events and unexplained illnesses. If requested by a state health agency, CDC will deploy response teams to investigate unexplained or suspicious illnesses or unusual etiologic agents and provide on-site consultation regarding medical management and disease control. To ensure the availability, procurement, and delivery of medical supplies, devices, and equipment that might be needed to respond to terrorist-caused illness or injury, CDC will maintain a national pharmaceutical stockpile.

Communication Systems

U.S. preparedness to mitigate the public health consequences of biological and chemical terrorism depends on the coordinated activities of well-trained health-care and public health personnel throughout the United States who have access to up-to-the minute emergency information. Effective communication with the public through the news media will also be essential to limit terrorists' ability to induce public panic and disrupt daily life.

Preparedness and Sheltering in Place

There are many options for members of the general public who wish to prepare for the effects of terrorist attacks involving the use of chemical, biological, or radiological weapons. In general, these options involve various implements or methods to avoid contact with the agents themselves, or with infected or contaminated individuals. One of the most effective means of preventing exposure to these weapons is to remain indoors after an attack has occurred, termed "sheltering in place," thereby avoiding the likelihood of coming into contact with the pathogen, chemical, or radiation by traveling unprotected through an area of contamination. The federal government, through the Ad Council, has developed and published several options for those wishing to take preparative measures on the Ready.Gov website, as have several other agencies including the Centers for Disease Control and Prevention, the Department of Energy, and many state and local offices of emergency management and homeland security. Levels of actual application of these measures by the general public are assumed to be very low, however, due to a combination of risk perception factors that generate a sense of inability to mitigate WMD effects, and a prioritization of risk reduction measures by these individuals that places such actions lower in priority ranking.

The "Preparedness and Response for a Bioterror or Chemical Attack" fact sheet discusses how the general population can prepare for a bioterror or chemical attack. Preparedness against dispersion of a chemical agent is further discussed in "Chemical Agents: Facts about Sheltering in Place." Both are available on the companion website for this book.

Source: CDC (2005b).

Another Voice: Why Is Mitigation and Preparedness the Only Sustainable, Cost-Effective Way of Dealing with Emergencies?

Pay Now or Later

Catastrophic disasters are associated with large losses of property and lives, where resources to cope with the disaster overwhelm local governments. Following such disasters, large amounts of capital in the form of disaster aid are necessary in order to put the physical infrastructure back to its original state. Even larger amounts—doubled, tripled, or sometimes quadrupled—are necessary to put the economic and social infrastructure back into a sustainable state. Therefore, local planners and policymakers should be extra careful when allowing settlements and the associated infrastructure systems in precarious zones such as active faults, coastal regions, flood zones, and nuclear power plants. These decisions should not only be based on scientific assessment of potential risks of failure (these are ideally embedded in building codes) but also "life cycle costs" of owning and operating infrastructure systems (LCCs are ideally factored into the "benefit-cost ratio" for capital allocation). LCCs should include allowances for scheduled and emergency maintenance for critical parts of the system, as well as economic allowances for failures.

Case in Point

In the immediate aftermath of Hurricane Katrina, the levees surrounding the city of New Orleans failed, causing the flooding of the entire city and incapacitating local response forces. The failure of the response is attributable, among other things, to the historic ill decision of settling in a very dangerous flood zone and continued expansion despite prior major flooding events, as well as the lack of funding that caused the poor maintenance and near-neglect of critical components of the levee structure which led to their compromise under extreme forces.

By Irmak Renda-Tanali, DSc, MSCE, Assistant Professor; Program Director, Homeland Security Management, Information and Technology Systems Department, Graduate School of Management and Technology, University of Maryland-University College.

Nuclear and Radiological Preparedness

The Nuclear Regulatory Commission (NRC) is the primary federal government agency in charge of regulating the commercial radiological operations within the United States. The NRC's mission is to regulate the nation's civilian use of by-product, source, and special nuclear materials to ensure adequate protection of public health and safety, to promote the common defense and security, and to protect the environment. The NRC's regulatory mission covers three main areas:

- *Reactors*: Commercial reactors for generating electric power and research and test reactors used for research, testing, and training
- *Materials*: Uses of nuclear materials in medical, industrial, and academic settings and facilities that produce nuclear fuel
- *Waste*: Transportation, storage, and disposal of nuclear materials and waste, and decommissioning of nuclear facilities from service

A key component of the mission of the NRC is to ensure that adequate preparedness measures are in place to protect the health and safety of the public. These actions are taken to avoid or reduce radiation dose exposure and are sometimes referred to as *protective measures*.

The overall objective of NRC's emergency preparedness (EP) program is to ensure that nuclear power plant operators are capable of implementing adequate measures to protect public health and safety in the event of a radiological emergency. As a condition of their license, operators of these nuclear power plants must develop and maintain EP plans that meet comprehensive NRC EP requirements. Increased confidence in public protection is obtained through the combined inspection of the requirements of emergency preparedness and the evaluation of their implementation.

The NRC maintains oversight of the capability of nuclear power plant operators to protect the public by conducting thorough inspections. The NRC maintains four regional offices (Region I in King of Prussia, Pennsylvania; Region II in Atlanta, Georgia; Region III in Lisle, Illinois; and Region IV in Arlington, Texas) that implement the NRC's inspection program. In addition to these regionally based inspectors, the NRC places "resident inspectors" at each of the nation's operating nuclear plants to carry out the inspection program on a day-to-day basis.

The NRC assesses the capabilities of nuclear power plant operators to protect the public by requiring the performance of a full-scale exercise at least once every 2 years that includes the participation of government agencies. These exercises are performed in order to maintain the skills of the emergency responders and to identify and correct weaknesses. They are evaluated by NRC regional inspectors and FEMA regional evaluators. Between the times when these 2-year exercises are conducted, additional drills are conducted by the nuclear power plant operators that are evaluated by the resident inspectors (Nuclear Regulatory Commission, 2014).

Terrorism Preparedness and Mitigation: Community Issues

The terrorism threat knows no geographic, social, or economic boundaries. Every citizen and every community is potentially at risk. Although the DHS focuses on federal and state efforts to prepare for and combat terrorism, local communities are struggling to address the terrorism risk. The following sections explain several initiatives that have been launched to deal with community issues concerning the terrorist threat.

Corporation for National and Community Service

The mission of the Corporation for National and Community Service (CNCS), an independent federal agency under the White House, is to provide opportunities for Americans of all ages and backgrounds to engage in service that addresses the nation's educational, public safety, environmental, and other human needs to achieve direct and demonstrable results. In doing so, the corporation fosters civic responsibility, strengthens the ties that bind citizens together, and provides educational opportunities for those who make a substantial commitment to service.

The CNCS provides opportunities for Americans to serve through three programs: Senior Corps, AmeriCorps, and Learn and Serve America. Members and volunteers serve with national and community nonprofit organizations, faith-based groups, schools, and local agencies to help meet community needs in education, the environment, public safety, homeland security, and other critical areas. The corporation is part of the USA Freedom Corps, a White House initiative to foster a culture of citizenship, service, and responsibility and help all Americans answer the president's call to service.

Senior Corps taps the skills, talents, and experiences of more than 360,000 Americans aged 55 years and older to meet a wide range of community challenges through three programs: RSVP, Foster Grandparents, and Senior Companions. RSVP volunteers conduct safety patrols for local police departments, participate in environmental projects, provide intensive educational services to children and adults, and respond to natural disasters, among other activities. Foster Grandparents serve one-on-one as tutors and mentors to young people with special needs. Senior Companions help homebound seniors and other adults maintain independence in their own homes.

More than 75,000 Americans are serving their communities 20–40 h a week through AmeriCorps. Most of AmeriCorps' members are selected by and serve with local and national nonprofit organizations such as Habitat for Humanity, the American Red Cross, City Year, Teach for America, and Boys and Girls Clubs of America and with a host of smaller community organizations, both secular and faith-based. According to the CNCS, "Since the program's founding in 1994, more than 900,000 AmeriCorps members have contributed more than 1.2 billion hours in service across America while tackling pressing problems and mobilizing millions of volunteers for the organizations they serve" (CNCS, 2014a).

AmeriCorps operates in a decentralized manner that gives a significant amount of responsibility to states and local nonprofit groups. Roughly three-quarters of all AmeriCorps grant funding goes to governor-appointed state service commissions, which award grants to nonprofit groups in responding to local needs. Most of the remainder of the grant funding is distributed by the corporation directly to multistate and national organizations through a competitive grants process. AmeriCorps NCCC (National Civilian Community Corps) is a residential program for more than 1200 members ages 18–24. Based on a military model, it sends members in teams of 10–14 to help nonprofit groups provide disaster relief, preserve the environment, build homes for low-income families, tutor children, and meet other challenges. Because members are trained in CPR, first aid, and mass care, and can be assigned to new duties on short notice, they are particularly well suited to meet the emerging homeland security needs of the nation.

In order to "strengthen the nation's disaster response capacity, the Federal Emergency Management Agency (FEMA) and the Corporation for National and Community Service have established FEMA Corps, a unit of 1600 service corps members within AmeriCorps NCCC solely devoted to disaster preparedness, mitigation, response, and recovery. This innovative partnership builds on the historic collaboration between the two agencies and enhances the federal government's disaster capabilities, increase the reliability and diversity of the disaster workforce, promote an ethic of service, expand education and economic opportunity for young people, and achieve an estimated cost savings of more than $350 million in the first five years" (CNCS, 2014b).

Learn and Serve America provides grants to schools, colleges, and nonprofit groups to support efforts to engage students in community service linked to academic achievement and the development of civic skills. This type of learning, referred to as *service learning*, improves communities while preparing young people for a lifetime of responsible citizenship. In addition to providing grants, Learn and Serve America serves as a resource on service and service learning to teachers, faculty members, schools, and community groups.

The CNCS is an important initiative for homeland security efforts at the local community level because it provides a significant portion of the total federal funding that goes to volunteer organizations and local communities that are trying to improve their homeland security capabilities.

On July 18, 2002, the CNCS announced that it had acquired more than $10.3 million in grants. These grants supported 37,000 volunteers for homeland security in public safety, public health, and disaster mitigation and preparedness. The corporation announced on September 10, 2003, the renewal of 17 of the grants from the previous year totaling nearly $4.5 million for homeland security volunteer projects that were developed in the aftermath of the 9/11 terrorist attacks.

In January 2004, the CNCS announced the availability of $3.2 million in funding for organizations addressing homeland security concerns by engaging students in service learning activities in their schools and communities. The funding was made available through the corporation's Learn and Serve America program, which provides grants to schools, colleges, and nonprofit groups to support programs that connect classroom learning with community service. The homeland security initiative aimed to engage young people aged 5–17 in planning for and responding to health, safety, and security concerns in their schools or communities, including natural disasters, school violence, medical emergencies, or terrorist acts. Examples of activities supported include engaging students in service learning projects to develop school crisis plans, distributing preparedness kits, conducting school safety audits and drills, providing health education, inventorying and maintaining emergency supplies, or providing language assistance to non-English-speaking populations.

In February 2004, the CNCS announced the renewal of 13 AmeriCorps homeland security grants to support 362 AmeriCorps members serving in public safety, public health, and disaster relief and preparedness projects across the country. The grants totaled $3.5 million and supported AmeriCorps projects in 20 states. The grantees included 12 state or local groups and one national organization, the American Red Cross. The grants supported AmeriCorps members' efforts to recruit volunteers, develop disaster response plans, teach disaster preparedness to students, assist firefighting and police operations, train people in first aid and CPR, respond to national and local disasters, and develop partnerships with organizations involved in homeland security such as Citizen Corps councils and Neighborhood Watch Programs. Results from the 2003 activities sponsored by the grants included the following:

- AmeriCorps members serving in a program sponsored by the Florida Department of Elder Affairs have recruited over 600 disaster service volunteers who contributed more than 12,000 h of service, distributed over 200,000 disaster service publications, and reached nearly 2500 residents with presentations on safety.
- Serving with the Green River Area Development District in rural Kentucky, AmeriCorps members have utilized data from a Global Positioning System to map out information about fire stations, emergency shelters, HAZMAT storage facilities, medical facilities, and nursing homes.
- Just blocks from the World Trade Center site, Pace University AmeriCorps members have trained 250 people in English, Chinese, and Spanish emergency preparedness techniques, created a resource

list that consolidates all important emergency numbers, and built a "Downtown Needs" website that serves as a volunteer clearinghouse for 2000 organizations in the downtown area.

- AmeriCorps members in the California Safe Corps have taught disaster preparedness classes to more than 1000 community members, recruited more than 100 new volunteers who have provided over 250 h of service, and assisted more than 200 victims of disasters.
- In Iowa, AmeriCorps members have made presentations on disaster preparedness at 400 schools across the state.
- In the summer of 2004, the devastation wrought by Hurricanes Charley and Frances in Florida prompted the CNCS to muster as much assistance as possible to the state. More than 600 national service volunteers have been deployed to both provide direct services and leverage the support of thousands of additional volunteers. The CNCS worked with state and federal disaster officials to deploy even more volunteers as needed.

AmeriCorps members and Senior Corps volunteers specially trained in disaster relief have responded to disasters in more than 30 states. The corporation has a long track record of working with FEMA and other relief agencies in helping run emergency shelters, assisting law enforcement, providing food and shelter, managing donations, and helping families and communities rebuild. Hundreds of national service volunteers have directly assisted victims of the 9/11 terrorist attacks by providing family services, organizing blood drives, raising funds, and counseling victims' families (from http://www.nationalservice.org/news/factsheets/homeland.html and http://www.nationalservice.org/news/homeland.html).

CNCS volunteers proved to be especially useful and valuable in the aftermath of Hurricane Katrina. The CNCS quickly activated its local volunteer base to join the response to the disaster and also deployed many of its volunteers from other states to take part in the response and recovery operations. Response to Hurricane Katrina constituted the single largest nonmilitary volunteer disaster response in the history of the United States. Close to 600,000 volunteers took part in the response and recovery to Hurricane Katrina of which approximately 35,000 were participants of various CNCS programs. Volunteers with diverse skills and training supported many important activities such as the management of evacuee shelter operations, food services, basic health-care services, informing disaster victims on available governmental and nongovernmental benefits, and general postincident counseling services. CNCS volunteers staffed the American Red Cross emergency call center in Fairfax, Virginia.

The CNCS did not suspend its efforts in the hurricane-hit region after the response transformed into a long-term recovery operation. The organization worked with established partners including but not limited to FEMA and the American Red Cross. Volunteers got involved with donation collection and warehouse management activities. The Alabama Emergency Management Agency's emergency phone answering system has been staffed by CNCS volunteers. The corporation funded volunteer-pilot-operated airlifts to transport patients out of the area, reunite families, and bring in medical supplies to the region. Trained and equipped members of the American Radio Relay League, a CNCS partner, have supported emergency radio communications. In the later phases of the recovery effort, volunteers collaborated with the federal, state, and local response units; military units were deployed to help with the recovery; and other nonprofit organizations and CNCS volunteers participated in debris removal, helped the elderly and the disabled, repaired damaged roofs, and staffed coordination offices. American Red Cross response vehicles such as mobile kitchens were also staffed by volunteers in many instances. The CNCS encouraged the volunteering of college students during their winter and spring breaks and created opportunities for their direct involvement in the hardest-hit areas as volunteers. Those students participated in repair and reconstruction projects and enjoyed supporting local communities as they helped them recover from the devastation caused by Hurricane Katrina (CNCS, 2006, 2007a,b).

The CNCS's FEMA Corps members responded to their first major disaster in 2013's Hurricane Sandy. In the year after Hurricane Sandy made landfall in 2012, over 3800 AmeriCorps members responded to Hurricane Sandy supporting more than 30,000 local Hurricane Sandy volunteers and providing over 400,000 h of service that included mucking out 3700 homes. Sidebar "FEMA Corps First Year Shaped by Sandy" provides a brief description of their efforts and their impact on the overall response to Hurricane Sandy (CNCS, 2014c).

FEMA Corps First Year Shaped by Sandy (by Greg Tucker)

> *In the month and a half my team was in New York, the progress I witnessed was absolutely incredible. Although we all were frequently exhausted by the various assignments we had been given each day, it truly makes it all worth it when you can step back and realize that you've played even a small part in such a huge recovery effort.*
>
> *FEMA Corps member Elizabeth McSherry. McSherry is part of disaster services history as one of first group of FEMA Corps members to experience the new program.*

When the Corporation for National and Community Service (CNCS) and the Federal Emergency Management Agency (FEMA) agreed to form the FEMA Corps national service program, the agencies had no idea how quickly its new program would be put to the test. Or that the test would come in the form of Hurricane Sandy.

AmeriCorps members have a strong history of responding to natural and manmade disasters, so it was a no-brainer to create a program dedicated to this purpose. The AmeriCorps NCCC members serving with FEMA Corps receive training that allow them to gain practical experience serving in the national emergency response network when disasters strike.

FEMA Corps members spend their 10-month terms focusing on disaster preparedness, mitigation, response, and recovery activities. They provide support in areas ranging from working directly with disaster survivors to supporting disaster recovering centers to sharing valuable disaster preparedness and mitigation information with the public.

During Hurricane Sandy operations, FEMA Corps members made their presence felt right away. Here are a few things we learned about FEMA Corps from its first year:

Ready and Willing: The first class of FEMA Corps teams was working on the Hurricane Isaac response before being dispatched to help with Hurricane Sandy days after the storm struck the northeast. Teams on the ground in New York and New Jersey provided direct assistance to disaster survivors by working at Disaster Recovery Centers and going door-to-door in impacted neighborhoods providing disaster information. See Figures 10-7 and 10-8.

Through mid-July, FEMA Corps teams provided 419,207 h of Hurricane Sandy assistance. (Other AmeriCorps NCCC teams served an additional 108,972 h related to the storm.) Examples of projects included connecting community members to local resources, developing resource guides to improve coordination efforts, registering hurricane victims at local shelters, and supporting numerous volunteer facilities.

Spreading the Word: FEMA Corps members helped educate the communities affected by Sandy by distributing more than 19,000 pieces of educational materials and preparedness kits. Additionally, members led FEMA for Kids programs in 21 schools across New Jersey to promote disaster awareness and helped develop the FEMA Connect program to reach high school audiences.

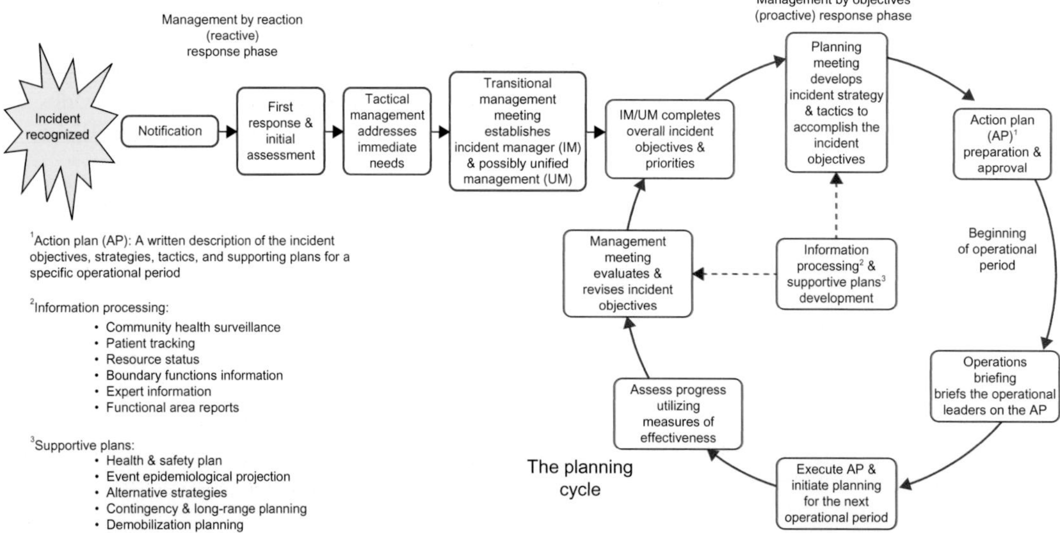

FIGURE 10-7 MaHIM management process. *Source: "Planning Cycle," US Coast Guard Incident Management Handbook, US Coast Guard COMDTPUB P3120, April 17, 2001.*

FIGURE 10-8 Anniston, AL, January 21, 2011—Health-care workers rush to decontaminate a simulated victim during an exercise at the Center for Domestic Preparedness, located in Anniston, Alabama. These students were attending the Hospital Emergency Response Training (HERT) for mass-casualty incidents course that places emergency response providers in a realistic mass-casualty training scenario. For more information on the CDP's more than 50 specialized programs and courses, please visit their website at http://cdp.dhs.gov.

Thinking Outside the Box: FEMA Corps Team Leader Ben Barron helped develop an initiative that used laptops and iPads to improve aid tracking and register storm survivors for disaster assistance. By embracing mobile technology, FEMA workers were able to make the disaster response process more efficient while maintaining face-to-face interactions. Barron discussed the initiative during a FEMA Think Tank on innovation in emergency management at the White House earlier this year.

They Said It: *"These FEMA Corps members have made a real difference in FEMA's disaster response and recovery efforts. They have brought incredible energy and enthusiasm for community service, directly impacting the lives of disaster survivors and paving a path for future FEMA Corps teams."*—FEMA Deputy Administrator Richard Serino.

Better Together: FEMA Corps couldn't have achieved any level of success without the cooperation between CNCS and FEMA that made it possible. The program's success is a model of interagency collaboration President Obama referenced when he established the Task Force on Expanding National Service led by White House Domestic Policy Council Director Cecilia Muñoz and CNCS CEO Wendy Spencer. CNCS hopes to expand models like this one to encourage more use of national service to solve our country's toughest challenges.

Source: CNCS (2014d).

Citizen Corps

Following the tragic events that occurred on September 11, 2001, state and local government officials have increased opportunities for citizens to become an integral part of protecting the homeland and supporting local first responders. Officials agree that the formula for ensuring a more secure and safer homeland consists of preparedness, training, and citizen involvement in supporting first responders. In January 2002, President George W. Bush launched the USA Freedom Corps to "capture the spirit of service that has emerged throughout our communities following the terrorist attacks."

Citizen Corps, a vital component of the USA Freedom Corps, was created to help coordinate volunteer activities that can make communities safer, stronger, and better prepared to respond to emergencies. It provides opportunities for people to participate in a range of measures to make their families, their homes, and their communities safer from the threats of crime, terrorism, and disasters of all kinds.

Citizen Corps is coordinated nationally by FEMA. In this capacity, FEMA works closely with other federal entities, state and local governments, first responders and emergency managers, the volunteer community, and the White House Office of the USA Freedom Corps. One of the initiatives supported by Citizen Corps is the Community Emergency Response Team (CERT). The program trains citizens to be better prepared to respond to emergency situations in their communities. When emergencies happen, CERT members can give critical support to first responders, provide immediate assistance to victims, and organize spontaneous volunteers at a disaster site. CERT members can also help with nonemergency projects that help improve the safety of the community.

The CERT course is taught in the community by a trained team of first responders who have completed a CERT Train-the-Trainer course conducted by their state training office for emergency management or FEMA's Emergency Management Institute (EMI), located in Emmitsburg, Maryland. CERT training includes disaster preparedness, disaster fire suppression, basic disaster medical operations, and light search and rescue operations. As of 2014, there were more than 2200 CERT registered programs active in many states, counties, and communities nationwide. For more information on CERT, see the CERT website https://www.fema.gov/community-emergency-response-teams.

Another important Citizen Corps initiative is the Medical Reserve Corps (MRC) program, which coordinates the skills of practicing and retired physicians, nurses, and other health-care professionals and other citizens interested in health issues who are eager to volunteer to address their community's ongoing public health needs and to help their community during large-scale emergency situations.

Local community leaders develop their own MRC units and identify the duties of the MRC volunteers according to specific community needs. For example, MRC volunteers may deliver necessary public health services during a crisis, assist emergency response teams with patients, and provide care directly to those with less serious injuries and other health-related issues. More information on the MRC program can be found at http://www.medicalreservecorps.gov.

The Neighborhood Watch Program (NWP) and Volunteers in Police Service (VIPS) programs are other Citizen Corps homeland security-related programs.

A relatively new partner program of the Citizen Corps initiative is the Fire Corps program. Launched in 2004, Fire Corps is a partnership between the International Association of Fire Chiefs' Volunteer and Combination Officers Section (IAFC/VCOS), the International Association of Fire Fighters (IAFF), the National Volunteer Fire Council (NVFC), and the US Fire Administration (USFA). Its mission is to help career, volunteer, and combination fire departments supplement existing personnel resources by recruiting citizen advocates. In June 2005, the program signed up its first 250 fire departments in its "citizen advocates" program. The purpose of the program is to help fire departments expand existing programs—or assist in developing new ones—that recruit citizens who donate their time and talents to support the fire service in nonoperational roles. As of 2014, there were 1098 established Fire Corps programs throughout the United States and US territories. More information about Fire Corps can be found at http://firecorps.org (Fire Corps, 2008).

The American Red Cross

The American Red Cross (ARC) has always been one of the most important partners of the federal, state, and local governments in disaster preparedness and relief operations. Some of the daily community operations of the Red Cross chapters include senior services, caregiver support, provision of hospital and nursing home volunteers, Lifeline (an electronic personal emergency response service), transportation to medical/doctor's appointments and other essential trips, food pantry and hot lunch programs, homeless shelters and transitional housing services, school clubs and community service learning programs and projects, youth programs (violence and substance abuse prevention, peer education and mentoring, and leadership development camps), food and rental assistance, language banks, and community information and referral.

From the first $10.3 million in federal grants provided to involve citizen volunteers in homeland security efforts in 2002, the ARC received $1,778,978, which was distributed by the national headquarters to many individual chapters. The recipient of the greatest portion of these funds was the Greater New York chapter, which received $500,000 of the funds for the recruitment, training, and mobilization of 5000 new disaster volunteers equipped to respond to another terrorist attack on a local level. These volunteers work with Red Cross service delivery units in New York to train additional volunteers, exponentially increasing the city's force of disaster relief workers.

In 2002, another $371,978 was given to the ARC National Headquarters for a nationwide program aimed at increasing volunteers in communities most vulnerable to terrorist attacks. The grant supported a yearlong program with 30 Community Preparedness Corps (CPC) members working in 19 chapters. Corps members worked in chapters to ensure that all community members—totaling some 27 million—have a "family disaster response plan." They tailored plans for those with language barriers and disabilities and for children and the elderly. At the same time, CPC volunteers focused on minimizing intolerance across the country by teaching international humanitarian law and the principles of the International Red Cross Movement (humanity, independence, neutrality, impartiality, voluntary service, unity, and universality).

Corps members also recruited and trained an estimated 400 new volunteers and instructors who made the educational programs available to additional vulnerable communities. Ultimately, corps members working through Red Cross chapters will create a network of hundreds of skilled volunteers across the country.

Additional grants have since been awarded to Red Cross chapters nationwide. In California, funds have been dedicated to the implementation of homeland security measures in Los Angeles, San Francisco, and Sacramento. The Oregon Trail Chapter that was awarded a grant funding 400 new volunteers will perform 1500 h of service to disaster preparedness. On the East Coast, the Red Cross developed "Disaster Resistant Neighborhood" programs across eight wards of Washington, DC. Through the program, these communities created disaster response plans. The southeast Pennsylvania chapter received a grant to create an alliance of more than 100 nonprofits in the Philadelphia area to form the Southeastern Pennsylvania Voluntary Organizations Active in Disaster (VOAD) to help citizens prevent, prepare for, and respond to disasters.

In 2003, the ARC participated in the TOPOFF 2 national training exercise. The Red Cross used this exercise to practice the screening of emergency shelter residents and supplies for radiation exposure, the logistic support when national stockpiles of medications were mobilized, and keeping the public informed as the national threat level reached the highest "red" alert. In the same year, the Red Cross was actively involved with the development of the new NRP. The ARC was the only nongovernmental organization that was invited to the discussions.

Throughout 2004, the Red Cross taught 11 million Americans critical lifesaving skills such as first aid, water safety, caregiving, CPR, and the use of automated external defibrillators (AEDs). In addition, the number of people attending presentations or demonstrations for Together We Prepare, community disaster education awareness, and the Masters of Disaster program climbed 6% to 3.9 million. Those programs aim to create safer families and communities.

Another 2004 initiative from the Red Cross involved expanding to diverse audiences with important preparedness and other information. To achieve this goal, the Red Cross expanded and detailed its Spanish language website and first-aid and preparedness print materials. In cooperation with the CDC, the Red Cross initiated a multiyear project to develop and disseminate terrorism preparedness materials to the public.

In 2005, the year of several major hurricanes, some criticism emerged regarding the way the ARC handled its duties during those disasters. In the days leading to the landfall of Hurricane Katrina at the shores of Florida, the ARC was initially praised for its proactive approach in prestaging volunteers and mass care resources, but as the disaster unfolded and showed its destructive face in larger geographies, issues concerning the ARC response to the disaster became more apparent. At the center of the problem were issues between FEMA and the ARC regarding rules of engagement as partners under the new NRP. A Government Accountability Office (GAO) study that looked at the relationship of the two agencies during and after Hurricane Katrina sheds light on some of the specific issues.

One major issue was the different interpretations of Emergency Support Function 6 (ESF #6) responsibilities and process flow by FEMA and the ARC. The ARC and FEMA are the designated primary agencies for ESF #6, in charge of mass care, housing, and human services. The ARC is directly responsible for mass care. The NRP tasks an ESF #6 coordinator, a FEMA official, with the oversight and coordination of all ESF #6 activities including mass care, which according to the ARC is not a perfect model since it designates the oversight of a core ARC competency to a non-ARC official. Therefore, during its response to Hurricane Katrina, the ARC in some instances bypassed the ESF #6 coordinator and tried to work with the FEMA Operations Section Chief. This resulted in tensions between the ARC and FEMA and in many instances undermined a very much needed partnership between the two agencies.

Another issue that the ARC was criticized for was the frequently changing personnel at facilities that required ongoing working relationships with the staff of other agencies, primarily FEMA. Those short shifts also reduced the exposure of ARC representatives to the operational environment of the ESF #6. The primary explanation for this problem was the ARC's predisposition for involvement in disasters with much shorter life spans and requiring shorter periods of continuous staffing—neither of which describe the needs of the Hurricane Katrina response where ESF #6 was active for more than 3 months. Also, since a significant portion of ARC personnel are volunteers, it is more difficult to engage those individuals in longer-term deployments than shorter ones.

In its response to GAO findings, the ARC underlined that it followed the guidance provided in the NRP as it worked with FEMA during Hurricane Katrina. Nevertheless, it is also mentioned that the ARC and FEMA are in the process of developing policies and procedures to formalize their agreement on seemingly gray areas of responsibility and ESF #6 operations. Regarding the issues of frequent ARC personnel changes in ESF #6, the ARC reports that it has improved the content of its ESF #6 training and hired 14 permanent employees to be trained in ESF #6 procedures and deployed at strategic locations in multiple states to coordinate with state emergency management agencies and officials (GAO, 2006; PBS, 2005; DHS, 2004).

Two other issues the ARC faced during its response to Hurricane Katrina were the fraudulent money transfers by some ARC subcontractors and unacceptably long wait times on phone-based services. The ARC provides cash payments to disaster victims to help them get through the first few days of a disaster until other means of relief become available. During Hurricane Katrina, the ARC established call centers manned by subcontractors to register and provide cash payments to hurricane victims using the money wiring services of a private contractor. The procedure did not have adequate checks and protection against fraudulent money transfers; therefore, a group of employees working for the subcontractor staffing the call center found loopholes to transfer money to themselves and their relatives who were not victims of the hurricane. None of those workers were actual ARC employees or volunteers. ARC has also been criticized by people trying to reach the call centers in that wait times were extremely long, and in many instances, hours. Some experts explain that those management problems are the result of the unique financial structure of the ARC, which heavily relies on donations; donors generally want their money spent strictly on direct assistance of hurricane victims rather than fixing administrative or managerial problems. This may minimize budgets to fix problems related to functions such as operations, finance, and accounting (Washington Post, 2005).

The Red Cross spent $310 million on disaster relief for the 2012 Hurricane Sandy. These costs were divided among several major work categories including individual casework and assistance (34% of total funds spent), food and shelter (30%), housing and community assistance (16%), relief items (11%), and other expenses (9%). The Red Cross mustered a total of 17,000 trained workers from all over the country, 90% of them were volunteers. The Red Cross provided 300+ emergency vehicles and 7 million relief items, served over 17 million meals and snacks, and financed over 74,000 overnight stays in shelters (American Red Cross, 2014b).

American Red Cross—Terrorism Preparedness

Terrorist attacks like the ones we experienced on September 11, 2001 have left many concerned about the possibility of future incidents of terrorism in the United States and their potential impact. They have raised uncertainty about what might happen next, increasing stress levels. There are things you can do to prepare for terrorist attacks and reduce the stress that you may feel now and later should another emergency arise. Taking preparatory action can reassure you and your children that you can exert a measure of control even in the face of such events.

What You Can Do to Prepare for Terrorism

Finding out what can happen is the first step. Once you have determined the events possible and their potential in your community, it is important that you discuss them with your family or household. Develop a disaster plan together.

What to Do If a Terrorism Event Occurs

- Remain calm and be patient.
- Follow the advice of local emergency officials.
- Listen to your radio or television for news and instructions.
- If the event occurs near you, check for injuries. Give first aid and get help for seriously injured people.
- If the event occurs near your home while you are there, check for damage using a flashlight. Do not light matches or candles or turn on electrical switches. Check for fires, fire hazards and other household hazards. Sniff for gas leaks, starting at the water heater. If you smell gas or suspect a leak, turn off the main gas valve, open windows, and get everyone outside quickly.
- Shut off any other damaged utilities.
- Confine or secure your pets.
- Call your family contact—do not use the telephone again unless it is a life-threatening emergency.
- Check on your neighbors, especially those who are elderly or disabled.

A Word on What Could Happen

As we've learned from previous events, the following things can happen after a terrorist attack:

- There can be significant numbers of casualties and/or damage to buildings and the infrastructure. So employers need up-to-date information about any medical needs you may have and on how to contact your designated beneficiaries.
- Heavy law enforcement involvement at local, state and federal levels follows a terrorist attack due to the event's criminal nature.
- Health and mental health resources in the affected communities can be strained to their limits, maybe even overwhelmed.
- Extensive media coverage, strong public fear and international implications and consequences can continue for a prolonged period.
- Workplaces and schools may be closed, and there may be restrictions on domestic and international travel.
- You and your family or household may have to evacuate an area, avoiding roads blocked for your safety.
- Clean-up may take many months.

Source: American Red Cross (2014a).

DIGGING DEEPER: INFLUENZA PANDEMIC MITIGATION AND PREPAREDNESS

An influenza pandemic is regarded as potentially the next large disaster that may threaten the entire globe and require the involvement of many nations and the international community for effective mitigation, prevention, preparedness, and response. Pandemic is the global outbreak of an infectious disease. The influenza pandemic is different from the seasonal flu in many ways. Among the differences are:

- Large or global geographic impact as opposed to local impacts of the seasonal flu
- Potential to quickly exhaust available resources of national health systems
- Potential to require medical supply and vaccine availability that is drastically different than what is required to deal with the seasonal flu to deal with a possible mandatory need to vaccinate masses of people within a very short time frame
- Long-lasting impact on the operations of the government, the general public, and the business sectors caused by drastic intervention measures, difficult to predict human response to those measures (such as risk perception and panic), suspended or delayed economic activity, and diminished confidence

Three influenza pandemics occurred during the twentieth century:

- **1918**: killed 675,000 in United States and around 50 million worldwide
- **1957**: killed at least 70,000 in United States and 1 to 2 million worldwide
- **1968**: killed about 34,000 in United States and 700,000 worldwide

The urgency for influenza pandemic mitigation and preparedness has increased in the past few years primarily due to two important medical incidents that at least partially shared the characteristics of an influenza pandemic or carried the potential to evolve into a serious global pandemic. These two incidents are SARS (severe acute respiratory syndrome) and avian influenza (bird flu). While some characteristics of the two diseases seem to be similar, essentially the root causes and the contagious behavior of those diseases are different. While both are potentially fatal respiratory infections that initiated in animals and then made the jump to humans with similar flu-like symptoms such as fever and difficulty breathing, there are two major differences. First, avian influenza is caused by a flu virus, whereas SARS has roots similar to the common cold. The second and more important difference is that SARS can be transmitted between humans, whereas in most cases of the avian flu, the transmission has occurred from a bird to a human.

SARS originated in southern China in late 2002. In February 2003, cases were reported in Hong Kong (China). In just a few days, cases were observed in Vietnam, Singapore, Canada, and Germany. Between November 2002 and July 2003, more than 8000 cases of SARS were reported globally. Those cases caused 774 deaths in 26 countries—most of which were in the Western Pacific.

Avian influenza is bird disease caused by type "A" strains of the influenza virus. While most birds are vulnerable to the virus, many wild bird species carry the viruses with no apparent symptoms. Of all strains of avian influenza "A" viruses, only four are known to have caused human infections: H5N1, H7N3, H7N7, and H9N2. H5N1 causes the most dangerous and fatal infections for humans. From 2003 to 2008, 349 human cases of the avian flu from 14 countries were reported to the World Health Organization, of which 216 were fatal. Indonesia and Vietnam had the highest numbers of human avian influenza deaths, with 94 and 47 lives lost, respectively. While H5N1 is still primarily a virus that can transmit from an infected bird to a human, cases of human-to-human transmission have been confirmed in at least three incidents in Thailand, Indonesia, and Pakistan. In all of those instances, the transmission occurred through extended close contact (caretaker and infected person). Scientists are not too concerned about this type of transmission, since it is highly preventable, but the possibility of a mutation in the virus genetic code that makes the transmission among humans much easier and faster is of real concern to public health officials (see the figure below).

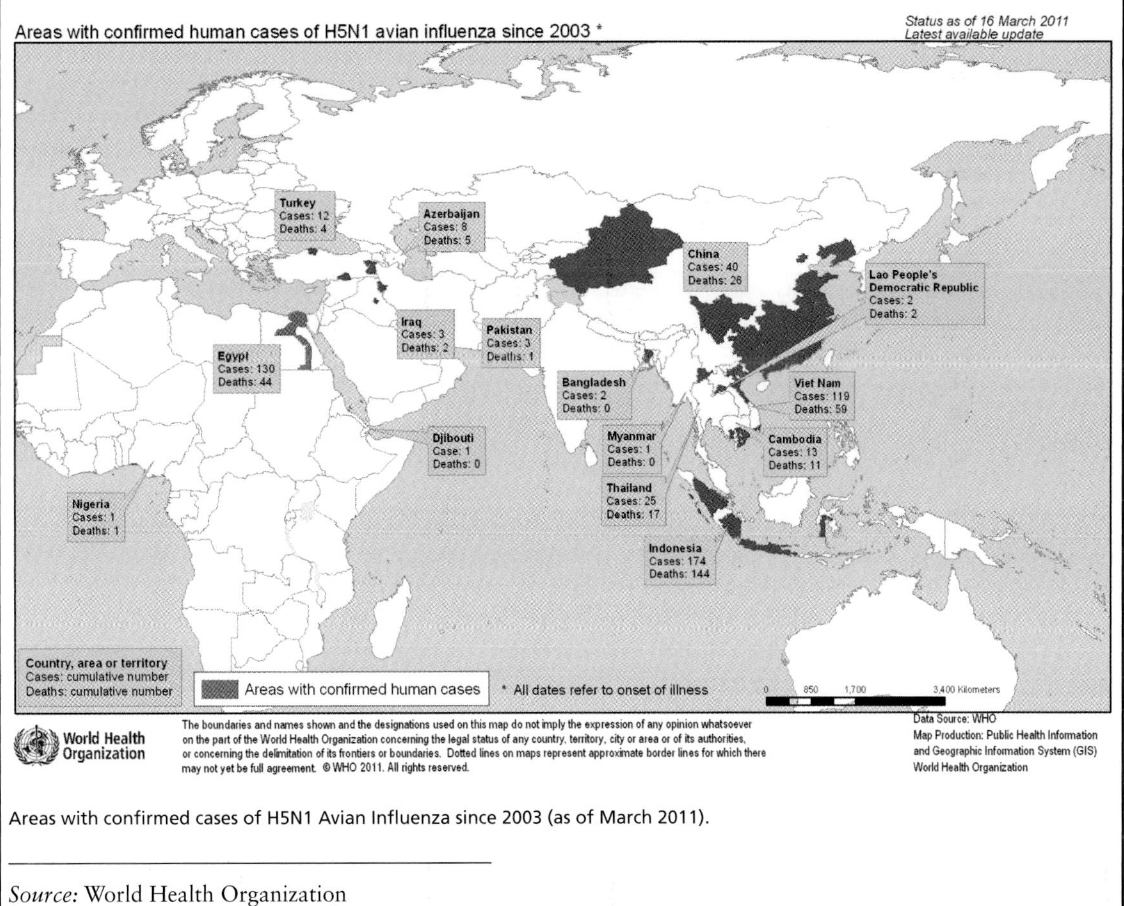

Areas with confirmed cases of H5N1 Avian Influenza since 2003 (as of March 2011).

Source: World Health Organization

(*Continued*)

DIGGING DEEPER: INFLUENZA PANDEMIC MITIGATION AND PREPAREDNESS—CONTINUED

Because the entire world is at risk of influenza pandemic, every country is expected to enable resources for preparedness and response in case of a potential outbreak. The World Health Organization supports those efforts by making information, data, knowledge, expertise, research, and guidelines available to the international community. In 2005, the World Health Organization released the "Checklist for Influenza Pandemic Preparedness Planning." The goal of the checklist is to provide national planning authorities a list of required and desired tasks to be completed to achieve a minimum level of preparedness that would increase the chance of success in an actual influenza pandemic response. The checklist is intentionally kept generic to ensure applicability in many nations with varying levels of resources and technical expertise. The checklist includes the following seven items:

1. *Preparing for an emergency*: This step involves the completion of preplanning activities such as the creation of political and public awareness regarding an influenza pandemic, the establishment of an overall preparedness strategy, and the appropriation of a budget adequate to sustain preparedness activities and to pay for resources deemed essential in the preparedness strategy.
2. *Surveillance*: Surveillance is one of the most critical steps of pandemic preparedness, as early detection of an outbreak is key to minimize further spread of the disease and initiation of a timely response. Unique and complex predictive procedures may be necessary to detect an outbreak in a timely fashion, which should effectively monitor and analyze multiple parameters that may be early signals of an upcoming influenza pandemic. For example, constant monitoring of daily cases that report to hospitals with flu-like symptoms may help in the creation of confidence intervals that designate normal conditions and abnormal conditions that may be associated with an uncommon demand for medical care related to a new flu outbreak.
3. *Case investigation and treatment*: This step ensures the creation of capability and resources to complete a first assessment of a virus when it shows signs of a known influenza strain. Adequate laboratory capability is mandatory. Established communication mechanisms with the World Trade Organization and other relevant organizations should occur to disseminate valuable new information in a timely fashion. Guidelines on clinical treatment of the new case should be established along with adequate training for first-response personnel.
4. *Preventing spread of the disease in the community*: Identification and initiation of postincident mitigation and prevention activities are crucial to stop dispersion of the disease to the general public, thus preventing an influenza pandemic outbreak. Some of the activities involved in this step are restrictions to mobility, setup of checkpoints, creation of rules for hospital admissions, creation of a communication system with the general public, and identification of priority rules in case vaccination becomes necessary with a limited supply of vaccine or other preventive medical supplies.
5. *Maintaining essential services*: Government organizations and other vital services should have internal organizational continuity plans to make sure that they can still provide the services the public expects from them even under the extreme operational conditions of an influenza pandemic outbreak. Government agencies in most nations have laws that require them to develop continuity plans, but those plans should be revised and improved based on the unique sets of challenges that may be posed as a direct consequence of the pandemic outbreak.
6. *Research and evaluation*: While countries dealing with an actual influenza pandemic outbreak are very likely to become stretched for resources, an actual outbreak is an

important opportunity for research and data collection to improve existing strategies and to test control measures applied for their level of effectiveness. Therefore, nations should make research and evaluation part of their response strategy and establish relationships and partnerships with other nations to ensure that scientific exchange among research communities is not impaired by the circumstances of the ongoing incident.

7. *Implementation, testing, and revision of national plan*: Revision of the national plan for applicability and testing it to improve its use during an actual outbreak are necessary. Make sure to set clear goals and measures of effectiveness that make progress evaluation of the plan easier during actual plan activation.

In the United States, the Department of Health and Human Services (HHS) holds primary responsibility for the coordination of influenza pandemic preparedness, as determined by the Homeland Security Council document, "National Strategy for Pandemic Influenza." The strategy identifies the following three pillars for effective management of a potential influenza pandemic:

- *Preparedness and communications*: Understand roles and responsibilities of different government agencies for the purposes of a potential influenza pandemic outbreak. Establish communications mechanisms and chain of command for effective incident management and decision making.
- *Surveillance and detection*: Ensure continuous "situational awareness" for timely identification outbreaks to limit the spread and to protect the public.
- *Response and containment*: Develop the capacity to effectively respond to an outbreak and establish mechanisms to minimize the spread of an overall economic and societal impact of an outbreak in progress.

Source: World Health Organization (2003), World Health Organization (2005), U.S. Department of Health and Services (2008), WikiBirdFlu.org (2007), World Health Organization (2008), Reuters (2007) and White House (2005).

Preparing for Ebola

In the summer of 2014, several individuals infected with the Ebola virus were hospitalized in the United States. The sometimes confused response (a summary of the Ebola response in the United States is presented in Chapter 9) to this situation and concerns about how to prepare to treat patients who present with Ebola-like symptoms prompted the Centers for Disease Control and Prevention (CDC) to develop a checklist for preparing for Ebola entitled "Detailed Emergency Medical Services (EMS) Checklist for Ebola Preparedness." According to the CDC, "Every EMS agency and system, including those that provide non-emergency and/or inter-facility transport, should ensure that their personnel can detect a person under investigation (PUI) for Ebola, protect themselves so they can safely care for the patient, and respond in a coordinated fashion. Many of the signs and symptoms of Ebola are non-specific and similar to those of other common infectious diseases such as malaria, which is commonly seen in West Africa. Transmission of Ebola can be prevented by using appropriate infection control measures" (CDC, 2014).

An important caveat is included in the CDC checklist that states, "The checklist format is not intended to set forth mandatory requirements or establish national standards. It is a list of activities that can help each agency prepare. Each agency is different and should adapt this document to meet its specific needs. In this checklist, EMS personnel refers to all persons, paid and volunteer who provide pre-hospital emergency medical services and have the potential for direct contact exposure (through broken skin or mucous membranes) with an Ebola patient's blood or body fluids, contaminated medical supplies and equipment, or contaminated environmental surfaces" (CDC, 2014).

The CDC checklist "is intended to enhance collective preparedness and response by highlighting key areas for EMS personnel to review in preparation for encountering and providing medical care to a person with Ebola. The checklist provides practical and specific suggestions to ensure the agency is able to help its personnel *detect* possible Ebola cases, *protect* those personnel, and *respond* appropriately" (CDC, 2014).

The CDC checklist includes the following sections, each complete with specific tasks that should be completed: prepare to detect, prepare to protect, and prepare to respond. A quick reference list is also included in the checklist (CDC, 2014).

A copy of the CDC checklist can be found at http://www.cdc.gov/vhf/ebola/pdf/ems-checklist-ebola-preparedness.pdf.

Critical Thinking

Should the CDC be allowed to mandate that health-care facilities and workers be required to follow CDC guidance on how to address Ebola and other potential infectious diseases? Will such a mandate be legal and would it improve preparedness in the public health community?

The Role of the Private Sector in Mitigation and Preparedness Activities

The events of September 11 brought to light the importance of private sector involvement in crisis, emergency, and disaster management. Since that time, an ever-expanding list of private entities has begun focusing on their needs in this area. This section discusses the essentials of private sector business continuity planning and disaster management. Most of the components discussed next have been learned as a result of experience with natural disasters or man-made accidents; however, the September 11 attacks have proved that those important components of classical crisis management are also important for terrorism risk management:

Business impact analysis (BIA): The management-level analysis by which an organization assesses the quantitative (financial) and qualitative (nonfinancial) impacts, effects, and loss that might result if the organization were to suffer a business-interrupting event. Performing BIA as a preparedness measure is important because findings from the BIA are used to make decisions concerning business continuity management strategies.

Crisis communications planning: Decision-making about how crisis communications will be performed during an emergency is important because communication is a critical success factor for effective crisis management. Preventing rumors about your corporation and telling your story before someone else does it for you are only possible via a predefined communication policy.

Information technology (IT) and systems infrastructure redundancy planning: There are different techniques and approaches regarding the enforcement of systems redundancy. Each company is unique, with its own IT and system needs and processes; therefore, customized approaches have to be employed to build more reliable systems infrastructure (e.g., backup databases, software, hardware, and network redundancy).

Geographic location and backup sites: The selection of the geographic location of headquarters and offices and the distribution of key executives in those buildings are strategically important decisions with regard to minimizing potential losses (both human and physical) during a disaster.

The availability of backup sites that allow employees to continue operations in case of physical loss of or damage to a primary facility is a key success factor but, unfortunately, is usually difficult to justify in terms of cost and benefit.

Transportation planning: The transportation infrastructure is one of the most sensitive infrastructures to emergency and disaster situations. Overloaded transportation infrastructure during crisis is usually a reason for microdisasters in the midst of bigger ones. Therefore, realistic transportation planning is important for a successful response.

Crisis leadership: Research and experience have shown that during crisis situations, people (e.g., employees, staff, and customers) need someone to tell them what is going on and explain what is being done about it, even if the information this person communicates is obsolete or redundant. Strong leadership also helps people to regain self-esteem and motivates them to commit to the efforts to overcome the crisis.

Insurance: It is important for companies to have a feasible but protective insurance policy. Realistic risk assessments and modeling are necessary to establish this economic feasibility.

There surely are other components of private sector risk mitigation and preparedness that are not mentioned in this text; however, these are the most important across the broad range of business types and sizes (Kayyem and Chang, 2002; Smith, 2002). See sidebar "Private-Sector Homeland Security Checklist" for assistance provided by the DHS.

Private-Sector Homeland Security Checklist

The Department of Homeland Security released the following anti-terror checklist for the private sector in its May 2003 Homeland Security Information Bulletin:

- Maintain situational awareness of world events and ongoing threats.
- Ensure all levels of personnel are notified via briefings, e-mail, voice mail, and signage of any changes in threat conditions and protective measures.
- Encourage personnel to be alert and immediately report any situation that may constitute a threat or suspicious activity.
- Encourage personnel to avoid routines, vary times and routes, preplan, and keep a low profile, especially during periods of high threat.
- Encourage personnel to take notice and report suspicious packages, devices, unattended briefcases, or other unusual materials immediately; inform them not to handle or attempt to move any such object.
- Encourage personnel to keep their family members and supervisors apprised of their whereabouts.
- Encourage personnel to know emergency exits and stairwells.
- Increase the number of visible security personnel wherever possible.
- Rearrange exterior vehicle barriers, traffic cones, and roadblocks to alter traffic patterns near facilities and cover by alert security forces.
- Institute/increase vehicle, foot, and roving security patrols varying in size, timing, and routes.
- Implement random security guard shift changes.
- Arrange for law enforcement vehicles to be parked randomly near entrances and exits.
- Review current contingency plans and, if not already in place, develop and implement procedures for receiving and acting on threat information; alert notification procedures; terrorist incident response procedures; evacuation procedures; bomb threat procedures; hostage and barricade

procedures; chemical, biological, radiological, and nuclear (CBRN) procedures; consequence and crisis management procedures; accountability procedures; and media procedures.
- When the aforementioned plans and procedures have been implemented, conduct internal training exercises and invite local emergency responders (fire, rescue, medical, and bomb squads) to participate in joint exercises.
- Coordinate and establish partnerships with local authorities to develop intelligence and information-sharing relationships.
- Place personnel on standby for contingency planning.
- Limit the number of access points, and strictly enforce access control procedures.
- Approach all illegally parked vehicles in and around facilities, question drivers, and direct them to move immediately; if the owner cannot be identified, have vehicle towed by law enforcement.
- Consider installing telephone caller ID; record phone calls, if necessary.
- Increase perimeter lighting.
- Deploy visible security cameras and motion sensors.
- Remove vegetation in and around perimeters; maintain regularly.
- Institute a robust vehicle inspection program to include checking the undercarriage of vehicles, under the hood, and in the trunk. Provide vehicle inspection training to security personnel.
- Deploy explosive detection devices and explosive detection canine teams.
- Conduct vulnerability studies focusing on physical security, structural engineering, infrastructure engineering, and power, water, and air infiltration, if feasible.
- Initiate a system to enhance mail and package screening procedures (both announced and unannounced).
- Install special locking devices on manhole covers in and around facilities.
- Implement a countersurveillance detection program.

Source: Continuity Central (May 21, 2003).

From its inception, DHS has worked to create a partnership with the private sector. This partnership is considered especially important because 85% of the critical infrastructure in the United States is held in the private sector. To date, DHS has had mixed results in creating and maintaining effective public-private sector partnerships. The 2014 Quadrennial Homeland Security Review (QHSR) calls for strengthening public-private partnerships and published a fact sheet entitled “Strengthening the Execution of Our Missions through Public-Private Partnerships” that is presented in the following sidebar.

Strengthening the Execution of Our Missions through Public-Private Partnerships

Homeland security is achieved through a shared effort among all partners, from corporations to nonprofits and American families. Together, we can harness common interests to achieve solutions beyond what any of us could do alone. At a time when we must do more with less, two guiding principles help public private partnerships maximize the investment by each partner and the success of the partnership: (1) aligning interests and (2) identifying shared outcomes.

A Structured Approach to Security and Resilience Partnerships
Although existing homeland security partnerships emerged from unique circumstances and specific challenges, there are important commonalities—models, lessons learned, and best practices—that can be applied to a range of other homeland security challenges. By using a structured approach to building and sustaining homeland security partnerships, the Department of Homeland Security (DHS) can begin to cross-apply lessons learned and best practices, spark partnership innovation, and engage with partners long before crises occur.

Partnership Archetypes for Homeland Security
Successful, well-organized partnership frameworks begin with a set of flexible models for current and future partnerships. The partnership archetypes for homeland security provide a foundation for thinking about partnership objectives, potential partners, and the resources and capabilities needed to address varying challenges.

- Information and Data Sharing—Engage and Disseminate
- Coordination—Align Complementary Activities
- Operational Linkages—Integrate Activities
- Co-Investment—Consolidate Financing and Resources
- Co-Production—Create New Products or Processes

Partnership Checklist
The Partnership Checklist provides a series of guideposts to anchor discussions around the most important elements of building a partnership.

- Identify the critical factors (context, capabilities, authorities, expertise, stakeholders, scope, and scale) that might impact the partnership
- Determine the value proposition of pursuing a partnership versus alternatives such as independent action or government procurement
- Define the outcomes the parties are trying to achieve
- Identify where public and private sector interests align
- Identify the range of challenges, opportunities, risks, and potential barriers to partnering assumed by the public and private sectors, in the near and long term
- Identify the partnership archetype that best fits the desired outcomes in the situation
- Identify and engage the relevant stakeholders and decision-makers to govern the partnership, and determine roles and responsibilities
- Determine how to measure success, for both the public and private sectors and, if applicable, the useful lifespan of the partnership

Partnering with DHS
For more information, please contact the DHS Private Sector Office at, partnerships@hq.dhs.gov, or visit https://www.dhs.gov/private-sector-office.

Source: DHS (2014b).

Critical Thinking

What do you think are the barriers to the establishment of effective public-private partnerships in homeland security? How can these barriers be overcome?

Corporate Preparedness and Risk Management in the Sarbanes-Oxley Era

The Sarbanes-Oxley Act of 2002, written by Senator Paul Sarbanes (D-MD) and Representative Michael Oxley (R-OH), was created to protect investors by improving the accuracy and reliability of corporate disclosures. The act is in direct response to financial fraud discovered in the cases of both Enron and WorldCom. However, it was created to cover issues beyond fraud (establishing a public company accounting oversight board, auditor independence, corporate responsibility, and enhanced financial disclosure) and is now a driving force behind corporate business continuity planning. Although the phrase *business continuity planning* is not once mentioned in the language of the act, continuity professionals claim that Section 404 of the act implies that such measures must be taken for compliance. Section 404 of the act reads as follows:

SEC. 404. MANAGEMENT ASSESSMENT OF INTERNAL CONTROLS.

(a) RULES REQUIRED—The Commission shall prescribe rules requiring each annual report required by Section 13(a) or 15(d) of the Securities Exchange Act of 1934 (15 U.S.C. 78 m or 78o(d)) to contain an internal control report, which shall

- state the responsibility of management for establishing and maintaining an adequate internal control structure and procedures for financial reporting; and
- contain an assessment, as of the end of the most recent fiscal year of the issuer, of the effectiveness of the internal control structure and procedures of the issuer for financial reporting.

(b) INTERNAL CONTROL EVALUATION AND REPORTING—With respect to the internal control assessment required by subsection (a), each registered public accounting firm that prepares or issues the audit report for the issuer shall attest to, and report on, the assessment made by the management of the issuer. An attestation made under this subsection shall be made in accordance with standards for attestation engagements issued or adopted by the Board. Any such attestation shall not be the subject of a separate engagement. (Sarbanes-Oxley Act of 2002, http://thomas.loc.gov/cgi-bin/query/F?c107:6:./temp/~c107*5GHak:e143423)

Section 404 of the Sarbanes-Oxley Act requires companies to include an internal control report that states the responsibility of management for establishing and maintaining an adequate internal control structure and procedures for financial reporting in their annual report. In addition, it requires management to ensure that the effectiveness of the internal control structure is assessed on an annual basis. The section also requires the external auditing entity to report on management's assessment of the effectiveness of the company's internal controls and procedures with respect to standards defined by the Public Company Accounting Oversight Board. Compliance with the act became effective in April 2005 for most companies.

Even though the section still focuses on financial record management and process control, in order to really ensure those things, it is almost a prerequisite for the company to ensure adequate protection and continuity of its entire core processes. This is where the "business continuity" aspect of the act becomes evident.

To protect the financial processes and records from misconduct or fraud and to ensure data integrity and resilience, the first step is to identify the risks, threats, and vulnerabilities that may endanger those expectations defined by the act. This is possible through a comprehensive risk and vulnerability assessment followed by a BIA to identify the business consequences of possible adverse incidents. The BIA is usually considered as one of the main building blocks of business continuity planning, because its findings usually help the corporations identify and prioritize the risks it has to mitigate and provide an understanding of recovery goals.

At present, it is too early to comment on whether there is full consensus between what the Sarbanes-Oxley Act demands from corporations and how the corporations interpret those expectations and what they are going to do about it. But it is true that business continuity concepts will adequately address some of the expectations of the act. Business continuity service providers seem to capitalize on this connection and enlarge the market for their services and products. The fact that the Sarbanes-Oxley Act places responsibility for compliance on top management makes it inevitable that these corporations will increase investments aimed at compliance. Business continuity is one of the answers.

A business continuity planning-focused journal article has indicated that compliance may require more than basic business continuity planning. The article explained that the act will make senior management involvement in the planning process inevitable and thus will require them to think about and find solutions beyond their organizations while paying more attention to service-level agreements, continuity of vendors, and suppliers (Benvenuto, 2004; Berman, 2004; Williams, 2005).

Critical Thinking

Should business sectors in addition to the financial services sector be required to develop business continuity plans per the Sarbanes-Oxley Act requirements?

DIGGING DEEPER: U.S. GOVERNMENT GUIDANCE ON PANDEMIC PREPAREDNESS PLANNING FOR BUSINESSES WITH OVERSEAS OPERATIONS

Due to the global nature of a potential pandemic influenza outbreak, a panel of representative U.S. agencies (i.e., Department of State, Department of Health and Human Services, Department of Commerce, and Centers for Disease Control and Prevention) have established pandemic planning guidelines for U.S. businesses with overseas operations. A summary of the guidelines follows. The full document can be found at http://www.pandemicflu.gov/plan/workplaceplanning/businessesoverseas.pdf.

- Plan for Maintaining Business Continuity during and after a Pandemic
- Plan for the Impact of a Pandemic on the Lives and Welfare of Your Employees
- Establish Policies and Guidelines to Be Implemented during a Pandemic to Avoid Creating Policies "On Demand" in the Midst of a Pandemic
- Determine Resources Required to Fulfill Actions in Your Pandemic Plan
- Create an Emergency Communications System
- Work to Coordinate with External Organizations and Your Community
- Prepare for Postpandemic Scenarios

Source: U.S. Department of Health and Services (2007). See the companion website for the full text of this document.

Best Practices

The nature of crisis, emergency, and risk management is very complicated: No matter how much one may discuss the process in the theoretical sense, the complexity of the actual environment in which they must try to implement practical applications cannot be fully appreciated. The three case studies that follow document private sector experience with disaster, individual mitigation and preparedness, and a governmental approach to mitigation and preparedness.

CASE STUDY 1: CANTOR FITZGERALD

For Joseph Noviello, September 11 began at 6:30am with a phone call confirming that an annual fishing trip with colleagues at the Cantor Fitzgerald bond trading firm was still on, despite some foul weather offshore. Minutes later, the most intense 2 days of his life would begin as the first plane hijacked by terrorists crashed into Cantor's building.

Watching on TV from his Manhattan apartment, Noviello had no way of knowing what lay in store. Clearly, this was a disaster of a proportion that neither he nor likely anyone in his position had dealt with before. Fortunately, he had a plan to follow.

That plan may have saved the company. No firm suffered a worse fate, in terms of lives lost on September 11, than Cantor Fitzgerald and its electronic marketplace unit, eSpeed. More than 700 employees of the two companies died in the destruction of the World Trade Center's north tower, where Cantor and eSpeed shared their headquarters and a vital computer center. Yet eSpeed was up and running when the bond market reopened at 8am on September 13, little more than 47h after the disaster.

"The difference for us was the planning we had in place," says Noviello, 36, who was promoted to eSpeed's chief information officer after the disaster. eSpeed's systems were built on a dual architecture that replicated all machines, connections, and functionality at the World Trade Center and at a Rochelle Park site, with a third facility in London.

eSpeed, which operates as a freestanding business and also serves as the trading engine for its parent company, lost 180 employees, including about half of its U.S.-based technology staff. But eSpeed had several important assets left. Most of the top technology executives had been out of the office, including Matt Claus, eSpeed's current CTO, and Noviello's right-hand man, who had been scheduled to go on the fishing trip.

The response atmosphere was tense, with people unsure as to what had happened to their friends or colleagues. "For days, every time a new face came in the door it was an emotional release," says Noviello. "There was a disaster-recovery contact list, but people were seeking to find each other not for work but to find out who was okay."

Beyond the technical questions were operational details such as advising staff on public transportation options to the suburban site, reestablishing shifts, and making sure there were counselors on duty. Conference calls every 2h kept track of milestones and objectives. "We were talking at 2am, at 4am," says Noviello. "Who is sleeping during something like this? Work is great therapy."

None of this effort would have succeeded without the duplicate architecture in Rochelle Park. Yet Cantor started moving into the facility only in February. From day one, Rochelle Park was seen as a concurrent system, not a disaster-recovery site.

All that redundancy would be stretched to the limit as eSpeed worked to overcome the technical hurdles before the opening of the bond market Thursday morning. Two of those hurdles were huge: the loss of eSpeed's private network connections and the destruction of the company's ability to handle fulfillment of trades.

The first problem was solved by allowing customers who had overseas offices connected to Cantor's London data center to reroute across their own networks to London. eSpeed worked with customers to reconfigure their servers to point to London and moved or expanded the permissions on customer accounts to connect to that site. For customers without overseas private networks, eSpeed worked to get them access over the Internet until the customers could get their high-speed connections hooked into the Rochelle Park facility.

To solve the second issue, help arrived in the form of one of eSpeed's competitors. ICI/ADP, another electronic trading company, offered to take care of eSpeed's clearing and settling of transactions through its own connection to banks. By Wednesday night, the eSpeed team had mapped its financial back-office system to ADP's system and had successfully sent test transactions to J.P. Morgan Chase & Co. and other banks. The cooperation of other companies, including vendors and fellow financial firms, turned out to be essential to Cantor/eSpeed's quick recovery.

The firm was weakened by the loss of so many people and the related shutdown of its voice-broker business. But it survived as a viable business. Thanks to planning, the company can keep operating, even if something should happen to Rochelle Park. Its data center in London will serve as the mirror site going forward.

And going forward, the company's systems should be even more resilient. "We are learning a lot of lessons as we are restoring the system," says Noviello, including how to automate more aspects of bringing systems back up. "And we are not restoring our bad habits" (Summarized from the original work of Cone and Gallagher, 2001).

Source: FEMA (2011b).

CASE STUDY 2: HOME ALONE ... EMERGENCY PLAN SAVES SISTERS

When the strongest tornado to hit Mississippi in more than 50 years tore through the small town of Smithville on April 27, 2011, 16-year-old Audrey Herren and her younger sister Cassidy, 11, knew what to do, and it probably saved their lives. They went into emergency mode—covered themselves with blankets and huddled on the floor of an inside hallway—and emerged virtually unscathed from a home that had disintegrated around them.

April 27 started off on an ominous note as the town's siren was sounded several times during the morning to warn residents of the approaching severe weather system. As the potential threat to Smithville became more certain, the 600 students in the town's K-12 school complex were released early, at approximately 2 pm. Parents Jim and Carol Herren were at work at the time, but they had learned via broadcast warnings and access to radar images of the storm that Smithville was in the path of a possible tornado. They called their daughters and told them to exercise their emergency plan, which they had put to use during earlier severe thunderstorms as recently as the previous week.

The tornado reached Smithville at 3:44 pm., roaring through the middle of town with peak winds estimated at 205 miles per hour. Most buildings were flattened, including more than 150 homes, 14 businesses, and 2 churches. Seventeen people lost their lives, either during the tornado or later as a result of injuries.

When the Herrens reached Smithville about an hour after the tornado struck, their daughters were not at their home (or what was left of it) as they had been told to move away from the area because of possible gas leaks. They connected with the girls later. The Herren family was able to save a bit of clothing from their home, but none of their furnishings could be salvaged. Most importantly their daughters had survived the storm.

"Everybody in town has a tornado story," said Carol Herren, "but unfortunately, many didn't turn out as positive as ours." And although her family didn't have a safe room at the time of the tornado, she is glad they had an emergency plan and that the plan likely saved her daughters.

(Continued)

CASE STUDY 2: HOME ALONE ... EMERGENCY PLAN SAVES SISTERS (CONTINUED)

The Herren family had occupied their home along Mississippi Highway 25, the main road through Smithville, for about 13 years. They are now living in a rented home that is just outside the tornado's path of destruction. They plan to begin construction of a safe room in a new home within the next few weeks that will specifically comply with the design criteria in FEMA 361, Design and Construction Guidance for Community Safe Rooms. They know several other neighbors who plan to do the same, and Jim Herren says he hopes that many others will decide to stay and rebuild in Smithville.

For additional information, contact the FEMA Safe Room Help Line at 866-222-3580 or at saferoom@dhs.gov. The help line provides information on where to go for assistance regarding hazard mitigation grants and other grant funding, project eligibility, and guidelines for safe room construction. FEMA's safe room website (http://www.fema.gov/plan/prevent/saferoom) is another source of information.

Source: FEMA (2011c).

CASE STUDY 3: SAFE ROOM WITHSTANDS EF-4 TORNADO, TUSCALOOSA COUNTY, ALABAMA

William Blakeney grew up in Tuscaloosa County and is well aware of the effects of disasters in the area. In an effort to prepare for disasters like the tornadoes in mid- and late April 2011, he built a safe room in his grandparents' home. Although they weren't home when the storms devastated the area, the only portion of their home left standing was the multipurpose safe room (see Figure 10-9).

FIGURE 10-9 Tuscaloosa, AL, June 12, 2011—A FEMA mitigation specialist conducts an interview with local media prior to the Safer Alabama Summit at the Bryant Auditorium on the University of Alabama campus. The summit provided information on how communities can best prepare for another catastrophic series of storms, and safe rooms will be on display to illustrate the building techniques required to withstand an F5 tornado. *Photo by FEMA/Tim Burkitt.*

Blakeney and his construction company had built a few safe rooms in the past, mainly in their family members' homes. While not built according to the design criteria of Federal Emergency

Management Agency's publication FEMA 320, Taking Shelter from the Storm: Building a Safe Room For Your Home or Small Business, this safe room was able to withstand the strong winds of the EF-4 tornado that ravaged the area.

FEMA 320 includes construction plans and cost estimates for building individual safe rooms. A safe room, built according to the standards outlined in FEMA 320, in a home or small business provides "near-absolute protection" for its occupants.

"We were not familiar with FEMA specifications, but we had built a few safe rooms," said Blakeney. "I was actually at the office and used the safe room we had built there when the tornado came through."

April's storms claimed over 40 lives in Tuscaloosa and left more than 2000 residents homeless. The area experiences tornadoes early spring and late fall each year, but never as severe as those on April 2011.

"Tornadoes usually hit the southern or northern parts of the town," said Blakeney about the recent events. His family had lived in Tuscaloosa County for more than 71 years. "In my time, we've never seen one come through the area like that!" The home was recently renovated so his grandparents could move from the outskirts of the city and live closer to other relatives. In the additional wing, the master bedroom closet was the perfect location to reinforce as the safe room.

"They had a basement in their old home and that made them feel secure," said Blakeney. "Here, they had nothing." The major home renovation was completed just 2 weeks before the storm hit the city and destroyed the home. His grandparents had not completely moved into the house and Blakeney was still adding finishing touches to the home. Fortunately, no one was home when the tornado struck because the entire neighborhood was destroyed.

Safe rooms provide homeowners, like Blakeney's grandparents, relief during times where they have to quickly seek shelter. Should homeowners decide to build a safe room in their new or existing home, FEMA 320 provides examples of proper installation techniques and designs. Safe rooms built to FEMA 320 standards have saved the lives of people affected by events like the one that destroyed many areas of Alabama.

"We just think it is a great investment for the sense of security," Blakeney added. "We will be building more in the future using FEMA 320." Building safe rooms according to FEMA specifications helps ensure that they will be able to withstand high winds and provide the ultimate protection. Not building according to FEMA specifications is risky and increases the likelihood of the safe room not providing the needed protection.

For additional information, contact the FEMA Safe Room Help Line at 866-222-3580 or at saferoom@dhs.gov. The help line provides information on where to go for assistance regarding hazard mitigation grants and other grant funding, project eligibility, and guidelines for safe room construction. FEMA's safe room website (http://www.fema.gov/plan/prevent/saferoom) is another source of information.

Exercises to Foster Preparedness

National Exercise Program

FEMA's National Exercise Division (NED) manages the National Exercise Program (NEP) "to test, assess and improve the nation's preparedness and resiliency. By assessing preparedness against a set of common national preparedness priorities, the Principals' Objectives, the NEP improves preparedness and resiliency and affects policy, priorities and fiscal decisions. The NEP is truly national in scope with the goal of fostering coordination and building relationships across the nation before an incident occurs. Each NEP cycle includes exercise types from drills to functional exercises and includes participants and exercises from all levels of government, non-governmental and private sector organizations and the Whole Community" (FEMA, 2014c).

A list of the national exercises conducted by the NEP to date is presented in sidebar "National Exercise Program Fast Facts," and a detailed description of the 2014 Capstone Exercise is presented in sidebar "National Exercise Program (NEP)—Capstone Exercise 2014."

National Exercise Program Fast Facts

Here's a look at what you need to know about the National Exercise Program, the U.S. system for emergency preparation drills. These exercises are mandated by Congress to test and strengthen federal, state, and local government ability to respond to potential catastrophic events.

The Federal Emergency Management Agency (FEMA) National Exercise Division (NED) oversees the National Exercise Program (NEP).

The first series of drills were called TOPOFF, which ran from 2000 to 2009.

The second series was called National Level Exercises (NLE), and ran from 2009 to 2012.

The National Exercise Program began Capstone Exercises in 2012.

TOPOFF Operations

TOPOFF—is short for TOP OFFICIALS. Governors, mayors, city managers, top federal and state officials, and others play active roles.

Sponsored by the U.S. Department of Homeland Security's Office for State and Local Government Coordination. Designed to involve all levels of government as well as emergency service responders including police, fire, public health workers and others.

States volunteer to participate in TOPOFF; two are chosen for each cycle.

TOPOFF 1: May 20, 2000—The first TOPOFF drill is mandated by Congress in 1998. It lasts 10 days and cost $3.5 million. The exercise features a bioterrorism attack in Denver, Colorado, a chemical warfare attack in Portsmouth, New Hampshire, and other activities in Washington, D.C. In New Hampshire, a mix of garlic and Gatorade is substituted for a bomb armed with mustard gas. Some lessons learned include: quick medical supplies depletion, hospitals filling to maximum capacity quickly, communication breakdowns (telephone lines), insufficient manpower, and poor decision-making skills. State officials say the drill taught them that rescue personnel need better training and protective gear.

TOPOFF 2: May 12–16, 2003—Takes place in Chicago and Seattle. TOPOFF 2 is a "five-day, full-scale exercise and simulation of how the Nation would respond in the event of a weapons of mass destruction (WMD) attack." TOPOFF 2 is the first large-scale counter-terrorism exercise since the September 11, 2001 terrorist attacks. Created by the Department of Homeland Security, the week long set of drills cost an estimated $16 million. More than 8500 people from 100 federal, state, and local agencies, as well as the American Red Cross and Canadian government, are involved. The simulated activities take place in Chicago and Seattle. The Seattle event is a dirty bomb, while the Chicago event is the release of a deadly biological agent.

TOPOFF 3: April 4–8, 2005—Takes place in Connecticut and New Jersey. Interrelated events take place in Canada (TRIPLE PLAY) and Great Britain (ATLANTIC BLUE).

The Connecticut event simulates a chemical weapons attack in New London; the New Jersey event simulates a vehicle-launched bioterror attack. Approximately 10,000 participants from 27 federal agencies, state, county, and local officials in Connecticut and New Jersey, and more than 150 private sector and non-government organizations take part in TOPOFF 3. In total, over 275 government and private organizations participate. TOPOFF 3 carries a budget of approximately $16 million.

TOPOFF 4: October 15–19, 2007—Takes place in Portland, Oregon; Phoenix, and the U.S. territory of Guam. The event is based on a scenario in which terrorists detonate a simulated "dirty bomb" in Guam, with similar, coordinated attacks later taking place in Phoenix and Portland. TOPOFF 4 involves more than 15,000 federal, state, territorial, and local participants. Of that number, approximately 4500 are involved in the activities in Oregon. This is the first TOPOFF event to include the participation of a U.S. territory. Dirty bombs, formally known as Radiological Dispersal Devices, are conventional explosives that release radioactive material upon explosion.

National Level Exercises

2009—It is announced that TOPOFF exercises will continue under a new name, Tier 1 National Level Exercise (NLE). These are conducted annually in accordance with the National Exercise Program (NEP). The exercises are still designed to provide all levels of government an opportunity to prepare for crises ranging from terrorism to natural disasters.

National Level Exercise 2009 (NLE 09): July 27–31, 2009—Takes place at federal headquarters facilities in the Washington D.C. area, and in federal, regional, state, tribal, local and private sector facilities in Arkansas, Louisiana, New Mexico, Oklahoma, Texas and California. Additionally, Australia, Canada, Mexico and the United Kingdom participate. The NLE 09 scenario begins in the aftermath of a national terrorist event outside of the United States, and the exercise centers on preventing efforts by the terrorists to enter the United States and carry out additional attacks. The exercise focuses exclusively on terrorism prevention and protection, as opposed to incident response and recovery.

National Level Exercise 2010 (NLE 10): May 17–18, 2010—NLE 2010 engages federal, state and local partners in a series of events to demonstrate and assess federal emergency preparedness capabilities pertaining to a simulated terrorist attack involving an improvised nuclear device. As part of NLE 2010, all federal agencies within the NCR participate in Eagle Horizon 2010, an exercise that requires federal departments and agencies to demonstrate their capability to perform mission essential functions in the event of a major emergency.

National Level Exercise 2011 (NLE 11): May 2011—Takes place at command posts, emergency operation centers and other locations, including federal facilities in the Washington D.C. area and federal, regional, state, tribal, local and private sector facilities in the eight member states of the Central United States Earthquake Consortium (CUSEC). The eight member states are: Alabama, Kentucky, Mississippi, Tennessee, Illinois, Indiana, Arkansas, and Missouri.

NLE 2011 simulates a major earthquake in the central United States region of the New Madrid Seismic Zone (NMSZ).

National Level Exercise 2012 (NLE 12): NLE 2012 is the first NLE that tests the existing plans and procedures to address the challenges in anticipating and responding to cyber incidents that have "virtual and real-world implications." NLE 2012 simulates a series of significant cyber incidents involving physical impacts on infrastructure, that require coordination among all levels of the U.S. government; various federal departments, agencies and cyber centers including the National Cybersecurity and Communications Integration Center (NCCIC) and the U.S. Computer Emergency Readiness Team (US-CERT); states; the private sector; higher education institutions and international partners.

- March 28–29, 2012—Exercise 1 involves the representatives sharing classified and unclassified information and building a Cyber Common Operational Picture (COP).
- April 25–27, 2012—In Exercise 2, participants focus on and evaluate the draft National Cyber Incident Response Plan (NCIRP). They also test the nation's operational capabilities among the governmental entities, the private sector partners and international partner nations.
- June 4–7, 2012—Exercise 3 addresses Whole Community cyber and physical response coordination, including a Cabinet meeting.
- June 19–21, 2012—Exercise 4 evaluates the continuity capability of federal departments and agencies during a significant cyber event.

Capstone Exercises

- 2012—The National Level Exercise (NLE) changes its name to the Capstone Exercise.
- 2013—The Capstone Exercise changes its format to a 2 year cycle.
- 2014—The Capstone Exercise includes the following multi-event exercises: The Alaska Shield 2014, Ardent Sentry 14, Nuclear Weapon Accident/Incident Exercise, Eagle Horizon 2014, and Silver Phoenix 2014.
- 2014—The Eagle Horizon 2014 exercise, which tests the government's response to potential attacks on public spaces like the DC Metro subway system, is canceled by the White House for undisclosed reasons. There are plans to resume the exercises with Eagle Horizon 2015.

Source: CNN (2014).

National Exercise Program (NEP)—Capstone Exercise 2014

The National Preparedness Goal (NPG) calls for a secure and resilient nation with the capabilities required across the whole community to prevent, protect against, mitigate, respond to and recover from the threats and hazards that pose the greatest risk. To achieve the Goal, the National Preparedness System (NPS) includes an integrated set of guidance, programs and processes that enable the nation to build, sustain and deliver the core capabilities within the context of the five mission areas: Prevention, Protection, Mitigation, Response, and Recovery. The NPS enables a collaborative, whole community approach to national preparedness that engages individuals, families, communities, the private and nonprofit sectors, faith-based organizations and all levels of government.

As a component of the NPS, the National Exercise Program (NEP) serves to test and validate core capabilities. Participation in exercises, simulations or other activities, including real world incidents, helps organizations validate their capabilities and identify shortfalls. Exercises also help organizations see their progress toward meeting their preparedness objectives.

The Capstone Exercise, formerly titled the National Level Exercise (NLE), is conducted every two years as the final component of each NEP progressive exercise cycle. The Capstone Exercise 2014 will examine the nation's collective ability to coordinate and conduct risk assessments and implement National Frameworks and associated plans to deliver core capabilities.

Further the Capstone Exercise 2014 will:
The Capstone Exercise 2014 will enable federal stakeholders to demonstrate operational coordination and information sharing capabilities with the private sector and other non-traditional partners as well as fulfill mandated exercise requirements or internal assessments to validate capabilities and identify key issues or potential shortfalls. The exercise will also encourage senior-level participation from all stakeholders, ensuring effective collaboration of decision-makers across the whole community.

The Capstone Exercise 2014 is a complex emergency preparedness exercise comprised of five distinct, but linked, component events. The Alaska Shield 2014 exercise, sponsored by the State of Alaska to commemorate the 50th anniversary of the 1964 Great Alaskan Earthquake, will provide the central scenario elements: significant damage from both the quake and the tsunami it triggers will affect the greater Pacific Northwest. Capstone Exercise 2014 incorporates several preparedness activities sponsored by other departments and agencies and is designed to educate and prepare the whole community for complex, large-scale disasters and emergencies.

The following component events are integrated into the Capstone Exercise to examine the core capabilities described in the National Preparedness Goal. This multi-event design recognizes the need for comprehensive all-hazards planning and the complexity to ensure exercise objectives are met.

- Assess the nation's performance against the 2013-14 NEP Principals' Objectives;
- Evaluate the readiness of local, state, territorial, tribal and federal officials to prevent, protect against, mitigate, respond to and recover from catastrophic incidents in a coordinated and unified manner; and
- Satisfy the requirements for a national level exercise as described in the Post Katrina Emergency Management Reform Act.

ALASKA SHIELD: Alaska Shield commemorates the anniversary of the 1964 9.2 magnitude Great Alaskan Earthquake by replicating the earthquake's effects and resulting tsunami.

ARDENT SENTRY 14: The Department of Defense aligned key components of the annual ARDENT SENTRY 14 exercise with ALASKA SHIELD, focusing on Defense Support to Civilian Authorities' mission.

Nuclear Weapon Accident/Incident Exercise: The Nuclear Weapon Accident/Incident Exercise (NUWAIX) 2014 accident occurs during a secure transportation convoy of nuclear weapons within the Continental United States. Intelligence and national leadership will need to quickly determine the cause and significance of the accident.

Eagle Horizon 2014: Eagle Horizon 2014 will focus on continuity of operations and reconstitution planning, requiring federal departments and agencies to activate continuity plans and perform their Primary Mission Essential Functions from their alternate facilities.

Silver Phoenix 2014: The Silver Phoenix combination of operations- and discussion-based exercises will examine the full range of recovery efforts and operations commencing upon the notification that a catastrophic incident has occurred. The exercises will explore the challenges associated with examining, prioritizing and conducting recovery activities involving multiple geographically dispersed and competing events using the National Disaster Recovery Framework.

The Great California ShakeOut: As stated on its website, "The Great California ShakeOut is an annual opportunity to practice how to be safer during big earthquakes: 'Drop,

Cover and Hold On.' The ShakeOut has also been organized to encourage you, your community, your school, or your organization to review and update emergency preparedness plans and supplies, and to secure your space in order to prevent damage and injuries. The main goal of the ShakeOut is to get Californians prepared for major earthquakes, so use the ShakeOut as an opportunity to learn what to do before, during, and after an earthquake." The most recent ShakeOut occurred on October 16, 2014 and approximately 10.4 million individuals participated in the exercise in California and over 26 million individuals across the country and worldwide in 2014. Individuals register on-line. For more information see Great California ShakeOut (2014).

Critical Thinking

How do the exercises managed by FEMA's National Exercise Program (NEP) differ from the Great California ShakeOut?

Conclusion

Mitigation, prevention, and preparedness programs are vital to the safety and security of the nation. Since the onset of civilization, people have worked to limit their vulnerability to hazards once they recognized that those hazards existed. Since the attacks of September 11, the focus of hazard mitigation in the United States shifted primarily to mitigation, prevention, and preparedness for terrorist attacks, but the real threat proved to be the traditional natural and man-made hazards that existed both before and after the attacks began. It is the responsibility of the government, which rests most clearly on the Department of Homeland Security, to protect the nation from the consequences of disastrous events. For that reason, it is vital that the all-hazards approach to mitigation, prevention, and preparedness be maintained.

Key Terms

All-Hazards Planning: The disaster planning and preparedness philosophy that advocates for holistic preparedness and flexible disaster planning to ensure the response can be improvised to deal with the many unknowns of any disaster situation. In one sense, it is the opposite of "scenario planning."

Avian Influenza: An infection typically seen in birds, although in rare cases human transmission has been observed. Among four strains of the virus known to be infectious for humans, H5N1 is the most dangerous one. Avian influenza is also called "bird flu" in daily use.

Bird Flu: Please refer to Avian Influenza.

Business Continuity Planning (BCP): The process of identification and remediation of commercial and organizational impacts of disasters through planning and strategy. Business continuity planning typically involves strategizing for the continuity and protection of the human resource, critical business processes, information systems, infrastructure, and organizational reputation.

Business Impact Analysis (BIA): The management-level analysis by which an organization assesses the quantitative (financial) and qualitative (nonfinancial) impacts, effects, and loss that might result if the organization were to suffer a business-interrupting event. Performing BIA as a preparedness measure is important because findings from the BIA are used to make decisions concerning business continuity management strategy.

Community Emergency Response Team (CERT): A community initiative of Citizen Corps to create disaster-resistant communities by training and disaster awareness. CERTs are composed of volunteers trained in basic disaster and medical response. As of 2008, there are more than 2800 CERT programs all over the United States.

Crisis Management: A proactive management effort to avoid crisis and the creation of strategy that minimizes adverse impacts of crisis to the organization when it could not be prevented. Effective crisis management requires a solid understanding of the organization, its strategy, liabilities, stakeholders, and legal framework combined with advanced communication, leadership, and decision-making skills to lead the organization through the crisis with minimizing potential loss.

Crisis: A critical turning point with impact to the future state of a given system. Although mostly signaling a deteriorating status of the system, if managed correctly, a crisis can be potentially beneficial. Example: increased customer confidence to a company that has managed to survive a major crisis in the industry provides competitive advantage.

Disaster Recovery Planning (DRP): The planning effort that primarily deals with the continuity and timely recovery of physical and logical components of information systems infrastructure and applications. The first goal in DRP is to ensure a redundant infrastructure that provides for continuity of information technology (IT) systems that support critical business processes. The second goal is to develop a prioritized recovery strategy for systems and applications based on their criticalities for the organization in case of an inevitable system failure or a catastrophic incident.

Epidemic: An infection that affects the public in a larger proportion than day-to-day diseases and infections to the degree that resources of national medical care systems are exhausted or significantly constrained. Epidemics also typically have impacts on the social and economic infrastructures.

Emergency Support Function (ESF): A specific area of expertise deemed critical for a successful disaster operation as identified by the federal disaster response framework. The Federal Response Plan (12 ESFs), the National Response Plan (15 ESFs), and the new National Response Framework (15 ESFs) each identify the various ESFs as appendixes. The ESFs in the National Response Framework are as follows: ESF #1, Transportation; ESF #2, Communications; ESF #3, Public Works and Engineering; ESF #4, Firefighting; ESF #5, Emergency Management; ESF #6, Mass Care, Emergency Assistance, Housing, and Human Services; ESF #7, Logistics Management and Resource Support; ESF #8, Public Health and Medical Services; ESF #9, Search and Rescue; ESF #10, Oil and Hazardous Materials Response; ESF #11, Agriculture and Natural Resources; ESF #12, Energy; ESF #13, Public Safety and Security; ESF #14, Long-Term Community Recovery; and ESF #15, External Affairs.

Federal Response Plan (FRP): A signed agreement among 27 federal departments and agencies, including the American Red Cross, that provided a mechanism for coordinating the delivery of federal assistance and resources to augment efforts of state and local governments overwhelmed by a major disaster or emergency, replaced by the National Response Plan.

Hazard: A potential source of danger or unsafe environment.

Influenza: A contagious infection of the respiratory tract. Common symptoms include fever, muscular pain, general tiredness, and chills. Symptoms are typically felt stronger than those caused by the common cold.

Man-Made Disaster: Sometimes also called *technological disaster*. Man-made disasters have two common elements: (1) They are not primarily induced by a naturally occurring process. (2) In most instances, the cause of the disaster is human error or failure of systems designed by humans. Examples of man-made disasters include oil spills, radiological incidents, chemical releases, and transportation disasters.

Mitigation: A sustained effort taken to reduce or eliminate risk to people and property from hazards and their effects.

Natural Disaster: A disaster that is primarily induced by the destructive power of nature. Examples of natural disasters include hurricane, earthquake, tsunami, and snowstorm.

National Planning Scenarios (NPS): Fifteen disaster scenarios, each corresponding to one particular natural, technological, or terrorist hazard threats, which together or individually allow for a standard against which plans, capabilities, and policies may be exercised and otherwise tested or measured.

National Response Framework (NRF): Presents the guiding principles that enable all response partners to prepare for and provide a unified national response to disasters and emergencies—from the smallest incident to the largest emergency catastrophe; defines key principles, roles, and structures that organize the way the nation responds; replaced the National Response Plan.

National Response Plan (NRP): A national-level plan that replaced the Federal Response Plan and was created in keeping with the National Incident Management System model to align federal coordination structures, capabilities, and resources into a unified, all-discipline, and all-hazards approach to domestic incident management.

Pandemic: An epidemic that impacts a large region or has global impacts.

Postdisaster Mitigation: Mitigation activities typically performed in the aftermath of a disaster either to provide a safer environment for the ongoing response or recovery effort or to mitigate potential impacts of the next disaster based on immediate lessons learned from a current one.

Predisaster Mitigation: Mitigation activities engaged prior to the occurrence of the disaster to minimize its impact when it occurs.

Preparedness: A state of readiness to respond to a disaster, crisis, or any other type of emergency situation.

Prevention: Actions taken to avoid an incident or to intervene in an effort to stop an incident from occurring for the purpose of protecting lives and property.

Risk: According to Stan Kaplan, risk is comprised of three components: scenario, probability of scenario, and consequence of scenario.

Tabletop Exercise: A mock disaster game in which participants playing different roles such as decision-maker, incident commander, or first responder typically gather around a table and discuss/decide their responses to the incident scenario presented by a moderator. The goal of a tabletop exercise is to simulate a disaster situation for the purposes of exposing the participant to the stressful decision-making conditions of a disaster. Tabletop exercises typically conclude with a debrief session where various parties discuss their respective roles, goals established, priorities, and challenges faced regarding the scenario played.

Terrorism: There are more than 100 definitions of terrorism in the literature. The United Nations defines terrorism as "an anxiety-inspiring method of repeated violent action, employed by (semi-) clandestine individual, group or state actors, for idiosyncratic, criminal or political reasons, whereby—in contrast to assassination—the direct targets of violence are not the main targets."

TOPOFF (abbreviation for "top officials"): TOPOFF is a congressionally mandated annual disaster preparedness and response exercise designed to improve the incident management/decision-making capability of the nation's top officials at every level of the government during an incident of national significance.

Review Questions

1. What are the initiatives that help local communities to mitigate/prepare against potential terrorist attacks? Why is community preparedness an important component of homeland security? Will FEMA's Whole Community concept work to help individuals and communities to be better prepared?
2. Discuss the content and potential benefits of the National Prevention Framework.
3. What mitigation/preparedness role does the private sector have in terms of homeland security? Do you believe that the private sector learned lessons from the 9/11 terrorist attacks?
4. What role do and/or should volunteer efforts such as the CNCS's FEMA Corps and the American Red Cross play in preparedness and mitigation activities?
5. Try to define terrorism mitigation using the common definition of mitigation in terms of the all-hazards approach. (Hint: Define risk as a combination of probability and consequence, and list all potential activities that can reduce both components of the potential terrorist event.)
6. Take a quick look at FEMA document, BIPS 06/FEMA 426: Reference Manual to Mitigate Potential Terrorist Attacks against Buildings (available at www.fema.gov). What are the two most important factors to minimize damage caused by car bombs to buildings?

References

American Red Cross, 2014a. Terrorism preparedness. http://www.redcross.org/prepare/disaster/terrorism.

American Red Cross, 2014b. Hurricane sandy response. http://www.redcross.org/support/donating-fundraising/where-your-money-goes/sandy-response.

American Society of Civil Engineers, 2007. Dam Safety Act signed by president. https://www.aawre.org/pressroom/news/grwk/event_release.cfm?uid53912.

Association of State Dam Safety Officials, 2005. What is the National Dam Safety & Security Program and why should it continue? http://www.damsafety.org/media/Documents/Legislative%20Handouts/NDSPA%20Handout.pdf.

Benvenuto, N., 2004. The relationship between business continuity and Sarbanes-Oxley. Protiviti KnowledgeLeader. http://www.protiviti.com/downloads/PRO/pro-us/articles/FeatureArticle_20040312.html.

Berman, A., 2004. Business continuity in a Sarbanes-Oxley world. Disaster Recovery Journal (Spring). http://www.drj.com/articles/spr04/1702-01.html.

Catalog of Federal Domestic Assistance, 2014. National Dam Safety Program. https://www.cfda.gov/index?s=program&mode=form&tab=core&id=ab7ea77994e6c0132e132c1aa73c26cf.

Centers for Disease Control and Prevention, 2005a. www.cdc.gov.

Centers for Disease Control and Prevention, 2005b. Biological and chemical terrorism: strategic plan for preparedness and response. http://emergency.cdc.gov/bioterrorism/prep.asp.

Centers for Disease Control and Prevention (CDC), 2014. Detailed Emergency Medical Services (EMS) checklist for ebola preparedness. http://www.cdc.gov/vhf/ebola/pdf/ems-checklist-ebola-preparedness.pdf.

Corporation for National Community Service, 2006. National service responds: the power of hope and help after Katrina. http://www.nationalservice.gov/pdf/katrina_report.pdf.

Corporation for National Community Service, 2007a. The power of help and hope after Katrina by the numbers: volunteers in the Gulf. http://www.nationalservice.gov/pdf/katrina_volunteers_respond.pdf.

Corporation for National Community Service, 2007b. A resource guide for the strategic initiatives. http://www.nationalservice.org/pdf/07_0913_resourceguide_strategicplan.pdf.

Corporation for National and Community Service (CNCS), 2014a. AmeriCorps. http://www.nationalservice.gov/programs/americorps.

Corporation for National and Community Service (CNCS), 2014b. AmeriCorps: FEMA Corps. http://www.nationalservice.gov/programs/americorps/americorps-nccc.

Corporation for National and Community Service (CNCS), 2014c. 6 Things to know about national service and Hurricane Sandy. http://www.nationalservice.gov/blogs/2013-10-29/6-things-know-about-national-service-and-hurricane-sandy.

CNCS, 2014d. http://www.nationalservice.gov/blogs/2013-10-25/fema-corps-first-year-shaped-sandy.

CNN, 2014. National exercise program fast facts. http://www.cnn.com/2013/10/30/us/operation-topoff-national-level-exercise-fast-facts/.

Committee on Homeland Security, 2014. U.S. House of Representatives. http://homeland.house.gov/hearing/hearingthe-boston-marathon-bombings-one-year-look-back-look-forward (April 9, 2014).

Cone, E., Gallagher, S., 2001. Cantor Fitzgerald—forty seven hours. www.baselinemag.com/print_article/0,3668,a517022,00.asp.

Congressional Research Service, 2007. Aging infrastructure: dam safety. www.fas.org/sgp/crs/homesec/RL33108.pdf.

Department of Homeland Security, 2004. National Response Plan Appendix ESF #6. Department of Homeland Security, Washington, DC. http://www.au.af.mil/au/awc/awcgate/nrp/esf06.pdf.

Department of Homeland Security, 2005. www.dhs.gov.

DHS, 2011a. http://www.dhs.gov/news/2011/04/20/secretary-napolitano-announces-implementation-national-terrorism-advisory-system.

DHS, 2011b. http://www.dhs.gov/xlibrary/assets/ntas/ntas-sample-alert.pdf.

Department of Homeland Security, 2013. National Prevention Framework. https://www.fema.gov/media-library/assets/documents/32196?id=7358 (May 2013).

Department of Homeland Security, 2014a. FY 2015 budget in brief. file:///Users/george_haddow/ihs5%20FY15-Budget%20in%20brief.pdf, http://www.dhs.gov/sites/default/files/publications/ntas-sample-alert.pdf.

Department of Homeland Security, 2014b. The 2014 Quadrennial Homeland Security Review. http://www.dhs.gov/sites/default/files/publications/qhsr/strengthening-the-execution-of-our-missions-through-public-private-partnerships.pdf.

DHS, 2014c. NTAS Guide: National Terrorism Advisory System Public Guide. http://www.dhs.gov/ntas-public-guide.

DHS, 2014d. http://www.dhs.gov/ntas-frequently-asked-questions.

Emergency Management Australia, 2000. Emergency Risk Management: Applications Guide. Emergency Management Australia, Sydney.

Federal Emergency Management Agency, 2005a. www.fema.gov.

Federal Emergency Management Agency, 2005b. National Flood Insurance Program.

Federal Emergency Management Agency, 2007a. Draft National Incident Management System. http://www.fema.gov/emergency/nims/.

Federal Emergency Management Agency, 2007b. Plan ahead for an earthquake. http://www.fema.gov/plan/prevent/earthquake/index.shtm.

Federal Emergency Management Agency, 2011a. Building and Infrastructure Protection Series (BIPS 06) Federal Emergency Management Agency (FEMA 426): Reference Manual to Mitigate Potential Terrorist Attacks against Buildings: Edition 2. http://www.dhs.gov/bips-06fema-426-reference-manual-mitigate-potential-terrorist-attacks-against-buildings-2nd-edition (October 2011).

FEMA, 2011b. FEMA mitigation best practices portfolio. http://www.fema.gov/mitigationbp/brief.do?mitssId=8410.

FEMA, 2011c. FEMA mitigation best practices portfolio. http://www.fema.gov/mitigationbp/bestPracticeDetail.do?mitssId=8390.

Federal Emergency Management Agency, 2013. Hazard Mitigation Assistance Unified Guidance: Hazard Mitigation Grant Program, Pre-Disaster Mitigation Program, and Flood Mitigation Assistance Program. http://www.fema.gov/media-library-data/15463cb34a2267a900bde4774c3f42e4/FINAL_Guidance:081213_508.pdf (July 12, 2103).

Federal Emergency Management Agency, 2014a. Written testimony of FEMA Administrator Craig Fugate for a Senate Committee on Homeland Security and Governmental Affairs, Subcommittee on Emergency Management, Intergovernmental Relations, and the District of Columbia hearing on FEMA's FY 2015 Budget Request. http://www.dhs.gov/news/2014/03/13/written-testimony-fema-administrator-senate-homeland-security-and-governmental (March 13, 2014).

Federal Emergency Management Agency, 2014b. Overview of the National Planning Frameworks. http://www.fema.gov/media-library/assets/documents/97352 (July 2014).

Federal Emergency Management Agency, 2014c. National Exercise Program (NEP) – Capstone Exercise 2014. https://www.fema.gov/national-exercise-program-nep-capstone-exercise-2014.

Federal Emergency Management Agency, 2014d. Federal Insurance and Mitigation Administration (FIMA). https://www.fema.gov/what-mitigation/federal-insurance-mitigation-administration.

Federal Emergency Management Agency, 2014e. Hazard mitigation grant program. https://www.fema.gov/hazard-mitigation-grant-program.

Federal Emergency Management Agency, 2014f. Louisiana's post-katrina recovery individuals & families. https://www.fema.gov/louisianas-post-katrina-recovery-individuals-families.

Federal Emergency Management Agency, 2014g. Sandy Recovery Office. https://www.fema.gov/sandy-recovery-office (October 6, 2014).

Federal Emergency Management Agency, 2014h. Flood Mitigation Assistance (FMA) Program. https://www.fema.gov/flood-mitigation-assistance-program.

Federal Emergency Management Agency, 2014i. Whole community. https://www.fema.gov/whole-community.

Federal Emergency Management Agency, 2014j. Losses paid (calendar/historical). https://www.fema.gov/statistics-calendar-year/number-losses-paid-calendar-year.

Federal Emergency Management Agency, 2014k. Total policies in force by calendar year. https://www.fema.gov/statistics-calendar-year/total-policies-force-calendar-year.

Fire Corps, 2008. Fire Corps National Advisory Committee Meets. http://firecorps.org/page/630/show_item/172/News.htm.

Government Accountability Office, 2006. Hurricanes Katrina and Rita: coordination between Federal Emergency Management Agency and the Red Cross should be improved for the 2006 hurricane season. http://www.gao.gov/new.items/d06712.pdf.

Great California ShakeOut, 2014. http://www.shakeout.org/california/index.html.

Kaplan, S., 1997. The words of risk analysis. Risk Analysis 17 (4), 408–409.

Kayyem, N.J., Chang, E.P., 2002. Beyond Business Continuity: The Role of the Private Sector in Preparedness

Planning. Belfer Center for Science and International Affairs, John F. Kennedy School of Government, Harvard University, Cambridge, MA.

National Commission on Terrorist Attacks upon the United States (9/11 Commission), 2004. What to Do? A Global Strategy. 9/11 Commission, Washington, DC (Chapter 12).

NEHRP, 2014. Agencies. http://www.nehrp.gov/about/agencies.htm.

Nuclear Regulatory Commission, 2014. Emergency preparedness and response. http://www.nrc.gov/about-nrc/emerg-preparedness/protect-public.html.

Partnership for Public Warning, 2003. A national Strategy for Integrated Public Warning Policy and Capability. http://www.google.com/search?client=safari&rls=en&q=partnership+for+public+warning+2003&ie=UTF-8&oe=UTF-8

Public Broadcasting Service, 2005. American Red Cross troubles. http://www.pbs.org/newshour/bb/health/july-dec05/redcross_12-14.html (December 14).

Public Safety Canada, 2008. Is your family prepared? http://www.emergencypreparednessweek.ca.

Reuters, 2007. WHO confirms human-to-human bird-flu case. http://www.reuters.com/article/scienceNews/idUSL2732429220071227 (December 27).

Smith, J.D., 2002. Business Continuity Management: Good Practice Guidelines. Business Continuity Institute, United Kingdom.

U.S. Department of Health and Human Services, 2007. Pandemic preparedness planning for US businesses with overseas operations. http://www.pandemicflu.gov/plan/workplaceplanning/businessesoverseaspdf.pdf.

U.S. Department of Health and Human Services, 2008. General information on pandemic and avian flu. http://www.pandemicflu.gov/general/index.html.

United Nations Development Programme, 1994. Vulnerability and Risk Assessment, second ed. Cambridge Architectural Research Limited, Cambridge.

Washington Post, 2005. Fraud alleged at Red Cross call centers. http://www.washingtonpost.com/wp-dyn/content/article/2005/12/26/AR2005122600654.html (December 27).

White House, 2005. National strategy for pandemic influenza. http://www.whitehouse.gov/homeland/nspi.pdf.

WikiBirdFlu.org., 2007. Relationship between bird flu and SARS. http://www.wikibirdflu.org/page/Relationship1between1Bird1Flu1and1SARS?t5anon.

Williams, B., 2005. Sarbanes-Oxley: another driver for business continuity management. http://www.disaster-resource.com/articles/03p_029.shtml.

World Health Organization, 2003. SARS. http://www.wpro.who.int/health_topics/sars/.

World Health Organization, 2005. WHO checklist for influenza pandemic preparedness planning. http://www.who.int/entity/csr/resources/publications/influenza/FluCheck6web.pdf.

World Health Organization, 2008. Cumulative number of confirmed human cases of avian influenza A/(H5N1) reported to WHO. http://www.who.int/csr/disease/avian_influenza/country/cases_table_2008_01_11/en/index.html.

11 Communications

What You Will Learn

- The mission and assumptions that serve as the basis of crisis communications
- How reporting the news by traditional media outlets has changed
- The growing role of social media and first informers in crisis communications
- How to build an effective disaster communications strategy
- How to communicate in the era of homeland security
- The role of social media in the Boston Marathon bombings

Communications is now universally accepted as a critical function in emergency management and homeland security. The dissemination of timely and accurate information to the general public, elected and community officials, and the media plays a major role in the effective management of disaster response and recovery activities. Communicating preparedness and mitigation information promotes actions that reduce the risk of future disasters. Communicating policies, goals, and priorities to staff, partners, and participants enhances support and promotes a more efficient disaster management operation. In communicating with the public, establishing a partnership with the media and actively participating in social media are key to implementing a successful strategy.

Communicating with the Public

FEMA's success in fulfilling its mission is highly dependent upon our ability to communicate with the individuals, families and communities we serve.

Shayne Adamski, Senior Manager of Digital Engagement, FEMA.

Source: Adamski (2013a).

Information sharing and its corollaries—collaboration and coordination—are key to effective, sustainable, timely, and participatory postdisaster recovery. "Unimpeded communication and the free flow of information are cornerstones of any post-disaster relief framework…" (Gillmor, 2006).

FIGURE 11-1 Forest Hills, NY, January 9, 2013—FEMA Federal Coordinating Officer Michael Byrne answers Hurricane Sandy disaster questions using Twitter at the Joint Field Office in Forest Hills, New York. *Source: Andrea Booher/FEMA.*

When that coordination doesn't occur, it hinders response and recovery efforts. "...[O]ne of the central facts documented in the aftermath of Katrina: the importance of maintaining a timely and accurate flow of information in a disaster zone. When information was neither timely nor accurate, people suffered" (May, 2006).

Communication failures by government responders in Hurricane Katrina were noted in the report prepared by the United States House of Representatives that stated, "The lack of a government public communications strategy and media hype of violence exacerbated public concerns and further delayed relief." The House report also asked, "Why coordination and information sharing between local, state, and federal governments was so dismal.... Why situational awareness was so foggy, for so long.... Why unsubstantiated rumors and uncritically repeated press reports—at times fueled by top officials—were able to delay, disrupt, and diminish the response" (Select Bipartisan Committee to Investigate the Preparation for and Response to Hurricane Katrina, 2006).

Many of these issues appear to have been addressed since 2005. FEMA, state and local emergency management agencies, and the voluntary agencies across the country have begun to recognize the importance of social media in their disaster communications. FEMA and the American Red Cross have invested heavily in social media, and state and local emergency management agencies are starting to catch up. See sidebars highlighting Representative Susan Brooks' comments on communications in Hurricane Sandy and the 2013 Boston Marathon bombings (Figure 11-1).

Emergency MGMT 2.0: How #SocialMedia & New Tech Are Transforming Preparedness, Response, and Recovery #Disasters #Part2 #Govt/NGOs

Statement of Susan Brooks (R-IN), Chairman of the Subcommittee on Emergency Preparedness, Response, and Communications, July 9, 2013

There is no doubt that social media and new technologies are playing an increasing role in the way we prepare for, respond to, and recover from disasters. As we have seen through recent events, such as

Hurricane Sandy and the Boston bombings, individuals and organizations, more than ever, are turning to social media and the Internet to obtain public safety information, to connect with friends and family, and to request assistance from emergency response organizations. In fact, in a 2012 survey conducted by the Red Cross, 70% of respondents suggested that emergency response agencies should regularly monitor their social media sites so they can promptly respond to any requests for help. In addition, an Infographic created by the University of San Francisco showed that during a disaster, one out of three citizens expects help to arrive within 60 min of posting a request on social media.[1]

Social media also enables response organizations to quickly push information to the public—something that has not been possible on such a wide scale until recently. A great example of this was after the Boston bombings when the first official announcement that Dzhokhar Tsarnaev had been captured came not at a traditional press conference, but through a tweet by the Boston Police Department. Also, during the search for the Tsarnaev brothers, individual citizens were able to tweet and post videos, photos, and other information to law enforcement officials, which served as a "force multiplier" and assisted in the hunt.

We have also seen similar examples in which response officials have leveraged information from social media to enhance response efforts during recent natural disasters, such as 2013 Hurricane Sandy and the 2012 Oklahoma tornadoes.

Two of the most prominent emergency management organizations are with us today, the American Red Cross and the Federal Emergency Management Agency. Earlier this year, I had the opportunity to visit both of their headquarters to learn more about their roles in preparing for, responding to, and recovering from disasters. I was impressed to see how they have incorporated twenty-first-century technology into their operations.

During my visit to the Red Cross, I learned how they partnered with Dell to develop a Digital Operations Center, which is the first social-media monitoring platform dedicated to humanitarian relief.[2] This center allows the Red Cross to crowdsource information from affected areas during a disaster; spot trends and better anticipate the public's needs; and connect people with the resources they need, such as food, water, shelter, or even emotional support.

In conjunction with the Digital Operations Center, the Red Cross has also developed a Digital Volunteer Program, which trains digital volunteers from across the country in how to use online applications to respond to questions from the public, distribute critical public safety information, and provide comfort and reassurance during emergencies.

During Hurricane Sandy, the digital volunteers played a critical role in enabling the Red Cross to actively monitor and verify social media posts around the clock and provide information to create situational awareness.

FEMA's Administrator, Craig Fugate, has been a big supporter of social media as well, and FEMA has been an active user of Facebook and Twitter to communicate with the public. I've also heard that FEMA is engaging with private sector companies, including Google[3] and Twitter.[4] to determine how best to take advantage of open data, social media, and two-way interaction to enhance their emergency management capabilities.

---

[1] *University of San Francisco Website:* http://onlinempa.usfca.edu/social-media/ (accessed on June 20, 2013).

[2] *American Red Cross Website:* http://www.redcross.org/news/press-release/The-American-Red-Cross-and-Dell-Launch-First-Of-Its-Kind-Social-Media-Digital-Operations-Center-for-Humanitarian-Relief (accessed on June 20, 2013).

[3] *FEMA Website:* http://www.fema.gov/medialibrary/media_records/1081 (accessed on June 21, 2013).

[4] *FEMA Website:* http://www.fema.gov/medialibrary/media_records/3581 (accessed on June 21, 2013).

We are also seeing a rise in the use of social media by state and local emergency management organizations. In a recent survey conducted by the National Emergency Management Association and CNA on the use of social media in the emergency management field, the majority of state, county, and local agencies reported using social media in their disaster preparedness and response efforts, but to varying degrees.

I think a good example of the use of social media at the local level is how the cities of Moore and Oklahoma City used their Twitter accounts during the devastating tornadoes last month. Both cities used Twitter to relay real-time updates on open shelters, road closures, lost and found pets, and personal items. They also actively monitored their accounts and responded to requests for assistance posted by disaster survivors.

In my home state of Indiana, MESH Coalition, a public health, non-profit, public-private partnership is using social media for, what they call, "infodemiology." They have dedicated staff monitoring social media as a disease surveillance tool and push information to hospitals and public health departments through Twitter. I had the opportunity to see this operation first hand last week. I am hopeful that this innovative use of social media and new technology will be replicated beyond the Hoosier state.

While I have highlighted some positive developments in the use of social media and new technology, I do realize that there are some challenges as well. For example, we must be mindful of how misleading, faulty, or malicious information or pictures can escalate quickly on social media sites and potentially negatively affect response efforts. In addition, as we learned from our private sector partners in the last hearing, there is a need to establish common standards and procedures to help make the sharing of data more efficient. Our private sector witnesses also agreed that there could be more done in the way of public/private sector partnerships to help maximize the use of social media for disaster purposes, and to leverage big data so response and recovery efforts can be focused on those areas most in need.

Source: Brooks (2013).

Boston Marathon Bombings: Testimony of Herman B. "Dutch" Leonard and Eliot I. Snider

On April 9, 2014 Harvard University Professors Herman B. "Dutch" Leonard and Eliot I. Snider testified before the US House of Representatives Committee on Homeland Security in a hearing on "The Boston Marathon Bombing, One Year On: A Look Back and to Look Forward." They testified about the results of the research they had conducted "to understand the sources of the strengths and weaknesses of the response to the marathon bombing." The excerpt from their testimony presented below focuses on recommendations concerning how to improve public communications by public officials in future response efforts.

Public Communication

- *Maintaining regular and open communication with the public—through traditional and social media—should be a high priority for senior officials, even when confidential investigations are ongoing*. When accurate, frequent, official communications were absent, news and social media filled the gap, sometimes with speculation and misinformation. Development of protocols for crisis communication, incorporating utilization of social media, should be part of the planning for fixed events. This should include improving practices for dispelling widely disseminated, inaccurate information or rumors.

- *Systems for coordinating and communicating information to families of individuals missing or injured in a crisis need to be improved*, perhaps including revision of HIPAA rules governing the release of personal information about patients receiving care during public safety emergencies.

Herman B. "Dutch" Leonard is the George F. Baker, Jr., professor of Public Management and faculty codirector of the Program on Crisis Leadership at the John F. Kennedy School of Government. At Harvard University, he is the Eliot I. Snider and Family professor of Business Administration and faculty cochair of the Social Enterprise Initiative at Harvard Business School.

Source: Committee on Homeland Security (2014).

Critical Thinking

Why is it critical that emergency and homeland security officials provide timely and accurate information to the public before, during, and after a natural man-made or terrorist incident?

This section defines the mission of an effective disaster communications strategy and outlines five critical assumptions that serve as the foundation for such a strategy. Examples of effective communications in disaster events and promoting disaster reduction efforts are included in this chapter; examples of ineffective communications and the effect these failures had on disaster response operations are also included.

Crisis Communications

Mission

The mission of an effective disaster communications strategy is to provide timely and accurate information to the public in all four phases of emergency management:

- *Mitigation*—to promote implementation of strategies, technologies, and actions that will reduce the loss of lives and property in future disasters
- *Preparedness*—to communicate preparedness messages that encourage and educate the public in anticipation of disaster events
- *Response*—to provide to the public notification, warning, evacuation, and situation reports on an ongoing disaster
- *Recovery*—to provide individuals and communities affected by a disaster with information on how to register for and receive disaster relief

Assumptions

The foundation of an effective disaster communications strategy is built on the following five critical assumptions:

- Customer focus
- Leadership commitment
- Inclusion of communications in planning and operations
- Situational awareness
- Media partnership

Five Critical Assumptions for a Successful Communications Strategy

1. *Customer focus*: Understand what information your customers and your partners need, and build communication mechanisms that deliver this information in a timely and accurate fashion.
2. *Leadership commitment*: The leader of the emergency operations must be committed to effective communications and must participate fully in the communications process.
3. *Inclusion of communications in planning and operations*: Communications specialists must be involved in all emergency planning and operations to ensure that communicating timely and accurate information is considered when action decisions are being considered.
4. *Situational awareness*: Effective communication is based on the timely collection, analysis, and dissemination of information from the disaster area in accordance with basic principles of effective communications, such as transparency and truthfulness.
5. *Media partnership*—Traditional media outlets (i.e., television, radio, the Internet, and newspapers) and social media outlets (i.e., Facebook, YouTube, and Twitter) are the most effective means for communicating timely and accurate information to the largest number of people. A partnership with the media involves understanding the needs of the media and employing trained staff who work directly with the media to get information to the public. Both traditional media and social media may also serve as information sources for emergency managers especially during the response and recovery phases.

Customer Focus

An essential element of any effective emergency management system is a focus on customers and customer service. This philosophy should guide communications with the public and with all partners in emergency management. A customer service approach includes placing the needs and interests of individuals and communities first, being responsive and informative, and managing expectations.

Customer Service and Emergency Management

We in the emergency management profession are about people and their capability to prepare for, respond to, recover from, and mitigate the damages these types of events produce. Our job, like all in a public service capacity, is one of customer service with our customers at the local level of government.

Albert Ashwood, Chairman, NEMA Legislative Committee Director, Oklahoma Department of Emergency Management.

Source: Ashwood (2013).

The customers for emergency management are diverse. They include internal customers, such as staff, other federal agencies, states, and other disaster partners. External customers include the general public, elected officials at all levels of government, community and business leaders, and the media. Each of these customers has special needs, and a good communications strategy considers and reflects their requirements.

Leadership Commitment

Recent examples of leadership commitment to effective disaster communications include the efforts of New York City Mayor Michael Bloomberg, New York State Governor Andrew Cuomo, and New Jersey Governor Chris Christie in Hurricane Sandy in 2012. All three public officials were very visible before, during, and after Sandy made landfall delivering regular updates and briefings for the media and the public. The staffs of all three officials made extensive use of social media to get information to the public during Sandy (Figure 11-2).

Good communication starts with a commitment by the leadership of the emergency management organization to sharing and disseminating information both internally and externally. One of the lessons learned from Hurricane Katrina according to a report authored by Donald F. Kettl of the Fels Institute of Government at the University of Pennsylvania in the report entitled *The Worst is Yet to Come: Lessons from September 11 and Hurricane Katrina* is "We need public officials to lead. Communicating confidence to citizens and delivering on promises are both critical in crises" (Kettl, 2005).

The leader of any disaster response and recovery effort must openly endorse and promote open lines of communications among the organization's staff, partners, and public in order to effectively communicate. This leader must model this behavior in order to clearly illustrate that communications is a valued function of the organization (see Figure 11-3).

FIGURE 11-2 Tuscaloosa, AL, April 28, 2011—At a press conference in Tuscaloosa, Administrator Craig Fugate praised the first responders, nonprofit and faith-based organizations, and members of the general public for their courage, their quick response, and tireless efforts to save lives and help the disaster survivors. *Source: Bradley Carroll/FEMA.*

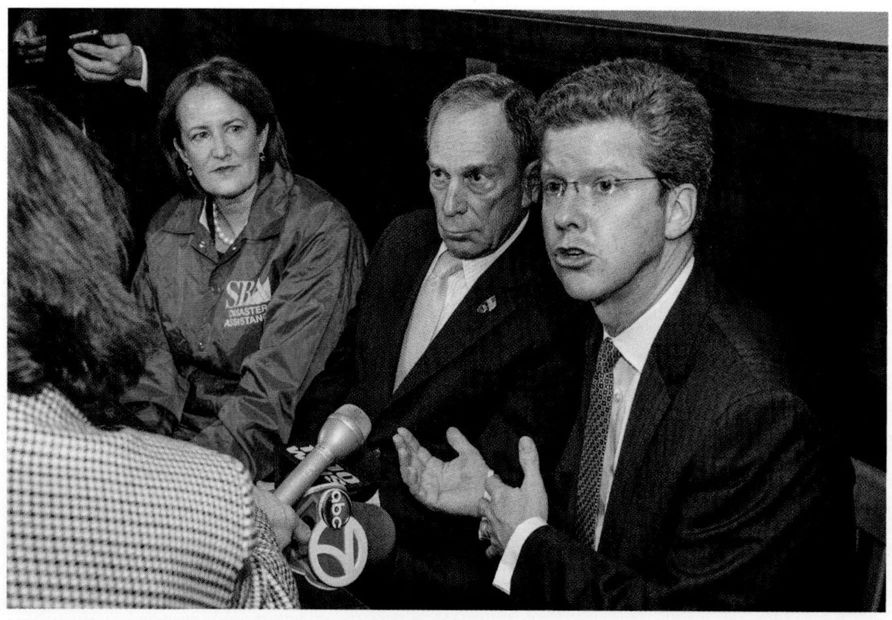

FIGURE 11-3 Staten Island, NY, February 6, 2013—Small Business Administration (SBA) Administrator Karen G. Mills, New York City Mayor Michael Bloomberg, and Secretary of Housing and Urban Development (HUD) Shaun Donovan met at Goodfella's Pizzeria in Dongan Hills, to announce the release of additional funding to aid homeowners and small business owners in their recovery efforts. Goodfella's was able to reopen quickly with the help a loan from the SBA. *Source: K.C. Wilsey/FEMA.*

In addition, FEMA Administrator Craig Fugate was involved in countless briefings, news conferences, and media interviews getting information to the public through the media concerning how to prepare for, respond to, and recover from Sandy. FEMA and other federal agencies involved in the federal response and recovery effort posted blogs on the FEMA Web site, photos and videos on YouTube, and daily messages on FEMA's Twitter account and Facebook page.

Five Things to Learn from Bloomberg About Crisis Communications

Writer Scott Eblin observed New York City's Mayor Bloomberg in the days before, during, and after Hurricane Sandy, and described several lessons he learned from the way Bloomberg handled the crisis.

Project Quiet Confidence: As I've written here before (long before Hurricane Sandy), leaders create the weather; not literally obviously, but leaders influence the response of others by how they show up. In all of his briefings, Bloomberg showed up prepared, appropriately concerned and quietly confident that his extended team and his citizens would respond to the storm in the most effective way possible. His quiet confidence likely gave confidence to others in a challenging situation.

Be Consistent and Frequent: I don't know the exact schedule that Bloomberg has had for his pressers but it looks like he was up for 20–30 min in the morning and afternoon each day before, during and after Sandy. Establishing an operating rhythm for his communications enabled him to get his team's messages out consistently. Keeping people informed helps keep them calm.

Be Relevant: Bloomberg and his staff have done a masterful job of talking about the things that matter most to people. He's kept his remarks relevant by providing information on preparation plans, evacuations, when the power will be back on, transportation updates and even the plans for Halloween post-Sandy.

Make Specific Requests: In a crisis, most people want to know what they can do to help or at least stay safe. (Then there are those who ignore all the requests at the peril of themselves and others.) Bloomberg has been very clear in asking people to do things that help themselves and the community—evacuate low lying areas, stay out of public parks until damaged trees are cleared, only use 911 for life threatening emergencies. Most people will honor specific, common sense requests. Leaders communicating in a crisis need to make them.

Put the Team Front and Center: In every press conference I saw, Bloomberg had the leaders of the relevant city agencies lined up behind him. They were there to answer questions but also to demonstrate that there was a unified effort to address the challenges at hand. Bloomberg went out of his way to recognize specific leaders and their agencies for the work they were doing. In a crisis, people want to know that qualified people have their backs. Bloomberg made sure that New Yorkers knew that.

Source: Eblin (2012).

Inclusion of Communications in Planning and Operations

The most important part of leadership's commitment to communications is the inclusion of communications in all planning and operations. This means that a communications specialist is included in the senior management team of any emergency management organization and operation. It means that communication issues are considered in the decision-making processes and that a communications element is included in all organizational activities, plans, and operations.

In the past, communicating with external audiences, or customers, and in many cases internal customers was not valued or considered critical to a successful emergency management operation. Technology has changed that equation. In today's world of 24-h television and radio news, the Internet, and social media, the demand for information is never-ending, especially in an emergency response situation. Emergency managers must be able to communicate critical information in a timely manner to their staff, partners, the public, and traditional and social media.

To do so, the information needs of the various customers and how best to communicate with these customers must be considered at the same time that planning and operational decisions are being made. For example, a decision process on how to remove debris from a disaster area must include the discussion of how to communicate information on the debris removal operation to community officials, the public, and the media.

Critical Thinking

Why is the director of an emergency management/homeland security organization so important to a successful crisis communications capability? What is this person's contribution(s) to keeping the public informed?

Situational Awareness

Situational awareness is key to an effective disaster response. Knowing the number of people killed and injured, the level of damage at the disaster site, the condition of homes and community infrastructure, and current response efforts provides decision makers with the situational awareness necessary to identify needs and appropriately apply available resources. The collection, analysis, and dissemination of information from the disaster site are the basis for an effective communications operation in a disaster response. This is also true during the disaster recovery phase, especially early in the recovery phase when the demand for information from the public, and therefore the media, is at its highest. Developing effective communication strategies to promote community preparedness and/or mitigation programs requires detailed information about the nature of the risks that impact the community and how the planned preparedness programs will help individuals and communities to be ready for the next disaster and the mitigation programs will reduce the impacts of future disasters.

Sharing this information is all-important and this will require creating a culture among emergency officials where information sharing is valued. Past research found that information available to citizens at times of crises—man-made or natural—is often inadequate, biased, incorrect, or late. "Studies show that the problem lies not with the technologies (or lack thereof) but with the culture of information sharing. The access, dissemination, and archiving of information is often controlled by government agencies, institutions who have a parochial interest in controlling its flow—what gets out where, to whom, how, and when" (Gillmor, 2006).

A glaring lack of situational awareness was identified as a severe hindrance to the government response to Hurricane Katrina. The US Senate report on the Hurricane Katrina response listed the following findings regarding situational awareness:

- The HSOC failed to take timely steps to create a system to identify and acquire all available, relevant information.
- The HSOC failed in its responsibility under the National Response Plan (NRP) to provide "general situational awareness" and a "common operational picture," particularly concerning the failure of the levees, the flooding of New Orleans, and the crowds at the Ernest N. Morial Convention Center.
- On the day of landfall (Monday), senior DHS officials received numerous reports that should have led to an understanding of the increasingly dire situation in New Orleans, yet they were not aware of the crisis until Tuesday morning.
- Louisiana was not equipped to process the volume of information received by its emergency operations center after landfall.
- Lack of situational awareness regarding the status of deliveries created difficulties in managing the provision of needed commodities in Louisiana and Mississippi (Senate Committee on Homeland Security and Governmental Affairs, 2006).

Critical Thinking

What are the many sources of information that can help emergency managers and homeland security officials build and maintain situational awareness? Consider both government, nongovernmental, media, and social media sources.

Public Information in the National Incident Management System (NIMS)

Public Information consists of the processes, procedures, and systems to communicate timely, accurate, and accessible information on the incident's cause, size, and current situation to the public, responders, and additional stakeholders (both directly affected and indirectly affected). Public information must be coordinated and integrated across jurisdictions, agencies, and organizations; among Federal, State, tribal, and local governments; and with NGOs and the private sector. Well-developed public information, education strategies, and communications plans help to ensure that lifesaving measures, evacuation routes, threat and alert systems, and other public safety information are coordinated and communicated to numerous audiences in a timely, consistent manner.

Source: FEMA (2008).

According to the most recent version of National Incident Management System (NIMS) document, "The PIO gathers, verifies, coordinates and disseminates accurate, accessible, and timely information on the incident's cause, size, and current situation; resources committed; and other matters of general interest for both internal and external use" (FEMA, 2008) (see Figure 11-4).

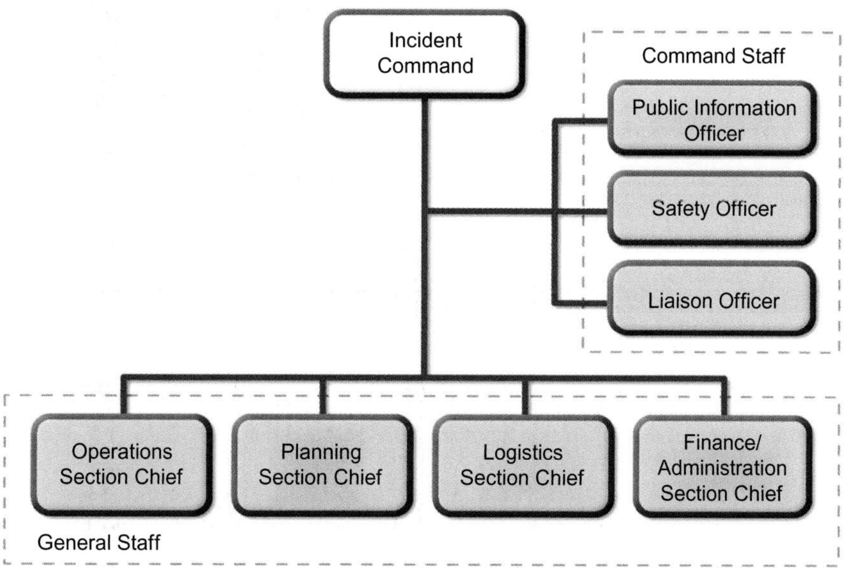

FIGURE 11-4 NIMS Command Staff Structure.

The duties of the PIO are defined as follows.

The public information officer supports the incident command structure as a member of the command staff. The public information officer advises the IC/UC on all public information matters relating to the management of the incident. The public information officer also handles inquiries from the media, the public, and elected officials; emergency public information and warnings; rumor monitoring and response; media relations; and other functions required to gather, verify, coordinate, and disseminate accurate, accessible, and timely information related to the incident. Information on public health, safety, and protection is of particular importance (see Figure 11-5). Public information officers are able to create coordinated and consistent messages by collaborating to the following:

- Identify key information that needs to be communicated to the public.
- Craft messages conveying key information that are clear and easily understood by all, including those with special needs.
- Prioritize messages to ensure timely delivery of information without overwhelming the audience.
- Verify accuracy of information through appropriate channels.
- Disseminate messages using the most effective means available (FEMA, 2008).

During a disaster response, an effective information management system involves three critical elements:

1. *Collection of information at the disaster site*: This effort may involve numerous groups including local first responders (police, fire, and emergency medical technicians), local and state emergency management staff, federal damage assessment teams, the local Red Cross chapter and other voluntary organizations on the ground, community leaders, and individuals. Increasingly, the public

FIGURE 11-5 Oceanport, NJ, November 9, 2012—Mark Strassmann of CBS Evening News interviews FEMA spokesperson Gene Romano at the Oceanport Camp where utility workers and some survivors of Hurricane Sandy are staying. *Photo by Liz Roll/FEMA.*

has been using online tools to share directly or through the traditional media information and images from the front lines, and information from "first informers" needs to be acknowledged and included.

2. *Analysis of information*: This effort is undertaken to identify immediate response support needs and early recovery phase needs and is used by decision makers to match available resources to these identified needs.
3. *Dissemination of information*: This involves sharing of this information internally with all stakeholders in a timely fashion and externally with the media and through the media with the public.

In the Incident Command System (ICS) as defined by FEMA, the Planning Section "is responsible for collecting, evaluating, and disseminating operational information pertaining to the incident. This Section maintains information and intelligence on the current and forecasted situation, as well as the status of resources assigned to the incident. The Planning Section prepares and documents Incident Action Plans and incident maps, and gathers and disseminates information and intelligence critical to the incident. The Planning Section has four primary Units and may also include technical specialists to assist in evaluating the situation and forecasting requirements for additional personnel and equipment" (FEMA, 2008).

Media Partnership

The media, both traditional media (TV, radio, and print) and social media (Facebook, YouTube, Twitter, etc.), plays a primary role in communicating with the public. No government emergency management organization could ever hope to develop a communications network comparable to those networks already established and maintained by television, radio, and newspapers. To effectively provide timely disaster information to the public, emergency managers must establish a partnership with their local media outlets.

The emergence of social media in recent years has provided emergency managers with a whole new set of opportunities and partners. Social media allows emergency managers to engage in a conversation with the individuals they serve that is ongoing before, during, and after a disaster event. Social media also presents a new source of real-time data and information from the field to emergency managers. Much of the rest of this book discusses how social media has changed disaster communications and its implications for the future of disaster communications.

In a June 7, 2013, post of the Scientific American Web site entitled "How Social Media Is Changing Disaster Response," author Dina Fine Maron noted, "When Hurricane Katrina ravaged the U.S. Gulf Coast in 2005, Facebook was the new kid on the block. There was no Twitter for news updates, and the iPhone was not yet on the scene. By the time Hurricane Sandy slammed the eastern seaboard last year, social media had become an integral part of disaster response, filling the void in areas where cell phone service was lost while millions of Americans looked to resources including Twitter and Facebook to keep informed, locate loved ones, notify authorities and express support. Gone are the days of one-way communication where only official sources provide bulletins on disaster news" (Maron, 2013).

The goal of a media partnership is to provide accurate and timely information to the public in both disaster and nondisaster situations. The partnership requires a commitment by both the emergency manager and the media to work together, and it requires a level of trust between both parties (see Figure 11-5).

Traditionally, the relationship between emergency managers and the media was strained at best. There was often a conflict between the need of the emergency manager to respond quickly and the need of the media to obtain information on the response so it can report it just as quickly. This conflict sometimes results in inaccurate reporting and tension between the emergency manager and the media. The loser in this conflict is always the public, which relies on the media for its information.

It is important for emergency managers to understand the needs of the media and the value they bring to facilitating response operations. An effective media partnership provides the emergency manager with a communications network to reach the public with vital information. Such a partnership provides the media with access to the disaster site, access to emergency managers and their staff, and access to critical information for the public that informs and ensures the accuracy of their reporting.

An effective media partnership helps define the roles of the emergency management organizations to manage public expectations and to boost the morale of the relief workers and the disaster victims. All these factors can speed the recovery of a community from a disaster event and promote preparedness and mitigation efforts designed to reduce the loss of life and property from the next disaster event.

Critical Thinking

Why would a traditional media outlet (e.g., television network, radio station newspaper, and magazine) enter into a media partnership with a government emergency management/homeland security agency?

The Power and Promise of Social Media in Emergency Management

Congressional Testimony by Shayne Adamski, Senior Manager of Digital Engagement, FEMA

FEMA's approach to emergency management recognizes that individuals, families and communities are our greatest assets and the keys to our success. In order to fulfill our mission, we must work together as one team—this notion is at the heart of our whole community approach to emergency management.

Social media is imperative to emergency management because the public uses these communication tools regularly. Rather than trying to convince the public to adjust to the way we at FEMA traditionally communicated, we have adapted to the way the public communicates, leveraging the tools they use on a daily basis. Millions of Americans use social media every day to check in on friends and family, learn about current events, and share their experiences. FEMA uses social media to be part of this ongoing dialogue and meet people where they are, using tools and platforms they are already familiar with.

FEMA also uses social media and other digital methods to communicate because as we have seen, information can lead to action. Our goal is for our safety-related information to have a real-world impact—to inspire actions that lead to more resilient families and communities. If someone sees a preparedness or safety tip from FEMA, the goal is that it will inspire them to prepare or empower them to tell a friend how to be more prepared or where to find help.

Finally, social media and technology allow us to reach more people more quickly during disasters, when they need accurate, timely and, authoritative information that helps ensure the protection of their life or livelihood. With one click of the mouse, or one swipe on their smartphone's screen, a message is capable of being spread to thousands of people and have a tangible impact.

Source: Adamski (2013a).

Finally, it is important to understand that social media is not be all and end all for communicating with the public. FEMA's senior manager of Digital Engagement Shayne Adamski noted in a recent interview, "Social media is but one of many tools that we use at FEMA to disseminate preparedness messages to the public before a disaster strikes, and we deliver timely and accurate information to the public in the immediate aftermath of a disaster event and the recovery period that follows" (Adamski, 2013b).

A November 12, 2012, post on the "Mindjet" Web site by Pete Hunt noted, "Three key media lessons emerged in the storm's wake: (1) Social media is invaluable, but its limitations are significant. Twitter is useless when your phone is out of batteries. (2) Radio and other traditional news outlets still have an important role to play in emergency broadcasting. But their reach is amplified when they embed themselves within the social media environment. (3) During a disaster, the best news is local news. People will track down local information on whatever platform they can find it" (Brown, 2012).

Whether dealing with the media, the public, or partners, effective communication is now accepted as a critical element of emergency management. Media relations should be open and cooperative; the information stream must be managed to provide a consistent, accurate message; and officials need to be proactive about telling their own story before it is done for them. A customer service approach is essential to communicate with the public, a collaborative approach should be taken to promoting programs, and great care should be given as to how and when risk is communicated to citizens. Multiple agencies and unclear lines of responsibility make communications among partners a challenge; political skill and acumen are needed to overcome such hurdles, and efforts are under way to improve communications in this area.

The Changing Media World

The Internet and social media have radically and irreversibly transformed the communications landscape. We are living through a media revolution that rivals the effects of earlier tectonic shifts—the inventions of the printing press, telephone, photograph, radio, and television.

The Internet has created a "new" news landscape and changed forever the way and speed news is produced and consumed. Former *The New York Times* columnist Frank Rich explained, "We didn't recognize we were up against change as sweeping as the building of the transcontinental railroad or the invention of electricity" (Rich, 2013).

The old communications paradigm—of professionals broadcasting one message to many—is dead. Now communications is a conversation between the many—we are all news producers and consumers, content creators, and curators (see Figure 11-6).

And the operating premise in this new media culture is now, according to Mark Glaser, executive editor of PBS MediaShift, "the audience knows more collectively than the reporter alone" (Glaser, 2006).

The emergence of Internet-based social media platforms such as Twitter and Facebook as news providers and the fact that four out of five (80% percent) of US adults now have a mobile connection to the Web through either a smartphone (56%) or tablet (34%) (Brenner, 2013) mean people can access, generate, influence, or share news wherever they are, anytime of day. "In this new multi-platform media environment," according to the Pew Research Center for the People and the Press, "people's relationship to news is becoming portable, personalized, and participatory" (Pew, 2010).

People's appetite for news has not dropped; in fact, there's evidence it may have increased (Pew, 2010). Most mobile users are not replacing one platform with another. According the Pew Research Center's Project for Excellence in Journalism, "they are consuming more news then they had in the past"

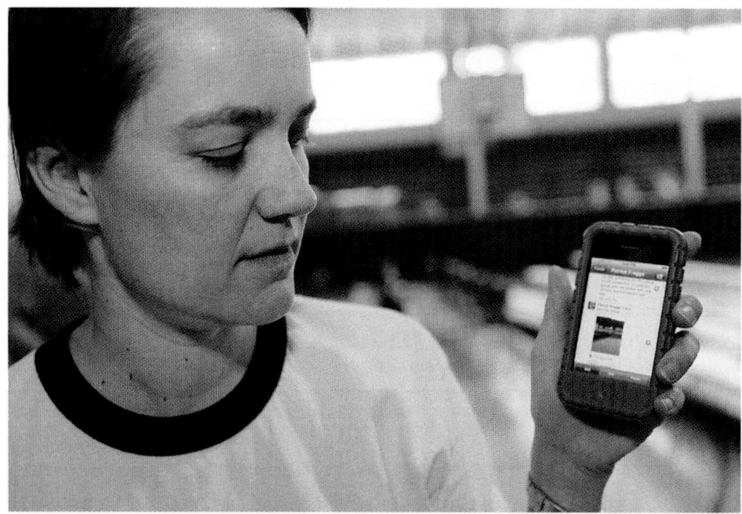

FIGURE 11-6 Nashville, TN, May 5, 2010—Nashville resident and disaster survivor Amy Frogge uses social media to display pictures that document the flood and damage to her home in Davidson County. FEMA is responding to the severe storms and flooding that damaged or destroyed thousands of homes in May 2010 across Tennessee. *Source: David Fine/FEMA.*

(Pew, 2013). It's that their consumption of news from traditional sources has declined and their reliance on the Internet and social media for news has increased dramatically. According to the Pew Research Center for the People and the Press's biennial study of news consumption habits, more Americans get news now online than from radios or newspapers and the number of people relying on social media as a news source doubled since 2010. For American adults under 30, social media has far surpassed newspapers and has equaled TV as a primary source of daily news (Pew Research Center, 2013).

Bottom line: the American news consumer has never had more news and information options. As Slate's Matthew Yglesias explains, "There's lots of competition and lots of stuff to read. A traditional newspaper used to compete with a single cross-town rival. *Time* would compete with *Newsweek*. *Time* doesn't compete with *Newsweek* anymore: Instead it competes with every single English-language website on the planet. It's tough, but it merely underscores the extent of the enormous advances in productivity that are transforming the industry.... Just as a tiny number of farmers now produce an agricultural bounty that would have amazed our ancestors, today's readers have access to far more high-quality coverage than they have time to read ... the American news consumer has never had it so good" (Yglesias, 2013).

This shift in the communications landscape is still sending out shock waves, and the consequences have yet to play out completely. According to former *The New York Times* columnist Rich, "Readers and practitioners alike have little choice but to hang on tight through the sublime and the ridiculous" (Rich, 2013). Cory Haik, the executive producer of digital news for *The Washington Post* agrees: "We don't know the future. We are always in beta. Everything we are doing now will be wrong in six months and we have to be okay with that" (Haik, 2013).

But changes have already occurred that have major implications for disaster communicators and their connections with the public. And before we can understand disaster communications in a changing media world, we need to better understand the change that is occurring in the media world.

Traditional media—newspapers, radio, and now television—is on the decline; online and digital news consumption, meanwhile, continues to increase.

The Pew Research Center's Project for Excellence in Journalism's annual report on the state of American journalism, the State of the News Media 2013, reported on significant changes in the print world:

- Estimates for newspaper newsroom cutbacks in 2012 put the industry down 30% since its peak in 2000 and below 40,000 full-time professional employees for the first time since 1978. Estimates are that number could go as low at 30,000.
- Cities in Michigan, Louisiana, Washington, and Alabama no longer have a daily newspaper.
- *Time* magazine, the only major print news weekly left standing, cut roughly 5% of its staff in early 2013 as a part of broader company layoffs.
- And in African-American news media, the Chicago Defender has winnowed its editorial staff to just four, while the Afro cut back the number of pages in its papers from a maximum of 32 in 2008 to 20 in 2012.
- A growing list of media outlets, such as Forbes magazine, uses technology by a company called Narrative Science to produce content by way of algorithm, no human reporting necessary.

On the TV side:

- Across the three cable channels, coverage of live events during the day, which often require a crew and correspondent, fell 30% from 2007 to 2012, while interview segments, which take fewer resources and can be scheduled in advance, were up by almost a third.
- On CNN, the cable channel that has branded itself around deep reporting, produced story packages were cut almost in half in length from 2007 to 2012.
- On local TV, sports, weather, and traffic now account on average for 40% of the content produced on the newscasts studied, while news story lengths shrink.

According to Pew's State of the Media 2013 report, "This adds up to a news industry that is undermanned and unprepared to cover and uncover stories or to verify information put into its hands" (Pew, 2013).

American's viewing and listening habits—the ways we consume news—are in transition too.

The Pew Research Center for the People and the Press's biennial survey on news consumption in the United States in 2012 provides a snapshot of what's changed and changing:

- Just 23% of Americans say they read a print newspaper yesterday, down by about half since 2000 (47%).
- The percentage saying they regularly watch local TV news has dipped below 50% for the first time (48%). And the percentage watching cable news channels has fallen five points since 2010 and 2008, from 39% to 34% currently.
- The decline in regular local TV viewership among Americans under age 30 is even more dramatic—down 14 points since 2006, from 42% just 28% in 2012, according to Pew Research Center survey data.
- Gauging the percentage of Americans who get some form of audio-based news—not just listening to the radio—is challenging because of the new forms of audio like satellite and online streaming. But according to Pew Research Center—one-third of adults report having listened to "news radio" yesterday. That's down considerably from 43% in 2000 and 52% in 1990.

Online news consumption rose sharply the last 2 years, following the rapid spread of digital platforms.

Online was the only category of news that showed growth in the 2012 Pew Research Center news consumption survey:

- In 2012, about 39% of respondents got news online or from a mobile device "yesterday" (the day before they participated in the survey), up from 34% in 2010.
- And when other online and digital news sources are included, the share of people who got news from one or more digital forms on an average day rises to 50%, just below the audience for television news (which combines cable, local, and network), but ahead of print newspapers and radio (29% and 33%, respectively).
- The second major trend in online news consumption is the rise of news consumption by users of all ages on social networks—Facebook, Google+, and many others. Today, 19% of the public says they saw news or news headlines on social networking sites yesterday, up from 9% 2 years ago. And the percentage regularly getting news or news headlines on these sites has nearly tripled, from 7% to 20%.
- This study measured Twitter separately from other social networks like Facebook, Google+, and LinkedIn. "That is unusual, as most studies lump all together as 'social media.' But it is probably useful, because Twitter functions more as an 'interest network' than a 'social network.' Follower relationships are based on shared interests, whereas the other networks tend to organize around personal relationships" (Sonderman, 2012).
  - One effect of that difference is that Twitter users connect more with journalists and news organizations. "More than a third (36%) of those with Twitter accounts use them to follow news organizations or journalists," the study says. "On social networking sites, 19% of users say they got information there from news organizations or journalists" (Pew, 2012).
- As news consumption on cell phones and other mobile devices has increased, so has the use of news apps. In the current survey, a quarter of all Americans, including 45% of mobile Internet users, say they have ever downloaded a news app to their cell phone, tablet, or another mobile device. That's up from 16% in 2010.

The proliferation in mobile devices is driving news consumption and "giving rise to a new multiplatform news consumer, one who accesses news through a combination of different devices and traditional sources" (Pew, 2013). According to a joint Pew Research Center and Economist Group study,

> *more than half of tablet news users, some 54%, say they also get news on a smartphone; 77% also get news on a desktop or laptop computer; 50% get news in print and a quarter get news on all four. Similarly, about three quarters of smartphone owners say they also get news on laptops or desktops, while a little over a quarter of them get news on a tablet. This same survey also found 31% of tablet news users said that they spend more time with news since getting their mobile devices. Another 43% said that the device is adding to the amount of news they consume.*
>
> *Social Media, News and Disasters.*

The growth in online—Internet and social media—news consumption is being driven by the growth of social media overall. 85% adults in the United States are now on the Internet.

The facts that four out of five (80%) of US adults now have a mobile connection to the Web through either a smartphone (56%) or a tablet (34%) (Brenner, 2013) and 67% of online adults are using social networking sites (Duggan and Johanna, 2013) have helped fuel the continued growth of social media and its use as news platform and as an interactive communications tool during disasters (Figure 11-7).

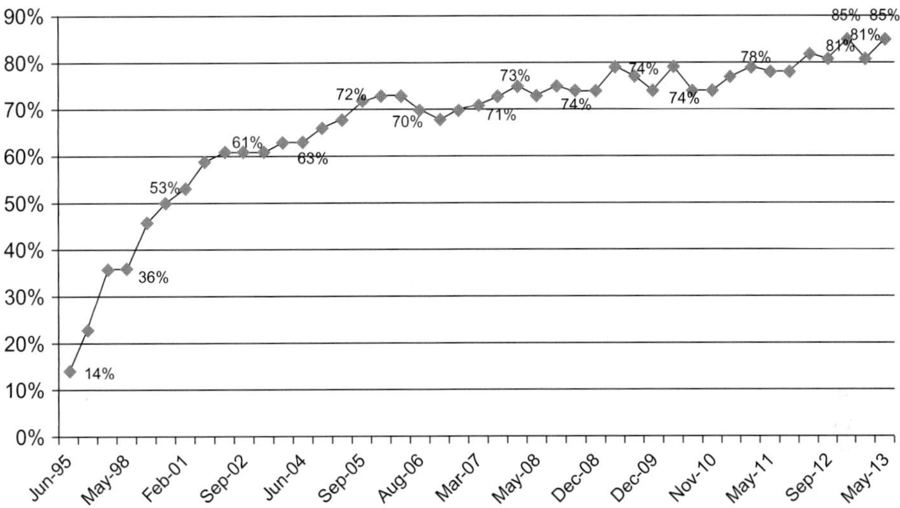

FIGURE 11-7 Internet Adoption, 1995–2013. *Source: Pew Research Center's Internet and American Life Project (2013).*

Critical Thinking

How have public viewing habits and new communications technologies changed the way news is collected and disseminated? What does this change mean for emergency management and homeland security officials?

What Are Social Media?

Social media are Internet-based tools, technologies, and applications that enable interactive communications and content exchange between users who move back and forth easily between roles as content creators and consumers (Figure 11-8).

While many traditional media (such as newspapers and television) remain important disaster communication channels, traditional media primarily facilitate one-way information dissemination. Social media provides the platform for real-time two-way dialogue and interaction between organizations, the public, and individuals (see Figure 11-9).

Social media outlets include, but are not limited to, the following groups:

- *Social networks*: A social network is a Web site that allows people to connect with friends and family and share photos, videos, music, and other personal data with either a select group of friends or a wider group of people based on shared or common interests. Common social networks include Facebook, Myspace, and LinkedIn.
- *Blogs*: Online journals that provide a platform for individuals and organizations to write and share content where readers can comment on the content as well as share that information with others. Examples include WordPress, Blogger, and TypePad.

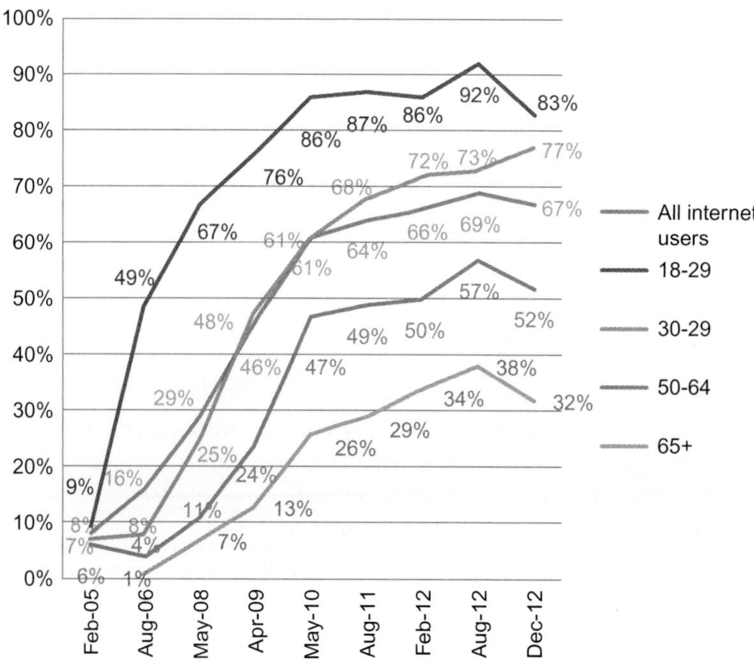

FIGURE 11-8 Social Networking Site Use by Age Group, 2005–2012. *Source: Pew Research Center's Internet & American Life Project surveys, 2005-2012.*

FIGURE 11-9 This year's Resolve to be Ready campaign focuses on "family connection" to reinforce the importance of parents including their children in preparedness conversations in advance of potential disasters. The Resolve to be Ready campaign makes an emergency preparedness resolution easy to keep by recommending families to consider these three ideas when making a plan: who to call, where to meet, and what to pack. Use this image as your Facebook and Twitter cover photo graphics to get your community prepared in 2014. *Source: Jana Baldwin/FEMA.*

- *Microblogs*: Sites that allow people to share limited amounts of information through posts, often with links to additional information. The best example of a microblog is Twitter, which allows sharing of bite-sized (140-character) content. Microblogs play an increasingly important role during breaking news events and disasters. Other examples include Tumblr and Yammer.
- *Crowdsourcing*: Crowdsourcing is making an open call to the public asking for solutions to a problem. These groups are being asked to use the Internet and its vast search and connective capabilities to gather and disseminate data and to help out an overloaded infrastructure that cannot or will not provide services needs in an emergency. Crowdsourcing social media sites have been used successfully in response to emergencies:
  - Managing traffic following natural disasters
  - Tracking food radiation contamination following the 2011 Japanese earthquake and tsunami (Safecast.org)
- *Digital mapping*: Data from many disasters such as fires, floods, and even disease outbreaks are compiled and turned into real-time, interactive visual images or digital maps. Google Maps and Ushahidi are examples of mapping programs used by the public.
- *Forums*: Online discussion groups focused on particular interests and topics. They have diverse topics of interest available for discussions. They can be powerful and popular elements of online communities during a public health emergency. LiveJournal and ProBoards are good examples.
- *Video sharing*: Online sites for sharing video—including YouTube and Vimeo.
- *Photo sharing*: Online sites for sharing photos multimedia content. Flickr and Pinterest are prime examples.
- *Wiki*: Web pages where people work together as a community to create and edit content. Wikipedia is an online encyclopedia that allows participants to add content or edit information included in the entries.

Two social media sites, Facebook and Twitter, dominate the competition in terms of their use as news distributors, especially during disasters.

Facebook

Facebook—which now has topped one billion users—is the most-used social networking site in the world and the second most-accessed site in the United States after Google. Facebook remains the most-used social networking platform, with two-thirds of online adults say that they are Facebook users (Duggan and Johanna, 2013).

Facebook allows registered users to create profiles, upload photos and video, send messages, and keep in touch with friends, family, and colleagues—in 37 different languages. Facebook also dominates the intersection of social media and news according to the Pew Research Center (Pew, 2012). Users "share" news stories and video through Facebook—with most links to news stories coming from friends and family. Facebook is considered a pathway to news, allowing users to "share" and "like" news stories and pointing users to content on news organizations' Web sites.

Twitter

For many breaking news events, it's now more likely that the first available description will be produced by a connected citizen than by a professional journalist. Twitter users were the first to report the Boston Marathon bombings, the death of Osama bin Laden, the Aurora, Colorado, movie theater shooting, Whitney Houston's death, and other news stories. Think of Twitter as the new newswire.

The percentage of Internet users who are on Twitter have doubled since November 2010, currently standing at 16% (Duggan and Johanna, 2013). Twitter users connect more with journalists and news organizations. "More than a third (36%) of those with Twitter accounts use them to follow news organizations or journalists," the study says. "On social networking sites, 19% of users say they got information there from news organizations or journalists" (Pew, 2012).

Twitter's role as a major news and political platform came to fruition during the Arab Spring when prodemocracy protestors relied on tweets to organize. NPR's Andy Carvin did pioneering work on Twitter, using the flood of tweets from places like Tahrir Square to question, verify, and report news live as it happened.

Video and Photo Sharing Sites

Concentrating on Facebook and Twitter alone is not enough. The growth in video and photo-sharing sites has been jaw-dropping:

- Between 1 and 2 million videos through Vine—Twitter's tool for posting six-second videos—are linked to Twitter each day (Shively, 2013b).
- In the year since Facebook bought Instagram—its photo (and as of June 2013 video) tool—it grew 500%, from 22 million active users to 100 million (Shively, 2013a).
- YouTube has gone from zero to a staggering 800 million monthly visitors and 4 billion hours of video viewed per month in 8 years (Bullas, 2013).
- Pew research shows an astounding 286% increase in Pinterest use in 2011–2012, from 700,000 users to more than 20 million, with 15% of Internet users now on Pinterest (Duggan and Johanna, 2013).

News organizations have found increasing use for Pinterest and Instagram. The Wall Street Journal uses Pinterest to highlight graphics; The Dallas Morning News and other papers use it for photos of everything from local storms and fires to mug shots of people wanted by the police (Pew State of Media, 2013). *Time* magazine used Instagram to document Hurricane Sandy, while NBC News reports "that all of its news shows now have Instagram accounts and that journalists embedded with presidential campaigns used them to post thousands of pictures from the campaign trail" (Pew State of Media, 2013).

Social Media and Disasters

Social media use rises during disasters. According to the START study on "Social Media Use during Disasters," "Research points to the rapt and sustained attention the public may give social media during disasters" (Fraustino et al., 2012).

- "According to Twitter, people sent more than 20 million tweets about the storm from Oct 27 through Nov 1. This was more than twice the usage from the two previous days. From the day the storm made landfall on Oct 29 through Wednesday the 31st, news, information, photos and video made up more than half of all the Twitter conversation" (PEW, 2013). Instagram's chief executive officer Kevin Systrom told the Associated Press that about 10 pictures per second were being uploaded to Instagram with the hashtag #sandy (Ngak, 2012).
- Twitter saw a 500% increase in Tweets from Japan as people reached out to friends, family and loved ones in the moments after the 3/11 earthquake and tsunami. According to Twitter, "during the initial stages of the Japanese earthquake, the volume of tweets being sent was up to 5000 tweets per second on five different occasions" (Richardson, 2011).

- The Boston Police Department's follower count spiked from 40,000 to more than 300,000 during coverage of the Marathon bombings and ensuring manhunt for the two terrorist suspects (Bar-Tur, 2013).
- "A quarter of Americans got information about the explosions and the hunt for the bombers on social networking sites such as Facebook and Twitter. Young Americans in particular kept up-to-date through social media. Slightly more than half (56%) of an 18-to-29 year subgroup polled by Pew got bombing-related news through social networking sites" (Pew Research Center, 2013).

News consumers turn to social media turning disasters because it provides:

Immediate access: Half of all Americans are now smartphone owners which means they can log onto social media with the tap of a finger. The proliferation of personal computers, laptops, tablets, and mobile phones provide previously unparalleled access to information through social media.

Familiarity in a frightening time: People are more likely to use a particular social media platform if their friends and family frequently use it and/or they trust and ascribe a high level of credibility to a social media platform. People are more likely to use social media if their friends and family are also users. People turn to existing social networks during disasters, including social media networks created before disasters (Fraustino et al., 2012).

Real time information and situational awareness: Social media use rises during disasters as people seek immediate and in-depth information. Information-seeking is a primary driver of social media use during routine times and spikes almost instantaneously during disasters. After the 2011 Japanese tsunami there were more than 5000 tweets per second about the disaster. And social media uniquely provides real-time disaster information. For example, during the 2007 California wildfires, the public turned to social media because they thought journalists and public officials were too slow to provide relevant information about their communities (Fraustino et al., 2012).

Tweets from hotelier *Richard Morse*, provided eyewitness, real time accounts of conditions In Port au Prince after the 2010 earthquake in Haiti:

> *Just about all the lights are out in Port au Prince ... people still screaming but the noise is dying as darkness sets.*
> *The Castel Haiti is a pile of rubble ... it was 8 stories high*
> *Our guests are sitting out in the driveway ... no serious damage here at the Oloffson but many large buildings nearby have collapsed*
> *The UNIBANK here on Rue Capois has collapsed*
>
> *Global Voices Online (2010)*

A way to reach rescuers and ask for help: More disaster victims are turning to social media for help and rescue—especially in events where loss of phone lines and cell towers make it impossible to call 911. Three out of four Americans (76%) expect help in less than three hours of posting a request on social media, up from 68% in 2011 (American Red Cross, 2012). And both the 2011 and 2012 Red Cross surveys confirm that the public overwhelming believes government agencies should be monitoring social media for distress calls and respond promptly.

After the 3/11 Japanese tsunami, 59-year old Naoko Utsami found herself on the rooftop of a community center with just one line of communication—the email on her mobile phone. She emailed her husband, who emailed their son in London who sent a Tweet to the deputy director of Tokyo who initiated the air rescue of Utsami and 400 others trapped on the roof (Perera, 2013).

Personal status information: In a 2012 survey, the American Red Cross found that three out of four (76%) say they've contacted friends and family to see if they were safe. let loved ones know they are safe during disasters (American Red Cross, 2012). Forty percent of those surveyed said they would use social tools to tell others they are safe, up from 24% in 2011 (American Red Cross, 2012). The top term employed by Facebook users in the United States the day after Hurricane Sandy hit was "we are ok."

A tool for reuniting families and friends: After devastating tornadoes hit Joplin, Missouri, dozens of Facebook pages, including "Joplin Tornado Citizen Checks," helped reunite friends and family and locate the missing. According to Time Magazine, these pages "quickly became the fastest way to get information, as survivors and their relatives relied on social media as they might once have leaned on the Red Cross or local relief agencies" (Skarada, 2011).

After the 2010 Haiti earthquake, Google worked with the United States Department of State to create Google Person Finder, an online registry and message board for survivors, family, and loved ones affected by a natural disaster allowing them to post and search for information about each other's status and whereabouts. Google Person Finder launched in English, French, and Haitian Creole on January 15, less than 3 days after the earthquake (Beckerman, 2013).

A way to meeting real time needs: After Hurricane Sandy hit the Northeast in October 2012, in addition to the obvious sources for information about food and shelter like the American Red Cross, FEMA, as well as the Ready.gov site, hashtags like #needgas[zipcode] #chargingstation #warmingshelter were created so the public could directly aid to the public. More than a third of the respondents surveyed by the Red Cross say social information has motivated them to gather supplies or seek safe shelter (American Red Cross, 2012).

Unfiltered information: Social media provides "raw" information unfiltered by traditional media, organizations, or politicians. It also provides authorities the opportunity to bypass the media and communicate directly with the public. One of the Boston police officers responsible for the social media content during the Boston Marathon bombings put it: "We don't break news. We are the news" (Keller, 2013).

A way to hold officials accountable: When the Japanese government would not admit the scope of the danger from leaking radiation at the Fukushima nuclear power plant after the 2011 earthquake, social media and crowd sourced information were used to create an accurate picture of the threat.

A platform for volunteering or donating: During disasters, people use social media to organize emergency relief and ongoing assistance efforts. Both Facebook and Twitter were used for disaster relief fundraising in Haiti. In the first 48 h following the Haitian Earthquake, the Red Cross raised more than $3 million from people texting a $10 donation. (Beckerman, 2013)

On Facebook's Disaster Relief site, a request to volunteer and donate in the wake of Hurricane Sandy:

> *"Making a difference & helping Sandy survivors. President Obama reminds us all how we can make a difference in helping our fellow Americans in the wake of a disaster" http://www.fema.gov/volunteer-donate-responsibly.*
> *"Help those affected by Hurricane Sandy in New Jersey." Click here to donate: https://sandynjrelieffund.org/.*

A tool for building community and resilience: As the public logs in online to share their feelings and thoughts, they build relationships and create a sense of community even when scattered across a vast geographic area. These virtual communities can be temporary or continue through recovery and beyond.

Emotional support and healing: Disasters are tragedies and they prompt people to seek not only information but also human contact, conversation, and emotional support.

Clearly, social media is already intertwined with disaster communications and information management and is now a critical element in preparedness and response communications. And as Americans are becoming increasingly reliant on social media and mobile devices during emergencies, so inescapably are the media and emergency managers.

Critical Thinking

Why is social media well suited for use by emergency and homeland security officials as well as the public? How does the technology meet the information needs of both groups?

The Emergence of Social Media as a Disaster Communications Tool

Even though the 1990s was a time of transformation in communications technology with the emergence of the World Wide Web, 24/7 cable television, and array of digital tools—from affordable and widely available wireless mobile devices and high-resolution satellite maps—digital media was not a factor in natural disaster coverage or recovery until 2001.

In the aftermath of the September 11, 2001, terrorist attacks, citizen-shot videos of the attacks on Twin Towers dominated news coverage and Americans turned to the Internet for information. But the sharp spike in traffic froze and crashed Web sites. In many ways, 9/11 was the last disaster covered under the old model of crisis communications: newspapers printed "extra" editions, people turned to television for news, and "the familiar anchors of the broadcast networks—Tom Brokaw, Peter Jennings, and Dan Rather—took on their avuncular roles of the past for a nation looking for comfort and reassurance" (May, 2006).

Television was the dominant source of news: More than half of Americans learned about the terrorist attacks from television, 1 in 4 from another person, 1 in 6 from radio, and only 1% from the Internet. After first learning about the crisis, 4 out of 5 Americans turned to TV to learn more (Fraustino et al., 2012).

Every disaster since September 11 has involved more "citizen journalists" and expanded the use and utility of the new media tools and technologies. An analysis of events traces the evolution of best practices and increasing reliance on social media.

China's SARS Epidemic (2003)

In 2003, during China's SARS epidemic, people used text messaging to exchange information the government tried to suppress (Hattotuwa, 2007).

Three major disasters within 9 months—the Asian tsunami (2004), the London transit bombings (2005), and Hurricane Katrina (2005)—marked the coming of age of participatory media.

The Asian Tsunami (2004)

Dan Gillmor, author of the seminal book on participatory journalism, *We the Media: Grassroots Journalism by the People, for the People*, called the December 26, 2004, Asian tsunami, "the turning point—a before-and-after moment for citizen journalism" (Cooper, 2007). Blogs, Web sites, and message boards provided news and aid—and in real time. One blog, "waveofdestruction.org" logged 682,366 unique visitors in 4 days (Cooper, 2007). Photo sharing capabilities and features were used to document events and to provide dramatic visual eyewitness accounts, including a poignant and frightening video of an incoming wave taken from the abandoned camera of one of the victims. This disaster also saw the initiation of the use of mobile technologies to solicit and receive donations for relief efforts.

The London Transit Bombings (2005)

Mobile devices played key communication roles in disseminating information primarily by text and photo during the terrorist attacks in the London subways. A cell phone photo taken by a commuter in a smoke-clogged tunnel in the Tube became the iconic image of the disaster. Londoners pooled their digital photos on Flickr—a photo-sharing site and service that allows people to tag pictures with comments and labels. Not only did Flickr host all of these images, but also they made them available for reuse, and bloggers writing about the bombings were able to use the Flickr images almost immediately, creating a kind of symbiotic relationship among social tools. Police asked people to supply them with cell phone pictures or videos because they might contain clues about the terrorists (Shirky, 2008).

Hurricane Katrina (2005)

In August 2005, Hurricane Katrina, a category three hurricane tore through New Orleans, LA; Mobile, AL; and Gulfport, MS. Over 1500 people were killed and tens of thousands left homeless. Blogs became the primary information-providing tool used by both traditional media and citizen journalists. Staff reporters for New Orleans' daily newspaper, *The Times-Picayune*, created a blog that for a time became the front page of their news operation. It enabled members of the community isolated by flood waters and debris to show and tell each other what they were seeing (May, 2006).

Cory Haik, who is now the executive producer of Digital News at *The Washington Post* but was the managing editor of NOLA.com, site of *The Times-Picayune* in New Orleans, where she shared in two Pulitzer Prizes with Picayune staff for breaking news coverage and public service during Katrina, explained, "We had to rely on community and user generated content out of necessity," (Because the paper's offices and printing plant were under water, the daily could not print in the weeks following the hurricane). "Swarms of people gave feedback to site via webform. It was not sophisticated—just cut and paste. We started by asking them to share the story of their commute—some of them had 17 hour commutes. Then we started getting stories from people left behind ... and then people started using the blog for rescue; sending us calls for help—my uncle is stuck in his attic..." (Haik, 2013).

Disaster survivors were also heavy users of location-specific media. For example, 75% of New Orleans residents responding to one survey visited online sites specific to their neighborhoods after Katrina (Fraustino et al., 2012).

Message boards provided critical information about shelter locations, family tracing, and missing persons. Internet expert Barbara Palser counted 60 separate online bulletin boards that were created to locate missing people within 2 weeks of the storm (May, 2006). Google Earth and Google Map, which provide and use online satellite imagery, were used to illustrate damage assessments—particularly to the Gulf Coast and barrier islands (May, 2006).

California Wildfires (2007)

In October 2007, wildfires in Southern California resulted in the loss of nearly 2200 homes and over $1 billion in damages. Residents with camera and video capacities on their cell phones were able to report on the fires' paths before first responders reached the disaster site (CDC, 2012). The wildfires marked a major step forward in the integration of mainstream media and citizen journalists. "Local media has been highlighting user-submitted photos and videos, and embedding new technology in their prime coverage. San Diego's public television station, KPBS, used Twitter to give its audience updates when its Web site went down, and the Twitter updates now have a prominent place on their home page" (Glaser, 2007).

San Diego TV station News 8 responded to the crisis by taking down its entire regular Web site and replacing it with a rolling news blog, linking to YouTube videos of its key reports, plus Google Maps showing the location of the fire (Stabe, 2007). Also on the site were links to practical information that viewers needed, including how to contact insurance companies, how to volunteer or donate to the relief efforts, evacuation information, and shelter locations. Local and national television stations asked for submissions from wildfire witnesses and victims. The NBC affiliate in San Diego received over 2000 submissions of pictures and video related to the wildfires (Glaser 2007).

"It's an exemplary case study in how a local news operation can respond to a major rolling disaster story by using all the reporting tools available on the Internet" (Catone, 2007).

Virginia Tech Shootings (2007) and Northern Illinois University (NIU) Shootings (2008)

People used mobile media extensively to communicate with others and give real-time accounts on what was going on during these traumatic events.

People used Facebook and other social networking sites to interact with others, seek information regarding the crisis, share experiences, form online relationships with others, and build community and awareness of the tragic events.

According to Digital Journalism Professor Sean Mussenden, coverage of the Virginia Tech shootings marked the first time traditional media, most particularly *The Washington Post*, "trolled Facebook and Twitter for information. It really was one of the first major examples of traditional media really relying on social media" (Mussenden, 2013).

Through Facebook messages posted by students, all 32 victims of the Virginia Tech shooting had been identified a full day before traditional journalistic sources had provided a list (CDC, 2012).

Myanmar Cyclone and China's Sichuan Earthquake (2008)

On May 2, 2008, Cyclone Nargis struck the Irrawaddy Delta region of Myanmar (Burma). The cyclone with winds of 120 mph made landfall at the mouth of the Irrawaddy River—a low-lying, densely populated region—and pushed a 12-foot wall of water 25 miles inland, killing at least 80,000 people, leaving as many as 2.5 million homeless.

Ten days later, on May 12, 2008, a 7.9 earthquake devastated China's Sichuan province, toppling buildings, collapsing schools, killing more than 69,000, injuring over 367,000, and displacing between 5 and 11 million people.

Two disasters, one common link: they demonstrated that new technologies—the Internet, text messaging systems, camera phones, Google Map mash-ups—and citizen journalists, especially bloggers, had irrevocably altered the nature of disaster reporting and replaced the top-down flow of information from repressive governments and the traditionally rigidly controlled media in times of crisis with a dynamic and democratic two-way exchange.

In Myanmar, where Internet and cell phone access were limited, the military government refused to allow aid workers or journalists to reach disaster areas and moved fast to restrict communications. In spite of these restrictions, Burmese blogs and news sites were quick to react by posting eyewitness accounts of the disaster and mobilizing fundraising efforts (BBC News, 2008). Twitter emerged quickly as an important medium for coverage of the crisis. Aid agencies working in Burma including AmeriCares and the Salvation Army used Twitter to disseminate information and coordinate activities. YouTube hosted scores of videos recording the devastation and feeble response (Rincon, 2008). Global Voices online and traditional media like *The New York Times*, BBC, and CNN featured, linked to, or aggregated coverage by bloggers and linked to videos and photos recorded by eyewitnesses.

Twitter broke the news of the Sichuan earthquake, according to several news accounts, before the US Geological Survey was able to perform its official role and report it (Washkuch, 2008).

A fast-moving network of text messages, instant messages, and blogs became a powerful source of firsthand accounts of the earthquake—testament to the fact that in the wake of disaster, the Chinese government gave reporters and bloggers unprecedented freedom (Global Voices Online, 2008). In addition to the broad use of Twitter, other online and new media tools included scores of user-shot videos on YouTube that captured the moments the quake struck, bulletin boards to help relatives and friends locate missing people, a channel on QQ Prayer to report fundraising scams, and a map mash-up on NetEase that allowed users in Wenchuan to report in live time what was happening in their area (Global Voices Online, 2008).

In addition to using online technology to report on the earthquake damage, Chinese citizens also used the same tools to expedite the recovery. According to *The Washington Post*, volunteers used e-mail, text messages, and cell phones to gather information on where help or supplies were needed and to direct relief. "No one from the government told us what to do. In this urgent situation, we decided to share some of the responsibility," one of the volunteer coordinators told *The Washington Post* (Fan, 2008).

Mumbai Terrorist Attacks (2008)

On November 27, 2008, a series of coordinated terrorist attacks across the city of Mumbai hit several hotels, a cafe, train station, and a Jewish center killing 173 people and injuring more than 300. Traditional news media took their lead and got most of their information from sources on the ground. The ten gunmen used new media—Google Earth maps to scout their locations (Tinker and Fouse, 2009). Eyewitnesses reported events during the 60 h terrorist ordeal using tweets, Flickr pictures, and videos posted on YouTube from their mobile devices (Tinker and Fouse, 2009). That user-generated content became the first reports of the attacks. According to ZDNet author Jennifer Leggio, Mumbai "is where social media grew up" (CDC, 2012).

Haiti Earthquake (2010)

On the January 12, 2010, a 7.0 magnitude earthquake scale struck near Port-au-Prince in Haiti killing more than 220,000 and displacing 1.7 million. Within minutes, Ushahidi, an organization that uses volunteers to gather data from text messages, e-mails, and social media—primarily Tweets and Facebook posts from eyewitnesses—began to pinpoint those reports on a Web-based, interactive map. Ushahidi, which is also the name of a crisis-mapping software first developed and used in Kenya, was used to capture, organize, map, and share critical information coming directly from Haitians during the initial disaster response phase.

The Haiti earthquake disaster highlighted the use of text messages and mapping software to communicate and track calls from people needing immediate medical attention or who were trapped under buildings and other fallen structures. "Haiti was a turning point in terms of the emergence of collaborative and distributed organizations and the recognition that social media serves a broader purpose for emergency managers than tweeting what you are eating about lunch," explained Dr. Jeannette Sutton, a disaster sociologist who studies the dynamics of online communications via Twitter across hazards and over time. Mobile phones were used to communicate first aid information and to provide information about where to go for shelter, food, water, and other health assistance (CDC, 2012).

An offering of medical care: "Hôspital Sacré Coeur in Milot says it has capacity for patients and asks people to make their own way there."

An announcement concerning search and rescue: "Though the government says the search and rescue phase is over, SAR teams are still available. If you know someone is trapped call +870 764 130 944, e-mail haiti.opc@gmail.com, or contact MINUSTAH."

The growing prevalence of mobile phone ownership and use, even in very poor countries like Haiti, made rescue efforts possible that would have been unthinkable in 2000 (CDC, 2012).

Following the earthquake, mobile devices allowed people from all over the world to donate to relief efforts using text messages. This type of fundraising effort, first seen following the 2004 tsunami disaster in Southeast Asia, increased the awareness of the power of nonprofit organizations as a communication channel in a disaster situation (CDC, 2012).

Japanese Earthquake and Tsunami (2011)

Crowdsourcing Web sites were used for monitoring traffic patterns out of affected regions and for tracking radiation contamination of food in the affected region and beyond (CDC, 2012).

Google Crisis Response site was one of the most visited social media sites used for sharing information on the crisis. It provided access to the company's Person Finder search program, which helps people reconnect after a disaster, using both personal descriptions and photos. They could connect with missing persons' phone lines and emergency voicemail message boards. They could also receive alerts and statuses from world health agencies, Japanese utility companies, government agencies services, and real-time updates of RSS feeds (CDC, 2012). (A detailed case study on the use of new media during this disaster is presented at the end of this chapter.)

Tuscaloosa and Joplin Tornadoes (2011)

2011 was the deadliest US tornado year on record, with more than 1665 tornadoes striking across the United States. Tuscaloosa, AL, and Joplin, MO, were especially hard hit. Social media were the public's first source of disaster information. For example, Twitter played a key role generating the first photos of the Tuscaloosa tornado devastation (Fraustino et al., 2012). The public also used social media to help find loved ones. A Facebook page named "Joplin, MO Tornado Recovery" gained 123,000 members in the days after the tornado and was used to help locate family members (Fraustino et al., 2012).

Social media also helped in the recovery and rebuilding. People monitored social media for volunteer opportunities. For example, the first Sunday after the storm in Tuscaloosa, one school system posted a request for volunteers to help clean up schools, and within 30 min, almost 80 people showed up. Similarly, on Craigslist, the "Joplin Tornado Volunteers List" aggregated volunteer opportunities. And in Tuscaloosa, the city created a social media Web site, Tuscaloosa Forward, for residents to share ideas for rebuilding; in less than 6 weeks, more than 4000 visitors provided more than 300 ideas (Fraustino et al., 2012).

Hurricane Sandy (2012)

From October 29 to 30, 2012, a category one hurricane swept across the US East Coast causing eight states to declare states of emergency and resulting in up to $50 billion in damage. Social media was widely used for information sharing: 1.1 million people mentioning the word "hurricane" on Twitter within a 21-h time period. Sandy became the number two most talked about topic on Facebook during 2012. For the first time, the photo-sharing site Instagram played a major role in information sharing during a disaster with ten storm-related pictures per second posted on the site (Fraustino et al., 2012).

Sandy also marked a shift in the use of social media by government agencies—an acknowledgment and embrace of social media's critical role in disasters in disseminating information, connecting people, and controlling rumors. In Sandy, more than ever before, government agencies turned to mobile and online technologies to communicate with the public and response partners:

- The New York Office of Emergency Management and New Jersey Governor Chris Christie used Twitter and Facebook to relay evacuation orders, direct resources where they were needed, and provide victims with updates about aid, shelter, and storm conditions (Cohen, 2013).
- On October 29, the day Sandy made landfall, FEMA reached more than 300,000 people on Facebook (up from an average of 12,000 per day) and reached 6 million Twitter users with one message (Cohen, 2013).
- Even before Sandy, New York City had 3 million followers across more than 300 city accounts on Facebook, Twitter (in both English and Spanish), Google+, Tumblr, YouTube, and more. Throughout response and recovery, these channels made it easy for the city to share information in various formats and enabled people to find and consume information in ways they preferred and were used to (Cohen, 2013).
- The public could also sign up to receive text alerts from the mayor's office Twitter account, @nycmayorsoffice, which served as a great alternative digital resource to the city's Web site, once people lost power and Internet access (Cohen, 2013).

Boston Marathon Bombings (2013)

At 2:49 p.m. on April 15, 2013, two bombs exploded near the finish line of the annual Boston Marathon killing three people and injuring 264. The first reports about the terrorist attack were spread through Twitter and Facebook. Even though television was the most widely used source of information about the bombing and its aftermath, it was social media that shaped the story and the response. While 80% of Americans followed the story on TV according to the Pew Research Center, about half (49%) say they kept up with news and information online or on a mobile device, and a quarter of Americans got information about the explosions and the hunt for the bombers on social networking sites such as Facebook and Twitter. Young Americans in particular kept up-to-date through social media. Slightly more than half (56%) of an 18-to-29-year subgroup polled by Pew got bombing-related news through social networking sites (Pew Research Center, 2013).

The Boston Marathon bombings were a watershed, a moment that marked forever the changed role of social media and the fully participatory public in breaking news events and coverage.

The New York Times wrote: "It is America's first fully interactive national tragedy of the social media age. The *Boston Marathon* bombings quickly turned into an Internet mystery that sent a horde of amateur sleuths surging onto the Web in a search for clues to the suspects' identity..." (Kakutani, 2013).

The two suspects in the Boston Marathon bombing were identified, cornered, and captured through the grand-scale dissemination and collection of information, photos, and videos through social media. Twitter, Facebook, and Internet Web sites all are credited with the effort (Presuitti, 2013). In the end, it was the public's connections to each other and to technology that broke the case.

The photos released by the FBI of suspect 1 and suspect 2, as they were known at the time, were instantaneously tweeted and retweeted, Facebooked, and Facebook-shared. "Thousands of marathon spectators flipped through their cell phone photos and videos—to see if they could match the suspects later identified as brothers Dzhokhar and Tamerlan Tsarnaev," according to the Voice of America News (Presuitti, 2013).

And finally, it was during the bombings the Boston Police Department set a new standard for government communications during a disaster—using social media to inform, correct inaccurate information, lead, and listen to the public conversation. During the event, the Boston Police Department's Twitter feed increased from about 35 thousand followers to near a quarter of a million (Glennon, 2013). Mashable—an online media company that focuses on innovation and technology—declared that during the crisis, the Boston Police Department "schooled us all on social media" (Bar-Tur, 2013) and asserted that "BPD's presence online helps reinvent the whole notion of community policing for the 21st century" (Bar-Tur, 2013). (A detailed case study on the use of new media during this disaster is presented at the end of this chapter.)

Critical Thinking

What do the previous case studies have in common in terms of crisis communications? Are there any significant differences between each of these events in terms of the information collection and dissemination needs of government officials and the public.

The Use of Digital Media During Disasters Will Continue to Skyrocket

What has driven the expanded use of and reliance on social media in disasters to date is the dramatic increase in the number of users and the explosion of tools at their disposal. The proliferation of mobile devices and connectivity has helped fuel the continued growth of social media—half of all US adults now have a mobile connection to the Web through either a smartphone or a tablet (Pew Research Center, 2012); 85% of adults in the United States are now on the Internet (Pew Research Center's Internet and American Life Project, 2013); and 67% of online adults are using social networking sites (Duggan and Johanna, 2013).

The number of social media networks has exploded, and countless sites are adding social features or integrations. And the number of app downloads from the Apple App store and the Google Play store for Android is staggering. "Since Apple officially opened the App Store, in 2008, its pool of titles has grown to eight hundred and fifty thousand, and more than fifty billion apps have been downloaded for use on iOS devices.... With Apple now at over fifty billion app downloads, and Google's Android apps having been downloaded nearly as many times, the two companies can count a hundred billion app installations between them" (Guerriero, 2013).

That trend is also playing out in the world of emergency management. According to the Center for Technology Innovation at Brookings, "In response to natural disasters such as Hurricane Katrina (2005), the earthquake in Haiti (2010), earthquake and tsunamis in Japan (2011), and the Oklahoma tornados (2013), mobile invention and application have skyrocketed. Mobile development has surged in reaction to the increase in need for instant and accurate information" (West and Valentini, 2013).

The report cites a range of innovations including the creation of *Aerial 3D* by Japanese developers, which uses laser beams to provide emergency response information to people in need of help and allows them to use mobile devices to pinpoint their locations and AT&T's *InstantAct*, "an application that provides public safety officials with an exact field location during disaster and a more robust, dependable way of communicating via voice" (West and Valentini, 2013).

After the Japanese tsunami, Apple featured a new section in its App Store called "Stay in Touch," providing a number of disaster relief applications such as the American Heart Association's *Pocket First Aid & CPR*; *Disaster Alert*, which provides information on instant global "active hazards"; and the American Red Cross's *Shelter View*, which helps users locate a nearby shelter. A number of government agencies including HHS, FEMA, and the USGS among others offer disaster relief apps (West and Valentini, 2013).

This profusion of new mobile tools should make accessing information before, during, and after disasters easier and indicates the reliance on digital and social media will continue its dramatic growth and evolution.

Building an Effective Disaster Communications Capability in a Changing Media World

Just as the media world is changing dramatically, the world of emergency management is changing rapidly. The onslaught of major catastrophic disasters around the world and the projected impact of global climate change have forced the emergency management community to reexamine all of its processes, including communications. Managing information before, during, and after a disaster has changed significantly in recent years, and emergency operations at all levels—local, state, and national—must recognize and acknowledge this change and adapt accordingly.

An article posted on The Guardian Web site entitled "Social media's crucial role in disaster relief efforts" noted, "Cities all over the world are at risk from extreme weather conditions and other infrastructure crises. That's one reason why, in recent years, a number of companies like Philips, Siemens and *Ideo* along with NGOs and groups like the *C40 Cities* have created dedicated research projects aimed at using big data and collaborative techniques (including crowdsourcing) to plan the future of sustainable cities. In one UN-funded project, researchers in Bangkok used a crowdsourcing mobile app to get local people to conduct real time flood monitoring" (Yeomans, 2012).

As we have noted throughout this book, the biggest change in disaster communications has come with the emergence of the public's use of social media outlets as partners in disaster coverage and communications. No organization working in the emergency management field—government and nongovernmental groups, voluntary agencies, and private sectors—can ignore the role that the public and their information networks will play in future disasters. On the contrary, it is incumbent on emergency management organizations to embrace digital and social media much the way traditional media outlets (i.e., television, radio, and newspapers) have already done and much to their benefit.

Emergency management organizations such as FEMA have established partnerships with both the traditional media outlets and social media in order to meet their primary communications mission of providing the public with timely and accurate information before, during, and after a disaster.

FEMA Administrator Talks About Social Media

In a May 7, 2012 interview conducted by The Weather Channel, current FEMA Administrator Craig Fugate had this to say about working with social media:

Question: You mentioned Social Media. It was around at the time of Hurricane Katrina. How has that phenomenon helped change what FEMA does?

Fugate: I think for government this has been a real challenge. We've been real good at broadcasting information out. But we've never been really good at understanding how the public took that information, whether they used it, nor did we do a good job of listening to people. I think Social Media has a dynamic there that is something that we have to learn how to do better. That is, we say we want you to do this as action is occurring, but then we can watch people as they communicate back to us and go, "Well, maybe we didn't do a good job here or maybe they didn't understand" and we need to re-emphasize that.

But the other thing is, listen to what people are telling us. Often times they are the best information coming out of a disaster area, well before any official reports come up. And even though you may have the rogue person out there putting out bad information, the general assumption that we find that holds true, if you are crowd-sourcing information, the truth will become known and often times the public knows better what is going on in the first hours of an event than even the official channel.

Question: Can you cite an example where Social Media helped FEMA?

Fugate: I think probably a real good case study of just one example is Joplin (Missouri). We were tracking that day. We knew we had severe weather outbreak potential. But when the original reports started coming up out of Joplin, the Social Media side was much more active, because again it is natural. Local responders are still responding to the initial impact. They don't necessarily have time to say and quantify, "How bad this is."

And so those initial reports, balanced against the reports of the tornado, really started painting a picture that this was much bigger than you would have assumed because the State had yet to request assistance; they were still responding. So well before the Governor was putting in a formal request—we had already begun moving assistance that way. And again, you are talking about maybe only hours, but that is critical in these types of events to get there as quickly as we can.

Source: The Weather Channel (2012).

The purpose of this section is to detail the seven elements that we believe will comprise an effective disaster communications capability in the future. These seven elements include the following:

- A communication plan
- Information coming in
- Information going out
- Messengers
- Staffing
- Training and exercises
- Monitor, update, and adapt

A Communication Plan

Disaster communication plans can take several forms. Planning for communicating in disaster response focuses on collecting, analyzing, and disseminating timely and accurate information to the public.

A disaster response communication plan should include protocols for

- collecting information from a variety of sources including citizen journalists and social media,
- analyzing these data in order to identify resource needs to match available resources to these needs and disseminating information concerning current conditions and actions to the public through both traditional and social media outlets,
- identifying trusted messengers who will deliver disaster response information to the public,
- identifying how disaster communications will be delivered to functional needs and non-English-speaking populations.

A disaster response communications plan should include a roster of local, state, and national media outlets, reporters, and first informers. This roster will be contacted to solicit information and to disseminate information back out to the public. Finally, the plan should include protocols for monitoring the media, identifying new sources of information collection or dissemination, and evaluating the effectiveness of the disaster communications. This information would be used to update the plan.

A communications plan for the recovery phase should look very similar to the disaster response plan. The recovery phase communications plan must also include protocols for collecting, analyzing, and disseminating timely and accurate information. During the recovery phase, much of the information to be disseminated to the public will come from government and other relief agencies and focus on available resources to help individuals and communities to rebuild. The communications plan must place a premium on delivering this information to the targeted audiences and must identify the appropriate communications mechanisms to communicate these messages. Information collection from the field from a wide variety of sources must be a priority in the communications plan for the recovery phase. Community relations staff, community leaders, and digital and social media are good sources of information on the progress of recovery activities and can provide valuable perspective on the mood of the individuals and communities impacted by the disaster. These sources are also effective in identifying communities, groups, and individuals who may have been passed over by recovery programs.

Communication plans for hazard mitigation and preparedness programs can be very similar and include the basics of a good communications plan including the following:

- Goal—what do you hope to accomplish? Preparedness campaigns seek to help individuals and communities to be ready for the next disaster, while the goal of most hazard mitigation programs is to promote community actions to reduce the impacts of future disasters as was the case in Napa, CA, with the Flood Reduction Program.
- Objectives—how will you achieve your goal? A common objective for a preparedness campaign is to help families to create a family disaster plan. A hazard mitigation program may seek the support of the voters to pass a bond issue such as the bond issues passed by voters in the city of Berkeley, CA, to retrofit critical buildings and infrastructure to resist earthquakes.
- Audiences—to whom will your communications plan be speaking? Target audiences for both preparedness and hazard mitigation communications campaigns may include residents in specific geographic locations; groups of individuals, such as homeowners, small business people, or families; functional needs populations such as children, elderly, disabled, and hearing-impaired; low-to-moderate income groups and neighborhoods; and individuals who own pets.

- Tools—what communications mechanisms will be used to communicate with the targeted audience(s)? These mechanisms should include working with traditional media outlets (television, radio, and newspapers), digital and social media outlets (Internet, Facebook, Twitter, YouTube, bloggers, and bulletin boards), and neighborhood communications networks.
- Messengers—who will deliver the messages? Potential messengers include elected and appointed officials, trusted community leaders, and, as is the case in communicating with children, animated characters.
- Timetable—the length of the communications program. Plot the various tasks to be undertaken to successfully implement the plan over a time frame including days, months, and years.
- Evaluate—how well did the communications plan work? Develop means for evaluating the effectiveness of the communications campaign. Success could be measured in terms of raising awareness, prompting action, or securing the votes needed to pass a bond issue.

In all four phases of emergency management, it is important to have a comprehensive communications plan.

Steps That Should Be Taken in Preparation for and in Response to a Crisis

1. Establish, communicate and enforce a customized Social Media Policy that specifies what employees are permitted and not permitted to do concerning social media.
2. Determine what engaging stakeholders via social media should accomplish.
3. Continuously monitor internet and especially social media content using free online tools such as Google alert, socialmention.com, touchgraph.com, and Twitter alert.
4. Engage a broad range of stakeholders by way of peer-to-peer conversation using various social media tools.
5. Carefully listen to and act upon stakeholder feedback provided via social media.
6. Identify and connect with key online influencers so they distribute your carefully crafted stakeholder messages.
7. Rebut false claims and accusations appearing in social media.
8. Refrain from engaging in pointless debate with negative posters (social media trolls).
9. Link up your organization's website and social media tools.
10. Evaluate your crisis response and make necessary social media adjustments.

Source: Disaster Resources Guide (2012).

Information Coming In

Information sharing is the basis of effective disaster communications. In disaster response, receiving and processing regular information concerning conditions at a disaster site and what is being done by agencies responding to the disaster allows disaster communicators to provide timely and accurate information to the public. In collecting this information, no potential source should be ignored and all possible sources should be encouraged to forward relevant information. To be successful in this task, you should identify all potential sources of information and develop working relationships with these various sources before the next disaster strikes. You must also be prepared to identify and partner with new sources of information as they come on the scene in the aftermath of a disaster.

Potential disaster information sources include the following:

- Government damage assessment teams—government disaster agencies at every level have staff responsible for assessing damages in the aftermath of a disaster. For a major disaster, a damage assessment team may include representatives from local, state, and federal response agencies. The information collected will include deaths; injuries; damages to homes, infrastructure, and the environment; and other critical data.
- First responders—among the first on the scene at any disaster, equipped with the necessary communications devices and trained to be observant.
- Voluntary agencies—these groups often have members or volunteers located in the disaster areas trained in damage assessment who can make first and ongoing assessments. For example, the Red Cross has extensive experience in reporting damage to homes and the number of people evacuated and in shelters.
- Community leaders—trusted leaders who have their own neighborhood network or work with community-based organizations with networks into the community can be a valuable source of on-the-ground information.
- First informers—individuals in the disaster site with the wherewithal to collect information and images and to communicate information and images by cell phones, handheld devices, or laptops.
- Social media—blogs (Web logs), Google Earth, Google Map, Wikis (Wikipedia), SMS (text messaging postings—Twitter), Flickr, Picasa (photo survey sites), and YouTube (video sharing sites).
- Online news sites—aggregate of community news, information, and opinion (ibrattleboro).
- Traditional media—television, radio, and newspaper reporters, editors, and news producers can be good sources of information, especially if they have deployed news crews to the disaster area before or just after a disaster strikes.

Having identified the potential information sources in your area, you must reach out to these sources to develop a working partnership and to put in place whatever protocols and technologies are needed to accept information from these sources. It is important that all potential sources of information understand what types of information you need from any situation so that they are looking for the information you need to make decisions. Government response agencies and voluntary agencies practicing National Information Management System (NIMS) and Incident Command System (ICS) will know what information to collect. You must reach out to the nongovernmental, nontraditional information sources before the next disaster to let them know what information you need and how to communicate that information to you.

Ideas for developing these working partnerships with nongovernmental, nontraditional information sources include the following:

- Build neighborhood communications networks—partner with community-based organizations, churches, and neighborhood associations to build neighborhood communications networks. Local residents can be trained in information collection, maybe as part of community emergency response team (CERT) training, and local community leaders can be entrusted to collect this information and forward it to emergency officials. These networks could also be used to send messages from emergency officials to neighborhood residents through trusted community leaders.

- Create and distribute a disaster information protocol for the public—list what information you will be seeking over the course of a disaster response and get this list out to the public. Make sure they know where to e-mail or post the information and images they collect.
- Establish a point of contact within your organization for information sources—designate staff that are accessible and will work with information sources during a disaster.
- Create an electronic portal for information from the field—wikis and Web logs (blogs) can accept and aggregate comments from users, set up a Twitter site that can be updated via text messages, and establish a YouTube and Facebook account.
- Include the public and traditional and social media outlets in disaster response training and exercises—incorporate these information sources into your disaster exercises to identify issues and gaps and to update plans accordingly. Media are not always included in exercises nor is the public, but by including these groups in your exercises, you make the exercise more authentic, you create an opportunity to identify difficult issues prior to facing them in the next disasters, and you can make appropriate adjustments. It is also a chance to get to know each other.
- Meet with traditional and new media types on a regular basis—another way to create personal relationships with these critical partners in any disaster response.
- Include information sources in your after-action debrief—their perspectives and experiences can be used to update the plan and operations.

Many of these information sources can be identified as part of hazard mitigation and preparedness campaigns. Working relationships can be developed during these nondisaster periods that will facilitate information collection and flow in disaster response.

Information Going Out

If information coming in is the basis for disaster communications, then information going out is the goal. Timely and accurate information can save lives in disaster response and in hazard mitigation and preparedness programs.

Historically, traditional media monopolized the dissemination of disaster information from public sources. Social media must now be added to the information dissemination mix. The Miami Herald reported in May 2012 that Florida Power & Light has "a Twitter account, Facebook posts, YouTube, a blog and also a new Power Tracker system for customers to monitor, in real time, power outages and restoration efforts" (Cohen, 2012).

In getting information to the public, you must use all the available communications mechanisms including the following:

- Traditional media—television, radio, and newspapers.
- Digital and social media—post new information on community Web sites, blogs, wikis, and bulletin boards, Facebook and Twitter; share timely photos and video online on YouTube; and tell traditional media that online outlets are being updated routinely (see Figure 11-10).
- Neighborhood communications networks—trusted community leaders who go door-to-door.

Historically, emergency officials have disseminated disaster information to the traditional media by means of press conferences, briefings, tours of the disaster site, one-on-one interviews with disaster officials,

FIGURE 11-10 National Severe Weather Preparedness Week Facebook Banner. *Source: Zachary Kittrie/FEMA.*

press releases, situation reports, and postings on the Internet. Radio actualities, photographs, and videotape have also been provided to traditional media. In major disasters, emergency management agencies have used satellite uplinks and video and audio press conferences to reach traditional media outlets across large sections of the country.

Disseminating information through social media outlets is growing and is certainly the wave of the future. Still, social media is something new for many emergency officials and will require patience and understanding of how these new media function with their audiences. Most of this work can occur during nondisaster periods. This is the time to learn more about Wikipedia, Twitter, blogs, Flickr, Facebook, YouTube, and social networking sites and to discover how you as an emergency manager can best use these new media to deliver preparedness and hazard mitigation messages as well as communicate with their target audiences in the disaster response and recovery phases.

Social Media Trends in the Emergency Management Community

Excerpts from Congressional Testimony by Albert Ashwood, Chairman, NEMA Legislative Committee and Director, Oklahoma Department of Emergency Management

Social Media incorporates various activities such as adapting technology and social interface. This has proven vital to the world of emergency management. Social networking can improve interaction between state agencies and the public. As real-time information is communicated to the public, the need to maintain accurate facts increases in urgency. The concept of using social media to communicate with the public remains a new phenomenon for many in the emergency management community. The idea of using social media to aid in preparing for, responding to, and recovering from disasters, has caught the attention of many in this field. Despite the benefits and shortfalls, social media continues to develop into an accepted form of communication. It has changed the way information is communicated and examined with citizens and the public. Two major trends seem to be forming as social media takes hold in the emergency management community:

- *Disseminating Information*: The first trend seen by emergency managers is the use of social media to convey information in or around an affected disaster area. The versatility of this method is recognized, yet it often lacks any guidelines to make an organized effort to reduce the amount of chaos after a disaster. With volumes of information potentially pouring into the EOC, important data can be overlooked. Reliability, coordination, and integration are three critical factors needed to determine how social media will be used from both a public-safety aspect and as an information sharing tool. As far as information sharing is concerned, social media is in its maturity. From a public-safety standpoint, social media is in its infancy.

- *Volunteer Mobilization*: Often after a disaster, volunteer work groups come in quickly to assist communities. Without a robust volunteer management system in place, the influx of personnel could become a management concern. Social media has been able to bridge the gap between the need for volunteers and the chaos which could occur in the absence of coordination. Although social media has reduced the amount of confusion that accompanies a disaster there are still many avenues to be explored. The emergency management community is still in the trial phase of using social media to assist in volunteer management.

To help assess the value and use of social media in the emergency management community, NEMA joined with the Center for Naval Analysis (CNA) last year to conduct a survey. To date, much of the data on social media and emergency management has been limited to anecdotal accounts or studies, so the CNA-NEMA study provided valuable information into the use of social media in emergency management. State emergency management directors and their Public Information Officers (PIO) were closely engaged in the development, distribution, and completion of the survey. Key findings of the survey included:

- *Familiarity with Social Media*: On average, respondents from state, county, and local levels of government all considered themselves at least "moderately familiar" with social media. Facebook, Twitter, and YouTube have become commonly associated with social media.
- *Use of Social Media*: Of those surveyed, all state emergency management agencies use social media in some capacity, as do 68% of county emergency management agencies and 85% of local response agencies. Of those surveyed, nearly all of the state emergency management agencies, half of the county emergency management agencies, and three-fifths of the local response agencies have used social media in response to a real-world event, primarily to push information out to the community. Over 90% of the events cited were from 2011 or 2012, underscoring the recent adoption of social media.
- *Determining Capabilities*: Respondents were asked to characterize their agency's social media capability along four dimensions:
  - *Governance*: Commitment and buy-in from senior leadership and political officials at the state level is more than double that at the county and local levels.
  - *Technology*: Technology used for other purposes in an agency is often used in an ad hoc fashion to support basic social media operations, such as posting status updates.
  - *Data/Analytics*: Data-extraction efforts at all levels are still reliant upon manual review, making monitoring efforts difficult to scale-up during large disasters.
  - *Processes*: Formally defined and tested processes and procedures lag behind social media use.
- *Trust but Verify*: Of those surveyed 59% of state emergency management agencies, 55% of county emergency management agencies, and 41% of local response agencies trust social media less than traditional media sources. Nearly all respondents agree that, on receiving information from social media sources, their agency would attempt to verify this information.
- *Barriers to Implementation*: Survey results indicate that the primary barrier to emergency management agencies' use of social media is a lack of dedicated personnel. While most respondents indicated that they would not necessarily look to the Federal Government to

play a large role in supporting the development of their agency's social media capabilities, they identified prime areas for potential support, including grant funding, training on how social media could be used, and the provision of guidance and standards.

As a result of this effort, the state PIOs developed work groups to examine the above findings. The work groups will:

- Develop best practices and goals for use of social media by state emergency managers to better target resources and funding towards implementation of social media;
- Develop and distribute a social media governing model that specifically addresses the public-safety responsibilities and the implications for emergency management and response entities;
- Create a template of standard operating procedures to manage social media information to more effectively integrate social media and public-sourced intelligence into emergency management information processes;
- Develop concepts for Virtual Operations Support Teams (VOST) that allows for rapid expansion of capabilities by leveraging trained and trusted personnel to respond both virtually via external monitoring and response and as teams with crucial skills for deployment to emergency operations center, and;
- The range of non-categorical issues raised in the report.

Conclusion

Social media has begun to play an integral role in emergency preparedness, response, and recovery. By understanding the way social media complements emergency management services, the future use of it can greatly enhance emergency management capabilities. Social media and its role in emergency management will continue to evolve. As the emergency management community shifts to accept this new form of communication, many aspects will need to be considered. A familiarity with social media will need to be established, the capabilities that pertain to emergency management will need to be identified and explored, verification of information will be a requirement and it will be critical to break down any barriers to implementation. Although the emergency management community is still in the experimental stages of using social media to convey important messages as well as receive information from the public, it represents the wave of the future.

Source: Ashwood (2013).

Prior to the next disaster, you should do the following:

- *Create a Twitter account*—This is an excellent platform for getting concise messages to the public. Predisaster is the time to establish a Twitter account and recruit followers. More and more emergency agencies use Twitter to communicate with their customers and to access information from local sources including FEMA, the Red Cross, and numerous state and local agencies.
- *Create a Facebook page*—Post information on how to prepare for future disasters and take mitigation actions that will reduce future disaster impacts. FEMA, other federal agencies, and many state and local emergency management agencies already have established a Facebook page.

- *Starting a blog*—Get your message out there about the risks your community faces; how to take action to reduce those risks and protect your family, home, and business; how to prepare for the next disaster; when to evacuate and how; what will happen when your organization responds; and how members of your community can become first informers. (see sidebar "Another Voice: Eric Holdeman" for comments on blogging).

Another Voice: Eric Holdeman

Eric Holdeman, former director of the King County (WA) Office of Emergency Management, is the principal for Eric Holdeman and Associates.

Blogging

We are living in the information age. The rise of computers and the Internet has provided the opportunity to now share information and knowledge like never before. Only the invention of the Gutenberg's printing press rivals the information availability explosion that we are currently living in.

The culture of professional emergency managers is to share information with other emergency managers and other professions. Emergency management crosses the entire spectrum of interests in communities. The private, public, and nonprofit sectors are all areas of interest to an emergency manager preparing a community for the next disaster.

With this in mind, it was only natural to begin blogging on the topic of emergency management and homeland security. It started innocently enough by establishing e-mail lists for the various disciplines. When I'd come across information that would be of interest, I'd share that with the appropriate spectrum of people and organizations that I had on my e-mail list. There were some days when I was sending 10 or more e-mails a day. Maintaining a viable e-mail list in our mobile society was also a time-consuming proposition. One of my staff who was administering our King County Office of Emergency Management (OEM) Web site suggested establishing an "Eric's Corner" Web link on our King County Web site and then inviting people to sign up to get weekly updates "pushed" out to them. Without knowing it, I had "backed into" the world of blogging. Besides sharing facts and documents, I was also providing a bit of commentary if I had an opinion on the information being shared.

Putting the mechanics of a blog in place was not that difficult, but establishing a listserv to push updates out proved more challenging. I found that King County did not have the capacity to do another listserv and I was stymied for a period of time. Then through casual conversations with staff from other organizations, one of them, the City of Seattle's Information Technology (IT) Office, offered to host the listserv that pushed the blog updates out—and for no charge, where in my own jurisdiction, I would have had to pay for the service. This is a great example of the level of cooperation that is needed if regional enterprises are to thrive.

After leaving King County, I was able to establish a new blog, "Disaster Zone," that operates on my company's Web site. The advantage in having a company sponsored Web presence is that it enables me to tap into the technical expertise of Web professionals, which I would not have if I were blogging on my own. It also has enabled the establishment of another listserv function that again pushes out information to people in "Weekly Updates." There are currently almost 1000 people who receive weekly Disaster Zone blog updates. Technology has also advanced so that people who want to be notified of updates as they occur can sign up for Really Simple Syndication (RSS), which is a blogging tool available to people who desire the updated blog postings as they happen.

Information is power. Some people chose to hoard it in order to maintain control over what gets done or doesn't get done. The opposite of that thinking, which I follow, is that if I share what I know with others, I empower them to become better informed and therefore more effective in how they prepare their organizations, communities, and regions. Sharing information in effect gives immortality to the person who is willing to share what they know. And what you know should not die with you. It would be such a waste of a precious resource, years, sometimes decades, of experience that mean hundreds or thousands of mistakes that you learned from.

People, when they have information, are empowered to make better decisions that may in some cases impact tens of thousands of people during disasters. I have found that blogging is a form of "mentoring" that allows a person to coach others in a profession that is still finding its way. If I can blog, anyone can! Try it and share what you know with others. Reap the rewards of knowing that together we are a stronger profession and one that is known for collaboration.

- *Post videos on YouTube*—Include features such as "how to" videos on how to disaster-proof your home, office, and business. Post videos that explain how to survive the next disaster (how much water and food to have on hand and where to go for information). Since Sandy, FEMA continues to regularly post videos on YouTube (see Figure 11-11).

FIGURE 11-11 LaPlace, LA, September 7, 2012—Mar Tobiason, Red Cross shelter volunteer, shows a YouTube video featuring a group of children living in a temporary shelter. The American Red Cross and FEMA are working with local, state, and other federal agencies to assist residents affected by Hurricane Isaac. *Photo by Patsy Lynch/FEMA.*

- *Create a Google Map*—of the locations of designated shelters and evacuation routes.
- *Create a cross agency team*—to coordinate social media protocols and processes for agreeing on a common Twitter hashtag, agreeing to retweet each other's tweets, etc.

How FEMA Uses Social Media

Excerpts from Congressional Testimony by Shayne Adamski, FEMA Senior Manager of Digital Engagement

FEMA uses multiple social media platforms to reach the public and to provide them with useful information. While no individual social media tool is exhaustive or all-encompassing, each allows us to communicate with the populations we serve. I would like to discuss a few of the social media tools we use at FEMA, and how we use them.

We are very active on two of the most popular social networks in America—Facebook and Twitter—where we are able to reach the greatest number of active, engaged users. We have three Facebook pages and 34 Twitter accounts. Collectively, our Twitter accounts have 400,000 followers, while our Facebook pages have 143,000 fans. FEMA also manages a YouTube channel as well as discussions on an online collaboration site called IdeaScale.

These numbers also show our growth and demonstrate our increasing ability to communicate with Americans online. When I started in my position in June 2010, we had 25,000 followers on all of our social media accounts combined. Today, FEMA has well over 500,000 users on these sites.

FEMA uses social media in five primary ways:

First, we use social media to provide up-to-date information about how the whole community emergency management team, including FEMA, is helping communities and individuals prepare for, respond to and recover from and mitigate disasters. At the onset of the recent Oklahoma tornadoes, one of the many messages that we tweeted was: "#Oklahoma: We're working closely with state emergency management & local officials. We stand ready to support as needed & requested."

We also leverage our social media accounts to help our federal, state, local, tribal, territorial, and private sector partners share key messages. For example, we shared many status updates from trusted sources before, during and after Hurricane Sandy, including from Governor Chris Christie, Mayor Michael Bloomberg and other governors and mayors throughout the affected region. Following the Oklahoma tornadoes in May, we amplified key messages from the Oklahoma state government and the city of Moore.

Second, we use social media to provide safety and preparedness tips. As the Subcommittee is aware, we are currently in the middle of the 2013 Atlantic hurricane season, so we recently posted tips regarding properly securing windows during a hurricane. Similar messages are posted regularly across all of our social media accounts to help ensure that Americans have actionable, specific ways to get themselves, their families, their business, and their communities better prepared for disasters.

Third, we use social media to inform the public of the most effective ways to help disaster survivors. Americans show tremendous generosity after disasters, so we provide tips on how that generosity could be most effective. For example, we encourage Americans to donate through trusted charities that know the specific needs of the impacted community.

Fourth, we tell disaster survivors where and how they are able to receive assistance—whether that be from FEMA or from another trusted source. To accomplish this, we leverage all of our social media accounts, including those managed in each of FEMA's regional offices. Our regional offices fill an important niche, providing useful information to local users, such as locations of FEMA's Disaster Recovery Centers or by highlighting local resources. We employed this tactic after Hurricane Sandy and during both the recent floods in Illinois and the tornadoes in Oklahoma.

Fifth, we tap into the potential of social media to gain valuable feedback. As I shared before, social media is at its essence a conversation and it is a conversation that we strive to be an active part of. Of course, in true conversation, both participants listen and respond in turn—social media is no different. This exchange is a critical component of being viewed as a responsive, authoritative source of information.

To further facilitate feedback and interaction from the online community, FEMA also holds the equivalent of "virtual town halls" using Twitter chats. Twitter chats are real-time conversations using the platform. One recent example came after Hurricane Sandy. Federal Coordinating Officer for New York, Mike Byrne, participated in a Twitter chat and fielded many questions, such as "How do homeowners get the amounts they need to rebuild?" and "Has @Fema spread into affected communities, holding open houses and is it better coordinated w/other agencies than 1 mo ago?". These online "townhalls" allow FEMA to answer questions in an open, public forum and contribute to growing our online following, which is essential to educating a greater number of Americans.

Source: Adamski (2013).

Messengers

The person who delivers the messages plays a critical role in disaster communications. The messengers put a human face on disaster response, and these people are critical to building confidence in the public that people will be helped and their community will recover. Public information officers (PIOs) regularly deliver information and messages to the media and the public. However, the primary face of the disaster response should be an elected or appointed official (i.e., mayor, governor, county administrator, or city manager) or the director of the emergency management agency or both. These individuals bring a measure of authority to their role as messenger and, in the case of the emergency management director, someone who is in charge of response and recovery operations.

The public wants to hear from an authority figure and the media wants to know that the person they are talking to is the one making the decisions. Elected officials who served as successful messengers in recent disasters include Boston Mayor Thomas Menino and Massachusetts Governor Deval Patrick in the aftermath of the 2013 Boston Marathon bombings, New Jersey Governor Chris Christie, and New York Governor Andrew Cuomo and NYC Mayor Bloomberg in Hurricane Sandy in 2012.

Prior to the next disaster, each emergency management agency should determine if an elected or appointed official will serve as the primary messenger alone or in tandem with the emergency agency director. It is best to work out in advance what types of information will be delivered by which messenger.

Protocols for briefing books and situational updates should be developed. A determination should be made as to who will lead press briefings and news conferences, who will be available to the media for one-on-one interviews, and who will be involved in communicating with the new media outlets. Again, all of these activities can be shared by the elected/appointed official and the emergency agency director.

Emergency management agencies should also designate appropriate senior managers who will be made available to both the traditional and new media to provide specific information on their activities and perspective. This is helpful in even the smallest disaster when persons with expertise in specific facets of the response can be very helpful in delivering disaster response information and messages.

Involving the designated elected/appointed officials and the agency director in hazard mitigation and preparedness communications will help them to prepare for communicating in disaster response and recovery and will make them familiar with the public as disaster communications messengers.

Staffing

Not many emergency management agencies have a single communications specialist much less a communications staff. Federal agencies such as FEMA, Department of Homeland Security (DHS), Health and Human Services (HHS), and others involved in disaster have extensive communications staff. Most state emergency management operations have at least a communications director/public information officer. The depth of staff support for communications varies widely. Emergency management agencies in major cities in the United States often have communications directors and in some cases extensive communications staff. Small-size to midsize cities and communities are unlikely to have a communications director or staff.

Albert Ashwood, Oklahoma state emergency management director, testified before Congress in July 2013 that, "Social media once again played an integral role in disaster communications following the tornadoes, flooding, and severe weather that occurred between May 18 and June 2 in Oklahoma. Due to limited staffing in the OEM, the use of social media was not active during the initial twenty days after the first tornado. Rotating shifts were constructed by public information officers (PIO) to assist along with other agencies in answering media calls during call-heavy time periods. An inadequate number of personnel made it difficult to consistently provide Twitter or Facebook updates" (Ashwood, 2013).

The survey of emergency management organizations conducted by the CNA for the National Emergency Management Association noted, "Less than one in six agencies surveyed that use social media have dedicated social media personnel" (Su, 2013).

Critical Thinking

Do you think that homeland security/emergency management agencies, especially at the local level, will have the human resources to build and maintain an effective crisis communications capability?

Implementing Social Media in Emergency Management

Often, an argument from emergency managers is that it will take a lot of staff time and effort to implement a successful social media program. However, with the advent of multiple free services, emergency managers can quickly disseminate, monitor and archive information via social media.

Additionally, as social media continue to mature, there will potentially be a reduced reliance on traditional public information and use of press releases, freeing up time for public information officers and joint information centers to devote to social media.

If emergency managers embrace the use of social media prior to a disaster, their use will become second nature, making the task of employing "new" communication options less daunting during an emergency. It also allows officials to become the authority during disasters and a source of information for their community. A simple plan for the use of social media along with constant use will make their integration into the public information arena and EOC seamless.

One obstacle that many emergency managers often cite is the inability to gain access to these systems due to local informational technology restrictions. It is important to gain the support of the local elected official or decision-maker of the community. By explaining to them the importance of these tools in disaster response and highlighting how they can help citizens, there are often ways to get access to social media. In general, having a good plan and protocol for social media use, identify how social media sites will be used and why it will be advantageous to make exceptions in their computer use policies or website restrictions, will help break down the technology restriction barrier.

Finally, even if emergency managers do not use social media, the community will continue to use them. Therefore, it benefits officials to embrace these platforms. By addressing false rumors and information as well as using social media to quickly disseminate important facts, social media can ultimately help emergency managers and organizations respond to critical requests. Social media and associated technology are the current situational awareness platform for many citizens and are changing the field of emergency management. Emergency managers and responders should embrace this movement and use it as another tool in their toolbox.

As more and more people gain access to mobile technology, social network usage will continue to rise. The use of mobile technology and social networks will make it easier for citizens to update emergency and disaster event information through posts, videos and pictures. It will be important for emergency managers to track and data mine social media for emergency preparedness and response. Establishing and implementing social media strategies and processes prior to an emergency event are key factors in increasing the validity and effectiveness of using social media for crisis communication.

Source: Smith et al. (2013).

The time has come for all organizations involved in emergency management to establish an ongoing communications staff capability. For agencies in small-size to midsize communities, this may require enlisting help from the local government's communications staff. One way to do this is to provide funding for a percentage of this individual's time each month. In this way, communications activities required during nondisaster periods could be acquired on a consistent basis. This will also allow for the local government communications staff and director to become better informed of the emergency management agency's activities and be better prepared to work with the emergency agency director during disaster response and recovery.

For large cities and federal and voluntary agencies with existing communications staff, it is now a matter of reordering priorities to meet the demands of working with the new media. Staff will be required to establish and maintain working relationships with new media outlets and to interact with various blogs, bulletin boards, social networking sites, and other new media outlets that serve their community. At minimum, there should be one designated staff person on the communications staff who is responsible for the day-to-day interaction with social media. Additional staff should be made available in a major disaster to work with these groups.

The social media designated staff would also work with social media outlets in promoting hazard mitigation and preparedness campaigns in the community and serve as the staff support for the establishment and maintenance of neighborhood communications networks working with trusted leaders in the community.

Social Media in Emergency Management: The Digital Public Information Officer (Author: Christopher Poirier)

The #*SMEM* (Social Media in Emergency Management) community is constantly abuzz on the values and challenges surrounding the use of social media by organizations to pass important emergency related information during a disaster. For the sake of this discussion, let's focus on the role of the PIO in keeping people informed through social media.

The PIO's primary job is to act as the "official voice" of an organization. In this case, we'll assume the PIO to be a part of a governmental function. This person and his or her team should be the official source of information during an emergency. However, in today's technology laden landscape, the PIOs in many jurisdictions have either entirely ignored the social media space, misused it, or are just starting to grasp it. To this end, I encourage PIOs to consider the following:

1. Be the Official Source
2. Open the Two-Way Street
3. Be Honest
4. Recruit, Standardize, and Innovate

Source: aNewDomain.net (2013).

Training and Exercises

An effective disaster communications operation requires well-trained messengers and staff and should be a vital part of all disaster exercises. Elected/appointed officials, agency directors, and PIOs should all receive formal media training in order to become comfortable working with the media to communicate disaster messages to the public. Media training teaches how to communicate a message effectively, techniques for fielding difficult questions, and provides the opportunity to practice delivery outside the crucible of a crisis. If possible, media training should be provided to senior staff who may appear in the media.

Staff training should come in several forms including:

- Media relations—learn how to work with traditional and new media including meeting deadlines, responding to inquiries, scheduling interviews, and understanding what types of information each media outlet requires and how a news operation works.

- Social media—learn what a blog is, how social networking works, and how to establish and maintain a neighborhood communications network.
- Marketing—learn how to pitch a story idea for a preparedness program or hazard mitigation project to all forms of media, how to develop supporting materials for preparedness and hazard mitigation campaigns, and how to evaluate the effectiveness of such efforts.

Staff Training in Social Media

GOHSEP Training Announcement

Training Course Announcement

Course Name: Social Media for Natural Disaster Response and Recovery

Date: August 7, 2012

Time: 9:00 a.m.–4:00 p.m.

Location: Jefferson Parish EOC 910 3rd Street, Gretna, LA 70053

Description: The course will provide participants with the knowledge and skills of social media and its uses, as well as the current tools, methods, and models to properly make use of social media for crisis communication. Participants will take part in facilitator-led activities. Through the use of social media tools, participants will learn and master skills to disseminate information and monitor, track, measure, and analyze social media traffic. Participants will be able to use social media as a method to identify warning signs that a crisis is developing. The use of social media for disaster preparedness has two components:

(1) As an effective means for providing updated information about a crisis, proactive steps must be taken prior to disasters in order for effective communications to occur.

(2) As a part of crisis observation, managers should be monitoring social media platforms and channels that may be relevant to their organization. Observing can be as simple as conducting regular searches and analyses of media platforms for keywords and phrases that may imply an emerging crisis or disaster. Monitoring of social media should extend into the crisis response and post-crisis phases to check how crisis management efforts are being received.

Source: Governor's Office of Homeland Security and Emergency Preparedness (GOHSEP). State of Louisiana.

Communications operations must always be included in future disaster exercises. It is highly recommended that these exercises include reporters from traditional media outlets and representatives from the new media, including bloggers and online news sites. Working with new media and online news sites should be included in exercises such as updating and correcting a Wikipedia site and posting information on a community bulletin board. Community leaders involved in neighborhood communications networks should also be included in the exercise.

Monitoring, Updating, and Adapting

Staff should be assigned to regularly monitor all media outlets. Summaries of news stories in the traditional media should be compiled regularly. Staff should routinely monitor new media outlets and provide regular summaries of news on these sites. This activity is especially important during a disaster response. Through monitoring, the media staff is capable of identifying problems and issues early in the process and can shape communications strategies to address these issues before they become big problems. This is also an opportunity to identify trends in how information flows through the media to the public and to identify areas for improvement of message development and delivery. Regular monitoring will identify rumors and misinformation and speed corrections.

FEMA's Hurricane Sandy: Rumor Control Initiative

From Congressional Testimony by FEMA's Senior Manager of Digital Engagement Shayne Adamski
This two-way flow of information had an impact after Hurricane Sandy. In the days following the hurricane, FEMA launched "Rumor Control," an initiative using all of our online platforms to dispel inaccurate information being shared online. We listened and identified rumors circulating online, from logistics information to specific disaster assistance programs, and moved to quickly correct the misinformation. This was done by creating a Rumor Control page on fema.gov and m.fema.gov (FEMA's mobile website), as well as through answering many questions received through our Facebook and Twitter accounts. FEMA receives questions almost daily on Facebook and Twitter, so we dedicate resources to answering them, thus helping to fulfill FEMA's mission of supporting America's citizens.

For more information see Hurricane Sandy: Rumor Control at http://www.fema.gov/hurricane-sandy-rumor-control.

Source: Adamski (2013).

The information collected as part of monitoring activities can be used to update communications plans, strategies, and tactics. These data can be used to determine how to allocate staff resources and to update training and exercise programs.

New media will continue to emerge as new technologies are developed and become widely accepted. Emergency management agencies must be constantly on the lookout for emerging communications technologies and opportunities. Agencies must adapt to changing media constantly and strive not to become fixed to any one media.

The use of mobile devices to disseminate and collect disaster information is growing that "more than 3 out of 4 crisis communications professionals view the ability to manage incident/emergency communications using mobile devices as a requirement … (the) challenge is to build a communications plan that includes the ability to gather intelligence and communicate with key stakeholders using social media and mobile technologies" (Everbridge, 2013).

Social Media: Part of FEMA's Larger Digital Presence

FEMA's digital presence extends beyond social media. FEMA also communicates with Americans via the web and various mobile platforms. These channels complement each other and allow us to reach a larger audience. FEMA runs several websites that serve as authoritative sources for information, including: fema.gov, ready.gov, and disasterasssitance.gov.

FEMA is also tapping into the importance that cell phones play in everyday life, specifically through our smartphone app, text message program and Wireless Emergency Alerts. In my experience, cell phones are often a lifeline after a disaster and many times are the only source of information in the hardest affected areas. As citizens continue to use smartphones more and more, those of us in emergency management should continually be looking for ways to share our message and make our services available through those devices.

In 2011, we also released our FEMA smartphone app, which provides information on how to: make a plan and build your emergency kit; stay safe and rebuild after a disaster; and lookup open disaster recovery centers and open shelters. We are very proud of the fact that the safety information in the FEMA app is accessible within the app even if the user does not have a cellular or Wi-Fi connection—making it a valuable tool during a disaster.

Text messaging is a form of communication that is particularly useful during and after a disaster when phone lines may be congested and voice calls often do not get through. Sending and receiving text messages requires less bandwidth and helps reduce the volume of phone calls in an area so that necessary communications are able to continue to be made.

After the May 20 tornadoes in Oklahoma, we posted a message to Facebook that reminded people to use text messaging to check in with friends/family in the impacted area, as well as the American Red Cross Safe and Well site. *The message* was seen by more than 230,000 people on Facebook.

In 2011, FEMA was the first federal agency to establish its own text message short code—meaning that anyone could text 43362 or 4FEMA to obtain valuable information. Texting this code allows people to search for open disaster recovery centers and shelters. During the height of Hurricane Sandy, our text message program received more than 10,000 requests in 1 day from people searching for shelter locations within a specific ZIP code. Citizens could also sign up to receive regular preparedness tips regarding the hazards that are most common in their area, such as earthquakes, wildfires, hurricanes, or tornadoes.

Local and state public safety officials can send Wireless Emergency Alerts directly to citizen's cell phones, utilizing FEMA's Integrated Public Alert & Warning System. These geographically targeted messages are sent from emergency managers, the National Weather Service, and the National Center for Missing and Exploited Children to warn citizens about severe weather, AMBER Alerts and other threats to safety. During national emergencies, the President can also communicate with citizens using Wireless Emergency Alerts.

Source: Adamski (2013).

The changing shape of homeland security and emergency management in the coming years will demand that communications take a larger role in all emergency operations and programming. Incorporating digital and social media forms and functions into communications plans and strategies and adapting to new technologies will be the order of the day for all emergency management agencies. Emergency and homeland security officials can no longer avoid communicating with the media and the public. Emergency agencies must accept the expanded role of communications in all four phases of emergency management and embrace it as a valuable tool in meeting the needs of the public.

Communicating in the Era of Homeland Security

In the fourth edition of this book, we included a section in the Communications chapter with the same title as this section "Communicating in the Era of Homeland Security." We noted that communicating with the public is an area that needs to be improved if the nation is going to have a truly effective homeland security system. From its inception, DHS has shown little interest in communicating with the public, and when it has, the results have not always been positive—the "duct tape and plastic" fiasco and past reports of former DHS Secretary Ridge questioning terror alert warnings serve as classic examples. DHS communications have improved during the Obama Administration, but DHS and its state and local partners still need to address three factors in order to further improve their communications with the American people. These three factors were as follows:

- A commitment from the leadership to communicate timely and accurate information to the public
- A resolution of the conflict between sharing data with the public in advance and in the aftermath of a terrorist incident that has value for intelligence or criminal prosecution purposes
- An investment in better understanding of the principal terrorist threats and developing communications strategies that educate and inform the public about these threats

What follows is a discussion of these three factors and what progress has been made by DHS and homeland security officials across the country in addressing the issues these factors present:

Factor 1. Leadership commitment: There must be a commitment from the leadership, not only at DHS and its state and local partners but also at all levels of government including the executive level to communicate timely and accurate information to the public. This is especially important in the response and recovery phases to a terrorist incident.

In a disaster scenario, the conventional wisdom that states information is power and that hoarding information helps to retain such power is almost categorically reversed. Withholding information during disaster events generally has an overall negative impact on the well-being of the public and on the impression the public forms about involved authorities. In practice, sharing of information is what generates authority and power, when that information is useful and relates to the hazard at hand. A good example of this fact is the actions of former New York City Mayor Rudy Giuliani after the September 11 attacks. Giuliani went to great lengths to get accurate and timely information to the public in a time of crisis, and his efforts both inspired the public and greatly enhanced the effectiveness of the response and recovery efforts he guided.

Historically, DHS leadership and the political leadership have been reluctant to make this commitment to share information with the public. This is something that must change if they expect the American people to fully comprehend the homeland security threat and to become actively engaged in homeland security efforts. Few citizens have any idea of what actual terrorism risks they face, and fewer can actually relate those risks in any comparable fashion to the risks they face every day.

Since the writing of this section in 2011, DHS and homeland security officials around the country have made progress in communicating with the public during and after a terrorist incident. The best example of this leadership commitment is the high-profile role law enforcement officials played in communicating with the public during the aftermath of the Boston Marathon bombings in 2013 and the subsequent capture of the second bombing suspect. Leaders from the Boston Police Department, the Massachusetts State Police, and federal law enforcement officials maintained a steady round of briefings and social media postings concerning their activities in responding to the injuries at the marathon finish line and in identifying and capturing the suspects. In fact, these officials set a standard for open communications and for engaging with the public through social media especially in the efforts to identify the suspects.

Factor 2. Resolve information sharing conflict: Homeland security officials at all levels must resolve the conflict between sharing data with the public in advance and in the aftermath of a terrorist incident that has value for intelligence or criminal prosecution purposes. This is directly linked to the commitment issue discussed in the previous paragraphs and has been repeatedly cited by homeland security officials as reasons for not sharing more specific information with the public.

Also at issue is the question of when to release relevant information to the public without compromising intelligence sources and/or ongoing criminal investigations. This is an issue that rarely if ever confronts emergency management officials dealing with natural and unintentional man-made disasters. Therefore, there is little precedent or experience for current homeland security officials to work with in crafting a communications strategy that balances the competing need for the public to have timely and accurate information with the need to protect intelligence sources and ongoing criminal investigations. To date, the needs of the intelligence and justice communities have clearly been judged to outweigh those of the public—but at a cost.

Withholding information leaves the public vulnerable and suspicious of the government. Lucy Dalglish, executive director of the Reporters Committee for the Freedom of the Press, said her task, and the task of journalists, was to convince government officials that over the long run, transparency can build trust and save lives: "The same information that a terrorist can use to do great damage can possibly give families information about which escape route to use to get away from a nuclear power plant. I think we're going to find that if we have a flu pandemic, the information that can be used to terrorize and scare people can also be used to save their lives. I think what we have to do is work very hard at convincing people that access to information is ultimately going to be our friend" (May, 2006).

The 2011 implementation by the Obama Administration of the National Terrorism Advisory System that replaced the much-maligned Homeland Security Advisory System (HSAS) was a critical first step in reestablishing trust with the public for the warning system. From this starting point, additional communications mechanisms can be developed to ensure that the public gets timely and accurate information both in advance of any terrorist incident and during the response and recovery phases in the aftermath of the next terrorist attack.

Overall progress on this front is more difficult to measure. The NTAS was a good step but nothing has been heard from the NTAS since its implementation in April 2011. While DHS encourages the public to engage with NTAS by reporting suspicious behavior, there is no indication that DHS is ready to use the NTAS to disseminate information on likely threats before they occur. Again, the public engagement through social media in the Boston Marathon bombing manhunt shows a willingness by homeland security and law enforcement authorities to gather information from the public. However, there has been no indication that these same authorities were willing to share the information they collected with the public beyond announcing when and where they captured the second suspect.

Factor 3. Invest in understanding the terror threats: More effort must be invested by federal departments and agencies to better understand the principal terrorist threats that our nation faces (i.e., biological, chemical, radiological, nuclear, and explosives) and to develop communications strategies that educate and inform the public about these threats with more useful information. The 2001 Washington, DC, anthrax incident is a perfect example of uninformed or misinformed public officials sharing what is often conflicting and, in too many instances, wrong information with the public.

The nation's public officials must be better informed about these principal risks and be ready and capable of explaining complicated information to the public. As the anthrax incident made clear, this is not a luxury, but a necessity if the response to similar incidents in the future is to be successful.

Decades of research and a new generation of technologies now inform emergency managers as they provide information about hurricanes, tornadoes, earthquakes, and hazardous materials incidents to the public. A similar research effort must be undertaken for these five new terrorist risks and communications strategies that will ensure that homeland security officials at all levels are capable of clearly explaining to the public the hazards posed by these threats.

These communications strategies must consider how to communicate to the public when incomplete information is all that is available to homeland security officials. In the vast majority of cases, this partiality of information is probable. A public health crisis will not wait for all the data to be collected and analyzed, nor will the public. Homeland security officials must develop strategies for informing the public effectively, as the crisis develops, by forming effective messages that are able to explain to the public how what is being said is the most accurate information available based on the information that, likewise, is available—despite its incomplete nature. Clearly, this is not an easy task, but it is not impossible. The public will increasingly expect such communications efforts, so the sooner such a system is in place, the better the next incident will be managed.

Progress here has been slow in addressing this factor. The 2014 Ebola scare clearly illustrates that the public remains uninformed about the threat of a pandemic. Few in the public and apparently in government quarters seemed to know what the procedures and protocols were for dealing with individuals infected by the Ebola virus. To further complicate the situation, public health and other government officials provided contradictory information to the public. And worst of all, these officials, who the public should be able to trust, left the stage to politicians and members of the pundit class to provide widely disparate versions of what should and should not be done to address this crisis. Obviously, more work needs to be done to better understand these new threats/hazards and to communicate that information responsibly to the public.

Critical Thinking

Do you think that there has been adequate progress in working to make crisis communications a priority and developing a functioning capability in emergency management/homeland security agencies? What do you think will happen in the future?

Conclusion

The experience of emergency managers with natural disasters provides at minimum a guide to the development of effective terrorism-related communications strategies. However, there is much work to be done to adapt existing and future crisis communications models to the new hazards, the new partners, and the new dynamic between response and recovery and criminal activity associated with the new terrorist threat. One thing will remain constant: communication with the public about the terrorist threat must receive the same attention and resources that are now going to new technologies, new training programs, and new organizations. It has never been more important that public officials talk to the public, and it has never been more difficult than it is now. If this problem is not addressed properly, it can only compound in the worst way the terrible consequences of any terrorist incident.

CASE STUDY 1

The Boston Marathon Bombings

America's first fully interactive national tragedy of the social media age.

At 2:49 p.m. on April 15, 2013, two bombs exploded near the finish line of the annual Boston Marathon killing three people and injuring 264. The first reports about the about the terrorist attack were spread through Twitter and Facebook.

At 2:59 p.m., the *Boston Globe* tweeted:

BREAKING NEWS: Two powerful explosions detonated in quick succession right next to the Boston Marathon finish line this afternoon.

Minutes later, the Boston Police Department confirmed the explosion in a tweet. And in a separate tweet soon after reported:

22 injured. 2 dead #tweetfromthebeat via @CherylFiandaca

According to Topsy, a Twitter analytics company, at around 4:10 p.m., there were more than 300,000 mentions on Twitter of "Boston explosions" (Stern, 2013). In a second wave of social media, details about the event spread. Media that included photos of blood covering the ground and a 6 s Vine video of the actual explosion was circulated, deepening people's sense of what had happened. Around 4:30 p.m., there were more than 700,000 mentions on Twitter of the "Boston Marathon" (Stern, 2013).

Even though television was the most widely used source of information about the bombing and its aftermath, it was social media that shaped the story and the response. While 80% of Americans followed the story on TV according to the Pew Research Center, about half (49%) say they kept up with news and information online or on a mobile device, and a quarter of Americans got information about the explosions and the hunt for the bombers on social networking sites such as Facebook and Twitter. Young Americans in particular kept up-to-date through social media. Slightly more than half (56%) of an 18-to-29-year subgroup polled by Pew got bombing-related news through social networking sites (Pew Research Center, 2013).

The Boston bombings and the manhunt that followed became the backdrop for the world to witness the transformation—for good and for bad—in news gathering and distribution and in disaster management and crises communications caused by social media platforms and technology. The Boston Marathon bombings were a watershed, a moment that marked forever the changed role of social media and the fully participatory public in breaking news events and coverage. *The New York Times* wrote: "It is America's first fully interactive national tragedy of the social media age" (Kakutani, 2013).

From marathon runners giving their accounts on Facebook, to law enforcement officials using Twitter to give real-time updates and asking for help identifying and capturing the suspects, to the *Boston Globe* converting its homepage to a live blog that pulled in Tweets from Boston authorities, news outlets, and ordinary citizens, social media showed itself to be an indispensible tool with a unique role to play and contribution to make in response to a terrorist attack. Boston also provided a cautionary tale when some journalists and members of the public opted to value speed over accuracy, using social media to spread incorrect, unverified information, causing a "misinformation disaster" (Ulanoff, 2013).

And finally, it was during the bombings the Boston Police Department set a new standard for government communications during a disaster—using social media to inform, correct inaccurate information, lead, and listen to the public conversation. Mashable—an online media company that focuses on innovation and technology—declared that during the crisis, the Boston Police Department "schooled us all on social media" (Bar-Tur, 2013) and asserted that "BPD's presence online helps reinvent the whole notion of community policing for the 21st century" (Bar-Tur, 2013).

How Social Media Was Used During the Boston Marathon Bombings

From the moment the two bombs went off on Boylston Street near the end of the Boston Marathon until the eventual capture of the surviving suspect, social media played a unique and complementary role in providing immediate access to the most up-to-date information and as a platform that made it possible for the public to be actively involved in the story as fully participating partners in the identification and hunt for the suspected terrorists.

According to Sean Mussenden, a professor of digital journalism at the University of Maryland, this is the new normal for investigations. "It's also the present, the modern media landscape in which we live. The audience is a huge active participant in these sorts of stories" (Presuitti, 2013).

Breaking News/Real-Time updates

Both the FBI and the Boston PD used Twitter to reach out to the public to inform them of what was going and what to do. The public found out in real time what was going on as soon as law enforcement did. They were given updates throughout the event. News conferences were tweeted out and shared on Facebook as they occurred.

According to Jason Fry writing for Poynter.org, the Web site of the Poynter Institute, a journalism school that owns the *Tampa Bay Times*, the biggest change in breaking disaster news coverage is that news gathering and reporting are now done in real time—in front of readers and viewers. "Instead of waiting for a carefully crafted report on the news or a front page, readers are now in the 'fog of war' with the participants and reporters and officials and everybody else ... given readers' hunger for news on such days, news organizations can't remain silent about reports until they've been verified with officials and subjected to the organization's own system of scrutiny. The chaos of breaking news is no longer something out of which coverage arises—it's the coverage itself" (Fry, 2013).

According to Fry, the *Boston Globe's* news coverage of the Boston Marathon bombing benefited from a marriage of "boots on the ground" and an "eye in the sky" (Fry, 2013). The *Boston Globe* had boots on the ground—quite literally, since the newspaper had reporters and photographers at the finish line very near the site of the two bombs.

But they also needed an eye in the sky—someone charged with gathering information from social media, deciding what's credible and what's not, and presenting it to readers "That meant incorporating what other journalists are seeing, hearing things and tweeting, keeping up with government officials, hospital spokespeople and other sources who now release information directly to the public, without funneling it through the media and staying abreast of what the public is reporting on social media" (Fry, 2013).

Situational Awareness

As soon as the bombs exploded, marathon participants and spectators turned to cell phones and social media to share photos and observations from the site and to let worried friends and family members know their condition and whereabouts.

Bruce Mendelsohn, a marketer who was attending a party just above the site of the first explosion, tweeted and uploaded photos from the bombing. According to Fry, "Mendelsohn is the kind of witness reporters hope to find but rarely do—a former Army medic with an eye for detail and the ability to assess spectators' injuries and what might have caused them" (Fry, 2013).

Mendelson's tweets:
Bruce Mendelsohn @brm90
I did see gruesome wounds and smelled cordite. My educated guess is that this was two bombs, detonated at ground level

(Continued)

CASE STUDY 1—CONTINUED

> *Bruce Mendelsohn @brm90*
> *Wounds commensurate with a ground-level detonation. I saw the wounds—mostly lower extremities.*

To help friends and families learn the fate of Marathon runners and spectators, Boston PD tweeted a number that family members looking for information related to injured individuals could call (Between the lines, 2013).

But heavy cell phone use caused slow and delayed service. The Massachusetts Emergency Management Agency sent a tweet telling people to try to use text messaging instead:

> *If you are trying to reach friends or family and can't get through via phone, try texting instead (less bandwidth).*
>
> *Thompson (2013)*

Google set up its Person Finder Web site in shortly after the twin bombings to make it easier to find and communicate with loved ones. The site allows users to enter the name of a person they are looking for or update information about someone who was there:

By the afternoon of April 16, information about some 5400 people had been entered into the database (Weiss, 2013) (Figure 11-12).

Law enforcement officials and other Boston institutions used social media to keep each other informed in real time. When the Boston PD tweeted about a third incident that occurred at JFK Presidential Library and Museum, they reported they were unsure if it was related or not to the two bombings. The JFK Presidential Library and Museum updated the Boston PD on Twitter: "The fire in the building is out. Appears to have started in the mechanical room. All staff and visitors are safe and accounted for" (Between the lines, 2013).

Help Identify the Suspects and Capture the Surviving Suspect

The two suspects in the Boston Marathon bombing were identified, cornered, and captured through the grand-scale dissemination and collection of information, photos, and videos through social media. Twitter, Facebook, and Internet Web sites all are credited with the effort (Presuitti, 2013). In the end, it was the public's connections to each other and to technology that broke the case.

"Today we are enlisting the public's help in identifying the two suspects," said FBI special agent Richard DesLauriers. The photos released by the FBI of suspect 1 and suspect 2, as they were known at the time, were instantaneously tweeted and retweeted, Facebooked, and Facebook-shared. "Thousands of marathon spectators flipped through their cell phone photos and videos—to see if they could match the suspects later identified as brothers Dzhokhar and Tamerlan Tsarnaev," according to the Voice of America News (Presuitti, 2013).

According to *The New York Times*, "The *Boston Marathon* bombings quickly turned into an Internet mystery that sent a horde of amateur sleuths surging onto the Web in a search for clues to the suspects' identity..." (Kakutani, 2013).

Boston PD used Twitter to provide a task force tip line number so people could call in if they had any tips on the case (Between the lines, 2013).

A gunfight in Watertown, Massachusetts, left one of the suspects Tamerlan Tsarnaev dead; his brother Dzhokhar was injured but escaped. A manhunt commenced and thousands of police officers searched Watertown. The FBI and Boston PD released several images of the subject of their manhunt

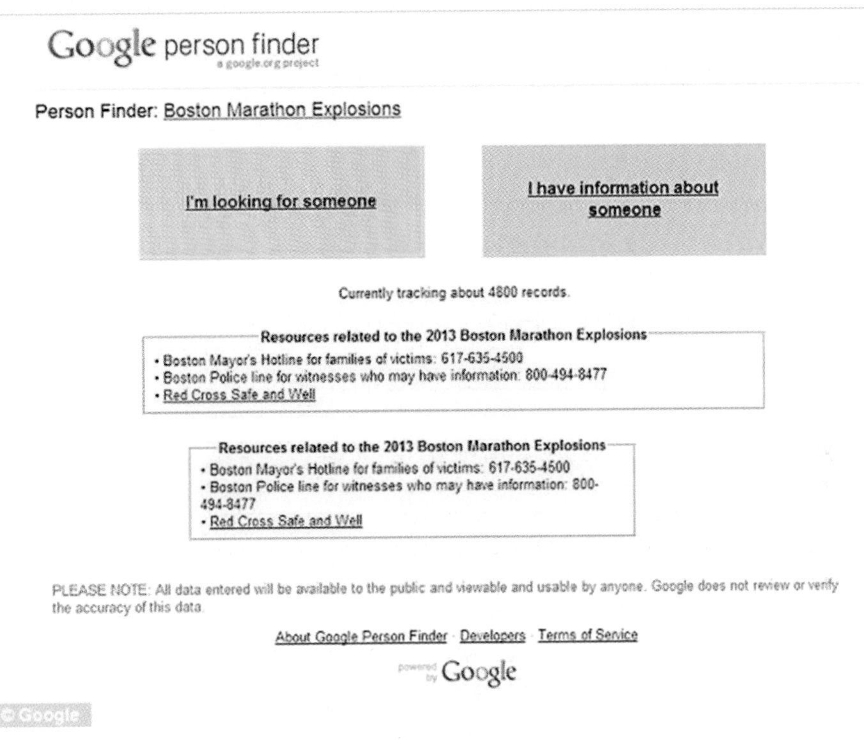

FIGURE 11-12 Google People Finder. *Source: Associated Press (2013).*

on social media (Figures 11-13 and 11-14) and tweeted and posted a license plate linked to the suspect (Figure 11-15) (Between the lines, 2013).

In the end, it was not a printed news release, phone calls, or a news conference that announced the capture of Dzhokhar Tsarnaev. It came in two tweets posted by the Boston Police Department:

Suspect in custody. Officers sweeping the area. Stand by for further info.

CAPTURED!!! The hunt is over. The search is done. The terror is over. And justice has won. Suspect in custody.

Keep People and Law Enforcement Officials Safe

Terrorism experts said that social media helped people in Boston and beyond determine their next steps after hearing about the explosions.

"Authorities have recognized that one the first places people go in events like this is to social media," said Bill Braniff, executive director of the National Consortium for the Study of Terrorism and Response to Terrorism. "We know from crisis communication research that people typically search for corroborating information before they take a corrective action—their TV tells them there's a tornado brewing and they talk to relatives and neighbors. And now they look at Twitter" (Gilgoff and Lee, 2013).

(Continued)

CASE STUDY 1—CONTINUED

FIGURE 11-13 Boston Bombing Suspect Picture.

FIGURE 11-14 Boston Police Department Tweet of Boston Bombing Suspect's Picture.

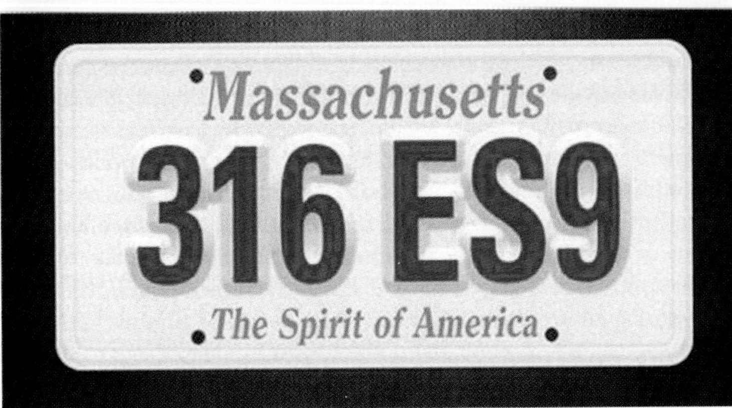

FIGURE 11-15 Image of Boston Bombing Suspect License Plate.

The Boston PD used Twitter to instruct the people of Boston on how to best remain safe and used Twitter and Facebook to tell the residents of Watertown to stay indoors and not answer the door unless they were instructed by a police officer to do so (Between the lines, 2013).

Social media was also used to keep law enforcement officials safe—after reporters and the public began tweeting from police scanner reports—giving away the location of officers involved in the manhunt. Cheryl Fiandaca—head of the Boston Police Department's Bureau of Public Information, the agency responsible for managing their social media accounts, said local media "know not to do that. They don't give away where officers are. But there were hundreds of reporters from all over the country here. We wanted to let other media folks who aren't as familiar know what's commonplace in Boston" (Keller, 2013). The police department sent the following alerts:

#MediaAlert: WARNING: Do Not Compromise Officer Safety by Broadcasting Tactical Positions of Homes Being Searched.

#MediaAlert: WARNING—Do Not Compromise Officer Safety/Tactics by Broadcasting Live Video of Officers While Approaching Search Locations.

This "polite scolding" to those tweeting information from police scanners was retweeted more than 20,000 times, higher than any other tweet at that time (Bar-Tur, 2013).

The University of Maryland digital journalism professor Sean Mussenden noted that "Journalists know not to tweet out police scanner—the public does not. Even cub reporters know you do not just write what's on the scanner." Boston proved it is "Dangerous to put speed over accuracy—especially in terrorist attack or a storm situation—it's essential to take time to be accurate" (Mussenden, 2013).

Correct Misinformation

Twitter was used aggressively to correct misinformation. The demand for constant updates and that fact that instant access to information is available through the smart phone led to the tweeting, posting, sharing, and broadcasting of inaccurate information during the event. The tension between speed and accuracy led to the communication of unverified information.

(Continued)

CASE STUDY 1—CONTINUED

After CNN and the Associated Press wrongly reported that the suspects were in custody, others picked up the news. Social media did the rest. "No one wants to be the second source to share this information, so thousands on social media, mostly Twitter, began sharing the news. It took almost an hour and a half for CNN to reverse its earlier report. The FBI even put out a statement begging the media to 'exercise caution'" (Ulanoff, 2013).

The social media site Reddit acknowledged its role in helping to disseminate false information, saying, "Some of the activity on Reddit fueled online witch hunts and dangerous speculation." Reddit also apologized to the family of the missing Brown University student Sunil Tripathi, who was misidentified on social media as a bombing suspect (Petrecca, 2013).

According to Fiandaca, the woman behind the Boston Police Department's Twitter account, "Twitter served as a great way to correct misinformation. We enhanced our reputation by putting out reliable and accurate information" (Solomonmccown&, 2013).

The Boston Police Department moved to counteract the false claims that were spreading across social networks. For example, on April 17, when, according to Businessweek, "The online news ecosystem was in the midst of a misinformation disaster, with rumors gleaned from the official police scanner and from inaccurate sources on major TV networks: A missing Brown student had been identified, inaccurately, as one of the suspects, and confusion reigned over the number of suspects involved in the massive manhunt," (Keller, 2013) and the Boston PD tweeted:

Despite reports to the contrary there has not been an arrest in the Marathon attack.

The department's tweet clarifying that there was no arrest shortly after the bombings saw more than 11,000 retweets. "By the end of the dramatic affair even the media was on board, as local reporters waited on a Boston Police tweet before officially announcing the capture of the elusive suspect" (Bar-Tur, 2013).

Ultimately, one of the lessons journalists learned from their coverage of Boston Marathon bombings is that "being right is better than being first." *The Boston Globe* local news editor Jen Peter, reflecting on media coverage of the bombings, noted that "on a normal day, being beaten on a scoop would be 'unpalatable' to her. But during high-pressure situations like the bombing and the events in Watertown, the *Globe* saw more outlets getting more negative feedback for spreading incorrect information than positive feedback for a scoop. Peter made the decision to 'verify, verify, verify,' even if the Globe didn't get it first" (Solomonmccown&, 2013).

Offer Community Support, Resources and Sympathy

Social media has the ability to create a sense of community during and after disasters. People used social media to offer strangers lodging, food or a hot shower when roads and hotels were closed. People also offered prayers and sympathy for the racers and the people of Boston. The hashtag #prayforboston trended on Twitter and Topsy reported that from 4:30 p.m. to 5:30 p.m., more than 75,000 tweets mentioned "Pray for Boston." People also shared photos of Boston on Instagram with the hashtag #prayforboston (Stern, 2013). Others started to find out how they could give in different ways, including donating blood (Stern, 2013).

"People were sharing as a community and grieving online. Social media brought people together. That wouldn't have happened a few years ago," according to Adam Gaffin, editor of Universal Hub, a community news and information site for the Boston area (Solomonmccown&, 2013). *The Boston Globe* social media editor Adrienne Lavidor-Berman was impressed that many more people read the positive stories of people helping each other than stories about the bombers (Solomonmccown&, 2013).

Boston Police Department: The Social Media Infrastructure and Community Relationship Were Built Long Before the Bombings

After Dzhokhar Tsarnaev was arrested, Mashable—an online media company that focuses on innovation and technology—declared that the Boston Police Department has "schooled us all on social media ... the Boston PD's presence online helps reinvent the whole notion of community policing for the 21st century" (Bar-Tur, 2013).

According to Businessweek, "That law enforcement agencies such as the Boston Police and Massachusetts State Police took to social media to deliver information in the wake of the twin explosions on Boylston Street is nothing special. The Aurora, Colo., police released breaking news through Twitter following the mass shooting in a movie theater. Virtually every police department now runs a Twitter feed for official communications. What is unusual is how adroitly the officials in charge of responding to the Boston tragedy took advantage of social media..." (Keller, 2013).

Noting that "true engagement does not arise in a time of crisis, but through preparation well ahead of the crisis," Mashable reported that "Even before the BPD's follower count spiked this week, from 40,000 to more than 300,000, the department boasted more Twitter followers than most of the area's local media" (Bar-Tur, 2013).

The department's Twitter account was created in 2009 and was first used to publish public safety instructions during the St. Patrick's Day parade. The department expanded its social-media presence onto Facebook and YouTube video-streaming site Ustream. These social media accounts are handled by the Bureau of Public Information, with three officers responsible for the content (Keller, 2013).

When the Marathon bombings occurred, the "infrastructure was in place for the department to effectively handle the situation on social media" (Keller, 2013). Bureau chief Cheryl Fiandaca explained "We staffed 24 hours. Someone was always here. We tried to put out as much information as we possibly could without jeopardizing the investigation" (Keller, 2013).

In the end, the Boston PD was credited with accomplishing "what no police department has done before: led conversation with citizens in a time of crisis. They also listened, a step that is more remarkable than it sounds for many large organizations, let alone law enforcement. They used Twitter to track and correct the misinformation that media outlets spread" (Bar-Tur, 2013).

One of the Boston police officers responsible for the social media content put it more succinctly: "We don't break news. We are the news" (Keller, 2013).

References

Associated Press, 2013. As cellphones fail, desperate people search for their loved ones after the Boston Marathon bombings using Google's 'person finder'. Daily Mail (April 15). http://www.dailymail.co.uk/news/article-2309733/Boston-Marathon-bombs-Desperate-people-search-loved-ones-using-Googles-person-finder.html.

Bar-Tur, Y., 2013. Boston police schooled us all on social media. Mashable (April 22). http://mashable.com/2013/04/22/boston-police-social-media/.

Between the Lines, 2013. How social media was used during the Boston Marathon bombings. http://abarbuto3.wordpress.com/2013/05/04/how-social-media-was-used-during-the-boston-marathon-bombings/ (May 4, 2013).

(Continued)

CASE STUDY 1—CONTINUED

Fry, J., 2013. Boston explosions a reminder how breaking news reporting is changing. Poynter.org. http://www.poynter.org/latest-news/making-sense-of-news/210471/boston-explosions-a-reminder-of-how-breaking-news-reporting-is-changing/ (April 16, 2013).

Gilgoff, D., Lee, J.J., 2013. Social media shapes Boston bombings response. National Geographic News (April 15). http://news.nationalgeographic.com/news/2013/13/130415-boston-marathon-bombings-terrorism-social-media-twitter-facebook/.

Kakutani, M., 2013. Unraveling Boston suspects' online lives, link by link. New York Times (April 23). http://www.nytimes.com/2013/04/24/us/unraveling-brothers-online-lives-link-by-link.html?pagewanted=all&_r=5&.

Keller, J., 2013. How Boston police won the Twitter wars during the Marathon bomber hunt. Bloomberg Businessweek Technology (April 26). http://www.businessweek.com/articles/2013-04-26/how-boston-police-won-the-twitter-wars-during-bomber-hunt#p2.

Mussenden, S., 2013. Interviewed by Kim Haddow (June 27, 2013).

Petrecca, L., 2013. After bombings, social media informs (and misinforms). USA Today (April 23). http://www.usatoday.com/story/news/2013/04/23/social-media-boston-marathon-bombings/2106701/.

Pew Research Center for the People & the Press, 2013a. Most expect 'occasional acts of terrorism' in the future. http://www.people-press.org/2013/04/23/most-expect-occasional-acts-of-terrorism-in-the-future/ (April 23, 2013).

Presuitti, C., 2013. Multi, social media play huge role in solving Boston bombings. Voice of America News (April 26). http://www.voanews.com/content/multi-social-media-play-huge-role-in-solving-boston-bombing/1649774.html.

SolomonMcCown&, 2013. Role of (social) media in Boston Marathon bombings. http://www.solomonmccown.com/our-news/2013/5/24/role-of-(social)-media-in-boston-marathon-bombings.aspx (May 24, 2013).

Stern, J., 2013. Boston Marathon bombing: the waves of social media reaction. ABC News Technology Review (April 16). http://abcnews.go.com/blogs/technology/2013/04/boston-marathon-bombing-the-waves-of-social-media-reaction/.

Thompson, C., 2013. Social media played critical role in Boston Marathon response. CNBC (April 16). http://www.cnbc.com/id/100645753.

Ulanoff, L., 2013. Boston bombings: truth, justice and the wild west of social media. Mashable (April 18). http://mashable.com/2013/04/18/boston-bombings-wild-west-of-social-media/.

Weiss, T.R., 2013. Google activates person finder in aftermath of Boston Marathon bombings. eWeek (April 16). http://www.eweek.com/cloud/google-activates-person-finder-in-aftermath-of-boston-marathon-bombings/.

CASE STUDY 2

Hurricane Sandy

Hurricane Sandy made landfall in the United States on the night of October 29, 2012 after first striking Jamaica, Hispaniola, the Bahamas, Cuba and Bermuda.

At its peak, Sandy was a Category 1 size hurricane and prior to making landfall in New Jersey. Sandy caused 72 deaths in the United States and has been ranked as the second most costly hurricane at an estimated $68 billion in damages according to the National Hurricane Center. Hurricane Katrina still ranks as the most costly hurricane at $125 billion in estimated damages (NOAA, 2013).

Sandy's major impacts in the United States occurred in the states of New York and New Jersey, and in New York City. New York City is the biggest media market in the United States and coverage of Sandy by traditional media was extensive and social media use during the storm set records.

Hurricane Sandy was the most social media covered disaster to date. A November 12, 2012 post on the Mindjet website by Pete Hunt entitled, "Hurricane #Sandy: Socializing Traditional Media" noted, "Sandy was the top phrase on Facebook, where users speculated about the storm's damage and provided updated information about their location and safety. More than 800,000 Instagram photos featured a "#Sandy" hashtag. Some 20 million tweets included storm-related terms. Social media's comparative advantage during Sandy was considerable. Emergency information from government officials and news sources was disseminated as quickly as people could retweet it" (Brown, 2012).

An infographic created by the Mindjet website vividly illustrates the extensive use of social media outlets including Facebook, Twitter and YouTube before, during and after Hurricane Sandy made landfall (see Figure 11-16).

FIGURE 11-16 Social Infographic: http://learn.mindjet.com/SuperstormSandy. Like the infographic? Feel free to use it.

(Continued)

CASE STUDY 2—CONTINUED

An article entitled, "Social Media and Hurricane Sandy" written by Allison Gilbert and posted on the digital Ethos website on November 15, 2012 stated, "Social media has been invaluable in the case of Hurricane Sandy, the worst storm to ever hit parts of Long Island, NY. Facebook has become an invaluable tool resulting in a means of communication, spreading information and fundraising. Ironically, the people with the least access to the Internet as a result of the storm are the ones who may benefit the most from social media. Those who have ventured into the devastated areas have been able to get information out so that help can come in from informing those outside of the devastated areas" (Gilbert, 2012).

Gilbert continued, "These Facebook groups and pages are accessible 24/7. They are alive long after televised bytes pass on as yesterday's news. Social media continues to be a source of support and assistance particularly to the residents of New York and New Jersey" (Gilbert, 2012).

Social media became the go to source for people looking for gasoline, shelter, food, water, and immediate assistance after Sandy made landfall.

In addition, FEMA set up a Hurricane Sandy landing page that "provided all of the specific relief, response and recovery information related to Sandy. Information for disaster survivors included how to get immediate help, how to locate a shelter, how to locate a FEMA Disaster Recovery Center, and access to the state-specific disaster declarations. This information was also ultimately provided in 18 languages aside from English. Links were provided to all applicable state and local websites, and information was provided for those who want to help (donations and volunteering)" (Virtual Social Media Working Group and DHS First Responders Group, 2013).

Hurricane Sandy also marked a shift in and an increased dependence on the use of social media by government agencies—an acknowledgement and embrace of social media's critical role in disasters in disseminating information, connecting people and controlling rumors. In Sandy—more than ever before government agencies turned to mobile and online technologies to communicate with the public and response partners (Cohen, 2013).

A report prepared by the Virtual Social Media Working Group and DHS First Responders Group noted that Sandy "marked a shift in the use of social media in disasters. More than ever before, government agencies turned to mobile and online technologies before, during, and after Sandy made landfall, to communicate with response partners and the public in order to share information, maintain awareness of community actions and needs, and more" (Virtual Social Media Working Group and DHS First Responders Group, 2013).

FEMA and FEMA Administrator Craig Fugate, the National Weather Service, the New Jersey Office of Emergency Management (NJOEM) and New Jersey Governor Chris Christie, the New York State Division of Homeland Security and Emergency Services (NYS DHSES) and New York Governor Andrew Cuomo, and the New York City Office of Emergency Management and Mayor Michael Bloomberg all used Twitter and Facebook to relay evacuation orders, direct resources where they were needed, provide victims with updates about aid, shelter and storm conditions.

On October 29, the day Sandy made landfall, FEMA reached more than 300,000 people on Facebook (up from an average of 12,000 per day) and reached 6 million Twitter users with one message (Cohen, 2013).

FEMA administrator Craig Fugate tweeted regularly before, during and after the storm at one point "providing more than 30,000 people with tips and links to help people sift through all the news about Sandy" (Baylon, 2012).

One report noted, "The National Weather Service also updates its Twitter feed with information from the National Hurricane Center, but NSW's Facebook page appears to have more traction, with more than 100 people clicking 'like' on every post. Facebook has been especially useful for the National Oceanic and Atmospheric Administration, which has been updating users with compelling pictures as well as satellite images and storm-tracking diagrams of Sandy" (Baylon, 2012).

The New Jersey Office of Emergency Management (NJOEM) has posted messages on their Facebook page continuously since the lead up to Hurricane Sandy making landfall. See examples of NJOEM tweets below (Figure 11-17):

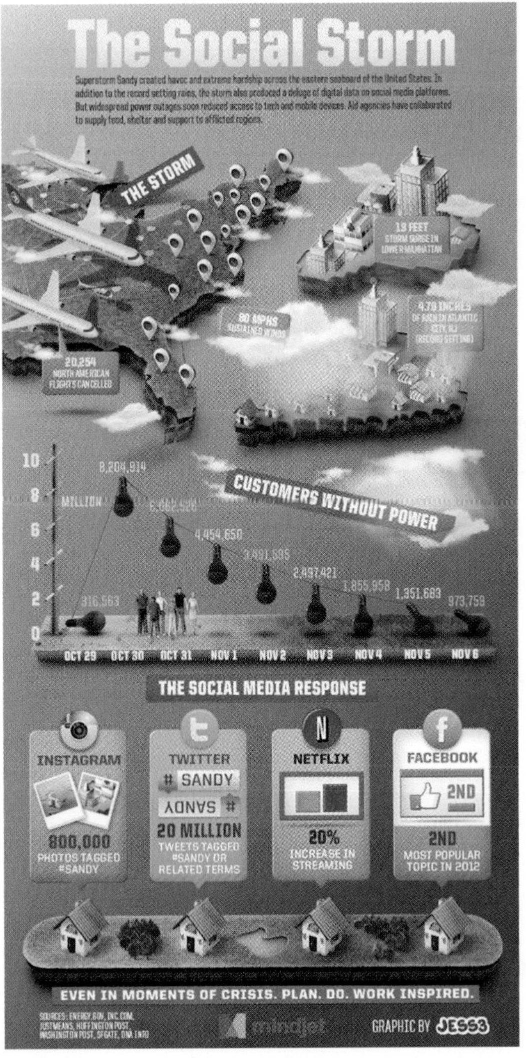

FIGURE 11-17 Hurricane Sandy Infographic.

(Continued)

CASE STUDY 2—CONTINUED

New Jersey Office of Emergency Management
October 29, 2012

Regarding travel on the road, please keep these points in mind:

- Don't go on the roads unless you are essential to the disaster response.

- There is no ban on driving, BUT there are travel restrictions in many counties e.g., Atlantic, Cumberland, Camden. The Parkway is closed from Exit 38 South and there is the possibility of expanding the closure.

- Regardless of current rain conditions, drive slower to avoid losing control when you drive into ponding and standing water that is already on every roadway.

- Never drive through standing water, even if you think your vehicle can clear the depth. Even if you have an SUV. You could stall and block access for emergency workers

- Expect that flash flooding can turn a stream under a roadway into a river, capable of washing vehicles right off the road. This resulted in a tragic death during Irene.

- If you don't have to be on the road, stay home. This is no time to venture out for sightseeing or taking photographs and videos.

Like · Comment · Share · 190 22 176

New Jersey Office of Emergency Management shared NOAA NWS National Hurricane Center's photo.
October 29, 2012

NOAA NWS National Hurricane Center

At 3 pm EDT, Hurricane Sandy was centered just 85 miles southeast of Atlantic City, New Jersey, moving toward the northwest at 28 mph. Landfall is expected this evening along the extreme southern New Jersey coastline or central Delaware. Get the latest at www.hurricanes.gov and, for local impacts, go to www.weather.gov

Like · Comment · Share · 48 3 155

Source: New Jersey Office of Emergency Management (NJOEM). https://www.facebook.com/READYNEWJERSEY.

New Jersey Office of Emergency Management
October 30, 2012 ·

SEG Cares @PSEGcares
PSE&G crews are working hard to restore power to customers without electricity. We know it's difficult and appreciate your patience

Like · Comment · Share · 143 55 4

New Jersey Office of Emergency Management
October 31, 2012 ·

RECOVERY BEGINS TODAY

Recovery begins today. We acknowledge and respect our feelings of sorrow and loss. At the same time, we draw on our resilience and remember that we are all in this together.

For now, a few items that residents are asking about:

- We'll have more about recovery programs after President Obama's visit and tour of impacted areas with Governor Christie. For now, a couple of items:

- The latest situation report is on our blog, http://readynj.posterous.com/state-eoc-situation-report-103...

- Halloween: As per last night's press conference, an announcement will be made regarding Halloween later today. There are trees and power lines down all over. Please keep the safety of your children as the first consideration surrounding this holiday.

- The Red Cross Safe and Well program can help you contact or locate loved ones: http://www.redcross.org/find-help/contact-family

- In some areas, cell and land line phone service is impacted. Try texting; it usually works when voice service is down.

Like · Comment · Share · 262 56 82

NJOEM was also very active on Twitter during Hurricane Sandy. On October 29 alone, NJOEM twitted 18 messages and retweeted over 75 messages from other emergency agencies and government officials including FEMA, CDC, NOAA, power companies, New Jersey Governor Christie, FEMA Administrator Craig Fugate, New Jersey Transit, New Jersey State Police, National Weather Service, and New Jersey Red Cross. NJOEM also retweeted numerous tweets generated by JSHurricaneNews a self described, "A bottom-up, two-way news outlet, JSHN is news for the people, by the people. JSHN covers news, traffic, and weather. News you can use" (New Jersey Office of Emergency Management, 2013).

(Continued)

CASE STUDY 2—CONTINUED

During the same day (October 29), the New York State Division of Homeland Security and Emergency Services (NYS DHSES) tweeted 39 messages and retweeted 13 messages from various other sources including New York Governor Andrew Cuomo, MTA, NWS, NY Department of Labor, CDC, and the New York City Office of Emergency Management (New York State Division of Homeland Security and Emergency Services, 2013).

Local governments in the disaster zone made use of social media outlets. The city of Summit, NJ, Public Information Annex posted 65 messages on the City Facebook Page and over 200 tweets on two accounts (City of Summit Office of Emergency Management, undated).

Voluntary agencies also made extensive use of social media. The American Red Cross offered the Hurricane app for both iPhone and Android device users to monitor conditions in their neighborhood and throughout the storm track, prepare their families and homes, find help, and let others know they are safe "even if the power is out" (Cohen, 2013).

One report noted on October 29 that "People have also been using the American Red Cross' application, The Hurricane, to update Twitter and Facebook, as well as to email and text family and friends that they are safe" (Baylon, 2012).

FEMA noted in its "Hurricane Sandy FEMA After-Action Report" that "Smartphone apps provide critical information to Sandy responders and survivors. Several organizations, including the American Red Cross, the U.S. Department of Veterans Affairs (VA), and FEMA have developed smartphone applications designed for rapid dissemination to survivors and disaster workers. Among the various applications used during Sandy were the American Red Cross's Hurricane app, the VA's Psychological First Aid (PFA) app, and FEMA's Emergency Preparedness app. Over 100,000 users downloaded the American Red Cross's Hurricane app to monitor and track the storm, prepare for the disaster, and locate shelters. The VA's PFA app—downloaded more than 1800 times—provides guidance on administering psychological first aid to adults, families, and children. The FEMA Emergency Preparedness app—downloaded by more than 50,000 users—provides an interactive checklist for emergency kits, maps with disaster recovery and shelter information, and an online application for assistance. Despite widespread power and cell phone outages, the use of smartphone applications provided necessary information to both survivors and responders" (FEMA Hurricane Sandy After Action Report, 2013).

Even before Sandy, New York City had 3 million followers across more than 300 city accounts on Facebook, Twitter (in both English and Spanish), Google+, Tumblr, YouTube, and more. Throughout response and recovery, these channels made it easy for the city to share information in various formats and enabled people to find and consume information in ways they preferred and were used to (Cohen, 2013).

The public could also sign up to receive text alerts from the mayor's office Twitter account, @nycmayorsoffice, which served as a great alternative digital resource to the city's Web site, once people lost power and Internet access (Cohen, 2013).

As noted in New York City's "Hurricane Sandy After-Action Report," "During the storm, the City pushed out information through as many channels as possible. Major television networks, radio channels, third-party Web sites, NYC.gov, and the Mayor's Office and Mike Bloomberg YouTube channels carried live press conferences while City Twitter feeds reinforced the most critical messages. OEM uses an additional set of tools to broadcast information to the general public, including Notify

NYC, the City's flagship emergency update system that sends alerts via landline, mobile, text, email, and Twitter to more than 165,000 registered users. Notify NYC's reach expanded by nearly 15% during Sandy, gaining more than 9600 direct subscribers and another 12,000 to the Notify NYC Twitter account" (NYC Hurricane Sandy After Action Report, 2013).

Government agencies posted short videos concerning Hurricane Sandy on YouTube. FEMA produced over 130 short videos concerning relevant to Sandy covering topics like how to register for FEMA assistance, FEMA's Public Assistance program, national guard efforts in Sandy, the role of voluntary agencies in Sandy recovery, mitigation and preparedness tips, beware of fraud, how to care for your pet, small business information assistance, and more (FEMA.gov, 2013).

A sampling of Hurricane Sandy YouTube videos can be accessed and found at http://www.youtube.com/results?search_query=hurricane+sandy+new+york+state+emergency+maangement&oq=hurricane+sandy+new+york+state+emergency+maangement&gs_l=youtube.3..33i21.37819.55497.0.55996.51.38.0.13.13.1.307.3745.34j2j1j1.38.0...0.0...1ac.1.11.youtube.ycNArQABcHU.

And the public used social media to update government agencies on conditions on the ground, to ask for help, and to inform deployment of resources decisions:

- Throughout the storm, Mayor Bloomberg's office monitored social media for public reactions to the storm, sending reports to city hall on a daily basis. Questions asked on Twitter were responded to directly.
- FEMA had a team watching the nearly 20 million Twitter messages posted about Sandy to better identify what was happening on the ground and put out timely safety information.
- Throughout the storm, the Red Cross pulled more than 2 million posts for review, using the word "shelter" and other specific keyword searches relevant to Red Cross services. Thirty-one digital volunteers responded to 2386 of the reviewed posts. About 229 posts were sent to mass care teams, and 88 resulted in a change in action on ground operations (Cohen, 2013).

FEMA used Crowd Sourcing technology for "Volunteers from across the country collaborated online to assist survivors in the immediate aftermath of Sandy. For the Humanitarian OpenStreetMap Team's MapMill project, volunteers used aerial imagery from the National Oceanic and Atmospheric Administration and the Civil Air Patrol to assess damages to buildings and infrastructure. Working mostly on November 1–3, over 6000 volunteers assessed the damage from aerial imagery as light, moderate, or heavy. Volunteers completed over 137,000 assessments of more than 35,000 images. The Humanitarian OpenStreetMap Team then used the results to create a color-coded grid map depicting damages throughout the area (see Figure 11-18). To expand distribution, Google included the map and images on its Sandy CrisisMap, and FEMA included it on the Agency's internal GeoPortal site. The effort provided a powerful example of the possibilities that crowd-sourcing holds for the future. The challenge for FEMA will be to determine how to further use crowd-sourced information to inform decision-making and disaster assistance programs" (FEMA Hurricane Sandy After Action Report, 2013).

Social media tools—including Twitter, Facebook and photo sharing platforms—were used to verify information and dispel rumors. For example—when false reports and images began circulating on the Internet, including a photo of the New York Stock Exchange under three feet of water, first responder agencies such as the New York City Fire Department posted messages on Twitter and other social media sites to correct misinformation (Cohen, 2013).

(Continued)

CASE STUDY 2—CONTINUED

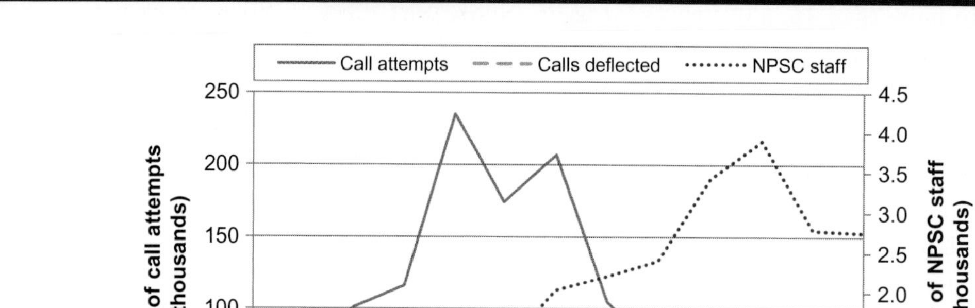

FIGURE 11-18 Crowd sourcing. Both FEMA and Google distributed the Humanitarian OpenStreetMap Team's grid map that showed the results of volunteers' damage assessments.

FEMA launched a Hurricane Sandy: Rumor Control page, which helped to distinguish the truth from false information about contractors, cash cards, food stamps and shelters (Cohen, 2013).

In the recovery period to Hurricane Sandy, the Federal government has established a Web page entitled "Hurricane Sandy Recovery" on its USA.gov Web site that provides links to a wide variety of government recovery programs and apps from agencies such as FEMA, HHS, HUD, USDA, the American Red Cross and others. This Web page provides updates on government recovery activity and links to how individuals can apply for government assistance, find temporary housing, and access health and safety information (USA.gov, 2013). New Jersey Office of Emergency Management, the New York State Division of Homeland Security and Emergency Services, and the New York City Office of Emergency Management also continue to post Hurricane Sandy recovery information on their Web sites and use social media outlets to get recovery news to the public.

References

Baylon, J., 2012. Hurricane Sandy: Authorities Use Social Media to Keep People Informed. Digital First Media. Accessed on the San Jose Mercury News website: http://www.mercurynews.com/breaking-news/ci_21880815/hurricane-sandy-social-media (October 29, 2012).

Cohen, S.E., 2013. Sandy marked a shift for social media use in disasters. Emergency Management (March 7). http://www.emergencymgmt.com/disaster/Sandy-Social-Media-Use-in-Disasters.html.

USA.gov, 2013. Hurricane Sandy Recovery: Resources to help you recover from Hurricane Sandy. http://www.

usa.gov/Topics/Weather/Hurricane/sandy.shtml (accessed August 28, 2013).

New Jersey Office of Emergency Management, 2013. https://twitter.com/ReadyNJ (accessed on August 28, 2013).

FEMA.gov, 2013. Hurricane Sandy YouTube videos. feed://www.fema.gov/medialibrary/tags/feed_video/2590 (accessed on August 28, 2013).

New York State Division of Homeland Security and Emergency Services, 2013. Twitter Messages. https://twitter.com/NYSDHSES (accessed on August 28, 2013).

NOAA, 2013. Billion Dollar Weather/Climate Disasters. National Climate Data Center. http://www.ncdc.noaa.gov/billions/events (accessed on July 31, 2013).

NYC Hurricane Sandy After Action Report, 2013. Deputy Mayor Linda I. Gibbs, Co-Chair Deputy Mayor Caswell F. Holloway, Co-Chair. http://www.nyc.gov/html/recovery/downloads/pdf/sandy_aar_5.2.13.pdf (May 2013).

City of Summit Office of Emergency Management, n.d. Hurricane Sandy October 2012 after action report. http://www.cityofsummit.org/filestorage/8242/8302/10255/11232/HURRICANE_SANDY_October_2012_After_Action_Report_Final_UPDATED.pdf.

FEMA Hurricane Sandy After Action Report, 2013. https://s3-us-gov-west-1.amazonaws.com/dam-production/uploads/20130726-1923-25045-7442/sandy_fema_aar.pdf (July 1, 2013).

Gilbert, A., 2012. Social Media and Hurricane Sandy. Digital Ethos. http://digitalethos.org/social-media-and-hurricane-sandy/ (posted on November 15, 2012).

Brown, P., 2012. Hurricane #Sandy: Socializing Traditional Media. Mindjet.com. http://blog.mindjet.com/2012/11/hurricane-sandy-socializing-traditional-media/ (posted on November 12, 2012).

Virtual Social Media Working Group and DHS First Responders Group, 2013. Lessons Learned: Social Media and Hurricane Sandy. https://communities.firstresponder.gov/DHS_VSMWG_Lessons_Learned_Social_Media_and_Hurricane_Sandy_Formatted_June_2013_FINAL.pdf (June 2013).

Key Terms

Comprehensive emergency management: An emergency management philosophy that seeks to reduce risk and prevent injuries, damages, and fatalities by treating hazards before, during, and after an event has occurred. There are generally four accepted functions performed in comprehensive emergency management: mitigation, preparedness, response, and recovery.

Crisis communication: The provision of timely, useful, and accurate information to the public during the response and recovery phases of a disaster event.

Mass media: Channels of communication for popular consumption, which could include books, magazines, advertisements, newspapers, newsletters, radio, television, the Internet, cinema, theater, and videos, among many others.

National Terrorism Advisory System: A robust terrorism advisory system that provides timely information to the public about credible terrorist threats and replaced the former color-coded Homeland Security Advisory System (HSAS).

Traditional news media: A subcomponent of the mass media focused on presenting current news to the public usually defined as television, radio, and print.

Ready.gov: A government-sponsored Web site developed by the Advertising Council to educate the public, businesses, and children about hazard risks in the United States.

Risk communication: Any communication intended to supply laypeople with the information they need to make informed, independent judgments about risks to health, safety, and the environment (Morgan et al., 2002).

Social media: Internet-based sites such as Facebook, Twitter, and YouTube where individuals share news about their lives, friends, and businesses and in disaster events about what is happening to them and their surroundings.

Warning: The delivery of notice of an actual impending threat with sufficient time to allow recipient individuals and communities to take shelter, evacuate, or take other mitigative actions in advance of a disaster event.

Review Questions

1. Identify and discuss the four critical assumptions underlying the crisis communications efforts of the Federal Emergency Management Agency (FEMA) in the 1990s.
2. Discuss how the role of the traditional media in crisis communications has changed.
3. Discuss the emergence of social media outlets such as Twitter, Facebook, and YouTube as a preferred means of communications before, during, and after a disaster event.
4. Discuss how information posted on social media sites might be harvested by government officials in order to increase their situational awareness and make resource allocation decisions.
5. Discuss how emergency managers or homeland security officials can build an effective crisis communications strategy in a changing media world.
6. Discuss what measures homeland security officials need to take in the future to improve how they communicate with the public.
7. What role did social media play in the response to the Boston Marathon bombings and the capture of the second suspect?

References

Adamski, S., 2013a. Statement of Shayne Adamski, Senior Manager of Digital Engagement, Federal Emergency Management Agency, U.S. Department of Homeland Security, Before the Committee on Homeland Security Subcommittee on Emergency Preparedness, Response and Communications, U.S. House of Representatives, Washington, DC. http://docs.house.gov/meetings/HM/HM12/20130709/101047/HHRG-113-HM12-Wstate-AdamskiS-20130709.pdf (July 9, 2013).

Adamski, S., 2013A. Interview with author conducted on July 23, 2013b.

American Red Cross, 2012. More Americans Using Mobile Apps in Emergencies. http://www.redcross.org/news/press-release/More-Americans-Using-Mobile-Apps-in-Emergencies (August 31, 2012).

aNewDomain.net, 2013. http://anewdomain.net/2013/04/11/social-media-in-emergency-management/ (accessed on July 31, 2013).

Ashwood, A., 2013. Albert Ashwood, Chairman, NEMA Legislative Committee Director, Oklahoma Department of Emergency Management, Statement for the Record on Behalf of the National Emergency management Association (NEMA), Submitted to the House Committee on Homeland Security Subcommittee on Emergency Preparedness, Response, and Communications United States House of Representatives. Emergency MGMT 2.0: How #SocialMedia & New Tech are Transforming Preparedness, Response, & Recovery #Disasters #Part2 #Govt/NGOs (July 9, 2013).

Bar-Tur, Y., 2013. Boston police schooled us all on schooled us all on social media. Mashable (April 22). http://mashable.com/2013/04/22/boston-police-social-media/.

BBC News, 2008. Burmese Blog the Cyclone. http://news.bbc.co.uk/2/hi/asia-pacific/7387313.stm (May 8, 2008).

Beckerman, M., 2013. Testimony of Michael Beckerman President and CEO of The Internet Association Before the United States House of Representatives Committee on Homeland Security, Subcommittee on Emergency Preparedness, Response and Communication. Emergency MGMT 2.0: How #SocialMedia & New Tech are Transforming Preparedness, Response, & Recovery #Disasters #Part1 #Privatesector. http://docs.house.gov/meetings/HM/HM12/20130604/100924/HHRG-113-HM12-Wstate-BeckermanM-20130604.pdf (June 4, 2013).

Brenner, J., 2013. Pew Internet: Mobile. http://pewinternet.org/Commentary/2012/February/Pew-Internet-Mobile.aspx (June 6, 2013).

Brooks, S., 2013. Statement of Chairman Susan Brooks (R-IN) Subcommittee on Emergency Preparedness, Response, and Communications. Emergency MGMT 2.0: How #SocialMedia & New Tech are Transforming Preparedness, Response, & Recovery #Disasters #Part2 #Govt/NGOs. http://homeland.house.gov/sites/homeland.house.gov/files/07-09-13-Brooks-Open_0.pdf (July 9, 2013 Remarks as Prepared).

Brown, P., 2012. Hurricane #Sandy: Socializing Traditional Media. Mindjet.com. http://blog.mindjet.com/2012/11/hurricane-sandy-socializing-traditional-media/ (posted on November 12, 2012).

Bullas, J., 2013. The Facts and Figures on You Tube in 2013. http://www.jeffbullas.com/2013/02/11/the-facts-and-figures-on-youtube-in-2013-infographic/#vhE36dwqCrxFWvr8.99 (February 11, 2013).

Catone, J., 2007. Online citizen journalism now undeniably mainstream. ReadWriteWeb (October 26). http://www.readwriteweb.com/archives/online_citizen_journalism_mainstream.php.

CDC, 2012. Crises and Emergency Risk Communications Manual, second ed. Centers for Disease Control and Prevention, Washington, DC. http://emergency.cdc.gov/cerc/pdf/CERC_2012edition.pdf.

Cohen, H., 2012. Stay on top of hurricane season with apps, email and web. Miami Herald (May 31). http://www.miamiherald.com/2012/05/31/2825810/stay-on-top-of-hurricane-season.html.

Cohen, S.E., 2013. Sandy marked a shift for social media use in disasters. Emergency Management (March 7). http://www.emergencymgmt.com/disaster/Sandy-Social-Media-Use-in-Disasters.html.

Committee on Homeland Security, 2014. U.S. House of Representatives. http://homeland.house.gov/hearing/hearingthe-boston-marathon-bombings-one-year-look-back-look-forward (April 9, 2014).

Cooper, G., 2007. Burma's Bloggers show power of citizen journalism in a crises. Alternet. http://permalink.gmane.org/gmane.culture.region.india.zestmedia/3925.

Disaster Resources Guide, 2012. Q&A on Social Media and Crisis Management. An Interview With Oliver S. Schmidt. http://www.disaster-resource.com/newsletter/2013/subpages/v431/meettheexperts.pdf (June, 2012).

Duggan, M., Johanna, B., 2013. Pew Research Center for the People & the Press, Internet & American Life Project. The Demographics of Social Media Users—2012. http://www.pewinternet.org/~/media//Files/Reports/2013/PIP_SocialMediaUsers.pdf (February 14, 2013).

Eblin, S., 2012. Five Things to Learn from Bloomberg About Crisis Communications. Government Executive. http://www.govexec.com/excellence/executive-coach/2012/10/five-things-learn-bloomberg-about-crisis-communications/59137/ (posted on October 31, 2012).

Everbridge, 2013. The Social Media Gap in Crisis Communications. Everbridge.com http://www.everbridge.com/everbridge-study-finds-58-of-organizations-lack-social-media-strategy-during-crises/ (accessed July 31, 2013).

Fan, M., 2008. Citizen groups step up in China. The Washington Post (May 29). http://www.washingtonpost.com/wp-dyn/content/article/2008/05/28/AR2008052803398_pf.html.

FEMA, 2008. National Incident Management System. FEMA, Washington, DC (December 2008).

Fraustino, J.D., Liu, B., Jin, Y., 2012. Social Media Use During Disasters: A Review of the Knowledge Base and Gaps. The National Consortium for the Study of Terrorism and Responses to Terrorism (START), College Park, MD. http://www.start.umd.edu/start/publications/START_SocialMediaUseduringDisasters_LitReview.pdf, Final report to Human Factors/Behavioral Sciences Division, Science and Technology Directorate, U.S. Department of Homeland Security.

Fry, K., 2004. Disasters and television. In: Newcomb, H. (Ed.), Encyclopedia of Television. Museum of Broadcast Communications.

Gillmor, D., 2004. We the Media: Grassroots Journalism By the People, For the People. O'Reilly Media Inc. http://oreilly.com/openbook/wemedia/book/.

Gillmor, D., 2006. We the Media: Grassroots Journalism by the People, for the People. O'Reilly Media Inc.

Gillmor, D., Hattotuwa, S., 2007. Citizen journalism and humanitarian aid: boon or bust? ICT for Peacebuilding. http://ict4peace.wordpress.com/2007/07/30/citizen-journalism-and-humanitarian-aid-bane-or-boon/.

Glaser, M., 2006. Your guide to citizen journalism. MediaShift PBS (September 27). http://www.pbs.org/mediashift/2006/09/your-guide-to-citizen-journalism270.

Glaser, M., 2007. California wildfire coverage by local media, blogs, twitter, maps and more. MediaShift (October 25). http://www.pbs.org/mediashift/2007/10/the_listcalifornia_wildfire_co_1.html.

Glennon, B., 2013. The role of technology in crisis management and how it could be done better. The Chicago Policy Review. http://chcicagopolicyreview.org/2013/05/07/the-role-of-technology-in-crisis-management-and-how-it-could-be-done-better/.

Global Voices Online, 2008a. Myanmar Cyclone 2008. http://www.globalvoicesonline.org/specialcoverage/myanmar-cyclone-2008/.

Global Voices Online, 2008b. Sichuan Earthquake 2008. http://www.globalvoicesonline.org/specialcoverage/sichuan-earthquake-2008/.

Global Voices Online, 2010. In aftermath of earthquake, eyewitness tweets from Haiti. January 13, 2010. http://globalvoicesonline.org/2010/01/13/in-aftermath-of-earthquake-eyewitness-tweets-from-haiti/.

Guerriero, M., 2013. Closing the App Gap: Google v. Apple. The New Yorker (June 6). http://www.newyorker.com/online/blogs/newsdesk/2013/06/google-apple-apps-mobile-downloads-gap.html.

Haik, C., 2013. Interviewed by Kim Haddow (July 12, 2013).

Hattotuwa, S., 2007. Who Is Afraid of Citizen Journalists? Communicating Disasters. TVA Asia Pacific and UNDP Regional Centre, Bangkok. http://www.tveap.org/disastercomm/Chapters_in_seperate_PDFs/Chap-14.pdf.

Hunt, P., 2012. Hurricane #Sandy: Socializing Traditional Media. Mindjet. http://blog.mindjet.com/2012/11/hurricane-sandy-socializing-traditional-media/ (November 12, 2012).

Kakutani, M., 2013. Unraveling Boston suspects' online lives, link by link. New York Times (April 23). http://www.nytimes.com/2013/04/24/us/unraveling-brothers-online-lives-link-by-link.html?pagewanted=all&_r=5&.

Keller, J., 2013. How Boston police won the Twitter wars during the Marathon bomber hunt. Bloomberg Businessweek Technology (April 26). http://www.businessweek.com/articles/2013-04-26/how-boston-police-won-the-twitter-wars-during-bomber-hunt#p2.

Kettl, D.F., 2005. The Worst is Yet to Come: Lessons from September 11 to Hurricane Katrina. Fels Institute of Government, University of Pennsylvania (September 2005).

Maron, D.F., 2013. How social media is changing disaster response. Scientific American (June 7). http://www.scientificamerican.com/article.cfm?id=how-social-media-is-changing-disaster-response.

May, A.L., 2006. First Informers in the Disaster Zone: The Lessons of Katrina. The Aspen Institute. http://www.aspeninstitute.org/publications/first-informers-disaster-zone-lessons-katrina.

Morgan, G., Fischhoff, B., Bostrom, A., Atman, C.J., 2002. Risk Communication: A Mental Models Approach. Cambridge University Press, Cambridge.

Mussenden, S., 2013. Interviewed by Kim Haddow (June 27, 2013).

Ngak, C., 2012. Social media a news sources and a tool during Superstorm Sandy. CBS News (October 30). http://www.cbsnews.com/8301-205_162-57542474/social-media-a-news-source-and-tool-during-superstorm-sandy/.

Perera, A., 2013. When a tsunami comes, tweet. Inter Press Service (April 2). http://www.ipsnews.net/2013/04/when-a-tsunami-comes-tweet/.

PEW, 2013. Pew Research Center's Project on Excellence in Journalism. http://www.journalism.org/index_report/hurricane_sandy_and_twitter (accessed July 31, 2013).

Pew Research Center, 2012a. The Number of Americans with Mobile Connections to the Web on the Rise. http://www.pewresearch.org/daily-number/number-of-americans-with-mobile-connections-to-the-web-on-the-rise/ (November 2, 2012).

Pew Research Center for Excellence in Journalism, 2013. The State of the News Media 2013: an annual report on American journalism. http://stateofthemedia.org/ (March 18, 2013).

Pew Research Center for the People and the Press, 2012. In a Changing Media Landscape, Even Television is Vulnerable. http://www.people-press.org/2012/09/27/in-changing-news-landscape-even-television-is-vulnerable/ (September 27, 2012).

Pew Research Center for the People & the Press, Internet & American Life Project, 2013b. Internet Adoption 1995–2013. http://www.pewinternet.org/Search.aspx?q=Internet%20Adoption%201995-2012 (May, 2013).

Pew Research Center for the People & the Press, 2013c. Most expect 'occasional acts of terrorism' in the future. http://www.people-press.org/2013/04/23/most-expect-occasional-acts-of-terrorism-in-the-future/ (April 23, 2013).

Pew Research Center's Project for Excellence in Journalism, 2010. Journalism.Org. Understanding the Participatory News Consumer: How Internet and cellphone users have turned news into a social experience. http://www.journalism.org/analysis_report/understanding_participatory_news_consumer (March 1, 2010).

Presuitti, C., 2013. Multi, social media play huge role in solving Boston bombings. Voice of America News (April 26). http://www.voanews.com/content/multi-social-media-play-huge-role-in-solving-boston-bombing/1649774.html.

Rich, F., 2013. The state of journalism: inky tears. New York Magazine (April 7). http://nymag.com/news/frank-rich/news-media-2013-4/index1.html.

Richardson, C., 2011. Visualizing twitter use during the Japanese earthquakes. WebProNews (June 30). http://www.webpronews.com/visualizing-twitter-use-during-the-japanese-earthquakes-2011-06.

Rincon, J., 2008. Myanmar: citizen videos in Cyclone Nargis aftermath. Reuters Global News Blog (May 16). http://blogs.reuters.com/global/tag/burma/.

Select Bipartisan Committee to Investigate the Preparation for and Response to Hurricane Katrina, 2006. A failure of initiative: final report of the special Bipartisan Committee to investigate the preparation for and response to Hurricane Katrina. Government Printing Office, http://www.gpoaccess.gov/congress/index.html (February 15, 2006).

Senate Committee on Homeland Security and Governmental Affairs, 2006. Hurricane Katrina: A Nation Still Unprepared. Government Printing Office, Washington, DC (S. Rept. 109-322).

Shirky, C., 2008. Here comes everybody: the power of organizing without organizations. The Penguin Press.

Shively, K., 2013a. How top brands are using instagram since the facebook buy. SimplyMeasured (May 9). http://simplymeasured.com/blog/2013/05/09/how-top-brands-are-using-instagram-since-the-facebook-buy-study/.

Shively, K., 2013b. Is vine growing faster than instagram did? SimplyMeasured (June 4). http://simplymeasured.com/blog/2013/06/04/is-vine-growing-quicker-than-instagram-did/.

Skarada, E., 2011. Facebook to the rescue: how social media is changing disaster response. Time (June 9). http://www.time.com/time/nation/article/0,8599,2076195,00.html.

Smith, A., Halstead, B., Esposito, L., Schlegelmilch, J., 2013. Social Media and Virtual Platforms: The New Situational Awareness for Emergency Management Professionals. Center for Emergency Preparedness and Disaster Response, Yale New Haven Health. http://ynhhs.org/emergency/PDFs/SocialMediaandVirtualPlatforms.pdf (accessed on July 31, 2013).

Sonderman, J., 2012. Poynter.org. One-third of all adults under 30 get news on social networks now. http://www.poynter.org/latest-news/mediawire/189776/one-third-of-adults-under-30-get-news-on-social-networks-now/ (September 27, 2012).

Stabe, M., 2007. California wildfires: a round up. OJB Online Journalism Blog (October 25). http://onlinejournalismblog.com/2007/10/25/california-wildfires-a-roundup/.

Stern, J., 2013. Boston Marathon bombing: the waves of social media reaction. ABC News Technology Review (April 16). http://abcnews.go.com/blogs/technology/2013/04/boston-marathon-bombing-the-waves-of-social-media-reaction/.

Su, S.Y., Wardell III, C., Thorkildsen, Z., 2013. Social Media in the Emergency Management Field. Center for Naval Analysis (CNA) and the National Emergency Management Association (NEMA). http://www.cna.org/sites/default/files/research/SocialMedia_EmergencyManagement.pdf (June, 2013).

Sutton, J., 2013. Interviewed by Kim Haddow on July 9, 2013.

The Weather Channel, 2012. http://www.weather.com/news/fema-fugate-interview-20120507 (May 7, 2012).

Tinker, T., Fouse, D., 2009. Expert Round Table on Social Media and Risk Communications During Times of Crisis: Strategic Challenges and Opportunities. Booz Allen Hamilton. http://www.boozallen.com/media/file/Risk_Communications_Times_of_Crisis.pdf (March 31, 2009).

Washkuch, F., 2008. Relief groups turn to Twitter amid crises. PR Week (May 20). http://www.prweekus.com/Relief-groups-turn-to-Twitter-amid-crises/article/110368/.

West, D.M., Valentini, E., 2013. How Mobile Devices are Transforming Disaster Relief and Public Safety. Center for Technology Innovation at Brookings. http://www.brookings.edu/~/media/research/files/papers/2013/07/16%20mobile%20technology%20disaster%20relief/west_valentini_mobile%20technology%20disaster%20relief_v20.pdf (July, 2013).

Yeomans, M., 2012. Social media's crucial role in disaster relief efforts. The Guardian.com. http://www.theguardian.com/sustainable-business/social-media-hurricane-sandy-emergency-planners (posted on November 6, 2012).

Yglesias, M., 2013. The glory days of American journalism. Slate (March 19). http://www.slate.com/articles/business/moneybox/2013/03/pew_s_state_of_the_media_ignore_the_doomsaying_american_journalism_has_never.html.

12 Science and Technology

What You Will Learn

- How homeland security research and development funding is distributed in DHS
- What research and development efforts are performed by the Department of Homeland Security and by what offices that work is done
- Where in the federal government structure research and development are performed in the areas of weapons of mass destruction and information and infrastructure
- The names and functions of the various government research facilities and laboratories
- Where homeland security research and development efforts are occurring outside the Department of Homeland Security

Introduction

The Department of Homeland Security (DHS) announced at the time of its establishment that it "is committed to using cutting-edge technologies and scientific talent" to create a safer country. In this vein, the Science and Technology (S&T) Directorate was formed, which still exists today despite the many iterations of DHS organizational change. The S&T Directorate was tasked under the original development plans with assuming the research needs of the new department and for organizing the scientific, engineering, and technological resources of the country in order to adapt their use to the newly recognized needs under the counterterrorism drive created by the September 11, 2001, terrorist attacks. Universities, the private sector, and federal laboratories have all become important DHS partners in this endeavor.

Tens of billions of dollars have already been spent by DHS and other agencies with related missions on developing and exploiting technologies for use in the fight against terrorism and, on occasion, for emergency management in general. As is true in all areas of research, not all of the technology developed has been successful, although many innovative and useful systems have resulted. These efforts come not without critics, and many people have expressed sentiments that the push toward increased use of technological solutions does not necessarily decrease vulnerabilities, but rather increases reliance on technologies that could fail. For this reason, there remains significant dissent over the actual overall value of technology as a homeland security tool.

Despite these controversies, it is undeniable that the way of life in the United States has changed as the result of a great investment in technology by the federal government. This chapter examines that investment and offers different views on its value.

Department of Homeland Security

Before the establishment of DHS, most R&D efforts dealing with issues relevant to homeland security were dispersed among a wide variety of agencies, and this situation remains. However, the clear trend since 2003 has been to make DHS a focus for such R&D, and as of 2008, over one-fifth of all R&D funding is managed by DHS (placing it second only after HHS). Inside DHS, the S&T Directorate has been established in order to coordinate and manage R&D efforts. For the first 3 years of the directorate's existence, R&D efforts were dispersed throughout the various directorates and independent agencies (e.g., the Coast Guard). However, as early as FY 2006, all R&D efforts were consolidated under S&T. A more detailed description of S&T and the research this directorate conducts follow.

DHS Science and Technology Directorate

The Science and Technology (S&T) Directorate, led by an undersecretary of homeland security, is the primary R&D office within the Department of Homeland Security. Since April 7, 2014, S&T has been led by Dr. Reginald Brothers, who previously served in the US Department of Defense's Office of the Assistant Secretary of Defense for Research and Engineering as the Deputy Assistant Secretary of Defense for Research (see sidebar "S&T Under Secretary Reginald Brothers").

S&T Under Secretary Reginald Brothers

The U.S. Senate confirmed Dr. Reginald Brothers on April 7, 2014, for the position of Under Secretary for Science and Technology at the U.S. Department of Homeland Security (DHS). As Under Secretary for Science and Technology, Dr. Brothers is the science adviser to the Secretary and Deputy Secretary of Homeland Security and is responsible for oversight and management of the Science and Technology Directorate (S&T), the Department's primary research and development arm and technical core. Through his leadership of S&T, Dr. Brothers is responsible for a science and technology portfolio that includes basic and applied research, development, demonstration, testing, and evaluation with the purpose of helping DHS operational elements and the Nation's first responders achieve their missions in the most effective, most efficient, and safest manner possible.

From December 2011 until April 2014, Dr. Brothers served in the U.S. Department of Defense's Office of the Assistant Secretary of Defense for Research and Engineering as the Deputy Assistant Secretary of Defense for Research. In this position, he was responsible for policy and oversight of the Department's science and technology programs from basic research through advanced technology development. Dr. Brothers was also responsible for the Department's laboratories and, as architect of the long-term strategic direction of the Department's science and technology programs, oversaw scientific advancements necessary for the continued technological superiority of U.S. Armed Forces.

Dr. Brothers is a science and technology leader and expert with more than 20 years of demonstrated success across the private and public sectors. He has held a variety of positions within the scientific and technological community that demonstrate his leadership and technical aptitude. This includes his prior service as a Technical Fellow and Director for Mission Applications in the Communications and Networking Business Area at BAE Systems, as a member of the Board on Army

Science and Technology within the National Academy of Sciences, and as a Program Manager for the Defense Advanced Research Projects Agency. This also includes his experience as a Group Leader at the Charles Stark Draper Laboratory and as Chief Architect at Envoy Networks, a successful 3G wireless start-up company.

Dr. Brothers received a B.S. in Electrical Engineering from Tufts University, an M.S. in Electrical Engineering from Southern Methodist University, and a Ph.D. in Electrical Engineering and Computer Science from the Massachusetts Institute of Technology.

Source: DHS (2014c).

One week after Dr. Brothers was confirmed as the leader of the S&T Directorate, the Congressional Research Service (CRS) released a report entitled "The DHS S&T Directorate: Selected Issues for Congress." The CRS report identified several issues that DHS and Congress needed to address in order to improve the effectiveness and efficiency of the work conducted by S&T. A summary of the report findings is presented in the sidebar "The DHS S&T Directorate: Selected Issues for Congress" (CRS, 2014).

The DHS S&T Directorate: Selected Issues for Congress

Summary

Policy makers generally believe that science and technology can and will play significant roles in improving homeland security. When Congress established the Department of Homeland Security (DHS), through the Homeland Security Act of 2002 (P.L. 107-296), it included the Directorate of Science and Technology (S&T) to ensure that the new department had access to science and technology advice and research and development (R&D) capabilities.

The S&T Directorate is the primary organization for R&D in DHS. It conducts R&D in several DHS laboratories and funds R&D conducted by other government agencies, the Department of Energy national laboratories, academia, and the private sector. Additionally, the directorate supports the development of operational requirements and oversees the operational testing and evaluation of homeland security systems for DHS. The Homeland Security Act of 2002 provided direction and broadly defined functions for the Under Secretary for Science and Technology and the S&T Directorate. Within this broad statutory framework, congressional and executive branch policy makers face many challenges, including balancing funding for R&D activities, which may not result in a deployable product for many years, with other near-term homeland security needs.

Despite several restructurings and close congressional oversight, the S&T Directorate continues to face difficulties in meeting congressional expectations. The 113th Congress may consider several policy issues related to the performance of the S&T Directorate. These include

- priority-setting mechanisms for the directorate's R&D programs, such as strategic planning and targeting high-priority investments;
- the scope of the directorate's R&D activities, such as balancing incremental efforts with efforts that offer high risk, but high reward;

- whether R&D efficiency and effectiveness could be enhanced through further consolidations of R&D activities into the S&T Directorate or through dispersing these activities to other entities; and
- the directorate's role in the DHS acquisition process, both in identifying operational requirements and assessing operational effectiveness.

Source: CRS (2014).

In his testimony at a congressional hearing held on September 9, 2014, Dr. Brothers outlined the current vision for S&T to achieve its mission to "strengthen America's security and resiliency by providing knowledge products and innovative technology solutions for the Homeland Security Enterprise." The following sidebar presents excerpts from Dr. Brother's testimony.

Excerpts from written testimony of S&T Under Secretary Dr. Reginald Brothers for a House Committee on Homeland Security, Subcommittee on Cybersecurity, Infrastructure Protection, and Security Technologies, and House Committee on Science, Space, and Technology, Subcommittee on Research and Technology hearing titled "Strategy and Mission of the DHS Science and Technology Directorate" on September 9, 2014.

A Strategic Focus for Homeland Security

Effective planning is how we as an organization will translate the basis for our work (e.g., Component priorities, the Secretary's initiatives, congressional mandates, White House policy) into functional programs that ultimately deliver novel or improved capability. This includes a strategic vision spanning the near term, including specific courses of action, through the long term and far horizon, including ambitious goals.

Four Visionary Goals

As a first step, one of my priorities coming on board was establishing visionary goals that would serve as 30-year horizon points to build toward. When Dr. George Heilmeier, one of the great technology leaders of our time, was Director of the Defense Advanced Research Projects Agency, the organization and its stakeholders were invigorated by his articulation of visionary goals, what he called his "silver bullets." *Make the oceans transparent. Create an invisible aircraft.* Heilmeier's visionary goals strove for previously unachieved capabilities and lower-cost equivalents to existing capabilities. They helped orient the organization and inspired stakeholders, including operators, end users, and performers in industry and academia.

R&D requires creativity and imagination, and we must tap into that enthusiasm to spur big thinking. At S&T, I tasked a working group with representatives from throughout the organization to draft vision statements for consumption and feedback from the rest of the directorate and our end user stakeholders. Building off of existing policy and doctrine (e.g., the Quadrennial Homeland

Security Review, Secretary Johnson's priorities, existing Homeland Security Presidential Directives), the group generated the four following draft goals:

- *Screening at Speed: Matching the Pace of Life*: Noninvasive screening at speed will provide for comprehensive threat protection while adapting security to the pace of life rather than life to security. Whether screening people, baggage or cargo, unobtrusive technologies and improved processes will enable the seamless detection of threats while respecting privacy, with minimal impact to the speed of travel and the pace of commerce.
- *A Trusted Cyber Future: Protecting Privacy, Commerce, and Community*: In a future of increasing cyber connections, users will trust that infrastructure is resilient, information is protected, illegal use is deterred, and privacy is not compromised. Frictionless security will operate seamlessly in the background, based on self-detecting, self-protecting, and self-healing cyber critical infrastructure—all without disruption.
- *Enable the Decision Maker: Providing Actionable Information Ahead of Incident Speed*: The decision maker has improved situational awareness and is better able to understand risks, weigh options, and take action—literally experience the information. The essential element to making informed decisions is access to timely, accurate, context-based information. Supported by new decision support, modeling and simulation systems, critical decisions can be made based on relevant information, transforming disparate data into proactive wisdom and ultimately improving operational effectiveness.
- *Responder of the Future: Protected, Connected, and Fully Aware*: The responder of the future is threat-adaptive, able to respond to all dangers safely and effectively. Armed with comprehensive physical protection; interoperable, networked tools; technology-enhanced threat detection and mitigation capabilities; and timely, actionable information, the responder of the future will be able to serve more safely and effectively as an integral part of the Nation's resiliency.

Following the development of the initial draft set of visionary goals by the working group, we opened them to Directorate-wide discussion and development. Based on that feedback, changes were made before a second wave of input from a wider group including the Department and external stakeholders outside DHS.

An Actionable Strategy

With the visionary goals as an ambitious end state, the next step is a narrower, 5–10 year strategic plan for S&T. This will be a nearer-term roadmap for how our organization seeks to achieve our visionary end goals. Development of a strategy is a platform to think through and communicate our plan internally and, as a result, make the most of our investments. Externally, a good strategy also provides critical signposts to industry, Congress, and other stakeholders for where our priorities lie and the path we seek to reach for long-time horizon deliverables. This is a standard tool in industry and elsewhere. I look forward to using the same approach at S&T to make us more accessible and to be the foundation for how we interface within the Department, as an interagency partner, and with industry and our other non-federal partners.

Delivering Force Multiplying Solutions

In order to position the Directorate more strategically, we are updating our approach to R&D programs. A new approach will allow a more focused, strategic relationship with our partners and will address the need for a jointly calibrated investment risk profile. At times, there will rightly be pressure to fill immediate needs or invest in incremental improvements, but a healthy portfolio must still allow for a portion of projects to carry more technical risk and offer proportionally greater potential returns. My vision for a balanced R&D portfolio is one that makes appropriate tradeoffs between technical feasibility and operational impact of projects, weighs potential event's probability and impact, and that distributes appropriately across types of performers (including non-traditional) and project timelines (<1 vs. 5 years).

As such, I plan for a portfolio that spans quick success projects integrating off-the-shelf technologies to potentially disruptive technologies that, out of necessity, will be high risk. S&T and our stakeholders have to embrace the risk-capability tradeoffs if we are to achieve our potential to deliver both near term and game-changing capabilities to our end users. There will also be three categories of programs, outlined below, that will ultimately reduce S&T's total number of programs but will increase overall impact, strategic focus, and sustainability of the R&D portfolio.

S&T's Process for Identifying Capability Gaps

There are two elements of S&T's work that are complementary but distinct. The first, requirements, is for acquisition programs and deals with physical characteristics and operational necessities (e.g., weight, dimension, ruggedness, look, and feel). S&T's contributions in this area include participation in the Department's joint capabilities and requirements process. Operational capability gaps, which are the second element, address missions, or subsets of missions that cannot be met currently or efficiencies which significantly enhance performance; these are based on customer and end user input. These operational capability gaps serve as S&T's primary driver for what we focus on in R&D programs.

Moving forward, S&T will formalize and integrate its framework for communicating, documenting, addressing, and reviewing capability gaps and R&D requirements. These generally grow from two complementary categories. The first is conceptual development through embedding directly with operators, analysis of future threats, or other interaction with operators. The second is through hands-on experimentation, also influenced by embedding with operators as well as through types of events like those in the Joint Interagency Field Exploration program. Those R&D requirements will then be the basis for S&T's technology roadmaps and new start programs.

A Twenty-First Century R&D Workforce

Going back to the lessons learned from corporate labs that have maintained their value to organizations, I look forward to implementation of a much more robust process for S&T's workforce to embed with operators and to allow operational staff to detail to S&T and provide direct input to our R&D projects. To function in the new digital age, we need scientists who break down firewalls between R&D and operations and who become fluent in the language of operators and end users. These "multi-lingual" program managers that can slide between operational and technical environments have the best track records for successful projects and transition to use.

Source: DHS (2014a).

The S&T Directorate current organizational chart is presented in Figure 12-1. The Science and Technology Directorate Organization is described in the sidebar "Science and Technology Directorate Organization."

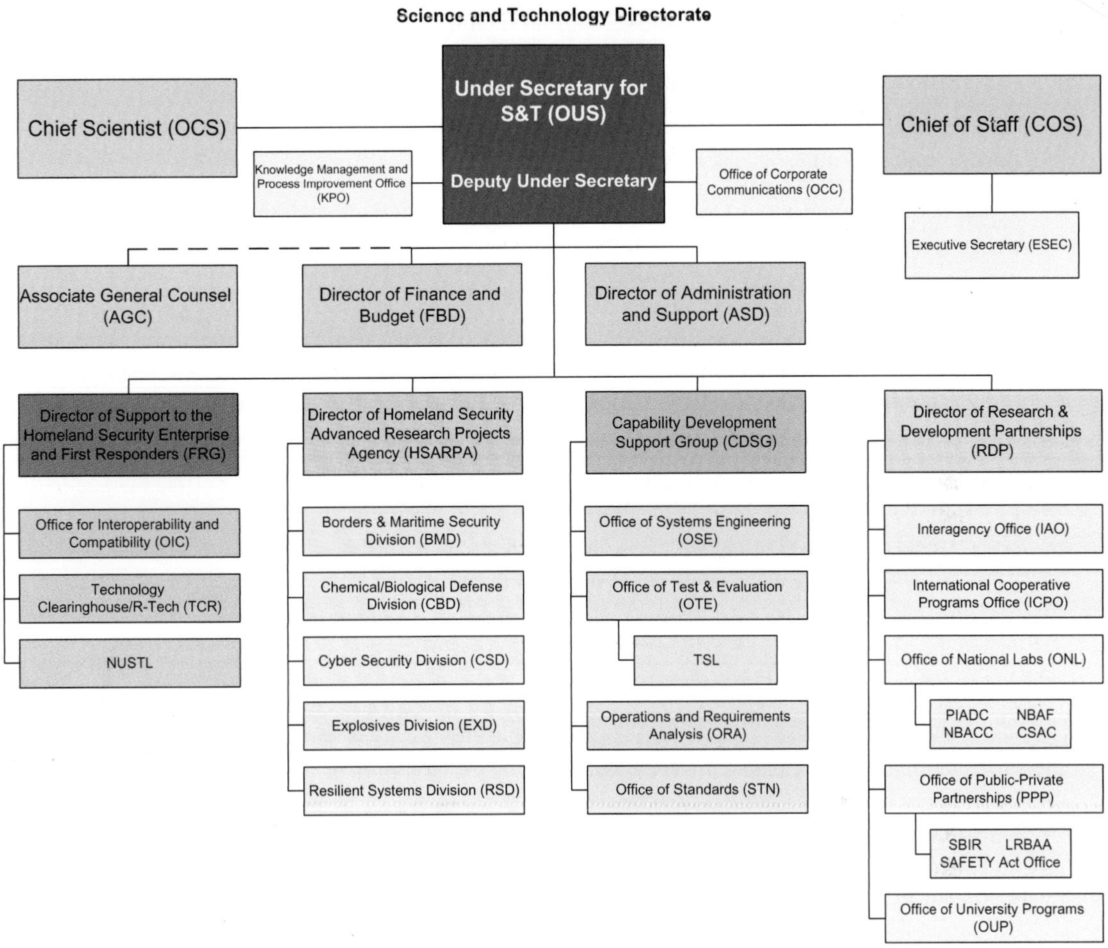

Science and Technology Directorate

Under Secretary for S&T (OUS)
Deputy Under Secretary
Chief Scientist (OCS)
Chief of Staff (COS)
Knowledge Management and Process Improvement Office (KPO)
Office of Corporate Communications (OCC)
Executive Secretary (ESEC)
Associate General Counsel (AGC)
Director of Finance and Budget (FBD)
Director of Administration and Support (ASD)
Director of Support to the Homeland Security Enterprise and First Responders (FRG)
Office for Interoperability and Compatibility (OIC)
Technology Clearinghouse/R-Tech (TCR)
NUSTL
Director of Homeland Security Advanced Research Projects Agency (HSARPA)
Borders & Maritime Security Division (BMD)
Chemical/Biological Defense Division (CBD)
Cyber Security Division (CSD)
Explosives Division (EXD)
Resilient Systems Division (RSD)
Capability Development Support Group (CDSG)
Office of Systems Engineering (OSE)
Office of Test & Evaluation (OTE)
TSL
Operations and Requirements Analysis (ORA)
Office of Standards (STN)
Director of Research & Development Partnerships (RDP)
Interagency Office (IAO)
International Cooperative Programs Office (ICPO)
Office of National Labs (ONL)
PIADC NBAF NBACC CSAC
Office of Public-Private Partnerships (PPP)
SBIR LRBAA SAFETY Act Office
Office of University Programs (OUP)

FIGURE 12-1 Science and Technology Directorate organizational chart. *Source: DHS (2014a,b).*

Science and Technology Directorate Organization

The S&T Directorate is organized into four groups that work together to ensure that each aspect of S&T's work (operational analyses, requirements generation, test and evaluation, technology development, and acquisition support) is given the appropriate amount of emphasis.

The Support to the Homeland Security Enterprise and First Responders Group (FRG) strengthens the response community's abilities to protect the homeland and respond to disasters. Three FRG divisions work together to carry out this mission:

- National Urban Security Technology Laboratory
- Office for Interoperability and Compatibility
- Technology Clearinghouse/R-Tech

The Homeland Security Advanced Research Projects Agency (HSARPA) focuses on identifying, developing, and transitioning technologies and capabilities to counter chemical, biological, explosive, and cyber terrorist threats and protecting our nation's borders and infrastructure. HSARPA manages six technical divisions to carry out this mission:

- Borders and Maritime Security Division
- Chemical and Biological Defense Division
- Cyber Security Division
- Explosives Division
- Resilient Systems Division

The Acquisition Support and Operations Analysis (ASOA) group strengthens the Homeland Security Enterprise mission to secure the nation by providing analyses, engineering, and test expertise and products connecting research, development, and acquisition to the operational end user. ASOA is of the following:

- Chief Systems Engineer
- Federally Funded Research and Development Centers Program Management Office
- Operational Test and Evaluation
- Research and Development Analysis and Assessment
- Standards

The Research and Development Partnerships (RDP) group builds enduring partnerships that deliver technology solutions to the HSE resourcefully and swiftly. It's an urgent mission that demands close cooperation across the HSE and among the group's six offices:

- Homeland Security Science and Technology Advisory Committee
- Interagency Office
- International Cooperative Programs Office
- Office of National Laboratories
  - Chemical Security Analysis Center
  - National Bio and Agro-Defense Facility
  - National Biodefense Analysis and Countermeasures Center
  - Plum Island Animal Disease Center
- Office of Public-Private Partnerships
  - Commercialization Office
  - Long-Range Broad Agency Announcement Office
  - Office of SAFETY Act Implementation
  - Small Business Innovative Research Office
- Office of University Programs
  - Special Projects Office

RDP also coordinates interactions with the White House through the Office of Science and Technology Policy.

Source: DHS (2014). http://www.dhs.gov/st-organization.

On October 24, 2014, Dr. Brothers unveiled new visionary goals for the S&T Directorate. In the announcement, Dr. Brothers stated, "As the primary research and development arm of DHS, S&T needs to look ahead—20–30 years out—to determine where we should be dedicating our research and development resources now." The announcement noted that "The long-term goals were finalized following an extensive collaboration effort that yielded input and suggestions from thousands of stakeholders in government, academia, and the nation's private sector industrial base" (DHS (2014d)).

S&T Visionary Goals

Screening at Speed: Security that Matches the Pace of Life

Noninvasive screening at speed will provide for comprehensive threat protection while adapting security to the pace of life rather than life to security. Unobtrusive screening of people, baggage, or cargo will enable the seamless detection of threats while respecting privacy, with minimal impact to the pace of travel and speed of commerce.

A Trusted Cyber Future: Protecting Privacy, Commerce, and Community

In a future of increasing cyber connections, underlying digital infrastructure will be self-detecting, self-protecting, and self-healing. Users will trust that information is protected, illegal use is deterred, and privacy is not compromised. Security will operate seamlessly in the background.

Enable the Decision Maker: Actionable Information at the Speed of Thought

Predictive analytics, risk analysis, and modeling and simulation systems will enable critical and proactive decisions to be made based on the most relevant information, transforming data into actionable information. Even in the face of uncertain environments involving chemical, biological, radiological, or nuclear incidents, accurate, credible, and context-based information will empower the aware decision maker to take instant actions to improve critical outcomes.

Responder of the Future: Protected, Connected, and Fully Aware

The responder of the future is threat-adaptive and cross functional. Armed with comprehensive physical protection, interoperable tools, and networked threat detection and mitigation capabilities, responders of the future will be better able to serve their communities.

Resilient Communities: Disaster-Proofing Society

Critical infrastructure of the future will be designed, built, and maintained to withstand naturally occurring and man-made disasters. Decision makers will know when disaster is coming, anticipate the effects, and use already-in-place or rapidly deployed countermeasures to shield communities from negative consequences. Resilient communities struck by disasters will not only bounce back but also bounce forward.

S&T Budget

The amount of funding under the overall DHS budget dedicated to R&D has steadily decreased from a high of $1.8 billion in FY 2006 to $876 million requested by the president in his FY 2015 budget (see Figure 12-2).

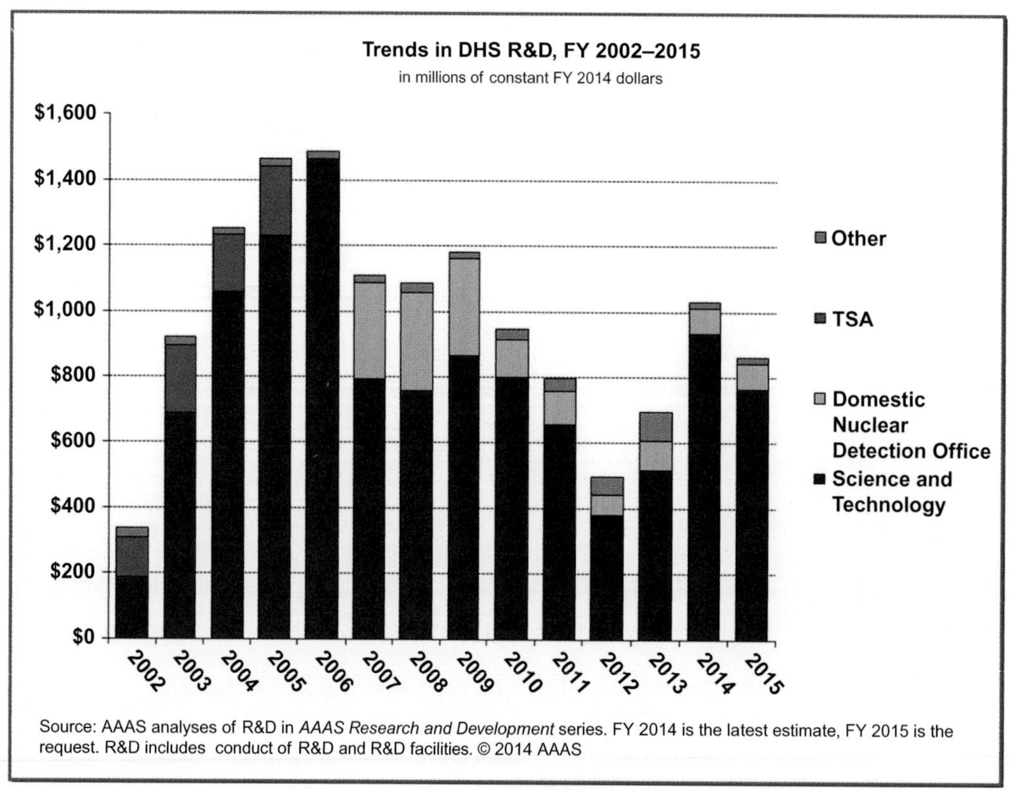

FIGURE 12-2 Trends in DHS R&D, FY 2002–2015. *Source: http://www.aaas.org/sites/default/files/DHS_0.jpg.*

According to a 2014 White House report entitled "The 2015 Budget: Science, Technology, and Innovation for Opportunity and Growth," "The Department of Homeland Security (DHS) Science and Technology (S&T) programs target opportunities in cybersecurity, explosives detection, nuclear detection, and chemical/biological detection and support ongoing enhancements of homeland security technology and development of state-of-the-art solutions for first responders. DHS R&D totals $876 million in the 2015 Budget, down 15.1% from the 2014 enacted level because of reduced construction funding. The Budget proposes $300 million to leverage previously appropriated resources to construct the National Bio- and Agro-Defense Facility (NBAF), a state-of-the-art laboratory to study and develop countermeasures for animal, emerging, and zoonotic diseases that threaten human health and the Nation's agricultural industry" (White House, 2014).

The American Association for the Advancement of Science in its report on the S&T FY 2015 budget request notes, "The FY 2015 Department of Homeland Security (DHS) Science and Technology Directorate (S&T) request totals $1.1 billion, a decrease of 12% from the FY 2014 enacted amount. It is the most significant cut in the DHS portfolio, followed by the 4.5% reduction in the Immigration and Customs Enforcement budget (ICE). A large portion of this decrease would come from the Laboratory Facilities account, with a $433 million adjustment-to-base. $300 million is included for the construction of the National Bio-Agro-Defense Facility (NBAF) in Kansas" (AAAS, 2014a). See Tables 12-1 and 12-2 and sidebar "Another Voice: Department of Homeland Security, By Jodi Lieberman, American Physical Society."

Table 12-1 Department of Homeland Security R&D (S&T Directorate) Budget ($ in Millions)

FY 2007	FY 2008	FY 2009	FY 2010	FY 2011	FY 2012	FY 2013	FY 2014	FY 2015
$846,916	$830,117	$932,587	$1,006,471	$1,006,471	$1,176,432	$508,000	$932,000 (estimate)	$776,000 (requested)

Source: American Association for the Advancement of Science (AAAS) (2014b).

Table 12-2 Department of Homeland Security (budget authority in millions of dollars)

	FY 2013	FY 2014	FY 2015	Change FY 14–15	
	Actual	Estimate	Budget	Amount	Percent
Domestic Nuclear Detection Office	92	79	80	1	1.3%
Science and Technology	508	932	776	−156	−16.7%
Coast Guard[a]	21	21	20	−1	−4.8%
Customs and Border Protection	63	0	0	0	-
Total DHS R&D	684	1032	876	−156	−15.1%
Select DHS Discretionary Budgets (include non-R&D components)					
Coast Guard	8459	8499	8135	−364	−4.3%
RDT&E	20	19	18	−1	−6.5%
Science & Technology	794	1220	1072	−148	−12.2%
Management and Admin	127	129	130	1	0.9%
Acquisition and Ops Support	46	42	42	0	0.0%
Laboratory Facilities	158	548	435	−113	−20.6%
Natl Bio and Agro-def Facil (NBAF)	31	404	300	−104	−25.7%
Research, Develop, and Innovation	425	462	434	−28	−6.1%
Apex R&D	-	15	15	0	0.0%
Border Security	-	44	51	7	16.5%
Chem/Bio/Expl	-	142	125	−16	−11.6%
Counterterrorist R&D	-	77	65	−12	−15.6%
Cybersecurity	-	80	77	−3	−4.0%
Disaster Resilience	-	104	101	−4	−3.6%
University Programs	38	40	31	−9	−22.0%
Domestic Nuclear Detection Office	303	285	304	19	6.7%
Management and Admin	38	37	37	0	0.4%
Research, Devel and Ops	215	205	199	−6	−3.0%
Transformational R&D	71	71	70	−2	−2.3%
Systems Acquisition	50	43	68	25	59.3%

All figures rounded to the nearest million. Changes calculated from unrounded figures.
[a]Includes contributions from the Oil Liability Trust Fund.
Source: OMB R&D data and agency budget justification. Does not include extra funding in the Opportunity, Growth, and Security Initiative (see Table II-20).

Another Voice: Department of Homeland Security, By Jodi Lieberman, American Physical Society

Highlights

- The FY 2015 Department of Homeland Security (DHS) Science and Technology Directorate (S&T) request totals $1.1 billion, a decrease of 12% from the FY 2014 enacted amount. It is the most significant cut in the DHS portfolio, followed by the 4.5% reduction in the Immigration and Customs Enforcement budget (ICE).
- A large portion of this decrease would come from the Laboratory Facilities account, with a $433 million adjustment-to-base. $300 million is included for the construction of the National Bio-Agro-Defense Facility (NBAF) in Kansas.
- The decrease also reflects a decrease in the CBE Defense, Counter Terrorist, Cyber Security/Information Analytics and First Responder/Disaster Resilience RDT&E thrust areas. Those reductions are 11.6%, 15.6%, 4.0%, and 3.6%, respectively.
- The Acquisitions and Operations Support Programs, Projects, and Activities (PPA) account is the only account not to be cut from the previous fiscal year; the Administration requests a flat line budget of $42 million.
- The request for the Laboratory Facilities PPA is reduced by 21%, mostly due to a 26% cut in the request for NBAF funding; this is likely due to the completion of site preparation and progress in construction of the central utility plant. NBAF construction received $404 million in FY2014; $300 million is requested in FY 2015.

Historical Trends, Impacts, and Context

Funding for the S&T Directorate has fluctuated over the last several years, partly due to Congressional concern over its inability to measure return on investment and for setting R&D priorities; these concerns and recommendations for addressing them were made by the National Association for Public Administration (NAPA) and the Government Accountability Office (GAO) as recently as 2013. A 2012 GAO report recommended that DHS develop "policies and guidance for defining, reporting, and coordinating R&D activities across the department, and that DHS establish a mechanism to track R&D projects." In its March 2013 explanatory statement for the Consolidated and Further Continuing Appropriations Act, 2013 (P.L. 113-6), Congress directed the Secretary of Homeland Security, through the Under Secretary for Science and Technology, to "establish a review process for all R&D work within DHS" and GAO once again pointed to this lack of review process in its April 2013 annual report on fragmented, overlapping, or duplicative federal programs.

Both the House and Senate, in their respective FY 2014 report language, address this concern again; the House bill directed DHS to "submit a report on reforms to its R&D programs, including a formal process for setting R&D priorities, a formal process for DHS-wide involvement in R&D decision-making and review, metrics for R&D program status and return on investment, and on the implementation of GAO's recommendations." It is unclear where the disconnect is between the significant changes made by former Under Secretary Tara O'Toole and Congress; it remains to be seen if the new Under Secretary for Science & Technology will finally bridge that gap. Doing so would likely go a long way in assuaging Congressional concerns and, as a result, minimizing fluctuations in funding for the Directorate.

In addition to the above Congressional concerns, the Senate noted that there remains no clear path to "bring innovative security technologies to the attention of Department decision makers, which may result in creative, cost-effective homeland security technology solutions being missed." In its language, the Senate once again underscores its desire to ensure that the DHS "customer" agencies are aware of cutting-edge technologies developed not only within the Department but also by industry and the university community through outreach by the S&T Directorate in order to stay ahead of evolving homeland security threats: in its FY 2014 appropriations report, the Senate requests that the Department submit a report to Congress detailing "efforts the agency is making to identify innovative technologies developed by industry, other Federal agencies, and universities that could improve the effectiveness, efficiency, and safety of DHS missions." This requirement underscores another ongoing theme in S&T activities: that the Directorate should serve as the principal conduit for innovative technologies and homeland security solutions for the mission agencies and to ensure that its activities are focused on identifying and providing those "customer-based" solutions.

Addressing Ongoing Issues

Basic Versus Applied Research

As his predecessor learned quickly, newly-confirmed Under Secretary for S&T Reggie Brothers must balance the need to respond to mission agency needs in the near term while ensuring that they have access to the latest in cutting-edge technologies and developments over the long term; that is, to balance basic research with applied research and "off-the-shelf" technologies. The challenge is being able to supply the latter while ensuring that the groundwork is laid for transformational innovations through the former. And Congress isn't a long-term institution. Legislators want results and they want them immediately, which does not lend itself well to long-term investments in basic research. That said, both Dr. Brothers and Anh Duong, the director of the Borders and Maritime Security Division under S&T, have both indicated that they intend to keep basic research in the S&T mix.

At a Border Security Expo in March, Duong stated that S&T's focus has definitely been on the "near-term stuff" for their customers but that the result has been an S&T Directorate with a "little S and big T." She continued that the agency intends, over the next 5 years, to lean more toward a balance between near-term and transformational, risky longer-term research.

Dr. Brothers is no stranger to this issue: in his previous position as Deputy Assistant Secretary of Defense for Research in the Office of the Assistant Secretary of Defense for Research and Engineering, as well at DARPA and BAE Systems, he was similarly challenged with this issue. In his confirmation hearing, Dr. Brothers also mentioned longer-term research: "With respect to balance in the science and technology portfolio, I believe the S&T Directorate should dedicate a significant portion of its portfolio to meeting the short-term needs of its customers....However, S&T should balance near-term investments with mid- and longer-term higher-payoff investments that provide new capabilities and new opportunities for customers."

Another persistent irritant for Congress has been the budget structure instituted by Under Secretary O'Toole beginning with the FY 2012 budget. The Directorate realigned its budget structure, putting all of its research and development activities into one Program, Project, and Activity (PPA) titled Research, Development, and Innovation (RD&I). Other activities were put into three other PPAs: Acquisition and Operations Support, Laboratory Support, and University Programs. S&T justified the realignment by stating that the new categories better aligned with the DHS Quadrennial Homeland Security Review priorities and, in its view, would provide more transparency. S&T also opined that the changes would make the budget "organizationally neutral." Both chambers objected, stating that the creation of the RD&I category was too large and too vague, and that it reduced transparency and accountability. They would object again in both the FY 2013 and FY 2014 appropriations bill language, directing S&T to divide the RD&I PPA into six PPAs: Apex, Border Security, Chem/Bio/Radiological/ Nuclear/Explosives Defense, Cybersecurity, and Disaster Resilience. Instead of creating six new PPAs, the Directorate instead created six "thrust" areas that correlate roughly with what Congress requested. It is unclear at this time whether that change adequately addressed Congressional concerns about clarity and transparency.

Addressing GAO Concerns

Since at least 2012, GAO has reported on the inability of DHS to account for its total investment in R&D agency-wide. Those concerns continue to plague DHS. Specifically, GAO has pointed out that "According to DHS budget officials, S&T, DNDO, and the U.S. Coast Guard are the only components that conduct R&D; they are also the only components that report budget authority, obligations, or outlays for R&D activities to OMB [the White House Office of Management and Budget]..." However, GAO also noted that the information reported to OMB by DHS underreported DHS R&D obligations because DHS components obligated money for R&D contracts that were not reported to OMB as R&D. According to GAO, DHS R&D budget accounts also mixed R&D and non-R&D spending, complicating its ability to identify its total R&D investment. In response to these concerns, DHS had reported that its Program Accountability and Risk Management office would evaluate "the most effective path forward to guide uniform treatment of R&D across the department in compliance with OMB rules" and would consider developing a new management directive, steering committee, or policy guidance to help better coordinate R&D. To date, DHS has not completed these actions. Moreover, while DHS has begun portfolio reviews related to R&D, it has not yet developed a policy to define who should coordinate R&D activities across the agency; doing so could, according to GAO, mitigate the risk of unnecessary overlap, fragmentation, or duplication.

In-Depth Review

The S&T Directorate has four RDT&E PPAs, and a number of thrust areas within each PPA. The FY 2015 request for the Research, Development, and Innovation (RD&I) PPA is $433.8 million, down 6% from FY 2014 enacted levels. RD&I has six thrust areas:

- APEX, which consists of crosscutting, multidisciplinary projects agreed to by the requesting DHS Component Head and the Under Secretary for Science and Technology;
- Border Security, which conducts R&D for technologies and solutions to prevent the illicit movement and illegal entry or exit of people, weapons, dangerous goods, and contraband, and to manage the risk posed by people and goods in transit;
- CBE Defense, which focuses on prevention of terrorism; reduction of vulnerability of critical infrastructure from terrorist attacks and other hazards; and prevention of the illicit movement and illegal entry or exit of people, weapons, dangerous goods, and contraband by providing technology, methods, and procedures to detect CBE threats;
- Counter Terrorist, which conducts R&D to identify individuals or groups that intend to conduct terrorist attacks or to illicitly move weapons, dangerous goods, and contraband. It also provides threat assessments of the high-consequence attack methods such as CBE that terrorists may use to attack the nation;
- Cyber Security/Information Analytics, which conducts and supports RDT&E and technology transition for advanced cybersecurity and information analytics technologies to secure the nation's current and future cyber and critical infrastructures, and to provide solutions for analyzing extremely large data sets to provide useful information for DHS Component use. This includes user identity and data privacy technologies, end system security, research infrastructure, law enforcement forensic capabilities, secure protocols, software assurance, cybersecurity education, and big data analytics and data manipulation; and
- First Responder/Disaster Resilience, which aims to reduce vulnerability of critical infrastructure, key leadership, and events to terrorist attacks and other hazards. The thrust

works with state, local, tribal, and territorial governments to secure their information systems; works with local and regional partners to identify hazards, assess vulnerabilities, and develop strategies to manage risks associated with all hazards; increases the state of preparedness of state, local, regional, tribal, and territorial partners, as well as nongovernmental organizations, the private sector, and the general public; advances and improves disaster emergency and interoperable communications capabilities; and improves the capabilities of DHS to lead in emergency management.

The FY 2015 request for Acquisition and Operations Support (AOS) is $41.7 million, the same as the FY 2014 enacted amount. AOS assists in the transition, acquisition, and deployment of technologies, information, and procedures that improve the efficiency and effectiveness of the operational capabilities across the HSE mission. It has five thrust areas: Operations Research and Analysis; SAFETY (Support Antiterrorism by Fostering Effective Technologies) Act; Standards; Technology Transition Support; and Testing and Evaluation.

The FY 2015 request for the Laboratory Facilities PPA is $435.2 million, a reduction of 21% from FY 2014 levels. Managed by the Office of National Laboratories (ONL), the Laboratory Facilities programs consist of Construction, Laboratory Infrastructure Upgrades, and Laboratory Operations. The reduction includes an adjustment-to-base of $433 million, and includes a current services request of $115 million, plus a $300 million request for continued construction activities at the NBAF.

The FY 2015 request for the University Programs PPA is $31 million, a 22% reduction below FY 2014 enacted levels. University Programs supports critical homeland security-related research and education at U.S. colleges and universities to address high-priority issues and to enhance homeland security capabilities over the long term. University Programs oversees the university-based Centers of Excellence and Minority Serving Institutions.

The two most significant reductions to the S&T account are under Explosives Detection (within CBE Defense), which is decreased by $15.5 million, and University Programs, which is reduced by $8.7 million.

The Explosives Detection cut decreases development of technologies for the Mass Transit and Dynamic X-Ray Imaging efforts, which provide screening and detection technologies for both aviation and surface mass transit. The decrease eliminates funding for the Algorithm & Analysis of Raw Images project. The University Programs cut reduces operational support to Centers of Excellence (COE) and will affect the number of future competitions for COEs.

Conclusion and Outlook

The confirmation of Dr. Reggie Brothers as Tara O'Toole's replacement to lead the S&T Directorate provides an opportunity to Dr. Brothers to finally put to rest ongoing Congressional and GAO concerns about coordination and management of R&D at the Department. Indeed, Dr. O'Toole took a very dysfunctional directorate and left it far better than when she began there in 2009. There is every indication that Dr. Brothers will continue down the path that O'Toole created for him. But it is clear there is far more work to be done to assuage those concerns. Dr. Brothers would do well to be mindful of Congressional concerns and to use every opportunity afforded him to make clear that the Directorate has a firm grasp on R&D being conducted throughout DHS.

With regard to appropriations, the 2-year Murray-Ryan budget deal has assured something close to regular order, so Dr. Brothers, as well as other Administration leaders, know the kinds of budgets they will have to work with. Constraints will continue to necessitate that he make the most of the budget he's got for S&T and to ensure not only coordination, but complementary R&D across the Department. The Directorate has regained some of the funding from the significant cuts leveled upon it in the enacted FY 2012 budget, in which Congress expressed its supreme displeasure with the path it was taking. But, if the most recent Congressional appropriations report language and GAO testimony are any indication, coordinating R&D activities at DHS, and in particular the S&T Directorate's role in keeping those activities straight, will continue to stymie efforts to turn the tide.

1. John F. Sargent Jr., Coordinator, November 5, 2013. Federal Research and Development Funding: FY2014. Congressional Research Service, R43086, p.21.
2. Ibid.
3. Ibid.
4. Dr. L. Reginald Brothers was nominated as Tara O'Toole's successor for Under Secretary for Science & Technology on January 30, 2014; his nomination hearing was held on March 5, 2014. He was confirmed on April 7, 2014.
5. Senate Report 113-77, Department of Homeland Security Appropriations Bill, 2014, p. 134.
6. Zach Rausnitz. S&T Ready to invest in riskier science, Fierce Homeland Security, March 20, 2014.
7. Statement of Dr. L. Reginald Brothers before the U.S. Senate Homeland Security and Governmental Affairs Committee, March 5, 2014.
8. Dana Shea. The DHS S&T Directorate: Selected Issues for Congress, Congressional Research Service, R43064, September 17, 2013, p. 4.
9. *"Oversight and Coordination of Research and Development Efforts Could be Strengthened,"* Statement of Dave C. Mauer, Director, Homeland Security and Justice, Government Accountability Office, before the Committee on Homeland Security and Governmental Affairs, U.S. Senate, July 17, 2013, p. 4.
10. Ibid, p. 4.
11. Ibid, p. 5.

Source: American Association for the Advancement of Science (AAAS) (2014b).

The S&T Directorate is responsible for setting the national agenda and giving direction and setting priorities for R&D efforts in other departments and agencies, regardless of the funding source. S&T is unique among federal R&D agencies in that it has responsibility for the entire cycle of science and technology (i.e., from product research to bringing the product to the market and deploying it).

The S&T Directorate established the Homeland Security Advanced Research Project Agency (HSARPA). This agency, based on the existing model of the Defense Advanced Research Project Agency (DARPA) in the Department of Defense (DOD), distributes resources within the directorate, awards money for the extramural grants, develops and tests potential technologies, and accelerates or prototypes development of technologies for deployment. The directorate has also created a Homeland Security Advisory Council consisting of 20 members appointed by the undersecretary representing first responders, citizen groups, researchers, engineers, and businesses to provide science and technology advice to the undersecretary. DHS has also created a new federally funded R&D center (FFRDC), the Homeland Security Institute, to act as a think tank for risk analyses, simulations of threat scenarios, analyses of possible countermeasures, and strategic plans for counterterrorism technology development. Table 12-3 presents the homeland security R&D budget for those departments and agencies currently involved in homeland security R&D. Various successes identified by DHS are listed in the sidebar "Science and Technology Directorate FY 2013 Accomplishments."

Table 12-3 Federal Homeland Security R&D Appropriations ($ in Millions)

Agency	FY 2006	FY 2007	FY 2008	FY 2009	FY 2010	FY 2011	FY 2012	FY 2013	FY 2014 (Estimate)	FY 2015 (Requested)
Agriculture	105	45	129	97	85	88	77	72	76	76
Commerce	62	59	68	76	135	177	178	174	188	183
DOD	1270	1175	1278	1506	2376	2115	2484	602	520	421
Energy	68	68	71	81	89	90	87	84	233	263
DHS	1300	1005	996	1033	887	1054	481	684	1032	876
EPA	40	41	53	74	66	42	42	40	39	40
HHS	1827	1829	1815	2106	1871	1929	1783	1773	1817	1845
NASA	93	97	94	109	20	6	14	13	13	13
NSF	329	329	357	358	370	395	396	389	398	379
DOT	3	1	2	1	0	0	0	0	0	0
All others	41	42	40	36	47	4	29	35	32	27
Total	5138	4691	4902	5475	5946	5900	5579	3865	4347	4122

Source: American Association for the Advancement of Science (AAAS) (2014b).

Science & Technology Directorate FY 2013 Accomplishments

- Detect to Protect Bio-Aerosol Detection Systems—This project advances biosensing by developing a number of innovative biosensors and a deployment architecture that can rapidly identify a biological organism and provide critical information, such as the size and rate of spread of an attack. This effort generated invaluable data that will inform the deployment of these sensor systems and future DHS biodetection efforts and strategic investments.
- Homemade Explosives (HME) Characterization—HMEs can be lethal and are designed to cause destruction or death when used in improvised explosive devices. S&T disseminates comprehensive safety data reports, providing standard operating procedures for the safe handling, preparation, and thermal stability of HMEs and conventional explosives by technicians, which, in turn, supports detection technology development.
- Checked Baggage—This project develops technologies and advanced system concepts for the Transportation Security Administration (TSA) to detect a wider range of explosives threat materials during the screening of checked baggage through commercial development of next-generation explosives detection systems and explosives trace detectors. This project delivered prototype fifth-generation X-ray computed tomography imaging systems with novel electron beam source for laboratory assessment.
- Wireless Emergency Alerts (WEA)—Mobile communications have become a critical media platform as our nation grows more dependent on mobile devices. The Office for Interoperable Communications (OIC) partnered with the New York City Office of Emergency Management and the Federal Emergency Management Agency to conduct an end-to-end demonstration of WEA, successfully originating, broadcasting, and delivering a WEA message to geo-targeted mobile devices.
- Resilient Electric Grid (REG)—S&T's REG uses super conducting technology to increase the reliability, flexibility, and resiliency of the nation's electric grid. REG developed a new cable that will allow distribution networks to interconnect and share power while eliminating the risk of cascading fault currents. The inherently fault current-limiting, high-temperature superconducting (IFCL-HTS) cable enables a more flexible architecture, making the grid more resilient. REG has successfully completed laboratory testing of a 25 m IFCL-HTS cable, and S&T is working on a pilot demonstration with the Department of Energy and Con Edison at substations in New York City in FY 2014.
- Finding Individuals for Disaster and Emergency Response (FINDER)—FINDER provides responders with a tool to maximize the window of time for rescue. This greatly increases a victim's chance of survival by quickly determining if a survivor is present in debris and then directing resources and manpower to facilitate a rescue. S&T and the Jet Propulsion Laboratory are now finalizing development of additional FINDER units that will be distributed to response agencies across the country for field testing during emergencies. OIC anticipates that a commercialized FINDER unit could be ready to be used in search and rescue operations as early as spring of 2014.

Source: DHS (2014b).

FY2015 Budget Highlights and Decreases

FY 2015 Highlights

- Rapid Biodetection $14.7M (0 FTE)

This project develops affordable and effective environmental/biological detection and collection systems that are suitable for urban environments' use for event detection and characterization purposes following an attack. The detection system outputs will feed into the emerging local-, state-, or national-level cloud processing architecture for rapid awareness and response in the event of a biological event/attack. The resulting advanced warning system will support indoor, outdoor, national security, and other biosurveillance monitoring in order to reduce the time it takes to identify biological threat agents in the field and increase effective response efforts.

- Checked Baggage $20.7M (0 FTE)

This project develops technologies and advanced system concepts for the Transportation Security Administration to detect a wider range of explosives threat materials during the screening of checked baggage through commercial development of next-generation explosives detection systems and explosives trace detectors. In addition, the next-generation checked baggage screening systems will operate with substantially reduced life cycle costs and false alarm rates, faster screening time, and reduced labor costs associated with screening of checked baggage, making the process more cost-effective.

- Integrated Passenger Screening Systems $19.2M (0 FTE)

This project allows for the application of innovative, compressive measurement techniques and advanced antenna components along with agile multiband imaging, which will provide higher imaging resolution and screening throughput while reducing system architecture complexity and product cost. Inexpensive, modular flat-panel advanced imaging technology systems will enable widespread deployment and improved threat detection capability at lower false alarm rates, thereby reducing airport operational costs. Reduced divestiture will lessen passenger inconvenience.

- Cyber Security Leap Ahead Technologies $12.8M (0 FTE)

This project identifies, incubates, and executes early research projects that may significantly advance current capabilities through moderate-risk and high-payoff outcomes in areas such as open-source technology development and mobile device security. These activities give organizations the ability to quickly shift and respond to new and potential threats by focusing attention on cutting-edge issues that are not currently being addressed.

- APEX Air Entry/Exit Re-Engineering $8.0M (0 FTE)

This project increases US Customs and Border Protection's ability to confirm the identity of persons entering and departing the United States, fulfill its obligation to implement a biometric air exit solution, and ensure that processes are efficient and keep pace with growth in international air travel. This project currently is building out a biometric test bed for scenario testing and demonstrations that will be critical to the operational and economic analysis and translating operational requirements.

- National Bio and Agro-Defense Facility (NBAF) $300.0M (0 FTE)

This allows S&T to execute the construction contract on the laboratory facility. This innovative federal-state partnership will support the first biosafety level 4 lab of its kind—a state-of-the-art biocontainment facility for the study of foreign animal and emerging zoonotic diseases that is central to the protection of the nation's food supply and to our national and economic security.

FY 2015 Major Decreases:

- Explosives Detection –$15.5M (0 FTE)

This decreases development of technologies for the mass transit and dynamic X-ray imaging efforts. These efforts provide screening and detection technologies for both aviation and surface mass transit, while maintaining efficient flow of passengers. This decrease eliminates funding for the Algorithm and Analysis of Raw Images project.

- University Programs –$8.7M (0 FTE)

This decrease will reduce operational support to Centers of Excellence (COE) and will affect the number of future competitions for COEs.

Source: DHS (2014b).

Critical Thinking

In your opinion, is federal funding better spent on all-hazards first-responder preparedness or on R&D efforts to find new emergency management solutions for terrorist hazards? Based on the FY 2015 funding levels for both of these activities (listed throughout this chapter), would the American public be better served by transferring funding from R&D to first-responder preparedness, or vice versa? Explain your answer.

R&D Efforts Focused on Weapons of Mass Destruction

The DHS website states, "The S&T Directorate will tap into scientific and technological capabilities to provide the means to detect and deter attacks using weapons of mass destruction. S&T will guide and organize research efforts to meet emerging and predicted needs and will work closely with universities, the private sector, and national and federal laboratories." This effort can be subdivided into two fields: chemical and biological and radiological and nuclear. In both fields, the directorate's aim is to carry research to develop sensors to detect such weapons from production to employment. The different organizations within the federal sector that will support and serve the R&D efforts of S&T are detailed in the following section.

Chemical, Biological, Radiological, and Nuclear Defense Information and Analysis Center

The Chemical, Biological, Radiological, and Nuclear Defense Information Analysis Center (CBRNIAC, http://www.cbrniac.apgea.army.mil/), formerly known as the CBIAC, is a full-service DOD Information Analysis Center (IAC). The CBRNIAC is the authoritative resource for DOD Chemical, Biological, Radiological and Nuclear (CBRN) Defense and Homeland Security scientific and technical (S&T) information.

The CBRNIAC generates, acquires, processes, analyzes, and disseminates CBRN Defense Science and Technology Information (STI) in support of the combatant commanders; war fighters; the reserve components; the CBRN Defense Research, Development, and Acquisition community; and other federal, state, and local government agencies. The CBRNIAC assists these agencies in implementing high-priority research and development (R&D) initiatives by

- identifying and acquiring relevant data and information from all available sources and in all media;
- processing data and acquisitions into suitable storage and retrieval systems;
- identifying, developing, and applying available analytic tools and techniques for the interpretation and application of stored data and acquisitions;
- disseminating focused information, datasets, and technical analyses to managers, planners, scientists, engineers, and military field personnel for the performance of mission-related tasks;
- anticipating requirements for CBRN Defense STI;
- identifying and reaching out to emerging CBRN Defense organizations (Department of Defense, 2011).

Defense Threat Reduction Agency

The Defense Threat Reduction Agency (DTRA, www.dtra.mil) safeguards national interests from weapons of mass destruction (WMDs) (chemical, biological, radiological, nuclear, and high explosives) by controlling and reducing the threat and providing quality tools and services for the war fighter. DTRA performs four essential functions to reach its mission: combat support, technology development, threat control, and threat reduction. Moreover, the agency's work covers a broad spectrum of activities:

- Shaping the international environment to prevent the spread of WMDs
- Responding to requirements to deter the use and reduce the impact of such weapons
- Preparing for the future as WMD threats emerge and evolve

The activities concerning homeland security are as follows:

- DTRA draws on the disparate chemical and biological weapons defense expertise within the DOD to increase response capabilities.
- The Advanced Systems and Concepts Office (ASCO) stimulates, identifies, and executes high-impact seed projects to encourage new thinking, address technology gaps, and improve the operational capabilities of DTRA.

Department of State

The Department of State (www.state.gov) contributes to the counterterror effort related to WMDs through diplomatic and intelligence-gathering efforts. The Department of State provides information and assessments of potential chemical and biological weapons sources throughout the world and analyzes what different countries and groups are doing to increase, decrease, or support WMD development and stockpiling.

Centers for Disease Control and Prevention

The Centers for Disease Control and Prevention (CDC, www.cdc.gov) is recognized as the lead federal agency for protecting the health and safety of people by providing credible information to enhance health decisions and promoting health through strong partnerships. CDC serves as the national focus for developing and applying disease prevention and control, environmental health, and health promotion and education activities designed to improve the health of the people of the United States, with the mission to promote health and quality of life by preventing and controlling disease, injury, and disability. CDC provides information about the effects and treatment for exposure to chemical and biological weapons and has valuable expertise in its 12 centers, institutes, and offices. The most prominent and relevant of the 12 follow:

- The National Center for Chronic Disease Prevention and Health Promotion prevents premature death and disability from chronic diseases and promotes healthy personal behaviors.
- The National Center for Health Statistics provides statistical information that will guide actions and policies to improve the health of the American people.
- The National Center for HIV/AIDS, Viral Hepatitis, STD, and TB Prevention provides national leadership in preventing and controlling human immunodeficiency virus infection, sexually transmitted diseases, and tuberculosis.
- The National Center for Infectious Diseases prevents illness, disability, and death caused by infectious diseases in the United States and around the world.
- The National Immunization Program prevents disease, disability, and death from vaccine-preventable diseases in children and adults.
- The Epidemiology Program Office strengthens the public health system by coordinating public health surveillance; providing support in scientific communications, statistics, and epidemiology; and training in surveillance, epidemiology, and prevention effectiveness.
- The Office of Science and Public Health Practice strengthens community practice of public health by creating an effective workforce, building information networks, conducting practice research, and ensuring laboratory quality.

Lawrence Livermore National Laboratory

The Lawrence Livermore National Laboratory (LLNL, www.llnl.gov) provides information about nuclear and radiological weapons. Its activities are explained more broadly in the R&D section.

US Nuclear Regulatory Commission

The US Nuclear Regulatory Commission (NRC, www.nrc.gov) is an independent agency established to regulate civilian use of nuclear materials. The NRC's mission is to regulate the nation's civilian use of by-product, source, and special nuclear materials to ensure adequate protection of public health and safety, to promote the common defense and security, and to protect the environment. The NRC's regulatory mission covers three main areas:

- *Reactors*: Commercial reactors for generating electric power and nonpower reactors used for research, testing, and training
- *Materials*: Uses of nuclear materials in medical, industrial, and academic settings and facilities that produce nuclear fuel
- *Waste*: Transportation, storage, and disposal of nuclear materials and waste and decommissioning of nuclear facilities from service

The NRC carries out its mission by conducting several activities, but most of them are not directly related to the homeland security purpose. The commission performs them as part of its mission to regulate the normal use of radiological material, but many of its capabilities and resources can be used during a radiological or nuclear incident. The major contribution fields are commission direction setting and policy making, radiation protection, establishment of a regulatory program, nuclear security and safeguards information on how to promote the common defense and security, public affairs, congressional affairs, state and tribal programs, and international programs.

Efforts Aimed at Information and Infrastructure

DHS has been given the primary responsibility for detecting and deterring attacks on the national information systems and critical infrastructures, and the S&T Directorate is developing a national R&D enterprise to support this mission. The three main issues concerning information and infrastructure are as follows: Internet security, telecommunication, and the security systems. The directorate coordinates and integrates several organizations to accomplish its mission, as discussed in the next sections.

SANS Institute

The SANS (Systems Administration, Audit, Network, Security) Institute (www.sans.org) is active in the fields of information security research, certification, and education and provides a platform for professionals to share lessons learned, conduct research, and teach the information security community. Besides the various training programs and resources aimed at informing its members and the community, the centers described below are part of SANS:

- *Internet Storm Center*: This center was created to detect rising Internet threats. It uses advanced data correlation and visualization techniques to analyze data from a large number of firewalls and intrusion detection systems in over 60 countries. Experienced analysts constantly monitor the Internet Storm Center data feeds and search for trends and anomalies in order to identify potential threats. When a potential threat is detected, the team immediately begins an intensive investigation to gauge the threat's severity and impact. The Internet Storm Center may request correlating data from an extensive network of security experts from across the globe and possesses the in-house expertise to analyze captured attack tools quickly and thoroughly. Critical information is then disseminated to the public in the form of alerts and postings.
- *Center for Internet Security (CIS) and SCORE*: CIS formalizes the best-practice recommendations once consensus between the SANS Institute and SCORE is reached and the practices are validated. The latter becomes the minimum standard benchmarks for general use by the industry. Both organizations rely on and have very broad contact with the field experts.

CERT Coordination Center

The CERT Coordination Center (CERT/CC, www.cert.org) is located at the Software Engineering Institute (SEI), an FFRDC at Carnegie Mellon University in Pittsburgh, PA. SEI was charged by DARPA in 1988 to set up a center to coordinate communication among experts during security emergencies and to help prevent future incidents.

The CERT/CC is part of the larger SEI Networked Systems Survivability Program, whose primary goals are to ensure that appropriate technology and systems management practices are used to resist attacks on networked systems and to limit damage and ensure continuity of critical services in spite of successful attacks, accidents, or failures. The center's research areas are summarized below:

- *Vulnerability analysis and incident handling*: The center analyzes the state of Internet security and conveys that information to the system administrators, network managers, and others in the Internet community. In these vulnerability and incident-handling activities, a higher priority is assigned to attacks and vulnerabilities that directly affect the Internet infrastructure (e.g., network service providers, Internet service providers, domain name servers, and routers).
- *Survivable enterprise management*: The center helps organizations protect and defend themselves. To this end, risk assessments that help enterprises identify and characterize critical information assets and then identify risks to those assets have been developed, and the enterprise can use the results of the assessment to develop or refine their overall strategy for securing their networked systems.
- *Education and training*: The center offers training courses to educate technical staff and managers of computer security-incident response teams and system administrators and other technical personnel within organizations to improve the security and survivability of each system. The center's staff also take part in developing curricula in information security and has compiled a guide, *The CERT® Guide to System and Network Security Practices*, published by Addison-Wesley.
- *Survivable network technology*: The center focuses on the technical basis for identifying and preventing security flaws and for preserving essential services if a system is penetrated and compromised. The center does research for new approaches to secure systems and analysis of how susceptible systems are to sophisticated attacks and find ways to improve the design of systems. Another focus is on modeling and simulation. The center has developed "Easel," a tool that is being used to study network responses to attacks and attack mitigation strategies. And finally, the center is also developing techniques that will enable the assessment and prediction of current and potential threats to the Internet. These techniques involve examining large sets of network data to identify unauthorized and potentially malicious activity.

Laboratories and Research Facilities

The R&D function is the most important aspect of the S&T Directorate. It relies on several existing agency programs to accomplish this task, including DOD, Department of Energy (DOE), and US Department of Agriculture (USDA) programs, among others. A significant portion of the funding attached to these programs comes from DOD's National Bioweapons Defense Analysis Center, responsible for nearly the entire biological countermeasures portfolio.

S&T's Office of National Laboratories coordinates DHS interactions with DOE national laboratories with expertise in homeland security. The office has the authority to establish a semi-independent DHS headquarters laboratory within existing federal laboratories, national laboratories, or FFRDC to supply scientific and technical knowledge to DHS and has done so with at least five national laboratories. In addition to

Livermore, DHS has established four other laboratories-within-laboratories at the Los Alamos, Sandia, Pacific Northwest, and Oak Ridge National Laboratories. DHS will also establish one or more university-based centers for homeland security.

The national and federal laboratory system possesses significant expertise in the area of WMDs in addition to massive computing power. These laboratories include the following:

- *DOE National Nuclear Security Administration laboratories*: Lawrence Livermore National Laboratory, Los Alamos National Laboratory, and Sandia National Laboratories.
- *DOE Office of Science laboratories*: Argonne National Laboratory, Brookhaven National Laboratory (BNL), Oak Ridge National Laboratory, Pacific Northwest National Laboratory, and other DOE laboratories.
- *Department of Homeland Security laboratories*: Environmental Measurements Laboratory (EML) and Plum Island Animal Disease Center.
- *Department of Health and Human Services laboratories*: HHS operates several laboratories focused on wide-ranging health and disease prevention issues.
- *US Customs and Border Protection Laboratories and Scientific Services*: The US Customs and Border Protection Laboratory and Scientific Services perform testing to determine the origin of agricultural and manufactured products.

This section starts with an overview of the facilities cited above and relevant programs and then discusses other R&D activities, such as the university-based center approach, and partnerships between DHS and other agencies.

Lawrence Livermore National Laboratory

The Homeland Security Organization at Lawrence Livermore National Laboratory (LLNL, www.llnl.gov) provides comprehensive solutions integrating threat, vulnerability, and trade-off analyses, advanced technologies, field-demonstrated prototypes, and operational capabilities to assist federal, state, local, and private entities in defending against catastrophic terrorism. The center is also dedicated to pursuing partnerships with universities and the private sector to fulfill its mission.

Los Alamos National Laboratory

Los Alamos National Laboratory (LANL, www.lanl.gov) is a DOE laboratory, managed by the University of California, and is one of the largest multidisciplinary institutions in the world. The Center for Homeland Security (CHS) was established in September 2002 to engage the laboratory's broad capabilities in the areas of counterterrorism and homeland security. It provides a single point of contact for all external organizations.

The organization's emphasis is on the key areas of nuclear and radiological science and technology, critical infrastructure protection, and chemical and biological science and technology. Current LANL projects with a key role in homeland security include the following:

- BASIS (the Biological Aerosol Sentry and Information System) is a biological early warning system that was tested and installed at the 2002 Salt Lake City Winter Olympics.
- A novel nuclear detector, the Palm Pilot CZT Spectrometer, is also in development and deployment, providing real-time gamma and neutron detection and isotope identification in a handheld device.
- LANL has also been active in the anthrax bacterial DNA analysis and the computerized feature identification tool known as GENIE, for Genetic Image Exploitation.

Sandia National Laboratory

The Sandia National Laboratory (www.sandia.gov) has been active since 1949 in the development of science-based technologies that support national security. Through science and technology, people, infrastructure, and partnerships, Sandia's mission is to meet national needs in the following six key areas:

- Nuclear weapons
- Nonproliferation
- Defense systems and assessments
- Homeland security
- Science, technology, and engineering
- Energy and infrastructure assurance

Argonne National Laboratory

Argonne National Laboratory (www.anl.gov) is one of the DOE's largest research centers. It is also the nation's first national laboratory, chartered in 1946. Argonne's research falls into four broad categories:

- *Basic science*: This program seeks solutions to a wide variety of scientific challenges. This includes experimental and theoretical work in materials science, physics, chemistry, biology, high-energy physics, and mathematics and computer science, including high-performance computing.
- *National security*: This program has increased in significance in recent years. This program uses Argonne capabilities developed over previous years for other purposes that help counter the terrorist threat. These capabilities include expertise in the nuclear fuel cycle, biology, chemistry, and systems analysis and modeling. This research is helping develop highly sensitive instruments and technologies to detect chemical, biological, and radioactive threats and identify their sources. Other research is helping to detect and deter possible weapons proliferation or actual attacks.
- *Energy resources*: This program helps to insure that a reliable supply of efficient and clean energy exists in the future. The laboratory's scientists and engineers are working to develop advanced batteries and fuel cells and advanced electric power generation and storage systems.
- *Environmental management*: This program includes work on managing and solving environmental problems and promoting environmental stewardship. Research includes alternative energy systems, environmental risk and economic impact assessments, hazardous waste site analysis and remediation planning, treatment to prepare spent nuclear fuel for disposal, and new technologies for decontaminating and decommissioning aging nuclear reactors.

Industrial technology development is an important activity in moving benefits of Argonne's publicly funded research to industry to help strengthen the nation's technology base.

Brookhaven National Laboratory

Established in 1947 on Long Island, New York, Brookhaven National Laboratory (BNL, www.bnl.gov) is a multiprogram national laboratory operated by Brookhaven Science Associates for the DOE. Six Nobel Prizes have been awarded for discoveries made at BNL. Brookhaven has a staff of approximately 3000 scientists, engineers, technicians, and support people and hosts more than 4000 guest researchers annually. BNL's role for the DOE is to produce excellent science and advanced technology with the cooperation, support, and appropriate involvement of our scientific and local communities. The fundamental elements of BNL's role in support of the four DOE strategic missions follow:

- To conceive, design, construct, and operate complex, leading edge, user-oriented facilities in response to the needs of the DOE and the international community of users
- To carry out basic and applied research in long-term, high-risk programs at the frontier of science
- To develop advanced technologies that address national needs and to transfer them to other organizations and to the commercial sector
- To disseminate technical knowledge, educate new generations of scientists and engineers, maintain technical capabilities in the nation's workforce, and encourage scientific awareness in the general public

Major programs that are managed at the laboratory include the following:

- Nuclear and high-energy physics
- Physics and chemistry of materials
- Environmental and energy research
- Nonproliferation
- Neurosciences and medical imaging
- Structural biology

Oak Ridge National Laboratory

The Oak Ridge National Laboratory (ORNL, www.ornl.gov) is a multiprogramming science and technology laboratory managed for the DOE by UT-Battelle, LLC. Scientists and engineers at ORNL conduct basic and applied R&D to create scientific knowledge and technological solutions that strengthen the nation's leadership in key areas of science; increase the availability of clean, abundant energy; restore and protect the environment; and contribute to national security. In their national security mission, ORNL provides federal, state, and local government agencies and departments with technology and expertise to support their national and homeland security needs. This technology and expertise are also shared with the private sector.

Pacific Northwest National Laboratory

The Pacific Northwest National Laboratory (PNNL, www.pnl.gov) is a DOE laboratory that delivers breakthrough science and technology to meet selected environmental, energy, health, and national security objectives; strengthen the economy; and support the education of future scientists and engineers.

PNNL's mission in national security supports the US government's objectives against the proliferation of nuclear, chemical, and biological WMDs and associated delivery systems. About one-third of PNNL's $600 million annual R&D budget reflects work in national security programs for the Departments of Energy and Defense and most other federal agencies. The focus is on issues that concern the Air Force, Army, Defense Advanced Research Projects Agency, Defense Threat Reduction Agency, Navy, and nuclear nonproliferation.

Scientists and engineers at PNNL are finding ways to diagnose the life of the Army's Abrams tank, developing technologies that verify compliance with the Comprehensive Nuclear-Test-Ban Treaty, helping North Korea secure spent nuclear fuel in proper storage canisters, and training border enforcement officials from the United States and foreign countries.

Other Department of Energy Laboratories and Objectives

The DOE (www.energy.gov) also has other affiliated organizations in addition to the ones cited above that focus on various homeland security issues. The topics addressed in these facilities include the following:

- *Cybersecurity protection*: These programs are aimed at protecting the information and systems that the DOE depends on, which only increases in scope as it grows in dependence on newer technologies.
- *Managing operations security*: This program seeks to manage security operations for DOE facilities in the national capital area and to develop policies designed to protect national security and other critical assets entrusted to DOE.
- *Preventing the spread of WMDs*: DOE plays an integral part in nuclear nonproliferation, countering terrorism, and responding to incidents involving WMDs. The department does this by providing technology, analysis, and expertise developed through this program.

Environmental Measurements Laboratory

The Environmental Measurements Laboratory (EML, www.eml.st.dhs.gov), a government-owned, government-operated laboratory, is directly part of the S&T Directorate. The laboratory advances and applies the science and technology required for preventing, protecting against, and responding to radiological and nuclear events in the service of homeland and national security.

EML's current programs focus on issues associated with environmental radiation and radioactivity. Specifically, EML provides DHS with environmental radiation and radioactivity measurements in the laboratory or field, technology development and evaluation, personnel training, instrument calibration, performance testing, data management, and data quality assurance.

The two unique facilities of the lab follow:

- *Environmental chamber*: A 25 m^3 facility, the only one in the United States that can generate atmospheres with controlled aerosols and gases for calibration and testing of new instruments
- *Gamma spectrometry laboratory*: A fully equipped laboratory with high-efficiency, high-resolution gamma sensors

Plum Island Animal Disease Center

The Plum Island Animal Disease Center (PIADC, www.ars.usda.gov/plum/) became part of DHS on June 1, 2003. Although the center remains an important national asset in which scientists conduct basic and applied research and diagnostic activities to protect the health of livestock on farms across the nation from foreign disease agents, it was also tasked with a new mission to help DHS to protect the country from terrorist threats, including those directed against agriculture.

The USDA is responsible for research and diagnosis to protect the nation's animal industries and exports from catastrophic economic losses caused by foreign animal disease (FAD) agents accidentally or deliberately introduced into the United States. While continuing its mission, it works closely with DHS personnel to fight agroterrorism.

On September 11, 2005, the Department of Homeland Security announced that the Plum Island Animal Disease Center would be replaced by a new federal facility, the National Bio and Agro-Defense Facility (NBAF). The NBAF will research high-consequence biological threats involving zoonotic (i.e., transmitted from animals to humans) diseases and FADs. It will allow basic research; diagnostic development, testing, and validation; advanced countermeasure development; and training for high-consequence livestock diseases. The new facility is being designed to

- integrate those aspects of public and animal health research that have been determined to be central to national security,
- assess and research evolving bioterrorism threats over the next five decades,
- enable the Departments of Homeland Security and Agriculture (USDA) to fulfill their related homeland defense research, development, testing, and evaluation (RDT&E) responsibilities.

Department of Health and Human Services Laboratories

The Department of Health and Human Services (www.hhs.gov) operates several laboratories focused on various health and disease prevention issues. The laboratories have extensive programs, and more details can be found later in this chapter.

US Customs and Border Protection Laboratories and Scientific Services

The DHS Customs and Border Protection Laboratories and Scientific Services (http://www.cbp.gov/about/labs-scientific-svcs) coordinates technical and scientific support with all CBP trade and border protection activities. According to DHS, this organization "is the forensic and scientific arm of U.S. Customs and Border Protection (CBP), providing forensic and scientific testing in the area of Trade Enforcement, Weapons of Mass Destruction, Intellectual Property Rights, and Narcotics Enforcement. Laboratories and Scientific Services coordinates technical and scientific support to all CBP Trade and Border Protection activities." The mission of the program is to provide rapid, quality scientific, forensic, and WMDs services to the CBP officials and other counterparts. One of the principal responsibilities of the CBP science officers is to manage the Customs Gauger/Laboratory Accreditation program. The program calls for the accreditation of commercial gaugers and laboratories so that their measurements and analytic results can be used by customs for entry and admissibility purposes. The staff edits and publishes the Customs Laboratory Bulletin, which, as a customs-scientific journal, is circulated internationally and provides a useful forum for technical exchange on subjects of general customs interest. US Customs and Border Protection maintains the following laboratory facilities:

- *Springfield (VA) Laboratory*: The Springfield Laboratory is a centralized facility that provides scientific support to CBP headquarters and the laboratories listed below. This facility provides analytic services to CBP legal and regulatory functions and to CBP offices that require scientific support and develops new analytic methods and evaluates new instrumentation. The activities of this facility vary in supporting CBP commercial and enforcement mission. The laboratory maintains the analytic uniformity among all CBP laboratories and maintains technical and scientific exchange with other federal enforcement agencies, technological branches of foreign customs agencies, and the military.
- *New York (NY) Laboratory*: The New York CBP services the greater New York City area including the New York Seaport, JFK Airport, the Port of Newark, and Perth Amboy. The laboratory provides scientific, forensic, and WMD services to CBP customers, including radiation detection, chemical WMD detection and identification, participation in the LSS national WMD strike team, and membership in the Food Emergency Response Network (FERN). This laboratory also trains DHS personnel on field radiation equipment.
- *Chicago (IL) Laboratory*: The Chicago Laboratory services all of the New England states, Illinois, Iowa, Nebraska, Wisconsin, Michigan, Kansas, Missouri, Indiana, part of Minnesota, and New York

except the New York City metropolitan area. This facility provides technical advice and analytic services to CBP officers, US Immigration and Customs Enforcement (ICE) agents, border patrol officers, and other entities on a wide range of issues. These services assist CBP officers in collecting revenue based on import duties and enforcing the law. The services provided to ICE agents and border patrol officers pertain primarily to law enforcement and forensics-related issues. The laboratory also provides training to its customers on interdiction, identification, and determination of WMDs.

- *Savannah (GA) Customs Laboratory*: The Savannah Customs Laboratory serves ports from Philadelphia, PA, to Key West, FL. The facility conducts chemical and physical testing of all types of commodities, narcotics, and other controlled substances. The Savannah Customs Laboratory operates two state-of-the art, custom-built mobile laboratories to meet the on-site testing needs of southeastern US ports used for the detection of materials for WMD.
- *Southwest Regional Science Center (Houston, TX)*: The Southwest Regional Science Center provides technical and scientific services to all of the ports of entry and border patrol sectors in the following eight states: Alabama, Tennessee, Mississippi, Louisiana, Arkansas, Oklahoma, Texas, and New Mexico. This geographic area contains 80% of the border between the United States and Mexico. This facility provides technical and scientific services to manage, secure, and control the nation's border and to prevent terrorists and terrorist weapons from entering the United States. Services provided include forensic crime scene investigation, WMD interdiction, and trade enforcement. Forensic scientists provide support to law enforcement investigations with the analysis of latent prints, controlled substances, pharmaceuticals, audio and video enhancements, accident investigation, and expert witness testimony.
- *Los Angeles (CA) Laboratory*: The Los Angeles Laboratory services all of southern California and southern Nevada, including Las Vegas, Arizona, and the California-Mexico border in these areas. The staff of chemists, textile analysts, and physical scientists is trained to assist in meeting the CBP mission in areas of trade, forensics, and WMDs. Among the laboratory's functions are forensic support such as evidence collection and analysis of trace, controlled substances and pharmaceuticals; technical support for chemical, biological, explosives, and radiation WMD issues; and latent print processing at the crime scene or in the laboratory. The laboratory has mobile vans equipped with field instrumentation to analyze and identify certain unknown chemicals, textile construction and applications on textiles, controlled substances, explosives, and WMD chemical agents and radiation. The Los Angeles Laboratory has vehicle-mounted and handheld detectors for rapid scan and identification of radiation sources from cargo containers.
- *San Francisco (CA) Laboratory*: The laboratory serves the northern two-thirds of California and the states of Oregon, Washington, North Dakota, South Dakota, Minnesota, Alaska, Hawaii, Colorado, Utah, Nevada, Montana, and Idaho. Major ports located in this service area include San Francisco, Portland, Seattle, Blaine, Anchorage, Honolulu, and Denver. This facility provides technical advice, forensic, and other scientific services to the CBP officials and other agencies on a wide range of imported and exported commodities. The laboratory also provides supports in WMDs, explosives, hazardous materials, and crime scene investigation. Several staff members are qualified radiation isotope identification device (RIID) trainers and continuously provide RIID operation trainings and CBP Radiation Detection Program and Response Protocol at the PNNL Radiation Academy (RADACAD) in Richland, Washington. The laboratory operates a small mobile unit that provides on-site examination and analyses of commercial shipments and training for local CBP officers and crime scene investigation (fingerprint collection) and examination and analysis on any suspicious illicit radioactive materials entering this country.

- *San Juan (PR) Laboratory*: The San Juan Laboratory serves the ports of Puerto Rico and the US Virgin Islands. This facility conducts chemical and physical testing of a wide variety of importations and forensic samples. Most of the facility's specialization has been in the area of controlled substances and other forensic samples. The San Juan Laboratory provides vital technical support and training to local and foreign law enforcement officials in areas such as WMD, radioactive material detection, crime scene management, and narcotics field test kits. The San Juan Laboratory mobile operations encompass active participation in WMD activities, forensic analysis, and crime scene management through all ports of Puerto Rico and the US Virgin Islands.
- *Teleforensic Center:* The Teleforensic Center provides scientific reachback support to field personnel on matters related to safeguarding of the nation's borders. The function of the Teleforensic Center (TC) operation is to provide field personnel with reachback access to scientific and technological resources. These resources help facilitate resolutions for field personnel in the performance of their duties. One of the field personnel's primary duties is detection, isolation, and control of potential threats that may result from the presence of chemical, biological, radiological or nuclear (CBRN) materials. TC scientists provide technical support to resolve threat issues related to the execution of this duty. The TC is staffed 24 h/day, 7 days per week.
- *Interdiction Technology Branch:* The Interdiction Technology Branch is a centralized facility that provides system acquisition and technical support to CBP Headquarters and field personnel. The LSS Interdiction Technology Branch (ITB) consists of general engineers, physical scientists, and project managers to provide CBP with an internal technical capability to ensure that field personnel have the best and most advanced high-technology enforcement equipment available. As the Department of Homeland Security and other organizations are conducting multiple research and development projects for next-generation equipment, ITB assists CBP in assessing the "readiness" of equipment proposed for field validation and/or deployment. ITB advises CBP executive management on high-technology enforcement and inspection technology and technically represents CBP on these issues with other domestic and foreign agencies, Congress, the media, industry, and academia. (CBP, 2014)

Academic Research Institutions

Universities and their research centers, institutes, and qualified staff represent a very important portion of the scientific research in the United States. These facilities account for an estimated one-third of the total federal budget available for R&D activities. The S&T Directorate has already started to show its recognition of the importance of these institutions in the overall homeland security R&D effort through both awarding them R&D grants and funding Homeland Security Centers of Excellence on their campuses.

Homeland Security Centers of Excellence

The S&T Directorate, through its Office of University Programs, is furthering the homeland security mission by engaging the academic community to create learning and research environments in areas critical to homeland security. Through the Homeland Security Centers of Excellence program, DHS has invested in university-based partnerships to develop centers of multidisciplinary research where important fields of inquiry can be analyzed and best practices developed, debated, and shared. The department's Homeland Security Centers of Excellence (HS-Centers) bring together the nation's best experts and focus its most talented researchers on a variety of threats that include agricultural, chemical, biological, nuclear/radiological, explosive, and cyberterrorism and the behavioral aspects of terrorism. The current

HS-Centers are listed in sidebar "Homeland Security Centers of Excellence." In FY 2012, $29.9 million in funding will be available for university programs.

DHS S&T Centers of Excellence

The DHS S&T Centers of Excellence (COEs) develop multidisciplinary, customer-driven, homeland security science and technology solutions and help train the next generation of homeland security experts.

The *COE network* is an extended consortium of hundreds of universities conducting groundbreaking research to address homeland security challenges. Sponsored by the *Office of University Programs*, the COEs work closely with the homeland security community to develop customer-driven, innovative tools and technologies to solve real-world challenges. COE partners include academic institutions; industry; national laboratories; DHS operational components; S&T divisions; other federal agencies; state, local, tribal and territorial homeland security agencies; and first responders. These partners work in concert to develop critical technologies and analyses to secure the nation.

DHS S&T Centers of Excellence

- *Center for Maritime, Island, and Remote and Extreme Environment Security (MIREES)*, co-led by the *University of Hawaii* and *Stevens Institute of Technology*, focuses on developing robust research and education programs addressing maritime domain awareness to safeguard populations and properties in geographical areas that present significant security challenges.
- *Center for Visualization and Data Analytics (CVADA)*, co-led by *Purdue University* (visualization sciences—VACCINE) and *Rutgers University* (data sciences—CCICADA), creates the scientific basis and enduring technologies needed to analyze large quantities of information to detect security threats to the nation.
- *Center of Excellence for Awareness and Localization of Explosives-Related Threats (ALERT)*, led by *Northeastern University*, develops new means and methods to protect the nation from explosives-related threats.
- *Center of Excellence for Zoonotic and Animal Disease Defense (ZADD)*, co-led by *Texas A&M University* and *Kansas State University*, protects the nation's agriculture and public health sectors against high-consequence foreign animal, emerging, and zoonotic disease threats.
- *Coastal Hazards Center of Excellence (CHC)*, co-led by the *University of North Carolina at Chapel Hill* and *Jackson State University*, performs research and develops education programs to enhance the nation's ability to safeguard populations, properties, and economies from catastrophic natural disasters.
- *National Center for Border Security and Immigration (NCBSI)*, co-led by the *University of Arizona* and the *University of Texas at El Paso*, develops novel technologies, tools, and advanced methods to balance immigration and commerce with effective border security.
- *National Center for Food Protection and Defense (NCFPD)*, led by the *University of Minnesota*, defends the safety and security of the food system by conducting research to protect vulnerabilities in the nation's food supply chain.
- *National Center for Risk and Economic Analysis of Terrorism Events (CREATE)*, led by the *University of Southern California*, develops advanced tools to evaluate the risks, costs, and consequences of terrorism.

- *National Center for the Study of Preparedness and Catastrophic Event Response (PACER)*, led by *Johns Hopkins University*, optimizes the nation's medical and public health preparedness, mitigation and recovery strategies in the event of a high-consequence natural or man-made disaster.
- *National Consortium for the Study of Terrorism and Responses to Terrorism (START)*, led by the *University of Maryland*, provides policy makers and practitioners with empirically grounded findings on the human elements of the terrorist threat and informs decisions on how to disrupt terrorists and terrorist groups.
- *National Transportation Security Center of Excellence (NTSCOE)* was established in accordance with H.R.1, Implementing the Recommendations of the 9/11 Commission Act of 2007, in August 2007. NTSCOE is a seven-institution consortium focused on developing new technologies, tools, and advanced methods to defend, protect, and increase the resilience of the nation's multimodal transportation infrastructure. The consortium comprises the following academic institutions:
  - Center for Transportation Safety, Security, and Risk at Rutgers University
  - Connecticut Transportation Institute at the University of Connecticut
  - Homeland Security Management Institute at Long Island University
  - Mack-Blackwell Rural Transportation Center at the University of Arkansas
  - Mineta Transportation Institute at San José State University
  - Texas Southern University
  - Tougaloo College
- *Center for Advancing Microbial Risk Assessment (CAMRA)*, co-led by *Michigan State University* and *Drexel University* and established jointly with the *U.S. Environmental Protection Agency*, fills critical gaps in risk assessments for mitigating microbial hazards.

Source: DHS (2014e). http://www.dhs.gov/science-and-technology/centers-excellence.

Maritime Research

The scope of the S&T Directorate encompasses the pursuit of a full range of research into the use, preservation, and exploitation of the national waterways and oceans. The US Coast Guard Research and Development Center is in charge of conducting research to support defense of this resource and of the homeland.

US Coast Guard

The Research and Development (R&D) Center is the Coast Guard's (www.uscg.mil) sole facility performing research, development, test, and evaluation (RDT&E) in support of the Coast Guard's major missions of maritime mobility, maritime safety, maritime security, national defense, and protection of natural resources. The center has as its mission "to be the Coast Guard's pathfinder, anticipating and meeting future technological challenges, while partnering with others to shepherd the best ideas into implementable solutions."

The Coast Guard RDT&E program produces two types of products: the development of hardware, procedures, and systems that directly contribute to increasing the quality and productivity of the operations and the expansion of knowledge related to technical support of operating and regulatory programs.

R&D Efforts External to the Department of Homeland Security

The majority of homeland security R&D funding is provided to federal agencies other than the DHS.

Department of Health and Human Services

National Institutes of Health

The National Institutes of Health's (NIH, www.nih.gov) most relevant effort in homeland security R&D is in bioterrorism-related research. It has conducted work in the field for much longer than the existence of the DHS, but it emerged as a high-priority R&D agency after the 2001 anthrax mail situation. Budget allocations, which tend to be a reliable predictor of federal priorities, have clearly indicated that this dedication to bioterrorism detection and countermeasures remains. In the FY 2014 budget, NIH saw a minor increase in homeland security research funding of 1.3% from the previous year, up to $1.805 billion. NIH is clearly the leader within the federal government for homeland security R&D efforts for its biodefense research portfolio. The biodefense priorities of NIAID include, in addition to biodefense research, the development of medical countermeasures against radiological and nuclear threats and medical countermeasures against chemical threats.

Centers for Disease Control and Prevention

The Centers for Disease Control and Prevention (CDC, www.cdc.gov) is another component of HHS that traditionally performed WMD terrorism R&D. However, with the opening of the Biodefense Advanced Research and Development Agency, CDC homeland security R&D funds have diminished. In fact, the majority of CDC terrorism activities, which are not R&D in nature, include the management of the Strategic National Stockpile (SNS) and funding for state and local responders to upgrade their abilities to prepare for and manage WMD events.

Biodefense Advanced Research and Development Agency

As part of its expanding effort to fund anthrax research and other R&D related to defenses against terrorist threats, the Office of the Secretary of Health and Human Services funded biodefense R&D in the Biodefense Advanced Research and Development Authority (BARDA, www.hhs.gov/aspr/barda/index.html). BARDA funds advanced R&D of new biodefense countermeasures as part of an HHS-wide effort to secure an adequate supply of such countermeasures for the SNS.

Department of Defense

The Department of Defense (DOD) has had a fluctuating budget for homeland security R&D since 2001. In FY 2014, DOD R&D funding decreased by 8%, to a total allocation of $2287 billion. The vast majority of DOD R&D funding is provided through the Defense Advanced Research Projects Agency (DARPA), which works mainly on applications that serve the needs of the military (e.g., biological warfare defense and the Chemical and Biological Defense Program). The outcome of this research, however, often has applications that can be applied by civilian first responders despite the military origin of the projects that generated them. The DOD Chemical and Biological Defense Program (CBDP) is another research-oriented agency that performs homeland security research activities.

Department of Agriculture

Even more so than DOD, the USDA has witnessed widely fluctuating R&D budgets since the September 11 terrorist attacks. Actual fiscal year funding amounts have varied from less than $50 million to over $232 million. Since 9/11, USDA has invested a considerable amount of research effort toward developing security mechanisms to protect dangerous pathogens, which could be used as terror weapons and are located in many laboratories dispersed throughout the United States. Increases in funding in FY 2006 and 2007 were dedicated to renovating facilities that performed animal research and diagnosis at the National Centers for Animal Health in Ames, Iowa. These efforts are aimed at protecting the US food supply from acts of sabotage and terrorism—both of which could have potentially devastating effects on the US economy. The FY 2014 funding for USDA homeland security R&D efforts was $232 million, an increase of almost 200% over the previous 2 years.

Environmental Protection Agency

The Environmental Protection Agency (EPA) has seen steady but small federal allocations of Homeland Security R&D funding since September 11. Since that year, EPA research related to homeland security has been focused primarily on drinking water security research (which would involve EPA efforts to develop better surveillance and laboratory networks for drinking water supplies to counter potential terrorist threats) and decontamination research (to develop better technologies and methods for decontaminating terrorist attack sites). EPA also conducts threat and consequence assessments and tests potential biodefense and other decontamination technologies. Much of this work is conducted at EPA's National Homeland Security Research Center (NHSRC) in Cincinnati (http://www.epa.gov/nhsrc/basicinfo.html). NHSRC develops expertise and products that are used to prevent, prepare for, and recover from public health and environmental emergencies arising from terrorist threats and incidents. Research and development efforts focus on the following five primary areas:

- *Securing and sustaining water systems* focuses on developing tools and applications to assist states, local municipalities, and utilities design and operate resilient systems. Some of the research includes developing products that can provide warnings to water utilities in the event of terrorist attacks with CBR agents, developing or testing methods for decontaminating water and wastewater infrastructure more rapidly and economically, and integrating water security technologies into drinking water distribution systems.
- *Characterizing contamination and determining risk* focuses on developing and evaluating or validating sampling, sample preparation protocols, and analytic methods for CBR agents. Risk communication tools are developed and evaluated. Some of the research includes evaluating sampling and analytic methods that would be used by multiple laboratories during a homeland security emergency, providing the scientific basis for establishing provisional exposure levels, and developing techniques for communicating risk to many different audiences by using structured and informative messages that have been researched and tested.
- *Remediating indoor and outdoor environments* focuses on developing and testing tools, applications, and methods to remediate sites contaminated during a CBR attack. Some of the research includes evaluating methods for effective decontamination of many types of surfaces that have been contaminated with CBR agents, investigating contaminant behavior under different environmental conditions, and identifying methods for disposing of contaminated materials generated during site cleanup.

National Institute of Standards and Technology

The Department of Commerce (DOC) is home to the National Institute of Standards and Technology (NIST), which funds R&D in cryptography and computer security and which provides scientific and technical support to DHS in these areas.

National Science Foundation

The National Science Foundation (NSF) funds research to combat bioterrorism in the areas of infectious diseases and microbial genome sequencing. These programs increased to $395 million in FY 2014.

Conclusion

Homeland security represents an entirely new spectrum of issues of R&D and technology and an opportunity to revitalize old issues under the homeland security umbrella. Establishing DHS and the S&T Directorate brought a new, major player into the federally supported R&D efforts. There was much discussion and disgruntlement within the research community concerning the lack of involvement of the NSF in the development of the homeland security R&D agenda. In fact, several people questioned the need for the S&T as opposed to just increasing the NSF's or NIST's portfolios.

With a spectrum of activity varying from research to development to deployment and a span of subjects from bioterrorism to personal protective equipment, from communication tools to nonproliferation, and from detection devices to mass production of vaccines, the S&T Directorate has been given a monumental task. The directorate not only coordinates the R&D facilities of many organizations but also has the authority to set priorities in others. The university-based HS-Centers provide a level of funding that has not been available for some time and provide one of the best funded opportunities for specific R&D to benefit emergency management.

Although the context of change leaves little room for conclusions, the budget given to the S&T Directorate either in existing programs or in new ones will provide the emergency management and first-responder communities new capabilities never before imagined. It is to be hoped that these technological "toys" do not give a false sense of confidence and overshadow the real requirements of building an improved capacity to mitigate, prepare for, respond to, and recover from the risks of terrorism (Figure 12-3).

FIGURE 12-3 New York City, NY, September 29, 2001—Lobby of hotel near the World Trade Center site. *Photo by Andrea Booher/ FEMA News Photo.*

Key Terms

BioWatch: A program aimed at detecting the release of pathogens into the air, thereby providing warning to the government and public health community of a potential bioterror event. This is performed through the use of aerosol samplers mounted on preexisting EPA air-quality monitoring stations that collect air, passing it through filters. These filters are manually collected at regular, reportedly 24 h intervals and are analyzed for potential biological weapon pathogens using polymerase chain reaction (PCR) techniques. Although filters from the BioWatch program were initially shipped to and tested at a federal laboratory in California, state and local public health laboratories now perform the analyses.

Man-portable air defense system (MANPADS): A missile firing device, used to destroy aircraft, that is easily carried or transported by a person.

SAFECOM: A communications program of the DHS Office for Interoperability and Compatibility that, with its federal partners, provides research, development, testing and evaluation, guidance, tools, and templates on communications-related issues to local, tribal, state, and federal emergency response agencies.

Review Questions

1. Identify the four lead groups of research in the DHS Science and Technology Directorate and explain what each does to contribute to counterterrorism efforts.
2. Define in your own words why HSARPA was established, and explain its scope and objectives.
3. What are the Homeland Security Centers of Excellence, and what are the research and development goals of each?
4. What government laboratories are working to develop WMD countermeasures? What specific areas of research is each focused on?
5. What government laboratories are working to protect critical information and infrastructure from terrorist attack? What specific areas of research is each focused on?

References

American Association for the Advancement of Science (AAAS), 2014a. AAAS report XXXIX: research and development FY 2015. http://www.aaas.org/page/aaas-report-xxxix-research-and-development-fy-2015.

American Association for the Advancement of Science (AAAS), 2014b. AAAS report XXXIX: research and development FY 2015. http://www.aaas.org/sites/default/files/HS%2015p.jpg.

CBP, 2014. Customs and Border Protection Laboratories and Scientific Services. http://www.cbp.gov/about/labs-scientific-svcs.

CRS, 2014. The DHS S&T Directorate: selected issues for congress. http://fas.org/sgp/crs/homesec/R43064.pdf.

Department of Defense, 2011. https://www.cbrniac.apgea.army.mil/About/Pages/default.aspx.

DHS, 2014a. Written testimony of S&T Under Secretary Dr. Reginald Brothers for a House Committee on Homeland Security, Subcommittee on Cybersecurity, Infrastructure Protection, and Security Technologies, and House Committee on Science, Space, and Technology, Subcommittee on Research and Technology hearing titled "Strategy and Mission of the DHS Science and Technology

Directorate." http://www.dhs.gov/news/2014/09/09/written-testimony-st-under-secretary-joint-subcommittee-hearing-house-committee (September 9, 2014).

DHS, 2014b. Department of Homeland Security – Budget in Brief FY2015. http://www.dhs.gov/publication/fy-2015-budget-brief.

DHS, 2014c. http://www.dhs.gov/person/dr-reginald-brothers.

DHS, 2014d. DHS science & technology directorate unveils new visionary goals. http://www.dhs.gov/dhs-science-technology-directorate-unveils-new-visionary-goals.

DHS, 2014e. http://www.dhs.gov/science-and-technology/centers-excellence.

White House, 2014. The 2015 budget: science, technology, and innovation for opportunity and growth. http://www.whitehouse.gov/sites/default/files/microsites/ostp/Fy%202015%20R&D.pdf.

13 The Future of Homeland Security

Introduction

Just as is true in many other fields and professions, the homeland security agenda has changed and continues to change in response to actual and perceived threats and identified needs, goals, and objectives. The Department of Homeland Security is still relatively new, yet it continues to assert itself as the leader in several areas that have proved highly volatile, including emergency management, immigration and border security, cybersecurity, and maritime protection. In the current budgetary and political climates, each of these issues is sure to present leadership at all government levels with a formidable challenge. This chapter is provided to identify and briefly explain several of the most pressing issues confronting those tasked with ensuring safety and security in the United States and the safety and security of US interests abroad.

It has been more than 13 years since the September 11 attacks in New York, Pennsylvania, and Virginia, and the means to measure how effectively DHS is performing in its leadership role—and exactly what role emergency management and disaster assistance functions will ultimately play within the department and the national homeland security system—are still evolving. The massive failure of the federal government's response to Hurricane Katrina in August 2005 has been tempered by the successful response to Hurricane Sandy in 2012 and other major disaster events since the Obama administration assumed office in 2009. This success is likely reflective of President Obama's decision to appoint seasoned Florida State Emergency Management director Craig Fugate to lead FEMA and an overall shift in homeland security policy that scaled back the dominant terrorism focus in favor of an all-hazards approach.

We believe that FEMA's history offers two important lessons for DHS as it progresses in its difficult mission. First, it is critical for DHS to take all the necessary steps to ensure that the nation's emergency management and disaster assistance capabilities, especially those at the federal government level, are not marginalized. Additionally, these emergency management agencies must be given the tools that enable them to effectively manage the new terrorist threat with which they are confronted. Second, the department's leadership must ensure that terrorism—in all of its forms—does not become the singular risk driving DHS policy. The policy agenda tends to be reactionary and moves in response to media and public sentiment—but rarely do these sentiments accurately match the statistical nature of the nation's all-hazards risk portfolio. In the absence of an all-hazards approach, coupled with the growing risk of many natural hazards that is driven by the changing climate, the scene will surely be set for a repeat of the Hurricane Katrina fiasco.

FEMA History Lesson

Prior to 1979, federal emergency management and disaster preparedness, response, and recovery programs and capabilities were scattered among numerous federal government agencies, including the White House. There was little, if any, coordination among these disparate parts. Communicating with the federal government during a disaster had become such a problem that the National Governors Association petitioned then-President Jimmy Carter to consolidate all federal programs into a single agency.

On April 1, 1979, President Carter signed the executive order that established the Federal Emergency Management Agency, moving federal disaster programs, agencies, and offices from across the federal government to a single executive branch agency. The director of FEMA was charged with integrating these diverse programs into one cohesive operation capable of delivering federal resources and assistance through a new concept called the *Integrated Emergency Management System*. This system was centered on an all-hazards approach.

With the election of President Ronald Reagan in 1980, the focus of FEMA's policies and programs shifted dramatically from an all-hazards approach to a single focus on nuclear attack planning through its Office of National Preparedness. At the same time, agency leadership and personnel struggled to integrate its many diverse programs. This focuses on a single low-probability/high-impact event and the inability of the agency's many parts to function effectively as one led to the disastrous responses to Hurricane Hugo, the Loma Prieta earthquake, and Hurricane Andrew. There were numerous calls for the abolition of FEMA, including from several members of Congress.

President Bill Clinton, elected in 1992, appointed the first FEMA director who was an experienced emergency manager. Under James Lee Witt's leadership, FEMA once again adopted an all-hazards approach, became a customer-focused organization that worked closely with its state and local emergency management partners, and effectively responded to an unprecedented series of major disasters across the country. These included not only major natural disasters but also terrorist events such as the first World Trade Center bombing and the Oklahoma City bombing.

The new FEMA successfully launched a national community-based disaster mitigation initiative, Project Impact, and for the first time reached out to the nation's business community to partner in emergency management at the national and community levels.

By the time of the election of President George W. Bush in 2000, FEMA had gained the trust of the public, the media, its partners, and elected officials in all levels of government. FEMA functioned as a single agency as envisioned when it was created in 1979 and possessed one of the most favorable brand names in government.

Upon taking office in 2001, the Bush administration began to deconstruct FEMA. It was assumed that a program like Project Impact, which focused on individual and private sector responsibility, would thrive under a Republican administration. Instead, it was eliminated (based on an argument that it was not effective), and funding for other natural disaster mitigation programs was dramatically reduced. However, the effect of Project Impact was given national media attention after an earthquake struck Seattle in February 2001, and the mayor of Seattle credited his city's participation in the Project Impact program for the minimal losses the city experienced as a result of that quake.

The emphasis on the national security functions of FEMA was highlighted when new FEMA director Joe Allbaugh was reinstated to the Office of National Preparedness, and all indications were that FEMA would once again focus on national security issues.

This process was accelerated after the September 11, 2001, terrorist attacks. FEMA became part of the new DHS, and the all-hazards approach, while acknowledged in speeches, was replaced by a single focus on terrorism. More importantly, the director of FEMA no longer reported directly to the president and was replaced in the president's cabinet by the DHS secretary. In the first major reorganization of DHS that began in July 2005, FEMA of the 1990s was disassembled and its parts spread throughout the department.

In August 2005, Hurricane Katrina struck the Gulf Coast and history repeated itself. DHS/FEMA was unable to provide the support needed by state and local officials for adequate response, and hundreds of Americans died as a result. This failure by FEMA in Hurricane Katrina mirrored the botched response by FEMA to Hurricane Andrew in 1992, as did the public's, the media's, and politicians' loss of confidence in FEMA that resulted. The effective responses to the tornadoes in Tuscaloosa, AL, and Joplin, MO, in 2011 and to Hurricane Sandy in 2012 indicated that the Obama/Fugate-led FEMA had regained its ability to successfully respond to major disasters. President Obama has shown that disaster response is a priority for his administration, and he has provided FEMA with the requisite leadership (Fugate is only the second experienced emergency manager to lead FEMA since its inception in 1979), resources, and other supports from the federal family to ensure that the full capability of the federal government is brought to bear when major disasters occur. It is now an accurate statement that the nation's emergency management system has again regained a secure footing and high degree of functional capacity with regard to all-hazards disaster response.

However, FEMA's focus on the response phase has to varying degrees diverted resources and commitments away from other phases of emergency management, namely, mitigation, preparedness, and recovery. Since the 2001 elimination of Project Impact under the George W. Bush administration, FEMA's hazard mitigation programs have suffered losses of both funding and staff support and have continued to suffer from reduced attention under the current FEMA administration. Congressional reform of the National Flood Insurance Program has backfired completely, and this valuable flood mitigation program that saves the federal government nearly $1 billion in disaster relief costs annually is in disarray. FEMA's Whole Community concept is a positive step in encouraging and guiding communities, individuals, and businesses on how to better prepare for disasters, but FEMA has failed to put any resources behind the concept beyond mentioning it in reports and press releases. FEMA has all but punted its role in recovery with the exception of continuing to manage its two disaster relief funding programs. In the aftermath of Hurricane Sandy (2012), HUD Secretary Shaun Donovan was tapped by the president to lead the federal recovery efforts, thus marking the first time since the 1993 Midwest floods that the FEMA administrator did assume this role.

The reduced focus by FEMA and by DHS on efforts in the nonresponse phases of emergency management is even more troubling on account of the relativity of risk in relation to the new terrorism hazard, as well as the potential impact of climate change, which threatens to cause more frequent and severe weather events for decades to come. Mitigating the impacts of these future events is critical to reducing their impacts on the nation's populations, communities, natural resources, and economy. Preparing the public and the business sector to deal with these events remains critical to achieving long-term reductions in life loss and physical harm. The actions taken prior to these future events to mitigate risk and prepare for disasters will have a direct impact on the time and resources needed to fully recover from future events. If FEMA is not willing or able to address what is needed in each of these other phases of emergency management, then consideration must be given to the idea of placing the responsibility for one or more of these functions into the hands of other federal departments (e.g., HUD).

Lessons for Homeland Security from the FEMA Experience

The writer George Santayana once famously said, "Those who ignore history are doomed to repeat it." There are two critical lessons to be learned from the FEMA experience that provide some perspective on how DHS may function in the future.

First and foremost, it will take time for DHS to become a functioning organization. DHS was cobbled together in much the same way that FEMA was bringing together an estimated 178,000 federal workers from 22 agencies and programs in a very short time period. It took FEMA nearly 15 years and several reorganizations to effectively coordinate and deliver the full resources of the federal government to support state and local governments in responding to major disasters. DHS is nearly 13 years old and has already undertaken three major reorganizations, and once the St. Elizabeths DHS headquarters facility is completed, there are likely no other major organizational changes at that time. If FEMA's experience is any kind of indicator, it will be at least 10 or more years before the department achieves a state of functional equilibrium.

Second, a fluctuating focus on low-probability/high-impact events (e.g., a major terrorist attack similar to September 11) will undermine the department's capabilities in responding to more common and overall more damaging high-probability/low-impact events (often called "extensive risk"). A FEMA staffer once said that you don't plan for the maximum event probable; you plan for the maximum event possible. This is especially critical for FEMA's response and recovery and preparedness and mitigation programs. In terms of natural and traditional man-made disasters (hurricanes, earthquakes, hazardous materials incidents, etc.), these programs' capabilities have been marginalized. The failure of FEMA to effectively respond to Hurricanes Andrew and Katrina is a clear example of the negative impact this single focus can have in an all-hazards world. DHS and FEMA must both maintain an all-hazards focus as long as the two are organizationally connected—but if history is any indication, it takes only one major terrorist event for the mission of both entities to shift back into a singular hazard perspective. The manner in which the government agencies from the national to the local levels diverted funding and attention to the Ebola virus—which is a serious threat yet pales in comparison with other hazards in the nation's risk profile—illustrates the degree and speed to which these focal changes occur.

The Future of Emergency Management in Homeland Security

At the time of the writing of the fourth edition of this book in 2011, we noted in this chapter that "rebuilding the nation's emergency management system, especially the role of the federal government in this system, does not conflict with the primary mission of DHS. In fact, it is a critical element in the overall homeland security strategy." We identified several steps that we felt needed to be taken to rebuild and enhance the nation's emergency management system and to strengthen and enhance DHS's efforts to build an effective homeland security system.

These recommended steps included the removal of FEMA from DHS in favor of its reestablishment as an executive branch agency reporting directly to the president. In 2011, we noted that "Moving FEMA out of DHS and consolidating its traditional mitigation, preparedness, response, and recovery programs will ensure that the all-hazards approach will be reinstated and that FEMA and its state and local partners will once again focus on dealing with all manners of disaster events including terrorist attacks. Emergency management professionals will once again be in charge of preparing the public, reducing future impacts through hazard mitigation, and managing the resources of the federal government in support of state and local governments in responding to major disasters and fostering a speedy and effective recovery from these events." As of November 2014, FEMA remains in DHS, and the calls for moving it out of DHS have quieted as a result of the success the agency has achieved in responding to a slew of major disasters since 2009.

However, we are now concerned that the mitigation and recovery programs at FEMA are being marginalized, and something needs to be done to strengthen these programs in light of the new terrorism threats and climate change hazards we now face and will continue to face in the future.

A second recommendation the authors proposed in the fourth edition of this book (2011) was the reinstatement of the Federal Response Plan (FRP) that from 1992 to 2002 had "successfully guided the federal government's response to over 350 presidentially declared disasters from Hurricane Andrew through the September 11 attacks." We noted then that "when the president declared a major disaster event, the FRP ensured that the full resources of the federal government would be brought to bear in support of state and local government and directed by FEMA. No single agency was expected to carry the full federal responsibility and everyone knew that the director of FEMA was in charge."

Currently, the National Response Framework (NRF) guides how the federal government works to support state and local governments in responding to presidentially declared major disasters. As of November 2014, FEMA appears to have regained its role as the leader in coordinating the federal response to major disasters as witnessed by the response to various major events since 2009 including Hurricane Sandy in 2012. There is no reason to believe that this capability will be diminished for the remainder of the current administration's tenure, and it would be very surprising if future presidents do not follow the lead of both President Clinton and President Obama in making disaster response a priority and appointing experienced emergency managers to lead FEMA.

A third recommendation that was made in the fourth edition of this book was that DHS takes a community-based approach to homeland security. We noted that "since September 11, 2001, the federal government has taken the lead in homeland security and the vast majority of policy and program initiatives have focused on federal capabilities and responsibilities. With the exception of the Citizen Corps program and Web-based awareness campaigns such as Ready.gov, very little has been done to effectively involve the American public in homeland security activities." We also noted that "[t]he 'Redefining Readiness' study conducted by the New York Academy of Medicine identified numerous problems with the assumptions of homeland security planners in developing smallpox and dirty bomb plans without input from the public. Involving the public in developing community-based homeland security plans is critical to the successful implementation of these plans." We remain convinced that "a large segment of the public is ready and willing to participate in these planning efforts and to be part of a community-based effort to deal with the new homeland security threats. Mechanisms for involving the public in this process are needed."

As of November 2014, we believe this issue has not been adequately addressed. The only significant example of engagement or partnership with the general public to address homeland security issues we are able to identify since the previous edition is the manner in which bystanders of the 2013 Boston Marathon bombings worked with local, state, and federal law enforcement to help identify the attackers (using photos and videos and calling in to report things they had witnessed when prompted by local police). Thousands of social media postings helped to keep all parties informed during the massive shelter-in-place/lockdown, the manhunt that ensued, and ultimately the capture of the surviving Tsarnaev brother.

DHS and FEMA must invest more resources and staff to engage the public in preparing for the next disaster event—whether a hurricane, chemical spill, or terrorist attack. This is happening at the local level in cities like Hartford, CT, and San Francisco, CA, both of which are designing and implementing community engagement programs that use a combination of training for community groups, local media, social media, and websites to spread homeland security and disaster preparedness messages. These local efforts deserve more resources and support from DHS and FEMA.

Our fourth recommendation in 2011 was for DHS to improve communications with the public. We noted that DHS had shown very little capacity to engage in meaningful communication with the public—and in those instances where engagement has occurred, the results have not always been positive—the "duct tape and plastic" fiasco serves as but one example. Others include FEMA's failed attempts at communications during Hurricane Katrina and the inability to provide meaningful information through the use of the Homeland Security Advisory System (HSAS). This is not to say that such capabilities do not exist, but rather that DHS and its state and local partners need to better embrace the concept of whole community in all aspects of homeland security other than where national security might be compromised.

Much has been done since in addressing the communications issue as we discussed in the "Communicating in the Era of Homeland Security" section located in Chapter 11 of this book. The communications conducted in the responses to Hurricane Sandy and the Boston Marathon bombings clearly indicate a newfound commitment by the leadership of DHS, FEMA, and local emergency management and law enforcement officials to getting timely and accurate information to the public in a crisis. The emergence of social media in these two events enabled public officials to actively engage the public in the response efforts. By fully embracing the use of social media, response officials were able to effectively get information directly to the public while at the same time receiving information posted by the public on social media sites valuable to the building of situational awareness and informing of resource allocation efforts. There are definitive indications that informing and engaging the public in disaster or terrorism response has improved in the changing media world.

One communications issue we raised in 2011 that has not been adequately addressed in the intervening years is that "more [...] must be invested by federal departments and agencies to better understand the principal terrorist threats that our nation faces (i.e., biological, chemical, radiological, nuclear, and explosives) and to develop communications strategies that educate and inform the public about these threats with more useful information." As the 2014/2015 Ebola epidemic indicated, the federal government has not been successful in first accurately and quickly assessing and appreciating new threats and subsequently providing the public with accurate information about their risk and how to manage it.

As we noted in the fourth edition of this book, "Decades of research and a new generation of technologies now inform emergency managers as they provide information about hurricanes, tornadoes, earthquakes, and hazardous materials incidents to the public. A similar research effort must be undertaken for [chemical, biological, radiological, and nuclear terrorist threats] and communications strategies that will ensure that homeland security officials at all levels are capable of clearly explaining to the public the hazards posed by these threats." Clearly, more resources must be invested in this critical task before the fear generated by what is unknown can be effectively mitigated.

Our final recommendation in 2011 concerned furthering the partnership between DHS and FEMA and the private sector. As we noted, "DHS and numerous business groups, such as the Business Roundtable, U.S. Chamber of Commerce, [and] ASIS International, acknowledge that an effective partnership between the government and business groups must be maintained as part of the nation's homeland security efforts. This is only logical considering that the nation's economic security depends in part on the success of the nation's national security policies."

The 2010 National Security Strategy, the 2010 Quadrennial Homeland Security Review, and the 2014 Quadrennial Homeland Security Review all noted that public-private partnerships are key to creating an effective homeland security system in this country and will enhance the response and recovery capabilities of the nation's emergency management system. However, as of November 2014, we see little progress in accomplishing this goal. As we noted in 2011, "A significant issue that must be addressed is how the government will protect and use confidential information that it is asking or requiring the business community to provide. The business community, which has vast institutional knowledge about this privacy issue as well as countless other issues that have been presented in the homeland security approach, must be included in the planning process not only for terrorism response planning but also for natural disaster management."

As we noted in the fourth edition of this book, "One possible avenue for establishing and nurturing an effective partnership with the business sector is to start at the community level. Issues such as what the government will do with confidential information are likely to be less critical at the community level, allowing for lessons to be learned in progressive steps. Additionally, there is an established history of public-private partnerships in emergency management at the community level, many of which started with FEMA's Project Impact program."

It is up to DHS and FEMA and the private sector to come up with a solution to the issues that keep effective public-private partnerships from becoming a reality. More focus and commitment from DHS/ FEMA must be directed to ensuring that the private sector is a ready and prepared partner for the next crisis. There have been some progress and cooperation, but it is imperative that an overall strategy be put in place to incorporate the business sector into the government's emergency management planning for homeland security.

Of course, since the writing of the last edition, there have been a number of incidents, issues, and events that have changed the homeland security landscape—not just relative to disasters and emergencies but in relation to the overall homeland security mission as described in the chapters of this book. Each of these will impact or otherwise define how the US government and its partners approach risk and how they choose to or are able to prevent, prepare for, respond to, and/or recover from safety- and security-disrupting events and situations.

For example, it is well known that the emergence of the Islamic State of Iraq and the Levant (ISIL—also called ISIS) has resulted in both radicalization of foreign nationals via internet engagement and also the training and extreme radicalization of foreign fighters who travel to Syria and Iraq to join ISIS in battle and return home as foreign terrorist fighters (FTFs). FTFs present a unique problem in that they are citizens of the countries they return home to and are therefore difficult to identify and track. They return equipped with the skills and motivation to plan and carry out an attack on their own fellow citizens and against their own government. Radicalization has led to a number of attacks, including the September 2014 beheading of a man in Oklahoma by a coworker and the 2013 beheading of a soldier in the United Kingdom by two individuals. None of the individuals in these incidents had attended any formal terror training or had engaged directly with terrorist organizations. However, there are thousands of foreign individuals who are currently fighting alongside terrorist groups in Syria and Iraq that will presumably return home without leaving their radicalized ideologies at the border. While it is estimated that less than one hundred of these are from the United States, other Western countries are experiencing a much higher number of FTFs among their citizenry, including Australia and the United Kingdom, which have approximately 250 and 400 FTF citizens, respectively (Markert, 2014).

The changing nature of the Internet as a terrorist recruiting ground and avenue for attack is another area where homeland security efforts must quickly adapt. At present, the laws dictating both the use of the Internet for illicit activities and the ability of law enforcement agencies to track and gather information are slow to respond to the nature of this emerging threat. For instance, the individual implicated in the September 2014 beheading in Oklahoma had proclaimed online that he intended to behead a random person for the purpose of waging a holy war. He had also used the Internet to try to recruit others, though he was ultimately unsuccessful in these attempts. Much has been discussed about the need to limit government surveillance of Internet communications since Edward Snowden shed light on various NSA programs—which have now been shuttered—but these programs were put in place for a reason even if they were not effective at protecting the innocent from possible exposure to surveillance. In their absence, the protections they offered are now nonexistent given that there is little the government can do to recreate them devoid of collateral exposure. Given the ability that ISIS and other groups have displayed to produce and broadcast professional-looking videos and other recruitment marketing products, the US government has no choice but to find ways to address this threat in a manner that protects privacy. This is no easy task.

The matter of cyberterrorism, cyberwarfare, cybercrime, and other cyber threats is probably the most significant problem facing the nation at the moment. A 2014 survey of technology experts conducted by the Pew Internet and American Life Project found that most believe a cyber-attack will occur between now and 2025 that will result in significant loss of life. While we traditionally think of cybersecurity as a matter of data loss and the theft of money and intellectual property, our modern reality is one in which almost every technology is connected to the Internet. Our homes are becoming automated—from our locks to our thermostats and lights. But for infrastructure, this means that dams, power grids, rail switches, air traffic control, sewers, and much more are all able to be tampered with from just about any location on the planet where an Internet connection exists. All of our hardening of perimeters and physical security enhancements will do nothing to prevent deadly attacks if the ability to prevent unauthorized control of such systems and devices is not developed and enabled. DHS leads the cybersecurity effort, but its priorities are set by Congress and the administration in power. It is incumbent upon the DHS leadership to ensure that the issue remains elevated and that those in decision-making positions are adequately informed in order to properly fund and authorize action.

Conclusion

We believe that FEMA experience from 1979 to the present may be a harbinger of the Department of Homeland Security's fate as it continues to struggle in the coming years to establish an integrated and effective national homeland security system. At a minimum, FEMA's experiences should serve as a cautionary tale for homeland security officials at the federal, state, and local levels of government.

Since the Hurricane Katrina experience, progress has been made in reestablishing FEMA's capabilities in responding to a major disaster and as the leader of the nation's emergency management system. Supporting community-based homeland security efforts involving the general public, continuing to communicate timely and accurate information to the public and taking full advantage of social media, investing in research about the new terrorist threats and climate change hazards, and working harder to establish a strong and vital partnership with the business sector could ease DHS's growing pains and pave the way for the establishment of a comprehensive homeland security system in this country. In this vein, we also believe that there are several areas relative to the new threats faced by the nation for which there is little our past can do to inform us. This includes such things as the return of radicalized FTFs who blend easily among the nation's citizenry and the recognition of grave vulnerabilities that are emerging on account of our vast cyber dependencies. We also must therefore recognize that DHS has to remain innovative and seek engagement with experts by forming and fostering partnerships outside of its traditional circles of intelligence and security. The government is behind on many of these issues, not always on account of technical capacity but rather because the statutory frameworks to guide action are either outdated or insufficient.

One final note on FEMA experience: At the core of FEMA's success in the 1990s was its focus on the needs of its customers, the American people. FEMA policies and programs from that period were driven by the needs of disaster victims and by the needs of community residents who wanted to reduce the terrible impacts of future events. Since its inception in 2002, DHS and its partners in the federal government have been focused almost exclusively on their own needs. Policies and programs have been designed and implemented that meet the needs of these governmental departments and agencies and that were not informed by the needs of the public, their supposed customers.

If the officials at DHS that work in homeland security at the state and local levels change one thing in the future, it is critical that they shift their focus from themselves to the public and that they plan and implement policies and programs with the full involvement of the public and their partners. It worked very well for FEMA, so there is no reason why it should not do the same for DHS.

Reference

Markert, J., 2014. ISIS attracts foreign fighters from across the globe: where do they come from and why? Curiousmatic. http://bit.ly/11SfXNQ (September 4).

Index

Note: Page numbers followed by *f* indicate figures, *b* indicate boxes, and *t* indicate tables.

C

D

F

G

I

M

N

P

S

T

U

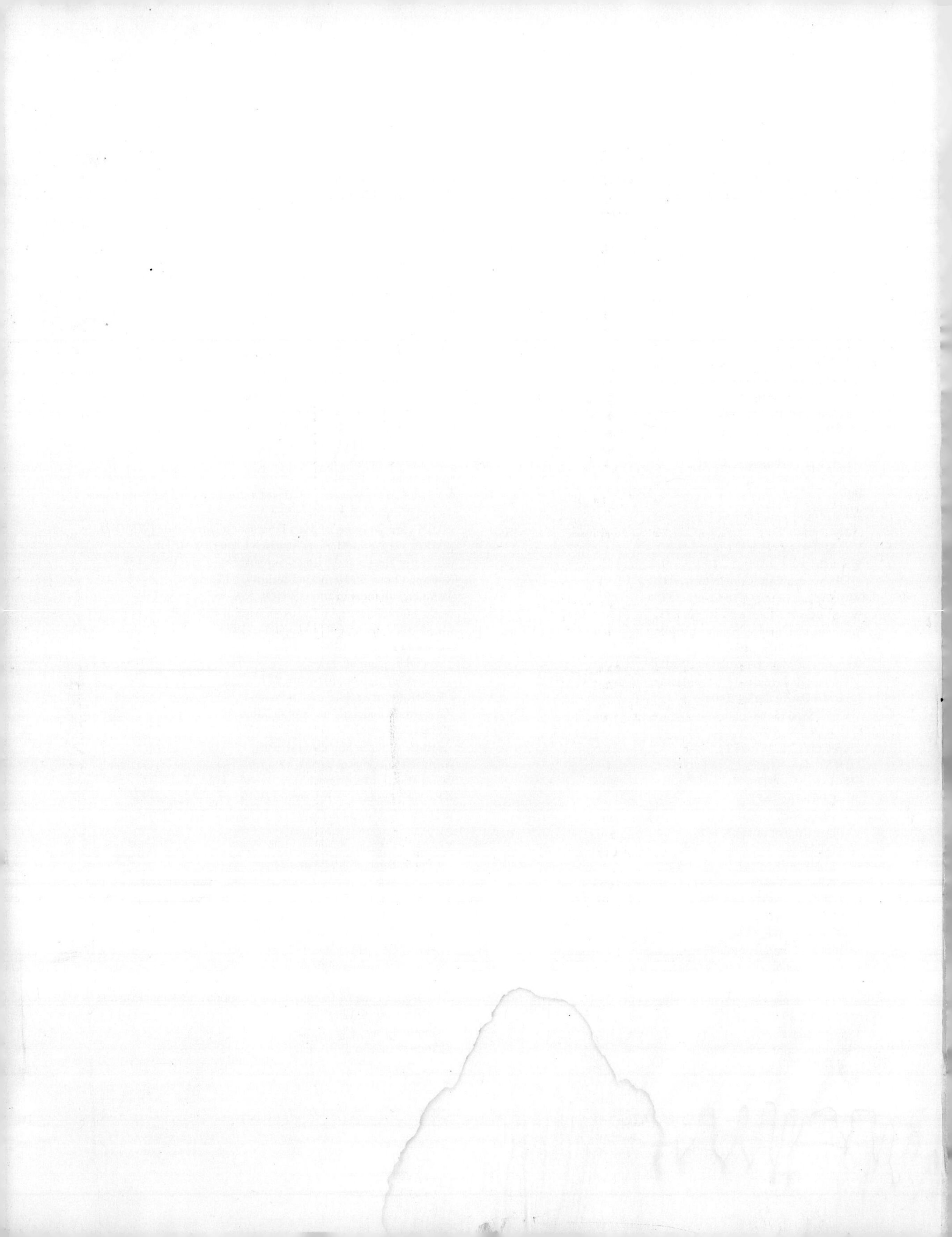